# CAMBRIDGE
## EDUCATIONAL SERVICES®

**AMERICA'S #1 CAMPUS-BASED TESTPREP.**

# GRE* Victory
# Student Text

GRE • LSAT • GMAT • MCAT • TOEFL • GED • PRAXIS • ACT • SAT • PSAT • PLAN • EXPLORE • PSAE • ITBS • CollegePrep™ • WorkKeys

**About Cambridge Educational Services:**

Cambridge Educational Services was founded in order to help all students, regardless of income, meet standards and perform to the best of their abilities on standardized tests and in the classroom. Our mission is to provide assessment services and program materials that make quality test preparation programs possible for a wide range of student ability levels. Our goal is to help students achieve test scores that reflect their true potential and ability. Our programs help thousands of students each year reach their goals, such as becoming National Merit Scholars, gaining admission to the colleges of their choice, and earning valuable scholarships. Cambridge publishes a variety of school improvement and preparation titles and products including student texts, teacher's guides, skills review manuals, software, and assessment services.

---

---

Cambridge Publishing, Inc., Chicago National Headquarters, Des Plaines, IL 60018

© 1991, 1993, 1996, 1998, 1999, 2001, 2002, 2003, 2008 by Cambridge Publishing, Inc.
All rights reserved. First edition 1991
Eighth edition 2008

Printed in the United States of America
**10 09 08 07   1 2 3 4 5**

ISBN-13: 978-1-58894-070-4

Portions reprinted from the GRE
© 2003 by Thomas H. Martinson.
All rights reserved

Dear Student,

The fact that you are reading this book means just one thing: you have a big, important test ahead of you. You want to do well, and we can help you. This course will assist you in building the skills and learning the test-taking strategies that are needed to succeed on the GRE.

The GRE can be a difficult test, requiring knowledge of concepts that you may have either forgotten or never learned. Full preparation, therefore, demands a targeted review.

Your *Cambridge GRE Victory Student Text, 8th Edition* contains all of the materials that you need in order to: (1) refresh or build your understanding of important skills; (2) apply those skills in the particular context of the GRE; and (3) reduce test anxiety through practice.

You have the tools to succeed. Attend class, participate in learning, do all of your assignments, and maintain a positive attitude. You can do it; we have confidence in you.

Good Luck!

*The Cambridge Curriculum Committee*

# TABLE OF CONTENTS

# HOW TO USE THIS BOOK

This book is organized into six parts:

1) setting a test score target and taking a diagnostic pre-assessment (Step One);
2) information to help you make sense of your pre-assessment results (Step Two);
3) skills review by test section, as well as problems resembling those found on the real GRE that your instructor will use to teach tested concepts and applicable strategies (Step Three);
4) four full-length GRE practice tests (Step Four);
5) taking a post-assessment and information to help you make sense of the results for final review (Step Five);
6) recommendations on application preparation, continuing your study after the course is done, and succeeding in graduate school (Step Six).

The following introduction will briefly explain how to use each part of this student text.

## SETTING A TEST SCORE TARGET AND TAKING A PRE-ASSESSMENT (STEP ONE)

Step One includes a section that describes how the admission process works, emphasizing the relationship between GPA and test scores and how these factors enter into deciding where to apply. With the help of your instructor, you will review this material and set realistic GRE target scores that will enable you to gain entrance into the school of your choice.

In order to know where to begin preparing for the GRE, you have to find out what you already do well and what you could learn to do better. The pre-assessment serves this purpose. You will take an official, retired GRE and Analytical Writing practice test under actual testing conditions. The pre-assessment answers and explanations are located in your student text, while sample essay responses are located in *Practicing to Take the GRE General Test, 10th Edition*.

If your program has not already done so, at this point in the course consider purchasing the Cambridge GRE CD-ROM, which is available at **www.CambridgeEd.com**. This CD provides timed tests with printable score reports, full explanations, and problem-solving strategies; an adaptive skill-builder that allows you to receive problems suited to your current skill level; and printable assessment reports.

## MAKING SENSE OF YOUR PRE-ASSESSMENT RESULTS (STEP TWO)

In order to succeed on the GRE, there are three areas on which you should focus: core skills, test mechanics, and concepts and strategies. With the help of your instructor, you will use the results of the pre-assessment to determine exactly which topics to review, for how long, and in what order.

Additionally, this step includes two sections that will help get you started: Time Management and Study Plan for the Course.

## TARGETED SKILLS, CONCEPTS, AND STRATEGIES (STEP THREE)

Step Three includes both a skills review and a test mechanics summary for each of the three GRE test sections:

- Verbal Reasoning
- Quantitative Reasoning
- Analytical Writing

This step also includes one lesson for each of the eight subject-areas covered on the test:

- Analogies
- Antonyms
- Sentence Completions
- Reading Comprehension
- Discrete Quantitative
- Quantitative Comparisons
- Graphs
- Writing

The Skills Review exercises contain problems that will enable you to do three things: (1) review material that you may have forgotten; (2) learn material that you may never have learned; and (3) master the skills required to answer real GRE items. At the beginning of each of the three skills reviews, there is a course outline. These outlines act as course syllabi, listing the related concepts and exercises.

The skills exercises cover a range of topics that are appropriate to the three sections of the test, but they do not necessarily contain problems that mimic GRE items. Rather, the skills problems are designed to help you learn a concept—not necessarily to help you learn about how the concepts appear on the actual exam. For example, the Careful Reading section in the Verbal Reasoning Skills Review helps you focus on the wording of item stems so as to better understand what is being asked by the test-writers. While such items do not appear on the actual test, the skill involved in these exercises is an invaluable tool for all subject-areas. Your instructor may either review the Skills Review material in class or have you complete the exercises as homework.

The test mechanics sections contain material on timing, pacing, and guessing that is relevant to each of the tested subject-areas. This material also presents a breakdown of the number of items and time restrictions for each test section.

After you have mastered the skills, you will be able to take full advantage of the concepts and test-taking strategies that are developed in the lessons, which make up the heart of this course and, in particular, this book. The lessons contain items that look like those found on the real GRE. When compared with items on the real tests, the items in this part of the book have similar content, represent the same difficulty levels, and can be solved by using the same problem-solving skills and test-taking strategies.

At the beginning of each of the eight lessons, there is a course outline. These outlines act as course syllabi, listing the related concepts that are tested for each item-type in each subject-area. The items in each lesson are organized to correspond with the respective outline. For each concept in the outline, there are various clusters of items. A cluster contains a greater number of items if the item-type appears with great frequency on the real test, and it contains a lesser number of items if the item-type appears with less frequency. Although the concepts are not arranged in clusters on the real GRE, we organize the problems in clusters so that the concepts are emphasized and reinforced. After you learn the concepts, you will be able to practice applying this conceptual knowledge on the practice tests.

Finally, Step Three includes a section that lists strategies for enhancing test performance: practical hints and methods to help alleviate debilitating test anxiety (Overcoming Test Anxiety).

## TAKING PRACTICE TESTS (STEP FOUR)

In the practice test section of the book, there are four full-length GRE practice tests. In these tests, the items not only mimic the real test in content and difficulty level, but they are also arranged in an order and with a frequency that simulates the real GRE.

Your instructor will either ask you to complete some or all of these items in class, or he or she will assign them as homework. If you are taking these four tests at home, you should take two *without* time restrictions and then two *with* time restrictions. Taking the test without time restrictions will help you get a sense of how long it would take for you to comfortably and accurately solve an item. Applying time pressure then forces you to pace yourself as you would on the real test. If you complete all four of the practice tests, any test anxiety you may have will be greatly reduced.

## TAKING A POST-ASSESSMENT AND MAKING SENSE OF YOUR RESULTS (STEP FIVE)

In order to know how far you have come since the pre-assessment, you need to take another official retired GRE and Analytical Writing practice test. You will take this post-assessment under actual testing conditions. You will use the results to evaluate your progress and to determine exactly what topics would be the most beneficial for you to review. The post-assessment answers, explanations, and sample essay responses are all located in *Practicing to Take the GRE General Test, 10th Edition*.

## FIGURING OUT WHAT TO DO NEXT (STEP SIX)

Step Six contains a short guide to help you design a study plan for the days or weeks between the end of the course and the official test. You will practice the test-taking and time management skills that you learned in Steps Two and Three to make the most of your remaining study time.

Additionally, this step includes two sections that will help you prepare for graduate school: Application Preparation and Succeeding in Graduate School.

# Step One: Setting a Test Score Target (Pre-Assessment)

Take an official test under real testing conditions to gain predictive data on which to base your study.

See what types of items and pacing you will encounter on your actual test.

Get inside tips for gaining admission to the graduate school of your choice.

## Step One Overview:

You start your course with an official test so that you know where you stand on the GRE. This diagnostic test tells you and your instructor where you need to focus to see the greatest improvement. You should complete this test under real testing conditions so you know what to expect on the day of the actual test. The structure of the course hinges on your pre-assessment performance, so try hard, but do not be too discouraged if you do not perform as well as you hoped. You will soon be learning the core curricular skills, test mechanics, and strategies to boost your score.

# SETTING A TEST SCORE TARGET

Helping you get into the graduate school of your choice is the goal of this section. We have advised tens of thousands of students, interviewed graduate school admissions officers across the country, and attended annual advisors' conferences. Thus, the descriptions, conclusions, and suggestions in this section have been distilled from a variety of sources.

This section is intended for a range of readers—for those who are already actively working on their applications as well as for those who are only thinking of applying to graduate school. Therefore, some of the points we make are very general and others are very specific. Some of the information may already be familiar, while other points and tips may surprise you. No matter what your status, you will find the following section immediately useful for applying to graduate school and getting into the graduate school of your choice.

## FUNCTION OF THE ADMISSION PROCESS

In order to set your graduate school target, you must understand and appreciate the function of the admission process as a social and economic process. Many prospective applicants view the filing of a graduate school application only from their own individual perspective and consider themselves outside spectators who merely benefit from (or are victims of) a bureaucratic juggernaut. For those who share this point of view, we offer the following comments:

> *Graduate schools only care about your GRE scores.*
> *You cannot get into a really good school unless you know someone.*
> *They really do not read your personal statement.*

Such comments reflect an attitude that is based on a misinterpretation of the admission process—not taking into consideration the social and economic factors. Let us examine this process from two perspectives: yours, and that of a graduate school.

First, from your perspective, you must keep in mind that the graduate school admission process is much more than merely answering a few questions about your educational background and employment history. Rather, the application process is just the first step on a career path that will last for most of the rest of your life. Decisions you make at this stage may have implications for your life 30 or 40 years from now. An easy way of realizing this is to imagine the different courses your life might follow if you do or do not get into graduate school, or to compare your career prospects if you are or are not accepted by your first choice school.

Now, this is not to say that not getting into a certain school spells disaster. Obviously, a variety of schools produce successful psychologists, engineers, biochemists, computer scientists, economists, chemists, teachers, historians, musicians, physicists, geologists, political scientists, sociologists, etc. Rather, we are simply trying to stress the importance of the admission process to you as an individual. Indeed, you do not have to look far into the future to appreciate the effect that the admission process will have on you. Your decisions at this point will determine where you are likely to live for the next two to four years.

Additionally, you must appreciate the financial commitment that you are making. In the first instance, the cost of the application process alone could be as much as $1,400. The fee that you pay Educational Testing Services to take the Graduate Record Examination with score reports could be as much as $152 ($140 for general test registration and $12 to receive scores over the phone). Up to four free test reports are included at the time that you take the test. If you need additional score reports, these are available for a fee of $15 per school, plus an additional $6 service fee if reports are ordered via telephone. Furthermore, the application fees charged by schools run between $35 and $90. If you apply to ten schools, you could easily spend $1,000 or more on application fees and score distribution charges. In addition, you will probably spend at least $100 on administrative details, such as document preparation, copying, postage, and long

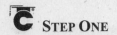 

distance telephone calls. Add another $300 or so for test preparation for the GRE, and you are already committed to $1,400 or more.

On top of application expenses, most schools require that you respond to an acceptance offer by a certain deadline with a non-refundable deposit. You may find yourself in the uncomfortable position of paying such a deposit to ensure that you have a graduate school seat even though you have not yet heard from some other schools. However, these sums pale in comparison to the cost of tuition. In-state tuition at a public school may be $10,000–$15,000 per year, while tuition at a top private school may be as much as $35,000–$40,000 per year. With the expense of room and board taken into consideration, (approximately $5,000–$19,000 per year, depending on the school), the entire expense to obtain your graduate degree could be anywhere from $30,000 to $235,000.

Do not let those numbers frighten you. We are not trying to dissuade you from pursuing a graduate degree. We are trying to dramatize a point: the decision to apply to graduate school has significant social and economic implications for you as an individual.

On the other side of the coin, from the perspective of the graduate school, there are also social and economic implications. A graduate school, like any educational institution, is a corporate entity, and its admission decisions reflect social and economic policies adopted by the corporation. Consider first some of the economic implications a graduate school faces in accepting or rejecting an applicant.

The graduate school has to be run as would any other business entity. It has employees; it owns or rents property; it operates a library; it buys furniture and office equipment; it pays utility bills; and so on. A large part of those expenses is paid using student tuition. A graduate school, therefore, is dependent on a steady flow of tuition income. So, admission decisions must be made in the context of budgetary constraints. A graduate school simply cannot afford to have large numbers of students dropping out of school. Therefore, one concern of a graduate school admissions officer is to ensure that those applicants who are accepted are committed to completing the course of study. Additionally— though this may not be an explicit concern—graduate schools rely heavily on alumni donations. Therefore, it would not be surprising to learn that an applicant who shows considerable professional promise would be considered favorably. Moreover, a school that graduates successful PhDs gets a reputation for being a good school and such a reputation in turn tends to attract highly qualified applicants.

We do not mean to give you the impression that an admission decision is made solely on economic considerations. That is far from the truth. Graduate schools also have a sense of the social responsibility they bear as educators of PhD students—one of the most influential groups of people in our society. They meet this responsibility in some obvious ways, such as actively seeking applicants from groups who are under-represented in the professional community and by establishing programs to train professionals for positions of special need.

The admission process, then, is the interface between these two perspectives. The process is designed to match individuals and institutions that can mutually satisfy each other's needs. This matching function, however, is somewhat skewed. For decades, there have been more people interested in pursuing professional careers than there are seats available at accredited graduate schools. Consequently, applicants are competing for graduate school entrance, especially at top schools.

Given the mismatch between the number of available slots and the number of applicants, the application process is turned into a competition. You will have to compete against others for a graduate school seat (or at least for a spot at the graduate school of your choice). To do this, you must make yourself attractive to a graduate school. You must persuade the admissions committee that you will help them satisfy their economic and social needs. That thought must guide you as you create your application (Step Six).

# HOW THE ADMISSION PROCESS WORKS

If we read the title of this section literally, then anything we say about it must be false. This is because there is no "the" admission process. Rather, each graduate school has its own individual admission process, and each process differs in ways more or less important from that of every other graduate school in the country.

On the other hand, we cannot talk about the details of the admission process at each of the more than 1,200 U.S. universities offering more than 500 graduate degree program areas. Indeed, almost all schools regard the mechanics of the decision-making process as a highly sensitive matter, and they do not share the details of that process with outsiders. In any event, you cannot exercise any control over the way a graduate school makes its decision. As you will see, you do not need "inside" information to create an effective application.

As noted above, the admission process varies from school to school. Faculty committees may be required to make the decisions by majority vote or unanimous agreement before an applicant is accepted. A professional admissions officer (who may not him or herself be a doctor) or a Dean of Admissions (who has a graduate degree but is not a faculty member) may make the decisions. A committee of members drawn from both administration and faculty may make the decisions. Finally, students themselves may have some input into the decisions.

We will not dwell on these different possibilities for two reasons. One, they are outside of your control. Two, regardless of the formal structure of the admission process, it is designed to satisfy the institution's social and economic goals—as we noted above.

Despite the variety of formal structures, one generalization is possible:

> *Every graduate school relies to some extent on the applicant's Grade Point Average (GPA) and GRE scores, but there are few (if any) graduate schools that rely only on these quantitative factors.*

This statement contains two ideas. Let us look at each.

The first idea is that every graduate school uses the GPA and GRE scores. While different graduate schools approach these numbers in unique ways, we can use a mathematical model to understand one way in which schools might take these factors into account. This sample formula is designed to weight the numbers approximately equally to give admissions officers some idea of how the applicant stacks up against other applicants. The following is a specific example:

The GRE is scored on a scale from 200 (the minimum) to 800 (the maximum) for the verbal and quantitative exam areas. Some schools will add both scores for a cumulative index; others will only consider the one area they deem more important. If you are quoted a required GRE index at a specific school it is important to inquire as to whether that index is the average or total of one or both of the 200–800 GRE scores.

The "200 to 800" point scale has a special relation to the "0 to 4" grading system used by most colleges: 800 equals 200 times 4. This permits the use of a formula to combine the two measures. For example:

$$(\text{Average GRE}) + (200 \cdot \text{GPA}) = \text{Index}$$

Let's look at an example: a student with a 3.5 grade point average and GRE scores of 700 (Quantitative Reasoning) and 650 (Verbal Reasoning):

$$\frac{(700 + 650)}{2} + (200 \cdot 3.5) = 1,375$$

What does the index signify? That brings us to the second idea, as the answer varies from school to school. Some schools have a fairly mechanical admission process that emphasizes the index (or some variation on it). The school may set a minimum index below which applications receive little or no study. An application with an index below the

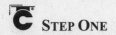
minimum is simply rejected. Such schools may also have a second, higher minimum that triggers an automatic acceptance. Students with indices that exceed the higher minimum are accepted unless there is some glaring weakness in the application that otherwise disqualifies them.

At the opposite extreme are schools that claim to minimize the importance of the GRE and the GPA. They claim that the GRE is the very last factor at which they look. Such schools have a very flexible admission process.

Many schools use the test scores and grades as a screening device to determine how much attention will be given to an application. Applications with very low test scores and grades will receive little attention. The schools reason that unless there is something obvious and compelling in the application to offset the low numbers, then the applicant should be rejected. Applications with very high test scores and grades will receive little attention. The reasoning is that unless there is something obvious and compelling in the application to reject it, it should be accepted. On this theory, the applications with test scores and grades in the middle receive the greatest attention. These are applications from candidates who are at least competitive for the school but who do not command an automatic acceptance. It is in this pool that competition is the most severe.

Here is a table that illustrates this principle:

| GPA | GRE SCORE (Percentile) | | | |
| --- | --- | --- | --- | --- |
|  | *61–70%* | *71–80%* | *81–90%* | *91–100%* |
| 3.75+ | $\frac{2}{19}$ | $\frac{49}{101}$ | $\frac{102}{116}$ | $\frac{72}{79}$ |
| 3.50–3.74 | $\frac{6}{112}$ | $\frac{75}{275}$ | $\frac{301}{361}$ | $\frac{120}{129}$ |
| 0–3.49 | $\frac{10}{160}$ | $\frac{90}{601}$ | $\frac{375}{666}$ | $\frac{201}{250}$ |

The fractions represent the total number of accepted applicants divided by the total number of applicants.

The categories in the table show what this graduate school did with applications with certain GRE scores (shown in percentile terms) and grade point averages. In the category in the upper right-hand corner are candidates with scores above the 90th percentile and GPAs above 3.75. The table shows that 72 of the 79 were accepted and seven were rejected.

What is obvious from the table is that some candidates with higher indices were rejected in favor of candidates with lower numbers. For example, of those candidates with scores between the 81st and 90th percentiles, 74 more candidates were accepted with a GPA below 3.50 than were students with a higher GPA between 3.50 and 3.74.

Why would a graduate school reject an applicant with higher numbers for one with lower numbers? The answer lies in our analysis of the admission process. Apparently, there were factors in the applications of those who were accepted that suggested to the admissions committee that those applicants would better meet the social and economic goals of the institution. Those factors are unquantifiable ones, such as motivation, commitment, leadership, experience, and so on.

As you prepare your graduate school applications, you are, of course, saddled with your GPA and your GRE scores, two factors that you cannot change. Therefore, the only real control that you will have over your application will consist of unquantifiable factors. We will show you later how to maximize their impact.

One final point about the mechanics of the application process is rolling admissions. Rolling admissions is a device used by some graduate schools that regulates the release of acceptances. A typical graduate school application season opens in October and closes in May or June. Applications are received throughout the application season, and decisions are made on an ongoing basis; this is achieved by targeting an entering class. Based on its admission history, a graduate school will estimate the expected range of GRE scores and GPAs of the students it will accept in the upcoming year. Then, as it receives applications (say, month by month), it will act on them. Students with very strong applications compared with the target group will receive acceptances; students with weak ones will receive rejections. Applications in the middle are carried over, and the applicants receive either no notification or notification that the application is still pending.

The rolling admissions process has advantages for both the graduate school and the applicant. From the applicant's point of view, the earlier the notification of the disposition of an application the better. That is, you know whether you were accepted or rejected and you can go on from there. From the graduate school's viewpoint, the entering class and therefore the stability of the budget begin to take shape as early as possible.

The rolling admissions process is also a tool you can use to your advantage: apply early. Obviously, schools have greater flexibility and there are more seats available earlier in the admission season than later. We do not mean to imply that if you apply late in the season you will be rejected. In fact, it is impossible to quantify exactly the advantage that applications received earlier, rather than later, enjoy. Still, if you want to maximize your chances of acceptance, apply early!

## WHERE TO APPLY

Given the economic commitment that you will be making, one of the obvious questions on your mind will be, "Where should I apply?" You should apply to a group of schools such that, given your economic resources, you maximize your chances of gaining admission to the graduate schools of your choice.

To apply to a graduate school, you must remit a non-refundable application fee. This means that you are, to speak crudely, gambling with your money. You pay the fee, but you do not know in advance whether you will win or lose. So, hedge your bets. In a gambling situation, a bettor will have several choices. Some will be long shots, others will be almost sure things, and the rest will lie somewhere in the middle. The long shots will pay handsome dividends and the sure things a reasonable return, while the others will pay in between.

Given these considerations, you should select two or perhaps three "long shot" schools. As the term "long shot" implies, the odds of your being accepted to these schools are not very good, but the potential payoff justifies the gamble. On the other hand, you should also select one or two "sure thing" schools. To do this, you may have to apply to a school in your geographical area that does not enjoy a particularly good reputation or to a school that is located in another part of the country. The rest of your applications should go to your "good bet" schools—schools for which the chances for acceptance are 40% to 75%.

Assume that you have the resources to apply to ten schools and that you have an above average GPA and GRE scores. Depending on the exact numbers, you may very well have a chance at one of the top graduate schools. However, those are your "long shot" schools. You are almost a sure thing at many schools (your "sure thing" schools). Finally, there is a long list of "good bet" schools in the middle. At each of these schools, your application will likely receive serious consideration, but it is not guaranteed for acceptance.

This strategy of "stacking" your applications will maximize your chances of acceptance at a school you want, while minimizing the chance that you will not get into any school. Of course, the way the strategy is implemented will vary from person to person. For people who are lucky enough to have a high GPA and top GRE scores, the middle and bottom tier schools collapse into a single tier. At the other extreme, those who are unlucky enough to have a GPA and GRE scores that are below what most schools accept will have to work with the second and third tiers.

As you prepare to implement this strategy, make a realistic assessment of your chances. Candidates unfortunately tend to overestimate the importance of what they believe to be their own interesting or unique factors. For example, we often hear candidates make statements such as, "Well sure my GPA is a little low, but I had to work part-time while I was in school"; and "I know my GRE scores are not that good, but I was a member of the university Student Council." These are valid points and are usually taken into consideration by admissions officers. However, the question is how much weight they will be given, for they (or some similar point) are true of most people applying to graduate school. For example, if you are thinking of applying to Harvard University with a GPA of 3.25 and GRE scores in the 75th percentile, then there had better be something really special in your background, such as an Olympic medal or Nobel Peace Prize!

A question related to the "Where should I apply?" question is, "What are the top graduate schools in the country?" Since there is no single criterion for "best graduate school" that would be accepted by everyone, it is arguable that this question simply cannot be given a meaningful answer. Nevertheless, it is possible to get an approximate answer. The *U.S. News & World Report* survey of graduate school deans lists the top twenty-five graduate schools in several disciplines and the specific areas of study that fall within each discipline. Listed here are the top three to five programs for several disciplines and areas of study. Note that more than one school may be number one, two, etc., indicating a tie. (Entries on the list may change each year, as may the rankings.)

| **BUSINESS** | **EDUCATION** | **ENGLISH** |
|---|---|---|
| 1. Harvard University (MA)<br>2. Stanford University (CA)<br>3. University of Pennsylvania (Wharton)<br>4. Mass. Institute of Technology (Sloan)<br>5. Northwestern University (Kellogg) (IL) | 1. Teachers College—Columbia University (NY)<br>2. Stanford University (CA)<br>3. Harvard University (MA)<br>3. Vanderbilt University (Peabody) (TN)<br>5. University of California—Los Angeles | 1. Harvard University (MA)<br>1. University of California—Berkeley<br>1. Yale University (CT) |
| **ENGINEERING** | **HISTORY** | **LAW** |
| 1. Mass. Institute of Technology<br>2. Stanford University (CA)<br>3. University of California—Berkeley<br>4. Georgia Institute of Technology<br>5. University of Illinois—Urbana-Champaign | 1. Yale University (CT)<br>2. Princeton University (NJ)<br>2. University of California—Berkeley | 1. Yale University (CT)<br>2. Harvard University (MA)<br>2. Stanford University (CA)<br>4. New York University<br>5. Columbia University (NY) |
| **MEDICINE (Primary Care)** | **MEDICINE (Research)** | **PHYSICS** |
| 1. University of Washington<br>2. University of North Carolina—Chapel Hill<br>3. University of Colorado—Denver and Health Sciences Center<br>4. Oregon Health Science University<br>5. Michigan State University College of Osteopathic Medicine | 1. Harvard University (MA)<br>2. Johns Hopkins University (MD)<br>3. University of Pennsylvania<br>4. Washington University in St. Louis<br>5. University of California—San Francisco | 1. Mass. Institute of Technology<br>1. Stanford University (CA)<br>3. California Institute of Technology |
| **POLITICAL SCIENCE** | **PSYCHOLOGY** | **SOCIOLOGY** |
| 1. Harvard University (MA)<br>2. Stanford University (CA)<br>3. University of Michigan—Ann Arbor | 1. Stanford University (CA)<br>2. University of California—Berkeley<br>2. University of Michigan—Ann Arbor | 1. University of Wisconsin—Madison<br>2. University of California—Berkeley<br>3. University of Michigan—Ann Arbor |

## TAKING THE GRE

Since the GRE plays an important role in the admission process, it is only common sense that you do everything you can to maximize your score. You should not take the GRE until you are certain that you are ready to do your best.

Graduate schools receive all of your GRE test scores—not just your best one. They also receive an average score calculated by ETS. You are already heading in the right direction by taking the Cambridge GRE Review Course—we will provide you with everything you need to succeed on the GRE. The rest is up to you. Good luck!

Name: _____  Date: _____

Student ID Number: _____

# PRE-ASSESSMENT

Start with number 1 for each new section. If a section has fewer items than answer spaces, leave the extra answer spaces blank. Be sure to erase any errors or stray marks completely.

**Section 1**

| 1 Ⓐ Ⓑ Ⓒ Ⓓ Ⓔ | 11 Ⓐ Ⓑ Ⓒ Ⓓ Ⓔ | 21 Ⓐ Ⓑ Ⓒ Ⓓ Ⓔ | 31 Ⓐ Ⓑ Ⓒ Ⓓ Ⓔ |
| 2 Ⓐ Ⓑ Ⓒ Ⓓ Ⓔ | 12 Ⓐ Ⓑ Ⓒ Ⓓ Ⓔ | 22 Ⓐ Ⓑ Ⓒ Ⓓ Ⓔ | 32 Ⓐ Ⓑ Ⓒ Ⓓ Ⓔ |
| 3 Ⓐ Ⓑ Ⓒ Ⓓ Ⓔ | 13 Ⓐ Ⓑ Ⓒ Ⓓ Ⓔ | 23 Ⓐ Ⓑ Ⓒ Ⓓ Ⓔ | 33 Ⓐ Ⓑ Ⓒ Ⓓ Ⓔ |
| 4 Ⓐ Ⓑ Ⓒ Ⓓ Ⓔ | 14 Ⓐ Ⓑ Ⓒ Ⓓ Ⓔ | 24 Ⓐ Ⓑ Ⓒ Ⓓ Ⓔ | 34 Ⓐ Ⓑ Ⓒ Ⓓ Ⓔ |
| 5 Ⓐ Ⓑ Ⓒ Ⓓ Ⓔ | 15 Ⓐ Ⓑ Ⓒ Ⓓ Ⓔ | 25 Ⓐ Ⓑ Ⓒ Ⓓ Ⓔ | 35 Ⓐ Ⓑ Ⓒ Ⓓ Ⓔ |
| 6 Ⓐ Ⓑ Ⓒ Ⓓ Ⓔ | 16 Ⓐ Ⓑ Ⓒ Ⓓ Ⓔ | 26 Ⓐ Ⓑ Ⓒ Ⓓ Ⓔ | 36 Ⓐ Ⓑ Ⓒ Ⓓ Ⓔ |
| 7 Ⓐ Ⓑ Ⓒ Ⓓ Ⓔ | 17 Ⓐ Ⓑ Ⓒ Ⓓ Ⓔ | 27 Ⓐ Ⓑ Ⓒ Ⓓ Ⓔ | 37 Ⓐ Ⓑ Ⓒ Ⓓ Ⓔ |
| 8 Ⓐ Ⓑ Ⓒ Ⓓ Ⓔ | 18 Ⓐ Ⓑ Ⓒ Ⓓ Ⓔ | 28 Ⓐ Ⓑ Ⓒ Ⓓ Ⓔ | 38 Ⓐ Ⓑ Ⓒ Ⓓ Ⓔ |
| 9 Ⓐ Ⓑ Ⓒ Ⓓ Ⓔ | 19 Ⓐ Ⓑ Ⓒ Ⓓ Ⓔ | 29 Ⓐ Ⓑ Ⓒ Ⓓ Ⓔ | |
| 10 Ⓐ Ⓑ Ⓒ Ⓓ Ⓔ | 20 Ⓐ Ⓑ Ⓒ Ⓓ Ⓔ | 30 Ⓐ Ⓑ Ⓒ Ⓓ Ⓔ | |

**Section 2**

| 1 Ⓐ Ⓑ Ⓒ Ⓓ Ⓔ | 9 Ⓐ Ⓑ Ⓒ Ⓓ Ⓔ | 17 Ⓐ Ⓑ Ⓒ Ⓓ Ⓔ | 25 Ⓐ Ⓑ Ⓒ Ⓓ Ⓔ |
| 2 Ⓐ Ⓑ Ⓒ Ⓓ Ⓔ | 10 Ⓐ Ⓑ Ⓒ Ⓓ Ⓔ | 18 Ⓐ Ⓑ Ⓒ Ⓓ Ⓔ | 26 Ⓐ Ⓑ Ⓒ Ⓓ Ⓔ |
| 3 Ⓐ Ⓑ Ⓒ Ⓓ Ⓔ | 11 Ⓐ Ⓑ Ⓒ Ⓓ Ⓔ | 19 Ⓐ Ⓑ Ⓒ Ⓓ Ⓔ | 27 Ⓐ Ⓑ Ⓒ Ⓓ Ⓔ |
| 4 Ⓐ Ⓑ Ⓒ Ⓓ Ⓔ | 12 Ⓐ Ⓑ Ⓒ Ⓓ Ⓔ | 20 Ⓐ Ⓑ Ⓒ Ⓓ Ⓔ | 28 Ⓐ Ⓑ Ⓒ Ⓓ Ⓔ |
| 5 Ⓐ Ⓑ Ⓒ Ⓓ Ⓔ | 13 Ⓐ Ⓑ Ⓒ Ⓓ Ⓔ | 21 Ⓐ Ⓑ Ⓒ Ⓓ Ⓔ | 29 Ⓐ Ⓑ Ⓒ Ⓓ Ⓔ |
| 6 Ⓐ Ⓑ Ⓒ Ⓓ Ⓔ | 14 Ⓐ Ⓑ Ⓒ Ⓓ Ⓔ | 22 Ⓐ Ⓑ Ⓒ Ⓓ Ⓔ | 30 Ⓐ Ⓑ Ⓒ Ⓓ Ⓔ |
| 7 Ⓐ Ⓑ Ⓒ Ⓓ Ⓔ | 15 Ⓐ Ⓑ Ⓒ Ⓓ Ⓔ | 23 Ⓐ Ⓑ Ⓒ Ⓓ Ⓔ | |
| 8 Ⓐ Ⓑ Ⓒ Ⓓ Ⓔ | 16 Ⓐ Ⓑ Ⓒ Ⓓ Ⓔ | 24 Ⓐ Ⓑ Ⓒ Ⓓ Ⓔ | |

**Section 3**

| 1 Ⓐ Ⓑ Ⓒ Ⓓ Ⓔ | 11 Ⓐ Ⓑ Ⓒ Ⓓ Ⓔ | 21 Ⓐ Ⓑ Ⓒ Ⓓ Ⓔ | 31 Ⓐ Ⓑ Ⓒ Ⓓ Ⓔ |
| 2 Ⓐ Ⓑ Ⓒ Ⓓ Ⓔ | 12 Ⓐ Ⓑ Ⓒ Ⓓ Ⓔ | 22 Ⓐ Ⓑ Ⓒ Ⓓ Ⓔ | 32 Ⓐ Ⓑ Ⓒ Ⓓ Ⓔ |
| 3 Ⓐ Ⓑ Ⓒ Ⓓ Ⓔ | 13 Ⓐ Ⓑ Ⓒ Ⓓ Ⓔ | 23 Ⓐ Ⓑ Ⓒ Ⓓ Ⓔ | 33 Ⓐ Ⓑ Ⓒ Ⓓ Ⓔ |
| 4 Ⓐ Ⓑ Ⓒ Ⓓ Ⓔ | 14 Ⓐ Ⓑ Ⓒ Ⓓ Ⓔ | 24 Ⓐ Ⓑ Ⓒ Ⓓ Ⓔ | 34 Ⓐ Ⓑ Ⓒ Ⓓ Ⓔ |
| 5 Ⓐ Ⓑ Ⓒ Ⓓ Ⓔ | 15 Ⓐ Ⓑ Ⓒ Ⓓ Ⓔ | 25 Ⓐ Ⓑ Ⓒ Ⓓ Ⓔ | 35 Ⓐ Ⓑ Ⓒ Ⓓ Ⓔ |
| 6 Ⓐ Ⓑ Ⓒ Ⓓ Ⓔ | 16 Ⓐ Ⓑ Ⓒ Ⓓ Ⓔ | 26 Ⓐ Ⓑ Ⓒ Ⓓ Ⓔ | 36 Ⓐ Ⓑ Ⓒ Ⓓ Ⓔ |
| 7 Ⓐ Ⓑ Ⓒ Ⓓ Ⓔ | 17 Ⓐ Ⓑ Ⓒ Ⓓ Ⓔ | 27 Ⓐ Ⓑ Ⓒ Ⓓ Ⓔ | 37 Ⓐ Ⓑ Ⓒ Ⓓ Ⓔ |
| 8 Ⓐ Ⓑ Ⓒ Ⓓ Ⓔ | 18 Ⓐ Ⓑ Ⓒ Ⓓ Ⓔ | 28 Ⓐ Ⓑ Ⓒ Ⓓ Ⓔ | 38 Ⓐ Ⓑ Ⓒ Ⓓ Ⓔ |
| 9 Ⓐ Ⓑ Ⓒ Ⓓ Ⓔ | 19 Ⓐ Ⓑ Ⓒ Ⓓ Ⓔ | 29 Ⓐ Ⓑ Ⓒ Ⓓ Ⓔ | |
| 10 Ⓐ Ⓑ Ⓒ Ⓓ Ⓔ | 20 Ⓐ Ⓑ Ⓒ Ⓓ Ⓔ | 30 Ⓐ Ⓑ Ⓒ Ⓓ Ⓔ | |

**Section 4**

| 1 Ⓐ Ⓑ Ⓒ Ⓓ Ⓔ | 9 Ⓐ Ⓑ Ⓒ Ⓓ Ⓔ | 17 Ⓐ Ⓑ Ⓒ Ⓓ Ⓔ | 25 Ⓐ Ⓑ Ⓒ Ⓓ Ⓔ |
| 2 Ⓐ Ⓑ Ⓒ Ⓓ Ⓔ | 10 Ⓐ Ⓑ Ⓒ Ⓓ Ⓔ | 18 Ⓐ Ⓑ Ⓒ Ⓓ Ⓔ | 26 Ⓐ Ⓑ Ⓒ Ⓓ Ⓔ |
| 3 Ⓐ Ⓑ Ⓒ Ⓓ Ⓔ | 11 Ⓐ Ⓑ Ⓒ Ⓓ Ⓔ | 19 Ⓐ Ⓑ Ⓒ Ⓓ Ⓔ | 27 Ⓐ Ⓑ Ⓒ Ⓓ Ⓔ |
| 4 Ⓐ Ⓑ Ⓒ Ⓓ Ⓔ | 12 Ⓐ Ⓑ Ⓒ Ⓓ Ⓔ | 20 Ⓐ Ⓑ Ⓒ Ⓓ Ⓔ | 28 Ⓐ Ⓑ Ⓒ Ⓓ Ⓔ |
| 5 Ⓐ Ⓑ Ⓒ Ⓓ Ⓔ | 13 Ⓐ Ⓑ Ⓒ Ⓓ Ⓔ | 21 Ⓐ Ⓑ Ⓒ Ⓓ Ⓔ | 29 Ⓐ Ⓑ Ⓒ Ⓓ Ⓔ |
| 6 Ⓐ Ⓑ Ⓒ Ⓓ Ⓔ | 14 Ⓐ Ⓑ Ⓒ Ⓓ Ⓔ | 22 Ⓐ Ⓑ Ⓒ Ⓓ Ⓔ | 30 Ⓐ Ⓑ Ⓒ Ⓓ Ⓔ |
| 7 Ⓐ Ⓑ Ⓒ Ⓓ Ⓔ | 15 Ⓐ Ⓑ Ⓒ Ⓓ Ⓔ | 23 Ⓐ Ⓑ Ⓒ Ⓓ Ⓔ | |
| 8 Ⓐ Ⓑ Ⓒ Ⓓ Ⓔ | 16 Ⓐ Ⓑ Ⓒ Ⓓ Ⓔ | 24 Ⓐ Ⓑ Ⓒ Ⓓ Ⓔ | |

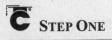 

## ISSUE TASK

**S T O P**

IF YOU FINISH BEFORE TIME IS CALLED, YOU MAY CHECK YOUR WORK ON THIS ESSAY ONLY.
DO NOT TURN TO ANY OTHER PORTION OF THE TEST.

## ARGUMENT TASK

_____

STOP

IF YOU FINISH BEFORE TIME IS CALLED, YOU MAY CHECK YOUR WORK ON THIS ESSAY ONLY.
DO NOT TURN TO ANY OTHER PORTION OF THE TEST.

# Step Two: Course Planning to Reach the Target

## Step Two Highlights:

Measure your baseline abilities so you can see how far you have come by the course's conclusion.

Examine a sample student summary report to learn how to analyze your pre-assessment data.

Learn the top areas where you should focus your efforts so that you will see the greatest score improvement.

Learn how to better manage your time and create a study plan for the course.

## Step Two Overview:

In Step Two, you will receive the results of your pre-assessment. Examine your score reports in detail in order to discover your strengths, as well as the areas in which you need to improve. Throughout the course, focus your review on the areas identified by the pre-assessment.

# SAMPLE STUDENT SUMMARY REPORT

The second step of the Cambridge Six-Step Approach is Course Planning to Reach the Target. During this step, you will receive the results of your official pre-assessment in the form of a student summary report. This report provides details about your performance and helps you determine where to focus your efforts during the course.

The student summary indicates your relative strengths and weaknesses and offers a snapshot of the level at which you have tested. The report indicates your score, as well as the number of right, wrong, and omitted items, in each tested area.

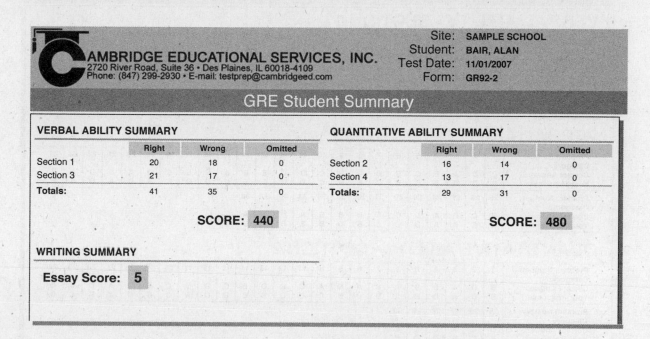

**CAMBRIDGE EDUCATIONAL SERVICES, INC.**
2720 River Road, Suite 36 • Des Plaines, IL 60018-4109
Phone: (847) 299-2930 • E-mail: testprep@cambridgeed.com

| | |
|---|---|
| Site: | SAMPLE SCHOOL |
| Student: | BAIR, ALAN |
| Test Date: | 11/01/2007 |
| Form: | GR92-2 |

## GRE Student Summary

**VERBAL ABILITY SUMMARY**

| | Right | Wrong | Omitted |
|---|---|---|---|
| Section 1 | 20 | 18 | 0 |
| Section 3 | 21 | 17 | 0 |
| Totals: | 41 | 35 | 0 |

SCORE: 440

**QUANTITATIVE ABILITY SUMMARY**

| | Right | Wrong | Omitted |
|---|---|---|---|
| Section 2 | 16 | 14 | 0 |
| Section 4 | 13 | 17 | 0 |
| Totals: | 29 | 31 | 0 |

SCORE: 480

**WRITING SUMMARY**

Essay Score: 5

It also provides an item analysis that includes the item number, the correct answer, and your response to each item. As you review the pre-assessment with your instructor, review this part of the report to reevaluate your original responses. (Note that the test sections are not necessarily listed in order on the report; rather, they are grouped by tested area.)

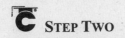

**CAMBRIDGE EDUCATIONAL SERVICES, INC.**
2720 River Road, Suite 36 • Des Plaines, IL 60018-4109
Phone: (847) 299-2930 • E-mail: testprep@cambridgeed.com

Site: **SAMPLE SCHOOL**
Student: **BAIR, ALAN**
Test Date: **11/01/2007**
Form: **GR92-2**

## GRE Student Summary

### VERBAL ABILITY - SECTION 1

| Problem Number: | 1 | 2 | 3 | 4 | 5 | 6 | 7 | 8 | 9 | 10 | 11 | 12 | 13 | 14 | 15 | 16 | 17 | 18 | 19 | 20 | 21 | 22 | 23 | 24 |
|---|---|---|---|---|---|---|---|---|---|---|---|---|---|---|---|---|---|---|---|---|---|---|---|---|
| Category: | | | | | | | | | | | | | | | | | | | | | | | | |
| Correct Answer: | A | D | A | C | E | B | D | C | B | E | D | D | E | D | C | B | B | E | A | B | A | C | B | C |
| Your Response: | A | D | A | E | E | B | B | C | C | B | E | E | D | A | C | C | B | B | E | D | C | E | B | D |

| Problem Number: | 25 | 26 | 27 | 28 | 29 | 30 | 31 | 32 | 33 | 34 | 35 | 36 | 37 | 38 |
|---|---|---|---|---|---|---|---|---|---|---|---|---|---|---|
| Category: | | | | | | | | | | | | | | |
| Correct Answer: | E | D | B | B | A | B | A | C | A | D | D | C | C | A |
| Your Response: | C | B | B | B | A | B | A | C | B | D | D | D | A | E |

### VERBAL ABILITY - SECTION 3

| Problem Number: | 1 | 2 | 3 | 4 | 5 | 6 | 7 | 8 | 9 | 10 | 11 | 12 | 13 | 14 | 15 | 16 | 17 | 18 | 19 | 20 | 21 | 22 | 23 | 24 |
|---|---|---|---|---|---|---|---|---|---|---|---|---|---|---|---|---|---|---|---|---|---|---|---|---|
| Category: | | | | | | | | | | | | | | | | | | | | | | | | |
| Correct Answer: | C | D | A | E | C | E | B | E | B | C | D | D | E | E | A | B | E | C | D | A | A | D | A | E |
| Your Response: | C | D | D | E | C | E | C | E | B | C | D | D | A | E | C | D | C | C | B | B | A | A | D | E |

| Problem Number: | 25 | 26 | 27 | 28 | 29 | 30 | 31 | 32 | 33 | 34 | 35 | 36 | 37 | 38 |
|---|---|---|---|---|---|---|---|---|---|---|---|---|---|---|
| Category: | | | | | | | | | | | | | | |
| Correct Answer: | B | C | D | A | D | C | E | D | B | B | A | D | E | A |
| Your Response: | D | C | A | A | D | C | A | B | D | B | E | C | D | C |

### QUANTITATIVE ABILITY - SECTION 2

| Problem Number: | 1 | 2 | 3 | 4 | 5 | 6 | 7 | 8 | 9 | 10 | 11 | 12 | 13 | 14 | 15 | 16 | 17 | 18 | 19 | 20 | 21 | 22 | 23 | 24 |
|---|---|---|---|---|---|---|---|---|---|---|---|---|---|---|---|---|---|---|---|---|---|---|---|---|
| Category: | | | | | | | | | | | | | | | | | | | | | | | | |
| Correct Answer: | B | D | A | D | B | A | B | A | D | A | C | B | D | B | C | D | D | C | B | D | A | D | B | E |
| Your Response: | B | D | A | D | B | A | B | D | B | C | C | D | B | C | B | D | A | C | B | D | A | D | C | C |

| Problem Number: | 25 | 26 | 27 | 28 | 29 | 30 |
|---|---|---|---|---|---|---|
| Category: | | | | | | |
| Correct Answer: | B | C | A | C | E | E |
| Your Response: | A | C | B | D | D | E |

### QUANTITATIVE ABILITY - SECTION 4

| Problem Number: | 1 | 2 | 3 | 4 | 5 | 6 | 7 | 8 | 9 | 10 | 11 | 12 | 13 | 14 | 15 | 16 | 17 | 18 | 19 | 20 | 21 | 22 | 23 | 24 |
|---|---|---|---|---|---|---|---|---|---|---|---|---|---|---|---|---|---|---|---|---|---|---|---|---|
| Category: | | | | | | | | | | | | | | | | | | | | | | | | |
| Correct Answer: | A | C | B | A | C | B | B | D | A | B | C | D | A | D | C | E | C | A | E | B | C | B | D | A |
| Your Response: | B | C | B | A | C | B | D | D | C | B | C | A | D | D | C | C | A | B | E | C | B | D | D | E |

| Problem Number: | 25 | 26 | 27 | 28 | 29 | 30 |
|---|---|---|---|---|---|---|
| Category: | | | | | | |
| Correct Answer: | C | C | E | A | D | C |
| Your Response: | D | ? | B | C | A | B |

Finally, the student summary provides a category key that describes the subject-areas within the Verbal and Quantitative test sections of the GRE.

## Category Key

The Education Testing Service (ETS) has established categories within the math, analytical writing and verbal sections of the GRE. These categories are used to help you improve your scores on the GRE by identifying your strongest and weakest areas of study. Below is a brief description of those categories as set forth by ETS, taken directly from their publication, "The Official Guide GRE: Practicing to Take the General Test."

### Verbal Ability

**Analogies (AY) -**

Analogy Questions measure your:

- Knowledge of the meanings of words
- Ability to see a relationship in a pair of words
- Ability to recognize a similar or parallel relationship

**Sentence Completions (SC) -**

Sentence Completion Questions measure your:

- Knowledge of the meanings of words
- Ability to understand how the different parts of a sentence fit logically together

**Reading Comprehension (RC) -**

The purpose of the reading comprehension questions is to measure the ability to read with understanding, insight, and discrimination. There are six types of reading comprehension questions: (1) the main idea or primary purpose of the passage, (2) information explicitly stated in the passage, (3) information or ideas implied or suggested by the author, (4) possible application of the author's ideas to other situations, (5) the author's reasoning or persuasive techniques, and (6) the tone of the passage or the author's attitude as it is revealed in the language used.

**Antonyms (AT) -**

The purpose of the antonym questions is to measure not merely the strength of one's vocabulary, but also the ability to reason from a given concept to its opposite.

### Quantitative Ability

**Arithmetic (AR) -**

Applications involving simple addition, subtraction, multiplication and division, percent, data interpretation (including mean, median, and mode), odd and even numbers, prime numbers, and divisibility.

**Algebra (AL) -**

Applications involving negative numbers, substitution, simplifying algebraic expressions, simple factoring, linear equations, inequalities, simple quadratic equations, positive integer exponents, roots of numbers, and sequences.

**Geometry (GM) -**

Applications involving area and perimeter of a polygon; area and circumference of a circle; volume of a box, cube, and cylinder; Pythagorean Theorem and special properties of isosceles, equilateral and right triangles; 30°-60°-90° and 45°-45°-90° triangles; properties of parallel and perpendicular lines; simple coordinate geometry; and slope, similarity, and geometric visualization.

**Quantitative Comparison (QC) -**

The quantitative comparison questions test the ability to reason quickly and accurately about the relative sizes of two quantities or to perceive that not enough information is provided to make such a decision.

**Other (OT) -**

Applications involving logical reasoning, newly defined symbols that are based on commonly used operation, probability, and counting.

# TIME MANAGEMENT

## INTRODUCTION

Graduate students live hectic and exciting lives. In order to succeed in graduate school, you must learn how to manage your time, which really means that you must learn how to manage yourself by becoming a proactive student. To be proactive means to act assertively and decisively in order to prepare for upcoming events or situations. To be proactive also means to make wise decisions about how to plan the use of your time. Therefore, a proactive student is a well-prepared student.

Work, family, school, and other obligations take up a great deal of time. Therefore, learning to manage your time and juggle multiple responsibilities is essential for succeeding in graduate school. This section focuses on how to better manage your time by using such powerful tools as the *PLAN* method and pyramid scheduling.

## SCHEDULING FOR SUCCESS—HAVE A PLAN

The *PLAN* method presents four elements for maximizing your time:

> *PRIORITIZE* tasks according to their long-term benefit.
> *LIST* those tasks according to their priority.
> *ARRANGE* those tasks on a schedule.
> *NEGOTIATE* your schedule if those tasks become overwhelming.

### P...PRIORITIZE

Though involvement in many activities is important, it is necessary to determine which of these activities are the most important. Students who *prioritize* their tasks arrange them in an optimum order that is based on level of importance: more important tasks take precedence over less important tasks. So, in order to prioritize, you need to identify activities that will benefit you most in the long run.

Different students have different priorities. While most graduate students do not study during all of their free time, successful students generally prioritize academics over other activities. These students devote a majority of their free time to studying so that they can reinforce what they have already learned in class. In order to effectively prioritize your tasks, you must first identify your own long-term goals. With a better understanding of your goals for the future, you can more effectively prioritize your activities in the present.

Here are some questions that you should ask yourself in order to better determine your long-term goals:

- What clubs or social service organizations would I like to join?
- What type of impact would I like to have on my community?
- What special accomplishments do I want to achieve?
- What types of positive things do I want people to say about me?
- Whom do I want to impress? How will I impress them?
- What will make me a happy and fulfilled person?
- In what additional ways can I prepare for the career I would like to pursue?

### L...LIST

Every week, make a *list* of the tasks that you want to accomplish, placing the most important tasks at the top of your list.

### A...ARRANGE

Each day, *arrange* all of your tasks on a daily schedule, prioritizing the most important tasks over tasks that are less important. The key to prioritization is to maintain a clear understanding of what is most important so that you can remain focused on the most significant tasks at hand.

### N...NEGOTIATE

In any given term, there are weeks that are especially busy and may prove to be overwhelming. Typically, chapter tests and final exams require considerable amounts of study time. The following are seven tips on how to better *negotiate* the details of your schedule in accordance with the potential added pressures of exam time.

1. Anticipate weeks with heavy workloads and note them on your schedule.
2. Meet with your professors to discuss any problems that you might have with completing class work.
3. Form a study group to help prepare for tests.
4. Get plenty of rest; you will need rest and energy during stressful times.
5. Do not wait until the last week of the term to complete major projects; procrastination is unproductive.
6. Attempt to get time off from your job during the most hectic times.
7. Say no to distractions such as watching television and reading books or magazines.

## MANAGE YOUR TIME BY USING PYRAMID SCHEDULING

A pyramid consists of a large base, or foundation, which transitions into progressively narrower levels until finally reaching a small point at the top. In a similar fashion, pyramid scheduling begins with organizing your long-term projects and then moves on to your more immediate tasks until finally reaching your daily schedule. Purchase an annual calendar or planner so that you can schedule months, weeks, and days, approaching your scheduling process in the following manner:

### SCHEDULE THE ENTIRE TERM

During the first week of each term, organize all of your major assignments and responsibilities on the calendar. After you have received a syllabus for each of your classes, reference all important dates that coincide with any of the following:

- Class assignments, such as reading selections and projects
- Tests and exams
- Quizzes
- Holidays and vacations
- Personal obligations, such as birthdays and family gatherings
- Job commitments
- Extracurricular activities

### SCHEDULE EACH MONTH

Two days before the beginning of each month, review your monthly schedule for all assignments, tests, and quizzes. Then, reference any important dates for monthly activities that do not already appear on your calendar, such as:

- Additional assignments
- Sporting events or concerts that you plan to attend
- Personal commitments, such as work schedule and social engagements

- Study blocks for major projects, exams, tests, or quizzes

### SCHEDULE EACH WEEK

On Sunday night of each week, review your weekly schedule for all assignments, tests, and quizzes. Look for any personal appointments or special commitments that may be scheduled for the upcoming week. Then, on a weekly calendar, outline a schedule for that upcoming week so that you will have sufficient time for studying and completing assignments. Each day of the weekly schedule should be divided up into mornings, afternoons, and evenings so that you can reference the most important times for certain daily activities, such as:

- Classes
- Class assignments, such as reading selections and projects
- Tests and exams
- Quizzes
- Holidays and vacation days
- Personal commitments, such as work schedule and social engagements
- Employment commitments
- Extracurricular activities
- Study sessions

### SCHEDULE EACH DAY

On the night before each school day, create a schedule that outlines important times for the following daily activities:

- Class schedule
- Study times
- Job schedule
- Free time
- Additional appointments, tasks, or responsibilities

### FINALLY, REMEMBER TO STICK TO YOUR SCHEDULE

Unless emergencies arise, stick to your schedule. Do not change your schedule unless it is absolutely necessary to accommodate and prioritize new activities. Remember that time management is really about self-management. So, remain disciplined so that you can follow your schedule without falling prey to distractions.

## CONCLUSION

Successful students are able to self-manage themselves by learning and using valuable time management tools. If you start to use these tools now, you can be successful in graduate school and beyond. Always remember to schedule your work and work your schedule!

# STUDY PLAN FOR THE COURSE

In order to be successful, it is important to have a plan. This rule applies in all areas of life, including the Cambridge GRE Review Course! The calendars below are examples of how you might develop a plan of action for success in the course. Remember that it is not necessary to do everything all at once. Instead, picking a few things to focus on each week helps to better manage your time.

## SAMPLE STUDY PLANNER

| Sunday | Monday | Tuesday | Wednesday | Thursday | Friday | Saturday |
|--------|--------|---------|-----------|----------|--------|----------|
| — | Verbal Reasoning Skills Review, Exercises 1–4 | Analogies Core Lesson, Review, and Timed-Practice Quizzes | Word Parts List and Vocabulary List | Antonyms Core Lesson, Review, and Timed-Practice Quizzes | Verbal Reasoning Skills Review, Exercises 5–6 | — |
| — | Sentence Completions Core Lesson, Review, and Timed-Practice Quizzes | Verbal Reasoning Skills Review, Exercises 7–12 | Reading Comprehension Core Lesson, Review, and Timed-Practice Quizzes | Quantitative Reasoning Skills Review, Exercises 9–12 | Discrete Quantitative Core Lesson | — |
| — | Discrete Quantitative Review and Timed-Practice Quizzes | Quantitative Comparisons Core Lesson | Quantitative Comparisons Review and Timed-Practice Quizzes | Graphs Summary (Quantitative Reasoning Express Skills Review) | Graphs Core Lesson and Review | — |
| — | Analytical Writing Skills Review, Exercises 1–5 | Analytical Writing Skills Review, Exercises 6–8 | Writing Core Lesson and Timed-Practice Quizzes | Practice Test I | Review Practice Test I | — |

| Sunday | Monday | Tuesday | Wednesday | Thursday | Friday | Saturday |
|--------|--------|---------|-----------|----------|--------|----------|
| — | Review Practice Test I (Cont'd.) | Practice Test II | Review Practice Test II | Review Practice Test II (Cont'd.) | Practice Test III | — |
| — | Review Practice Test III | Review Practice Test III (Cont'd.) | Practice Test IV | Review Practice Test IV | Review Practice Test IV (Cont'd.) | — |
| — | — | — | — | — | — | — |
| — | — | — | — | — | — | Test Day |

On the following page are empty calendars. Make copies of this page and fill in the assignments for each day until the actual test. Use the tips from the sample calendar on the previous page to create your own plan. Your teacher can help you set goals for each subject-area.

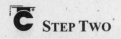 

| Sunday | Monday | Tuesday | Wednesday | Thursday | Friday | Saturday |
|--------|--------|---------|-----------|----------|--------|----------|
|        |        |         |           |          |        |          |
|        |        |         |           |          |        |          |
|        |        |         |           |          |        |          |
|        |        |         |           |          |        |          |

| Sunday | Monday | Tuesday | Wednesday | Thursday | Friday | Saturday |
|--------|--------|---------|-----------|----------|--------|----------|
|        |        |         |           |          |        |          |
|        |        |         |           |          |        |          |
|        |        |         |           |          |        |          |
|        |        |         |           |          |        |          |

| Sunday | Monday | Tuesday | Wednesday | Thursday | Friday | Saturday |
|--------|--------|---------|-----------|----------|--------|----------|
|        |        |         |           |          |        |          |
|        |        |         |           |          |        |          |
|        |        |         |           |          |        |          |
|        |        |         |           |          |        |          |

# Step Three: Targeted Skills, Concepts, and Strategies

## Step Three Highlights:

Practice skills that are foundational to success on the GRE.

Review test mechanics that are specific to each subject-area.

Discover the powerful alternative test-taking strategies that will give you an edge when taking the test.

Measure progress on tested concepts with timed-practice quizzes.

Learn how to overcome test anxiety.

## Step Three Overview:

In this textbook, Step Three contains skills review exercises and test mechanics summaries that are representative of each of the three tested areas, as well as lesson items that look like those found on the real GRE. The skills review items will help you build foundational skills. When compared to the test, the lesson items have the same content, represent similar difficulty levels, and are solved by using the same problem-solving and alternative test-taking strategies. You will go over these items alongside similar official items with your instructor in class. Use the Strategy Summary Sheets located throughout this step to record the alternative test-taking strategies taught during the lessons.

# Verbal Reasoning Skills Review

# CAMBRIDGE TESTPREP™

## VERBAL REASONING SKILLS REVIEW OUTLINE

## XVIII.  Exercise 12—Item-Type Coding (Items #1–22, p. 94)

# Vocabulary

Students often believe that if they do not know what a certain word means, then they will not be able to correctly answer an item that requires them to understand the meaning of that word. The first section of the Verbal Reasoning Skills Review contains lesson material with six corresponding exercises that will help you focus on recognizing word parts, becoming more familiar with challenging vocabulary words, and using context clues to determine what difficult words mean. In addition to understanding context, this section emphasizes the importance of understanding the logical structure of a sentence and applying that understanding to anticipate appropriate words in succeeding on Analogies, Antonyms, and Sentence Completions items, as well as certain Reading Comprehension items that test the implied meaning of words. Although identifying Analogies item-types (Exercise 2) is a strategy that is discussed later in the course (Verbal Reasoning Concepts and Strategies, Analogies Core Lesson), knowing how to recognize an item stem as fitting into a certain pattern is a fundamental skill that applies to all subjects and therefore should be reinforced in the Skills Review.

## Diagnostic Sentences

For Analogies items, the starting point is to understand the relationship between the two words that are provided in the item stem. For example, an Analogies item stem might be worded as follows:

LINGUISTICS : LANGUAGE

This item stem literally reads "Linguistics is to language." The idea behind an Analogies item is that there is a necessary relationship between the two words in its stem. Constructing a "diagnostic sentence" helps provide an understanding of such a relationship. In the case of the item stem LINGUISTICS : LANGUAGE, a diagnostic sentence might be worded as follows:

Linguistics is the study of language.

Alternatively, the diagnostic sentence might read:

Language is the defining characteristic, or feature, of linguistics.

What is most important in these diagnostic sentences are the phrases "study of" and "defining characteristic," which indicate the analogy relationship that is being tested. Once the relationship has been established, it can then be applied to each of the five answer choices to determine which one most closely shares its quality. Exercise 1 will help you become familiar with the relationships between ideas that are necessary in solving Analogies items.

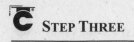 

EXERCISE 1

# Creating Diagnostic Sentences

**DIRECTIONS:** Exactly 28 of the following pairs of words are possible Analogies item stems because a necessary relationship can be drawn between the two words. For each of these 28 items, construct a "diagnostic sentence" that may help provide an understanding of the type of analogy that is being tested. For the remaining 28 items, simply place a large "X" in the space provided. Answers are on page 885.

1. CRUSADER : CAUSE

_____
_____

2. CONFIDENCE : POSSESSION

_____
_____

3. DEBUT : BEGINNING

_____
_____

4. IMPULSE : DELIBERATION

_____
_____

5. PASSIVE : LONGING

_____
_____

6. DISASTER : PREDICTION

_____
_____

7. NOMAD : MOUNTAINS

_____
_____

8. LANGUISH : PROCUREMENT

_____
_____

9. IMITATION : ORIGINALITY

_____
_____

10. VOLATILE : VAPORIZATION

_____
_____

11. DAIS : SPEAKER

_____
_____

12. PHOTOSYNTHESIS : TROPICS

_____
_____

13. EPAULET : SHOULDER

_____
_____

14. APPROBATION : COMPLIMENT

_____
_____

15. INTREPID : FEAR

_____
_____

16. OPULENCE : WEALTH

_____
_____

17. IMPERATIVE : ILL-FATED

_____
_____

18. MALADROIT : SKILL

_____
_____

19. LEVITY : CONFUSION

_____
_____

20. MOTLEY : VARIETY

_____
_____

21. TACIT : SOLICITUDE

_____
_____

22. REVOLUTION : MONARCH

_____
_____

23. ANNOYANCE : DISSOLUTION

_____
_____

24. EQUIVOCATE : CLARITY

_____
_____

25. ODIOUS : REPULSION

_____
_____

26. FUTURE : SOOTHSAYER

_____
_____

27. HAPLESS : MERCENARY

_____
_____

28. PAINFUL : EXCRUCIATING

_____
_____

29. GARGOYLE : PHLEGMATIC

_____
_____

30. SINECURE : EMPLOYMENT

_____
_____

31. OAR : BOAT

_____
_____

32. KNIFE : TRUCK

_____
_____

33. HORSE : TREE

_____
_____

34. CASINO : GAMBLING

_____
_____

35. SYRUP : APPLES

_____
_____

36. ROOF : CURTAIN

_____
_____

37. LISP : SPEECH

_____
_____

38. JOG : SPRINT

_____
_____

39. PAINT : DRAWER

_____
_____

40. ROCK : QUARRY

_____
_____

41. SCRIBBLE : WRITE

_____
_____

42. BLINK : LISTEN

_____
_____

43. UNICORN : CATASTROPHE

_____
_____

44. PASTEL : COLOR

_____
_____

45. ROGUE : MARKET

_____
_____

46. TARGET : WOUND

_____
_____

47. KEYSTONE : ARCH

_____
_____

48. IMPOSTER : CHEAPSKATE

_____
_____

49. BRAZEN : TRUSTWORTHY

_____
_____

50. RESTIVE : AGREEMENT

_____

_____

51. ARROW : QUIVER

_____

_____

52. MELT : LIQUID

_____

_____

53. CHAOS : ORDER

_____

_____

54. PLATEAU : RIVER

_____

_____

55. CREDENTIALS : COMMERCE

_____

_____

56. ADMIRATION : COMPETITOR

_____

_____

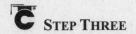 

## Analogy Relationships

For Analogies items, you must not only read the item correctly, but you must also correctly identify the item-type. Every Analogies item will be from one of ten basic types. Some of these types are more common than others. You can avoid memorizing information that is not needed to answer an item by focusing only on information that is needed to identify the analogy relationship that is being tested by that specific item-type. Remember that many more questions could be asked on any given passage than are actually asked. If you do not identify the correct item-type, then there is a good chance that you will not use the appropriate strategy for finding the correct answer. You must therefore know the characteristics of the correct answer that are associated with each item-type.

---

### TEN TYPES OF ANALOGIES ITEMS

**Defining Characteristic (DC)** – X is a defining characteristic of Y.

**Lack of Defining Characteristic (LO)** – Lack of X is a defining characteristic of Y.

**Type Of (TO)** – X is a type of Y.

**Part Of (PO)** – X is a part of Y.

**Place For (PF)** – X is a place for Y.

**Degree (D)** – X is a more (or less) extreme form of Y.

**Tools (T)** – X is a tool used by Y, or X is a tool used to do Y.

**Sign Of (SO)** – X is a sign of Y.

**Sequence (S)** – X is the cause (or result) of Y.

**Spurious Form (SF)** – X is a spurious form of Y.

---

Exercise 2 will help you to immediately recognize all ten item-types and therefore the analogy relationships that are being tested based on the wording of the item stem. In Exercise 3, you will then apply this understanding in order to complete parallel relationships as they would appear in correctly constructed Analogies items.

# Understanding Analogy Relationships

**DIRECTIONS:** For each of the Analogies item stems, determine the item-type and construct a diagnostic sentence for each of the pairs of words. Possible item-types are listed in the box on the previous page. Use the abbreviations listed in that box. Answers are on page 887.

1. CONDEMNED : EXECUTED

   _____

   _____

2. INVENTION : ORIGINALITY

   _____

   _____

3. ALIEN : CITIZENSHIP

   _____

   _____

4. FALLACIOUS : ERROR

   _____

   _____

5. MORTIFICATION : EMBARRASSMENT

   _____

   _____

6. INEFFABLE : EXPRESS

   _____

   _____

7. EPHEMERAL : PERISH

   _____

   _____

8. ARACHNID : TARANTULA

   _____

   _____

9. PROCRASTINATION : HASTE

   _____

   _____

10. PROSELYTIZE : CONVERSION

    _____

    _____

11. PARIAH : SCORN

    _____

    _____

12. DELIRIUM : SENSE

    _____

    _____

13. PROTAGONIST : CHARACTER

    _____

    _____

14. NEGLIGENCE : CARE

_____
_____

15. RECOVERY : RELAPSE

_____
_____

16. IDLE : CARE

_____
_____

17. GARRULOUS : TALK

_____
_____

18. DEFAULT : FORECLOSURE

_____
_____

19. ENTHUSIASM : MANIA

_____
_____

20. SOOTHSAYER : PROPHECY

_____
_____

21. COMA : CONSCIOUSNESS

_____
_____

22. PUNDIT : KNOWLEDGE

_____
_____

23. PHILANTHROPIST : BENEVOLENCE

_____
_____

24. AUSTERITY : ORNAMENTATION

_____
_____

25. EVICTION : RESIDENCE

_____
_____

26. JUDGE : COURTROOM

_____
_____

27. STAR : GALAXY

_____
_____

28. NOTE : SCALE

_____
_____

29. SCULPTOR : CHISEL

_____
_____

30. SNIFTER : BRANDY

_____
_____

31. OBEDIENCE : OBSEQUIOUSNESS

_____
_____

32. GRIMACE : PAIN

_____

_____

33. VACCINATION : IMMUNITY

_____

_____

34. BUFFER : SHOCK

_____

_____

35. WORKDAY : LUNCH

_____

_____

36. SIP : GUZZLE

_____

_____

37. LUMBERJACK : AX

_____

_____

38. TIFF : BATTLE

_____

_____

39. MAST : SHIP

_____

_____

40. CITADEL : ATTACK

_____

_____

41. APPETIZER : DESSERT

_____

_____

42. JOY : EMOTION

_____

_____

43. CELLO : BOW

_____

_____

44. SEMINARY : THEOLOGIAN

_____

_____

45. SAND : SMOOTHNESS

_____

_____

46. CROUCH : SPRING

_____

_____

47. EROSION : GULLY

_____

_____

48. COLANDER : CHEF

_____

_____

49. TERMITE : INSECT

_____

_____

# Creating Parallel Relationships

**DIRECTIONS:** Find a word that, when substituted for the underlined word, will complete the analogy between the two pairs of words. Possible answers are on page 889.

1. SWAGGER : WALK :: BRAG : <u>LISTEN</u>

   _____
   _____

2. RULER : CENTIMETER :: <u>ALARM</u> : MINUTE

   _____
   _____

3. LAWYER : CLIENT :: DOCTOR : <u>CURE</u>

   _____
   _____

4. RACQUET : TENNIS :: <u>GLOVE</u> : BASEBALL

   _____
   _____

5. DRIZZLE : CLOUDBURST :: <u>CANDLE</u> : CONFLAGRATION

   _____
   _____

6. SHED : HAIR :: MOLT : <u>BIRD</u>

   _____
   _____

7. CONDOLENCE : LOSS :: CONGRATULATION : <u>FAME</u>

   _____
   _____

8. ARID : MOISTURE :: BANKRUPT : <u>PLANS</u>

   _____
   _____

9. BEAR : HIBERNATE :: BIRD : <u>FLY</u>

   _____
   _____

10. INN : TRAVELER :: DORM : <u>COLLEGE</u>

    _____
    _____

11. SUPERSTITIOUS : SECRECY :: ALACRITY : <u>SATISFACTION</u>

    _____
    _____

12. CUPIDITY : DESIRE :: MISERLINESS : <u>GENEROSITY</u>

    _____
    _____

13. IRREVERENT : BLASPHEMOUS :: DISAPPROVING : <u>CONSISTENT</u>

    _____
    _____

14. GUEST : INVITATION :: <u>JURY</u> : SUBPOENA

_____

_____

15. BOLD : BRAZEN :: SHY : <u>HOPEFUL</u>

_____

_____

16. ZOOLOGY : ANIMAL :: BOTANY : <u>ATOM</u>

_____

_____

17. TRIAL : ATTORNEY :: SURGERY : <u>CLERK</u>

_____

_____

18. SCROLL : BOOK :: PARCHMENT : <u>LIBRARY</u>

_____

_____

19. GALOSHES : SHOES :: <u>LAUNDRY</u> : SUIT

_____

_____

20. BRANCH : TREE :: <u>FACE</u> : HUMAN

_____

_____

21. ANCIENT : AGE :: HEAVY : <u>SKILL</u>

_____

_____

22. TERMITE : WOOD :: ANT : WOOL

_____

_____

23. TEPID : SCALDING :: COOL : <u>INTERESTED</u>

_____

_____

24. LUSH : VEGETATION :: CROWDED : <u>TRAFFIC</u>

_____

_____

25. CISTERN : WATER :: <u>LEAF</u> : TEA

_____

_____

26. LAWN : GRASS :: PELT : <u>SCALP</u>

_____

_____

27. SCORE : SYMPHONEY :: <u>DEVELOPER</u> : BUILDING

_____

_____

28. PAINTING : MUSEUM :: <u>HUNTER</u> : MENAGERIE

_____

_____

29. MALADROIT : SKILL :: TENUOUS : <u>QUALITY</u>

_____

_____

30. INTRODUCTION : CONCLUSION :: <u>SALUTATION</u> : GREETING

_____

_____

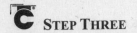
## Word Parts List

Review the following word parts lists to familiarize yourself with the meanings of certain prefixes, suffixes, and roots.

| Prefix | Meaning | Examples |
| --- | --- | --- |
| a | in, on, of, to | abed—in bed |
| a, ab, abs | from, away | abrade—wear off |
| | | absent—away, not present |
| ad, ac, af, ag, al, an | to, toward | accost—approach and speak to |
| ap, ar, as, at | | adjunct—something added to |
| | | aggregate—bring together |
| ambi, amphi | around, both | ambidextrous—using both hands equally |
| | | amphibious—living both in water and on land |
| ana | up, again, anew, throughout | analyze—loosen up, break up into parts |
| | | anagram—word spelled from letters of other word |
| ante | before | antediluvian—before the Flood |
| anti | against | anti-war—against war |
| arch | first, chief | archetype—first model |
| auto | self | automobile—self-moving vehicle |
| circum | around | circumnavigate—sail around |
| contra, contro, counter | against | contradict—speak against |
| | | counterclockwise—against the clock |
| de | away from, down, opposite of | detract—draw away from |
| di | twice, double | dichromatic—having two colors |
| dia | across, through | diameter—measurement across |
| dis, di | not, away from | dislike—to not like |
| | | digress—turn away from the subject |
| equi | equal | equivalent—of equal value |
| ex, e, ef | from, out | expatriate—one living outside native country |
| | | emit—send out |
| hyper | too much, over | hyperactive—overly active |
| hypo | too little, under | hypothermia—having too little body heat |
| in, il, ig, im, ir | not | innocent—not guilty |
| | | ignorant—not knowing |
| | | irresponsible—not responsible |
| in, il, im, ir | on, into, in | impose—place on |
| | | invade—go into |
| mis | badly, wrongly | misunderstand—understand incorrectly |
| mis, miso | hatred | misogyny—hatred of women |
| mono | single, one | monorail—train that runs on a single rail |
| non | not | nonentity—a nobody |
| omni | all | omnipresent—present in all places |
| pan | all | panorama—a complete view |
| poly | many | polygonal—many-sided |
| post | after | postmortem—after death |
| pre | before, earlier than | prejudice—judgment in advance |
| pro | in favor of, forward, in front of | proceed—go forward |
| | | pro-war—in favor of war |
| retro | backward | retrospective—looking backward |
| se | apart, away | seclude—keep away |
| semi | half | semiconscious—half conscious |

| super | above, greater | superfluous—beyond what is needed |
| syn, sym, syl, sys | with, at the same time | synthesis—a putting together |
| | | sympathy—a feeling with |
| tele | far | television—machine for seeing far |
| trans | across | transport—carry across a distance |
| un | not | uninformed—not informed |
| vice | acting for, next in rank to | vice president—second in command |

| *Suffix* | *Meaning* | *Examples* |
| --- | --- | --- |
| able, ble | able, capable | acceptable—able to be accepted |
| acious, cious | characterized by, having the quality of | spacious—having the quality of space |
| age | sum, total | mileage—total number of miles |
| al | of, like, suitable for | theatrical—suitable for theater |
| ance, ancy | act or state of | disturbance—act of disturbing |
| ary, ar | having the nature of, concerning | military—relating to soldiers |
| | | polar—relating to a pole |
| er, or | one who, that which | doer—one who does |
| | | conductor—that which conducts |
| escent | becoming | obsolescent—becoming obsolete |
| ic, ac | of, like | demonic—of or like a demon |
| ion | act or condition of | operation—act of operating |
| ious | having, characterized by | anxious—characterized by anxiety |
| ish | like, somewhat | foolish—like a fool |
| ism | belief or practice of | racism—belief in racial superiority |
| ist | one who does, makes, or is concerned with | scientist—one concerned with science |
| ity, ty, y | character or state of being | amity—friendship |
| | | jealousy—state of being jealous |
| ive | of, relating to, tending to | destructive—tending to destroy |
| logy | speech, study of | geology—study of the earth |
| ment | act or state of | abandonment—act of abandoning |
| ory | having the quality of | compensatory—quality of compensation |
| | a place or thing for | lavatory—place for washing |
| some | full of, like | frolicsome—playful |

| *Root* | *Meaning* | *Examples* |
| --- | --- | --- |
| acr | bitter | acrid, acrimony |
| act, ag | do, act, drive | action, react, agitate, agent |
| acu | sharp, keen | acute, acumen |
| agog | leader | pedagogue, demagogic |
| agr | field | agronomy, agriculture |
| ali | other | alias, alienate, inalienable |
| alt | high | altitude, contralto |
| alter, altr | other, change | alternative, altercation, altruism |
| am, amic | love, friend | amorous, amiable |
| anim | mind, life, spirit | animism, animate, animosity |
| annu, enni | year | annual, superannuated, biennial |
| anthrop | man | anthropoid, misanthropy |
| apt, ept | fit | apt, adapt, ineptitude |
| aqu | water | aquatic, aquamarine |
| arbit | arm, weapon | army, armature, disarm |
| art | skill, a fitting together | artisan, artifact, articulate |
| aster, astr | star | asteroid, disaster, astral |
| aud, audit, aur | hear | auditorium, audition, auricle |

| | | |
|---|---|---|
| aur | gold | aureate, aureomycin |
| aut | self | autism, autograph |
| bell | war | anti-bellum, belligerent |
| brev | short | brevity, abbreviation, abbreviate |
| cad, cas, cid | fall | cadence, casualty, accident |
| cand | white, shining | candid, candle, incandescent |
| cant, chant | sing, charm | cantor, recant, enchant |
| capit | head | capital, decapitate, recapitulate |
| cede, ceed, cess | go, yield | secede, exceed, process, intercession |
| cent | hundred | century, percentage, centimeter |
| cern, cert | perceive, make certain, decide | concern, certificate, certain |
| chrom | color | monochrome, chromatic |
| chron | time | chronometer, anachronism |
| cide, cis | cut, kill | genocide, incision, suicide |
| cit | summon, impel | cite, excite, incitement |
| civ | citizen | uncivil, civilization |
| clam, claim | shout | clamorous, proclaim, claimant |
| clar | clear | clarity, clarion, declare |
| clin | slope, lean | inclination, recline |
| clud, clus, clos | close, shut | seclude, recluse, closet |
| cogn | know | recognize, incognito |
| col, cul | prepare | colony, cultivate, agriculture |
| corp | body | incorporate, corpse |
| cosm | order, world | cosmetic, cosmos, cosmopolitan |
| crac, crat | power, rule | democrat, theocracy |
| cre, cresc, cret | grow | increase, crescent, accretion |
| cred | trust, believe | credit, incredible |
| crux, cruc | cross | crux, crucial, crucifix |
| crypt | hidden | cryptic, cryptography |
| cur, curr, curs | run, course | occur, current, incursion |
| cura | care | curator, accurate |
| dem | people | demographic, demagogue |
| dent | tooth | dental, indentation |
| derm | skin | dermatitis, pachyderm |
| di, dia | day | diary, quotidian |
| dic, dict | say, speak | indicative, edict, dictation |
| dign | worthy | dignified, dignitary |
| doc, doct | teach, prove | indoctrinate, docile, doctor |
| domin | rule | predominate, domineer, dominion |
| dorm | sleep | dormitory, dormant |
| du | two | duo, duplicity, dual |
| duc, duct | lead | educate, abduct, ductile |
| dyn | force, power | dynamo, dynamite |
| equ | equal | equation, equitable |
| erg, urg | work, power | energetic, metallurgy, demiurge |
| ev | time, age | coeval, longevity |
| fac, fact, fect, fic | do, make | facility, factual, perfect, artifice |
| fer | bear, carry | prefer, refer, conifer, fertility |
| ferv | boil | fervid, effervesce |
| fin | end, limit | finite, confine |
| firm | strong | reaffirm, infirmity |
| flect, flex | bend | reflex, inflection |
| flor | blossom | florescent, floral |
| flu, fluct, flux | flow | fluid, fluctuation, influx |
| form | shape | formative, reform, formation |

| | | |
|---|---|---|
| fort | strong | effort, fortitude |
| frag, fract | break | fragility, infraction |
| fug | flee | refuge, fugitive |
| gam | marry | exogamy, polygamous |
| ge, geo | earth | geology, geode, perigee |
| gen | birth, kind, race | engender, general, generation |
| gest | carry, bear | gestation, ingest, digest |
| gon | angle | hexagonal, trigonometry |
| gram, graph | writing | cryptogram, telegraph |
| grat | pleasing, agreeable | congratulate |
| grav | weight, heavy | grave (situation), gravity |
| greg | flock, crowd | gregarious, segregate |
| habit, hibit | have, hold | habitation, inhibit, habitual |
| her, hes | stick, cling | adherent, cohesive |
| hydr | water | dehydration, hydrofoil |
| iatr | heal, cure | pediatrics, psychiatry |
| it | journey, go | itinerary, exit |
| ject | throw | reject, subjective, projection |
| jud | judge | judicial, adjudicate |
| jur | swear | perjure, jurisprudence |
| labor | work | laborious, belabor |
| leg | law | legal, illegitimate |
| lev | light, rise | levity, alleviate |
| liber | free | liberal, libertine |
| liter | letter | literate, alliterative |
| lith | rock, stone | Neolithic, lithograph |
| loc | place | locale, locus, allocate |
| log | word, study | logic, biology, dialogue |
| loqu, locut | talk, speech | colloquial, loquacious, interlocutor |
| luc, lum | light | translucent, pellucid, illumine |
| lud, lus | play | allusion, ludicrous, interlude |
| magn | large, great | magnificent, magnitude |
| mal | bad, ill | malodorous, malady |
| man, manu | hand | manifest, manicure, manuscript |
| mar | sea | maritime, submarine |
| mater, matr | mother | matrilocal, maternal |
| ment | mind | demented, mental |
| merg, mers | plunge, dip | emerge, submersion |
| meter, metr, mens | measure | chronometer, metronome, geometry |
| micr | small | microfilm, micron |
| min | little | minimum, minute |
| mit, miss | send | remit, admission, missive |
| mon, monit | warn | admonish, monument, monitor |
| mor | custom | mores, immoral |
| mor, mort | death | mortify, mortician |
| morph | shape | amorphous, anthropomorphic |
| mov, mob, mot | move | removal, automobile, motility |
| mut | change | mutable, transmute, mutation |
| necr | dead, die | necropolis, necrosis |
| neg | deny | renege, negative |
| nom, noun, nown, | name, order, rule | anonymous, antinomy, misnomer |
| nam, nym, nomen, nomin | name | nomenclature, cognomen, nominate |
| nomy | law, rule | astronomy, antinomy |
| nov | new | novice, innovation |
| ocul | eye | binocular, oculist |

| | | |
|---|---|---|
| onym | name | pseudonym, antonym |
| ora | speak, pray | oracle, oratory |
| orn | decorate | adorn, ornate |
| orth | straight, correct | orthodox, orthopedic |
| pan | all | panacea, pantheon |
| pater, patr | father | patriot, paternity |
| ped | child | pedagogue, pediatrics |
| ped, pod | foot | pedestrian, impede, tripod |
| pel, puls | drive, push | impel, propulsion |
| pend, pens | hang | pendulous, suspense |
| pet, peat | seek | petition, impetus, repeat |
| phil | love | philosopher, Anglophile |
| phob | fear | phobic, agoraphobia |
| phon | sound | phonograph, symphony |
| phor | bearing | semaphore, metaphor |
| phot | light | photograph, photoelectric |
| pon, pos | place, put | component, repose, postpone |
| port | carry | report, portable, deportation |
| pot | power | potency, potential |
| press | press | pressure, impression |
| prim, proto, prot | first | primal, proton, protagonist |
| psych | mind | psychic, metempsychosis |
| rid, ris | laugh | deride, risible, ridiculous |
| rog | ask | rogation, interrogate |
| rupt | break | erupt, interruption, rupture |
| sanct | holy | sacrosanct, sanctify, sanction |
| sci, scio | know | nescient, conscious, omniscience |
| scop | watch, view | horoscope, telescopic |
| scrib, script | write | scribble, proscribe, description |
| sed, sid, sess | sit, seat | sediment, sedate, session |
| seg, sect | cut | segment, section, intersect |
| sent, sens | feel, think | nonsense, sensitive, sentient |
| sol | alone | solitary, solo, desolate |
| solv, solu, solut | loosen | dissolve, soluble, absolution |
| somn | sleep | insomnia, somnolent |
| son | sound | sonorous, unison |
| soph | wise, wisdom | philosophy, sophisticated |
| spec, spic, spect | look | specimen, conspicuous, spectacle |
| spir | breathe | spirit, conspire, respiration |
| stab, stat | stand | unstable, status, station |
| stead | place | instead, steadfast |
| string, strict | bind | astringent, stricture, restrict |
| stru, struct | build | construe, structure, destructive |
| sum, sumpt | take | presume, consumer, assumption |
| tang, ting, tact, tig | touch | tangent, contingency, contact |
| tax, tac | arrange, arrangement | taxonomy, tactic |
| techn | skill, art | technique, technician |
| tele | far | teletype, telekinesis |
| tempor | time | temporize, extemporaneous |
| ten, tain, tent | hold | tenant, tenacity, retention |
| tend, tens, tent | stretch | contend, extensive, intent |
| tenu | thin | tenuous, attenuate |
| test | witness | attest, testify |
| the | god | polytheism, theologist |
| tom | cut | atomic, appendectomy |

| tort, tors | twist | tortuous, torsion, contort |
|---|---|---|
| tract | pull, draw | traction, attract, protract |
| trib | assign, pay | attribute, tribute, retribution |
| trud, trus | thrust | obtrude, intrusive |
| urb | city | urbane, suburb, urban |
| vac | empty | vacuous, evacuation |
| vad, vas | go | invade, evasive |
| val, vail | strength, worth | valid, avail, prevalent |
| ven, vent | come | advent, convene, prevention |
| ver | true | aver, veracity, verity |
| verb | word | verbose, adverb, verbatim |
| vert, vers | turn | revert, perversion, versatile |
| vest | dress | vestment |
| vid, vis | see | video, evidence, vision, revise |
| vinc, vict | conquer | evince, convict, victim |
| viv, vit | life | vivid, revive, vital |
| vo, voc, vok, vow | call | vociferous, provocative, equivocate |
| volv, volut | roll, turn | involve, convoluted, revolution |
| vulg | common | divulge, vulgarity |
| zo | animal | zoologist, Paleozoic |

# Understanding Word Parts

**DIRECTIONS:** For items #1–14, write down a few words in which the respective prefix is used. Three possible answers and their definitions are on page 889.

1. **a, an – lacking, not**

   _____

   _____

2. **bene, ben – good, well**

   _____

   _____

3. **co, col, con – with, together**

   _____

   _____

4. **dys – bad, poor**

   _____

   _____

5. **extra – outside, beyond**

   _____

   _____

6. **fore – in front of, previous**

   _____

7. **homo – same, like**

   _____

   _____

8. **intra, intro – within, inside**

   _____

   _____

9. **mal, male – bad, wrong, poor**

   _____

   _____

10. **neo – new**

    _____

    _____

11. **ob – over, against, toward**

    _____

    _____

12. **peri – around, near**

    _____

    _____

13. **re – back, again**

    _____

    _____

14. **sub, suf, sus – under, beneath**

_____

_____

**DIRECTIONS:** For items #15–28, write down a few words in which the respective suffix is used. Three possible answers and their definitions are on page 890.

15. **ant, ent – one who**

_____

16. **cy – act, state, or position of**

_____

17. **dom – state, rank, that which belongs to**

_____

_____

18. **ence – act, state, or quality of**

_____

_____

19. **fy – to make**

_____

_____

20. **il, ile – having to do with, like, suitable for**

_____

_____

21. **logue, loquy – speech or writing**

_____

_____

22. **mony – a resulting thing, condition, or state**

_____

_____

23. **ness – act or quality**

_____

_____

24. **ous, ose – full of, having**

_____

_____

25. **ship – skill, state of being**

_____

_____

26. **tude – state or quality of**

_____

_____

27. **ward – in the direction of**

_____

_____

28. **y – full of, like, somewhat**

_____

_____

**DIRECTIONS:** For items #29–48, write down a few words in which the respective root is used. Three possible answers and their definitions are on page 891.

29. **arch – chief**

_____

_____

30. **capt, ceipt, cept – take, seize, hold**

   _____

   _____

31. **dur – hard, lasting**

   _____

   _____

32. **err – wander**

   _____

   _____

33. **fid – belief, faith**

   _____

   _____

34. **grad, gress – step, go**

   _____

   _____

35. **heli – sun**

   _____

   _____

36. **iso – same, equal**

   _____

   _____

37. **jug, junct – join**

   _____

   _____

38. **leg, lig, lect – choose, gather, read**

   _____

   _____

39. **medi – middle**

   _____

   _____

40. **nasc, nat – born**

   _____

   _____

41. **oper – work**

   _____

   _____

42. **path, pat, pass – feel, suffer**

   _____

   _____

43. **quer, quir, quis – question, seek**

   _____

   _____

44. **reg, rig, rect – straight, rule**

   _____

   _____

45. **sequ, secut – follow**

   _____

   _____

46. **turb – agitate**

   _____

   _____

47. **umbr – shade**

   _____

   _____

48. **vol – wish**

_____

_____

# Vocabulary List

Review the following vocabulary list to familiarize yourself with the meanings of words of varied difficulty.

## —Difficulty Level 1—

**abacus**—a frame with beads or balls used for doing or teaching arithmetic

**abash**—disconcert; to make embarrassed and ill at ease

**abate**—to deduct; to make less

**abduction**—to carry off by force

**aberration**—a deviation from the normal or the typical

**abeyance**—temporary suspension

**abhor**—detest; to shrink from in disgust or hatred

**abhorrence**—loathing; detestation

**abide**—to stay; stand fast; remain

**abjure**—recant; to give up (opinions) publicly

**abominate**—loathe; to dislike very much

**abrade**—to scrape or rub off

**abridge**—shorten; to reduce in scope or extent

**abrogate**—cancel; call off

**abscond**—to go away hastily and secretly

**absolve**—acquit; to pronounce free from guilt or blame

**abstinence**—the act of voluntarily doing without pleasures

**abstruse**—hard to understand; deep; recondite

**absurdity**—nonsense

**abyss**—chasm; a deep fissure in the earth; bottomless gulf

**acclaim**—to greet with loud applause or approval

**accretion**—growth in size by addition or accumulation

**acerbic**—sharp, bitter, or harsh in temper and language

**acquisition**—something or someone acquired or added

**acrimony**—asperity; bitterness or harshness of temper, manner, or speech

**acute**—shrewd; keen or quick of mind

**adapt**—adjust; to make fit or suitable by changing

**adjunct**—connected or attached in a secondary or subordinate way

**adorn**—ornament; to put decorations on something

**adroit**—expert; clever; skillful in a physical or mental way

**adulterate**—not genuine; to make inferior or impure

**adversary**—opponent; a person who opposes or fights against another

**advocate**—a person who pleads another's cause

**aesthete**—a person who artificially cultivates artistic sensitivity or makes a cult of art and beauty

**aesthetic**—artistic; sensitive to art and beauty

**affable**—gentle and kindly

**affinity**—connection; close relationship

**afflict**—to cause pain or suffering to; distress very much

**affluent**—plentiful; abundant; flowing freely

**aggrandize**—to make seem greater

**alias**—assumed name

**allegiance**—loyalty or devotion

**alleviate**—to reduce or decrease; lighten or relieve

**allocate**—allot; to distribute in shares or according to a plan

**alloy**—the relative purity of gold or silver; fineness

**allude**—to refer in a casual or indirect way

**altercation**—an angry or heated argument

**amalgamate**—unite; combine

**ambiguous**—not clear; having two or more possible meanings

**ambivalence**—simultaneously conflicting feelings toward a person or thing

**amble**—to go easily and unhurriedly

**ameliorate**—improve; to make or become better

**amenable**—willing to follow advice or suggestion; answerable

**amiable**—good-natured; having a pleasant and friendly disposition

**amicable**—peaceable; showing good will

**amphibious**—can live both on land and in water

**anagram**—a word or phrase made from another by rearranging its letters

**analogy**—partial resemblance; similarity in some respects between things otherwise unlike

**anarchy**—the complete absence of government

**anathema**—a thing or person greatly detested

**anatomist**—a person who analyzes in great detail

**anecdote**—a short, entertaining account of some happening

**anhydrous**—without water

**animosity**—hostility; a feeling of strong dislike or hatred

**annexation**—attachment; adding on

**anomalous**—abnormal; deviating from the regular arrangement, general rule, or usual method

**anthology**—a collection of poems, stories, songs, or excerpts

**antidote**—a remedy to counteract a poison

**antigen**—a protein, toxin, or other substance to which the body reacts by producing antibodies

**antipathy**—strong or deep-rooted dislike

**anvil**—an iron or steel block on which metal objects are hammered into shape

**apathetic**—feeling little or no emotion; unmoved

**apocryphal**—not genuine; spurious; counterfeit; of doubtful authorship or authenticity

**appease**—to satisfy or relieve

**appraise**—to set a price for; decide the value of

**apprehension**—an anxious feeling of foreboding; dread

**apprentice**—novice; any learner or beginner

**arabesque**—a complex and elaborate decorative design

**arbitrary**—unreasonable; unregulated; despotic

**arbitrate**—to decide a dispute

**arboreal**—of or like a tree

**arcane**—hidden or secret

**ardor**—passion; emotional warmth

**arduous**—difficult to do; laborious; onerous

**arid**—dry and barren; lacking enough water for things to grow

**aromatic**—smelling sweet or spicy; fragrant or pungent

**arouse**—to awaken, as from sleep

**articulate**—expressing oneself easily and clearly

**artisan**—craftsman; a worker in a skilled trade

**aspiration**—strong desire or ambition

**assail**—assault; to attack physically and violently

**assay**—an examination or testing

**assert**—to state positively; declare; affirm

**assimilate**—to absorb and incorporate into one's thinking

**astound**—amaze; to bewilder with sudden surprise

**astute**—cunning; having or showing a clever or shrewd mind

**atrocity**—brutality; a very displeasing or tasteless thing

**auditor**—a hearer or listener

**augment**—enlarge; to make greater, as in size, quantity, or strength

**auspicious**—successful; favored by fortune

**austere**—forbidding; having a severe or stern look or manner

**avid**—eager and enthusiastic

**avow**—to declare openly or admit frankly

**ballad**—a romantic or sentimental song

**banal**—commonplace; dull or stale because of overuse

**bane**—ruin; death; deadly harm

**barrage**—a heavy, prolonged attack of words or blows

**barren**—empty; devoid

**barrio**—in Spanish-speaking countries, a district or suburb of a city

**bask**—to warm oneself pleasantly, as in the sunlight

**baste**—to sew with long, loose stitches

**beacon**—any light for warning or guiding

**bedazzle**—to dazzle thoroughly

**bedizen**—to dress or decorate in a cheap, showy way

**belated**—tardy; late or too late

**belligerent**—at war; showing a readiness to fight or quarrel

**beneficent**—doing good

**benevolence**—a kindly, charitable act or gift

**benign**—good-natured; kindly

**bequeath**—to hand down; pass on

**berate**—to scold or rebuke severely

**bewilder**—puzzle; to confuse hopelessly

**bias**—a mental leaning or inclination; partiality; bent

**bilge**—the bulge of a barrel or cask

**bilk**—to cheat or swindle; defraud

**blandishment**—a flattering act or remark meant to persuade

**blatant**—disagreeably loud or boisterous

**blithe**—carefree; showing a gay, cheerful disposition

**boisterous**—rowdy; noisy and unruly

**bolster**—a long, narrow cushion or pillow; to support

**boon**—blessing; welcome benefit

**boor**—a rude, awkward, or ill-mannered person

**bourgeois**—a person whose beliefs, attitudes, and practices are conventionally middle-class

**brazen**—like brass in color, quality, or hardness; impudent

**breach**—a breaking or being broken

**breadth**—width; lack of narrowness

**brevity**—the quality of being brief

**buttress**—a projecting structure built against a wall to support or reinforce it

**cadet**—a student at a military school; younger son or brother

**cadge**—to beg or get by begging

**cajole**—to coax with flattery and insincere talk

**calk**—a part of a horseshoe that projects downward to prevent slipping

**callous**—unfeeling; lacking pity or mercy

**camaraderie**—loyal, warm, and friendly feeling among comrades

**candid**—honest or frank

**capacious**—roomy; spacious

**caprice**—whim; a sudden, impulsive change

**capricious**—erratic; flighty; tending to change abruptly

**caption**—a heading or title, as of an article

**carping**—tending to find fault

**cartographer**—a person whose work is making maps or charts

**castigate**—to punish or rebuke severely

**catalyst**—a person or thing acting as the stimulus in bringing about or hastening a result

**catapult**—a slingshot or type of launcher

**catastrophe**—any great and sudden disaster or misfortune

**caustic**—corrosive; that which can destroy tissue by chemical action

**cavern**—a cave

**cerebral**—intellectual; appealing to the intellect rather than the emotions

**charlatan**—a person who pretends to have expert knowledge or skill

**chary**—careful; cautious

**chasten**—to punish; to refine; to make purer in style

**chide**—to scold

**chivalrous**—gallant; courteous; honorable

**circuitous**—roundabout; indirect; devious

**circumlocution**—an indirect way of expressing something

**circumspect**—cautious; careful

**circumvent**—entrap; to surround or encircle with evils

**citizenry**—all citizens as a group

**clairvoyant**—having the power to perceive that which is outside of the human senses

**clamor**—a loud outcry; uproar

**clamorous**—noisy; loudly demanding or complaining

**clandestine**—kept secret or hidden

**cleave**—split; to divide by a blow

**cliché**—an expression or idea that has become trite

**coalesce**—to grow together; to unite or merge

**coddle**—to treat tenderly

**codicil**—an appendix or supplement

**coerce**—enforce; to bring about by using force

**coeval**—of the same age or period

**cognizance**—perception or knowledge

**cognizant**—aware or informed

**coherent**—clearly articulated; capable of logical, intelligible speech and thought

**colloquial**—conversational; having to do with or like conversation

**combustion**—the act or process of burning

**commend**—praise; to express approval of

**commensurate**—proportionate; corresponding in extent or degree

**commingle**—intermix; blend; to mingle together

**commodity**—anything bought and sold

**communicable**—that which can be communicated

**compassion**—deep sympathy; sorrow for the sufferings of others

**compatible**—that which can work well together, get along well together, combine well

**compelling**—captivating; irresistibly interesting

**competent**—well qualified; capable; fit

**complacency**—quiet satisfaction; contentment

**complacent**—self-satisfied; smug

**complaisant**—willing to please; obliging

**compliance**—a tendency to give in readily to others

**compliant**—yielding; submissive

**comprehensive**—able to understand fully

**comprise**—to include; contain

**compulsion**—that which compels; driving force

**computation**—calculation; a method of computing

**concession**—an act or instance of granting or yielding

**conciliatory**—tending to reconcile

**concise**—brief and to the point; short and clear

**concoct**—devise; invent; plan

**condemn**—censure; disapprove of strongly

**condescension**—a patronizing manner or behavior

**condolence**—expression of sympathy with another in grief

**condone**—forgive; pardon; overlook

**conduit**—a channel conveying fluids; a tube or protected trough for electric wires

**confiscate**—to seize by authority

**conformity**—action in accordance with customs, rules, and prevailing opinion

**congregation**—a gathering of people or things

**congruent**—in agreement; corresponding; harmonious

**conjoin**—to join together; unite; combine

**conjunction**—a joining together or being joined together

**consensus**—an opinion held by all or most

**conspire**—to plan and act together secretly

**consternation**—great fear or shock that makes one feel helpless or bewildered

**constituent**—component; a necessary part or element

**consummate**—supreme; complete or perfect in every way

**contemn**—scorn; to view with contempt

**contemporaneous**—existing or happening in the same period of time

**contemptuous**—scornful; disdainful

**contentious**—always ready to argue; quarrelsome

**contentment**—the state of being satisfied

**context**—the whole situation, background, or environment relevant to a particular event, personality, creation, etc.

**contrite**—penitent; feeling sorry for sins

**contumacious**—disobedient; obstinately resisting authority

**conventional**—customary; of, sanctioned by, or growing out of custom or usage

**conversion**—a change from one belief, religion, doctrine, opinion, etc. to another

**convey**—to make known

**conviction**—a strong belief

**convoluted**—extremely involved; intricate; complicated

**copious**—very plentiful; abundant

**coronation**—act or ceremony of crowning a sovereign

**corpuscle**—a very small particle

**corroborate**—confirm; to make more certain the validity of

**countenance**—facial expression; composure

**coup**—a sudden, successful move or action

**covert**—concealed; hidden; disguised

**covet**—to want ardently; long for with envy

**crass**—tasteless; insensitive; coarse

**craven**—very cowardly; abjectly afraid

**credence**—belief, especially in the reports or testimony of another

**credulity**—a tendency to believe too readily

**crescendo**—any gradual increase in force, intensity

**criterion**—a standard on which judgment can be based

**critique**—a critical analysis or evaluation

**cryptic**—mysterious; having a hidden or ambiguous meaning

**culmination**—climax; the highest point

**culpable**—deserving blame; blameworthy

**cultivate**—to promote development or growth

**cumulative**—accumulated; increasing in effect, size, quantity, etc.

**cunning**—skillful or clever

**curator**—a person in charge of a museum, library, etc.

**cynical**—sarcastic; sneering

**daunt**—intimidate; to make afraid or discouraged

**dearth**—any scarcity or lack

**debacle**—an overwhelming defeat

**debase**—cheapen; to make lower in value, quality, character, or dignity

**debilitate**—to make weak or feeble

**decelerate**—to reduce speed; slow down

**decipher**—decode; to make out the meaning of

**decisive**—showing determination or firmness

**decry**—denounce; to speak out against strongly and openly

**deference**—courteous regard or respect

**defiance**—open, bold resistance to authority or opposition

**defiant**—openly and boldly resisting

**defunct**—no longer living or existing; dead or extinct

**defuse**—to render harmless

**degenerate**—having sunk below a former or normal condition

**delegate**—to send from one place to another; appoint; assign

**deleterious**—injurious; harmful to health or well-being

**delineate**—describe; to depict in words

**delirium**—uncontrollably wild excitement or emotion

**demagogue**—a leader who gains power using popular prejudices and false claims; a leader of the common people in ancient times

**demise**—a ceasing to exist; death

**demure**—affectedly modest or shy; coy

**denouement**—the outcome, solution, unraveling, or clarification of a plot in a drama, story

**denounce**—to condemn strongly

**despotic**—of or like a despot; autocratic; tyrannical

**destitute**—living in complete poverty

**desuetude**—disuse; the condition of not being used

**detonate**—to explode violently and noisily

**detumescence**—a gradual shrinking of a swelling

**devastate**—to make helpless; overwhelm

**devious**—not straightforward or frank

**diction**—manner of expression in words

**diminutive**—very small; tiny

**disabuse**—to rid of false ideas or misconceptions

**discern**—make out clearly

**discombobulate**—upset the composure of

**discomfit**—make uneasy

**disconcert**—embarrass; confuse

**discord**—disagreement; conflict

**discordant**—disagreeing; conflicting

**discourteous**—impolite; rude; ill-mannered

**discrepancy**—difference; inconsistency

**disinter**—bring to light

**disparage**—show disrespect for; belittle

**dissident**—not agreeing

**distillate**—the essence; purified form

**distraught**—extremely troubled

**divergence**—separating; branching off

**divergent**—deviating; different

**diverse**—different; dissimilar

**diversion**—distraction of attention

**divination**—the art of foretelling future events; clever conjecture

**doggerel**—trivial, awkward, satirical verse

**dogma**—a doctrine; tenet; belief

**dolt**—a stupid, slow-witted person; blockhead

**dormant**—as if asleep; quiet; still

**dross**—waste matter; worthless stuff; rubbish

**drub**—to defeat soundly in a fight or contest

**dubious**—feeling doubt; hesitating; skeptical

**dulcet**—sweet-sounding; melodious

**duress**—constraint by threat; imprisonment

**eccentricity**—irregularity; oddity

**eclectic**—selecting from various systems, doctrines, or sources

**efficacious**—having the intended result; effective

**effusive**—expressing excessive emotion

**embellish**—decorate by adding detail; ornament

**embodiment**—concrete expression of an idea

**emend**—correct or improve

**eminent**—rising above other things or places

**emissary**—a person sent on a specific mission

**emollient**—softening; soothing

**empathy**—ability to share in another's emotions, thoughts, or feelings

**emulate**—imitate

**enamor**—fill with love and desire; charm

**encroach**—trespass or intrude

**endow**—provide with some talent or quality

**enigma**—riddle; a perplexing and ambiguous statement

**enmity**—hostility; antagonism

**enthrall**—captivate; fascinate
**enumerate**—count; determine the number of
**epigram**—a short poem with a witty point
**epithet**—a descriptive name or title
**epitome**—a person or thing that shows typical qualities of something
**equipoise**—state of balance or equilibrium
**equivocal**—having two or more meanings
**equivocate**—to be deliberately ambiguous
**eradicate**—wipe out; destroy; to get rid of
**erroneous**—mistaken; wrong
**espionage**—the act of spying
**espouse**—support or advocate
**euphoria**—feeling of vigor or well-being
**evocation**—calling forth
**ewe**—female sheep
**exalt**—elevate; to praise; glorify
**exasperate**—irritate or annoy very much; aggravate
**excoriate**—denounce harshly
**exemplary**—serving as a model or example
**expunge**—erase or remove completely
**extant**—still existing; not extinct
**extol**—praise highly
**extrapolate**—arrive at conclusions or results
**exuberance**—feeling of high spirits

**faddish**—having the nature of a fad
**fallacious**—misleading or deceptive
**famine**—hunger; a withering away
**feckless**—weak; ineffective
**feint**—a false show; sham
**feral**—untamed; wild
**fervent**—hot; burning; glowing
**fervid**—impassioned; fervent
**finite**—having measurable or definable limits; not infinite
**fissure**—a long, narrow, deep cleft or crack
**flippant**—frivolous and disrespectful; saucy
**florid**—highly decorated; gaudy; showy; ornate
**flout**—show scorn or contempt
**forage**—search for food or provisions
**forbearance**—patience
**forbid**—not permit; prohibit
**forensics**—debate or formal argumentation
**forge**—a furnace for heating metal to be wrought; to advance
**forlorn**—without hope; desperate
**formidable**—causing fear or dread
**forthright**—straightforward; direct; frank
**fortify**—strengthen
**fracas**—a noisy fight or loud quarrel; brawl
**fractious**—hard to manage; unruly
**fraught**—emotional; tense; anxious; distressing
**frenetic**—frantic; frenzied

**frieze**—ornamental band formed by a series of decorations
**froward**—not easily controlled; stubbornly willful
**fulsome**—offensively flattering
**futile**—ineffectual; trifling or unimportant

**genial**—cheerful; friendly; sympathetic
**germinate**—start developing or growing
**glib**—done in a smooth, offhand fashion
**goad**—driving impulse; spur
**gouge**—scrape or hollow out
**gourmand**—a glutton; one who indulges to excess
**gregarious**—fond of the company of others; sociable
**gristle**—cartilage found in meat
**grouse**—complain; grumble
**grovel**—behave humbly or abjectly

**hackney**—make trite by overuse
**hapless**—unfortunate; unlucky; luckless
**haste**—the act of hurrying; quickness of motion
**haughty**—proud; arrogant
**heed**—take careful notice of
**hence**—thereafter; subsequently
**herbaceous**—like a green leaf in texture, color, shape
**heroine**—girl or woman of outstanding courage and nobility
**hew**—chop or cut with an ax or knife; hack; gash
**hierarchy**—an arrangement in order of rank, grade, class
**hindsight**—ability to see, after the event, what should have been done
**hirsute**—hairy; shaggy; bristly
**homogeneous**—of the same race or kind
**hone**—to perfect; sharpen; yearn
**hoodwink**—mislead or confuse by trickery
**hue**—a particular shade or tint of a given color
**humble**—not proud; not self-assertive; modest
**humdrum**—lacking variety; dull; monotonous
**humility**—absence of pride or self-assertion
**hybrid**—anything of mixed origin; unlike parts
**hypocrisy**—pretending to be what one is not
**hypothesis**—unproved theory

**idealist**—visionary or dreamer
**idiosyncrasy**—personal peculiarity or mannerism
**idol**—object of worship; false god
**idolatrous**—given to idolatry or blind adoration
**idolatry**—worship of idols
**immaculate**—perfectly clean; unsoiled
**impart**—make known; tell; reveal
**impeccable**—without defect or error; flawless
**impede**—obstruct or delay
**impenitent**—without regret, shame, or remorse
**imperturbable**—cannot be disconcerted, disturbed, or excited; impassive

**impervious**—not affected
**impetuous**—moving with great, sudden energy
**impinge**—to make inroads or encroach
**impious**—lacking respect or dutifulness
**implacable**—unable to be appeased or pacified; relentless
**implicate**—to involve or concern
**imposture**—fraud; deception
**inadvertent**—not attentive or observant; heedless
**incantation**—chanted words or formula
**incarcerate**—imprison; confine
**incessant**—continual; never ceasing
**incinerate**—burn up; cremate
**incongruous**—lacking harmony or agreement
**incontrovertible**—not disputable or debatable
**incorrigible**—unable to be corrected, improved, or reformed
**incumbent**—lying, resting on something; imposed as a duty
**indignation**—righteous anger
**indignity**—unworthiness or disgrace
**indiscernible**—imperceptible
**indiscriminate**—confused; random
**indispensable**—absolutely necessary or required
**indomitable**—not easily discouraged, defeated, or subdued
**industrious**—diligent; skillful
**ineffable**—too overwhelming to be expressed in words
**inefficacious**—unable to produce the desired effect
**infallible**—incapable of error; never wrong
**infamy**—bad reputation; notoriety; disgrace
**ingratiate**—to achieve one's good graces by conscious effort
**inimical**—hostile; unfriendly
**innate**—existing naturally rather than through acquisition
**innocuous**—harmless; not controversial, offensive, or stimulating
**inquisitor**—harsh or prying questioner
**insipid**—not exciting or interesting; dull
**insouciant**—calm and untroubled; carefree
**insularity**—detachment; isolation
**intelligible**—clear; comprehensible
**intemperate**—lacking restraint; excessive
**interstellar**—between or among the stars
**inveterate**—habitual; of long standing; deep-rooted
**irascible**—easily angered; quick-tempered

**jaunty**—gay and carefree; sprightly; perky
**jubilant**—joyful and triumphant; elated; rejoicing
**jurisprudence**—a part or division of law

**kernel**—the most central part; a grain

**lackluster**—lacking energy or vitality

**lambaste**—scold or denounce severely
**lament**—mourn; grieve
**languid**—without vigor or vitality; drooping; weak
**laudable**—praiseworthy; commendable
**laudatory**—expressing praise
**legion**—a large number; multitude
**lethargic**—abnormally drowsy or dull; sluggish
**limerick**—nonsense poem of five anapestic lines
**limn**—describe
**lionize**—treat as a celebrity
**listless**—spiritless; languid
**literati**—scholarly or learned people
**lithe**—bending easily; flexible; supple
**litigant**—a party to a lawsuit
**liturgy**—ritual for public worship in any of various religions or churches
**livid**—grayish-blue; extremely angry
**loquacious**—fond of talking
**loquacity**—talkativeness
**lucid**—transparent
**lummox**—a clumsy, stupid person

**magnanimous**—noble in mind
**magnitude**—greatness; importance or influence
**malevolence**—malice; spitefulness; ill will
**malfeasance**—wrongdoing or misconduct
**malinger**—pretend to be ill to escape duty or work; shirk
**masque**—dramatic composition
**maverick**—a person who takes an independent stand
**maxim**—statement of a general truth
**mazurka**—a lively Polish folk dance
**meager**—thin; lean; emaciated
**medieval**—characteristic of the Middle Ages
**mellifluous**—sounding sweet and smooth; honeyed
**menace**—threaten harm or evil
**mercenary**—motivated by a desire for money or other gain
**merriment**—gaiety and fun
**metamorphose**—transform
**metaphor**—a figure of speech containing an implied comparison
**methodology**—system of procedures
**meticulous**—extremely careful about details
**minatory**—menacing; threatening
**miser**—a greedy, stingy person
**mitigate**—make less rigorous or less painful; moderate
**mnemonic**—helping, or meant to help, the memory
**modicum**—small amount
**monarch**—hereditary head of a state
**mordant**—biting; cutting; caustic; sarcastic
**morose**—ill-tempered; gloomy
**myriad**—indefinitely large number
**mythical**—imaginary; fictitious

**narcissism**—self-love
**negate**—make ineffective
**nexus**—a connected group or series
**nib**—point of a pen
**nocturnal**—active during the night
**noisome**—having a bad odor; foul-smelling
**nomad**—one who has no permanent home, who moves about constantly
**nostalgia**—longing for things of the past
**notoriety**—prominence or renown, often unfavorable
**novice**—apprentice; beginner
**nuance**—a slight or delicate variation

**obliterate**—erase; efface
**obsequious**—compliant; dutiful; servile
**obsolete**—no longer in use or practice
**obstinate**—unreasonably determined to have one's own way; stubborn
**obtuse**—not sharp or pointed; blunt
**occult**—secret; esoteric
**odium**—disgrace brought on by hateful action
**officious**—ready to serve; obliging
**ominous**—threatening; sinister
**omnipotent**—unlimited in power or authority
**onerous**—burdensome; laborious
**opulent**—very wealthy or rich
**oration**—a formal public speech
**orator**—eloquent public speaker
**ornate**—heavily ornamented or adorned
**orthodox**—strictly conforming to the traditional
**oscillate**—to be indecisive in purpose or opinion; vacillate
**ossify**—settle or fix rigidly
**ostracism**—rejection or exclusion by general consent
**overwrought**—overworked; fatigued

**paean**—a song of joy, triumph, praise
**palliate**—relieve without curing; make less severe
**pallid**—faint in color; pale
**palpable**—tangible; easily perceived by the senses
**pantomime**—action or gestures without words as a means of expression
**paradigm**—example or model
**paradox**—a statement that seems contradictory
**paramount**—ranking higher than any other
**parch**—dry up with heat
**pariah**—outcast
**parody**—a poor or weak imitation
**pathology**—conditions, processes, or results of a particular disease
**peccadillo**—minor or petty sin; slight fault
**pellucid**—transparent or translucent; clear
**penchant**—strong liking or fondness
**penitent**—truly sorry for having sinned and willing to atone

**peremptory**—intolerantly positive or assured
**peril**—exposure to harm or injury; danger
**peripheral**—outer; external; lying at the outside
**pervade**—to become prevalent throughout
**petrous**—of or like rock; hard
**petulant**—peevish; impatient or irritable
**philistine**—a person smugly narrow and conventional in views and tastes
**pinion**—confine or shackle
**placate**—stop from being angry; appease
**platitude**—commonplace, flat, or dull quality
**plethora**—overabundance; excess
**poignant**—emotionally touching or moving
**poseur**—a person who assumes attitudes or manners merely for their effect upon others
**postulate**—claim; demand; require
**pragmatic**—busy or active in a meddlesome way; practical
**preclude**—shut out; prevent
**precocious**—exhibiting premature development
**predilection**—preconceived liking; partiality or preference
**presage**—sign or warning of a future event; omen
**prescience**—foreknowledge
**preside**—exercise control or authority
**prig**—annoyingly pedantic person
**proclivity**—natural or habitual inclination
**procure**—obtain; secure
**profane**—show disrespect for sacred things; irreverent
**profuse**—generous, often to excess
**proliferate**—to reproduce (new parts) in quick succession
**prolific**—turning out many products of the mind
**prolix**—wordy; long-winded
**propagate**—reproduce; multiply
**propinquity**—nearness of relationship; kinship
**propriety**—properness; suitability
**prosaic**—matter of fact; ordinary
**prose**—ordinary speech; dull
**protuberance**—projection; bulge
**provocative**—stimulating; erotic
**prudence**—careful management
**pugnacious**—eager and ready to fight; quarrelsome
**pundit**—actual or self-professed authority
**punitive**—inflicting, concerned with, or directed toward punishment

**quaff**—drink deeply in a hearty or thirsty way
**quell**—crush; subdue; put an end to
**querulous**—full of complaint; peevish
**quotidian**—everyday; usual or ordinary

**ramify**—divide or spread out into branches
**rancor**—deep spite or malice
**rapacious**—taking by force; plundering

**rasp**—rough, grating tone
**ratify**—approve or confirm
**raucous**—loud and rowdy
**reciprocate**—cause to move alternately back and forth
**recluse**—secluded; solitary
**recompense**—repay; compensate
**regale**—delight with something pleasing or amusing
**relegate**—exile or banish
**relinquish**—give up; abandon
**remedial**—providing a remedy
**reparation**—restoration to good condition
**replete**—well-filled or plentifully supplied
**reprieve**—give temporary relief to, as from trouble or pain
**reprobate**—disapprove of strongly
**repugnant**—contradictory; inconsistent
**requiem**—musical service for the dead
**resplendent**—dazzling; splendid
**restitution**—return to a former condition or situation
**reticent**—habitually silent; reserved
**rhapsodize**—to describe in an extravagantly enthusiastic manner
**rogue**—a rascal; scoundrel
**rubric**—a category or section heading, often in red; any rule or explanatory comment
**ruffian**—brutal, violent, lawless person
**ruse**—trick or artifice

**sacred**—holy; of or connected with religion
**salutary**—healthful; beneficial
**salutation**—greeting, addressing, or welcoming by gestures or words
**salve**—balm that soothes or heals
**sanctimonious**—pretending to be very holy
**sanction**—support; encouragement; approval
**savant**—learned person; eminent scholar
**scrupulous**—having principles; extremely conscientious
**scurvy**—low; mean; vile; contemptible
**semaphore**—system of signaling
**seminal**—of reproduction; germinal; originative
**serene**—calm; peaceful; tranquil
**servile**—humbly yielding or submissive; of a slave or slaves
**shroud**—covers, protects, or screens; veil; shelter
**signatory**—joined in the signing of something
**sinister**—wicked; evil; dishonest
**sinuous**—not straightforward; devious
**slake**—make less intense by satisfying
**snide**—slyly malicious or derisive
**sodden**—filled with moisture; soaked
**solace**—comfort; consolation; relief
**soluble**—able to be dissolved
**somber**—dark and gloomy or dull
**soporific**—pertaining to sleep or sleepiness

**sporadic**—occasional; not constant or regular
**spurious**—not true or genuine; false
**squalid**—foul or unclean
**stealth**—secret, furtive, or artfully sly behavior
**stigma**—mark or sign indicating something not considered normal or standard
**stint**—restrict or limit
**stolid**—unexcitable; impassive
**stymie**—situation in which one is obstructed or frustrated
**subliminal**—on the threshold of consciousness; under the surface
**submission**—resignation; obedience; meekness
**suffice**—be adequate
**sully**—soil; stain; tarnish by disgracing
**sunder**—break apart; separate; split
**superfluous**—excessive
**supine**—sluggish; listless; passive
**surfeit**—too great an amount or supply; excess
**surreptitious**—acting in a secret, stealthy way
**symbiosis**—relationship of mutual interdependence
**syntax**—orderly or systematic arrangement of words

**tactile**—perceived by touch; tangible
**tangible**—having actual form and substance
**tawdry**—cheap and showy; gaudy; sleazy
**tedium**—tediousness
**tempt**—persuade; induce; entice
**tenet**—principle, doctrine, or belief held as a truth
**tenuous**—slender or fine; not dense
**terrestrial**—worldly; earthly
**throng**—crowd
**timorous**—subject to fear; timid
**toupee**—a man's wig
**tractable**—easily worked; obedient; malleable
**tranquil**—calm; serene; peaceful
**transcend**—exceed; surpass; excel
**transgress**—go beyond a limit
**translucent**—partially transparent or clear
**transmute**—transform; convert
**treacherous**—untrustworthy or insecure
**treachery**—perfidy; disloyalty; treason
**trepidation**—fearful uncertainty; anxiety
**trite**—no longer having originality
**troubadour**—minstrel or singer
**truncate**—cut short
**tumultuous**—wild and noisy; uproarious
**turgid**—swollen; distended
**turmoil**—commotion; uproar; confusion
**tyranny**—very cruel and unjust use of power or authority

**uncanny**—inexplicable; preternaturally strange; weird
**underling**—one in a subordinate position; inferior
**unfeigned**—genuine; real; sincere

**unfetter**—free from restraint; liberate
**unification**—state of being unified
**unintelligible**—unable to be understood; incomprehensible
**unity**—oneness; singleness
**univocal**—unambiguous
**unscrupulous**—not restrained by ideas of right and wrong
**untenable**—incapable of being occupied
**untoward**—inappropriate; improper
**unwitting**—not knowing; unaware
**upbraid**—rebuke severely or bitterly
**uproarious**—loud and boisterous
**usury**—interest at a high rate
**utilitarian**—stressing usefulness over beauty
**utopia**—idealized place

**vacillate**—sway to and fro; waver; totter
**vacuum**—completely empty space
**vagabond**—wandering; moving from place to place
**vagrant**—a person who lives a wandering life
**valiant**—brave
**vapid**—tasteless; flavorless; flat
**variegate**—vary; diversify
**veer**—change direction; shift
**vehement**—acting or moving with great force
**venerate**—show feelings of deep respect; revere
**vengeance**—revenge
**vestige**—a trace of something that once existed

**vex**—distress; afflict; plague
**vicarious**—serving as a substitute
**villainous**—evil; wicked
**vitiate**—spoil; corrupt
**vivacious**—full of life and animation; lively
**vocation**—trade; profession; occupation
**volatile**—flying or able to fly
**voluble**—talkative
**voluminous**—large; bulky; full
**voracious**—ravenous; gluttonous

**waft**—float, as on the wind
**wane**—grow dim or faint
**wary**—cautious; on one's guard
**welter**—to become soaked; stained; bathed
**wheedle**—coax; influence or persuade by flattery
**whet**—make keen; stimulate
**wile**—sly trick
**wither**—shrivel; wilt
**witty**—cleverly amusing
**wrath**—intense anger; rage; fury
**wrench**—sudden, sharp twist or pull

**yacht**—small vessel for pleasure cruises or racing
**yearn**—to have longing or desire
**yielding**—submissive; obedient

**zeal**—intense enthusiasm
**zenith**—highest point; peak

—*Difficulty Level 2*—

**abstemious**—exercising moderation; self-restraint
**aggregation**—gathered together; accumulated
**alacrity**—cheerful promptness; eagerness
**ambient**—surrounding
**amorphous**—shapeless; formless
**antediluvian**—before the flood; antiquated
**apostate**—fallen from the faith
**arrogate**—to claim or seize as one's own
**ascetic**—practicing self-denial; austere
**ascribe**—attribute to a cause
**asperity**—having a harsh temper; roughness
**assuage**—lessen; soothe
**assiduous**—diligent
**attenuation**—a thinning out
**august**—great dignity or grandeur
**aver**—affirm; declare to be true

**bacchanalian**—drunken
**baleful**—menacing; deadly
**beguile**—to deceive; cheat; charm; coax
**beleaguer**—besiege or attack; harass
**bellicose**—belligerent; pugnacious; warlike
**belie**—misrepresent; be false to

**bombastic**—pompous; puffed up with conceit; using inflated language
**bovine**—resembling a cow; placid or dull
**bucolic**—rustic; pastoral
**burgeon**—grow forth; send out buds

**cacophony**—harsh or discordant sound; dissonance
**calumny**—slander
**capitulate**—surrender
**cathartic**—purgative; inducing a figurative cleansing
**cavil**—disagree; nit-pick; make frivolous objections
**celerity**—swiftness
**chassis**—framework and working parts of an automobile
**chimerical**—fantastically improbable; highly unrealistic
**churlish**—rude; surly
**circumscribe**—limit
**cogent**—convincing
**collusion**—conspiring in a fraudulent scheme
**comely**—attractive; agreeable
**compendium**—brief, comprehensive summary
**concord**—harmony

**confluence**—flowing or coming together
**consecrate**—induct into a religious office; declare sacred
**consonance**—agreement; harmony
**contrite**—penitent; repentant; feeling sorry for sins
**contumely**—insult; contemptuous treatment
**conundrum**—riddle; difficult problem
**cosset**—pamper
**cupidity**—excessive desire for money; avarice
**cursory**—hasty; done without care

**decimate**—destroy a great number
**defer**—yield; delay
**demur**—to take exception; object
**denigrate**—blacken someone's reputation or character
**derision**—ridicule
**desiccate**—dry up; drain
**desultory**—aimless; unmethodical; unfocused
**diaphanous**—translucent; see-through
**diatribe**—speech full of bitterness
**didactic**—intended primarily to instruct
**diffidence**—modesty; shyness; lack of confidence
**dilatory**—given to delay or procrastination
**dilettante**—aimless follower of the arts; amateur; dabbler
**din**—loud confusing noise
**disaffection**—lack of trust; to cause discontent
**disarming**—deprive of resentment; peaceable or friendly; win over
**discursive**—rambling; passing from one topic to another
**disingenuous**—deceitful; lacking in candor; not frank
**disparate**—basically different; unrelated
**disputatious**—argumentative
**disquietude**—uneasiness; anxiety
**dissemble**—conceal true motives; pretend
**dissolute**—loose in morals or conduct
**dissonant**—lacking in harmony; discordant
**dogmatic**—adhering to a tenet
**dolorous**—sorrowful; having mental anguish
**duplicity**—deception by pretending to feel and act one way while acting another; bad faith; double dealing

**ebullient**—greatly excited
**edify**—instruct; correct morally
**efface**—erase; obliterate as if by rubbing it out
**efficacy**—power to produce desired effect
**effrontery**—shameless boldness; impudence; temerity
**egregious**—notorious; shocking
**encomium**—glowing praise
**encumber**—hinder
**endemic**—prevailing among a specific group
**enervate**—weaken; debilitate
**engender**—cause; produce
**ensconce**—settle in; hide; conceal
**ephemeral**—fleeting; short-lived

**equanimity**—calmness; composure
**erudite**—learned; scholarly
**eschew**—shun
**esoteric**—hard to understand
**etymology**—study of word parts
**evanescent**—tending to vanish like vapor
**evince**—show clearly
**exacerbate**—worsen; embitter
**exculpate**—clear from blame
**execrable**—detestable
**exegesis**—explanation, especially of biblical passages
**exhort**—urge
**exigency**—urgent situation
**expatriate**—one choosing to live abroad

**facile**—easily accomplished; ready or fluent
**fatuous**—foolish or inane
**fealty**—loyalty; allegiance
**felicitous**—well chosen; apt; suitable
**ferment**—agitation; commotion
**fetid**—malodorous
**filial**—pertaining to a son or daughter
**flaccid**—flabby
**foment**—stir up; instigate
**fortuitous**—accidental; by chance
**fulminate**—to thunder; explode
**fungible**—capable of being used in place of something else

**gainsay**—contradict; speak or act against
**galvanize**—stimulate by shock; stir up; revitalize
**gambol**—romp; to skip about
**garrulous**—loquacious; wordy; talkative
**gossamer**—sheer, like cobwebs
**gratuitous**—given freely; unwarranted
**guile**—slyness and cunning

**hackles**—hairs on back and neck
**halcyon**—calm; peaceful
**harbinger**—one that announces or foreshadows what is coming; precursor; portent
**hummock**—small hill
**hedonist**—one who believes pleasure is sole aim in life
**hegemony**—dominance, especially of one nation over another
**heinous**—atrocious; hatefully bad
**hermetic**—obscure and mysterious; relating to the occult
**hubris**—arrogance; excessive self-conceit
**humus**—substance formed by decaying vegetable matter

**iconoclastic**—attacking cherished traditions
**ignominious**—dishonorable; disgraceful
**imbroglio**—complicated situation
**immolate**—offer as a sacrifice

**immutable**—unchangeable
**impalpable**—imperceptible; intangible
**impecunious**—without money
**importune**—repeatedly urge
**impuissance**—powerlessness; feebleness
**impunity**—freedom from punishment or harm
**inchoate**—recently begun; rudimentary
**incipient**—becoming apparent; beginning
**incisive**—sharply expressive
**inculcate**—impress on the mind by admonition
**incursion**—temporary invasion
**indelible**—not able to be removed or erased
**indemnify**—make secure against loss
**indigent**—poor
**indite**—write; compose
**indolent**—lazy
**ineluctable**—irresistible; not to be escaped
**inexorable**—not to be moved by entreaty; unyielding;
  relentless
**iniquitous**—wicked; immoral
**insidious**—deceitful; treacherous
**internecine**—mutually destructive
**interpolate**—insert between other things
**intractable**—stubborn
**intransigence**—refusal to compromise
**intrepid**—brave
**inure**—make accustomed to something difficult
**invective**—abuse
**inveigh**—condemn; censure

**jaundice**—prejudice; envious; yellow
**jettison**—throw overboard
**jocose**—given to joking
**jocund**—merry
**juggernaut**—irresistible, crushing force
**juxtapose**—place side by side

**ken**—range of knowledge
**kinetic**—producing motion
**kismet**—fate
**knell**—tolling of a bell
**knoll**—little round hill

**lachrymose**—producing tears
**laconic**—using few words
**largess**—liberal giving; generous gift
**lascivious**—lustful
**lassitude**—weariness; debility
**latent**—potential but undeveloped; dormant
**laxity**—carelessness
**legerdemain**—sleight of hand
**licentious**—amoral; lewd and lascivious
**Lilliputian**—extremely small
**limpid**—clear
**lugubrious**—mournful, often to an excessive degree

**maelstrom**—whirlpool
**maladroit**—clumsy; bungling
**malediction**—curse
**malleable**—capable of being shaped
**malignant**—growing worse
**maraud**—rove in search of plunder
**martinet**—one who issues orders
**masticate**—chew
**maudlin**—effusively sentimental
**megalomania**—mania for doing grandiose things
**melee**—fight
**mendacity**—untruthfulness
**mendicant**—beggar
**mercurial**—volatile; changeable; fickle
**meretricious**—flashy; tawdry
**miasma**—a poisonous atmosphere
**misanthrope**—a person who hates mankind
**miscreant**—villain
**mollify**—soothe
**monolithic**—consisting of a single character; uniform;
  unyielding
**moribund**—dying
**myopic**—nearsighted; lacking foresight
**munificent**—generous

**nadir**—lowest point
**nascent**—incipient; coming into being
**nebulous**—unclear; vague; hazy; cloudy
**necromancy**—black magic; dealing with the dead
**nefarious**—wicked
**nostrum**—questionable medicine
**nubile**—marriageable
**nugatory**—futile; worthless

**obdurate**—stubborn; unyielding
**obfuscate**—make obscure; confuse
**obloquy**—slander; disgrace; infamy
**obstreperous**—unruly; boisterous; noisy
**obviate**—make unnecessary
**occlude**—shut; close
**odious**—hateful; vile
**oligarchy**—government by a privileged few
**opprobrium**—infamy; vilification
**ostensible**—apparent; showing outwardly; professed

**panegyric**—formal praise
**paragon**—model of perfection
**parlance**—language; idiom
**parlay**—exploit successfully
**parsimonious**—stingy
**paucity**—scarcity
**pecuniary**—obsessed by money
**pedantic**—bookish
**pejorative**—negative in connotation; having a
  tendency to make worse; disparaging

**penurious**—marked by penury; stingy
**perdition**—eternal damnation; complete ruin
**perfidy**—treacherous; betrayal of trust
**perfunctory**—indifferent; done merely as a duty; superficial
**pernicious**—fatal; very destructive or injurious
**perspicacious**—having insight; penetrating; astute
**perspicuous**—plainly expressed
**phlegmatic**—calm; not easily disturbed
**piebald**—of different colors; mottled; spotted
**piety**—devoutness; reverence for God
**pillory**—criticize or ridicule
**piquancy**—something that stimulates taste; tartness
**pithy**—essential; brief and to the point
**polemic**—controversy; argument in support of a point of view
**polyglot**—speaking several languages
**portent**—sign; omen; something that foreshadows a coming event
**precipitous**—abrupt or hasty
**probity**—honesty; integrity
**prodigal**—wasteful; reckless with money
**prodigious**—marvelous; enormous
**profligate**—dissolute; reckless; loose in morals; wanton
**profundity**—intellectual depth
**promulgate**—proclaim; make public; put into effect
**propitious**—favorable; timely
**proscribe**—outlaw; ostracize; banish
**protract**—prolong in time or space; extend; lengthen
**puerile**—childish; lacking in maturity
**pungent**—stinging; sharp in taste; caustic
**pusillanimous**—cowardly

**quiescent**—at rest; dormant; temporarily inactive
**quixotic**—idealistic but impractical

**raconteur**—someone who is skilled at telling stories or anecdotes
**raffish**—vulgar; crude
**raiment**—clothing
**recalcitrant**—stubborn; refractory; reluctant; unwilling; refusing to submit
**recidivism**—habitual return to crime
**recondite**—abstruse; profound; secret
**recumbent**—reclining; lying down
**redolent**—suggestive of an odor; fragrant
**redoubtable**—formidable; causing fear
**refractory**—stubborn; obstinate
**remand**—order back; return to service
**remonstrate**—object; protest
**remunerative**—compensating; rewarding for service
**repine**—complain; mourn; fret
**ribald**—wanton; profane or coarse; joking or mocking

**sagacious**—perceptive; shrewd; having insight

**salacious**—lustful; lecherous; lascivious
**salient**—standing out conspicuously; prominent
**salubrious**—healthful
**sanguine**—having a ruddy complexion; cheerful; hopeful
**sardonic**—sneering; sarcastic; cynical
**sartorial**—tailored
**saturnine**—sullen; sardonic; gloomy
**sedition**—resistance to authority
**sedulous**—diligent; persevering
**sententious**—terse; concise; aphoristic
**sophistry**—seemingly plausible but fallacious reasoning
**specious**—seeming reasonable but incorrect
**spendthrift**—one who spends money extravagantly
**splenetic**—bad-tempered; irritable
**static**—showing a lack of motion
**stentorian**—powerful in sound; extremely loud
**stringent**—vigorous; rigid; binding
**succor**—aid; assistance; comfort
**supercilious**—contemptuous; arrogant
**sycophant**—one who seeks favor by flattering; a parasite

**taciturn**—quiet; habitually silent
**tangential**—peripheral; only slightly connected
**temerity**—foolish or rash boldness
**temporal**—not lasting forever; limited by time
**tenacity**—holding fast
**toady**—servile flatterer; a "yes man"
**tome**—large book
**torpor**—lack of activity; lethargy
**tortuous**—winding; full of curves
**traduce**—to speak falsely
**transcendent**—exceeding usual limits; incomparable; beyond ordinary existence; peerless
**trenchant**—effective; thorough; cutting; keen
**truculent**—threatening; aggressively self-assertive; savage
**turbid**—muddy
**turpitude**—depravity

**ubiquitous**—being everywhere; omnipresent
**unctuous**—oily; suave
**undulating**—moving with a wavelike motion
**unequivocal**—plain; obvious

**vacuity**—emptiness
**vainglorious**—boastful
**vanguard**—forerunner; advance forces
**venal**—capable of being bribed
**venial**—forgivable; trivial
**veracious**—truthful
**verbose**—wordy
**verdant**—green; lush in vegetation

**verisimilitude**—appearance of truth
**veritable**—actual; being truly so
**vicissitude**—change of fortune
**viscid**—having a cohesive and sticky fluid
**vitriolic**—corrosive; sarcastic
**vituperative**—abusive; scolding
**vociferous**—clamorous; noisy
**vouchsafe**—bestow condescendingly; guarantee

**waggish**—mischievous; humorous; tricky
**wanton**—excessively merry; frolicsome; having no
    regard for others
**winnow**—sift; separate good parts from bad
**winsome**—agreeable; gracious
**wizen**—wither; shrivel

**xenophobia**—fear or hatred of foreigners

**zealous**—fervent; enthusiastic
**zephyr**—gentle breeze; west wind

# Vocabulary in Context

**DIRECTIONS:** The following is a vocabulary exercise. After reading the passage, choose the *best* answer to each item. Answer all items on the basis of what is suggested by adjacent material in the passage. Answers are on page 893.

"Heartily tired" from the brutal, almost daily conflicts that erupted over questions of national policy between himself and Alexander Hamilton, Thomas Jefferson resigned his position as Secretary of State in 5 1793. Although his Federalist opponents were convinced that this was merely a strategic withdrawal to allow him an opportunity to plan and promote his candidacy for the Presidency should Washington step down in 1796, Jefferson insisted that this retirement 10 from public life was to be final.

But even in retirement, the world of politics pursued him. As the election grew nearer and it became apparent that Washington would not seek a third term, rumors of Jefferson's Presidential ambitions grew in 15 intensity. Reacting to these continuous insinuations in a letter to James Madison, Jefferson allowed that while the idea that he coveted the office of chief executive had been originated by his enemies to impugn his political motives, he had been forced to examine his 20 true feelings on the subject for his own peace of mind. In so doing he concluded that his reasons for retirement—the desire for privacy, and the delight of family life—coupled with his now failing health were insuperable barriers to public service. The "little spice 25 of ambition" he had in his younger days had long since evaporated and the question of his Presidency was forever closed.

Jefferson did not actively engage in the campaign on his own behalf. The Republican party, anticipating 30 modern campaign tactics, created grass roots sentiment for their candidate by directing their efforts toward the general populace. In newspapers, Jefferson was presented as the uniform advocate of equal rights among the citizens while Adams was portrayed as the 35 champion of rank, titles, heredity, and distinctions. Jefferson was not certain of the outcome of the election

until the end of December. Under the original electoral system established by the Constitution, each Presidential elector cast his ballot for two men without 40 designating between them as to office. The candidate who received the greater number of votes became the President; the second highest, the Vice President. Jefferson foresaw on the basis of his own calculations that the electoral vote would be close. He wrote to 45 Madison that in the event of a tie, he wished for the choice to be in favor of Adams. In public life, the New Englander had always been senior to Jefferson; and so, he explained, the expression of public will being equal, Adams should be preferred for the higher honor. 50 Jefferson, a shrewd politician, realized that the transition of power from the nearly mythical Washington to a lesser luminary in the midst of the deep and bitter political divisions facing the nation could be perilous, and he had no desire to be caught in 55 the storm that had been brewing for four years and was about to break. "This is certainly not a moment to covet the helm," he wrote to Edward Rutledge. When the electoral vote was tallied, Adams emerged the victor. Rejoicing at his "escape," Jefferson was completely 60 satisfied with the decision. Despite their obvious and basic political differences, Jefferson genuinely respected John Adams as a friend and compatriot. Although Jefferson believed that Adams had deviated from the course set in 1776, in Jefferson's eyes he 65 never suffered diminution; and Jefferson was quite confident that Adams would not steer the nation too far from its Republican tack. Within two years, Jefferson's views would be drastically altered as measures such as the Alien and Sedition Acts of 1798 convinced him of 70 the need to wrest control of the government from the Federalists.

1. In line 1, the word "heartily" most nearly means

   (A) sincerely
   (B) vigorously
   (C) zealously
   (D) gladly
   (E) completely

2. In line 10, the word "public" most nearly means

   (A) communal
   (B) open
   (C) official
   (D) people
   (E) popular

3. In line 10, the word "final" most nearly means

   (A) last
   (B) closing
   (C) ultimate
   (D) eventual
   (E) conclusive

4. In line 16, the word "allowed" most nearly means

   (A) permitted
   (B) admitted
   (C) tolerated
   (D) granted
   (E) gave

5. In line 29, the word "anticipating" most nearly means

   (A) expecting
   (B) presaging
   (C) awaiting
   (D) inviting
   (E) hoping

6. In line 33, the word "uniform" most nearly means

   (A) standard
   (B) unchanging
   (C) militant
   (D) popular
   (E) honest

7. In line 35, the word "champion" most nearly means

   (A) victor
   (B) opponent
   (C) colleague
   (D) embodiment
   (E) defender

8. In line 47, the word "senior" most nearly means

   (A) older in age
   (B) higher in rank
   (C) graduate
   (D) mentor
   (E) director

9. In line 52, the word "luminary" most nearly means

   (A) bright object
   (B) famous person
   (C) office holder
   (D) candidate
   (E) winner

10. In line 65, the word "diminution" most nearly means

   (A) foreshortening
   (B) shrinkage
   (C) abatement
   (D) ill health
   (E) degradation

# Vocabulary Completions

**DIRECTIONS:** For items #1–12, select an appropriate completion for each blank in the following paragraph from the corresponding numbered lists provided below. Answers are on page 894.

Today, the Surgeon General announced the

findings of a new —— that concludes that smoking
$\phantom{aaa}$ 1

1. (A) movie
   (B) election
   (C) report
   (D) advertisement
   (E) plan

represents a serious —— to non-smokers as well as to
$\phantom{aaaaaa}$ 2

2. (A) consciousness
   (B) hazard
   (C) remedy
   (D) possibility
   (E) treatment

——. According to the Surgeon General, disease risk
$\phantom{a}$ 3

3. (A) cigarettes
   (B) fumes
   (C) alcoholics
   (D) pipes
   (E) smokers

due to —— of tobacco smoke is not limited to the
$\phantom{aaaaa}$ 4

4. (A) observation
   (B) criticism
   (C) improvement
   (D) inhalation
   (E) cessation

—— who is smoking, but it can also extend to those
$\phantom{aa}$ 5

5. (A) individual
   (B) doctor
   (C) campaign
   (D) reporter
   (E) objector

who —— tobacco smoke in the same room. Simple
　6

6. (A) create
   (B) breathe
   (C) enjoy
   (D) ban
   (E) control

—— of smokers and non-smokers within the same
　7

7. (A) encouragement
   (B) prohibition
   (C) separation
   (D) intermingling
   (E) prosecution

airspace may reduce, but does not ——, exposure of
　　　　　　　　　　　　　　8
non-smokers to environmental smoke. A spokesperson

8. (A) imagine
   (B) increase
   (C) prepare
   (D) eliminate
   (E) satisfy

for the tobacco industry —— the report, saying the
　　　　　　　　　　9

9. (A) purchased
   (B) prepared
   (C) understood
   (D) criticized
   (E) worshipped

available —— does not support the conclusion that
　　　　10
environmental tobacco smoke is a hazard to non-

smokers. On the other hand, the Coalition for

Smoking on Health, an anti-smoking organization,

10. (A) alibi
    (B) publicity
    (C) evidence
    (D) reaction
    (E) resources

11. (A) praised
    (B) rejected
    (C) prolonged
    (D) denied
    (E) proclaimed

—— the report and called for —— government action
　11　　　　　　　　　　　　12
to ensure a smoke-free environment for all non-

smokers.

12. (A) minimal
    (B) immediate
    (C) reactionary
    (D) uncontrolled
    (E) theoretical

**DIRECTIONS:** For items #13–22, write down a few *possible* words that you anticipate could be used to fill in the blank and complete the sentence. Possible answers are on page 894.

13. Stress is the reaction an individual feels when he believes the demands of a situation —— his ability to meet them.

    _____

    _____

    _____

14. The —— of his career, capturing the coveted "Most Valuable Player" award, came at a time of deep personal sadness.

    _____

    _____

    _____

15. Martin's opponent is a(n) —— speaker who is unable to elicit a reaction from a crowd on even the most emotional of issues.

    _____

    _____

    _____

16. The cold weather caused —— damage to the Florida citrus crop, prompting growers to warn that the reduced yield is likely to result in much higher prices.

    _____

    _____

    _____

17. The report is so —— that it covers all of the main points in detail and at least touches on everything that is even remotely connected with its topic.

    _____

    _____

    _____

18. The Constitution sets up a system of checks and balances among the executive, the legislative, and the judicial branches to ensure that no one branch can establish —— control over the government.

    _____

    _____

    _____

19. The females of many common species of birds have dull coloring that —— them when they are sitting on a nest in a tree or other foliage.

    _____

    _____

    _____

20. She was one of the most —— criminals of the 1930s, her name a household word and her face in every post office.

    _____

    _____

    _____

21. Although he had not been physically injured by the explosion, the violence of the shock left him temporarily ——.

    _____

    _____

    _____

22. Good teachers know that study habits learned as a youngster stay with a student for life, so they try to find ways to —— enthusiasm for studies.

    _____

    _____

    _____

**DIRECTIONS:** For items #23–32, underline a few words or phrases that provide clues for the completion of the sentences. Then, write down a few *possible* words that you anticipate could be used to fill in the blanks and complete the sentences. Possible answers are on page 894.

23. The survivors had been drifting for days in the lifeboat, and in their weakness, they appeared to be —— rather than living beings.

_____
_____
_____

24. The guillotine was introduced during the French Revolution as a(n) ——, an alternative to other less humane means of execution.

_____
_____
_____

25. Because of the —— nature of the chemical, it cannot be used near an open flame.

_____
_____
_____

26. The Mayor's proposal for a new subway line, although a(n) ——, is not a final solution to the city's transportation needs.

_____
_____
_____

27. In a pluralistic society, policies are the result of compromise, so political leaders must be —— and must accommodate the views of others.

_____
_____
_____

28. The committee report vigorously expounded the bill's strengths but also acknowledged its ——.

_____
_____
_____

29. Because there is always the danger of a power failure and disruption of elevator service, high-rise buildings, while suitable for younger persons, are not recommended for ——.

_____
_____
_____

30. For a child to be happy, his day must be very structured; when his routine is ——, he becomes nervous and irritable.

_____
_____
_____

31. The current spirit of —— among different religions has led to a number of meetings that their leaders hope will lead to better understanding.

_____
_____
_____

32. Our modern industrialized societies have been responsible for the greatest destruction of nature and life; indeed, it seems that more civilization results in greater ——.

_____
_____
_____

# Reading

The remainder of the Verbal Reasoning Skills Review is a unique set of lesson material with six corresponding exercises that will not only help you to read carefully on the GRE, in general, but also, more specifically, to help you develop the ability to grasp the meaning behind Reading Comprehension item stems.

Both the Careful Reading and Coding exercises provide item stems that resemble those found on an actual standardized test. With the former, you are asked to choose the answer choice that best restates this original item stem, which forces you to focus on the exact meaning of the question that is being asked. As for the latter, you are asked to code the item stems, allowing for a more attentive and productive reading of the passage, with an understanding of the reasoning behind what is being asked by each of the item stems. Although coding item stems (Exercises 11 and 12) is a strategy that is discussed later in Step Three (Verbal Reasoning Concepts and Strategies, Reading Comprehension Core Lesson), knowing how to recognize an item stem as fitting into a certain pattern is a fundamental skill that applies to all subjects and therefore should be reinforced in the Skills Review.

## Careful Reading of Item Stems

After surveying thousands of students, we found that up to one-third of the time, an item was answered incorrectly because the student misinterpreted the item. In other words, students could have answered the item correctly had they understood what the test writers were really asking. You must read the item carefully and correctly, or you will get it wrong.

It may seem that this sort of error would only affect your ability to correctly answer Verbal Reasoning items. In fact, if you cannot read with enough precision to comprehend the exact question that is being asked, you are also limiting your potential to correctly answer Quantitative Reasoning items. An inability to focus on the actual question means that you would most likely have problems in both of these areas on the exam. In order to receive points for a correct answer, you must first be able to understand exactly what the test-writer is asking in each item stem. When you have become proficient at careful reading, you will no longer waste valuable time on an individual item trying to determine exactly what the item is asking.

Exercises 7–10 are designed to reinforce careful reading of the item stems on the actual test. Although some of the items in these exercises may seem to require knowledge of basic math and verbal concepts, it will not be necessary to "solve" an item. Do not be confused by distracting terminology or by an answer that "might" qualify as a correct restatement of the item stem. The correct answer choice to a Careful Reading item is the most specifically accurate, and therefore the *best*, restatement of the question that is being asked by the test-writers.

For each item in the Careful Reading exercises, you are asked to determine which of the given answer choices is the best restatement of the original item stem. On the following page you will find Careful Reading item stems that are representative of the two disciplines that are covered in the exercises.

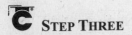 

| | | |
|---|---|---|
| *Verbal Reasoning:* | According to the passage, which of the following statements is true? | |
| | According to the passage, what is true? | ✓ |
| | According to the passage, what is not true? | ✗ |
| | | |
| *Quantitative Reasoning:* | After the area of a given figure is increased, what is the percent increase in the area of the figure? | |
| | What is the percentage change in area? | ✓ |
| | What is the new total area after the increase in area? | ✗ |

(Note that since Analytical Writing item stems consist of Issue and Argument prompts rather than actual questions, they are not included in the Careful Reading section.)

On the GRE, the Verbal Reasoning sections include Reading Comprehension and Sentence Completions items. Exercises 7 and 9 will help you focus on the exact questions that are being asked by Reading Comprehension item stems. There is no need for you to see the entire selection as it would appear on the actual exam. (Note that since Sentence Completions item stems consist of incomplete sentences rather than actual questions, they are not included in these exercises.) Exercises 8 and 10 will help you focus on the exact questions that are being asked by Quantitative Reasoning item stems. It is not necessary to worry about your math skills; these skills are addressed in the Quantitative Reasoning Skills Review. In these exercises, focus on the actual question that is being asked by the Quantitative Reasoning item stems.

# Careful Reading of Verbal Reasoning Item Stems, Pt. I

**DIRECTIONS:** Choose the *best* restatement of the item stem. Answers are on page 895.

1.  What is the main idea of the passage?

    (A) What is the central theme of the passage?
    (B) Which specific detail is mentioned in the first sentence of the passage?
    (C) Which idea is always stated in the last sentence of the passage?
    (D) Which idea is a supporting detail in the passage?

2.  The author of the passage would most likely agree with which of the following statements about words and art?

    (A) How do words relate to art?
    (B) Which statement pertains to words and art?
    (C) Which of the author's statements about words is not necessarily true of art?
    (D) Which statement does the author hold to be true about both words and art?

3.  As used in this context, "address" most nearly means

    (A) What is the most common definition of "address"?
    (B) What is the only definition of "address"?
    (C) How would "address" be defined as it is used in the passage?
    (D) Who does the author address in the passage?

4.  The primary purpose of the passage is to

    (A) What is the first specific detail?
    (B) What is the author's tone in the passage?
    (C) How does this passage make you feel?
    (D) What is the main objective of the passage?

5.  The main point of the storyteller's interpretation is that

    (A) How does the storyteller interpret the main point of the passage?
    (B) Which of the storyteller's interpretations addresses the main point of the passage?
    (C) What is the central focus of the storyteller's interpretation?
    (D) Which of the following is not included in the storyteller's interpretation?

6.  It can be inferred from the passage that the term "Monocrats" means

    (A) What does the term "Monocrats" mean?
    (B) What does the author infer about Monocrats?
    (C) Why does the author refer to Monocrats?
    (D) Where does the author refer to Monocrats in the passage?

7.  It can be inferred that the author regards the Hudson Bay Company as a

    (A) Why does the author refer to the Hudson Bay Company?
    (B) What are the author's feelings about the Hudson Bay Company?
    (C) In what way is the author associated with the Hudson Bay Company?
    (D) What can you infer about the Hudson Bay Company?

8. According to the author of Passage 1, it is difficult to formulate a general historical law about revolution because

   (A) Why does the author of Passage 1 find it difficult to formulate plans for a revolution?
   (B) Why is it difficult to formulate a general historical law about revolution?
   (C) Why does the author of Passage 1 formulate a general law?
   (D) Why is it easy to formulate a general law?

9. In line 17, the phrase "adequately articulated" means

   (A) What does "adequately articulated" mean in general?
   (B) Which phrase adequately articulates line 17 in the passage?
   (C) What does "adequately articulated" mean in the context of the passage?
   (D) Which phrase is adequately articulated in the passage?

10. According to Passage 2, any disappointment at the failure of general laws to explain historical events is due to

   (A) Which laws explain historical events?
   (B) Why don't the general laws fail to explain historical events?
   (C) What causes the disappointment at the failure of general laws to explain events?
   (D) What causes the failure of general laws to explain historical events?

11. Passage 2 explains that the technique of Verstehen is used to enable the historian to study

   (A) Which historian in Passage 2 explains the technique of Verstehen?
   (B) According to Passage 2, what can historians study by means of the Verstehen technique?
   (C) According to Passage 2, what can't historians study by means of the Verstehen technique?
   (D) Which technique do historians use to study Verstehen?

12. In order to account for what Passage 2 calls the "inside" of a historical event, the author of Passage 1 would most likely refer to

   (A) Why does the author of Passage 1 refer to the "inside" of a historical event?
   (B) What would the author of Passage 1 refer to in order to account for the "inside" of a historical event?
   (C) Why does the author of Passage 2 refer to the "inside" of a historical event?
   (D) What would the author of Passage 2 refer to in order to account for the "inside" of a historical event?

13. The author's list of regions through which the cultivation of maize spread assumes that

   (A) Why does the author's list pertain to the cultivation of maize?
   (B) What assumption can be made by the author's list of regions?
   (C) The cultivation of maize spread through which of the regions listed by the author?
   (D) What assumption can be made about the cultivation of maize?

14. The author introduces the examples of wheat and barley in order to

   (A) Wheat and barley are examples of what?
   (B) In what order does the author refer to wheat and barley?
   (C) Where does the author refer to wheat and barley in the passage?
   (D) For what reason does the author mention wheat and barley?

15. What is the author's primary purpose?

   (A) Which of the author's purposes is listed in the first sentence of the passage?
   (B) Which purpose may be considered secondary to the author's purpose?
   (C) As a reader, which of the author's purposes do you first detect when reading the passage?
   (D) Which of the following is the author's primary reason for writing the passage?

# Careful Reading of Quantitative Reasoning Item Stems, Pt. I

**DIRECTIONS:** Choose the *best* restatement of the item stem. Answers are on page 898.

1. If a machine produces 240 thingamabobs per hour, how many minutes are needed for the machine to produce 30 thingamabobs?

   (A) How many minutes does it take to make 270 thingamabobs?
   (B) How many minutes does it take to make 8 sets of 30 thingamabobs each?
   (C) How many minutes does it take to make 240 thingamabobs at 30 thingamabobs per hour?
   (D) How many minutes does it take to make 30 thingamabobs at 240 thingamabobs per hour?

2. After a 20-percent decrease in price, the cost of an item is *D* dollars. What was the price of the item before the decrease?

   (A) What was the original price of the item?
   (B) What was the price before the 80-percent decrease?
   (C) What was the price before the $20 decrease?
   (D) What was the price before the 80-percent increase?

3. If the price of candy increases from 5 pounds for $7 to 3 pounds for $7, how much *less* candy, in pounds, can be purchased for $3.50 at the new price than at the old price?

   (A) How much less candy can be purchased for $3.50 at the old price?
   (B) How much candy can be purchased for $3.50 at the new price?
   (C) How much less candy can be purchased for $3.50 at the new price?
   (D) How much candy can be purchased for $3.50 at the old price?

4. A jar contains 24 white marbles and 48 black marbles. What percent of the marbles in the jar are black?

   (A) What percent of the 72 marbles in the jar are white?
   (B) How many more black marbles than white marbles are in the jar?
   (C) What percent of all the marbles in the jar are not black?
   (D) Of the 72 white and black marbles in the jar, what percent are not white?

5. Twenty students attended Professor Rodriguez's class on Monday and twenty-five students attended on Tuesday. The number of students who attended on Tuesday was what percent of the number of students who attended on Monday?

   (A) 45 students are what percent of 20 students?
   (B) 45 students are what percent of 25 students?
   (C) 25 students are what percent of 20 students?
   (D) 20 students are what percent of 25 students?

6. Willie's monthly electric bills for last year were as follows: $40, $38, $36, $38, $34, $34, $30, $32, $34, $37, $39, and $40. What was the mode?

   (A) What number is the average of the series?
   (B) What number occurs least frequently?
   (C) What number occurs most frequently?
   (D) What number is the median of the series?

7. If 4.5 pounds of chocolate cost $10, how many pounds of chocolate can be purchased for $12?

   (A) At the given price, how much more chocolate can be purchased for $12 than $10?
   (B) At the given price, what is the cost of 12 pounds of chocolate?
   (C) At the given price, how many pounds can be purchased for $12?
   (D) At the given price, how many pounds can be purchased for $10?

8. At Star Lake Middle School, 45 percent of the students bought a yearbook. If 540 students bought yearbooks, how many students did NOT buy a yearbook?

   (A) How many students bought a yearbook?
   (B) How many students did not buy a yearbook if 45% bought yearbooks?
   (C) How many of the 540 students bought a yearbook if 45% bought yearbooks?
   (D) How many of the 540 students did not buy a yearbook?

9. Walking at a constant rate of 4 miles per hour, it took Jill exactly 1 hour to walk home from school. If she walked at a constant rate of 5 miles per hour, how many minutes did the trip take?

   (A) How long was the trip if Jill walked at a rate of 1 mile per hour when it takes 4 hours to walk home at a rate of 5 miles per hour?
   (B) How long was the trip if Jill walked at a rate of 4 miles per hour when it takes 1 hour to walk home at a rate of 5 miles per hour?
   (C) How long was the trip if Jill walked at a rate of 5 miles per hour when it takes 1 hour to walk home at a rate of 4 miles per hour?
   (D) How long was the trip if Jill walked at a rate of 5 miles per hour when it takes 4 hours to walk home at a rate of 1 mile per hour?

10. If the sum of 5 consecutive integers is 40, what is the smallest of the 5 integers?

    (A) What is the smallest of 5 integers that equal 40 when added together?
    (B) What is the smallest of 10 consecutive integers that equal 40 when added together?
    (C) What is the largest of 5 consecutive integers that equal 40 when added together?
    (D) What is the smallest of 5 consecutive integers that equal 40 when added together?

11. Which of the following equations correctly describes the relationship between the values $x$ and $y$ in the table?

    (A) According to the table, what is the relationship between x and y as expressed in an equation?
    (B) How much larger than x is y?
    (C) How much smaller than x is y?
    (D) According to the table, what is the relationship between x and z?

12. The quadratic equation $x^2 - 3x = 4$ can be solved by factoring. Which of the following states the complete solution?

    (A) What is the complete solution to the quadratic equation $x^2 - 4x = 3$?
    (B) What is the complete solution to the quadratic formula?
    (C) What is the complete solution to the quadratic equation $x^2 - 3x = 4$?
    (D) What is one of the values of x for the given quadratic equation?

13. In a card game, a player had 5 successful turns in a row, and after each one, the number of points added to his total score was double what was added the preceding turn. If the player scored a total of 465 points, how many points did he score on the first turn?

    (A) How many points did he score on the fifth turn?
    (B) How many total points did he score after all five turns?
    (C) How many points did he score after the first turn?
    (D) On the first turn, how many points did the player score?

14. At a certain firm, *d* gallons of fuel are needed per day for each truck. At this rate, *g* gallons of fuel will supply *t* trucks for how many days?

    (A) How many t trucks will g gallons supply for d days?
    (B) d gallons will supply t trucks for how many days if g gallons of fuel are needed per day for each truck?
    (C) g gallons will supply t trucks for how many days if d gallons of fuel are needed per day for each truck?
    (D) g gallons and d gallons together will supply t trucks for how many days?

15. A merchant increased the price of a $25 item by 10 percent. If she then reduces the new price by 10 percent, the final result is equal to which of the following?

    (A) What is the final price of a $25 item after its price has been decreased by 10% and the resulting price is then increased by 10%?
    (B) What is 10% of ten $25 items?
    (C) What is the final price of a $25 item after its price has been increased by 10% and the resulting price is then decreased by 10%?
    (D) How much is 20% of a $25 item?

16. If a train travels *m* miles in *h* hours and 45 minutes, what is its average speed in miles per hour?

    (A) How long does it take the train to travel 45 miles?
    (B) What is the average speed if a train travels h miles in m hours and 45 minutes?
    (C) What is the average speed, in miles per hour, if a train travels 45 miles in h hours and m minutes?
    (D) What is the average speed if a train travels m miles in h hours and 45 minutes?

17. In a right isosceles triangle, the hypotenuse is equal to which of the following?

    (A) What is the hypotenuse of a right triangle?
    (B) What is the hypotenuse of a right triangle in which two sides are equal?
    (C) What is the hypotenuse of an isosceles triangle in which all three sides are equal?
    (D) What is the hypotenuse of a 30°-60°-90° triangle?

18. If a line intersects two points that are plotted at (3,6) and (7,9), what is its slope?

    (A) What are the slopes of two lines that include points (3,6) and (7,9), respectively?
    (B) What is the slope of a line that includes points (3,6) and (7,−9)?
    (C) What is the slope of a line that includes points (6,3) and (9,7)?
    (D) What is the slope of a line that includes points (3,6) and (7,9)?

19. The average of 8 numbers is 6; the average of 6 other numbers is 8. What is the average of all 14 numbers?

    (A) What is the average of 8 numbers?
    (B) What is the average of 14 numbers?
    (C) What is the average of 8 numbers plus the other average of 6 numbers?
    (D) What is the average of the other 6 numbers?

20. If the fourth term in a geometric sequence is 125 and the sixth term is 3,125, what is the second term of the sequence?

    (A) What is the second term in the periodic sequence?
    (B) What value is represented between the first and third terms in the geometric sequence?
    (C) What geometric term represents the process that is necessary to determine the value of the given sequence?
    (D) What is the difference between 3,125 and 125?

# Careful Reading of Verbal Reasoning Item Stems, Pt. II

**DIRECTIONS:** Choose the *best* restatement of the actual item that is being asked. Answers are on page 902.

1. The word "tacitly" in line 19 means

   (A) What is the tacit meaning of line 19?
   (B) In the context of line 19, what does the word "tacitly" mean?
   (C) In the context of line 19, what does the word "tacit" mean?
   (D) What is the tacit meaning of the first word in line 19?

2. Between the first and second paragraphs, Stanton changes her tone from

   (A) How does Stanton's tone in the second paragraph differ from that in the first?
   (B) What is Stanton's initial tone?
   (C) Why is Stanton's tone in the second paragraph more negative than in the first?
   (D) In what way does Stanton's tone remain unchanged?

3. Unlike Dante, Madame de Staël is

   (A) In what way is Madame de Staël like Dante?
   (B) In what way is Dante disliked by Madame de Staël?
   (C) Does Madame de Staël like Dante?
   (D) In what way is Madame de Staël unlike Dante?

4. Sun Yat-sen uses the example of Hong Kong to show

   (A) Is Sun Yat-sen from Hong Kong?
   (B) Why does Sun Yat-sen use Hong Kong as an example?
   (C) Why does Sun Yat-sen use Hong Kong as an example of Chinese culture?
   (D) Which statement is an example of Sun Yat-sen's relationship to Hong Kong?

5. How does Gandhi feel about the charge leveled against him?

   (A) Are Gandhi's charges on the level?
   (B) How does Gandhi exhibit his opposition to the charges leveled against him?
   (C) How does Gandhi feel about leveling charges against others?
   (D) What are Gandhi's feelings about the charge leveled against him?

6. Madame d'Épinay feels that Rousseau's complaints are

   (A) Why does Rousseau complain to Madame d'Épinay?
   (B) How does Rousseau feel about Madame d'Épinay's complaints?
   (C) How does Madame d'Épinay feel about Rousseau's complaints?
   (D) In what way does Madame d'Épinay feel that Rousseau's complaints are similar to her own?

7. Which of these best summarizes the difference between Rousseau's and Madame d'Épinay's philosophy of friendship?

   (A) Which statement summarizes Rousseau's feelings toward Madame d'Épinay's philosophy of friendship?
   (B) Which statement summarizes how Rousseau's and Madame d'Épinay's philosophies of friendship are distinct from one another?
   (C) How are Rousseau's and Madame d'Épinay's philosophies of friendship similar to one another?
   (D) What is the difference between Rousseau's philosophy of friendship and Madame d'Épinay's philosophy of rivalry?

8. Galileo includes the second paragraph in order to

   (A) For what reason does Galileo include the second paragraph?
   (B) How does the second paragraph relate to the rest of the passage?
   (C) In the second paragraph, why are the sentences arranged in that particular order?
   (D) Why is Galileo mentioned in the second paragraph?

9. Chekhov expresses definite opinions on each of the following points EXCEPT:

   (A) Which of the following points made by Chekhov is not based on fact?
   (B) On which of the following points does Chekhov express a definite opinion?
   (C) On which of the following points does Chekhov not express a definite opinion?
   (D) Which of the following points made by Chekhov is based only on opinion?

10. The narrative of Sojourner Truth implies that slaveholders' cruelty is based on

   (A) How is Sojourner Truth's cruelty implied in the narrative between slaves and slaveholders?
   (B) How do Sojourner Truth's slaveholders express their cruelty?
   (C) According to Sojourner Truth, what is the basis for justifying the cruelty of slaveholders?
   (D) What does Sojourner Truth imply as the basis for slaveholders' cruelty?

11. Would you expect Sojourner Truth to approve of the Declaration of Sentiments?

   (A) Did Sojourner Truth approve of the Declaration of Sentiments?
   (B) Did Sojourner Truth expect the Declaration of Sentiments to be approved?
   (C) Would Sojourner Truth approve of the Declaration of Sentience?
   (D) Would Sojourner Truth approve of the Declaration of Sentiments?

12. Which of the following most accurately summarizes the main idea of the passage?

   (A) What is the main point of the second paragraph?
   (B) What is the main idea of the passage?
   (C) Which point is a specific detail in the passage?
   (D) Which of the following points is not mentioned in the passage?

13. The author of the passage seems to value the Vignes/Wolfskill site most for

   (A) Why is the Vignes site valued more highly than the Wolfskill site?
   (B) Why is the Vignes/Wolfskill site not valued as highly as other sites listed by the author?
   (C) What is the most significant reason for why the author values the Vignes/Wolfskill site?
   (D) For what reason does the author most value the Vignes/Wolfskill site?

14. In line 52, "appropriate" most nearly means

   (A) Is the quote included by the author appropriate to the passage?
   (B) What word in line 52 most nearly means the same thing as "appropriate"?
   (C) Is line 52 appropriate to the passage?
   (D) What is the best definition for the word "appropriate" as it is used in the context of line 52?

15. The chief characteristic of Lady Bertram exposed in this excerpt is her

   (A) What main quality of Lady Bertram's is exposed in this excerpt?
   (B) Is Lady Bertram the main character in this excerpt?
   (C) Does Lady Bertram expose the main character's chief characteristic in this excerpt?
   (D) Which of Lady Bertram's characteristics is not exposed in this excerpt?

16. The author of Passage 1 creates an analogy between a novel and a(n)

   (A) What does the author of Passage 1 contrast to a novel?
   (B) What does the author of Passage 2 make analogous to a novel?
   (C) What does the author of Passage 1 make analogous to a novel?
   (D) The author of Passage 1 creates an analogy between which two novels?

17. The authors of both passages would be most likely to agree with which of the following statements?

   (A) With which statement would neither author agree?
   (B) With which statement would both authors agree?
   (C) With which statement would only one of the two authors agree?
   (D) With which statement would both authors disagree?

18. According to the third paragraph, an "allergen" differs from "antigens" in that an allergen

   (A) How are "antigens" different from an "allergen"?
   (B) How are "antigens" similar to an "allergen"?
   (C) How is an "antigen" similar to "allergens"?
   (D) How is an "allergen" different from "antigens"?

19. Austen's description of Mrs. Norris's many occupations (third paragraph) depicts her as a

   (A) In describing Austen's many occupations, how does Mrs. Norris depict her?
   (B) Which of Mrs. Norris's occupations does Austen describe in the third paragraph?
   (C) How many of Mrs. Norris's occupations are described in the third paragraph?
   (D) In describing Mrs. Norris's many occupations, how does Austen depict her?

20. The passage relies upon an extended metaphor of an immune response as a

   (A) To what does the passage metaphorically compare an immune response?
   (B) What is the best definition of an immune response as it is referred to in the passage?
   (C) The metaphor of an immune response extends through how many paragraphs?
   (D) How does the author of the passage respond to commonly accepted metaphorical explanation as it is used to describe an immune response?

21. The passage suggests that which of the following would deter a child from regarding an incident of television violence as real?

   (A) What would convince a child that television violence is real?
   (B) What would prevent a child from accepting the reality of violence on television?
   (C) What type of television violence would children be most likely to regard as real?
   (D) Under what conditions would a child not be deterred from watching television violence?

22. Which of the following best describes the
function of the final paragraph?

    (A) Which statement best summarizes the
    content of the final paragraph?
    (B) What is the function of the paragraph that
    precedes the final paragraph?
    (C) What purpose does the final paragraph serve?
    (D) What is the function of the first paragraph?

23. With which of the following statements about the
use of dialogue in novels would the author of
Passage 2 most likely agree?

    (A) With which statement about dialogue would
    the author of Passage 2 agree?
    (B) With which statement about dialogue would
    the author of Passage 2 disagree?
    (C) With which statement about dialogue would
    the author of Passage 1 disagree?
    (D) With which statement about dialogue in
    novels would the author of Passage 2 agree?

24. Austen undercuts her description of the lovely
Miss Bertrams by pointing out that they

    (A) How do the Miss Bertrams undercut their
    description of Austen?
    (B) How do the Miss Bertrams undercut Austen's
    description of them?
    (C) How does Austen undermine her description
    of the Miss Bertrams?
    (D) How does Austen undermine the Miss
    Bertrams description of her?

25. The word "asserting" in line 30 means

    (A) Which of the following statements is asserted
    in line 30?
    (B) What is the most common definition of the
    word "asserting"?
    (C) Which definition of the word "asserting" is
    mentioned in line 30?
    (D) What is the word "asserting" intended to
    mean in the context of line 30?

26. In quoting Gertrude Stein's saying, "There's no
there, there" (lines 8–9), Dolores Hayden most
likely means to say that

    (A) What is the meaning behind Gertrude Stein's
    saying?
    (B) What is the meaning behind Dolores
    Hayden's saying?
    (C) What is the meaning behind Dolores
    Hayden's use of Gertrude Stein's saying?
    (D) What is the meaning behind Gertrude Stein's
    use of Dolores Hayden's saying?

27. The author is primarily concerned with

    (A) What does the author suggest in the first
    paragraph of the passage?
    (B) What idea does the author chiefly regard in
    the passage?
    (C) Toward what dilemma does the author
    exhibit genuine concern?
    (D) Which topic does the author refer to before
    any other in the passage?

# Careful Reading of Quantitative Reasoning Item Stems, Pt. II

**DIRECTIONS:** Choose the *best* restatement of the item stem. Answers are on page 907.

1. What number increased by 25 equals twice the number?

   (A) What number is twice 25?
   (B) 25 is two times what number?
   (C) What number provides the same result when either increased by 25 or multiplied by 2?
   (D) What number provides the same result when either increased by 2 or multiplied by 25?

2. At State College, one-fourth of the students are from abroad. Of those, one-eighth are from China. What fraction of the student body is from China?

   (A) What fraction of the students are Chinese if they make up $\frac{1}{4} \div \frac{1}{8}$ of the student body?
   (B) What fraction of the students are Chinese if they make up $\frac{1}{8} \cdot \frac{1}{4}$ of the student body?
   (C) What fraction of the students are Chinese if they make up $\frac{1}{8} \div \frac{1}{4}$ of the student body?
   (D) What fraction of the students are Chinese if they make up $\frac{1}{4} + \frac{1}{8}$ of the student body?

3. If the average of 8, 10, 15, 20, and $x$ is 11, what is $x$?

   (A) What is x if the average of 15, 20, 8, 10, and y is 11?
   (B) What is x if the average of 15, 20, 8, 10, and x is 15?
   (C) What is x if the average of 15, 20, 10, 8, and x is 11?
   (D) What is x if the average of 11, 20, 8, 10, and x is 11?

4. Jane and Hector have the same birthday. When Hector was 36, Jane was 30. How old was Jane when Hector was twice her age?

   (A) How old was Jane when Hector was 12?
   (B) How old will Jane be when Hector is 60?
   (C) How old was Jane when Hector was 36?
   (D) How old was Hector when Jane was 12?

5. If the price of a book increases from $10.00 to $12.50, what is the percent increase in price?

   (A) What is the percent decrease in price of a book that originally cost $12.50 and now costs $10.00?
   (B) What is the percent increase in price of a book that originally cost $10.00 and now costs $22.50?
   (C) The difference in price between a book that had cost $10.00 and now costs $12.50 is what percentage of the new price?
   (D) The difference in price between a book that had cost $10.00 and now costs $12.50 is what percentage of the old price?

6. Boys and girls belong to the chess club. There are 36 people in the club, 15 of whom are girls. In lowest terms, what fraction of the club is boys?

   (A) With 15 girls in a club of 51 total people, what fraction (in lowest terms) of the club is boys?
   (B) With 21 boys in a club of 36 people, what fraction (in lowest terms) of the club is not girls?
   (C) With 15 girls in a club of 36 people, what fraction (in lowest terms) of the club is girls?
   (D) With 21 boys in a club of 36 people, what fraction (in lowest terms) of the club is girls?

7. If the sum of two consecutive integers is 29, what is the least of these integers?

   (A) What is the smaller of two consecutive integers that when added together total 29?
   (B) What is the smaller of two non-consecutive integers that when subtracted from the larger of those two integers results in 29?
   (C) What is the larger of two consecutive integers that when added together total 29?
   (D) What is the smaller of two consecutive integers that when added together total 92?

8. If a jar of 300 black and white marbles contains 156 white marbles, what percent of the marbles is black?

   (A) 156 is what percent of 300?
   (B) 144 is what percent of 300?
   (C) 300 is what percent of 456?
   (D) 144 is what percent of 456?

9. If 0.129914 is rounded off to the nearest hundredth, how many of its digits change?

   (A) How many digits change in 0.129914 if it is rounded off to the nearest tenth?
   (B) How many digits change in 0.129414 if it is rounded off to the nearest thousandth?
   (C) How many digits change in 0.129941 if it is rounded off to the nearest hundredth?
   (D) How many digits change in 0.129914 if it is rounded off to the nearest hundredth?

10. Ray is now 10 years older than Cindy. If in 8 years Ray will be twice as old as Cindy, how old is Cindy now?

   (A) How old will Cindy be in 8 years?
   (B) What is Cindy's current age?
   (C) If Ray is currently 8 years older than Cindy, what is Cindy's current age?
   (D) When Ray is 16 years older than Cindy, how old will Cindy be?

11. Let the "JOSH" of a number be defined as 3 less than 3 times the number. What number is equal to its "JOSH"?

   (A) What value for x is equal to $3x - 3$?
   (B) What value for x is equal to $3x + 3$?
   (C) What value for y is equal to $3x + 3$?
   (D) What value for y is equal to $3x - 3$?

12. What is the area of a circle with center $O$?

   (A) What is the area of circle $O$?
   (B) The circle with center $O$ has an area of what value?
   (C) Circle $O$ has a center with an area of what value?
   (D) What is the circumference of circle $O$?

13. In the country of Glup, 1 glop is 3 glips, and 4 glips are 5 globs. How many globs are 2 glops?

   (A) 4 glips are how many globs?
   (B) 2 glops are how many glups?
   (C) 2 glops are how many globs?
   (D) 3 glips are how many globs?

14. If $\frac{4}{5}$ is subtracted from its reciprocal, then what value is the result?

   (A) What is the result of $\frac{4}{5} - \frac{5}{4}$?
   (B) What is the result of $\frac{4}{5} - \frac{4}{5}$?
   (C) What is the result of $\frac{5}{4} - \frac{4}{5}$?
   (D) What is the result of $\frac{1}{5} - \frac{4}{5}$?

15. What is the value of $\frac{2}{3} - \frac{5}{8}$?

   (A) In decimal form, what is the result of $\frac{2}{3} - \frac{5}{8}$?
   (B) By subtracting $\frac{5}{8}$ from $\frac{2}{3}$, what value is yielded?
   (C) By subtracting $\frac{2}{3}$ from $\frac{5}{8}$, what value is yielded?
   (D) By subtracting $\frac{8}{5}$ from $\frac{3}{2}$, what value is yielded?

16. What is the average of 8.5, 7.8, and 7.7?

    (A) When 8.5, 7.8, and 7.7 are placed in
        sequential order, which number would be in
        the middle?
    (B) After dividing the sum total of 8.5, 7.7, and
        7.5 by 3, what is the result?
    (C) After multiplying the sum total of 8.5, 7.8,
        and 7.7 by 3, what is the result?
    (D) After dividing the sum total of 7.7, 8.5, and
        7.8 by 3, what is the result?

17. What is the area of square *PQRS*?

    (A) What is the area of square *QSPR*?
    (B) What is the area of quadrilateral *PQRS*?
    (C) What is the area of rectangle *PQRS*?
    (D) What is the area of square *SRQP*?

18. The average of 4, 5, $x$, and $y$ is 6, and the average
    of $x$, $z$, 8, and 9 is 8. What is the value of $z - y$?

    (A) What is the value of $z - y$ if 8 is the average
        of 9, $x$, 8, and $z$, and 6 is the average of 5, $y$,
        $x$, and 4?
    (B) What is the value of $z - y$ if the average of 4,
        5, $x$, and $y$ is 8, and the average of $x$, $z$, 8, and
        9 is 6?
    (C) What is the value of $z - y$ if 6 is the average
        of 9, $x$, 8, and $z$, and 8 is the average of 5, $y$,
        $x$, and 4?
    (D) What is the value of $y - z$ if the average of 4,
        5, $x$, and $y$ is 6, and the average of $x$, $z$, 8, and
        9 is 8?

19. 0.01 is the ratio of 0.1 to what number?

    (A) What is the value of $x$ if $0.01 : x$ is 0.1?
    (B) What is the value of $0.01 \div 0.1$?
    (C) What is the value of $x$ if $.1 : x$ is .01?
    (D) What is the value of $.001 \div 0.1$?

20. $\overline{AB}$ is parallel to $\overline{ED}$, and $\overline{AC}$ is equal to $\overline{BC}$. If
    $\angle BED$ is 50°, then what is the value of $x$?

    (A) What is the value of $x$ if $\angle BED = 50°$, $\overline{CB}$ is
        parallel to $\overline{CA}$, and $\overline{DE}$ is equal to $\overline{BA}$?
    (B) What is the value of $x$ if $\angle EDB = 50°$, $\overline{AB}$ is
        parallel to $\overline{ED}$, and $\overline{AC}$ is equal to $\overline{BC}$?
    (C) What is the value of $x$ if $\angle BED = 50°$, $\overline{AB}$ is
        parallel to $\overline{AC}$, and $\overline{ED}$ is equal to $\overline{BC}$?
    (D) What is the value of $x$ if $\angle DEB = 50°$, $\overline{CB}$ is
        equal to $\overline{CA}$, and $\overline{DE}$ is parallel to $\overline{BA}$?

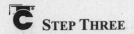 

## Coding of Item Stems

Most students are pressed for time on the Reading Comprehension items. You can save time by looking for the correct answers to items as you read the passage for the first time. Reading a passage and answering several corresponding items at the rate of less than one item per minute requires a very different skill than what you would typically use when reading a book, newspaper, or magazine.

For Reading Comprehension items, you must not only read the item correctly, but you must also correctly identify the item-type. Every Reading Comprehension item, regardless of the corresponding passage format, will be from one of six basic types. You can avoid memorizing information that is not needed to answer an item by focusing only on information that is needed to answer the question that is being asked by that specific item-type. Remember that many more questions could be asked on any given passage than are actually asked. If you do not identify the correct item-type, then there is a good chance that you will not use the appropriate strategy for finding the correct answer. You must therefore know the characteristics of the correct answer that are associated with each item-type.

Reading Comprehension items are designed to test three levels of comprehension: appreciation of the general theme, understanding of specific points, and evaluation of the text. Exercises 11 and 12 are designed to help you immediately recognize both the level of comprehension and the item-type, respectively, that are being tested based on the wording of the item stem. Each of the three levels of comprehension is represented by at least one of the six types of Reading Comprehension items. The following are descriptions of the three levels of reading comprehension:

### GENERAL THEME

The first level of reading is the most basic. *Main Idea* items and items about the overall development of the selection test whether you understand the passage at the most general level. The first and/or last sentences of paragraphs may be helpful in understanding either the content of particular paragraph or the general theme of the passage.

### SPECIFIC POINTS

The second level of reading takes you deeper into the selection. *Specific Detail* items and items about the logical roles of details (*Logical Structure*) help you understand specific points in the passage and test your ability to read carefully.

### EVALUATION

The third level of reading takes you even deeper into the selection. *Implied Idea*, *Further Application*, and *Attitude/Tone* items require, in addition to an understanding of the material, a judgment or an evaluation of what you have read. As a result, these items tend to be the most difficult.

---

## SIX TYPES OF READING COMPREHENSION ITEMS

**Main Idea** – What is the unifying theme?

**Specific Detail** – What is explicitly mentioned?

**Logical Structure** – How are the ideas constructed and arranged?

**Implied Idea** – What can be inferred?

**Further Application** – How can the information be applied to new situations?

**Attitude/Tone** – What does the writer reveal through attitude, voice, or tone?

---

When taking the test, read each passage slowly and carefully as you search for clues that will help answer each item. The faster you read the passage, the less likely you are to pick the correct answer choice. Most answer choices require careful reading, analysis, and an application of the facts to the exact question that is being asked.

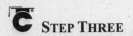 

EXERCISE **11**

# Comprehension Level Coding

**DIRECTIONS:** Code each Reading Comprehension item stem according to one of the three levels of comprehension: General Theme (GT), Specific Points (SP), or Evaluation (E). Answers are on page 910.

1. According to the passage, tears and laughter have all of the following in common EXCEPT

   _____

   _____

2. The author implies that animals lack the ability to

   _____

   _____

3. The word "ludicrous" in line # most nearly means

   _____

   _____

4. The author develops the passage primarily by

   _____

   _____

5. In the second paragraph, the author

   _____

   _____

6. Which of the following titles best describes the content of the selection?

   _____

   _____

7. The author is primarily concerned with discussing the

   _____

   _____

8. The passage states that the open government statute is intended to accomplish all of the following EXCEPT

   _____

   _____

9. The passage most strongly supports which of the following conclusions about a decision that is within the authority of the executive director of an agency?

   _____

   _____

10. In the final paragraph, the author discusses

   _____

   _____

11. The author makes all of the following points about the rules governing the commission EXCEPT

   _____

   _____

12. It can be inferred from the passage that the executive director is authorized to make certain purchases costing less than $5,000 in order to

   _____

   _____

13. Which of the following statements about a "review and comment" session can be inferred from the selection?

_____

_____

14. According to the passage, all of the following are true of metamorphic rock EXCEPT

_____

_____

15. As described by the selection, the sequence of events leading to the present landscape was

_____

_____

16. The author regards the explanation he gives as

_____

_____

17. The author provides information that defines which of the following terms?

_____

_____

18. The author would most likely agree with which of the following statements?

_____

_____

19. The passage supports which of the following conclusions about the writings of Yevgeny Zamyatin?

_____

_____

20. The author's treatment of James Burnham's writing can best be described as

_____

_____

21. The statement that Burnham inverted the logical priority of the individual over the state means that Burnham believed that

_____

_____

22. The author criticized Burnham for

_____

_____

# Item-Type Coding

**DIRECTIONS:** Code each Reading Comprehension item stem according to one of the six item-types: Main Idea (MI), Specific Detail (SD), Logical Structure (LS), Implied Idea (II), Further Application (FA), or Attitude/Tone (AT). Answers are on page 912.

1. According to Burnham, in the completely autocratic state, history will have come to an end because

———————————————————
———————————————————

2. It can be inferred from the passage that the physical features of a galaxy that do not belong to a rich cluster are determined primarily by the

———————————————————
———————————————————

3. The author implies that the currently accepted theories on galaxy formation are

———————————————————
———————————————————

4. According to the passage, a cluster with a central, supergiant galaxy will

———————————————————
———————————————————

5. According to the passage, the outcome of a collision between galaxies depends on which of the following?

———————————————————
———————————————————

6. According to the passage, as a galaxy falls inward toward the center of a cluster, it

———————————————————
———————————————————

7. According to the passage, a star such as our Sun would probably not be found in a cluster such as Virgo because

———————————————————
———————————————————

8. The phrase "nature never became a toy to the wise spirit" means which of the following?

———————————————————
———————————————————

9. The author implies that the difference between farms and the landscape is primarily a matter of

———————————————————
———————————————————

10. The author uses the word "property" in the phrase "property in the horizon" (line #) to mean

———————————————————
———————————————————

11. The phrase "color of the spirit" in line # means

———————————————————
———————————————————

12. The main purpose of this passage is to

_____

_____

13. Which of the following best explains the distinction between a life circumstance and a life event?

_____

_____

14. The author uses all of the following techniques EXCEPT

_____

_____

15. Which of the following best explains the relationship between the first paragraph and the second paragraph of the passage?

_____

_____

16. The passage provides information that defines which of the following terms?

_____

_____

17. According to the passage, Wineland was characterized by which of the following geographical features?

_____

_____

18. It can be inferred from the passage that scholars who doubt the authenticity of the Biarni narrative make all of the following objections EXCEPT

_____

_____

19. The author mentions the two high mountains in order to show that it is unlikely to be true that

_____

_____

20. All of the following are mentioned as similarities between Leif Erikson's voyage and Biarni's voyage EXCEPT

_____

_____

21. It can be inferred that the author regards the historicity of the Biarni narrative as

_____

_____

22. The author's attitude toward the Aleuts can best be described as one of

_____

_____

# Verbal Reasoning Test Mechanics

# CAMBRIDGE TESTPREP™

## Test Mechanics
# VERBAL REASONING

### ANATOMY OF THE VERBAL REASONING TEST SECTION:

The computer-adaptive GRE has one "live" Verbal Reasoning test section. This section contains Analogies, Antonyms, Sentence Completions, and Reading Comprehension items. (Remember that the test could include an experimental section which might contain Verbal Reasoning items, but that section would NOT be scored.) According to Educational Testing Service, Verbal Reasoning items test the following skills:

- Ability to analyze and evaluate written material and synthesize information obtained from it
- Ability to analyze relationships among component parts of sentences
- Ability to recognize relationships between words and concepts

Typically, the Verbal Reasoning test section contains 30 items broken down approximately as follows: 7 Analogies, 9 Antonyms, 6 Sentence Completions, and 8 Reading Comprehension items. (Note: The ratio of items for each subject-area is approximately the same on both the computer-based version and the paper-and-pencil test.)

Due to a peculiarity in the algorithm for the GRE computer-adaptive test, you are able to attain your top score only if you answer all of the items in a test section (e.g., 30 in Verbal Reasoning). You might think that you could score an 800 by answering the first five or six items correctly and then refusing to respond to any more items—thus claiming for yourself a "perfect score." However, this simply is not the way the test is designed. This observation also explodes the myth that you need to answer perfectly on the first few items to avoid becoming "trapped in the basement" of the scoring scale from which you can never escape. This can lead to the mistake of spending so much time on the first few items that you do not finish the test section. Instead, you have to find the appropriate balance between speed and accuracy. The following guidelines will help you strike such a balance.

### VERBAL REASONING PACING AND GUESSING TECHNIQUES:

On average, you will need to spend differing amounts of time on the various items due to the inherent features of each subject-area—the least amount of time on an Antonyms item, a bit more time on an Analogies item, even more time on a Sentence Completions item, and finally, the most amount of time on a Reading Comprehension item. The relative times to be allocated to each of these items are summarized in the following table:

| Subject-Area | Average Time per Item |
| --- | --- |
| Antonyms | 40 seconds |
| Analogies | 50 seconds |
| Sentence Completions | 1 minute |
| Reading Comprehension | 1.5 minutes |

Remember that these times are *averages*. The items become more difficult as you progress through the test and move up the ladder of difficulty, so you do not want to get "bogged down" on an item. Therefore, you should keep an eye on the time clock. A properly paced exam will develop as follows:

| Item Currently Working On | Items Remaining | Time Remaining |
| --- | --- | --- |
| 1 | 29 | 29 minutes |
| 8 | 22 | 22.5 minutes |
| 15 | 15 | 15 minutes |
| 22 | 8 | 7.5 minutes |
| 30 | 0 | 1 minute |

In the Verbal Reasoning Concepts and Strategies portion of this course, you will learn techniques for handling these different verbal items that will help you maintain the right pace, but some of the more important techniques are worth mentioning right now:

*Analogies*:

- Analogies items, like Antonyms items, are short, but they are as much a test of relationships between concepts as they are of vocabulary, so you may need a little more time, on average, to answer these items than you would to answer Antonyms items.

- If you do not know one or more of the key words in the Analogies item, then you are "flying blind." Do not wait for the lightning to strike because it will not. Instead, eliminate any "non-answers" (discussed in the Analogies Core Lesson), guess, and continue on to the next item.

*Antonyms*:

- Antonyms are the shortest Verbal Reasoning items, so it stands to reason that they should take the least amount of time to answer. So, make up your mind in advance not to spend more than 45 seconds on a single Antonyms item.

- Antonyms items are mainly a test of vocabulary. There are some techniques to fall back on, in general, if you have no idea of the meaning of the key word. However, if your back-up strategies have failed, guess and keep moving. Again, do not wait for the lightning to strike because it will not. You must stay on track. Plus, the time that you save can be invested in a later item.

*Sentence Completions*:

- While Sentence Completions items are partly a test of vocabulary, they also involve a fair bit of logic. Since logic requires a greater effort than does vocabulary, you can expect to spend more time on Sentence Completions than on either Antonyms or Analogies items.

- The logic of a Sentence Completions item is dictated by certain key words such as "because," "although," "therefore," and "so" (discussed in the Sentence Completions Core Lesson). If a sentence is completely devoid of logical clues and you cannot get any traction on it, guess and go on to the next item.

*Reading Comprehension*:

- Reading Comprehension items are the longest Verbal Reasoning items. Often, the item stem and answer choices contain 75 to 100 total words, or even more. So, you should expect to spend more time answering one of these items than you would answering any one of the other Verbal Reasoning items—plus, you need to read the passage!

- A Reading Comprehension passage usually consists of 250 to 300 words, and you need to read it before you can answer the items. Do NOT, however, study the passage as you would a college textbook. Instead, read the passage for the main point and overall structure. Remember that this is an "open-book" test, so you can go back to find details.

# Verbal Reasoning Concepts and Strategies

# Analogies

# CAMBRIDGE TESTPREP™

## ANALOGIES OUTLINE

## I. Core Lesson (p. 107)

### A. Analogies Preliminaries

### B. Facts About Analogies Items

1. Parts of Speech
2. Nature of Difficult Items
3. Wrong Answer Choices Are Wrong for One of Two Reasons

### C. Basic Strategies

1. Creating Diagnostic Sentences
2. Tinkering with Diagnostic Sentences
3. Fine-Tuning Diagnostic Sentences

### D. Ten Most Common Item-Types

1. Defining Characteristic (Items #1–8, p. 107)
2. Lack of Defining Characteristic (Items #9–13, p. 107)
3. Type Of (Item #14, p. 108)
4. Part Of (Items #15–17, p. 108)
5. Place For (Items #18–21, p. 108)
6. Degree (Items #22–26, p. 109)
7. Tools (Items #27–29, p. 109)
8. Sign Of (Items #30–32, p. 109)
9. Sequence (Items #33–35, p. 109)
10. Spurious Form (Items #36–37, p. 110)

### E. Additional Strategies

1. Customizing Diagnostic Sentences (Items #38–43, p. 110)
2. Tough Calls (Items #44–45, p. 110)
3. Shooting in the Dark

## II. Review (Items #1–50, p. 111)

## III. Timed-Practice Quizzes (p. 116)

### A. Quiz I (Items #1–22, p. 116)

### B. Quiz II (Items #1–22, p. 118)

### C. Quiz III (Items #1–22, p. 120)

## IV.  Strategy Summary Sheet (p. 122)

# CORE LESSON

The items in this section accompany the Core Lesson section of the Analogies Lesson. You will work through the items with your instructor in class.

**DIRECTIONS:** Each of the following items consists of a related pair of words or phrases presented in capital letters, followed by five lettered pairs of words or phrases presented in lowercase letters. For each item, choose the lettered pair that expresses a relationship that is most nearly like that expressed in the capitalized pair. Answers are on page 914.

1. CONCILIATORY : FRIENDLINESS ::

   (A) peaceful : litigation
   (B) oblivious : awareness
   (C) inventive : practicality
   (D) toxic : antidote
   (E) rueful : sorrow

2. TANGLED : KNOT ::

   (A) snarled : rope
   (B) crumpled : wrinkle
   (C) mussed : hair
   (D) empty : hole
   (E) canned : preserves

3. TRANQUILITY : PEACE ::

   (A) chaos : disorder
   (B) retraction : indictment
   (C) combustion : waste
   (D) miracle : belief
   (E) tension : relaxation

4. PICKPOCKET : WALLET ::

   (A) burglar : night
   (B) embezzler : funds
   (C) detective : fugitive
   (D) merchant : expenses
   (E) innkeeper : guest

5. HEAR : INAUDIBLE ::

   (A) touch : intangible
   (B) mumble : praiseworthy
   (C) spend : wealthy
   (D) prepare : ready
   (E) enjoy : illegal

6. BLAME : SCAPEGOAT ::

   (A) explain : answer
   (B) convict : punishment
   (C) lionize : hero
   (D) appreciate : art
   (E) relate : secret

7. TRAITOR : DISLOYALTY ::

   (A) rebel : defiance
   (B) general : army
   (C) executioner : reliability
   (D) artist : business
   (E) banker : marketing

8. BETRAY : TREACHERY ::

   (A) acknowledge : infamy
   (B) amuse : horror
   (C) abandon : desertion
   (D) inflate : reduction
   (E) contend : victory

9. ACCIDENTAL : INTENTION ::

   (A) voluntary : requirement
   (B) anticipated : performance
   (C) interesting : feeling
   (D) practical : knowledge
   (E) insane : correction

10. ANONYMOUS : IDENTITY ::

   (A) amorphous : form
   (B) masked : party
   (C) wealthy : income
   (D) motivated : goal
   (E) infamous : report

11. VACUUM : AIR ::

   (A) invitation : host
   (B) vacancy : occupant
   (C) love : passion
   (D) literacy : writing
   (E) bait : trap

12. OBSCURITY : INTELLIGIBILITY ::

   (A) ambiguity : clarity
   (B) redundancy : repetition
   (C) novelty : experimentation
   (D) cynicism : philosophy
   (E) insight : communication

13. KNOW : IGNORANCE ::

   (A) cure : health
   (B) construct : school
   (C) invite : party
   (D) educate : graduation
   (E) breathe : suffocation

14. BALLAD : SONG ::

   (A) spire : church
   (B) ode : poem
   (C) novel : chapter
   (D) envelope : letter
   (E) leopard : jaguar

15. SINGER : CHORUS ::

   (A) architect : blueprint
   (B) teacher : student
   (C) author : publisher
   (D) driver : highway
   (E) actor : cast

16. FOREST : TREES ::

   (A) fleet : ships
   (B) lumber : wood
   (C) rose : thorns
   (D) shelf : books
   (E) camera : film

17. VERDICT : TRIAL ::

   (A) audience : play
   (B) finish : race
   (C) overture : opera
   (D) recovery : operation
   (E) act : drama

18. BEE : HIVE ::

   (A) horse : carriage
   (B) rider : bicycle
   (C) sheep : flock
   (D) cow : barn
   (E) dog : show

19. BEE : APIARY ::

   (A) horse : carriage
   (B) rider : bicycle
   (C) sheep : flock
   (D) cow : barn
   (E) dog : show

20. DRUGGIST : PHARMACY ::

   (A) librarian : catalogue
   (B) physician : patient
   (C) chef : restaurant
   (D) carpenter : wood
   (E) musician : nightclub

21. ROUSTABOUT : CIRCUS ::

   (A) electrician : kitchen
   (B) dean : classroom
   (C) stevedore : dock
   (D) engineer : library
   (E) ruffian : factory

22. ECSTASY : PLEASURE ::

    (A) hatred : affection
    (B) condemnation : approval
    (C) rage : anger
    (D) difficulty : understanding
    (E) privacy : invasion

23. PIT : ABYSS ::

    (A) defeat : rout
    (B) impasse : detour
    (C) hurdle : clearance
    (D) improvement : practice
    (E) ambition : success

24. NOISE : DIN ::

    (A) utterance : voice
    (B) celebration : revelry
    (C) motion : traction
    (D) sanity : treatment
    (E) remonstrance : sin

25. MOISTEN : DRENCH ::

    (A) pump : replenish
    (B) chill : freeze
    (C) deny : pretend
    (D) dance : rejoice
    (E) announce : suppress

26. BOOK : TOME ::

    (A) page : binding
    (B) plot : character
    (C) omission : diligence
    (D) library : borrower
    (E) story : saga

27. INCISION : SCALPEL ::

    (A) hospital : patient
    (B) playground : swing
    (C) kitchen : knife
    (D) electricity : wire
    (E) hole : drill

28. SCYTHES : REAPING ::

    (A) screws : turning
    (B) crops : planting
    (C) lights : reading
    (D) shears : cutting
    (E) saws : gluing

29. BICYCLIST : PEDAL ::

    (A) referee : contest
    (B) singer : piano
    (C) rower : oar
    (D) runner : marathon
    (E) jockey : horse

30. CRINGE : FEAR ::

    (A) gasp : breath
    (B) think : conclusion
    (C) yawn : boredom
    (D) enhance : nobility
    (E) announce : reaction

31. BOAST : VANITY ::

    (A) gloat : satisfaction
    (B) write : novel
    (C) primp : humility
    (D) apologize : profit
    (E) mail : photograph

32. CORNUCOPIA : ABUNDANCE ::

    (A) chameleon : lizard
    (B) insignia : banner
    (C) gargoyle : edifice
    (D) phoenix : rebirth
    (E) idolatry : religion

33. EXTINGUISHED : RELIT ::

    (A) completed : discouraged
    (B) announced : publicized
    (C) collapsed : rebuilt
    (D) evicted : purchased
    (E) imagined : denied

34. REMISSION : DISEASE ::

    (A) reduction : procedure
    (B) transportation : goods
    (C) assignment : position
    (D) stay : execution
    (E) impression : security

35. CHECKPOINT : HIGHWAY ::

    (A) postponement : delay
    (B) map : route
    (C) detour : destination
    (D) advertisement : product
    (E) valve : pipe

36. PLAGIARIZE : TEXT ::

    (A) pirate : software
    (B) question : source
    (C) insist : favor
    (D) ignore : background
    (E) withdraw : effort

37. PSEUDONYM : NAME ::

    (A) alibi : crime
    (B) sailboat : wind
    (C) mountain : valley
    (D) church : state
    (E) mask : face

38. LOW : CATTLE ::

    (A) run : horses
    (B) grunt : hogs
    (C) scratch : chickens
    (D) plant : crops
    (E) store : grain

39. PLANT : FERTILIZER ::

    (A) animal : food
    (B) rose : thorn
    (C) harvest : plenty
    (D) season : hunting
    (E) restaurant : menu

40. SCRIPT : DRAMA ::

    (A) writing : page
    (B) photograph : magazine
    (C) lyric : note
    (D) chapter : book
    (E) score : symphony

41. HAND : WRIST ::

    (A) muscle : bone
    (B) tendon : finger
    (C) foot : ankle
    (D) skull : brain
    (E) ear : hair

42. ANNEX : BUILDING ::

    (A) bedroom : apartment
    (B) fountain : park
    (C) epilogue : novel
    (D) dining car : train
    (E) memory : computer

43. RAMPART : FORTRESS ::

    (A) bicycle : wheel
    (B) river : lake
    (C) cage : animal
    (D) ladder : roof
    (E) fence : house

44. SUNDIAL : TIME ::

    (A) balance : weight
    (B) pyramid : worship
    (C) umpire : score
    (D) thermometer : illness
    (E) metronome : music

45. SUPPORT : PATRON ::

    (A) acceptance : donor
    (B) loyalty : patriot
    (C) apathy : zealot
    (D) deception : anarchist
    (E) entertainment : narrator

# REVIEW

This section contains Analogies items for further practice.

**DIRECTIONS:** Each of the following items consists of a related pair of words or phrases presented in capital letters, followed by five lettered pairs of words or phrases presented in lowercase letters. For each item, choose the lettered pair that expresses a relationship that is most nearly like that expressed in the capitalized pair. Answers are on page 914.

1. CACHE : HIDE ::

   (A) forgiveness : punish
   (B) stockpile : accumulate
   (C) testimony : falsify
   (D) ignition : extinguish
   (E) intimidation : fear

2. LOQUACITY : TALK ::

   (A) garrulity : listen
   (B) piety : disregard
   (C) gluttony : eat
   (D) tenacity : resign
   (E) simplicity : understand

3. GROTESQUE : DISTORTED ::

   (A) fabricated : efficient
   (B) monotonous : constant
   (C) trustworthy : optimistic
   (D) imagined : permanent
   (E) mature : young

4. SVELTE : EMACIATED ::

   (A) enriched : impoverished
   (B) large : gargantuan
   (C) still : profound
   (D) routine : inspiring
   (E) permanent : transitory

5. REDUNDANT : REPETITIOUS ::

   (A) written : oral
   (B) incomplete : developed
   (C) censured : obscene
   (D) wise : understandable
   (E) verbose : wordy

6. LAPIDARY : GEMS ::

   (A) carpenter : stones
   (B) biologist : laboratories
   (C) numismatist : coins
   (D) aviator : students
   (E) cardiologist : hearts

7. INTERLOPER : CONSENT ::

   (A) investor : return
   (B) referee : game
   (C) translator : language
   (D) missionary : commitment
   (E) intruder : invitation

8. GARGOYLE : GROTESQUE ::

   (A) magician : elegant
   (B) boulevard : serene
   (C) government : amicable
   (D) miser : affectionate
   (E) philanthropist : benevolent

9. LIBEL : DEFAMATORY ::

   (A) praise : laudatory
   (B) option : selective
   (C) value : sparse
   (D) insult : apologetic
   (E) struggle : victorious

10. GREGARIOUSNESS : SOCIABILITY ::

    (A) courageousness : fearfulness
    (B) reliability : esteem
    (C) forgetfulness : memorability
    (D) affability : friendliness
    (E) gullibility : believability

11. MAVERICK : STRAY ::

    (A) hermit : recluse
    (B) expert : ignorance
    (C) trickster : payment
    (D) miser : money
    (E) rumor : truth

12. PLATITUDE : TRITE ::

    (A) axiom : geometrical
    (B) prescription : medical
    (C) cuisine : international
    (D) boredom : friendly
    (E) innovation : novel

13. MOTLEY : COLOR ::

    (A) bovine : herd
    (B) cacophonous : sound
    (C) legal : codification
    (D) miraculous : apathy
    (E) remedial : expertise

14. BELIE : TRUTH ::

    (A) convey : idea
    (B) mask : face
    (C) invite : attention
    (D) succumb : illness
    (E) dawdle : tardiness

15. HARBINGER : BEGINNING ::

    (A) ordain : decree
    (B) herald : advent
    (C) amend : correction
    (D) emancipate : freedom
    (E) commiserate : news

16. ELEGIAC : MOURNING ::

    (A) contemptuous : disdain
    (B) rambunctious : enervation
    (C) profligate : lassitude
    (D) amorphous : spontaneity
    (E) deferential : veracity

17. MOUNTAIN : TUNNEL ::

    (A) window : frame
    (B) river : bridge
    (C) door : handle
    (D) charcoal : fire
    (E) wall : window

18. FRIGHTEN : SCARE ::

    (A) question : ask
    (B) look : see
    (C) terrorize : startle
    (D) brave : fear
    (E) upset : calm

19. DOOR : OPEN ::

    (A) cap : remove
    (B) knife : cut
    (C) blackboard : erase
    (D) gift : wrap
    (E) car : speed

20. PUERILE : MATURITY ::

    (A) pungent : poignancy
    (B) poised : serenity
    (C) obscure : clarity
    (D) ostentatious : pretension
    (E) profuse : extravagance

21. INFINITE : BOUNDS ::

    (A) intangible : property
    (B) kinetic : motion
    (C) nebulous : clarity
    (D) ponderous : bulk
    (E) propitious : favor

22. SOAR : ALIGHT ::

   (A) hop : stumble
   (B) crawl : run
   (C) lift : carry
   (D) walk : hike
   (E) sail : moor

23. COTTON : SOFT ::

   (A) wool : warm
   (B) iron : hard
   (C) nylon : strong
   (D) wood : polished
   (E) silk : expensive

24. MULE : INTRACTABLE ::

   (A) horse : turbulent
   (B) fox : wily
   (C) dog : candid
   (D) wolf : fickle
   (E) tiger : inexorable

25. DISAGREEMENT : CONCORD ::

   (A) limitation : restriction
   (B) impartiality : bias
   (C) advantage : agreement
   (D) predicament : dilemma
   (E) predictability : routine

26. BEEF : JERKY ::

   (A) corn : flake
   (B) ham : pork
   (C) grape : raisin
   (D) meat : sausage
   (E) flesh : bone

27. MAGNANIMOUS : PETTY ::

   (A) arrogant : insolent
   (B) valiant : belligerent
   (C) passionate : blasé
   (D) munificent : generous
   (E) circumspect : prudent

28. HILT : BLADE ::

   (A) holster : gun
   (B) sheath : knife
   (C) leash : dog
   (D) stem : leaf
   (E) petal : branch

29. BRAGGART : DIFFIDENCE ::

   (A) benefactor : generosity
   (B) pariah : esteem
   (C) partisan : partiality
   (D) savant : wisdom
   (E) sycophant : flattery

30. DIATRIBE : BITTERNESS ::

   (A) dictum : injury
   (B) critique : even-handedness
   (C) polemic : consonance
   (D) encomium : praise
   (E) concordance : disagreement

31. TRAVESTY : RIDICULE ::

   (A) reproduction : provoke
   (B) forgery : deceive
   (C) imitation : feign
   (D) treachery : reprieve
   (E) poetry : comprehend

32. VOLATILE : STABILITY ::

   (A) spontaneous : enthusiasm
   (B) voluble : glibness
   (C) wanton : restraint
   (D) reverent : respect
   (E) servile : humility

33. MUNIFICENT : GENEROSITY ::

   (A) dolorous : sorrow
   (B) domineering : timidity
   (C) indisputable : doubt
   (D) fortunate : haplessness
   (E) beguiled : judiciousness

34. JOCULAR : SOLEMNITY ::

    (A) latent : visibility
    (B) pompous : spectacle
    (C) ruined : demolition
    (D) vindictive : enmity
    (E) lonely : insularity

35. GATE : PLANE ::

    (A) latch : door
    (B) fence : yard
    (C) track : train
    (D) highway : car
    (E) driver : bus

36. DIFFUSE : CONCENTRATION ::

    (A) spread : expansion
    (B) diffident : shyness
    (C) indelicate : coarseness
    (D) incongruous : harmony
    (E) anger : resentment

37. DETRIMENTAL : PERNICIOUS ::

    (A) delightful : delicious
    (B) cheerful : exuberant
    (C) painful : sore
    (D) helpful : useful
    (E) fearful : timid

38. ROBUST : VIGOR ::

    (A) massive : strength
    (B) sick : illness
    (C) farsighted : glasses
    (D) full : appetite
    (E) sanguine : hope

39. TRAITOROUS : PERFIDY ::

    (A) despicable : country
    (B) envious : green
    (C) devious : dourness
    (D) loyal : steadfastness
    (E) smart : average

40. DEMUR : HESITATION ::

    (A) attract : agreeability
    (B) equivocate : conviction
    (C) denounce : insensitivity
    (D) facilitate : action
    (E) question : knowledge

41. DISCERNING : PERCEPTION ::

    (A) moribund : defilement
    (B) oblivious : forgetfulness
    (C) interminable : brevity
    (D) ambiguous : clarity
    (E) loathsome : decrepitude

42. PROSELYTIZE : CONVERT ::

    (A) argue : persuade
    (B) digress : disturb
    (C) abide : forego
    (D) deflect : condone
    (E) dissemble : abet

43. BALEFUL : EVIL ::

    (A) fulsome : refinement
    (B) disjointed : compatibility
    (C) mandatory : requirement
    (D) literate : obstreperousness
    (E) dogmatic : hostility

44. AMBIVALENCE : COMMIT ::

    (A) perfidy : profit
    (B) gullibility : discern
    (C) travesty : judge
    (D) enthusiasm : predict
    (E) conundrum : outwit

45. AMBULATORY : MOBILITY ::

    (A) cantankerous : foolishness
    (B) frolicsome : insight
    (C) venial : goodness
    (D) salubrious : decay
    (E) loquacious : speech

46. THWART : ACHIEVE ::

   (A) retain : submit
   (B) couch : conceal
   (C) silence : speak
   (D) pretend : inherit
   (E) permeate : infiltrate

47. PRESTIDIGITATION : DECEPTION ::

   (A) adulation : enemy
   (B) legerdemain : illusion
   (C) solemnity : funeral
   (D) inexorability : chronology
   (E) procrastination : deadline

48. MAELSTROM : WHIRLPOOL ::

   (A) catastrophe : reminder
   (B) horizon : crepuscule
   (C) tempest : delight
   (D) inferno : fire
   (E) explosion : concentration

49. APOCRYPHAL : GENUINE ::

   (A) spurious : authentic
   (B) labored : relieved
   (C) fragmented : riddled
   (D) enigmatic : rambunctious
   (E) credulous : flagrant

50. DISAPPROBATION : CONDEMN ::

   (A) solvency : deploy
   (B) calumny : laud
   (C) enigma : enlighten
   (D) fallacy : disseminate
   (E) exhortation : urge

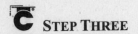 

# TIMED-PRACTICE QUIZZES

**DIRECTIONS:** This section contains three Analogies quizzes. While being timed, complete each quiz. Each of the following items consists of a related pair of words or phrases presented in capital letters, followed by five lettered pairs of words or phrases presented in lowercase letters. For each item, choose the lettered pair that expresses a relationship that is most nearly like that expressed in the capitalized pair. Answers are on page 915.

## QUIZ I (22 items; 15 minutes)

1. VALVE : PIPE ::

   (A) switch : wire
   (B) map : detour
   (C) menu : diner
   (D) dam : electricity
   (E) cap : jacket

2. LANDSLIDE : EARTH ::

   (A) growth : soil
   (B) flood : water
   (C) building : plan
   (D) bladder : air
   (E) ignition : fire

3. RECIPE : FOOD ::

   (A) blueprint : building
   (B) formula : scientist
   (C) ingredient : concoction
   (D) liquid : consumption
   (E) score : performer

4. EVERGREEN : TREE ::

   (A) carrot : vegetable
   (B) wildlife : forest
   (C) lake : ocean
   (D) nightfall : daybreak
   (E) ice : glacier

5. HONE : KNIFE ::

   (A) tune : instrument
   (B) count : money
   (C) waste : energy
   (D) paint : brush
   (E) polish : glint

6. PIROUETTE : BALLET ::

   (A) coach : diving
   (B) market : farming
   (C) swirl : painting
   (D) fame : acting
   (E) somersault : tumbling

7. PRESUME : DETERMINE ::

   (A) theorize : prove
   (B) beautify : recall
   (C) authorize : detain
   (D) frustrate : prefer
   (E) believe : accept

8. DEBATER : ARGUMENT ::

   (A) minister : congregation
   (B) poet : artist
   (C) chauffeur : passenger
   (D) boxer : ring
   (E) musician : instrument

9. INFLATE : MAGNITUDE ::

   (A) measure : weight
   (B) extend : duration
   (C) magnify : coin
   (D) limit : speed
   (E) legislate : crime

10. SLANDER : PEJORATIVE ::

    (A) ingratiate : miraculous
    (B) revere : condemning
    (C) extol : laudatory
    (D) ruminate : superficial
    (E) reward : grateful

11. WEB : ENTANGLE ::

(A) spider : spin
(B) trap : ensnare
(C) treason : betray
(D) ransom : kidnap
(E) grid : delineate

12. IMPROMPTU : PLANNING ::

(A) gratuitous : ticket
(B) dramatic : rehearsal
(C) cursory : care
(D) ravenous : appetite
(E) enlightened : knowledge

13. LACONIC : WORDS ::

(A) affable : friends
(B) hesitant : action
(C) monotonous : address
(D) tolerant : laughter
(E) ambitious : calamity

14. STATIC : MOTION ::

(A) lengthy : time
(B) arid : moisture
(C) cautious : bravery
(D) gentle : impulse
(E) careless : danger

15. VALISE : LUGGAGE ::

(A) passport : travel
(B) bracelet : jewelry
(C) wrapping : present
(D) receipt : money
(E) warranty : electronics

16. RECLUSIVE : SOLITUDE ::

(A) miserly : generosity
(B) inventive : reward
(C) meticulous : order
(D) compassionate : aid
(E) visionary : past

17. RECIDIVISM : CRIMINAL ::

(A) justice : plaintiff
(B) bankruptcy : lawyer
(C) condemnation : authority
(D) finesse : magician
(E) relapse : patient

18. EQUIVOCATION : MEANING ::

(A) feint : intention
(B) secrecy : stealth
(C) geniality : amiability
(D) travesty : insight
(E) refinement : innovation

19. SYLLABUS : COURSE ::

(A) dean : university
(B) nutrition : study
(C) sketch : portrait
(D) agenda : conference
(E) schedule : ticket

20. REGRETTABLE : LAMENT ::

(A) praiseworthy : applaud
(B) verbose : rejoice
(C) incongruous : detect
(D) reliable : defend
(E) obnoxious : boast

21. EMBARRASSMENT : MORTIFICATION ::

(A) mistake : error
(B) faith : doubt
(C) pain : agony
(D) favor : bias
(E) worry : cause

22. CORPULENT : WEIGHT ::

(A) extravagant : expenditure
(B) illustrious : prediction
(C) insensitive : sympathy
(D) ill-advised : diet
(E) ambivalent : conviction

## QUIZ II (22 items; 15 minutes)

1. GRAIN : SAND ::

   (A) ounce : flour
   (B) speck : dust
   (C) bottle : liquid
   (D) link : chain
   (E) coal : oil

2. HANDSHAKE : TRUST ::

   (A) medal : victory
   (B) smoke : fire
   (C) flag : enemy
   (D) walking stick : limp
   (E) olive branch : peace

3. NEST : SPARROW ::

   (A) cave : drawing
   (B) flight : wing
   (C) lair : lion
   (D) meadow : lake
   (E) pond : water

4. WATERFALL : CASCADE ::

   (A) snow : freeze
   (B) missile : launch
   (C) tree : exfoliate
   (D) wave : undulate
   (E) monarch : reign

5. UNIFORM : SOLDIER ::

   (A) silks : jockey
   (B) leash : dog
   (C) pasture : cow
   (D) farmer : tractor
   (E) costume : scenery

6. LIAR : MENDACITY ::

   (A) swindler : burglary
   (B) glutton : appetite
   (C) philistine : knowledge
   (D) soldier : orders
   (E) diplomat : nationalism

7. EXPEL : SCHOOL ::

   (A) inquire : question
   (B) deport : country
   (C) accept : application
   (D) embrace : wonder
   (E) divide : celebration

8. DETENTION : RELEASE ::

   (A) viciousness : attack
   (B) calamity : repair
   (C) qualification : employ
   (D) induction : discharge
   (E) therapy : confuse

9. MOCK : DERISION ::

   (A) despise : contempt
   (B) reject : account
   (C) repair : corruption
   (D) inspire : muse
   (E) observe : refinement

10. DOODLE : AIMLESSNESS ::

    (A) revive : substantial
    (B) inform : success
    (C) blurt : planning
    (D) exile : competition
    (E) waver : indecision

11. PEAR : FRUIT ::

    (A) flower : seed
    (B) baseball : sport
    (C) building : windows
    (D) street : pavement
    (E) youth : juvenile

12. DISCIPLINARIAN : OBEDIENCE ::

   (A) principal : school
   (B) fireman : hose
   (C) parent : children
   (D) perfectionist : flawlessness
   (E) picture : colors

13. DECIBEL : LOUDNESS ::

   (A) gram : ounce
   (B) meter : yard
   (C) length : width
   (D) carat : weight
   (E) gallon : mile

14. JOURNEYMAN : APPRENTICE ::

   (A) colleague : pedagogue
   (B) salesclerk : merchandise
   (C) veteran : rookie
   (D) voter : registration
   (E) champion : practice

15. UNFATHOMABLE : COMPREHEND ::

   (A) gullible : distract
   (B) discreet : falsify
   (C) desired : obtain
   (D) untenable : maintain
   (E) secure : revolt

16. WOOD : CARVE ::

   (A) paper : burn
   (B) pipe : blow
   (C) clay : mold
   (D) tree : grow
   (E) brick : build

17. GALLERY : ARTWORK ::

   (A) museum : children
   (B) zoo : animals
   (C) theater : exhibits
   (D) stadium : field
   (E) forest : park

18. FADE : VANISH ::

   (A) abate : diminish
   (B) meander : wander
   (C) chide : reprimand
   (D) deplete : replenish
   (E) infer : imply

19. BOOK : CHAPTER ::

   (A) film : projector
   (B) thesis : doctorate
   (C) prelude : piano
   (D) sculpture : chisel
   (E) symphony : movement

20. ROOTS : TREE ::

   (A) foundation : building
   (B) chimney : smoke
   (C) exit : entrance
   (D) engine : automobile
   (E) sleeve : shirt

21. LUBRICANT : FRICTION ::

   (A) machine : operator
   (B) spasm : muscle
   (C) dessert : sugar
   (D) balm : pain
   (E) drawer : chest

22. INSOMNIA : SLEEP ::

   (A) starvation : famine
   (B) enlightenment : data
   (C) hypochondria : physician
   (D) inattention : negligence
   (E) disaffection : trust

## QUIZ III (22 items; 15 minutes)

1. SCRIBBLING : WRITING ::

   (A) pen : pencil
   (B) sound : vibration
   (C) walking : jogging
   (D) mumbling : speaking
   (E) seeing : vision

2. URGE : INSIST ::

   (A) refuse : deny
   (B) request : demand
   (C) deserve : receive
   (D) infer : imply
   (E) inspire : revoke

3. SCREAM : FRIGHT ::

   (A) moan : loudness
   (B) sweat : drops
   (C) groan : pain
   (D) fly : plane
   (E) cry : tears

4. PROGRESS : IMPASSE ::

   (A) fire : residue
   (B) speed : location
   (C) circulation : tourniquet
   (D) disciple : leader
   (E) captain : ship

5. MURAL : WALL ::

   (A) pen : letter
   (B) tree : forest
   (C) painting : canvas
   (D) tobacco : smoke
   (E) museum : curator

6. HYPOCRITE : DUPLICITOUS ::

   (A) partisan : impartial
   (B) traitor : disloyal
   (C) soldier : tough
   (D) tailor : prosperous
   (E) prisoner : repentant

7. SOAR : HOVER ::

   (A) trail : hike
   (B) sing : harmonize
   (C) fall : trip
   (D) help : aid
   (E) swim : float

8. CARPENTER : CABINET ::

   (A) gardener : tree
   (B) musician : clarinet
   (C) cobbler : boot
   (D) banker : deposit
   (E) potter : kiln

9. BICEP : MUSCLE ::

   (A) cobra : snake
   (B) pump : heart
   (C) bat : bird
   (D) cup : mug
   (E) ball : rubber

10. POVERTY : MONEY ::

    (A) elation : joy
    (B) despair : remorse
    (C) veracity : honesty
    (D) erudition : learning
    (E) darkness : light

11. ENGAGEMENT : MARRIAGE ::

    (A) overture : opera
    (B) night : darkness
    (C) failure : success
    (D) demands : destitution
    (E) ballgame : umpire

12. IMPORTANT : PIVOTAL ::

    (A) major : minimal
    (B) robust : strong
    (C) stern : draconian
    (D) salient : compulsory
    (E) impetuous : perfect

13. GRAIN : SILO ::

   (A) vitamin : nutrition
   (B) farm : tractor
   (C) van : warehouse
   (D) water : reservoir
   (E) money : investor

14. SQUANDER : ASSETS ::

   (A) pronounce : judgment
   (B) exhaust : resources
   (C) fulfill : dream
   (D) accumulate : balance
   (E) obtain : goods

15. COMMENCE : PROCRASTINATION ::

   (A) terminate : prolongation
   (B) show : demonstration
   (C) frighten : terror
   (D) guarantee : refund
   (E) capture : torture

16. LETHARGY : ENERGY ::

   (A) appetite : hunger
   (B) redemption : sacrament
   (C) sorrow : pity
   (D) merit : remuneration
   (E) apathy : interest

17. INAUGURATE : BEGINNING ::

   (A) encapsulate : thought
   (B) advise : dissension
   (C) prevaricate : prank
   (D) forbid : sanction
   (E) consecrate : dedication

18. EVANESCENT : VANISH ::

   (A) effervescent : corrode
   (B) iridescent : shine
   (C) expressive : admonish
   (D) fluorescent : disappear
   (E) vacuous : expedite

19. DISINGENUOUS : DECEIVE ::

   (A) contemptuous : praise
   (B) creative : stabilize
   (C) accommodating : compromise
   (D) inactive : healthy
   (E) hereditary : transmit

20. FASTIDIOUS : CLEANLINESS ::

   (A) pliant : fabrication
   (B) meticulous : detail
   (C) timorous : hostility
   (D) bereft : animosity
   (E) enervated : activity

21. SOLICITOUS : ATTENTION ::

   (A) rebellious : compliance
   (B) tepid : maturity
   (C) corrosive : chemical
   (D) ingenuous : naïveté
   (E) mischievous : disregard

22. IMPULSIVE : SPONTANEITY ::

   (A) overwrought : procrastination
   (B) succinct : brevity
   (C) ignoble : simultaneity
   (D) pretentious : modesty
   (E) fallow : fecundity

# CAMBRIDGE TESTPREP™

## Strategy Summary Sheet
# ANALOGIES

In general, an analogy is a parallel that is drawn between two different, but sufficiently similar, events, situations, or circumstances. Analogies draw a parallel between one pair of words or phrases and another pair of words or phrases. A few Analogies items are not based upon actual dictionary definitions, but there is nonetheless a tight connection between the two words or phrases. With such a connection, you do not need to know anything about the particular facts of the case to understand the connection. Instead, you are expected to simply consider the meanings of the words or phrases. For example, consider the following sentences: "This bachelor is not married," and "This clerk is not married." The first sentence is necessarily true because part of the meaning of "bachelor" is that such a person is "not married." The second sentence may or may not be true, depending on the clerk's marital status. For this reason, CLERK : MARRIED would never appear as a capitalized pair of words. BACHELOR : MARRIED, however, could be the basis for an Analogies item because of the tight connection between the words.

**BASIC STRATEGIES:** Complexity arises due to advanced vocabulary, parts of speech, and abstract relationships. The correct answer must contain the same grammatical linkage as the pair of words in the item stem, so determine the parts of speech of XXXX : YYYY in cases of ambiguity. "Non-answers" exhibit either no tight relationship or one that is dissimilar to that of the stimulus pair.

1.  *Creating Diagnostic Sentences*: Formulate a diagnostic sentence (DXS) that expresses the connection between the two capitalized words and then test each answer choice to find the pair of words that best fits the sentence.

2.  *Tinkering with Diagnostic Sentences*: If necessary, reverse the order of the capitalized pair of words (e.g., YYYY is a defining characteristic of XXXX) to make the analogy relationship more obvious. Likewise, alter the diagnostic sentence (DXS) or parts of speech to render the analogy less obscure.

3.  *Fine-Tuning Diagnostic Sentences*: After eliminating "non-answers" (no tight relationship), if more than one possible answer choice satisfies the initial diagnostic sentence (DXS), consider further refining/sharpening the sentence to discriminate among the remaining answer choices.

**ITEM-TYPES:** The following are the ten most common types of analogy relationships and corresponding examples of diagnostic sentences (DXS):

1.  *Defining Characteristic*: WISDOM is a defining characteristic of a SAGE.

2.  *Lack Of*: Lack of RAIN is the defining characteristic of a DROUGHT.

3.  *Type Of*: A SONNET is a type of POEM.

4.  *Part Of*: A BRANCH is a part of a TREE.

5.  *Place For*: A PULPIT is a place for a MINISTER.

6.  *Degree*: AN EPIC is a lengthy STORY.

7.  *Tools*: A SCALPEL is a tool used by a SURGEON.

8.  *Sign Of*: A SIGH is a sign of RELIEF.

9.  *Sequence*: A VIRUS precedes or causes an ILLNESS.

10. *Spurious Form*: A STAGGER is a spurious (defective) form of a WALK.

## ADDITIONAL STRATEGIES:

1.  *Customizing Diagnostic Sentences*: The ten item-types described above are simply the most common. When the analogy relationship does not fit neatly into any of these ten types, you should not be afraid to create your own diagnostic sentence (DXS).

2.  *Tough Calls*: When tinkering with the diagnostic sentence (DXS) proves inconclusive, improve words among the remaining possible answer choices; if a substitute word more closely parallels the relationship in the item stem, that answer is comparatively defective.

3.  *Shooting in the Dark*: As always, eliminate any answer choice pair that does not express a tight relationship (e.g., CHAUVINIST : IMAGINATION). A CHAUVINIST may, but does not necessarily, have a lack of IMAGINATION. Modify the unknown vocabulary or use it in a sentence to determine if the word and its terms are truly unknown. If unknown words are within the item stem pair (XXXX : YYYY), you may have to guess. If unknown words fall within the remaining answer choices, construct a diagnostic sentence (DXS). Eliminate answer choices that do not express the proper corresponding relationship. Do not eliminate an answer choice because the vocabulary is unknown.

NOTES: _____

_____

_____

_____

_____

_____

_____

_____

_____

_____

_____

_____

_____

_____

# Antonyms

# CAMBRIDGE TESTPREP™

## ANTONYMS OUTLINE

# CORE LESSON

The items in this section accompany the Core Lesson section of the Antonyms Lesson. You will work through the items with your instructor in class.

**DIRECTIONS:** Each of the following items consists of a word printed in capital letters, followed by five lettered words or phrases in lowercase letters. Choose the lettered word or phrase that is most nearly <u>opposite</u> in meaning to the word in capital letters. Answers are on page 915.

1. EXPERT:

   (A) flatterer
   (B) novice
   (C) victor
   (D) enemy
   (E) borrower

2. FORBID:

   (A) misuse
   (B) denounce
   (C) remind
   (D) allow
   (E) conform

3. NEBULOUS:

   (A) very clear
   (B) highly unusual
   (C) openly hostile
   (D) lightly used
   (E) overly indulgent

4. INCIPIENCE:

   (A) piquancy
   (B) culmination
   (C) tenacity
   (D) aggregation
   (E) eccentricity

5. ORNAMENTAL:

   (A) ferocious
   (B) hospitable
   (C) insincere
   (D) devious
   (E) essential

6. PRECIPITOUS:

   (A) well-planned
   (B) gargantuan
   (C) prolific
   (D) short-lived
   (E) extremely hostile

7. ENIGMATIC:

   (A) talkative
   (B) oppressed
   (C) easily understood
   (D) easily avoided
   (E) very common

8. AIR:

   (A) revoke
   (B) cleanse
   (C) suppress
   (D) initiate
   (E) confirm

9. LAVISH:

   (A) conclude
   (B) hoard
   (C) proclaim
   (D) distinguish
   (E) settle

10. PILLORY:

(A) edify
(B) truncate
(C) magnify
(D) venerate
(E) delineate

11. DERELICT:

(A) ungrateful
(B) decisive
(C) protective
(D) secluded
(E) attentive

12. RAIL:

(A) speak well of
(B) refuse to accept
(C) make note of
(D) return to
(E) pass over

13. CONVICTION:

(A) adversity
(B) prejudice
(C) allegiance
(D) victory
(E) doubt

14. TEDIOUS:

(A) unlimited
(B) confined
(C) enthralling
(D) appetizing
(E) illuminating

15. SQUANDER:

(A) whisper
(B) conserve
(C) import
(D) deny
(E) quarrel

16. ACCESSORIAL:

(A) persistent
(B) conclusive
(C) distinguished
(D) partial
(E) essential

17. LUCIDITY:

(A) unintelligibility
(B) capriciousness
(C) frugality
(D) moroseness
(E) inescapability

18. CONTAMINATION:

(A) ingenuousness
(B) miserliness
(C) purification
(D) forgetfulness
(E) prejudice

19. INEBRIATION:

(A) sobriety
(B) felicity
(C) jollity
(D) gravity
(E) piety

20. ACQUIESCENCE:

(A) rebellion
(B) distillation
(C) inquisition
(D) revision
(E) contrivance

21. PUNCTUALITY:

(A) frailty
(B) veracity
(C) effectiveness
(D) tardiness
(E) rigidity

22. COGNOSCIBLE:

    (A) inviting
    (B) unknowable
    (C) forlorn
    (D) expensive
    (E) withdrawn

23. CONFLUENCE:

    (A) sensitivity
    (B) separation
    (C) increase
    (D) encouragement
    (E) maturity

24. PROXIMATE:

    (A) purposefully designed
    (B) nontransferable
    (C) distant
    (D) insincere
    (E) inquisitive

25. INDEFATIGABLE:

    (A) redolent
    (B) exhausted
    (C) famished
    (D) regrettable
    (E) ignorant

26. INANIMATE:

    (A) convicted
    (B) progressive
    (C) insane
    (D) lively
    (E) charming

27. DISSONANT:

    (A) thoughtful
    (B) forbidden
    (C) harmonious
    (D) enviable
    (E) candid

28. QUAINT:

    (A) wealthy
    (B) ordinary
    (C) difficult
    (D) worrisome
    (E) horrendous

29. CHERUBIC:

    (A) foolish
    (B) erroneous
    (C) nasty
    (D) calm
    (E) imagined

30. PIQUANT:

    (A) shocking
    (B) jovial
    (C) rigorous
    (D) merry
    (E) bland

# REVIEW

This section contains Antonyms items for further practice.

**DIRECTIONS:** Each of the following items consists of a word printed in capital letters, followed by five lettered words or phrases in lowercase letters. Choose the lettered word or phrase that is most nearly <u>opposite</u> in meaning to the word in capital letters. Answers are on page 916.

1. ENERVATE:

   (A) invigorate
   (B) contemplate
   (C) necessitate
   (D) evaluate
   (E) elucidate

2. NOISOME:

   (A) luxurious
   (B) beneficial
   (C) idyllic
   (D) moronic
   (E) sedate

3. RECALCITRANT:

   (A) polished
   (B) feckless
   (C) yielding
   (D) somber
   (E) miserly

4. ABSTEMIOUS:

   (A) self-indulgent
   (B) terse
   (C) obstreperous
   (D) finite
   (E) contrite

5. TORPOR:

   (A) lucidity
   (B) cohesion
   (C) activity
   (D) sobriety
   (E) upshot

6. MUNIFICENT:

   (A) miserly
   (B) grandiose
   (C) faulty
   (D) perplexing
   (E) rudimentary

7. INVEIGH:

   (A) forswear
   (B) barter
   (C) laud
   (D) misuse
   (E) remand

8. ABROGATE:

   (A) enact
   (B) disinfect
   (C) replenish
   (D) entice
   (E) tarnish

9. LACONIC:

   (A) wordy
   (B) inconsistent
   (C) morose
   (D) merciful
   (E) contrite

10. ENSCONCE:

(A) uncover
(B) enthrall
(C) exceed
(D) include
(E) rely

11. APOSTATE:

(A) believer
(B) magician
(C) functionary
(D) trainer
(E) vendor

12. CAVIL:

(A) incite
(B) arrest
(C) refund
(D) assent
(E) withhold

13. GARRULOUS:

(A) grisly
(B) fervent
(C) youthful
(D) cautious
(E) silent

14. IMPERVIOUS:

(A) gallant
(B) brazen
(C) penetrable
(D) coherent
(E) intense

15. NADIR:

(A) calamity
(B) perdition
(C) apex
(D) nexus
(E) self-control

16. SALUBRIOUS:

(A) unhealthful
(B) in short supply
(C) out of date
(D) poorly planned
(E) gradual

17. MOTILITY:

(A) laxness
(B) insanity
(C) wisdom
(D) salvation
(E) paralysis

18. PROCLIVITY:

(A) prodigality
(B) avoidance
(C) credence
(D) calumny
(E) inception

19. TENUOUS:

(A) unseemly
(B) inherited
(C) substantial
(D) forlorn
(E) awkward

20. NEFARIOUS:

(A) virtuous
(B) pedestrian
(C) resourceful
(D) sordid
(E) potent

21. DESICCATE:

(A) reclaim
(B) proliferate
(C) refrain
(D) inundate
(E) defer

22. VACILLATE:

   (A) rise above
   (B) remain constant
   (C) laugh heartily
   (D) attempt unsuccessfully
   (E) incur expenses

23. IGNOMINIOUS:

   (A) uneducated
   (B) resilient
   (C) vigorous
   (D) honorable
   (E) dangerous

24. LASSITUDE:

   (A) aptitude
   (B) civility
   (C) strength
   (D) jollity
   (E) largess

25. SEDULOUS:

   (A) imposing
   (B) fluctuating
   (C) lazy
   (D) ample
   (E) exemplary

26. CONTROVERT:

   (A) predict
   (B) bemuse
   (C) intend
   (D) agree
   (E) rectify

27. INSOUCIANT:

   (A) amiable
   (B) fretful
   (C) swift
   (D) inferior
   (E) formidable

28. SALACIOUS:

   (A) forthright
   (B) disreputable
   (C) prudish
   (D) tolerant
   (E) impatient

29. LANGUOROUS:

   (A) frenetic
   (B) corporeal
   (C) explicit
   (D) recondite
   (E) anomalous

30. PROLIX:

   (A) obtuse
   (B) terse
   (C) sinuous
   (D) slothful
   (E) vacuous

31. CONTUMACIOUS:

   (A) dauntless
   (B) obsequious
   (C) euphonic
   (D) hirsute
   (E) prodigal

32. SPLENETIC:

   (A) taciturn
   (B) enigmatic
   (C) complacent
   (D) contrite
   (E) mischievous

33. OBDURATE:

   (A) ambiguous
   (B) demoralized
   (C) vitriolic
   (D) malleable
   (E) inimitable

34. SYCOPHANT:

(A) mentor
(B) pundit
(C) esthete
(D) dissenter
(E) dilettante

35. PERSPICACIOUS:

(A) of indefinite duration
(B) lacking intrinsic value
(C) insufficiently precise
(D) condemnatory
(E) dull-witted

36. PARSIMONY:

(A) contraband
(B) stealth
(C) torpor
(D) generosity
(E) defoliation

37. SAGACITY:

(A) willingness
(B) idiocy
(C) relentlessness
(D) speculation
(E) fame

38. TEMERITY:

(A) fortitude
(B) capacity
(C) interest
(D) caution
(E) relevance

# TIMED-PRACTICE QUIZZES

**DIRECTIONS:** This section contains three Antonyms quizzes. While being timed, complete each quiz. Each of the following items consists of a word printed in capital letters, followed by five lettered words or phrases in lowercase letters. Choose the lettered word or phrase that is most nearly <u>opposite</u> in meaning to the word in capital letters. Answers are on page 916.

## QUIZ I (20 items; 10 minutes)

1. DISRUPT:

   (A) enhance
   (B) atone
   (C) renovate
   (D) move forward
   (E) join together

2. EVACUATE:

   (A) veer off
   (B) extinguish
   (C) replenish
   (D) strain
   (E) withstand

3. LACKLUSTER:

   (A) frivolous
   (B) brilliant
   (C) complicated
   (D) temperate
   (E) sensible

4. LACERATE:

   (A) sew together
   (B) pack tightly
   (C) push aside
   (D) rap sharply
   (E) learn fast

5. PROFUSION:

   (A) paucity
   (B) remuneration
   (C) coherence
   (D) inception
   (E) remonstrance

6. CARDINAL:

   (A) successful
   (B) developing
   (C) devastating
   (D) wholesome
   (E) insignificant

7. EERIE:

   (A) elusive
   (B) irreverent
   (C) mature
   (D) normal
   (E) confused

8. REJUVENATE:

   (A) entertain
   (B) embattle
   (C) frighten
   (D) age
   (E) refuse

9. ECLECTIC:

   (A) uniform
   (B) righteous
   (C) courteous
   (D) relieved
   (E) relentless

10. AMELIORATION:

(A) reduction
(B) involvement
(C) reception
(D) worsening
(E) enthusiasm

11. MUTINOUS:

(A) routine
(B) clever
(C) obedient
(D) helpful
(E) pitiful.

12. UPBRAID:

(A) sever
(B) conjoin
(C) defer
(D) vacillate
(E) laud

13. BANE:

(A) stagnation
(B) altercation
(C) witty pun
(D) good fortune
(E) lassitude

14. TEMPER:

(A) prepare
(B) intensify
(C) generate
(D) whisper
(E) sugarcoat

15. DIVESTITURE:

(A) competition
(B) reconciliation
(C) acquisition
(D) precondition
(E) investigation

16. FULMINATE:

(A) weaken
(B) fall into
(C) inflate
(D) neglect
(E) remain quiet

17. QUIXOTIC:

(A) practical
(B) formative
(C) treacherous
(D) infallible
(E) fleeting

18. AVER:

(A) repay
(B) calm
(C) amass
(D) concede
(E) deny

19. SOLICITOUSNESS:

(A) disregard
(B) sincerity
(C) fealty
(D) curiosity
(E) testimony

20. EXONERATE:

(A) testify
(B) engender
(C) accuse
(D) inundate
(E) abrogate

## QUIZ II (20 items; 10 minutes)

1. RALLY:

   (A) refute
   (B) belittle
   (C) fulfill
   (D) forget
   (E) disband

2. PROFOUND:

   (A) whimsical
   (B) precise
   (C) restless
   (D) shallow
   (E) toxic

3. MOROSE:

   (A) intense
   (B) careful
   (C) joyous
   (D) untried
   (E) worrisome

4. GUILE:

   (A) abundance
   (B) forbidden
   (C) treasure
   (D) naiveté
   (E) impression

5. MALIGN:

   (A) refuse
   (B) constrain
   (C) praise
   (D) demand
   (E) reply

6. LOUTISH:

   (A) boisterous
   (B) provocative
   (C) calamitous
   (D) sophisticated
   (E) insightful

7. ASSUAGE:

   (A) aggravate
   (B) purify
   (C) consecrate
   (D) rehabilitate
   (E) denounce

8. FORBEARANCE:

   (A) indulgence
   (B) piety
   (C) endurance
   (D) extension
   (E) reliance

9. METICULOUS:

   (A) uniform
   (B) educated
   (C) consigned
   (D) forbidden
   (E) careless

10. ESOTERIC:

    (A) widely known
    (B) able-bodied
    (C) strong-willed
    (D) well-developed
    (E) ill-conceived

11. REFRACTORY:

    (A) corrosive
    (B) inebriated
    (C) punitive
    (D) extenuating
    (E) zealous

12. VOLUBLE:

(A) intermittent
(B) elastic
(C) refined
(D) reticent
(E) forgone

13. BUCOLIC:

(A) urban
(B) redundant
(C) well-mannered
(D) reconditioned
(E) ebullient

14. RECONDITE:

(A) evident
(B) cheerful
(C) healthful
(D) former
(E) earnest

15. TRACTABLE:

(A) incoherent
(B) advisable
(C) simplistic
(D) influential
(E) uncooperative

16. RECIDIVISM:

(A) effective rehabilitation
(B) deep depression
(C) unique talent
(D) sufficient funds
(E) truthful accusation

17. MULTIFARIOUS:

(A) voluminous
(B) mundane
(C) noble
(D) monolithic
(E) unsurpassable

18. FOMENT:

(A) enjoin
(B) assuage
(C) sequester
(D) remand
(E) console

19. MERCURIAL:

(A) tactful
(B) stable
(C) spiritual
(D) flagrant
(E) inept

20. OBFUSCATE:

(A) suppress
(B) elucidate
(C) reprimand
(D) absolve
(E) protract

## QUIZ III (20 items; 10 minutes)

### 1. VALID:

(A) incongruous
(B) illicit
(C) fallacious
(D) intrinsic
(E) despicable

### 2. RAMPANT:

(A) controlled
(B) reviewed
(C) rebuffed
(D) amended
(E) discarded

### 3. TRANSIENT:

(A) movable
(B) insistent
(C) permanent
(D) callous
(E) defensive

### 4. RECANT:

(A) assert
(B) predict
(C) rescue
(D) entangle
(E) fail

### 5. MUNDANE:

(A) perverse
(B) spiritual
(C) complex
(D) difficult
(E) formal

### 6. ABATE:

(A) pretend
(B) foretell
(C) concede
(D) regress
(E) increase

### 7. TREPIDATION:

(A) contempt
(B) restlessness
(C) rancor
(D) vigilance
(E) courage

### 8. DIAPHANOUS:

(A) concise
(B) diminutive
(C) heroic
(D) remiss
(E) opaque

### 9. ATTENUATION:

(A) concentration
(B) distraction
(C) remission
(D) vindictiveness
(E) generosity

### 10. WHIMSICAL:

(A) chivalrous
(B) perfect
(C) predictable
(D) hidden
(E) backward

### 11. PLENITUDE:

(A) richness
(B) scarcity
(C) luxury
(D) contentment
(E) magnificence

### 12. DISINTER:

(A) confine
(B) lend
(C) bury
(D) attach
(E) remain

13. DISAPPROBATION:

    (A) inconstancy
    (B) veneration
    (C) temerity
    (D) pliability
    (E) despotism

14. DESULTORY:

    (A) considerate
    (B) weakened
    (C) victorious
    (D) illustrious
    (E) focused

15. INCITE:

    (A) forget
    (B) calm
    (C) change
    (D) involve
    (E) produce

16. CONTENTIOUS:

    (A) moronic
    (B) sophomoric
    (C) permanent
    (D) compliant
    (E) inventive

17. SALIENT:

    (A) concealed
    (B) inclined
    (C) stagnant
    (D) blameworthy
    (E) omnipotent

18. RAFFISH:

    (A) tyrannical
    (B) august
    (C) simplified
    (D) questionable
    (E) moronic

19. DOGMATIC:

    (A) urgent
    (B) insightful
    (C) flexible
    (D) moral
    (E) resourceful

20. WINSOME:

    (A) elegant
    (B) intrepid
    (C) distinctive
    (D) sincere
    (E) disagreeable

# CAMBRIDGE TESTPREP™

## Strategy Summary Sheet
# ANTONYMS

Although Antonyms items test knowledge of vocabulary more directly than the other types of Verbal Reasoning items, they are not designed *only* to test the strength of one's vocabulary. These items also test the ability to reason and determine the opposite meaning of a word. Regardless, your ability to do well on an Antonyms item has a great deal to do with whether you know the meaning of the capitalized word. If the capitalized word is a part of your vocabulary, you will have a good chance of answering correctly. Otherwise, you may be forced to guess. However, there are some helpful strategies that you can use even when you do not know the meaning of the item stem word. And, of course, as mentioned above, knowing the vocabulary is not the only important component—you must also reason through the answer choices to find the best opposite.

## ANTONYMS CONCEPTS AND STRATEGIES:

1. *Opposite Meaning*: As already indicated, while Antonyms items test vocabulary, they essentially test the ability to reason and determine the opposite meaning of a word.

2. *Vocabulary*: With Antonyms items, difficulty is determined primarily by vocabulary.

3. *Shades of Meaning*: Relationships of opposites may depend upon shades of meaning; in these cases, you should select the word or phrase *most nearly* opposite in meaning.

4. *Parts of Speech*: Since the exam may test different parts of speech of the same word, look at the answer choices to determine what part of speech is intended.

5. *Secondary Meanings*: Be alert for tested secondary meanings—if an easy item stem word appears in a problem that should be difficult, ask yourself: "Does this word have a secondary meaning?"

## GENERAL STRATEGIES:

1. *Anticipate and Match*: The "Anticipate and Match" strategy is executed in three stages. First, read the capitalized item stem word. Second, based on your understanding of its meaning, you should *anticipate* one or two words that might be used as opposites. Third, attempt to match the anticipated opposite(s) with one of the five answer choices. Given that Antonyms items often depend upon shades of meaning, you cannot expect to find the anticipated opposite very often. Instead, this strategy becomes effective on the chance that you are able to match either the anticipated opposite(s) or a synonym of those opposites with an actual answer choice.

2. *Change Parts of Speech*: There are many words with which you might be slightly familiar but of whose usage you are uncertain. In these situations, it is helpful for you to change the part of speech to one with which you are more familiar and that you can use in a sentence to aid in determining the meaning.

3. *Dissect the Word*: Another approach to solving Antonyms items is to try to dissect the word. Take the capitalized item stem word apart, isolating the root word and its prefix and/or suffix. You should refer to the Word Parts List in this student text (p. 46). Your knowledge of similar words can make a significant impact, and familiarity is the key to reasoning the answers for difficult items.

4. *Place the Word in a Context*: In some cases, you may have seen a word before but are not entirely sure of its meaning; therefore, you should try to place the word into a context.

**NOTES:** _____

_____

_____

_____

_____

_____

_____

_____

_____

_____

_____

_____

_____

_____

_____

_____

_____

_____

_____

_____

_____

_____

_____

_____

_____

_____

_____

# Sentence Completions

# CAMBRIDGE TESTPREP™

## SENTENCE COMPLETIONS OUTLINE

# CORE LESSON

The items in this section accompany the Core Lesson section of the Sentence Completion Lesson. You will work through the items with your instructor in class.

**DIRECTIONS:** Each sentence or paragraph in this section has one or more missing elements, as indicated by a blank or blanks. Choose the word or set of words that best fits the meaning of the text. Answers are on page 917.

1. The terms "toad" and "frog" refer to two different animals belonging to different genera, and careful students —— between the two.

   (A) intermingle
   (B) ignore
   (C) distinguish
   (D) confuse
   (E) dispute

2. Since the evidence of the manuscript's —— is ——, its publication will be postponed until a team of scholars has examined it and declared it to be genuine.

   (A) authenticity. .inconclusive
   (B) truthfulness. .tarnished
   (C) veracity. .indubitable
   (D) legitimacy. .infallible
   (E) profundity. .forthcoming

3. If we continue to consume our fossil fuel supply without restraint, then someday it will be ——.

   (A) replenished
   (B) limited
   (C) useless
   (D) available
   (E) exhausted

4. The critics must have detested the play, for the review was not merely ——, it was ——.

   (A) unhappy. .miserable
   (B) laudatory. .enthusiastic
   (C) sincere. .long
   (D) appreciative. .stinging
   (E) critical. .scathing

5. The judge, after ruling that the article had unjustly —— the reputation of the architect, ordered the magazine to —— its libelous statements in print.

   (A) praised. .communicate
   (B) injured. .retract
   (C) sullied. .publicize
   (D) damaged. .disseminate
   (E) extolled. .produce

6. Joyce's novel *Finnegan's Wake* continues to —— critics, including those who find it incomprehensible and call it ——.

   (A) appall. .genial
   (B) captivate. .nonsensical
   (C) baffle. .transparent
   (D) bore. .compelling
   (E) entertain. .monotonous

7. People who use their desktop computers for writing can become almost hypnotized by the unbroken succession of letters and text; in such cases, a computer video game can supply a welcome ——.

   (A) burden
   (B) diversion
   (C) handicap
   (D) predicament
   (E) insight

8. There is no necessary connection between a dollar and what can be purchased for a dollar; the value of money is —— and can be —— by supply and demand.

    (A) arbitrary. .altered
    (B) predetermined. .overruled
    (C) conventional. .inspired
    (D) lackluster. .improved
    (E) optional. .prevented

9. His —— should not be confused with cowardice; during the war, I saw him on several occasions risk his own life while rescuing members of his unit.

    (A) heroism
    (B) indifference
    (C) caution
    (D) notoriety
    (E) confidence

10. Her acceptance speech was ——, eliciting thunderous applause at several points.

    (A) tedious
    (B) well-received
    (C) cowardly
    (D) uninteresting
    (E) poorly written

11. The public debates were often ——, finally deteriorating into mudslinging contests.

    (A) informative
    (B) bitter
    (C) theoretical
    (D) inspiring
    (E) insightful

12. The ease with which the candidate answers difficult questions creates the impression that she has been a public servant for years, but in reality she entered politics only ——.

    (A) securely
    (B) enthusiastically
    (C) frequently
    (D) needfully
    (E) recently

13. The ascent of the mountain is ——, but anyone who makes it to the top is rewarded by a spectacular view.

    (A) helpful
    (B) easy
    (C) unique
    (D) unpleasant
    (E) automatic

14. Although the terms "toad" and "frog" refer to two different animals belonging to different genera, some students —— the two.

    (A) distinguish
    (B) confuse
    (C) respect
    (D) observe
    (E) mention

15. While Barbara argues strongly that current policies are unjust, she does not —— any particular changes.

    (A) reject
    (B) presume
    (C) advocate
    (D) remember
    (E) oppose

16. Although there are more female students at the college than male students, the women seem to have a(n) —— influence on the student government.

    (A) enormous
    (B) negligible
    (C) provocative
    (D) venerable
    (E) active

17. Unless we —— our water resources, there may come a time when our supplies of clean water are completely depleted.

    (A) predict
    (B) use
    (C) conserve
    (D) replace
    (E) tap

18. For Thomas Aquinas, the Scholastic thinker and author of the *Summa Theologica*, the question of angels dancing on a pinhead was not —— but a —— issue of vital import to his project of reconciling Aristotelian metaphysics with medieval Church doctrine.

    (A) whimsical. .profound
    (B) insightful. .complex
    (C) comical. .superficial
    (D) premeditated. .serious
    (E) capricious. .fanciful

19. Despite the fact that they had clinched the divisional title long before the end of regular season play, the team continued to play every game as though it were ——.

    (A) superfluous
    (B) irrational
    (C) lengthy
    (D) hopeless
    (E) vital

20. Nutritionists have found that certain elements long known to be —— in large quantities are —— to life in small amounts.

    (A) lethal. .essential
    (B) deadly. .painful
    (C) healthful. .pleasurable
    (D) fatal. .unbearable
    (E) unfashionable. .important

21. Though afflicted by headaches, nausea, and respiratory difficulties, Nietzsche —— to let his —— problems prevent him from writing.

    (A) hoped. .imaginary
    (B) opted. .financial
    (C) failed. .emotional
    (D) decided. .theoretical
    (E) refused. .physical

22. Although critics denounced the film as silly and inane, people flocked to the theater to see it, guaranteeing its —— success.

    (A) scholarly
    (B) hypothetical
    (C) critical
    (D) financial
    (E) eventual

23. Elementary school children, who have not yet been repeatedly disappointed by other people, are much more —— than older and more cynical high school students.

    (A) inquisitive
    (B) relaxed
    (C) enjoyable
    (D) trusting
    (E) enlightened

24. Even the most arbitrary and —— corporation today must be aware of the attitudes of its employees; management may at times be more or less ——, but all must respect the power of an organized workforce.

    (A) influential. .outraged
    (B) prosperous. .precipitous
    (C) flexible. .patronizing
    (D) authoritarian. .responsive
    (E) susceptible. .permanent

25. The university should —— the function of the alumni fund so that its importance will be better appreciated by the school's graduates who are asked to contribute to it.

    (A) revoke
    (B) elucidate
    (C) ascertain
    (D) prescribe
    (E) entice

26. In spite of the —— of the minister's sermon, when it was finished, most of the congregation was ——.

    (A) passion. .fidgety
    (B) tedium. .fearful
    (C) understanding. .merciful
    (D) obtrusiveness. .hurt
    (E) veracity. .inspired

27. Although this disease threatens the lives of several thousand people every year, the —— of supplies and equipment has —— the progress of medical research for a cure.

    (A) discontinuance. .ensured
    (B) scarcity. .hampered
    (C) rationing. .enhanced
    (D) squandering. .facilitated
    (E) financing. .neglected

28. The passage of the mass transit bill over the Governor's veto, despite opposition by key leaders in the legislature, was a devastating —— for the party machinery and suggests that other, much-needed legislation may receive similar treatment in the future.

    (A) victory
    (B) optimism
    (C) compromise
    (D) slap
    (E) setback

29. The rocket scientists had fully expected the thermothrockle to hydrolyze under the intense ionizing radiation requiring the mission to be aborted; but the astronauts —— the problem by tekelating the suborbital flexion, and the mission continued.

    (A) recreated
    (B) transmitted
    (C) misjudged
    (D) circumvented
    (E) proscribed

30. It is highly characteristic of business' —— attitude that little or no interest was evinced in urban renewal until similar undertakings elsewhere proved that such projects could be ——.

    (A) prestigious. .feasible
    (B) capitalistic. .rigid
    (C) degrading. .completed
    (D) mercantile. .insensitive
    (E) pragmatic. .profitable

31. George Bernard Shaw expressed his —— for technological progress when he said that the human race is just interested in finding more —— ways of exterminating itself.

    (A) hope. .impartial
    (B) regard. .remote
    (C) preference. .violent
    (D) support. .effective
    (E) contempt. .efficient

32. The committee's report is not as valuable as it might have been because it addresses only the symptoms and not the —— causes of the problem.

    (A) unimpeachable
    (B) ephemeral
    (C) underlying
    (D) incipient
    (E) superficial

33. Calvin had long been known for his mendacity, but even those who knew him well were surprised at the —— explanation he gave for the shortage of funds.

    (A) elegant
    (B) disingenuous
    (C) sincere
    (D) dogmatic
    (E) bitter

34. A good mystery writer knows how to lose the reader in a (i)—— from which there is no easy exit by anticipating and encouraging seemingly plausible theories only to show, at the appropriate juncture, that these are dead ends; to truly enjoy the book, you have to accept this (ii)—— and admire the architecture of the twists and turns and cul-de-sacs.

| (i) | (ii) |
| --- | --- |
| chamber | manipulation |
| prison | inequity |
| labyrinth | clarification |

35. Economic protectionism is seductive, but countries that succumb to its allure soon find that it makes (i)—— promises; conversely, countries that commit to economic (ii)—— ensure a brighter economic future for their citizens.

| (i) | (ii) |
| --- | --- |
| false | sanctity |
| sincere | competition |
| intrepid | rigidity |

36. The book's treatment of vegetarianism reveals immense learning, the advantage of having read obscure pamphlets alongside literary masterworks, (i)—— mystical treatises alongside widely distributed political manifestos, and the theories of crackpots alongside the meditations of respected scholars. It traces the origins of vegetarianism to (ii)—— times: the ancient Greek Pythagoras eschewed meat and is often mentioned as (iii)—— a vegetarian diet. By the middle of the 18<sup>th</sup> century, vegetarianism had become a secular religion, and by the mid-19<sup>th</sup> century, it was associated with French revolutionaries, British nudists, and Romantics from across Europe.

| (i) | (ii) | (iii) |
| --- | --- | --- |
| arcane | unsettled | placating |
| inflamed | classical | advocating |
| precocious | contemporary | reviling |

37. As we age, the brain shrinks, the distance between neurons increases, and connections become (i)——. Still, a surprising number of mental functions not only remain (ii)——, they actually improve with age. More mature brains store more expert knowledge. As a consequence, older professionals can more readily distinguish what is important from what is not. This helps to explain why a senior partner in a law firm is better able to handle (iii)—— litigation involving boxes and boxes of documents, only a few of which are relevant.

| (i) | (ii) | (iii) |
| --- | --- | --- |
| compressed | compromised | complex |
| attenuated | insubstantial | hostile |
| inelastic | unimpaired | worrisome |

# REVIEW

This section contains Sentence Completions items for further practice.

**DIRECTIONS:** Each sentence or paragraph in this section has one or more missing elements, as indicated by a blank or blanks. Choose the word or set of words that best fits the meaning of the text. Answers are on page 917.

1. Marxist revolution directly challenged the bourgeois order, and Communism explicitly endeavored to destroy traditional religion and to —— itself as an alternative faith.

   (A) repudiate
   (B) enshrine
   (C) undermine
   (D) illuminate
   (E) placate

2. The judge shouted to counsel on both sides that he would —— no argument on the issue and enjoined them to ——.

   (A) hear. .vote
   (B) accept. .speculation
   (C) brook. .silence
   (D) entertain. .toleration
   (E) contrive. .cease

3. In order to —— the deadline for submitting the research paper, the student tried to —— additional time from the professor.

   (A) extend. .wheedle
   (B) accelerate. .obtain
   (C) postpone. .forego
   (D) sustain. .imagine
   (E) conceal. .procure

4. Due to the —— of the materials needed to manufacture the product and the ever-increasing demand for it, it is highly probable that the final cost to the consumer will ——.

   (A) immensity. .evolve
   (B) paucity. .escalate
   (C) scarcity. .relax
   (D) acuity. .stabilize
   (E) certainty. .fluctuate

5. After the —— journey, the President sent a request to the Prime Minister asking that they —— their meeting until he had had an opportunity to refresh himself.

   (A) exhilarating. .commence
   (B) lengthy. .defray
   (C) exhausting. .defer
   (D) dilatory. .reschedule
   (E) leisurely. .accelerate

6. Following the aborted Bay of Pigs invasion, Congressional opinion about the CIA shifted from almost universal —— of the agency as both essential and highly professional to widespread —— its value as a national policy tool and the integrity of its members.

   (A) endorsement. .skepticism about
   (B) acceptance. .control over
   (C) knowledge. .doubt about
   (D) condemnation. .destruction of
   (E) praise. .victimization of

7. Jazz is an American art form that is now —— in Europe through the determined efforts of —— in France, Scandinavia, and Germany.

   (A) foundering. .governments
   (B) diminishing. .musicians
   (C) appreciated. .opponents
   (D) waning. .novices
   (E) flourishing. .expatriates

8. One of the kidnappers, when left alone with the hostage, attempted to persuade him that they were neither —— nor ——, but only interested in calling international attention to their cause.

(A) impeccable. .sincere
(B) redoubtable. .condescending
(C) antagonistic. .vindictive
(D) recalcitrant. .clandestine
(E) intrepid. .compliant

9. Although the comedian was very clever, many of his remarks were —— and —— lawsuits against him for slander.

(A) derogatory. .resulted in
(B) pithy. .came upon
(C) protracted. .forestalled
(D) depraved. .assuaged
(E) recanted. .sparked

10. Because the disease is relatively rare and doctors know little about it, any treatment prescribed can —— the pain but cannot —— the patient.

(A) alleviate. . infect
(B) palliate. .cure
(C) abate. .affect
(D) minimize. .revive
(E) intensify. .rejuvenate

11. The —— customer was —— by the manager's prompt action and apology.

(A) pecuniary. .appalled
(B) weary. .enervated
(C) sedulous. .consoled
(D) intrepid. .mortified
(E) irate. .mollified

12. You must act with —— if you want to buy your airline ticket before tomorrow's price increase.

(A) celerity
(B) clemency
(C) facility
(D) lassitude
(E) laxity

13. The —— background music hinted of the dangers threatening the movie's heroine.

(A) trenchant
(B) ebullient
(C) sardonic
(D) portentous
(E) precocious

14. The junta's promise of free elections was ——, a mere sop to world opinion.

(A) spurious
(B) contentious
(C) unctuous
(D) lucid
(E) presumptuous

15. His —— manner served to hide the fact that he secretly indulged in the very vices he publicly ——.

(A) sedulous. .dispelled
(B) sanctimonious. .condemned
(C) dogmatic. .espoused
(D) stentorian. .prescribed
(E) candid. .promulgated

16. The Eighteenth Amendment, often called the Prohibition Act, —— the sale of alcoholic beverages.

(A) prolonged
(B) preempted
(C) sanctioned
(D) proscribed
(E) encouraged

17. The —— attitudes politicians have today cause them to —— at the slightest hint of controversy.

(A) dauntless. .recoil
(B) craven. .cower
(C) pusillanimous. .prevail
(D) undaunted. .quail
(E) fractious. .grovel

18. Mrs. Jenkins, upon hearing that her arm was broken, looked —— at the doctor.

    (A) jovially
    (B) plaintively
    (C) fortuitously
    (D) serendipitously
    (E) opportunely

19. Even —— pleasures may leave —— memories.

    (A) ephemeral. .lasting
    (B) emphatic. .stalwart
    (C) transitory. .fleeting
    (D) surreptitious. .secret
    (E) enigmatic. .mysterious

20. Unsure of her skills in English, the young girl was —— when called on to speak in class.

    (A) remunerative
    (B) transient
    (C) reticent
    (D) sartorial
    (E) resilient

21. Each spring, the —— tree put out fewer and fewer leaves.

    (A) ambient
    (B) malignant
    (C) desultory
    (D) moribund
    (E) reclusive

22. The bully's menacing, —— manner was actually just for show; in reality, it was entirely ——.

    (A) imperturbable. .vapid
    (B) truculent. .affected
    (C) stringent. .credulous
    (D) supercilious. .blatant
    (E) parsimonious. .contentious

23. A public official must be —— in all his or her actions to avoid even the appearance of impropriety.

    (A) redolent
    (B) unctuous
    (C) baleful
    (D) circumspect
    (E) propitious

24. She was —— as a child, accepting without question everything she was told.

    (A) obstreperous
    (B) recalcitrant
    (C) credulous
    (D) truculent
    (E) tearful

25. Warned by smoke alarms that a widespread fire was ——, the ushers —— the theatre immediately.

    (A) expected. .filled
    (B) ubiquitous. .purged
    (C) eminent. .checked
    (D) imminent. .evacuated
    (E) insidious. .obviated

26. The municipality attracted the country's scientific elite and —— them, insulating them entirely from the problems of ordinary civilian life.

    (A) cajoled
    (B) muted
    (C) mused
    (D) cosseted
    (E) impeded

27. Although the bank executive gave the appearance of a(n) —— businessman, he was really a ——.

    (A) dedicated. .capitalist
    (B) respectable. .reprobate
    (C) depraved. .profligate
    (D) empathetic. .philanthropist
    (E) churlish. .miscreant

28. During a campaign, politicians often engage in —— debate, attacking each other's proposals in a torrent of —— words.

(A) acerbic. .amiable
(B) acrimonious. .malicious
(C) intensive. .nebulous
(D) garrulous. .inarticulate
(E) impassioned. .vapid

29. —— by her family, the woman finally agreed to sell the farm.

(A) Decimated
(B) Importuned
(C) Encumbered
(D) Interpolated
(E) Designated

30. The ghost of his royal father —— the young Hamlet to avenge his murder.

(A) enervates
(B) parlays
(C) marauds
(D) exhorts
(E) inculcates

31. A life of hardship and poverty has —— them to petty physical discomforts.

(A) ascribed
(B) inured
(C) remonstrated
(D) deferred
(E) impugned

32. Although he was known as a —— old miser, his anonymous gifts to charity were always ——.

(A) grasping. .tasteless
(B) spendthrift. .gracious
(C) gregarious. .selfish
(D) penurious. .generous
(E) stingy. .mangy

33. The composer was —— enough to praise the work of a musician he detested.

(A) magnanimous
(B) loquacious
(C) munificent
(D) parsimonious
(E) surreptitious

34. Though the law's —— purpose was to curtail false advertising, its actual result was to —— free speech.

(A) potential. .preclude
(B) mendacious. .eschew
(C) ostensible. .circumscribe
(D) illicit. .reconcile
(E) recalcitrant. .repress

35. The royal astrologers were commanded to determine the most —— date for the king's coronation.

(A) propitious
(B) ostensible
(C) aberrant
(D) resplendent
(E) obsequious

36. The poem by the great satirist was dripping with venom and was —— with scorn.

(A) contentious
(B) discordant
(C) redolent
(D) sardonic
(E) vicarious

37. The new regime immediately —— laws implementing the promised reforms.

(A) vouchsafed
(B) ensconced
(C) augmented
(D) promulgated
(E) parlayed

38. A long illness can —— even the strongest constitution.

    (A) obviate
    (B) inculcate
    (C) bolster
    (D) enervate
    (E) disparage

39. The city —— to the advancing invaders without firing a single shot.

    (A) extolled
    (B) regressed
    (C) equivocated
    (D) dissembled
    (E) capitulated

40. If you find peeling potatoes to be ——, perhaps you would prefer to scrub the floors?

    (A) felicitous
    (B) remunerative
    (C) onerous
    (D) vilifying
    (E) redundant

41. To strengthen her client's case, the lawyer sought to put the —— of the witness in doubt.

    (A) laxity
    (B) posterity
    (C) probity
    (D) onus
    (E) sensitivity

42. His —— CD collection included everything from Bach to rock.

    (A) divisive
    (B) effusive
    (C) eclectic
    (D) intrinsic
    (E) laconic

43. Her statements were so —— that we were left in doubt as to her real intentions.

    (A) equitable
    (B) equivocal
    (C) innocuous
    (D) dogmatic
    (E) incisive

44. Blue whales grow to —— size and must eat tons of plankton to —— their huge appetites.

    (A) prodigious. .satiate
    (B) effusive. .assuage
    (C) colossal. .deplete
    (D) fortuitous. .exhort
    (E) obstreperous. .vanquish

45. Both coffee and tea have beneficial as well as —— side-effects; while they stimulate the heart and help overcome fatigue, they also —— insomnia and other nervous disorders.

    (A) injurious. .exacerbate
    (B) malignant. .interrupt
    (C) salutary. .heighten
    (D) negligible. .forestall
    (E) specious. .prevent

46. The Parks Department claims that there is a —— of wildlife in the New York City area, and that species that have not lived in the area for most of the century are once again being sighted.

    (A) resurgence
    (B) paucity
    (C) superstructure
    (D) prototype
    (E) compendium

47. Although he had inherited a substantial amount of money, his —— soon led to his filing for bankruptcy.

    (A) prodigality
    (B) volubility
    (C) tenacity
    (D) fastidiousness
    (E) animosity

48. Although the faculty did not always agree with the chairperson of the department, they —— her ideas, mostly in —— her seniority and out of respect for her previous achievements.

   (A) scoffed at. .fear of
   (B) harbored. .defense of
   (C) implemented. .deference to
   (D) marveled at. .lieu of
   (E) ignored. .honor of

49. According to recent studies, prices in supermarkets are considerably higher in the inner city, thus —— the poor who receive assistance to buy the food.

   (A) reprimanding
   (B) intimidating
   (C) alleviating
   (D) assuaging
   (E) exploiting

50. Legislation to stop smoking in public places has been —— by some as a move to save lives, while it is —— by the tobacco industry, which calls the action "alarmist."

   (A) heralded. .condemned
   (B) thwarted. .buffered
   (C) initiated. .condoned
   (D) prejudiced. .supported
   (E) extolled. .elicited

51. Critics are divided in their views on O'Keeffe's art, some admiring her abstractions, others esteeming her figurative works; the first group presents the artist as a progressive while the second places her within the —— tradition.

   (A) conservative
   (B) abstract
   (C) conciliatory
   (D) innovative
   (E) victorious

52. The public quite naturally expects that the Picassos and Rembrandts of the museum's painting collection will be on display at all times, but the lack of well-known masterpieces in the photographic collection gives the curator uncommon —— in deciding which works to exhibit.

   (A) leeway
   (B) guidance
   (C) confidence
   (D) sensitivity
   (E) flair

53. Cultural weightlessness is a defining characteristic of Los Angeles, and each new fashion trend or food fad that emanates from its environs causes its —— to despair of ever hearing Easterners retract their sneering view of the place as nothing more than a disordered set of clogged freeways.

   (A) detractors
   (B) designers
   (C) loyalists
   (D) expatriates
   (E) imitators

54. Prior to the formation of the Central Intelligence Agency, intelligence-gathering functions were ——, with several departments of the executive branch independently engaged in such activities and refusing to share information with each other.

   (A) reliable
   (B) constricted
   (C) fragmented
   (D) precarious
   (E) indigenous

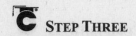 

# TIMED-PRACTICE QUIZZES

**DIRECTIONS:** This section contains three Sentence Completions quizzes. While being timed, complete each quiz. Each sentence or paragraph has one or more missing elements, as indicated by a blank or blanks. Choose the word or set of words that best fits the meaning of the text. Answers are on page 918.

## QUIZ I (20 items; 15 minutes)

1. —— the activities of her employees, the director refused to —— their methods.

   (A) Disarming. .condone
   (B) Applauding. .question
   (C) Repudiating. .punish
   (D) Handling. .oversee
   (E) Approving. .arrogate

2. The —— soldier —— at the idea that he was to go to battle.

   (A) luckless. .rejoiced
   (B) youthful. .retired
   (C) unwilling. .recoiled
   (D) frail. .relapsed
   (E) vigorous. .repined

3. Although the jury thought the defendant had been somewhat less than —— in his testimony, the —— summary of the defense attorney finally convinced them of her client's innocence.

   (A) interesting. .lackluster
   (B) candid. .persuasive
   (C) convincing. .inordinate
   (D) honest. .confusing
   (E) forthright. .irrational

4. The guests invited to meet the famous critic were —— by a charm that contrasted sharply with the —— of his writing.

   (A) appalled. .inadequacy
   (B) frustrated. .wittiness
   (C) deceived. .elegance
   (D) delighted. .venom
   (E) enthralled. .lucidity

5. The critic thought the film was completely unrealistic; he termed the plot —— and the acting ——.

   (A) contrived. .unbelievable
   (B) imaginative. .genuine
   (C) ambitious. .courageous
   (D) artificial. .unparalleled
   (E) absorbing. .uninspiring

6. Dedicated wildlife photographers willingly travel great distances and gladly endure considerable hardship to share with audiences their —— for the natural world.

   (A) distaste
   (B) contempt
   (C) preference
   (D) expectations
   (E) enthusiasm

7. In his private life he was quite ——, but he gave large sums of money to charities, so most people thought of him as a ——.

   (A) pusillanimous. .charlatan
   (B) immodest. .chauvinist
   (C) flamboyant. .savant
   (D) sinister. .mercenary
   (E) miserly. .philanthropist

8. The term "Indian," introduced by Columbus and —— by historians, is a misnomer for the Native American.

   (A) eradicated
   (B) arbitrated
   (C) infiltrated
   (D) perpetuated
   (E) coerced

9. Though the story is set in a small village in a remote area of South America, the novel's themes are so —— that its events could have occurred anywhere and involved any of us at any time.

(A) mythical
(B) universal
(C) overstated
(D) anguished
(E) complex

10. A good historian merely makes —— and accumulates facts; a great historian uses —— to understand why events occurred the way they did.

(A) statements. .research
(B) references. .evidence
(C) observations. .imagination
(D) arguments. .texts
(E) errors. .sympathy

11. Because the poet was restless and uneasy in society, he sought a —— existence and a life of ——.

(A) stable..pleasure
(B) claustrophobic..frivolity
(C) materialistic..urbanity
(D) conservative..squalor
(E) nomadic..solitude

12. Because he was —— and the life of the party, his friends thought that he was happy, but his wife was —— and shy and was thought to be unhappy.

(A) melancholy..sympathetic
(B) philanthropic..conciliatory
(C) vitriolic..sophomoric
(D) garrulous..taciturn
(E) inimical..gregarious

13. The goal of the archaeological dig is to recover as many artifacts as possible before they are —— by the construction of the new bridge.

(A) preserved
(B) revived
(C) reproduced
(D) obliterated
(E) illustrated

14. The experienced ambassador was generally an —— person who regained her composure quickly even on those —— occasions when she was close to losing her temper.

(A) articulate. .momentous
(B) imperturbable. .infrequent
(C) unforgiving. .numerous
(D) idealistic. .rare
(E) insistent. .trying

15. In Doyle's famous detective stories, Mycroft, the brother of Sherlock Holmes, is described as quite ——, going only from his apartment to his office to his club and back to his apartment.

(A) illustrious
(B) omnivorous
(C) loquacious
(D) spontaneous
(E) sedentary

16. Determinist philosophers have argued that our moral intuitions are —— rather than learned and that they are dictated by genetic makeup.

(A) transcendental
(B) fortuitous
(C) innate
(D) contingent
(E) empirical

17. The rescue workers' gnawing sense of —— developed into concern and ultimately despair as they gradually approached the remote site of the car crash.

(A) resignation
(B) foreboding
(C) anticipation
(D) urgency
(E) duplicity

18. Karen was —— in her vindictiveness, frequently feigning disarming warmth while —— waiting for an opportunity to strike back.

    (A) confident. .foolishly
    (B) open. .cautiously
    (C) withdrawn. .overtly
    (D) secure. .immodestly
    (E) ruthless. .secretly

19. The sonatas of Beethoven represent the —— of classicism, but they also contain the seeds of its destruction, romanticism, which —— the sonata form by allowing emotion rather than tradition to shape the music.

    (A) denigration. .perpetuates
    (B) pinnacle. .shatters
    (C) plethora. .heightens
    (D) fruition. .restores
    (E) ignorance. .encumbers

20. In the Middle Ages, the Benedictine monasteries were often —— of civilization and a refuge for science in an otherwise —— and superstitious world.

    (A) arbiters. .scholarly
    (B) brethren. .sanctimonious
    (C) forerunners. .erudite
    (D) conservators. .barbarous
    (E) advocates. .rarefied

## QUIZ II (20 items; 15 minutes)

1. The —— treatment of the zoo animals resulted in community-wide ——.

   (A) curious. .apathy
   (B) popular. .neglect
   (C) critical. .distention
   (D) adequate. .revulsion
   (E) inhumane. .criticism

2. Unlike gold, paper money has no —— value; it is merely a representation of wealth.

   (A) financial
   (B) inveterate
   (C) economic
   (D) intrinsic
   (E) fiscal

3. The history book, written in 1880, was tremendously ——, unfairly blaming the South for the Civil War.

   (A) biased
   (B) objective
   (C) suppressed
   (D) questionable
   (E) complicated

4. Contrary to popular opinion, bats are not generally aggressive and rabid; most are shy and ——.

   (A) turgid
   (B) disfigured
   (C) punctual
   (D) innocuous
   (E) depraved

5. As science progresses, observations that at one time seemed to conflict with one another can sometimes be —— by a more advanced theory.

   (A) established
   (B) inferred
   (C) detected
   (D) reconciled
   (E) delimited

6. Carling, a political appointee who was not really able to run the agency, tended to promote others even less —— than himself who would not question his authority.

   (A) competent
   (B) likable
   (C) honest
   (D) wholesome
   (E) envied

7. It is no longer possible to regard one nation's economy as an —— system; we are now moving toward becoming a global village with international markets.

   (A) ineffective
   (B) opportunistic
   (C) equitable
   (D) irrational
   (E) isolated

8. Attorneys would be extremely unlikely to boast that no one can hear a word they say, but some doctors seem to be quite proud of their —— handwriting.

   (A) elegant
   (B) unique
   (C) cultivated
   (D) illegible
   (E) handsome

9. The farm consisted of land that was barely —— with poor soil made —— by the almost total lack of spring rains.

   (A) cultivated. .productive
   (B) fertile. .rich
   (C) profitable. .consistent
   (D) teeming. .desirable
   (E) arable. .arid

10. The phrase "physical law" is merely a metaphor, for physical laws do not compel objects to behave in a certain way but simply —— the way they do behave.

    (A) suggest
    (B) describe
    (C) finish
    (D) become
    (E) condition

11. Because the orchestra's conductor is an intensely private person, he —— making the appearances at fund-raising functions that are part of the job.

    (A) loathes
    (B) anticipates
    (C) excuses
    (D) prepares
    (E) convenes

12. It is ironic and even tragic that people who have relatively little are generous to those who have even less while the wealthy can be totally ——.

    (A) fortunate
    (B) elite
    (C) selfish
    (D) stylish
    (E) active

13. Unfortunately, Professor Greentree has the unusual ability to transform a lively discussion on a central issue into a dreadfully boring —— on a —— point.

    (A) discourse. .significant
    (B) textbook. .single
    (C) monologue. .tangential
    (D) treatise. .useful
    (E) critique. .stimulating

14. Although for centuries literature was considered something that would instruct as well as entertain, many modern readers have little patience with —— works and seek only to be ——.

    (A) epic..demoralized
    (B) didactic..distracted
    (C) bawdy..absorbed
    (D) superficial..enlightened
    (E) ambiguous..misled

15. Treason is punishable by death because —— constitutes a threat to the very —— of the state.

    (A) perfidy..survival
    (B) grief..existence
    (C) veracity..foundation
    (D) pacifism..dismantling
    (E) patriotism..well-being

16. Hot milk has long been a standard cure for insomnia because of its —— quality.

    (A) malevolent
    (B) amorphous
    (C) soporific
    (D) plaintive
    (E) desultory

17. His untimely death, at first thought to be due to a —— fever, was later —— to poison.

    (A) degenerative. .relegated
    (B) debilitating. .ascribed
    (C) raging. .reduced
    (D) sanguine. .abdicated
    (E) pernicious. .prescribed

18. Psychologists believe that modern life —— neurosis because of the —— of traditional values that define acceptable behavior.

    (A) copes with..inundation
    (B) strives for..condoning
    (C) concentrates on..plethora
    (D) fosters..disappearance
    (E) corroborates..dispelling

19. Although Mozart's music suggests a composer of great —— and seriousness, his letters imply that he was naïve and ——.

(A) erudition. .grave
(B) sophistication. .uncouth
(C) fortitude. .macabre
(D) levity. .sanctimonious
(E) fragility. .pensive

20. Recent studies demonstrate that personal memory is actually quite ——, subject to contamination and reshaping so that aspects of a person's memory are apt to be —— or erroneous.

(A) implausible. .inaccurate
(B) volatile. .subjective
(C) malleable. .insensitive
(D) inhibited. .recalcitrant
(E) comprehensive. .reflective

## QUIZ III (20 items; 15 minutes)

1. The football team was —— by injuries: of the 53 members, only 40 were fit to play.

   (A) truncated
   (B) decimated
   (C) invaded
   (D) ostracized
   (E) reviled

2. In the Middle Ages, scientists and clergymen thought the universe was well-ordered and ——; today scientists are more likely to see the world as ——.

   (A) baffling..dogmatic
   (B) harmonious..chaotic
   (C) transient..predictable
   (D) emancipated..intriguing
   (E) divergent..galling

3. The actress owed her reputation to her —— public and not to the —— reviews that bordered on being cruel.

   (A) diffident..approbatory
   (B) congenial..simpering
   (C) trusting..didactic
   (D) adoring..scathing
   (E) innocent..deferential

4. Since the city cannot ticket their cars, the diplomats can park anywhere with ——.

   (A) penury
   (B) impunity
   (C) precision
   (D) languor
   (E) ignominy

5. If you —— the charges instead of —— them, people may conclude that you are guilty.

   (A) delegate. .enumerating
   (B) preempt. .disclaiming
   (C) efface. .disavowing
   (D) reduce. .mitigating
   (E) ignore. .rebutting

6. On the narrow and —— mountain road, the truck skidded when it rounded a curve.

   (A) pejorative
   (B) salutary
   (C) propitious
   (D) sedulous
   (E) tortuous

7. Since the results of the experiment were —— the body of research already completed, the committee considered the results to be ——.

   (A) similar to..speculative
   (B) inconsistent with..anomalous
   (C) compounded by..heretical
   (D) dispelled by..convincing
   (E) contradicted by..redundant

8. Although scientists have sought to measure time, only writers and poets have truly —— its quality and our —— experience of it.

   (A) neglected..uniform
   (B) understood..benign
   (C) captured..ephemeral
   (D) belied..credulous
   (E) devised..fractious

9. Although her acting was ——, she looked so good on stage that the audience applauded anyway.

   (A) dynamic
   (B) laudable
   (C) implacable
   (D) execrable
   (E) intrepid

10. Because of her unpopular opinions, she was unable to —— broad support among the voters; however, those who did support her were exceptionally ——.

   (A) alienate. .many
   (B) survey. .divided
   (C) cut across. .quiet
   (D) amass. .loyal
   (E) evoke. .languid

11. While scientists continue to make advances in the field of ——, some members of the clergy continue to oppose the research, arguing that it is —— for human beings to tamper with life.

(A) psychology..imperative
(B) astronomy..fallacious
(C) genetics..immoral
(D) geology..erroneous
(E) botany. .unethical

12. Although a gala performance, the conducting was ——, and the orchestra less than enthusiastic, but the audience seemed —— the defects and was enthralled.

(A) auspicious..sensitive to
(B) perfunctory..oblivious to
(C) decimated..mindful of
(D) voracious..excited by
(E) animated..impaired by

13. Philosophical differences —— the unification of the two parties into one.

(A) delegated
(B) legislated
(C) impeded
(D) enacted
(E) entrusted

14. When a job becomes too ——, workers get ——, their attention wanders, and they start to make careless errors.

(A) diverse. .busy
(B) hectic. .lazy
(C) tedious. .bored
(D) fascinating. .interested
(E) rewarding. .sloppy

15. His —— of practical experience and his psychological acuity more than —— his lack of formal academic training.

(A) claims. .compromise
(B) background. .repay
(C) breadth. .account for
(D) wealth. .compensate for
(E) fund. .elucidate

16. The merchant —— a small neighborhood business into a citywide chain of stores.

(A) appraised
(B) transferred
(C) parlayed
(D) redeemed
(E) instilled

17. It is not always easy to —— one's mistakes, but it is inevitably more —— to try to hide them.

(A) cover. .suspect
(B) confess. .difficult
(C) cancel. .attractive
(D) solve. .satisfying
(E) anticipate. .circumspect

18. A professional journalist will attempt to —— the facts learned in an interview by independent ——.

(A) endorse. .questioning
(B) query. .study
(C) garnish. .sources
(D) verify. .investigation
(E) embellish. .scrutiny

19. With the evidence —— from numerous x-ray studies, scientists are beginning to form a picture of the atomic structure of the cell.

(A) remanded
(B) gleaned
(C) pilfered
(D) atrophied
(E) implored

20. His offhand, rather —— remarks —— a character that was really rather serious and not at all superficial.

(A) flippant..masked
(B) pernicious..betrayed
(C) bellicose..belied
(D) controversial..revealed
(E) shallow..enlivened

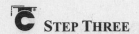
# CAMBRIDGE TESTPREP™

## Strategy Summary Sheet
# SENTENCE COMPLETIONS

Sentence Completions items measure your understanding of both reading comprehension and vocabulary. A *typical* Sentence Completions item consists of a sentence with either one or two blanks provided for missing material and five words or pairs of words presented as answer choices. You must select the word or pair of words that will best complete the intended meaning of the sentence. An answer choice may also be in the form of a phrase (or phrases).

The new Text Completions items include a short text of one to five sentences in length with two or three numbered blanks, each blank indicating that something has been omitted. With these items, you are required to fill all the blanks (choosing from three answer choices per blank) in the way that best completes the meaning of the text as a whole.

Virtually any subject area may be covered, but no special outside knowledge is required. Complex vocabulary and sentence structure increase item difficulty. Answer choices are incorrect when the resulting sentences are not idiomatically valid or when the overall meaning becomes illogical. While an answer choice may be eliminated because the completed sentence fails to make sense, you must not discard an alternative on the basis of grammatical syntax because such syntax will always be correct.

**ITEM-TYPE STRATEGIES:** For Sentence Completions items, it is quite useful to analyze the logical pattern of the sentence. While a countless number of sentences are possible, logical structure falls into two basic categories (Thought Extension and Thought Reversal) that are often signaled via key words or punctuation. More complex sentences may not contain pure extensions or reversals of thought but may have a mixture of both elements (Combined Reasoning). There are a variety of strategies that can be used to solve each of the three types of Sentence Completions items: Thought Extension (Coordinate Conjunctions, Subordinate Conjunctions, Key Adjectives and Adverbs, Punctuation, and Phrases), Thought Reversal (Coordinate Conjunctions, Subordinate Conjunctions, Key Adjectives and Adverbs, and Phrases), and Combined Reasoning (various elements of Thought Extension and Thought Reversal).

1.  *Thought Extension*: In Thought Extension items, missing words may parallel or serve to extend another thought in the sentence. The following are the most important thought extension clues:

    - *Coordinate Conjunctions*: Conjunctions are words that join together words, phrases, clauses, or sentences. They indicate to the reader how the joined elements are related to each other. With Thought Extension items, coordinate conjunction clues continue or reinforce/strengthen the underlying logic (e.g., "and," "or").

    - *Subordinate Conjunctions*: A subordinate conjunction joins together two ideas in a sentence and indicates that one idea is subordinate to, or dependent upon, the other idea. Since they have to indicate the way in which the subordinate clause depends upon the main clause, subordinate conjunctions serve as important verbal clues. With Thought Extension items, subordinate conjunction clues continue or reinforce/strengthen the underlying logic (e.g., "since," "if," "for," "because," "so").

    - *Key Adjectives and Adverbs*: In many cases, the elements of the sentence that provide descriptive detail (adjectives and adverbs) are important clues. With Thought Extension items, look for terminology that continues or reinforces/strengthens the underlying logic.

    - *Punctuation*: Sometimes, a punctuation mark will serve as an important clue. Commas, semicolons, and colons indicate the continuation of a thought.

- *Phrases*: With Thought Extension items, phrase clues consist of any additional information that serves to continue or reinforce/strengthen the underlying logic.

2. *Thought Reversal*: In Thought Reversal items, missing word(s) are the reverse, or opposite, of ideas that are presented elsewhere in the sentence. The following are the most important thought reversal clues:

   - *Coordinate Conjunctions*: Coordinate conjunction clues that set up a contrast with or diminish/weaken the underlying logic (e.g., "but," "or," "yet")

   - *Subordinate Conjunctions*: Subordinate conjunction clues that set up a contrast with or diminish/weaken the underlying logic (e.g., "although," "while," "unless")

   - *Key Adjectives and Adverbs*: Terminology that sets up a contrast with or diminishes/weakens the underlying logic (e.g., "however," "instead," "not," "large/small")

   - *Phrases*: Any additional information that serves to set up a contrast with or diminish/weaken the underlying logic

3. *Combined Reasoning*: Sometimes, a single strand of reasoning may not be sufficient to dispose of an item. Combined Reasoning items consist of complex sentences that contain a mixture of extensions and reversals of thought. To correctly answer these items, it is important to first understand the overall logical structure of the sentence, identifying the ideas and thoughts that are extended and those that are reversed.

**GENERAL STRATEGIES:** There are also a variety of general strategies that can be used to solve Sentence Completions items: "Anticipate and Test," "Simplify Your Life," and Hard Cases ("Go to Pieces" and Difficult Answers). With Text Completions items, read through the text completely to get an overall sense of the material, identifying any of the above reasoning clues that are indicative of the logical structure (e.g., conjunction clues, punctuation, etc.).

1. *"Anticipate and Test"*: You should read the sentence through for understanding, trying to *anticipate* what word or words would effectively complete the sentence. Then, you should look at the answer choices to find the one that comes closest to your initial prediction. Occasionally, you will find the very word or words that you anticipated, but most of the time the answer choices will include words that are similar to those that came to mind when you initially read the sentence. After picking the answer choice that matches your anticipated guesses, insert the selection into the sentence to *test* it and then read the sentence through to make sure that the answer choice reads smoothly and correctly. Upon reading it, you should be convinced that this is the correct answer choice. If that does not work, test the remaining answer choices. The anticipation part of this strategy does not apply when sentences are open-ended, that is, when they allow for multiple possible completion scenarios. In this event, you should directly substitute the various answer choices into the blank(s) and test for validity.

2. *"Simplify Your Life"*: The difficulty of Sentence Completions items is based on the number of details that are included. In general, the more details there are in a sentence, the harder the item is to answer. You can eliminate unnecessary details to make the item easier.

3. *Hard Cases*: There are Sentence Completions items on the test that are very difficult due to complex logical structures and difficult vocabulary. While the strategies presented above will still be helpful, these items often require a more sophisticated approach. Here are two strategies for handling these "hard cases." The first strategy is for handling sentences with complex logical structures; the second strategy is for handling sentences with difficult vocabulary.

   - *"Go to Pieces"*: When approaching Sentence Completions items with complex logical structures, you should try to simplify the task by breaking the sentence into pieces and isolating a small part of the sentence that you understand; this part of the sentence must contain an omitted word. Then, test the answer choices, eliminating as many of them as possible. This strategy is most useful for items that have two blanks because if either of the two resulting constructions lacks meaning, then you may discard that answer choice. Remember that an answer choice may be incorrect because it does not create an idiomatic construction. (Note that this strategy is not an effective method for solving the new Text Completions items that contain two or three numbered blanks since the answer choices for different blanks function independently; that is, selecting one answer choice for one blank does not affect what answer choices you can select for another blank.)

- *Difficult Answers*: Remember that difficult items have difficult answers. The more difficult Sentence Completions items tend to be near the end of a group, but they can be anywhere, depending on your vocabulary skills. In fact, you may know all of the words in a more difficult item but not all of the words in an easier item. If forced to guess, you should not choose an easy answer choice. Instead, choose the answer choice with the most difficult vocabulary word(s).

**NOTES:** _____

_____

_____

_____

_____

_____

_____

_____

_____

_____

_____

_____

_____

_____

_____

_____

_____

_____

# Reading Comprehension

# CAMBRIDGE TESTPREP™

## READING COMPREHENSION OUTLINE

### I. Core Lesson (p. 177)

**A. Facts About Reading Comprehension Items**

**B. Facts About Reading Comprehension Passages**

1. Passages Can Treat Any Subject
2. Material Is Taken out of Context
3. Passages Are Edited
4. Passages Test Comprehension, Not "Speed-Reading"
5. Careful Reading Is Required

**C. The Item Stems**

1. Three Comprehension Levels
   a. General Theme
   b. Specific Points
   c. Evaluation
2. Six Item-Types
   a. Main Idea (Item #1, p. 177)
   b. Specific Detail (Item #2, p. 177)
   c. Logical Structure (Item #3, p. 178)
   d. Implied Idea (Item #4, p. 178)
   e. Further Application (Item #5, p. 178)
   f. Attitude/Tone (Item #6, p. 178)
3. Coding Practice

**D. The Answer Choices**

1. Main Idea Item Choices (Item #7, p. 179)
2. Specific Detail Item Choices (Items #8–9, p. 179)
3. Logical Structure Item Choices (Items #10–11, p. 180)
4. Implied Idea Item Choices (Item #12, p. 180)
5. Further Application Item Choices (Item #13, p. 180)
6. Attitude/Tone Item Choices (Item #14, p. 180)

**E. Further Use of Reading Comprehension Strategies** (Items #15–26, p. 181)

**F. Pre-Assessment Examples**

### II. Review (Items #1–32, p. 185)

### III. Timed-Practice Quizzes (p. 196)

**A. Quiz I** (Items #1–8, p. 196)

# CORE LESSON

The passages and items in this section accompany the Core Lesson of the Reading Comprehension Lesson. You will work through the items with your instructor in class.

**DIRECTIONS:** Each reading selection in this group is followed by questions based on its content. Answer the questions following a selection on the basis of what is stated or implied in that selection, choosing the best answer to each question. Answers are on page 919.

Items 1–6 are based on the following passage.

The liberal view of democratic citizenship that developed in the 17th and 18th centuries was fundamentally different from that of the classical Greeks. The pursuit of private interests with as little
5 interference as possible from government was seen as the road to human happiness and progress rather than the public obligations and involvement in the collective community that were emphasized by the Greeks. Freedom was to be realized by limiting the scope of
10 governmental activity and political obligation and not through immersion in the collective life of the *polis*. The basic role of the citizen was to select governmental leaders and keep the powers and scope of public authority in check. In the liberal view, the rights of
15 citizens against the state were the focus of special emphasis.

Over time, the liberal democratic notion of citizenship developed in two directions. First, there was a movement to increase the proportion of members of
20 society who were eligible to participate as citizens— especially through extending the right of suffrage—and to ensure the basic political equality of all. Second, there was a broadening of the legitimate activities of government and a use of governmental power to redress
25 imbalances in social and economic life. Political citizenship became an instrument through which groups and classes with sufficient numbers of votes could use the state's power to enhance their social and economic well-being.
30 Within the general liberal view of democratic citizenship, tensions have developed over the degree to which government can and should be used as an instrument for promoting happiness and well-being. Political philosopher Martin Diamond has categorized
35 two views of democracy as follows. On the one hand, there is the "libertarian" perspective that stresses the private pursuit of happiness and emphasizes the necessity for restraint on government and protection of individual liberties. On the other hand, there is the
40 "majoritarian" view that emphasizes the "task of the government to uplift and aid the common man against the malefactors of great wealth." The tensions between these two views are very evident today. Taxpayer revolts and calls for smaller government and less
45 government regulation clash with demands for greater government involvement in the economic marketplace and the social sphere.

1. The author's primary purpose is to

   (A) study ancient concepts of citizenship
   (B) contrast different notions of citizenship
   (C) criticize modern libertarian democracy
   (D) describe the importance of universal suffrage
   (E) introduce means of redressing an imbalance of power

2. According to the passage, all of the following are characteristics that would distinguish the liberal idea of government from the Greek idea of government EXCEPT

   (A) The emphasis on the rights of private citizens
   (B) The activities that government may legitimately pursue
   (C) The obligation of citizens to participate in government
   (D) The size of the geographical area controlled by a government
   (E) The definition of human happiness

3. The author cites Martin Diamond in the last paragraph because the author

   (A) regards Martin Diamond as an authority on political philosophy
   (B) wishes to refute Martin Diamond's views on citizenship
   (C) needs a definition of the term "citizenship"
   (D) is unfamiliar with the distinction between libertarian and majoritarian concepts of democracy
   (E) wants voters to support Martin Diamond as a candidate for public office

4. It can be inferred from the passage that the Greek word "*polis*" means

   (A) family life
   (B) military service
   (C) marriage
   (D) private club
   (E) political community

5. A majoritarian would be most likely to favor legislation that would

   (A) eliminate all restrictions on individual liberty
   (B) cut spending for social welfare programs
   (C) provide greater protection for consumers
   (D) lower taxes on the wealthy and raise taxes on the average worker
   (E) raise taxes on the average worker and cut taxes on business

6. The tone of the passage can best be described as

   (A) argumentative
   (B) morose
   (C) scholarly
   (D) frivolous
   (E) technical

Items 7–14 are based on the following passage.

Because some resources must be allocated at the national level, we have created policies that reflect the aggregated attributes of our society. The federal budget determines the proportion of federal resources to be
5 invested in social welfare programs and how these resources are distributed among competing programs. This budget is arrived at through a reiterative aggregative political process which mediates the claims of groups interested in health, education, welfare, and
10 so on, thus socializing the continuing conflict generated by their separate aspirations. The test of whether a policy is "good" under this system is whether it can marshal sufficient legitimacy and consent to provide a basis for cohesion and action. Technical criteria may
15 play a role in the process, but the ultimate criteria are political and social.

Whether a policy that is "good" in the aggregate sense is also "good" for a particular person, however, is a different matter. If everyone had identical attributes,
20 these criteria of goodness would produce identical outcomes. With any degree of complexity or change, however, these criteria will always produce different outcomes. Any policy negotiated to attain an aggregate correctness will be wrong for every individual to whom
25 the policy applies. The less a person conforms to the aggregate, the more wrong it will be.

When a policy is not working, we normally assume that the policy is right in form but wrong in content. It has failed because insufficient intelligence
30 has informed its construction or insufficient energy its implementation. We proceed to replace the old policy with a new one of the same form. This buys time, since some time must elapse before the new policy can fully display the same set of symptoms of failure as the old.
35 We thus continue to invest our time, energy, and other resources as if every new discovery of a non-working policy is a surprise, and a surprise that can be corrected with some reorganized model. But if policies based on complex, aggregated information are always wrong
40 with respect to the preferences of every person to whom they apply, we should concentrate on limiting such policies to minima or "floors." Rather than trying for better policies, we should try for fewer policies or more limited aggregated ones. Such limitations could
45 be designed to produce policies as spare and minimal as possible, for the resources not consumed in their operation would then be usable in non-aggregative, person-specific ways—that is, in a disaggregated fashion. This will require more than just strengthened
50 "local" capacity; it will require the development of new procedures, institutions, roles, and expectations.

7. Which of the following best states the central theme of the passage?

(A) Policies designed to meet the needs of a large group of people are inherently imperfect and should be scaled down.
(B) Policies created by the democratic process are less effective than policies designed by a single, concentrated body of authority.
(C) The effectiveness of a social policy depends more upon the manner in which the policy is administered than upon its initial design.
(D) Since policies created on the federal level are inherently ineffective, all federal social welfare programs should be discontinued.
(E) Because state, county, and city officials are more knowledgeable about local conditions, responsibility for all social welfare programs should be shifted to the local level.

8. According to the passage, the test of whether a policy is successful in the aggregate sense is whether or not it

(A) applies to a large number of people
(B) satisfies the needs of the people to whom it applies
(C) appeals to a sufficiently large number of people
(D) can be revised periodically in response to changing conditions
(E) can be administered by existing federal agencies

9. According to the passage, a policy based on aggregation will be wrong for every person to whom it applies because

(A) many individuals are unaware of the existence of such programs
(B) technical criteria are not given sufficient emphasis
(C) individuals who have no need for a program may still fit its eligibility criteria
(D) some administrators may not apply policies uniformly to all
(E) no individual fits precisely the group profile

10. Which of the following, if true, would most weaken the author's argument?

    (A) Many aggregative social welfare policies enacted during the 1930s are still in effect even though they have been modified several times.
    (B) A study by the General Services Administration of the federal government concluded that waste and mismanagement in government programs has declined in recent years.
    (C) Many government programs can be made more efficient by applying sophisticated computer models and other advanced technology to the problems they are designed to solve.
    (D) The individuals who are the targets of aggregative policies are not required by law to accept the benefits offered by those programs.
    (E) The resources that would be freed by limiting aggregative policies exist only as tax revenues, which cannot be distributed except through aggregative policies.

11. The author places the word "good" in both lines 17 and 18 of the second paragraph in order to

    (A) emphasize that the word is ambiguous when applied to public policies
    (B) stress that no two people will agree on what is "good" and what is not
    (C) minimize the need to describe public policies in value terms
    (D) point out that the word can be applied to individuals but not to groups
    (E) remind the reader that the word is a technical term

12. Which of the following words, when substituted for the word "aggregate" (line 26), would LEAST change the meaning of the sentence?

    (A) extreme
    (B) group
    (C) average
    (D) quantity
    (E) difference

13. Which of the following would the author probably agree is NOT an example of a policy based on a process of aggregation?

    (A) A school dietician prepares menus based on a survey of the taste preferences of students.
    (B) A state requires licensed drivers to take an eye examination only once every ten years because most people's eyes do not change radically in a shorter period of time.
    (C) The trainer for a baseball team prescribes exercises for injured team members according to the nature of the injury and the physical makeup of the player.
    (D) The Senate passed a law lowering the legal driving limit to 0.08, based on studies that determined impairment as a function of blood-alcohol levels.
    (E) The new presidential candidate promised universal healthcare when the majority of Americans reported this as their main concern on recent surveys.

14. The author regards the use of aggregative policies as

    (A) enlightened but prohibitively expensive
    (B) undesirable but sometimes necessary
    (C) wasteful and open to corruption
    (D) essential and praiseworthy
    (E) ill-conceived and unnecessary

Items 15–21 are based on the following passage.

Traditional strategies for controlling insect-pests tend to rely on the use of non-selective insecticides that cause extensive ecological disruption. The alternative sterile-insect technique, in which members of the target
5 species are irradiated to cause sterility, has enjoyed some modest success. When released into an infested area, the sterile insects mate with normal insects but produce no offspring. Unfortunately, the irradiation weakens the insects, making it less likely that they will
10 mate; and, in any event, sterile insects do not search selectively for non-sterile mates. A third, newly developed strategy is based on parasite release.

Pest hosts and their associated parasites have evolved biological and behavioral characteristics that
15 virtually ensure that the relative numbers of hosts and parasites in the ecosystem they inhabit remain within relatively narrow limits—even though coexisting populations may fluctuate up to 100-fold during a single season. The close numerical relationships are
20 entirely consistent with nature's balancing mechanisms, which permit closely associated organisms to live together in harmony. Thus, in natural populations, the ratios of parasites to hosts are not high enough to result in dependable control. However, it is
25 possible to mass-rear parasites so that they can be released at strategic times and in numbers that result in parasite-to-host ratios sufficient to control host populations.

*Biosteres tryoni,* for example, has a strong
30 affinity for medfly larvae. Let us assume that a new medfly infestation is discovered. It is likely to have originated from a single female and, even in an area with a good surveillance program, to be in the third reproductive cycle. The rate of population increase is
35 tenfold per generation; so at the time the infestation comes to light, about 1,000 males and 1,000 females are emerging and will produce a total of approximately 80,000 larvae. Reproduction will be concentrated in an area of about one square mile, but scattered
40 reproduction will occur anywhere within a 25-square-mile area. At first glance, the odds of controlling the infestation by parasite release seem low; but with new techniques for mass-producing parasites, it is possible to release one million males and one million females
45 into the infested area. This would mean an average of 62 females per acre, and the average female parasitizes about 30 host larvae during its lifetime. Additionally, the parasites actively search for host habitats by using the kairomone signals emanating from infested fruit.
50 Even assuming that only ten percent of the released females are successful and, further, that they parasitize

an average of only ten larvae, they could still parasitize one million larvae. Only 80,000 larvae are available, however; so the actual ratio would be 12.5:1. A ratio as
55 low as 5:1 results in 99 percent parasitism.

This method of pest eradication presents no health or environmental problems and is actually cheaper. The cost of mass-rearing and distributing *B. tryoni* is about $2,000 per million. So, even if six
60 million parasites of both sexes are released during a period corresponding to three medfly reproductive cycles, the total cost of the treatment would be $12,000—compared to $25,000 for a single insecticide spray application to the same 25-square-mile area.

15. The author implies that the sterile-insect release strategy is not completely effective because

(A) some sterile insects mate with other sterile insects
(B) weakened sterile insects refuse to mate with healthy insects
(C) the cost of producing a sufficient number of sterile insects is prohibitive
(D) sterile insects are incapable of producing offspring
(E) irradiation leaves a radioactive residue offensive to healthy insects

16. According to the passage, *Biosteres tryoni* is effective in controlling medfly infestations because

(A) female B. tryoni feed on adult medflies
(B) male and female B. tryoni parasitize medfly larvae
(C) male and female B. tryoni mate with medflies
(D) male B. tryoni prevent male medflies from mating
(E) female B. tryoni parasitize medfly larvae

17. It can be inferred that if *B. tryoni* were not attracted by kairomone signals from medfly-infested fruit that the parasite release strategy would be

    (A) less effective because some B. tryoni would remain in areas not infested
    (B) less effective because none of the B. tryoni would parasitize medfly larvae
    (C) equally effective because B. tryoni do not damage fruit crops
    (D) more effective because some B. tryoni would fail to reproduce
    (E) more effective because the B. tryoni would remain more widely dispersed

18. In the development of the passage, the author

    (A) explains a scientific theory and then offers evidence to refute it
    (B) cites statistics to compare the relative effectiveness of different strategies
    (C) speculates on the probable course of scientific developments
    (D) states a general principle and then provides an example of its application
    (E) poses a question and then provides a detailed answer to it

19. Which of the following statements about medfly reproduction can be inferred from the passage?

    (A) The medfly is capable of reproducing asexually.
    (B) A typical generation contains ten times as many females as males.
    (C) A new generation of medfly is produced once a year.
    (D) A medfly colony will reproduce for only three generations.
    (E) Only about 25 percent of larvae reach adulthood.

20. It can be inferred that an insecticide application for the hypothetical infestation would treat a 25-square-mile area because

    (A) the cost for a single spray application to the area is $25,000
    (B) B. tryoni would tend to concentrate themselves in infested areas
    (C) medfly reproduction might occur anywhere within that region
    (D) the spray would repel medflies from fruit not already infested
    (E) medflies from another, yet undiscovered infestation might be in the area

21. The author is primarily concerned with

    (A) criticizing the use of non-selective insecticides
    (B) defending the use of parasite release programs
    (C) explaining the workings of a new pest-control method
    (D) refuting the suggestion that parasite release is costly
    (E) analyzing the reproductive habits of the medfly

Items 22–26 are based on the following passage.

Two techniques have recently been developed to simplify research and reduce the number of non-human primates needed in studies of certain complex hormonal reactions. One technique involves the
5 culturing of primate pituitary cells and the cells of certain human tumors. In the other, animal oviduct tissue is transplanted under the skin of laboratory primates. Both culturing techniques complement existing methods of studying intact animals.
10 With an *in vitro* culturing technique, researchers are deciphering how biochemical agents regulate the secretion of prolactin, the pituitary hormone that promotes milk production. The cultured cells survive for as long as a month, and they do not require serum, a
15 commonly used culture ingredient that can influence cellular function and confound study results. One primate pituitary gland may yield enough cells for as many as 72 culture dishes, which otherwise would require as many animals.
20 The other technique allows scientists to monitor cellular differentiation in the reproductive tracts of female monkeys. While falling short of the long-sought goal of developing an *in vitro* model of the female reproductive system, the next best alternative was
25 achieved. The method involves transplanting oviduct tissue to an easily accessible site under the skin, where the grafted cells behave exactly as if they were in their normal environment. In about 80 percent of the grafts, blood vessels in surrounding abdominal skin grow into
30 and begin nourishing the oviduct tissue. Otherwise, the tissue is largely isolated, walled off by the surrounding skin. A cyst forms that shrinks and swells in tandem with stages of the menstrual cycle. With about 80 percent of the grafts reestablishing themselves in the
35 new site, a single monkey may bear as many as 20 miniature oviducts that are easily accessible for study. Because samples are removed with a simple procedure requiring only local anesthesia, scientists can track changes in oviduct cells over short intervals. In
40 contrast, repeated analysis of cellular changes within the oviduct itself would require abdominal surgery every time a sample was taken—a procedure that the animals could not tolerate.
Scientists are using the grafting technique to
45 study chlamydia infections, a leading cause of infertility among women. By infecting oviduct tissues transplanted into the abdominal skin of rhesus monkeys, researchers hope to determine how the bacteria cause pelvic inflammatory disease and lesions
50 that obstruct the oviduct. Such research could eventually lead to the development of antibodies to the infectious agent and a strategy for producing a chlamydia vaccine.

22. This passage deals primarily with

   (A) reproductive organs of non-human primates
   (B) diseases of the pituitary glands
   (C) in vitro studies of pituitary hormones
   (D) techniques for studying hormonal reactions
   (E) new anesthesia techniques

23. According to the passage, the primary benefit of the new research is that

   (A) scientists can study the pituitary gland for the first time
   (B) the procedures are simpler and require fewer laboratory animals
   (C) the study of intact laboratory animals has now been rendered obsolete
   (D) researchers were able to discover prolactin
   (E) an in vitro model of the reproductive system was developed

24. All of the following are true of the transplantation technique EXCEPT

   (A) It avoids the need for subjecting a laboratory subject to repeated major surgery.
   (B) It permits scientists to monitor changes frequently.
   (C) The transplanted cells grow as they would in their normal site.
   (D) The transplanted cells can be easily grown in vitro.
   (E) The transplant operation is usually successful.

25. According to the passage, chlamydia causes infertility in women by

   (A) causing tissue changes that block the oviduct
   (B) shrinking and swelling tissues in conjunction with the menstrual cycle
   (C) allowing skin tissue to encyst reproductive tissue
   (D) necessitating abdominal surgery to remove damaged tissue
   (E) diverting the blood supply from the reproductive organs to the skin

26. It can be inferred from the passage that an *in vitro* model of the female reproductive system is

    (A) currently available but prohibitively expensive
    (B) currently available and widely used
    (C) theoretically possible but of no scientific value
    (D) theoretically possible but as yet technically impossible
    (E) theoretically impossible

# REVIEW

This section contains Reading Comprehension items for further practice.

**DIRECTIONS:** Each reading selection in this group is followed by questions based on its content. Answer the questions following a selection on the basis of what is stated or implied in that selection, choosing the best answer to each question. Answers are on page 919.

Items 1–6 are based on the following passage.

At Nuremberg, 210 individuals were tried before thirteen military tribunals. The International Military Tribunal (IMT) tried the major German war criminals, including Hermann Goering, Rudolph Hess, and
5 Joachim von Ribbentrop, from November 1945 to October 1946. Subsequently, another 185 defendants, grouped by organization or by type of crime, were tried before twelve United States military tribunals. Robert H. Jackson, the United States chief of counsel and an
10 associate justice of the United States Supreme Court, decided for the IMT that in order to obtain convictions of the officials who gave the orders but did not themselves execute them, the prosecution would rely heavily upon documentary evidence. Such evidence
15 was presumably more persuasive than affidavits and direct testimony of witnesses who might easily be brought by defense lawyers to waver in their statements.

In the course of the various trials, the prosecution
20 chose from the millions of records available to them about 18,000 records to be presented as evidence. Only 2,500 of these were affidavits or interrogation transcripts. Of the total number of defense exhibits, about one-half were affidavits. The rest of the
25 documentary evidence came from a variety of sources, often from the defendant's personal files, the materials in the tribunal library file, and prosecution records and resources. Heavy reliance on the latter often placed the defense in a position of dependence on the good will of
30 the prosecution.

The prosecution staff of the IMT established an elaborate system requiring the cooperation of many government agencies for processing documents, and the prosecution at the 12 United States trials at
35 Nuremberg inherited this system. The resources of the defense were, of course, considerably more limited. Though defendants were given the right to present evidence to the tribunal, they were often compelled to engage in a long and often futile struggle to obtain
40 records. Rulings were often affected by factors not directly related to courtroom and document-handling procedures. Some former members of the IMT defense counsel had acquired more expertise than others by defending several of the accused before the various
45 United States tribunals at different times. As the crimes of the Nazis became more remote in time and the differences among the Allies in the cold-war period increased, a strong, rearmed Germany that could serve as an integral part of Western European defense
50 became desirable. Correspondingly, it became difficult to try German military leaders before United States military tribunals while reestablishing a German military force. Sentences were progressively lightened and procedures softened. Sometimes, however, the
55 nature of the crimes committed precluded the chance of the defendants to receive lighter sentences. Many harsh sentences resulted from the trial of 24 SS Einsatzgruppen for exterminating approximately one million Soviet citizens. In general, SS defendants
60 received severe sentences, often the death penalty, and had greater difficulty in obtaining documents than other defendants.

The judges themselves were also of considerable importance. Judge Toms, from Michigan's third
65 judicial district, Judge Phillips, from North Carolina's thirteenth district, Judge Musamanno, from the court of common pleas in Pennsylvania, and John J. Speight, admitted to the bar of Alabama, adjudicated the Milch and Pohl cases. In addition, judges Musamanno and
70 Speight were on the bench in the Ohlendorf case. Their rulings on document-handling procedures were often more rigid and disadvantageous to defendants than were those of other judges. Among the latter were judges Wennerstrum, Shake, and Christianson of the
75 Supreme Court of Minnesota, who presided over the Weizaecker case.

Although one might say that greater leniency in document procedures might have resulted in better defense, considering the crimes charged, there is no
80 assurance that even the most liberal procedure would have produced exonerating records. The prosecution's greater control of documents in the earlier cases, acting under rules similar to adversary proceedings, tainted the trials. Yet, despite these flaws, the procedures

85 devised at Nuremberg pioneered the massive use of
records as court evidence with large groups of
defendants. In the face of the terrible hatred
engendered by the inhumanities of the Second World
War, the tribunals succeeded in dispensing, essentially,
90 justice.

1. The author is primarily concerned with

   (A) describing a historical event
   (B) developing a theory of jurisprudence
   (C) analyzing courtroom procedures
   (D) criticizing a government policy
   (E) interpreting a legal principle

2. The author's attitude toward the military tribunals
   can best be described as

   (A) restrained contempt
   (B) evident awe
   (C) uncontrolled rage
   (D) profound amusement
   (E) qualified endorsement

3. Which of the following conclusions can be
   inferred about the Milch, Pohl, Ohlendorf, and
   Weizaecker cases?

   (A) Milch, Pohl, and Ohlendorf were convicted,
       but Weizaecker was acquitted.
   (B) Although all four defendants were convicted,
       Weizaecker received a lighter sentence.
   (C) The Milch, Pohl, and Ohlendorf trials took
       place before the Weizaecker trial.
   (D) The defense attorneys in the Weizaecker case
       were given more liberal access to documents
       than in the other cases.
   (E) Milch, Pohl, and Ohlendorf were tried by the
       IMT, but Weizaecker was not.

4. According to the passage, defendants at the
   Nuremberg trials

   (A) were not given the opportunity to present
       evidence
   (B) frequently had difficulty obtaining
       documents
   (C) were not represented by counsel
   (D) were tried in absentia
   (E) were prosecuted by officers of the United
       States military

5. It can be inferred from the selection that
   defendants

   (A) called more witnesses than the prosecution
   (B) submitted more affidavits than the
       prosecution
   (C) did not have access to the tribunal libraries
   (D) were not permitted to testify on their own
       behalf
   (E) relied more heavily on affidavits than the
       prosecution

6. The author would be most likely to agree with
   which of the following statements?

   (A) Members of the SS were unfairly punished
       more severely than other war criminals.
   (B) The IMT was more effective than the 12
       United States military tribunals.
   (C) Many war criminals would have received
       harsher sentences had they been tried earlier.
   (D) Counsel who represented the defendants at
       Nuremberg were often incompetent.
   (E) Trial by documentary evidence is inherently
       prejudicial to the rights of a defendant.

Items 7–13 are based on the following passage.

Depletion is a natural phenomenon that characterizes the development of all non-renewable resources and oil in particular. Broadly speaking, depletion is a progressive reduction of the overall stock
5 of a resource as the resource is produced; narrowly, the term refers to the decline of production associated with a particular field, reservoir, or well. Typically, production from a given well increases to a peak and then declines over time until some economic limit is
10 reached and the well is shut in. If it were not for changes in prices, costs, and technology, depletion of the world's resources would resemble the simple decline curve of a single well.

Geologists and engineers routinely make
15 estimates of oil resources by field, but the estimates are a "best guess" given the available data, and they are revised as more knowledge becomes available. There is no time frame or probability associated with estimates of total resources in place. In contrast, proved reserves
20 of crude oil are the estimated quantities that, on a particular date, are demonstrated with reasonable certainty to be recoverable in the future from known reservoirs under existing economic and operating conditions. Generally, there is at least a 90 percent
25 probability that, at a minimum, the estimated volume of proved reserves in the reservoir can be recovered under existing economic and operating conditions.

Each year, production is taken from proved reserves, reducing both proved reserves and the total
30 resource. Innovative production techniques such as well recompletions, secondary and tertiary enhanced recovery techniques, and expanded production of unconventional resources have reduced net depletion rates at the well and field levels. Advanced exploration
35 and drilling techniques, such as 3-D seismic imaging, directional drilling, and multiple wells from single boreholes, have reduced the cost of finding new pools, reduced the risk of dry holes and dry hole costs, and allowed new pools to be developed and produced more
40 quickly. Lower exploration, drilling, and dry hole costs increase the return on capital by lowering costs. More rapid production of resources from a field increases the return on capital because earnings are realized sooner in the project's life, and therefore, they are discounted
45 less.

Higher returns make some fields that are too expensive to develop under "normal" circumstances economically feasible, because reduced costs allow firms to make profits where they could not before. On
50 the other hand, more rapid development and production of a field by definition increases the rate of depletion.

If an operator produces a field more quickly, the rate of depletion must rise. While the rate of depletion increases with technological progress, the adverse
55 effects of depletion are diminished, and higher levels of production can be maintained for longer periods of time. As depletion leads producers to abandon older fields and develop new ones, the process of developing domestic oil resources leads producers to find and
60 develop the larger, more economical fields first. Later, fields tend to be less desirable, because they are farther away from existing infrastructure or they are smaller in size. Thus, as time progresses, more effort is required to produce the same level of the resource from the
65 same exploration area.

While the frontier for new resources is diminishing, increased innovation has, thus far, served to offset depletion at least partially, keeping production stronger than it would have been in the absence of the
70 innovations. Technological progress is expected to continue to enhance exploration, reduce costs, and improve production technology. But eventually, as field sizes decrease, the ultimate recovery from discovered fields will shrink. Thus, despite
75 technological improvements, ultimate recovery from the average field of the future will be smaller than that from the average field today.

7. The passage is primarily concerned with

(A) sketching a plan to prolong production of existing oil resources
(B) warning of the consequences of overexploiting oil resources
(C) discussing economic factors influencing oil production and depletion
(D) describing methods of extracting oil resources more efficiently
(E) proposing alternative energy sources to replace dependence on oil

8. According to the passage, the most important difference between total oil resources and proved reserves is that proved reserves

   (A) are determined by geological principles probably found to be present beneath the surface
   (B) require the use of advanced production techniques for recovery
   (C) cannot be known for certain to exist until their existence has been verified by experts
   (D) can be produced at a cost comparable to that required for resources currently being recovered
   (E) do not presuppose the existence of advanced technologies for their extractions from the ground

9. Which of the following best explains why the author puts the word "normal" in quotation marks (line 47)?

   (A) Baseline conditions are not natural but are artificially defined by economic factors.
   (B) Reduced costs make oil production operations more profitable than other economic activities.
   (C) Oil is strictly a nonrenewable energy resource in spite of technological advances.
   (D) Existing oil production infrastructure eventually wears out and needs to be replaced.
   (E) Oil reserves are gradually being depleted, making it more and more difficult to find proved reserves.

10. The passage implies that an oil well is removed from production when

   (A) the supply of oil it produces is completely exhausted
   (B) the cost of operating the well exceeds the return
   (C) new wells have been bored to replace the capacity of the existing well
   (D) the cost of capital required to open the well has been recovered
   (E) it is no longer possible to accelerate oil production by the well

11. According to the passage, technological innovation offsets natural depletion because it

   (A) makes it profitable to locate and extract more oil resources
   (B) reduces the ratio of proved reserves to actual oil resources
   (C) replenishes oil resources even as it extracts them from the ground
   (D) permits the exploitation of more expansive oil fields with large resources
   (E) minimizes the need to invest in capital expenditures in order to produce oil

12. Which of the following would be most likely to result in an increase in proved reserves in the United States?

   (A) Increased oil production by foreign sources
   (B) A significant rise in the price of crude oil
   (C) A reduction in estimates of total oil resources
   (D) New federal regulations requiring cleaner engines
   (E) Discovery of a large field of clean-burning coal

13. With which one of the following statements would the author of the passage be most likely to agree?

   (A) Rising capital costs associated with the search for new oil fields will cause proved oil reserves to decline sharply in the short-run.
   (B) Continued reliance on oil as an energy source for the long-term is foolhardy because depletion will consume existing stocks of oil.
   (C) Past production of oil has proceeded at such a rapid rate that future reserves of oil as fuel are now threatened.
   (D) Technological innovation will likely continue to ensure adequate oil resources for use in the foreseeable future.
   (E) The cost of recovery of oil resources is in large part irrelevant because of the importance of oil as an energy source.

Items 14–19 are based on the following passage.

Integrating defense technology with commercial technology can reduce fixed costs and result in other significant economic efficiencies by the use of common processes, labor, equipment, material, and
5 facilities. This includes cooperation between government and private facilities in research and development, manufacturing, and maintenance operations; combined production of similar military and commercial items, including components and
10 sub-systems, side-by-side on a single production line or within a single firm or facility; and use of commercial off-the-shelf items directly within military systems. However, several factors determine the extent to which such integration is possible and the ease with which it
15 can be accomplished. It is useful to compare the experience of the United States with its clear separation of the commercial and defense sectors with that of the People's Republic of China (PRC).

In the United States, one of the biggest obstacles
20 to integrating civil and military procurement is the body of laws governing military procurement. In large part, due to past accounting and acquisitions scandals, myriad reporting requirements frequently deter commercially successful firms from bidding on
25 military contracts. Additionally, the Department of Defense (DOD) demands extensive rights to technical data to ensure that production of a system continues even in the event of a serious business disruption such as bankruptcy. DOD may request not only data about
30 the system itself but also information on proprietary manufacturing processes that commercial firms are anxious to protect. The private-public dichotomy that gives rise to these barriers has no parallel in the PRC because the state owns the bulk of the means of
35 production in the first place.

Additionally, the American military emphasizes high performance, even marginal improvements, regardless of cost. Not only is this additional performance not necessarily sought in commercial
40 products (e.g., commercial jetliners have little need for an afterburner), but it also is usually not cost-effective. In the PRC, although operational parameters are set by the People's Liberation Army (PLA), the standards involved in actual production are set by central
45 managers. The latter are far more versed in engineering, whereas the former have generally been capable only of setting out operational requirements without necessarily understanding the industrial demands involved. Thus, production standards have
50 been the responsibility of the producers rather than the users. Consequently, in the PRC, little effort is made to acquire or develop the very latest state-of-the art weapons technologies.

Yet another obstacle to commercial-military
55 integration involves militarily unique technologies (e.g., ballistic missiles and electronic warfare programming have no civilian applications). In the PRC, military technologies have tended to be rendered "unique" only because certain resources have been in
60 limited supply. That is, the PLA has priority for receiving many of the more advanced and expensive technologies and facilities, but these are in relatively short supply. It is likely, for example, that the Chinese air-defense network has a more advanced set of air-
65 traffic control capabilities than does the Chinese civilian air-traffic net simply because of the scarcity of such equipment.

In general, the PRC appears to have been more successful in integrating military and commercial
70 technology, but it is difficult to assess the extent to which this success is due to the relatively primitive state of technology or to political and economic conditions. It is likely a combination of both. Certainly, replicating in the United States the full degree of
75 integration in the PRC would entail unacceptable political and economic costs. In particular, it is unlikely that the American political system would accept the ambiguity inherent in the commercial use of public facilities and, perhaps more importantly, the conflict of
80 public appropriation of private resources.

14. The primary purpose of the passage is to

(A) compare the integration of military and commercial technology in the United States and the People's Republic of China
(B) use the Chinese political system as the basis for critiquing policies in the United States
(C) criticize the United States for failing to completely integrate military and commercial technology
(D) assess the extent to which military procurement procedures in the People's Republic of China would be useful in the United States
(E) analyze the causes of the failure of the United States to achieve a complete integration of technology between the military and commercial sectors

15. According to the passage, proprietary rights do not present a barrier to integration of commercial and military technology in the People's Republic of China because

    (A) the state controls the means of production
    (B) commercial and military sectors rely on similar technology
    (C) military weapons are not permitted in the commercial sector
    (D) the PRC does not pursue state-of-the-art weapons systems
    (E) the army of the People's Republic of China does not control defense manufacturing

16. It can be inferred that an increase in the availability of high technology air-traffic control equipment in the People's Republic of China would result in

    (A) considerable simplification of the procurement policies for both the civilian and military components of air-traffic control
    (B) less effective performance on the part of air-traffic controllers because of unfamiliarity with new technology
    (C) increased waste and redundancy as the civilian and military sectors competed for the rights to develop new equipment
    (D) cost savings that would be achieved by shifting technicians into lower paying positions
    (E) greater disparity between the capabilities of the civilian air-traffic control system and its military counterpart

17. The passage mentions all of the following as economic efficiencies that could be achieved by the integration of commercial and military technology EXCEPT

    (A) Production lines creating parts for both the commercial and military sectors
    (B) Manufacturing facilities producing sub-systems with civilian and military uses
    (C) Research and development facilities working on problems of both commercial and military significance
    (D) Store housed items originally manufactured for commercial use that also have military applications
    (E) Defense control of commercial manufacturing facilities producing military components

18. The experience of the People's Republic of China, when compared to that of the United States, most strongly supports which of the following conclusions?

    (A) Advanced technologies for weapons systems are adopted more rapidly in countries with planned economies than in nations with capitalistic systems.
    (B) Uniquely material applications of advanced technology are less likely to be developed by military forces that are under the close supervision of civilian authorities.
    (C) Costs of technologically advanced acquisitions tend to be lower when procurement decisions are made by managers with engineering backgrounds.
    (D) Private firms that operate with little or no government oversight prefer to bid on government contracts rather than to produce commercial products for the private sector.
    (E) Economies that are controlled by central planners operate less efficiently than economies in which decision-making authority is widely dispersed.

19. Which of the following best states the conclusion of the passage?

   (A) Attempts at integrating commercial and military technology in the People's Republic of China have been more successful than those in the United States.

   (B) Economic and political differences would make it difficult for the United States to achieve the same integration of commercial and military technology as the People's Republic of China.

   (C) Political factors are more important determinants of a nation's ability to integrate its military and commercial technology sectors than economic considerations.

   (D) Close integration of technological breakthroughs in the civilian and military sectors frequently results in important economic advantages.

   (E) The strength of a country's military posture is in large part determined by the ability of the country's military to incorporate cutting-edge technology into its weapons systems.

Items 20–25 are based on the following passage.

Since 1994, the International Monetary Fund (IMF) has functioned as a quasi-lender of last resort to developing nations. The principles for operating as a lender of last resort were systematically expounded by Henry Thornton in 1802 and reformulated independently by Walter Bagehot in 1873: lend liberally, on good collateral, to the market, for a short term, and at a penalty rate of interest. These recommendations ensure that panic is quelled while the central bank discourages borrowing except by fundamentally solvent parties willing to pay a premium. It is generally accepted that a financial institution other than an aid institution should avoid lending at subsidized (below-market) rates of interest.

It has been a matter of debate whether the IMF honors this important principle. Contributor nations to the IMF do earn interest and can withdraw funds at any time (features that suggest the IMF is like a savings bank), but this ignores the risk involved in IMF loans. Because defaults have been rare, the IMF has not imposed costs in the sense of a nominal operating loss that would reduce the value of the contributions of the members, but a single default by a large borrower would show clearly that the IMF's status does not exclude it from the kinds of risks that the private sector faces when lending to governments. Even in the absence of serious defaults, the U.S. and other contributors have, from time to time, found it necessary to make supplemental contributions to the fund.

Additionally, contributors pay an "opportunity cost." Suppose the IMF pays interest of 2 percent a year for funds it lends to other countries, but a contributor country could earn 6 percent a year lending the funds directly to the same countries. The opportunity cost of the contribution to the IMF is the difference, which amounts to 4 percent a year. Indeed, if participation in the IMF costs nothing at all, contributors would not need to supplement their positions from time to time; the IMF could instead borrow from international financial markets and lend the funds at a suitable mark-up, as banks do.

It has been suggested that conditions imposed on loans by the IMF justify lower rates. Typically, the IMF will require that borrowing governments reduce their budget deficits and rate of money growth (inflation); eliminate monopolies, price controls, interest-rate ceilings, and subsidies; and in some cases, devalue their currencies. Often, these conditions are unpopular, but setting aside the wisdom of the content of conditionality, the important question is regarding the effect on the prospect of repayment. Banks, for example, require mortgage loans to be collateralized by houses. This type of conditionality improves the prospect of repayment and enables banks to make a profit, charging lower interest rates than they otherwise could. The IMF does not require collateral. IMF conditionality, therefore, does not significantly improve the prospects for repayment, and conditionality does not reduce the element of subsidy.

Giving a subsidy is undesirable because instead of making borrowers pay penalty rates of interest when they make mistakes, the IMF allows borrowers to pay lower interest rates during crises than they pay to borrow from the private sector in normal, non-crisis periods. Local taxpayers, rather than taxpayers in countries that are net lenders to the IMF, pay most of the cost of a crisis, so the possibility of obtaining loans from the IMF at subsidized rates of interest is not a positive inducement for a crisis; but all things being equal, subsidized interest rates reduce the incentive to take politically painful measures that may prevent a crisis. Subsidized rates also make countries more inclined to turn to the IMF rather than to the private sector for financing. In this sense, the IMF's subsidized loans create a "moral hazard" (reduced vigilance against imprudent behavior because one does not pay its full costs).

20. Which of the following best describes the development of the passage?

(A) The author reviews two different interpretations of a set of facts and rejects one while accepting the other.
(B) The author reviews two different interpretations of a set of facts and concludes that neither is valid.
(C) The author outlines a list of principles and then demonstrates that the principles are outdated.
(D) The author proposes a new economic theory and argues its advantages over the accepted theory.
(E) The author sketches a theory and offers various objections to it without endorsing them.

21. According to the passage, opportunity cost is the difference between the

    (A) value received and the cost of pursuing a foregone opportunity
    (B) value received and savings realized by not pursuing a foregone opportunity
    (C) value received and the value that would have been received from the foregone opportunity
    (D) cost of pursuing one option and the cost of pursuing a foregone alternative
    (E) cost of pursuing one option and the value that would have been received from a foregone opportunity

22. According to the passage, the IMF sometimes uses conditionality for the purpose that a private bank requires

    (A) payment of interest
    (B) pledge of collateral
    (C) deposits from investors
    (D) proof of solvency
    (E) repayment of loans

23. The author mentions the possibility of precipitating a financial crisis in order to obtain loans on favorable terms (lines 62–65) in order to

    (A) dispose of a weak argument that might otherwise cloud the analysis
    (B) isolate one of the hidden assumptions of a possible counterargument
    (C) uncover a hidden contradiction in a competing line of analysis
    (D) clarify the meaning of a key term used in more than one sense
    (E) demonstrate that a line of reasoning leads to an absurd conclusion

24. With which of the following statements would the author of the passage most likely agree?

    (A) The IMF could reduce the moral hazard attached to lending at below-market interest by exacting promises from borrowers to improve the efficiency of their markets.
    (B) The IMF should lend freely at below-market interest rates because any losses incurred due to default can be offset by supplemental contributions from depositor nations.
    (C) The IMF could minimize the danger of default of loans by requiring debtor nations to pledge collateral that is sufficient to secure the value of the loan.
    (D) For the IMF to function as a sound financial institution, it must reform its lending practices so that it charges interest that reflects the risk attendant on its loans.
    (E) It is immoral for any institution to lend funds to a borrower at below-market interest because the subsidy encourages the borrower to assume excessive risk.

25. The passage suggests that if the IMF charged interest rates that are commensurable with the risks of its loans, then

    (A) more borrowers would wish to obtain loans from the IMF
    (B) borrowers would be more receptive to conditionality
    (C) rates of default on outstanding loans would decline
    (D) private lenders would relax conditions imposed on loans
    (E) contributors would no longer need to make supplemental contributions

Items 26–32 are based on the following passage.

Meteorite ALH84001 is a member of a family of meteorites, half of which were found in Antarctica, that are believed to have originated on Mars. Oxygen isotopes, as distinctive as fingerprints, link these
5 meteorites and clearly differentiate them from any Earth rock or other kind of meteorite. Another family member, ETA79001, was discovered to contain gas trapped by the impact that ejected it from Mars. Analysis of the trapped gas shows that it is identical to
10 atmosphere analyzed by the spacecraft that landed on Mars in 1976.

The rock of ALH84001 was formed 4.5 billion years ago, and 3.6 billion years ago, it was invaded by water containing mineral salts precipitated out to form
15 small carbonate globules with intricate chemical zoning. These carbonates are between 1 and 2 billion years old. 16 million years ago, an object from space, possibly a small asteroid, impacted Mars and blasted off rocks. One of these rocks traveled in space until it
20 was captured by the Earth's gravity and fell on Antarctica. Carbon-14 dating shows that this rock has been on Earth about 13,000 years.

The carbonate globules contain very small crystals of iron oxide (magnetite) and at least two kinds
25 of iron sulfide (pyrrhotite and another mineral, possibly greigite). Small crystals of these minerals are commonly formed on Earth by bacteria, although inorganic processes can also form them. In addition, manganese is concentrated in the center of each
30 carbonate globule, and most of the larger globules have rims of alternating iron-rich and magnesium-rich carbonates. The compositional variation of these carbonates is not what would be expected from high temperature equilibrium crystallization but is more like
35 low temperature crystallization. It is consistent with formation by non-equilibrium precipitation induced by microorganisms.

There are also unusually high concentrations of PAH-type hydrocarbons. These PAHs are unusually
40 simple compared to most PAHs, including PAHs from the burning of coal, oil, or gasoline or the decay of vegetation. Other meteorites contain PAHs, but the pattern and abundances are different. Of course, PAHs can be formed by strictly inorganic reactions, and
45 abundant PAHs were produced in the early solar system and are preserved on some asteroids and comets. Meteorites from these objects fall to Earth and enable us to analyze the PAHs contained within the parent bodies. While some of these are similar to the
50 PAHs in the Martian meteorite, all show some major

differences. One reasonable interpretation of the PAHs is that they are decay products from bacteria.

Also present are unusual, very small forms that could be the remains of microorganisms. These
55 spherical, ovoid, and elongated objects closely resemble the morphology of known bacteria, but many of them are smaller than any known bacteria on Earth. Furthermore, microfossil forms from very old Earth rocks are typically much larger than the forms that we
60 see in the Mars meteorite. The microfossil-like forms may really be minerals and artifacts that superficially resemble small bacteria. Or, perhaps lower gravity and more restricted pore space in rocks promoted the development of smaller forms of microorganisms. Or,
65 maybe such forms exist on Earth in the fossil record but have not yet been found. If the small objects are microfossils, are they from Mars or from Antarctica? Studies so far of the abundant microorganisms found in the rocks, soils, and lakes near the coast of Antarctica
70 do not show PAHs or microorganisms that closely resemble those found in the Martian meteorite.

There is considerable evidence in the Martian meteorite that must be explained by other means if we are to definitely rule out evidence of past Martian life
75 in this meteorite. So far, we have not seen a reasonable explanation by others that can explain all of the data.

26. The main purpose of the passage is to

(A) argue that the available data support the conclusion that life once existed on Mars
(B) examine various facts to determine what thesis about ALH84001 is most strongly supported
(C) answer objections to the contention that Martian meteorites contain evidence of primitive life
(D) pose challenges to scientists who hope to prove that ALH84001 proves that life exists on Mars
(E) explore different scientific theories as to the origin of life on Earth

27. According to the passage, what evidence most strongly establishes that meteorite ALH84001 originated on Mars?

    (A) comparison of trapped gases and the Martian atmosphere
    (B) presence of alternating iron and magnesium carbonates
    (C) evidence of shapes that resemble known bacteria
    (D) pattern of carbonate globules with unusual zoning
    (E) discovery of unusual PAHs in unusual abundances

28. It can be inferred that the discovery in Antarctica of fossils of tiny microorganisms the size of the objects noted in meteorite ALH84001 (lines 53–54) would tend to show that the objects

    (A) are the remains of bacteria that lived on Mars
    (B) were produced by inorganic processes
    (C) are the remains of bacteria that lived in Antarctica
    (D) were present in the rock when it broke from Mars' surface
    (E) are the decay products from once living organisms

29. The passage mentions all of the following as tending to prove that ALH84001 may once have contained primitive life EXCEPT

    (A) Presence of objects resembling the morphology of known bacteria
    (B) Extraordinarily high concentrations of unusual PAHs
    (C) Presence of iron oxide and iron sulfide crystals
    (D) Unusual zonings of carbonate globules
    (E) Distinctive oxygen isotopes trapped in gases

30. According to the passage, the compositional variation of the carbonate deposits (lines 23–26) and the PAH–type hydrocarbons (line 28) both

    (A) result from chemical processes more likely to occur on Mars than on Earth
    (B) might be the product of an organic reaction or the product of an inorganic process
    (C) tend to occur at relatively cooler temperatures than other, similar reactions
    (D) are evidence of chemical processes that occurred during the formation of the solar system
    (E) are byproducts of organic processes and cannot result from inorganic reactions

31. The author mentions lower gravity and restricted pore space (lines 62–63) in order to explain why

    (A) bacteria on Mars might be smaller than ones found on Earth
    (B) no microfossil record of bacteria has yet been found in Antarctica
    (C) the spherical, ovoid, and elongated shapes in ALH84001 cannot be bacteria
    (D) restricted pore space in Martian rocks would hinder bacterial growth
    (E) non-equilibrium precipitation is probably not the result of an organic reaction

32. With which of the following conclusions about the possibility of life on Mars would the author most likely agree?

    (A) The available evidence strongly suggests that conditions on Mars make it impossible for life to have developed there.
    (B) The scientific evidence is ambiguous and supports no conclusion about the possibility of life on Mars.
    (C) Scientific evidence cannot, in principle, ever demonstrate that life existed on Mars.
    (D) Scientific data derived from ALH84001 is consistent with the proposition that life once existed on Mars.
    (E) It is as likely that life developed in a hostile environment such as Antarctica as on Mars.

# TIMED-PRACTICE QUIZZES

**DIRECTIONS:** This section contains three Reading Comprehension quizzes. While being timed, complete each quiz. Each reading selection in this group is followed by questions based on its content. Answer the questions following a selection on the basis of what is <u>stated</u> or <u>implied</u> in that selection, choosing the best answer to each question. Answers are on page 919.

## QUIZ I (8 items; 10 minutes)

<u>Items 1–4</u> are based on the following passage.

In a recent survey, Garber and Holtz concluded that the average half-hour children's television show contains 47 violent acts. When asked about the survey, network television executive Jean Pater responded, "I
5  sure as heck don't think that Bugs Bunny's pouring a glass of milk over a chipmunk's head is violence." Unfortunately, both Garber and Holtz and Pater beg the question. The real issue is whether children view such acts as violence.
10     The violence programming aimed at children almost always appears in the context of fantasy. Cartoon violence generally includes animation, humor, and a remote setting; make-believe violence generally uses only the first two cues; realistic, acted violence,
15  which is not used in programming for children, depends entirely on the viewer's knowledge that the portrayal is fictional. Most children as young as four years can distinguish these three contexts, though there is no support for the idea that children, especially
20  young children, can differentiate types of violence on a cognitive or rational basis (e.g., by justification of motives for the violent behavior).
     There is no evidence of direct imitation of television violence by children, though there is
25  evidence that fantasy violence can energize previously learned aggressive responses such as a physical attack on another child during play. It is by no means clear, however, that the violence in a portrayal is solely responsible for this energizing effect. Rather, the
30  evidence suggests that any exciting material can trigger subsequent aggressive behavior and that it is the excitation rather than the portrayal of violence that instigates or energizes any subsequent violent behavior. "Cold" imitation of violence by children is extremely
35  rare, and the very occasional evidence of direct, imitative associations between television violence and aggressive behavior has been limited to extremely novel and violent acts by teenagers or adults with already established patterns of deviant behavior. The

40  instigational effect means, in the short term, that exposure to violent portrayals could be dangerous if shortly after the exposure (within 15 to 20 minutes), the child happens to be in a situation that calls for interpersonal aggression as an appropriate response—
45  for example, an argument between siblings or among peers. This same instigational effect, however, could be produced by other exciting but nonviolent television content or by any other excitational source, including, ironically enough, a parent's turning off the set.
50     So, there is no convincing causal evidence of any cumulative instigational effects such as more aggressive or violent dispositions in children. In fact, passivity is a more likely long-term result of heavy viewing of television violence. The evidence does not
55  warrant the strong conclusions advanced by many critics who tend to use television violence as a scapegoat to draw public attention away from the real causes of violence—causes like abusive spouses and parents and a culture that celebrates violence generally.

1. According to the passage, all of the following would deter a child from regarding an incident of television violence as real EXCEPT

  (A) including easily recognized cartoon characters
  (B) explaining that characters mean to do no harm
  (C) having characters laugh at their misfortunes
  (D) using a futuristic setting with spaceships and robots
  (E) setting the action in prehistoric times

2. The author implies that a child who has an argument with a sibling two to three hours after watching fantasy violence on television would

    (A) almost surely be more aggressive than usual
    (B) tend to act out the fantasy violence on the sibling
    (C) probably not be unusually violent or aggressive
    (D) likely lapse into a state of total passivity
    (E) generally, but not always, be more violent

3. The author mentions the possible effect of a parent's turning off a television (line 49) in order to

    (A) demonstrate that children are able to distinguish fantasy violence from real violence
    (B) highlight the fact that it is not violence but energy level that stimulates behavior
    (C) refute the suggestion that children are able to understand the motive for a violent action
    (D) question the evidence for the proposition that television violence causes violent behavior
    (E) show that reducing the number of hours a child watches television effectively eliminates passivity

4. Which of the following best describes the author's attitude toward the claim that television violence has a negative effect on children?

    (A) personal displeasure
    (B) fervent support
    (C) reluctant agreement
    (D) impartial disputation
    (E) passive acceptance

Items 5–8 are based on the following passage.

The two principal ways in which immigrant groups adjust to the dominant culture of the host country are assimilation and acculturation. Some ethnic groups appear to have been almost completely
5 assimilated, but Puerto Ricans remain a clearly identifiable minority community.

Puerto Ricans have followed the examples of previous immigrant groups by clustering in their own ethnic communities. They have created islands within a
10 city where Spanish is spoken, native foods are available, Latin music is heard, and other elements of the island lifestyle are evident. The cultural familiarity of the barrio keeps many Puerto Ricans from leaving even when they can find better housing elsewhere, and
15 this slows the process of assimilation.

Additionally, Puerto Ricans are a short plane trip from their homeland. There is a constant two-way flow between this country and the island that disrupts the assimilation process. And with the trend toward ethnic
20 pride and cultural pluralism, pride in Puerto Rican cultural roots has been strengthened. Had the extreme anti-foreigner sentiment of the 1940s persisted, Puerto Ricans may well have had to assimilate sooner, as did many other ethnic groups.
25 The term acculturation rather than assimilation would be used to describe the Puerto Rican experience on the mainland of the United States. Genuine assimilation has not taken place until an immigrant is able to function in the host community without
30 encountering prejudice or discrimination. The problem of hostility in an alien world does not disappear with acculturation; there remains the painful reality of deprivation of status and social rejection.

5. The author is primarily concerned with

   (A) explaining why Puerto Ricans have not been assimilated
   (B) analyzing the process of acculturation of immigrant groups
   (C) discussing social problems created by discrimination against Puerto Ricans
   (D) comparing the experience of Puerto Ricans with that of other immigrant groups
   (E) describing some of the important features of Puerto Rican culture

6. According to the passage, Puerto Ricans have not been assimilated for which of the following reasons?

   I. The physical proximity of Puerto Rico helps to maintain strong ties to their homeland.
   II. The prevailing social and political climate is conducive to the survival of a distinct ethnic identity.
   III. Puerto Ricans prefer to live in cultural enclaves where elements of the Puerto Rican lifestyle abound.

   (A) I only
   (B) III only
   (C) I and II only
   (D) II and III only
   (E) I, II, and III

7. Which of the following is true of the development of the passage?

   (A) The author proposes a theory and then rejects it.
   (B) The author bases a general conclusion on a few examples.
   (C) The author uses technical terms without defining them.
   (D) The author suggests a plan for solving a problem.
   (E) The author contrasts two different explanations.

8. Which of the following statements can be inferred from the passage?

   (A) Assimilation eventually eliminates any discrimination against an immigrant group.
   (B) Acculturation cannot be effective so long as an immigrant group persists in maintaining its own ethnic identity.
   (C) Assimilation can never begin if an immigrant group establishes its own ethnic communities.
   (D) Assimilation is a more complete absorption of an immigrant group by the dominant country than acculturation.
   (E) Acculturation gradually eliminates the barriers that prevent assimilation of an immigrant group.

## QUIZ II (8 items; 10 minutes)

Items 1–4 are based on the following passage.

Literary critics are fond of referring to a work as a "musical novel" whenever a writer employs techniques that can be conveniently described in musical terminology, but the notion that all such works
5 are of the same genre is an oversimplification. In *The Waves,* Virginia Woolf uses musical techniques to evoke imagery. In *Moderato Cantabile,* Marguerite Duras follows the form of the first movement of a sonata. When most literary critics pronounce both
10 *The Waves* and *Moderato Cantabile* "musical novels," it is these gross features that they have in mind; and so they overlook what makes *Moderato Cantabile* a truly musical novel: It is actually "heard" by the reader. The novel is mostly dialogue punctuated by the sounds of a
15 radio, boats, and crowds, like musical phrases defined by rests; all that we know and all that we need to know of Anne and Chauvin is what we hear them say. Ironically, this technique that makes *Moderato Cantabile* more successful than *The Waves* as a
20 "musical novel" may account for Duras' relative lack of success as a filmmaker. Despite the great success of her screenplay for "Hiroshima, Mon Amour," few of the 19 films that she wrote and directed did well, primarily because words often replaced action entirely.

1. The author's primary concern is to

   (A) provide a definition for the phrase "musical novel"
   (B) compare the literary works of Virginia Woolf to those of Marguerite Duras
   (C) show that the term "musical novel" does not have a clear, unambiguous meaning
   (D) provide guidelines for interpreting musical novels
   (E) evaluate the relative effectiveness of different literary techniques

2. The author mentions Duras' lack of success as a filmmaker in order to

   (A) prove that good novelists do not necessarily make good filmmakers
   (B) help show that dialogue has a different effect than imagery
   (C) demonstrate that Duras was an artist who was more than just a writer
   (D) suggest that a successful filmmaker needs to use action as well as dialogue
   (E) suggest that most great novels cannot be made into great films

3. With which of the following statements would the author be most likely to agree?

   (A) The musical form of the sonata is ideal for exploring the complexities of human feelings.
   (B) Music is a more effective art form for expressing the duality of experience than literature.
   (C) Unless a novel has a title and subject matter that suggest musical form, it cannot be "heard" by the reader.
   (D) Novels with musical structures are interesting experiments but will not likely produce serious literature.
   (E) Musical structures and techniques can be used to enhance the effectiveness of a literary work.

4. The author's attitude to Duras' work can best be described as

   (A) studied neutrality
   (B) muted criticism
   (C) scholarly indifference
   (D) qualified admiration
   (E) unbridled enthusiasm

Items 5–8 are based on the following passage.

Conventional echocardiography provides highly detailed, two-dimensional pictures of the heart's anatomy and motion by using high-frequency sound reflected off anatomic surfaces. Cardiologists have
5 even been able to measure the direction and magnitude of blood flow within the heart. But conventional echocardiography provides no direct information about tissue structure or the healing process that follows a heart attack.

10 Recently, it has been learned that the acoustic properties of healthy tissue differ from those of injured tissue, and investigators anticipate that these differences can be diagnostically useful. Research is currently focused on ischemic injury, which occurs
15 when the blood supply to part of the heart is obstructed. Ischemia often occurs when the disease process atherosclerosis causes coronary arteries to become narrowed by fatty plaques, which can eventually cause a myocardial infarction, or heart attack.

20 Ischemia and infarction can be studied in the laboratory by blocking one of the coronary arteries of an animal. Deprived of blood, portions of the myocardium die. As the injured heart heals over a period of weeks, scar tissue forms at the damaged site,
25 or infarct zone.

The degree of attenuation, or loss of signal strength, is different for healthy and damaged tissue and varies according to frequency for damaged tissue. By compiling data associating the quantitative measure
30 of attenuation with the qualitative features of heart tissues, researchers hope to develop a valuable complement to existing echocardiography techniques.

5. The author is primarily concerned with discussing

   (A) the causes of heart disease
   (B) a new technique for studying the heart
   (C) laboratory studies of heart attacks
   (D) procedures of conventional echocardiography
   (E) the process by which the heart heals following myocardial infarction

6. The author mentions that cardiologists have been able to measure the direction and magnitude of the flow of blood in the heart in order to

   (A) prove that atherosclerosis can lead to heart attack
   (B) illustrate a method of doing research with laboratory animals
   (C) acquaint the reader with the functioning of the heart
   (D) demonstrate that conventional echocardiography is very sophisticated
   (E) illustrate for the reader the meanings of some unfamiliar medical terms

7. The passage implies that the use of high frequency sound to characterize the physical state of tissues is

   (A) widely used
   (B) very reliable
   (C) extremely dangerous
   (D) still experimental
   (E) theoretically impossible

8. According to the passage, data on the relationship between the qualitative features of tissue and attenuation

   (A) will render conventional echocardiography obsolete
   (B) is available in already published materials
   (C) could be used in conjunction with conventional echocardiography
   (D) should be used only in a medical emergency
   (E) will have little clinical value

## QUIZ III (8 items; 10 minutes)

Items 1–4 are based on the following passage.

Synchrotron radiation is the name given to pulses of intense x-rays created by electrons circulating within a large evacuated storage ring at nearly the speed of light. Compared with conventional sources, these
5  electron rings produce a much more intense, highly collimated beam of x-rays. Additionally, synchrotron radiation is tunable. By using a monochromonator, a researcher can select x-rays of specific wavelengths or energies.
10  Synchrotron radiation can decipher structural changes during a reaction such as cellular respiration. Data gathered with an array of time-resolved spectroscopic methods, for example, can provide glimpses of local molecular events—the breaking of
15  chemical bonds and the formation of intermediate compounds—that may transpire within a few millionths of a second.
The biggest payoff from the gain in beam intensity, however, will be the enhanced sensitivity of
20  measurements that will maintain the high precision in the high-resolution data of atomic distances on the order of 0.02 to 0.05 angstroms. When working with less powerful machines, researchers compensate for deficiencies in beam intensity by preparing samples
25  that contain high concentrations of protein. The high concentration increases the strength of the signals emanating from the sample when it is exposed to a beam. But many macromolecules cannot be highly concentrated; and when extracted proteins can be
30  concentrated, the sample is not likely to represent conditions in the living membranes, where proteins are scattered over a large area.

1.  The author is primarily concerned with describing

    (A) a new scientific theory
    (B) the properties of x-rays
    (C) the structure of proteins
    (D) the functioning of cells
    (E) an instrument for scientific research

2.  In developing the passage, the author utilizes which of the following devices?

    I.   Statistics to prove a theory
    II.  A contrast of technique
    III. An example to illustrate a point

    (A) I only
    (B) II only
    (C) III only
    (D) II and III only
    (E) I, II, and III

3.  According to the passage, researchers using conventional x-ray sources to study proteins use highly concentrated samples in order to

    (A) simulate the conditions in living cells
    (B) obtain a larger picture of the sample
    (C) condense several experiments into a short span of time
    (D) allow for respiration by sample components
    (E) compensate for the inadequacy of the x-ray beam

4.  The passage makes all of the following statements about synchrotron radiation EXCEPT

    (A) The length of the waves that make up the beam can be controlled.
    (B) The beam is more intense than that of conventional x-ray sources.
    (C) It yields more precise data than conventional x-ray sources.
    (D) It is less dangerous to researchers than conventional x-ray sources.
    (E) It is composed of pulsating x-rays.

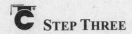
<u>Items 5–8</u> are based on the following passage.

    The geological story of the Rocky Mountains is a long one, the details of which are lost in the passage of hundreds of millions of years. Scientists have put together some of the story from bits of scattered
5  evidence that strongly indicate a certain chain of events, few of which can be proved to everyone's satisfaction. Most of the rocks in the Colorado region are crystalline and ancient. The gneiss and schist were, in part, once sediments formed in the seas—perhaps a
10  billion years ago. These sediments were buried beneath thousands of feet of other sediments, cemented and hardened into layers of sedimentary rock and later squeezed, crushed, and elevated by slow, ceaselessly working earth forces that produced mountains. During
15  this period, the sedimentary rocks were changed to harder metamorphic rocks, probably because of deep burial under tremendous pressure and considerable heat. Masses of molten rock welled up into these earlier deposits and hardened under the Earth's surface.
20  This later intrusive material is now exposed granite in many parts of the Rocky Mountains.

    These ancient mountains were gradually worn away by wind, rain, and other agents of erosion, which must have attacked the surface of the Earth as
25  vigorously then as now. With the passage of millions of years, these mountains were gradually worn away until a new sea lapped over the land where mountains had been, and once again sediments were dropped in its bottom. This new invasion of the ocean affected the
30  Colorado region during the many millions of years in which dinosaurs dominated the Earth.

    In response to little-understood rhythms of the Earth's crust, which have lifted mountains ever so slowly at great intervals all over the world, the seas
35  drained away as the crust rose again, and the rising land once more became subject to the ceaseless attack of erosion. This uplift—which began 60 million years ago—originated the system of mountain ranges and basins that today gives Colorado its spectacular scenery
40  and much of its climate.

5. The passage deals primarily with the

    (A) scenic beauty of Colorado's mountains
    (B) geological history of Colorado's mountains
    (C) classification of rock types
    (D) rhythms of the Earth's crust
    (E) era of the dinosaurs

6. According to the passage, all of the following are true of metamorphic rock EXCEPT

    (A) It is harder than sedimentary rock.
    (B) It is formed from sedimentary rock.
    (C) It is extremely old.
    (D) It is a preliminary form of granite.
    (E) It is created by extreme temperatures and high pressure.

7. The author regards the explanation he gives as

    (A) conclusively proven
    (B) complete fiction
    (C) highly tentative and unsupported by evidence
    (D) speculative but supported by evidence
    (E) certain but unprovable

8. Based on the author's description of the geological process, it can be inferred that the gneiss and schist are

    (A) types of sedimentary rock
    (B) types of granite
    (C) types of metamorphic rock
    (D) types of crystal
    (E) types of igneous rock

# CAMBRIDGE TESTPREP™

## Strategy Summary Sheet
# READING COMPREHENSION

Reading Comprehension items, in particular, require you to understand, analyze, and apply information and concepts presented in written form. All items are to be answered on the basis of what is stated or implied in the reading material, and no specific knowledge of the material is required. Reading Comprehension material can treat any subject, and material will be taken out of context and edited. Passages test comprehension, not "speed-reading." A "mental magnifying glass" is required to study the passages and corresponding items, for they test careful reading as well as logical relationships.

**READING COMPREHENSION STRATEGIES:** Understanding the three levels of reading comprehension and how they relate to the six Reading Comprehension item-types will help you to quickly identify the question that is being asked by a particular item.

1.  *General Theme*: **Main Idea** items represent the first and most basic level of reading: appreciation of the general theme. These items ask about the overall development of the selection and test whether you understand the passage at the most general level. The first sentence of a paragraph—often the topic sentence—may provide a summary of the content of that paragraph. Also, the last sentence of a paragraph usually provides concluding material that may also be helpful in understanding the central theme that unifies the passage. The following are examples of Main Idea item stems:

    *   *Which of the following is the main point of the passage?*
    *   *The primary purpose of the passage is to....*

2.  *Specific Points*: The second level of reading, understanding specific points, takes you deeper into the selection. Specific Detail and Logical Structure items represent this comprehension level. These items test your ability to read carefully. Since this is a computer-adaptive format test, you cannot return to the selection. Therefore, if something is highly technical or difficult to understand, do not dwell on it for too long—guess if necessary.

    **Specific Detail** items ask about details that are explicitly mentioned in the passage. This type of item differs from a Main Idea item in that explicit details are points provided by the author in developing the main idea of the passage. Specific Detail items provide "locator words" that identify the required information in the passage. The following are examples of Specific Detail item stems:

    *   *The author mentions which of the following?*
    *   *According to the passage,...?*

    **Logical Structure** items ask about the overall structure of the passage or the logical role played by a specific part of the passage. The following are examples of Logical Structure item stems:

    *   *The author develops the passage primarily by....*
    *   *The author mentions...in order to....*

3.  *Evaluation*: The third level of reading, evaluation of the text, takes you even deeper into the selection. Implied Idea, Further Application, and Attitude/Tone items represent this comprehension level. These items ask not just for understanding, but require a judgment or an evaluation of what you have read. For this reason, they are usually the most difficult.

**Implied Idea** items do not ask about what is specifically stated in the passage. Rather, these items ask about what can be logically inferred from what is stated in the passage. For example, the passage might explain that a certain organism ($X$) is found only in the presence of another organism ($Y$). An accompanying Implied Idea item might ask the following question: "If organism $Y$ is not present, what can be inferred?" Since the passage implies that in the absence of $Y$, $X$ cannot be present, the answer would be "$X$ is not present." Since this type of item generally builds on a specific detail, "locator words" for identifying information in the passage are often provided in the item stem.

Implied Idea items may also test the understanding of a word or phrase in context. In addition to testing vocabulary, these items incorporate elements that are similar to Sentence Completions items. The nature of these items indicates two points. First, the correct answer will provide the appropriate meaning in the context of the passage. Second, the correct answer may not be the most commonly used meaning of the word; in fact, if it were, then what would be the point of including the item on the test? Thus, the general strategy for this type of item is to favor the less commonly used meaning. The following are examples of Implied Idea item stems:

- *The passage implies that....*
- *The author uses the phrase "..." to mean....*
- *The word —— in line ## means....*
- *In line ##, what is the best definition of —— ?*

**Further Application** items are similar to Implied Idea items, but they go one step further: you must apply what you have learned from the passage to a new situation. The following are examples of Further Application item stems:

- *With which of the following statements would the author most likely agree?*
- *The passage is most probably taken from which of the following sources?*

**Attitude/Tone** items ask about the author's attitude toward a specific detail or the overall voice of the passage. The following are examples of Attitude/Tone item stems:

- *The tone of the passage can best be described as....*
- *The author regards...as....*

If you are unable to immediately determine the correct answer, eliminate as many answer choices as possible and then guess from the remaining answer choices. Remember that you will not be able to move around and answer items randomly since the test is administered on a computer.

**NOTES:** _____

_____

_____

_____

_____

_____

_____

_____

_____

# Quantitative Reasoning Skills Review

# CAMBRIDGE TESTPREP™

## QUANTITATIVE REASONING SKILLS REVIEW OUTLINE

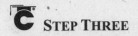

# Exercise 12—Solving Story Problems (Items #1–81, p. 401)

# Numbers

## Real Number System

All *real numbers* correspond to points on the number line and vice versa. Real numbers include whole numbers, integers, fractions, decimals, and irrational numbers. All real numbers, except zero, are either positive or negative. On the number line, numbers corresponding to points to the left of zero are negative and numbers corresponding to point to the right of zero are positive.

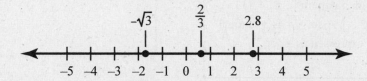

For any two numbers on the number line, the number to the left is *less than* the number to the right. Note that this is the same as saying that for any two numbers on the number line, the number to the right is *greater than* the number to the left. The symbol "<" is used to mean "less than," and the symbol ">" is used to mean "greater than." If a number $n$ is "between 1 and 3" on the number line, than $n > 1$ and $n < 3$; that is, $1 < n < 3$.

*Examples:*

1. $-5 < -\frac{5}{2}$

2. $-0.8 < \frac{3}{2} < 2$

3. $2.4 > -\frac{1}{4}$

4. $1 > 0.2 > -\sqrt{2}$

The symbol "≤" is used to mean "less than or equal to," and the symbol "≥" is used to mean "greater than or equal to." Therefore, if a number $n$ is "between 1 and 3, inclusive" on the number line, $1 \leq n \leq 3$.

The following diagram outlines the subsets of the *real number system*. You should be familiar with the terminology and numbers contained in several of these subsets. Each set is a subset of the one above it; for example, the set of natural numbers is a subset of the set of whole numbers, integers, rational numbers, and real numbers. Natural numbers are whole numbers, integers, rational numbers, and real numbers. Refer back to this diagram as often as necessary.

---

**Real Numbers**

Real numbers are all the numbers on the number line including fractions, integers, radicals, negatives, and zero.

**Rational Numbers**

Rational numbers can be expressed as a ratio of two integers (e.g., $\frac{2}{7}$, $-\frac{8}{2}$, $\frac{9}{10}$). A rational number can be expressed as a number that terminates (e.g., $-1$, $0$, $35$, $-5.25$, $8.0262$) or as a non-terminating decimal with a pattern (e.g., $4.333\ldots$, $3.2525\ldots$, $-0.19621962\ldots$). Also, $\sqrt{4}$ is a rational number since it can be expressed as $\frac{2}{1}$, or 2.

**Irrational Numbers**

Irrational numbers cannot be expressed as a ratio of two integers. No pattern exists when irrational numbers are expressed as decimals and they do not terminate (e.g., $\sqrt{2}$, $-\sqrt{3}$, $\pi$).

**Integers**

Integers are signed (positive and negative) whole numbers and the number zero: $\{\ldots, -2, -1, 0, 1, \ldots\}$.

**Whole Numbers**

Whole numbers are the numbers used for counting and the number zero: $\{0, 1, 2, 3, \ldots\}$.

**Natural or Counting Numbers**

Natural numbers are the numbers used for counting: $\{1, 2, 3, \ldots\}$.

## Terms and Operations

For simplicity, we will introduce the terms and operational concepts associated with all numbers using **whole numbers**. **Whole numbers** are the numbers used for counting, plus the number zero: $\{0, 1, 2, 3, 4, \ldots\}$. Later we will return to the other numbers of the real number system, including fractions, signed numbers, and irrational numbers.

### Basic Terms

**sum (total):** The result of adding numbers together. The **sum**, or total, of 2 and 3 is 5: $2 + 3 = 5$.

**difference:** The result of subtracting one number from another. The **difference** between 5 and 2 is 3: $5 - 2 = 3$.

**product:** The result of multiplying numbers together. The **product** of 2 and 3 is 6: $2 \cdot 3 = 6$.

**quotient:** The result of dividing one number by another. The **quotient** when 6 is divided by 2 is 3: $6 \div 2 = 3$.

**remainder:**  In division, if the quotient is not itself a whole number, the result can be written as a whole number quotient plus a whole number remainder. For example, $7 \div 3 = 2$, plus a ***remainder*** of 1.

## Symbols of Inclusion

Sets of ***parentheses***, ***brackets***, and ***braces*** indicate the order in which operations are to be performed. The innermost symbol of inclusion indicates which operation should be executed first. Generally, operations in parentheses are done first, operations in brackets are done second, and operations in braces are done third. Parentheses, brackets, and braces have the same meaning—three different symbols are used for clarity.

*Examples:*

1. $(2+3) \cdot 4 = 20$

2. $2 + (3 \cdot 4) = 14$

3. $\frac{(2 \cdot 3) \cdot (2+1)}{3 \cdot (5-4)} = \frac{(6) \cdot (3)}{3 \cdot (1)} = \frac{18}{3} = 6$

A particularly complex statement might use parentheses, brackets, and even braces if necessary. With problems such as these, work from the inside out. Start with the operations within parentheses; then do the operations within the brackets; and finally complete the indicated operations.

*Example:*

$$\{[(2 \cdot 3) - 5] \cdot 1\} + [2 \cdot (4-1)] = (6-5) + (2 \cdot 3) = 1 + 6 = 7$$

## Order of Operations

Parentheses, brackets, and braces eliminate ambiguity, but they do not always dictate the order in which operations must be done. Use this mnemonic to remember the order of operations for simplifying expressions: *Please Excuse My Dear Aunt Sally*.

| | |
|---|---|
| Please: | **Parentheses, brackets, braces** |
| Excuse: | **Exponents, radicals** |
| My: | **Multiplication*** |
| Dear: | **Division*** |
| Aunt: | **Addition*** |
| Sally: | **Subtraction*** |

*Remember: add/subtract and multiply/divide in expressions as the operations occur from left to right.

*Examples:*

1. $6 + 4 \cdot 3 - 5 = 6 + 12 - 5 = 18 - 5 = 13$

2. $[2(3+4)](3 \cdot 2) = [2(7)](6) = (14)(6) = 84$

3. $\{(2+7) - [(8 \cdot 6) \div 2] + 25\}\{[2 + 3(2-1)] \div 5\} = [(2+7) - (48 \div 2) + 25]\{[2 + 3(1)] \div 5\} =$
   $[(2+7) - 24 + 25](5 \div 5) = (9 + 25 - 24)(1) = (9 + 1) = 10$

## Factoring and Canceling

An important point to make is that even when multiplication and addition are combined, you have a choice about order of operations. In the following example, most people would probably do the addition first and then the multiplication. It is also permissible, however, to do the multiplication first.

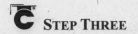 

*Example:*

$$5(2+3+4) = 5(9) = 45$$
$$5(2+3+4) = 5(2)+5(3)+5(4) = 10+15+20 = 45$$

Thus, $10+15+20$ is equal to $5(2)+5(3)+5(4)$, which in turn equals $5(2+3+4)$. This reverse multiplication process is called *factoring*. Factoring can be a tremendous labor-saving device. It is almost always more efficient to first simplify expressions by factoring.

*Example:*

$$(723)(34) - (723)(33) = 24,582 - 23,859 = 723$$
$$(723)(34) - (723)(33) = 723(34-33) = 723(1) = 723$$

Factoring can be combined with division for even greater simplifying power. Division of factors common to both the numerator and the denominator is called *canceling*.

*Example:*

$$\frac{24+36}{12} = \frac{12(2+3)}{12} = (1)(2+3) = 5$$

➤ In this case, 12 can be factored from both 24 and 36. It is then possible to divide 12 by 12, which is 1.

---

## Properties of the Integers 0 and 1

The integers 0 and 1 have special properties that differ from other integers. First, the integer 0 is neither positive nor negative. If $n$ is any number, then $n \pm 0 = n$ and $n \cdot 0 = 0$. Also, division by 0 is not defined. Therefore, it is never allowable to divide anything by 0. The integer 1 multiplied by any number $n$ is equal to the original number; that is, $1 \cdot n = n$. Also, for any number $n \neq 0$, $n \cdot \frac{1}{n} = 1$. Note that the number 1 can be expressed in many ways; for example, $\frac{n}{n} = 1$ for any number $n \neq 0$. Finally, multiplying or dividing an expression by 1, in any form, does not change the value of that expression.

*Examples:*

1. $4+0=4$
2. $4-0=4$
3. $3 \cdot 0 = 0$
4. $1 \cdot 5 = 5$
5. $2 \cdot \frac{1}{2} = 1$
6. $\frac{4}{4} = 1$

## Factors, Multiples, and Primes

Numbers that evenly divide another number are called the **factors** of that number. If a number is evenly divisible by another number, it is considered a **multiple** of that number. 1, 2, 3, 4, 6, and 12 are all factors of 12: 12 is a multiple of 2, a multiple of 3, and so on. Some numbers are not evenly divisible except by 1 and themselves. A number such as this is called a **prime** number. For example, 13 is evenly divisible by 1 and 13 but not by 2 through 12. Note: 1 is NOT considered a prime number even though it is not evenly divisible by any other number. The following are examples of prime numbers: 2, 3, 5, 7, 11, 13, 17, 19, and 23.

*Example:*

Let $D = 120$. How many positive factors, including 1 and 120, does $D$ have?

➤ Express 120 using prime factors: $120 = 2(2)(2)(3)(5) = 2^3(3)(5)$. The exponents of the prime factors 2, 3, and 5, are 3, 1, and 1, respectively. Add 1 to each exponent and multiple the results together: $(3+1)(1+1)(1+1) = (4)(2)(2) = 16$.

## Odd and Even Numbers

An **odd number** is not evenly divisible by 2; an **even number** is a number that is divisible by 2. Any number with a last digit that is 0, 2, 4, 6, or 8 is divisible by 2 and is even. Any number with a last digit that is 1, 3, 5, 7, or 9 is not evenly divisible by 2 and is odd. Zero is considered an even number. The following are important principles that govern the behavior of odd and even numbers.

**PRINCIPLES OF ODD AND EVEN NUMBERS**
1. EVEN ± EVEN = EVEN
2. EVEN ± ODD = ODD
3. ODD ± EVEN = ODD
4. ODD ± ODD = EVEN
5. EVEN • EVEN = EVEN
6. EVEN • ODD = EVEN
7. ODD • EVEN = EVEN
8. ODD • ODD = ODD

*Examples:*

1. $2 + 4 = 6$; $2 - 4 = -2$
2. $4 + 3 = 7$; $4 - 3 = 1$
3. $3 + 4 = 7$; $3 - 4 = -1$
4. $3 + 5 = 8$; $3 - 5 = -2$
5. $2 \cdot 4 = 8$
6. $2 \cdot 3 = 6$
7. $3 \cdot 2 = 6$
8. $3 \cdot 5 = 15$

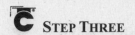 

The rules for multiplication DO NOT apply to division. For example, if you divide the even number 4 by the even number 8, the result is $\frac{1}{2}$. Odd and even are characteristics of whole numbers and negative integers, but not fractions. A fraction is neither odd nor even.

## Consecutive Integers

*Consecutive integers* immediately follow one another. For example, 3, 4, 5, and 6 are consecutive integers, but 3, 7, 21, and 45 are not. In a string of consecutive integers, the next number is always one more than the preceding number. Thus, if $n$ is the first number in a string of consecutive integers, the second number is $n+1$, the fourth number is $n+3$, and so on.

| 1st | 2nd | 3rd | 4th |
|---|---|---|---|
| $n$ | $n+1$ | $n+2$ | $n+3$ |
| 3 | 4 | 5 | 6 |

We can also speak of *consecutive even integers* and *consecutive odd integers*. 2, 4, 6, and 8 are consecutive even integers; 3, 5, 7, and 9 are consecutive odd integers. If $n$ is the first number in a string of consecutive even or odd integers, the second number is $n+2$, the third number is $n+4$, the fourth number is $n+6$, and so on.

| 1st | 2nd | 3rd | 4th |
|---|---|---|---|
| $n$ | $n+2$ | $n+4$ | $n+6$ |
| 3 | 5 | 7 | 9 |
| 4 | 6 | 8 | 10 |

Do not be confused by the fact that the sequence for consecutive odd integers proceeds as $n$, $n+2$, $n+4$, etc. Even though 2, 4, etc. are even numbers, $n+2$, $n+4$, etc. will be odd numbers when the starting point, $n$, is odd.

## Working with Signed Numbers

Numbers are just positions in a linear system. Each whole number is one greater than the number to its left and one less than the number to its right. The following number line represents the *integer number system*, which consists of the signed (positive and negative) whole numbers and zero:

$$-15 \quad -10 \quad -5 \quad 0 \quad 5 \quad 10 \quad 15$$
$$(-) \longleftarrow|\!|\!|\!|\!|\!|\!|\!|\!|\!|\!|\!|\!|\!|\!|\!|\!|\!|\!|\!|\!|\!|\!|\!|\!|\!|\!|\!|\!|\!|\!|\!|\!|\!|\!|\!|\!|\longrightarrow (+)$$

With both positive and negative integers, each position is one more than the position before it and one less than the position after it: $-1$ is one less than zero and one more than $-2$; $-2$ is one less than $-1$ and one more than $-3$. The minus sign indicates the direction in which the number system is moving with reference to zero. If you move to the right, you are going in the positive direction; to the left, in the negative direction.

It is natural to use negative numbers in everyday situations, such as games and banking: An overdrawn checking account results in a minus balance. You can manipulate negative numbers using the basic operations (addition, subtraction, multiplication, and division). To help explain these operations, we introduce the concept of absolute value.

## Absolute Value

The *absolute value* of a number is its value without any sign and so it is always a positive numerical value: $|x| \geq 0$. Therefore, $|x| = x$ if $x \geq 0$ and $|x| = -x$ if $x < 0$. A number's absolute value is its distance on the number line from the origin, without regard to direction: $|x| = |-x|$.

*Examples:*

1. $|4| = 4$

2. $|-10| = 10$

3. $|5| - |3| = 5 - 3 = 2$

4. $|-2| + |-3| = 2 + 3 = 5$

This idea of value, without regard to direction, helps to clarify negative number operations.

## Adding Negative Numbers

To add negative numbers to other numbers, subtract the absolute value of the negative numbers.

*Example:*

$$10 + (-4) = 10 - |-4| = 10 - 4 = 6$$

➤ The number line illustrates the logic: Start at 10 and move the counter four units in the negative direction. The result is 6:

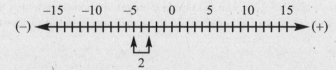

Follow this procedure even if you wind up with a negative result, as illustrated in the following example.

*Example:*

$$10 + (-12) = 10 - |-12| = 10 - 12 = -2$$

➤ Start at 10 and move the counter 12 units in a negative direction. The result is two units to the left of zero, or −2.

Similarly, the procedure works when you add a negative number to another negative number.

*Example:*

$$-3 + -2 = -3 - |-2| = -3 - 2 = -5$$

➤ Begin at −3, and move the counter two units in the negative direction. The result is −5:

**Any addition of a negative number is equivalent to subtraction of a positive number.**

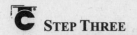 

*Examples:*

1. $5 + (-2) = 5 - 2 = 3$
2. $7 + (-7) = 7 - 7 = 0$

## Subtracting Negative Numbers

Subtracting negative numbers is a little different. When you subtract a negative number, you are really adding, since the number itself has a negative value. It is like a double negative: "It is not true that Bob's not here" means that Bob is here. To subtract a negative number from another quantity, add the absolute value of the negative number to the other quantity.

*Example:*

$10 - (-5) = 10 + \left| -5 \right| = 10 + 5 = 15$

➢ Start at 10: Since the minus signs cancel each other out, move the counter in the positive direction. The result is 15:

Follow this procedure no matter where you start, even if you are subtracting a negative number from zero or from another negative number.

*Example:*

$-5 - (-10) = -5 + \left| -10 \right| = -5 + 10 = 5$

➢ Start at −5: Since the minus signs cancel each other out, move the counter in the positive direction. The result is 5:

**Any subtraction of a negative number is equivalent to addition of a positive number.**

*Examples:*

1. $4 - (-4) = 4 + 4 = 8$
2. $0 - (-7) = 0 + 7 = 7$
3. $-8 - (-4) = -8 + 4 = -4$

## Multiplying Negative Numbers

We can also explain the rules for multiplying negative numbers through the concept of absolute value. To multiply a positive number by a negative number, simply multiply together the absolute values of the two numbers, and then make the sign of the resultant value negative. The product of two numbers with the same sign is always positive, and the product of two numbers with different signs is always negative.

*Examples:*

1. $3 \cdot -6 = -(|3| \cdot |-6|) = -(3 \cdot 6) = -18$
2. $-2 \cdot 4 = -(|-2| \cdot |4|) = -(2 \cdot 4) = -8$

A way of remembering this is to think that the minus sign has "tainted" the problem, so the result must be negative.

To multiply a negative number by a negative number, multiply together the absolute values of the two numbers. The product of two negative numbers is always positive.

*Example:*

$$-3 \cdot -6 = |-3| \cdot |-6| = 3 \cdot 6 = 18$$

This is like saying that two wrongs DO make a right—a negative times a negative produces a positive.

***Any product involving an odd number of negatives will be negative. Any product involving an even number of negatives will be positive.***

*Examples:*

1. $-1 \cdot -2 = 2$
2. $-1 \cdot -2 \cdot -3 = -6$
3. $-1 \cdot -2 \cdot -3 \cdot -4 = 24$
4. $-1 \cdot -2 \cdot -3 \cdot -4 \cdot -5 = -120$

## Dividing Negative Numbers

When dividing negative numbers, the same rules apply as with multiplication. If the division involves a positive number and a negative number, divide using the absolute values of the numbers, and then make the sign of the resultant value negative.

*Examples:*

1. $6 \div -3 = -(|6| \div |-3|) = -(6 \div 3) = -2$
2. $-8 \div 2 = -(|-8| \div |2|) = -(8 \div 2) = -4$

For division involving two negative numbers, divide using the absolute values of the numbers, and then make the sign of this value positive.

*Example:*

$$-8 \div -4 = |-8| \div |-4| = 8 \div 4 = 2$$

*Any quotient involving an odd number of negatives will be negative. Any quotient involving an even number of negatives will be positive.*

*Examples:*

1. $\frac{4}{-2} = -2$

2. $\frac{(-2)(6)}{-4} = \frac{-12}{-4} = 3$

3. $\frac{(3)(-2)(-4)}{(-1)(2)} = -(3 \bullet 4) = -12$

**Summary of Signed Numbers**

---

**PRINCIPLES FOR WORKING WITH NEGATIVE NUMBERS**

1. *Subtraction* of a *negative* number is equivalent to *addition* of a *positive* number.

2. *Addition* of a *negative* number is equivalent to *subtraction* of a *positive* number.

3. *Multiplication* or *division* involving an *odd* number of *negative* numbers always results in a *negative* number.

4. *Multiplication* or *division* involving an *even* number of *negative* numbers always results in a *positive* number.

---

These rules govern operations with all signed numbers. Be careful how you apply the rules to complicated expressions; just take each item step by step.

*Example:*

$$\frac{(2 \bullet -3) - (-2 + -12)}{(-8 \div 2) \bullet (2 + -4)} = \frac{(-6) - (-14)}{(-4) \bullet (-2)} = \frac{-6 + 14}{4 \bullet 2} = \frac{14 - 6}{8} = \frac{8}{8} = 1$$

## Properties of Real Numbers

The following is a list of the properties of real numbers encountered in this review. Note that these properties apply to all real numbers, not just whole and signed numbers.

## PROPERTIES OF REAL NUMBERS
($x$, $y$, and $z$ represent real numbers)

1. $x + y = y + x$ and $xy = yx$.

2. $(x + y) + z = x + (y + z)$ and $(xy)z = x(yz)$

3. $x(y + z) = xy + yz$

4. If $x$ and $y$ are both positive, then $x + y$ and $xy$ are positive

5. If $x$ and $y$ are both negative, then $x + y$ is negative and $xy$ is positive

6. If $x$ is positive and $y$ is negative, then $xy$ is negative

7. If $xy = 0$, then $x = 0$ and $y = 0$

8. $|x + y| \leq |x| + |y|$

*Examples:*

1. $2 + 4 = 4 + 2 = 6$

2. $(2)(4) = (4)(2) = 8$

3. $(3 + 5) + 6 = 3 + (5 + 6) = 3 + 11 = 14$

4. $(2\sqrt{3})(3) = 2(3\sqrt{3}) = 6\sqrt{3}$

5. $\frac{1}{2}(2 + 4) = \frac{1}{2}(2) + \frac{1}{2}(4) = 1 + 2 = 3$

6. $2x = 0 \Rightarrow x = 0$

7. $|5 + 2| \leq |5| + |2| \Rightarrow |7| \leq 7 \Rightarrow 7 = 7$

8. $|3 + (-2)| \leq |3| + |-2| \Rightarrow |3 - 2| \leq 3 + 2 \Rightarrow 1 \leq 5$

# Numbers

**DIRECTIONS:** Choose the correct answer to each of the following items. Answers are on page 923.

1. Subtracting 1 from which digit in the number 12,345 will decrease the value of the number by 1,000?
   A. 1    C. 3    E. 5
   B. 2    D. 4

2. Adding 3 to which digit in the number 736,124 will increase the value of the number by 30,000?
   A. 7    C. 6    E. 4
   B. 3    D. 2

3. Adding 1 to each digit of the number 222,222 will increase the value of the number by how much?
   A. 333,333    C. 100,000    E. 1
   B. 111,111    D. 10

4. $(1 \cdot 10,000) + (2 \cdot 1,000) + (3 \cdot 100) + (4 \cdot 10) + (5 \cdot 1) = ?$
   A. 5,000    C. 12,345    E. 543,210
   B. 15,000    D. 54,321

5. $(1 \cdot 1) + (1 \cdot 10) + (1 \cdot 100) + (1 \cdot 1,000) + (1 \cdot 10,000) = ?$
   A. 5    C. 11,111    E. 1,111,100
   B. 5,000    D. 111,110

6. $(1 \cdot 100,000) + (2 \cdot 10,000) + (3 \cdot 1,000) = ?$
   A. 123    C. 12,300    E. 1,230,000
   B. 1,230    D. 123,000

7. $(2 \cdot 1,000) + (3 \cdot 100) + (1 \cdot 10,000) + (2 \cdot 10) + 1 = ?$
   A. 11,223    C. 12,321    E. 32,121
   B. 12,132    D. 23,121

8. $(9 \cdot 10,000) + (9 \cdot 100) = ?$
   A. 99    C. 90,009    E. 90,900
   B. 9,090    D. 90,090

9. $(2 \cdot 10,000) + (8 \cdot 1,000) + (4 \cdot 10) = ?$
   A. 284    C. 2,084    E. 28,040
   B. 482    D. 2,840

10. What is the sum of 2 and 3?
    A. 1    C. 6    E. 10
    B. 5    D. 8

11. What is the sum of 5, 7, and 8?
    A. 12    C. 20    E. 28
    B. 15    D. 25

12. What is the sum of 20, 30, and 40?
    A. 60    C. 80    E. 100
    B. 70    D. 90

13. What is the difference between 8 and 3?
    A. 24    C. 8    E. 3
    B. 11    D. 5

14. What is the difference between 28 and 14?
    A. 2    C. 14    E. 392
    B. 7    D. 42

15. What is the product of 2 and 8?
    A. 4    C. 10    E. 24
    B. 6    D. 16

16. What is the product of 20 and 50?
    A. 70    C. 1,000    E. 100,000
    B. 100    D. 10,000

17. What is the product of 12 and 10?
    A. 2    C. 120    E. 300
    B. 22    D. 240

18. What is the sum of $(5 + 1)$ and $(2 + 3)$?
    A. 4    C. 24    E. 40
    B. 11    D. 33

19. What is the difference between $(5+2)$ and $(3 \cdot 2)$?

   A. 0     C. 3     E. 14
   B. 1     D. 10

20. What is the product of the sum of 2 and 3 and the sum of 3 and 4?

   A. 6     C. 35     E. 72
   B. 12     D. 48

21. What is the sum of the product of 2 and 3 and the product of 3 and 4?

   A. 6     C. 18     E. 72
   B. 12     D. 35

22. What is the difference between the product of 3 and 4 and the product of 2 and 3?

   A. 2     C. 6     E. 36
   B. 3     D. 12

23. What is the remainder when 12 is divided by 7?

   A. 1     C. 3     E. 5
   B. 2     D. 4

24. What is the remainder when 18 is divided by 2?

   A. 0     C. 3     E. 9
   B. 1     D. 6

25. What is the remainder when 50 is divided by 2?

   A. 0     C. 3     E. 50
   B. 1     D. 25

26. What is the remainder when 15 is divided by 8?

   A. 0     C. 4     E. 89
   B. 1     D. 7

27. What is the remainder when 15 is divided by 2?

   A. 0     C. 7     E. 14
   B. 1     D. 8

28. When both 8 and 13 are divided by a certain number, the remainder is 3. What is the number?

   A. 4     C. 6     E. 8
   B. 5     D. 7

29. When both 33 and 37 are divided by a certain number, the remainder is 1. What is the number?

   A. 4     C. 10     E. 18
   B. 9     D. 16

30. When both 12 and 19 are divided by a certain number, the remainder is 5. What is the number?

   A. 3     C. 5     E. 9
   B. 4     D. 7

31. $(4 \cdot 3) + 2 = ?$

   A. 6     C. 12     E. 26
   B. 9     D. 14

32. $(2 \cdot 3) \div (2 + 1) = ?$

   A. 0     C. 2     E. 6
   B. 1     D. 3

33. $[2 \cdot (12 \div 4)] + [6 \div (1 + 2)] = ?$

   A. 4     C. 8     E. 24
   B. 6     D. 18

34. $[(36 \div 12) \cdot (24 \div 3)] \div [(1 \cdot 3) - (18 \div 9)] = ?$

   A. 3     C. 16     E. 24
   B. 8     D. 20

35. $[(12 \cdot 3) - (3 \cdot 12)] + [(8 \div 2) \div 4] = ?$

   A. 0     C. 4     E. 16
   B. 1     D. 8

36. $(1 \cdot 2 \cdot 3 \cdot 4) - [(2 \cdot 3) + (3 \cdot 6)] = ?$

   A. 0     C. 6     E. 24
   B. 1     D. 16

37. Which of the following statements is (are) true?

   I. $(4 + 3) - 6 = 4 + (6 - 2)$
   II. $3(4 + 5) = (3 \cdot 4) + (3 \cdot 5)$
   III. $(3 + 5) \cdot 4 = 4 \cdot (5 + 3)$

   A. I only     D. II and III only
   B. II only     E. I, II, and III
   C. III only

38. $12 + 24 + 36 = ?$

   A. $3 \cdot 12$     D. $6(2) + 6(3) + 6(4)$
   B. $12(1 + 2 + 3)$     E. $12 \cdot 24 \cdot 36$
   C. $12(3 + 4 + 5)$

39. $25 + 50 + 100 = ?$

   A. $5(1 + 2 + 3)$     D. $25(1 + 2 + 4)$
   B. $5(1 + 2 + 4)$     E. $25(1 + 5 + 10)$
   C. $25(1 + 2 + 3)$

40. $\frac{9(121) - 99(120)}{33} = ?$

    A. 1        C. 33        E. 120
    B. 3        D. 99

41. $1,234(96) - 1,234(48) = ?$

    A. $1,234 \cdot 48$        D. $(1,234 \cdot 1,234)$
    B. $1,234 \cdot 96$        E. $2 \cdot 1,234$
    C. $1,234(48 + 96)$

42. How many prime numbers are greater than 20 but less than 30?

    A. 0        C. 2        E. 4
    B. 1        D. 3

43. How many prime numbers are greater that 50 but less than 60?

    A. 0        C. 2        E. 4
    B. 1        D. 3

44. Which of the following numbers is (are) prime?

    I. 11
    II. 111
    III. 1,111

    A. I only        D. I and III only
    B. II only        E. I, II, and III
    C. I and II only

45. Which of the following numbers is (are) prime?

    I. 12,345
    II. 999,999,999
    III. 1,000,000,002

    A. I only        D. I, II, and III
    B. III only        E. Neither I, II, nor III
    C. I and II only

46. What is the largest factor of both 25 and 40?

    A. 5        C. 10        E. 25
    B. 8        D. 15

47. What is the largest factor of both 6 and 9?

    A. 1        C. 6        E. 12
    B. 3        D. 9

48. What is the largest factor of both 12 and 18?

    A. 6        C. 36        E. 216
    B. 24        D. 48

49. What is the largest factor of 18, 24, and 36?

    A. 6        C. 12        E. 18
    B. 9        D. 15

50. What is the largest factor of 7, 14, and 21?

    A. 1        C. 14        E. 35
    B. 7        D. 21

51. What is the smallest multiple of both 5 and 2?

    A. 7        C. 20        E. 40
    B. 10        D. 30

52. What is the smallest multiple of both 12 and 18?

    A. 36        C. 72        E. 216
    B. 48        D. 128

53. Which of the following is (are) even?

    I. 12
    II. 36
    III. 101

    A. I only        D. I and III only
    B. II only        E. I, II, and III
    C. I and II only

54. Which of the following is (are) odd?

    I. $24 \cdot 31$
    II. $22 \cdot 49$
    III. $33 \cdot 101$

    A. I only        D. I and III only
    B. II only        E. I, II, and III
    C. III only

55. Which of the following is (are) even?

    I. $333,332 \cdot 333,333$
    II. $999,999 + 101,101$
    III. $22,221 \cdot 44,441$

    A. I only        D. I and III only
    B. II only        E. I, II, and III
    C. I and II only

56. If $n$ is an even number, then which of the following MAY NOT be even?

    A. $(n \cdot n) + n$    C. $n + 2$    E. $\frac{n}{2}$
    B. $n \cdot n - n$    D. $3(n + 2)$

57. For any whole number $n$, which of the following MUST be odd?

  I. $3(n+1)$
  II. $3n+2n$
  III. $2n-1$

  A. I only
  B. II only
  C. III only
  D. I and II only
  E. I, II, and III

58. If 8 is the third number in a series of three consecutive whole numbers, what is the first number in the series?

  A. 0
  B. 1
  C. 6
  D. 7
  E. 11

59. If 15 is the fifth number in a series of five consecutive odd numbers, what is the third number in the series?

  A. 5
  B. 7
  C. 9
  D. 11
  E. 13

60. If $m$, $n$, and $o$ are consecutive whole numbers that total 15, what is the largest of the three numbers?

  A. 4
  B. 5
  C. 6
  D. 14
  E. 17

61. If $A = 2^2(3)(7) = 84$, how many positive factors, including 1 and 84, does $A$ have?

  A. 12
  B. 24
  C. 36
  D. 42
  E. 84

62. If $B = 5(8)(11) = 440$, how many positive factors, including 1 and 440, does $B$ have?

  A. 8
  B. 10
  C. 12
  D. 16
  E. 24

63. If $ab(c - d + 2e) = -6$, which of the numbers $a$, $b$, $c$, $d$, and $e$ CANNOT be 0?

  A. $a$ and b only
  B. $b$ only
  C. $c$ only
  D. $d$ only
  E. $c$ and d only

64. If $[a - 2(b + c - 3d)]e = 3$ which of the numbers $a$, $b$, $c$, $d$, and $e$ CANNOT be 0?

  A. $a$
  B. $b$
  C. $c$
  D. $d$
  E. $e$

Items #65–79: Each of the following items includes a number line and a counter. Select the letter of the correct position for the counter after the indicated operations.

*Example:*

  $2 + 3 = ?$

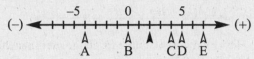

The original position of the counter is 2. If you move it three units in the positive direction, the result is 5, (D).

65. $3 + 1 = ?$

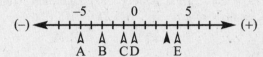

66. $5 - 2 = ?$

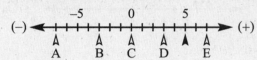

67. $5 + (-2) = ?$

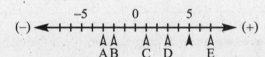

68. $3 + 2 + (-7) = ?$

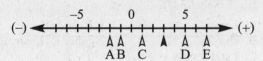

69. $2 + (-4) = ?$

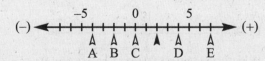

70. $-2 + (-2) = ?$

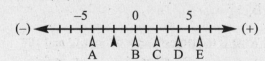

71. $4 + (-2) + (-2) = ?$

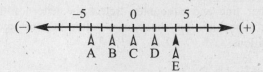

72. $-4 + (-1) + (-1) = ?$

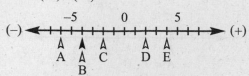

73. $-4 + 8 = ?$

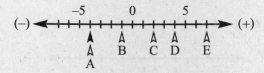

74. $-2 + 2 + (-1) = ?$

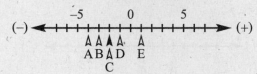

75. $2 - (-1) = ?$

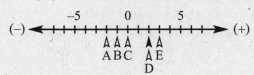

76. $5 - (-2) = ?$

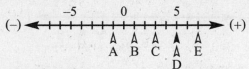

77. $0 - (-4) = ?$

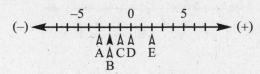

78. $-2 - (-1) = ?$

79. $-3 - (-1) - (-2) = ?$

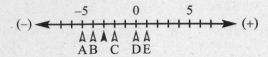

Items #80–116: Determine the correct answer for each of these problems without the aid of a number line.

80. $5 + 8 + (-2) + (-1) = ?$

   A. 3          C. 10          E. 23
   B. 7          D. 13

81. $12 - 7 + 6 + (-1) = ?$

   A. 2          C. 10          E. 18
   B. 6          D. 14

82. $3 + (-3) = ?$

   A. −6         C. 0           E. 6
   B. −3         D. 3

83. $0 + (-12) = ?$

   A. −12        C. −1          E. 12
   B. −6         D. 0

84. $-3 + 1 = ?$

   A. −4         C. 2           E. 8
   B. −2         D. 4

85. $-2 + (-6) = ?$

   A. −8         C. −2          E. 4
   B. −4         D. 2

86. $-2 + (-3) + (-4) = ?$

   A. −24        C. −6          E. 6
   B. −9         D. 0

87. $100 + (-99) = ?$

   A. −199       C. −1          E. 99
   B. −99        D. 1

88. $14 - (-2) = ?$

   A. 16         C. 4           E. −14
   B. 12         D. −2

89. $2 - (-5) = ?$

   A. 7          C. −2          E. −7
   B. 3          D. −3

90. $0 - (-4) = ?$

    A. $-8$      C. $0$      E. $8$
    B. $-4$      D. $4$

91. $-2 - (-3) = ?$

    A. $-6$      C. $-1$      E. $3$
    B. $-5$      D. $1$

92. $-5 - (-1) - 1 = ?$

    A. $-7$      C. $-3$      E. $2$
    B. $-5$      D. $-1$

93. $(5 - 1) + (1 - 5) = ?$

    A. $-5$      C. $0$      E. $5$
    B. $-3$      D. $3$

94. $[2 - (-6)] - [-2 + (-1)] = ?$

    A. $-2$      C. $1$      E. $11$
    B. $-1$      D. $5$

95. $1 \cdot -2 = ?$

    A. $-2$      C. $-\frac{1}{2}$      E. $2$
    B. $-1$      D. $1$

96. $-8 \cdot 6 = ?$

    A. $-48$      C. $2$      E. $48$
    B. $-2$      D. $14$

97. $-10 \cdot -10 = ?$

    A. $-100$      C. $0$      E. $100$
    B. $-20$      D. $20$

98. $-2 \cdot -1 \cdot 1 = ?$

    A. $-3$      C. $1$      E. $4$
    B. $-2$      D. $2$

99. $-10 \cdot -10 \cdot -10 = ?$

    A. $-1,000$      C. $-1$      E. $1,000$
    B. $-30$      D. $1$

100. $-2 \cdot -2 \cdot -2 \cdot -2 = ?$

    A. $-32$      C. $4$      E. $32$
    B. $-8$      D. $16$

101. $-1 \cdot -1 \cdot -1 \cdot -1 \cdot -1 \cdot -1 \cdot -1 \cdot -1 \cdot -1 \cdot -1 = ?$

    A. $-10$      C. $0$      E. $10$
    B. $-1$      D. $1$

102. $4 \div -2 = ?$

    A. $-8$      C. $-\frac{1}{2}$      E. $8$
    B. $-2$      D. $2$

103. $-12 \div 4 = ?$

    A. $-4$      C. $-2$      E. $4$
    B. $-3$      D. $3$

104. $-12 \div -12 = ?$

    A. $-144$      C. $1$      E. $144$
    B. $-1$      D. $24$

105. $[7 - (-6)] + [3 \cdot (2 - 4)] = ?$

    A. $-2$      C. $7$      E. $23$
    B. $0$      D. $12$

106. $[2 \cdot (-3)][1 \cdot (-4)][2 \cdot (-1)] = ?$

    A. $-48$      C. $2$      E. $56$
    B. $-16$      D. $28$

107. $(6 \cdot -2) \div (3 \cdot -4) = ?$

    A. $-12$      C. $1$      E. $24$
    B. $-1$      D. $3$

108. $\{[4 - (-3)] + [7 - (-1)]\}[-3 - (-2)] = ?$

    A. $-25$      C. $-7$      E. $8$
    B. $-15$      D. $-1$

109. $[(2 \cdot -1) + (4 \div -2)][(-6 + 6) - (2 - 3)] = ?$

    A. $5$      C. $-2$      E. $-23$
    B. $2$      D. $-4$

110. $(2 - 3)(3 - 2)(4 - 3)(3 - 4)(5 - 4)(4 - 5) = ?$

    A. $-625$      C. $1$      E. $625$
    B. $-1$      D. $50$

111. $[2(3 - 4)] + [(125 \div -25)(1 \cdot -2)] = ?$

    A. $-12$      C. $2$      E. $125$
    B. $-8$      D. $8$

112. $-\frac{1}{2} \cdot 2 \cdot -\frac{1}{2} \cdot 2 \cdot -\frac{1}{2} \cdot 2 = ?$

    A. $-16$      C. $-1$      E. $2$
    B. $-8$      D. $1$

113. $[(2 \cdot 3) \div (-6 \cdot 1)][(21 \div 7) \cdot \frac{1}{3}] = ?$

    A. $-5$      C. $1$      E. $36$
    B. $-1$      D. $12$

114. $(-5 \cdot -2)-(-2 \cdot -5) = ?$

    A. 0          C. 10         E. 18
    B. 2          D. 12

115. $6 \div -\frac{1}{3} = ?$

    A. −18         C. 2          E. 18
    B. $-\frac{1}{2}$      D. 3

116. $[-3-(-3)]-[-2-(-2)]-[-1-(-1)] = ?$

    A. −12         C. 0          E. 12
    B. −6          D. 6

117. If $n$ is any negative number, which of the following must also be negative?

    I. $n+n$
    II. $n \cdot n$
    III. $n-n$

    A. I only              D. II and III only
    B. II only             E. I, II, and III
    C. I and III only

118. If $n$ is any negative number, which of the following must also be negative?

    I. $n \cdot -n$
    II. $-n \cdot -n$
    III. $-n+n$

    A. I only              D. II and III only
    B. II only             E. I, II, and III
    C. III only

119. If $n$ is any positive number, which of the following must be negative?

    I. $n \cdot -n$
    II. $-n+-n$
    III. $n-(-n)$

    A. I only              D. I and III only
    B. II only             E. I, II, and III
    C. I and II only

120. If $n$ is any positive number, which of the following must be positive?

    I. $-n-(-n)$
    II. $-n \cdot -n$
    III. $n \div (-n \cdot -n)$

    A. I only              D. I and III only
    B. II only             E. II and III only
    C. III only

121. Given any number such that $n \neq 0$, which of the following must be equal to 0?

    I. $-n \cdot -n \cdot -n \cdot -n \cdot -n \cdot -n$
    II. $[(n-n)-n]-[(n-n)-n]$
    III. $n \div [(n \div n) \div n]$

    A. I only              D. I and III only
    B. II only             E. I, II, and III
    C. I and II only

122. In the figure below, what point between $A$ and $B$ is two times as far from $A$ as from $B$?

    $\overset{\overset{A}{\bullet}}{_{-10}}$ ———— $\overset{\overset{B}{\bullet}}{_{41}}$

    A. 7          C. 17         E. 31
    B. 10         D. 24

123. In the figure below, what point between $A$ and $B$ is three times as far from $A$ as from $B$?

    $\overset{\overset{A}{\bullet}}{_{-12}}$ ———— $\overset{\overset{B}{\bullet}}{_{28}}$

    A. 12         C. 20         E. 24
    B. 18         D. 21

124. $|1|+|-2|+|3|+|-4|+|5|+|-6|+|7|+|-8|+$ $|9|+|-10|+|11|+|-12| = ?$

    A. −12         C. 6          E. 78
    B. −6          D. 12

# Fractions

When one whole number is divided by another whole number and the result is not a third whole number, the result is a *fraction*. For example, when 2 is divided by 3, the result is not a whole number, but rather it is the fraction $\frac{2}{3}$. Note that any whole number can also be expressed as a fraction; e.g., $\frac{12}{3} = 4$, $7 = \frac{7}{1}$.

The number above the division line in the fraction is called the *numerator*; the number below the line is called the *denominator*. In a *proper fraction*, the numerator is less than the denominator, so the fraction has a value of less than 1, e.g., $\frac{1}{2}$ and $\frac{3}{4}$, which are both less than 1. In an *improper fraction*, the numerator is greater than the denominator, so the fraction has a value greater than 1, e.g., $\frac{3}{2}$ and $\frac{4}{3}$, which are both greater than 1. A *mixed number* consists of both a whole number and a fraction written together. For example, $2\frac{1}{2}$ is equivalent to $2 + \frac{1}{2}$, and $3\frac{4}{5}$ is equivalent to $3 + \frac{4}{5}$.

## Converting Mixed Numbers to Improper Fractions

Before you add, subtract, multiply, or divide, convert *mixed numbers* to *improper fractions*. To convert a mixed number to an improper fraction, use the following procedure.

Step 1: Use the denominator of the old fractional part of the mixed number as the new denominator.

Step 2: Multiply the whole number part of the mixed number by the denominator of the old fractional part and add to that product the numerator of the old fractional part. This is the new numerator.

*Examples:*

1. Rewrite $2\frac{3}{7}$ as an improper fraction.

   ➤ The denominator of the improper fraction is 7. The numerator is determined by multiplying 7 by 2 and adding 3 to the result. To summarize: $2\frac{3}{7} \Rightarrow \frac{(2 \cdot 7) + 3}{7} = \frac{14 + 3}{7} = \frac{17}{7}$.

2. $3\frac{1}{4} = \frac{(3 \cdot 4) + 1}{4} = \frac{13}{4}$

3. $6\frac{2}{5} = \frac{(6 \cdot 5) + 2}{5} = \frac{32}{5}$

4. $2\frac{12}{13} = \frac{(2 \cdot 13) + 12}{13} = \frac{38}{13}$

## Converting Improper Fractions to Mixed Numbers

To convert an improper fraction to a mixed number, reverse the process described above.

Step 1: Divide the denominator into the numerator. The quotient becomes the whole number part of the mixed number.

Step 2: Use the same denominator for the fraction; the numerator is the remainder of the division process in Step 1.

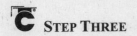 

*Examples:*

1. Convert $\frac{30}{7}$ into a mixed number.

   ➢ Divide 7 into 30; the result is 4 with a remainder of 2. The 4 is the whole number part of the mixed number. Next, the numerator of the fraction is the remainder 2, and the denominator is 7. Therefore, $\frac{30}{7} = 4\frac{2}{7}$.

2. $\frac{29}{5} = 29 \div 5 = 5$ with a remainder of $4 = 5\frac{4}{5}$

3. $\frac{31}{6} = 31 \div 6 = 5$ with a remainder of $1 = 5\frac{1}{6}$

4. $\frac{43}{13} = 43 \div 13 = 3$ with a remainder of $4 = 3\frac{4}{13}$

## Reducing Fractions to Lowest Terms

For reasons of convenience, it is customary to reduce all fractions to their lowest terms. When you reduce a fraction to lowest terms, you really are doing nothing but rewriting it in an equivalent form. This is accomplished by eliminating common factors in both the numerator and the denominator of the fraction.

*Example:*

$\frac{8}{16} = \frac{1(8)}{2(8)} = \frac{1}{2}$

   ➢ There are various ways of describing what goes on when you reduce a fraction. You might think of taking out a common factor, such as 8 in this example, and then dividing 8 into 8 (canceling). It is also possible to think of the process as dividing both the numerator and the denominator by the same number: $\frac{8}{16} = \frac{8 \div 8}{16 \div 8} = \frac{1}{2}$.

It does not matter how you describe the process, so long as you know how to reduce a fraction to its lowest terms. A fraction is expressed in lowest terms when there is no number (other than 1) that can be evenly divided into both the numerator and the denominator. For example, the fraction $\frac{8}{15}$ is in lowest terms, since there is no number (other than 1) that evenly goes into 8 that also evenly goes into 15. On the other hand, the fraction $\frac{8}{12}$ is not in lowest terms, since both 8 and 12 can be evenly divided by 4. Reducing $\frac{8}{12}$ by a factor of 4 gives $\frac{2}{3}$, which is in lowest terms since nothing (other than 1) evenly divides into both 2 and 3.

*Examples:*

1. $\frac{12}{36} = \frac{1 \cdot 12}{3 \cdot 12} = \frac{1}{3}$

2. $\frac{42}{48} = \frac{7 \cdot 6}{8 \cdot 6} = \frac{7}{8}$

3. $\frac{50}{125} = \frac{2 \cdot 25}{5 \cdot 25} = \frac{2}{5}$

If a fraction is particularly large, you may need to reduce it in steps. The process is largely a matter of trial and error, but there are a couple of rules that can guide you. Remember that if both the numerator and the denominator are even numbers, you can reduce the fraction by a factor of 2. Finally, if both the numerator and the denominator end in either 0 or 5, they are both divisible by 5.

*Examples:*

1. $\dfrac{32}{64} = \dfrac{16(2)}{32(2)} = \dfrac{8(2)}{16(2)} = \dfrac{4(2)}{8(2)} = \dfrac{2(2)}{4(2)} = \dfrac{1(2)}{2(2)} = \dfrac{1}{2}$

2. $\dfrac{55}{100} = \dfrac{11(5)}{20(5)} = \dfrac{11}{20}$

## Common Denominators

A **common denominator** is a number that is a multiple of the denominators of two or more fractions. For example, 12 is a multiple of both 3 and 4 (both 3 and 4 divide evenly into 12), so it is a suitable common denominator for $\frac{1}{3}$ and $\frac{1}{4}$. Converting a fraction to one with another denominator is the reverse of reducing it to lowest terms. When you multiply both the numerator and the denominator by the same number, you are really just multiplying the fraction by 1, so its value is not changed; e.g., $\frac{3}{3} = 1$.

In grade school, you were taught to find the lowest common denominator for fractions. In truth, any common denominator will work. The easiest way to find a common denominator is to multiply the different denominators together. For example, a common denominator for 2 and 3 is $2 \cdot 3$, or 6; a common denominator for 3 and 4 is $3 \cdot 4$, or 12; a common denominator for 2 and 5 is $2 \cdot 5$, or 10.

What was the big deal about lowest common denominators? It is the same as reducing fractions to lowest terms: It is easier to work with smaller numbers. A common denominator for 2 and 8 is 16, but 8 is also a possibility. It is easier to deal with a fraction of denominator 8 than 16. In the final analysis, you can use any common denominator, because you can always reduce a fraction to its lowest terms.

To reduce a fraction to its lowest terms, divide the numerator and the denominator by their **greatest common factor**. If you cannot find the greatest common factor, divide both numbers by a common factor. Keep dividing by common factors until the only common factor of the numerator and the denominator is 1.

## Operations of Fractions

### Adding Fractions

The procedure for adding fractions depends on whether or not the fractions share the same denominator. To add fractions with the same denominator, create a new fraction using that denominator. The new numerator is the sum of the old numerators.

*Examples:*

1. $\frac{3}{7} + \frac{2}{7} = \frac{5}{7}$

2. $\frac{2}{5} + \frac{2}{5} = \frac{4}{5}$

3. $\frac{1}{7} + \frac{2}{7} + \frac{3}{7} = \frac{6}{7}$

To add fractions with different denominators, you must first find a common denominator and convert the fractions in the manner described above. For example, $\frac{1}{3}$ and $\frac{1}{5}$. Since these fractions have unlike denominators, you must find a common denominator such as 15. Next, you convert each fraction to a fraction with a denominator of 15.

*Examples:*

1. $\frac{1}{3} + \frac{1}{5} = \frac{1(5)}{3(5)} + \frac{1(3)}{5(3)} = \frac{5}{15} + \frac{3}{15} = \frac{8}{15}$

2. $\frac{1}{3} + \frac{2}{7} = \frac{1(7)}{3(7)} + \frac{2(3)}{7(3)} = \frac{7}{21} + \frac{6}{21} = \frac{13}{21}$

3. $\frac{2}{9} + \frac{4}{5} = \frac{2(5)}{9(5)} + \frac{4(9)}{5(9)} = \frac{10}{45} + \frac{36}{45} = \frac{46}{45}$

To add a fraction and a whole number, you can treat the whole number as a fraction with a denominator of 1.

*Example:*

$2 + \frac{1}{5} + \frac{1}{2} = \frac{2}{1} + \frac{1}{5} + \frac{1}{2} = \frac{2(10)}{1(10)} + \frac{1(2)}{5(2)} + \frac{1(5)}{2(5)} = \frac{20}{10} + \frac{2}{10} + \frac{5}{10} = \frac{27}{10}$

To add a fraction and a mixed number, change the mixed number to an improper fraction and add together the two fractions.

*Example:*

$2\frac{1}{3} + \frac{1}{3} = \frac{7}{3} + \frac{1}{3} = \frac{8}{3} = 2\frac{2}{3}$

## Subtracting Fractions

Follow the same procedures for subtraction of fractions as for addition, except subtract rather than add. When the fractions have the same denominators, simply subtract one numerator from the other.

*Examples:*

1. $\frac{5}{7} - \frac{2}{7} = \frac{3}{7}$

2. $\frac{4}{5} - \frac{3}{5} = \frac{1}{5}$

When fractions have different denominators, it is first necessary to find a common denominator.

*Examples:*

1. $\frac{7}{8} - \frac{3}{5} = \frac{7(5)}{8(5)} - \frac{3(8)}{5(8)} = \frac{35}{40} - \frac{24}{40} = \frac{11}{40}$

2. $\frac{5}{6} - \frac{1}{5} = \frac{5(5)}{6(5)} - \frac{1(6)}{5(6)} = \frac{25}{30} - \frac{6}{30} = \frac{19}{30}$

3. $2 - \frac{7}{6} = \frac{2}{1} - \frac{7}{6} = \frac{2(6)}{1(6)} - \frac{7(1)}{6(1)} = \frac{12}{6} - \frac{7}{6} = \frac{5}{6}$

## *"Flying-X" Method*

You do not need to worry about finding a lowest common denominator as long as you remember to reduce the result of an operation to lowest terms. This sets up a little trick for adding and subtracting fractions that makes the process a purely mechanical one—one you do not even have to think about. The trick is called the "flying-x."

To add (or subtract) any two fractions with unlike denominators use the following procedure.

Step 1: Multiply the denominators to get a new denominator.
Step 2: Multiply the numerator of the first fraction by the denominator of the second.
Step 3: Multiply the denominator of the first fraction by the numerator of the second.
Step 4: The new numerator is the sum (or difference) of the results of Steps 2 and 3.

Once again, it is more difficult to describe the process than it is to do it. Perhaps the easiest way to learn it is to see it done. To add two fractions: $\frac{a}{b} + \frac{c}{d} = \frac{a}{b} \diagdown\diagup \frac{c}{d} = \frac{ad + bc}{bd}$.

*Example:*

$$\frac{2}{7} + \frac{1}{5} = \frac{2}{7} \diagdown\diagup \frac{1}{5} = \frac{10 + 7}{35} = \frac{17}{35}$$

As you can see, the connecting arrows make a figure that looks like an "x" floating above the ground, or a "flying x."

The "flying-x" method also works for subtracting fractions.

*Examples:*

1.  $\frac{3}{5} - \frac{1}{3} = \frac{3}{5} \diagup\diagdown \frac{1}{3} = \frac{9 - 5}{15} = \frac{4}{15}$

2.  $\frac{6}{7} - \frac{5}{6} = \frac{6}{7} \diagup\diagdown \frac{5}{6} = \frac{36 - 35}{42} = \frac{1}{42}$

Of course, this may not give you the lowest terms of the fractions, so it may be necessary to reduce.

*Examples:*

1.  $\frac{3}{4} - \frac{1}{8} = \frac{3}{4} \diagup\diagdown \frac{1}{8} = \frac{24 - 4}{32} = \frac{20}{32} = \frac{5}{8}$

2.  $\frac{2}{3} - \frac{1}{6} = \frac{2}{3} \diagup\diagdown \frac{1}{6} = \frac{12 - 3}{18} = \frac{9}{18} = \frac{1}{2}$

## Multiplying Fractions

Multiplication of fractions does not require a common denominator. To multiply fractions, just multiply numerators to create a new numerator, and multiply denominators to create a new denominator.

*Examples:*

1.  $\frac{3}{4} \cdot \frac{1}{5} = \frac{3 \cdot 1}{4 \cdot 5} = \frac{3}{20}$

2.  $\frac{2}{3} \cdot \frac{2}{5} = \frac{2 \cdot 2}{3 \cdot 5} = \frac{4}{15}$

## Dividing Fractions

Division of fractions is the opposite of multiplication. To divide by a fraction, you invert the divisor (the fraction by which you are dividing) and then multiply the two together.

*Examples:*

1.  $2 \div \frac{1}{4} = \frac{2}{1} \cdot \frac{4}{1} = \frac{8}{1} = 8$

2. $\dfrac{\frac{2}{3}}{\frac{5}{6}} = \dfrac{2}{3} \cdot \dfrac{6}{5} = \dfrac{12}{15} = \dfrac{4}{5}$

3. $\dfrac{1}{3} \div \dfrac{5}{6} = \dfrac{1}{3} \cdot \dfrac{6}{5} = \dfrac{6}{15} = \dfrac{2}{5}$

4. $\dfrac{2}{7} \div 2 = \dfrac{2}{7} \div \dfrac{2}{1} = \dfrac{2}{7} \cdot \dfrac{1}{2} = \dfrac{2}{14} = \dfrac{1}{7}$

5. $\dfrac{1}{5} \div \dfrac{1}{2} = \dfrac{1}{5} \cdot \dfrac{2}{1} = \dfrac{2}{5}$

6. $3 \div \dfrac{1}{5} = \dfrac{3}{1} \cdot \dfrac{5}{1} = \dfrac{15}{1} = 15$

## Comparing Fractions

### Comparing Decimal Equivalents

We can compare the values of fractions in several different ways. The first method is the one most commonly used but which often takes up valuable time. Convert the fractions to decimal equivalents and compare these values.

*Example:*

Find the largest value of the following fractions: $\frac{1}{2}$, $\frac{2}{3}$, $\frac{1}{8}$, and $\frac{2}{11}$.

➢ Convert the fractions to decimal equivalents: $0.5$, $0.6\overline{6}$, $0.125$, and $0.18\overline{18}$. Compare the values: $0.6\overline{6}$ is the largest.

### Upward Cross-Multiplication

The second method of comparing fractions is often faster. We use ***upward cross-multiplication***—multiply the denominator of the one fraction with the numerator of the other fraction in an upward direction. The fraction with the greatest product above it has the greatest value.

*Example:*

Find the largest value of the following fractions: $\frac{1}{2}$, $\frac{2}{3}$, $\frac{1}{8}$, and $\frac{2}{11}$.

➢ Compare $\frac{1}{2}$ with $\frac{2}{3}$ by multiplying $(3)(1)$ and $(2)(2)$ and place the value above each fraction:

$\overset{③}{\underset{}{\frac{1}{2}}} \bowtie \overset{④}{\underset{}{\frac{2}{3}}} \Rightarrow 4$ is larger than 3, so $\frac{2}{3}$ is larger than $\frac{1}{2}$. Now, compare $\frac{2}{3}$ with the other two remaining

fractions: $\overset{⑯}{\frac{2}{3}} \bowtie \overset{③}{\frac{1}{8}} \Rightarrow \frac{2}{3}$ is larger. $\overset{㉒}{\frac{2}{3}} \bowtie \overset{⑥}{\frac{2}{11}} \Rightarrow \frac{2}{3}$ is larger. Therefore, $\frac{2}{3}$ is the largest value.

Alternatively, you can directly compare fractions by converting all of the fractions to fractions with the same denominator. The fraction with the largest numerator is then the largest value.

*Example:*

Find the smallest value of the following fractions: $\frac{1}{4}$, $\frac{5}{14}$, $\frac{3}{7}$, and $\frac{1}{2}$.

➢ Convert the fractions to fractions with the same denominator: $\frac{1}{4} \cdot \frac{7}{7} = \frac{7}{28}$; $\frac{5}{14} \cdot \frac{2}{2} = \frac{10}{28}$; $\frac{3}{7} \cdot \frac{4}{4} = \frac{12}{28}$; $\frac{1}{2} \cdot \frac{14}{14} = \frac{14}{28}$. Since $\frac{7}{28}$ is the rewritten fraction with the smallest numerator, the fraction equivalent $\frac{1}{4}$ is the smallest value of the given fractions.

# Fractions

**DIRECTIONS:** Choose the correct answer to each of the following items. Answers are on page 929.

1. $5\frac{3}{8} = ?$

   A. 1         C. $\frac{23}{8}$         E. $\frac{43}{8}$

   B. $\frac{15}{8}$        D. $\frac{35}{8}$

2. $2\frac{3}{4} = ?$

   A. $\frac{1}{4}$        C. $\frac{9}{4}$         E. $\frac{15}{4}$

   B. $\frac{3}{4}$        D. $\frac{11}{4}$

3. $3\frac{1}{2} = ?$

   A. $\frac{13}{2}$       C. $\frac{41}{12}$      E. $\frac{71}{12}$

   B. $\frac{37}{12}$      D. $\frac{53}{12}$

4. $1\frac{1}{65} = ?$

   A. $\frac{64}{65}$       C. $\frac{66}{65}$      E. $\frac{67}{66}$

   B. $\frac{65}{66}$       D. $\frac{66}{64}$

5. $5\frac{2}{7} = ?$

   A. $\frac{5}{14}$       C. $\frac{37}{7}$      E. $\frac{110}{7}$

   B. $\frac{35}{7}$       D. $\frac{70}{7}$

6. $\frac{12}{8} = ?$

   A. 4         C. $2\frac{1}{2}$      E. $1\frac{1}{4}$

   B. 3         D. $1\frac{1}{2}$

7. $\frac{20}{6} = ?$

   A. $3\frac{1}{3}$      C. $4\frac{1}{6}$      E. 6

   B. $3\frac{2}{3}$      D. $4\frac{1}{3}$

8. $\frac{23}{13} = ?$

   A. 10       C. $1\frac{10}{13}$     E. $\frac{7}{13}$

   B. $7\frac{7}{13}$     D. $\frac{13}{23}$

9. $\frac{25}{4} = ?$

   A. $\frac{4}{25}$      C. $1\frac{1}{8}$      E. $6\frac{1}{4}$

   B. $\frac{4}{12}$      D. $1\frac{1}{4}$

10. $\frac{201}{100} = ?$

   A. $1\frac{1}{100}$    C. $2\frac{1}{100}$    E. 101

   B. $1\frac{1}{50}$     D. $2\frac{1}{50}$

11. $\frac{3}{12} = ?$

   A. $\frac{1}{6}$       C. $\frac{1}{3}$       E. $\frac{3}{4}$

   B. $\frac{1}{4}$       D. $\frac{1}{2}$

12. $\frac{27}{81} = ?$

   A. $\frac{1}{9}$       C. $\frac{1}{3}$       E. $\frac{2}{3}$

   B. $\frac{2}{9}$       D. $\frac{4}{9}$

13. $\frac{125}{625} = ?$

   A. $\frac{1}{10}$      C. $\frac{2}{5}$       E. $\frac{4}{5}$

   B. $\frac{1}{5}$       D. $\frac{7}{10}$

14. $\frac{39}{52} = ?$

   A. $\frac{1}{5}$       C. $\frac{1}{3}$       E. $\frac{3}{4}$

   B. $\frac{1}{4}$       D. $\frac{1}{2}$

15. $\frac{121}{132} = ?$

   A. $\frac{1}{11}$      C. $\frac{9}{10}$      E. $\frac{11}{12}$

   B. $\frac{1}{10}$      D. $\frac{10}{11}$

16. Which of the following is equal to $\frac{4}{25}$?

   A. $\frac{8}{50}$   C. $\frac{12}{150}$   E. $\frac{200}{250}$

   B. $\frac{8}{100}$   D. $\frac{160}{200}$

17. Which of the following is NOT equal to $\frac{3}{8}$?

   A. $\frac{6}{16}$   C. $\frac{31}{81}$   E. $\frac{120}{320}$

   B. $\frac{15}{40}$   D. $\frac{33}{88}$

18. Which of the following is NOT equal to $\frac{3}{4}$?

   A. $\frac{6}{8}$   C. $\frac{20}{24}$   E. $\frac{300}{400}$

   B. $\frac{12}{16}$   D. $\frac{36}{48}$

19. Which of the following is NOT equal to $\frac{5}{6}$?

   A. $\frac{25}{30}$   C. $\frac{50}{60}$   E. $\frac{100}{120}$

   B. $\frac{45}{50}$   D. $\frac{55}{66}$

20. Which of the following is NOT equal to $\frac{1}{6}$?

   A. $\frac{2}{12}$   C. $\frac{4}{24}$   E. $\frac{6}{40}$

   B. $\frac{3}{18}$   D. $\frac{5}{30}$

21. $\frac{1}{7}+\frac{2}{7}=?$

   A. $\frac{2}{7}$   C. $\frac{6}{7}$   E. $\frac{12}{7}$

   B. $\frac{3}{7}$   D. $\frac{8}{7}$

22. $\frac{5}{8}+\frac{1}{8}=?$

   A. $\frac{1}{2}$   C. $\frac{7}{8}$   E. $\frac{4}{3}$

   B. $\frac{3}{4}$   D. $\frac{8}{5}$

23. $\frac{12}{13}+\frac{12}{13}=?$

   A. 0   C. $\frac{12}{26}$   E. $\frac{26}{13}$

   B. 1   D. $\frac{24}{13}$

24. $\frac{3}{8}+\frac{5}{8}=?$

   A. $\frac{2}{8}$   C. $\frac{5}{4}$   E. $\frac{12}{5}$

   B. 1   D. $\frac{8}{5}$

25. $\frac{1}{11}+\frac{2}{11}+\frac{7}{11}=?$

   A. $\frac{4}{11}$   C. $\frac{10}{11}$   E. $\frac{11}{7}$

   B. $\frac{7}{11}$   D. $\frac{11}{10}$

26. $\frac{3}{8}+\frac{5}{6}=?$

   A. $\frac{8}{48}$   C. $\frac{29}{24}$   E. $\frac{14}{8}$

   B. $\frac{8}{14}$   D. $\frac{3}{2}$

27. $\frac{1}{8}+\frac{1}{7}=?$

   A. $\frac{1}{56}$   C. $\frac{1}{15}$   E. $\frac{15}{56}$

   B. $\frac{1}{27}$   D. $\frac{1}{5}$

28. $\frac{1}{12}+\frac{1}{7}=?$

   A. $\frac{19}{84}$   C. $\frac{10}{19}$   E. $\frac{5}{4}$

   B. $\frac{19}{42}$   D. $\frac{20}{19}$

29. $\frac{3}{5}+\frac{2}{11}=?$

   A. $\frac{43}{110}$   C. $\frac{54}{55}$   E. $\frac{100}{43}$

   B. $\frac{43}{55}$   D. $\frac{55}{54}$

30. $\frac{1}{2}+\frac{1}{3}+\frac{1}{6}=?$

   A. $\frac{1}{36}$   C. 1   E. $\frac{7}{3}$

   B. $\frac{1}{12}$   D. $\frac{7}{6}$

31. $\frac{2}{3}+\frac{3}{6}+\frac{4}{6}=?$

   A. $\frac{9}{20}$   C. $\frac{7}{6}$   E. $\frac{16}{3}$

   B. $\frac{6}{7}$   D. $\frac{11}{6}$

32. $\frac{2}{3}-\frac{1}{3}=?$

   A. $\frac{1}{6}$   C. $\frac{2}{3}$   E. $\frac{6}{3}$

   B. $\frac{1}{3}$   D. $\frac{4}{3}$

33. $\frac{5}{7}-\frac{4}{7}=?$

   A. $\frac{9}{7}$   C. $\frac{5}{7}$   E. $\frac{1}{49}$

   B. 1   D. $\frac{1}{7}$

34. $\frac{9}{10} - \frac{1}{5} = ?$

   A. $\frac{7}{10}$       C. $\frac{10}{7}$       E. $\frac{20}{7}$

   B. $\frac{7}{5}$        D. $\frac{18}{7}$

35. $\frac{3}{2} - \frac{1}{4} = ?$

   A. $\frac{5}{4}$       C. $\frac{3}{4}$       E. $\frac{1}{3}$

   B. $\frac{4}{5}$       D. $\frac{2}{3}$

36. $2\frac{1}{2} - \frac{7}{8} = ?$

   A. $\frac{9}{2}$       C. $\frac{13}{8}$       E. $\frac{4}{5}$

   B. $\frac{5}{2}$       D. $\frac{5}{4}$

37. $2\frac{2}{3} - 1\frac{1}{6} = ?$

   A. $1\frac{1}{6}$       C. $1\frac{1}{2}$       E. $2$

   B. $1\frac{1}{3}$       D. $1\frac{2}{3}$

38. $\frac{1}{2} \cdot \frac{2}{3} = ?$

   A. $\frac{1}{6}$       C. $\frac{1}{2}$       E. $\frac{3}{4}$

   B. $\frac{1}{3}$       D. $\frac{2}{3}$

39. $\frac{2}{7} \cdot \frac{1}{4} = ?$

   A. $\frac{1}{63}$       C. $\frac{1}{4}$       E. $\frac{5}{9}$

   B. $\frac{1}{14}$       D. $\frac{3}{8}$

40. $\frac{1}{3} \cdot \frac{1}{3} = ?$

   A. $\frac{1}{9}$       C. $\frac{1}{3}$       E. $\frac{3}{2}$

   B. $\frac{1}{6}$       D. $\frac{2}{3}$

41. $\frac{1}{2} \cdot \frac{1}{2} \cdot \frac{1}{2} = ?$

   A. $\frac{1}{16}$       C. $\frac{3}{16}$       E. $\frac{2}{3}$

   B. $\frac{1}{8}$       D. $\frac{3}{8}$

42. $\frac{2}{3} \cdot \frac{3}{4} \cdot \frac{4}{5} = ?$

   A. $\frac{2}{5}$       C. $\frac{2}{3}$       E. $\frac{4}{5}$

   B. $\frac{3}{5}$       D. $\frac{3}{4}$

43. $\frac{1}{4} \cdot \frac{1}{8} \cdot 3 = ?$

   A. $\frac{3}{32}$       C. $\frac{1}{4}$       E. $\frac{3}{4}$

   B. $\frac{1}{8}$       D. $\frac{1}{2}$

44. $\frac{1}{3} \cdot \frac{1}{6} \cdot 12 = ?$

   A. $\frac{1}{3}$       C. $1$       E. $2$

   B. $\frac{2}{3}$       D. $\frac{3}{2}$

45. $\frac{7}{8} \div \frac{3}{4} = ?$

   A. $\frac{7}{6}$       C. $\frac{3}{4}$       E. $\frac{1}{8}$

   B. $1$          D. $\frac{1}{3}$

46. $\frac{5}{7} \div \frac{1}{7} = ?$

   A. $\frac{1}{7}$       C. $5$       E. $12$

   B. $\frac{1}{5}$       D. $7$

47. $\frac{1}{12} \div \frac{1}{12} = ?$

   A. $\frac{1}{144}$       C. $12$       E. $144$

   B. $1$          D. $18$

48. $2 \div \frac{1}{11} = ?$

   A. $22$       C. $\frac{11}{2}$       E. $\frac{1}{22}$

   B. $11$       D. $\frac{11}{22}$

49. $\frac{8}{9} \div \frac{7}{8} = ?$

   A. $\frac{64}{63}$       C. $\frac{7}{9}$       E. $\frac{1}{3}$

   B. $\frac{9}{7}$       D. $\frac{1}{2}$

50. $\frac{1}{10} \div \frac{3}{5} = ?$

   A. $\frac{1}{6}$       C. $\frac{3}{10}$       E. $\frac{5}{3}$

   B. $\frac{1}{5}$       D. $\frac{3}{5}$

51. $(\frac{1}{4} + \frac{2}{3}) \cdot (\frac{3}{2} + \frac{1}{4}) = ?$

   A. $\frac{21}{47}$       C. $\frac{51}{48}$       E. $\frac{105}{51}$

   B. $\frac{33}{49}$       D. $\frac{77}{48}$

52. $(\frac{2}{3} \cdot \frac{1}{6}) \div (\frac{1}{2} \cdot \frac{1}{4}) = ?$

    A. $\frac{1}{18}$    C. $\frac{8}{9}$    E. $\frac{15}{75}$

    B. $\frac{2}{9}$    D. $\frac{11}{8}$

53. $[(\frac{1}{3} + \frac{1}{2}) \cdot (\frac{2}{3} - \frac{1}{3})] \cdot 18 = ?$

    A. 5    C. $\frac{5}{6}$    E. $\frac{2}{3}$

    B. $\frac{7}{8}$    D. $\frac{4}{5}$

54. $[(\frac{1}{3} \div \frac{1}{6}) \cdot (\frac{2}{3} \div \frac{1}{3})] \cdot (\frac{1}{2} + \frac{3}{4}) = ?$

    A. 5    C. 3    E. 1

    B. 4    D. 2

55. $8(\frac{1}{3} + \frac{3}{4}) = ?$

    A. $\frac{1}{3}$    C. $\frac{16}{3}$    E. $\frac{26}{3}$

    B. $\frac{4}{3}$    D. $\frac{19}{3}$

56. $\frac{1}{4} - \frac{1}{5} = ?$

    A. $\frac{1}{5}$    C. $\frac{1}{20}$    E. $\frac{4}{5}$

    B. $\frac{1}{3}$    D. $\frac{3}{4}$

57. $\frac{\frac{4}{9}}{\frac{2}{5}} = ?$

    A. $\frac{1}{2}$    C. $\frac{8}{45}$    E. $1\frac{1}{9}$

    B. $\frac{3}{4}$    D. $\frac{11}{9}$

58. $(-\frac{1}{2})^2 + (\frac{1}{4})^2 + (-2)(\frac{1}{2})^2 = ?$

    A. $-\frac{3}{16}$    C. $\frac{1}{3}$    E. $\frac{4}{5}$

    B. $-\frac{1}{5}$    D. $\frac{3}{4}$

59. Which fraction is the largest?

    A. $\frac{9}{16}$    C. $\frac{5}{8}$    E. $\frac{1}{2}$

    B. $\frac{7}{10}$    D. $\frac{4}{5}$

60. Jughead eats $\frac{2}{5}$ of a pound of cake each day. How many pounds of cake does Jughead eat in 3 weeks?

    A. $4\frac{1}{2}$    C. $5\frac{1}{5}$    E. 10

    B. $5\frac{3}{4}$    D. $8\frac{2}{5}$

61. Chompa eats $\frac{3}{8}$ of a bag of candy per day. How many weeks will 42 bags of candy last Chompa?

    A. 4    C. 9    E. 16

    B. 5    D. 12

62. If Bruce can eat $2\frac{1}{2}$ bananas per day, how many bananas can Bruce eat in 4 weeks?

    A. 70    C. 80    E. 90

    B. 75    D. 85

63. One brass rod measures $3\frac{5}{16}$ inches long and another brass rod measures $2\frac{3}{4}$ inches long. What is the total length, in inches, of the two rods combined?

    A. $6\frac{9}{16}$    C. $5\frac{1}{2}$    E. $5\frac{1}{32}$

    B. $6\frac{1}{16}$    D. $5\frac{1}{16}$

64. Which of the following equals the number of half-pound packages of tea that can be taken out of a box that holds $10\frac{1}{2}$ pounds of tea?

    A. 5    C. 11    E. 21

    B. $10\frac{1}{2}$    D. $20\frac{1}{122}$

65. If each bag of tokens weighs $5\frac{3}{4}$ pounds, how many pounds do 3 bags weigh?

    A. $7\frac{1}{4}$    C. $16\frac{1}{2}$    E. $17\frac{1}{2}$

    B. $15\frac{3}{4}$    D. $17\frac{1}{4}$

66. During one week, a man traveled $3\frac{1}{2}$, $1\frac{1}{4}$, $1\frac{1}{6}$, and $2\frac{3}{8}$ miles. The next week, he traveled $\frac{1}{4}$, $\frac{3}{8}$, $\frac{9}{16}$, $3\frac{1}{16}$, $2\frac{5}{8}$, and $3\frac{3}{16}$ miles. How many more miles did he travel the second week than the first week?

    A. $1\frac{37}{48}$    C. $1\frac{3}{4}$    E. $\frac{47}{48}$

    B. $1\frac{1}{2}$    D. 1

67. A certain type of board is sold only in lengths of multiples of 2 feet. The shortest board sold is 6 feet and the longest is 24 feet. A builder needs a large quantity of this type of board in $5\frac{1}{2}$-foot lengths. To minimize waste, which of the following board lengths should be ordered?

    A. 6-foot    C. 22-foot    E. 26-foot

    B. 12-foot    D. 24-foot

68. A man spent $\frac{15}{16}$ of his entire fortune in buying a car for $7,500. How much money did he possess?

    A. $6,000  C. $7,000  E. $8,500
    B. $6,500  D. $8,000

69. The population of a town was 54,000 in the last census. Since then it has increased by two-thirds. Which of the following equals its present population?

    A. 18,000  C. 72,000  E. 108,000
    B. 36,000  D. 90,000

70. $\frac{1}{3}$ of the liquid contents of a can evaporates on the first day and $\frac{3}{4}$ of the remainder evaporates on the second day. Which of the following equals the fractional part of the original contents remaining at the close of the second day?

    A. $\frac{5}{12}$  C. $\frac{1}{6}$  E. $\frac{4}{7}$
    B. $\frac{7}{12}$  D. $\frac{1}{2}$

71. A car is run until the gas tank is $\frac{1}{8}$ full. The tank is then filled to capacity by putting in 14 gallons. What is the gas tank's capacity, in gallons?

    A. 14  C. 16  E. 18
    B. 15  D. 17

# Decimals

A *decimal* is nothing more than a special way of writing fractions using a denominator of ten, or one hundred, or one thousand, and so on. Decimals are written with a decimal point to the left of the decimal digits in order to distinguish them from whole numbers.

*Examples:*

1. The fraction $\frac{3}{10}$ written as a decimal is 0.3.

2. The fraction $\frac{72}{100}$ written as a decimal is 0.72.

The positions to the right of the decimal point are called decimal places. Decimal places are analogous to the positions of the digits in whole numbers (units column, tens column, etc.). The number of decimal places indicates the denominator of the fraction. One decimal place indicates a denominator of 10; two places indicate a denominator of 100; three indicate a denominator of 1,000; and so on. 0.335 is read as three hundred thirty-five thousandths and 0.12345 as twelve thousand three hundred forty-five hundred thousandths.

$$0 \quad . \quad 1 \quad 2 \quad 3 \quad 4 \quad 5$$

TENTHS | HUNDREDTHS | THOUSANDTHS | TEN THOUSANDTHS | HUNDRED THOUSANDTHS

When a decimal does not include a positive or negative whole number, a zero is placed to the left of the decimal point. This has no mathematical significance; it is there just to make the decimals more readable. Without the zero, someone might fail to see the decimal and read .335 as 335. On the exam, all decimals that do not include a positive or negative whole number are written with a zero to the left of the decimal point.

## Converting Fractions to Decimals

If the fraction already has a denominator that is ten, one hundred, one thousand, etc., the conversion is very easy. The numerator of the fraction becomes the decimal. The number of zeros in the denominator governs the placement of the decimal point. Starting just to the right of the last digit of the numerator, you count over one digit to the left for each zero in the denominator. For example, to express $\frac{127}{1,000}$ in decimal form, take the numerator, 127, as the decimal. Then, starting just to the right of the 7, count over three places to the left (one for each zero in 1,000). The decimal equivalent is 0.127.

*Examples:*

1. $\frac{3}{10} = 0.3$ (One zero in the denominator indicates one decimal place.)

2. $\frac{13}{100} = 0.13$ (Two zeros in the denominator indicate two decimal places.)

3. $\frac{522}{1,000} = 0.522$ (Three zeros in the denominator indicate three decimal places.)

If there are fewer digits in the numerator than zeros in the denominator, add zeros to the left of the number until you have enough decimal places. For example, consider $\frac{53}{1,000}$: the denominator contains three zeros, but 53 is only a two-digit number. Therefore, add one zero to the left of the 5: $\frac{53}{1,000} = 0.053$.

*Examples:*

1. $\frac{3}{100} = 0.03$ (Two zeros mean two decimal places.)

2. $\frac{71}{10,000} = 0.0071$ (Four zeros mean four decimal places.)

3. $\frac{9}{100,000} = 0.00009$ (Five zeros mean five decimal places.)

To convert a proper fraction with a denominator other than 10, 100, etc., convert the fraction to an equivalent form using a denominator such as ten, one hundred, etc. For example, to convert $\frac{3}{4}$ to a decimal, change it into a fraction with a denominator of 100: $\frac{3}{4} = \frac{3 \cdot 25}{4 \cdot 25} = \frac{75}{100}$. Then, $\frac{75}{100}$ is written as 0.75, as described in the previous section.

*Examples:*

1. $\frac{2}{5} = \frac{2 \cdot 2}{5 \cdot 2} = \frac{4}{10} = 0.4$

2. $\frac{1}{4} = \frac{1 \cdot 25}{4 \cdot 25} = \frac{25}{100} = 0.25$

3. $\frac{3}{8} = \frac{3 \cdot 125}{8 \cdot 125} = \frac{375}{1,000} = 0.375$

4. $\frac{1}{50} = \frac{1 \cdot 2}{50 \cdot 2} = \frac{2}{10} = 0.02$

To determine which denominator you should use, divide the denominator of the fraction into 10, then into 100, then into 1,000, until you find the first denominator that is evenly divisible by the denominator of the fraction. For example, $\frac{3}{8}$ does not have an equivalent form with a denominator of 10, but it does have an equivalent form with a denominator of 1,000. This is the same process used above to find common denominators for fractions. (Note: You can also convert a fraction into a decimal by dividing the numerator of the fraction by its denominator. However, this method obviously presupposes that you know how to divide decimals. We will come back to the topic of converting to decimals when we discuss how to divide decimals.)

## Converting Mixed Numbers to Decimals

To change a mixed number to a decimal, convert the fractional part of the mixed number to a decimal as discussed above, and then place the whole number part of the mixed number to the left of the decimal point.

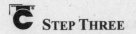 

*Examples:*

1. Convert the mixed number $2\frac{3}{4}$ to a decimal.

   ➤ First, convert $\frac{3}{4}$ to a decimal: $\frac{3}{4} = 0.75$. Then, place the whole-number part to the left of the decimal point: 2.75. Notice that the extra zero is dropped—there is no reason to write 02.75.

2. $6\frac{1}{10} = 6.1$

3. $12\frac{1}{2} = 12.5$

4. $3\frac{7}{8} = 3.875$

## Converting Improper Fractions to Decimals

To convert an improper fraction to a decimal, just treat the improper fraction as a mixed number and follow the procedure just outlined.

*Examples:*

1. $\frac{9}{4} = 2\frac{1}{4} = 2.25$

2. $\frac{7}{2} = 3\frac{1}{2} = 3.5$

3. $\frac{8}{5} = 1\frac{3}{5} = 1.6$

It is also possible, and often easier, to convert fractions to decimals by dividing the numerator by the denominator. Again, we will postpone this part of the discussion until we have studied division of decimals.

## Converting Decimals to Fractions and Mixed Numbers

To convert a decimal back to a fraction, it is necessary only to create a fraction using the digits of the decimal number as a numerator and a denominator of 1 followed by a number of zeros equal to the number of decimal places.

*Examples:*

1. Convert 0.125 to a fraction.

   ➤ Use 125 as the numerator and 1,000 as the denominator: $\frac{125}{1,000}$. Reduce the fraction to lowest terms: $\frac{125}{1,000} = \frac{1}{8}$.

2. $0.04 = \frac{4}{100} = \frac{1}{25}$

3. $0.25 = \frac{25}{100} = \frac{1}{4}$

4. $0.005 = \frac{5}{1,000} = \frac{1}{200}$

Finally, if the decimal consists of both a whole part and a fraction, the conversion will result in a mixed number. The whole part of the mixed number will be the whole part of the decimal. Then, convert the fractional part of the decimal as just shown.

*Examples:*

1. Convert 2.05 to a mixed number.
   - ➢ Write 0.05 as a fraction: $0.05 = \frac{5}{100} = \frac{1}{20}$. The whole number part is 2, so $2.05 = 2\frac{1}{20}$.

2. $1.75 = 1 + \frac{75}{100} = 1 + \frac{3}{4} = 1\frac{3}{4}$

3. $32.6 = 32 + \frac{6}{10} = 32 + \frac{3}{5} = 32\frac{3}{5}$

4. $2.05 = 2 + \frac{5}{100} = 2 + \frac{1}{20} = 2\frac{1}{20}$

5. $357.125 = 357 + \frac{125}{1,000} = 357 + \frac{1}{8} = 357\frac{1}{8}$

## Operations of Decimals

### Adding and Subtracting Decimals

Decimals can be manipulated in very much the same way as whole numbers. You can add and subtract decimals.

*Examples:*

1. $0.2 + 0.3 + 0.1 = 0.6$
2. $0.7 - 0.2 = 0.5$

Adding zeros to the end of a decimal number does not change the value of that number. If the decimals do not have the same number of decimal places, add zeros to the right of those that do not until every number has the same number of decimal places. Then, line up the decimal points and combine the decimals as indicated. Follow the same process for subtracting decimals.

*Examples:*

1. $0.75 - 0.1125 \Rightarrow$
$$\begin{array}{r} 0.7500 \\ -0.1125 \\ \hline 0.6375 \end{array}$$

2. $0.125 + 0.6 + 0.115 \Rightarrow$
$$\begin{array}{r} 0.125 \\ 0.600 \\ +0.115 \\ \hline 0.840 \end{array}$$

3. $0.999 - 0.000001 \Rightarrow$
$$\begin{array}{r} 0.999000 \\ -0.000001 \\ \hline 0.998999 \end{array}$$

4. $2.14 + 0.125 + 0.0005 \Rightarrow$
$$\begin{array}{r} 2.1400 \\ 0.1250 \\ +0.0005 \\ \hline 2.2655 \end{array}$$

5. $0.8 - 0.1111 \Rightarrow$
$$\begin{array}{r} 0.8000 \\ -0.1111 \\ \hline 0.6889 \end{array}$$

6. $0.11 + 0.9 + 0.033 \Rightarrow$
$$\begin{array}{r} 0.110 \\ 0.900 \\ +0.033 \\ \hline 1.043 \end{array}$$

## Multiplying Decimals

As with fractions, there is no need to find a common denominator when multiplying decimals: The multiplication process generates its own. Simply multiply as with whole numbers and then adjust the decimal point. To find the correct position for the decimal point first, count the total number of decimal places in the numbers that are being multiplied. Then, in the final product, place the decimal point that many places to the left, counting from the right side of the last digit.

*Examples:*

1. $0.25 \cdot 0.2 = ?$

   ➤ Ignore the decimals and multiply: $25 \cdot 2 = 50$. Now, adjust the decimal point. Since 0.25 has two decimal places, and 0.2 has one decimal place, count three places to the left, starting at the right side of the 0 in 50; the final product is $0.050 = 0.05$.

2. $0.1 \cdot 0.2 \cdot 0.3 = 0.006$ ($1 \cdot 2 \cdot 3 = 6$, and there are three decimal places in the multiplication.)

3. $0.02 \cdot 0.008 = 0.00016$ ($2 \cdot 8 = 16$, and there are five decimal places in the multiplication.)

4. $2 \cdot 0.5 = 1$ ($2 \cdot 5 = 10$, and there is one decimal place in the multiplication.)

5. $2.5 \cdot 2.5 = 6.25$ ($25 \cdot 25 = 625$, and there are two decimal places in the multiplication.)

6. $0.10 \cdot 0.10 \cdot 0.10 = 0.001$ ($10 \cdot 10 \cdot 10 = 1,000$, and there are six decimal places in the multiplication.)

To simplify the process of multiplying decimals, drop any final zeros before multiplying. Thus, in the case of the last example, $0.10 \cdot 0.10 \cdot 0.10 = 0.1 \cdot 0.1 \cdot 0.1 = 0.001$ since there are three decimal places in the multiplication.

## Dividing Decimals

Like multiplication, division generates a common denominator by a suitable adjustment of zeros. However, there are two situations in which division of decimals is a little tricky. Let's review them one at a time.

First, when the divisor (the number doing the dividing) is a whole number, place the decimal point in the quotient (result of division) immediately above the decimal point in the dividend (the number being divided). Then, keep dividing until there is no remainder, adding zeros as needed to the right of the dividend. This is the procedure whenever the divisor is a whole number—even if the dividend is also a whole number.

*Examples:*

1. $0.25 \div 5 \Rightarrow$
$$\begin{array}{r} 0.05 \\ 5\overline{)0.25} \\ \underline{-25} \\ 0 \end{array}$$

2. $2.5 \div 2 \Rightarrow$
$$\begin{array}{r} 1.25 \\ 2\overline{)2.50} \\ \underline{-2} \\ 0\ 5 \\ \underline{-4} \\ 10 \\ \underline{-10} \\ 0 \end{array}$$

3. $1.75 \div 25 \Rightarrow$
$$\begin{array}{r} 0.07 \\ 25\overline{)1.75} \\ \underline{-1\ 75} \\ 0 \end{array}$$

4. $1.44 \div 12 \Rightarrow$
$$\begin{array}{r} 0.12 \\ 12\overline{)1.44} \\ \underline{-1\ 44} \\ 0 \end{array}$$

5. $0.1 \div 250 \Rightarrow$
$$\begin{array}{r} 0.0004 \\ 250\overline{)0.1000} \\ \underline{-1000} \\ 0 \end{array}$$

6. $9 \div 2 \Rightarrow$
$$\begin{array}{r} 4.5 \\ 2\overline{)9.0} \\ \underline{-8} \\ 10 \\ \underline{-10} \\ 0 \end{array}$$

The second tricky situation occurs when the divisor is a decimal. In these cases, "clear" the fractional part of the decimal by moving the decimal point to the right. For example, if dividing by 0.1, change 0.1 to 1; if dividing by

2.11, convert that to 211 by moving the decimal point two places to the right. However, you must also move the decimal point of the dividend by the same number of places to ensure that their relative values are not changed. Notice that in the following examples both decimal points are moved the same number of places to the right.

*Examples:*

$$
\begin{array}{r}
2. \\
2.\underline{5.})\overline{5.\underline{0.}} \\
\end{array}
$$

1. $5 \div 2.5 \Rightarrow$ $\quad \underline{-5\ 0}$
$\qquad\qquad\qquad 0$

$$
\begin{array}{r}
8. \\
1.\underline{25.})\overline{10.\underline{00.}} \\
\end{array}
$$

2. $10 \div 1.25 \Rightarrow$ $\quad \underline{-10\ 00}$
$\qquad\qquad\qquad\quad 0$

$$
\begin{array}{r}
1000. \\
0.\underline{05.})\overline{50.\underline{00.}} \\
\end{array}
$$

3. $50 \div 0.05 \Rightarrow$ $\quad \underline{-50\ 00}$
$\qquad\qquad\qquad\quad 0$

There are two final things to say about dividing decimals. First, as mentioned previously, you can use division of decimals to convert fractions to decimals. For example, to convert $\frac{9}{2}$ to a decimal number, simply divide 9 by 2.

*Examples:*

1. $\frac{9}{2} = 2\overline{)9} \Rightarrow$
$$
\begin{array}{r}
4.5 \\
2\overline{)9.0} \\
\underline{-8} \\
1\ 0 \\
\underline{-1\ 0} \\
0 \\
\end{array}
$$

2. $\frac{3}{4} = 4\overline{)3} \Rightarrow$
$$
\begin{array}{r}
0.75 \\
4\overline{)3.00} \\
\underline{-2\ 8} \\
20 \\
\underline{-20} \\
0 \\
\end{array}
$$

Second, some fractions do not have exact decimal equivalents. Try converting $\frac{1}{3}$ to a decimal using the division route. You will be at it forever, because you get an endless succession of "3"s. Try converting $\frac{1}{9}$ a decimal using the division method. Again, you will get an endless succession, this time of repeating "1"s. By convention, repeating decimals are indicated using an overbar: $0.1\overline{1}$.

# Decimals

**DIRECTIONS:** Choose the correct answer to each of the following items. Answers are on page 934.

1. What is $\frac{7}{10}$ expressed as a decimal?

   A. 70      C. 0.7      E. 0.0007
   B. 7       D. 0.007

2. What is $\frac{73}{100}$ expressed as a decimal?

   A. 73      C. 0.73     E. 0.0073
   B. 7.3     D. 0.073

3. What is $\frac{21}{1,000}$ expressed as a decimal?

   A. 0.21    C. 0.0021   E. 0.000021
   B. 0.021   D. 0.00021

4. What is $\frac{557}{1,000}$ expressed as a decimal?

   A. 5.57    C. 0.0557   E. 0.00057
   B. 0.557   D. 0.0057

5. What is $\frac{34}{10,000}$ expressed as a decimal?

   A. 0.00034 C. 0.034    E. 3.4
   B. 0.0034  D. 0.34

6. What is $\frac{1}{1,000,000}$ expressed as a decimal?

   A. 0.01    C. 0.0001   E. 0.000001
   B. 0.001   D. 0.00001

7. What is $\frac{30}{100}$ expressed as a decimal?

   A. 3       C. 0.03     E. 0.0003
   B. 0.3     D. 0.003

8. What is $\frac{1,000}{4,000}$ expressed as a decimal?

   A. 0.25    C. 0.0025   E. 0.000025
   B. 0.025   D. 0.00025

9. Which of the following is (are) equal to $\frac{1}{10}$?

   I. 1.0
   II. 0.1
   III. 0.1000

   A. I only              D. II and III only
   B. II only             E. I, II, and III
   C. III only

10. Which of the following is (are) equal to $\frac{25}{100}$?

    I. 0.25
    II. 0.025
    III. 0.0025

    A. I only             D. II and III only
    B. I and II only      E. I, II, and III
    C. I and III only

11. What is $\frac{257}{100}$ expressed as a decimal?

    A. 25.7    C. 0.257    E. 0.00257
    B. 2.57    D. 0.0257

12. What is $\frac{57}{10}$ expressed as a decimal?

    A. 57      C. 0.57     E. 0.0057
    B. 5.7     D. 0.057

13. What is $\frac{5}{8}$ expressed as a decimal?

    A. 0.125   C. 0.850    E. 5.80
    B. 0.625   D. 1.25

14. What is $\frac{4}{5}$ expressed as a decimal?

    A. 0.4     C. 0.8      E. 2.4
    B. 0.6     D. 1.2

15. What is $\frac{1}{20}$ expressed as a decimal?

    A. 0.05    C. 0.0005   E. 0.000005
    B. 0.005   D. 0.00005

16. What is $\frac{1}{50}$ expressed as a decimal?

    A. 0.2     C. 0.002    E. 0.00002
    B. 0.02    D. 0.0002

17. What is $\frac{3}{200}$ expressed as a decimal?

    A. 0.15       C. 0.0015     E. 0.000015
    B. 0.015     D. 0.00015

18. What is $\frac{9}{500}$ expressed as a decimal?

    A. 0.000018   C. 0.0018     E. 0.18
    B. 0.00018    D. 0.018

19. What is $\frac{17}{500}$ expressed as a decimal?

    A. 0.175    C. 0.0175    E. 0.00034
    B. 0.034    D. 0.0034

20. What is $\frac{123}{200}$ expressed as a decimal?

    A. 0.615    C. 0.0615    E. 0.00615
    B. 0.256    D. 0.0256

21. $0.1 + 0.1 = ?$

    A. 0.002    C. 0.2     E. 20
    B. 0.02     D. 2

22. $0.27 + 0.13 + 0.55 = ?$

    A. 0.21    C. 0.47    E. 0.95
    B. 0.36    D. 0.85

23. $0.528 + 0.116 + 0.227 = ?$

    A. 0.871    C. 0.243    E. 0.0012
    B. 0.583    D. 0.112

24. $0.7 + 0.013 + 0.028 = ?$

    A. 0.741    C. 1.02    E. 2.553
    B. 0.988    D. 1.224

25. $1.23 + 0.00001 = ?$

    A. 1.24    C. 1.23001   E. 1.230000001
    B. 1.2301   D. 1.2300001

26. $57.1 + 23.3 + 35.012 = ?$

    A. 412.115   C. 115.0412  E. 1.15412
    B. 115.412   D. 11.5412

27. $0.01 + 0.001 + 0.0001 + 0.00001 = ?$

    A. 1     C. 0.1111    E. 0.001111
    B. 0.10    D. 0.01111

28. $0.9 + 0.09 + 0.009 + 0.0009 = ?$

    A. 0.9999   C. 0.009999  E. 0.0000999
    B. 0.09999  D. 0.0009999

29. $0.27 + 0.36 + 2.1117 + 3.77777 + 1.42 = ?$

    A. 5.44    C. 8.11143   E. 14.002785
    B. 7.93947  D. 12.223479

30. $12,279.1 + 3,428.01 + 3,444.99 = ?$

    A. 19,151.99  C. 19,152.09  E. 19,152.11
    B. 19,152    D. 19,152.1

31. $0.7 - 0.3 = ?$

    A. 0.004    C. 0.04    E. 0.4
    B. 0.021    D. 0.21

32. $0.75 - 0.25 = ?$

    A. 5     C. 0.5    E. 0.005
    B. 1     D. 0.25

33. $1.35 - 0.35 = ?$

    A. 1     C. 0.1    E. 0.00001
    B. 0.35    D. 0.0035

34. $25.125 - 5.357 = ?$

    A. 19.768   C. 12.115   E. 2.288
    B. 15.432   D. 4.108

35. $1 - 0.00001 = ?$

    A. 0.9    C. 0.999   E. 0.99999
    B. 0.99   D. 0.9999

36. $0.2 \cdot 0.1 = ?$

    A. 0.3    C. 0.1    E. 0.006
    B. 0.2    D. 0.02

37. $0.1 \cdot 0.1 \cdot 0.1 = ?$

    A. 0.3    C. 0.01    E. 0.0001
    B. 0.1    D. 0.001

38. $1.1 \cdot 1.1 \cdot 1.1 = ?$

    A. 1.331   C. 0.111   E. 0.00111
    B. 1.111   D. 0.0111

39. $0.11 \cdot 0.33 = ?$

    A. 0.363   C. 0.00363  E. 0.0000363
    B. 0.0363  D. 0.000363

40. $0.2 \cdot 0.5 \cdot 0.2 \cdot 0.5 = ?$

    A. 0.1    C. 0.001   E. 0.00001
    B. 0.01    D. 0.0001

41. $5 \cdot 0.25 = ?$

    A. 1.25      C. 0.0125     E. 0.000125
    B. 0.125    D. 0.00125

42. $10 \cdot 0.000001 = ?$

    A. 0.00001   C. 0.001      E. 0.1
    B. 0.0001    D. 0.01

43. $100 \cdot 0.00052 = ?$

    A. 0.0052   C. 5.2       E. 520
    B. 0.052    D. 52

44. $1.2 \cdot 1.2 = ?$

    A. 0.144    C. 14.4     E. 1,444
    B. 1.44     D. 144

45. $1.000 \cdot 1.000 \cdot 1.000 \cdot 1.000 = ?$

    A. 1        C. 0.01     E. 0.0001
    B. 0.1     D. 0.001

46. $6 \div 0.2 = ?$

    A. 0.03    C. 3       E. 300
    B. 0.3     D. 30

47. $0.2 \div 5 = ?$

    A. 0.4    C. 0.004    E. 0.00004
    B. 0.04   D. 0.0004

48. $1 \div 0.001 = ?$

    A. 10,000  C. 100     E. 0.0001
    B. 1,000   D. 0.001

49. $25.1 \div 2.51 = ?$

    A. 100    C. 0.1     E. 0.001
    B. 10     D. 0.01

50. $0.25 \div 8 = ?$

    A. 4      C. 0.03125  E. 0.003125
    B. 0.4    D. 0.004

51. $0.005 \div 0.005 = ?$

    A. 1      C. 0.005    E. 0.00005
    B. 0.5    D. 0.0005

52. $2 \div 2.5 = ?$

    A. 8      C. 0.8     E. 0.008
    B. 5     D. 0.5

53. $111 \div 0.111 = ?$

    A. 1      C. 11     E. 1,000
    B. 10    D. 110

54. $0.12345 \div 0.012345 = ?$

    A. 100    C. 1      E. 0.01
    B. 10     D. 0.1

55. $0.002 \div 0.00002 = ?$

    A. 100    C. 0.1     E. 0.001
    B. 10     D. 0.01

56. Express as a decimal: $\frac{3}{5} + \frac{5}{8}$.

    A. 1.00    C. 1.225   E. 1.75
    B. 1.115   D. 1.50

57. Find the average of $\frac{2}{3}$ and 0.75.

    A. $\frac{9}{24}$    C. $\frac{17}{24}$    E. $\frac{23}{24}$

    B. $\frac{14}{24}$   D. $\frac{21}{24}$

58. Find the average of 0.1, 0.01, and $\frac{1}{4}$.

    A. 0.10    C. 0.50    E. 1.0
    B. 0.12    D. 0.75

59. $\dfrac{12\frac{1}{3}}{0.2} = ?$

    A. $\frac{1}{50}$    C. $\frac{85}{2}$    E. $\frac{225}{4}$

    B. $\frac{3}{40}$    D. $\frac{185}{3}$

60. $0.1[\frac{1}{3} - 2(\frac{1}{2} - \frac{1}{4})] = ?$

    A. $-\frac{2}{15}$    C. $-\frac{1}{90}$    E. $\frac{3}{4}$

    B. $-\frac{1}{60}$    D. $\frac{1}{2}$

61. For three months, Pete saved part of his monthly allowance. He saved $4.56 the first month, $3.82 the second month, and $5.06 the third month. How much did Pete save altogether?

    A. $12.04   C. $13.04   E. $14.44
    B. $12.44   D. $13.44

62. From an employee's salary of $190.57, an employer deducts $3.05 for social security and $5.68 for pension. What is the final amount of the check?

    A. $180.84   C. $181.84   E. $182.84
    B. $181.04   D. $182.04

63. If the outer radius of a metal pipe is 2.84 inches and the inner radius is 1.94 inches, what is the thickness, in inches, of the metal?

   A. 0.85     C. 1.00     E. 1.25
   B. 0.90     D. 1.18

64. Pete earns $20.56 on Monday, $32.90 on Tuesday, and $20.78 on Wednesday. He spends half of all that he earned during the 3 days. How much does he have left?

   A. $36.12     C. $37.12     E. $38.12
   B. $36.72     D. $37.72

65. What is the total cost of $3\frac{1}{2}$ pounds of meat at $1.69 per pound and 20 lemons at $0.60 per dozen?

   A. $5.92     C. $6.92     E. $7.92
   B. $6.42     D. $7.42

66. A reel of cable weighs 1,279 pounds. If the empty reel weighs 285 pounds and the cable weighs 7.1 pounds per foot, how many feet of cable are on the reel?

   A. 140     C. 160     E. 180
   B. 150     D. 170

67. How much will 345 fasteners at $4.15 per hundred cost?

   A. $13.12     C. $14.12     E. $14.82
   B. $13.82     D. $14.32

# Percents

A *percent* is a special type of fraction that always has a denominator equal to 100. The percent sign, "%," is shorthand for "$\frac{x}{100}$." For example, $67\% = \frac{67}{100}$.

## Converting to and from Percents

Since percents are simply a special type of fraction, both fractions and decimals can be converted to percents, and vice versa. The easiest conversion is to change a decimal to a percent: Move the decimal point two places to the right and add the percent sign.

*Examples:*

1. $0.27 = 27\%$
2. $0.50 = 50\%$
3. $0.275 = 27.5\%$

This substitutes "%" for two decimal places—simply a matter of changing things from one form into an equivalent form, which is a process we have already used in several ways. To change a percent back to a decimal, move the decimal point two places to the left and drop the percent sign.

*Examples:*

1. $27\% = 0.27$
2. $50\% = 0.50$
3. $27.5\% = 0.275$

You already know the rules for converting fractions to decimals, and vice versa. To convert a fraction to a percent, just convert the fraction to a decimal and follow the rule above.

*Examples:*

1. $\frac{3}{4} = 0.75 = 75\%$
2. $\frac{5}{8} = 0.625 = 62.5\%$
3. $\frac{1}{10} = 0.10 = 10\%$

To reverse the process, follow the rule given above for turning percentages back into decimals, and then use the procedure outlined in the previous section for converting decimals to fractions.

*Examples:*

1. $75\% = 0.75 = \frac{75}{100} = \frac{3}{4}$
2. $62.5\% = 0.625 = \frac{625}{1,000} = \frac{5}{8}$
3. $10\% = 0.1 = \frac{1}{10}$

There are two tricky types of percents: those greater than 100% and those less than 1%. First, it is possible to have a percent that is larger than 100. This would be the result of converting a mixed number, such as $2\frac{3}{4}$, to a percent: $2\frac{3}{4} = 2.75 = 275\%$. Second, percents can also be less than 1, in which case they are written with decimals; for example, 0.5%. However, these numbers follow the general rules outlined above. To convert 0.5% to a fraction: $0.5\% = 0.005 = \frac{5}{1,000} = \frac{1}{200}$. Similarly, fractions smaller than $\frac{1}{100}$ will yield a percent less than 1: $\frac{1}{2,500} = 0.0004 = 0.04\%$.

## Operations of Percents

### Adding and Subtracting Percents

Percents are fractions, so they can be manipulated like other fractions. All percents have 100 as the denominator. It is easy to add and subtract percents because you already have a common denominator.

*Examples:*

1. Paul originally owned 25 percent of the stock of a certain company. He purchased another 15 percent of the stock privately, and he received a gift of another 10 percent of the stock. What percent of the stock of the company does Paul now own?

   ➤  $25\% + 15\% + 10\% = 50\%$

2. In a certain election, Peter and Mary received 50 percent of all the votes that were cast. If Peter received 20 percent of the votes cast in the election, what percent of the votes did Mary receive?

   ➤  $50\% - 20\% = 30\%$

### Multiplying Percents

To multiply percents, first convert them to decimals and then multiply. For example, $60\% \cdot 80\% = 0.60 \cdot 0.80 = 0.48 = 48\%$.

*Example:*

In a certain group, 80 percent of the people are wearing hats. If 60 percent of those wearing hats are also wearing gloves, what percent of the entire group is wearing both a hat and gloves?

   ➤  $60\%$ of $80\% = 60\% \cdot 80\% = 0.60 \cdot 0.80 = 0.48 = 48\%$

### Dividing Percents

To divide percents, first convert them to decimals and then divide. For example, $100\% \div 12.5\% = 1 \div 0.125 = 8$.

*Example:*

Peter is purchasing an item on a lay-away plan. If he pays weekly installments of 8% of the purchase price, how many weeks will it take for Peter to payoff the entire purchase price?

   ➤  $100\% \div 8\% = 1 \div 0.08 = 12.5$ weeks

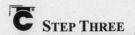 

**Percent Story Problems**

Four basic variations of percent problems appear on the exam as story problems:

- What is *x* percent of something?
- This is what percent of that?
- This is a given percent of what?
- What is the percent change from this quantity to that quantity?

***"What Is X Percent of Some Quantity?"***

Percents are fractions, so in the question, "What is *x* percent of some quantity?", the *of* indicates multiplication.

*Examples:*

1. A certain class is made up of 125 students. If 60 percent of the students are men, how many men are in the class?

   ➢  60% of 125 = 60% • 125 = 0.06 • 125 = 75

2. If Sam originally had $25 and gave 25 percent of that amount to his friend Samantha, how much money did Sam give to Samantha?

   ➢  25% of $25 = 25% • 25 = 0.25 • 25 = $6.25

3. If Paula had 50 marbles and gave 20 percent of them to her friend Paul, how many marbles did Paula give to Paul?

   ➢  20% of 50 = 20% • 50 = 0.20 • 50 = 10

***"What Percent Is This of That?"***

A second common item involving percents has the form, "What percent is this of that?"

*Example:*

What percent is 3 of 12?

➢  Convert $\frac{3}{12}$ to a decimal by dividing 3 by 12 and then change that decimal number to a percent: $\frac{3}{12} = \frac{1}{4} = 0.25 = 25\%$.

There are other ways of phrasing the same question:

- 3 is what percent of 12?
- Of 12, what percent is 3?

Note that all three of the above questions are equivalent and represent the three following general forms:

- What percent is this of that?
- This is what percent of that?
- <u>Of that</u>, <u>what percent</u> is this?

Although the order of words is different, these three questions ask the same thing: to express a fraction as a percent. Here is a little trick to help you avoid confusion. Notice that in each question form, there is the phrase "*of* that" and the phrase "*is* this" ("this *is*"). When you set up a fraction for the percent, always place the "*is* this" value over the "*of* that" value. We call this the "*is* over *of*" method for percents: $\frac{is}{of} = \frac{\%}{100}$.

*Example:*

5 is what percent of 25? Of 25, what percent is 5? What percent is 5 of 25?

➤ Notice that these questions are equivalent. $\frac{is}{of} = \frac{\%}{100} \Rightarrow \frac{5}{25} = \frac{1}{5} = 0.2 = \frac{\%}{100} \Rightarrow \% = (0.2)(100) = 20\%$.

As long as you place the "*is* this" value in the numerator and the "*of* that" value in the denominator, you cannot make a mistake.

*Examples:*

1. What percent is 20 of 50?

   ➤ $\frac{20}{50} = \frac{2}{5} = 0.40 = 40\%$

2. Of 125, what percent is 25?

   ➤ $\frac{25}{125} = \frac{1}{5} = 0.20 = 20\%$

3. 12 is what percent of 6?

   ➤ $\frac{12}{6} = 2 = 200\%$

The "*is* over *of*" method can be used to attack any item that presents a variation on this theme. For example, what number is 20% of 25? This is similar to the previous examples, except in this case, the percent is given and one of the two numbers is missing. Still, the "*is* over *of*" method works; "*is* this" is represented by "what number"— simply a slight variation in wording.

*Examples:*

1. What number is 20% of 25?

   ➤ $\frac{is}{of} = \frac{\%}{100} \Rightarrow \frac{is}{25} = \frac{20}{100} \Rightarrow is = \frac{500}{100} = 5$

2. 5 is 20% of what number?

   ➤ $\frac{is}{of} = \frac{\%}{100} \Rightarrow \frac{5}{of} = \frac{20}{100} \Rightarrow of = \frac{500}{20} = 25$

Notice that in the second example, the method still applies. No matter how wordy or otherwise difficult such items get, they are all answerable using this method.

*Example:*

John received a paycheck for $200. Of that amount, he paid Ed $25. What percent of the paycheck did John give Ed?

➤ $200 is the *of* value; $25 is the *is* value: $\frac{is}{of} = \frac{\%}{100} \Rightarrow \frac{25}{200} = \frac{\%}{100} \Rightarrow \% = \frac{25 \cdot 100}{200} = \frac{25}{2} = 12.5\%$.

### *"This Is X Percent of What?"*

In the third type of percent problem, the task is to manipulate a given value and percent to determine the unknown total value. The "*is* over *of*" equation, $\frac{is}{of} = \frac{\%}{100}$, can also be used for this variation.

*Examples:*

1. Seven students attended a field trip. If these 7 students were $6\frac{1}{4}\%$ of all the $9^{th}$-graders, find the total number of $9^{th}$-graders.

   ➤ $\frac{is}{of} = \frac{\%}{100} \Rightarrow \frac{7}{x} = \frac{6.25\%}{100} \Rightarrow 7 \cdot 100 = 6.25 \cdot x \Rightarrow x = \frac{7 \cdot 100}{6.25} = 112.$

2. A television set discounted by 18% was sold for \$459.20. What was the price of the set before the discount?

   ➤ Simplified: "\$459.20 is $100\% - 18\%$, or 82%, of what?" $\frac{\$459.20}{x} = \frac{82}{100} \Rightarrow \$459.20 \cdot 100 = x \cdot 82 \Rightarrow$ $x = \frac{\$459.20 \cdot 100}{82} = \$560.$

## Percent Change

The fourth percent item involves a quantity change over time. This type of item asks you to express the relationship between the change and the original amount in percent terms. To solve, create a fraction that is then expressed as a percent. Think of this as the "*change* over *original*" trick, because the fraction places the change over the original amount.

*Examples:*

1. The price of an item increased from \$20 to \$25. What was the percent increase in the price?

   ➤ $\frac{Change}{Original\ Amount} = \frac{25 - 20}{20} = \frac{5}{20} = \frac{1}{4} = 0.25 = 25\%$

2. Mary was earning \$16 per hour when she received a raise of \$4 per hour. Her hourly wage increased by what percent?

   ➤ $\frac{Change}{Original\ Amount} = \frac{4}{16} = 0.25 = 25\%$

The "*change* over *original*" trick works for decreases as well.

*Examples:*

1. A stock's value declined from \$50 per share to \$45 per share. What was the percent decline in the value of a share?

   ➤ $\frac{Change}{Original\ Amount} = \frac{5}{50} = \frac{1}{10} = 0.10 = 10\%$

2. Student enrollment at City University dropped from 5,000 students in 1990 to 4,000 students in 2000. What was the percent drop in the number of students enrolled at City University?

   ➤ $\frac{Change}{Original\ Amount} = \frac{1,000}{5,000} = \frac{1}{5} = 0.20 = 20\%$

# Percents

**DIRECTIONS:** Choose the correct answer to each of the following items. Answers are on page 938.

1. What is 0.79 expressed as a percent?

    A. 0.0079%  C. 0.79%  E. 79%
    B. 0.079%  D. 7.9%

2. What is 0.55 expressed as a percent?

    A. 55%  C. 0.55%  E. 0.0055%
    B. 5.5%  D. 0.055%

3. What is 0.111 expressed as a percent?

    A. 111%  C. 1.11%  E. 0.0111%
    B. 11.1%  D. 0.111%

4. What is 0.125 expressed as a percent?

    A. 125%  C. 1.25%  E. 0.0125%
    B. 12.5%  D. 0.125%

5. What is 0.5555 expressed as a percent?

    A. 5,555%  C. 55.55%  E. 0.555%
    B. 555.5%  D. 5.555%

6. What is 0.3 expressed as a percent?

    A. 30%  C. 0.30%  E. 0.003%
    B. 3%  D. 0.03%

7. What is 0.7500 expressed as a percent?

    A. 7,500%  C. 75%  E. 0.75%
    B. 750%  D. 7.5%

8. What is 2.45 expressed as a percent?

    A. 2,450%  C. 24.5%  E. 0.245%
    B. 245%  D. 2.45%

9. What is 1.25 expressed as a percent?

    A. 125%  C. 1.25%  E. 0.0125%
    B. 12.5%  D. 0.125%

10. What is 10 expressed as a percent?

    A. 1,000%  C. 10%  E. 0.1%
    B. 100%  D. 1%

11. What is 0.015 expressed as a percent?

    A. 15%  C. 0.15%  E. 0.0015%
    B. 1.5%  D. 0.015%

12. What is 0.099 expressed as a percent?

    A. 99%  C. 0.99%  E. 0.0099%
    B. 9.9%  D. 0.099%

13. What is 0.0333 expressed as a percent?

    A. 3.33%  C. 0.0333%  E. 0.000333%
    B. 0.333%  D. 0.00333%

14. What is 0.001 expressed as a percent?

    A. 0.1%  C. 0.001%  E. 0.00001%
    B. 0.01%  D. 0.0001%

15. What is 0.0100 expressed as a percent?

    A. 1%  C. 0.001%  E. 0.1%
    B. 0.01%  D. 0.0001%

16. What is 25% expressed as a decimal?

    A. 25.0  C. 0.25  E. 0.0025
    B. 2.5  D. 0.025

17. What is 56% expressed as a decimal?

    A. 5.6  C. 0.056  E. 0.00056
    B. 0.56  D. 0.0056

18. What is 10% expressed as a decimal?

    A. 100.0  C. 1.0  E. 0.001
    B. 10.0  D. 0.1

19. What is 100% expressed as a decimal?

    A. 100.0  C. 1.0  E. 0.001
    B. 10.0  D. 0.1

20. What is 250% expressed as a decimal?

    A. 250.0  C. 2.5  E. 0.025
    B. 25.0  D. 0.25

21. What is 1,000% expressed as a decimal?

    A. 1,000.0  C. 10.0  E. 0.01
    B. 100.0  D. 1.0

22. What is 0.25% expressed as a decimal?

    A. 25.0      C. 0.025      E. 0.00025
    B. 0.25      D. 0.0025

23. What is 0.099% expressed as a decimal?

    A. 99      C. 0.099      E. 0.00099
    B. 0.99      D. 0.0099

24. What is 0.0988% expressed as a decimal?

    A. 0.988      C. 0.00988      E. 9.8
    B. 0.0988      D. 0.000988

25. What is 0.00100% expressed as a decimal?

    A. 0.01      C. 0.0001      E. 0.000001
    B. 0.001      D. 0.00001

26. What is $\frac{1}{10}$ expressed as a percent?

    A. 100%      C. 1%      E. 0.01%
    B. 10%      D. 0.1%

27. What is $\frac{3}{100}$ expressed as a percent?

    A. 300%      C. 3%      E. 0.03%
    B. 30%      D. 0.3%

28. What is $\frac{99}{100}$ expressed as a percent?

    A. 99%      C. 0.99%      E. 0.0099%
    B. 9.9%      D. 0.099%

29. What is $\frac{100}{1,000}$ expressed as a percent?

    A. 0.1%      C. 10%      E. 1,000%
    B. 1.0%      D. 100%

30. What is $\frac{333}{100}$ expressed as a percent?

    A. 333%      C. 3.33%      E. 0.0333%
    B. 33.3%      D. 0.333%

31. What is $\frac{9}{1,000}$ as a percent?

    A. 9%      C. 0.09%      E. 0.0009%
    B. 0.9%      D. 0.009%

32. What is $\frac{3}{4}$ expressed as a percent?

    A. 0.0075%      C. 0.75%      E. 75%
    B. 0.075%      D. 7.5%

33. What is $\frac{4}{5}$ expressed as a percent?

    A. 4.5%      C. 45%      E. 450%
    B. 8%      D. 80%

34. What is $\frac{3}{50}$ expressed as a percent?

    A. 60%      C. 0.6%      E. 0.0006%
    B. 6%      D. 0.006%

35. What is $\frac{3}{75}$ expressed as a percent?

    A. 0.004%      C. 0.4%      E. 40%
    B. 0.04%      D. 4%

36. What is $\frac{6}{500}$ expressed as a percent?

    A. 0.012%      C. 1.2%      E. 120%
    B. 0.12%      D. 12%

37. What is $\frac{111}{555}$ expressed as a percent?

    A. 222%      C. 22%      E. 2%
    B. 200%      D. 20%

38. What is $\frac{8}{5,000}$ expressed as a percent?

    A. 16%      C. 0.016%      E. 0.00016%
    B. 0.16%      D. 0.0016%

39. What is $1\frac{1}{10}$ expressed as a percent?

    A. 110%      C. 1.1%      E. 0.011%
    B. 11%      D. 0.11%

40. What is $9\frac{99}{100}$ expressed as a percent?

    A. 999%      C. 9.99%      E. 0.0999%
    B. 99.9%      D. 0.999%

41. What is $3\frac{1}{2}$ expressed as a percent?

    A. 0.35%      C. 35%      E. 3,500%
    B. 3.5%      D. 350%

42. What is $1\frac{3}{4}$ expressed as a percent?

    A. 175%      C. 17.5%      E. 1.75%
    B. 134%      D. 13.4%

43. What is $10\frac{1}{5}$ expressed as a percent?

    A. 10.02%      C. 100.2%      E. 1,020%
    B. 10.2%      D. 102%

44. What is $3\frac{1}{50}$ expressed as a percent?

    A. 302%      C. 3.02%      E. 0.00302%
    B. 30.2%      D. 0.0302%

45. What is $\frac{111}{100}$ expressed as a percent?

    A. 1,110%    C. 11.1%    E. 0.0111%
    B. 111%      D. 1.11%

46. What is $\frac{7}{2}$ expressed as a percent?

    A. 0.35%    C. 35%    E. 3,500%
    B. 3.5%     D. 350%

47. What is $\frac{13}{15}$ expressed as a percent?

    A. 260%    C. 2.6%    E. 0.026%
    B. 26%     D. 0.26%

48. What is $\frac{9}{8}$ expressed as a percent?

    A. 1,125%    C. 11.25%    E. 0.1125%
    B. 112.5%    D. 1.125%

49. What is $\frac{22}{5}$ expressed as a percent?

    A. 440%    C. 4.4%    E. 0.044
    B. 44%     D. 0.44%

50. What is $\frac{33}{6}$ expressed as a percent?

    A. 550%    C. 5.5%    E. 0.55%
    B. 53%     D. 5.3%

51. Which of the following is equal to 18%?

    A. $\frac{18}{1}$    C. $\frac{18}{100}$    E. $\frac{18}{10,000}$
    B. $\frac{18}{10}$    D. $\frac{18}{1,000}$

52. Which of the following is equal to 80%?

    A. 80    C. 0.8    E. 0.008
    B. 8     D. 0.08

53. Which of the following is equal to 45%?

    A. $\frac{1}{9}$    C. $\frac{11}{19}$    E. $\frac{9}{10}$
    B. $\frac{9}{20}$    D. $\frac{3}{4}$

54. Which of the following is equal to 7%?

    A. 0.007    C. 0.7    E. 70
    B. 0.07     D. 7

55. Which of the following is equal to 13.2%?

    A. 0.0132    C. 1.32    E. 132
    B. 0.132     D. 13.2

56. Which of the following is equal to 1.111%?

    A. 0.001111    C. 0.11111    E. 11.11
    B. 0.01111     D. 1.111

57. Which of the following is equal to 10.101%?

    A. 0.0010101    C. 0.10101    E. 10.101
    B. 0.010101     D. 1.0101

58. Which of the following is equal to 33%?

    A. $\frac{1}{3}$    C. $\frac{33}{111}$    E. $\frac{33}{10,000}$
    B. $\frac{33}{100}$    D. $\frac{33}{1,000}$

59. Which of the following is equal to 80.1%?

    A. $80\frac{1}{10}$    C. $\frac{801}{1,000}$    E. 0.00801
    B. 8.01     D. 0.0801

60. Which of the following is equal to 0.02%?

    A. $\frac{1}{5}$    C. $\frac{1}{500}$    E. $\frac{1}{50,000}$
    B. $\frac{1}{50}$    D. $\frac{1}{5,000}$

61. Which of the following is equal to 250%?

    A. $\frac{25}{1,000}$    C. $\frac{1}{4}$    E. 25
    B. $\frac{25}{100}$    D. 2.5

62. Which of the following is equal to 1,000%?

    A. $\frac{1}{10}$    C. 10    E. 1,000
    B. 1     D. 100

63. 37% + 42% = ?

    A. 6%    C. 106%    E. 154%
    B. 79%    D. 110%

64. 210% + 21% = ?

    A. 21,021%    C. 23.1%    E. 0.231%
    B. 231%    D. 2.31%

65. 8% + 9% + 10% + 110% = ?

    A. 17%    C. 180%    E. 18,000%
    B. 137%    D. 1,800%

66. 254% + 166% + 342% = ?

    A. 900%    C. 432%    E. 92%
    B. 762%    D. 111%

67. 0.02% + 0.005 = ?

    A. 7%    C. 1%    E. 0.025%
    B. 2.5%    D. 0.07%

68. 33% − 25% = ?

  A. 0.08%      C. 8%       E. 800%
  B. 0.8%       D. 80%

69. 100% − 0.99% = ?

  A. 1%         C. 11%      E. 99.99%
  B. 9.9%       D. 99.01%

70. 222% − 22.2% = ?

  A. 221.88%    C. 22.188%  E. 1.998%
  B. 199.8%     D. 19.98%

71. If John read 15 percent of the pages in a book on Monday and another 25 percent on Tuesday, what percent of the book did he read on Monday and Tuesday combined?

  A. 7.5%       C. 55%      E. 80%
  B. 40%        D. 75%

72. If from 9:00 a.m. to noon Mary mowed 35 percent of a lawn, and from noon to 3:00 p.m. she mowed another 50 percent of the lawn, what percent of the lawn did she mow between 9:00 a.m. and 3:00 p.m.?

  A. 17.5%      C. 74.3%    E. 98%
  B. 60%        D. 85%

Items #73–75 refer to the following table.

| Schedule for Completing Project X | | | | | |
| --- | --- | --- | --- | --- | --- |
|  | Mon. | Tues. | Wed. | Thurs. | Fri. |
| % of work to be completed each day | 8% | 17% | 25% | 33% | 17% |

73. By the end of which day is one-half of the work scheduled to be completed?

  A. Monday     C. Wednesday  E. Friday
  B. Tuesday    D. Thursday

74. By the end of Tuesday, what percent of the work is scheduled to be completed?

  A. 8%         C. 25%      E. 88%
  B. 17%        D. 50%

75. If production is on schedule, during which day will $\frac{2}{3}$ of the project have been completed?

  A. Monday     C. Wednesday  E. Friday
  B. Tuesday    D. Thursday

76. A bucket filled to 33% of its capacity has an amount of water equal to $\frac{1}{4}$ of the bucket's capacity added to it. The bucket is filled to what percent of its capacity?

  A. 8%         C. 33%      E. 75%
  B. 25%        D. 58%

77. If Edward spends 15% of his allowance on a book and another 25% on food, what percent of his allowance remains?

  A. 10%        C. 45%      E. 80%
  B. 40%        D. 60%

78. 50% of 50% = ?

  A. 1%         C. 25%      E. 250%
  B. 2.5%       D. 100%

79. 1% of 100% = ?

  A. 0.01%      C. 1%       E. 100%
  B. 0.1%       D. 10%

80. If a jar contains 100 marbles and 66% of those marbles are red, how many marbles in the jar are red?

  A. 6          C. 66       E. 6,660
  B. 34         D. 660

81. If 75% of 240 cars in a certain parking lot are sedans, how many of the cars in the parking lot are sedans?

  A. 18         C. 60       E. 210
  B. 24         D. 180

82. If 0.1% of the 189,000 names on a certain mailing list have the initials *B.D.*, how many names on the list have the initials *B.D.*?

  A. 1.89       C. 189      E. 189,000
  B. 18.9       D. 18,900

83. What percent of 10 is 1?

  A. 0.1%       C. 10%      E. 1,000%
  B. 1%         D. 100%

84. What percent of 12 is 3?

  A. 2.5%       C. 25%      E. 400%
  B. 3.6%       D. 36%

85. 50 is what percent of 40?

  A. 125%       C. 80%      E. 8%
  B. 90%        D. 12.5%

86. What number is 10% of 100?

    A. 0.01        C. 1        E. 1,000
    B. 0.1        D. 10

87. What number is 250% of 12?

    A. 3        C. 24        E. 36
    B. 15        D. 30

88. If Patty's age is 48 and Al's age is 36, then Al's age is what percent of Patty's age?

    A. 7.5%        C. 75%        E. 175%
    B. 25%        D. $133\frac{1}{3}$%

89. If 25 of the employees at a bank are women and 15 are men, then what percent of the bank's employees are women?

    A. 37.5%        C. 60%        E. 90%
    B. 40%        D. 62.5%

90. If the price of an item increases from $5.00 to $8.00, the new price is what percent of the old price?

    A. 20%        C. 62.5%        E. 160%
    B. 60%        D. 92.5%

91. If the price of an item increases from $5.00 to $8.00, the old price is what percent of the new price?

    A. 20%        C. 62.5%        E. 160%
    B. 60%        D. 92.5%

92. If the price of a share of stock drops from $200 to $160, the new price is what percent of the old price?

    A. 20%        C. 50%        E. 125%
    B. 25%        D. 80%

93. If the price of a share of stock drops from $200 to $160, the old price is what percent of the new price?

    A. 20%        C. 50%        E. 125%
    B. 25%        D. 80%

94. If the price of a share of stock drops from $200 to $160, what was the percent decline in the price?

    A. 20%        C. 50%        E. 125%
    B. 25%        D. 80%

Items #95–99 refer to the following table.

| Enrollments for a One-Week Seminar | |
| --- | --- |
| Week Number | Number of Enrollees |
| 1 | 10 |
| 2 | 25 |
| 3 | 20 |
| 4 | 15 |
| 5 | 30 |

95. The number of people who enrolled for the seminar in Week 1 was what percent of the number of people who enrolled in Week 2?

    A. 5%        C. 50%        E. 250%
    B. 40%        D. 80%

96. The number of people who enrolled for the seminar in Week 4 was what percent of the number of people who enrolled in Week 5?

    A. 15%        C. 50%        E. 200%
    B. 25%        D. 100%

97. The number of people who enrolled for the seminar in Week 5 was what percent of the number of people who enrolled in Week 4?

    A. 15%        C. 50%        E. 200%
    B. 25%        D. 100%

98. What was the percent increase in the number of people enrolled for the seminar from Week 1 to Week 2?

    A. 40%        C. 100%        E. 250%
    B. 80%        D. 150%

99. What was the percent decrease in the number of people enrolled for the seminar from Week 3 to Week 4?

    A. 25%        C. 75%        E. $133\frac{1}{3}$%
    B. $33\frac{1}{3}$%        D. 125%

100. If a textbook costs $35, what is 8% sales tax on the textbook?

    A. $1.20        C. $2.00        E. $3.20
    B. $1.80        D. $2.80

101. If a textbook costs $30 plus 8.5% sales tax, what is the total cost of one textbook?

    A. $3.55        C. $23.55        E. $33.55
    B. $12.55        D. $32.55

102. How much is 25% of 80?

    A. 2          C. 20          E. 45
    B. 8          D. 40

103. How much is 2.3% of 90?

    A. 1.07       C. 2.17        E. 2.3
    B. 2.07       D. 2.7

104. On a test that had 50 items, Gertrude got 34 out of the first 40 correct. If she received a grade of 80% on the test, how many of the last 10 items did Gertrude have correct?

    A. 6          C. 10          E. 34
    B. 8          D. 12

105. The number of the question you are now reading is what percent of 1,000?

    A. 0.1%       C. 10.5%       E. 1,050%
    B. 10%        D. 100%

106. 40 is what percent of 50?

    A. 5%         C. 80%         E. 95%
    B. 25%        D. 90%

107. 80 is what percent of 20?

    A. 4%         C. 40%         E. 400%
    B. 8%         D. 200%

108. In the junior class, 300 enrolled in a test preparation course, while 500 did not. What percent of the junior class did not enroll in a test preparation course?

    A. 7%         C. 62.5%       E. 90%
    B. 35%        D. 75%

109. Mary's factory produces pencils at a cost to her company of $0.02 per pencil. If she sells them to a wholesaler at $0.05 each, what is her percent of profit based on her cost of $0.02 per pencil?

    A. 25%        C. 75%         E. 150%
    B. 50%        D. 100%

110. In a certain class of 30 students, 6 received A's. What percent of the class did not receive an A?

    A. 8%         C. 60%         E. 90%
    B. 40%        D. 80%

111. If the Wildcats won 10 out of 12 games, to the nearest whole percent, what percentage of their games did the Wildcats win?

    A. 3          C. 38          E. 94
    B. 8          D. 83

112. On Thursday, Hui made 86 out of 100 free throws. On Friday, she made 46 out of 50 free throws. What was Hui's free throw percentage for the two days?

    A. 8.8%       C. 28%         E. 88%
    B. 12.8%      D. 82%

113. A stereo was discounted by 20% and sold at the discount price of $256. Which of the following equals the price of the stereo before the discount?

    A. less than $300
    B. between $300 and $308
    C. between $308 and $316
    D. between $316 and $324
    E. more than $324

114. In a bag of red and black jellybeans, 136 are red jellybeans and the remainder are black jellybeans. If 15% of the jellybeans in the bag are black, what is the total number of jellybeans in the bag?

    A. 151        C. 175         E. 906
    B. 160        D. 200

115. The regular price of a TV set is $118.80. Which of the following equals the price of the TV set after a sale reduction of 20%?

    A. $158.60    C. $138.84     E. $29.70
    B. $148.50    D. $95.04

116. A circle graph of a budget shows the expenditure of 26.2% for housing, 28.4% for food, 12% for clothing, 12.7% for taxes, and the balance for miscellaneous items. Which of the following equals the percent for miscellaneous items?

    A. 79.3       C. 68.5        E. 20.7
    B. 70.3       D. 29.7

117. Two dozen shuttlecocks and four badminton rackets are to be purchased for a playground. The shuttlecocks are priced at $.35 each and the rackets at $2.75 each. The playground receives a discount of 30% from these prices. Which of the following equals the total cost of this equipment?

    A. $7.29      C. $13.58      E. $19.40
    B. $11.43     D. $18.60

118. A piece of wood weighing 10 ounces is found to have a weight of 8 ounces after drying. Which of the following equals the moisture content?

   A. 80%          C. $33\frac{1}{3}$%          E. 20%

   B. 40%          D. 25%

119. A bag contains 800 coins. Of these, 10 percent are dimes, 30 percent are nickels, and the rest are quarters. Which of the following equals the amount of money in the bag?

   A. less than $150
   B. between $150 and $300
   C. between $301 and $450
   D. between $450 and $800
   E. more than $800

120. Six quarts of a 20% solution of alcohol in water are mixed with 4 quarts of a 60% solution of alcohol in water. Which of the following equals the alcoholic strength of the mixture?

   A. 80%          C. 36%          E. 10%

   B. 40%          D. 25%

121. A man insures 80% of his property and pays a $2\frac{1}{2}$% premium amounting to $348. What is the total value of his property?

   A. $19,000          C. $18,000          E. $13,920

   B. $18,400          D. $17,400

122. A clerk spent his 35-hour work week as follows: $\frac{1}{5}$ of his time he sorted mail, $\frac{1}{2}$ of his time he filed letters, and $\frac{1}{7}$ of the time he did reception work. The rest of his time was devoted to messenger work. Which of the following approximately equals the percent of time spent on messenger work by the clerk during the week?

   A. 6%          C. 14%          E. 20%

   B. 10%          D. 16%

123. In a school in which 40% of the enrolled students are boys, 80% of the boys are present on a certain day. If 1,152 boys are present, which of the following equals the total school enrollment?

   A. 1,440          C. 3,600          E. 5,760

   B. 2,880          D. 5,400

124. Mrs. Morris receives a salary raise from $25,000 to $27,500. Find the percent of increase.

   A. 19%          C. 90%          E. $12\frac{1}{2}$%

   B. 10%          D. 151%

125. The population of Stormville has increased from 80,000 to 100,000 in the last 20 years. Find the percent of increase.

   A. 20%          C. 80%          E. 10%

   B. 25%          D. 60%

126. The value of Super Company Stock dropped from $25 a share to $21 a share. Find the percent of decrease.

   A. 4%          C. 12%          E. 20%

   B. 8%          D. 16%

127. The Rubins bought their home for $30,000 and sold it for $60,000. Find the percent of increase.

   A. 100%          C. 200%          E. 150%

   B  50%          D. 300%

128. During the pre-holiday rush, Martin's Department Store increased its sales staff from 150 to 200 persons. By what percent must it now decrease its sales staff to return to the usual number of salespersons?

   A. 25%          C. 20%          E. 75%

   B. $33\frac{1}{3}$%          D. 40%

129. If enrollment at City University grew from 3,000 to 12,000 in the last 10 years, what was the percent of increase in enrollment?

   A. 25%          C. 300%          E. 400%

   B. 125%          D. 330%

# Statistical Measures

*Mean* (or average), *median*, *mode*, *range*, *standard deviation*, and *frequency distribution* are types of statistics that can be determined for a given set of numbers. These statistics provide particular information about a particular set of data.

### Mean

### Calculating a Mean (Average)

To calculate an *average (arithmetic mean)*, just add the quantities contributing to the average and then divide that sum by the number of quantities involved. For example, the average of 3, 7, and 8 is 6: $3+7+8=18$, and $18 \div 3 = 6$. Typically, on the exam, the term "average" is used instead of "mean" or "arithmetic mean."

*Example:*

A student's final grade is the average of her scores on five exams. If she receives scores of 78, 83, 82, 88, and 94, what is her final grade?

➤ To find the average, add the five grades and divide that sum by 5: $\frac{78+83+82+88+94}{5} = \frac{425}{5} = 85$.

It is possible that an easy item might ask that you find the average of a few numbers, as above; however, items about averages can take several other forms. The generalized formula for an average (arithmetic mean) is given by the following equation.

### EQUATION FOR FINDING AN AVERAGE

  Average (Arithmetic Mean) $= \overline{x} = \frac{x_1 + x_2 + x_3 + ... + x_n}{n}$

### Determining Missing Elements

Some items provide the average of a group of numbers and some—but not all—of the quantities involved. You are then asked to find the *missing element(s)*. For example, if the average of 3, 8, and $x$ is 6, what is the value of $x$? Since the average of the three numbers is 6, the sum or total of the three numbers is $3 \cdot 6 = 18$. The two given numbers are equal to $3+8=11$, so the third number must be $18-11=7$. Check the solution by averaging 3, 8, and 7: $3+8+7=18$, and $18 \div 3 = 6$.

*Examples:*

1. For a certain five-day period, the average high temperature (in degrees Fahrenheit) for Chicago was 30°. If the high temperatures recorded for the first four of those days were 26°, 32°, 24°, and 35°, what was the high temperature recorded on the fifth day?

   ➤ The sum of the five numbers is $5 \cdot 30 = 150$. The sum for the four days we know about is: $26+32+24+35=117$. Thus, the fifth day must have had a high temperature of $150-117=33$.

2. The average of Jose's scores on four tests is 90. If three of those scores are 89, 92, and 94, what is his fourth score?

   ➤ The sum of all four scores must be $4 \cdot 90 = 360$. The three known scores sum to: $89 + 92 + 94 = 275$. Thus, the remaining score must be $360 - 275 = 85$.

3. The average of a group of eight numbers is 9. If one of these numbers is removed from the group, the average of the remaining numbers is 7. What is the value of the number removed?

   ➤ The sum of the original numbers is $8 \cdot 9 = 72$. The sum of the remaining numbers is $7 \cdot 7 = 49$, so the value of the number that was removed must be $72 - 49 = 23$.

A variation on this type of an item might ask about more than one missing element.

*Example:*

   In a group of children, three of the children are ages 7, 8, and 10, and the other two are the same age. If the average of the ages of all five children is 7, what is the age of the other two children?

   ➤ The total sum of the five ages must be $5 \cdot 7 = 35$. The known ages total only $7 + 8 + 10 = 25$, so the ages of the two other children must total 10. Since there are two of them, each one must be 5 years old.

### Calculating Weighted Averages

In the average problems discussed thus far, each element in the average has been given equal weight. Sometimes, averages are created that give greater weight to one element than to another.

*Example:*

   Cody bought 4 books that cost $6.00 each and 2 books that cost $3.00 each. What is the average cost of the 6 books?

   ➤ The average cost of the 6 books is not just the average of $6.00 and $3.00, which is $4.50. He bought more of the higher priced books, so the average must reflect that fact. One method is to treat each book as a separate expense: $\frac{6+6+6+6+3+3}{6} = \frac{30}{6} = 5$. Another method is to "weigh" the two different costs: $6(4) + 3(2) = 30$ and $\frac{30}{6} = 5$.

## Median

The *median* of an odd number of data values is the middle value of the data set when it is arranged in ascending or descending order. The median of an even number of data values is the average of the two middle values of the data set when it is arranged in ascending or descending order.

*Examples:*

1. What is the median of $\{1, 1, 2, 3, 4, 5, 6, 7, 7, 7, 8, 8, 9\}$?

   ➤ The set contains an odd number of data values, so the median is the middle value: 6.

2. What is the median of $\{7, 9, 10, 16\}$?

   ➤ The set contains an even number of data values, so the median is the average of the two middle values: $\frac{9+10}{2} = 9.5$.

## Mode

The **mode** is the value that appears most frequently in a set of data. Some data sets have multiple modes, while other data sets have no modes.

*Examples:*

1. The mode of $\{2, 4, 5, 5, 5, 6, 6, 19, 2\}$ is 5.
2. The group of numbers $\{-3, 5, 6, -3, -2, 7, 5, -3, 6, 5, 5, -3\}$ is bimodal since $-3$ and 5 each occur four times.

## Range

There are several ways to measure the degree to which numerical data are spread out or dispersed. The **range** of a set of numbers is the simplest measure of the spread of the data. The range is the difference between the highest and lowest numbers in the set. Note that the range depends on only these two values in the data. The greater the range, the greater the spread in the data.

*Example:*

The range of $\{5, 10, 3, 24, 11, 4\}$ is $24 - 3 = 21$.

## Standard Deviation

Another common measure of dispersion is **standard deviation**. Generally, the greater the spread of the data away from the mean, the greater the standard deviation. The standard deviation of *n* numbers can be calculated using the following steps.

Step 1: Calculate the arithmetic mean (average) of the n numbers.
Step 2: Calculate the differences between the mean and each of the n numbers.
Step 3: Square each of the differences.
Step 4: Calculate the average of the squared differences.
Step 5: Take the nonnegative square root of the average from Step 4. This is the standard deviation of the *n* numbers.

Unlike the range of a data set, the standard deviation depends on every data value, though it depends most on values that are farthest from the mean. Therefore, a data set distributed closely around the mean will have a smaller standard deviation than will data spread far from the mean.

*Example:*

What is the standard deviation of the data set $\{0, 2, 2, 5, 7, 8\}$ ?

➤ Calculate the average of the 6 numbers: $\text{average}_{\text{data set}} = \frac{0+2+2+5+7+8}{6} = \frac{24}{6} = 4$. Next, calculate the differences between the average (4) and each of the 6 numbers, and square each of these differences:

$x = 0$: $\quad 0 - 4 = -4 \Rightarrow (-4)^2 = 16$

$$x = 2: \quad 2 - 4 = -2 \Rightarrow (-2)^2 = 4$$
$$x = 5: \quad 5 - 4 = 1 \Rightarrow 1^2 = 1$$
$$x = 7: \quad 7 - 4 = 3 \Rightarrow 3^2 = 9$$
$$x = 5: \quad 5 - 4 = 1 \Rightarrow 1^2 = 1$$
$$x = 8: \quad 8 - 4 = 4 \Rightarrow 4^2 = 16$$

Calculate the average of the 8 squared differences: $\text{average}_{\text{squared differences}} = \frac{16 + 4 + 4 + 1 + 9 + 16}{6} = \frac{50}{6} = \frac{25}{3}$. The standard deviation is equal to the nonnegative square root of this average: standard deviation $= \sqrt{\frac{25}{3}} \approx 2.9$.

Note that on the actual exam, it is unlikely that knowledge of the formula for standard deviation will be tested. Rather, understanding of the concept behind standard deviation—that it is a measure of how the data values vary from the mean—is tested.

*Example:*

Arrange the following data sets from greatest standard deviation to least standard deviation: $\{12, 13, 14, 15, 16\}$, $\{12, 13, 14, 15, 16\}$, $\{14, 14, 14, 14, 14\}$, and $\{6, 14, 14, 14, 24\}$.

➤ The second data set has no variation, so the standard deviation is 0. The first data set has small deviations from the mean of 14, so the standard deviation in this set is greater than in the second set. Because of the extreme values 6 and 24, the variation in the third set is clearly greater than the variation in the first set. Thus, the standard deviation in the third set is greater than the standard deviation in 1.

## Frequency Distribution

Finally, a frequency distribution is a simple way of displaying how numerical data are distributed. This method arranges the data according to the varying frequencies with which the data occurs.

*Example:*

Display the following 15 numbers using a frequency distribution: $\{-2, 0, 2, 0, 1, -1, 2, -1, 4, 0, -2, 2, -1, -1, 1\}$.

➤ Simply create a table that lists the different numerical values, $x$, in the data set and the frequencies, $f$, with which they occur:

| $x$ | $F$ |
|------|-----|
| −2 | 2 |
| −1 | 4 |
| 0 | 3 |
| 1 | 2 |
| 2 | 3 |
| 4 | 1 |
| Total | 15 |

# Statistical Measures

**DIRECTIONS:** Choose the correct answer to each of the following items. Answers are on page 947.

1. What is the average of 8, 6, and 16?

   A. 10     C. 13     E. 18
   B. 12     D. 15

2. What is the average of 0 and 50?

   A. 0     C. 10     E. 50
   B. 5     D. 25

3. What is the average of 5, 11, 12, and 8?

   A. 6     C. 9     E. 12
   B. 8     D. 10

4. What is the average of 25, 28, 21, 30, and 36?

   A. 25     C. 29     E. 44
   B. 28     D. 34

5. What is the average of $\frac{1}{4}$, $\frac{3}{4}$, $\frac{5}{8}$, $\frac{1}{2}$, and $\frac{3}{8}$?

   A. $\frac{3}{32}$     C. $\frac{1}{2}$     E. $\frac{27}{32}$
   B. $\frac{5}{16}$     D. $\frac{5}{8}$

6. What is the average of $0.78, $0.45, $0.36, $0.98, $0.55, and $0.54?

   A. $0.49     C. $0.56     E. $0.61
   B. $0.54     D. $0.60

7. What is the average of 0.03, 0.11, 0.08, and 0.5?

   A. 0.18     C. 0.28     E. 1.0
   B. 0.25     D. 0.50

8. What is the average of 1,001, 1,002, 1,003, 1,004, and 1,005?

   A. 250     C. 1,003     E. 5,000
   B. 1,000     D. 2,500

9. What is the average of −8, −6, and −13?

   A. −8     C. −13     E. −9
   B. −15     D. −12

10. Jordan receives test scores of 79, 85, 90, 76, and 80. What is the average of these test scores?

    A. 82     C. 84     E. 86
    B. 83     D. 85

11. Mr. Whipple bought five different items costing $4.51, $6.25, $3.32, $4.48, and $2.19. What is the average cost of the five items?

    A. $3.40     C. $3.90     E. $4.15
    B. $3.80     D. $4.00

12. Nadia received scores of 8.5, 9.3, 8.2, and 9.0 in four different gymnastics events. What is the average of her scores?

    A. 8.5     C. 8.9     E. 9.1
    B. 8.75     D. 9

13. Five people have ages of 44, 33, 45, 44, and 29 years. What is the average of their ages in years?

    A. 36     C. 40     E. 43
    B. 39     D. 41

14. In a certain government office, if 360 staff hours are needed to process 120 building permit applications, on the average how long (in hours) does it take to process one application?

    A. 3     C. 12     E. 36
    B. 6     D. 24

15. In a chemical test for Substance $X$, a sample is divided into five equal parts. If the purity of the five parts is 84 percent, 89 percent, 87 percent, 90 percent, and 80 percent, then what is the overall purity of the sample (expressed as a percent of Substance $X$)?

    A. 83     C. 86     E. 88
    B. 84     D. 87

16. The average of three numbers is 24. If two of the numbers are 21 and 23, what is the third number?

    A. 20     C. 26     E. 30
    B. 24     D. 28

17. The average of three numbers is 5. If two of the numbers are zero, what is the third number?

    A. 1      C. 5      E. 15
    B. 3      D. 10

18. The average of the weight of four people is 166 pounds. If three of the people weigh 150 pounds, 200 pounds, and 180 pounds, what is the weight of the fourth person?

    A. 134      C. 155      E. 165
    B. 140      D. 161

19. For a certain student, the average of five test scores is 83. If four of the scores are 81, 79, 85, and 90, what is the fifth test score?

    A. 83      C. 81      E. 79
    B. 82      D. 80

20. Sue bought ten items at an average price of $3.60. The cost of eight of the items totaled $30. If the other two items were the same price, what was the price she paid for each?

    A. $15.00      C. $6.00      E. $1.50
    B. $7.50      D. $3.00

21. In a certain shipment, the weights of twelve books average 2.75 pounds. If one of the books is removed, the weights of the remaining books average 2.70 pounds. What was the weight, in pounds, of the book that was removed?

    A. 1.7      C. 3.0      E. 4.5
    B. 2.3      D. 3.3

22. The average of a group of seven test scores is 80. If the lowest and the highest scores are thrown out, the average of the remaining scores is 78. What is the average of the lowest and highest scores?

    A. 100      C. 90      E. 85
    B. 95      D. 88

23. In a certain group, twelve of the children are age 10, and eight are age 15. What is the average of the ages of all the children in the group?

    A. 9.5      C. 11      E. 12
    B. 10.5      D. 11.5

24. Robert made the following deposits in a savings account:

| Amount | Frequency |
| --- | --- |
| $15 | 4 times |
| $20 | 2 times |
| $25 | 4 times |

What was the average of all the deposits Robert made?

    A. $18.50      C. $21.50      E. $22.50
    B. $20.00      D. $22.00

25. The average of the weights of six people sitting in a boat is 145 pounds. After a seventh person gets into the boat, the average of the weights of all seven people in the boat is 147 pounds. What is the weight, in pounds, of the seventh person?

    A. 160      C. 155      E. 147
    B. 159      D. 149

26. Find the mean of the following 5 numbers: 2, 3, 13, 15, and 1.

    A. 4.6      C. 6.8      E. 16.8
    B. 6.2      D. 8.6

27. Find the mean of the following 6 numbers: $-3$, 2, 6, 5, 2, and 0.

    A. 1      C. 5      E. 8
    B. 2      D. 6

28. If the mean of 6 numbers is 10, what is the sixth number if the five given numbers are $-3$, 5, 6, 13, and 17?

    A. 12      C. 18      E. 22
    B. 16      D. 20

29. The average of 5 numbers is 56. If two new numbers are added to the list, the average of the 7 numbers is 58. Which of the following equals the average of the two new numbers?

    A. 64      C. 62      E. 60
    B. 63      D. 61

30. Arranged in some order, $3x+1$, $2x+4$, and $x+10$ represent 3 consecutive whole numbers. If $x$ represents a whole number and the average of the 3 numbers is 13, then solve for $x$.

    A. 2      C. 6      E. 10
    B. 4      D. 8

31. Arthur interviewed 100 female corporate officers and found that 34 of them were 55 years old, 28 were 45 years old, 26 were 35 years old, and 12 of them were 25 years old. What was the average of the women's ages?

    A. 16          C. 43.4          E. 45
    B. 43          D. 44.3

Items #32–34 refer to the following information.

During the last 14 games, a basketball player scored the following points per game: 42, 35, 29, 42, 33, 37, 26, 38, 42, 47, 51, 33, 30, and 40.

32. What is the median score?

    A. 35.4          C. 36          E. 38
    B. 35.7          D. 37.5

33. What is the mode?

    A. 35.4          C. 38          E. 44
    B. 37.5          D. 42

34. If after one more game, the player's average for points per game is exactly 37, how many points did the player score in the fifteenth game?

    A. 30          C. 37.5          E. 44
    B. 37          D. 42

35. Find the median of the following 5 numbers: 1, 3, 7, 2, and 8.

    A. 1          C. 3          E. 7
    B. 2          D. 4.2

36. Find the median for the following data set: $\{2, -3, 8, 4, 9, -16, 12, 0, 4, 2, 1\}$.

    A. 4          C. 2          E. 0
    B. 2.1          D. 1

37. Find the median for the following data set: $\{2, -3, 8, 4, 9, -16, 12, 8, 4, 2\}$.

    A. 2          C. 3.5          E. 4.2
    B. 3          D. 4

38. Find the mode of the following 5 numbers: 4, 8, 10, 8, and 15.

    A. 4          C. 9          E. 15
    B. 8          D. 10

39. Find the mode of the following data set: $\{6, 8, 10, 2, -2, 2, 8, 4, 2\}$.

    A. 6          C. 4          E. 1
    B. 4.4          D. 2

40. A set of seven numbers contains the numbers: 1, 4, 5, and 6. The other three numbers are represented by $2x + 8$, $x - 4$, and $7x - 4$. If the mode of these seven numbers is a negative even integer, then what is a possible value for $x$?

    A. 0          C. 2          E. 5
    B. 1          D. 4

41. The grades received on a test by twenty students were 100, 55, 75, 80, 65, 65, 95, 90, 80, 45, 40, 50, 85, 85, 85, 80, 80, 70, 65, and 60. What is the average of these grades?

    A. 70.5          C. 77          E. 100
    B. 72.5          D. 80.3

42. Arthur purchased 75 six-inch rulers costing 15¢ each, 100 one-foot rulers costing 30¢ each, and 50 one-yard rulers costing 72¢ each. What was the average price per ruler?

    A. $26\frac{1}{8}$¢          C. 39¢          E. $77\frac{1}{4}$¢
    B. $34\frac{1}{3}$¢          D. 42¢

43. What is the average grade for a student who received 90 in English, 84 in algebra, 75 in French, and 76 in music, if the subjects have the following weights: English 4, algebra 3, French 3, and music 1?

    A. 81          C. 82          E. 83
    B. $81\frac{1}{2}$          D. $82\frac{1}{2}$

Items #44–46 refer to the following information.

A census shows that on a certain neighborhood block the number of children in each family is 3, 4, 4, 0, 1, 2, 0, 2, and 2, respectively.

44. Find the average number of children per family.

    A. 4          C. $3\frac{1}{2}$          E. $1\frac{1}{2}$
    B. 3          D. 2

45. Find the median number of children.

    A. 1          C. 3          E. 5
    B. 2          D. 4

46. Find the mode of the number of children.

   A. 0       C. 2       E. 4
   B. 1       D. 3

47. The diameter of a rod is required to be
   $1.5 \pm 0.015$ inches. Which of the following
   represents the possible range of measurements for
   the rod's diameter?

   A. 1.490 inches to 1.520 inches
   B. 1.495 inches to 1.520 inches
   C. 1.495 inches to 1.525 inches
   D. 1.495 inches to 1.530 inches
   E. 1.500 inches to 1.530 inches

48. $A$ is a set containing 5 different numbers, $B$ is a
   set containing 4 different numbers, all of which
   are members of $A$. Which of the following
   statements CANNOT be true?

   A. The mean of $A$ is equal to the mean of $B$.
   B. The median of $A$ is equal to the median of $B$.
   C. The range of $A$ is equal to the range of $B$.
   D. The mean of $A$ is greater than the mean of $B$.
   E. The range of $A$ is less than the range of $B$.

49. If a set of data values has a mean of 10.0 and a
   standard deviation of 1.5, which of the following
   values is more than 1.0 standard deviations from
   the mean?

   A. 8.0       C. 9.5       E. 12.0
   B. 8.5       D. 11.5

50. The arithmetic mean and standard deviation of a
   certain normal distribution are 15.5 and 3.0,
   respectively. What value is exactly 1.5 standard
   deviations less than the mean?

   A. 10.5       C. 12.5       E. 14
   B. 11.0       D. 13.0

51. If the variables $A$, $B$, and $C$ take on only the
   values 1, 2, 3, 4, 5, or 6 with frequencies
   indicated by the shaded regions below, for which
   of the frequency distributions is the mean equal to
   the median?

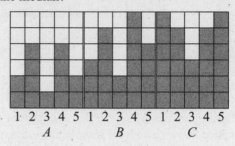

   A. $A$ only
   B. $B$ only
   C. $C$ only
   D. $A$ and $C$ only
   E. $A$, $B$, and $C$

# Ratios and Proportions

## Working with Ratios

### Two-Part Ratios

A *ratio* is a statement about the relationship between any two quantities, or we might say a ratio is a statement that compares any two quantities. Suppose that in an English class there are five girls and eight boys. We can compare those quantities by saying that the ratio of girls to boys is 5 to 8. Conversely, the ratio of boys to girls is 8 to 5. Notice that order is very important in stating a ratio. The order of the numbers in the ratio must reflect the order of the categories being compared. In our example, it would be incorrect to say that the ratio of girls to boys is 8 to 5.

A phrase such as "5 to 8" is one way of stating a ratio, but there are several other ways. A ratio can also be described using a colon: "the ratio of girls to boys is $5:8$" or "the ratio of boys to girls is $8:5$." Alternatively, the ratio can be written in fraction form: "the ratio $\frac{girls}{boys}$ is $\frac{5}{8}$" and "the ratio $\frac{boys}{girls}$ is $\frac{8}{5}$."

Ratios of the form $a:b$ or $a/b$ can also refer to numbers instead of a number of objects. We can speak abstractly of the ratio $5:8$, which is the ratio of any set of five things to any set of eight things. Consequently, ratios can be manipulated in the same way as fractions. Just as you could rewrite a fraction to get a form with a different denominator, you can convert a ratio to an equivalent form by multiplying both terms of the ratio by the same number. For example, $\frac{5}{8} = \frac{5 \cdot 2}{8 \cdot 2} = \frac{10}{16}$ and $\frac{8}{5} = \frac{8 \cdot 3}{5 \cdot 3} = \frac{24}{15}$.

It is customary to reduce a ratio to its lowest terms just as you would reduce fractions to their lowest terms. For example, in a certain classroom, there are ten girls and sixteen boys; the ratio of girls to boys is $\frac{10}{16}$, which is $\frac{5}{8}$. Although you may not be aware of it, you probably also use ratios informally in ordinary conversation. A common phrase that signifies a ratio is "for every (number)...there are (number)...." For example, in the classroom just described, for every 10 girls there are 16 boys, or in lowest terms, for every 5 girls there are 8 boys, and for every 8 boys there are 5 girls.

Finally, a ratio can also be stated as a rate using the word "per." If a car travels 200 miles and uses 10 gallons of fuel, the car gets 200 miles per 10 gallons, or 20 miles per gallon. Cost, too, is often described as a ratio. If it is possible to purchase a dozen greeting cards for $2.40, the cost of the cards is $2.40 per dozen, or 20 cents per card.

### Three-Part Ratios

When three quantities are to be compared, they can be stated using ordinary ratios. For example, if a bowl of fruit contains two apples, three pears, and five oranges, the ratio of apples to pears is $2:3$; the ratio of apples to oranges is $2:5$; and the ratio of pears to oranges is $3:5$. This same information can also be conveyed in a single statement. The ratio of apples to pears to oranges is $2:3:5$.

A *three-part ratio* depends on the middle term to join the two outside terms. Above, the ratio of apples to pears is $2:3$, and the ratio of pears to oranges is $3:5$. Since 3 is common to both ratios, it can be the middle term. Sometimes it will be necessary to find a common middle term.

*Example:*

On a certain day, a bank has the following rates of exchange: $\frac{\text{dollar}}{\text{mark}} = \frac{1}{3}$ and $\frac{\text{mark}}{\text{pound}} = \frac{6}{1}$. What is the ratio of dollars to pounds?

> To find the ratio dollars : pounds, we will use marks as the middle term. However, the ratio of dollars to marks is $1:3$, and the ratio of marks to pounds is $6:1$. We must change the first ratio to express it in terms of six marks rather than three marks. This is like finding a common denominator before adding fractions: $\frac{1}{3} = \frac{1 \cdot 2}{3 \cdot 2} = \frac{2}{6}$, so the ratio of dollars to marks is $2:6$, and the ratio of dollars to marks to pounds is $2:6:1$. Thus, the ratio of dollars to pounds is $2:1$.

### Using Ratios to Divide Quantities

An item may require that you divide a quantity according to a certain ratio.

*Examples:*

1. A \$100 prize is divided between two contestants according to the ratio $2:3$. How much does each contestant receive?

   > Add the terms of the ratio to determine by how many parts the prize is to be divided. Divide the prize by that many parts, and multiply the result by the number of parts to be given to each contestant. $2 + 3 = 5$, so the prize is to be divided into five parts. Each part is: $\$100 \div 5 = \$20$. One contestant gets $2 \cdot \$20 = \$40$, and the other contestant receives $3 \cdot \$20 = \$60$.

2. Bronze is 16 parts tin and 9 parts copper. If a bronze ingot weighs 100 pounds, how much does the tin weigh (in pounds)?

   > First, the number of parts in the ratio is: $16 + 9 = 25$. Second, $100 \div 25 = 4$, so each part is worth 4 pounds. Since there are 16 parts of tin, the tin must weigh $16 \cdot 4 = 64$ pounds.

## Working with Proportions

A ***proportion*** is the mathematical equivalent of a verbal analogy. For example, $2:3::8:12$ is equivalent to "two is to three as eight is to twelve." The main difference between an analogy and a proportion is the precision. A verbal analogy depends upon words that do not have unique and precise meanings, while mathematical proportions are made up of numbers, which are very exact.

In a mathematical proportion, the first and last terms are called the "extremes" of the proportion because they are on the extreme outside, and the two middle terms are called the "means" (mean can mean "middle"). In a mathematical proportion, the product of the extremes is always equal to the product of the means. For example, $2:3::8:12$ and $2 \cdot 12 = 3 \cdot 8$.

### Determining the Missing Elements in Proportions

Since any ratio can be written as a fraction, a proportion, which states that two ratios are equivalent, can also be written in fractional forms as an equation. This is the foundation for the process called cross-multiplication, a process that is useful in solving for an unknown element in a proportion.

*Examples:*

1. $\frac{2}{3} = \frac{8}{12} \Rightarrow \frac{2}{3} \succ=\prec \frac{8}{12} \Rightarrow 2 \cdot 12 = 3 \cdot 8$

2. $\frac{6}{9} = \frac{12}{x} \Rightarrow \frac{6}{9} \succ=\prec \frac{12}{x} \Rightarrow 6x = 108 \Rightarrow x = \frac{108}{6} = 18$.

   ➢ After cross-multiplying, divide both sides of the equality by the numerical coefficient of the unknown. Then, check the correctness of this solution by substituting 18 back in to the original proportion: $\frac{6}{9} = \frac{12}{18} \Rightarrow \frac{6}{9} \succ=\prec \frac{12}{18} \Rightarrow 6 \cdot 18 = 9 \cdot 12$.

3. $\frac{3}{15} = \frac{x}{45} \Rightarrow \frac{3}{15} \succ=\prec \frac{x}{45} \Rightarrow 3 \cdot 45 = 15x \Rightarrow x = \frac{135}{15} = 9$

   ➢ Check the solution by substitution: $\frac{3}{15} = \frac{9}{45} \Rightarrow \frac{3}{15} \succ=\prec \frac{9}{45} \Rightarrow 3 \cdot 45 = 15 \cdot 9 \Rightarrow 135 = 135$.

## Direct Proportions

The use of proportions can be a powerful problem-solving tool. ***Direct proportions*** equate ratios of two quantities having a direct relationship. The more there is of one quantity, the more there is of the other quantity, and vice versa.

*Example:*

If the cost of a dozen donuts is $3.60, what is the cost of 4 donuts? Assume there is no discount for buying in bulk.

   ➢ One method for solving this item is to calculate the cost of one donut ($3.60 ÷ 12 = $0.30), and then multiply that cost by four ($0.30 • 4 = $1.20). While this approach is not incorrect, the same result can be reached in a conceptually simpler way. The more donuts being purchased, the greater the total cost, and vice versa. Relate the quantities using a direct proportion:

   $\frac{\text{Total Cost } X}{\text{Total Cost } Y} = \frac{\text{Number } X}{\text{Number } Y} \Rightarrow \frac{\$3.60}{x} = \frac{12}{4} \Rightarrow 12x = \$3.60 \cdot 4 \Rightarrow x = \frac{\$14.40}{12} = \$1.20$.

In the previous example, we set up the proportion by grouping like terms: "cost" is on one side of the proportion and "number" is on the other side. It is equally correct to set up the proportion as $\frac{\text{Total Cost } X}{\text{Number } X} = \frac{\text{Total Cost } Y}{\text{Number } Y}$. Additionally, it does not matter which quantity is on top or bottom: $\frac{\text{Number } X}{\text{Total Cost } X} = \frac{\text{Number } Y}{\text{Total Cost } Y}$ is equally correct. However, it is generally a good idea to group like terms to avoid confusion.

***The LONGER the travel time, the GREATER the distance traveled (assuming a CONSTANT speed).***

*Example:*

If a plane moving at a constant speed flies 300 miles in 6 hours, how far will the plane fly in 8 hours?

   ➢ Group like terms:

   $\frac{\text{Time } X}{\text{Time } Y} = \frac{\text{Output } X}{\text{Output } Y} \Rightarrow \frac{6}{8} = \frac{300}{x} \Rightarrow \frac{6}{8} \succ=\prec \frac{300}{x} \Rightarrow 6x = 8 \cdot 300 \Rightarrow x = \frac{2,400}{6} = 400$.

*The LONGER the time of operation, the GREATER the output.*

*Example:*

If an uninterrupted stamping machine operating at a constant rate postmarks 320 envelopes in 5 minutes, how long will it take the machine to postmark 480 envelopes?

➢ Group like terms:

$$\frac{\text{Time } X}{\text{Time } Y} = \frac{\text{Output } X}{\text{Output } Y} \Rightarrow \frac{5}{x} = \frac{320}{480} \Rightarrow \frac{5}{x} \succ = \prec \frac{320}{480} \Rightarrow 5(480) = x(320) \Rightarrow x = \frac{5(480)}{320} = 7.5 \text{ minutes.}$$

*The GREATER the number of items, the GREATER the weight.*

*Example:*

If 20 jars of preserves weigh 25 pounds, how much do 15 jars of preserves weigh?

➢ Group like terms:

$$\frac{\text{Weight of Jars } X}{\text{Weight of Jars } Y} = \frac{\text{Jars } X}{\text{Jars } Y} \Rightarrow \frac{25}{x} = \frac{20}{15} \Rightarrow \frac{25}{x} \succ = \prec \frac{20}{15} \Rightarrow 25(15) = x(20) \Rightarrow x = \frac{25(15)}{20} = 18.75 \text{ pounds.}$$

### Inverse Proportions

In some situations, quantities are related inversely; that is, an increase in one results in a decrease in the other. For example, the more workers, or machines, doing a job, the less time it takes to finish. In this case, quantities are related inversely to each other. To solve problems involving inverse relationships, use the following procedure to set up an inverse proportion.

Step 1: Set up an ordinary proportion—make sure to group like quantities.
Step 2: Invert the right side of the proportion.
Step 3: Cross-multiply and solve for the unknown.

*Example:*

Traveling at a constant rate of 150 miles per hour, a plane makes the trip from Phoenix to Grand Junction in 4 hours. How long will the trip take if the plane flies at a constant rate of 200 miles per hour?

➢ First, set up a proportion, grouping like terms: $\frac{\text{Speed } X}{\text{Speed } Y} = \frac{\text{Time } X}{\text{Time } Y} \Rightarrow \frac{150}{200} = \frac{4}{x}$. Then, invert the right side of the proportion: $\frac{150}{200} = \frac{x}{4} \Rightarrow \frac{150}{200} \succ = \prec \frac{x}{4} \Rightarrow 150(4) = 200(x) \Rightarrow x = \frac{150(4)}{200} = 3 \text{ hours.}$

While it is possible, though not advised, to set up a direct proportion without grouping like terms, with an inverse proportion, it is essential to group like terms. This is sufficient reasoning to always group like terms: You will not make a mistake if the item involves an inverse proportion.

# Ratios and Proportions

**DIRECTIONS:** Choose the correct answer to each of the following items. Answers are on page 950.

1. If a jar contains 3 blue marbles and 8 red marbles, what is the ratio of blue marbles to red marbles?

A. 3:11     C. 8:3     E. 4:1
B. 3:8      D. 11:3

2. If a school has 24 teachers and 480 students, what is the ratio of teachers to students?

A. $\frac{1}{20}$     C. $\frac{1}{48}$     E. $\frac{1}{200}$
B. $\frac{1}{24}$     D. $\frac{1}{56}$

3. If a library contains 12,000 works of fiction and 3,000 works of nonfiction, what is the ratio of works of fiction to works of nonfiction?

A. $\frac{1}{9}$     C. $\frac{1}{4}$     E. $\frac{5}{1}$
B. $\frac{1}{5}$     D. $\frac{4}{1}$

4. Which of the following is (are) equivalent to $\frac{1}{3}$?

I. $\frac{4}{120}$

II. $\frac{75}{100}$

III. $\frac{120}{360}$

A. I only            D. II and III only
B. III only          E. I, II, and III
C. I and III only

Items #5–6 refer to the following table.

| Students at Tyler Junior High School | | |
|---|---|---|
| | 7th Grade | 8th Grade |
| Girls | 90 | 80 |
| Boys | 85 | 75 |

5. What is the ratio of seventh-grade girls to the total number of girls at Tyler Junior High School?

A. $\frac{9}{17}$     C. $\frac{18}{17}$     E. $\frac{17}{9}$
B. $\frac{8}{9}$      D. $\frac{9}{8}$

6. What is the ratio of eighth-grade girls to the total number of students at Tyler Junior High School?

A. $\frac{8}{33}$     C. $\frac{8}{15}$     E. $\frac{17}{30}$
B. $\frac{9}{33}$     D. $\frac{8}{17}$

7. If an airplane flies 275 miles on 25 gallons of fuel, then what is the average fuel consumption for the entire trip expressed in miles per gallon?

A. 25     C. 15     E. 7
B. 18     D. 11

8. An assortment of candy includes 12 chocolates, 6 caramels, and 9 mints. What is the ratio of chocolates : caramels : mints?

A. 4:3:2     C. 3:4:2     E. 2:4:3
B. 4:2:3     D. 3:2:4

9. If Lucy has twice the amount of money that Ricky has, and Ricky has three times the amount of money that Ethel has, then what is the ratio of the amount of money Ethel has to the amount of money Lucy has?

A. $\frac{1}{8}$     C. $\frac{1}{4}$     E. $\frac{2}{1}$
B. $\frac{1}{6}$     D. $\frac{1}{2}$

10. If three farkels buy two kirns, and three kirns buy five pucks, then nine farkels buy how many pucks?

A. 2     C. 8     E. 17
B. 5     D. 10

11. If Machine $X$ operates at twice the rate of Machine $Y$, and Machine $Y$ operates at $\frac{2}{3}$ the rate of Machine $Z$, then what is the ratio of the rate of operation of Machine $X$ to the rate of operation of Machine $Z$?

A. $\frac{4}{1}$     C. $\frac{4}{3}$     E. $\frac{1}{3}$
B. $\frac{3}{1}$     D. $\frac{3}{4}$

12. If 48 marbles are to be divided between Bill and Carl in the ratio of $3 : 5$, how many marbles should Bill get?

   A. 6       C. 18       E. 30
   B. 8       D. 24

13. If $10 is to be divided between Janeway and Nelix so that Nelix receives $\frac{1}{4}$ of what Janeway receives, then how much should Janeway receive?

   A. $10.00       C. $7.50       E. $2.00
   B. $8.00       D. $6.00

14. If a $1,000 reward is to be divided among three people in the ratio of $2 : 3 : 5$, what is the largest amount that will be given to any one of the three recipients?

   A. $200       C. $500       E. $900
   B. $300       D. $750

15. If $\frac{6}{8} = \frac{x}{4}$, then $x = ?$

   A. 12       C. 4       E. 2
   B. 6       D. 3

16. If $\frac{14}{x} = \frac{2}{7}$, then $x = ?$

   A. 7       C. 28       E. 343
   B. 14       D. 49

17. If $\frac{3}{4} = \frac{4}{x}$, then $x = ?$

   A. $\frac{3}{16}$       C. $\frac{4}{3}$       E. $\frac{16}{3}$
   B. $\frac{3}{4}$       D. $\frac{7}{3}$

18. If 240 widgets cost $36, what is the cost of 180 widgets?

   A. $8       C. $24       E. $32
   B. $16       D. $27

19. If a kilogram of a certain cheese costs $9.60, what is the cost of 450 grams of the cheese? (1 kilogram $= 1,000$ grams)

   A. $2.78       C. $3.88       E. $5.12
   B. $3.14       D. $4.32

20. If 50 feet of electrical wire cost $4.80, then $10.80 will buy how many feet of the wire?

   A. 60       C. 67.25       E. 112.5
   B. 62.5       D. 75

21. In a certain group of people, 100 people have red hair. If only 25 percent of the people have red hair, then how many people do not have red hair?

   A. 75       C. 300       E. 500
   B. 125       D. 400

22. If a certain fundraising project has raised $12,000, which is 20 percent of its goal, how much money will have been raised when 50 percent of the goal has been reached?

   A. $60,000       C. $18,000       E. $4,800
   B. $30,000       D. $15,000

23. If 48 liters of a certain liquid weigh 50 kilograms, then how much, in kilograms, will 72 liters of the liquid weigh?

   A. 25       C. 75       E. 120
   B. 60       D. 90

24. If the trip from Soldier Field to Wrigley Field takes two hours walking at a constant rate of four miles per hour, how long (in hours) will the same trip take walking at a constant rate of five miles per hour?

   A. 2.5       C. 1.6       E. 1.25
   B. 1.75       D. 1.5

25. A swimming pool is filled by either of two pipes. Pipe A supplies water at the rate of 200 gallons per hour and takes eight hours to fill the pool. If Pipe B can fill the pool in five hours, what is the rate (in gallons per hour) at which Pipe B supplies water?

   A. 125       C. 360       E. 575
   B. 320       D. 480

26. What is the ratio of 3 to 8 expressed as a decimal?

   A. 0.125       C. 0.375       E. 1
   B. 0.25       D. 0.50

27. If the ratio of 3 to 4 is the same as the ratio of 15 to $x$, find $x$.

   A. 5       C. 15       E. 25
   B. 10       D. 20

28. Annika can solve 10 math problems in 30 minutes. At this rate, how many math problems can she solve in 48 minutes?

   A. 8       C. 32       E. 56
   B. 16       D. 46

29. Seung can walk up 6 flights of stairs in 4 minutes. At this rate, how many flights of stairs could he walk up in 18 minutes?

A. 4      C. 14      E. 27
B. 10     D. 20

30. If 4 candy bars cost $1.04, how much should 6 candy bars cost?

A. $0.96   C. $1.56   E. $2.06
B. $1.25   D. $1.85

31. If Baby Andrew takes 8 steps to walk 2 yards, how many steps will he take to walk 5 yards?

A. 5      C. 15      E. 25
B. 10     D. 20

32. If a 40-inch stick is divided in a $3:5$ ratio, how long, in inches, is the shorter piece?

A. 5      C. 15      E. 25
B. 10     D. 20

33. Orville claims that 3 bags of his popcorn will yield 28 ounces when popped. If this is the case, how many ounces will 5 bags of his popcorn yield when popped?

A. 23        C. $54\frac{1}{2}$   E. $64\frac{2}{3}$
B. $46\frac{2}{3}$   D. 64

34. In a poll of 1,000 people, 420 said they would vote for Mason. Based on this poll, how many people would be expected to vote for Mason if 60,000,000 people actually vote?

A. 25,200,000   C. 26,000,000   E. 26,500,000
B. 25,500,000   D. 26,200,000

35. In 4 days, a worm grew from 5 centimeters to 12 centimeters. At this rate, how long, in centimeters, will the worm be in another 6 days?

A. 21      C. 22.25   E. 23
B. 22      D. 22.5

36. Elan can mow 3 lawns in 85 minutes. At this rate, how long would he need to mow 5 lawns?

A. 140 minutes, 20 seconds
B. 141 minutes
C. 141 minutes, 40 seconds
D. 142 minutes
E. 142 minutes, 50 seconds

37. Sarah does $\frac{1}{5}$ of a job in 6 minutes. At this rate, what fraction of the job will she do in 10 minutes?

A. $\frac{1}{4}$   C. $\frac{1}{2}$   E. $\frac{3}{2}$
B. $\frac{1}{3}$   D. $\frac{3}{4}$

38. A snapshot measures $2\frac{1}{2}$ inches by $1\frac{7}{8}$ inches. If it is enlarged so that the longer dimension is 4 inches, what is the length, in inches, of the enlarged shorter dimension?

A. $2\frac{1}{2}$   C. $3\frac{3}{8}$   E. 5
B. 3          D. 4

39. Three of the men's white handkerchiefs cost $2.29. How much will a dozen of those handkerchiefs cost?

A. $27.48   C. $9.16   E. $4.58
B. $13.74   D. $6.87

40. A certain pole casts a 24 foot long shadow. At the same time another pole that is 3 feet high casts a 4 foot long shadow. How high, in feet, is the first pole, given that the heights and shadows are in proportion?

A. 18      C. 20      E. 24
B. 19      D. 21

41. If a drawing is scaled $\frac{1}{8}$ inch to the foot, what is the actual length, in feet, represented by $3\frac{1}{2}$ inches on the drawing?

A. 3.5     C. 21      E. 120
B. 7       D. 28

42. Aluminum bronze consists of copper and aluminum, usually in the ratio of $10:1$ by weight. If an object made of this alloy weighs 77 pounds, how many pounds of aluminum does it contain?

A. 0.7     C. 7.7     E. 77.0
B. 7.0     D. 70.7

43. It costs 31 cents per square foot to lay vinyl flooring. How much will it cost to lay 180 square feet of flooring?

A. $16.20   C. $55.80   E. $180.00
B. $18.60   D. $62.00

44. If Tuvak earns $352 in 16 days, how much will he earn in 117 days?

    A. $3,050      C. $2,285      E. $1,170
    B. $2,574      D. $2,080

45. Assuming that on a blueprint $\frac{1}{8}$ inch equals 12 inches of actual length, what is the actual length, in inches, of a steel bar represented on the blueprint by a line $3\frac{3}{4}$ inches long?

    A. $3\frac{3}{4}$      C. 36      E. 450
    B. 30         D. 360

46. Blake, James, and Staunton invested $9,000, $7,000, and $6,000, respectively. Their profits were to be divided according to the ratio of their investments. If James uses his share of the firm's profit of $825 to pay a personal debt of $230, how much will he have left?

    A. $30.50      C. $34.50      E. $37.50
    B. $32.50      D. $36.50

47. If on a road map $1\frac{5}{8}$ inches represents 10 miles, how many miles does 2.25 inches represent?

    A. $\frac{180}{13}$ miles   C. $\frac{57}{4}$ miles   E. 3 miles
    B. $\frac{53}{4}$ miles     D. $\frac{27}{2}$ miles

48. Jake and Jessie are standing next to each other in the sun. If Jake's shadow is 48 inches long, and he is 72 inches tall, how long is Jessie's shadow, in inches, if she is 66 inches tall?

    A. 42      C. 44      E. 46
    B. 43      D. 45

49. A blueprint allows 1 inch for every 12 feet. At that rate, 7 inches represents how many yards?

    A. $\frac{28}{3}$   C. 84      E. 336
    B. 28        D. 252

50. A bug crawls clockwise around the outside rim of a clock from the 12 to the 4 and travels 7 inches. If a second bug crawls around the outside rim from the 6 to the 11, in the same direction, how many inches did the bug travel?

    A. 7.75      C. 8.25      E. 8.75
    B. 8         D. 8.5

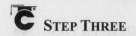 

# Exponents and Radicals

## Powers and Exponents

### Powers of Numbers

A **power** of a number indicates repeated multiplication. For example, "3 to the fifth power" means $3 \cdot 3 \cdot 3 \cdot 3 \cdot 3$, which equals 243. Therefore, 3 raised to the fifth power is 243.

*Examples:*

1. 2 to the second power $= 2 \cdot 2 = 4$.

2. 2 to the third power $= 2 \cdot 2 \cdot 2 = 8$.

3. 2 to the fourth power $= 2 \cdot 2 \cdot 2 \cdot 2 = 16$.

4. 3 to the second power $= 3 \cdot 3 = 9$.

5. 3 to the third power $= 3 \cdot 3 \cdot 3 = 27$.

The second power of a number is also called the square of the number. This refers to a square with sides equal in length to the number; the square of the number is equal to the area of the aforementioned square.

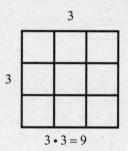

$$3 \cdot 3 = 9$$

The third power of a number is also called the cube of the number, which refers to a cube with sides equal in length to the number; the cube of the number is equal to the volume of the cube with sides equal in length to that number.

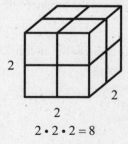

$$2 \cdot 2 \cdot 2 = 8$$

Beyond the square and the cube, powers are referred to by their numerical names, e.g., fourth, fifth, sixth, and so on.

## Exponential Notation

The notation system for designating the power of a number is a superscript following the number. The number being multiplied is the **base,** and the superscript is the **exponent**. The exponent indicates the operation of repeated multiplication.

*Examples:*

1. The third power of 2 is written as $2^3$: base $\rightarrow 2^{3 \ \leftarrow \text{exponent}} = 2 \cdot 2 \cdot 2$.

2. The fifth power of 2 is written as $3^5$: base $\rightarrow 3^{5 \ \leftarrow \text{exponent}} = 3 \cdot 3 \cdot 3 \cdot 3 \cdot 3$.

A base without an exponent is unchanged and represents the *first power* of the number. Since $x^1 = x$, the exponent 1 is not explicitly noted.

*Examples:*

1. $2^1 = 2$
2. $1,000^1 = 1,000$

---

## Operations Involving Exponents

There are special rules that apply to operations involving exponents. When you begin working with radicals (fractional exponents) and algebraic expressions, these same rules will apply.

### Multiplication Involving Exponents

The **product rule** is used to multiply two identical bases with similar or different exponents. To multiply powers of the same base, add the exponents: $x^m \cdot x^n = x^{m+n}$. To better understand this rule, explicitly write out the multiplication indicated by the exponents.

*Example:*

$$2^2 \cdot 2^3 = 2^{2+3} = 2^5 = (2 \cdot 2)(2 \cdot 2 \cdot 2)$$

> ➢ Writing out the expression and using the product rule give you the same result, but it is much faster to apply the latter.

Therefore, the product rule provides an easy shortcut for multiplying identical bases with exponents.

*Examples:*

1. $3^2 \cdot 3^5 = 3^{(2+5)} = 3^7$
2. $5^2 \cdot 5^3 \cdot 5^5 = 5^{(2+3+5)} = 5^{10}$
3. $x^3 \cdot x^4 = x^{(3+4)} = x^7$
4. $y^7 \cdot y^2 \cdot y^4 = y^{(7+2+4)} = y^{13}$

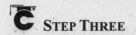 

Notice that each of these examples has only one base. The product rule does NOT apply to terms with different bases.

*Example:*

$2^4 \cdot 3^4 = ?$

> The product rule cannot be used since 2 and 3 are not equal bases. You must explicitly multiply all of the numbers: $2^4 \cdot 3^4 = (2 \cdot 2 \cdot 2 \cdot 2)(3 \cdot 3 \cdot 3 \cdot 3 \cdot) = 16 \cdot 81 = 1,296$.

Finally, the product rule does NOT apply to addition or subtraction of bases with exponents, even if the bases are identical.

*Example:*

$2^2 + 2^3 \neq 2^5$, since $2^2 + 2^3 = (2 \cdot 2) + (2 \cdot 2 \cdot 2) = 4 + 8 = 12$ and $2^5 = 2 \cdot 2 \cdot 2 \cdot 2 \cdot 2 = 32$.

### Division Involving Exponents

The **quotient rule** is used for division involving identical bases with exponents. When dividing similar bases, subtract the exponent in the denominator from the exponent in the numerator: $\frac{x^m}{x^n} = x^{m-n}$. As with the product rule, the quotient rule can be verified by explicitly carrying out the indicated operations, as illustrated in the first of the following examples.

*Examples:*

1. $\frac{2^5}{2^3} = 2^{(5-3)} = 2^2$

> Writing out the expression and using the quotient rule give you the same result:
> $\frac{2^5}{2^3} = \frac{2 \cdot 2 \cdot 2 \cdot 2 \cdot 2}{2 \cdot 2 \cdot 2} = \frac{32}{8} = 4 = 2^2$.

2. $\frac{5^{10}}{5^9} = 5^{(10-9)} = 5^1 = 5$

3. $\frac{x^8}{x^6} = x^{(8-6)} = x^2$

4. $\frac{y^3}{y^2} = y^{(3-2)} = y^1 = y$

An **exponent of zero** results whenever a quantity is divided into itself. Since a quantity divided into itself is equal to 1, any base (except zero) with an exponent of zero is also equal to 1: $x^0 = 1$ if $x \neq 0$. $0^0$ is an undefined operation in math.

*Examples:*

1. $\frac{5^3}{5^3} = 5^{(3-3)} = 5^0 = 1$

2. $\frac{x^{12}}{x^{12}} = x^{(12-12)} = x^0 = 1$

### Raising a Power to a Power

The **power rule** is used when a power of a number is raised to another power. This is done by multiplying the exponents together: $(x^m)^n = x^{mn}$. Again, we can prove the validity of this shortcut by explicitly carrying out the indicated multiplications.

*Examples:*

1. $(2^2)^3 = 2^{(2 \cdot 3)} = 2^6$

   ➢ Writing out the expression and using the power rule give you the same result:
   $(2^2)^3 = (2 \cdot 2)^3 = 4^3 = 4 \cdot 4 \cdot 4 = 64 = 2^6$.

2. $(x^3)^4 = x^{(3 \cdot 4)} = x^{12}$

### Raising a Product to a Power

The **product power rule** is used when a product with exponents is raised to a power. The exponent outside the parentheses governs all the factors inside the parentheses. When raising a product to a power, first multiply the exponent on the outside by each exponent on the inside: $(x^m y^p)^n = x^{mn} \cdot y^{pn}$.

*Examples:*

1. $(2 \cdot 3)^2 = 2^2 \cdot 3^2 = 4 \cdot 9 = 36$

   ➢ Writing out the expression and using the product power rule give you the same result: $(2 \cdot 3)^2 = (6)^2 = 36$.

2. $(2^2 \cdot 3^3)^2 = 2^{(2 \cdot 2)} \cdot 3^{(3 \cdot 2)} = (2^4)(3^6) = (16)(729) = 11,664$

3. $(x^2 \cdot y^3)^4 = x^{(2 \cdot 4)} \cdot y^{(3 \cdot 4)} = x^8 y^{12}$

### Raising a Quotient to a Power

The **quotient power rule** is used when a quotient with exponents is raised to a power. It is essentially the same as the previous rule for determining the power of a product. The exponent outside the parentheses governs all the factors inside the parentheses. Determine the power of a quotient by multiplying the exponent on the outside by each exponent on the inside: $\left(\frac{x^m}{y^p}\right)^n = \frac{x^{mn}}{y^{pn}}$.

*Examples:*

1. $\left(\frac{2}{3}\right)^3 = \frac{2^3}{3^3} = \frac{8}{27}$

   ➢ Writing out the expression and using the quotient power rule give you the same result: $\left(\frac{2}{3}\right)^3 = \frac{2}{3} \cdot \frac{2}{3} \cdot \frac{2}{3} = \frac{2 \cdot 2 \cdot 2}{3 \cdot 3 \cdot 3} = \frac{8}{27}$.

2. $\left(\frac{1^2}{3^3}\right)^2 = \frac{1^{(2 \cdot 2)}}{3^{(3 \cdot 2)}} = \frac{1^4}{3^6} = \frac{1}{729}$

3. $\left(\frac{x^2}{y^3}\right)^2 = \frac{x^{(2 \cdot 2)}}{y^{(3 \cdot 2)}} = \frac{x^4}{y^6}$

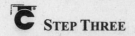 

## Negative Exponents

**Negative exponents** do not signify negative numbers. Instead, they signify fractions. Specifically, a negative exponent indicates the power of the **reciprocal** of the base: $x^{-n} = \frac{1}{x^n}$.

*Examples:*

1. $\frac{2^2}{2^3} = 2^{(2-3)} = 2^{-1} = \frac{1}{2^1} = \frac{1}{2}$

2. $\frac{2^2}{2^3} = \frac{2 \cdot 2}{2 \cdot 2 \cdot 2} = \frac{4}{8} = \frac{1}{2}$

3. $3^{-2} = (\frac{1}{3})^2 = \frac{1}{9}$

4. $x^{-3} = (\frac{1}{x})^3 = \frac{1}{x^3}$

## Rational (Fractional) Exponents

Exponents are not restricted to integer values. **Rational (fractional) exponents** are also possible. Later in this chapter, we will use rational exponents when working with radicals. Rational exponents also appear in algebraic expressions, functions, and equations. The rules for working with rational exponents are the same as those for integer exponents.

*Examples:*

1. $2^{\frac{1}{2}} \cdot 2^{\frac{1}{2}} = 2^1 = 2$

2. $(x^2 y^4)^{\frac{1}{4}} = x^{\frac{1}{2}} y$

## Working with Exponents

Complex expressions may require the application of two or more operations involving exponents. No matter how complex an item gets, it can be solved by a series of simple steps following the five rules that are explained above for working with exponents. Remember to follow the rules for order of operations. Also, be careful when negative signs are involved.

*Examples:*

1. $(2^3 \cdot 3^2)^2 = 2^{3 \cdot 2} \cdot 3^{2 \cdot 2} = 2^6 \cdot 3^4$

2. $(\frac{3^3 \cdot 5^5}{3^2 \cdot 5^2})^2 = (3^{3-2} \cdot 5^{5-2})^2 = (3^1 \cdot 5^3)^2 = 3^2 \cdot 5^6$

3. $(\frac{x^2 \cdot y^3}{x \cdot y^2})^2 = (x^{2-1} \cdot y^{3-2})^2 = (x \cdot y)^2 = x^2 y^2$

4. $(-3)^3 (-2)^6 = (-27)(64) = -1,728$

5. $-2^4 (-3)^2 = -(2^4)(-3)^2 = -(16)(9) = -144$

These rules for working with exponents provide simple shortcuts, as verified by explicitly executing all indicated operations. When you begin to manipulate algebraic expressions, not only will these same shortcuts apply, but they will become indispensable.

---

**SUMMARY OF OPERATIONS INVOLVING EXPONENTS**

$$x^1 = x; \; x^0 = 1$$

$$\text{Product Rule: } x^m \cdot x^n = x^{m+n}$$

$$\text{Quotient Rule: } \frac{x^m}{x^n} = x^{m-n}$$

$$\text{Power Rule: } (x^m)^n = x^{m \cdot n}$$

$$\text{Product Power Rule: } (x^m \cdot y^p)^n = x^{mn} \cdot y^{pn}$$

$$\text{Quotient Power Rule: } \left(\frac{x^m}{y^p}\right)^n = \frac{x^{mn}}{y^{pn}}$$

$$\text{Negative Exponents: } x^{-n} = \left(\frac{1}{x}\right)^n = \frac{1}{x^n}$$

## Roots and Radicals

### Roots of Numbers

A **square root** of a number $x$ is a solution to the equation $\sqrt{x} = b$, in which $x = b^2$. When you perform the multiplication indicated by an exponent, you are in effect answering the question, "What do I get when I multiply this number by itself so many times?" Now ask the opposite question, "What number, when multiplied by itself so many times, will give me a certain value?" For example, when you raise 2 to the third power, you find out that $2^3 = 8$. Now, ask the question in the other direction. What number, when raised to the third, is equal to 8?

This reverse process is called "finding the root of a number." Why roots? Look at the following diagram; since $2^6 = 64$, the sixth root of 64 is 2. The picture resembles plant roots.

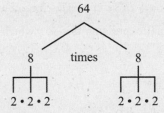

Of course, we rarely deal with sixth roots. Mostly, we deal with two roots: $2 \cdot 2 = 4$, so the second or **square root** of 4 is 2; and occasionally with numbers having three roots: $2 \cdot 2 \cdot 2 = 8$, so the third or **cube root** of 8 is 2.

The operation of taking a square root of a number is signaled by the **radical** sign, $\sqrt{\phantom{x}}$. **Radical** comes from the Latin word "rad," which means "root."

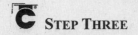 

*Examples:*

1. $\sqrt{1} = 1$  
2. $\sqrt{4} = 2$  
3. $\sqrt{9} = 3$  
4. $\sqrt{16} = 4$  
5. $\sqrt{25} = 5$  
6. $\sqrt{36} = 6$  
7. $\sqrt{49} = 7$  
8. $\sqrt{64} = 8$  
9. $\sqrt{81} = 9$  
10. $\sqrt{100} = 10$  
11. $\sqrt{121} = 11$  
12. $\sqrt{144} = 12$  

The symbol $\sqrt{\phantom{x}}$ always denotes a positive number. Later, when we get to the topic of quadratic equations in algebra, we will run across a "$\pm$" sign preceding the radical; this signifies both the positive and negative values of the root.

If a radical sign is preceded by a superscript number, then the number, or **index**, indicates a root other than the square root. In the notation $\sqrt[n]{a}$, $n$ is the root or index, $\sqrt{\phantom{x}}$ is the radical, and $a$ is the radicand.

*Examples:*

1. $\sqrt[3]{8} = 2 \Rightarrow$ The cube root of 8 is 2.
2. $\sqrt[4]{81} = 3 \Rightarrow$ The fourth root of 81 is 3.
3. $\sqrt[6]{64} = 2 \Rightarrow$ The sixth root of 64 is 2.

### Determining Square Roots

If a number is a perfect square (e.g., 4, 9, 16, etc.), then extracting its square root is easy. Simply use the values given in the examples of square roots above. Not every number, however, has an exact square root. In such cases, you can do one of two things. First, you may be able to find in the number a factor that does have an exact square root and extract that factor from under the radical sign.

*Examples:*

1. $\sqrt{125} = ?$

   ➢ 125 does not have a perfect square root. However, 25 has a perfect square and is a factor of 125, so factor 125 into 25 and 5: $\sqrt{125} = \sqrt{25 \cdot 5}$. Then, take the square root of 25, which is 5; $\sqrt{25} \cdot \sqrt{5} = 5 \cdot \sqrt{5}$. The final expression is $5\sqrt{5}$, which means 5 multiplied by the square root of 5: $\sqrt{125} = 5\sqrt{5}$.

2. $\sqrt{27} = \sqrt{9 \cdot 3} = \sqrt{9} \cdot \sqrt{3} = 3 \cdot \sqrt{3} = 3\sqrt{3}$

3. $\sqrt{32} = \sqrt{16 \cdot 2} = \sqrt{16} \cdot \sqrt{2} = 4 \cdot \sqrt{2} = 4\sqrt{2}$

4. $\sqrt{52} = \sqrt{4 \cdot 13} = \sqrt{4} \cdot \sqrt{13} = 2 \cdot \sqrt{13} = 2\sqrt{13}$

For the purposes of the exam, knowledge of the approximate values for common square roots may save valuable test time. For example, it is useful to know that $\sqrt{2}$ is approximately 1.4 and that $\sqrt{3}$ is approximately 1.7. Other values can be approximated by using ranges; e.g., $\sqrt{7}$ must be between 2 and 3 ($\sqrt{4} < \sqrt{7} < \sqrt{9}$). Since 7 is closer to 9 than to 4, a good approximation of $\sqrt{7}$ is 2.6 to 2.7.

## Operations Involving Radicals
## (Rational Exponents)

Radicals can be rewritten using **rational (fractional) exponents**. This simplifies the process of working with radicals, since all of the rules for exponents apply to fractional exponents and thus to radicals. The relationship between a rational exponent and the radical representing a given root is: $\sqrt[n]{x^m} = x^{\frac{m}{n}}$, where $m$ and $n$ are integers, and $n \neq 0$.

*Examples:*

1. $\sqrt{4} = 4^{\frac{1}{2}} = 2$
2. $\sqrt[3]{8} = 8^{\frac{1}{3}} = 2$

When you multiply a square root by itself, the result is the radicand: $(\sqrt{x})(\sqrt{x}) = x$. This can be explained using the product rule for exponents as illustrated in the following example.

*Example:*

$$(\sqrt{2})(\sqrt{2}) = 2^{\frac{1}{2}} \cdot 2^{\frac{1}{2}} = 2^1 = 2$$

The power rules for working with exponents are the ones you are most likely to use when working with radicals. The following example illustrates how the product power rule applies to radicals.

*Example:*

$$\sqrt{125} = 125^{\frac{1}{2}} = (25 \cdot 5)^{\frac{1}{2}} = 25^{\frac{1}{2}} \cdot 5^{\frac{1}{2}} = (\sqrt{125})(\sqrt{5}) = 5\sqrt{5}$$

Notice that this is just the process of extracting a square root by finding a factor, but what makes this process work is the product power rule of exponents. The quotient power rule is used in the following example.

*Example:*

$$\sqrt{\frac{4}{9}} = \left(\frac{4}{9}\right)^{\frac{1}{2}} = \frac{4^{\frac{1}{2}}}{9^{\frac{1}{2}}} = \frac{\sqrt{4}}{\sqrt{9}} = \frac{2}{3}$$

Importantly, since radicals are fractional exponents and obey the rules for exponents, you cannot simply add radicals. $\sqrt{4} + \sqrt{9}$ is not equal to $\sqrt{13}$, and you can prove this by taking the square root of 4, which is 2, and the square root of 9, which is 3. $2+3$ is 5, which does not equal $\sqrt{13}$.

### OPERATIONS INVOLVING RADICALS (RATIONAL EXPONENTS)

*Product Rule:* $\sqrt{x} \cdot \sqrt{x} = x^{\frac{1}{2}} x^{\frac{1}{2}} = x^1 = x$

*Quotient Rule:* $\dfrac{\sqrt[m]{x}}{\sqrt[n]{x}} = \dfrac{x^{\frac{1}{m}}}{x^{\frac{1}{n}}} = x^{(\frac{1}{m} - \frac{1}{n})}$

*Power Rule:* $(\sqrt[m]{x})^n = (x^{\frac{1}{m}})^n = x^{\frac{n}{m}}$

*Product Power Rule:* $\sqrt[m]{x^n y^p} = (x^n y^p)^{\frac{1}{m}} = x^{\frac{n}{m}} y^{\frac{p}{m}} = \sqrt[m]{x^n} \cdot \sqrt[m]{y^p}$

*Quotient Power Rule:* $\sqrt[m]{\dfrac{x^n}{y^p}} = \left(\dfrac{x^n}{y^p}\right)^{\frac{1}{m}} = \dfrac{x^{\frac{n}{m}}}{y^{\frac{p}{m}}} = \dfrac{\sqrt[m]{x^n}}{\sqrt[m]{y^p}}$

# Exponents and Radicals

**DIRECTIONS:** Choose the correct answer to each of the following items. Answers are on page 953.

1. What is the third power of 3?
   A. 1     C. 9     E. 27
   B. 3     D. 15

2. What is the fourth power of 2?
   A. 2     C. 8     E. 32
   B. 4     D. 16

3. What is the first power of 1,000,000?
   A. 0     C. 1     E. 1,000,000
   B. $\frac{1}{1,000,000}$     D. 10

4. $100^0 = ?$
   A. 0     C. 10     E. 100,000
   B. 1     D. 100

5. $2^3 \cdot 2^2 = ?$
   A. 6     C. $2^5$     E. $4^6$
   B. 8     D. $2^6$

6. $3^{10} \cdot 10^3 = ?$
   I. $30^{30}$
   II. $300 \cdot 1,000$
   III. $30 + 30$
   A. I only     D. II and III only
   B. II only     E. Neither I, II, nor III
   C. I and III only

7. $5^4 \cdot 5^9 = ?$
   A. $25^{36}$     C. $5^{13}$     E. 5
   B. $5^{36}$     D. $5^5$

8. $2^3 \cdot 2^4 \cdot 2^5 = ?$
   A. $2^{12}$     C. $8^{12}$     E. $8^{60}$
   B. $2^{60}$     D. $4^{60}$

9. $(2+3)^{20} = ?$
   A. $5^{20}$     C. $6^{20}$     E. $20^6$
   B. $2^{20} + 3^{20}$     D. $20^5$

10. $\frac{2^5}{2^3} = ?$
    A. $2^2$     C. $2^8$     E. $2^{15}$
    B. $4^4$     D. $4^8$

11. $\frac{3^{10}}{3^8} = ?$
    A. 3     C. $9^2$     E. $3^{80}$
    B. $3^2$     D. $3^{18}$

12. $\frac{5^2}{5^2} = ?$
    I. 0
    II. 1
    III. $5^0$
    A. I and II only     D. III only
    B. I and III only     E. Neither I, II, nor III
    C. II and III only

13. $\frac{3^2}{3^3} = ?$
    I. $3^{-1}$
    II. $\frac{1}{3}$
    III. $-1$
    A. I only     D. I and III only
    B. II only     E. I, II, and III
    C. I and II only

14. $(2^2)^3 = ?$
    A. $2^5$     C. $4^5$     E. $6^5$
    B. $2^6$     D. $4^6$

15. $(5^2)^6 = ?$
    A. $5^8$     C. $10^4$     E. $10^{12}$
    B. $5^{12}$     D. $10^8$

16. $(7^7)^7 = ?$

    A. 21     C. $7^{49}$     E. $49^{49}$
    B. $7^{14}$     D. $21^7$

17. $(3 \cdot 2)^2 = ?$

    I. 36
    II. $3 \cdot 3 \cdot 2 \cdot 2$
    III. $3^2 \cdot 2^2$

    A. I only            D. I and III only
    B. II only          E. I, II, and III
    C. III only

18. $(5 \cdot 3)^2 = ?$

    I. $15^2$
    II. $5^2 \cdot 3^2$
    III. $8^2$

    A. I only            D. I and II only
    B. II only          E. I, II, and III
    C. III only

19. $(\frac{8}{3})^2 = ?$

    I. $\frac{64}{9}$
    II. $\frac{8^2}{3^2}$
    III. $11^2$

    A. I only            D. I and III only
    B. II only          E. I, II, and III
    C. I and II only

20. $(\frac{4}{9})^2 = ?$

    A. $\frac{2}{3}$     C. $\frac{16}{81}$     E. $\frac{4}{9^2}$
    B. $\frac{4}{9}$     D. $\frac{4^2}{9}$

21. $(2 \cdot 2^2 \cdot 2^3)^2 = ?$

    A. $2^8$     C. $2^{12}$     E. $2^{18}$
    B. $2^{10}$     D. $2^{16}$

22. $(\frac{2^4 \cdot 5^4}{2^2 \cdot 5^2}) = ?$

    A. $2^4 \cdot 5^4$     C. $4^6$     E. 24
    B. $2^6 \cdot 2^6$     D. $4^8$

23. $\frac{3^6 \cdot 5^3 \cdot 7^9}{3^4 \cdot 5^3 \cdot 7^8} = ?$

    A. $3^2 \cdot 5 \cdot 7$     C. $3 \cdot 5 \cdot 7$     E. $3^2 \cdot 7$
    B. $3^2 \cdot 5 \cdot 7^2$     D. $3^2 \cdot 5$

24. $(\frac{5^{12} \cdot 7^5}{5^{11} \cdot 7^5})^2 = ?$

    A. 25     C. $5^7$     E. $7^5$
    B. 49     D. $5^{11}$

25. $(\frac{12^{12} \cdot 11^{11} \cdot 10^{10}}{12^{12} \cdot 11^{11} \cdot 10^9})^2 = ?$

    A. 0     C. 10     E. 1,000
    B. 1     D. 100

26. $\sqrt{36} = ?$

    I. 6
    II. $-6$
    III. $3\sqrt{3}$

    A. I only            D. II and III only
    B. I and II only     E. I, II, and III
    C. I and III only

27. $\sqrt{81} + \sqrt{4} = ?$

    I. $\sqrt{85}$
    II. $\sqrt{9} + \sqrt{2}$
    III. 11

    A. I only            D. I and II only
    B. II only          E. II and III only
    C. III only

28. $\sqrt{27} = ?$

    A. 3     C. $3\sqrt{9}$     E. 81
    B. $3\sqrt{3}$     D. 27

29. $\sqrt{52} = ?$

    A. $\sqrt{5} + \sqrt{2}$     C. $2\sqrt{13}$     E. $13^2$
    B. 7     D. $13\sqrt{4}$

30. $\sqrt{\frac{9}{4}} = ?$

    A. $\frac{\sqrt{3}}{2}$     C. $\frac{3}{2}$     E. $\sqrt{5}$
    B. $\frac{3}{\sqrt{2}}$     D. 5

31. $\frac{\sqrt{81}}{\sqrt{27}} = ?$

    A. $\sqrt{3}$     C. $3\sqrt{3}$     E. $9\sqrt{3}$
    B. 3     D. 9

32. $2\sqrt{2}$ is most nearly equal to which of the following?

    A. 2.8     C. 4     E. 12
    B. 3.4     D. 7

33. $\sqrt{27}$ is approximately equal to which of the following?

    A. 3     C. 4.5     E. 9
    B. 4     D. 5.1

34. $\sqrt{12}$ is approximately equal to which of the following?

    A. 2     C. 4     E. 8
    B. 3.4     D. 6

35. $\sqrt{23}$ is approximately equal to which of the following?

    A. 4     C. 6     E. 8
    B. 4.8     D. 7

36. $\sqrt{45}$ is approximately equal to which of the following?

    A. 5     C. 6.6     E. 7.5
    B. 5.5     D. 7

37. $(7+\sqrt{5})(3-\sqrt{5}) = ?$

    A. $4+4\sqrt{5}$     C. $16+4\sqrt{5}$     E. 16
    B. $4-\sqrt{5}$     D. $16-4\sqrt{5}$

38. $(5-\sqrt{2})(3-\sqrt{2}) = ?$

    A. $17+\sqrt{2}$     C. $17+\sqrt{8}$     E. 25
    B. $17-8\sqrt{2}$     D. $17+8\sqrt{2}$

39. $(3+\sqrt{1})(2-\sqrt{3}) = ?$

    A. $-1$     C. $-1+\sqrt{3}$     E. $1+\sqrt{3}$
    B. $-1-\sqrt{3}$     D. 1

40. $\sqrt{2} \cdot 2\sqrt{3} = ?$

    A. $-2\sqrt{6}$     C. 2     E. $2\sqrt{6}$
    B. $-\sqrt{6}$     D. $\sqrt{6}$

41. $\sqrt{8}+\sqrt{50} = ?$

    A. $-7\sqrt{2}$     C. $\sqrt{2}$     E. 7
    B. $-\sqrt{2}$     D. $7\sqrt{2}$

42. $\sqrt{3^2+5^2} = ?$

    A. 6     C. 7     E. 8
    B. $\sqrt{34}$     D. $\sqrt{51}$

43. $\sqrt{(2\sqrt{3})^2+2^2} = ?$

    A. 1     C. 3     E. 5
    B. 2     D. 4

44. Is $(5+\sqrt{2})(5-\sqrt{2})$ rational?

    A. Yes
    B. No
    C. Cannot be determined from the given information

45. Is $\frac{(5+\sqrt{2})}{(5-\sqrt{2})}$ rational?

    A. Yes
    B. No
    C. Cannot be determined from the given information

46. $\frac{\sqrt{2}}{2}(\sqrt{6}+\frac{\sqrt{2}}{2}) = ?$

    A. $\sqrt{3}+\frac{1}{2}$     C. $\sqrt{6}+1$     E. $\sqrt{6}+2$
    B. $\frac{\sqrt{3}}{2}$     D. $2\sqrt{3}+\frac{1}{2}$

47. $\frac{15\sqrt{96}}{5\sqrt{2}} = ?$

    A. $7\sqrt{3}$     C. $11\sqrt{3}$     E. $40\sqrt{3}$
    B. $7\sqrt{12}$     D. $12\sqrt{3}$

48. Which of the following radicals is a perfect square?

    A. $\sqrt{0.4}$     C. $\sqrt{0.09}$     E. $\sqrt{0.025}$
    B. $\sqrt{0.9}$     D. $\sqrt{0.02}$

49. $(-\frac{1}{3})^4 = ?$

    A. $-\frac{1}{81}$     C. $-\frac{1}{12}$     E. $-\frac{1}{64}$
    B. $\frac{1}{81}$     D. $\frac{1}{12}$

50. $-4^4 = ?$

    A. $-256$     C. $-16$     E. $-8$
    B. 256     D. 16

51. $\sqrt[12]{x^6} = ?$

    A. $x^6$     C. $x^2$     E. $x^{-2}$

    B. $x^{-6}$     D. $x^{\frac{1}{2}}$

52. $\sqrt[k]{6^{2km}}$ MUST be a positive integer if:

    A. $k$ is a positive integer
    B. $k$ is a multiple of 3
    C. $k < 0$
    D. $m$ is a non-negative common fraction
    E. $m$ is a non-negative integer

53. If $n$ is an integer and $0.012345 \times 10^n$ is greater than 10,000, what is the least possible value of $n$?

    A. 2     C. 4     E. 6
    B. 3     D. 5

# Algebraic Operations

Algebra is the branch of mathematics that uses letter symbols to represent numbers. The letter symbols are, in essence, placeholders. They function somewhat like "someone" or "somewhere." For example, in the sentence "Someone took the book and put it somewhere," neither the identity of the person in question nor the new location of the book is known. We can rewrite this sentence in algebraic terms: "$x$ put the book in $y$ place." The identity of $x$ is unknown, and the new location of the book is unknown. It is for this reason that letter symbols in algebra are often referred to as "unknowns."

Algebra, like English, is a language, and for making certain statements, algebra is much better than English. For example, the English statement "There is a number such that, when you add 3 to it, the result is 8" can be rendered more easily in algebraic notation: $x + 3 = 8$. In fact, learning the rules of algebra is really very much like learning the grammar of any language. Keeping this analogy between algebra and English in mind, let's begin by studying the components of the algebraic language.

## Elements of Algebra

### *Algebraic Terms*

The basic unit of the English language is the word. The basic unit of algebra is the **term**. In English, a word consists of one or more letters. In algebra, a term consists of one or more letters or numbers. For example, $x$, $2z$, $xy$, $N$, $2$, $\sqrt{7}$, and $\pi$ are all algebraic terms. A term can be a product, quotient, or single symbol.

In English, a word may have a root, a prefix, a suffix, an ending, and so on. In algebra, a term may have a coefficient, an exponent, and a sign, etc. Of course, algebraic terms also include a variable, also referred to as the base.

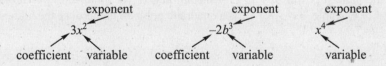

Just as with numbers, when the sign of an algebraic term is positive, the "+" is not written; e.g., $3x$ is equivalent to $+3x$. Additionally, when the coefficient is 1, it is understood to be included and is not written out; e.g., $x$ rather than $1x$.

The elements in an algebraic term are all joined by the operation of multiplication. The coefficient and its sign are multiplied by the variable. For example: $-3x = (-3)(x)$; $5a = (+5)(a)$; and $\frac{1}{2}N = (+\frac{1}{2})(N)$.

The exponent, as you have already learned, also indicates multiplication. Thus, $x^2$ means $x$ times $x$; $a^3$ means $a$ times $a$ times $a$; and $N^5$ means $N$ times $N$ times $N$ times $N$ times $N$. Be careful not to confuse the coefficient with the exponent. $3x$ means "$+3$ times $x$," while $x^3$ means "$x$ times $x$ times $x$." Of course, many terms have both a coefficient and an exponent. Thus, $3x^2$ means "$+3$ times $x$ times $x$," and $-5a^3$ means "$-5$ times $a$ times $a$ times $a$."

## Algebraic Expressions

In English, words are organized into phrases. In algebra, terms are grouped together in *expressions*. An expression is a collection of algebraic terms that are joined by addition, subtraction, or both.

*Examples:*

1. $x + y$
2. $-2x + 3y + z$
3. $3x^2 - 2y^2$
4. $x^2 + y^{20}$

A *rational expression* is a fraction containing algebraic terms. In other words, rational expressions are algebraic fractions.

*Examples:*

1. $\frac{1}{x}$
2. $\frac{x^2}{xy - y^2}$
3. $\frac{3 + \frac{1}{x}}{9 - \frac{1}{x^2}}$

Algebraic expressions are classified according to the number of terms the expression contains. A *monomial* is an algebraic expression with exactly one term. A *polynomial* is an algebraic expression with more than one term. A *binomial* is a polynomial with exactly two terms. A *trinomial* is a polynomial with exactly three terms.

The highest power of the variable term in any polynomial expression determines the degree of the polynomial. A *first degree* (or *linear*) *polynomial* has 1 as the highest power of its variable. For example, $y + 3$ is a linear polynomial because the highest power of $y$ is 1. A *second degree* (or *quadratic*) *polynomial* has 2 as the highest power of its variable. For example, $3x^2 - 8x - 3$ is a quadratic polynomial because the highest power of $x$ is 2.

## Algebraic Equations

In algebra, a complete sentence is called an equation. An equation asserts that two algebraic expressions are equal. Equations involving rational expressions are called *rational equations.*

*Examples:*

1. $2x + 4 = 3x - 2$
2. $\frac{y^2 - 5y}{y^2 - 4y - 5} = \frac{y}{y + 1}$

## *Adding and Subtracting Algebraic Terms*

Addition and subtraction are indicated in algebra, as they are in arithmetic, with the signs "+" and "−." In arithmetic, these operations combine the numbers into a third number. For example, the addition of 2 and 3 is equivalent to combining 2 and 3 to form the number 5: $2 + 4 = 5$.

In algebra, however, only *similar (like) terms* may be combined. Similar terms are terms with the same variables having the same exponent values. Coefficients do not factor into whether or not terms are similar.

*Examples:*

1. $3x^2$, $40x^2$, $-2x^2$, and $\sqrt{2}x^2$ are similar terms.

2. $xy$, $5xy$, $-23xy$, and $\pi xy$ are similar terms.

3. $10xyz$, $-xyz$, and $xyz$ are similar terms.

4. $3x$ and $3x^2$ are NOT similar terms.

5. $xy$ and $x^2y$ are NOT similar terms.

6. $xy$, $yz$, and $xz$ are NOT similar terms.

To simplify an algebraic expression, group similar terms and add/subtract the numerical coefficients of each group. Variables and exponents of combined similar terms remain unchanged.

*Examples:*

1. $x^2 + 2x^2 + 3x^2 = ?$

   ➤ All three terms are similar since each includes $x^2$. Combine the terms by adding the coefficients: $1 + 2 + 3 = 6$. Thus, the result is $6x^2$.

2. $y + 2x + 3y - x = ?$

   ➤ With two different types of terms, group the similar terms together: $(2x - x) + (y + 3y)$. Add the coefficients for each type of term. For the $x$ terms, the combined coefficient is $2 - 1 = 1$; for the $y$ terms, $1 + 3 = 4$. The result is $x + 4y$.

3. $x - 3x + 5x - 2x = (1 - 3 + 5 - 2)x = x$

4. $2x - y - 3x + 4y + 5x = (2x - 3x + 5x) + (4y - y) = 4x + 3y$

5. $5x^2 + 3x^3 - 2x^2 + 4x^3 = (5x^2 - 2x^2) + (3x^3 + 4x^3) = 3x^2 + 7x^3$

Notice that when you have combined all similar terms, it is not possible to carry the addition or subtraction any further.

## *Multiplying and Dividing Algebraic Terms*

Use the arithmetic *rules of exponents* to multiply or divide algebraic terms. Remember that $x^0 = 1$ when $x \neq 0$, and $x^1 = x$.

---

**OPERATIONS OF ALGEBRAIC TERMS**

$Product\ Rule$: $x^m \cdot x^n = x^{m+n}$

$ax^m \cdot bx^n = abx^{m+n}$

$Quotient\ Rule$: $\frac{x^m}{x^n} = x^{m-n}$

$Power\ Rule$: $(x^m)^n = x^{mn}$

$Product\ Power\ Rule$: $(x^m \cdot y^p)^n = x^{mn} \cdot y^{pn}$

$Quotient\ Power\ Rule$: $(\frac{x^m}{y^p})^n = \frac{x^{mn}}{y^{pn}}$

$Negative\ Exponents$: $x^{-n} = \frac{1}{x^n}$

*Examples:*

1. *Product Rule:*

    a. $(x^2)(x^3) = x^{(2+3)} = x^5$

    b. $(3x^2)(xy) = (3 \cdot 1)(x^2 \cdot xy) = 3 \cdot x^{(2+1)} \cdot y = 3x^3 y$

    c. $(2xyz)(3xy)(4yz) = (2 \cdot 3 \cdot 4)(xyz \cdot xy \cdot yz) = 24 \cdot x^{(1+1)} \cdot y^{(1+1+1)} \cdot z^{(1+1)} = 24x^2 y^3 z^2$

2. *Quotient Rule:*

    a. $\frac{x^3}{x^2} = x^{(3-2)} = x^1 = x$

    b. $\frac{2x^4 y^3}{x^2 z} = \frac{2}{1} \cdot \frac{x^4 y^3}{x^2 z} = 2 \cdot \frac{x^{(4-2)} y^3}{z} = \frac{2x^2 y^3}{z}$

3. *Power Rule:* $(x^2)^3 = x^{(2)(3)} = x^6$

4. *Product Power Rule:* $(x^2 y^3)^2 = x^{(2)(2)} y^{(3)(2)} = x^4 y^6$

5. *Quotient Power Rule:* $(\frac{x^2}{y^3})^2 = \frac{x^{(2)(2)}}{y^{(3)(2)}} = \frac{x^4}{y^6}$

---

## Operations of Algebraic Fractions

### Adding and Subtracting Algebraic Fractions

Adding and subtracting algebraic fractions, like adding and subtracting numerical fractions, require common denominators. If the denominators are the same, simply add/subtract the numerators: $\frac{a}{x} \pm \frac{b}{x} = \frac{a \pm b}{x}$.

*Examples:*

1. $\frac{5}{x} + \frac{3}{x} = \frac{5+3}{x} = \frac{8}{x}$

2. $\frac{2x}{y} - \frac{x}{y} = \frac{2x-x}{y} = \frac{x}{y}$

3. $\frac{a}{cd} + \frac{x}{cd} = \frac{a+x}{cd}$

To add or subtract algebraic fractions with unlike denominators, you must first find a common denominator. Usually, this can be accomplished by using the same method as with numerical fractions: $\frac{a}{x} \pm \frac{b}{y} = \frac{ay}{xy} \pm \frac{bx}{xy} = \frac{ay \pm bx}{xy}$.

*Example:*

$$\frac{2x}{y} + \frac{3y}{x} = \frac{2x}{y} \geq + \leq \frac{3y}{x} = \frac{2x^2 + 3y^2}{xy}$$

### Multiplying and Dividing Algebraic Fractions

To multiply algebraic fractions, follow the rule for multiplying numeric fractions. Multiply terms in the numerators to create a new numerator, and multiply terms in the denominator to create a new denominator: $\frac{a}{c} \bullet \frac{b}{d} = \frac{ab}{cd}$.

*Examples:*

1. $\frac{2}{x} \bullet \frac{3}{y} = \frac{6}{xy}$

2. $\frac{x^2 y^3}{z} \bullet \frac{x^3 y^2}{wz} = \frac{x^5 y^5}{wz^2}$

To divide algebraic fractions, follow the rule for dividing numeric fractions. Invert the divisor, or second fraction, and multiply: $\frac{a}{c} \div \frac{b}{d} = \frac{a}{c} \bullet \frac{d}{b} = \frac{ad}{cb}$.

*Examples:*

1. $\frac{2}{y} \div \frac{3}{x} = \frac{2}{y} \bullet \frac{x}{3} = \frac{2x}{3y}$

2. $\frac{2x^2}{y} \div \frac{y}{x} = \frac{2x^2}{y} \bullet \frac{x}{y} = \frac{2x^3}{y^2}$

## Multiplying Algebraic Expressions

A *polynomial* is an algebraic expression with one or more terms involving only the operations of addition, subtraction, and multiplication of variables. Polynomial means "many terms," although it is possible to get a monomial by adding two polynomials. A multiplication item such as $(x + y)(x + y)$ requires a special procedure. The fundamental rule for multiplying is that every term of one expression must be multiplied by every term of the other expression.

### Distributive Property

First, let's look at the case in which a polynomial is to be multiplied by a single term. One way of solving the item is to first add and then multiply. Alternatively, we can use the ***distributive property*** to multiply every term inside the parentheses by the term outside the parentheses, and then we can add the terms: $x(y + x) = xy + xz$. The result is the same regardless of the method used. The following example illustrates these two methods using real numbers.

*Example:*

$$2(3+4+5) = 2(12) = 24$$

➤ The distributive property returns the same result:

$$2(3+4+5) = (2 \cdot 3) + (2 \cdot 4) + (2 \cdot 5) = 6 + 8 + 10 = 24.$$

When working with algebraic expressions, use the distributive property, since you cannot add unlike terms. The following examples apply the distributive property to algebraic expressions.

*Examples:*

1. $x(y+z) = xy + xz$

2. $a(b+c+d) = ab + ac + ad$

To multiply two polynomials, either add the polynomials before multiplying them, or reverse the order of operations using the distributive property.

*Example:*

$$(2+3)(1+3+4) = (5)(8) = 40$$

➤ The distributive property returns the same result:

$$(2+3)(1+3+4) = (2 \cdot 1) + (2 \cdot 3) + (2 \cdot 4) + (3 \cdot 1) + (3 \cdot 3) + (3 \cdot 4) = 2 + 6 + 8 + 3 + 9 + 12 = 40.$$

**FOIL Method**

To multiply two binomials using the **FOIL method**, follow these steps for combining the binomial terms: (1) multiply the first terms, (2) multiply the outer terms, (3) multiply the inner terms, (4) multiply the last terms, and (5) combine like terms. The FOIL method is simply a mnemonic shortcut derived from the distributive property. The following diagram illustrates application of the FOIL method.

**MULTIPLYING TWO BINOMIALS**
**(FOIL: First, Outer, Inner, Last)**

$$(x+y)(x+y) = x^2 + xy + xy + y^2 = x^2 + 2xy + y^2$$

*Examples:*

1. $(x+y)(x+y) = ?$

➤ First: $(x)(x) = x^2$; Outer: $(x)(y) = xy$; Inner: $(y)(x) = xy$; Last: $(y)(y) = y^2$. Add: $x^2 + xy + xy + y^2 = x^2 + 2xy + y^2$.

2. $(x-y)(x-y) = ?$

➤ First: $(x)(x) = x^2$; Outer: $(x)(-y) = -xy$; Inner: $(-y)(x) = -xy$; Last: $(-y)(-y) = y^2$. Add: $x^2 - xy - xy + y^2 = x^2 - 2xy + y^2$.

Three situations, one in addition to the two illustrated in the previous examples, arise with such frequency that you should memorize the results to simplify the calculation.

---

**THREE COMMON MULTIPLICATIONS INVOLVING POLYNOMIALS**

1. $(x+y)^2 = (x+y)(x+y) = x^2 + 2xy + y^2$
2. $(x-y)^2 = (x-y)(x-y) = x^2 - 2xy + y^2$
3. $(x+y)(x-y) = x^2 - y^2$

---

You might be asked to multiply something more complex than two binomials. The process is tedious and time-consuming, but ultimately it is executed the same way.

*Example:*

$(x+y)^3 = ?$

➤ Apply the FOIL method to the first two binomials, then multiply the last binomial to the resultant trinomial of the first two binomials:

$$(x+y)^3 = (x+y)(x+y)(x+y)$$
$$= (x^2 + 2xy + y^2)(x+y)$$
$$= x(x^2) + x(2xy) + x(y^2) + y(x^2) + y(2xy) + y(y^2)$$
$$= x^3 + 2x^2y + xy^2 + x^2y + 2xy^2 + y^3$$
$$= x^3 + 3x^2y + 3xy^2 + y^3$$

## Factoring Algebraic Expressions

Although the term *factoring* intimidates many students, factoring is really nothing more than reverse multiplication. For example, if $(x+y)(x+y) = x^2 + 2xy + y^2$, then $x^2 + 2xy + y^2$ can be factored into $(x+y)(x+y)$. Fortunately, for the purposes of taking the test, any factoring you might need to do will fall into one of three categories.

### Finding a Common Factor

If all the terms of an algebraic expression contain a common factor, then that term can be factored out of the expression.

*Examples:*

1. $ab + ac + ad = a(b + c + d)$
2. $abx + aby + abz = ab(x + y + z)$
3. $x^2 + x^3 + x^4 = x^2(1 + x + x^2)$
4. $3a + 6a^2 + 9a^3 = 3a(1 + 2a + 3a^2)$

### Reversing a Known Polynomial Multiplication Process

Three patterns recur with such frequency on the exam that you should memorize them. These patterns are the same as the ones you were encouraged to memorize in the discussion of the FOIL method.

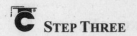 

### THREE COMMON POLYNOMIAL MULTIPLICATION REVERSALS

1. Perfect square trinomial: $x^2 + 2xy + y^2 = (x+y)(x+y)$
2. Perfect square trinomial: $x^2 - 2xy + y^2 = (x-y)(x-y)$
3. Difference of two squares: $x^2 - y^2 = (x+y)(x-y)$

### *Reversing an Unknown Polynomial Multiplication Process*

Occasionally, you may find it necessary to factor an expression that does not fall into one of the three categories presented above. The expression will most likely have the form $ax^2 + bx + c$; e.g., $x^2 + 2x + 1$. To factor such expressions, set up a blank diagram: ( )( ). Then, fill in the diagram by answering the following series of questions.

1. What factors will produce the first term, $ax^2$?
2. What possible factors will produce the last term, $c$?
3. Which of the possible factors from step 2, when added together, will produce the middle term, $bx$

*Examples:*

1. Factor $x^2 + 3x + 2$.
   - ➤ What factors will produce the first term, $ax^2$, where $a = 1$? $x$ times $x$ yields $x^2$, so the factors, in part, are $(x\ )(x\ )$. What possible factors will produce the last term? The possibilities are $\{2,1\}$ and $\{-2,-1\}$. Which of the two sets of factors just mentioned, when added together, will produce a result of $+3x$? The answer is $\{2,1\}$: $2 + 1 = 3$, as the FOIL method confirms: $(x+2)(x+1) = x^2 + x + 2x + 2 = x^2 + 3x + 2$.

2. Factor $x^2 + 4x - 12$.
   - ➤ What factors will generate $ax^2$? $(x\ )(x\ )$.

     What factors will generate $-12$? $\{1,-12\}$, $\{12,-1\}$, $\{2,-6\}$, $\{6,-2\}$, $\{3,-4\}$, and $\{4,-3\}$. Which factors, when added together, will produce the middle term of $+4x$? The answer is $\{6,-2\}$: $6 + (-2) = 4$. Thus, the factors are $(x+6)$ and $(x-2)$, as the FOIL method confirms: $(x+6)(x-2) = (x+6)(x-2) = x^2 - 2x + 6x - 12 = x^2 + 4x - 12$.

## Absolute Value in Algebraic Expressions

Algebraic terms involving absolute values are treated the same way as numeric absolute values. Remember that the absolute value of any term is always a positive numerical value.

---

**PRINCIPLES OF ABSOLUTE VALUE**

1. $|x| = x$ if $x \geq 0$; $|x| = -x$ if $x < 0$
2. $|x| = |-x|$
3. $|x| \geq 0$
4. $|x - y| = |y - x|$

*Examples:*

1.  If $w = -3, |w| = ?$

    ➢ Since the value of $w$ is less than zero, $|w| = -w = -(-3) = 3$.

2.  Let $x$ be a member of the following set: $\{-11, -10, -9, -8, -7, -6, -5, -4, -3, -2, -1, 0, 1, 2, 3, 4\}$. $\frac{|2x - |x||}{3}$ is a positive integer for how many different numbers in the set?

    ➢ If $x < 0$, then $|x| = -x$: $\frac{|2x - |x||}{3} = \frac{|2x - (-x)|}{3} = \frac{|2x + x|}{3} = \frac{|3x|}{3} = |x|$, which is always a positive. Therefore, $\frac{|2x - |x||}{3}$ is a positive integer for all numbers in the set less than zero. If $x \geq 0$, then $|x| = x$: $\frac{|2x - |x||}{3} = \frac{|2x - x|}{3} = \frac{|x|}{3} = \frac{x}{3}$. Thus, the only other number in the set that returns a positive integer is 3. The total number of values in the set that satisfy the condition is: $11 + 1 = 12$.

## Radicals in Algebraic Expressions

Radicals in algebraic expressions are manipulated in the same way as numeric radicals using the rules of exponents.

*Example:*

Does $\frac{3\sqrt{x} + \sqrt{x^3}}{x} = \frac{3}{\sqrt{x}} + \sqrt{x}$?

➢ $\frac{3\sqrt{x} + \sqrt{x^3}}{x} = \frac{3\sqrt{x}}{x} + \frac{\sqrt{x^3}}{x} = \frac{3x^{\frac{1}{2}}}{x} + \frac{x^{\frac{3}{2}}}{x} = 3x^{(\frac{1}{2} - 1)} + x^{(\frac{3}{2} - 1)} = 3x^{-\frac{1}{2}} + x^{\frac{1}{2}} = \frac{3}{\sqrt{x}} + \sqrt{x}$.

When simplifying expressions containing roots and radicals that are inverse operations of one another, it is important to note that the sign of the variable impacts the sign of the result. Consider $\sqrt{x^2}$. If $x \geq 0$, then $\sqrt{x^2} = x$; if $x < 0$, then $\sqrt{x^2} = -x$.

*Examples:*

1.  $\sqrt{2^2} = 2$.
2.  $\sqrt{(-2)^2} = -(-2)^2 = 2$.

# Algebraic Operations

**DIRECTIONS:** Choose the correct answer to each of the following items. Answers are on page 956.

1. Which of the following is (are) like terms?

   I. $34x$ and $-18x$
   II. $2x$ and $2xy$
   III. $x^3$ and $3x$

   A. I only
   B. II only
   C. I and III only
   D. II and III only
   E. I, II, and III

2. Which of the following is (are) like terms?

   I. $\sqrt{2x}$ and $\sqrt{3x}$
   II. $\pi$ and $10$
   III. $x^2$ and $2x^2$

   A. I only
   B. II only
   C. I and II only
   D. I and III only
   E. I, II, and III

3. $x + 2x + 3x = ?$

   A. $6x^6$
   B. $x^6$
   C. $6x$
   D. $x + 6$
   E. $x - 6$

4. $2x + 3x - x + 4x = ?$

   A. $8x^8$
   B. $x^8$
   C. $8x$
   D. $x + 8$
   E. $x - 8$

5. $a^3 + a^2 + a = ?$

   A. $3a^3$
   B. $a^3$
   C. $2a^2$
   D. $a^2$
   E. $a^3 + a^2 + a$

6. $z^2 + 2z^2 - 5z^2 = ?$

   A. $-9z^2$
   B. $-2z^2$
   C. $0$
   D. $2z^2$
   E. $2z^2$

7. $a^3 - 12a^3 + 15a^3 + 2a^3 = ?$

   A. $6a^3$
   B. $2a^2$
   C. $6a$
   D. $3a$
   E. $a$

8. $3c + 2a - 1 + 4c - 2a + 1 = ?$

   A. $2a + 4c + 12$
   B. $4a + 3c - 2$
   C. $a + c - 1$
   D. $2a + 1$
   E. $7c$

9. $-7nx + 2nx + 2n + 7x = ?$

   A. $0$
   B. $-5nx + 2n + 7x$
   C. $18nx$
   D. $9nx + 9xn$
   E. $4nx$

10. $c^2 + 2c^2d^2 - c^2 = ?$

   A. $4c^2d^2$
   B. $2c^2d^2$
   C. $c^2d^2$
   D. $2cd$
   E. $cd$

11. $2x^2 + 2x^2 + 2x^2 = ?$

   A. $6x^6$
   B. $2x^6$
   C. $6x^2$
   D. $6x$
   E. $6$

12. $3xy + 3x^2y - 2xy + y = ?$

   A. $6xy - y$
   B. $x + xy + y$
   C. $3x^2y + xy + y$
   D. $x^2y^2 + xy$
   E. $3xy + x$

13. $x^2 + 2xy - 3x + 4xy - 6y + 2y^2 + 3x - 2xy + 6y = ?$

   A. $x^2 - 2xy + y^2$
   B. $x^2 + y^2 + 3x + 2y$
   C. $x^2 + 2y^2 + 4xy + 6x + 6y$
   D. $x^2 + 2y + 4xy + 6x$
   E. $x^2 + 2y + 4xy$

14. $8p + 2p^2 + pq - 4p^2 - 14p - pq = ?$

   A. $-2p^2 - 6p$
   B. $-p^2 + 6p$
   C. $2p^2 + 6p$
   D. $p^2 + 3pq$
   E. $3p^2 - pq$

15. $pqr + qrs + rst + stu = ?$

   A. $pqrst$
   B. $pq + qr + rs + st + tu$
   C. $pqr + rst$
   D. $4pqrst$
   E. $pqr + qrs + rst + stu$

16. $(x^2)(x^3) = ?$

   A. $x^{\frac{2}{3}}$   C. $x^{\frac{3}{2}}$   E. $x^6$
   B. $x$   D. $x^5$

17. $(a)(a^2)(a^3)(a^4) = ?$

   A. $10a$   C. $a^5$   E. $a^{24}$
   B. $24a$   D. $a^{10}$

18. $y^5 \div y^2 = ?$

   A. $3y$   C. $y^{\frac{5}{2}}$   E. $y^7$
   B. $7y$   D. $y^3$

19. $(x^2 y)(xy^2) = ?$

   A. $4xy$   C. $xy^4$   E. $xy^{16}$
   B. $x^3 y^3$   D. $x^4 y^4$

20. $(abc)(a^2 bc^2) = ?$

   A. $4abc$   C. $a^3 b^2 a^3$   E. $abc^6$
   B. $a^2 bc^2$   D. $a^3 b^3 c^3$

21. $(xy^2)(x^2 z)(y^2 z) = ?$

   A. $8xyz$   C. $x^3 y^4 z^2$   E. $x^3 y^3 z^3$
   B. $x^2 y^4 z$   D. $x^3 y^3 z^2$

22. $\frac{x^2 y^4}{xy} = ?$

   A. $y^3$   C. $x^2 y^3$   E. $xy^8$
   B. $xy^3$   D. $x^3 y^5$

23. $\frac{a^3 b^4 c^5}{abc} = ?$

   A. $a^2 b^3 c^4$   C. $(abc)^3$   E. $(abc)^{60}$
   B. $a^3 b^4 c^5$   D. $(abc)^{12}$

24. $(x^2 y^3)^4 = ?$

   A. $(xy)^9$   C. $x^8 y^{12}$   E. $xy^{24}$
   B. $x^6 y^7$   D. $xy^{20}$

25. $(\frac{a^2}{b^3})^3 = ?$

   A. $\frac{a^5}{b}$   C. $a^5 b$   E. $a^6 b^9$
   B. $\frac{a^6}{b^9}$   D. $a^6 b$

26. $\frac{x^3 y^4 z^5}{x^4 y^2 z} = ?$

   A. $y^2 z^4$   C. $\frac{y^2 z^4}{x}$   E. $\frac{y^6 z^6}{x}$
   B. $xy^2 z^4$   D. $\frac{y^2 z^5}{x}$

27. $(\frac{c^4 d^2}{c^2 d})^3 = ?$

   A. $c^5 d^3$   C. $c^6 d^3$   E. $c^6 d^6$
   B. $c^5 d^5$   D. $c^6 d^4$

28. $(\frac{x^2 y^3}{xy})(\frac{x^3 y^4}{xy}) = ?$

   A. $x^2 y^3$   C. $x^3 y^5$   E. $x^6 y^7$
   B. $x^3 y^4$   D. $x^5 y^6$

29. $(\frac{abc^2}{abc^3})(\frac{a^2 b^2 c}{ab}) = ?$

   A. $\frac{ab}{c}$   C. $ab$   E. $1$
   B. $\frac{bc}{a}$   D. $c$

30. $(\frac{x^5 y^3 z^2}{x^4 y^2 z})(\frac{x^2 y^3 z^5}{xy^2 z^4})^3 = ?$

   A. $xyz$   C. $x^5 y^5 z^5$   E. $xyz^{12}$
   B. $x^2 y^2 z^2$   D. $x^6 y^6 z^6$

31. $\frac{a}{c} + \frac{d}{c} = ?$

   A. $\frac{ab}{c}$   C. $\frac{a+b}{2c}$   E. $\frac{a+b}{abc}$
   B. $\frac{a+b}{c}$   D. $\frac{a+b}{c^2}$

32. $\frac{x}{2} + \frac{y}{2} + \frac{z}{2} = ?$

   A. $\frac{x+y+z}{2}$   C. $\frac{x+y+z}{8}$   E. $\frac{xyz}{8}$
   B. $\frac{x+y+z}{6}$   D. $\frac{xyz}{2}$

33. $\frac{ab}{x} + \frac{bc}{x} + \frac{cd}{x} = ?$

    A. $\frac{abcd}{x}$     C. $\frac{ab+bc+cd}{x}$     E. $\frac{ab+bc+cd}{x^3}$

    B. $\frac{a+b+c+d}{x}$     D. $\frac{ab+bc+cd}{3x}$

34. $\frac{x^2}{k} + \frac{x^3}{k} + \frac{x^4}{k} = ?$

    A. $\frac{x^9}{k}$     C. $\frac{x^{24}}{k}$     E. $\frac{x^2+x^3+x^4}{3k}$

    B. $\frac{x^9}{3k}$     D. $\frac{x^2+x^3+x^4}{k}$

35. $\frac{2x}{z} - \frac{y}{z} = ?$

    A. $\frac{2x-y}{z}$     C. $\frac{2x-y}{x^2}$     E. $\frac{2xy}{2z}$

    B. $\frac{2x-y}{2z}$     D. $\frac{2xy}{z}$

36. $\frac{x}{y} + \frac{y}{x} = ?$

    A. $\frac{xy}{x+y}$     C. $\frac{x+y}{xy}$     E. $\frac{x^2+y^2}{xy}$

    B. $\frac{x+y}{y+x}$     D. $\frac{xy+yx}{xy}$

37. $\frac{a}{b} - \frac{b}{a} = ?$

    A. $\frac{ab}{a-b}$     C. $\frac{a-b}{ab}$     E. $\frac{a^2-b^2}{ab}$

    B. $\frac{a-b}{b-a}$     D. $\frac{ab-ba}{ab}$

38. $\frac{x^2}{y} + \frac{x^3}{z} = ?$

    A. $\frac{x^2+x^3}{yz}$     C. $\frac{x^6}{yz}$     E. $\frac{x^2z+x^3y}{yz}$

    B. $\frac{x^5}{yz}$     D. $\frac{x^2+x^3}{yz}$

39. $\frac{x}{a} + \frac{y}{b} + \frac{z}{c} = ?$

    A. $\frac{xyz}{abc}$           D. $\frac{xbc+yac+zab}{a+b+c}$

    B. $\frac{x+y+z}{a+b+c}$      E. $\frac{xa+yb+zc}{abc}$

    C. $\frac{xbc+yac+zab}{abc}$

40. $\frac{x^2}{y^2} - \frac{y^3}{x^3} = ?$

    A. $\frac{x^2-x^3}{y^5}$     C. $\frac{x^2-y^3}{x^2-y^2}$     E. $\frac{x^6-y^6}{x^3y^2}$

    B. $\frac{x^3-x^2}{y^6}$     D. $\frac{x^5-y^5}{x^3y^2}$

41. $2(x+y) = ?$

    A. $2xy$     C. $2+x+2y$     E. $2x^2+2y^2$

    B. $2x+2y$     D. $4x$

42. $a(b+c) = ?$

    A. $ab+bc$     C. $2abc$     E. $ab+ac+bc$

    B. $ab+ac$     D. $ab^2+b^2c$

43. $3(a+b+c+d) = ?$

    A. $3abcd$
    B. $3a+b+c+d$
    C. $3a+3b+3c+3d$
    D. $3ab+3bc+3cd$
    E. $12a+12b+12c+12d$

44. $2x(3x+4x^2) = ?$

    A. $x^{10}$     C. $5x^2+6x^3$     E. $6(x^2+x^3)$

    B. $6x+8x^2$     D. $6x^2+8x^3$

45. $3a^2(ab+ac+bc) = ?$

    A. $3a^3b^2c$          D. $3a^3b+3a^3c+3a^2bc$

    B. $3a^3+3b^3+3c$    E. $3a^5b+3a^5c$

    C. $3a^2b+3a^2c+3a^2bc$

46. $(x+y)(x+y) = ?$

    A. $x^2+y^2$          D. $x^2-2xy+y^2$

    B. $x^2-y^2$         E. $x^2+2xy+y^2$

    C. $x^2+2xy-y^2$

47. $(a+b)^2 = ?$

    A. $a^2+b^2$         D. $a^2-2ab+b^2$

    B. $a^2-b^2$         E. $a^2+2ab+b^2$

    C. $a^2+2ab-b^2$

48. $(x-y)^2 = ?$

    A. $x^2+2xy-y^2$    D. $x^2-2xy-y^2$

    B. $x^2+2xy+y^2$    E. $x^2+y^2$

    C. $x^2-2xy+y^2$

49. $(a+b)(a-b) = ?$

    A. $a^2-b^2$         D. $a^2-2ab+b^2$

    B. $a^2+b^2$         E. $a^2+2ab-b^2$

    C. $a^2+2ab+b^2$

50. $(x-2)^2 = ?$

    A. $2x$      C. $x^2 - 4$      E. $x^2 - 4x - 4$
    B. $4x$      D. $x^2 - 4x + 4$

51. $(2-x)^2 = ?$

    A. $4 - x^2$      C. $x^2 + 4x + 4$      E. $x^2 - 4x - 4$
    B. $x^2 + 4$      D. $x^2 - 4x + 4$

52. $(ab + bc)(a + b) = ?$

    A. $a^2 b + ab^2 + b^2 c + abc$
    B. $a^2 b + ab^2 + abc$
    C. $a^2 b + ab^2 + a^2 bc$
    D. $a^2 b + ab + bc + abc$
    E. $a^2 + b^2 + c^2 + abc$

53. $(x - y)(x + 2) = ?$

    A. $x^2 + 2xy + 2y$      D. $x^2 - xy + 2x - 2y$
    B. $x^2 + 2xy + x + y$      E. $x^2 + 2x + 2y - 2$
    C. $x^2 + 2xy + x - 2y$

54. $(a + b)(c + d) = ?$

    A. $ab + bc + cd$      D. $ac + ad + bc + bd$
    B. $ab + bc + cd + ad$      E. $ab + ac + ad$
    C. $ac + bd$

55. $(w + x)(y - z) = ?$

    A. $wxy - z$      D. $wy + wz + xy - xz$
    B. $wy + xy - yz$      E. $wy - wz + xy - xz$
    C. $wy - wz + xy + xz$

56. $(x + y)(w + x + y) = ?$

    A. $x^2 + wx + wy + xy$
    B. $x^2 + y^2 + wx + wy + 2xy$
    C. $x^2 + y^2 + wxy$
    D. $x^2 + y^2 + wx^2 y^2$
    E. $x^2 y^2 + wxy$

57. $(2 + x)(3 + x + y) = ?$

    A. $x^2 + 6xy + 6$
    B. $x^2 + 6xy + 3x + 2y + 6$
    C. $x^2 + 2xy + 6x + 6y + 6$
    D. $x^2 + xy + 5x + 2y + 6$
    E. $x^2 + 3xy + 2x + y + 6$

58. $(x + y)^3 = ?$

    A. $x^3 + 5x^2 y + y^2 z + xyz$
    B. $x^3 + 3x^3 y + 3xy^3 + y^3$
    C. $x^3 + 3x^2 y + 3xy^2 + y^3$
    D. $x^3 + 6x^2 y^2 + y^3$
    E. $x^3 + 12x^2 y^2 + y^3$

59. $(x - y)^3 = ?$

    A. $x^3 - 3x^2 y + 3xy^2 - y^3$
    B. $x^3 + 3x^3 y + 3xy^3 + y^3$
    C. $x^3 + 3x^2 y - 3xy^2 - y^3$
    D. $x^3 + 6x^2 y^2 + y^3$
    E. $x^2 + 6x^2 y^2 - y^3$

60. $(a + b)(a - b)(a + b)(a - b) = ?$

    A. $1$      D. $a^4 - 2a^2 b^2 + b^4$
    B. $a^2 - b^2$      E. $a^4 + 2a^2 b^2 + b^4$
    C. $a^2 + b^2$

61. $2a + 2b + 2c = ?$

    A. $2(a + b + c)$      D. $6(a + b + c)$
    B. $2(abc)$      E. $8(a + b + c)$
    C. $2(ab + bc + ca)$

62. $x + x^2 + x^3 = ?$

    A. $x(x + 2x + 3x)$      D. $x(1 + x + x^2)$
    B. $x(1 + 2x + 3x)$      E. $x(1 + 3x)$
    C. $x(1 + 2 + 3)$

63. $2x^2 + 4x^3 + 8x^4 = ?$

    A. $2x^2(1 + 2x + 4x^2)$      D. $2x^2(x + 2x^2 + 4x^3)$
    B. $2x^2(1 + 2x + 4x^3)$      E. $2x^2(x^2 + 2x^3 + 4x^4)$
    C. $2x^2(x + 2x + 4x^2)$

64. $abc + bcd + cde = ?$

    A. $ab(c + d + e)$      D. $c(ab + bd + de)$
    B. $ac(b + e)$      E. $d(a + b + c + e)$
    C. $b(a + c + de)$

65. $x^2 y^2 + x^2 y + xy = ?$

    A. $(x+y)^2$              D. $xy(xy+x+y)$

    B. $x^2 + y^2$             E. $xy(x+y+1)$

    C. $x^2 y^2 (x+y)$

66. $p^2 + 2pq + q^2 = ?$

    A. $(p+q)(p-q)$      D. $p^2 + q^2$

    B. $(p+q)(p+q)$      E. $(p-q)^2$

    C. $p^2 - q^2$

67. $144^2 - 121^2 = ?$

    A. $23$

    B. $(144+121)(144-121)$

    C. $(144+121)(144+121)$

    D. $23^2$

    E. $(144+121)^2$

68. $x^2 - y^2 = ?$

    A. $(x+y)(x-y)$      D. $x^2 + y^2$

    B. $(x+y)(x+y)$      E. $2xy$

    C. $(x-y)(x-y)$

69. $x^2 + 2x + 1 = ?$

    A. $(x+1)(x-1)$      D. $x^2 - 1$

    B. $(x+1)(x+1)$      E. $x^2 + 1$

    C. $(x-1)(x-1)$

70. $x^2 - 1 = ?$

    A. $(x+1)(x+1)$      D. $(x-1)^2$

    B. $(x-1)(x-1)$      E. $(x+1)^2$

    C. $(x+1)(x-1)$

71. $x^2 + 3x + 2 = ?$

    A. $(x+1)(x-2)$      D. $(x-2)(x-1)$

    B. $(x+2)(x+1)$      E. $(x+3)(x-1)$

    C. $(x+2)(x-1)$

72. $a^2 - a - 2 = ?$

    A. $(a+2)(a-1)$      D. $(a+2)(a-2)$

    B. $(a-2)(a+1)$      E. $(a+1)(a-1)$

    C. $(a+1)(a+2)$

73. $p^2 + 4p + 3 = ?$

    A. $(p+3)(p+1)$      D. $(p+3)(p+4)$

    B. $(p+3)(p-1)$      E. $(p+3)(p-4)$

    C. $(p-3)(p-1)$

74. $c^2 + 6c + 8 = ?$

    A. $(c+2)(c+4)$      D. $(c+3)(c+5)$

    B. $(c+2)(c-4)$      E. $(c+8)(c-1)$

    C. $(c+4)(c-2)$

75. $x^2 + x - 20$

    A. $(x+5)(x-4)$      D. $(x+10)(x-2)$

    B. $(x+4)(x-5)$      E. $(x+20)(x-1)$

    C. $(x+2)(x-10)$

76. $p^2 + 5p + 6 = ?$

    A. $(p+1)(p+6)$      D. $(p-3)(p-2)$

    B. $(p+6)(p-1)$      E. $(p+5)(p+1)$

    C. $(p+2)(p+3)$

77. $x^2 + 8x + 16 = ?$

    A. $(x+2)(x+8)$      D. $(x+4)(x-4)$

    B. $(x+2)(x-8)$      E. $(x+4)(x+4)$

    C. $(x-4)(x-4)$

78. $x^2 - 5x - 6 = ?$

    A. $(x+1)(x+6)$      D. $(x-6)(x+1)$

    B. $(x+6)(x-1)$      E. $(x-2)(x-3)$

    C. $(x+2)(x+3)$

79. $a^2 - 3a + 2 = ?$

    A. $(a-2)(a-1)$      D. $(a-3)(a+1)$

    B. $(a-2)(a+1)$      E. $(a+3)(a+1)$

    C. $(a+1)(a-2)$

80. $x^2 + x - 12 = ?$

    A. $(x+6)(x+2)$      D. $(x-4)(x-3)$

    B. $(x+6)(x-2)$      E. $(x+12)(x+1)$

    C. $(x+4)(x-3)$

81. $x^2 - 8x + 16 = ?$

    A. $x+2$      C. $(x+2)^2$      E. $(x+4)^3$

    B. $x+4$      D. $(x-4)^2$

82. What number must be added to $12x + x^2$ to make the resulting trinomial expression a perfect square?

   A. 4        C. 25        E. 49
   B. 16       D. 36

83. What number must be added to $4x^2 - 12x$ to make the resulting trinomial expression a perfect square?

   A. 2        C. 9         E. 16
   B. 4        D. 12

84. $x^2 - 8x + 15 = ?$

   A. $(x+5)(x+3)$      D. $(x-5)(x-3)$
   B. $(x-5)(x+3)$      E. $(x-15)(x-1)$
   C. $(x+5)(x-3)$

85. $2x^2 + 5x - 3 = ?$

   A. $(x-1)(x+3)$      D. $(3x+1)(x+3)$
   B. $(2x-1)(x+3)$     E. $(3x-1)(2x+3)$
   C. $(2x+1)(x-3)$

86. $21x + 10x^2 - 10 = ?$

   A. $(5x-2)(2x+5)$     D. $(8x+2)(4x+5)$
   B. $(5x+2)(2x+5)$     E. $(10x-4)(2x-5)$
   C. $(5x+2)(2x-5)$

87. $ax^2 + 3ax = ?$

   A. $3ax$       C. $ax(x+3)$     E. $ax^2(x+3)$
   B. $ax(x-3)$    D. $ax^2(-3)$

88. $2x^2 - 8x + 3 - (x^2 - 3x + 9) = ?$

   A. $(x-6)(x-1)$      D. $(2x-6)(x-1)$
   B. $(x-6)(x+1)$      E. $(2x+6)(x-1)$
   C. $(x+6)(x+1)$

89. If $15x^2 + ax - 28 = (5x-4)(3x+7)$, then $a = ?$

   A. 7        C. 23        E. 33
   B. 14       D. 28

90. $x^2 - 9 = ?$

   A. $x^2 - 3$         D. $(x+3)(x-10)$
   B. $(x-3)(x-3)$    E. $x-3$
   C. $(x+3)(x+3)$

91. $x^2 - 9y^4 = ?$

   A. $(x+3y^2)(x-3y^2)$     D. $(2x+3y^2)(2x+3y^2)$
   B. $(x-3y^2)(x-3y^2)$     E. $(2x-3y^2)(2x-3y^2)$
   C. $(x+3y^2)(x+3y^2)$

92. $x^2 + 6x - 27 = ?$

   A. $(x-9)(x-9)$      D. $(x+9)(x+3)$
   B. $(x-9)(x-3)$      E. $(x+9)(x-3)$
   C. $(x-3)(x-3)$

93. $\frac{8x^{-4}}{2x} = ?$

   A. $\frac{2}{x^5}$       C. $\frac{3}{x^5}$       E. $\frac{8}{x^5}$
   B. $\frac{4}{x^4}$       D. $\frac{4}{x^5}$

94. $\frac{3^{-1}x^5y^2}{2xy} = ?$

   A. $\frac{x^2y}{6}$       C. $\frac{x^6y^2}{8}$       E. $\frac{x^6y^2}{10}$
   B. $\frac{x^4y}{6}$       D. $\frac{x^6y^4}{6}$

95. $\frac{6x^{-5}y^2}{3^{-1}x^{-4}y} = ?$

   A. $\frac{12y^4}{x^4}$       C. $\frac{16y^5}{x^4}$       E. $\frac{18y^5}{x^6}$
   B. $\frac{16y^4}{x^5}$       D. $\frac{18y}{x}$

96. $\frac{9^2x^3y}{3^{-1}x^{-4}y} = ?$

   A. $243x^7$      C. $248x^7$      E. $256x$
   B. $244x^3$      D. $252x^2$

97. If $x = -2$, $x^2 = ?$

   A. $-4$       C. 6        E. 10
   B. 4        D. 8

98. If $x = -3$ and $y = 5$, then $x^2y = ?$

   A. $-50$      C. 45        E. 55
   B. $-45$      D. 50

99. If $x = -2$ and $y = -3$, then $x^2 - 4xy - x = ?$

   A. $-24$      C. $-18$      E. $-14$
   B. $-20$      D. $-16$

100. $(x-y)(x^2-2x+5)=?$

    A. $x^3-2x^2+5x-x^2y+2xy-5y$
    B. $x^3+2x^2+5x-x^2y+2xy-5y$
    C. $x^3-2x^2-5x-x^2y+2xy-5y$
    D. $x^3-2x^2+5x+x^2y+2xy-5y$
    E. $x^3-2x^2+5x-x^2y-2xy-5y$

101. $(2x+\sqrt{3})^2=?$

    A. $3x^2+3x\sqrt{3}+3$       D. $-4x^2+4x\sqrt{3}+3$
    B. $4x^2-4x\sqrt{3}+3$       E. $4x^2+4x\sqrt{3}+3$
    C. $4x^2-4x\sqrt{3}-3$

102. If $x=-2$ and $y=3$, then $2x^2-xy=?$

    A. 10       C. 14       E. 18
    B. 12       D. 16

103. $(\frac{x^2y^3x^5}{2^{-1}})^2=?$

    A. $4x^{12}y^4$       C. $4x^{14}y^4$       E. $4x^{14}y^6$
    B. $4x^{12}y^{66}$      D. $4x^{12}y^6$

104. Does $\sqrt{x^2+y^2}=x+y$?

    A. Yes
    B. No
    C. Cannot be determined from the given information

105. Does $\sqrt{(x+y)^2}=\sqrt{x^2+2xy+y^2}$?

    A. Yes
    B. No
    C. Cannot be determined from the given information

106. Does $\frac{x}{\sqrt{2x-y}}=x\sqrt{2x+y}$?

    A. Yes
    B. No
    C. Cannot be determined from the given information

107. Does $\frac{6}{\sqrt{2a-3c}}=\frac{6\sqrt{2a-3c}}{(2a-3c)}$?

    A. Yes
    B. No
    C. Cannot be determined from the given information

108. $\frac{n}{6}+\frac{2n}{5}=?$

    A. $\frac{13n}{30}$       C. $\frac{3n}{30}$       E. $\frac{3n}{11}$
    B. $17n$        D. $\frac{17n}{30}$

109. $1-\frac{x}{y}=?$

    A. $\frac{1-x}{y}$       C. $\frac{x-y}{y}$       E. $\frac{y-x}{xy}$
    B. $\frac{y-x}{y}$       D. $\frac{1-x}{1-y}$

110. $\frac{x-y}{x+y}\div\frac{y-x}{y+x}=?$

    A. 1       C. $\frac{(x-y)^2}{(x+y)^2}$       E. 0
    B. $-1$       D. $-\frac{(x-y)^2}{(x-y)^2}$

111. $\frac{1+\frac{1}{x}}{\frac{y}{x}}=?$

    A. $\frac{x+1}{y}$       C. $\frac{x+1}{xy}$       E. $\frac{y+1}{y}$
    B. $\frac{x+1}{x}$       D. $\frac{x^2+1}{xy}$

112. $(\frac{2x^2}{y})^3=?$

    A. $\frac{8x^5}{3y}$       C. $\frac{6x^5}{y^3}$       E. $\frac{8x^6}{y^3}$
    B. $\frac{6x^6}{y^3}$       D. $\frac{8x^5}{y^3}$

113. $\frac{\frac{1}{x}+\frac{1}{y}}{3}=?$

    A. $\frac{3x+3y}{xy}$       C. $\frac{xy}{3}$       E. $\frac{y+x}{3}$
    B. $\frac{3xy}{x+7}$       D. $\frac{y+x}{3xy}$

114. If $b\geq0$, then $\frac{\sqrt{32b^3}}{\sqrt{8b}}=?$

    A. $2\sqrt{b}$       C. $2b$       E. $b\sqrt{2b}$
    B. $\sqrt{2b}$       D. $\sqrt{2b^2}$

115. If $x\geq0$, then $\sqrt{\frac{x^2}{9}+\frac{x^2}{16}}=?$

    A. $\frac{25x^2}{144}$       C. $\frac{5x^2}{12}$       E. $\frac{7x}{12}$
    B. $\frac{5x}{12}$       D. $\frac{x}{7}$

116. $\sqrt{36y^2 + 64x^2} = ?$

    A. $6y + 8x$          D. $10x^2y^2$

    B. $10xy$            E. Cannot be simplified

    C. $10x^2y^2$

117. If $x \geq 0$, then $\sqrt{\frac{x^2}{64} - \frac{x^2}{100}} = ?$

    A. $\frac{x}{40}$        C. $\frac{x}{2}$        E. $\frac{3x}{80}$

    B. $-\frac{x}{2}$       D. $\frac{3x}{40}$

118. If $y \geq 0$, then $\sqrt{\frac{y^2}{2} - \frac{y^2}{18}} = ?$

    A. $\frac{2y}{3}$          D. $\frac{y\sqrt{3}}{6}$

    B. $\frac{y\sqrt{5}}{5}$        E. None of these

    C. $\frac{10y}{3}$

119. $\sqrt{a^2 + b^2} = ?$

    A. $a + b$           D. $(a+b)(a-b)$

    B. $a - b$           E. None of these

    C. $\sqrt{a^2} + \sqrt{b^2}$

120. Given every pair $(x, y)$ of negative numbers and resulting value $\frac{x}{|x|} + \frac{xy}{|xy|}$ , what is the set of all numbers formed?

    A. $\{0\}$       C. $\{2\}$       E. $\{0, 2\}$

    B. $\{-2\}$     D. $\{0, -2\}$

121. When factored as completely as possible with respect to the integers, $16x^4 - 81y^{16} = ?$

    A. $(4x^2 + 9y^4)(4x^2 - 9y^4)$

    B. $(4x^2 + 9y^8)(4x^2 - 9y^8)$

    C. $(4x^2 + 9y^4)(2x + 3y)(2x - 3y)$

    D. $(4x^2 + 9y^8)(2x + 3y^4)(2x - 3y^4)$

    E. $16x^4 - 81y^{16}$

# Algebraic Equations and Inequalities

Pursuing the analogy between English and algebra as a language, the algebraic analogue of a complete sentence in English (with subject and verb) is an equation. An **algebraic equation** is a statement that two algebraic expressions are equivalent.

*Examples:*

| *English* | *Algebra* |
|---|---|
| Ed is three years older than Paul..........................| $E = P + 3$ |
| Paul is twice as old as Mary...............................| $P = 2M$ |
| Ned has $2 more than Ed...................................| $N = E + \$2$ |
| Bill has three times as much money as does Ted......| $B = 3T$ |

## Solving Algebraic Formulas

An **algebraic formula** is an equation that typically involves a relationship between literal quantities. Problems that involve formulas often ask you to solve for a particular unknown (variable) using substitution. Algebraic formulas can take many different forms, including function math, scientific equations, geometric formulas, and story-problems. Regardless of the format, the concept is the same: Replace the variables for which values are given and solve for the unknown variable.

*Examples:*

1. For all real numbers $x$ and $y$, $x \oplus y = 2x + y^2$. What is the value of $3 \oplus 7$?

   ➤ Substitute 3 for $x$ and 7 for $y$ in the given expression: $x \oplus y = 2x + y^2 \Rightarrow 3 \oplus 7 = 2(3) + (7)^2 = 6 + 49 = 55$.

2. The formula that relates Fahrenheit temperature to Celsius temperature is: $F = 1.8C + 32$, where $F$ is Fahrenheit degrees (°F) and $C$ is Celsius degrees (°C). What is the temperature, in Fahrenheit degrees, if the temperature is $25°C$?

   ➤ Substitute 25 for $C$ in the given equation and solve for $F$: $F = 1.8C + 32 = 1.8(25) + 32 = 45 + 32 = 77°F$.

3. The volume of a sphere is: $V = \frac{4\pi r^3}{3}$, where $r$ is the radius of the sphere. Find the volume of a sphere with a radius of 6.

   ➤ Substitute 6 for $r$ in the given formula and solve for $V$: $V = \frac{4\pi r^3}{3} = \frac{4\pi(6)^3}{3} = 4\pi \cdot 72 = 288\pi$.

4. If a person must pick one object from a group of $x$ objects and then one object from a group of $y$ objects, the number of possible combinations is $xy$. Jan must select 1 candy bar from 7 different candy bars and 1 pack of gum from 3 different packs of gum. What is the maximum number of combinations available to Jan?

   ➤ Substitute 7 for $x$ and 3 for $y$ in the given expression: # of combinations $= xy = (7)(3) = 21$.

Formulas that represent real-life situations often involve variables with units of measure, such as inches or gallons. You must ensure that all variables have similar units on both sides of the equation in order for the equality to remain true. To maintain consistency, it may be necessary to convert units using equivalent expressions (e.g., 12 inches/foot, 1 foot/12 inches, 60 minutes/hour, 1 hour/60 minutes). Thus, when dealing with quantities given in units of any type, it helps to explicitly write out the units in the expressions.

*Example:*

If string costs $k$ cents per foot at the hardware store, how much will $w$ feet and $j$ inches of the string cost?

➢ Explicitly write out the units in the expression and cancel like units in the numerator and denominator:

$$\text{Cost of string (cents)} = \frac{k \text{ cents}}{1 \text{ ft. of string}} \bullet \text{length of string (ft.)}$$

$$= \frac{k \text{ cents}}{1 \text{ ft.}} \bullet [w \text{ ft.} + (j \text{ in.} \bullet \frac{1 \text{ ft.}}{12 \text{ in.}})]$$

$$= \frac{k \text{ cents}}{1 \text{ ft.}} \bullet [w \text{ ft.} + (j \text{ in.} \bullet \frac{1 \text{ ft.}}{12 \text{ in.}})]$$

$$= \frac{k \text{ cents}}{1 \text{ ft.}} \bullet (w + \frac{j}{12})(\text{ft.})$$

Therefore, the cost of the string, in cents, is: $k(w + \frac{j}{12})$.

---

## Basic Principle of Equations

The fundamental rule for working with any equation is: Whatever you do to one side of an equation, you must do exactly the same thing to the other side of the equation. This rule implies that you can add, subtract, multiply, and divide both sides of the equality by any value without changing the statement of equality. The only exception is that you cannot divide by zero. The following example illustrates the validity of this principle using an equation containing only real numbers.

*Example:*

$5 = 5$

➢ This is obviously a true statement. You can add any value to both sides of the equation, say 10, and the statement will remain true. Add 10: $5 + 10 = 5 + 10 \Rightarrow 15 = 15$. You can also subtract the same value from both sides, e.g., 7: $15 - 7 = 15 - 7 \Rightarrow 8 = 8$. You can multiply both sides by the same value, e.g., $-2$: $8 \bullet -2 = 8 \bullet -2 \Rightarrow -16 = -16$. Finally, you can divide both sides by the same value (except zero); e.g., $-4$: $-16 \div -4 = -16 \div -4 \Rightarrow 4 = 4$.

This principle for manipulating equations applies to algebraic equations with variables, as the following example illustrates.

*Example:*

$5 + x = 5 + x$

➢ Add $x$: $5 + x + x = 5 + x + x \Rightarrow 5 + 2x = 5 + 2x$. Whatever $x$ is, since it appears on both sides of the equation, both sides of the equation must still be equal. Now, subtract a value, e.g., $y$: $5 + 2x - y = 5 + 2x - y$. Again, since $y$ appears on both sides of the equation, the statement that the two expressions are equal remains true.

DO NOT multiply both sides of an equation by zero if the equation contains a variable. You may lose special characteristics of the variable. For example, the equation $2x = 8$ is true only if $x = 4$. However, the equation $0(2x) = 0(8)$ is true for any value of $x$.

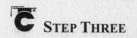 

## Solving Linear Equations

Equations that have only variables of the first power are called equations of the first degree or *linear equations*. While a linear equation can have any number of different variables, equations with one or two variables are most common on the exam.

The fundamental rule of equations is the key to solving linear equations. To solve for an unknown variable, identically manipulate both sides of the equation to isolate the variable on one side. Be sure to reduce the other side of the equation by combining similar terms.

*Examples:*

1. If $2x+3 = x+1$, then what is the value of $x$?

   ➢ To solve for $x$, manipulate the equation to isolate $x$. Subtract $x$ from both sides: $2x+3-x = x+1-x \Rightarrow x+3 = 1$. Next, subtract 3 from both sides: $x+3-3 = 1-3 \Rightarrow x = -2$.

2. If $4x+2 = 2x+10$, then what is the value of $x$?

   ➢ Subtract $2x$ from both sides of the equation: $4x+2-2x = 2x+10-2x \Rightarrow 2x+2 = 10$. Then, subtract 2 from both sides: $2x+2-2 = 10-2 \Rightarrow 2x = 8$. Divide both sides by 2: $2x \div 2 = 8 \div 2 \Rightarrow x = 4$.

3. If $3y-2x = 12$, then what is the value of $y$?

   ➢ Add $2x$ to both sides of the equation: $3y-2x+2x = 12+2x \Rightarrow 3y = 12+2x$. Divide both sides by 3: $y = \frac{2x}{3}+4$.

So far, we have been very formal in following the fundamental rule for working with equations. The process is simplified using a shortcut called *transposition*. Transposing is the process of moving a term or a factor from one side of the equation to the other by changing it into its mirror image. Perform these "inverse operations" until the variable is isolated. Note that this shortcut does not change the fundamental rule or its outcome: it simply bypasses the formal steps.

To transpose a term that is added or subtracted, move it to the other side of the equation and change its sign. Thus, a term with a positive sign on one side is moved to the other side and becomes negative, and vice versa. It is imperative when using transposition that you do not forget to change signs when terms change sides.

*Examples:*

1. $x+5 = 10$

   ➢ Rather than going through the formal steps of subtracting 5 from both sides of the equality, simply transpose the 5: move it from the left side to the right side and change its sign from "+" to "−": $x = 10-5 \Rightarrow x = 5$.

2. $x-5 = 10 \Rightarrow x = 10+5 \Rightarrow x = 15$
3. $3x = 5+2x \Rightarrow 3x-2x = 5 \Rightarrow x = 5$

To transpose a multiplicative factor, move the factor to the opposite side of the equation and invert it; that is, replace it with its reciprocal.

*Example:*

$$\frac{2x+5}{3}=9$$

> ➤ $2x$ and 5 are both divided by 3; in other words, they are both multiplied by $\frac{1}{3}$. Therefore, the $\frac{1}{3}$ must be transposed first. Move it to the opposite side of the equation and invert it: $2x+5 = 9(3) = 27$. Now the 5 can be transposed: $2x = 27 - 5 = 22$. Finally, solve for $x$ by transposing the 2: $x = 22 \cdot \frac{1}{2} = 11$.

## Solving Simultaneous Equations

Ordinarily, if an equation has more than one variable, it is not possible to determine the unique numeric solution for any individual variable. For example, the equation $x + y = 10$ does not have one unique solution set for $x$ and $y$: $x$ and $y$ could be 1 and 9, 5 and 5, −2 and 12, and so on. However, if there are as many equations as there are variables, the equations can be manipulated as a system to determine the value of each variable. This technique is called *solving simultaneous equations* because the equations are taken to be true at the same time, or simultaneously, in order to determine the variable value. On the exam, simultaneous equations are typically limited to two equations and two unknowns.

*Example:*

Given $x + y = 10$ and $x - y = 6$, solve for $x$ and $y$.

> ➤ If we treat both of the equations as making true statements at the same time, then there is only one solution set for $x$ and $y$, for there is only one pair of numbers that will satisfy both equations, $x = 8$ and $y = 2$.

It is easy to see the answer to the previous example, but solutions will not always be this obvious. How do you find the specific solution for a given set of equations? There are two methods for solving simultaneous equations: substitution and linear combination (elimination).

### Substitution

The steps for *substitution* are as follows:

Step 1: Pick one of the two given equations and define one variable in terms of the other.
Step 2: Substitute the defined variable into the other equation and solve.
Step 3: Substitute the solution back into either equation and solve for the remaining variable.

*Examples:*

1. If $2x + y = 13$ and $x - y = 2$, what are the values of $x$ and $y$?

> ➤ Redefine one variable in terms of the other. Since $y$ is already a single variable in both equations, define $y$ in terms of $x$: $y = 13 - 2x$. Substitute $13 - 2x$ for $y$ in the second equation and solve for $x$: $x - (13 - 2x) = 2 \Rightarrow 3x = 15 \Rightarrow x = 5$. Finally, solve for $y$ by substituting 5 for $x$ in either equation: $2x + y = 13 \Rightarrow 2(5) + y = 13 \Rightarrow y = 3$.

2. If $3x + 2y = 16$ and $2x - y = 6$, what are the values of $x$ and $y$?

> ➤ Since $y$ is a simple term in the second equation, define $y$ in terms of $x$: $2x - y = 6 \Rightarrow y = 2x - 6$. Substitute this expression for $y$ in the first equation and solve for $x$: $3x + 2(2x - 6) = 16 \Rightarrow$

$7x = 28 \Rightarrow x = 4$. Finally, solve for $y$ by substituting 4 for $x$ in either equation: $2x - y = 6 \Rightarrow$ $2(4) - y = 6 \Rightarrow y = 2$.

3. If $y = 7 + x$ and $3x + 2y = 4$, what are the values of $x$ and $y$?

➤ Substitute $7 + x$ for $y$ in the second equation and solve for $x$: $3x + 2y = 4 \Rightarrow 3x + 2(7 + x) = 4 \Rightarrow$ $5x = -10 \Rightarrow x = -2$. Substitute $-2$ for $x$ in the first equation and solve for $y$: $y = 7 + x = 7 - 2 = 5$.

### Linear Combination (Elimination)

The second method for solving simultaneous equations is **linear combination** or **elimination**. Eliminate one of the two variables by adding or subtracting the two equations. If necessary, division of one equation by another may eliminate one of two variables. This is the case when solving equations containing variables with exponents.

*Examples:*

1. If $2x + y = 8$ and $x - y = 1$, what are the values of $x$ and $y$?

➤ In this pair of simultaneous equations, there is a "$+y$" term in one equation and a "$-y$" term in the other. Since $+y$ and $-y$ added together yields zero, eliminate the $y$ term by adding the two equations together. (Actually, you will be adding the left side of the second equation to the left side of the first equation and the right side of the second to the right side of the first, but it is easier to speak of the process as "adding equations.") $[2x + y = 8] + [(x - y = 1)] = [3x = 9] \Rightarrow x = 3$. Find the value of $y$ by substituting 3 for $x$ in either equation: $2x + y = 8 \Rightarrow 2(3) + y = 8 \Rightarrow y = 8 - 6 = 2$.

2. If $4x + 3y = 17$ and $2x + 3y = 13$, what are the values of $x$ and $y$?

➤ In this pair, each equation has a $+3y$ term, which you can eliminate by subtracting the second equation from the first. $[4x + 3y = 17] - [2x + 3y = 13] = [2x = 4] \Rightarrow x = 2$. Solve for $y$ by substituting 2 for $x$ in either equation: $4x + 3y = 17 \Rightarrow 4(2) + 3y = 17 \Rightarrow 8 + 3y = 17 \Rightarrow 3y = 9 \Rightarrow y = 3$.

3. $x^5 = 6y$ and $x^4 = 2y$; $x$ is a real number such that $x \neq 0$ and $y$ is a real number. Solve for $x$.

➤ The system of equations is reduced to one equation and one variable by dividing the first equation by the second equation: $\frac{x^5}{x^4} = \frac{6y}{2y} \Rightarrow x = 3$.

If a system of equations has more variables than equations, then not every variable value can be determined. Instead, you will be asked to solve for one or more variables in terms of another variable.

*Examples:*

1. If $y = 2a$ and $3x + 8y = 28a$, find $x$ in terms of $a$.

➤ Substitute $2a$ for $y$ and solve for $x$: $3x + 8y = 28a \Rightarrow 3x + 8(2a) = 28a \Rightarrow 3x = 28a - 16a \Rightarrow$: $x = \frac{12a}{3} = 4a$.

2. In terms of $a$, solve the following pair of equations for $x$ and $y$: $3x - 4y = 10a$ and $5x + 2y = 8a$.

➤ First, solve for either $x$ or $y$ in terms of $a$ alone. To find $x$ in terms of $a$, multiply the second equation by 2 and add the result to the first equation. $[2(5x + 2y = 8a)] + [3x - 4y = 10a] = [13x = 26a] \Rightarrow$ $x = 2a$. To find $y$ in terms of $a$, substitute $2a$ for $x$ in either equation: $5x + 2y = 8a \Rightarrow y = \frac{8a - 5(2a)}{2} \Rightarrow$ $y = \frac{-2a}{2} = -a$.

## Solving Equations by Factoring

Factoring is an alternative short-cut method for solving some equations. Before factoring, rewrite the equation with all of the terms on one side of the equation and 0 on the other side. If the nonzero side of the equation can be factored into a product of expressions, then use the following property to yield simpler equations that can be solved: if $xy = 0$, then $x = 0$ or $y = 0$. The solutions of the simpler equations will be solutions of the factored equation. The solutions of an equation are also called the *roots* of the equation.

*Examples:*

1.  $\dfrac{(4x^2 - 1)(x + 2)}{x + 4} = 0$

    ➤ Either $4x^2 - 1 = 0$ or $x + 2 = 0$. In each instance, solve for $x$:

    $$4x^2 - 1 = 0$$
    $$x^2 = \tfrac{1}{4}$$
    $$x = \pm\tfrac{1}{2}$$

    $$x + 2 = 0$$
    $$x = -2$$

    Therefore, the set of all possible values for $x$ is $\{-2, -\tfrac{1}{2}, \tfrac{1}{2}\}$.

2.  Solve for $x$: $x^3 + 2x^2 + x = 3(x + 1)^2$

    ➤ Move all the terms to one side of the equality and simplify by factoring like terms:

    $$x^3 + 2x^2 + x - 3(x + 1)^2 = 0$$
    $$x(x^2 + 2x + 1) - 3(x + 1)^2 = 0$$
    $$x(x + 1)^2 - 3(x + 1)^2 = 0$$
    $$(x - 3)(x + 1)^2 = 0$$
    $$x = \{-1, 3\}$$

## Solving Quadratic Equations

Equations that involve variables of the second power (e.g., $x^2$) are called **quadratic equations**. Unlike a linear equation with a single variable, which has a single solution, a quadratic may have two solutions. By convention, quadratic equations are written so that the right side of the equation is equal to zero. The general form is: $\boldsymbol{ax^2 + bx + c = 0}$.

*Example:*

Solve for $x$: $x^2 + x - 2 = 0$.

➤ To solve the quadratic equation, factor the left side of the equation: $x^2 + x - 2 = 0 \Rightarrow (x + 2)(x - 1) = 0$. For the equality to hold true, $x + 2$ or $x - 1$ must equal zero. Therefore, $x = -2$ or $1$, so this quadratic equation has two solutions.

This last example illustrates the *zero product property*: if $xy = 0$, then $x = 0$ or $y = 0$.

*Example:*

$$x^2 - 3x - 4 = 0$$

> Factor the left side of the equation: $(x+1)(x-4) = 0$. Either $x+1 = 0$, in which case $x = -1$, or $x - 4 = 0$, in which case $x = 4$. Therefore, the solution set for this quadratic equation is $\{-1, 4\}$.

However, not every quadratic equation has two different solutions.

*Example:*

$$x^2 + 2x + 1 = 0$$

> Factor the left side of the equation: $(x+1)(x+1) = 0$. Since the two factors are the same, the equation has one solution: $-1$.

For quadratic equations not in standard form, you must first group like terms and rearrange the equation into standard form.

*Examples:*

1. Solve for $x$: $2x^2 + 12 - 3x = x^2 + 2x + 18$.

   > Rewrite the equation by grouping like terms and simplifying:

   $$2x^2 + 12 - 3x = x^2 + 2x + 18$$
   $$(2x^2 - x^2) + (-3x - 2x) + (12 - 18) = 0$$
   $$x^2 - 5x - 6 = 0$$
   $$(x - 6)(x + 1) = 0$$

   Either $x - 6 = 0$ or $x + 1 = 0$. Therefore the set of all possible values for $x$ is $\{-1, 6\}$.

2. Solve for $x$: $x(8 + x) = 2x + 36 + 6x$.

   > Rewrite the equation by grouping like terms and simplifying:

   $$x(8 + x) = 2x + 36 + 6x$$
   $$8x + x^2 = 8x + 36$$
   $$x^2 = 36$$

   Since squaring a negative number yields a positive and squaring a positive number yields a positive, $x = \pm 6$.

Some higher degree equations can also be solved if they can be written in quadratic form.

*Example:*

Solve for $x$: $x^4 - 13x^2 + 36 = 0$.

> Factor: $(x^2 - 9)(x^2 - 4) = 0$. Factor again: $(x+3)(x-3)(x+2)(x-2) = 0$. To find the four possible values of $x$, set each factor equal to zero and solve each for $x$: $x + 3 = 0 \Rightarrow x = -3$; $x - 3 = 0 \Rightarrow x = 3$; $x + 2 = 0 \Rightarrow x = -2$; and $x - 2 = 0 \Rightarrow x = 2$. Therefore, the solution set is: $\{-3, 3, -2, 2\}$.

Alternatively, you can use the quadratic formula, $x = \dfrac{-b \pm \sqrt{b^2 - 4ac}}{2a}$, to solve quadratic equations.

*Example:*

Solve for $x$: $3 - x = 2x^2$.

➤ $3 - x = 2x^2 \Rightarrow 2x^2 + x - 3 = 0$. $a = 2, b = 1, c = -3$. $x = \frac{-b \pm \sqrt{b^2 - 4ac}}{2a} = \frac{-1 \pm \sqrt{1^2 - 4(2)(-3)}}{2(2)} = \frac{-1 \pm \sqrt{1 + 24}}{4} = \frac{-1 \pm 5}{4}$. Therefore, $x = \{1, -\frac{3}{2}\}$.

## Algebraic Inequalities

An ***inequality*** is very much like an equation except, as the name implies, it is a statement that two quantities are not equal. Four different symbols are used to make statements of inequality:

- $>$ greater than
- $<$ less than
- $\geq$ greater than or equal to
- $\leq$ less than or equal to

*Examples:*

$5 < 1$ .................. 5 is greater than 1.
$2 > -2$ .............. 2 is greater than $-2$.
$x > 0$ ................. $x$ is greater than zero.
$x > y$ ................. $x$ is greater than $y$.
$8 < 9$ ................. 8 is less than 9.
$-4 < -1$ ............. $-4$ is less than $-1$.
$x < 0$ ................. $x$ is less than zero.
$y < x$ ................. $y$ is less than $x$.
$x \geq 0$ ................. $x$ is greater than or equal to zero. ($x$ could be zero or any number larger than zero.)
$x \geq y$ ................. $x$ is greater than or equal to $y$. (Either $x$ is greater than $y$, or $x$ and $y$ are equal.)
$x \leq 0$ ................. $x$ is less than or equal to zero. ($x$ could be zero or any number less than zero.)
$x \leq y$ ................. $x$ is less than or equal to $y$. (Either $x$ is less than $y$, or $x$ and $y$ are equal.)

The fundamental rule for working with inequalities is similar to that for working with equalities: Treat each side of the inequality exactly the same. You can add or subtract the same value to each side of an inequality without changing the inequality, and you can multiply or divide each side of an inequality by any *positive* value without changing the inequality.

*Example:*

$$5 > 2$$
Add 25 to both sides. $5 + 25 > 2 + 25$
$$30 > 27$$
Subtract 6 from both sides. $30 - 6 > 27 - 6$
$$24 > 21$$
Multiply both sides by 2. $24 \cdot 2 > 21 \cdot 2$
$$48 > 42$$
Divide both sides by 6. $48 \div 6 > 42 \div 6$
$$8 > 7$$

However, if you multiply or divide an inequality by a *negative* number, the direction of the inequality is reversed. Therefore, remember to change the direction of the inequality when multiplying or dividing by a negative number.

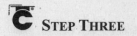
*Example:*

$$4 > 3$$
Multiply both sides by -2.  $4(-2) < 3(-2)$
$$-8 < -6$$

These properties hold true for inequalities containing variables, as the following two examples illustrate.

*Examples:*

1.  For what values of $x$ is $3(2-x)+7x > 30$?

    ➤ Solve for $x$:

    $$3(2-x)+7x > 30$$
    $$6-3x+7x > 30$$
    $$6+4x > 30$$
    $$4x > 24$$
    $$x > 6$$

2.  For what values of $x$ is $3(2-x)+x > 30$?

    ➤ Solve for $x$:

    $$3(2-x)+x > 30$$
    $$6-3x+x > 30$$
    $$6-2x > 30$$
    $$-2x > 24$$
    $$x < -12$$

## Exponents in Equations and Inequalities

### Integer and Rational Exponents

Algebraic equations and inequalities can include terms with integer and rational exponents. The rules of exponents apply when manipulating these terms.

*Examples:*

1.  If $x = 2$, then what is the value of $(x^{-2x})^{x^{-x}}$?

    ➤ Substitute $x = 2$ into the given expression:

    $$(x^{-2x})^{x^{-x}} = [(2)^{-2(2)}]^{2^{-2}} = [(2)^{-4}]^{(\frac{1}{2})^2} = 2^{(-4)(\frac{1}{4})} = 2^{-1} = \frac{1}{2}.$$

2.  Find the value of $2x^0 + x^{\frac{2}{3}} + x^{-\frac{2}{3}}$ when $x = 27$.

    ➤ Substitute $x = 27$:

    $$2x^0 + x^{\frac{2}{3}} + x^{-\frac{2}{3}} = 2(27)^0 + (27)^{\frac{2}{3}} + (27)^{-\frac{2}{3}} = 2(1) + (\sqrt[3]{27})^2 + \frac{1}{27^{\frac{2}{3}}} = 2 + 9 + \frac{1}{9} = 11\frac{1}{9}.$$

### Algebraic Exponentials

When solving equations that involve algebraic exponential terms, try to find a common base to use throughout the problem.

*Example:*

Solve for $x$: $4^{x+2} = 8^{3x-6}$

➤ Since $4 = 2^2$ and $8 = 2^3$, the common base in this item is 2. Thus:

$$4^{x+2} = 8^{3x-6}$$
$$(2^2)^{x+2} = (2^3)^{3x-6}$$
$$2^{2x+4} = 2^{9x-18}$$

Now, drop the common base and solve for $x$:

$$2x + 4 = 9x - 18$$
$$22 = 7x$$
$$x = \frac{22}{7}$$

## Exponential Growth

Items that involve exponential growth test knowledge of exponential growth sequences, also called geometric sequences. In a geometric sequence, the ***ratio***, $r$, of any term to its preceding term is constant. If the terms of a geometric sequence are designated by $a_1, a_2, a_3...a_n$, then $\boldsymbol{a_n = a_1 r^{n-1}}$. Sequences that involve exponential growth have real-life applications, such as determining population growth over a specific period.

*Examples:*

1. Find the $5^{\text{th}}$ term of the geometric sequence $\{4, 12, 36,...\}$.

   ➤ In this geometric sequence, the ratio between the terms is 3. The $5^{\text{th}}$ term is: $a_n = a_1 r^{n-1} \Rightarrow a_5 = 4(3)^{5-1} = 4(3)^4 = 4 \cdot 81 = 324$.

2. On June 1, 1990, the population of Grouenphast was 50,250. If the population is increasing at an annual rate of 8.4%, what is the approximate population of Grouenphast on June 1, 2010?

   ➤ An annual increase of 8.4% means that each year the population will be 108.4% of the previous year's population. Thus, the ratio between terms, $r$, is 1.084. The population on June 1, 1990 is the starting term: $a_1 = 50,250$. Since June 1, 2010 is 20 years later, the population at that time is the $21^{\text{st}}$ term in the sequence: $n = 21$. Therefore, the population on June 1, 2010 is: $a_n = a_1 r^{n-1} \Rightarrow a_{21} = 50,250(1.084)^{20} \approx 252,186$.

The previous example involving growth over time suggests an alternate form of the geometric sequence equation called the ***exponential growth equation***: $a_t = a_0 r^{\frac{t}{T}}$. In this equation, $a_t$ is the amount after time $t$; $a_0$ is the initial amount ($t = 0$), $r$ is the proportionality constant, $t$ is the total period of growth, and $T$ is the time per cycle of growth. Note that this equation also applies to exponential decay, where the initial amount is larger than the amount after time $t$.

*Example:*

The number of rabbits in a certain population doubles every 3 months. Currently, there are 5 rabbits in the population. How many rabbits will there be 3 years from now?

➤ In this case, the total time of growth is 3 years. Since the population doubles every 3 months, the time per cycle of growth is one-fourth of a year. Using the formula for exponential growth: $a_t = a_0 r^{\frac{t}{T}} \Rightarrow a_3 = (5)(2)^{\frac{3}{0.25}} = (5)(2)^{12} = 20,450$. We can verify this solution by working out the values, allowing the population to double every 3 months.

| Period (months) | 0 | 3 | 6 | 9 | 12 | 15 | 18 | 21 | 24 | 27 | 30 | 33 | 36 |
|---|---|---|---|---|---|---|---|---|---|---|---|---|---|
| Population Size | 5 | 10 | 20 | 40 | 80 | 160 | 320 | 640 | 1,280 | 2,560 | 5,120 | 10,240 | 20,480 |

## Properties of Functions

A function is a set of ordered pairs $(x, y)$ such that for each value of $x$, there is exactly one value of $y$. By convention, we say that "$y$ is a function of $x$," which is written as: $y = f(x)$ or $y = g(x)$, etc. The set of $x$-values for which the set is defined is called the **domain** of the function. The set of corresponding values of $y$ is called the **range** of the function.

*Example:*

What are the domain and range of the function $y = |x|$?

➤ The function is defined for all real values of $x$. Hence the domain is the set of all real numbers. Since $y = |x|$ can only be a positive number or zero, the range of the function is given by the set of all real numbers equal to or greater than zero.

When we speak of $f(a)$, we mean the value of $y = f(x)$ when $x = a$ is substituted in the expression for $f(x)$. If $z = f(y)$ and $y = g(x)$, we say that $z = f[g(x)]$. Thus, $z$ is in turn a function of $x$.

This function notation is a short way of writing the result of substituting a value for a variable. Once a function $f(x)$ is defined, think of the variable $x$ as an input and $f(x)$ as the corresponding output. In any function, there can be no more than one output for a given input. Note, however, that there may be more than one input that returns the same output.

*Examples:*

1. If $f(x) = 2x^x - 3x$, find the value of $f(3)$.

   ➤ Substitute 3 for $x$ in the given expression:
   $$f(x) = 2x^x - 3x \Rightarrow f(3) = 2(3)^3 - 3(3) = 2(27) - 9 = 54 - 9 = 45.$$

2. If $f(x) = 2x - 9^{\frac{1}{x}}$, what is $f(-2)$?

   ➤ $f(-2) = 2(-2) - 9^{-\frac{1}{2}} = -4 - \frac{1}{\sqrt{9}} = -4 - \frac{1}{3} = -\frac{13}{3}$.

3. If $z = f(y) = 3y + 2$ and $y = g(x) = x + 2$, then $z = ?$

   ➤ $z = f[g(x)] = 3[g(x)] + 2 = 3(x + 2) + 2 = 3x + 6 + 2 = 3x + 8$.

In the previous chapter we introduced geometric sequences as an example of working with exponents. Note that a geometric sequence ($a_n = a_1 r^{n-1}$) is actually a function. In general, a **sequence**, $a_n$, is any function $a(n)$ with a domain consisting of only the positive integers and possibly zero; that is, $n = 0, 1, 2, 3, \ldots$, or $n = 1, 2, 3, \ldots$. Note that a sequence is often written by listing its values in the order $a_1, a_2, a_3, \ldots, a_n, \ldots$. For example, $a_n = (-1)^n (n!)$ for $n = 1, 2, 3, \ldots$, is written as $-1, 2, -6, \ldots, (-1)^n (n!), \ldots$.

*Example:*

1. What is the $5^{th}$ term of the sequence defined by $a_n = 3n^2 + 2$ for $n = 1, 2, 3, \ldots$?

   ➤ The fifth term of the sequence is for $n = 5$. Substitute 5 for $n$ in the function $3n^2 + 2$: $3(5)^2 + 2 = 77$.

2. Find the $4^{th}$ term of the sequence with values $-1, 2, -6, \ldots, (-1)^n(n!), \ldots$.

   ➤ The values of $n$ for any sequence are consecutive integers, so determine the value of $n$ for the $4^{th}$ term of the sequence by finding the first $n$ value. Test $n = 1$: $(-1)^1(1) = -1$. Therefore, the $4^{th}$ value of $n$ must be 4: $(-1)^4(4!) = 4 \cdot 3 \cdot 2 \cdot 1 = 24$.

## Rational Equations and Inequalities

Algebraic equations and inequalities may include rational (fractional) expressions. When manipulating rational expressions, follow the same rules as discussed with equations, inequalities, and algebraic fractions.

*Examples:*

1. If $\dfrac{x}{x+6} = \dfrac{y^3 - 1}{(y+1)(y^2 - y + 1) + 4}$, then $x = ?$

   ➤ $\dfrac{x}{x+6} = \dfrac{y^3 - 1}{y^3 - y^2 + y + y^2 - y + 1 + 4} = \dfrac{y^3 - 1}{y^3 + 5} = \dfrac{y^3 - 1}{y^3 - 1 + 6} = \dfrac{y^3 - 1}{(y^3 - 1) + 6}$. Therefore, $x = y^3 - 1$.

2. Let $x$ represent a positive whole number. Given the two inequalities, $\dfrac{1}{x} > \dfrac{1}{4}$ and $\dfrac{x-3}{x^2 - 3x} < \dfrac{1}{7}$, how many more values for $x$ satisfy the second equality than satisfy the first inequality?

   ➤ For the first inequality: $\dfrac{1}{x} > \dfrac{1}{4} \Rightarrow x < 4$. Thus, the set of satisfying values for $x$ is $\{1, 2, 3\}$. For the second inequality, $\dfrac{x-3}{x(x-3)} < \dfrac{1}{7}$, since it is not possible to divide by zero, $x \neq 3$. Reduce the equation: $\dfrac{x-3}{x(x-3)} < \dfrac{1}{7} \Rightarrow \dfrac{1}{x} < \dfrac{1}{7} \Rightarrow 7 > x$. Since $x < 7$ and $x \neq 3$, the set of satisfying values for the second inequality is $\{1, 2, 4, 5, 6\}$. Thus, two more whole numbers satisfy the second inequality than the first.

## Radical Equations and Inequalities

Expressions in algebraic equations and inequalities may include radicals. The same principles for working with equations and inequalities apply when manipulating radicals.

*Example:*

$5\sqrt{x-4} - 28 = 12$ for what value of $x$?

   ➤ Solve for $x$:

$$5\sqrt{x-4} - 28 = 12$$
$$5\sqrt{x-4} = 40$$
$$\sqrt{x-4} = 8$$
$$x - 4 = 64$$
$$x = 68$$

## Absolute Value in Equations and Inequalities

Expressions in algebraic equations and inequalities may include absolute values. The same principles for working with equations and inequalities apply when manipulating absolute values.

*Examples:*

1. What is the sum of all different integers that can be substituted for $x$ such that $|x| + |x - 3| = ?$

   ➤ The absolute value of any real number, including integers, is always zero or more. Therefore, try only $-3, -2, -1, 0, 1, 2, 3$. The last four work in the equality: $|0| + |0 - 3| = 0 + 3 = 3$; $|1| + |1 - 3| = 1 + 2 = 3$; $|2| + |2 - 3| = 2 + 1 = 3$; $|3| + |3 - 3| = 3 + 0 = 3$. Thus, $0 + 1 + 2 + 3 = 6$.

2. If $x$ represents an integer, $|x - 3| + |x + 2| < 7$ for how many different values of $x$?

   ➤ Absolute values are always equal to or greater than zero. Thus, if $x = -4$, $|x - 3| = |-4 - 3| = 7$; there is no need to try any integers less than $-3$. Similarly, if $x = 5$, $|x + 2| = |5 + 2| = 7$, there is no need to try any integers greater than 4. Therefore, test only the integers between $-3$ and 4. Six integers satisfy the inequality: $\{-2, -1, 0, 1, 2, 3\}$.

# Algebraic Equations and Inequalities

**DIRECTIONS:** Choose the correct answer to each of the following items. Answers are on page 963.

1. If $3x = 12$, then $x = ?$
   A. 2      C. 4      E.10
   B. 3      D. 6

2. If $2x + x = 9$, then $x = ?$
   A. 0      C. 3      E.9
   B. 1      D. 6

3. If $7x - 5x = 12 - 8$, then $x = ?$
   A. 0      C. 2      E.4
   B. 1      D. 3

4. If $3x + 2x = 15$, then $x = ?$
   A. 2      C. 5      E.9
   B. 3      D. 6

5. If $a - 8 = 10 - 2a$, then $a = ?$
   A. −2     C. 2      E.6
   B. 0      D. 4

6. If $p - 11 - 2p = 13 - 5p$, then $p = ?$
   A. −4     C. 1      E.6
   B. −1     D. 2

7. If $12x + 3 - 4x - 3 = 8$, then $x = ?$
   A. −5     C. 0      E.5
   B. −1     D. 1

8. If $5x - 2 + 3x - 4 = 2x - 8 + x + 2$, then $x = ?$
   A. −5     C. 1      E.6
   B. 0      D. 3

9. If $a + 2b - 3 + 3a = 2a + b + 3 + b$, then $a = ?$
   A. −1     C. 2      E.6
   B. 0      D. 3

10. If $4y + 10 = 5 + 7y + 5$, then $y = ?$
    A. −2     C. 0      E.8
    B. −1     D. 4

11. If $-4 - x = 12 + x$, then $x = ?$
    A. −8     C. 1      E.4
    B. −2     D. 2

12. If $\frac{x}{2} + x = 3$, then $x = ?$
    A. $\frac{1}{2}$      C. 1      E.3
    B. $\frac{2}{3}$      D. 2

13. If $\frac{2x}{3} + \frac{x}{4} + 4 = \frac{x}{6} + 10$, then $x = ?$
    A. $\frac{11}{12}$      C. 5      E.20
    B. $\frac{3}{2}$      D. 8

14. If $\frac{a}{2} - \frac{a}{4} = 1$, then $a = ?$
    A. $\frac{1}{2}$      C. 1      E.4
    B. $\frac{2}{3}$      D. 2

15. If $\frac{1}{p} + \frac{2}{p} + \frac{3}{p} = 1$, then $p = ?$
    A. $\frac{2}{3}$      C. 1      E.6
    B. $\frac{3}{4}$      D. 2

16. If $\frac{2x - 6}{3} = 8$, then $x = ?$
    A. 1      C. 6      E.18
    B. 3      D. 15

17. If $\frac{5 - x}{5} = 1$, then $x = ?$
    A. −5     C. 0      E.5
    B. −1     D. 1

18. If $\frac{2 - x}{10} = 1$, then $x = ?$
    A. −8     C. $-\frac{1}{5}$      E.5
    B. −1     D. 1

19. If $\frac{5}{x+1} + 2 = 5$, then $x = ?$

    A. $-\frac{2}{7}$     C. $\frac{7}{2}$     E. 10
    B. $\frac{2}{3}$     D. 7

20. If $\frac{x}{2} + \frac{x}{3} = \frac{1}{2} + \frac{1}{3}$, then $x = ?$

    A. $\frac{1}{3}$     C. 1     E. 3
    B. $\frac{2}{3}$     D. 2

21. If $3x + y = 10$ and $x + y = 6$, then $x = ?$

    A. 1     C. 3     E. 5
    B. 2     D. 4

22. If $2x + y = 10$ and $x + y = 7$, then $y = ?$

    A. 3     C. 5     E. 9
    B. 4     D. 6

23. If $x + 3y = 5$ and $2x - y = 3$, then $x = ?$

    A. 2     C. 5     E. 9
    B. 4     D. 6

24. If $x + y = 2$ and $x - y = 2$, then $y = ?$

    A. −2     C. 0     E. 2
    B. −1     D. 1

25. If $a + b = 5$ and $2a + 3b = 12$, then $b = ?$

    A. 1     C. 3     E. 6
    B. 2     D. 4

26. If $5x + 3y = 13$ and $2x = 4$, then $y = ?$

    A. 1     C. 3     E. 5
    B. 2     D. 4

27. If $k - n = 5$, and $2k + n = 16$, then $k = ?$

    A. −3     C. 1     E. 7
    B. 0     D. 5

28. If $t = k - 5$ and $k + t = 11$, then $k = ?$

    A. 2     C. 8     E. 14
    B. 3     D. 11

29. If $a + 5b = 9$ and $a - b = 3$, then $a = ?$

    A. 1     C. 5     E. 11
    B. 4     D. 7

30. If $8 + x = y$ and $2y + x = 28$, then $x = ?$

    A. 2     C. 6     E. 18
    B. 4     D. 12

31. If $\frac{x+y}{2} = 4$ and $x - y = 4$, then $x = ?$

    A. 1     C. 4     E. 8
    B. 2     D. 6

32. If $\frac{x+y}{2} = 7$ and $\frac{x-y}{3} = 2$, then $x = ?$

    A. 2     C. 8     E. 14
    B. 4     D. 10

33. If $x + y + z = 10$ and $x - y - z = 4$, then $x = ?$

    A. 2     C. 6     E. 12
    B. 3     D. 7

34. If $x + 2y - z = 4$ and $2x - 2y + z = 8$, then $x = ?$

    A. −2     C. 4     E. 8
    B. 0     D. 6

35. If $x + y + z = 6$, $x + y - z = 4$, and $x - y = 3$, then $x = ?$

    A. −2     C. 4     E. 8
    B. 0     D. 6

36. If $x^2 - 5x + 4 = 0$ then $x = ?$

    A. −2 or 1     C. −1 or 2     E. 4 or 2
    B. 4 or 1     D. −4 or −1

37. If $x^2 - 3x - 4 = 0$, then $x = ?$

    A. −4 or 1     C. −1 or 2     E. 6 or −1
    B. −2 or 2     D. 4 or −1

38. If $x^2 + 5x + 6 = 0$, then $x = ?$

    A. −3 or −2     C. −1 or 6     E. 6 or −2
    B. −3 or 2     D. 1 or −6

39. If $x^2 - 3x + 2 = 0$, then $x = ?$

    A. −2 or −1     C. 1 or 2     E. 3 or 5
    B. −1 or 2     D. 2 or 3

40. If $x^2 + 3x + 2 = 0$, then which of the following values is (are) possible for $x$?

    I. 1
    II. −1
    III. −2

    A. I only          D. I and II only
    B. II only         E. II and III only
    C. III only

41. If $x^2 + 5x = -4$, then $x = ?$
   A. $-1$ or $-4$    C. 1 or 2    E. 2 or 6
   B. $-1$ or $-2$    D. 1 or 4

42. If $x^2 - 8 = 7x$, then $x = ?$
   A. $-8$ and $-1$    C. $-1$ and 8    E. 1 and 8
   B. $-4$ and 1    D. 1 and 4

43. If $k^2 - 10 = -3k$, then $k = ?$
   A. $-10$ and $-1$    C. $-5$ and 3    E. 2 and $-5$
   B. $-10$ and 1    D. $-3$ and 5

44. If $x^2 = 12 - x$, then $x = ?$
   A. $-4$ and $-3$    C. $-3$ and 4    E. 1 and 6
   B. $-4$ and 3    D. $-2$ and 6

45. If $3x^2 = 12x$, then $x = ?$
   A. 0 or 3    C. $-2$ or 2    E. 3 or 12
   B. 0 or 4    D. 2 or 4

46. If $4(5-x) = 2(10-x^2)$, then $x = ?$
   A. 0 or 2    C. $-2$ or 4    E. 4 or 5
   B. 2 or 4    D. 0 or $-2$

47. For what values of $x$ is $3 + 4x < 28$?
   A. $x < 4$    C. $x < 6.25$    E. $x \geq 0$
   B. $x > 4$    D. $x > 6.25$

48. For what values of $x$ is $5(3x-2) \geq 50$?
   A. $x \geq 4$    C. $x \geq 10$    E. $x > 8$
   B. $x \leq 4$    D. $x \leq 10$

49. For what values of $x$ is $8 - 3x > 35$?
   A. $x > 0$    C. $x \geq 0$    E. $x \geq 9$
   B. $x > -3$    D. $x < -9$

50. If $x^2 = 6x - 8$, then $x = ?$
   A. $-8$ and $-2$    C. $-2$ and 2    E. 2 and 8
   B. $-4$ and $-2$    D. 2 and 4

51. If $(x-8)(x+2) = 0$, then $x = ?$
   A. $-8$ or $-2$    C. 4 or $-2$    E. 10 or $-5$
   B. $-4$ or $-2$    D. 8 or $-2$

52. If $9 - 3(6-x) = 12$, then $x = ?$
   A. 4 or $-2$    C. 4    E. 7
   B. 7 or $-2$    D. 6

53. If $\frac{x+5}{4} = 17$, then $x = ?$
   A. 13 or 25    C. 63    E. 124
   B. 54    D. 75 or $-24$

54. If $\frac{x}{2} - \frac{x-2}{3} = 0.4$, then $x = ?$
   A. $-1$ or 1.4    C. 2 or $-1.6$    E. 2.6
   B. $-1.6$    D. 2.4

55. If $0.02x + 1.44 = x - 16.2$, then $x = ?$
   A. 18    C. 14    E. 10
   B. 16    D. 12

56. If $3 - 2(x-5) = 3x + 4$, then $x = ?$
   A. $\frac{1}{2}$ or $\frac{1}{4}$    C. $\frac{9}{5}$    E. 5
   B. $-\frac{9}{5}$    D. 1 or 3

57. If $x^2 - 9x = 22$, then $x = ?$
   A. $-11$ or 2    C. 2 or 3    E. 11
   B. 3    D. 11 or $-2$

58. If $(x+8)(x+1) = 78$, then $x^2 + 9x = ?$
   A. 50    C. 60    E. 70
   B. 55    D. 65

59. If $2x + 3y = 12$ and $x = -6$, then $y = ?$
   A. 2    C. 8    E. 12
   B. 4    D. 10

60. At what point does the line $5x + 2y = 20$ intersect the $x$-axis? (Hint: What must the $y$-coordinate be?)
   A. $(-4,0)$    C. $(0,0)$    E. $(4,2)$
   B. $(-2,0)$    D. $(4,0)$

61. If $3x + 5y = 10$, then $y = ?$
   A. $-0.6x - 2$    C. $0.5x - 4$    E. $-0.6x + 2$
   B. $-0.4x + 2$    D. $0.6x - 2$

62. If $x = ay + 3$, then $y = ?$
   A. $\frac{x-2}{4a}$    C. $\frac{a}{x-3}$    E. $\frac{a}{3x}$
   B. $\frac{x-3}{a}$    D. $\frac{x+a}{3}$

63. If $8x + 16 = (x+2)(x+5)$, then $x = ?$
   A. 3 or $-2$    C. $-2$    E. 3
   B. $-3$    D. 2 or 3

64. If $\frac{x+5}{0.2} = 0.3x$, then $x = ?$

   A. $-\frac{125}{23}$      C. $-\frac{250}{47}$      E. $\frac{250}{47}$

   B. $-76$         D. $\frac{47}{250}$

65. If $\frac{0.2+x}{3} = \frac{5}{4}$, then $x = ?$

   A. $-\frac{40}{17}$      C. $0$        E. $\frac{40}{17}$

   B. $-\frac{17}{40}$      D. $\frac{17}{40}$

66. If $x$ is an integer and $6 < x < 8$, then what is the value of $x$?

   A. 4         C. 7        E. 10

   B. 5         D. 9

67. If $x$ is an integer and $5 \le x \le 7$, then which of the following values is (are) possible for $x$?

   I. 5
   II. 6
   III. 7

   A. II only        D. II and III only
   B. I and II only    E. I, II, and III
   C. I and III only

68. If $x$ and $y$ are integers, $2 < x < 4$, and $8 > y > 6$, then what is the value of $xy$?

   A. 12        C. 21       E. 32
   B. 16        D. 24

69. If $x$ and $y$ are integers, $5 > x \ge 2$, and $6 < y \le 9$, then which of the following is the *minimum* value of $xy$?

   A. 14        C. 20       E. 54
   B. 18        D. 45

70. If $1 \le x \le 3$, then which of the following values is (are) possible for $x$?

   I. $\frac{5}{2}$
   II. $\frac{7}{2}$
   III. $\frac{3}{2}$

   A. I only       D. I and III only
   B. II only      E. I, II, and III
   C. I and II only

71. If $3^{8x+4} = 27^{2x+12}$, then $x = ?$

   A. $\frac{1}{4}$       C. 4        E. 16

   B. $\frac{1}{9}$       D. 9

72. If $(3+x)x = 2x + x + 16$, then which of the following is (are) the possible value(s) for $x$?

   A. 2         C. 2 or –2    E. 8 or –8
   B. 4         D. 4 or –4

73. If $10x^2 = 30$ and $(6+y)y = 6y + 52$, then $2x^2 + 2y = ?$

   A. 110      C. 82       E. 55
   B. 96       D. 72

74. If $|x| = 5$, then $x = ?$

   A. 5
   B. 5 or –5
   C. Any real number less than 5
   D. No real number
   E. Any real number greater than zero

75. The commutative property states that if a final result involves two procedures or objects, then the final result is the same regardless of which procedure or object is taken first and which is taken second. Which of the following is an example of the commutative property of addition?

   A. $xy = yx$         D. $7 - 3 = 3 - 7$

   B. $5 + 4 = 4 + 5$     E. $\frac{x}{y} = \frac{y}{x}$

   C. $2a + b = 2b + a$

76. If $x = 3a$ and $y = 5x + 6$, then $y = ?$

   A. 21        C. $6a + 15$    E. $21a$
   B. $15a + 6$    D. $3a + 15$

77. If $2(x+3) = 18a + 10$, then $x = ?$

   A. $9a + 2$     C. $16a + 4$    E. 11
   B. $9a + 5$     D. $9a + 3.5$

78. The formula that relates Fahrenheit temperature to Celsius temperature is $F = 1.8C + 32$, where $F$ is the temperature in Fahrenheit degrees and $C$ is the temperature in Celsius degrees. What is the temperature, in Celsius degrees, if the temperature in Fahrenheit degrees is 41°?

   A. 5         C. 9        E. 73
   B. 7.2      D. 10.8

79. If $x$ is a real number such that $x \neq 0$, $y$ is a real number, $x^5 = 8y$, and $x^4 = y$, then which of the following is true?

   A. $x = 7y$     C. $x = 8y^2$     E. $x = 8$

   B. $x = 8y$     D. $x = 7y^2$

80. The commutative property states that if a final result involves two procedures or objects, then the final result is the same regardless of which procedure or object is taken first and which is taken second. Which of the following is an example of the commutative property of multiplication?

   A. $xy = yx$         D. $7 - 3 = 3 - 7$

   B. $5 + 4 = 4 + 5$     E. $\frac{x}{y} = \frac{y}{x}$

   C. $2a + b = 2b + a$

81. What is the tenth term of the sequence $\{1, 4, 9, 16, \ldots\}$?

   A. 25     C. 49     E. 100

   B. 36     D. 81

82. If a sequence is defined by the rule $a_n = (a_{n-1} - 3)^2$, what is $a_4$ (the fourth term of the sequence) if $a_1$ is 1?

   A. 1     C. 3     E. 5

   B. 2     D. 4

83. A geometric sequence is a sequence of numbers formed by continually multiplying by the same number; e.g., $\{81, 27, 9, 3 \ldots\}$ is a geometric sequence formed by continually multiplying by $\frac{1}{3}$. What is the next term in the geometric sequence of $\{2, 8, 32, 128, \ldots\}$?

   A. 132     C. 384     E. 1,024

   B. 256     D. 512

84. A sequence is formed by substituting consecutive whole numbers in the expression $x^3 + x^2 - 2x + 1$. What is the next term in the sequence of $\{1, 9, 31, 73, \ldots\}$?

   A. 115     C. 135     E. 141

   B. 125     D. 137

85. Which of the following values for $c$ returns two distinct real solutions to the equation $x^2 - 8x + c = 0$?

   A. −20     C. 18     E. 20

   B. 17     D. 19

86. Which of the following values for $b$ returns two distinct real solutions to the equation $x^2 + bx + 8 = 0$?

   A. 6     C. 4     E. 1

   B. 5     D. $\sqrt{2}$

87. The cost of buying a certain material is $k$ cents per yard. What is the cost, in cents, of $x$ yards and $y$ inches of the material?

   A. $kx + y$     C. $x + 36y$     E. $xk + 26yk$

   B. $36x + y$     D. $xk + \frac{yk}{36}$

88. If $x^2 - 14k^2 = 5kx$, what are the 2 solutions for $x$ in terms of $k$?

   A. $2k$ and $7k$     C. $k$ and $5k$     E. $k$ and $-5k$

   B. $-2k$ and $7k$     D. $-k$ and $5k$

89. An arithmetic sequence is a sequence of numbers formed by continually adding the same number; e.g., $\{1, 3, 5, 7, 9, 11, \ldots\}$ is an arithmetic sequence formed by continually adding 2. What is the ninth term in the arithmetic sequence of $\{1, 4, 7, 10, 13, \ldots\}$?

   A. 16     C. 19     E. 25

   B. 17     D. 21

90. $\frac{1}{a} + \frac{1}{b} = 7$ and $\frac{1}{a} - \frac{1}{b} = 3$ Find $\frac{1}{a^2} - \frac{1}{b^2}$.

   A. 10     C. 3     E. 4

   B. 7     D. 21

91. If $\frac{3x}{4} = 1$, then $\frac{2x}{3} = ?$

   A. $\frac{1}{3}$     C. $\frac{2}{3}$     E. 2

   B. $\frac{1}{2}$     D. $\frac{8}{9}$

92. If $x = \frac{y}{7}$ and $7x = 12$, then $y = ?$

   A. 3     C. 7     E. 72

   B. 5     D. 12

93. If $x = k + \frac{1}{2} = \frac{k+3}{2}$, then $x = ?$

    A. $\frac{1}{3}$      C. 1      E. $\frac{5}{2}$

    B. $\frac{1}{2}$      D. 2

94. If $7 - x = 0$, then $10 - x = ?$

    A. $-3$      C. 3      E. 10
    B. 0      D. 7

95. If $x = 7 - \sqrt{3}$ and $y = 7 + \sqrt{3}$, which of the following must be rational?

    I. $xy$
    II. $x + y$
    III. $\frac{x}{y}$

    A. I only      D. I and II only
    B. III only      E. I, II, and III
    C. I and III only

96. $\frac{2^{x+4} - 2(2^x)}{2(2^{x+3})} = ?$

    A. $\frac{1}{2}$      C. $\frac{3}{4}$      E. $\frac{7}{8}$

    B. $\frac{1}{4}$      D. $\frac{5}{8}$

97. Let $y = 2^x$ and $w = 8^x$. For what value of $x$ does $w = 2y$?

    A. a rational number between 0 and 2
    B. a whole number between 2 and 8
    C. a irrational number between 2 and 8
    D. no such value of $x$ exists
    E. more than one such value of $x$ exists

98. A population that starts at 16 and doubles every 30 months can be expressed as $16\left(2^{\frac{2x}{5}}\right)$, where $x$ is the number of elapsed years. What is the approximate population size after 105 months have elapsed?

    A. $11\sqrt{2}$      C. 128      E. 192
    B. 27      D. $128\sqrt{2}$

99. Let $n$ be a member of the set $\{5, 6, 7, 8, 9, 10, 11, 12, 13, 14, 15, 16\}$. For how many different values of $n$ is the following equation true?

$$\frac{1 + 2 + \ldots + n}{2 + 4 + \ldots + 2n} = \frac{1}{2}$$

    A. 0      C. 6      E. 12
    B. 1      D. 11

100. Which of the following statements is always correct?

    A. If $x < 0$, then $x^2 > -x$
    B. If $x > 0$, then $(x+3)(x+2) > x^2 + 4x + 3$
    C. If $x > 0$, then $x^3 + 8 > (x+2)(x^2 - 2x + 4)$
    D. If $x = 8$, then $1 + 2 + 3 + \ldots + x > x(x+1)$
    E. If $x = 6$, then $\frac{2^x}{2^{x-1}} > 4$

101. A prime number is defined as a whole number that is greater than 1 whose only divisors are 1 and the number itself. Examples of prime numbers are 13, 17, and 29. What is the smallest prime number that divides the sum of $3^3 + 5^5 + 7^7 + 11^{11}$?

    A. 2      C. 5      E. 11
    B. 3      D. 7

102. Let $x$ represent a positive odd integer. The smallest value of $x$ such that $3\frac{1}{4}, 3\frac{3}{4}, 3\frac{5}{4}, \ldots, 3\frac{x}{4}$ is greater than $2^x$ is:

    A. a multiple of 3
    B. a multiple of 5 but not a multiple of 3
    C. a multiple of 7 but not a multiple of either 3 or 5
    D. 11
    E. 13

103. If $x$ represents a real number, how many different values of $x$ satisfy the equation $x^{128} = 16^{32}$?

    A. 0
    B. 1
    C. 2
    D. more than 2, but infinite
    E. infinite

104. How many of the following five numerical expressions represent whole numbers?

$$8^0, \; 9^{-2}, \; \left(\tfrac{1}{9}\right)^{-2}, \; \left(\tfrac{1}{8}\right)^{\frac{2}{3}}, \; \left(\tfrac{1}{16}\right)^{-\frac{1}{4}}$$

    A. 0      C. 3      E. 4
    B. 2      D. 4

105. If $y = 3x$, $3^{x+2} = ?$

    A. $y^2$      C. $y + 3$      E. $y + 9$
    B. $2^y$      D. $9y$

106. How many real values of $x$ exist such that $x = \sqrt{x} + 20$?

    A. 0
    B. 1
    C. 2
    D. more than 2, but not infinite
    E. infinite

107. Let $x$ be an element of $\{-6,-5,-4,-3,-2,-1,0,2,$ $6,8,10,12\}$ and $x = 3k$, where $k$ is an integer. Find the sum of all different values of $x$ such that $\sqrt{2x+8} = \sqrt{y}$ for some value of $y$ if $y$ is an element of $\{-2,0,2,4,6,8,10,12,14,16,18,20,22,$ $24,26,28\}$.

    A. 3          C. 9          E. 15
    B. 6          D. 12

108. Let $k$ be a positive whole number such that $11 < k < 15$. If $\sqrt{8x} + 6 = 18$, for how many different values of $k$ will the solution set for $x$ contain an even integer?

    A. 0          C. 2          E. 4
    B. 1          D. 3

109. Let $f(x) = \frac{x-2}{2x-13}$. If $x$ represents a whole number, what is the largest value of $x$ such that $f(x) < 0$?

    A. −1          C. 1          E. 8
    B. 0          D. 6

110. If $f(x) = 8$ when $x = 2$ and $f(x) = 20$ when $x = 6$, then $f(x) = kx + w$. The value of $k + w$ is:

    A. 2          C. 5          E. 20
    B. 4          D. 8

111. If $-5 < x < -1$, and $f(x) = \left|14 - |1 + 2x|\right|$, then $f(x)$ equals:

    A. $13 - 2x$          C. $13 + 2x$          E. $13 + 3x$
    B. $15 + 2x$          D. $2x - 13$

112. If $f(x) = 3 + 2^x$ and $g(x) = (2+3)^x$, then what is the value of $f(2) + g(3)$?

    A. 36          C. 150          E. 300
    B. 132          D. 225

113. If $f(x) = \frac{kx}{3x+5}$, $x \neq -\frac{5}{3}$, $k$ is a constant, and $f(x)$ satisfies the equation $f(f(x)) = x$ for all real values of $x$ except for $x = -\frac{5}{3}$, what is the value of $k$?

    A. $k$ cannot be uniquely determined.
    B. $k$ does not equal any real value.
    C. $k = -\frac{5}{3}$
    D. $k = -\frac{3}{5}$
    E. $k = -5$

114. The range of the relation $\{(x,y) \mid y^2 = 4x\}$ is $\{0,9,16\}$. Which of the following is the domain?

    A. $\{0, 20.25, 64\}$
    B. $\{0, 3, 4\}$
    C. $\{0, 36, 64\}$
    D. $\{-4, -3, 0, 3, 4\}$
    E. $\{0, 2.25, 4\}$

115. If $y = 2x + 1$ and the domain for $x$ is the set of all non-negative integers, then the range for $y$ is the set of which of the following?

    A. non-negative integers
    B. non-negative even integers
    C. odd integers
    D. positive odd integers
    E. real numbers equal to or greater than 1

116. If $7x + 4y = 218$, and both $x$ and $y$ are positive integers, what is the sum of the two largest values in the range of $y$?

    A. 433          C. 427          E. 95
    B. 428          D. 101

117. How many whole numbers are not in the domain of values for $x$ if $y = \frac{(x-1)(x-2)(x-3)}{x^2 - 11 + 30}$?

    A. 1          C. 3          E. 5
    B. 2          D. 4

118. If $f(x) = 17x + 14$, then $f(2) + f(3) + f(4)$ is:

    A. 195          C. 126          E. 51
    B. 153          D. 102

119. $f(x)$ and $g(x)$ represent linear functions. If $f(x) = 5$ for $x = 1$, $g(x) = 3x + 8$, and $f(x) = g(x)$ for $x = 2$, then what is the value of $f(4)$?

    A. 12          C. 20          E. 32
    B. 16          D. 24

# Geometry

If you have ever taken a basic course in geometry, you probably remember having to memorize theorems and do formal proofs. Fortunately, you will not be asked to do any formal proofs on the exam, and the formulas you need to know are few and relatively simple. Most often, test items ask you to find the measure of an angle, the length of a line, or the area of a figure.

## Geometric Notation

You should be familiar with basic geometric notation. The line segment with points $P$ and $Q$ as endpoints is represented by $\overline{PQ}$. $PQ$ represents the length of $\overline{PQ}$. A line passing through points $P$ and $Q$ is represented by $\overleftrightarrow{PQ}$. $\overrightarrow{PQ}$ represents the ray beginning at point $P$ and passing through point $Q$. Finally, the symbol "$\cong$" is used to represent the term "congruent."

*Example:*

If $\overleftrightarrow{AB}$ does not contain point $C$, but it does contain point $D$, what is the maximum number of points in the intersection of $\overleftrightarrow{AB}$ and $\overleftrightarrow{CD}$?

➢ $\overleftrightarrow{AB}$ and $\overleftrightarrow{CD}$ are different lines, so the maximum number of points at which they can intersect is one point, point $D$.

## Line and Angle Properties

For the purposes of this review and the test, the word *line* means a straight line:

$$P \qquad Q$$
$$\bullet \qquad \bullet \qquad l$$

The line above is designated line $l$. The portion of line $l$ from point $P$ to point $Q$ is called "line segment $PQ$," or "$\overline{PQ}$."

When two lines intersect, they form an *angle*, and their point of intersection is called the *vertex* of that angle.

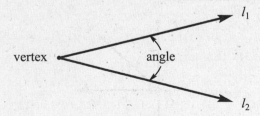

The size of an angle is measured in **degrees**. Degrees are defined in reference to a circle. By convention, a circle is divided into 360 equal parts, or degrees.

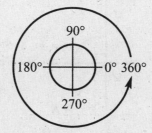

A 90° angle is also called a **right angle**. A right angle is often indicated in the following way:

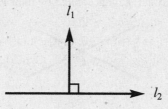

Two right angles form a straight line:

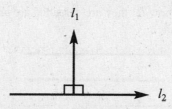

Since two right angles form a straight line, the degree measure of the angle of a straight line is $90° + 90° = 180°$:

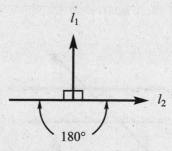

An angle that is less than 90° is called an **acute angle**:

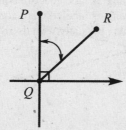

In the figure above, $\angle PQR$ is an acute angle.

An angle that is greater than 90° but less than 180° is called an **obtuse angle**:

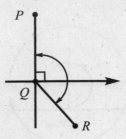

In the figure above, $\angle PQR$ is an obtuse angle.

When two lines intersect, the opposite (or vertical) angles created by their intersection are congruent, or equal:

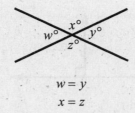

$$w = y$$
$$x = z$$

Two lines that do not intersect regardless of how far they are extended are **parallel** to each other. In the following figure, the symbol ∥ indicates that $l_1$ and $l_2$ are parallel.

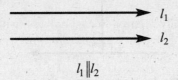

$$l_1 \parallel l_2$$

When parallel lines are intersected by a third line, a **transversal**, the following angle relationships are created:

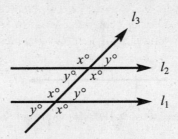

All angles labeled $x$ are equal.
All angles labeled $y$ are equal.
Any $x$ plus any $y$ totals 180.

Two lines that are **perpendicular** to the same line are parallel to each other:

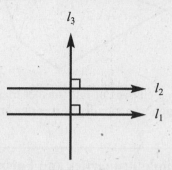

Since $l_1$ and $l_2$ are both perpendicular to $l_3$, we can conclude that $l_1$ and $l_2$ are parallel to each other.

## Polygon Properties

- A **polygon** is a closed figure created by three or more lines.
- A **triangle** is any polygon with exactly three sides.
- A **quadrilateral** is any polygon with exactly four sides.
- A **pentagon** is any polygon with exactly five sides.
- A **hexagon** is any polygon with exactly six sides.

A polygon with more than six sides is usually referred to as a polygon with a certain number of sides; for example, a polygon with ten sides is called a ten-sided polygon. A **regular polygon** is a polygon with equal sides and equal angles (e.g., a square). The sum of the degree measures of the **exterior angles** of a polygon is 360. The sum of the degree measures of the **interior angles** of a polygon can be expressed as $180(n-2)$, where $n$ is the number of sides in the polygon.

Furthermore, note that any polygon is made up of a number of smaller triangles: a quadrilateral consists of two triangles, a pentagon consists of three triangles, an octagon consists of six triangles, etc. Therefore, the sum of the angles of a polygon can be found by partitioning the polygon into triangles and summing the angle measures of those triangles, each of which is equal to $180°$.

*Example:*

What is the sum of the degree measures of the interior angles of the following six-sided pentagon?

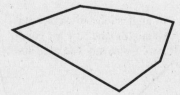

➢ If you remember the formula, use it: $180(n-2) = 180(6-2) = 180 \cdot 4 = 720°$. Otherwise, partition the polygon into smaller triangles:

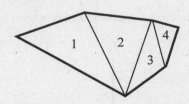

Since the six-sided polygon consists of four smaller triangles, each of which has an interior degree measure of 180°, the polygon's interior degree measure must be $4 \cdot 180 = 720°$.

## Triangle Properties and Formulas

### Properties of Triangles

A *triangle* is a three-sided figure. Within a given triangle, the larger an angle is, the longer the opposite side of the angle is; conversely, the longer a side is, the larger the opposite angle is.

*Examples:*

1.  In the figure below, since $\overline{PR} > \overline{QR} > \overline{PQ}$, $\angle Q > \angle P > \angle R$.

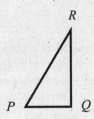

2.  In the figure below, since $\angle P > \angle Q > \angle R$, $\overline{QR} > \overline{PR} > \overline{PQ}$.

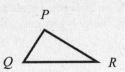

Within a given triangle, if two sides are equal, then the angles opposite the two sides are equal, and vice versa:

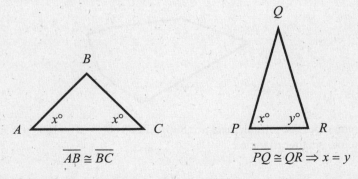

A triangle with exactly two equal sides is called an *isosceles triangle*. A triangle with exactly three equal sides is called an *equilateral triangle*.

*Example:*

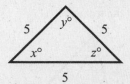

> ➢ An equilateral triangle has three equal sides and therefore three equal angles: $x = y = z$. Thus, each angle must be 60°.

A triangle with a right angle is called a ***right triangle***. The longest side of the right triangle, which is opposite the 90° angle, is called the ***hypotenuse***.

### Pythagorean Theorem

The sides of every right triangle fit a special relationship called the ***Pythagorean theorem***: the square of the hypotenuse is equal to the sum of the squares of the other two sides. This is easier to understand when it is summarized in a formula.

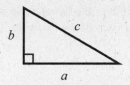

***Pythagorean Theorem:*** $c^2 = a^2 + b^2$

### Formulas of Triangles

The ***perimeter*** of a triangle is the sum of the lengths of the three sides:

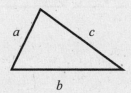

***Perimeter*** $= P = a + b + c$

The ***altitude*** of a triangle is a line drawn from a vertex perpendicular to the opposite side. The formula for finding the ***area*** of a triangle is equal to one-half multiplied by the altitude and the base.

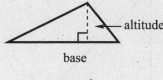

***Area*** $= \frac{ab}{2}$

*Example:*

In the figure below, what is the area of the triangle?

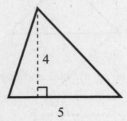

➤ $A_{\text{triangle}} = \frac{ab}{2} = \frac{4 \cdot 5}{2} = 10$

## Special Properties of 45°-45°-90° Triangles

In a triangle with angles of 45°-45°-90°, the length of the hypotenuse is equal to the length of either side multiplied by the square root of two. Conversely, the length of each of the two sides is equal to one-half the length of the hypotenuse multiplied by the square root of two.

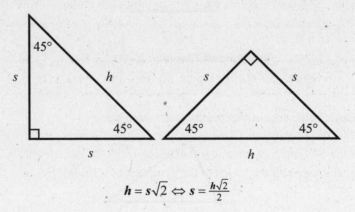

$$h = s\sqrt{2} \Leftrightarrow s = \frac{h\sqrt{2}}{2}$$

*Examples:*

1. In $\triangle ABC$, both $\angle A$ and $\angle C$ are 45°. If the length of $\overline{AB}$ is 3, what is the length of $\overline{AC}$?

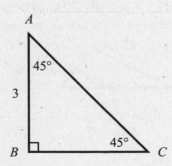

➤ $h = s\sqrt{2} \Rightarrow AC = AB(\sqrt{2}) = 3\sqrt{2}$

2. In $\triangle LMN$, both $\angle L$ and $\angle N$ are $45°$. If the length of $\overline{LN}$ is 4, what is the length of $\overline{MN}$?

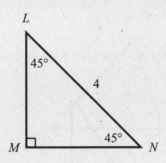

➤ $s = \frac{h\sqrt{2}}{2} \Rightarrow MN = LN(\frac{\sqrt{2}}{2}) = (4)(\frac{\sqrt{2}}{2}) = 2\sqrt{2}$

3. In the figure below, FGHJ is a square. What is the value of $\sin \angle FHJ$?

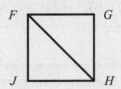

➤ In the square, diagonal $\overline{FH}$ bisects right angle $\angle GHJ$. Thus, $\angle FHJ = 45°$. Use the properties of $45°$-$45°$-$90°$ triangles: let $FJ = x$; then, $JH = x$, and $FH = x\sqrt{2}$. Thus, $\sin \angle FHJ = \frac{FJ}{FH} = \frac{x}{x\sqrt{2}} = \frac{1}{\sqrt{2}}$.

## Special Properties of 30°-60°-90° Triangles

Similarly, the sides of 30°-60°-90° triangles also share special relationships. In triangles with angles of 30°-60°-90°, the length of the side opposite the 30° angle is equal to one-half the length of the hypotenuse, and the length of the side opposite the 60° angle is equal to one-half the length of the hypotenuse multiplied by $\sqrt{3}$.

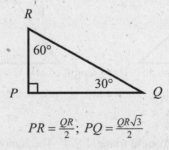

$$PR = \frac{QR}{2}; \; PQ = \frac{QR\sqrt{3}}{2}$$

*Examples:*

1. In $\triangle ABC$, $\angle A = 60°$ and $\angle C = 40°$. If the length of $\overline{AC}$ is 6, what are the lengths of $\overline{AB}$ and $\overline{BC}$?

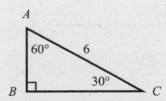

➤ $AB = \frac{AC}{2} = \frac{6}{2} = 3$

$BC = \frac{AC\sqrt{3}}{2} = \frac{6\sqrt{3}}{2} = 3\sqrt{3}$

2. In $\triangle FGH$, $\angle F = 60°$. If the length of $\overline{FH}$ is 14, what is the length of $\overline{FG}$?

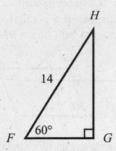

➤ The length of the side opposite the 30° angle, $\overline{FG}$, is equal to one-half the length of the side opposite the 90° angle, $\overline{FH}$: $FG = \frac{FH}{2} = \frac{14}{2} = 7$.

## Similar Triangles

"Real world" items such as blueprints, scale drawings, microscopes, and photo enlargements involve similar figures. **Similar triangles** are frequently encountered on the exams. The symbol for similarity is "~." If two triangles are similar, the corresponding sides have the same ratio, and their matching angles are **congruent**; that is, they have the same number of degrees. The symbol for congruency is "≅."

*Examples:*

1. In the figure below, $\triangle ABC \sim \triangle DEF$. Find the length of $\overline{AC}$.

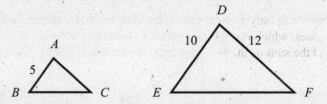

➤ The triangles are similar, so create a proportion relating the similar sides: $\frac{AC}{5} = \frac{12}{10} \Rightarrow 10(AC) = 5(12) = 60 \Rightarrow AC = 6$.

2. Right triangle $PQR$ is similar to right triangle $STV$. The hypotenuse of $\triangle PQR$ is 12 units long and one of the legs is 6 units long. Find the smallest angle of $\triangle STV$.

➤ Any right triangle in which one leg is equal to one-half the hypotenuse must be a 30°-60°-90° triangle. Since the two triangles are similar, the matching angles are congruent. Therefore, the smallest angle of $\triangle STV$ is 30°.

## Quadrilateral Properties and Formulas

A *quadrilateral* is a closed, four-sided figure in two dimensions. Common quadrilaterals are the parallelogram, rectangle, and square. The sum of the four angles of a quadrilateral is 360°. A *parallelogram* is a quadrilateral in which both pairs of opposite sides are parallel. Opposite sides of a parallelogram are equal, or congruent. Similarly, opposite angles of a parallelogram are also equal, or congruent. Again, the symbol for congruency is "≅."

$$\overline{DC} \cong \overline{AB};\ \overline{DA} \cong \overline{CB}$$
$$\angle D \cong \angle B;\ \angle A \cong \angle C$$

The area of a parallelogram is found by multiplying the base times its height. The height must be measured at a right angle.

*Example:*

In the figure below, find the area of the parallelogram.

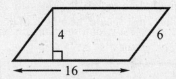

➤ The base of the parallelogram is 16 and the height is 4 (not 6). Remember, the height must be measured at a right angle to the base. Therefore, the area is: $16 \cdot 4 = 64$.

A *trapezoid* is a quadrilateral with only two parallel sides. The area of a trapezoid is equal to one-half of the height times the sum of the two bases, which are the two parallel sides. Alternatively, a trapezoid can be broken down into triangles and rectangles, and the sum of these areas equals the trapezoid's area. The following example illustrates both methods.

*Example:*

In the figure below, find the area of the trapezoid.

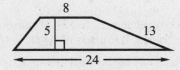

➤ The area of a trapezoid is: $\frac{(b_1 + b_2)h}{2} = \frac{(8 + 24)(5)}{2} = 80$. However, if you do not remember the formula, simply break down the trapezoid into two triangles and a rectangle:

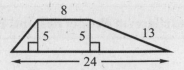

Use the Pythagorean theorem to find the base of the right-hand triangle: $x^2 + 5^2 = 13^2 \Rightarrow x = \sqrt{169-25} = \sqrt{144} = 12$. This implies that the base of the left-hand triangle is: $24 - 12 - 8 = 4$. Thus, the left-hand triangle's area is: $\frac{4 \cdot 5}{2} = 10$; the right-hand triangle's area is: $\frac{12 \cdot 5}{2} = 30$; and the rectangle's area $= 8 \cdot 5 = 40$. The trapezoid area is: $10 + 30 + 40 = 80$.

---

### FORMULAS FOR PARALLELOGRAMS AND TRAPEZOIDS

$$Parallelogram\ Area = b \cdot h$$
$$Trapezoid\ Area = \frac{(b_1 + b_2)h}{2}$$

---

A **rectangle** is any four-sided figure that has four right angles. Since the opposite sides of a rectangle are congruent, it is customary to speak of the two dimensions of a rectangle: width and length. A **square** is a rectangle with four congruent sides.

To find the **perimeter** of either a rectangle or a square, simply add the lengths of the four sides. To find the **area** of a rectangle, multiply the width times the length. In a square, the sides are all congruent, so there is no difference between length and width. To find the area of a square, just square the length of one side.

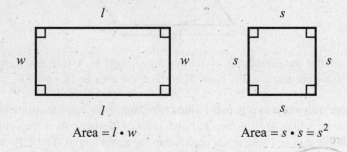

Area $= l \cdot w$          Area $= s \cdot s = s^2$

---

### FORMULAS FOR RECTANGLES AND SQUARES

$$Rectangle\ Perimeter\ = 2(\text{width}) + 2(\text{length})$$
$$= 2w + 2l = 2(w + l)$$
$$Rectangle\ Area\ = w \cdot l$$
$$Square\ Perimeter\ = 4(\text{side}) = 4s$$
$$Square\ Area\ = s \cdot s = s^2$$

---

## Circle Properties and Formulas

### Properties of Circles

A *circle* is a closed plane curve, all points of which are equidistant from the center. A complete circle contains 360°, and a semicircle contains 180°. The distance from the center of the circle to any point on the circle is called the *radius*:

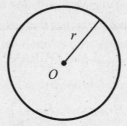

A line segment that passes through the center of the circle and that has endpoints on the circle is called the *diameter*. The diameter of a circle is twice the radius.

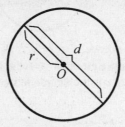

A *chord* is a line segment that connects any two points on a circle. A *secant* is a chord that extends in either one or both directions. A *tangent* is a line that touches a circle at one and only one point. A line that is tangent to a circle is perpendicular to a radius drawn to the point of tangency. The *circumference*, or perimeter, is the curved line that bounds the circle. An *arc* of a circle is any part of the circumference. The symbol for arc is "⌒."

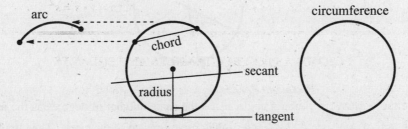

### Example:

Two different circles lie in a flat plane. The circles may or may not intersect, but neither circle lies entirely within the other. What is the difference between the minimum and maximum number of lines that could be common tangents to both circles?

> Three cases are possible for the orientation of the two circles:

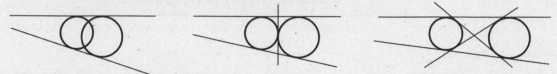

The difference between the minimum and maximum number of tangents that could be common to both circles is: $4 - 2 = 2$.

A **central angle**, such as $\angle AOB$ in the next figure, is an angle with a vertex at the center of the circle and with sides that are radii. A central angle is equal to, or has the same number of degrees as, its intercepted arc. An **inscribed angle**, such as $\angle MNP$, is an angle with a vertex on the circle and with sides that are chords. An inscribed angle has half the number of degrees of its intercepted arc. $\angle MNP$ intercepts $\overparen{MP}$ and has half the degrees of $\overparen{MP}$.

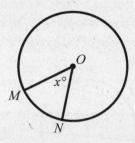

Since the number of degrees of arc in an entire circle is 360, the length of the intercepted arc of a central angle is $\frac{x}{360}$ of the circumference of the circle, where $x$ is the degree measure of the central angle.

*Example:*

In the following circle with center $O$, if $x = 60$ and the diameter of the circle is 12, what is the length of $\overparen{MN}$?

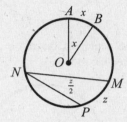

> Since the $\angle MON$ is a central angle, it has the same number of degrees as the intercepted $\overparen{MN}$. Thus, the length of $\overparen{MN}$ is: $\frac{x}{360} = \frac{60}{360} = \frac{1}{6}$ of the circumference of the circle. The circumference of the circle is: $C = 2\pi r = 2\pi \cdot \frac{d}{2} = \pi d = 12\pi$. Therefore, the length of $\overparen{MN}$ is: $\frac{12\pi}{6} = 2\pi$.

If each side of a polygon is tangent to a circle, the polygon is **circumscribed** about the circle and the circle is **inscribed** in the polygon. Conversely, if each vertex of a polygon lies on a circle, then the polygon is **inscribed** in the circle and the circle is **circumscribed** about the polygon.

*Example:*

In the figure below, △*ABC* is circumscribed about a circle and □*DEFG* is inscribed in a circle.

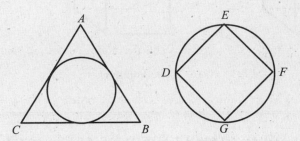

An angle inscribed in a semicircle is a right angle because the semicircle has a measure of 180°, and the measure of the inscribed angle is one half of that.

*Example:*

In the figure below, $\overset{\frown}{NP}$ has a degree measure of 180°; therefore, the degree measure of ∠*NMP* must be 90°.

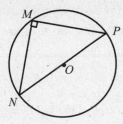

**Formulas for Circles**

**FORMULAS FOR CIRCLES**

*Circumference*: $C = 2\pi r$; $r$ = radius

*Area*: $A = \pi r^2$

$\pi(\text{pi}) \approx \frac{22}{7} \approx 3.14$

## Surface Area and Volume of Solids

In a three-dimensional figure, the total space contained within the figure is called the ***volume***; it is expressed in ***cubic denominations*** (e.g., cm$^3$). The total outside surface is called the ***surface area***; it is expressed in ***square denominations*** (e.g., cm$^2$). In computing volume and surface area, express all dimensions in the same denomination.

A ***rectangular solid*** is a figure of three dimensions having six rectangular faces that meet each other at right angles. The three dimensions are length, width, and height. A ***cube*** is a rectangular solid whose edges are equal. A ***cylinder*** is a solid composed of two circular, parallel planes joined at the edges by a curved surface. The centers of the circular planes both lie in a line perpendicular to either plane.

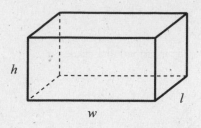 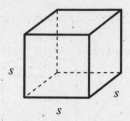 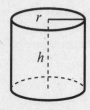

Volume $= w \cdot l \cdot h$          Cube Volume $= s^3$          Cylinder Volume $= h\pi r^2$

---

### FORMULAS FOR RECTANGULAR SOLIDS, CUBES, AND CYLINDERS

*Rectangular Solid Volume* $=$ width $\cdot$ length $\cdot$ height $= w \cdot l \cdot h$
*Rectangular Solid Surface Area* $= 2(w \cdot l) + 2(l \cdot h) + 2(h \cdot w)$

*Cube Volume* $=$ side$^3 = s^3$
*Cube Surface Area* $= 6s^2$

*Cylinder Volume* $=$ height $\cdot$ end area $= h(\pi r^2)$
*Cylinder Surface Area* $= (2\pi r \cdot h) + 2(\pi r^2)$

---

*Examples:*

1. What is the volume and surface area of the following rectangular solid?

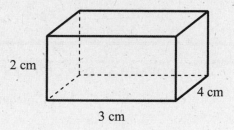

2 cm

4 cm

3 cm

➤ Volume $= w \cdot l \cdot h = 3 \cdot 4 \cdot 2 = 24$ cm$^3$

Surface Area $= 2(w \cdot l) + 2(l \cdot h) + 2(h \cdot w) = 2(3 \cdot 4) + 2(4 \cdot 2) + 2(2 \cdot 3) = 24 + 16 + 12 = 52$ cm$^2$

2. What is the volume and surface area of the following cube?

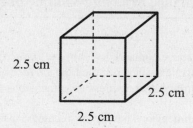

2.5 cm

2.5 cm

2.5 cm

➤ Volume $= s^3 = (2.5)^3 = 15.625$ cm$^3$

Surface Area $= 6s^2 = 6(2.5)^2 = 37.5$ cm$^2$

3.  What is the volume and surface area of the following cylindrical solid?

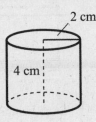

2 cm

4 cm

> Volume $= h(\pi r^2) = 4(\pi \cdot 2^2) = 16\pi\,\text{cm}^3$
>
> Surface Area $= (2\pi r \cdot h) + 2(\pi r^2) = (2\pi \cdot 2 \cdot 4) + 2(\pi \cdot 2^2) = 16\pi + 8\pi = 24\pi\,\text{cm}^2$

The **surface area of a sphere** is $4\pi$ multiplied by the radius squared. The **volume of a sphere** is $\frac{4\pi}{3}$ multiplied by the radius cubed.

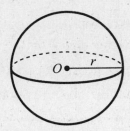

$O \bullet \quad r$

---

**FORMULAS FOR SPHERES**

*Sphere Surface Area* $= 4\pi^2$
*Sphere Volume* $= \frac{4\pi r^3}{3}$

---

# Geometry

**DIRECTIONS:** Choose the correct answer to each of the following items. Answers are on page 972.

1. In the figure below, $x = ?$

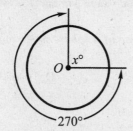

*O* is the center of the circle.

  A. 30       C. 90       E. 270
  B. 60       D. 120

2. In the figure below, $x = ?$

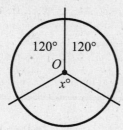

*O* is the center of the circle.

  A. 45       C. 90       E. 150
  B. 60       D. 120

3. In the figure below, $x = ?$

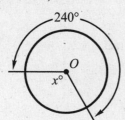

  A. 60       C. 120      E. 180
  B. 90       D. 150

4. In the figure below, $x = ?$

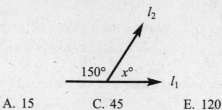

  A. 15       C. 45       E. 120
  B. 30       D. 90

5. In the figure below, $x = ?$

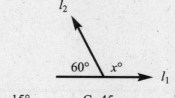

  A. 15°      C. 45       E. 120
  B. 30       D. 90

6. In the figure below, $x = ?$

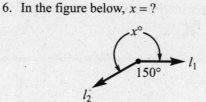

  A. 210      C. 150      E. 120
  B. 180      D. 135

7. In the figure below, $x = ?$

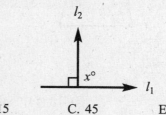

  A. 15       C. 45       E. 90
  B. 30       D. 60

8. In the figure below, $x = ?$

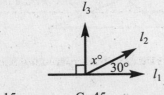

A. 15     C. 45     E. 90
B. 30     D. 60

9. In the figure below, $x = ?$

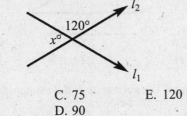

A. 45     C. 75     E. 120
B. 60     D. 90

10. In the figure below, $x = ?$

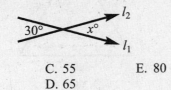

A. 30     C. 55     E. 80
B. 45     D. 65

11. Which of the following is (are) true of the figure below?

I. $\overline{AB} \cong \overline{BC}$
II. $\overline{BC} \cong \overline{AC}$
III. $\overline{AC} \cong \overline{AB}$

A. I only
B. II only
C. I and II only
D. I and III only
E. I, II, and III

Items #12–16 are based on the following figure.

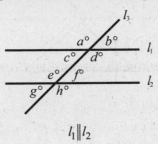

$l_1 \| l_2$

12. Which of the following is (are) necessarily true?

  I. $a = b$
  II. $b = c$
  III. $g = h$

A. I only
B. II only
C. I and II only
D. II and III only
E. I, II, and III

13. Which of the following is (are) necessarily true?

  I. $b = c$
  II. $d = c$
  III. $g = e$

A. I only
B. III only
C. I and III only
D. II and III only
E. I, II, and III

14. Which of the following is (are) necessarily true?

  I. $c + d = 180$
  II. $c + a = 180$
  III. $b + g = 180$

A. I only
B. III only
C. I and II only
D. II and III only
E. I, II, and III

15. If $e = 120$, then $g = ?$

A. 60     C. 120     E. 180
B. 90     D. 150

16. If $h = 60$, then $d = ?$

A. 60     C. 120     E. 180
B. 90     D. 150

17. Which of the following is (are) true of the figure below?

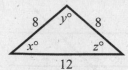

   I. $x = y$
   II. $y = z$
   III. $z = x$

A. I only       D. I and II only
B. II only      E. I, II, and III
C. III only

18. Which of the following is (are) true of the figure below?

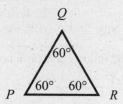

   I. $\overline{PQ} \cong \overline{QR}$
   II. $\overline{QR} \cong \overline{PR}$
   III. $\overline{PR} \cong \overline{PQ}$

A. I only       D. II and III only
B. III only      E. I, II, and III
C. I and II only

19. Which of the following is (are) true of the figure below?

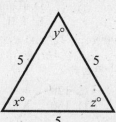

   I. $x = y$
   II. $y = z$
   III. $z = x$

A. I only       D. II and III only
B. I and II only   E. I, II, and III
C. I and III only

20. What is the perimeter of the triangle below?

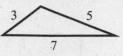

A. 3       C. 15       E. 30
B. 5       D. 20

21. What is the perimeter of the triangle below?

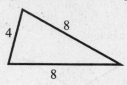

A. 20      C. 12       E. 8
B. 18      D. 10

22. What is the perimeter of the triangle below?

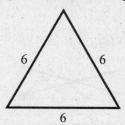

A. 6       C. 18       E. 24
B. 12      D. 21

23. What is the area of the triangle below?

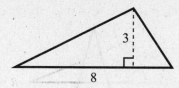

A. 3       C. 12       E. 24
B. 6       D. 18

24. What is the area of the triangle below?

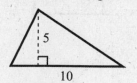

A. 5       C. 12       E. 25
B. 10      D. 15

25. What is the area of the triangle below?

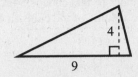

A. 6     C. 15     E. 24
B. 12    D. 18

26. In the figure below, what is the length of $\overline{RS}$?

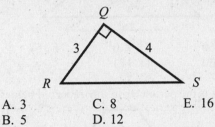

A. 3     C. 8     E. 16
B. 5     D. 12

27. In the figure below, what is the length of $\overline{AB}$?

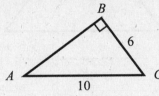

A. 4     C. 12    E. 24
B. 8     D. 16

28. In the figure below, what is the length of $\overline{PR}$?

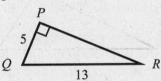

A. 12    C. 27    E. 48
B. 23    D. 36

29. In the figure below, what is the length of $\overline{AC}$?

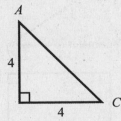

A. 2     C. 4     E. 8
B. $2\sqrt{2}$   D. $4\sqrt{2}$

30. In the figure below, what is the length of $\overline{JL}$?

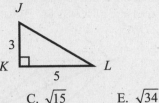

A. $\sqrt{2}$    C. $\sqrt{15}$    E. $\sqrt{34}$
B. $2\sqrt{2}$   D. $2\sqrt{6}$

31. What is the area of the parallelogram below?

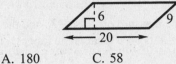

A. 180   C. 58   D. 29
B. 120   E. 15

32. What is the area of the parallelogram below?

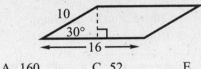

A. 160   C. 52   E. 16
B. 80    D. 26

33. What is the area of the parallelogram below?

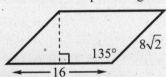

A. $128\sqrt{3}$   C. 128   E. 64
B. $128\sqrt{2}$   D. $64\sqrt{2}$

34. In the figure below, $\overline{AC}$ and $\overline{BD}$ are diameters, and the measure of $\angle ABO$ is 70°. What is the measure of $\angle COD$?

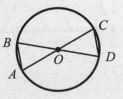

A. 110°   C. 40°   E. 30°
B. 70°    D. 35°

35. In the figure below, $\overline{AC}$ and $\overline{DE}$ bisect each other at point $B$. The measure of $\angle A$ is 20° and the measure of $\angle D$ is 86°. What is the measure of $\angle DBC$

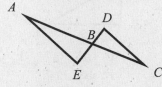

   A. 106°      C. 66°      E. 33°
   B. 74°       D. 45°

36. In $\triangle ABC$, the measure of $\angle A$ is 23° and the measure of $\angle B$ is 84°. What is the longest side of $\triangle ABC$?

   A. $\overline{AC}$
   B. $\overline{AB}$
   C. $\overline{BC}$
   D. $\overline{AC} \cong \overline{AB}$ (there is no longest side)
   E. $\overline{AC} \cong \overline{BC}$ (there is no longest side)

37. In $\triangle ABC$, the measure of $\angle A$ is 40° and the measure of $\angle B$ is 70°. What is the longest side of $\triangle ABC$?

   A. $\overline{AC}$
   B. $\overline{AB}$
   C. $\overline{BC}$
   D. $\overline{AC} \cong \overline{AB}$ (there is no longest side)
   E. $\overline{AC} \cong \overline{BC}$ (there is no longest side)

38. $\triangle ABC$ has three sides with lengths $\overline{AB} = 19$, $\overline{BC} = 20$, and $\overline{AC} = 21$. What is the smallest angle of $\triangle ABC$?

   A. $\angle A$
   B. $\angle B$
   C. $\angle C$
   D. $\angle A \cong \angle B$ (there is no smallest angle)
   E. $\angle A \cong \angle B \cong \angle C$ (there is no smallest angle)

39. Each side of a cube is a square with an area of 49 square centimeters. What is the volume of the cube, in cubic centimeters?

   A. 49       C. $7^4$      E. $7^{49}$
   B. $7^3$      D. $49^7$

40. Each side of a cube is a square. The total surface area of all sides of this cube is 54 square inches. What is the volume of the cube, in cubic inches?

   A. $54^3$      C. $9^3$      E. 9
   B. $(\sqrt{54})^3$    D. 27

41. What is the area of the trapezoid below?

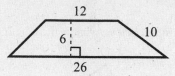

   A. 260      C. 130      E. 58
   B. 130      D. 114

42. What is the perimeter of the trapezoid below?

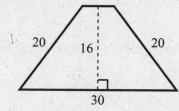

   A. 70       C. 80       E. 100
   B. 76       D. 90

43. The volume of a sphere is $V = \frac{4}{3}\pi r^3$, where $r$ is the radius of the sphere. If the surface area of the sphere is $324\pi$, what is the sphere's volume?

   A. $243\pi$      C. $729\pi$      E. $1,296\pi$
   B. $324\pi$      D. $972\pi$

44. What is the perimeter of the figure below?

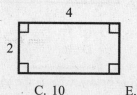

   A. 6       C. 10       E. 16
   B. 8       D. 12

45. What is the perimeter of the figure below?

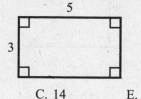

   A. 8       C. 14       E. 16
   B. 12      D. 15

46. What is the area of the figure below?

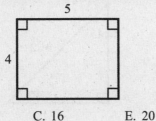

A. 10    C. 16    E. 20
B. 15    D. 18

47. What is the area of the figure below?

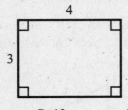

A. 6    C. 12    E. 24
B. 8    D. 16

48. What is the area of the figure below?

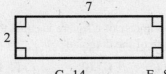

A. 5    C. 14    E. 81
B. 9    D. 25

49. In the figure below, $\overline{AB} = 5$. What is the area of square $ABCD$?

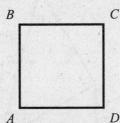

A. 5    C. 20    E. 40
B. 10    D. 25

50. If the radius of a circle is 2, what is the diameter?

A. 1    C. 3    E. 8
B. 2    D. 4

51. If the diameter of a circle is 10, what is the radius?

A. 2    C. 8    E. 20
B. 5    D. 15

52. If the radius of a circle is 3, what is the circumference?

A. $2\pi$    C. $6\pi$    E. $12\pi$
B. $3\pi$    D. $9\pi$

53. If the radius of a circle is 5, what is the circumference?

A. $5\pi$    C. $15\pi$    E. $24\pi$
B. $10\pi$    D. $20\pi$

54. If the diameter of a circle is 8, what is the circumference?

A. $8\pi$    C. $4\pi$    E. $\pi$
B. $6\pi$    D. $2\pi$

55. If the radius of a circle is 3, what is the area?

A. $\pi$    C. $6\pi$    E. $12\pi$
B. $3\pi$    D. $9\pi$

56. If the radius of a circle is 5, what is the area?

A. $25\pi$    C. $18\pi$    E. $\pi$
B. $21\pi$    D. $2\pi$

57. If the diameter of a circle is 8, what is the area?

A. $16\pi$    C. $10\pi$    E. $4\pi$
B. $12\pi$    D. $8\pi$

58. If the diameter of a circle is 12, what is the area?

A. $18\pi$    C. $30\pi$    E. $36\pi$
B. $24\pi$    D. $32\pi$

59. In the figure below, what are $a$ and $b$?

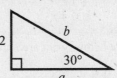

A. $a = \sqrt{3}, b = 2$    D. $a = 4, b = 2\sqrt{3}$
B. $a = 2\sqrt{3}, b = 4$    E. $a = 4, b = 4\sqrt{3}$
C. $a = 2, b = 2$

60. In the figure below, what are $c$ and $d$?

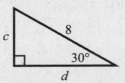

A. $c = 2, d = \sqrt{3}$    D. $c = 4\sqrt{2}, d = 2$
B. $c = 2\sqrt{2}, d = 3$    E. $c = 3, d = 2\sqrt{3}$
C. $c = 4, d = 4\sqrt{3}$

61. In the figure below, what are *e* and *f*?

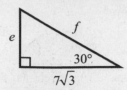

A. $e = 2$, $f = 6$     D. $e = 7$, $f = 10$

B. $e = \sqrt{2}$, $f = 8$     E. $e = 7$, $f = 14$

C. $e = 4$, $f = 3\sqrt{5}$

62. In the figure below, what are *g* and *h*?

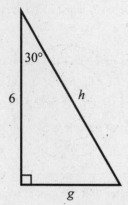

A. $g = \sqrt{3}$, $h = \sqrt{3}$     D. $g = 4$, $h = 4\sqrt{3}$

B. $g = 2\sqrt{2}$, $h = 2\sqrt{3}$     E. $g = 6$, $h = 7$

C. $g = 2\sqrt{3}$, $h = 4\sqrt{3}$

63. What is the altitude of an equilateral triangle with a perimeter of 24?

A. $2\sqrt{3}$     C. 6     E. 8

B. $4\sqrt{3}$     D. $4\sqrt{5}$

64. In the figure below, what are *i* and *j*?

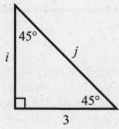

A. $i = 3$, $j = 3\sqrt{2}$     D. $i = 5$, $j = 3\sqrt{3}$

B. $i = 3$, $j = 3$     E. $i = 4$, $j = 5$

C. $i = 4\sqrt{2}$, $j = 4$

65. In the figure below, what are *k* and *m*?

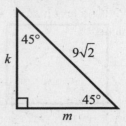

A. $k = 3$, $m = 3$     D. $k = 9$, $m = 9$

B. $k = 2\sqrt{3}$, $m = 3$     E. $k = 3$, $m = 9$

C. $k = 4$, $m = 6$

66. In the figure below, $AB = BC = \sqrt{6}$. What is the length of $\overline{AC}$? Note that the triangle is not drawn to scale.

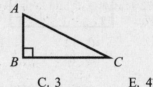

A. 2     C. 3     E. 4

B. $2\sqrt{3}$     D. $3\sqrt{2}$

67. If the perimeter of a square is equal to 40, what is the length of the diagonal?

A. $10\sqrt{2}$     C. 10     E. 14

B. $5\sqrt{3}$     D. $3\sqrt{5}$

68. In the figure below, what is *p* equal to?

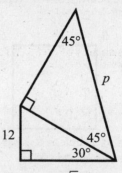

A. $2\sqrt{2}$     C. $10\sqrt{2}$     E. $24\sqrt{2}$

B. $2\sqrt{3}$     D. $20\sqrt{3}$

69. In the circle below, $\overline{RS}$ is parallel to diameter $\overline{PQ}$, and $\overline{PQ}$ has a length of 12. What is the length of minor $\overparen{RS}$?

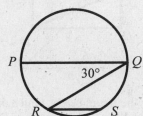

A. $\frac{\pi}{2}$  C. $2\pi$  E. $\frac{7\pi}{2}$

B. $\pi$  D. $\frac{3\pi}{2}$

70. What is the number of degrees in the angle formed by the minute and hour hands of a clock at 2:20?

A. 90  C. 60  E. 30

B. 70  D. 50

71. What is the radius of a circle with an area of 49?

A. 7  C. $\frac{7}{\sqrt{\pi}}$  E. $\pi^2$

B. $7\pi$  D. $\frac{7}{\pi}$

72. What is the area of a circle with a circumference of $\frac{22\pi}{30}$?

A. $\frac{484\pi}{9}$  C. $\frac{121\pi}{3}$  E. $\frac{556\pi}{4}$

B. $\frac{121\pi}{9}$  D. $\frac{484\pi}{3}$

73. A circle has an area of $36\pi^3$. What is the radius of the circle?

A. 6  C. $6\pi^2$  E. $6\pi^4$

B. $6\pi$  D. $6\pi^3$

74. If the radius of a circle is 8, what is the circumference of the circle?

A. $4\pi$  C. $12\pi$  E. $16\pi$

B. $8\pi$  D. $14\pi$

75. In the figure below, what is the value of the shaded area?

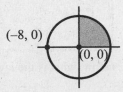

A. $16\pi$  C. $64\pi$  E. $16\pi^2$

B. $32\pi$  D. $66\pi$

76. In the figure below, the length of $\overline{OA}$ is 2 and the length of $\overline{OB}$ is 3. What is the area between the two circles?

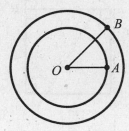

A. $4\pi$  C. $6\pi$  E. $8\pi$

B. $5\pi$  D. $7\pi$

77. In the figure below, a circle with an area of $144\pi$ is inscribed in a square. What is the area of the shaded region?

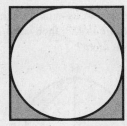

A. $576 - 144\pi$  D. $1,728 - 144\pi$

B. $216 - 72\pi$  E. $256 - 24\pi$

C. $144 - 24\pi$

78. A square has a perimeter of 40. A second square has an inscribed circle with an area of $64\pi$. What is the ratio of the length of a side of the first square to the length of a side of the second square?

A. $5:8$  C. $5:16$  E. $12:\pi$

B. $5:4$  D. $10:8\pi$

79. The area of a square is $64x^2y^{16}$. What is the length of a side of the square?

    A. $8xy^8$    C. $8x^2y^{16}$    E. $20x^2y^4$
    B. $8xy^4$    D. $16x^2y^{16}$

80. In the figure below, what is the area of square *BCDE*?

    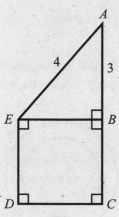

    A. 5    C. 12    E. 49
    B. 7    D. 24

81. What is the area of a right triangle with legs of lengths 4 and 5?

    A. 6    C. 12    E. 24
    B. 10    D. 20

82. In the figure below, assume *O* is the center of the circle. If $\angle OAB$ is 45°, then what is the area of the shaded segment?

    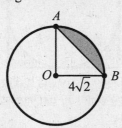

    A. $32\pi - 16\sqrt{2}$    D. $8\pi - 16$
    B. $32\pi - 8$    E. $8\pi - 8$
    C. $4\pi - 8$

83. In the figure below, rectangle *ABCD* has an area of 15. What is the length of the diagonal $\overline{AC}$?

    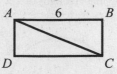

    A. 4    C. 6.5    E. 7.5
    B. 5    D. 7

84. Regarding the figure below, which one of the following statements is true?

    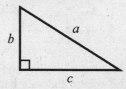

    A. $a^2 + b^2 = c^2$    D. $b^2 + c^2 = a^2$
    B. $a + b = c$    E. $a + c = b$
    C. $b + c = a$

85. At 12 cents per square foot, how much will it cost to paint the rectangular slab in the figure below?

    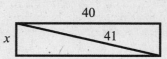

    A. $43.20    C. $98.40    E. $201.50
    B. $46.40    D. $196.80

86. In the figure below, what is the length of $\overline{BC}$?

    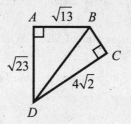

    A. 1    C. 3    E. 5
    B. 2    D. 4

87. If the diagonal of a square is $5\sqrt{2}$, what is the area of the square?

    A. 10    C. 25    E. 35
    B. 20    D. 30

88. What is the area of the rectangle in the figure below?

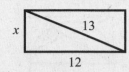

A. 156    C. 72    E. 60
B. 78    D. 66

89. In the figure below, what is $x$ equal to?

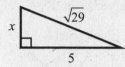

A. $\sqrt{29}-5$    C. 24    E. $\sqrt{2}$
B. $\sqrt{24}$    D. 2

90. If $2\sqrt{3}$ is the diagonal of a square, then what is the perimeter of the square?

A. $4\sqrt{6}$    C. $6\sqrt{3}$    E. 14
B. 8    D. 12

91. In the figures below, what is the ratio of the perimeter of $\triangle ABC$ to the perimeter of $\triangle DEF$?

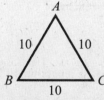

A. 1:1    C. 15:16    E. 7:3
B. 5:6    D. 6:5

92. In terms of $\pi$, what is the area of a circle whose radius is $2\sqrt{5}$?

A. $\pi$    C. $10\pi$    E. $40\pi$
B. $4\pi$    D. $20\pi$

93. What is the radius of a circle whose area is $12\pi$?

A. $40\pi$    C. $2\sqrt{3}$    E. 3
B. 1    D. 2

94. What is the radius of a circle if the distance to walk halfway around the rim of the circle is $\sqrt{6}\pi$?

A. $\sqrt{2}$    C. 2    E. 3
B. $\sqrt{3}$    D. $\sqrt{6}$

95. If the legs of a right triangle are 2 and 5, what is the hypotenuse?

A. $\sqrt{22}$    C. $5\sqrt{2}$    E. 6
B. $\sqrt{29}$    D. $\sqrt{35}$

96. If the hypotenuse of a right triangle is 37 and one leg is 35, what is the length of the other leg?

A. $4\sqrt{3}$    C. 12    E. 16
B. $6\sqrt{2}$    D. $14\sqrt{2}$

97. If $2\sqrt{12}$, $3\sqrt{6}$, and $4\sqrt{3}$ are the dimensions of a rectangular solid, what is the volume of the solid?

A. $216\sqrt{24}$    C. $144\sqrt{6}$    E. $\sqrt{24}$
B. $\sqrt{5,184}$    D. 5,184

98. What is the volume of a cylinder with an altitude of 10 and a circumference of $\sqrt{128\pi}$?

A. $\sqrt{1,280\pi}$    C. $640\pi$    E. $3,460\pi$
B. $320\pi$    D. $1,280\pi$

99. In the figure below, what is $x$ equal to?

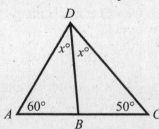

A. 30    C. 35    E. 70
B. 32    D. 40

100. If the ratio of the sides of a triangle are $x : x\sqrt{3} : 2x$, and the length of the smallest side is 5, what is the length of the largest side?

A. 10    C. $8\sqrt{3}$    E. 20
B. 12    D. 15

101. In the figure below, what is the length of $\overline{JK}$?

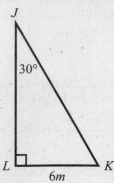

A. $6m\sqrt{3}$  C. $12m$  E. $14m$
B. $9m$  D. $12m\sqrt{3}$

102. In the figure below, $\Delta DEF$ is an isosceles triangle. What is the length of $\overline{DF}$?

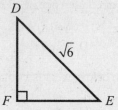

A. $2\sqrt{6}$  C. $\sqrt{3}$  E. $12\sqrt{2}$
B. $6\sqrt{2}$  D. $12$

103. If the longest side of a 30°-60°-90° triangle is $2\sqrt{3}$, what is the area of the triangle?

A. 8  C. $1.5\sqrt{3}$  E. 1
B. 4  D. 2

104. In the figure below, what is the length of the diagonal $\overline{AC}$ of square $ABCD$?

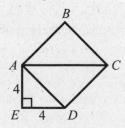

A. $4\sqrt{2}$  C. $8\sqrt{2}$  E. $32\sqrt{2}$
B. 8  D. 16

105. In the figure below, if $\overset{\frown}{BC}$ equals 60°, then what is the area of $\Delta ABC$?

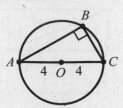

A. 16  C. $8\sqrt{3}$  E. $10\sqrt{2}$
B. $4\sqrt{3}$  D. 12

106. In the figure below, what is $2x - 60$ equal to?

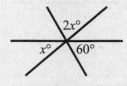

A. 80  C. 30  E. 10
B. 40  D. 20

107. In the figure below, $a$ equals all of the following EXCEPT

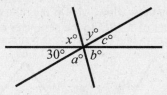

A. $y$  C. $180 - b - c$  E. $180 - x - y$
B. $150 - x$  D. $150 - b$

108. In the figure below, $\overline{EC} \parallel \overline{AB}$ and $\overline{AD} \cong \overline{BD}$. What is the sum of the degree measures of $\angle A + \angle B + \angle BCE$?

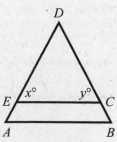

A. $(x + y)°$  C. $(180 + x)°$  E. $(90 - y)°$
B. $3x°$  D. $-2x°$

109. In the figure below, if $\overline{AE} \parallel \overline{BD}$ and $\overline{BD} \cong \overline{DC}$, then what is $\angle BDC$ equal to?

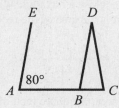

A. 10°          C. 18°          E. 24°
B. 15°          D. 20°

110. In the figure below, if $l_1 \parallel l_2$ and $\angle 7 = 117°$, which other angles must also equal 117°?

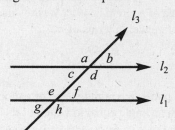

A. $a, e, h$          C. $c, e, f$          E. $a, c, e, g$
B. $a, c, b$          D. $h, f, b$

111. In the figure below, what is the value of $x$?

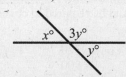

A. 30          C. 60          E. 80
B. 45          D. 65

112. In the figure below, which of the following statements is true?

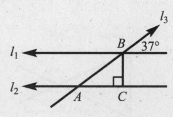

$l_1 \parallel l_2$

A. $\overline{AC} > \overline{BC}$          D. $\overline{AC} + \overline{BC} = \overline{AB}$
B. $\overline{AC} < \overline{BC}$          E. $\overline{AC} - \overline{BC} = \overline{AB}$
C. $\overline{AC} = \overline{BC}$

113. In the figure below, $\overline{OM} \parallel \overline{PJ}$, and $\overline{FG}$ and $\overline{EG}$ divide $\angle CGO$ into 3 congruent angles. What is the degree measure of $\angle EGC$?

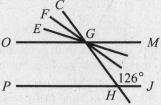

A. 18°          C. 42°          E. 63°
B. 36°          D. 54°

114. In the figure below, $\triangle ABE \sim \triangle ACD$. What is the length of $\overline{CD}$?

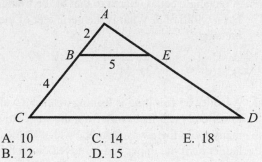

A. 10          C. 14          E. 18
B. 12          D. 15

115. A triangle with sides of 12, 14, and 20 is similar to a second triangle that has one side with a length of 40. What is the smallest possible perimeter of the second triangle?

A. 48          C. 120          E. 180
B. 92          D. 160

116. A right circular cylinder has a base whose diameter is $8x$; the height of the cylinder is $3y$. What is the volume of the cylinder?

A. $24xy$          C. $48\pi xy$          E. $48\pi x^2 y$
B. $24\pi x^2 y$          D. $96\pi xy$

117. If the perimeter of a rectangle is 68 yards and the width is 48 feet, what is the length?

A. 10 yards          C. 20 feet          E. 54 feet
B. 18 feet          D. 46 feet

118. What is the total length of fencing, in yards, needed to enclose a rectangular area that measures 46 feet long by 34 feet wide?

A. $26\frac{1}{3}$          C. 48          E. $53\frac{1}{3}$
B. $26\frac{2}{3}$          D. $52\frac{2}{3}$

119. An umbrella 50" long can lie diagonally on the bottom of a trunk with a length and width that are which of the following, respectively?

    A. 26", 30"    C. 31", 31"    E. 40", 30"
    B. 30", 36"    D. 40", 21"

120. A road runs 1,200 feet from point $A$ to point $B$, and then makes a right angle going to point $C$, a distance of 500 feet. A new road is being built directly from $A$ to $C$. How many feet shorter will the new road be than the old road?

    A. 400    C. 850    E. 1,300
    B. 609    D. 1,000

121. A certain triangle has side lengths of 6, 8, and 10. A rectangle equal in area to that of the triangle has a width of 3. What is the perimeter of the rectangle?

    A. 11    C. 22    E. 30
    B. 16    D. 24

122. A ladder 65 feet long is leaning against a wall. Its lower end is 25 feet away from the wall. How many more feet away from the wall will the ladder be if the upper end is moved down 8 feet?

    A. 60    C. 14    E. 8
    B. 52    D. 10

123. A rectangular bin 4 feet long, 3 feet wide, and 2 feet high is solidly packed with bricks whose dimensions are 8 inches × 4 inches × 2 inches What is the number of bricks in the bin?

    A. 54
    B. 320
    C. 648
    D. 848
    E. Cannot be determined from the given information

124. If the cost of digging a trench is $2.12 per cubic yard, what would be the cost of digging a trench that is 2 yards long, 2 yards wide, and 2 yards deep?

    A. $21.20    C. $64.00    E. $104.80
    B. $40.00    D. $84.80

125. A piece of wire is shaped to enclose a square, whose area is 121 square inches. It is then reshaped to enclose a rectangle whose length is 13 inches. What is the area of the rectangle, in square inches?

    A. 64    C. 117    E. 234
    B. 96    D. 144

126. What is the area, in square feet, of a 2-foot-wide walk around the outside of a garden that is 30 feet long and 20 feet wide?

    A. 104    C. 680    E. 1,416
    B. 216    D. 704

127. The area of a circle is $49\pi$. What is its circumference, in terms of $\pi$?

    A. $14\pi$    C. $49\pi$    E. $147\pi$
    B. $28\pi$    D. $98\pi$

128. In two hours, the minute hand of a clock rotates through an angle equal to which of the following?

    A. 90°    C. 360°    E. 1,080°
    B. 180°    D. 720°

129. A box is 12 inches in width, 16 inches in length, and 6 inches in height. How many square inches of paper would be required to cover it on all sides?

    A. 192    C. 720    E. 1,440
    B. 360    D. 900

130. If the volume of a cube is 64 cubic inches, the sum of the lengths of its edges is how many inches?

    A. 48    C. 24    E. 12
    B. 32    D. 16

131. In the figure below, $x = ?$

    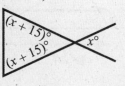

    A. 20    C. 50    E. 90
    B. 35    D. 65

132. What is the difference of the areas of two squares with sides of 5 and 4, respectively?

    A. 3    C. 9    E. 91
    B. 4    D. 16

133. A triangle with sides of 4, 6, and 8 has the same perimeter as an equilateral triangle with sides of length equal to which of the following?

 A. 2  C. 3  E. 8
 B. $\frac{3}{2}$  D. 6

134. In the figure below, $x = ?$

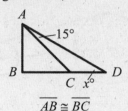

$\overline{AB} \cong \overline{BC}$

 A. 15°  C. 40°  E. 75°
 B. 30°  D. 60°

135. If the area of the rectangle shown below is equal to 1, then $l = ?$

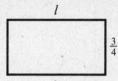

 A. $\frac{4}{9}$  C. $\frac{4}{3}$  E. 2
 B. 1  D. $\frac{9}{4}$

136. A semicircle is divided into three arcs with respective lengths $2\pi$, $6\pi$, and $14\pi$. The semicircle is a part of a circle with which of the following radii?

 A. 44  C. 22  E. 6
 B. 33  D. 11

137. In the figure below, $x = ?$

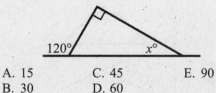

 A. 15  C. 45  E. 90
 B. 30  D. 60

138. In the figure below, $\angle A \cong \angle B$.

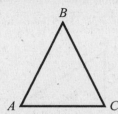

Which of the following statements must be true?

 A. $\angle A \cong \angle B \cong \angle C$
 B. $\angle A \not\cong \angle C$
 C. $\overline{AC} \cong \overline{BC}$
 D. $\overline{BC} \cong \overline{AB}$
 E. $\overline{AB} \cong \overline{AC}$

139. In the incomplete figure below, the circle and $\overrightarrow{AB}$ have how many points of intersection?

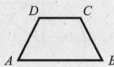

 A. 0
 B. 1
 C. 2
 D. 3
 E. An infinite number

140. In the figure below, which is not necessarily drawn to scale, $\angle A \cong \angle C$ and $\angle B \cong \angle D$.

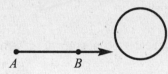

How many of the following four statements of congruence must be true?

$\angle A \cong \angle B$
$\overline{AB} \cong \overline{DC}$
$\overline{AD} \cong \overline{BC}$
$\overline{AB} \cong \overline{BC} \cong \overline{CD} \cong \overline{AD}$

 A. 0  C. 2  E. 4
 B. 1  D. 3

141. In the diagram below, $\angle ABC = 90°$, $\overline{AC} = 10\sqrt{2}$, and $\overline{AB} + \overline{BC} = 3\sqrt{38}$. What is the area of $\triangle ABC$?

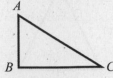

A. 19     C. 32     E. 40
B. 29     D. 35.5

142. In the diagram below, $\overline{AD} \cong \overline{AE}$ and $\overline{AB} \cong \overline{BF} \cong \overline{CE} \cong \overline{CF} \cong \overline{DE}$.

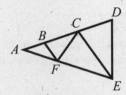

What is the degree measure of $\angle DAE$?

A. 20°     C. 25°     E. 35°
B. 24°     D. 30°

143. In the figure below, $\triangle ABC$ intersects a circle with center $O$. $\overline{AB}$ is tangent to the circle at $A$. If $\overline{AB} = 8$ and $\overline{BO} = 10$, what is the area of the circle?

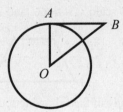

A. $4\pi$     C. $36\pi$     E. $100\pi$
B. $6\pi$     D. $64\pi$

144. The figure below shows a circle with center $O$, two radii $\overline{OA}$ and $\overline{OB}$, and two tangents $\overline{AC}$ and $\overline{BC}$. What is the area of the shaded region?

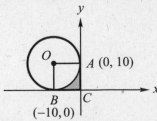

A. $100 - 100\pi$   C. $50 - 50\pi$   E. $100 - 25\pi$
B. $50 - 100\pi$    D. $50 - 25\pi$

145. The figure below shows two circles lying in the same plane with respective centers at $O$ and $P$. $\overline{AB}$ is a common external tangent segment to the two circles at $A$ and $B$, respectively. If $\overline{OA} = 13$, $\overline{PB} = 3$, and $\overline{OP} = 26$, then what is the length of $\overline{AB}$?

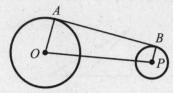

A. 26     C. 24     E. 18
B. 25     D. 20

146. The figure below shows a circle of area $144\pi$ square inches with a radius drawn to the point of tangency of the circle on the $x$-axis.

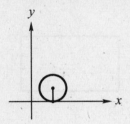

If this point of tangency is 16 inches from the origin, then the number of inches from the origin to the center of the circle is:

A. 12     C. 16     E. 20
B. $12\sqrt{2}$     D. $16\sqrt{2}$

147. In the figure below, $\overline{TP} \cong \overline{RA}$, and $\overline{TR} \parallel \overline{PA}$. $\overline{TR} = 12$, $\overline{PA} = 44$. If $\angle P = 45°$, what is the area of $TRAP$?

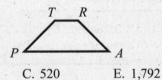

A. 448     C. 520     E. 1,792
B. 464     D. 896

148. In the figure below, which is not necessarily drawn to scale, $\angle ABC = 90°$, $\overline{AB} = 10$, and $\frac{\overline{AB}}{\overline{BC}} = 1$. What is the length of $\overline{AC}$?

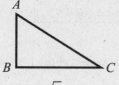

A. 10     C. $10\sqrt{2}$     E. $20\sqrt{3}$

B. 20     D. $10\sqrt{3}$

149. In the figure below, $B$ and $E$ lie on $\overline{AC}$ and $\overline{AD}$, respectively, of $\triangle ACD$, such that $\overline{BE} \parallel \overline{CD}$. $\overline{BD} \perp \overline{AC}$, and $\overline{BC} \cong \overline{ED}$. If $\overline{BC} = 10$ and $\overline{CD} = 20$, what is the area of $\triangle ABE$?

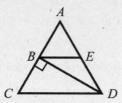

A. 100

B. $50\sqrt{3}$

C. 50

D. $25\sqrt{3}$

E. Cannot be determined from the given information

150. The figure below shows three acute angles and two obtuse angles.

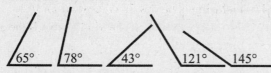

If two different angles are created randomly using the five angles shown, what is the probability that both angles are acute?

A. $\frac{1}{10}$     C. $\frac{2}{5}$     E. $3\frac{3}{10}$

B. $\frac{1}{5}$     D. $\frac{3}{5}$

151. The perimeter of a regular hexagon is given by the formula $P = 6s$, where $P$ is the perimeter and $s$ is the length of one side. If one side of a regular hexagon has a length of 3, what is the perimeter?

A. 12     C. 18     E. 30

B. 15     D. 21

152. The volume of a cone is $\frac{\pi r^2 h}{3}$, where r is the radius of the cone base and $h$ is the cone height. What is the volume, in cubic inches, of a cone of height 12 inches that has a base of radius 3 inches?

A. $144\pi$     C. $72\pi$     E. $36\pi$

B. $108\pi$     D. $54\pi$

# Coordinate Geometry

## Coordinate Axis System

The easiest way to understand the coordinate axis system is as an analog to the points of the compass. If we take a plot of land, we can divide it into quadrants:

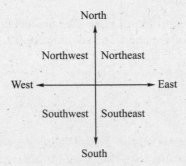

Now, if we add measuring units along each of the directional axes, we can actually describe any location on this piece of land by two numbers.

*Example:*

Point $P$ is located at 4 units East and 5 units North. Point $Q$ is located at 4 units West and 5 units North. Point $R$ is located at 4 units West and 2 units South. Point $T$ is located at 3 units East and 4 units South.

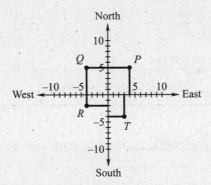

The coordinate system used in coordinate geometry differs from our map of a plot of land in that it uses $x$- and $y$-axes divided into negative and positive regions.

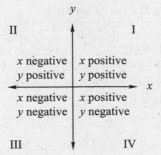

It is easy to see that **Quadrant I** corresponds to our Northeast quarter, in which the measurements on both the $x$- and $y$-axes are positive. **Quadrant II** corresponds to our Northwest quarter, in which the measurements on the $x$-axis are negative and the measurements on the $y$-axis are positive. **Quadrant III** corresponds to our Southwest quarter, in which both the $x$-axis measurements and the $y$-axis measurements are negative. Finally, **Quadrant IV** corresponds to our Southeast quarter, in which the $x$-values are positive while the $y$-values are negative.

## Ordered Pairs

An **ordered pair** of coordinates has the general form $(x, y)$. The first element refers to the **x-coordinate**: the distance left or right of the **origin**, or intersection of the axes. The second element gives the **y-coordinate**: the distance up or down from the origin.

*Example:*

Plot $(3, 2)$.

➤ Move to the positive 3 value on the $x$-axis. Then, from there move up two units on the $y$-axis, as illustrated by the graph on the left. The graph on the right demonstrates an alternative method: the point $(3, 2)$ is located at the intersection of a line drawn through the $x$-value 3 parallel to the $y$-axis and a line drawn through the $y$-value 2 parallel to the $x$-axis.

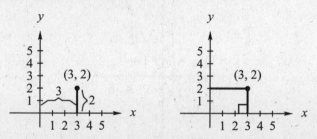

## Plotting Equations

The coordinate axis system provides a framework for plotting equations. Simply plot several pairs of points for the given equation.

*Examples:*

1. Plot the equation $x = y$.

   ➤ This equation has an infinite number of solutions:

   | $x$ | 1 | 2 | 3 | 5 | 0 | −3 | −5 | ... |
   |---|---|---|---|---|---|---|---|---|
   | $y$ | 1 | 2 | 3 | 5 | 0 | −3 | −5 | ... |

   Plot these pairs of $x$ and $y$ on the axis system. Draw a line through them to produce a plot of the original equation. The complete picture of the equation $x = y$ is a straight line including all the real numbers such that $x$ is equal to $y$.

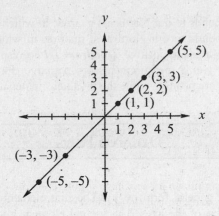

2. Plot the equation $y = 2x$.

   ➤ This equation has an infinite number of solutions:

| $x$ | −4 | −2 | −1 | 0 | 1 | 2 | 4 | ... |
|---|---|---|---|---|---|---|---|---|
| $y$ | −8 | −4 | −2 | 0 | 2 | 4 | 8 | ... |

   After entering the points on the graph, complete the picture. It is a straight line, but it rises more rapidly than does $x = y$.

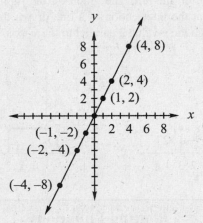

## Midpoint of Line Segments

For a line segment between two points, $(x_1, y_1)$ and $(x_2, y_2)$, the ***midpoint*** $= (\frac{x_1 + x_2}{2}, \frac{y_1 + y_2}{2})$. The $x$-coordinate of the midpoint is the average of the two $x$-axis endpoints and the $x$-coordinate of the midpoint is the average of the two $y$-axis endpoints.

*Examples:*

1. Find the midpoint between $(-5, 8)$ and $(11, 34)$.

   ➤ The midpoint is $(\frac{x_1 + x_2}{2}, \frac{y_1 + y_2}{2}) = (\frac{-5 + 11}{2}, \frac{8 + 34}{2}) = (\frac{6}{2}, \frac{42}{2}) = (3, 21)$.

2. One endpoint of a circle diameter is located at (13,1). If the center of the circle is (15,10), find the other endpoint.

➢ The midpoint of the diameter is (15,10), so $15 = \frac{x_1 + x_2}{2} = \frac{13 + x_2}{2}$ and $10 = \frac{y_1 + y_2}{2} = \frac{1 + y_2}{2}$. $x_2 = (15 \cdot 2) - 13 = 17$ and $y_2 = (10 \cdot 2) - 1 = 19$. Thus, $(x_2, y_2) = (17,19)$.

## Distance between Two Points

To determine the distance between two points on a coordinate graph, consider points $P$ and $Q$. For simplicity's sake, we will confine the discussion to the first quadrant, but the method generally works in all quadrants and even with lines covering two or more quadrants. Assign the value $(x_1, y_1)$ to point $P$ and $(x_2, y_2)$ to point $Q$:

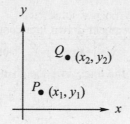

To find distance between points $P$ and $Q$, construct a triangle:

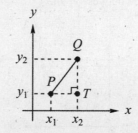

Point $T$ now has the coordinates $(x_2, y_1)$. To calculate the length of $\overline{PT}$, find the distance moved on the $x$-axis: $x_2 - x_1$ units. The $y$-coordinate does not change. Similarly, the length of $\overline{QT}$ will be $y_2 - y_1$ since the distance is purely vertical, moving up from $y_1$ to $y_2$, with no change in the $x$-value. Apply the Pythagorean theorem:

$$(PQ)^2 = (PT)^2 + (QT)^2 = (x_2 - x_1)^2 + (y_2 - y_1)^2$$

$$PQ = \sqrt{(x_2 - x_1)^2 + (y_2 - y_1)^2}$$

*Example:*

In the figure below, what is the length of $\overline{PQ}$?

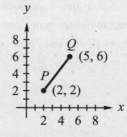

> Find the length of $\overline{PQ}$ by constructing a triangle:

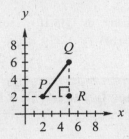

$\overline{QR}$ runs from $(5,6)$ to $(5,2)$, so it must be 4 units long. $\overline{PR}$ runs from $(2,2)$ to $(5,2)$, so it is 3 units long. Use the Pythagorean theorem: $(\overline{PQ})^2 = (\overline{QR})^2 + (\overline{PR})^2 = 4^2 + 3^2 = 16 + 9 = 25$. Therefore, $\overline{PQ} = \sqrt{25} = 5$.

Therefore, you can find the length of any line segment drawn in a coordinate axis system between points $(x_1, y_1)$ and $(x_2, y_2)$ using this ***distance formula***: $d = \sqrt{(x_2 - x_1)^2 + (y_2 - y_1)^2}$. Notice that it does not actually matter which point is considered the start of the line and the end of the line, since the change in each coordinate is squared in the distance formula.

*Example:*

In the figure below, what is the distance between $P$ and $Q$?

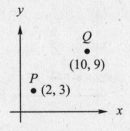

> The distance between $P$ and $Q$ is: $\sqrt{(x_2 - x_1)^2 + (y_2 - y_1)^2} = \sqrt{(10 - 2)^2 + (9 - 3)^2} = \sqrt{64 + 36} = \sqrt{100} = 10$.

## Linear Functions

### Slope-Intercept Form

If $x$ and $y$ are related by a linear equation, then $y$ is a ***linear function***. Except for a vertical line, every line equation is a linear function that can be represented in ***slope-intercept form***: $y = mx + b$. $m$ is the slope of the line and $b$ is the $y$-intercept. The $y$-intercept is the $y$-coordinate of the point where the line intersects the $y$-axis, or where $x = 0$. The ***slope***, $m$, of a line describes the steepness of the line. It is defined as the change in $y$-values divided by the change in $x$-values, or rise over run: ***slope*** $= m = \frac{y_2 - y_1}{x_2 - x_1} = \frac{rise}{run}$.

*Examples:*

1. Find the slope of the line containing $(3, 2)$ and $(8, 22)$.

   ➤ $m = \frac{y_2 - y_1}{x_2 - x_1} = \frac{22 - 2}{8 - 3} = \frac{20}{5} = 4$.

2. Find the slope of the line given by the equation $6x + 12y = 13$.

   ➤ $6x + 12y = 13 \Rightarrow 12y = -6x + 13 \Rightarrow y = \frac{-6x + 13}{12} \Rightarrow y = -\frac{x}{2} + \frac{13}{12}$. Therefore, the slope is $-\frac{1}{2}$.

3. The points $(-5, 12)$, $(0, 7)$ and $(10, -3)$ lie on a line. What is the *y*-intercept of this line?

   ➤ The *x*-coordinate of the second point is 0. Therefore, this point's *y*-coordinate, 7, is the *y*-intercept of the line.

## Parallel Lines

The equation of a line that is parallel to the *x*-axis is $y = k$, where is a constant. The equation of a line that is parallel to the *y*-axis is $x = c$, where $c$ is a constant. If two lines are parallel, their slopes are equal and vice versa.

*Example:*

Find the equation for a line that passes through the point $(0, 12)$ and is parallel to the line $y = 7x - 15$.

   ➤ A line has slope-intercept form $y = mx + b$. If the line passes through the *y*-axis at $(0, 12)$, then the *y*-intercept $b = +12$. If the two lines are parallel, then the slopes are equal and $m = +7$. Therefore, the line equation is $y = mx + b \Rightarrow y = 7x + 12$.

## Perpendicular Lines

If two perpendicular lines have slopes $m_1$ and $m_2$, then $m_1 = -\frac{1}{m_2}$ and vice versa.

*Example:*

The equation of a line is $y = \frac{x}{4} + 10$. If a second line is perpendicular to the line, what is the slope of this line?

   ➤ If two lines are perpendicular to one another, their slopes are opposite reciprocals of one another. Thus, if a line has a slope of $\frac{1}{4}$, then the line perpendicular to it has a slope of $-4$.

## Quadratic Functions

If $y$ is expressed in the form $y = ax^2 + bx + c$, where $a \neq 0$ and $b$ is any real number, $y$ is a ***quadratic function***. Graphs of quadratic functions are called parabolas. The basic graph that you need to know is $f(x) = x^2$, as illustrated in the first of the following examples.

*Examples:*

1. Which of the following graphs depicts a quadratic function?

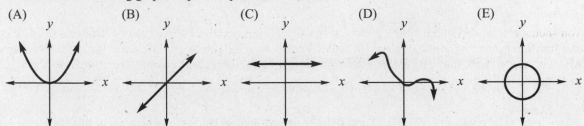

(A)   (B)   (C)   (D)   (E)

> All quadratic equations can be written in the form $y = ax^2 + bx + c$. (B) is a linear plot with the $y$-intercept equal to 0: $y = ax$. (C) is a constant value for $y$: $y = k$. (E) is a plot of a circle: $x^2 + y^2 = k$, where $k$ is a constant. (D) is a complicated function without a standard form of equation. Only (A) is a quadratic equation: $y = ax^2$.

2. A quadratic function of the form $y = ax^2 + bx + c$ includes the following ordered pairs of $(x, y)$: $(1, 17)$, $(5, 61)$, and $(7, 95)$. What is the value of $c$ for this quadratic function?

> Solve the system of three simultaneous equations that are generated by the three ordered pairs: $17 = a(1)^2 + b(1) + c$, $61 = a(5)^2 + b(5) + c$, and $95 = a(7)^2 + b(7) + c$. The quadratic function is $y = x^2 + 5x + 11$.

## Identifying Graphs of Functions

You may be asked simply to identify graphs of linear and quadratic functions. The graph of a linear function is a straight line, while the graph of a quadratic function is called a parabola and always has the shape of a curve about the $y$-axis.

*Example:*

The line of best fit for $y = f(x)$ for the ordered pairs $(-4, -18)$, $(1, 3)$, $(2, 6)$, $(3, 8)$, and $(4, 14)$ is best represented by which of the following graphs?

(A)   (B)   (C)   (D)   (E)

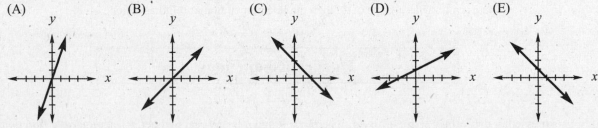

> The correct answer is (A). Both $x$ and $y$ increase in value for each ordered pair, so eliminate (C) and (E). You can eliminate (B) since the values of $x$ and $y$ in the given ordered pairs clearly indicate that $x \neq y$. Finally, eliminate (D) because when $x = 1$, $y = 3$, whereas in the graph of (D), $y < 3$ when $x = 1$.

Functions can be also mathematical models of real-life situations. For example, an item might present information about the projected sales of a product at various prices and ask for a mathematical model in the form of a graph or equation that represents projected sales as a function of price.

## Qualitative Behavior of Graphs

You should also understand how the graphs of functions behave qualitatively. Items on the exam might show the graph of a function in the $xy$-coordinate plane and ask for the number of values of $x$ for which $f(x)$ equals a particular value. Alternatively, an item may present a graph with numerical values, requiring you to recognize the form of the graphed function.

*Examples:*

1. The figure below shows a graph of the function $y = x^2 + 2x + 6$. What is the smallest possible integer value of $y$?

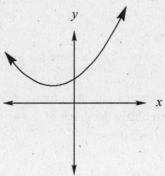

➢ The lowest point on the function occurs when $x < 0$. Find the symmetry by substitution: if $x = 1$, $y = 9$; if $x = 0$, $y = 6$; if $x = -1, y = 5$; if $x = -2$, $y = 6$; if $x = -3$, $y = 9$. The coordinates of these points are $(-3, 9)$, $(-2, 6)$, $(-1, 5)$, $(0, 6)$, and $(1, 9)$, respectively. Thus, the lowest point occurs at $(-1, 5)$. Alternatively, solve for the vertex using the properties of parabolas. The standard form of a parabola is: $y = a(x - h)^2 + k$, where the vertex is at $(h, k)$. Write the equation in standard form: $y = (x^2 + 2x + 1) + 6 - 1 = (x + 1)^2 + 5 = [x - (-1)]^2 + 5$. Therefore, the vertex is at $(-1, 5)$.

2. What is the sum of all distinct integer y-values for the graph of the absolute value function in the figure below?

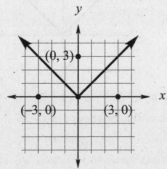

➢ Each negative y-value has a canceling positive y-value. Therefore, the answer is zero.

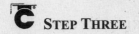 

## Transformation Effects on Graphs

When you alter a graph, you transform it. If you transform a graph without changing its shape, you translate it. Vertical and horizontal transformations are translations. Items on the exam may test knowledge of the effects of simple translations of graphs of functions. For example, the graph of a function $f(x)$ could be given and you might be asked items about the graph of the function $f(x+2)$.

### Vertical Translations

To move a function up or down, you add or subtract outside the function. That is, $f(x)+b$ is $f(x)$ moved up $b$ units, and $f(x)-b$ is $f(x)$ moved down $b$ units.

*Example:*

In order to obtain the graph of $y=(x+2)^2+6$ from the graph of $y=x^2+4x+11$, how should the graph of $y=x^2+4x+11$ be moved?

➤ Rewrite the original function in the form $f(x)+b$: $y=x^2+4x+11 \Rightarrow y=x^2+4x+4+7 = (x+2)^2+7$. Therefore, to obtain the graph of $y=(x+2)^2+6$ from the graph of $y=(x+2)^2+7$, the graph must be moved one unit down.

### Horizontal Translations

To shift a function to the left or to the right, add or subtract inside the function. That is, $f(x+b)$ is $f(x)$ shifted $b$ units to the left, and $f(x-b)$ is $f(x)$ shifted $b$ units to the right.

*Example:*

The graph below is of the function $y=|x|$.

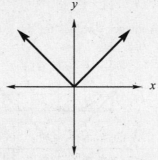

Which of the following is a graph of the function $y=|x+3|$?

(A) 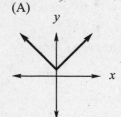  (B) 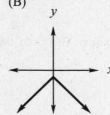  (C) 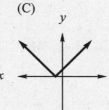  (D) 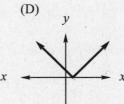  (E)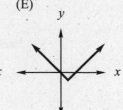

➤ By translation of the original graph from $y = |x|$ to $y = |x+3|$, the original graph is moved three units to the left, (C). Alternatively, substitute values for $x$ and $y$: $y = 0$ for $x = -3$. (C) is the only graph that contains the point $(-3, 0)$.

## Graphing Geometric Figures

You can also use the coordinate system for graphing geometric figures. The following figure is a graph of a square whose vertices are at coordinates $(0, 0)$, $(4, 0)$, $(4, 4)$, and $(0, 4)$.

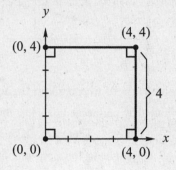

Each side of the square is equal to 4 since each side is 4 units long and parallel to either the $x$- or $y$-axis. Since every coordinate point is the perpendicular intersection of two lines, it is possible to measure distances in the coordinate system.

*Examples:*

1. In the figure below, what is the area of the circle?

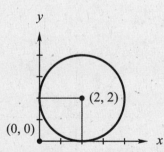

➤ To solve this problem, find the radius of the circle. The center of the circle is located at the intersection of $x = 2$ and $y = 2$, or the point $(2, 2)$. Thus, the radius is 2 units long and the area is $4\pi$.

2. $\triangle ABC$ has coordinates $A$, $B$, and $C$ equal to $(5,3)$, $(19,7)$ and $(17,25)$, respectively. By how much does the largest slope for any median of $\triangle ABC$ exceed the largest slope for any altitude of $\triangle ABC$?

   ➢ The largest slope occurs for the steepest ascent for increasing values of $x$. Draw a figure of the given information in the coordinate plane:

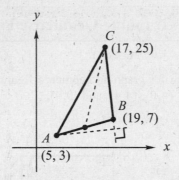

A median is drawn from one angle of a triangle to the midpoint of the opposite side. Of the three possible medians, the median that connects $C$ to the midpoint of $\overline{AB}$ has the largest slope. The midpoint of $\overline{AB}$ is $(\frac{5+19}{2}, \frac{7+3}{2}) = (12,5)$. Therefore, the slope of the median is $\frac{25-5}{17-12} = 4$. An altitude is drawn from one angle of a triangle to the opposite side at a right angle. Of the three possible altitudes, the altitude that connects $A$ to $\overline{BC}$ has the largest slope. Since this altitude is perpendicular to $\overline{BC}$, its slope is the opposite reciprocal of the slope of $\overline{BC}$. The slope of $\overline{BC}$ is $\frac{25-7}{17-19} = \frac{18}{-2} = -9$, so the slope of the altitude $\frac{1}{9}$. Therefore, the amount by which the slope of the median is larger than the slope of the altitude is: $4 - \frac{1}{9} = \frac{36}{9} - \frac{1}{9} = \frac{35}{9}$.

EXERCISE **11**

# Coordinate Geometry

**DIRECTIONS:** Choose the correct answer to each of the following items. Answers are on page 983.

1. Which of the following graphs represents a relation of which the domain is the set of all real numbers and the range is the set of all non-negative real numbers?

A.
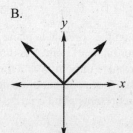

D.
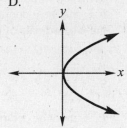

B.
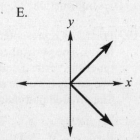

E.

C.
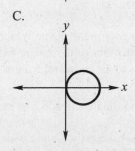

2. Which of the lettered points on the number line below could represent the result when the coordinate of point $F$ is divided by the coordinate of point $X$?

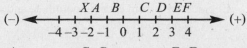

A. A     C. C     E. E
B. B     D. D

3. $\overline{AB}$ is the diameter of a circle whose center is point $O$. If the coordinates of point $A$ are $(2,6)$ and the coordinates of point $B$ are $(6,2)$, find the coordinates of point $O$.

A. $(4,4)$    C. $(2,-2)$    E. $(2,2)$
B. $(4,-4)$    D. $(0,0)$

4. $\overline{AB}$ is the diameter of a circle whose center is point $O$. If the coordinates of point $O$ are $(2,1)$ and the coordinates of point $B$ are $(4,6)$, find the coordinates of point $A$.

A. $(3,3\frac{1}{2})$    C. $(0,-4)$    E. $(-1,-2\frac{1}{2})$
B. $(1,2\frac{1}{2})$    D. $(2\frac{1}{2},1)$

5. Find the distance from the point whose coordinates are $(4,3)$ to the point whose coordinates are $(8,6)$.

A. 5    C. $\sqrt{7}$    E. 15
B. 25    D. $\sqrt{67}$

6. The vertices of a triangle are $(2,1)$, $(2,5)$, and $(5,1)$. What is the area of the triangle?

A. 12    C. 8    E. 5
B. 10    D. 6

7. The area of a circle whose center is at $(0,0)$ is $16\pi$. The circle does NOT pass through which of the following points?

A. $(4,4)$    C. $(4,0)$    E. $(0,-4)$
B. $(0,4)$    D. $(-4,0)$

8. What is the slope of a line that passes through $(0,-5)$ and $(8,27)$?

A. 4    C. $\frac{8}{32}$    E. $-4$
B. 2    D. $-\frac{8}{32}$

9. The slope of a line that passes through points $(3,7)$ and $(12,y)$ is $\frac{1}{3}$. What is the value of $y$?

A. 2    C. $6\frac{2}{3}$    E. 10
B. 4    D. $7\frac{1}{3}$

10. What is the slope of the line $y = 5x + 7$?

    A. 7     C. 2     E. $\frac{1}{5}$

    B. 5     D. $\frac{7}{5}$

11. A line passes through points $(3, 8)$ and $(w, 2k)$. If $w \neq 3$, what is the slope of the line?

    A. $\frac{8 - 2k}{3 + w}$     C. $\frac{2k - 8}{w - 3}$     E. $\frac{3}{8}$

    B. $\frac{2k + 8}{w + 3}$     D. $\frac{w - 3}{2k - 8}$

12. What is the equation of the line that passes through the point $(0, 13)$ and is parallel to the line $4x + 2y = 17$?

    A. $4x + 2y = 13$

    B. $4x + 2y = -13$

    C. $y = -2x + 13$

    D. $y = 2x + 13$

    E. Cannot be determined from the given information

13. A line passes through the point $(0, -5)$ and is perpendicular to the line $y = -\frac{x}{2} + 5$. What is the equation of the line?

    A. $y = -\frac{x}{2} - 5$

    B. $y = 2x - 5$

    C. $y = -2x - 5$

    D. $y = -\frac{x}{2} + 13$

    E. Cannot be determined from the given information

14. If point $P$ has coordinates $(-2, 2)$ and point $Q$ has coordinates $(2, 0)$, what is the distance from point $P$ to point $Q$?

    A. $-4$     C. $4\sqrt{5}$     E. 6

    B. $2\sqrt{5}$     D. 4

15. If point $R$ has coordinates $(x, y)$ and point $S$ has coordinates $(x + 1, y + 1)$, what is the distance between point $R$ and point $S$?

    A. $\sqrt{2}$          D. $\sqrt{x^2 + y^2 + 2}$

    B. 2            E. $x + y + 1$

    C. $\sqrt{x^2 + y^2}$

16. Will is standing 40 yards due north of point $P$. Grace is standing 60 yards due west of point $P$. What is the shortest distance between Will and Grace?

    A. 20 yards       D. 80 yards

    B. $4\sqrt{13}$ yards    E. $80\sqrt{13}$ yards

    C. $20\sqrt{13}$ yards

17. On a coordinate graph, what is the distance between points $(5, 6)$ and $(6, 7)$?

    A. $\sqrt{2}$     C. 2     E. $6\sqrt{2}$

    B. 1     D. 4

18. On a coordinate plane, point $B$ is located 7 units to the left of point $A$. The $x$-coordinate of point $A$ is $x$, and the $y$-coordinate of point $A$ is $y$. What is the $x$-coordinate of point $B$?

    A. $x - 7$

    B. $x + 7$

    C $y + 7$

    D. $y - 7$

    E. Cannot be determined from the given information

19. Point $R$ is represented on the coordinate plane by $(x, y)$. The vertical coordinate of point $S$ is three times the vertical coordinate of point $R$ and the two points have the same horizontal coordinate. The ordered pair that represents point $S$ is:

    A. $(3x, y)$     C. $(x, y - 3)$     E. $(x, 3y)$

    B. $(x, y + 3)$     D. $(3x, 3y)$

20. A square is drawn in a coordinate plane. Which of the following transformations of the square will shift the square 7 units to the right and 5 units downward?

    A. Add 7 to each $x$-coordinate and add 5 to each $y$-coordinate.

    B. Multiply each $x$-coordinate by 7 and divide each $y$-coordinate by 5.

    C. Add 7 to each $x$-coordinate and subtract 5 from each $y$-coordinate.

    D. Subtract 7 from each $x$-coordinate and subtract 5 from each $y$-coordinate.

    E. Subtract 7 from each $x$-coordinate and add 5 to each $y$-coordinate.

21. In the rectangular coordinate system below, if $x = 4.2$, then $y$ equals which of the following?

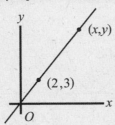

A. 2.8    C. 4.8    E. 6.3
B. 3.4    D. 6.2

22. Points $(x, -4)$ and $(-1, y)$ (not shown in the figure below) are in Quadrants III and II, respectively. If $x$ and $y \neq 0$, in which quadrant is point $(x, y)$?

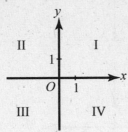

A. I
B. II
C. III
D. IV
E. Cannot be determined from the given information

23. If Sam lives 8 miles west of Jeni, and Molly lives 10 miles north of Jeni, approximately how many miles less would Molly walk if she walks directly to Sam's house, rather than first to Jeni's house and then to Sam's house?

A. 1    C. 3    E. 5
B. 2    D. 4

24. If point $B$ (not shown in the figure below) lies below the $x$-axis at point $(4, -4)$, what is the area of $\triangle ABC$?

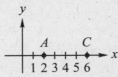

A. 2    C. 6    E. 16
B. 4    D. 8

25. On a coordinate graph, what is the distance between points $(-1, 4)$ and $(2, 8)$?

A. 3    C. 5    E. 8
B. 4    D. 6

26. In the figure below, $\overline{AB}$ is the base of a water ski ramp and is 18 feet long. The slope (rise divided by run) of the ramp is $m$. If the ramp is $y$ feet high, then what is the value of $y$?

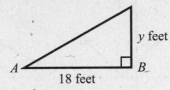

A. $\frac{m}{18}$    C. $18 - m$    E. $m + 18$
B. $18m$    D. $m - 18$

27. What is the midpoint between $(-2, 15)$ and $(8, 17)$?

A. $(6, 16)$    C. $(5, 16)$    E. $(6, 32)$
B. $(3, 16)$    D. $(5, 32)$

28. In the figure below, $\overline{AB}$ is the diameter of a circle whose center is at point $P$. What are the coordinates for point $B$?

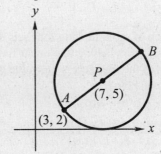

A. $(10, 7)$    C. $(12, 7)$    E. $(11, 7)$
B. $(5, 2.5)$    D. $(11, 8)$

29. How many of the following graphs are graphs of linear functions?

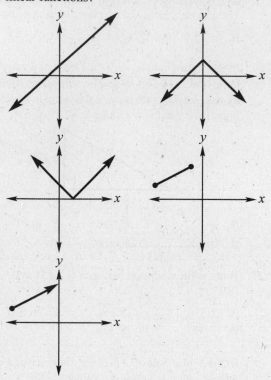

A. 1     C. 3     E. 5
B. 2     D. 4

30. In each of the following four sets, the three ordered pairs belong to a linear function. In how many of the four sets is the value of the variable $x$ less than zero?

$\{(0,1),(-4,7),(x,0)\}$
$\{(0,2),(-5,52),(x,12)\}$
$\{(2,-5),(-2,-17),(x,13)\}$
$\{(6,17),(8,25),(x,4)\}$

A. 0     C. 2     E. 4
B. 1     D. 3

31. If $y = mx + b$, $x = 5$ for $y = 20$, and $x = 9$ for $y = 32$, then $m + b$ is:

A. 76     C. 14     E. 3
B. 52     D. 8

32. Which of the following graphs depicts the quadratic functions $y = \frac{x^2}{2}$ and $y = -\frac{x^2}{2}$?

A.

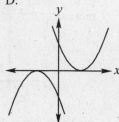

D.

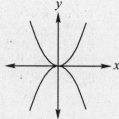

B.

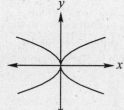

E.

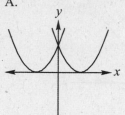

C.

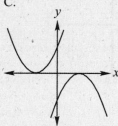

33. If $y = -2x^2 + 16x - 1$, what is the largest possible value for $y$?

A. −1
B. 13
C. 31
D. 32
E. Cannot be determined from the given information

34. The graph of $y = 4x^2$ intersects the graph of $y = x^2 + 3x$ at how many points?

A. 0     C. 2     E. 4
B. 1     D. 3

35. A student noted that the graph of the following ordered points for $(x, y)$ appeared to approximate a parabolic curve: $(1, 7)$, $(-1, 0)$, $(2, 12)$, $(4, 29)$, $(5, 42)$. Which of the following equations best represents the curve?

    A. $y = x^2 + 6$

    B. $y = x^2 + 3x + 2$

    C. $y = 2x^2 + x + 4$

    D. $y = x^2 - x + 8$

    E. $y = 2x^2 + x + 4$

36. The graph of the following ordered pairs for $(x, y)$ is approximately a straight line of the form $y = mx + b$: $(1, 18)$, $(2, 23)$, $(3, 27)$, $(4, 32)$, $(5, 38)$. Which of the following best approximates the value of $b$?

    A. 13      C. 20      E. 25
    B. 18      D. 23

37. A scientist studying insect movement observes that in a day, each insect travels a particular geometric pattern and the distance traveled by each insect is directly proportional to the insect's length. The values for insect length and distance traveled in a day, in inches, for four insects are: $(1, 1.57)$, $(1.5, 2.36)$, $(2, 3.14)$, and $(3, 4.71)$. The geometric pattern traveled by the four insects is a:

    A. square
    B. equilateral triangle
    C. circle
    D. semicircle
    E. regular polygon of five sides

38. The figure below shows two parallel lines with coordinates of points as shown. What is the slope of the line passing through point $(6, 0)$?

    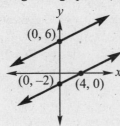

    A. $\frac{1}{2}$      C. $\frac{1}{4}$      E. $\frac{1}{6}$

    B. $\frac{1}{3}$      D. $\frac{1}{5}$

39. The center of a circle is located at $(19, 7)$. One end of a diameter of the circle is located at $(4, 6)$. The second end of the diameter is located at:

    A. $(11.5, 6.5)$      C. $(34, 8)$      E. $(38, 8)$
    B. $(11.5, 13)$      D. $(38, 14)$

40. In the figure below, which is not necessarily drawn to scale, $ABCD$ is a square and $\angle FGH \cong \angle A$.

    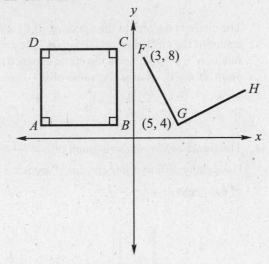

    If points $F$ and $G$ have the coordinates as indicated in the figure, how many of the following four ordered pairs could possibly represent point $H$?

    $(8, 6)$, $(9, 6)$, $(11, 7)$, $(13, 8)$

    A. 0      C. 2      D. 3
    B. 1      E. 4

41. The line that passes through $(1, 5)$ and $(-2, 17)$ is parallel to the line that passes through $(17, 6)$ and $(13, y)$. What is the value of $y$?

    A. 10      C. 16      E. 22
    B. 14      D. 18

42. What is the distance from the point $(-2, 5)$ to the point $(7, -7)$?

    A. 9      C. 15      E. 24
    B. 12      D. 18

43. The figure below shows a circle with an area of $9\pi$.

The circle is tangent to the $x$-axis at $(0,0)$ and the center of the circle lies on the $y$-axis. The constant function $y = k$ intersects the circle at exactly one point. If $k > 0$, what is the value of $k$?

A. 1      C. 3      E. 9
B. 2      D. 6

44. The figure below shows a graph of $y = \dfrac{12}{x^2 + 6x + 7}$. How many different integers for $y$ are not a part of the graph of $y = \dfrac{12}{x^2 + 6x + 7}$?

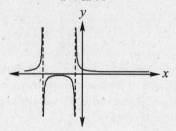

A. 2      C. 7      E. 13
B. 6      D. 12

45. The graph below shows two different parabola functions: $y = (x-1)^2 + 4$ and $y - 2 = -(x+5)^2$.

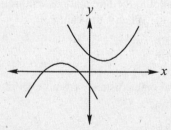

The values of $y$ that are not on either of the parabolas are all values of $y$ such that:

A. $-5 \le y \le 1$    C. $1 < y < 4$    E. $4 < y < 5$
B. $2 < y < 4$    D. $1 \le y \le 5$

46. The graph below is of the function $y = (x-2)^2 + 3$.

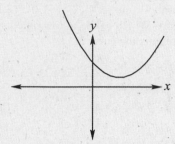

If a horizontal shift of four units to the left were performed on the original graph, at what point $(x, y)$ would the transformed graph intersect the original graph?

A. $(2, 7)$    C. $(6, 3)$    E. $(0, 3)$
B. $(2, -1)$    D. $(-2, 3)$

47. The graph of $y = 3x^2$ can be produced from the graph of $y = x^2$ by performing a vertical stretch by a factor of three. The graph of $y = 2x^2 + 12x + 1$ can be produced from the graph of $y = x^2$ by performing a vertical stretch by a factor of two, a horizontal shift of three units to the left, and a vertical shift of:

A. 17 units down.
B. 12 units down.
C. 1 unit down.
D. 1 unit up.
E. 12 units up.

48. The following ordered pairs for $(x, y)$ represent points on a graph: $(5, 15)$, $(10, 28)$, $(11, 27)$, $(25, 47)$, $(40, 76)$, $(50, 111)$, and $(60, 129)$. Which of the following equations represents the line of best fit (the line that most closely approximates the set of points)?

A. $y = \frac{x}{3}$    C. $y = 3x - 6$    E. $y = 5x - 4$
B. $y = \frac{x}{3} - 2$    D. $y = 2x + 3$

49. The graph below shows a circle whose equation
    is $x^2 + y^2 = 16$.

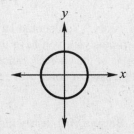

The graph is moved by the following
transformations: four units to the right and two
units up. Which of the following is the correctly
transformed graph?

A.

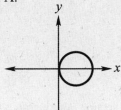

D.

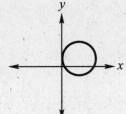

B.

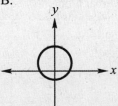

E.

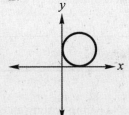

C.

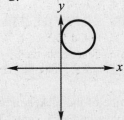

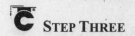 

# Solving Story Problems

**Story problems** may test arithmetic, algebra, or geometry in the context of a "story." You should have everything you need to solve these problems. However, remember that if a math story item stumps you, you have the answer at hand. Simply work backwards from the answer choices—the right answer has to be one of the choices. Since quantitative (i.e., numerical value) choices are arranged in size order, starting with the middle answer choice will result in the fewest calculations.

In solving story problems, the most important technique is to read accurately. Be sure you clearly understand what you are asked to find. Then, evaluate the item in common sense terms and to eliminate answer choices. For example, if two people are working together, their combined speed is greater than either individual speed, but not more than twice as fast as the fastest speed. Finally, be alert for the "hidden equation"—some necessary information so obvious that the item assumes that you know it.

*Examples:*

1. boys + girls = total class

2. imported wine + domestic wine = all wine

3. wall + floor = right angle (Pythagorean theorem)

Some of the frequently encountered types of problem-solving problems are described in this section, although not every item you may encounter will fall into one of these categories. However, thoroughly familiarizing yourself with the types of problems that follow will help you to develop the skills to translate and solve all kinds of verbal problems.

---

## Coin Problems

---

For coin **problems**, change the value of all monies involved to cents before writing an equation. The number of nickels must be multiplied by 5 to give their value in cents; dimes must be multiplied by 10; quarters by 25; half-dollars by 50; and dollars by 100.

*Example:*

Richard has $3.50 consisting of nickels and dimes. If he has 5 more dimes than nickels, how many dimes does he have?

➤ Let $x$ = the number of nickels; $x + 5$ = the number of dimes; $5x$ = the value of the nickels in cents; $10x + 50$ = the value of the dimes in cents; and $350$ = the value of the money he has in cents. Thus: $5x + 10x + 50 = 350 \Rightarrow 15x = 300 \Rightarrow x = 20$. Therefore, Richard has 20 nickels and 25 dimes.

In an item such as this, you can be sure that 20 would be among the multiple-choice answers. You must be sure to read carefully what you are asked to find and then continue until you have found the quantity sought.

## Number and Set Problems

Number problems can be story problems that require knowledge of the properties of numbers in order to solve the item. Typically, number problems involve **consecutive integers** or **consecutive odd/even numbers**. Consecutive integers are one number apart and can be represented by $x$, $x+1$, $x+2$, etc. Consecutive even or odd integers are two numbers apart and can be represented by $x$, $x+2$, $x+4$, etc.

*Example:*

Three consecutive odd integers have a sum of 33. Find the average of these integers.

➢ Represent the integers as $x$, $x+2$, and $x+4$. Write an equation indicating the sum is 33: $3x+6=33 \Rightarrow 3x=27 \Rightarrow x=9$. Thus, the integers are 9, 11, and 13. In the case of evenly spaced numbers such as these, the average is the middle number, 11. Since the sum of the three numbers was given originally, all we really had to do was to divide this sum by 3 to find the average, without ever knowing what the numbers were.

Set problems test understanding of relationships between different sets of numbers or **elements**. A **set** is a collection of things; e.g., the set of positive integers.

---

### DEFINITIONS FOR WORKING WITH SETS

The **number of elements** in set $P$ is: $n(P)$.

The **union** of two sets $P$ and $Q$ is the set of all elements in *either* $P$ or $Q$, or both: $P \cup Q$.

The **intersection** of two sets $P$ and $Q$ is the set of all elements in *both* $P$ and $Q$: $P \cap Q$.

The **cardinal number theorem** is used find the number of elements in a union of two sets.
$$n(P \cup Q) = n(P) + n(Q) - n(P \cap Q)$$

---

*Examples:*

1. Let $S = \{3, 5, x\}$. If exactly one subset of $S$ contains two different elements whose sum is 12, what value(s) can $x$ be?

   ➢ Since either $3+x=12$ or $5+x=12$, then $x=9$ or $x=7$.

2. In a class of 30 students, 15 students are learning French, 11 students are learning Spanish, and 7 students are learning neither French nor Spanish. How many students in the class are learning both French and Spanish?

   ➢ Use the cardinal number theorem:
   $$n(F \cup S) = n(F) + n(S) - n(F \cap S)$$
   $$30 - 7 = 15 + 11 \cdot n(F \cap S)$$
   $$(F \cap S) = 3$$

The cardinal number theorem is also known as the **addition principle for counting** and is the first of several useful methods for counting objects and sets of objects without actually listing the elements to be counted. According to the theorem, if set $A$ contains $m$ objects, set $B$ contains $n$ objects, and there are no objects common to the two sets, then the total number of objects in the two sets combined is $m+n$. However, if there are $k$ objects common to the two sets, then the total in the combined set is $m+n-k$. In other words, you must take into account the double-counting of objects common to both sets.

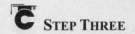 

*Example:*

Of a group of students at a campus cafe, 9 ate pizza and 5 had salad. If 3 had both pizza and salad, how many had either pizza or salad?

➤ The question describes two sets: one consisting of students that ate pizza (set $P$: $m = 9$), and one consisting of students that had salad (set $S$: $n = 5$). Since the question states that 3 students had both pizza and salad, the number of students common to the two sets is 3 ($k = 3$). Therefore, the total in the combined set (number of students who had either pizza or salad) is: $m + n - k = 9 + 5 - 3 = 11$.

This kind of situation involving sets that overlap is most easily handled by displaying the given information in a *Venn diagram*.

*Example:*

Two circles are drawn on a floor. 20 people are standing in circle $A$. 15 people are standing in circle $B$. 9 people are standing in both circles. Find the total number of people standing in the two circles.

➤ The item can be symbolized with a Venn diagram:

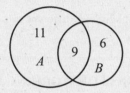

From the diagram, it can be seen that there are a total of $11 + 9 + 6$ or 26 people.

## Age Problems

*Age* problems involve a comparison of ages at the present time, several years from now, or several years ago. A person's age $x$ years from now is found by adding $x$ to his present age. A person's age $x$ years ago is found by subtracting $x$ from his present age.

*Examples:*

1. Michelle was 12 years old $y$ years ago. What is her age $b$ years from now?

   ➤ Michelle's present age is $12 + y$. In $b$ years, her age will be $12 + y + b$.

2. Logan is 5 years older than Florencia. Three years ago, Logan was twice as old as Florencia. How old is Logan?

   ➤ If you have trouble setting up the equations, use numbers. Suppose that Florencia is 11. If Logan is 5 years older than Florencia, then Logan must be $11 + 5 = 16$. Thus, if $L$ is Logan's age and $F$ is Florencia's age, $L = F + 5$. Three years ago, Logan was $L - 3$ and Florencia was $F - 3$. Therefore, since 3 years ago, Logan was twice as old as Florencia, $L - 3 = 2(F - 3) \Rightarrow L - 3 = 2F - 6 \Rightarrow L = 2F - 3$. Substitute $L = F + 5 \Rightarrow F = L - 5$ for $F$ in the equation $L = 2F - 3$ to find Logan's current age: $L = 2F - 3 = 2(L - 5) - 3 = 2L - 13 \Rightarrow L = 13$.

## Interest Problems

### Simple Interest

**Simple interest** is computed on the principal (amount of initial investment) only. To calculate the amount of simple interest paid on an investment, multiply the principal invested by the rate (percent) of interest paid and the time of the investment: **Simple interest income = principal • rate • time**.

*Examples:*

1. If \$4,000 is invested at 3% simple annual interest, how much interest is earned in 4 months?

   ➤ Since the annual interest is 3%, the interest for 1 year is: $\$4,000(0.03) = \$120$. Thus, the interest earned in 4 months, or $\frac{1}{3}$ of a year is: $(\frac{\$120}{3}) = \$40$.

2. Mr. Krecker invests \$4,000, part at 6% and part at 7%; the first year return is \$250. Find the amount invested at 7%.

   ➤ Let $x$ equal the amount invested at 7%. Thus, $4,000 - x$ equals the amount invested at 6%; $0.07x$ equals the income from the 7% investment; and $0.06(4,000 - x)$ equals the income from the 6% investment. Therefore:
   $$0.07x + 0.06(4,000 - x) = 250$$
   $$7x + 6(4,000 - x) = 25,000$$
   $$7x + 24,000 - 6x = 25,000$$
   $$x = 1,000 \ (\$1,000 \text{ invested at } 7\%)$$

### Compound Interest

**Compound interest** is computed on the principal as well as on any interest already earned. The interest already earned is determined as simple interest for each period that the interest is compounded with the principal increasing to include the previously earned interest.

*Example:*

If \$2,000 is invested at 5% annual interest, compounded quarterly, what is the balance after 9 months?

   ➤ Since the interest is compounded quarterly, figure the interest for the four periods, with each successive interest computed for the principal plus all prior interest income. The balance after the first 3 months (one-quarter of a year) would be: $\$2,000 + (\$2,000)(0.05) = \$2,000 + \$100 = \$2,100$. The balance after the second 3 months would be: $\$2,100 + (\$2,100)(0.05) = \$2,100 + \$105 = \$2,205$. The total balance after the final third 3 months would be: $\$2,205 + (\$2,205)(0.05) = \$2,205 + \$110.25 = \$2,315.25$.

The previous example illustrates how if interest is compounded, the interest is computed on the principal as well as on any interest earned. The general formula for compounded interest follows:

$$\text{Final Balance} = \text{Principal} \cdot (1 + \tfrac{\text{interest rate}}{C})^{(\text{time})(C)}$$

where $C$ is the number of times the interest is compounded annually.

*Example:*

If \$12,000 is invested at 8% annual interest, compounded semiannually, what is the balance after 1 year?

> The interest is compounded twice a year, so $C = 2$: Final Balance $= 12,000(1 + \frac{0.08}{2})^{(1)(2)} = 12,000(1.04)^2 = \$12,979.20$.

## Mixture Problems

You should be familiar with two kinds of **mixture problems**. The first type is sometimes referred to as dry mixture, in which dry ingredients of different values, such as nuts or coffee, are mixed. The second type of mixture item deals with different priced tickets. For this type of problem, it is best to organize the data in a chart of three rows and three columns labeled as illustrated in the following problem.

*Example:*

A dealer wishes to mix 20 pounds of nuts selling for 45 cents per pound with some more expensive nuts selling for 60 cents per pound to make a mixture that will sell for 50 cents per pound. How many pounds of the more expensive nuts should he use?

> Create a table summarizing the provided information:

|          | No. of lbs. × | Price/lb.= | Total Value |
|----------|---------------|------------|-------------|
| Original | 20            | 0.45       | 0.45(20)    |
| Added    | $x$           | 0.60       | 0.60($x$)   |
| Mixture  | $20 + x$      | 0.50       | 0.50($20 + x$) |

The value of the original nuts plus the value of the added nuts must equal the value of the mixture:

$$0.45(20) + 0.60(x) = 0.50(20 - x)$$
$$45(20) + 60(x) = 50(20 + x)$$
$$900 + 6x = 1,000 + 5x$$
$$10x = 100$$
$$x = 10$$

Therefore, he should use 10 lbs. of 60-cent nuts.

The second type of mixture item deals with percents and amounts rather than prices and value.

*Example:*

How much water must be added to 20 gallons of solution that is 30% alcohol to dilute it to a solution that is only 25% alcohol?

> Create a table summarizing the provided information:

|          | No. of gals. × | % alcohol = | Amt. alcohol |
|----------|----------------|-------------|--------------|
| Original | 20             | 0.30        | 0.30(20)     |
| Added    | $x$            | 0           | 0            |
| Mixture  | $20 + x$       | 0.25        | 0.25($20 + x$) |

Note that the percent of alcohol in water is zero. Had pure alcohol been added to strengthen the solution, the percent would have been 100. Thus, the amount of alcohol added (none) plus the original amount must equal the amount of alcohol in the new solution:

$$0.30(20 = 0.25(20 + x)$$
$$30(20) = 25(20 + x)$$
$$600 = 500 + 25x$$
$$100 = 25x$$
$$x = 4 \text{ gallons}$$

## Motion Problems

The fundamental relationship in all *motion problems* is *distance = rate • time*. The problems at the level of this examination usually derive their equation from a relationship concerning distance. Most problems fall into one of three types.

### Motion in Opposite Directions

When two objects moving at the same speed start at the same time and move in opposite directions, or when two objects start at points at a given distance apart and move toward each other until they meet, then the distance the second travels will equal one-half the total distance covered. Either way, the total distance $= d_1 + d_2$:

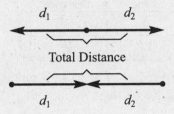

### Motion in the Same Direction

This type of item is sometimes called the "catch-up" problem. Two objects leave the same place in the same direction at different times and at different rates, but one "catches up" to the other. In such a case, the two distances must be equal.

### Round Trip

In this type of problem, the rate going is usually different from the rate returning. The times are also different. But if we go somewhere and then return to the starting point, the distances must be the same.

To solve any motion problem, it is helpful to organize the data in a box with columns for rate, time, and distance. A separate line should be used for each moving object. Remember that if the rate is given in *miles per hour*, the time must be in *hours* and the distance in *miles*.

*Examples:*

1. Two cars leave a restaurant at 1 p.m., with one car traveling east at 60 miles per hour and the other west at 40 miles per hour along a straight highway. At what time will they be 350 miles apart?

   ➢ Create a table summarizing the provided information:

   |  | Rate | × | Time | = | Distance |
   |---|---|---|---|---|---|
   | Eastbound | 60 | | $x$ | | $60x$ |
   | Westbound | 40 | | $x$ | | $40x$ |

   Notice that the time is unknown, since we must determine the number of hours traveled. However, since the cars start at the same time and stop when they are 350 miles apart, their times are the same: $60x + 40x = 350 \Rightarrow 100x = 350 \Rightarrow x = 3.5$. Therefore, in 3.5 hours, it will be 4:30 p.m.

2. Gloria leaves home for school, riding her bicycle at a rate of 12 miles per hour. Twenty minutes after she leaves, her mother sees Gloria's English paper on her bed and leaves to bring it to her. If her mother drives at 36 miles per hour, how far must she drive before she reaches Gloria?

   ➢ Create a table summarizing the provided information:

| | Rate | × | Time | = | Distance |
|---|---|---|---|---|---|
| Gloria | 12 | | $x$ | | $12x$ |
| Mother | 36 | | $x - \frac{1}{3}$ | | $36(x - \frac{1}{3})$ |

The 20 minutes has been converted to $\frac{1}{3}$ of an hour. In this problem, the times are not equal, but the distances are: $12x = 36(x - \frac{1}{3}) = 36x - 12 \Rightarrow 12 = 24x \Rightarrow x = \frac{1}{2}$. Thus, if Gloria rode for $\frac{1}{2}$ hour at 12 miles per hour, the distance covered was 6 miles.

3. Nisha leaves home at 11 a.m. and rides to Andrea's house to return her bicycle. She travels at 12 miles per hour and arrives at 11:30 a.m. She turns right around and walks home. How fast does she walk if she returns home at 1 p.m.?

➤ Create a table summarizing the provided information:

| | Rate | × | Time | = | Distance |
|---|---|---|---|---|---|
| Going | 12 | | $\frac{1}{2}$ | | 6 |
| Return | $x$ | | $1\frac{1}{2}$ | | $\frac{3x}{2}$ |

The distances are equal: $6 = \frac{3x}{2} \Rightarrow 12 = 3x \Rightarrow x = 4$ miles per hour.

## Rate and Work Problems

### Rate Problems

We introduced rate problems in the section above on motion problems, since distance traveled per unit time is a rate. Anytime you compare two quantities with different units, you are finding a *rate*. To find a rate, look for the different units and their corresponding numbers. Rate problems can be solved by using ratios.

*Examples:*

1. If Save-A-Lot Grocery advertises 2 pounds of cherries for $2.20, how much would 3 pounds of cherries costs?

➤ Create two ratios corresponding to the different units and their corresponding numbers. Set the ratios equal to one another and solve for the unknown quantity. The rate in the question is quantity of cherries per price (or price per quantity of cherries), and the unknown is the cost of 3 pounds of cherries: $\frac{2 \text{ pounds}}{\$2.20} = \frac{3 \text{ pounds}}{x} \Rightarrow x = \frac{3}{2}(\$2.20) = \$3.30$.

2. During a 4-hour party, 5 adults consumed drinks costing $120. For the same drink costs per person per hour, what would be the cost of drinks consumed by 4 adults during a 3-hour party?

➤ The ratio in question is drink costs per person per hour, so equate two ratios and solve for the missing value: $\frac{\$120}{5 \text{ adults/4 hours}} = \frac{x}{4 \text{ adults/3hours}} \Rightarrow \frac{120 \cdot 4}{5} = \frac{x \cdot 3}{4} \Rightarrow x = \frac{120 \cdot 16}{15} = 8 \cdot 16 = \$128$.

Note that the following words are frequently used in rate problems: *for, in, per, to, each*. For example: $100 *for* 5 hours of work, 3 widgets produced *in* 5 minutes, 55 miles *per* hour, 13 floors *to* a building, 7 cards *to each* person.

## Work Problems

*Combined rate*, or *work*, problems concern the speed with which work can be accomplished and the time necessary to perform a task, if the size of the workforce is change. Thus, work problems involve combining individual rates into a combined rate.

*Example:*

If Tess alone can weed a garden in 3 days and Rio can weed the same garden in 5 days, how long will it take them to weed the garden if they work together?

➢ Let $x$ equal number of days required if Tess and Rio work together to weed the garden and create a table summarizing the given information:

|  | Tess | Rio | Together |
|---|---|---|---|
| Days to weed garden | 3 | 5 | $x$ |
| Part weeded in 1 day | $\frac{1}{3}$ | $\frac{1}{5}$ | $\frac{1}{x}$ |

Since the part done by Tess in one day plus the part done by Rio in one day equals the part done by both in one day, we have: $\frac{1}{3} + \frac{1}{5} = \frac{1}{x}$. Multiply each part of the equation by $15x$ to clear the fractions: $\frac{1}{3}(15x) + \frac{1}{5}(15x) = \frac{1}{x}(15x) \Rightarrow 5x + 3x = 15 \Rightarrow 8x = 15 \Rightarrow x = 1\frac{7}{8}$ days.

From the previous example, we can see that the basic formula for solving work problems is: $\frac{1}{a} + \frac{1}{b} = \frac{1}{c}$, where $a$ and $b$ are the number of minutes, days, hours, etc. that it takes the two individuals, respectively, to complete a job when working alone, and $c$ is the number of minutes, days, hours, etc. that it takes the two individuals to do the job when working together.

*Example:*

When working alone, machine $X$ can fill a production order in 4 hours, and machine $Y$ can fill the same order in $x$ hours. When the two machines operate simultaneously to fill the production order, it takes them 2.5 hours to complete the job. What is the value of $x$?

➢ $\frac{1}{4} + \frac{1}{Y} = \frac{1}{2.5} \Rightarrow \frac{1}{4}(10Y) + \frac{1}{Y}(10Y) = \frac{1}{2.5}(10Y) \Rightarrow 2.5Y + 10 = 4Y \Rightarrow \frac{3}{2}(Y) = 10 \Rightarrow Y = \frac{20}{3} = 6\frac{2}{3}$. Working alone, machine $Y$ can fill the production order in $6\frac{2}{3}$ hours.

## Variation Problems

Variation in mathematics refers to the interrelationship of variables in such a manner that a change of value for one variable produces a corresponding change in another. There are three basic types of variation: *direct*, *inverse*, and *joint*.

### Direct Variation

The expression "$x$ varies directly with $y$" can be described by any of the following equations.

**DIRECT VARIATION RELATIONSHIPS**

$y = kx$, $k$ is a constant      $\frac{x_1}{y_1} = \frac{x_2}{y_2}$

Two quantities are said to vary directly if they change in the same direction. As one increases, the other increases and their ratio is equal to the positive constant.

For example, the amount you must pay for milk varies directly with the number of quarts of milk you buy. The amount of sugar needed in a recipe varies directly with the amount of butter used. The number of inches between two cities on a map varies directly with the number of miles between these cities.

*Example:*

If $x$ varies directly as $y^2$, and $x = 12$ when $y = 2$, what is the value of $x$ when $y = 3$?

➤ Notice that the variation involves the square of $y$. Therefore: $\frac{x_1}{y_1^2} = \frac{x_2}{y_2^2} \Rightarrow \frac{12}{2^2} = \frac{x}{3^2} \Rightarrow \frac{12}{4} = \frac{x}{9} \Rightarrow x = 27$.

### *Inverse Variation*

The expression "$x$ varies inversely as $y$" can be described by any of the following equations.

---
**INVERSE VARIATION RELATIONSHIPS**

$xy = k$, $k$ is a constant $\qquad \frac{x_1}{y_2} = \frac{x_2}{y_1}$

---

Two quantities vary inversely if they change in opposite directions. As one quantity increases, the other quantity decreases.

For example, the number of people hired to paint a house varies inversely with the number of days the job will take. A doctor's stock of flu vaccine varies inversely with the number of patients she injects. The number of days a given supply of cat food lasts varies inversely with the number of cats being fed.

*Example:*

The time $t$ to empty a container varies inversely with the square root of the number of men $m$ working on the job. If it takes 3 hours for 16 men to do the job, how long will it take 4 men working at the same rate to empty the container?

➤ $\frac{t_1}{\sqrt{m_2}} = \frac{t_2}{\sqrt{m_1}} \Rightarrow t_1\sqrt{m_1} = t_2\sqrt{m_2} \Rightarrow 3\sqrt{16} = t\sqrt{4} \Rightarrow t = 3 \cdot \frac{\sqrt{16}}{\sqrt{4}} = 3(\sqrt{4}) = 3 \cdot 2 = 6$.

### *Joint Variation*

The expression "$x$ varies jointly as $y$ and $z$" can be described by any of the following equations.

---
**JOINT VARIATION RELATIONSHIPS**

$\frac{x}{yz} = k$, $k$ is a constant $\qquad \frac{x_1}{y_1 z_1} = \frac{x_2}{y_2 z_2} \qquad \frac{x_1}{x_2} = \left(\frac{y_1}{y_2}\right)\left(\frac{z_1}{z_1}\right)$

---

*Example:*

The area, $A$, of a triangle varies jointly as the base $b$ and the height h. If $A = 20$ when $b = 10$ and $h = 4$, what is the value of $A$ when $b = 6$ and $h = 7$?

➤ $\frac{A_1}{b_1 h_1} = \frac{A_2}{b_2 h_2} \Rightarrow \frac{20}{(10)(4)} = \frac{A_2}{(6)(7)} \Rightarrow A_2 = 21$.

## Percent Problems

Many problem-solving items involve percents as they apply to certain types of business situations.

### Percent Increase or Decrease

Percent increase or decrease is found by putting the amount of increase or decrease over the original amount and changing this fraction to a percent.

*Example:*

A company normally employs 100 people. During a slow spell, it fired 20% of its employees. By what percent must it now increase its staff to return to full capacity?

➢ $20\% = \frac{1}{5} \cdot 100 = 20$. The company now has $100 - 20 = 80$ employees. If it then increases by 20 employees, the percent of increase is $\frac{20}{80} = \frac{1}{4}$, or 25%.

### Discounts

A discount is expressed as a percent of the original price that will be deducted from that price to determine the sale price.

*Examples:*

1. Bill's Hardware offers a 20% discount on all appliances during a sale week. How much must Mrs. Russell pay for a washing machine marked at $280?

   ➢ $20\% = \frac{1}{5} \Rightarrow \frac{1}{5} \cdot \$280 = \$56$ discount $\Rightarrow \$280 - \$56 = \$224$ sale price. Alternatively, the following shortcut simplifies the solution: if there is a 20% discount, Mrs. Russell will pay 80% of the marked price: $80\% = \frac{4}{5} \Rightarrow \frac{4}{5} \cdot \$280 = \$224$ sale price.

2. A store offers a television set marked at $340 less consecutive discounts of 10% and 5%. Another store offers the same set with a single discount of 15%. How much does the buyer save buying at the better price?

   ➢ In the first store, the initial discount means the buyer pays 90%, or $\frac{9}{10}$ of $340, which is $306. The second discount must be figured on the first sale price. The additional 5% discount means the buyer pays 95% of $306, or $290.70. A 5% discount on $306 is less than an additional 5% discount on $340. Thus, the second store will have a lower sale price. In the second store, the buyer will pay 85% of $340, or $289—$1.70 less than the price at the first store.

### Profit

*Gross profit* is equal to revenues minus expenses, that is, the selling price minus cost.

*Example:*

A used car lot paid $5,000 for a trade-in car. At what price should the salesman sell the used car in order to make a gross profit of 60% of the cost of the car?

➢ The cost of the car is $5,000, so the gross profit is 60% of $5,000, or $0.6(5,000) = \$3,000$. Since the gross profit is equal to the selling price minus cost, the selling price of the car must be gross profit plus cost, or $\$3,000 + \$5,000 = \$8,000$.

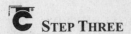 

## Commission

Many salespeople earn money on a commission basis. In order to inspire sales, they are paid a percentage of the value of goods that they personally sell. This amount is called a commission.

*Examples:*

1.  Mr. Saunders works at Brown's Department Store, where he is paid $80 per week in salary plus a 4% commission on all his sales. How much does he earn in a week in which he sells $4,032 worth of merchandise?

    ➢ Find 4% of $4,032 and add this amount to $80: $4,032 \cdot 0.04 = \$161.28 \Rightarrow \$161.28 + \$80 = \$241.28$.

2.  Bill Olson delivers newspapers for a dealer and keeps 8% of all money collected. In one month, he was able to keep $16. How much did he forward to the dealer?

    ➢ First, find how much he collected by asking $16 is 8% of what number: $\$16 = 0.08x \Rightarrow$ $\$1,600 = 8x \Rightarrow x = \$200$. Then, subtract the amount Bill kept ($16) from the total collected ($200). Therefore, Bill forwarded $184 to the dealer.

## Taxes

Taxes are a percent of money spent or money earned.

*Examples:*

1.  Dane County collects a 7% sales tax on automobiles. If the price of a used Ford is $5,832 before taxes, what will it cost when the sales tax is added in?

    ➢ Find 7% of $5,832 to determine the amount of tax and then add that amount to $5,832. This can be done in one step by finding 107% of $5,832: $\$5,832 \cdot 1.07 = \$6,240.24$.

2.  If income is taxed at the rate of 10% for the first $10,000 of earned income, 15% for the next $10,000, 20% for the next $10,000, and 25% for all earnings over $30,000, how much income tax must be paid on a yearly income of $36,500?

    ➢ Find the income tax collected at each percentage rate and add them:

    $$
    \begin{aligned}
    10\% \text{ of first } \$10,000 &= \$1,000 \\
    15\% \text{ of next } \$10,000 &= \$1,500 \\
    20\% \text{ of next } \$10,000 &= \$2,000 \\
    + \quad 25\% \text{ of next } \$6,500 &= \$1,625 \\
    \hline
    \text{Total Tax} &= \$6,125
    \end{aligned}
    $$

## Measurement Problems

Some questions may involve different units of measure. For any problem requiring conversion from one unit of measure to another, other than for units of time, the relationship between those units will be given.

*Example:*

A car travels at a constant rate of 37 miles per hour. If 1 kilometer is equal to 0.62 miles, approximately how many kilometers does the car travel in 20 minutes?

> ➤ 1 kilometer equals 0.62 miles, so multiply the given speed by $\frac{1 \text{ kilometer}}{0.62 \text{ miles}}$ to convert it to kilometers per hour: $\frac{37 \text{ miles}}{\text{hour}} \cdot \frac{1 \text{ kilometer}}{0.62 \text{ miles}} \approx 60$ kilometers per hour. Thus, in 20 minutes, or one-third of an hour, the car travels $\frac{60}{3} = 20$ kilometers.

## Counting Methods

### *The Multiplication Principle for Counting*

The ***multiplication principle for counting*** states that if an object is to be chosen from a set of $m$ objects and a second object is to be chosen from a different set of $n$ objects, then the total number of ways of choosing both object simultaneously is $mn$. In other words, if an operation takes two steps and the first step can be performed in $m$ ways, and if, for each of those ways, the second step can be performed in $n$ ways, then the total number of ways of performing the operation is $mn$.

*Examples:*

1. A litter of boxer puppies contains 4 with brindle coloring and 5 with fawn coloring. In how many ways can one choose a pair of one brindle puppy and one fawn puppy from this litter of puppies?

   > ➤ You have 4 choices for a brindle puppy and 5 choices for a fawn puppy. By the multiplication principle, the total number of possible pairs is: $4 \cdot 5 = 20$.

2. From a garden with 6 flower varieties, a bouquet of 3 different types of flowers is to be picked. How many different possible bouquets are there?

   > ➤ Extend the multiplication principle to a three-step process: there are 6 choices of flower for the first pick of the bouquet, for each of which there are 5 choices for the second flower (because one flower type has been eliminated, having been picked as the first flower in the bouquet). Furthermore, for each of these pairs, there are 4 remaining flower choices for the third pick (because two flower types have been eliminated, having been picked as the first and second flowers in the bouquet). Therefore, the total number of possible bouquets is: $6 \cdot 5 \cdot 4 = 120$.

### *Permutations*

A natural extension of the multiplication principle is the concept of ***permutations***, or orderings in distinct arrangements of $n$ distinguishable objects in a row. If a set of $n$ objects is to be ordered from 1$^{\text{st}}$ to $n^{\text{th}}$, then there are $n$ choices for the first object, $n-1$ choices for the second object, $n-2$ choices for the third object, and so on, until there is only one choice for the $n^{\text{th}}$ object. Therefore, the number of ways of ordering the $n$ objects, also called ***n factorial***, is as follows:

$$n! = n(n-1)(n-2)\ldots(3)(2)(1)$$

*Examples:*

1. If 5 spices (rosemary, oregano, basil, sage, and pepper) are arranged randomly on a shelf, what is the chance that they will be in alphabetical order from left to right?

   > ➤ There are 5 distinguishable objects that can be arranged in $5! = 5 \cdot 4 \cdot 3 \cdot 2 \cdot 1 = 120$ ways. In only one of these ways will they be in alphabetical order. Therefore, the chance is $\frac{1}{120}$ that the spices will be arranged in alphabetical order from left to right.

2. In how many ways can 5 spices (rosemary, oregano, basil, sage, and pepper) be arranged on the shelf if the oregano and the basil must be next to each other?

  ➢ Since the oregano and the basil must be next to each other, treat the two together as one spice, thereby reducing the total number of spices to be arranged from 5 to 4. These 4 spices—rosemary, oregano/basil, sage, and pepper—can be arranged in $4! = 4 \cdot 3 \cdot 2 \cdot 1 = 24$ ways. However, for each of these ways, we could have set up the "glued" spices in two sequences: oregano/basil or basil/oregano. Therefore, there is a total of $2 \cdot 24 = 48$ ways in which the spices can be arranged with the oregano and basil next to each other.

If you are asked to find the number of ways to arrange a smaller group that is being drawn from a larger group, you can use the following *permutation formula*:

$$P = \frac{n!}{(n-k)!}$$

where $n$ is the number of elements in the larger set and $k$ is the number of elements being arranged.

*Example:*

  Five candidates are running for office. The candidates who come in first, second, and third place will be elected president, vice-president, and treasurer, respectively. How many outcomes for president, vice-president, and treasurer are there?

  ➢ Using the permutation formula: $P = \frac{n!}{(n-k)!} = \frac{5!}{(5-3)!} = \frac{5!}{2!} = \frac{5 \cdot 4 \cdot 3 \cdot 2 \cdot 1}{2 \cdot 1} = 5 \cdot 4 \cdot 3 = 60$. Notice that the formula is the same as applying the following logic: Any of the 5 candidates could come in first place, leaving 4 candidates who could come in second place, leaving 3 candidates who could come in third place, for a total of $5 \cdot 4 \cdot 3 = 60$ possible outcomes for president, vice-president, and treasurer.

## Combinations

A *combination* problem is one in which the order or arrangement of the smaller group that is being drawn from the larger group does NOT matter. Rather than the permutation formula, use the following *combination formula*:

$$C = \frac{n!}{k!(n-k)!}$$

where $n$ is the number of elements in the larger set and $k$ is the number of elements being arranged.

*Example:*

  How many different ways are there to choose 4 socks from a drawer containing 9 socks?

  ➢ Since the order or arrangement of the 4 socks being drawn from the drawer containing 9 socks does not matter, use the combination formula: $C = \frac{9!}{4!(9-4)!} = \frac{9!}{4! \cdot 5!} = \frac{9 \cdot 8 \cdot 7 \cdot 6 \cdot 5!}{4 \cdot 3 \cdot 2 \cdot 1 \cdot 5!} = \frac{9 \cdot 8 \cdot 7}{4} = 126$.

## Probability

## Single-Event Probability

*Probability* is concerned with experiments that have a finite number of outcomes. Probabilities occur in games, sports, weather reports, etc. The probability that some particular outcome or set of outcomes (called an *event*) will occur is expressed as a ratio. The numerator of a probability ratio is the number of ways that the event of interest can occur. The denominator is the total number of outcomes that are possible. This **probability ratio** is true for experiments in which all of the individual outcomes are equally likely:

$$\text{Probability of event} = \frac{\text{number of ways that event can happen}}{\text{number of outcomes possible}}$$

*Example:*

If a six-sided die is tossed, what is the probability that you will get a number greater than 4?

➤ There are a total of 6 ways a die can land: 1, 2, 3, 4, 5, or 6. Each of these 6 events are equally likely. There are 2 possible outcomes that are greater than 4: 5 or 6. Therefore, the probability of the die landing with a number greater than 3 is $\frac{2}{6} = \frac{1}{3}$.

Note that the probability that an event occurs is a number between 0 and 1, inclusive. If the event has no outcomes, then it is impossible and its probability is 0. If the event is the set of all possible outcomes, then it is certain to occur and its probability is 1.

### Multiple-Event Probability

Another type of probability involves finding the probability of a certain outcome after multiple events. One type of **multiple-event probability** involves individual events that must occur a certain way. For these experiments, figure out the probability for each individual event and multiply the individual probabilities together.

*Example:*

If 2 marbles are randomly chosen from a jar with 3 red marbles and 7 black marbles, what is the probability that both marbles will be red?

➤ Since 3 out of the 10 marbles are red, the probability that the first marble chosen is red is $\frac{3}{10}$. After choosing 1 red marble, this leaves 2 red marbles in the jar out of 9. Therefore, the probability that the second marble chosen will also be red is $\frac{2}{9}$. The probability that both marbles chosen will be red is: $\frac{3}{10} \cdot \frac{2}{9} = \frac{6}{90} = \frac{1}{15}$.

A second type of multiple-event probability involves individual events that can have different outcomes. For these experiments, create a probability ratio by dividing the number of desired outcomes by the total number of possible outcomes. The total number of possible outcomes is found by multiplying together the number of possible outcomes for each individual event. The number of desired outcomes can be determined by counting the possibilities.

*Example:*

If a dime is tossed 3 times, what is the probability that at least 2 of the 3 tosses will be heads up?

➤ There are 2 possible outcomes for each toss (heads or tails), so after 3 tosses there are a total of $2^3 = 2 \cdot 2 \cdot 2 = 8$ possible outcomes. Next, list all the possibilities where at least 2 of the 3 tosses are heads up: H, H, H; H, H, T; H, T, H; T, H, H. Thus, the total number of desired outcomes is 4. Therefore, the probability that at least 2 of the 3 tosses will be heads up is: $\frac{4}{8} = \frac{1}{2}$.

Probabilities can also be determined for an experiment with two different events, $A$ and $B$. The probability of $A$ occurring is denoted by $P(A)$, and the probability of $B$ occurring is denoted by $P(B)$. Given these two events, there are three additional events that can be defined. "*Not A*" is the set of outcomes that are not outcomes in $A$; "*A or B*" is the set of outcomes in $A$ or $B$ or both ($A \cup B$); "*A and B*" is the set of outcomes in both $A$ and $B$ ($A \cap B$). If the event "*A and B*" is impossible, then *A* and *B* are said to be **mutually exclusive**. If the occurrence of either event *A* or *B* does not alter the probability that the other event occurs, then *A* and *B* are said to be **independent**.

---

### PROBABILITIES FOR MULTIPLE-EVENT EXPERIMENTS
(An experiment with events *A* and *B*)

"*Not A*": $P(\text{not } A) = 1 - P(A)$

"*A or B*": $P(A \text{ or } B) = P(A) + P(B) - P(A \text{ and } B)$

"*A and B*" (*A* and *B* are mutually exclusive): $P(A \text{ and } B) = 0$

"*A and B*" (*A* and *B* are independent): $P(A \text{ and } B) = P(A)P(B)$

---

*Example:*

If a six-sided die is tossed, what is the probability that you will a prime number or an even number?

➤ Let *A* be the event that the outcome is a prime number, $\{2,3,5\}$, and let *B* be the event that the outcome is an even number, $\{2,4,6\}$. Since 3 outcomes are prime, $P(A) = \frac{3}{6} = \frac{1}{2}$. Similarly, $P(B) = \frac{1}{2}$. $P(A \text{ and } B)$, or the probability that the outcome is both even and prime, is $\frac{1}{6}$ since only 2 is both even and prime. Therefore, $P(A \text{ or } B) = \frac{1}{2} + \frac{1}{2} - \frac{1}{6} = \frac{5}{6}$. Note that this is the same as reasoning that the set of prime and even numbers on the die is $\{2,3,4,5,6\}$, so the probability of getting one of these numbers is $\frac{5}{6}$.

#### Geometric Probability

Some items on the exam may involve geometric probability. For example, if a point is to be chosen at random from the interior of a region, part of which is shaded, you might be asked to find the probability that the point chosen will be from the shaded portion of the region. Such an item might be presented in a specific context, such as throwing darts at a target.

*Examples:*

1. The figure below shows a circle inscribed in a square. The area of the square is 324. If a point is selected at random in the interior of the square, what is the approximate probability that the point also lies in the interior of the circle?

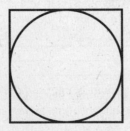

➤ Since the area of the square is 324, $A_{\text{square}} = s^2 \Rightarrow s = 18$. The side of the square is equal to the diameter of the circle, so the radius of the circle is $18 \div 2 = 9$. The area of the circle is: $A_{\text{circle}} = \pi r^2 = \pi (9)^2 = 81\pi$. Therefore, the probability that a point chosen at random in the interior of the square will also be in the interior of the circle is: $\frac{A_{\text{circle}}}{A_{\text{square}}} = \frac{81\pi}{324} = \frac{\pi}{4} \approx 0.785$.

2. The figure below shows a rectangle that is bounded by the two axes and two lines whose respective equations are $y = 8$ and $x = 6$. The shaded trapezoidal region is bounded on three sides by portions of

three sides of the rectangle. The fourth unbounded side of the shaded trapezoidal region is a line segment that is a portion of the line whose equation is $2y = x + 4$. If a point is selected at random in the interior of the rectangle, what is the probability that the point also lies in the shaded region?

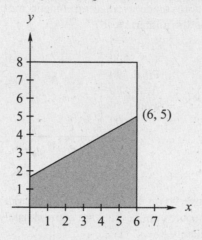

> For the line $2y = x + 4$, substitute values for $x$ and solve for $y$. If $x = 0, 2y = 0 + 4 \Rightarrow y = 2$. If $x = 6$, $2y = 6 + 4 \Rightarrow y = 5$. The parallel sides of the trapezoid have lengths of 2 and 5; the altitude of the trapezoid is 6. Therefore, the probability that the point will be in both the interior of the rectangle and the interior of the shaded region is: $\dfrac{A_{\text{shaded}}}{A_{\text{rectangle}}} = \dfrac{\frac{6(2+5)}{2}}{6 \cdot 8} = \dfrac{3 \cdot 7}{48} = \dfrac{21}{48} = \dfrac{7}{16}$.

## Data Interpretation: Tables and Graphs

You are expected to be able to interpret data displayed in tables, charts, and graphs.

*Example:*

The tables below show the number, type, and cost of candy bars bought during one week at two local drugstores.

| | Number of Candy Bars Bought | | | | | |
| --- | --- | --- | --- | --- | --- | --- |
| | Type A | | Type B | | Type C | |
| | Large | Giant | Large | Giant | Large | Giant |
| Drugstore P | 60 | 20 | 69 | 21 | 43 | 17 |
| Drugstore Q | 44 | 18 | 59 | 25 | 38 | 13 |

| Cost per Candy Bar | | |
| --- | --- | --- |
| | Large | Giant |
| Type A | $0.45 | $0.69 |
| Type B | $0.45 | $0.79 |
| Type C | $0.55 | $0.99 |

What is the total cost of all Type B candy bars bought at these two drugstores during the week?

> Total the cost of all Type B bars bought at the two drugstores:
> $69(0.45) + 21(0.79) + 59(0.45) + 25(0.79) = \$93.94$.

The test may also ask about the line of best fit for a scatterplot. A scatterplot is really just a plot of various data points for which a line of best fit can be drawn.. For example, an item may require you to identify that a line of best fit for a scatterplot has a slope that is positive but less than 1. You are not expected to use formal methods for finding the equation of a line of best fit.

*Example:*

The points in the scatterplot below show the relationship between 14 students' test scores on a mid-term test and a final test. What is the approximate average (arithmetic mean) of the scores on the final test for all students who scored above 90 on the midterm test?

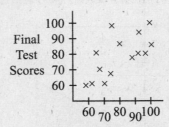

Mid-Term Test Scores

➤ Five students scored above 90 on the mid-term. Their marks are the five to the right on the scatterplot. The five corresponding scores on the final are approximately 80, 80, 85, 95, and 100. The average of these scores is approximately 88.

# Solving Story Problems

**DIRECTIONS:** Choose the correct answer to each of the following items. Answers are on page 988.

1.  A suit is sold for $68 while marked at $80. What is the rate of discount?

    A. 15%     C. $17\frac{11}{17}$%     E. 24%

    B. 17%     D. 20%

2.  Lilian left home with $60 in her wallet. She spent $\frac{1}{3}$ of that amount at the supermarket, and she spent $\frac{1}{2}$ of what remained at the drugstore. If Lilian made no other expenditures, how much money did she have when she returned home?

    A. $10     C. $20     E. $50

    B. $15     D. $40

3.  In the figure below, circle $O$ and circle $P$ are tangent to each other. If the circle with center $O$ has a diameter of 8 and the circle with center $P$ has a diameter of 6, what is the length of $\overline{OP}$?

    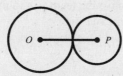

    A. 7     C. 14     E. 28

    B. 10     D. 20

4.  A man buys a radio for $70 after receiving a discount of 20%. What was the marked price?

    A. $56     C. $87.50     E. $92

    B. $84.50     D. $90

5.  Colin and Shaina wish to buy a gift for a friend. They combine their money and find they have $4.00, consisting of quarters, dimes, and nickels. If they have 35 coins and the number of quarters is half the number of nickels, how many quarters do they have?

    A. 5     C. 20     E. 36

    B. 10     D. 23

6.  Willie receives $r$% commission on a sale of $s$ dollars. How many dollars does he receive?

    A. $rs$     C. $100rs$     E. $\frac{rs}{100}$

    B. $\frac{r}{s}$     D. $\frac{r}{100s}$

7.  Three times the smallest of three consecutive odd integers is 3 more than twice the largest. Find the largest integer.

    A. 9     C. 13     E. 17

    B. 11     D. 15

8.  A refrigerator was sold for $273, yielding a 30% profit on the cost. For how much should it be sold to yield only a 10% profit on the cost?

    A. $210     C. $235     E. $241

    B. $231     D. $240

9.  If 60 feet of uniform wire weigh 80 pounds, what is the weight, in pounds, of 2 yards of the same wire?

    A. $2\frac{2}{3}$     C. 80     E. 2,400

    B. 8     D. 120

10. What single discount is equivalent to two successive discounts of 10% and 15%?

    A. 25%     C. 24%     E. 22%

    B. 24.5%     D. 23.5%

11. Robert is 15 years older than Stan. However, $y$ years ago Robert was twice as old as Stan. If Stan is now $b$ years old and $b > y$, find the value of $b - y$.

    A. 13     C. 15     E. 17

    B. 14     D. 16

12. The net price of a certain article is $306 after successive discounts of 15% and 10% are taken off the marked price. What is the marked price?

   A. $408
   B. $400
   C. $382.50
   D. $234.09
   E. None of the above

13. A gear 50 inches in diameter turns a smaller gear 30 inches in diameter. If the larger gear makes 15 revolutions, how many revolutions does the smaller gear make in that time?

   A. 9      C. 20     E. 30
   B. 12     D. 25

14. If a merchant makes a profit of 20% based on the selling price of an article, what percent does he make on the cost?

   A. 15     C. 25     E. 45
   B. 20     D. 40

15. How many ounces of pure acid must be added to 20 ounces of a solution that is 5% acid to strengthen it to a solution that is 24% acid?

   A. $2\frac{1}{2}$     C. 6      E. 10
   B. 5                   D. $7\frac{1}{2}$

16. If $x$ men can do a job in $h$ days, how long would $y$ men take to do the same job?

   A. $\frac{x}{h}$     C. $\frac{hy}{x}$     E. $\frac{x}{y}$
   B. $\frac{xh}{y}$    D. $xyh$

17. A certain radio costs a merchant $72. At what price must he sell it if he is to make a profit of 20% of the selling price?

   A. $86.40     C. $90     E. $148
   B. $88        D. $144

18. A dealer mixes $a$ pounds of nuts that cost $b$ cents per pound with $c$ pounds of nuts that cost $d$ cents per pound. At what price should he sell a pound of the mixture if he wishes to make a profit of 10 cents per pound?

   A. $\frac{ab+cd}{a+c}+10$

   B. $\frac{ab+cd}{a+c}+0.1$

   C. $\frac{b+d}{a+c}+10$

   D. $\frac{b+d}{a+c}+0.10$

   E. $\frac{b+d+10}{a+c}$

19. If a furnace uses 40 gallons of oil in a week, how many gallons, to the nearest gallon, does it use in 10 days?

   A. 57     C. 28     E. 4
   B. 44     D. 20

20. Nell invests $2,400 in the Security National Bank at 5%. How much additional money must she invest at 8% so that the total annual income will be equal to 6% of her entire investment?

   A. $4,400     C. $3,000     E. $1,200
   B. $3,600     D. $2,400

21. A baseball team has won 40 games out of 60 played. It has 32 more games to play. How many of these must the team win to make its record 75% for the season?

   A. 28     C. 30     E. 34
   B. 29     D. 32

22. A recipe requires 13 ounces of sugar and 18 ounces of flour. If only 10 ounces of sugar are used, how much flour, to the nearest ounce, should be used?

   A. 11     C. 13     E. 15
   B. 12     D. 14

23. Ivan left Austin to drive to Boxville at 6:15 p.m. and arrived at 11:45 p.m. If he averaged 30 miles per hour and stopped one hour for dinner, how many miles is Boxville from Austin?

   A. 120     C. 180     E. 190
   B. 135     D. 185

24. If prices are reduced 25% and sales increase 20%, what is the net effect on gross receipts?

    A. They increase by 5%.
    B. They decrease by 5%.
    C. They remain the same.
    D. They increase by 10%.
    E. They decrease by 10%.

25. If a car can drive 25 miles on two gallons of gasoline, how many gallons will be needed for a trip of 150 miles?

    A. 12     C. 16     E. 20
    B. 13     D. 17

26. A plane traveling 600 miles per hour is 30 miles from Kennedy Airport at 4:58 p.m. At what time will it arrive at the airport?

    A. 5:00 p.m.     C. 5:02 p.m.     E. 5:23 p.m.
    B. 5:01 p.m.     D. 5:20 p.m.

27. A salesperson earns a commission of 5% on all sales between $200 and $600, and 8% on all sales over $600. What is the commission earned in a week in which sales total $800?

    A. $20     C. $48     E. $88
    B. $36     D. $78

28. A school has enough bread to last 30 children 4 days. If 10 children are added, how many days will the bread last?

    A. $\frac{1}{3}$     C. $2\frac{1}{3}$     E. 3
    B. $1\frac{1}{3}$     D. $2\frac{2}{3}$

29. Mr. Bridges can wash his car in 15 minutes, while his son Dave takes twice as long to do the same job. If they work together, how many minutes will the job take them?

    A. 5     C. 10     E. 30
    B. $7\frac{1}{2}$     D. $22\frac{1}{2}$

30. A train travels from Madison to Chicago at an average speed of 50 miles per hour and returns immediately along the same route at an average speed of 40 miles per hour. Of the following, which is closest to the average speed, in miles per hour, for the round-trip?

    A. 43.0     C. 44.4     E. 45.0
    B. 44.0     D. 44.5

31. At $c$ cents per pound, what is the cost of $a$ ounces of salami?

    A. $\frac{c}{a}$     C. $ac$     E. $\frac{16c}{a}$
    B. $\frac{a}{c}$     D. $\frac{ac}{16}$

32. If 3 miles are equivalent to 4.83 kilometers, then 11.27 kilometers are equivalent to how many miles?

    A. $2\frac{1}{3}$     C. 7     E. $7\frac{1}{2}$
    B. 5     D. $7\frac{1}{3}$

33. If 4 workers take an hour to pave a road, how long should it take 12 workers to pave the same road?

    A. $\frac{1}{4}$ hour     C. $\frac{1}{2}$ hour     E. 1 hour
    B. $\frac{1}{3}$ hour     D. $\frac{3}{4}$ hour

34. At a certain printing plant, each of $m$ machines prints 6 newspapers every $s$ seconds. If all machines work together but independently without interruption, how many minutes will it take to print an entire run of 18,000 newspapers?

    A. $\frac{180s}{m}$     C. $50ms$     E. $\frac{300m}{s}$
    B. $\frac{50s}{m}$     D. $\frac{ms}{50}$

35. If $p$ pencils cost $d$ dollars, how many pencils can be bought for $c$ cents?

    A. $\frac{100pc}{d}$     C. $\frac{pd}{c}$     E. $\frac{cd}{p}$
    B. $\frac{pc}{100d}$     D. $\frac{pc}{d}$

36. Gerard takes 6 hours to do a job. Leo takes 8 hours to do the same job. How many hours should it take Gerard and Leo working together to do the same job?

    A. $\frac{7}{24}$     C. 3     E. 7
    B. $2\frac{3}{7}$     D. $3\frac{3}{7}$

37. There are two drains, drain 1 and drain 2, in a pool. If both drains are opened, the pool is emptied in 20 minutes. If drain 1 is closed and drain 2 is open, the pool will be emptied in 30 minutes. If drain 2 is closed and drain 1 is open, how many minutes will it take to empty the pool?

    A. 20     C. 50     E. 120
    B. 30     D. 60

38. Working alone, machines X, Y, and Z can do a certain job in 3, 5, and 6 hours, respectively. What is the ratio of the time it takes machine X to do the job, working alone at its rate, to the time it takes machines Y and Z to do the job, working together at their individual rates?

    A. $\frac{11}{33}$     C. $\frac{30}{33}$     E. $\frac{30}{11}$
    B. $\frac{11}{30}$     D. $\frac{33}{30}$

39. If the number $n$ of newspapers sold per week varies with the price $p$ in dollars according to the equation $n = 40 - 3p$, what would be the total weekly revenue from the sale of $1 newspapers?

    A. $30     C. $35     E. $40
    B. $33     D. $37

40. A car dealer who gives a customer a 20% discount on the list price of a car still realizes a net profit of 25% of cost. If the dealer's cost is $4,800, what is the usual list price of the car?

    A. $6,000     C. $7,200     E. $8,001
    B. $6,180     D. $7,500

41. A candy manufacturer produces 400 bars of a certain chocolate each month at a cost to the manufacturer of 25 cents and all the produced chocolate bars are sold each month. What is the minimum selling price per bar that will ensure that the monthly profit on the sales of these chocolate bars will be at least $420?

    A. $1.00     C. $1.20     E. $1.30
    B. $1.10     D. $1.25

42. Acme Auto Parts manufactures car parts for which the production costs consist of annual fixed costs totaling $120,000 and variable costs averaging $6 per item. If Acme Auto Parts sells each item for $12, how many items must it manufacture and sell to earn an annual profit of $60,000?

    A. 6,000     C. 15,000     E. 30,000
    B. 12,000     D. 20,000

43. The variable $m$ varies directly as the square of $t$. If $m$ is 7 when $t = 1$, what is the value of $m$ when $t = 2$?

    A. 28     C. 7     E. 2
    B. 14     D. $3\frac{1}{2}$

44. 6 students in a class failed algebra, representing $16\frac{2}{3}\%$ of the class. How many students passed the course?

    A. 48     C. 33     E. 28
    B. 36     D. 30

45. If the value of a piece of property decreases by 10% while the tax rate on the property increases by 10%, what is the effect on taxes?

    A. Taxes increase by 10%.
    B. Taxes increase by 1%.
    C. There is no change in taxes.
    D. Taxes decrease by 1%.
    E. Taxes decrease by 10%.

46. The variable $m$ varies jointly as $r$ and $l$. If $m$ is 8 when $r$ and $l$ are each 1, what is the value of $m$ when $r$ and $l$ are each 2?

    A. 64     C. 16     E. 2
    B. 32     D. 4

47. 95% of the residents of Coral Estates live in private homes. 40% of those live in air-conditioned homes. What percent of the residents of Coral Estates live in air-conditioned homes?

    A. 3%     C. 30%     E. 38%
    B. 3.8%     D. 34%

48. Exactly three years before the year in which Anna was born, the year was $1980 - x$. In terms of $x$, what is the year of Anna's twentieth birthday?

    A. $1977 + x$     C. $2003 - x$     E. $2006 + x$
    B. $1997 + x$     D. $2003 + x$

49. Mr. Carlson receives a salary of $500 a month and a commission of 5% on all sales. What must be the amount of his sales in July so that his total monthly income is $2,400?

    A. $48,000     C. $7,600     E. $2,000
    B. $38,000     D. $3,800

50. John can wax his car in 3 hours. Jim can do the same job in 5 hours. How long will it take them if they work together?

    A. $\frac{1}{2}$ hour     C. 2 hours     E. 8 hours
    B. $1\frac{7}{8}$ hours     D. $2\frac{7}{8}$ hours

51. In a run/walk marathon, Weber runs $x$ miles in $h$ hours, then walks the remainder of the marathon route, $y$ miles, in the same number of hours. Which of the following represents Weber's average speed, in miles per hour, for the entire marathon?

    A. $\frac{x-y}{h}$    C. $\frac{2(x+y)}{h}$    E. $\frac{x+y}{2h}$

    B. $\frac{x-y}{2h}$    D. $\frac{2(x+y)}{2h}$

52. In the junior class at Shawnee High School, 168 students took the SAT, 175 students took the ACT, 80 students took both, and 27 students did not take either one. What is the total number of students in the junior class at Shawnee High School?

    A. 440    C. 290    E. 248
    B. 343    D. 282

53. Let $R = \{3, 5, 6, 7, 9\}$. How many different subsets of $R$ with 1, 2, 3, or 4 elements contain one or more odd numbers?

    A. 31    C. 29    E. 27
    B. 30    D. 28

54. A survey of 51 students was conducted concerning each student's favorite flavors of ice cream. Of the 51 students, 10 students liked only vanilla, 12 students liked only strawberry, and 15 students liked only chocolate. Every student liked at least one of the three flavors. 7 students liked both vanilla and strawberry, and 9 students liked both vanilla and chocolate. The largest possible number of students who could have liked both chocolate and strawberry is:

    A. 2    C. 7    E. 14
    B. 3    D. 12

55. Sixty students are enrolled in French, Spanish, or German. Forty-five students are in French, 35 are in Spanish, and 20 are in German. Fifteen students are enrolled in all three of the courses. How many of the students are enrolled in exactly two of the courses?

    A. 5    C. 12    E. 20
    B. 10    D. 15

56. If there are 3 different roads from Seattle to Olympia and 4 different roads from Olympia to Portland, how many different routes are there from Seattle to Portland that pass through Olympia?

    A. 1    C. 10    E. 24
    B. 7    D. 12

57. Set $X$ is the set of all positive integral multiples of 8: $X = \{8, 16, 24, 32, ...\}$. Set $Y$ is the set of all positive integral multiples of 6: $Y = \{6, 12, 18, 24, ...\}$. The intersection of these two sets is the set of all positive integral multiples of:

    A. 2    C. 14    E. 48
    B. 4    D. 24

58. In how many arrangements can a theater usher seat 4 men and 3 women in a row of 7 seats if the men are to have the first, third, fourth, and seventh seats?

    A. 6    C. 24    E. 840
    B. 12    D. 144

59. Of the 50 children in a school sports program, 40 percent will be assigned to softball, and the remaining 60 percent to baseball. However, 70 percent of the children prefer softball and 30 percent prefer baseball. What is the least possible number of children who will NOT be assigned to the sport they prefer?

    A. 10    C. 20    E. 35
    B. 15    D. 30

60. Recipes are filed in a recipe book according to at least 12 different color codes. If combination of three different colors is chosen to represent each color code and if each color code is uniquely represented by that choice of three colors, what is the minimum number of colors needed for the coding? (Assume that the order of the colors in a combination does not matter.)

    A. 3    C. 5    E. 10
    B. 4    D. 6

61. If $y$ varies directly with $x$ and the constant of variation is 3, then $y = 12.3$ when $x = 4.1$. If $y$ varies directly with $x$ and $y = 6.72$ when $x = 4.2$, then what is the constant of variation?

    A. 3.1    C. 2.52    E. 2.50
    B. 4.2    D. 1.6

62. Each of the following choices is comprised of three equations relating $x$ and $y$. Identify the set of equations that demonstrates direct variation, inverse variation, and neither direct nor inverse variation, respectively?

    A. $y = 3x; x^2 + y^2 = x + 5; y = \frac{4}{x}$

    B. $y = 3x; x^2 + y^2 = x + 5; y = \frac{x}{4}$

    C. $x = \frac{y}{3}; xy = 7; x^2 + y^2 = \frac{x}{5}$

    D. $y = 3x; y = \frac{4}{x}; x = 5y$

    E. $y = \frac{2x}{3}; x = 5y; x^2 + y^2 = x + 7$

63. At a constant temperature, the resistance of a wire varies directly with length and inversely with the square of the wire diameter. A piece of wire that is 0.1 inch in diameter and 50 feet long has a resistance of 0.1 ohm. What is the resistance, in ohms, of a wire of the same material that is 9,000 feet long and 0.3 inches in diameter?

    A. 0.3    C. 2    E. 9
    B. 0.9    D. 3

64. Let $y$ vary directly as $x$, and let $w$ vary directly as the square of $x$. If $y = 10$ for $x = 1.25$ and $w = 8$ for $x = \sqrt{2}$, then for what positive value of $x$ will $y = w$?

    A. 1    C. 2    E. 5
    B. $1\frac{1}{2}$    D. 4

65. The perimeter of a square varies directly as the length of one side of the square with a constant of variation of 4. The circumference of a circle varies directly as the circle's radius and a constant of variation equal to:

    A. $\pi$    C. 1    E. $\frac{1}{\pi}$
    B. $2\pi$    D. 2

66. If $x$ and $y$ vary inversely, then for any ordered pair $(x, y)$, the value of $xy$ is a constant number. The ordered pairs $(-12, -3)$ and $(6, 6)$ represent an example of inverse variation for $x$ and $y$. Which of the following graphs represents a possible inverse variation relationship between $x$ and $y$?

A.

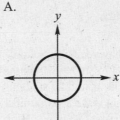

D.

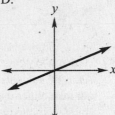

B.

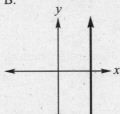

E.

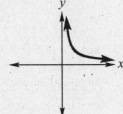

C.

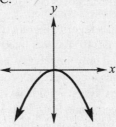

67. The formula for compound interest is $A = P(1 + \frac{r}{n})^{nt}$, where $A$ is the final amount, $P$ is the initial investment, $r$ is the annual percentage interest rate, $t$ is the time period, and $n$ is the number of times per year that the interest is compounded. If an initial investment of $10,000 accrues compound interest at a percentage rate of 4.16% and is worth $10,424.02, $10,866.03, $11,326.77, and $11,807.06 after 1, 2, 3, and 4 years, respectively, then $n$ is approximately equal to:

    A. 1    C. 4    E. 12
    B. 2    D. 6

68. The simple interest earned on an investment is given by the formula $I = prt$, where $I$ is the amount of interest, $p$ is the amount invested, $r$ is the yearly percentage rate of interest, and $t$ is the number of years for the investment. What is the simple interest earned on an investment of $1,000 for 2 years at a yearly percentage rate of interest of 6%?

    A. $6     C. $60     E. $600
    B. $12     D. $120

69. The probability that an event will happen can be shown by the fraction $\frac{\text{winning events}}{\text{total events}}$ or $\frac{\text{favorable events}}{\text{total events}}$. From the 8 digit number 12,344,362, Helen selects a digit at random. What is the probability that she selected 4?

    A. $\frac{1}{8}$     C. $\frac{1}{4}$     E. $\frac{4}{1}$
    B. $\frac{1}{5}$     D. $\frac{1}{2}$

70. Last night, Dave and Kathy both arrived at Pizza Palace at two different random times between 10:00 p.m. and midnight. They had agreed to wait exactly 15 minutes for each other to arrive before leaving. What is the probability that Dave and Kathy were together at Pizza Palace last night between 10:00 p.m. and midnight?

    A. $\frac{1}{8}$     C. $\frac{15}{64}$     E. $\frac{31}{64}$
    B. $\frac{1}{4}$     D. $\frac{3}{8}$

71. George must select 1 pencil from 6 different pencils and 1 pen from 5 different pens. How many different combinations can George make?

    A. 5     C. 30     E. 65
    B. 11     D. 56

72. A letter is selected at random from the word "DAVID." What is the probability that the letter selected is "D"?

    A. $\frac{1}{5}$     C. $\frac{1}{3}$     E. $\frac{3}{5}$
    B. $\frac{1}{4}$     D. $\frac{2}{5}$

73. One of the letters in the alphabet is selected at random. What is the probability that the letter selected is a letter found in the word "MATHEMATICS"?

    A. $\frac{1}{26}$     C. $\frac{5}{13}$     E. $\frac{6}{13}$
    B. $\frac{4}{13}$     D. $\frac{11}{26}$

74. Two integers are to be randomly selected from the sets below, one integer from each set. What is the probability that the sum of the two integers will equal 11?

    $$X = \{2, 4, 5, 8, 9\}$$
    $$Y = \{2, 3, 4, 7\}$$

    A. 0.10     C. 0.20     E. 0.30
    B. 0.15     D. 0.25

75. If 6 books are lined up in random order on a shelf, what is the probability that the oldest book will be on the left end and the newest book will be on the right end?

    A. $\frac{1}{8}$     C. $\frac{1}{5}$     E. $\frac{1}{4}$
    B. $\frac{1}{6}$     D. $\frac{2}{5}$

76. If a fair coin is to be tossed 3 times, what is the probability that on at least 1 of the tosses the coin will turn up heads?

    A. $\frac{1}{8}$     C. $\frac{1}{2}$     E. $\frac{31}{64}$
    B. $\frac{1}{4}$     D. $\frac{7}{8}$

77. In the figure below, two sides of the rectangle $ABGF$ lie on two sides of the square $ACDE$. $\overline{AF} = 9$, $\overline{BC} = 8$, and $\overline{FE} = 1$.

    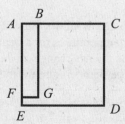

    If a point is chosen at random in the interior of the square, what is the probability that the point also lies in the interior of the rectangle?

    A. $\frac{1}{50}$     C. $\frac{7}{50}$     E. $\frac{11}{50}$
    B. $\frac{3}{50}$     D. $\frac{9}{50}$

78. The stronger the relationship between two variables, the more closely the points on a scatter plot will approach some linear or curvilinear pattern. Which of the scatter plots below represents the strongest relationship between the two variables?

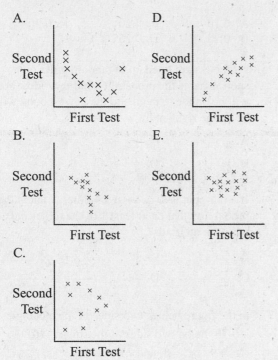

A.

Second Test

First Test

B.

Second Test

First Test

C.

Second Test

First Test

D.

Second Test

First Test

E.

Second Test

First Test

79. The table below shows the daily change in the weather temperatures for a certain city last week. What was the net change, in degrees Celsius, in the weather temperature for the week?

| Day | Daily Change in Temperature (° C) |
|---|---|
| Sunday | +5.5 |
| Monday | +1.7 |
| Tuesday | −3.9 |
| Wednesday | −3.3 |
| Thursday | −0.5 |
| Friday | +0.8 |
| Saturday | −0.2 |

A. −5.7　　C. 0.1　　E. 5.7
B. −0.1　　D. 5.3

80. The table below represents the number of voters in five counties that voted in a general election and the percent change in the number of voters from the previously held primary election. Which county had the greatest net increase in voters between the primary and the general elections?

| County | Number of Voters in General Election (in millions) | Percent Change from Primary Election |
|---|---|---|
| M | 5.67 | −23% |
| N | 2.34 | +14% |
| O | 1.25 | −2% |
| P | 4.56 | +4% |
| Q | 6.23 | +8% |

A. County M
B. County N
C. County O
D. County P
E. County Q

81. The table below shows the number of students in three sports at East High School. 8 students are in both basketball and tennis, 5 students are in both basketball and volleyball, and 3 students are in both volleyball and tennis. No student is in all three sports. How many different students are in the three sports? What is the total number of students that participate only in basketball or tennis?

| Sport | Number of Students |
|---|---|
| Basketball | 35 |
| Volleyball | 15 |
| Tennis | 40 |

A. 22　　　C. 50　　　E. 75
B. 29　　　D. 51

# Quantitative Reasoning Express Skills Review

# CAMBRIDGE TESTPREP™

## QUANTITATIVE REASONING EXPRESS SKILLS REVIEW OUTLINE

# Arithmetic Summary

1. **Real Numbers:** Real numbers are all the numbers on the number line, including integers, decimals, fractions, and radical numbers.

   e.g., $-\frac{1}{2}, 0, \frac{2}{3}, \sqrt{2}, \pi$

   A real number is *rational* if it can be written as the ratio of two integers, where the denominator does not equal zero. Natural numbers, whole numbers, integers, common fractions, and repeating decimals are some examples of rational numbers.

   e.g., $-\frac{1}{2}, 0, 0.75, \frac{2}{3}$

   A real number is *irrational* if it cannot be written as the ratio of two integers. Irrational numbers have infinite non-repeating decimal representations.

   e.g., $\sqrt{2}, \pi$

   *Properties of real numbers:*

   $(+)(+) = (+)$
   $(-)(-) = (+)$
   $(+)(-) = (-)$
   $(-)^2 = (+)$

   $m + 0 = m$, where $m$ is a real number
   $m \cdot 0 = 0$, where $m$ is a real number

   e.g., 1. $(\frac{1}{2})(4) = 2$
   2. $(-2)(-\frac{4}{5}) = (\frac{8}{5})$
   3. $(2)(-4) = (-8)$
   4. $(-\frac{3}{4})(4) = -3$
   5. $(-2)^2 = 4$
   6. $2 + 0 = 2$
   7. $(2)(0) = 0$

2. **Natural Numbers:** *Natural* numbers are the set of positive integers and are also referred to as counting numbers: 1, 2, 3, 4, 5, ....

3. **Whole Numbers:** *Whole* numbers are the numbers used for counting, plus the number zero: 0, 1, 2, 3, 4, 5....

4. **Integers:** *Integers* are positive or negative whole numbers.

   e.g., $-568, -45, 0, 6, 67, \frac{16}{2}, 345$

5. **Positive and Negative Integers:** If the signs of the two numbers being added or subtracted are *different*, disregard the signs temporarily, subtract the smaller number from the larger number, and keep the sign attached to the larger number.

   e.g., $-3 + -2 = -1$
   $-4 + 6 = 2$

   If the signs of the two numbers being added or subtracted are the *same*, disregard the signs temporarily, add the two numbers, and keep the sign attached to each number.

   e.g., 1. $-5 - 3 = -8$
   2. $4 + 8 = 12$

6. **Even and Odd Integers:** An *even* integer is evenly divisible by 2, whereas an *odd* integer is not evenly divisible by 2. 0 is an even integer.

   e.g., $-50, -4, 0, 2, 34$ are even integers.
   $-45, -3, 9, 15$ are odd integers.

   *Important properties of even and odd integers:*

   | | |
   |---|---|
   | even + even = even | e.g., $2 + 4 = 6$ |
   | even + odd = odd | e.g., $4 + 3 = 7$ |
   | odd + odd = even | e.g., $3 + 5 = 8$ |
   | odd + even = odd | e.g., $3 + 4 = 7$ |
   | even • even = even | e.g., $2 \cdot 4 = 8$ |
   | even • odd = even | e.g., $2 \cdot 3 = 6$ |
   | odd • odd = odd | e.g., $3 \cdot 5 = 15$ |
   | odd • even = even | e.g., $3 \cdot 2 = 6$ |

7. **Factor:** A *factor* is a number that divides evenly into another number.

   e.g., 1, 2, 3, 4, 6, and 12 are factors of 12

8. **Prime:** A *prime* number is any natural number (except 1) that is divisible only by 1 and itself.

   e.g., 2, 3, 5, 7, 11, 13, 17, and 19 are all prime numbers

9. **Prime Factors:** All natural numbers can be expressed as the product of prime numbers, which are called the *prime factors* of that number.

   e.g., 1. $3 = (3)(1)$
   2. $12 = (2)(2)(3)$

**10. Consecutive Integers:** *Consecutive* integers are in continuous sequence. If the first integer of a consecutive sequence is $m$, the sequence is $m$, $m+1$, $m+2$, etc.

e.g., 1. $\{4,5,6,7, ...\}$
2. $\{-10,-9,-8,-7 ...\}$

Consecutive *even* or *odd* integers are in continuous sequence of even or odd integers, respectively. An even or odd sequence is $m$, $m+2$, $m+4$, $m+6$, etc.

e.g., 1. $\{-4,-2,0,2, ...\}$
2. $\{7,9,11,13, ...\}$

**11. Miscellaneous Symbols:**

"$=$" means "is equal to"
"$\neq$" means "is not equal to"
"$<$" means "is less than"
"$>$" means "is greater than"
"$\leq$" means "is less than or equal to"
"$\geq$" means "is greater than or equal to"
"$|\ |$" means "absolute value (always non-negative)"

e.g., 1. $3 = 3$
2. $\frac{3}{4} \neq \frac{5}{6}$
3. $-3 < 6$
4. $5 > 4$
5. $m - 3 \leq -3$, for $m = ...,-3,-2,-1,0$
6. $m + 3 \geq 3$, for $m = 0, 1, 2, 3, ...$
7. $\left|-5\right| = 5$

**12. Terms:** The *sum* or *total* is the result of adding numbers together. The *difference* is the result of subtracting one number from another. The *product* is the result of multiplying numbers together. The *quotient* is the result of dividing one number by another. The *remainder* is the number remaining after one number is divided into another number.

e.g., 1. The sum (or total) of 2 and 3 is 5: $2 + 3 = 5$.
2. The difference between 5 and 2 is 3: $5 - 2 = 3$.
3. The product of 2 and 3 is 6: $(2)(3) = 6$.
4. The quotient of 6 divided by 2 is 3: $6 \div 2 = 3$.
5. The remainder of 7 divided by 3 is 1: $7 \div 3 = 2$ plus a remainder of 1.

**13. Fractions:** When one whole integer is divided by another whole integer (other than zero) and the result is not a third whole integer, the result is a fraction, or ratio. The top number is called the *numerator*; the bottom number is called the *denominator*.

e.g., 2 divided by 3 results in a fraction, not a whole number: $2 \div 3 = \frac{2}{3}$.

*Proper fractions* have a numerator of lower value than the denominator and thus have a value less than 1.

e.g., $\frac{1}{2}$ and $\frac{3}{4}$ are both less than 1.

*Improper fractions* have a numerator of greater value than the denominator, and thus have a value greater than 1.

e.g., $\frac{3}{2}$ and $\frac{4}{3}$ are both greater than 1.

A *mixed number* consists of both a whole number and a fraction written together.

e.g., 1. $2\frac{1}{2} = 2 + \frac{1}{2}$
2. $3\frac{4}{5} = 3 + \frac{4}{5}$

To add, subtract, multiply, or divide fractions, convert mixed numbers to improper fractions as follows:

a. The new denominator is the denominator of the fractional part of the mixed number.
b. The new numerator is the whole number of the mixed number multiplied by the denominator of the fractional part and then added to its numerator.

e.g., 1. $3\frac{1}{4} = \frac{(3 \cdot 4) + 1}{4} = \frac{13}{4}$
2. $6\frac{2}{5} = \frac{(6 \cdot 5) + 2}{5} = \frac{32}{5}$
3. $2\frac{12}{13} = \frac{(2 \cdot 13) + 12}{13} = \frac{38}{13}$

To convert an improper fraction to a mixed number, reverse the process as follows:

a. Divide the denominator into the numerator. The integer part of the quotient becomes the whole number part of the mixed number.
b. With the same denominator, create a fraction with the numerator equal to the remainder of the first step.

e.g., 1. $\frac{29}{5} = 29 \div 5 = 5$ with a remainder of $4 = 5\frac{4}{5}$.
2. $\frac{31}{6} = 31 \div 6 = 5$ with a remainder of $1 = 5\frac{1}{6}$.
3. $\frac{43}{13} = 43 \div 13 = 3$ with a remainder of $4 = 3\frac{4}{13}$.

14. **Reducing Fractions:** It is conventional to reduce all fractions to lowest terms. To reduce a fraction to lowest terms, eliminate redundant factors that are in both the numerator and the denominator. Either factor or divide out the redundant factors from both.

e.g., $\frac{8}{16} = \frac{1(8)}{2(8)} = \frac{1}{2}$, or $\frac{8}{16} = \frac{8 \div 8}{16 \div 8} = \frac{1}{2}$.

A fraction is expressed in *lowest terms* when there is no natural number (other than 1) that can be divided evenly into both the numerator and the denominator.

e.g., $\frac{8}{15}$ is in lowest terms, as there is no natural number (other than 1) that divides evenly into 8 and 15.

15. **Complex Fractions:** A *complex fraction* is a fraction in which either the numerator or the denominator, or both, contains fractions. There are two methods for simplifying complex fractions.

*Method 1*: Multiply the numerator by the reciprocal of the denominator and simplify.

e.g., $\frac{\frac{1}{2}}{\frac{3}{4}} = \left(\frac{1}{2}\right)\left(\frac{4}{3}\right) = \frac{4}{6} = \frac{2}{3}$

*Method 2*: Multiply both the numerator and the denominator by the least common denominator for the terms in the numerator and the denominator of the complex fraction and simplify.

e.g., $\frac{\frac{1}{2}}{\frac{3}{4}} \cdot \frac{(4)}{(4)} = \frac{\frac{4}{2}}{\frac{12}{4}} = \frac{2}{3}$

16. **Common Denominators:** A *common denominator* is a number that is a multiple of the denominators of two or more fractions.

e.g., Since 12 is an even multiple of both 3 and 4, it is a common denominator for $\frac{1}{3}$ and $\frac{1}{4}$.

*Converting a fraction to another denominator* is the reverse of reducing it to lowest terms. Multiplying the numerator and the denominator of a fraction by the same number is equal to multiplying it by 1, which means that the value is unchanged.

e.g., 1. $\frac{1}{4} = \frac{(1)(3)}{(4)(3)} = \frac{3}{12}$

2. $\frac{2}{3} = \frac{(2)(4)}{(3)(4)} = \frac{8}{12}$

17. **Adding Fractions:** The procedure for adding fractions varies depending on whether or not the fractions already share the same denominator.

*To add fractions with the same denominator*, create a new fraction using the common denominator. The new numerator is the sum of the old numerators.

e.g., $\frac{3}{7} + \frac{2}{7} = \frac{5}{7}$

*To add fractions with different denominators*, find a common denominator and convert the fractions.

e.g., 1. $\frac{1}{3} + \frac{1}{5} = \frac{1(5)}{3(5)} + \frac{1(3)}{5(3)} = \frac{5}{15} + \frac{3}{15} = \frac{8}{15}$

2. $\frac{1}{3} + \frac{2}{7} = \frac{1(7)}{3(7)} + \frac{2(3)}{7(3)} = \frac{7}{21} + \frac{6}{21} = \frac{13}{21}$

*To add a fraction and a whole number*, treat the whole number as a fraction with a denominator of 1.

e.g., $2 + \frac{1}{5} + \frac{1}{2} = \frac{2}{1} + \frac{1}{5} + \frac{1}{2} = \frac{2(10)}{1(10)} + \frac{1(2)}{5(2)} + \frac{1(5)}{2(5)} = \frac{20}{10} + \frac{2}{10} + \frac{5}{10} = \frac{27}{10}$

*To add a fraction and a mixed number*, change the mixed number to an improper fraction and then add.

e.g., $2\frac{1}{3} + \frac{1}{3} = \frac{7}{3} + \frac{1}{3} = \frac{8}{3} = 2\frac{2}{3}$

18. **Subtracting Fractions:** Follow the same procedure for addition, except subtract rather than add.

*To subtract fractions with the same denominator*, simply subtract the second numerator from the first.

e.g., $\frac{5}{7} - \frac{2}{7} = \frac{3}{7}$

*To subtract fractions with different denominators*, first find a common denominator.

e.g., $\frac{7}{8} - \frac{3}{5} = \frac{7(5)}{8(5)} - \frac{3(8)}{5(8)} = \frac{35}{40} - \frac{24}{40} = \frac{11}{40}$

19. **"Flying-X" Method for Adding and Subtracting Fractions:** It is not necessary to find the least common denominator when adding or subtracting fractions if you reduce the result to lowest terms. Any common denominator will work—simply use the "flying-x" method.

$$\frac{a}{b} + \frac{c}{d} = \frac{a}{b} \gtrless \frac{c}{d} = \frac{ad + bc}{bd}$$

a. Multiply the denominators together to get a new denominator.

b. Multiply the numerator of the first fraction by the denominator of the second.

c. Multiply the denominator of the first fraction by the numerator of the second.

d. The new numerator is the sum (or difference) of the results of steps 2 and 3.

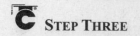
e.g., 1. $\frac{2}{7} + \frac{1}{5} = \frac{2}{7} \gtreqless + \lesseqgtr \frac{1}{5} = \frac{10+7}{35} = \frac{17}{35}$

2. $\frac{3}{5} + \frac{1}{3} = \frac{3}{5} \gtreqless + \lesseqgtr \frac{1}{3} = \frac{9+5}{15} = \frac{14}{15}$

20. **Multiplying Fractions:** Multiplication of fractions does not require a common denominator. Just multiply numerators to create a new numerator, and multiply denominators to create a new denominator.

e.g., 1. $\frac{3}{4} \cdot \frac{1}{2} = \frac{(3)(1)}{(4)(2)} = \frac{3}{8}$

2. $\frac{2}{3} \cdot \frac{2}{5} = \frac{(2)(2)}{(3)(5)} = \frac{4}{15}$

21. **Dividing Fractions:** To divide by a fraction, take the reciprocal of the divisor (the fraction doing the dividing) and then multiply the two terms.

e.g., 1. $2 \div \frac{1}{4} = 2 \cdot \frac{4}{1} = \frac{8}{1} = 8$

2. $\frac{\frac{2}{3}}{\frac{5}{6}} = \frac{2}{3} \cdot \frac{6}{5} = \frac{12}{15} = \frac{4}{15}$

22. **Converting Fractions to Decimals:** If the fraction already has a denominator that is 10, 100, 1,000, etc., the conversion is easy. The numerator of the fraction becomes the decimal. The placement of the decimal point is governed by the number of zeros in the denominator.

e.g. Express $\frac{127}{1,000}$ in decimal form.

In the numerator, count three places to the left of the 7—one for each zero in 1,000: $\frac{127}{1,000} = 0.127$.

If there are fewer numbers in the numerator than there are decimal places, add zeros to the left of the number until there are enough decimal places.

e.g., $\frac{3}{100} = 0.03$

*To convert a proper fraction with a denominator other than 10, 100, etc.,* first convert the fraction to the equivalent form using a denominator such as 10, 100, etc. To determine which denominator to use, divide the denominator of the fraction into 10, then into 100, then into 1,000, until a denominator that is evenly divisible by the denominator of the original fraction is found.

e.g., 1. $\frac{2}{5} = \frac{(2)(2)}{(5)(2)} = \frac{4}{10} = 0.4$

2. $\frac{1}{4} = \frac{(1)(25)}{(4)(25)} = \frac{25}{100} = 0.25$

3. $\frac{3}{8} = \frac{(3)(125)}{(8)(125)} = \frac{375}{1,000} = 0.375$

To convert proper fractions to decimals, dividing the denominator into the numerator is usually easier.

e.g., 1. $\frac{2}{5} = 5\overline{)2.0}^{0.4} = 0.4$

2. $\frac{3}{8} = 8\overline{)3.000}^{0.375} = 0.375$

*To convert a mixed number into a decimal,* convert the fractional part of the mixed number to a decimal as just discussed, and then place the whole number part of the mixed number to the left of the decimal point.

e.g., 1. $6\frac{1}{10} = 6.1$ (Convert $\frac{1}{10}$ to 0.1 and then place the 6 to the left of the decimal point.)

2. $3\frac{7}{8} = 3.875$ (Convert $\frac{7}{8}$ to 0.875 and then place the 3 to the left of the decimal point.)

*To convert an improper fraction to a decimal,* convert it to a mixed number and follow the procedure just outlined.

e.g., $\frac{9}{4} = 2\frac{1}{4} = 2.25$

23. **Converting Decimals to Fractions:** The numerator of the fraction is the digit(s) to the right of the decimal point. The denominator is a 1 followed by the same number of zeros as the number of decimal places to the right of the decimal point.

e.g., $0.005 = \frac{5}{1,000} = \frac{1}{200}$ (0.005 has three decimal places, so the new denominator is 1 followed by 3 zeroes).

If a decimal has numbers to both the right and left of the decimal point, the conversion to a fraction results in a mixed number. The whole part of the mixed number is the whole part of the decimal.

e.g., 1. $1.75 = 1 + \frac{75}{100} = 1 + \frac{3}{4} = 1\frac{3}{4}$

2. $357.125 = 357 + \frac{125}{1,000} = 357 + \frac{1}{8} = 357\frac{1}{8}$

*Memorize these decimal equivalents:*

$\frac{1}{2} = 0.50$  $\quad$  $\frac{1}{3} = 0.33\overline{3}$  $\quad$  $\frac{1}{4} = 0.25$

$\frac{1}{5} = 0.20$  $\quad$  $\frac{1}{6} = 0.16\overline{6}$  $\quad$  $\frac{1}{7} = 0.142857$

$\frac{1}{8} = 0.125$  $\quad$  $\frac{1}{9} = 0.1\overline{11}$  $\quad$  $\frac{1}{10} = 0.10$

(Note: A bar over a digit or digits indicates that the digit or group of digits repeats.)

**24. Adding and Subtracting Decimals:** To add or subtract decimals, line up the decimal points, fill in the appropriate number of zeros, and then add or subtract.

e.g., $0.25 + 0.1 + 0.825 = 0.25$
$$\begin{array}{r} 0.1 \\ + \ 0.825 \\ \hline = 0.250 \\ 0.100 \\ + \ 0.825 \\ \hline 1.175 \end{array}$$

**25. Multiplying Decimals:** To multiply decimals, first multiply as with whole numbers and then adjust the decimal point. Count the total number of decimal places in the numbers being multiplied, count that many places to the left from the right of the final number in the product, and put the decimal point there.

e.g., 1. $(0.1)(0.2)(0.3) = 0.006$ $(1 \cdot 2 \cdot 3 = 6$, and there are three decimal places in the multiplication.)

2. $(0.10)(0.10)(0.10) = 0.001000 = 0.001$ $(10 \cdot 10 \cdot 10 = 1,000$, and there are six decimal places in the problem.)

**26. Dividing Decimals:** When the divisor is a whole number, place a decimal point in the quotient immediately above the decimal point in the dividend. Keep dividing until there is no remainder, adding zeros as needed to the right of the divisor.

e.g., $2.5 \div 2 = 2\overline{)\begin{array}{l} 1.25 \\ 2.50 \end{array}}$
$$\begin{array}{r} -2 \\ \hline 0\ 5 \\ -\ 4 \\ \hline 10 \\ -\ 10 \\ \hline 0 \end{array}$$

When the divisor is a *decimal*, "clear" the fractional part of the decimal by moving both the divisor and dividend decimal points the same number of spaces to the right.

e.g., $5 \div 2.5 = 50 \div 25 = 25\overline{)\begin{array}{l} 2 \\ 50 \end{array}}$
$$\begin{array}{r} -50 \\ \hline 0 \end{array}$$

**27. Ratios:** A *ratio* is a statement about the relationship between two quantities. The ratio of two quantities, $x$ and $y$, can be expressed as $x \div y$, $x / y$, or $x : y$.

e.g., 1. $\frac{2}{5} = 2.5$

2. $\frac{\text{boys}}{\text{girls}} = $ boys : girls = ratio of boys to girls

3. $\frac{\text{miles}}{\text{hour}} = $ miles : hour = miles per hour

**28. Proportions:** A *proportion* is a statement of equality between two ratios.

e.g., $\frac{3}{4} = \frac{9}{12}$

With *direct variation*, ratios are directly related: The more of one quantity, the more of the other, and vice versa.

e.g., If 12 donuts cost $3.60, how much do 4 donuts cost?

$\frac{\text{Total Cost for } X}{\text{Total Cost for } Y} = \frac{X}{Y} \Rightarrow \frac{\$3.60}{Y} = \frac{12}{4} \Rightarrow \$3.60(4) = 12Y$
$Y = 3.60(4) \div 12 = \$1.20$

With *inverse variation*, ratios are inversely related: An increase in one quantity is a decrease in the other. Use this method to solve inverse variation problems: first, set up an ordinary proportion, making sure that you group like quantities; then, take the reciprocal of the proportion's right side; and finally, cross-multiply and solve for the unknown.

e.g., Traveling at a constant rate of 150 mph, a plane makes the trip from City P to City Q in four hours. How long will the trip take if the plane flies at a constant rate of 200 mph?

$\frac{\text{Speed } X}{\text{Speed } Y} = \frac{\text{Time } X}{\text{Time } Y} = \frac{150 \text{ mph}}{200 \text{ mph}} = \frac{4 \text{ hours}}{Y \text{ hours}} \Rightarrow \frac{150}{200} = \frac{Y}{4}$
$Y = 4(150) \div 200 = 3 \text{ hours}$

**29. Percentage Conversions:** *To change any decimal to a percent*, move the decimal point two places to the right and add a percent sign. To change a percent to a decimal, reverse the process.

e.g., 1. $0.275 = 27.5\%$
2. $0.03 = 3\%$
3. $0.02\% = 0.0002$
4. $120\% = 1.20$

*To convert a fraction to a percent*, first convert the fraction to a decimal. Reverse the process for converting percents to fractions.

e.g., 1. $\frac{3}{4} = 0.75 = 75\% = 0.75 = \frac{75}{100} = \frac{3}{4}$

2. $\frac{5}{8} = 0.625 = 62.5\% = \frac{625}{1,000} = \frac{5}{8}$

30. **Common Percent Problems:** All percent problems have the same three components: *is*, *of*, and %. Depending on the form of the question, one of these three components is the unknown variable.

*"What is x% of that?"*
*"This is what percent of that?"*
*"This is x% of what?*

Percentage problems can be solved using several different methods. Two methods are outlined below.

*Method 1*: Write the statement as an equation, rewrite the percent as $\frac{\%}{100}$, and solve for the unknown.

e.g., 5 is 20% of what number?
$5 = \frac{20x}{100} \Rightarrow x = \frac{(5)(100)}{20} = 25$. Thus, 5 is 20% of 25.

*Method 2*: Since there are three parts to all percent problems (*is*, *of*, and %), use the following equation to solve for the unknown: $\frac{is}{of} = \frac{\%}{100}$.

e.g., 1. 20 is what percent of 50?
$\% = x$, $is = 20$, $of = 50$
$\frac{is}{of} = \frac{\%}{100} \Rightarrow \frac{20}{50} = \frac{x}{100} \Rightarrow \frac{(20)(100)}{50} = 40$

2. What number is 20% of 25?
$\% = 20$, $is = x$, $of = 25$
$\frac{is}{of} = \frac{\%}{100} \Rightarrow \frac{x}{25} = \frac{20}{100} \Rightarrow x = \frac{(20)(25)}{100} = 5$

Another common percent item is *change in amount*.

$$\text{Percent Change} = \frac{|\text{New Amount} - \text{Original Amount}|}{\text{Original Amount}}$$

The absolute value allows for percent decreases as well.

e.g., An item's price is increased from \$3 to \$5. What is the percent increase in the price?

$$\frac{|\text{New Amount} - \text{Original Amount}|}{\text{Original Amount}} = \frac{5-3}{3} = \frac{2}{3} = 66\%$$

31. **Averages:** To calculate an *average* (or mean), add together the quantities to be averaged; then divide that sum by the number of quantities added.

e.g., The average of 3, 7, and 8 is 6: $3 + 7 + 8 = 18$ and $18 \div 3 = 6$.

If solving for a *missing element* of an average, set up the average equation and solve for the unknown.

e.g., The average score on four tests is 90. If three scores are 89, 92, and 94, what is the fourth score?

$\frac{89 + 92 + 94 + x}{4} = 90 \Rightarrow x = 85$

In *weighted averages*, greater weight is given to one element than to another.

e.g., Four books cost \$6.00 each and two books cost \$3.00 each. What is the average cost of a book?

$\frac{(4)(6) + (2)(3)}{4 + 2} = \frac{24 + 6}{6} = \frac{30}{6} = 5$

32. **Median:** The *median* is the middle value of a number set when arranged in ascending or descending order. The median of an even numbered set is the average of the two middle values, when the numbers are arranged in ascending or descending order.

e.g., The median of $\{8, 6, 34, 5, 17, 23\}$ is: $\frac{8 + 17}{2} = 12.5$.

33. **Mode:** The value that appears most frequently in a set of numbers is the *mode*.

e.g., The mode of 4, 5, 3, 4, 5, 1, 2, 3, 6, 4, and 6, is 4.

34. **Counting Principle:** To determine the number of ways that particular events can occur, multiply the number of ways that each event can occur.

e.g., 1. How many ways can you select one boy and one girl from a class of 15 girls and 13 boys?

$(15)(13) = 195$ ways

2. In how many ways can 5 students sit in a row with 5 chairs?

$(5)(4)(3)(2)(1) = 120$ ways

3. In how many ways can you fill three chairs given five students?

$(5)(4)(3) = 60$ ways

35. **Probability Principle:** The probability that an event will happen can be found from the fraction $\frac{\text{winning events}}{\text{total events}}$ or $\frac{\text{favorable events}}{\text{total events}}$.

e.g., From the set $\{-4, -3, -2, 0, 1, 6, 8, 1002\}$, a number is selected at random. Find the probability that the selected number is an even integer.

There are 6 even integers $(-4, -2, 0, 6, 8, 1002)$ out of a total of 8 integers, so the probability is: $\frac{6}{8} = \frac{3}{4}$.

# Algebra Summary

1. **Basic Operations:**

   *Addition*: $n + n = 2n$
   $n + m = n + m$

   *Subtraction*: $3n - 2n = n$
   $n - m = n - m$

   *Multiplication*: $n \cdot m = (n)(m) = nm$
   $(n)(0) = 0$

   *Division*: $n \div m = \frac{n}{m}$
   $n \div 0 = \text{undefined}$

2. **Powers:** A *power* of a number indicates repeated multiplication.

   e.g., 3 raised to the fifth power is
   $(3)(3)(3)(3)(3) = 243$

3. **Exponents:** An *exponent* is a number that indicates the operation of repeated multiplication. Exponents are notated as superscripts. The number being multiplied is the *base*.

   e.g., 1. $2^3 = (2)(2)(2) = 8$
   2. $5^4 = (5)(5)(5)(5) = 625$

   *Exponent Rules*:

   1. $x^m \cdot x^n = x^{m+n}$
   2. $x^m \div x^n = x^{m-n}$
   3. $(x^m)^n = x^{mn}$
   4. $(xy)^m = x^m y^m$
   5. $\left(\frac{x}{y}\right)^m = \frac{x^m}{y^m}$
   6. $x^1 = x$, for any number $x$
   7. $x^0 = 1$, for any number $x$, such that $x \neq 0$
   8. $0^0$ is undefined.

   e.g., 1. $(2^3)(2^2) = (2 \cdot 2 \cdot 2)(2 \cdot 2) = 2^{3+2} = 2^5$
   $(3^2)(3^3)(3^5) = 3^{2+3+5} = 10$

   2. $2^4 \div 2^2 = \frac{(2)(2)(2)(2)}{(2)(2)} = 2^{4-2} = 2^2$
   $5^3 \div 5^5 = 5^{3-5} = 5^{-2} = \left(\frac{1}{5}\right)^2 = \frac{1}{25}$

   3. $(2^2)^3 = (2 \cdot 2)^3 =$
   $(2 \cdot 2)(2 \cdot 2)(2 \cdot 2) = 2^{2 \cdot 3} = 2^6$

   4. $(2 \cdot 3)^2 = (2 \cdot 3)(2 \cdot 3) = (2 \cdot 2)(3 \cdot 3) =$
   $2^2 \cdot 3^2 = 4 \cdot 9 = 36$

$(2^3 \cdot 3^2)^2 = 2^{3 \cdot 2} \cdot 3^{2 \cdot 2} = 2^6 \cdot 3^4$

5. $\left(\frac{2}{3}\right)^2 = \frac{2^2}{3^2} = \frac{4}{9}$

$\left(\frac{3^3 \cdot 5^2}{3^2 \cdot 5^2}\right) = (3^{3-2} \cdot 5^{5-2})^2 = (3^1 \cdot 5^3)^2 = (3^2)(5^6)$

A negative exponent signifies a fraction, indicating the *reciprocal* of the base.

e.g., 1. $x^{-1} = \frac{1}{x}$
2. $2x^{-1} = 2\left(\frac{1}{x}\right) = \frac{2}{x}$
3. $4^{-2} = \left(\frac{1}{4}\right)^2 = \frac{1}{16}$

4. **Roots:** The *root* of a number is a number that is multiplied a specified number of times to give the original number. Square root $= m^{\frac{1}{2}} = \sqrt{m}$. Cube root $= m^{\frac{1}{3}} = \sqrt[3]{m}$.

   e.g., 1. $\sqrt{4} = 4^{\frac{1}{2}} = 2$
   2. $\sqrt[3]{8} = 8^{\frac{1}{3}} = 2$
   3. $\sqrt{125} = 125^{\frac{1}{2}} = (25 \cdot 5)^{\frac{1}{2}}(5^{\frac{1}{2}}) = (\sqrt{25})(\sqrt{5}) = 5\sqrt{5}$
   4. $\sqrt{\frac{4}{9}} = \left(\frac{4}{9}\right)^{\frac{1}{2}} = \frac{4^{\frac{1}{2}}}{9^{\frac{1}{2}}} = \frac{\sqrt{4}}{\sqrt{9}} = \frac{2}{3}$

5. **Basic Algebraic Operations:** Algebraic operations are the same as for arithmetic, with the addition of unknown quantities. Manipulate operations in the same way, combining (adding and subtracting) only like terms. Like terms have the same variables with the same exponents.

   e.g., 1. $x^2 - 3x + 5x - 3x^2 = -2x^2 + 2x$
   2. $(x^2)(x^3) = x^{2+3} = 5$
   3. $4x^3 y^4 \div 2xy^3 = 2x^2 y$
   4. $\frac{5}{x} + \frac{3}{x} = \frac{5+3}{x} = \frac{8}{x}$
   5. $\left(\frac{x^2 y^3}{z}\right)\left(\frac{x^3 y^2}{wz}\right) = \frac{x^5 y^5}{wz^2}$

**6. Multiplying Polynomials:** A *polynomial* is an algebraic expression with more than one term. A binomial is a polynomial consisting of exactly two terms. When multiplying two binomials, use the *FOIL* (*F*irst, *O*uter, *I*nner, *L*ast) *method*:

$(x + y)(x + y) = ?$

Multiply the *first* terms: $x \cdot x = x^2$

Multiply the *outer* terms: $x \cdot y = xy$

Multiply the *inner* terms: $y \cdot x = yx = xy$

Multiply the *last* terms: $y \cdot y = y^2$

Combine like terms:

$(x + y)(x + y) = x^2 + 2xy + y^2$

e.g., $(x - y)(x - y) = ?$

First: $(x)(x) = x^2$

Outer: $(x)(-y) = -xy$

Inner: $(-y)(x) = -xy$

Last: $(-y)(-y) = y^2$

Combine: $x^2 - xy - xy + y^2 = x^2 - 2xy + y^2$

If the two polynomials are not binomials, do the following:

e.g., $(x + y)(x^2 + 2xy + y^2)$

$= x(x^2) + x(2xy) + x(y^2) + y(x^2) +$

$\quad y(2xy) + y(y^2)$

$= x^3 + 2x^2y + xy^2 + x^2y + 21xy^2 + y^3$

$x^3 + 3x^2y + 3xy^2 + y^3$

*Memorize these common patterns:*

$(x + y)^2 = (x + y)(x + y) = x^2 + 2xy + y^2$

$(x - y)^2 = (x - y)(x - y) = x^2 - 2xy + y^2$

$(x + y)(x - y) = x^2 - y^2$

**7. Factoring:** *Factoring* is the reverse of multiplication. There are three factoring situations.

a. If all of the terms in an expression contain a common factor, then it can be factored out of each term. Do this first, if possible.

e.g., 1. $ab + ac + ad = a(b + c + d)$

2. $x^2 + x^3 + x^4 = x^2(1 + x + x^2)$

3. $3xy + xz + 4x = x(3y + z + 4)$

b. Algebraic expressions are often one of three common patterns.

e.g., 1. $x^2 + 2xy + y^2 = (x + y)(x + y) = (x + y)^2$

2. $x^2 - 2xy + y^2 = (x - y)(x - y) = (x - y)^2$

3. $x^2 - y^2 = (x - y)(x + y)$

c. Occasionally, expressions do not fall into one of the two categories above. To factor the expression, which is usually in the form $ax^2 + bx + c$, set up the following blank diagram: ( )( ). Fill in the diagram by answering the following questions:

- What factors produce the first term, $ax^2$?
- What factors produce the last term, $c$?
- Which of the possible factors, when added together, produce the middle term, $bx$?

e.g., 1. $x^2 + 3x + 2 = (x + 2)(x + 1)$

2. $x^2 + 4x - 12 = (x + 6)(x - 2)$

**8. Solving Linear Equations:** An equation that contains variables only of the first power is a linear equation. You can add, subtract, multiply, and divide both sides of an equation by the same value without changing the statement of equality. (You cannot multiply or divide by zero.) To find the value of a variable, isolate the variable on one side of the equation and solve.

e.g., 1. $4x + 2 = 2x + 10$

$4x + 2 - 2x = 2x + 10 - 2x$

$2x + 2 = 10$

$2x + 2 - 2 = 10 - 2$

$2x = 8$

$\frac{2x}{2} = \frac{8}{2}$

$x = 4$

2. $\frac{2x + 6}{2} = 9$

$x = \frac{9(2) - 6}{2} = 6$

**9. Solving Quadratic Equations:** Equations that involve variables of the second power are called quadratic equations and may have zero, one, or two real solutions.

a. If possible, take the square root of both sides.

e.g., $x^2 = 25 \Rightarrow x \pm 5$

b. Otherwise, arrange all terms on the left side of equation so that the right side of equation is zero: $ax^2 + bx + c = 0$. Factor the left side of the equation and set each binomial equal to zero. Solve for the unknown.

e.g., 1. Solve for $x : x^2 - 2x = 3$.

$x^2 - 2x = 3 \Rightarrow (x-3)(x+1) = 0$
$x = 3$ or $x = -1$

2. Solve for $x : x^2 - 3x = 4$.

$x^2 - 3x - 4 = 0 \Rightarrow (x-4)(x+1) = 0$
$x = 4$ or $x = -1$

c. The quadratic formula, $x = \dfrac{-b \pm \sqrt{b^2 - 4ac}}{2a}$, may also be used to solve quadratic equations.

e.g., Solve for $x : 3 - x = 2x^2$.

$3 - x = 2x^2 \Rightarrow 2x^2 + x - 3 = 0$
$a = 2, b = 1, c = -3$.
$x = \dfrac{-b \pm \sqrt{b^2 - 4ac}}{2a} = \dfrac{-1 \pm \sqrt{1^2 - 4(2)(-3)}}{2(2)} =$
$\dfrac{-1 \pm \sqrt{1 + 24}}{4} = \dfrac{-1 \pm 5}{4} = 1$ or $-\dfrac{3}{2}$

10. **Solving Simultaneous Equations:** Given two equations with two variables, the equations may be solved simultaneously for the values of the two variables. There are several methods for solving simultaneous equations.

*Method 1—Substitution*: Solve one equation for one variable and substitute this into the other equation to find the other variable. Plug back into the first equation.

e.g., If $2x - y = 6$ and $3x + 2y = 16$, solve for $x$ and $y$.

Solve for $y$: $2x - y = 6$
$y = 6 - 2x = 2x - 6$
Substitute: $3x + 2y = 16$
$3x + 2(2x - 6) = 16$
$3x + 4x - 12 = 16$
$x = 4$
Substitute: $y = 2x - 6 = 2(4) - 6 = 2$

*Method 2—Elimination*: Make the coefficients of one variable equal and then add (or subtract) the two equations to eliminate one variable.

e.g., If $2x - y = 6$ and $3x + 2y = 16$, solve for $x$ and $y$.

Combine: $2[2x - y = 6]$
$\underline{+3x + 2y = 16}$
$7x = 28 \Rightarrow x = 4$

Substitute: $2x - y = 6$
$2(4) - y = 6$
$y = 2$

11. **Inequalities:** The fundamental rule for working with inequalities is similar to that for working with equalities. The same value may be added or subtracted to each side of an inequality without changing the inequality. Each side may be multiplied or divided by the same *positive* value without changing the direction of the inequality.

e.g., 1. $5 > 2$
$5 + 25 > 2 + 25$
$30 > 27$

2. $24 > 20$
$24(2) > 20(2)$
$48 > 40$

3. $24 > 20$
$24 \div 4 > 20 \div 4$
$6 > 5$

To multiply or divide by a *negative* number, reverse the direction of the inequality.

e.g., 1. $4 > 2$
$4(-2) < 2(-2)$
$-8 < -4$

2. $4 > 2$
$4 \div (-2) < 2 \div (-2)$
$-2 < -1$

12. **Slope:** The *slope*, $m$, of a line describes its steepness. It is defined as the change in $y$-values divided by the change in $x$-values, or rise over run.

$$m = \frac{\Delta y}{\Delta x} = \frac{y_2 - y_1}{x_2 - x_1} = \frac{\text{rise}}{\text{run}}$$

e.g., The slope of the line that contains points $(-3,5)$ and $(2,7)$ is: $m = \frac{y_2 - y_1}{x_2 - x_1} = \frac{7-5}{2-(-3)} = \frac{2}{5}$.

13. **Linear Equations:**

*Slope-Intercept Form:*  $y = mx + b$; $m = \text{slope} = \frac{\Delta y}{\Delta x} = \frac{y_2 - y_1}{x_2 - x_1}$

*Point-Slope Form:*  $y - y_1 = m(x - x_1)$

*Standard Form:*  $Ax + By = C$, $m = -\frac{a}{b}$

14. **Distance Formula:** The distance between two points can be found using the *distance formula*:

$$d = \sqrt{(x_2 - x_1)^2 + (y_2 - y_1)^2}$$

where $(x_1, y_1)$ and $(x_2, y_2)$ are the given points.

e.g., The distance between $(-1,4)$ and $(7,3)$ is equal to:

$$d = \sqrt{[7-(-1)]^2 + (3-4)^2} = \sqrt{64+1} = \sqrt{65}$$

15. **Midpoint Formula:** The midpoint between two points, $(x_1; y_1)$ and $(x_2, y_2)$, is found using the *midpoint formula*:

$$\text{midpoint} = \left(\frac{x_1 + x_2}{2}, \frac{y_1 + y_2}{2}\right)$$

e.g., The midpoint between points $(-3,6)$ and $(4,-9)$ is $\left(\frac{x_1 + x_2}{2}, \frac{y_1 + y_2}{2}\right) = \left(\frac{-3+4}{2}, \frac{6+(-9)}{2}\right) = \left(\frac{1}{2}, -\frac{3}{2}\right)$.

16. **Functions:** A function is a set of ordered pairs $(x, y)$ such that for each value of $x$, there is exactly one value of $y$. The set of $x$-values for which the set is defined is called the domain of the function. The set of corresponding values of $y$ is called the range of the function.

e.g., What is the domain and range for $f(x) = x^2$?

$f$ represents the function. $x$ represents values in the domain of the function. $f(x)$ represents values in the range of the function. Since $x$ can be any real number, the domain is the set of all real numbers. We square the value of $x$ to obtain $f(x)$. Squaring any real number yields a number of zero or more. Thus, the range is the set of all non-negative numbers.

# **Common Equations Summary**

1. **Distance:** $\text{Distance} = (\text{Rate})(\text{Time})$. Given two of the three values, any unknown may be solved for by rearranging the equation.

   e.g., After driving constantly for four hours, Olivia reached her destination—200 miles from where she started. What was her average rate of travel?

   $\text{Distance} = (\text{Rate})(\text{Time})$

   $\text{Rate} = \frac{\text{Distance}}{\text{Time}} = \frac{200 \text{ miles}}{4 \text{ hours}} = 50 \text{ mph}$

2. **Simple Interest:** $I_{simple} = Prt$, where $P$ is the principal, $r$ is the rate, and $t$ is the time period.

   e.g., With a principal of $1,200 and a rate of 10% per year, what was the interest earned over one month?

   $I_{simple} = Prt = (\$1,200)(\frac{0.10}{\text{year}})(\frac{1 \text{ year}}{12 \text{ months}}) = \$10$

3. **Compound Interest:** $I_{compound} = P(1+r)^n - P$, where $P$ is the principal, $r$ is the rate, and $n$ is the number of periods.

   e.g., With a principal of $1,000 and a compound interest rate of 15% per year, how much compound interest was earned over 5 years?

   $I_{compound} = P(1+r)^n - P$

   $= (\$1,000)(1+0.15)^5 - (\$1,000)$

   $\approx \$2,011 - \$1,000 = \$1,011$

4. **Combined Work Rates:** $Rate_1 + Rate_2 = Rate_3$

   e.g., Machine I washes four loads in 60 minutes and Machine II washes one load in 30 minutes. How many loads will both machines working together wash in 20 minutes?

   $\frac{x \text{ loads}}{20 \text{ min.}} = \frac{4 \text{ loads}}{60 \text{ min.}} + \frac{1 \text{ load}}{30 \text{ min.}} = \frac{4 \text{ loads}}{60 \text{ min.}} + \frac{2 \text{ loads}}{60 \text{ min.}}$

   $x = 20(\frac{4}{60} + \frac{2}{60}) = \frac{6(20)}{60} = 2 \text{ loads}$

5. **Mixed Denominations:** When an item gives information that involves *mixed denominations* (e.g., different prices for same item, tickets, colors, etc.), set up simultaneous equations and solve the system of equations for the desired unknown quantity.

   e.g., The store sold apples for $0.20 and oranges for $0.50 each. A total of 50 apples and oranges were bought for $19. How many apples and how many oranges were bought?

   $x = \text{\# of apples}; \ y = \text{\# of oranges}$

   $x + y = 50 \Rightarrow x = 50 - y$

   $(0.20)x + (0.50)y = 19$

   $0.2(50 - y) + 0.5y = 19$

   $10 - 0.2y + 0.5y = 19$

   $0.3y = 30 \text{ oranges}$

   $y = 30 \text{ oranges}$

   $x = 50 - y = 50 - 30 = 20 \text{ apples}$

6. **Mixture of Concentrations or Values:** A *mixture item* is one in which two quantities of different items with different concentrations or values are mixed together and a new quantity (the sum of the two) and concentration or value are created.

   $$Q_1 C_1 + Q_2 C_2 = (Q_1 + Q_2)C_3$$

   e.g., How many liters of a juice that is 10% orange juice must be added to three liters of another juice that is 15% orange juice to produce a mixture that is 12% orange juice?

   $Q_1 C_1 + Q_2 C_2 = (Q_1 + Q_2)C_3$

   $Q(0.10) + (3)(0.15) = (Q + 3)(0.12)$

   $0.1Q + 0.45 = 0.12Q + 0.36$

   $0.45 - 0.36 = 0.12Q - 0.1Q$

   $0.09 = 0.02Q$

   $Q = 4.5$

7. **Markup, Cost, and Revenue:** $R = (1+M)C$, where $R$ is the revenue, $M$ is the markup, and $C$ is the cost.

   e.g., The revenue from an item is $120. With a markup in cost of 25%, what is the original cost?

   $C = \frac{R}{1+M} = \frac{120}{1+0.25} = \$96$

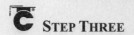

STEP THREE

# Geometry Summary

**1. Lines and Angles:**

**a. Symbols:**

$\overline{AB}$: line segment with endpoints $A$ and $B$
$\overrightarrow{AB}$: infinite ray from $A$ through $B$
$\overleftrightarrow{AB}$: infinite line through $A$ and $B$
$l_1 \| l_2$: parallel lines
$\perp$: perpendicular
⌐: right angle

**b. Facts About Lines and Angles:**

*Vertical angles* are equal:

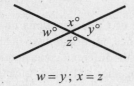

$$w = y;\ x = z$$

Two extended lines that do not intersect regardless of length are *parallel* to each other:

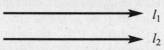

Parallel lines intersected by a third line, the transversal, create the following angles:

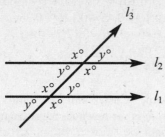

$$x = x,\ y = y,\ x + y = 180$$

Two lines *perpendicular* to the same line are parallel to each other:

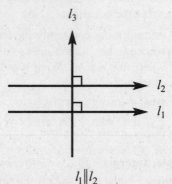

$$l_1 \| l_2$$

There are 180° in a straight line:

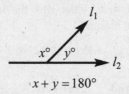

$$x + y = 180°$$

There are 90° in a *right angle* and two right angles form a straight line:

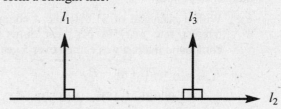

An angle less than 90° is an *acute angle*. In the following figure, $\angle PQR$ is an acute angle:

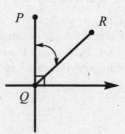

An angle greater than 90° is an *obtuse angle*. In the following figure, $\angle PQR$ is an obtuse angle:

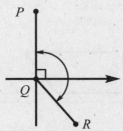

**2. Polygons:** A *polygon* is a closed figure created by three or more lines. The sum of the interior angles of any polygon is $180(n-2)$, where $n$ = the number of sides of the polygon. The sum of the measures of the exterior angles of a polygon is 360° for all polygons.

A *triangle* is any polygon with exactly three sides.

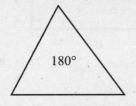

$$180(n-2) = 180(3-2) = 180$$

A *quadrilateral* is any polygon with exactly four sides. Opposite sides of a *parallelogram* are equal and parallel.

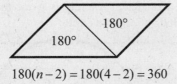

$$180(n-2) = 180(4-2) = 360$$

A *pentagon* is any polygon with exactly five sides.

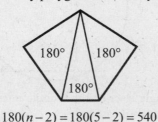

$$180(n-2) = 180(5-2) = 540$$

A *hexagon* is any polygon with exactly six sides.

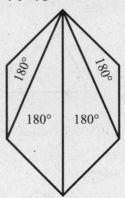

$$180(n-2) = 180(6-2) = 720$$

**3. Triangles:** A *triangle* is a 3-sided figure. Within a given triangle, the larger the angle, the longer the opposite side; conversely, the longer the side, the larger the opposite angle.

A triangle with two equal sides is an *isosceles* triangle. A triangle with three equal sides is an *equilateral* triangle.

Within a given triangle, if two sides are equal, their opposite angles are equal, and vice versa:

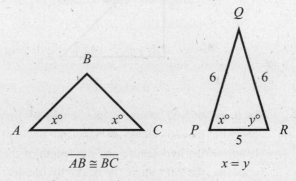

$$\overline{AB} \cong \overline{BC} \qquad\qquad x = y$$

The sides of every right triangle follow the *Pythagorean theorem*: the square of the hypotenuse is equal to the sum of the squares of the other two sides.

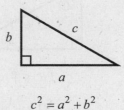

$$c^2 = a^2 + b^2$$

The *perimeter of a triangle* is the sum of the lengths of the three sides:

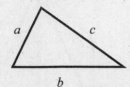

$$\text{Perimeter}_{\text{triangle}} = a + b + c$$

The *area of a triangle* is one-half times the base times the height:

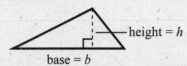

$$\text{Area}_{\text{triangle}} = \tfrac{1}{2}(bh) = \tfrac{bh}{2}$$

In a *45°-45°-90° triangle*, the length of the hypotenuse is equal to the length of either side multiplied by the square root of two:

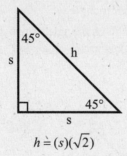

$$h \doteq (s)(\sqrt{2})$$

In a *30°-60°-90° triangle*, the length of the side opposite the 30° angle is equal to one-half the length of the hypotenuse and the length of the side opposite the 60° angle is equal to one-half the length of the hypotenuse multiplied by $\sqrt{3}$:

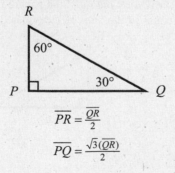

$$\overline{PR} = \frac{\overline{QR}}{2}$$

$$\overline{PQ} = \frac{\sqrt{3}(\overline{QR})}{2}$$

4. **Parallelograms and Trapezoids:** A *parallelogram* is a quadrilateral in which both pairs of opposite sides are parallel. A *trapezoid* is a quadrilateral with only two parallel sides.

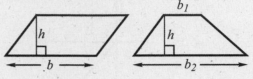

$$\text{Area}_{\text{parallelogram}} = bh \quad \text{Area}_{\text{trapezoid}} = \tfrac{1}{2}(h)(b_1 + b_2)$$

5. **Rectangles and Squares:** A *rectangle* is any four-sided figure that has four right angles. A *square* is a rectangle with four equal sides:

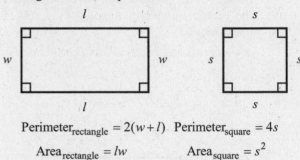

$$\text{Perimeter}_{\text{rectangle}} = 2(w+l) \quad \text{Perimeter}_{\text{square}} = 4s$$

$$\text{Area}_{\text{rectangle}} = lw \qquad \text{Area}_{\text{square}} = s^2$$

6. **Circles:** The distance from the center of a circle to any point on the circle is the *radius*. A line segment that passes through the center of a circle and that has endpoints on the circle is called the *diameter*. The diameter of a circle is twice the radius. There are 360° of *arc* in a circle:

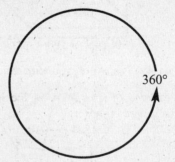

An angle inscribed in a circle intercepts an arc that is twice its measure:

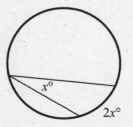

An angle whose vertex is at the center of a circle intercepts an arc of the same measure:

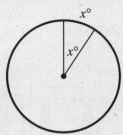

The *circumference of a circle* is the radius times $2\pi$. The *area of a circle* is the radius squared times $\pi$.

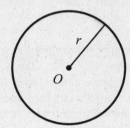

$$C_{\text{circle}} = 2\pi r ; \quad A_{\text{circle}} = \pi r^2$$

7. **Solid Geometry:** Solid geometry refers to three-dimensional figures. *Volume* is a three-dimensional quantity. The *volume of a rectangular solid* is the length times the width times the height:

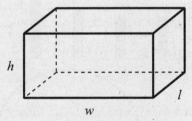

$$V_{\text{solid}} = lwh$$

The *volume of a cylinder* is the height times the radius squared times $\pi$.

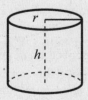

$$V_{\text{cylinder}} = h(\pi r^2)$$

The *volume of a right circular cone* is one-third of the height times the radius squared times $\pi$.

$$\text{Volume}_{\text{right circular cone}} = \frac{h(\pi r^2)}{3}$$

The *surface area of a sphere* is four times $\pi$ times the radius squared. The *volume of a sphere* is four-thirds times $\pi$ times the radius cubed.

$$\text{Area}_{\text{surface of sphere}} = 4\pi r^2 ; \quad \text{Volume}_{\text{sphere}} = \frac{4\pi r^3}{3}$$

# Graphs Summary

1. **Table Charts:** The simplest type of graph, which is actually a chart, is the table. The following table chart contains data regarding the number of persons using City Library from 1991 to 1995:

Number of Persons Using City Library
(Tens of Thousands)

|  | 1991 | 1992 | 1993 | 1994 | 1995 |
|---|---|---|---|---|---|
| Adults | 8 | 10 | 10 | 12 | 15 |
| Students | 10 | 12 | 15 | 19 | 20 |
| Preschoolers | 12 | 2 | 3 | 4 | 6 |

2. **Bar Graphs:** The same data might be presented in what is called a bar graph. In a bar graph, the length of a bar represents quantity.

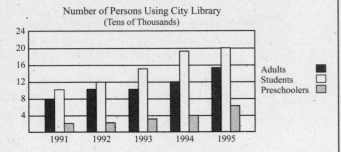

Number of Persons Using City Library
(Tens of Thousands)

Thus, the bar for "adults in 1991" covers the distance from the base line of the graph (zero) to 8:

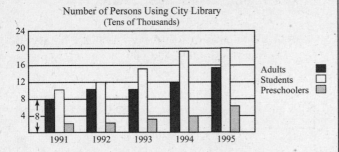

Number of Persons Using City Library
(Tens of Thousands)

Since each unit represents ten thousand people, $8 \cdot 10,000 = 80,000$ adults used the library in 1991. Similarly, the bar for "students in 1995" covers the distance from the base line (zero) to 20 units:

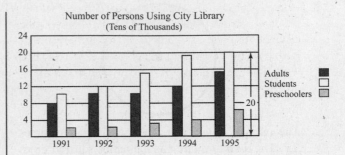

Number of Persons Using City Library
(Tens of Thousands)

So, $20 \cdot 10,000 = 200,000$ students used the library in 1995.

Our bar graph is not quite as precise as the table. For example, the table clearly indicates that the number of preschoolers who used the library in 1991 was 20,000, but the "preschoolers in 1991" bar does not fall on any line. It appears, however, to end about halfway between the base line (zero) and the first scale line (four):

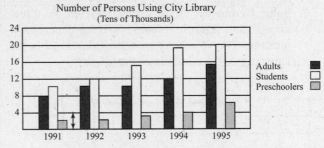

Number of Persons Using City Library
(Tens of Thousands)

So, we would conclude that the number of preschoolers who used the library in 1991 was approximately 20,000. In any event, a GRE item would never ask for more precision than actually provided by the graph.

There is, however, an advantage to the bar graph presentation over the prose presentation or even the table presentation. You can make cross-comparisons at a glance! For example, since distance on the graph represents quantity, you can see that the number of students using the library increased in every year (because the bar for students in each year subsequent to 1991 is longer than the one for the year preceding it). You can see at a glace that in 1991, the number of adults who used the library was about four times the number of preschoolers who used the library, and that the number of adults who used the library in 1992 was the same as the number of adults who used the library in 1993.

3. **Line Graphs:** In the bar graphs just shown, the bars are not, strictly speaking, necessary. It is the distance from the base line to the top of the bar that is important, and this distance could be indicated with a single point as is shown in the following graph:

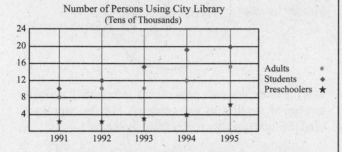

This graph displays the same data as the bar graph. However, it is difficult to read. The bars help you visualize relationships among the data. Bars, however, are not the only device that an artist can use. A graphic artist might opt to create a line graph:

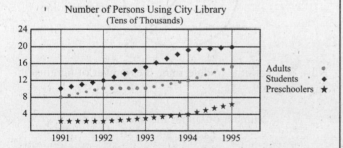

Again, it is the distance between the base line and any point on a line that represents the quantity. For example, the number of students who used the library in 1993 was 150,000:

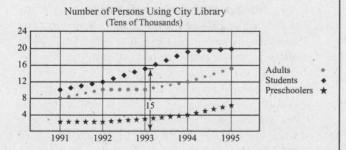

4. **Cumulating Bar Graphs:** Sometimes, an artist may want to use a graph to show a total as well as individual categories. In that case, he or she could use a cumulating bar graph, so-called because the bars used to represent the individual categories are "stacked up" to reach a total:

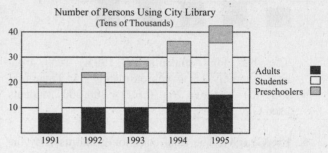

(Notice that we have changed the scale because we need larger numbers to accommodate the totals.)

In this bar graph, distance also represents quantity. For example, the total number of people to use the library in 1991 was $20 \cdot 10,000 = 200,000$:

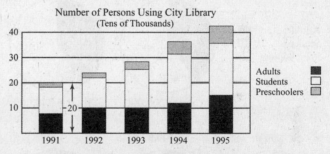

And the number of adults who used the library in 1993 was $10 \cdot 10,000 = 100,000$:

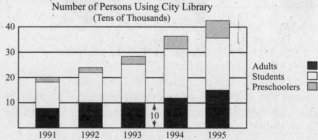

The one thing that is a little tricky about a cumulating bar graph is that only the bottom category (in this case, "Adults") and the overall total can be read by referring to the base line (zero). To determine the quantity of any other category, you must find the length of that particular bar. For example, how many students used the library in 1995?

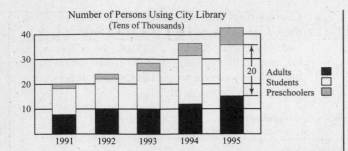

Number of Persons Using City Library
(Tens of Thousands)

The bar for "students in 1995" runs from approximately 15 to approximately 35. Therefore, $(35-15) \cdot 10,000 = 20 \cdot 10,000 = 200,000$ students used City Library in 1995.

**5. Pie Graphs:** The final common graph used by the GRE is the pie graph, so called because it has the shape of a pie and each slice of the pie shows the portion of the entire pie allocated to each category:

Number of Persons Using City Library

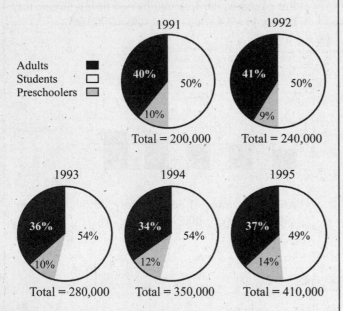

For example, the pie graph for 1991 shows you at a glance that student users accounted for half of all users in that year and that preschoolers accounted for a relatively small share, only one-tenth.

The most important characteristic of a pie graph is that the pie itself gives you only relative shares, not actual quantities:

Distribution of Family Income in County X

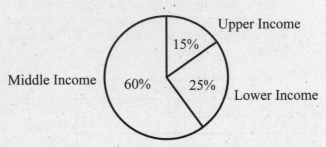

This pie alone does not provide any information about the number of families in any category. For that you would need the total quantity represented by the pie:

Distribution of Family Income in County X
Total Number of Families = 1,200

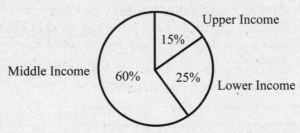

Now, it is possible to determine the number of families in any category:

Number of Upper Income Families
15% of $1,200 = 180$

Number of Middle Income Families
60% of $1,200 = 720$

Number of Lower Income Families
25% of $1,200 = 300$

## ARITHMETIC, ALGEBRA, AND COORDINATE GEOMETRY FORMULAS

$$\text{Average} = \frac{x_1 + x_2 + x_3 \ldots + x_n}{n}; \; x_1, x_2, x_3 \ldots x_n = \text{values}; \; n = \text{total numbers}$$

$$\text{Finding Percent: } \frac{\text{is}}{\text{of}} = \frac{\%}{100}$$

$$\text{Percent Change} = \frac{\left| \text{New Amount} - \text{Original Amount} \right|}{\text{Original Amount}}$$

$$\text{Distance} = \text{Rate} \cdot \text{Time}$$

$$\text{Combined Work Rate: } \text{Rate}_3 = \text{Rate}_1 + \text{Rate}_2$$

$$\text{Mixture Problems: } (Q_1 + Q_2)C_3 = Q_1 C_1 + Q_2 C_2; \; Q = \text{quantities}; \; C = \text{concentrations}$$

$$\text{Interest}_{\text{simple}} = \text{Principal} \cdot \text{Rate} \cdot \text{Time}$$

$$\text{Interest}_{\text{compound}} = (\text{Principal})(1 + \text{Rate})^{\# \text{ of periods}} - \text{Principal}$$

$$\text{Revenue} = (1 + \text{Markup})(\text{Cost})$$

$$\text{Slope-Intercept Linear Equation: } y = mx + b$$

$$\text{Slope of a Line: } m = \frac{y_2 - y_1}{x_2 - x_1}$$

## GEOMETRY FORMULAS

$$\text{Perimeter}_{\text{square}} = 4s; \; s = \text{side}$$

$$\text{Perimeter}_{\text{rectangle}} = 2l + 2w; \; l = \text{length}; \; w = \text{width}$$

$$\text{Perimeter}_{\text{triangle}} = a + b + c; \; a, b, \text{ and } c \text{ are the sides}$$

$$\text{Circumference}_{\text{circle}} = 2\pi r; \; \pi \approx 3.14; \; r = \text{radius}$$

$$\text{Area}_{\text{square}} = s^2; \; s = \text{length of side}$$

$$\text{Area}_{\text{rectangle}} = lw; \; l = \text{length}; \; w = \text{width}$$

$$\text{Area}_{\text{parallelogram}} = bh; \; b = \text{base}; \; h = \text{height}$$

$$\text{Area}_{\text{trapezoid}} = \frac{(b_1 + b_2)h}{2}; \; b = \text{base}; \; h = \text{height}$$

$$\text{Area}_{\text{triangle}} = \frac{bh}{2}; \; b = \text{base}; \; h = \text{height}$$

$$\text{Area}_{\text{circle}} = \pi r^2; \; \pi \approx 3.14; \; r = \text{radius}$$

$$\text{Volume}_{\text{cube}} = s^3; \; s = \text{side}$$

$$\text{Volume}_{\text{rectangular solid}} = lwh; \; l = \text{length}; \; w = \text{width}; \; h = \text{height}$$

$$\text{Volume}_{\text{cylinder}} = \pi r^2 h; \; \pi \approx 3.14; \; r = \text{radius}; \; h = \text{height}$$

$$\text{Volume}_{\text{cone}} = \frac{\pi r^2 h}{3}; \; \pi \approx 3.14; \; r = \text{radius}; \; h = \text{height}$$

$$\text{Area}_{\text{surface of sphere}} = 4\pi r^2; \; \pi \approx 3.14; \; r = \text{radius}$$

$$\text{Volume}_{\text{sphere}} = \frac{4\pi r^3}{3}; \; \pi \approx 3.14; \; r = \text{radius}$$

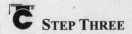
# POLYGON FORMULAS

45°-45°-90° Triangle: $h = s\sqrt{2}$; $h$ = hypotenuse; $s$ = length of either leg

30°-60°-90° Triangle: $a = \frac{h}{2}$; $a$ = side opposite $\angle 30°$; $h$ = hypotenuse

30°-60°-90° Triangle: $b = \frac{\sqrt{3}(h)}{2}$; $b$ = side opposite $\angle 60°$; $h$ = hypotenuse

Pythagorean Theorem (Right Triangles): $c^2 = a^2 + b^2$; $c$ = hypotenuse; $a$ and $b$ = legs

Sum of Interior Angles of Polygon: $S = 180(n-2)$; $n$ = number of sides of the polygon

# Glossary of Terms

**Absolute Value**—the value of a number when the sign is not considered

**Acute Angle**—an angle with a measure of less than 90°

**Adjacent Angles**—angles that share a common side and a common vertex

**Area**—the space within a closed plane figure, measured in square units

**Binomial**—an algebraic expression with two terms

**Circle**—the set of all points in a plane that are equidistant from a center point

**Circumference**—the distance around a circle

**Coefficient**—the number in front of a term

**Complementary Angles**—two angles with a sum of 90°

**Composite Numbers**—a number that can be divided evenly by more than itself and one

**Cube (1)**—a six-sided solid with all six faces being equal-sized squares

**Cube (2)**—the result when a number is multiplied by itself twice

**Cube Root**—a number that when raised to the third power will yield a second given number

**Denominator**—the bottom term of a fraction

**Diameter**—a line segment extending from one side of a circle to the opposite, through the center point

**Difference**—the result of subtraction

**Domain**—the set of all $x$-values for a function

**Equilateral Triangle**—a triangle with all three sides equal and all three angles being 60°

**Evaluate**—to determine the value of an expression

**Exponent**—used to indicate the operation of repeated multiplication

**Factor**—an integer that divides into another equally

**Function**—ordered pairs $(x, y)$ with exactly one $y$-value for any $x$-value

**Hypotenuse**—the side opposite the right angle of a right triangle

**Improper Fraction**—a fraction where the numerator is larger than the denominator

**Integers**—the set of numbers divisible by one without producing a remainder

**Irrational Numbers**—any number that cannot be expressed as a fraction

**Isosceles Triangle**—a triangle with two equal sides and equal opposite angles

**Least Common Denominator**—the smallest natural number that can be divided evenly by all denominators in the equation

**Legs**—in a right triangle, the two sides that are not the hypotenuse

**Mean**—the sum of all items divided by the number of items

**Median**—in a set of numbers arranged in order, the middle value or the mean of the two middle values

**Mixed Number**—a term that has both a whole number part and a fractional part

**Mode**—the most commonly occurring value in a set of values

**Monomial**—an algebraic expression with only one term

**Natural Numbers**—the set of positive integers starting with 1

**Numerator**—the top term of a fraction

**Obtuse Angle**—an angle with a measure between 90° and 180°

**Origin**—the intersection between the $x$- and $y$-axes of a coordinate graph

**Parallel Lines**—lines that never intersect regardless of how far they are extended

**Parallelogram**—a four-sided closed figure with opposite sides that are parallel and of equal length

**Percentage**—a fraction with a denominator of 100

**Perimeter**—the total distance around the outside of a polygon

**Perpendicular Lines**—two lines that intersect at a 90°angle

**Polygon**—a multi-sided plane closed figure

**Polynomial**—an algebraic expression with two or more terms

**Power**—used to indicate repeated multiplication

**Prime Numbers**—numbers that are evenly divisible only by themselves and one

**Product**—the result of multiplication

*Proper Fraction*—a fraction where the denominator is larger than the numerator

*Quadrants*—the four sections of a coordinate graph

*Quadrilateral*—a four-sided plane closed figure

*Quotient*—the result of division

*Radius*—a line segment extending from the center of a circle to any point on the circle

*Range* (1)—the difference between the largest and smallest numbers in a set

*Range* (2)—the set of all *y*-values for a function

*Rational Number*—any number that can be expressed as a fraction

*Real Numbers*—the set of rational and irrational numbers

*Rectangle*—a four-sided plane closed figure with opposite sides equal and 90°angles

*Right Triangle*—a triangle with a 90°angle

*Root*—a number that when raised to a certain power will yield a second given number

*Scientific Notation*—a number written as the product of a real number between 1 and 10 and a power of 10

*Set*—a group of numbers, elements, objects, etc.

*Square* (1)—the result when a number is multiplied by itself

*Square* (2)—a four-sided plane closed figure with all four sides equal and 90°angles

*Square Root*—a number that when raised to the second power will yield a second given number

*Sum*—the result of addition

*Supplementary Angles*—two angles with a sum of 180°

*Term*—an expression, either numerical or literal

*Triangle*—a three-sided plane closed figure

*Variable*—a symbol that is used to stand for a number

*Vertex*—a point at which two rays or sides of a polygon meet to form an angle

*Volume*—the space inside a solid, measured in cubic units

*Whole Numbers*—the set of positive integers including zero

*X-axis*—the horizontal axis of a coordinate graph

*Y-axis*—the vertical axis of a coordinate graph

# Quantitative Reasoning Test Mechanics

# CAMBRIDGE TESTPREP™

## Test Mechanics
## QUANTITATIVE REASONING

### ANATOMY OF THE QUANTITATIVE REASONING TEST SECTION:

The computer-adaptive GRE has one "live" Quantitative Reasoning test section. This section contains Discrete Quantitative, Quantitative Comparisons, and Graphs items. (Remember that the test could include an experimental section which might contain Quantitative Reasoning items, but that section would NOT be scored.) According to Educational Testing Service, Quantitative Reasoning items test the following skills:

- Ability to understand basic concepts of arithmetic, algebra, geometry, and data analysis
- Ability to reason quantitatively
- Ability to solve problems in a quantitative setting

Typically, the Quantitative Reasoning test section contains 28 items broken down approximately as follows: 9 Discrete Quantitative, 14 Quantitative Comparisons, and 5 Graphs. (Note: The ratio of items for each subject-area is approximately the same on both the computer-based version and the paper-and-pencil test.)

As noted in Verbal Reasoning Test Mechanics (p. 99), due to a peculiarity in the algorithm for the GRE computer-adaptive test, you can attain your top score only if you answer all of the items in a test section. You might think that you could score an 800 on the computer-adaptive test by answering the first five or six items correctly and then refusing to respond to any more items—claiming for yourself a "perfect score." However, this simply is not the way the test is designed. This observation also explodes the myth that you need to answer perfectly on the first few items to avoid becoming "trapped in the basement" of the scoring scale from which you can never escape. This can lead to the mistake of spending so much time on the first few items that you do not finish the test section. Instead, you have to find the appropriate balance between speed and accuracy. The following guidelines will help you strike such a balance.

### QUANTITATIVE REASONING PACING AND GUESSING TECHNIQUES:

On average, you will need to spend differing amounts of time on the various items due to the inherent features of each subject-area—the least amount of time on a Quantitative Comparisons item, more time on a Discrete Quantitative item, and the most time on a Graphs item. The relative times to be allocated to each of these items are summarized in the following table:

| Subject-Area | Average Time per Item |
| --- | --- |
| Quantitative Comparisons | 1 minute, 20 seconds |
| Discrete Quantitative | 1 minute, 40 seconds |
| Graphs | 2 minutes |

Remember that these times are *averages*. The items become more difficult as you progress through the test and move up the ladder of difficulty, so you do not want to get "bogged down" on an item. Therefore, you should keep an eye on the time clock. A properly paced exam will develop as follows:

| Item Currently Working On | Items Remaining | Time Remaining |
| --- | --- | --- |
| 1 | 27 | 45 minutes |
| 7 | 21 | 33.75 minutes |
| 14 | 14 | 22.5 minutes |
| 21 | 7 | 11.25 minutes |
| 28 | 0 | 1 minute |

In the Quantitative Reasoning Concepts and Strategies portion of this course, you will learn techniques for handling these different math items that will help you maintain the right pace, but some of the more important techniques are worth mentioning right now:

*Quantitative Comparisons:*

Quantitative Comparisons are the simplest of the Quantitative Reasoning items, so it stands to reason that they should take the least amount of time to answer. Additionally, the math required for these types of items is fairly simple. This is not to say that Quantitative Comparisons items are all easy. Rather, the point is that if you are having trouble with an item, it's probably not because you're struggling with a manipulation and you need just another minute to figure out the answer. Instead, you're most likely waiting for the lightning to strike—that flash of insight needed to solve the problem. But the lightning won't come. So, just make up your mind in advance that you're not going to spend more than 1 minute and 20 seconds on any one item. When you've put in that much time, you're probably not going to make any more progress, so guess and move along.

*Discrete Quantitative:*

Discrete Quantitative items can sometimes require manipulations, for example, a series of algebraic steps needed to "solve for $x$." If an item is giving you trouble because you're making an error somewhere along the way, you may be tempted to "try just once more"—and again, and again, and again. However, do NOT take this approach; the chances are that you're just going to repeat your mistake the next time around. Instead, guess and go on. You'll also find that Discrete Quantitative items can sometimes be solved by estimating quantities and by employing time-saving techniques, such as reducing and canceling, instead of performing lengthy operations. Note that you'll be more likely to use these techniques if you rigidly enforce the time limit, an approach that is beneficial in and of itself.

*Graphs:*

Graphs problems are the fly in the ointment. In the first place, you need to invest some time familiarizing yourself with the graph(s) before you can even start to answer the accompanying items. Fortunately, a set of graphs may support two or three items. Unfortunately, these items vary in difficulty. Some Graphs items require nothing more than extracting a number from the corresponding figure(s). More difficult Graphs items require the use of two or three numbers and perhaps even some manipulation. And the most difficult items often require matching data from two sources, and that is time-consuming. So, while 2 minutes per Graphs item is the general rule, that estimate includes the time you need to read the graphs themselves. In the Graphs Core Lesson, you'll be shown techniques for organizing this "reading" to save yourself time. Then, remember that some items, by themselves, may take only 15 or 20 seconds each, while some others may need 1.5 minutes or maybe even a little longer. That means that with a Graphs problem that consists of one graph and three items, you can spend 2 minutes reading the graph and then 30 seconds, 1.5 minutes, and 2 minutes on the three items (according to difficulty) and still come in at 6 minutes, the time allotted for 3 Graphs items $(2 \cdot 3 = 6)$.

# Quantitative Reasoning Concepts and Strategies

# Discrete Quantitative

# CAMBRIDGE TESTPREP™

## DISCRETE QUANTITATIVE OUTLINE

# CORE LESSON

The items in this section accompany the Core Lesson section of the Discrete Quantitative Lesson. You will work through the items with your instructor in class.

**DIRECTIONS:** Each of the following questions has five answer choices. Select the best of the available choices. For Numeric Entry items, enter the answer in the box provided.

Notes: All numbers used are real numbers.

All angle measures are positive.

A figure accompanying a question is included to provide information useful in answering that question. However, unless a note explicitly states that a figure is drawn to scale, you should answer a question not by estimating the magnitudes of various aspects, but by using your knowledge of the principles of mathematics. You can assume, however, that the positions of points, angles, regions, etc. are in the order shown, that lines shown as straight are straight, and that all figures lie in the plane unless otherwise noted.

Answers are on page 997.

1. What is the average of 8.5, 7.8, and 7.7?

2. If the price of fertilizer has been decreased from 3 pounds for $2 to 5 pounds for $2, how many more pounds of fertilizer can be purchased for $10 than could have been purchased before?

   (A) 2
   (B) 8
   (C) 10
   (D) 12
   (E) 15

3. If $\frac{2x-5}{3} = -4x$, then $x =$

   (A) $-1$
   (B) $-\frac{5}{14}$
   (C) 0
   (D) $\frac{5}{14}$
   (E) 1

4. A vending machine dispenses $k$ cups of coffee, each at a cost of $c$ cents, every day. During a period $d$ days long, what is the amount of money in dollars taken in by the vending machine from the sale of coffee?

   (A) $\frac{100kc}{d}$
   (B) $kcd$
   (C) $\frac{dk}{c}$
   (D) $\frac{kcd}{100}$
   (E) $\frac{kc}{100d}$

5. If a circle has a radius of 1, what is its area?

   (A) $\frac{\pi}{2}$
   (B) $\pi$
   (C) $2\pi$
   (D) $4\pi$
   (E) $\pi^2$

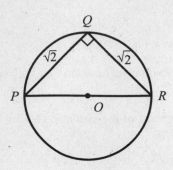

6. In the figure above, a triangle is inscribed in a circle with center $O$. What is the area of the circle?

(A) $\frac{\pi}{2}$

(B) $\frac{\pi}{\sqrt{2}}$

(C) $\pi$

(D) $\pi\sqrt{2}$

(E) $2\pi$

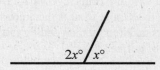

7. In the figure above, $x =$

(A) 15
(B) 30
(C) 45
(D) 60
(E) 120

Items 8–9 refer to the following figure.

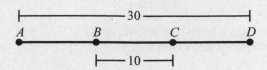

8. In the figure above, $\overline{AB} =$

(A) 5
(B) 10
(C) 15
(D) 20
(E) Cannot be determined from the information given

9. In the figure above, $\overline{AB} + \overline{CD} =$

(A) 5
(B) 10
(C) 15
(D) 20
(E) Cannot be determined from the information given

Items 10–11 refer to the following figure.

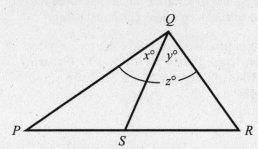

10. Which of the following must be true?

   I.   $\overline{PS} < \overline{SR}$
  II.   $z = 90$
 III.   $x > y$

(A) I only
(B) I and II only
(C) I and III only
(D) I, II, and III
(E) Neither I, II, nor III

11. Which of the following must be true?

    I. $\overline{PR} > \overline{PS}$
    II. $z > x$
    III. $x + y = z$

    (A) I only
    (B) I and II only
    (C) I and III only
    (D) I, II, and III
    (E) Neither I, II, nor III

12. In a certain year, the number of girls who graduated from City High School was twice the number of boys. If $\frac{3}{4}$ of the girls and $\frac{5}{6}$ of the boys went to college immediately after graduation, what fraction of the graduates that year went to college immediately after graduation?

    (A) $\frac{5}{36}$
    (B) $\frac{16}{27}$
    (C) $\frac{7}{9}$
    (D) $\frac{29}{36}$
    (E) $\frac{31}{36}$

13. A jar contains black and white marbles. If there are ten marbles in the jar, which of the following could NOT be the ratio of black to white marbles?

    (A) $9:1$
    (B) $7:3$
    (C) $1:1$
    (D) $1:4$
    (E) $1:10$

14. If $n$ is a negative number, which of the following is the LEAST?

    (A) $-n$
    (B) $n - n$
    (C) $n + n$
    (D) $n^2$
    (E) $n^4$

15. If a machine produces 240 thingamabobs per hour, how many <u>minutes</u> are needed for the machine to produce 30 thingamabobs?

    (A) 6
    (B) 7.5
    (C) 8
    (D) 12
    (E) 12.5

16. Of the 120 people in a room, $\frac{3}{5}$ are women. If $\frac{2}{3}$ of the people are married, what is the maximum number of women in the room who could be <u>unmarried</u>?

    (A) 80
    (B) 72
    (C) 48
    (D) 40
    (E) 32

17. Three friends are playing a game in which each person simultaneously displays one of three hand signs: a clenched fist, an open palm, or two extended fingers. How many different combinations of the signs are possible?

    (A) 3
    (B) 9
    (C) 10
    (D) 12
    (E) 27

18. If $\frac{1}{3}$ of the girls at a school equals $\frac{1}{5}$ of the total number of students, then what is the ratio of girls to boys at the school?

    (A) $5:3$
    (B) $3:2$
    (C) $2:5$
    (D) $1:3$
    (E) $1:5$

19. Peter walked from point $P$ to point $Q$ and back again, a total distance of 2 miles. If he averaged 4 miles per hour on the trip from $P$ to $Q$ and 5 miles per hour on the return trip, what was his average walking speed for the entire trip?

   (A) 4
   (B) $4\frac{2}{9}$
   (C) $4\frac{4}{9}$
   (D) $4\frac{1}{2}$
   (E) $4\frac{4}{5}$

20. After a 20 percent decrease in price, the cost of an item is $D$ dollars. What was the price of the item before the decrease?

   (A) $0.75D$
   (B) $0.80D$
   (C) $1.20D$
   (D) $1.25D$
   (E) $1.5D$

21. On a certain trip, a motorist drove 10 miles at 30 miles per hour, 10 miles at 40 miles per hour, and 10 miles at 50 miles per hour. What portion of her total driving time was spent driving 50 miles per hour?

   Give your answer as a fraction.

   ```
   ┌─────────────────┐
   │                 │
   └─────────────────┘
   ┌─────────────────┐
   │                 │
   └─────────────────┘
   ```

22. What is the largest number of non-overlapping sections that can be created when a circle is crossed by three straight lines?

   (A) 3
   (B) 4
   (C) 5
   (D) 6
   (E) 7

23. At Glen Ridge High School, 20 percent of the students are seniors. If all of the seniors attended the school play, and 60 percent of all the students attended the play, what percent of the non-seniors attended the play?

   ```
   ┌─────────────────┐
   │                 │ %
   └─────────────────┘
   ```

**Water Usage in Cubic Feet**

24. The water meter at a factory displays the reading above. What is the MINIMUM number of cubic feet of water the factory must use before four of the five digits on the meter are again the same?

   (A) 10,000
   (B) 1,000
   (C) 999
   (D) 666
   (E) 9

25. A telephone call from City X to City Y costs $1.00 for the first three minutes and $0.25 for every minute thereafter. What is the maximum length of time (in minutes) that a caller could talk for $3.00?

   (A) 8
   (B) 10
   (C) 11
   (D) 12
   (E) 13

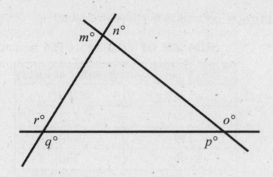

26. In the figure above, $m + n + o + p + q + r =$

(A) 360
(B) 540
(C) 720
(D) 900
(E) Cannot be determined from the information given

27. $\frac{8}{9} - \frac{7}{8} =$

(A) $\frac{1}{72}$
(B) $\frac{1}{8}$
(C) $\frac{1}{7}$
(D) $\frac{15}{72}$
(E) $\frac{15}{7}$

28. $\sqrt{1 - (\frac{2}{9} + \frac{1}{36} + \frac{1}{18})} =$

(A) $\frac{1}{5}$
(B) $\sqrt{\frac{2}{3}}$
(C) $\frac{5}{6}$
(D) $1$
(E) $\sqrt{3}$

29. $\frac{1}{2} \cdot \frac{2}{3} \cdot \frac{3}{4} \cdot \frac{4}{5} \cdot \frac{5}{6} \cdot \frac{6}{7} \cdot \frac{7}{8} =$

(A) $\frac{1}{56}$
(B) $\frac{1}{8}$
(C) $\frac{28}{37}$
(D) $\frac{41}{43}$
(E) $\frac{55}{56}$

30. $86(37) - 37(85)$

(A) 0
(B) 1
(C) 37
(D) 85
(E) 86

31. $\frac{0.2521 \cdot 8.012}{1.014}$ is approximately equal to

(A) 0.25
(B) 0.5
(C) 1.0
(D) 1.5
(E) 2.0

32. Which of the following fractions is the largest?

(A) $\frac{111}{221}$
(B) $\frac{75}{151}$
(C) $\frac{333}{998}$
(D) $\frac{113}{225}$
(E) $\frac{101}{301}$

33. If the senior class has 360 students, of whom $\frac{5}{12}$ are women, and the junior class has 350 students, of whom $\frac{4}{7}$ are women, how many more women are there in the junior class than in the senior class?

(A) $(360 - 350)(\frac{4}{7} - \frac{5}{12})$
(B) $\frac{(360 - 350)(\frac{4}{7} - \frac{5}{12})}{2}$
(C) $(\frac{4}{7} \cdot \frac{5}{12})(360 - 350)$
(D) $(\frac{4}{7} \cdot 350) - (\frac{5}{12} \cdot 360)$
(E) $(\frac{5}{12} \cdot 360) - (\frac{4}{7} \cdot 350)$

34. If the price of candy increases from 5 pounds for $7 to 3 pounds for $7, how much less candy (in pounds) can be purchased for $3.50 at the new price than at the old price?

    (A) $\frac{2}{7}$
    (B) 1
    (C) $1\frac{17}{35}$
    (D) 2
    (E) $3\frac{34}{35}$

35. If $n$ is any integer, which of the following is always an odd integer?

    (A) $n-1$
    (B) $n+1$
    (C) $n+2$
    (D) $2n+1$
    (E) $2n+2$

36. If $0 < x < 1$, which of the following is the largest?

    (A) $x$
    (B) $2x$
    (C) $x^2$
    (D) $x^3$
    (E) $x+1$

Items 37–39 refer to the following table.

**NUMBER OF FIRES IN CITY Y**

| Year | Number of Fires |
|------|-----------------|
| 1992 | 100 |
| 1993 | 125 |
| 1994 | 140 |
| 1995 | 150 |
| 1996 | 135 |

37. The number of fires in 1992 was what percent of the number of fires in 1993?

    [    ] %

38. The number of fires in 1996 was what percent of the number of fires in 1995?

    [    ] %

39. What was the percent decrease in the number of fires from 1995 to 1996?

    [    ] %

40. A groom must divide 12 quarts of oats between two horses. If Dobbin is to receive twice as much as Pegasus, how many quarts of oats should the groom give to Dobbin?

    (A) 4
    (B) 6
    (C) 8
    (D) 9
    (E) 10

41. If the ratio of John's allowance to Lucy's allowance is $3:2$, and the ratio of Lucy's allowance to Bob's allowance is 3:4, what is the ratio of John's allowance to Bob's allowance?

    (A) $1:6$
    (B) $2:5$
    (C) $1:2$
    (D) $3:4$
    (E) $9:8$

42. For a certain student, the average of ten test scores is 80. If the high and low scores are dropped, the average is 81. What is the average of the high and low scores?

    (A) 76
    (B) 78
    (C) 80
    (D) 81
    (E) 82

43. In a certain course, a student's final exam grade is weighted twice as heavily as his midterm grade. If a student receives a score of 84 on his final exam and 90 on his midterm, what is his average for the course?

    (A) 88
    (B) 87.5
    (C) 86
    (D) 85.5
    (E) 85

44. The number of employment applications received by a certain firm per month during 1994 was:

    $$8, 3, 5, 3, 4, 3, 1, 0, 3, 4, 0, 7$$

    What is the median number of applications?

    (A) 3
    (B) 4
    (C) 5
    (D) 6
    (E) 7

45. The monthly electric bills for a given year were as follows: $40, 38, 36, 38, 34, 34, 30, 32, 34, 37, 39, and 40. What is the mode?

    (A) $33
    (B) $34
    (C) $35
    (D) $36
    (E) $37

46. If 4.5 pounds of chocolate cost $10, how many pounds of chocolate can be purchased for $12?

    (A) $4\frac{3}{4}$
    (B) $5\frac{2}{5}$
    (C) $5\frac{1}{2}$
    (D) $5\frac{3}{4}$
    (E) 6

47. At a certain school, 45 percent of the students bought a yearbook. If 540 students bought yearbooks, how many students did not buy yearbooks?

    (A) 243
    (B) 540
    (C) 575
    (D) 660
    (E) 957

48. Walking at a constant rate of 4 miles per hour, it takes Jill exactly one hour to walk home from school. If she walks at a constant rate of 5 miles per hour, how many *minutes* will the trip take?

    (A) 48
    (B) 54
    (C) 56
    (D) 72
    (E) 112

49. Which of the following is the larger of two numbers the product of which is 600 and the sum of which is five times the difference between the two?

    (A) 10
    (B) 15
    (C) 20
    (D) 30
    (E) 50

50. If $\frac{1}{3}$ of a number is 3 more than $\frac{1}{4}$ of the number, then what is the number?

    (A) 18
    (B) 24
    (C) 30
    (D) 36
    (E) 48

51. If $\frac{3}{5}$ of a number is 4 more than $\frac{1}{2}$ of the number, then what is the number?

    (A) 20
    (B) 28
    (C) 35
    (D) 40
    (E) 56

52. When both 16 and 9 are divided by $n$, the remainder is 2. What is $n$?

    (A) 3
    (B) 4
    (C) 5
    (D) 6
    (E) 7

53. The sum of the digits of a three-digit number is 16. If the tens digit of the number is 3 times the units digit, and the units digit is $\frac{1}{4}$ of the hundreds digit, then what is the number?

    (A) 446
    (B) 561
    (C) 682
    (D) 862
    (E) 914

54. If the sum of five consecutive integers is 40, what is the smallest of the five integers?

    (A) 4
    (B) 5
    (C) 6
    (D) 7
    (E) 8

55. If $a^3 + b = 3 + a^3$, then $b =$

    (A) $3^3$
    (B) $3\sqrt{3}$
    (C) 3
    (D) $\sqrt[3]{3}$
    (E) $-\sqrt{3}$

56. If $n+1+n+2+n+3 = 1+2+3$, then $n =$

    (A) $-3$
    (B) $-1$
    (C) 0
    (D) 1
    (E) 3

57. If $x = 2$, what is the value of $x^2 + 2x - 2$?

    (A) $-2$
    (B) 0
    (C) 2
    (D) 4
    (E) 6

58. If $x = 2$, then $\frac{1}{x^2} + \frac{1}{x} - \frac{x}{2} =$

    Give your answer as a fraction.

59. $\dfrac{9(x^2y^3)^6}{(3x^6y^9)^2} =$

(A) 1
(B) 3
(C) $x^2y^3$
(D) $3x^2y^3$
(E) $x^{12}y^{12}$

60. $\dfrac{x^2-y^2}{x+y} =$

(A) $x^2-y^2$
(B) $x^2+y^2$
(C) $x^2+y$
(D) $x+y^2$
(E) $x-y$

61. $\dfrac{x^2-x-6}{x+2} =$

(A) $x^2-\frac{1}{2}(x)-3$
(B) $x^2-2$
(C) $x-2$
(D) $x-3$
(E) $x$

62. The function $[x]$ is defined by $[x]=x^2-x$ for all integers. What is the value of the function $[-2]$?

63. The function $[x]$ is defined by $[x]=x^2-x$ for all integers. What is the value of the function $[[3]]$?

64. If $(2+3)(1+x)=25$, then $x=$

(A) $\frac{1}{5}$
(B) $\frac{1}{4}$
(C) 1
(D) 4
(E) 5

65. After filling the car's fuel tank, a driver drove from $P$ to $Q$ and then to $R$. She used $\frac{2}{5}$ of the fuel driving from $P$ to $Q$. If she used another 7 gallons to drive from $Q$ to $R$ and still had $\frac{1}{4}$ of a tank left, how many gallons does the tank hold?

☐ gallons

66. If $x+y=3$, then $2x+2y=$

(A) $\frac{1}{3}$
(B) $\frac{1}{2}$
(C) $\frac{2}{3}$
(D) 6
(E) Cannot be determined from the information given

67. If $2x+y=8$ and $x-y=1$, then $x=$

(A) $-2$
(B) $-1$
(C) 0
(D) 1
(E) 3

68. If $x^2-3x=4$, then which of the following shows all possible values of $x$?

(A) 4, 1
(B) 4, $-1$
(C) $-4$, 1
(D) $-4$, $-1$
(E) $-4$, 1, 4

69. Diana spent $\frac{1}{2}$ of her allowance on a book and another $3 on lunch. If she still had $\frac{1}{6}$ of her original allowance, how much is Diana's allowance?

    (A) $24
    (B) $18
    (C) $15
    (D) $12
    (E) $9

70. In a certain game, a player had five successful turns in a row, and after each one, the number of points added to his total score was double what was added the preceding turn. If the player scored a total of 465 points, how many points did he score on the first play?

    (A) 15
    (B) 31
    (C) 93
    (D) 155
    (E) 270

71. At a certain firm, $d$ gallons of fuel are needed per day for each truck. At this rate, $g$ gallons of fuel will supply $t$ trucks for how many days?

    (A) $\frac{dt}{g}$
    (B) $\frac{gt}{d}$
    (C) $dgt$
    (D) $\frac{t}{dg}$
    (E) $\frac{g}{dt}$

72. $Y$ years ago, Paul was twice as old as Bob. If Bob is now 18 years old, how old is Paul in terms of $Y$?

    (A) $36 + Y$
    (B) $18 + Y$
    (C) $18 - Y$
    (D) $36 - Y$
    (E) $36 - 2Y$

73. If pencils cost $x$ cents each, how many pencils can be purchased for $y$ dollars?

    (A) $\frac{100}{xy}$
    (B) $\frac{xy}{100}$
    (C) $\frac{100y}{x}$
    (D) $\frac{y}{100x}$
    (E) $100xy$

74. A merchant increased the original price of an item by 10 percent. If she then reduces the new price by 10 percent, the final result in terms of the original price is

    (A) a decrease of 11 percent
    (B) a decrease of 1 percent
    (C) no net change
    (D) an increase of 1 percent
    (E) an increase of 11 percent

75. Harold is twice as old as Jack, who is three years older than Dan. If Harold's age is five times Dan's age, how old in years is Jack?

    (A) 2
    (B) 4
    (C) 5
    (D) 8
    (E) 10

76. A tank with capacity $T$ gallons is empty. If water flows into the tank from Pipe X at the rate of $X$ gallons per minute, and water is pumped out by Pipe Y at the rate of $Y$ gallons per minute, and $X$ is greater than $Y$, in how many minutes will the tank be filled?

    (A) $\frac{T}{Y - X}$
    (B) $\frac{T}{X - Y}$
    (C) $\frac{T - X}{Y}$
    (D) $\frac{X - Y}{60T}$
    (E) $\frac{60T}{XY}$

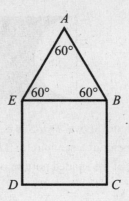

77. Machine X produces *w* widgets in five minutes. Machine X and Machine Y, working at the same time, produce *w* widgets in two minutes. How long will it take Machine Y working alone to produce *w* widgets?

    (A) 2 minutes, 30 seconds
    (B) 2 minutes, 40 seconds
    (C) 3 minutes, 20 seconds
    (D) 3 minutes, 30 seconds
    (E) 3 minutes, 40 seconds

78. If a train travels *m* miles in *h* hours and 45 minutes, what is its average speed in miles per hour?

    (A) $\frac{m}{h+\frac{3}{4}}$

    (B) $\frac{m}{1\frac{3}{4}h}$

    (C) $m(h+\frac{3}{4})$

    (D) $\frac{m+45}{h}$

    (E) $\frac{h}{m+45}$

79. On a playground, there are *x* seesaws. If 50 children are all riding on seesaws, two to a seesaw, and five seesaws are not in use, what is *x*?

    (A) 15
    (B) 20
    (C) 25
    (D) 30
    (E) 35

80. If *BCDE* is a square with an area of 4, what is the perimeter of $\triangle ABE$?

    (A) 3
    (B) 4
    (C) 6
    (D) 8
    (E) 12

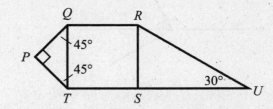

81. In the figure above, if *QRST* is a square and $\overline{PQ} = \sqrt{2}$, what is the length of $\overline{RU}$?

    (A) $\sqrt{2}$
    (B) $\sqrt{6}$
    (C) $2\sqrt{2}$
    (D) 4
    (E) $4\sqrt{3}$

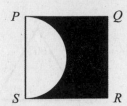

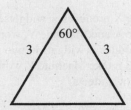

82. In the figure above, $PQRS$ is a square, and $\overline{PS}$ is the diameter of a semicircle. If $\overline{PQ} = 2$, what is the area of the shaded portion of the diagram?

(A) $4 - 2\pi$
(B) $4 - \pi$
(C) $4 - \frac{\pi}{2}$
(D) $8 - \pi$
(E) $8 - \frac{\pi}{2}$

85. The perimeter of the triangle shown above is

(A) $3\sqrt{2}$
(B) 6
(C) 7.5
(D) 9
(E) $9\sqrt{2}$

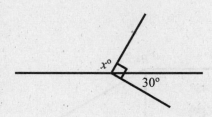

83. In the figure above, what is the value of $x$?

(A) 30
(B) 65
(C) 120
(D) 150
(E) 170

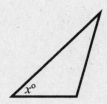

86. In the figure above, $x =$

(A) 30
(B) 45
(C) 60
(D) 75
(E) 90

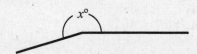

84. In the figure above, $x =$

(A) 120
(B) 150
(C) 180
(D) 210
(E) 240

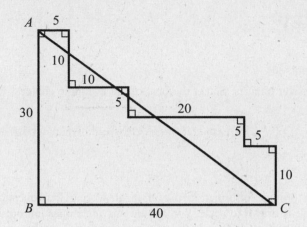

87. In the figure above, $\overline{AC} =$

(A) $30\sqrt{2}$
(B) 50
(C) 75
(D) $60\sqrt{2}$
(E) 100

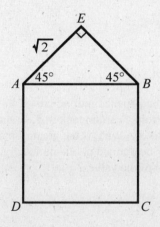

88. In the figure above, what is the area of square *ABCD*?

(A) 2
(B) $2\sqrt{2}$
(C) 4
(D) $4\sqrt{2}$
(E) 8

# REVIEW

This section contains Discrete Quantitative items for further practice.

**DIRECTIONS:** Each of the following questions has five answer choices. Select the best of the available choices. For Numeric Entry items, enter the answer in the box provided.

Notes:  All numbers used are real numbers.

All angle measures are positive.

A figure accompanying a question is included to provide information useful in answering that question. However, unless a note explicitly states that a figure is drawn to scale, you should answer a question not by estimating the magnitudes of various aspects, but by using your knowledge of the principles of mathematics. You can assume, however, that the positions of points, angles, regions, etc. are in the order shown, that lines shown as straight are straight, and that all figures lie in the plane unless otherwise noted.

Answers are on page 997.

1. A company bought a load of water-damaged copy paper, estimating that $\frac{2}{3}$ of the reams could be salvaged, in which case the cost per salvageable ream would be $0.72. If it later turned out that $\frac{3}{4}$ of the reams were salvageable, then what was the actual cost per salvageable ream?

   (A) $0.56
   (B) $0.60
   (C) $0.64
   (D) $0.68
   (E) $0.80

2. A cube has an edge that is four inches long. If the edge is increased by 25%, then the volume is increased by approximately

   (A) 25%
   (B) 48%
   (C) 73%
   (D) 95%
   (E) 122%

3. If each of the dimensions of a rectangle is increased 100%, the area is increased by

   (A) 100%
   (B) 200%
   (C) 300%
   (D) 400%
   (E) 500%

4. Three valves, when opened individually, can drain the water from a certain tank in 3, 4, and 5 minutes, respectively. What is the greatest part of the tank that can be drained in one minute by opening just two of the valves?

   (A) $\frac{3}{20}$
   (B) $\frac{1}{5}$
   (C) $\frac{7}{12}$
   (D) $\frac{2}{3}$
   (E) $\frac{3}{4}$

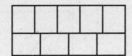

5. Nine playing cards from the same deck are placed as shown in the figure above to form a large rectangle of area 180 sq. in. How many inches are there in the perimeter of this large rectangle?

(A) 29
(B) 58
(C) 64
(D) 116
(E) 210

6. What is 10% of $\frac{1}{3}(x)$ if $\frac{2}{3}(x)$ is 10% of 60?

(A) 0.1
(B) 0.2
(C) 0.3
(D) 0.4
(E) 0.5

7. A pound of water is evaporated from 6 pounds of seawater containing 4% salt. The percentage of salt in the remaining solution is

(A) 3.6%
(B) 4%
(C) 4.8%
(D) 5.2%
(E) 6%

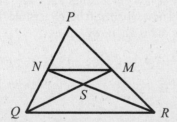

8. In the figure above, $M$ and $N$ are midpoints of $\overline{PR}$ and $\overline{PQ}$, respectively, of $\triangle PQR$. What is the ratio of the area of $\triangle MNS$ to that of $\triangle PQR$?

(A) 2:5
(B) 2:9
(C) 1:4
(D) 1:8
(E) 1:12

9. The average of 8 numbers is 6; the average of 6 other numbers is 8. What is the average of all 14 numbers?

(A) 6
(B) $6\frac{6}{7}$
(C) 7
(D) $7\frac{2}{7}$
(E) $8\frac{1}{7}$

10. The front wheels of a wagon are 7 feet in circumference and the back wheels are 9 feet in circumference. When the front wheels have made 10 more revolutions than the back wheels, what distance, in feet, has the wagon gone?

(A) 126
(B) 180
(C) 189
(D) 315
(E) 630

11. Doreen can wash her car in 15 minutes, while her younger brother Dave takes twice as long to do the same job. If they work together, how many minutes will the job take them?

(A) 5
(B) $7\frac{1}{2}$
(C) 10
(D) $22\frac{1}{2}$
(E) 30

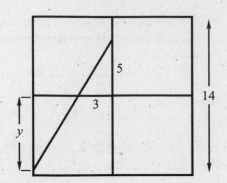

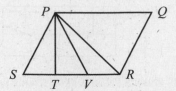

12. In the figure above, the side of the large square is 14. The four smaller squares are formed by joining the midpoints of opposite sides. Find the value of $Y$.

   (A) 5
   (B) 6
   (C) $6\frac{5}{8}$
   (D) $6\frac{2}{3}$
   (E) 6.8

13. A cylindrical container has a diameter of 14 inches and a height of 6 inches. Since one gallon equals 231 cubic inches, the capacity of the tank in gallons is approximately

   (A) $\frac{2}{3}$
   (B) $1\frac{1}{7}$
   (C) $2\frac{2}{7}$
   (D) $2\frac{2}{3}$
   (E) 4

14. In the figure above, $PQRS$ is a parallelogram, and $\overline{ST} = \overline{TV} = \overline{VR}$. What is the ratio of the area of $\triangle SPT$ to the area of the parallelogram?

   (A) $\frac{1}{6}$
   (B) $\frac{1}{5}$
   (C) $\frac{2}{7}$
   (D) $\frac{1}{3}$
   (E) Cannot be determined from the information given

15. If $p > q$ and $r < 0$, which of the following is (are) true?

   I.  $pr < qr$
   II. $p + r > q + r$
   III. $p - r < q - r$

   (A) I only
   (B) II only
   (C) I and II only
   (D) I and III only
   (E) I, II, and III

16. John is now three times Pat's age. Four years from now, John will be $x$ years old. In terms of $x$, how old is Pat now?

   (A) $\frac{x+4}{3}$
   (B) $3x$
   (C) $x + 4$
   (D) $x - 4$
   (E) $\frac{x-4}{3}$

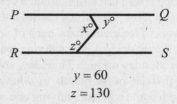

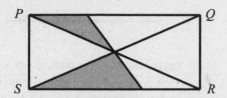

17. In the figure above, what percent of the area of rectangle *PQRS* is shaded?

    (A) 20
    (B) 25
    (C) 30
    (D) $33\frac{1}{3}$
    (E) 35

18. A train running between two towns arrives at its destination 10 minutes late when it goes 40 miles per hour and 16 minutes late when it goes 30 miles per hour. The distance in miles between the towns is

    (A) $8\frac{6}{7}$
    (B) 12
    (C) 192
    (D) 560
    (E) 720

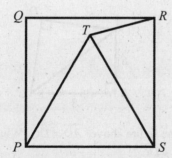

19. In the figure above, *PQRS* is a square and $\triangle PTS$ is an equilateral triangle. How many degrees are there in $\angle TRS$?

    (A) 60
    (B) 75
    (C) 80
    (D) 90
    (E) Cannot be determined from the information given

$y = 60$
$z = 130$

20. In the figure above, $\overline{PQ}$ is parallel to $\overline{RS}$. How many degrees are there in $\angle x$?

    (A) 90
    (B) 100
    (C) 110
    (D) 120
    (E) 130

21. If Paul can paint a fence in 2 hours and Fred can paint the same fence in 3 hours, Paul and Fred working together can paint the fence in how many hours?

    (A) 5
    (B) $2\frac{1}{2}$
    (C) $1\frac{1}{5}$
    (D) 1
    (E) $\frac{5}{6}$

22. A motorist drives 60 miles to her destination at an average speed of 40 miles per hour and makes the return trip at an average speed of 30 miles per hour. Her average speed in miles per hour for the entire trip is

    (A) 17
    (B) $34\frac{2}{7}$
    (C) 35
    (D) $43\frac{1}{3}$
    (E) 70

23. If $(x+1)(x-2)$ is positive, then

    (A) $x < -1$ or $x > 2$
    (B) $x > -1$ or $x < 2$
    (C) $-1 < x < 2$
    (D) $-2 < x < 1$
    (E) $x = -1$ or $x = 2$

24. An ice cream truck runs down a certain street 4 times a week. This truck carries 5 different flavors of ice cream bars, each of which comes in 2 different designs. Considering that the truck runs Monday through Thursday, and Monday was the first day of the month, by what day of the month could a person, buying one ice cream bar each truck-run, purchase all of the different varieties of ice cream bars?

    (A) 11$^{th}$
    (B) 16$^{th}$
    (C) 21$^{st}$
    (D) 24$^{th}$
    (E) 30$^{th}$

25. If $N! = N(N-1)(N-2)\ldots[N-(N-1)]$, what does $\frac{N!}{(N-2)!}$ equal?

    (A) $N^2 - N$
    (B) $N^5 + N^3 - N^2 + \frac{N}{N^2}$
    (C) $N + 1$
    (D) $1$
    (E) $6$

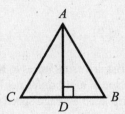

26. In the figure above, $\triangle ABC$ is equilateral and has a perpendicular line drawn from point $A$ to point $D$. If the triangle is "folded over" on the perpendicular line so that points $B$ and $C$ meet, the perimeter of the new triangle is approximately what percent of the perimeter of the triangle before the fold?

    (A) 100%
    (B) 78%
    (C) 50%
    (D) 32%
    (E) Cannot be determined from the information given

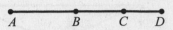

27. In the figure above, $\overline{AB}$ is three times longer than $\overline{BC}$, which is two times as long as $\overline{CD}$. If $\overline{BC}$ is removed from the line and the other two segments are joined to form one line, then what is the ratio of the original $\overline{AD}$ to the new $\overline{AD}$?

    (A) $3:2$
    (B) $9:7$
    (C) $5:4$
    (D) $7:6$
    (E) $11:10$

28. If $s$, $t$, and $u$ are different positive integers and $\frac{s}{t}$ and $\frac{t}{u}$ are also positive integers, which of the following CANNOT be a positive integer?

    (A) $\frac{s}{u}$
    (B) $s \cdot t$
    (C) $\frac{u}{s}$
    (D) $(s+t)u$
    (E) $(s-u)t$

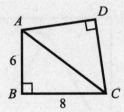

29. In the figure above, $\overline{AD} = \overline{DC}$. What is $\overline{AD} + \overline{DC}$?

    (A) $18\sqrt{2}$
    (B) $18$
    (C) $10\sqrt{2}$
    (D) $10$
    (E) $6\sqrt{2}$

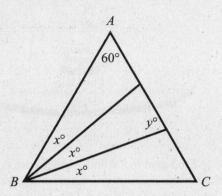

30. In the figure above, $\overline{AB} = \overline{BC} = \overline{CA}$. What is the value of $y$?

(A) 20
(B) 60
(C) 80
(D) 100
(E) 120

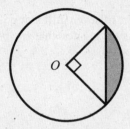

31. In the figure above, $O$ is the center of the circle with radius 1. What is the area of the shaded region?

(A) $\frac{3\pi}{4} + \frac{1}{2}$

(B) $\frac{3\pi}{4} - \frac{1}{2}$

(C) $\frac{\pi}{4} + \frac{1}{2}$

(D) $\frac{\pi}{4} - \frac{1}{2}$

(E) $\pi - 1$

32. If $z = \frac{x+y}{x}$, $1 - z =$

(A) $\frac{1-x+y}{x}$

(B) $\frac{x+y-1}{x}$

(C) $\frac{1-x-y}{x}$

(D) $-\frac{y}{x}$

(E) $1 - x - y$

33. In a list of the first one hundred positive integers, the digit 9 appears how many times?

(A) 9
(B) 10
(C) 11
(D) 19
(E) 20

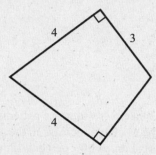

34. In the figure above, what is the area of the quadrilateral?

(A) 18
(B) 15
(C) 12
(D) 9
(E) 8

35. The average weight of the 8 packages in a certain shipment is 6 pounds. If the heaviest package is removed, the average weight of the remaining packages is 5 pounds. What is the weight, in pounds, of the heaviest package?

(A) 6
(B) 8
(C) 10
(D) 13
(E) 15

36. In the Excel Manufacturing Company, 46 percent of the employees are men. If 60 percent of the employees are unionized and 70 percent of these are men, what percent of the non-union employees are women?

(A) 90%
(B) 87.5%
(C) 66.7%
(D) 50%
(E) 36%

37. An accrediting agency set up a proficiency test for a lab in which 20 percent of the samples were injected with a contaminant. If the lab correctly labeled 80 percent of the contaminated samples but incorrectly labeled 5 percent of the uncontaminated samples, then what percent of the samples labeled by the lab as uncontaminated were actually contaminated?

    (A) 4%
    (B) 5%
    (C) 10%
    (D) 20%
    (E) 25%

38. A study of a city's water-use patterns shows that for every $8x$ percent increase in the price of water, usage drops by $x$ percent. If the price of water is currently $1.05 per 1,000 cubic feet, by how much should the price per 1,000 cubic feet be raised in order to obtain a reduction in usage of 2 percent?

    (A) $0.042
    (B) $0.105
    (C) $0.168
    (D) $0.199
    (E) $0.225

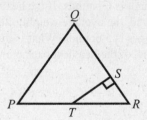

39. In the figure above, each side of $\triangle PQR$ has a length of 4. If $\overline{QS} = 3$, what is the area of $PQST$?

    (A) $\frac{9}{2}$
    (B) $\frac{9\sqrt{3}}{2}$
    (C) $\frac{7\sqrt{3}}{2}$
    (D) $\frac{9\sqrt{3}}{4}$
    (E) $\frac{7\sqrt{3}}{4}$

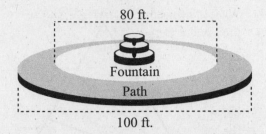

40. The fountain in the illustration above is located exactly at the center of the circular path. How many cubic feet of gravel are required to cover the circular garden path twelve inches deep with gravel?

    (A) $10\pi$
    (B) $900\pi$
    (C) $2,500\pi$
    (D) $4,500\pi$
    (E) $5,400\pi$

41. The average of seven different positive integers is 12. What is the greatest that any one of the integers could be?

    (A) 19
    (B) 31
    (C) 47
    (D) 54
    (E) 63

42. If $5x = 3y = z$, and $x, y,$ and $z$ are positive integers, all of the following must be integers EXCEPT

    (A) $\frac{z}{xy}$
    (B) $\frac{z}{5}$
    (C) $\frac{z}{3}$
    (D) $\frac{z}{15}$
    (E) $\frac{x}{3}$

43. What is the width of a rectangle with an area of $48x^2$ and a length of $24x$?

(A) 2
(B) $2x$
(C) $24x$
(D) $2x^2$
(E) $2x^3$

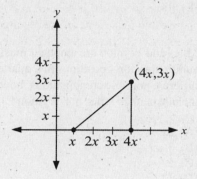

44. In the figure above, if the area of the triangle is 54, then $x =$

(A) $3\sqrt{3}$
(B) 3
(C) $2\sqrt{3}$
(D) 2
(E) Cannot be determined from the information given

45. If $x = \frac{1}{y+1}$ and $y \neq -1$, then $y =$

(A) $x+1$
(B) $x$
(C) $\frac{x+1}{x}$
(D) $\frac{x-1}{x}$
(E) $\frac{1-x}{x}$

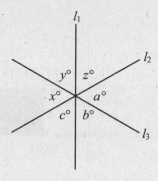

46. In the figure above, three lines intersect as shown. Which of the following must be true?

   I.  $a = x$
   II. $y + z = b + c$
   III. $x + a = y + b$

(A) I only
(B) II only
(C) I and II only
(D) I and III only
(E) I, II, and III

47. If $a^2 b^3 c < 0$, then which of the following must be true?

(A) $b^3 < 0$
(B) $b^2 < 0$
(C) $b < 0$
(D) $c < 0$
(E) $bc < 0$

48. If $\frac{2}{3}$ of a number is 5 more than $\frac{1}{4}$ of the number, what is the number?

(A) 12
(B) 15
(C) 18
(D) 24
(E) 36

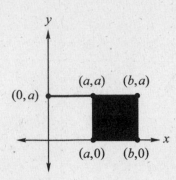

49. What is the area of the shaded portion of the figure above, expressed in terms of *a* and *b*?

(A) $a(b-a)$
(B) $a(a-b)$
(C) $b(a-b)$
(D) $b(b-a)$
(E) $ab$

50. If the distances between points *P*, *Q*, and *R* are equal, which of the following could be true?

  I.  *P*, *Q*, and *R* are points on a circle with center *O*.
  II.  *P* and *Q* are points on a circle with center *R*.
  III.  *P*, *Q*, and *R* are vertices of an equilateral triangle.

(A) I only
(B) II only
(C) III only
(D) II and III only
(E) I, II, and III

51. Thirty percent of the candidates who passed the written part of the hiring test for a certain city's police force were men. If forty percent of the candidates were women, what was the ratio of the pass rate for men to the pass rate for women?

(A) $\frac{3}{28}$
(B) $\frac{2}{7}$
(C) $\frac{3}{8}$
(D) $\frac{6}{7}$
(E) $\frac{12}{13}$

52. A company purchased 120 Model M computers and 50 Model N computers. If the cost of a Model N computer was 160 percent of the cost of a Model M computer, then what percent of the total purchase was the cost of one Model M computer?

(A) 0.5%
(B) 0.625%
(C) 0.8%
(D) 1.25%
(E) 8%

53. Miles and Wynton are among 7 musicians auditioning for 4 positions in a quartet. Of the different possible combinations, how many include neither Miles nor Wynton?

(A) 2
(B) 3
(C) 5
(D) 12
(E) 21

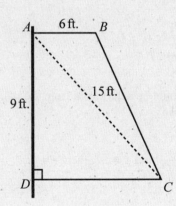

54. The figure above represents a sail on a mast with dimensions shown. If $\overline{AB}$ is parallel to $\overline{DC}$, what is the area, in square feet, of the sail?

(A) 54
(B) 56
(C) 64
(D) 72
(E) 81

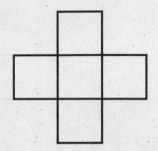

55. The figure above is composed of five squares, each with a side of *s* units. If the number of units in the perimeter of the figure is equal to the number of square units in the area of the figure, then *s* =

(A) $\frac{1}{5}$

(B) $\frac{3}{4}$

(C) $\frac{8}{5}$

(D) 2

(E) $2\frac{2}{5}$

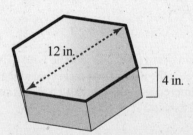

12 in.

4 in.

56. The figure above represents a hexagonal paving stone of dimensions shown. If the block is of uniform thickness, what is the volume of the material contained in the block expressed in cubic inches?

(A) $18\sqrt{3}$

(B) $36\sqrt{3}$

(C) $54\sqrt{3}$

(D) $108\sqrt{3}$

(E) $216\sqrt{3}$

57. A music store purchased *c* copies of a particular CD for *d* dollars per copy. If the store gave away *p* copies for promotional purposes and sold the remaining copies for *k* dollars each, which of the following represents the gross profit on the sale of the CDs?

(A) $k(c-p)-dc$

(B) $d(c-p)-kc$

(C) $c(k-p)-cd$

(D) $p(k-c)-d$

(E) $pk-cd$

58. Of the 2,400 students at John Jay High School, $\frac{1}{4}$ are seniors. If, due to overcrowding, $\frac{1}{3}$ of the seniors is transferred to other schools, what fraction of the remaining students at John Jay High School would be seniors?

(A) $\frac{1}{12}$

(B) $\frac{1}{8}$

(C) $\frac{1}{6}$

(D) $\frac{2}{11}$

(E) $\frac{3}{7}$

59. An airline offers three different fares on a commuter flight, Y, K, and P, for $100, $200, and $500, respectively. If the plane has 16 seats and a fully booked flight generated $2,500 in revenue, and if there were twice as many Y fares as there were K fares, how many P fares were sold on the plane?

(A) 1

(B) 2

(C) 4

(D) 5

(E) 6

60. Metal X costs twice as much as Metal Y. If a certain amalgam is $\frac{1}{4}$ Metal X and $\frac{3}{4}$ Metal Y, what fraction of the cost of the amalgam is attributable to the cost of Metal X?

(A) $\frac{1}{8}$

(B) $\frac{1}{5}$

(C) $\frac{1}{4}$

(D) $\frac{2}{5}$

(E) $\frac{3}{5}$

61. A manager has been instructed to reduce the cost of a manufacturing process by 40%. Materials account for $\frac{2}{5}$ of the cost, and labor accounts for $\frac{3}{5}$ of the cost. If it is possible to cut materials costs by $\frac{1}{2}$, by what percent must labor costs be reduced in order to achieve the goal?

(A) 20%

(B) 25%

(C) 33.3%

(D) 50%

(E) 66.6%

62. If $0 < kn < 1$, then which of the following could be true?

(A) $k < 0$ and $n > 0$

(B) $k > 0$ and $n < 0$

(C) $k < -1$ and $n > 1$

(D) $k < -1$ and $n > -1$

(E) $k < -1$ and $n < -1$

63. The cost to a certain company, in dollars, of producing $n$ number of CD players is $15,000 + 10n$. If the company sells the CD players for $25n$, what is the number of CD players that it must sell in order to cover exactly the cost of producing $n$ number of CD players?

(A) 15,000

(B) 10,000

(C) 7,500

(D) 5,000

(E) 1,000

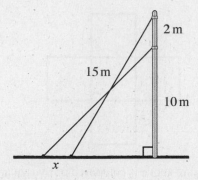

64. The figure above represents a pole steadied by a guy wire 15 meters long. Originally, the wire is anchored in the ground and fastened 2 meters below the top of the pole and 10 meters above the bottom of the pole. If the wire is refastened to the top of the pole and the ground anchor is moved as shown, what is the value, in meters, of $x$?

(A) $5\sqrt{5}$

(B) 5

(C) 3

(D) $5\sqrt{5} - 9$

(E) $\sqrt{5}$

65. If $P$ and $Q$ are points on a circle with a radius of 2, what is the distance as measured along the circumference of the circle such that $P$ and $Q$ are furthest apart?

(A) 1

(B) $\frac{\pi}{2}$

(C) $\pi$

(D) 2

(E) $2\pi$

66. Charles spent $\frac{2}{5}$ of the money that he had saved to start a new business on renovating a store and $\frac{2}{3}$ of what remained on inventory. If he still had $2,000, how much had Charles saved to start the new business?

(A) $10,000

(B) $8,000

(C) $7,500

(D) $5,000

(E) $4,000

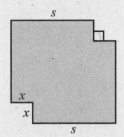

67. The figure above shows two overlapping and superimposed squares, both with side $s$. If $x = \frac{1}{4}s$, what is the area of the figure?

(A) $\frac{23s^2}{16}$

(B) $s^2$

(C) $\frac{3s^2}{4}$

(D) $\frac{5s^2}{8}$

(E) $\frac{9s^2}{16}$

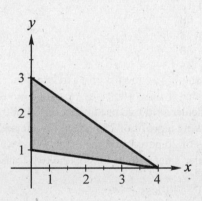

68. In the figure above, what is the area of the shaded region?

(A) 2
(B) $2\sqrt{2}$
(C) 3
(D) 4
(E) $4\sqrt{2}$

69. An investment fund manager is considering three stocks, P, Q, and R, for her portfolio. For the cost of 1 share of P, she could buy 3 shares of Q or 5 shares of R. If she invested an amount equal to the cost of 4,500 shares of Q but purchased equal numbers of shares of P and R and no shares of Q, how many shares of R did she buy?

(A) 250
(B) 625
(C) 1,250
(D) 3,650
(E) 3,750

70. Three students from among a group of five nominees are to be named to a committee. How many different groups of three students are available to be named?

(A) 3
(B) 6
(C) 10
(D) 20
(E) 60

71. If $3x + 5y = 24$ and $3y = 2x$, what is the value of $\frac{x}{y}$?

(A) $-\frac{1}{3}$

(B) $\frac{1}{3}$

(C) $\frac{2}{3}$

(D) $\frac{3}{2}$

(E) 3

72. A printing press produced $k$ books during the first 80 minutes of a run. If it produced another 24,000 books in the remaining $w$ minutes of the run, what was the machine's average operating speed, expressed in books per hour, for the entire run?

(A) $60(kw + 3,000)$

(B) $\frac{kw}{60} + 5,000$

(C) $\frac{kw + 80(24,000)}{60}$

(D) $\frac{kw + 24,000}{(80)(60)}$

(E) $\frac{60(k + 24,000)}{80 + w}$

73. At a certain college, 25 percent of the students pay out-of-state tuition while the other 75 percent pay in-state tuition. Half of the students are enrolled in the College of Arts and Sciences while the other half are enrolled in technical schools. If 10 percent of the students enrolled in technical schools pay out-of-state tuition, what percent of the students enrolled in the College of Arts and Sciences pay in-state tuition?

    (A) 15%
    (B) 30%
    (C) 40%
    (D) 50%
    (E) 60%

74. What is the ratio of the area of an equilateral triangle inscribed in a circle to the area of the circle?

    (A) $\pi\sqrt{3}$
    (B) $\frac{\pi\sqrt{3}}{2}$
    (C) $\frac{\sqrt{3}}{2}$
    (D) $\frac{\sqrt{3}}{4\pi}$
    (E) $\frac{3\sqrt{3}}{4\pi}$

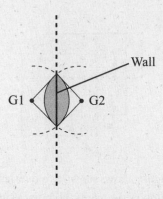

75. In the figure above, two guard stations, G1 and G2, are both 80 yards from the wall on either side, as shown. The line segment between the two guard stations is perpendicular to the wall. Each station has a spotlight projected onto the wall that illuminates a circular region with a radius of 100 yards. What is the length, in yards, of the portion of the wall that is illuminated by both security lights?

    (A) 120
    (B) 90
    (C) 75
    (D) 60
    (E) 45

76. A dealer sold two used boats for $3,600 each, making a profit of 25 percent on one and taking a loss of 20 percent on the other. What was the dealer's net gain or loss on the two transactions?

    (A) $540-loss
    (B) $180-loss
    (C) $90-loss
    (D) $120-gain
    (E) $360-gain

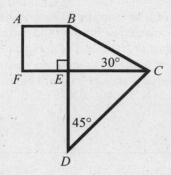

77. In the figure above, square $ABEF$ has an area of 9. What is the area of $\triangle ECD$?

   (A) $3\sqrt{2}$
   (B) $3\sqrt{3}$
   (C) $6$
   (D) $\frac{9\sqrt{3}}{2}$
   (E) $\frac{27}{2}$

78. During a three-hour rush, the average number (arithmetic mean) of vehicles passing through a particular toll plaza was 3,000 vehicles per hour. The number of cars passing through the toll plaza during the second hour of the rush was 1.5 times that of the number passing through the toll plaza during the first hour, and the number during the third hour was 2.5 times that of the number of the first hour. How many vehicles passed through the toll plaza during the second hour?

   (A) 1,500
   (B) 2,700
   (C) 3,000
   (D) 3,600
   (E) 4,500

79. If $x$ is not equal to 2, and $\frac{(x^2-4)}{3y} = \frac{(x-2)}{2}$, then, in terms of $y$, $x =$

   (A) $2y-3$
   (B) $3y-2$
   (C) $\frac{2y-3}{3}$
   (D) $\frac{3y-4}{2}$
   (E) $\frac{y}{2}$

80. A vat contains 8 kilograms of solution, S, that is, by weight, 30 percent Chemical X and 70 percent solvent. If 3 kilograms of the solvent are evaporated from the solution and an additional 4 kilograms of S are added back to the vat, what percent of the new solution, by weight, is Chemical X?

   (A) 20%
   (B) 25%
   (C) 36%
   (D) 40%
   (E) 50%

81. In a clinical trial of an experimental drug, 4 out of 5 patients were given the drug while the other 1 out of 5 were given a placebo. Of the patients given the drug, 95 percent showed significant improvement; the other 5 percent did not show significant improvement. Of the patients given the placebo, 20 percent showed significant improvement; the others did not. What percent of the patients who showed significant improvement were given the placebo?

   (A) 4%
   (B) 5%
   (C) 8%
   (D) 16%
   (E) 25%

82. Pipe P can drain the liquid from a tank in $\frac{3}{4}$ the time that it takes Pipe Q to drain it and in $\frac{2}{3}$ the time that it takes Pipe R to drain it. If all three pipes operating simultaneously but independently are used to drain liquid from the tank, then Pipe Q drains what portion of the liquid from the tank?

(A) $\frac{9}{29}$

(B) $\frac{8}{23}$

(C) $\frac{3}{8}$

(D) $\frac{17}{29}$

(E) $\frac{3}{4}$

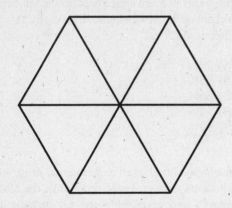

83. In the figure above, if each line segment has a length of 1, what is the area of the hexagonal region?

(A) $\frac{\sqrt{3}}{2}$

(B) $\sqrt{3}$

(C) $2\sqrt{3}$

(D) $\frac{3\sqrt{3}}{2}$

(E) $6\sqrt{3}$

84. A store sells an item at a 20 percent discount off the price marked on the item and makes a gross profit equal to 20 percent of the cost of the item. If the item were sold without any discount, what would be the store's gross profit on the item?

(A) 50%
(B) 40%
(C) 33.3%
(D) 25%
(E) 10%

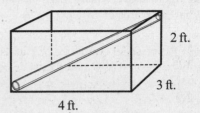

85. A glass tube used in scientific experiments is packed in a crate of dimensions shown. Which of the following measurements, in feet, most closely approximates the length of the tube?

(A) $\sqrt{13}$
(B) $\sqrt{29}$
(C) $\sqrt{41}$
(D) $2\sqrt{13}$
(E) 24

86. When the integer $n$ is divided by 4, the remainder is 2. Which of the following is NOT a multiple of 4?

(A) $n-2$
(B) $n+2$
(C) $2n$
(D) $3n$
(E) $4n$

87. Today, Maria is three times as old as Fernando. In 20 years, Maria's age will be ten years less than twice the age that Fernando will be then. How many years old is Fernando today?

(A) 10
(B) 12
(C) 15
(D) 30
(E) 40

88. The Adams Gift Company sold 4,800 deluxe castings of a bronze statue of Pegasus before offering collectors the regular edition. After its release, the regular edition outsold the deluxe edition by a ratio of 4 : 1. If a total of 17,400 statues were sold, how many of the deluxe editions were sold?

(A) 2,520
(B) 7,320
(C) 10,080
(D) 12,600
(E) 13,180

89. Originally, an order consisting of $T$ units was to have been shipped in $N$ crates with $x$ units in each crate. If new shipping regulations require the use of an additional $S$ crates, and the order will be shipped with $y$ units in each crate, which of the following represents the difference between $x$ and $y$?

(A) $\frac{N}{T}$
(B) $\frac{S}{T}$
(C) $\frac{(N+S)}{T}$
(D) $\frac{TS}{N(N+S)}$
(E) $\frac{TS}{N(N-S)}$

90. If $K$ and $N$ are positive integers that have remainders of 2 and 3 when divided by 6, respectively, which of the following is NOT a possible value of $K + N$?

(A) 11
(B) 23
(C) 41
(D) 59
(E) 124

# TIMED-PRACTICE QUIZZES

This section contains three Discrete Quantitative quizzes. Complete each quiz while being timed.

**DIRECTIONS:** Each of the following questions has five answer choices. Select the best of the available choices. For Numeric Entry items, enter the answer in the box provided.

Notes:   All numbers used are real numbers.

All angle measures are positive.

A figure accompanying a question is included to provide information useful in answering that question. However, unless a note explicitly states that a figure is drawn to scale, you should answer a question not by estimating the magnitudes of various aspects, but by using your knowledge of the principles of mathematics. You can assume, however, that the positions of points, angles, regions, etc. are in the order shown, that lines shown as straight are straight, and that all figures lie in the plane unless otherwise noted.

Answers are on page 998.

## QUIZ I (20 items; 30 minutes)

1. A jar contains between 50 and 60 marbles. If the marbles are counted out 3 at a time, 1 is left over; if they are counted out 4 at a time, 3 are left over. How many marbles are in the jar?

   (A) 52
   (B) 54
   (C) 55
   (D) 58
   (E) 59

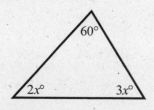

2. In the triangle above, $x =$

   (A) 24
   (B) 20
   (C) 16
   (D) 12
   (E) 10

3. A normal dozen contains 12 items, and a baker's dozen contains 13 items. If $x$ is the number of items that could be measured either in a whole number of normal dozens or in a whole number of baker's dozens, what is the minimum value of $x$?

   (A) 1
   (B) 12
   (C) 13
   (D) 25
   (E) 156

4. Starting from points 200 kilometers apart, two trains travel toward each other along two parallel tracks. If one train travels at 70 kilometers per hour and the other at 80 kilometers per hour, how much time, in hours, will elapse before the trains pass each other?

   (A) $\frac{3}{4}$
   (B) 1
   (C) $\frac{4}{3}$
   (D) $\frac{3}{2}$
   (E) 2

5. A student begins heating a certain substance with a temperature of 50 degrees Celsius over a Bunsen burner. If the temperature of the substance will rise 20 degrees Celsius for each 24 minutes it remains over the burner, what will be the temperature, in degrees Celsius, of the substance after 18 minutes?

(A) 52
(B) 56
(C) 60
(D) 65
(E) 72

6. How many two-element subsets of the set below do NOT contain the pair red and green?

{red, green, yellow, blue}

(A) 2
(B) 4
(C) 5
(D) 6
(E) 10

7. If the ratio of men to women in a meeting is 8 to 7, what fractional part of the people at the meeting are women?

(A) $\frac{1}{56}$
(B) $\frac{1}{15}$
(C) $\frac{1}{7}$
(D) $\frac{7}{15}$
(E) $\frac{8}{7}$

8. In a certain direct mail center, each of $x$ computers addresses $y$ letters every $z$ minutes. If every computer works without interruption, how many hours are required for the center to address 100,000 letters?

(A) $\frac{100,000z}{60xy}$
(B) $\frac{100,000x}{60yz}$
(C) $\frac{100,000xy}{60z}$
(D) $\frac{60xy}{100,000z}$
(E) $\frac{60y}{100,000xz}$

9. The object of a certain board game is to use clues to identify a suspect and the weapon used to commit a crime. If there are three suspects and six weapons, how many different possible solutions to the game are there?

(A) 2
(B) 3
(C) 9
(D) 12
(E) 18

10. The average weight of three boxes is $25\frac{1}{3}$ pounds. If each box weighs at least 24 pounds, what is the greatest possible weight, in pounds, of any one of the boxes?

(A) 25
(B) 26
(C) 27
(D) 28
(E) 29

11. If $n$ subtracted from $\frac{13}{2}$ is equal to $n$ divided by $\frac{2}{13}$ what is the value of $n$?

(A) $\frac{2}{3}$
(B) $\frac{13}{15}$
(C) 1
(D) $\frac{13}{11}$
(E) 26

12. If $x = 6 + y$ and $4x = 3 - 2y$, what is the value of $x$?

(A) 4
(B) $\frac{11}{13}$
(C) $\frac{5}{2}$
(D) $-\frac{2}{3}$
(E) $-\frac{7}{2}$

13. If $\frac{2}{3}$ is written as a decimal to 101 places, what is the sum of the first 100 digits to the right of the decimal point?

(A) 66
(B) 595
(C) 599
(D) 600
(E) 601

14. A jar contains 5 blue marbles, 25 green marbles, and $x$ red marbles. If the probability of drawing a red marble at random is $\frac{1}{4}$, what is the value of $x$?

(A) 25
(B) 20
(C) 15
(D) 12
(E) 10

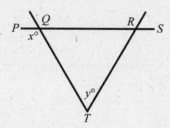

15. In the figure above, $\overline{QT} = \overline{QR}$. If $x = 120$ then $y =$

(A) 30
(B) 60
(C) 75
(D) 90
(E) 120

16. If $\frac{x}{y} = -1$ then $x + y =$

(A) 2
(B) 1
(C) 0
(D) -1
(E) -2

17. $\frac{1}{10^{25}} - \frac{1}{10^{26}} =$

(A) $\frac{9}{10^{25}}$
(B) $\frac{9}{10^{26}}$
(C) $\frac{1}{10^{25}}$
(D) $-\frac{9}{10^{25}}$
(E) $-\frac{1}{10}$

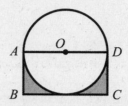

18. In the figure above, $ABCD$ is a rectangle with sides $\overline{AB}$, $\overline{BC}$, and $\overline{CD}$ touching the circle with center $O$. If the radius of the circle is 2, what is the area of the shaded region?

(A) $\frac{3\pi}{2}$
(B) $\frac{3\pi}{4}$
(C) $8 - 2\pi$
(D) $2 - \pi$
(E) $\pi - 1$

19. If Yuriko is now twice as old as Lisa was 10 years ago, how old is Lisa today if Yuriko is now $n$ years old?

(A) $\frac{n}{2} + 10$
(B) $\frac{n}{2} - 10$
(C) $n - 10$
(D) $2n + 10$
(E) $2n - 10$

20. In a certain community, the property tax is solely a function of the tax rate and the assessed value of the property. If the assessed value of a property is increased by 25 percent while the tax rate is decreased by 25 percent, what is the net effect on the taxes on the property?

(A) An increase of 18.75 percent
(B) An increase of 6.25 percent
(C) No net change
(D) A decrease of 6.25 percent
(E) A decrease of 18.75 percent

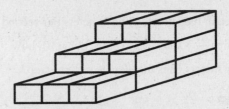

## QUIZ II (20 items; 30 minutes)

1. If $x + 3 = 3 + 12$ what is the value of $x$?

   (A) 0
   (B) 3
   (C) 6
   (D) 9
   (E) 12

2. Which of the following CANNOT be written as the sum of two negative numbers?

   (A) $-5$
   (B) $-3\sqrt{2}$
   (C) $-1$
   (D) $-\frac{1}{2}$
   (E) 0

3. If $x + 2y = 3$, what is the value of $2x + 4y$?

   (A) $-3$
   (B) 0
   (C) 2
   (D) 6
   (E) 9

4. The average (arithmetic mean) of three numbers is 6. If the sum of two of the numbers is 11, then the third number is

   (A) 5
   (B) 6
   (C) 7
   (D) 8
   (E) 9

5. Joan had exactly $9 before Jerry repaid her $6 that he had borrowed. After the debt was repaid, both Joan and Jerry had the same amount of money. How much money did Jerry have before the debt was repaid?

   (A) $3
   (B) $9
   (C) $15
   (D) $21
   (E) $24

6. The figure above is a plan that shows one view of a solid set of steps to be constructed from concrete blocks of equal size. How many blocks are needed to construct the steps?

   (A) 12
   (B) 15
   (C) 18
   (D) 21
   (E) 24

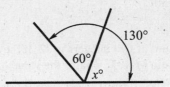

7. In the figure above, what is the value of $x$?

   (A) 70
   (B) 60
   (C) 50
   (D) 40
   (E) 30

8. If $2^{x+1} = 4^{x-1}$, what is the value of $x$?

   (A) 1
   (B) 2
   (C) 3
   (D) 4
   (E) 5

9. Of the actors in a certain play, 5 are in Act I, 12 are in Act II, and 13 are in Act III. If 10 of the actors are in exactly two of the three acts and all of the other actors are in just one act, how many actors are in the play?

   (A) 17
   (B) 20
   (C) 24
   (D) 30
   (E) 38

10. A certain bicycle traveling $k$ meters per second requires $\frac{k^2}{20} + k$ meters to stop. If $k = 10$, how many meters does the bicycle need to stop?

    (A) 10
    (B) 12
    (C) 15
    (D) 20
    (E) 30

11. What percent of 125 is 100?

    (A) 75%
    (B) 80%
    (C) 120%
    (D) 125%
    (E) 150%

12. The sum of two integers is 72. If the integers are in a ratio of $4 : 5$, what is the value of the smaller integer?

    (A) 32
    (B) 36
    (C) 40
    (D) 42
    (E) 48

13. If $n = \frac{x}{12} + \frac{x}{12} + \frac{x}{12} + \frac{x}{12}$ and $n$ is a positive integer, then the least possible value of $x$ is

    (A) 2
    (B) 3
    (C) 4
    (D) 5
    (E) 6

14. $\dfrac{10^3 (10^5 + 10^5)}{10^4} =$

    (A) $10^4$
    (B) $10^6$
    (C) $2(10^2)$
    (D) $2(10^4)$
    (E) $2(10^9)$

15. An album contains $x$ black-and-white photographs and $y$ color photographs. If the album contains a total of 24 photographs, then all of the following can be true EXCEPT

    (A) $x = y$
    (B) $x = 2y$
    (C) $x = 3y$
    (D) $x = 4y$
    (E) $x = 5y$

Items 16–17 refer to the following number line in which the letters represent a series of consecutive integers.

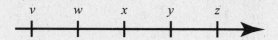

16. $y - w =$

    (A) 0
    (B) 1
    (C) 2
    (D) 3
    (E) 4

17. In terms of $v$, $v + x + z =$

    (A) $3v + 2$
    (B) $3v + 3$
    (C) $3v + 4$
    (D) $3v + 5$
    (E) $3v + 6$

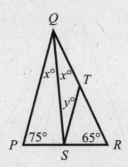

18. In $\triangle PQR$ above, if $\overline{PQ} \parallel \overline{ST}$, then $y =$

(A) 20
(B) 40
(C) 45
(D) 50
(E) 55

19. For all positive integers $x$:

$$\clubsuit(x) = x^2 \text{ if } x \text{ is even}$$
$$\clubsuit(x) = \sqrt{x} \text{ if } x \text{ is odd}$$

What is the value of $\clubsuit(7+1)$?

(A) 64
(B) 50
(C) 25
(D) $2\sqrt{2}$
(E) $\sqrt{7}$

20. If $2a = 3b = 4c$, then what is the average (arithmetic mean) of $a$, $b$, and $c$, in terms of $a$?

(A) $\frac{13a}{18}$
(B) $\frac{13a}{9}$
(C) $\frac{8a}{3}$
(D) $\frac{4a}{3}$
(E) $2a$

## QUIZ III (20 items; 30 minutes)

1. If a recipe that will produce 8 servings of a dish uses 2 eggs, then how many eggs are needed to produce 12 servings of the dish?

   (A) 12
   (B) 8
   (C) 6
   (D) 4
   (E) 3

2. If $x + 5$ is an even integer, then $x$ could be which of the following?

   (A) –4
   (B) –1
   (C) 0
   (D) 2
   (E) 4

3. If $(x + 2)(9 - 4) = 25$, then $x =$

   (A) 1
   (B) 2
   (C) 3
   (D) 4
   (E) 5

4. $\sqrt{1+2+3+4+1+2+3+4+1+2+3+4+1+2+3} =$

   (A) $3\sqrt{2}$
   (B) $3\sqrt{3}$
   (C) 4
   (D) 5
   (E) 6

5. What is the average (arithmetic mean) of all integers 6 through 15 (including 6 and 15)?

   (A) 6
   (B) 9
   (C) 10.5
   (D) 11
   (E) 21

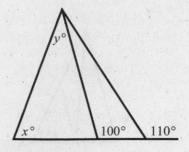

6. In the figure above, if $x = 50$, then $y =$

   (A) 30
   (B) 45
   (C) 50
   (D) 60
   (E) 75

7. Of the following, which number is the greatest?

   (A) 0.08
   (B) 0.17
   (C) 0.171
   (D) 0.1077
   (E) 0.10771

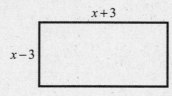

8. If the rectangle above has an area of 72, then $x =$

   (A) 3
   (B) 4
   (C) 6
   (D) 8
   (E) 9

9. Machine X produces 15 units per minute and Machine Y produces 12 units per minute. In one hour, Machine X will produce how many more units than will Machine Y?

(A) 90
(B) 180
(C) 240
(D) 270
(E) 360

10. Two circles with radii $r$ and $r+3$ have areas that differ by $15\pi$. What is the radius of the *smaller* circle?

(A) 4
(B) 3
(C) 2
(D) 1
(E) $\frac{1}{2}$

11. The average (arithmetic mean) of Pat's scores on three tests was 80. If the average of her scores on the first two tests was 78, what was her score on the third test?

(A) 82
(B) 84
(C) 86
(D) 88
(E) 90

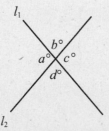

12. In the figure above, $a+c-b$ is equal to which of the following?

(A) $2a-d$
(B) $2a+d$
(C) $2d-a$
(D) $2a$
(E) 180

13. If $3a+6b=12$, then $a+2b=$

(A) 1
(B) 2
(C) 3
(D) 4
(E) 6

14. If $p, q, r, s$, and $t$ are whole numbers and the expression $2(p(q+r)+s)+t$ is even, which of the numbers *must* be even?

(A) $p$
(B) $q$
(C) $r$
(D) $s$
(E) $t$

15. If $x, y$, and $z$ are integers, $x > y > z > 1$, and $xyz = 144$, then what is the greatest possible value of $x$?

(A) 8
(B) 12
(C) 16
(D) 24
(E) 36

16. On the first day after being given an assignment, a student read one-half the number of pages assigned and read three more pages on the second day. If the student still has six more pages to read, how many pages were assigned?

(A) 15
(B) 18
(C) 24
(D) 30
(E) 36

17. For all integers, $x \spadesuit y = 2x + 3y$. Which of the following must be true?

    I.   $3 \spadesuit 2 = 12$

    II.  $x \spadesuit y = y \spadesuit x$

    III. $0 \spadesuit (1 \spadesuit 2) = (0 \spadesuit 1) \spadesuit 2$

    (A) I only
    (B) I and II only
    (C) I and III only
    (D) II and III only
    (E) I, II, and III

18. The sum, the product, and the average (arithmetic mean) of three different integers are equal. If two of the integers are $x$ and $-x$, the third integer is

    (A) $\frac{x}{2}$
    (B) $2x$
    (C) 1
    (D) 0
    (E) Cannot be determined from the information given

19. The sum of two positive consecutive integers is $n$. In terms of $n$, what is the value of the larger of the two integers?

    (A) $\frac{n-1}{2}$
    (B) $\frac{n+1}{2}$
    (C) $\frac{n}{2}+1$
    (D) $\frac{n}{2}-1$
    (E) $\frac{n}{2}$

20. If a polygon with all equal sides is inscribed in a circle, then the measure in degrees of the minor arc created by adjacent vertices of the polygon could be all of the following EXCEPT

    (A) 30
    (B) 25
    (C) 24
    (D) 20
    (E) 15

# CAMBRIDGE TESTPREP™

## Strategy Summary Sheet
# DISCRETE QUANTITATIVE

Discrete Quantitative items are multiple-choice math problems that test arithmetic, algebra, and geometry concepts. NO trigonometry or calculus will be on the exam. ETS states that data analysis concepts such as standard deviation and probability are tested, yet these items occur very infrequently and less than any other tested concept. So, rather than spend valuable class time reviewing such a rare type of item, simply refer to the *GRE Bulletin of Information* and the test materials available online at **www.gre.org** for further discussion. Concentrate on mastering the rest of the more commonly tested concepts.

Some Discrete Quantitative items will look as though they might have been taken from math textbooks; others will require application of math knowledge to new situations. Therefore, Discrete Quantitative items may be classified according to whether they just test ability to do mathematical manipulations or require some original thinking (application). Methods for attacking a particular item depend on the type of item.

## GENERAL STRATEGIES:

Pay attention to thought-reversers (capitalized and underlined words). When guessing on difficult items, eliminate "simple answer choices" and the "cannot be determined" response, (E). Do not hastily choose an easy answer choice unless it has been reasoned. Answering difficult items correctly counts more towards your score than answering easy items correctly, and answering difficult items incorrectly subtracts less from your score than answering easy items incorrectly. So, do not be afraid of working your way into difficult territory. If you can see your way to a quick and elegant solution, solve the problem directly, based on your knowledge of the subject. Translate, use pictures, and substitute useful numbers into story problems. Use the "plug-and-chug" strategy (especially on Algebra items), but look for tricks in difficult problem presentation that allow for easy problem-solving. Since the correct answer is among the answer choices, use the "good enough" principle and approximation to your advantage. Since answer choices are arranged in ascending or descending order, "test-the-test," starting with (C). Remember to guess quickly if you do not understand an item or cannot think of a way to solve the problem. As for the Numeric Entry items, since there are no answer choices to guide you, read the material carefully, watching for labels or designated units that indicate the appropriate type of answer. Using estimation or some other appropriate test-taking strategy, you should double-check your answers to these types of items, making sure that they are reasonable with respect to the information given.

## CHECKLIST OF SKILLS AND CONCEPTS TESTED BY CATEGORY:

*Arithmetic*:

- Simplifying: Fractions, Collecting Terms
- Factoring
- Approximation
- The "Flying-X" Method
- Decimal/Fraction Equivalents
- Properties of Numbers: Odd, Even, Negative, Positive, Sequential
- Percentages: Change, Original Amount, Price Increase
- Ratios: Two-Part, Three-Part, Weighted
- Averages: Simple, Weighted
- Proportions: Direct, Indirect

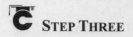 

*Algebra*:

- Evaluation of Expressions
- Exponents
- Factoring
- Picture Math
- Solving Equations: Linear, Quadratic, Multiple
- Special Problems: Work, Averages

*Geometry*:

- Lines and Angles: Perpendicular, Parallel, Intersecting
- Triangles: Equilateral, Isosceles, Acute, Obtuse, Perimeter, Area, Altitude, Pythagorean Theorem
- Quadrilaterals: Squares, Rectangles, Rhombi, Parallelograms, Trapezoids, Perimeter, Area
- Polygons: Sum of Interior Angles
- Circles: Radius, Diameter, Circumference, Area, Chords, Tangents
- Solids (Three-Dimensional): Cubes, Cylinders, Spheres, Volumes, Surface Areas
- Complex Figures

**NOTES:** _____

_____

_____

_____

_____

_____

_____

_____

_____

_____

_____

_____

_____

_____

_____

_____

_____

_____

_____

_____

# Quantitative Comparisons

# CAMBRIDGE TESTPREP™

## QUANTITATIVE COMPARISONS OUTLINE

# CORE LESSON

The items in this section accompany the Core Lesson section of the Quantitative Comparisons Lesson. You will work through the items with your instructor in class.

All numbers used are real numbers.

All angle measures are positive.

A figure accompanying a question is included to provide information useful in answering that question. However, unless a note explicitly states that a figure is drawn to scale, you should answer a question not by estimating the magnitudes of various aspects, but by using your knowledge of the principles of mathematics. You can assume, however, that the positions of points, angles, regions, etc. are in the order shown, that lines shown as straight are straight, and that all figures lie in the plane unless otherwise noted.

Directions: Each of the questions 1 through 96 consists of two quantities, one in Column A and one in Column B. Choose:

A if the quantity in Column A is greater
B if the quantity in Column B is greater
C if the two quantities are equal
D if the relationship cannot be determined from the information given

Notes: If information is centered above the two quantities to be compared, then that information is true of both quantities.

A symbol that appears in both columns represents the same thing in both columns.

The only possible choices are (A), (B), (C), and (D). Do not choose (E).

Answers are on page 999.

| Column A | Column B |
|---|---|
| **1.** 2 dozen | 23 |
| **2.** $0.5 \cdot 0.2$ | $0.5 + 0.2$ |
| **3.** $48^2 + 2(48)(52) + 52^2$ | $(100)(100)$ |
| **4.** $x + 1$ | $x$ |

| Column A | Column B |
|---|---|
| $p > 0$ | |
| **5.** $p$ | $2p$ |
| $2x - 4 = 10$ | |
| **6.** $x$ | $7$ |
| **7.** $x^3$ | $x^4$ |

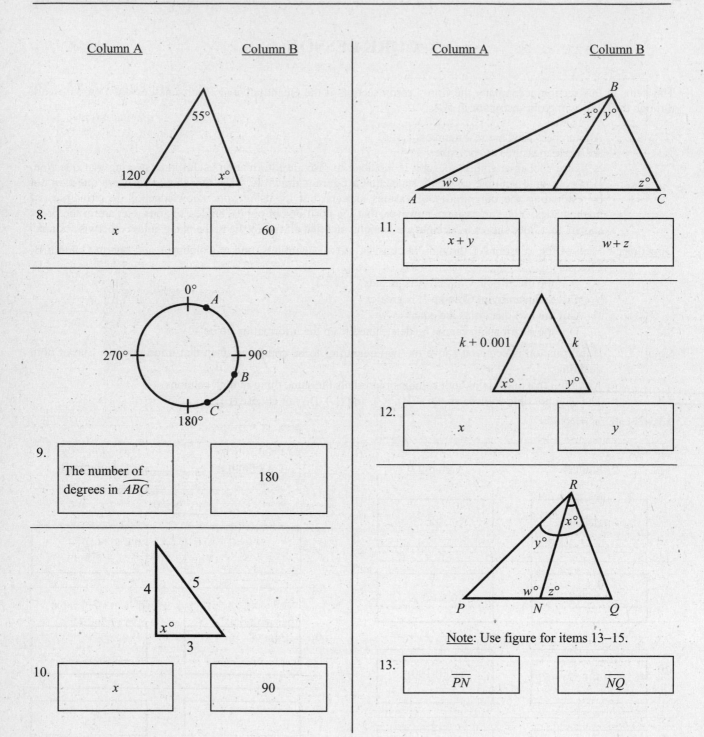

Column A        Column B        Column A        Column B

55°

120°        x°

8.

| x | 60 |

0°   A

270°        90°

B

180°   C

9.

| The number of degrees in $\overset{\frown}{ABC}$ | 180 |

4    5

x°

3

10.

| x | 90 |

B

x°  y°

w°              z°

A                 C

11.

| x + y | w + z |

k + 0.001        k

x°        y°

12.

| x | y |

R

x°

y°

w° z°

P      N        Q

Note: Use figure for items 13–15.

13.

| $\overline{PN}$ | $\overline{NQ}$ |

Column A | Column B | Column A | Column B

**14.**

| $x$ | $y$ |

**15.**

| $w + z$ | 180 |

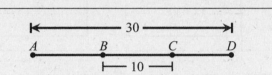

Note: Use figure for items 16–17.

**16.**

| $\overline{AB}$ | 10 |

**17.**

| $\overline{AB} + \overline{CD}$ | 20 |

**18.**

| $\frac{2}{3} + \frac{5}{6}$ | $\frac{2+5}{3+6}$ |

**19.**

| 0.333 | $\frac{1}{3}$ |

$x$ is positive.

**20.**

| $x$ | $x^2$ |

**21.**

| $0.64x + 0.65y$ | $0.64(x + y)$ |

John's birthday is separated from
Pat's birthday by three days and
Pat's birthday is separated from
Ellen's birthday by six days.

**22.**

| The number of days separating John's birthday from Ellen's | 10 |

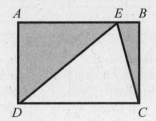

$\triangle DEC$ is inscribed in rectangle $ABCD$.

**23.**

| Area of shaded part of the figure | Area of unshaded part of the figure |

Three pounds of Brand X laundry
powder cost $12.33. Four pounds of
Brand Y laundry powder cost $16.44.

**24.**

| The average cost per pound of Brand X | The average cost per pound of Brand Y |

**25.**

| $-3 \cdot -4 \cdot 3$ | $2 \cdot 0 \cdot 5$ |

**26.**

| $2,000 \cdot 0.05$ | $20 \cdot 5$ |

| | Column A | Column B |
|---|---|---|
| 27. | $100 - 0.009$ | $99 + 0.0001$ |

Medium eggs cost $0.80 per dozen, and large eggs cost $0.90 per dozen.

| | Column A | Column B |
|---|---|---|
| 28. | The cost of nine dozen medium eggs | The cost of eight dozen large eggs |
| 29. | The distance traveled in 7 hours and 30 minutes by a train moving at a constant speed of 115 miles per hour | The distance traveled in 5 hours and 30 minutes by a train moving at a constant speed of 150 miles per hour |
| 30. | The average age of ten people | The average age of twelve people |
| 31. | $3(x+3)$ | $3x+3$ |
| 32. | $2(x+2)$ | $2x+4$ |
| 33. | $t+t+t$ | $3t$ |
| 34. | $x+x+x$ | $x^3$ |

| | Column A | Column B |
|---|---|---|
| 35. | $(x^2 y^3)^4$ | $(x^4 y^6)^2$ |

$xy = 0$

| | Column A | Column B |
|---|---|---|
| 36. | $(x+y)^2$ | $x^2 + y^2$ |

$xy = 2$

| | Column A | Column B |
|---|---|---|
| 37. | $(x+y)^2$ | $x^2 + y^2 + 2$ |
| 38. | $(x+2)(y+3)$ | $(x+3)(y+2)$ |
| 39. | Combined weight of $p$ packages weighing $k$ kilograms each | Combined weight of $k$ packages weighing $p$ kilograms each |

$a > b > 0$

| | Column A | Column B |
|---|---|---|
| 40. | $(60\%$ of $a) + (40\%$ of $b)$ | $50\%(a+b)$ |
| 41. | The average of 7, 8, and 6 | The average of 7, 8, 6, and 0 |
| 42. | $2 \cdot (13 - \frac{14}{19})$ | $(13 - \frac{14}{19}) + (13 - \frac{14}{19})$ |

|  | Column A | Column B |
| --- | --- | --- |

**43.** $\dfrac{111}{221}$ ⟷ $\dfrac{222}{445}$

**44.** $\left(-\dfrac{1}{2}\right)^{23}$ ⟷ $\left(\dfrac{1}{2}\right)^{23}$

**45.** $0.123 \div 123$ ⟷ $123 \div 0.123$

**46.** $x^2$ ⟷ $x^3$

$x \neq 0$

**47.** $x^2$ ⟷ $x^3$

$x \neq 0$
$x \neq 1$

**48.** $x^2$ ⟷ $x^3$

$x > 0$
$x \neq 1$

**49.** $x^2$ ⟷ $x^3$

$x > 1$

**50.** $x^2$ ⟷ $x^3$

|  | Column A | Column B |
| --- | --- | --- |

**51.** $x^2$ ⟷ $2x$

$x^2 = y^2$

**52.** $x^2$ ⟷ $xy$

$x$ and $y$ are positive integers.
$x$ is greater than $y$.

**53.** $x^y$ ⟷ $y^x$

The average (arithmetic mean) of
26, 14, $x$, and $y$ is 10.

$y > 0$

**54.** $x$ ⟷ $0$

$w > 1$

**55.** The number of widgets produced in an hour if the average rate of production is $w$ widgets per hour ⟷ The number of widgets produced in an hour if the average rate of production is 1 widget per $w$ hours

After Diana spent $\frac{1}{2}$ of her allowance on a book and another $3 on lunch, $\frac{1}{6}$ of her allowance remained.

**56.** Diana's allowance ⟷ $18

| Column A | Column B |
|---|---|
| **57.** $5 \cdot 6 \cdot 7 \cdot 8 \cdot 9 \cdot 10$ | $50 \cdot 54 \cdot 56$ |
| **58.** $\dfrac{13}{14}$ | $\dfrac{14}{15}$ |
| **59.** $\dfrac{9}{11}$ | $\sqrt{\dfrac{9}{11}}$ |
| **60.** $10^{11} - 10^{10}$ | $10^{10}$ |
| **61.** $\dfrac{1}{\sqrt{3}}$ | $\sqrt{3}$ |
| **62.** $\dfrac{101}{102} \cdot \dfrac{102}{103} \cdot \dfrac{103}{104} \cdot \dfrac{104}{105} \cdot \dfrac{105}{106}$ | $\dfrac{101}{106}$ |
| **63.** $3x + 2x + 2$ | $2x + 3$ |

$m > 1$

| Column A | Column B |
|---|---|
| **64.** $\dfrac{m + m + m + m}{m \cdot m}$ | $\dfrac{4}{m^2}$ |
| **65.** $2x$ | $x$ |

| Column A | Column B |
|---|---|
| **66.** $\dfrac{x+2}{2}$ | $\dfrac{x+4}{5}$ |
| **67.** $25(1) + 25(2) + 25(3) + 25(4)$ | $250$ |
| **68.** $36(437)$ | $37(436)$ |
| **69.** $3{,}250^2 - 3{,}249^2$ | $7{,}000$ |

$x - 1 \le 0$

| Column A | Column B |
|---|---|
| **70.** $\dfrac{x^2 - 1}{x - 1}$ | $x + 1$ |

$x + 1 \ne 0$

| Column A | Column B |
|---|---|
| **71.** $\dfrac{x^2 - 1}{x + 1}$ | $x - 1$ |

$2x + y = 7$
$x + y = 4$

| Column A | Column B |
|---|---|
| **72.** $x$ | $y$ |

$x + y = 5$
$x - y = 1$

| Column A | Column B |
|---|---|
| **73.** $x$ | $y$ |

Column A          Column B          Column A          Column B

$$3x = 4y$$

74.

| 0 | $4y - 3x$ |

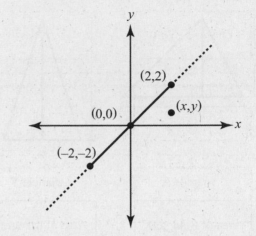

An investor bought two CDs. CD X paid 4% interest, and CD Y paid 6% interest. Combined interest from the two CDs was $2,960.

75.

| Amount invested in CD X | Amount invested in CD Y |

78.

| $x$ | $y$ |

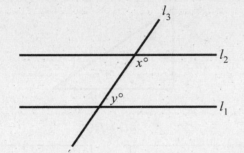

$l_1$ and $l_2$ are parallel.

76.

| $x + y$ | 180 |

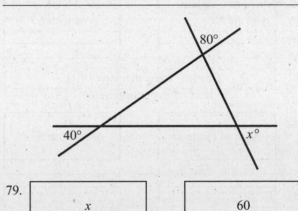

79.

| $x$ | 60 |

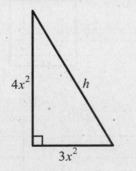

77.

| $h$ | $5x^2$ |

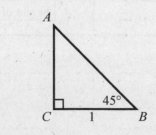

80.

| $\overline{AB}$ | $\sqrt{2}$ |

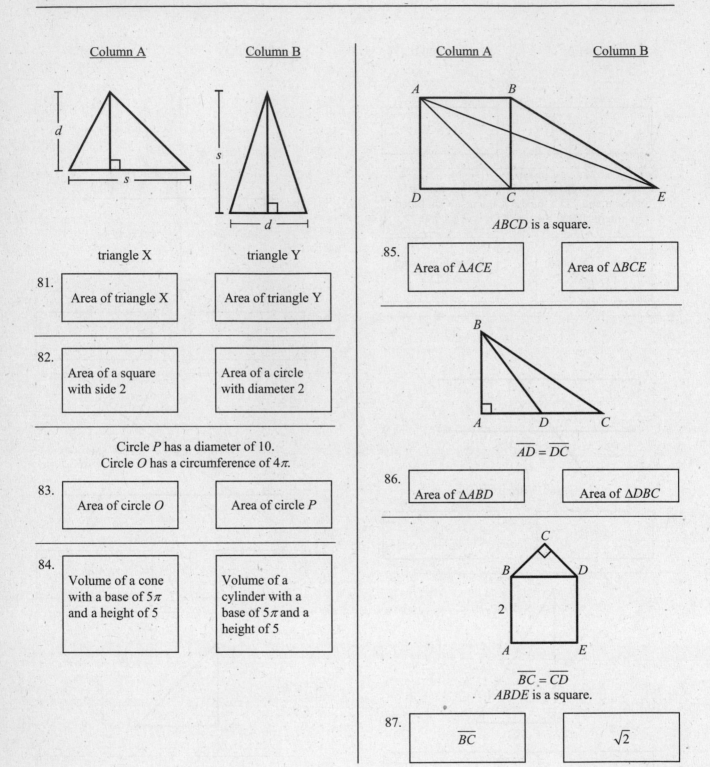

Column A    Column B

triangle X    triangle Y

81. Area of triangle X | Area of triangle Y

82. Area of a square with side 2 | Area of a circle with diameter 2

Circle P has a diameter of 10.
Circle O has a circumference of $4\pi$.

83. Area of circle O | Area of circle P

84. Volume of a cone with a base of $5\pi$ and a height of 5 | Volume of a cylinder with a base of $5\pi$ and a height of 5

Column A    Column B

ABCD is a square.

85. Area of $\triangle ACE$ | Area of $\triangle BCE$

$\overline{AD} = \overline{DC}$

86. Area of $\triangle ABD$ | Area of $\triangle DBC$

$\overline{BC} = \overline{CD}$
ABDE is a square.

87. $\overline{BC}$ | $\sqrt{2}$

Column A          Column B          Column A          Column B

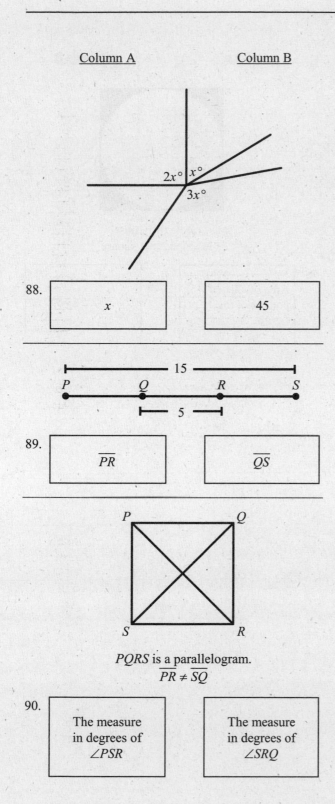

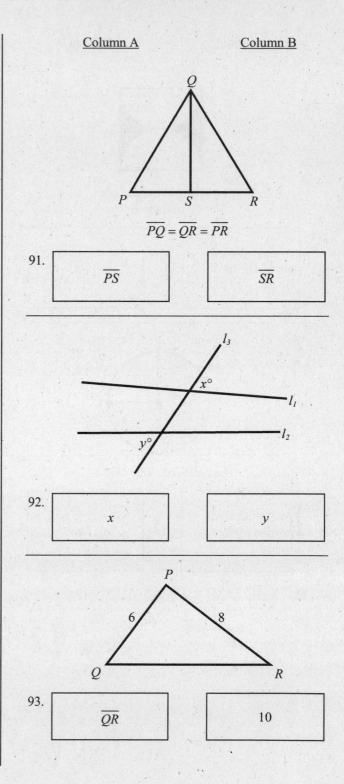

$\overline{PQ} = \overline{QR} = \overline{PR}$

88.

| $x$ | 45 |

89.

| $\overline{PR}$ | $\overline{QS}$ |

PQRS is a parallelogram.
$\overline{PR} \neq \overline{SQ}$

90.

| The measure in degrees of $\angle PSR$ | The measure in degrees of $\angle SRQ$ |

91.

| $\overline{PS}$ | $\overline{SR}$ |

92.

| $x$ | $y$ |

93.

| $\overline{QR}$ | 10 |

| Column A | Column B | | Column A | Column B |
|---|---|---|---|---|

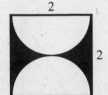

2

2

The square above contains
two semicircles.

94.

| Area of shaded portion of the figure | $4 - \pi$ |
|---|---|

A circle of radius 2
is inscribed in a square.

96.

| Area of shaded portion of the figure | $16 - 4\pi$ |
|---|---|

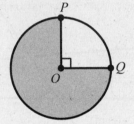

*P*

*O*

*Q*

The radius of circle *O* is 2.

95.

| Area of shaded portion of the figure | $2\pi$ |
|---|---|

# REVIEW

This section contains Quantitative Comparisons items for further practice.

All numbers used are real numbers.

All angle measures are positive.

A figure accompanying a question is included to provide information useful in answering that question. However, unless a note explicitly states that a figure is drawn to scale, you should answer a question not by estimating the magnitudes of various aspects, but by using your knowledge of the principles of mathematics. You can assume, however, that the positions of points, angles, regions, etc. are in the order shown, that lines shown as straight are straight, and that all figures lie in the plane unless otherwise noted.

Directions: Each of the questions 1 through 76 consists of two quantities, one in Column A and one in Column B. Choose:

A if the quantity in Column A is greater

B if the quantity in Column B is greater

C if the two quantities are equal

D if the relationship cannot be determined from the information given

Notes: If information is centered above the two quantities to be compared, then that information is true of both quantities.

A symbol that appears in both columns represents the same thing in both columns.

The only possible choices are (A), (B), (C), and (D). Do not choose (E).

Answers are on page 999.

| Column A | Column B |
|---|---|

Hector is $x$ years old, and
Maria is $y$ years younger than Hector.

1. $x$ | $y$

$$x = \frac{1}{y}$$

2. $x^2 + x^3 + x^4$ | $y^2 + y^3 + y^4$

| Column A | Column B |
|---|---|

$$x + y = 7$$
$$xy = 6$$
$x$ and $y$ are integers.

3. $x$ | $y$

$N$ is a two-digit number.
The sum of the digits of $N$ is 9.
The product of the digits of $N$ is 20.

4. $N$ | $54$

| Column A | Column B | | Column A | Column B |
|---|---|---|---|---|

**5.**

$(x^2 - y^2)^2$ | $(y^2 - x^2)^2$

---

$x(y + z) = 0$
$y = -z$

**12.**

$x$ | $y + z$

---

$x$ is a 2-digit number
divisible by 2, 3, and 5.

**6.**

$x$ | $60$

---

**13.**

The number of prime numbers between 1 and 25 | $9$

---

$\frac{a}{b} = 1$
$\frac{b}{a} = 1$

**7.**

$a$ | $1$

---

$s > 1$

**14.**

The volume of a cube with a side of $s$ | The volume of a rectangular solid with sides of $s$, $s+1$, and $s-1$

---

$x < 0$
$y > 0$

**8.**

$x^2 + y^2$ | $(x + y)^2$

---

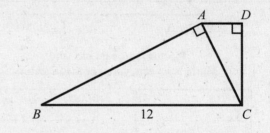

**9.**

$\frac{x}{9} = \frac{y}{17}$

$x$ and $y$ are positive integers.

$9x$ | $17y$

---

**15.**

$12$ | $\overline{CD}$

---

$5^{m - n} = 5$

**10.**

$m$ | $n$

---

**16.**

The average of the degrees in all the angles of a quadrilateral | The average of the degrees in all the angles of *two* triangles

---

**11.**

$(a - b)(a + c)$ | $a(a + c) - b(a + c)$

| Column A | Column B |
|---|---|

The total cost of $m$ items is $21.
The total cost of $n$ items is $25.

**17.**

| The average cost of the $m$ items | The average cost of the $n$ items |
|---|---|

$s > t$

**18.**

| $s^2$ | $t^2$ |
|---|---|

Items 19–20 refer to the following figure.

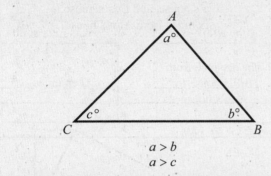

$a > b$
$a > c$

**19.**

| $\overline{AC}$ | $\overline{AB}$ |
|---|---|

**20.**

| $\overline{AB}$ | $\overline{CB}$ |
|---|---|

| Column A | Column B |
|---|---|

$O$ is the center of the circle.

**21.**

| The distance from point $P$ to a point $Q$ (not shown) on the circle | The radius of the circle |
|---|---|

$n$ is a positive integer.

**22.**

| Remainder when $2n + 1$ is divided by 2 | Remainder when $3n + 1$ is divided by 2 |
|---|---|

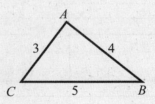

**23.**

| Area of $\triangle ABC$ | 6 |
|---|---|

$< x >$ denotes the greatest integer less than or equal to $x$.

**24.**

| $< 3\frac{1}{16} > + < -3\frac{1}{16} >$ | 0 |
|---|---|

| Column A | Column B | | Column A | Column B |
|---|---|---|---|---|

*x* and *y* are positive integers.

25.

$$\frac{x}{y}$$

$$\frac{x+1}{y+1}$$

$S_1 = \{1,3,5,7,9\}$
$S_2 = \{2,4,6,8\}$

26.

The sum of any 3 different numbers from $S_1$

The sum of any 2 different numbers from $S_2$

A dress originally priced at $120 is reduced by 10 percent. The price of the dress is then increased by 10 percent to *x* dollars.

27.

*x*

120

$x + y + z = 5$
$x + y - z = 2$

28.

*x*

*z*

$\overline{PQ}$ and $\overline{RS}$ are diameters of the same circle.

29.

$\overline{PR}$

$\overline{QS}$

Kim has more than twice the number of marbles that Amanda and Jeff have together.

30.

Three times the number of marbles that Amanda has

The number of marbles that Kim has

31.

The number of different duos that can be formed from a group of five singers

The number of different trios that can be formed from a group of five singers

$0 < x < y$

32.

$(x+3)(y+4)$

$(y+3)(x+4)$

Bill's house is four miles from Eva's house, and Eva's house is six miles from Ann's house.

33.

The distance from Bill's house to Ann's house

Ten miles

$x \cdot 1 = \frac{1}{x}$

34.

*x*

1

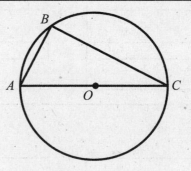

*O* is the center of the circle.
$\overline{AC} = 4$

35.

Area of $\triangle ABC$

1

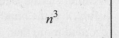
| Column A | Column B |
|---|---|

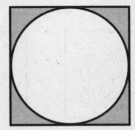

A circle is inscribed in a square, and
the area of the circle is $36\pi$.

**36.**

| Perimeter of the square | 48 |
|---|---|

$2x - 4 = 10$

**37.**

| The cost of $x$ copies of a *book* at $y$ dollars per copy | The cost of $y$ gallons of fuel at $x$ dollars per gallon |
|---|---|

**38.**

| The average (arithmetic mean) of 23, 19, and 12 | The median of 23, 19, and 13 |
|---|---|

$\frac{2}{x} + \frac{1}{5} = \frac{1}{3x}$

**39.**

| $x$ | $-8$ |
|---|---|

$x > 0$
$y > 0$

**40.**

| The time required to travel $x$ kilometers at $y$ kilometers per hour | The time required to travel $\frac{x}{2}$ kilometers at $2y$ kilometers per hour |
|---|---|

| Column A | Column B |
|---|---|

**41.**

| $(n-1)(n)(n+1)$ | $n^3$ |
|---|---|

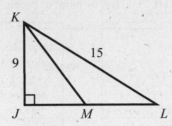

The area of $\triangle KLM$ is 27.

**42.**

| The length of $\overline{JM}$ | The length of $\overline{ML}$ |
|---|---|

$x$ is not equal to 0.

**43.**

| $\dfrac{|x|}{x}$ | 1 |
|---|---|

**44.**

| The sum of all the integers from 33 to 91, inclusive | The sum of all the integers from 34 to 92, inclusive |
|---|---|

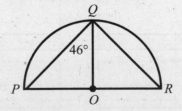

$O$ is the center of the circle.

**45.**

| $\overline{PQ}$ | $\overline{QR}$ |
|---|---|

| Column A | Column B | | Column A | Column B |
|---|---|---|---|---|

Weather station L recorded precipitation for every day in July. $x$ is the number of days during July for which L recorded more than 0.0 inches but less than 0.15 inches of precipitation, and $y$ is the number of days for which L recorded 0.15 inches or more of precipitation.

**46.**

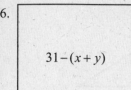

$31-(x+y)$ | Number of days during July for which L recorded no precipitation

In 1999, University U first enrolled part-time students. In 2000, and again in 2001, the number of part-time students enrolled at University U increased by 1,250.

**47.** Percent increase in the number of part-time students from 1999 to 2000 | Percent increase in the number of part-time students from 2000 to 2001

$$2^{3x} = 64$$
$$3^{2y} = 81$$

**48.** $x$ | $y$

**49.** $(x+2)^2$ | $(x-2)^2$

**50.** $0.9$  | $\sqrt{0.9}$

**51.** The average (arithmetic mean) cost of 24 books costing $3x$ dollars | The average (arithmetic mean) cost of 2 books costing $\frac{x}{4}$ dollars

$P > 0$

**52.** The total interest due on a loan of $P$ dollars on which a 4 percent simple annual interest is charged for a term of 5 months | $\frac{5}{3}(\frac{P}{100})$

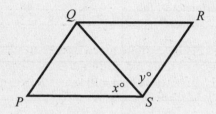

*PQRS* is a parallelogram.

**53.** $x$ | $y$

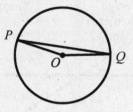

$O$ is the center of the circle.
$\overline{PQ} = 6$

**54.** The area of circle $O$ | $9\pi$

| Column A | Column B |
|---|---|

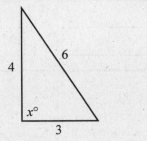

**55.**

| $x$ | 90 |
|---|---|

The ratio of blue marbles to red marbles in a box is $1:2$. After two more red marbles and one more blue marble are added to the box, the ratio of red marbles to blue marbles is $x:y$.

**56.**

| $x$ | $y$ |
|---|---|

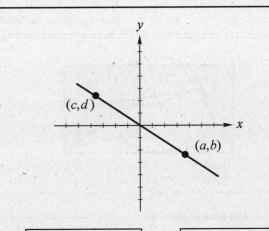

**57.**

| $a+d$ | $b+c$ |
|---|---|

| Column A | Column B |
|---|---|

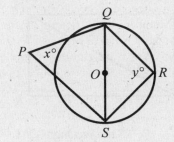

$O$ is the center of the circle.

**58.**

| $x$ | $y$ |
|---|---|

In a taste-test, matching soft drink P against soft drink Q, each participant chose either P or Q, and P was chosen by $\frac{2}{5}$ more people than those who chose Q.

**59.**

| The fraction of test participants who chose P | $\frac{7}{12}$ |
|---|---|

$$x^2 + 3x - 4 = 0$$

**60.**

| Three times the sum of the roots of the equation | $-9$ |
|---|---|

$$xy = 0$$

**61.**

| $(x+y)^2$ | $x^2 + y^2$ |
|---|---|

$$\frac{1}{x} \div \frac{1}{y} = \frac{2}{7}$$

**62.**

| $\frac{x}{y}$ | $\frac{y}{x}$ |
|---|---|

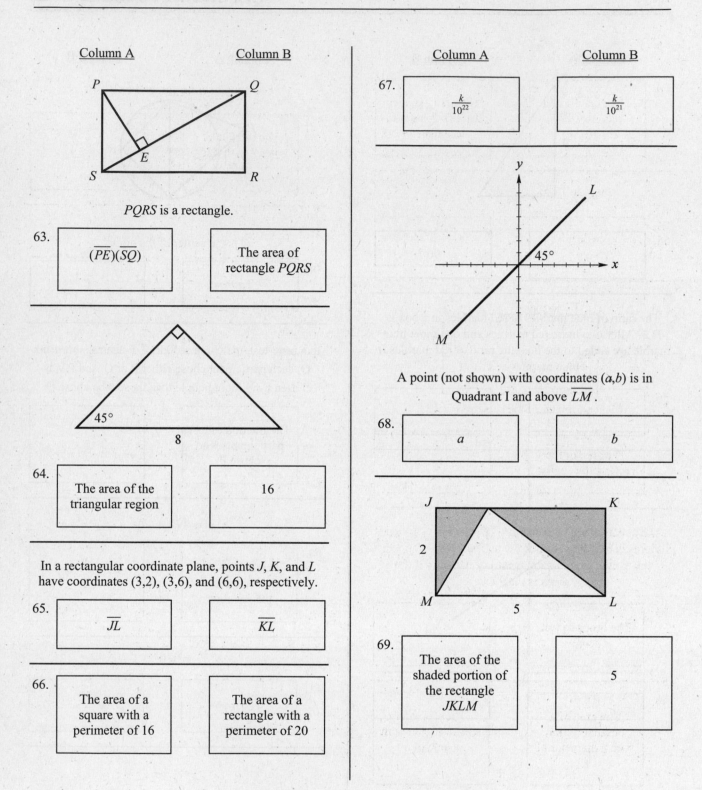

Column A     Column B

*PQRS* is a rectangle.

**63.**
$(\overline{PE})(\overline{SQ})$     The area of rectangle *PQRS*

**64.**
The area of the triangular region     16

In a rectangular coordinate plane, points *J*, *K*, and *L* have coordinates (3,2), (3,6), and (6,6), respectively.

**65.**
$\overline{JL}$     $\overline{KL}$

**66.**
The area of a square with a perimeter of 16     The area of a rectangle with a perimeter of 20

Column A     Column B

**67.**
$\dfrac{k}{10^{22}}$     $\dfrac{k}{10^{21}}$

A point (not shown) with coordinates (*a*,*b*) is in Quadrant I and above $\overline{LM}$.

**68.**
*a*     *b*

**69.**
The area of the shaded portion of the rectangle *JKLM*     5

| Column A | Column B | | Column A | Column B |
|---|---|---|---|---|

**70.**

| The greatest odd factor of 120 | The greatest even factor of 120 that is less than 24 |
|---|---|

For all numbers $n$, $\clubsuit n = k - n$.

**71.**

| $\clubsuit(\clubsuit n)$ | $n$ |
|---|---|

$l$

2.5

The perimeter of the rectangle is 15.

**72.**

| The area of the rectangular region | 12.5 |
|---|---|

The average (arithmetic mean) of a student's 10 test scores is 88. When one of the test scores is dropped, the average (arithmetic mean) of the other 9 test scores is 90.

**73.**

| The dropped test score | 70 |
|---|---|

**74.**

| The area of a circular region with a diameter of $n$ | The area of a square region with a side of $n$ |
|---|---|

$k$ is a positive integer, and $(-1)^k = 1$.

**75.**

| The remainder when $k$ is divided by 2 | 0 |
|---|---|

$-\sqrt{x} + y = \sqrt{x} - 1$

**76.**

| $2\sqrt{x}$ | $y$ |
|---|---|

# TIMED-PRACTICE QUIZZES

This section contains three Quantitative Comparisons quizzes. Complete each quiz while being timed.

All numbers used are real numbers.
All angle measures are positive.
A figure accompanying a question is included to provide information useful in answering that question. However, unless a note explicitly states that a figure is drawn to scale, you should answer a question not by estimating the magnitudes of various aspects, but by using your knowledge of the principles of mathematics. You can assume, however, that the positions of points, angles, regions, etc. are in the order shown, that lines shown as straight are straight, and that all figures lie in the plane unless otherwise noted.

Directions:   Each of the questions below consists of two quantities, one in Column A and one in Column B. Choose:
  A if the quantity in Column A is greater
  B if the quantity in Column B is greater
  C if the two quantities are equal
  D if the relationship cannot be determined from the information given

Notes:   If information is centered above the two quantities to be compared, then that information is true of both quantities.
  A symbol that appears in both columns represents the same thing in both columns.
  The only possible choices are (A), (B), (C), and (D). Do not choose (E).

Answers are on page 1000.

## QUIZ I (22 items; 30 minutes)

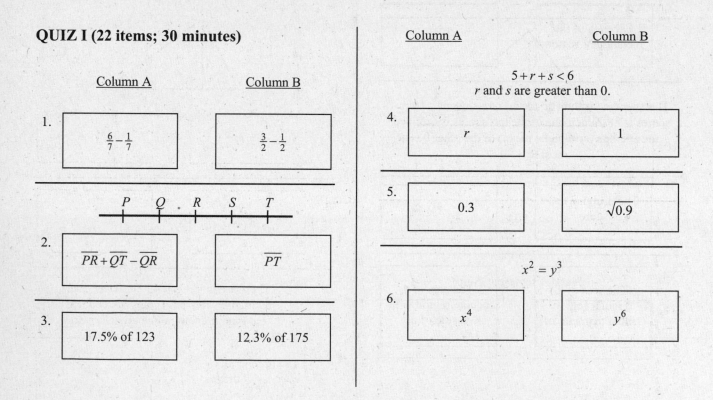

Column A | Column B

1.   $\frac{6}{7} - \frac{1}{7}$   |   $\frac{3}{2} - \frac{1}{2}$

$P \quad Q \quad R \quad S \quad T$

2.   $\overline{PR} + \overline{QT} - \overline{QR}$   |   $\overline{PT}$

3.   17.5% of 123   |   12.3% of 175

Column A | Column B

$5 + r + s < 6$
$r$ and $s$ are greater than 0.

4.   $r$   |   1

5.   0.3   |   $\sqrt{0.9}$

$x^2 = y^3$

6.   $x^4$   |   $y^6$

| Column A | Column B |
|---|---|

Point $P$ with coordinates $(x, y)$ is exactly 3 units from the origin.

**7.**

| $x$ | 3 |
|---|---|

The perimeter of square $PQRS$ is $12\sqrt{3}$.

**8.**

| Length of a side of square $PQRS$ | $4\sqrt{3}$ |
|---|---|

$n$ is a positive integer.

**9.**

| Remainder when $3n + 4$ is divided by 3 | 0 |
|---|---|

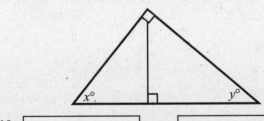

**10.**

| $x$ | $y$ |
|---|---|

$$\frac{\begin{array}{r} 50M \\ \bullet\ \ 7 \end{array}}{3{,}56N}$$

$M$ and $N$ represent digits.

**11.**

| $M$ | $N$ |
|---|---|

---

| Column A | Column B |
|---|---|

For all positive integers $f$ and $g$, $f \infty g$ is defined by the equation $f \infty g = fg - (f + g)$.

**12.**

| $f \infty g$ | $g \infty f$ |
|---|---|

$x$ is a positive integer.

**13.**

| Remainder when $2x + 2$ is divided by 2 | 1 |
|---|---|

**14.**

| 2 multiplied by the average of $x$ and $y$ | The average of $2x$ and $2y$ |
|---|---|

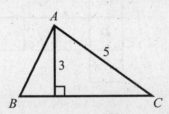

**15.**

| Area of $\triangle ABC$ | 6 |
|---|---|

**16.**

| $\dfrac{0.667}{0.166}$ | $\dfrac{\frac{2}{3}}{\frac{1}{6}}$ |
|---|---|

There are more than 40 but fewer than 50 marbles in a jar. If they are counted out four at a time, three are left over.

**17.**

| The number of marbles in the jar | 47 |
|---|---|

|         Column A          |        Column B        |
| :-----------------------: | :--------------------: |

**18.**

| Twice the area of a circle with radius $r$ | Half the area of a circle with radius $2r$ |

$$x - 1 \neq 0$$

**19.**

| $\dfrac{x^2 - 2x + 1}{x - 1}$ | $x - 1$ |

$$x = 1 - y$$

**20.**

| $x$ | $y$ |

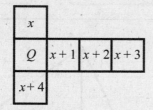

The sum of the terms in the
column is equal to the sum
of the terms in the row.

**21.**

| $x$ | $-2$ |

**22.**

| The value of the units digit in $6^{21}$ | The value of the units digit in $5^{21}$ |

## QUIZ II (22 items; 30 minutes)

| Column A | Column B |
|---|---|

$s > t$

1.

| $s - t$ | $t - s$ |

---

The cost of three apples
and two pears is $2.50.

2.

| The cost of one apple | The cost of one pear |

---

The regular price of a CD is $x$ dollars, but it has been discounted by $y$ percent.

3.

| $x$ | $y$ |

---

$p > 0$
$q < 0$

4.

| $p + q$ | $p - q$ |

---

The distance from City A to City B is 12 miles.
The distance from City A to City C is 10 miles.

5.

| Distance from City A to City B | Distance from City B to City C |

---

| Column A | Column B |
|---|---|

The seating capacity of the Red Room is less than the seating capacity of the Blue Room. The seating capacity of the Blue Room is greater than the seating capacity of the Green Room.

6.

| The seating capacity of the Red Room | The seating capacity of the Green Room |

---

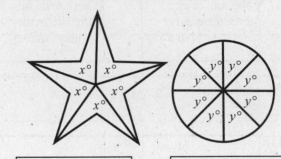

7.

| The value of $x$ | The value of $y$ |

---

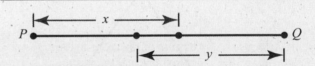

8.

| Length of $\overline{PQ}$ | $x + y$ |

---

9.

| The number of which 63 is 7% | 7% of 63 |

---

$r = \frac{1}{2}$

10.

| $2r^3 - 12r + 7$ | $r^2 + 1$ |

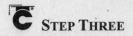 

| Column A | Column B |
|---|---|

$x \neq 0$

**11.**

| $\dfrac{1}{x^2}$ | $x^2$ |
|---|---|

$S_1 = \{3,6,9,12,15,18\}$
$S_2 = \{4,8,12,16,20,24\}$

**12.**

| The sum of any three different numbers from $S_1$ | The sum of any three different numbers from $S_2$ |
|---|---|

$m^3 = 64$
$\sqrt{n} = 16$

**13.**

| $m$ | $n$ |
|---|---|

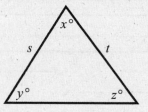

$x = y = z$

**14.**

| $s$ | $t$ |
|---|---|

**15.**

| Area of a rectangle with a length of 4 and a width of $\pi$ | Area of a circle with radius 4 |
|---|---|

| Column A | Column B |
|---|---|

**16.**

| The surface area of a cube with edge of length 4 | Twice the surface area of a cube with edge of length 2 |
|---|---|

$r < 0 < s$

**17.**

| $r^5$ | $s^4$ |
|---|---|

$x^2 = 25$
$2y + 3 = 27$

**18.**

| $x$ | $y$ |
|---|---|

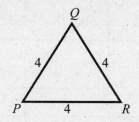

**19.**

| Area of $\triangle PQR$ | $4\sqrt{3}$ |
|---|---|

Column A          Column B

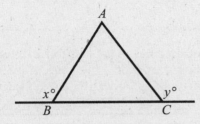

$$\overline{AB} = \overline{AC}$$

20.

| x | y |
|---|---|

---

*m* and *n* are positive integers.

21.

| $(5^m)^n$ | $5^m \cdot 5^n$ |
|---|---|

---

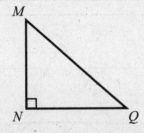

22.

| $\angle M + \angle Q$ | $45°$ |
|---|---|

## QUIZ III (22 items; 30 minutes)

<u>Column A</u>    <u>Column B</u>

**1.**

| The sum of all angles of a square | The sum of all angles of a polygon with sides of equal length |

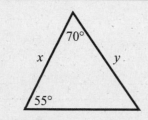

**2.**

| $x$ | $y$ |

Smithtown is 20 kilometers from Jamestown.
Jamestown is 50 kilometers from Charlestown.

**3.**

| Distance in kilometers from Smithtown to Charlestown | 70 |

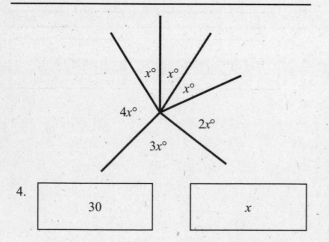

**4.**

| 30 | $x$ |

<u>Column A</u>    <u>Column B</u>

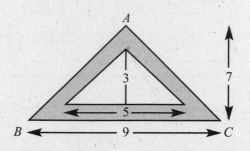

**5.**

| Area of the smaller triangle | Shaded area |

$x > 0$

**6.**

| $\frac{1}{x}$ | $x$ |

$x = \frac{1}{3}$
$y = \frac{1}{6}$

**7.**

| $\frac{x}{y}$ | $\frac{y}{x}$ |

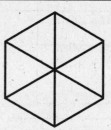

The two-dimensional figure above consists of six equilateral triangles, each with a perimeter of 6.

**8.**

| 36 | The sum of the lengths of all the line segments in the figure |

Column A          Column B                    Column A          Column B

**9.**

$(a+3)(a-4)$          $a^2-7a+12$

**10.**

Circumference of     Perimeter of square
circle with radius    with side $\pi r$
$2r$

**11.**

          $\sqrt{\frac{1}{3}+\frac{1}{6}}$

Items 12–13 refer to the following definition.

$$*x = (x-1)^2 + x$$

**12.**

$*{-2}$          $*2$

**13.**

$*1$          $*0$

**14.**

Remainder when       1
$11,111^{20}$ is divided
by 10

**15.**

$(a+b)(c+d)$          $(d+c)(b+a)$

**16.**

42% of 165          The number of
which 80 is 20%

$$\frac{30\heartsuit \cdot 6}{1,85\blacklozenge}$$

**17.**

$\heartsuit$          $\blacklozenge$

$x \neq 0$

**18.**

The reciprocal of          $x$
$\frac{1}{x}$

$M > 0$
$N < 0$

**19.**

$M \cdot N$          $\frac{-M}{N}$

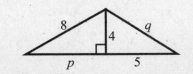

**20.**

$p$          $q$

**21.**

$16 + 3(-2)[4+6]$          $-4[3(9+5)]$

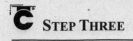

Column A          Column B

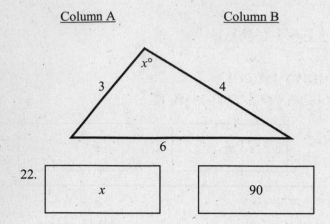

22.

| x | 90 |
|---|----|

# CAMBRIDGE TESTPREP™

## Strategy Summary Sheet
# QUANTITATIVE COMPARISONS

## GENERAL STRATEGIES:

Never choose answer choice (E).

Never guess answer choice (D) to an item that will have numerical solutions.

*"Good Enough" Principle*: Do only as much work as needed to conserve time.

*Simplifying Comparisons*: You may add or subtract the same thing to both sides to simplify a comparison; you may also multiply or divide by the same <u>positive</u> value.

*"Test-the-Test" Strategy*: If the problem involves an unknown, you may benefit by substituting numbers. One or two substitutions can eliminate two of the four answer choices.

## ARITHMETIC COMPARISON STRATEGIES:

Perform the arithmetic operations if they are manageable, that is, not too time-consuming or complicated (e.g., division and averages).

If the manipulations would take too long, look for one of the shortcuts (e.g., simplifying expressions, factoring, approximations).

## ALGEBRA COMPARISON STRATEGIES:

When dealing with variables, remember that negative numbers and fractions sometimes exhibit peculiar behavior. Pay particular attention to the seven regions on the number line, some of which may be excluded from consideration when the problem's additional information so stipulates: $x < -1$, $x = -1$, $-1 < x < 0$, $x = 0$, $0 < x < 1$, $x = 1$, $x > 1$.

If the item uses algebraic expressions, do whatever operations are indicated, if possible (e.g., distributive law).

If equation(s) are involved, solve for the unknown(s). For example, addition/subtraction or substitution may be used to solve a system of two linear equations with two unknowns.

Employ techniques based on the premise that "it must be one of the guilty suspects." By substituting meaningful numbers for variables, you may gain insight into the appropriate answer or at least eliminate some of the impossible ones. If one of the columns has numerical data, while the other column has a variable, substitute the numerical values for the variable into the scenario presented.

## GEOMETRY COMPARISON STRATEGIES:

Use knowledge of geometry principles, such as parallel lines or the Pythagorean theorem.

Quantitative Comparisons items also employ composite figures and figures with shaded areas. So, combine strategies.

Do NOT trust the figures. Do NOT assume that sides are equal, parallel, or at right angles to one another simply because of their appearance. You *are* entitled, however, to assume that lines drawn as straight are straight and that points, angles, and regions are in the relative positions shown.

**NOTES:** _____

# Graphs

# CAMBRIDGE TESTPREP™

## GRAPHS OUTLINE

### I. Core Lesson (p. 527)

# CORE LESSON

The items in this section accompany the Core Lesson section of the Graphs Lesson. You will work through the items with your instructor in class.

**DIRECTIONS:** Each of the following questions has five answer choices. Select the best of the available choices. Answers are on page 1001.

Items 1–4 refer to the following graph.

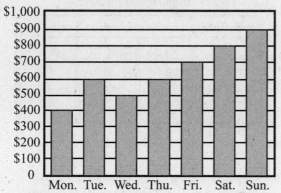

**GROSS RECEIPTS OF STORE X**

1. During the week shown, what was the greatest increase in sales from one day to the next?

   (A) $50
   (B) $100
   (C) $150
   (D) $200
   (E) $250

2. What was the difference between Tuesday's sales and Wednesday's sales?

   (A) $10
   (B) $50
   (C) $100
   (D) $200
   (E) $500

3. Average daily sales for the week were approximately

   (A) $275
   (B) $400
   (C) $550
   (D) $650
   (E) $850

4. Monday's sales were what percent of Saturday's sales?

   (A) 20%
   (B) $33\frac{1}{3}\%$
   (C) 40%
   (D) 50%
   (E) 60%

Items 5–9 refer to the following graph.

**SALES OF COMPANY Z BY CITY**
(Thousands of Dollars)

| | 1st Quarter | | 2nd Quarter | | 3rd Quarter | | 4th Quarter | |
| --- | --- | --- | --- | --- | --- | --- | --- | --- |
| | Total | High Week | Total | High Week | Total | High Week | Total | High Week |
| Atlanta | 90.1 | 10.5 | 100.3 | 23.4 | 60.4 | 10.6 | 84.5 | 12.3 |
| Boston | 100.2 | 14.9 | 84.7 | 16.3 | 120.3 | 20.7 | 110.2 | 23.4 |
| Chicago | 151.0 | 30.1 | 120.2 | 33.2 | 110.7 | 15.4 | 118.0 | 16.3 |
| Detroit | 66.2 | 12.4 | 48.2 | 9.5 | 56.7 | 8.2 | 60.2 | 12.4 |
| Houston | 48.9 | 6.5 | 40.3 | 5.4 | 36.3 | 6.5 | 22.1 | 3.4 |
| Los Angeles | 123.7 | 22.5 | 116.7 | 23.4 | 140.2 | 22.2 | 110.4 | 20.0 |
| Miami | 89.2 | 18.1 | 76.3 | 11.1 | 56.5 | 8.1 | 48.2 | 7.1 |
| New York | 220.1 | 35.2 | 198.7 | 26.4 | 178.3 | 18.4 | 199.2 | 17.6 |
| Seattle | 43.2 | 6.0 | 38.2 | 4.5 | 33.5 | 3.8 | 40.1 | 6.5 |
| Washington, D.C. | 76.3 | 18.1 | 56.2 | 8.8 | 64.2 | 9.2 | 53.1 | 6.6 |

5. For the first quarter, what was the ratio of the high week to total sales for Chicago?

   (A) 1:7
   (B) 1:6
   (C) 1:5
   (D) 1:4
   (E) 1:3

6. For the three cities with the highest total sales for the third quarter, approximately what was the average (arithmetic mean) of the total third-quarter sales of those three cities in thousands of dollars?

   (A) 110
   (B) 128
   (C) 135
   (D) 146
   (E) 158

7. For how many cities shown were highest total quarterly sales for the year recorded in the third quarter?

   (A) 2
   (B) 3
   (C) 4
   (D) 5
   (E) 6

8. For which of the following cities was the difference in dollar value of total sales recorded between the first quarter and the fourth quarter the least?

   (A) Atlanta
   (B) Boston
   (C) Detroit
   (D) Houston
   (E) Seattle

9. Which of the following conclusions can be inferred from the data?

   I. The lowest high week for the entire year was recorded in Seattle.
   II. The difference between Atlanta's highest quarterly total for the year and its lowest quarterly total was less than that for Washington, D.C.
   III. For Houston, the lowest ratio of total quarterly sales to high week was recorded in the third quarter.

   (A) III only
   (B) I and II only
   (C) I and III only
   (D) II and III only
   (E) I, II, and III

Items 10–14 refer to the following graphs.

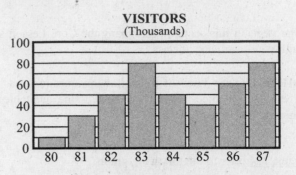

**VISITORS**
(Thousands)

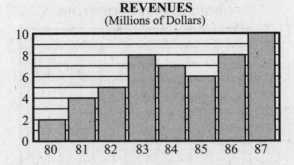

**REVENUES**
(Millions of Dollars)

10. For the entire period, what was the greatest increase in visitors from one year to the next?

    (A) 10,000
    (B) 20,000
    (C) 30,000
    (D) 70,000
    (E) 80,000

11. For the period of 1982–86 inclusive, what was the average (mean) number of visitors per year?

    (A) 48,000
    (B) 56,000
    (C) 59,250
    (D) 75,000
    (E) 84,000

12. From 1981 to 1985, which year showed the greatest percentage increase in visitors over the previous year in that period?

    (A) 1981
    (B) 1982
    (C) 1983
    (D) 1984
    (E) 1985

13. If, in 1984, 20 percent of all visitors accounted
for 50 percent of the revenues, what was the
average (arithmetic mean) amount of revenue
derived from each of those visitors?

(A) $185
(B) $215
(C) $280
(D) $350
(E) $385

14. Before the start of 1980, the management of
Hotel Convention Center K set what it considered
to be an acceptable dollars-of-revenue to number-
of-visitors ratio. If the acceptable ratio is $135 per
visitor, in how many of the years shown did the
convention center attain an acceptable ratio?

(A) 5
(B) 4
(C) 3
(D) 2
(E) 1

Items 15–19 refer to the following graph.

**ANNUAL DISTRIBUTION OF THREE CHARITIES FROM 1966 TO 1985**
(Millions of Dollars)

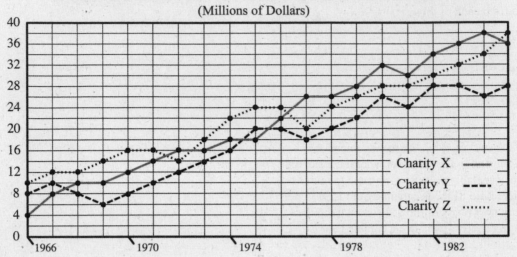

15. For how many years was the annual distribution of Charity X greater than those of both Charity Y and Charity Z?

   (A) 4
   (B) 9
   (C) 11
   (D) 14
   (E) 15

16. From 1971 to 1982, by how many millions of dollars did the annual distribution of Charity Z increase?

   (A) 8
   (B) 12
   (C) 14
   (D) 16
   (E) 18

17. From 1970 to 1981, by what percent did the annual distribution of Charity X increase?

   (A) 100%
   (B) 150%
   (C) 200%
   (D) 250%
   (E) 300%

18. In 1977, what were the combined annual distributions of Charity X and Z (in millions)?

   (A) 38
   (B) 44
   (C) 46
   (D) 52
   (E) 64

19. Which of the following statements can be inferred from the information given?

   I. Between 1969 and 1979, total annual distributions by all three charities combined increased by more than 150%.
   II. For each year after the first year shown, annual distributions by Charity Y failed to increase.
   III. For the years 1978 and 1979 combined, Charity X accounted for greater than one-third of all monies distributed by all charities.

   (A) I only
   (B) II only
   (C) I and II only
   (D) I and III only
   (E) I, II, and III

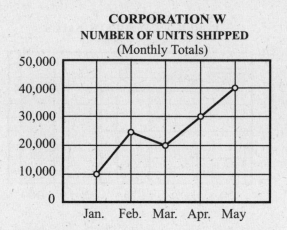

Items 20–24 refer to the following graphs.

### CORPORATION W
### NUMBER OF WORKERS EMPLOYED

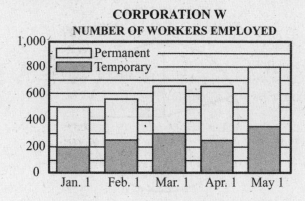

### CORPORATION W
### NUMBER OF UNITS SHIPPED
(Monthly Totals)

20. What was the total number of workers employed by Corporation W on February 1$^{st}$?

(A) 500
(B) 550
(C) 600
(D) 650
(E) 700

21. By what percent did the number of temporary workers employed by Corporation W increase from April 1$^{st}$ to May 1$^{st}$?

(A) 12%
(B) 20%
(C) 25%
(D) $33\frac{1}{3}$%
(E) 40%

22. What was the difference, if any, between the number of permanent workers employed by Corporation W on March 1$^{st}$ and on April 1$^{st}$?

(A)   0
(B)   50
(C)  100
(D)  150
(E)  200

23. Approximately what was the total number of units shipped by Corporation W for the months of January, February, and March, inclusive?

(A) 40,000
(B) 55,000
(C) 60,000
(D) 70,000
(E) 85,000

24. If, on May 1$^{st}$, 60 percent of the permanent workers and 40 percent of the temporary workers employed by Corporation W were women, how many of the workers employed by Corporation W at that time were women?

(A) 180
(B) 200
(C) 260
(D) 410
(E) 800

Items 25–29 refer to the following graphs.

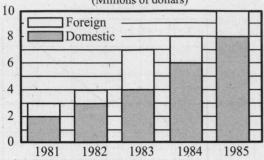

**COMPANY T**
**FOREIGN & DOMESTIC SALES**
(Millions of dollars)

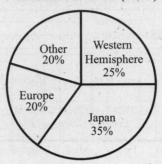

**COMPANY T**
**FOREIGN SALES (1985)**

25. What was the total dollar value of foreign sales by Company T in 1981 and 1982?

   (A) $1,000,000
   (B) $2,000,000
   (C) $3,000,000
   (D) $7,000,000
   (E) $12,000,000

26. What was the difference in the value of foreign sales by Company T between 1983 and 1985?

   (A) $1,000,000
   (B) $2,000,000
   (C) $3,000,000
   (D) $5,000,000
   (E) $6,000,000

27. In 1984, foreign sales accounted for what percent of total sales by Company T?

   (A) 15%
   (B) 20%
   (C) 25%
   (D) $33\frac{1}{3}$%
   (E) 40%

28. In 1985, what was the dollar value of sales by Company T to Europe?

   (A) $200,000
   (B) $400,000
   (C) $1,200,000
   (D) $1,600,000
   (E) $2,000,000

29. If sales to the Western Hemisphere in 1983 accounted for the same percent of foreign sales as to Japan in 1985, what was the dollar value of sales to the Western Hemisphere in 1983?

   (A) $1,050,000
   (B) $1,250,000
   (C) $1,375,000
   (D) $1,425,000
   (E) $1,555,000

# REVIEW

This section contains Graphs items for further practice.

**DIRECTIONS:** Each of the following questions has five answer choices. Select the best of the available choices. Answers are on page 1001.

<u>Items 1–5</u> refer to the following graphs.

**STUDENT ENROLLMENTS AND TEACHERS ON STAFF FOR SELECTED HIGH SCHOOLS**

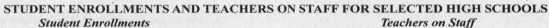

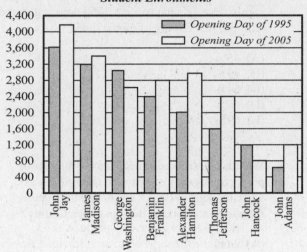

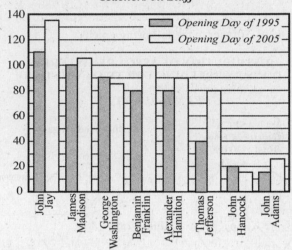

1. At how many of the schools shown did the number of students enrolled on opening day decline from 1995 to 2005?

   (A) 0
   (B) 1
   (C) 2
   (D) 3
   (E) 4

2. From 1995 to 2005, what was the largest increase in the number of students enrolled on opening day at any high school shown?

   (A)   250
   (B)   500
   (C)   600
   (D)   800
   (E) 1,000

3. Which of the following high schools shown had the highest teacher-to-student ratio on opening day of 1995?

   (A) Benjamin Franklin
   (B) Alexander Hamilton
   (C) Thomas Jefferson
   (D) John Hancock
   (E) John Adams

4. Which of the high schools shown had the greatest percent increase in the number of students enrolled on opening day from 1995 to 2005?

   (A) John Jay
   (B) Alexander Hamilton
   (C) Thomas Jefferson
   (D) John Hancock
   (E) John Adams

5. For the school that had the greatest percent increase in the number of teachers on staff on opening day from 1995 to 2005, the number of students enrolled on opening day increased by what percent?

(A) 20%
(B) 25%
(C) $33\frac{1}{3}\%$
(D) 50%
(E) 60%

Items 6–10 refer to the following graphs.

**DISTRIBUTION OF ASPCA REGISTERED DOGS BY BREEDING FOR TWO COUNTIES**

*GREEN COUNTY*

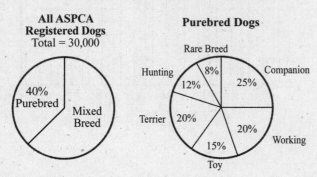

*POPE COUNTY*

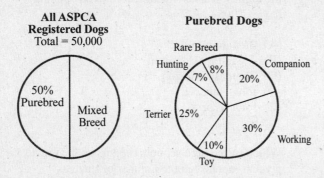

6. How many more purebred dogs are registered with the ASPCA in Pope County than in Green County?

(A) 6,000
(B) 7,500
(C) 10,400
(D) 13,000
(E) 15,500

7. How many more of the purebred dogs registered with the ASPCA in Green County are registered as companion dogs than as working dogs?

(A) 600
(B) 800
(C) 1,600
(D) 2,500
(E) 5,000

8. For Green County and Pope County combined, approximately what percent of all dogs registered with the ASPCA are of mixed breed?

(A) 45%
(B) 49%
(C) 54%
(D) 60%
(E) 69%

9. What is the difference between the number of purebred dogs registered with the ASPCA as working dogs in Pope County and the number registered as working dogs in Green County?

(A) 2,600
(B) 5,100
(C) 6,600
(D) 8,300
(E) 9,000

10. Which of the following statements can be inferred from the data?

I. More mixed-breed dogs are registered with the ASPCA in Green County than in Pope County.
II. More rare-breed purebred dogs are registered with the ASPCA in Green County than in Pope County.
III. In Pope County, twice as many companion dogs are registered with the ASPCA as toy dogs.

(A) I only
(B) III only
(C) I and II only
(D) I and III only
(E) II and III only

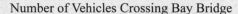

Items 11–13 refer to the following graph.

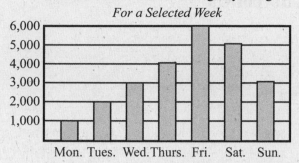

Number of Vehicles Crossing Bay Bridge
*For a Selected Week*

11. How many more vehicles crossed Bay Bridge on Saturday than on Sunday?

    (A) 1,000
    (B) 1,500
    (C) 2,000
    (D) 2,500
    (E) 3,000

12. During the week shown, the average number of vehicles crossing Bay Bridge each day was approximately

    (A) 2,100
    (B) 2,400
    (C) 2,800
    (D) 3,000
    (E) 3,500

13. The greatest percent increase in the number of vehicles crossing Bay Bridge occurred between

    (A) Monday and Tuesday
    (B) Tuesday and Wednesday
    (C) Wednesday and Thursday
    (D) Thursday and Friday
    (E) Friday and Saturday

Items 14–16 refer to the following graphs.

**NUMBER OF ENROLLED STUDENTS**

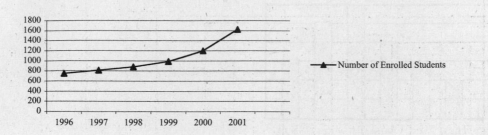

**BUDGET (IN CURRENT DOLLARS)**

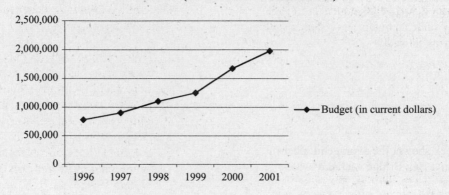

14. The average annual increase in the budget from 1996 to 2001 was approximately

   (A) $1,200,000
   (B) $750,000
   (C) $500,000
   (D) $240,000
   (E) $25,000

15. For which year did the budget show the greatest percent increase over the previous year?

   (A) 1997
   (B) 1998
   (C) 1999
   (D) 2000
   (E) 2001

16. The average per student expenditure was greatest in which year?

   (A) 1997
   (B) 1998
   (C) 1999
   (D) 2000
   (E) 2001

Items 17–19 refer to the following graph.

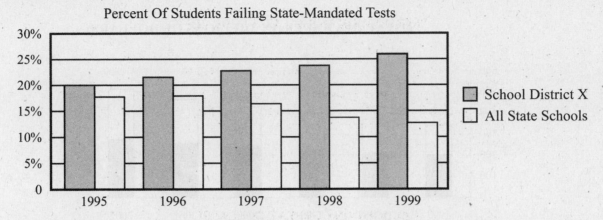

Percent Of Students Failing State-Mandated Tests

17. If School District X had 1,000 students in 1995, then how many students in District X failed state-mandated tests in that year?

(A) 220
(B) 200
(C) 180
(D) 80
(E) 20

18. If the state classifies as "failing" any school district in which the percent of students failing state-mandated tests exceeds that of all state schools by 50%, in which year was School District X first classified as "failing"?

(A) 1995
(B) 1996
(C) 1997
(D) 1998
(E) 1999

19. Which of the following statements is supported by the data in the graph?

(A) The percent of students in School District X failing state-mandated tests increased by more than 25% from 1995 to 1999.
(B) The number of students in all state schools failing state-mandated tests fell by 50% from 1995 to 1999.
(C) The number of students in all state schools failing state-mandated tests dropped from 1996 to 1999.
(D) The number of students failing state-mandated tests in School District X increased in each of the years between 1996 and 1999.
(E) The number of schools in District X with students failing state-mandated tests exceeded the number of schools statewide in each year shown.

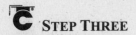

Items 20–22 refer to the following graphs.

## TOTAL REVENUES (IN MILLIONS OF DOLLARS)

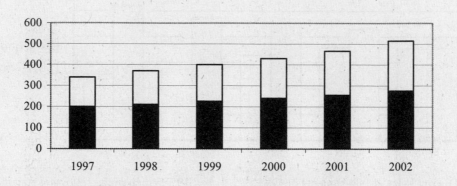

## SOURCES OF CONSULTING SERVICES REVENUES—2002

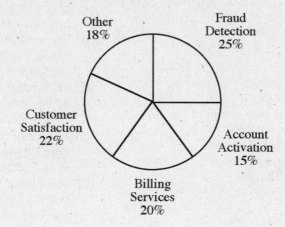

20. Total revenues were approximately how much greater in 2001 than in 1998?

(A) $40 million
(B) $75 million
(C) $95 million
(D) $110 million
(E) $125 million

21. From 1998 to 2002, the percent increase in revenues derived from consulting services increased by approximately what percent?

(A) 18%
(B) 33.3%
(C) 40%
(D) 50%
(E) 95%

22. In 2002, the amount of revenue derived from consulting on account activation accounted for what percent of the total revenue for that year?

(A) 3%
(B) 7%
(C) 11%
(D) 18%
(E) 23%

Items 23–25 refer to the following graphs.

**STUDENT ENROLLMENT AT UNIVERSITY X**

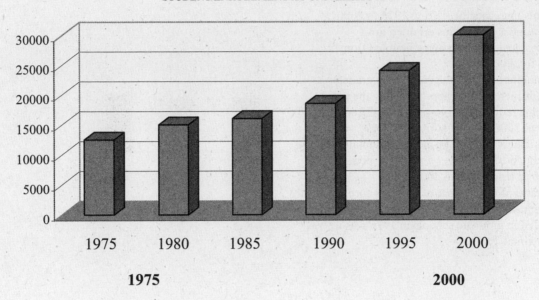

**1975**

**2000**

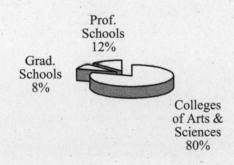

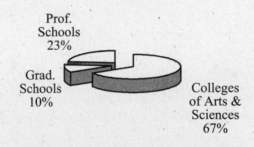

23. In 1975, the number of students enrolled in professional schools at University X was approximately

  (A) 1,000
  (B) 1,500
  (C) 1,800
  (D) 2,400
  (E) 10,000

24. Approximately how many more students were enrolled in the College of Arts & Sciences in 2000 than in 1975?

  (A) 12,500
  (B) 10,000
  (C) 8,500
  (D) 7,500
  (E) 6,000

25. The graphs provide support for which of the
    following conclusions?

    (A) The number of students enrolled in graduate
        schools increased by $\frac{1}{5}$ from 1975 to 2000.
    (B) The number of students enrolled in
        professional schools almost doubled from
        1975 to 2000.
    (C) The number of students enrolled in graduate
        schools increased by approximately the same
        percentage for each five-year period from
        1980 to 2000.
    (D) The greatest percentage increase in total
        student enrollment over a five-year period
        occurred from 1995 to 2000.
    (E) The ratio of the number of students enrolled
        in graduate schools in 2000 to the number
        enrolled in graduate schools in 1975 was
        approximately 3 : 1.

Items 26–28 refer to the following graph.

**Number of Households in County X by Income**

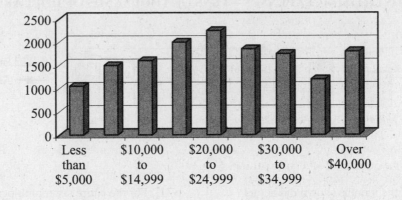

26. How many households in County X had incomes between $20,000 and $29,999?

(A) 1,850
(B) 2,250
(C) 4,100
(D) 4,500
(E) 4,800

27. By approximately what percent did the number of households in County X with incomes between $15,000 and $19,999 exceed the number with incomes between $10,000 and $14,999?

(A) 10%
(B) 15%
(C) 20%
(D) 25%
(E) 33.3%

28. According to the graph, which of the following statements must be true?

(A) The number of people living in County X in households with incomes greater than $30,000 but less than $34,999 is 1,750.
(B) The median income for households in County X is between $20,000 and $24,999.
(C) The total income of all households in County X with incomes below $5,000 is less than $25,000.
(D) More households in County X earned between $15,000 and $19,999 than earned between $5,000 and $14,999.
(E) Total household income for those households in County X with incomes between $35,000 and $39,999 was greater than for those households with incomes between $30,000 and $34,999.

Items 29–31 refer to the following graph.

**ADVERTISING EXPENSES—TENS OF THOUSANDS OF DOLLARS**

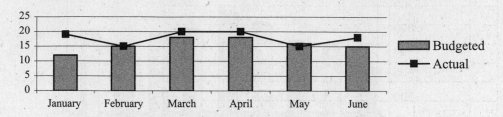

29. For how many of the months shown did actual advertising expenses exceed budgeted advertising expenses?

   (A) 2
   (B) 3
   (C) 4
   (D) 5
   (E) 6

30. In which of the following months was the ratio of actual advertising expenses to budgeted expenses the highest?

   (A) January
   (B) February
   (C) March
   (D) May
   (E) June

31. For the entire six-month period shown, total actual advertising expenses exceeded budgeted advertising expenses by

   (A) $1,300
   (B) $9,400
   (C) $10,700
   (D) $13,000
   (E) $100,700

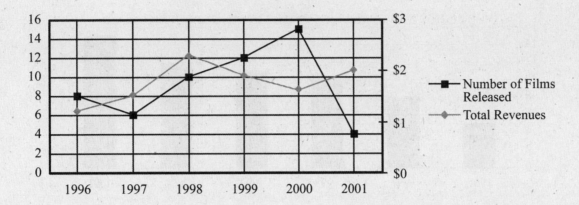

Items 32–34 refer to the following graph.

**ACTIVITY OF FILM STUDIO F**
(REVENUES IN MILLIONS)

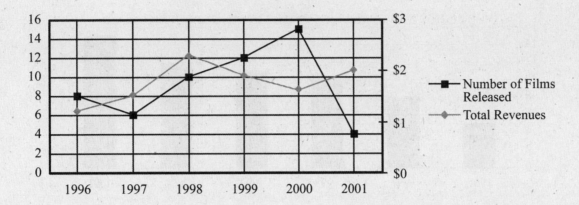

32. For the period between 1996 and 2001, Film Studio F released how many films?

(A) 40
(B) 46
(C) 49
(D) 52
(E) 55

33. In which year did the films released by Film Studio F generate the greatest revenues per film?

(A) 1997
(B) 1998
(C) 1999
(D) 2000
(E) 2001

34. In how many of the years shown was the average revenue per film released greater than $200,000?

(A) 0
(B) 1
(C) 2
(D) 3
(E) 4

Items 35–37 refer to the following graphs.

**SALES IN THE UNITED STATES (BILLIONS OF DOLLARS)**

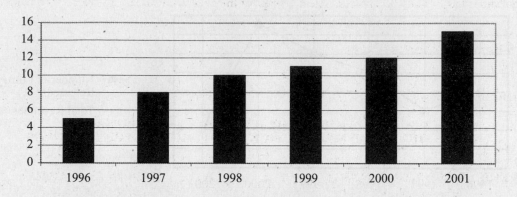

**SALES OF COMPANY X BY REGION—2001**

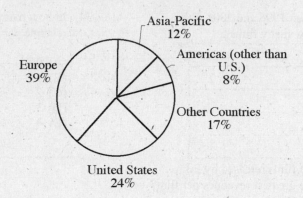

35. Average annual sales by Company X in the United States for the period between 1996 and 2001 was most nearly

    (A) $4.5 billion
    (B) $6 billion
    (C) $7.5 billion
    (D) $8.2 billion
    (E) $10 billion

36. In which year did the annual sales of Company X in the United States show the greatest percentage increase over the previous year?

    (A) 1997
    (B) 1998
    (C) 1999
    (D) 2000
    (E) 2001

37. Sales of Company X for 2001 in Europe were most nearly

    (A) $12 billion
    (B) $18 billion
    (C) $21 billion
    (D) $24 billion
    (E) $27 billion

# TIMED-PRACTICE QUIZZES

**DIRECTIONS:** This section contains three Graphs quizzes. Complete each quiz while being timed. Each of the following questions has five answer choices. Select the best of the available choices. Answers are on page 1001.

## QUIZ I (5 items; 7 minutes)

Items 1–5 refer to the following graphs.

### NEW AND PREVIOUSLY OWNED VEHICLES REGISTERED IN
### KING COUNTY AND MEDIAN DECLARED PURCHASE PRICE, 1991-1995

**VEHICLE REGISTRATIONS**
(Thousands)

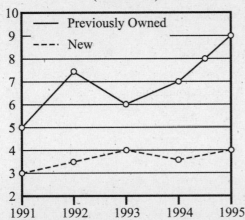

**MEDIAN DECLARED
PURCHASE PRICE**

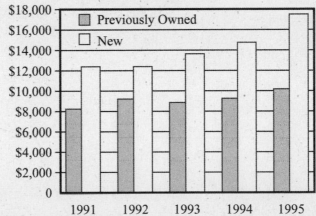

1. According to the information in the graph, the number of new vehicles registered in 1992 was approximately

   (A)  2,500
   (B)  3,500
   (C)  5,000
   (D)  7,500
   (E) 12,500

2. From 1991 to 1995, for how many years was there an increase over the previous year in the number of registrations of both "Previously Owned" vehicles and "New" vehicles?

   (A) 0
   (B) 1
   (C) 2
   (D) 3
   (E) 4

3. From 1993 to 1995, the percent increase in the number of registrations of previously owned vehicles was closest to

   (A)  30%
   (B)  50%
   (C)  60%
   (D)  80%
   (E) 125%

4. In the year in which the median declared purchase price for previously owned vehicles was closest to that for new vehicles, there were how many registrations of previously owned vehicles?

   (A) 5,000
   (B) 6,000
   (C) 7,500
   (D) 8,000
   (E) 9,000

5. In 1991, the median declared purchase price of a previously owned vehicle was approximately what percent of the median declared purchase price of a new vehicle?

(A) 25%
(B) 40%
(C) 50%
(D) 65%
(E) 80%

## QUIZ II (5 items; 7 minutes)

Items 1–5 refer to the following graphs.

DISTRIBUTION OF PRIVATE SECTOR WORKFORCE
FOR WASHINGTON AND
WARREN COUNTIES

WASHINGTON COUNTY
Total = 120,000

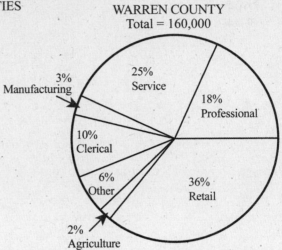

WARREN COUNTY
Total = 160,000

1.  In Washington County, how many workers are
    employed in the professional sector?

    (A) 14,400
    (B) 16,000
    (C) 17,500
    (D) 25,600
    (E) 30,100

2.  For Warren County, how many employment
    categories include more than 24,000 people?

    (A) 1
    (B) 2
    (C) 3
    (D) 4
    (E) 5

3.  Warren County has how many more people in the
    Clerical category than Washington County?

    (A) 8,800
    (B) 7,000
    (C) 5,600
    (D) 4,500
    (E) 3,200

4.  The ratio of the number of persons in the Service
    category in Washington County to the number of
    persons in the Service category in Warren County
    is

    (A) 1 : 2
    (B) 3 : 4
    (C) 1
    (D) 4 : 3
    (E) 2

5. For how many of the categories is the number of people employed in Washington County greater than the number of people employed in Warren County?

(A) 0
(B) 1
(C) 2
(D) 3
(E) 4

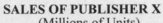

## QUIZ III (5 items; 7 minutes)

Items 1–5 refer to the following graphs.

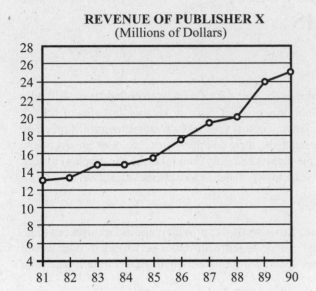

**REVENUE OF PUBLISHER X**
(Millions of Dollars)

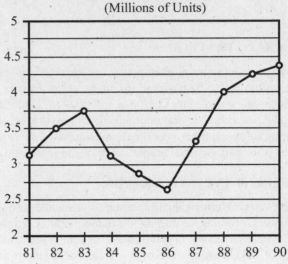

**SALES OF PUBLISHER X**
(Millions of Units)

1. Revenues of Publisher X were most nearly equal in which of the following years?

   (A) 1981 and 1982
   (B) 1982 and 1983
   (C) 1983 and 1984
   (D) 1984 and 1985
   (E) 1985 and 1986

2. Publisher X sold approximately how many more units in 1988 than in 1984?

   (A)   800,000
   (B) 1,100,000
   (C) 1,400,000
   (D) 1,800,000
   (E) 2,200,000

3. In 1982, Publisher X sold 700,000 units from its fiction line. The fiction line accounted for what percent of the total number of units sold?

   (A)   5%
   (B) 10%
   (C) 15%
   (D) 20%
   (E) 25%

4. How many years after the year 1981 show both an increase in unit sales and an increase in revenues?

   (A) 2
   (B) 3
   (C) 4
   (D) 5
   (E) 6

5. What was the approximate difference between the average revenue per unit generated in 1988 and in 1982?

   (A) $1.20
   (B) $1.70
   (C) $2.50
   (D) $3.25
   (E) $4.10

# Cambridge TestPrep™

## Strategy Summary Sheet
# GRAPHS

## GENERAL STRATEGIES:

Graphs provide pictorial information accompanied by mathematical problems. An extremely steep ladder of difficulty holds within a five-item group of Graphs items. Graphs consist not only of lines, bars, or sectors, but also of title(s), legends, scales, and other clarifying information. Understanding data in context thus takes an investment of time. You may need to calculate minimum/maximum, averages, ratios/percentages, increases/decreases, etc. Get an overview, scanning titles and other verbal cues to understand context. Read the item(s) carefully, and return to the graph(s) to seek needed information. Since graphs are drawn to scale, you can use your answer sheet as a crude measuring device.

## DIFFERENT TYPES OF GRAPHS:

*Table Charts*: Numerical information is presented in matrix form. Rows (records) provide various occurrences (e.g., customers, locations, or accounting transactions). Columns (fields) contain specific attributes pertaining to each record (e.g., purchases, sales, or payments over time). Items may ask for specific information about data within a particular record or field, a group of records or fields, or the entire table.

*Bar Graphs*: A set of vertical bars denotes comparative numerical values (*y*-axis values). The horizontal (*x*-axis) labels, along with graph title(s), indicate the information being tracked (e.g., days of the week, locations of sales, or names of customers). Information may be statistical (histogram or frequency chart). More complicated graphs may contain a group of bars arranged by sets, described via a legend (e.g., sales within specific territories over varying points in time). Alternatively, this type of information could be handled via stacked bar graphs.

*Line Graphs*: When the horizontal axis is time-related, a series of points may be plotted to denote level of activity over time for various parties. To distinguish the different parties being tracked, the points and/or the lines connecting them will have distinct formats, as indicated by the legend. While discerning trends and intersections is easy, reading values can become somewhat difficult. Using the edge of a piece of paper as a straight-edge may prove valuable.

*Cumulating Bar Graphs*: Cumulating bar graphs are more complex bar graphs. A set of elements is tracked at each instance along the horizontal axis, as described in the legend. The height/value of the lowest component and the entire bar can be directly read from the vertical scale. Otherwise, specific values can be calculated by subtraction or by using your answer sheet to construct a linear scale.

*Pie Graphs*: Pie graphs best describe percentages of resource allocation over various parties at a specific point in time. The percentages must total 100%. These graphs are often used in combination with another type of graph, such as a stacked bar graph. In these cases, you need to find the link between the two different graphs (e.g., a particular point in time).

NOTES: _____

_____

_____

_____

_____

# Analytical Writing Skills Review

# CAMBRIDGE TESTPREP™

## ANALYTICAL WRITING SKILLS REVIEW OUTLINE

# Common Grammatical Errors

## Subject-Verb Agreement

One common grammatical error is lack of agreement between subject and verb. The simplest subject-verb disagreements are usually obvious, as in the following examples. Note: Throughout this Analytical Writing Skills Review, ✓ = correct, and ✗ = wrong.

*Examples:*

The books <u>is</u> on the shelf. ✗

The books <u>are</u> on the shelf. ✓

The teacher <u>admonish</u> the class to calm down. ✗

The teacher <u>admonished</u> the class to calm down. ✓

In order to test your ability to spot such errors, test-writers may use one of the three following tricks:

**WHAT OBSCURES SUBJECT-VERB AGREEMENT**

1. Material Inserted Between Subject and Verb

2. Inverted Sentence Structure

3. Use of Compound Subjects

### Material Inserted Between Subject and Verb

*Examples:*

Star <u>performers</u> in the movies or on television usually <u>earns</u> substantial income from royalties. ✗

One school of thought maintains that the federal <u>deficit</u>, not exorbitant corporate profits or excessively high wages, <u>cause</u> most of the inflation we are now experiencing. ✗

A recent survey shows that a <u>household</u> in which both the wife and the husband are pursuing careers <u>stand</u> a better chance of surviving intact than one in which only the husband works. ✗

In each of these three sentences, the subject and verb do not agree: "performers…earns," "deficit…cause," and "household…stand." However, the errors may not be immediately evident because of the intervening material. In the first sentence, the subject is separated from the verb by prepositional phrases. In the second sentence, the subject and the verb are separated by a parenthetical expression. In the third sentence, a clause intervenes between the subject and the verb.

The plausibility of the incorrect verb choice, and therefore the chance that the error will go unnoticed, is strengthened when test-writers place a word or phrase near the verb that might be mistaken for the subject: "television…earns," "profits and wages…cause," and "careers…stand." If the first word of each of these pairs had been the subject, then there would have been no failure of agreement.

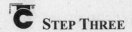 

*Inverted Sentence Structure*

A second common problem of subject-verb agreement is ***inverted sentence structure***. In an inverted sentence, the verb precedes the subject. You should pay careful attention to the agreement between subject and verb, no matter how those elements are ordered.

*Examples:*

> Although the first amendment to the Constitution does guarantee freedom of speech, the Supreme Court has long recognized that there has to be some restrictions on the exercise of this right. ✖
>
> Jennifer must have been doubly pleased that day, for seated in the gallery to watch her receive the award was her brother, her parents, and her husband. ✖

In both of these sentences, the subjects and verbs do not agree. The relationships are obscured by the order in which the elements appear in the sentence—the verbs come before the subjects. These sentences should read:

> Although the first amendment to the Constitution does guarantee freedom of speech, the Supreme Court has long recognized that there <u>have</u> to be some restrictions on the exercise of this right. ✓
>
> Jennifer must have been doubly pleased that day, for seated in the gallery to watch her receive the award <u>were</u> her brother, her parents, and her husband. ✓

---

### WATCH FOR INVERTED SENTENCE STRUCTURES

 Regardless of the order of the sentence—subject-verb or verb-subject—the verb must always agree with its subject. If a sentence has a complex structure, it often helps to look at each element in isolation.

---

*Use of Compound Subjects*

Finally, be alert for ***compound subjects***. Usually, when the subject of a sentence consists of two or more elements joined by the conjunction "and," the subject is considered plural and requires a plural verb. Consider the following example:

*Example:*

> Of the seven candidates, only John, Bill, and Jim <u>was</u> past office holders. ✖

The subject, "John, Bill, and Jim," is compound (joined by "and") and requires the plural verb "were"—even though the individual nouns are singular.

---

### WATCH FOR COMPOUND SUBJECTS

 Compound subjects, typically two or more subjects joined by "and," are plural and need a plural verb.

---

Be careful not to confuse the compound subject with the disjunctive subject. When elements of the subject are joined by "or," the verb must agree with the element nearest to it. Replacing "and" with "or" changes our previous example:

*Example:*

Of the seven candidates, John, Bill, or Jim <u>is</u> likely to win. ✓

The elements are joined by "or," so the verb must agree with "John" or "Bill" or "Jim." The verb "is" correctly agrees with the disjunctive subject.

Additionally, watch out for subjects that are designed to look like compound subjects but which are actually singular. Typically, these subjects are disguised using pronouns.

*Example:*

Neither one of those fools even <u>know</u> how to change a light bulb. ✖

The subject is not "those fools"; instead, it is the singular subject "Neither one." Thus, the singular verb "knows" is required.

---

### WATCH FOR DISJUNCTIVE AND SINGULAR SUBJECTS

1. If the elements of the subject are joined by "or," the subject is disjunctive. The verb must agree with the closest element of the subject.

2. Be alert for singular subjects that appear to be plural (typically pronouns).

---

## Pronoun Usage

The rules for ***pronoun usage*** are summarized below.

---

### PRONOUN USAGE RULES

1. A pronoun must have an antecedent (referent) to which it refers.

2. The pronoun must refer clearly to the antecedent.

3. The pronoun and antecedent must agree.

4. The pronoun must have the proper case.

---

### *Pronouns Must Have Antecedents*

A ***pronoun*** is used as a substitute for a noun. The noun that it replaces is called the ***antecedent*** (referent). With the exception of certain idioms such as "It is raining," a pronoun that does not have an antecedent is used incorrectly.

*Examples:*

Although Glen is president of the student body, he has not yet passed his English exam, and because of <u>it</u>, he will not graduate with the rest of his class. ✖

The damage done by Senator Smith's opposition to the policy of equal employment is undeniable, but <u>that</u> is exactly what he attempted to do in his speech on Thursday. ✘

In the first example, what is the antecedent of "it"? It is not "he has not yet passed his English exam," because that is a complete thought, or clause, not just a noun. "It" is not a pronoun substitute for that entire thought. Rather, "it" refers to Glen's "failure" to pass the exam, thereby providing "it" with the required antecedent. However, "failure" does not appear in noun form in the sentence. In other words, "it" wants to refer to a noun, but there is no noun to function as its point of reference. The sentence must be rewritten: "because of that fact, he will not graduate…."

In the second example, "that" functions as a relative pronoun—it relates something in the first clause to the second clause. However, to what does "that" refer? Test possibilities by substituting them for "that" in the second clause. The sentence should make sense when you replace the pronoun with its antecedent. Is the antecedent "damage"?

but <u>damage</u> is exactly what he attempted to do…. ✘

Perhaps, then, the antecedent is <u>opposition</u> or <u>undeniable</u>:

but <u>opposition</u> is exactly what he attempted to do…. ✘

but <u>undeniable</u> is exactly what he attempted to do…. ✘

There are no other candidates for the antecedent, so we must conclude that the use of "that" is incorrect. Most likely, what the writer intended to say was that the Senator attempted to deny the damage:

The damage done by Senator Smith's opposition to the policy of equal employment is undeniable, but he attempted to deny that damage in his speech on Thursday. ✔

---

### PRONOUNS MUST HAVE ANTECEDENTS

 Except for a few idiomatic expressions ("It" is getting late, "It" will be sunny today), every pronoun must have an antecedent. An antecedent must be a noun, not a thought or phrase. Identify a pronoun's antecedent and then check that it is correct by substituting it for the pronoun in the sentence.

---

### Antecedents Must Be Clear

The antecedent of a pronoun must be made clear from the structure of the sentence. Consider these examples:

*Examples:*

Edward's father died before <u>he</u> reached his 20<sup>th</sup> birthday, so <u>he</u> never finished his education. ✘

In 1980, the University Council voted to rescind Provision 3, <u>which</u> made it easier for some students to graduate. ✘

In the first example, it is not clear whether the father died before he reached the age of 20 or before Edward reached the age of 20. Furthermore, it is not clear whose education remained unfinished. Similarly, in the second example, the antecedent of "which" is not clear. "Which" may refer to Provision 3 or it may refer to the University Council's vote to rescind Provision 3.

## WATCH FOR UNCLEAR ANTECEDENTS

The antecedent of a pronoun must be clearly identified by the structure of the sentence.

*Example:*

The letter is on the desk <u>that</u> we received yesterday. ✗

The letter <u>that</u> we received yesterday is on the desk. ✓

Finally, the impersonal use of "it," "they," and "you" tends to produce vague, wordy sentences.

*Examples:*

In the manual <u>it</u> says to make three copies. ✗

The manual says to make three copies. ✓

<u>They</u> predict we are in for a cold, wet winter. ✗

The almanac predicts a cold, wet winter. ✓

### *Pronoun-Antecedent Agreement*

The pronoun must agree with its antecedent. Consider the following example:

*Example:*

Historically, the college dean was also a professor, but today <u>they</u> are usually administrators. ✗

In the example, "they" must refer to "dean," but "dean" is singular and "they" is plural. The sentence can be corrected in one of two ways: by changing the first clause to the plural or by changing the second clause to the singular.

Historically, college deans were also professors, but today they are usually administrators. ✓

Historically, the college dean was also a professor, but today the dean is usually an administrator. ✓

## WATCH FOR PRONOUN-ANTECEDENT AGREEMENT

If the antecedent is singular, the pronoun must be singular; if the antecedent is plural, the pronoun must be plural.

Finally, it is incorrect to use different forms of the same pronoun to refer to an antecedent. This error results in the sentence having different antecedents and therefore a *shifting subject*.

## WATCH FOR SHIFTING SUBJECTS

Watch for shifting subject errors. These errors occur if different forms of the same pronoun are used to refer to the antecedent.

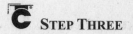 

*Example:*

> The teacher told John that <u>he</u> thought <u>his</u> work was improving. ✘

Does the teacher think that his own work is improving or that John's work is improving? The correct sentence reads: "The teacher told John that John's work was improving."

***Pronouns Must Have Proper Case***

A pronoun must agree with its antecedent in case, number, and person. The pronoun's function in a sentence determines which case should be used. You should be familiar with the following three categories of pronoun case: nominative (or subjective), objective, and possessive.

---

**TYPES OF PRONOUN CASE**

✎ *Nominative (subjective)* case pronouns are used as subjects of sentences.

✎ *Objective* case pronouns are used as objects: direct objects, indirect objects, and objects of prepositions. If a prepositional phrase ends with a pronoun, it must be an objective pronoun.

✎ *Possessive* case pronouns are used to show possession. Use a possessive pronoun preceding a gerund. A gerund is the "-ing" form of a verb that is used as a noun.

✎ *Interrogative* pronouns stand in for the answer to a question.

---

The following examples illustrate correct usage of pronoun case.

*Examples:*

> *Nominative*: <u>I</u> thought <u>he</u> would like the gift <u>we</u> bought. ✔
>
> *Objective*: The choice for the part is between Bob and <u>me</u>. ✔ (The object pronoun <u>me</u> follows the preposition <u>between</u>.)
>
> *Possessive*: Do you mind <u>my</u> using your computer? ✔ (The possessive pronoun <u>my</u> precedes the gerund <u>using</u>.)
>
> *Interrogative*: <u>Who</u> is the starting pitcher for the Orioles today? ✔

---

**EXAMPLES OF PRONOUN CASE**

| | Nominative Case | | Objective Case | | Possessive Case | |
|---|---|---|---|---|---|---|
| | *Singular* | *Plural* | *Singular* | *Plural* | *Singular* | *Plural* |
| 1st Person: | I | we | me | us | my | our |
| 2nd Person: | you | you | you | you | your | your |
| 3rd Person: | he, she, it | they | him, her, it | them | his, her, its | their |
| *Interrogative:* | who | who | whom | whom | whose | whose |

---

The following are additional examples of the *nominative*, or subjective, pronoun case.

*Examples:*

> John and <u>him</u> were chosen. ✘
>
> John and <u>he</u> were chosen. ✔ (<u>He</u> is the subject of the verb; we certainly would not say that <u>him</u> was chosen.)
>
> It was <u>her</u> who was chosen. ✘
>
> <u>She</u> was chosen. ✔
>
> <u>Us</u> student-workers decided to organize into a union. ✘
>
> <u>We</u> student-workers decided to organize into a union. ✔
>
> He is as witty as <u>her</u>. ✘
>
> He is as witty as <u>she</u> is. ✔
>
> <u>Whom</u> do you suppose will win the election? ✘
>
> <u>Who</u> do you suppose will win the election? ✔

The following are additional examples of the *objective* pronoun case.

*Examples:*

> They accused Tom and <u>he</u> of stealing. ✘
>
> They accused Tom and <u>him</u> of stealing. ✔ (<u>Him</u> is the object of the verb <u>accused</u>; they accused <u>him</u>, not <u>he</u>.)
>
> The tickets were given to Bill and <u>I</u>. ✘
>
> The tickets were given to Bill and <u>me</u>. ✔ (<u>Me</u> is the object of <u>to</u>; the tickets were given to <u>me</u>, not to <u>I</u>.)
>
> <u>Who</u> did you see? ✘
>
> <u>Whom</u> did you see? ✔ (Hint: Make this a declarative sentence: "You saw <u>him</u>." You would not say, "You saw <u>he</u>.")

An easy way to remember when to use "who" versus "whom" is that in those situations that "him" (or "her") would be appropriate, "whom" should be used; in those situations that "he" (or "she") would be appropriate, "who" should be used.

Finally, personal pronouns that express ownership never require an apostrophe. Also, a pronoun that precedes a gerund ("-ing" verb form used as a noun) is usually the possessive case.

*Examples:*

> This book is <u>your's</u>, not <u>her's</u>. ✘
>
> This book is <u>yours</u>, not <u>hers</u>. ✔
>
> He rejoiced at <u>him</u> going to the party. ✘
>
> He rejoiced at <u>his</u> going to the party. ✔

Some pronouns are either singular or plural, while others can be both. The structure and intended meaning of the sentence indicate whether the pronoun is singular or plural.

 **SINGULAR AND/OR PLURAL PRONOUNS**

*Singular*: anybody, another, everybody, everything, somebody, something, nobody, one, anyone, everyone, someone, no one, each, every, neither, either, much

*Plural*: both, few, many, most, several

*Singular & Plural*: all, any, half, more, none, some

Technically, pronouns are divided into eight formal categories:

 **FORMAL CATEGORIES OF PRONOUNS**

*Personal*: I, we, my, mine, our, ours, me, us, you, your, yours, he, she, it, they, his, hers, its, their, theirs, him, her, them

*Demonstrative*: this, these, that, those

*Indefinite*: all, any, anything, both, each, either, one, everyone, everybody, everything, few, many, more, neither, none, somebody, someone, something

*Relative*: who, whose, whom, which, of which, that, of that, what, of what

*Interrogative*: who, whose, whom, which, of which, what, of what

*Numerical*: one, two, three, first, second, third

*Reflexive/Intensive*: myself, ourselves, yourself, yourselves, himself, herself, itself, themselves

*Reciprocal*: each other, one another

*Example:*

Many of the students <u>which</u> were participating in the spelling bee had been finalists last year. ✖

In the above example, the pronoun "which" refers to "Many of the students" and it is the incorrect pronoun choice. Instead, the sentence should read: "Many…who were participating…."

## Adjectives vs. Adverbs

*Adjectives Modify Nouns, Adverbs Modify Verbs*

*Adjectives* are used to modify nouns, while *adverbs* are used to modify verbs, adjectives, or other adverbs.

*Example:*

No matter how <u>quick</u> he played, Rich never beat Julie when playing the card game "speed." ✗

In the above example, "quick" is intended to modify the speed with which Rich played cards. However, "quick" is an adjective and therefore cannot be used to modify a verb. By adding "-ly" to the end of "quick," we can transform it into an adverb and the sentence reads: "No matter how quickly he played...."

The following examples further illustrate the proper use of adjectives and adverbs.

*Examples:*

*Adjectives*: Mr. Jackson is a <u>good</u> teacher. ✓

He is a <u>bad</u> driver. ✓

There has been a <u>considerable</u> change in the weather. ✓

My sister is a <u>superb</u> dancer. ✓

The teacher gave a <u>quick</u> explanation of the problem. ✓

This is a <u>slow</u> exercise. ✓

*Adverbs*: Mr. Jackson teaches <u>well</u>. ✓

He drives <u>badly</u>. ✓

The weather has changed <u>considerably</u>. ✓

My sister dances <u>superbly</u>. ✓

The teacher explained the problem <u>quickly</u>. ✓

This exercise must be done <u>slowly</u>. ✓

The first three of the following examples underscore that adjectives, not adverbs, must be used to modify nouns. The remaining examples show that adverbs, not adjectives, must be used to modify verbs and adjectives.

*Examples:*

He said that the medicine tasted <u>terribly</u>. ✗
He said that the medicine tasted <u>terrible</u>. ✓

The dog remained <u>faithfully</u> to its master until the end. ✗
The dog remained <u>faithful</u> to its master until the end. ✓

I felt <u>badly</u> about forgetting the appointment. ✗
I felt <u>bad</u> about forgetting the appointment. ✓

He can do the job <u>easier</u> than you can. ✗
He can do the job more <u>easily</u> than you can. ✓

The problem seemed <u>exceeding</u> complex to me. ✘

The problem seemed <u>exceedingly</u> complex to me. ✔

It rained <u>steady</u> all day yesterday. ✘

It rained <u>steadily</u> all day yesterday. ✔

The professor presented an <u>obvious</u> important point in class. ✘

The professor presented an <u>obviously</u> important point in class. ✔

We all agreed that the new film was <u>real</u> funny. ✘

We all agreed that the new film was <u>really</u> funny. ✔

The students found the physics examination <u>extreme</u> difficult. ✘

The students found the physics examination <u>extremely</u> difficult. ✔

If you speak <u>firm</u>, he will listen to you. ✘

If you speak <u>firmly</u>, he will listen to you. ✔

He made <u>considerable</u> more progress than I did. ✘

He made <u>considerably</u> more progress than I did. ✔

### Linking Verbs

**Linking verbs** are followed by adjectives, not adverbs. The following is a list of common linking verbs.

| | COMMON LINKING VERBS | | | |
|---|---|---|---|---|
| be | become | appear | look | seem |
| remain | feel | smell | sound | taste |

Note that some of the verbs listed as linking verbs may sometimes function as verbs of action. The following examples illustrate this point.

*Examples:*

*Adjectives*:  I feel <u>tired</u>. ✔

He looked <u>angry</u>. ✔

The pie tastes <u>delicious</u>. ✔

*Adverbs*:  I felt my way <u>slowly</u> in the darkness. ✔

He looked about the room <u>angrily</u>. ✔

She tasted the pie <u>cautiously</u>. ✔

*Watch for Adjectives Posing as Adverbs*

> ### WATCH FOR ADJECTIVE-ADVERB SWITCHING
>
> Be alert for adjectives posing in place of adverbs and vice versa. Adjectives can usually be transformed into adverbs by adding "-ly." However, verbs must be modified by adverbs, not simply an adjective posing as an adverb.

*Examples:*

The girl looks <u>intelligently</u>. ✘
The girl looks <u>intelligent</u>. ✓

That perfume smells <u>sweetly</u>, doesn't it? ✘
That perfume smells <u>sweet</u>, doesn't it? ✓

The physician appeared <u>nervously</u> when he talked to the patient. ✘
The physician appeared <u>nervous</u> when he talked to the patient. ✓

This bed seems very <u>comfortably</u>. ✘
This bed seems very <u>comfortable</u>. ✓

Several people arrived too <u>lately</u> to be admitted to the performance. ✘ ("Lately" is not an adverb for "late." Instead, "lately" means "as of late.")
Several people arrived too <u>late</u> to be admitted to the performance. ✓

The horse ran <u>fastly</u> enough to win the race. ✘ ("Fastly" is not a word!)
The horse ran <u>fast</u> enough to win the race. ✓

The architect worked <u>hardly</u> to finish his drawings by the next day. ✘ ("Hardly" is not an adverb for "hard." Instead, "hardly" means "barely.")
The architect worked <u>hard</u> to finish his drawings by the next day. ✓

## Double Negatives

It is true that we all hear and sometimes say *double negatives* in daily conversation. However, double negatives are NOT acceptable in standard written English.

*Example:*

I <u>hadn't hardly</u> begun to understand Spanish when I had to move again. ✘

The phrase "hadn't hardly" is a double negative. The sentence should read: "I had hardly begun to understand...."

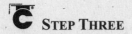 

---

**WATCH FOR DOUBLE NEGATIVES**

Watch for double negatives ("not barely," "hardly nothing")—they are always incorrect.

---

## Nouns and Noun Clauses

*Nouns* are names of people, places, things, or ideas; they are used to indicate the subject of a sentence. Like pronouns, nouns have a case.

---

**TYPES OF NOUN CASE**

🖊 *Nominative (Subjective)* case is used when the noun is the subject of the sentence.

🖊 *Objective* case is used when the noun is an indirect or direct object or is the object of a preposition.

🖊 *Possessive* case is used when nouns are intended to show possession.

---

Sometimes the place of the noun in a sentence is filled by a *noun clause* instead of a single noun. A noun clause is a dependent clause.

*Example:*

<u>That Judy was chosen for the promotion</u> is not surprising. ✔

The failure to properly introduce a noun clause is an error of sentence structure. "That" by itself is not the noun, nor is "Judy was chosen for the promotion" a noun. However, the two combined create a noun clause and function as the noun.

---

**RULE FOR INTRODUCING NOUN CLAUSES**

 A noun clause is a group of words that functions as the subject (or another noun usage) of a sentence. "That" is often the best word to use to introduce noun clauses.

---

*Examples:*

The reason the saxophone is popular is <u>because</u> its timbre can approximate that of the human voice. ✖

The reason the saxophone is popular is <u>that</u> its timbre can approximate that of the human voice. ✓

<u>Why</u> American car manufacturers did not reduce car sizes earlier than they did is a mystery to most market experts. ✖

<u>That</u> American car manufacturers did not reduce car sizes earlier than they did is a mystery to most market experts. ✓

The above examples make the error of introducing noun clauses with <u>because</u> and <u>why</u>. In both sentences, a noun clause is required; <u>that</u> should be used in both cases.

---

**WATCH FOR "BECAUSE" AND "WHY" AS NOUN CLAUSE INTRODUCTIONS**

 Noun clauses must be introduced by "that," not "because" or "why."

---

Additionally, DO NOT use "where" for "that" in object clauses.

*Example:*

I saw in the bulletin <u>where</u> Mrs. Wagner's retirement was announced. ✖

I saw in the bulletin <u>that</u> Mrs. Wagner's retirement was announced. ✓

However, if the subject of the sentence actually is about where something is, then use "where."

*Examples:*

<u>Where</u> the wedding had initially been scheduled is not where it ended up being held. ✓

All I want to know is <u>where</u> we are supposed to go for homeroom attendance. ✓

# Common Grammatical Errors

**DIRECTIONS:** For items #1–25, circle the letter of the underlined part of the sentence containing the grammatical error. Answers are on page 1005.

1. The professor deals <u>harsh</u> with students <u>who are</u>
                     A                   B
   <u>not prepared</u>, and <u>he is</u> even <u>more severe</u> with
    B            C           D
   those who plagiarize.

2. A recent study <u>indicates</u> that the average person
                  A
   <u>ignores</u> most commercial advertising and <u>does</u>
    B                            C
   <u>not buy</u> products <u>because of them</u>.
    C            D

3. <u>Despite the fact</u> that New York City is <u>one of the</u>
       A                           B
   <u>most</u> densely populated areas in the world, <u>there</u>
    B                          C
   <u>are</u> many parks where one can sit on a bench
    C
   under the trees and <u>you can</u> read a book.
                      D

4. Charles Dickens <u>wrote</u> about the <u>horrifying</u>
                A             B
   conditions in the English boarding <u>schools that</u> he
                             C
   learned about on one <u>of his</u> trips to Yorkshire.
                  D

5. André Breton <u>initiated</u> the Surrealist movement
            A
   <u>with the publication</u> of a manifesto, <u>and it</u>
    B                      C
   incorporated the theories of Freud <u>as well as</u> his
                          D
   own.

6. The review of the concert <u>published</u> in the
                         A
   morning's paper mentioned that the soloist <u>is a</u>
                                       B
   very promising talent and <u>that</u> the orchestra
                         C
   <u>played capable</u>.
    D

7. During <u>the war</u>, there were many people in the
         A
   Polish countryside <u>that</u> sheltered <u>those</u> who <u>had</u>
                   B           C         D
   <u>escaped</u> from concentration camps.
    D

8. The dean <u>lectured to we students</u> <u>on the privilege</u>
              A        B              C
   <u>and</u> responsibility <u>of attending</u> the university.
    C                 D

9. <u>You taking the initiative</u> <u>in the negotiations</u> <u>will</u>
              A                B         C
   <u>profit</u> the company <u>to a great degree</u>.
    C                  D

10. The members of the club <u>insisted that</u> <u>I be</u> the
                          A      B
    representative of the organization at the
    conference <u>which</u> was something <u>I had hoped</u> to
               C                   D
    avoid.

11. <u>No one</u> knows for sure <u>whether there was</u> a real
      A                    B
    <u>person about which</u> Shakespeare <u>wrote</u> his
          C                   D
    sonnets.

12. <u>Although</u> the director of the zoo <u>takes</u> great pains
     A                      B
<u>to recreate</u> the natural habitats of the animals, few
   C
of the exhibits <u>is completely</u> accurate in every
                D
detail.

13. Climatic differences between the north and south

of <u>some</u> countries <u>helps to</u> <u>account for the</u>
    A           B         C
<u>differences</u> in temperament of the inhabitants <u>of</u>
   C                                    D
<u>the two</u> regions.
   D

14. The month of August <u>was particularly cold;</u>
                        A
<u>hardly no daily temperatures</u> <u>were recorded</u> above
         B                C
80 degrees, and <u>only one was</u> recorded above 90
               D
degrees.

15. The diaries of Stendhal, <u>which make entertaining</u>
                                 A
<u>reading</u>, <u>also provides</u> a great wealth of
   A       B
information <u>about musical taste</u> and performance
             C
practice <u>in the last century.</u>
             D

16. <u>Given the evidence</u> of the existence of a
     A
complicated system of communication <u>used by</u>
                               B
<u>whales</u>, it is <u>necessary to</u> acknowledge <u>its</u>
  B         C                D
intelligence.

17. <u>Him being at the rally does not necessarily mean</u>
        A              B
<u>that</u> the congressman <u>agrees</u> with the president's
 C             D
entire platform.

18. Although there is no perfect form of government,

representative democracy, <u>as it is practiced in</u>
                         A
America, <u>is a system</u> that is <u>working well</u> and
 A      B            C
<u>more than satisfactory.</u>
     D

19. George <u>hired</u> a caterer, <u>who</u> <u>he</u> <u>later</u>
     A           B  C  D
<u>recommended</u>, after tasting her specialty—spring
   D
rolls.

20. <u>After driving past Trinity Church</u>, the bus <u>stopped</u>
          A                              B
<u>at the recent constructed</u> Exposition Tower, the
         B
<u>tallest</u> building in the city, <u>to allow the passengers</u>
  C                           D
<u>to take</u> the special elevators to the observation
  D
tower.

21. The student senate <u>passed</u> the resolution <u>banning</u>
                 A                  B
<u>smoking in the cafeteria</u> <u>with scarcely any</u>
        B             C
dissenting <u>votes which angered</u> many members of
              D
the faculty.

22. Most employers <u>assume</u> that one's professional
            A
personality and work habits <u>are formed</u> <u>as a result</u>
                     B        C
<u>of</u> <u>your</u> early work experience.
 C  D

23. <u>Only a small number</u> of taxi drivers <u>fail to insure</u>
           A                                  B

    their vehicles, but usually <u>these are the ones</u> who
                                       C

    need <u>it</u> most.
          D

24. <u>Angered</u> by the double standard society <u>imposed</u>
      A                                B

    <u>on</u> women, Edna St. Vincent Millay <u>wrote candid</u>
    B                                   C

    <u>about</u> <u>her</u> opinions and her personal life.
    C   D

25. Unless <u>they hire players</u> <u>who</u> <u>are</u> better hitters, the
             A         B   C

    fans <u>will gradually lose</u> interest in the team
             D

    despite the fine efforts of the pitching staff.

**DIRECTIONS:** For items #26–41, after identifying each answer choice as an adjective or adverb, determine whether the blank should be filled in with the adjective choice or the adverb choice. Answers are on page 1006.

26. Kathy does her homework _____.

    slow _____      slowly _____

27. We understand each other _____.

    really well _____  real good _____

28. Students should be _____ to their professors at all times.

    polite _____     politely _____

29. Paula has adjusted to her new school. She is doing _____.

    good _____      well _____

30. I think the cake is done. It smells _____.

    good _____      well _____

31. Your room is a _____ mess. Clean it up at once!

    terrible _____   terribly _____

32. When I found out that the accident was my fault, I felt _____.

    awfully _____   awful _____

33. The movie we saw last night wasn't _____ exciting.

    terrible _____   terribly _____

34. Doing a job _____ right away saves time in the long run.

    well _____      good _____

35. Cats have a developed sense of smell. They can smell _____.

    well _____      good _____

36. "Mrs. Chang, your son works _____ in class. You can be proud of him."

    hard _____      hardly _____

37. In order to deliver the package on time, the messenger biked _____.

    fast _____      quick _____

38. The college I will be attending in September is _____.

    nearly _____   near _____

39. After contracting the disease, Marc's symptoms appeared _____.

    slow _____     slowly _____

40. Doctors need to remain _____ even during an epidemic.

    healthy _____    healthily _____

41. Leo's stomach felt _____ after the terrific Thanksgiving feast.

    heavy _____    heavily _____

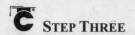 

# Analyzing Sentence Structure

When analyzing the structure of a sentence, ask yourself the following four questions.

**CHECKLIST FOR ANALYZING SENTENCE STRUCTURE**

1. Is the sentence a run-on sentence?

2. Are the elements of the sentence parallel?

3. Are there any incomplete split constructions?

4. Do the verb tenses correctly reflect the sequence of events?

## Run-on Sentences

Be aware of sentences that carelessly run main clauses together without appropriate punctuation or connectors. ***Run-on sentences*** can be corrected in one of three ways: "end-stop" punctuation, a semicolon, or a connector.

The most common way to correct a run-on sentence is to divide the sentence using "end-stop" punctuation.

*Examples:*

The lecture was dull you almost fell asleep. ✘
The lecture was dull. You almost fell asleep. ✓

Was the lecture dull you almost fell asleep. ✘
Was the lecture dull? You almost fell asleep. ✓

The lecture was incredibly dull you almost fell asleep. ✘
The lecture was incredibly dull! You almost fell asleep. ✓

The comma is not an end-mark. DO NOT use a comma by itself to separate two sentences.

*Example:*

Close the window, there is a draft in the room. ✘
Close the window. There is a draft in the room. ✓

Sometimes, two sentences are very closely related in meaning, and full "end-stop" punctuation may seem too strong. A semicolon can then be used to divide the two sentences.

*Example:*

It was a beautiful day there was not a cloud in the sky. ✘
It was a beautiful day; there was not a cloud in the sky. ✓

A third way to correct the run-on is to use a connector (conjunction) such as "and," "but," "for," "or," and "nor" if the two sentences are equally important. It is usually advisable to place a comma before these connectors.

*Example:*

I like to ski, my friend prefers to sit by the fire. ✖

I like to ski, but my friend prefers to sit by the fire. ✓

Particular problem words that may cause run-ons are "however," "therefore," "consequently," and "moreover." These words are not sentence connectors, and when they follow a complete thought, either a period or a semicolon should precede them.

## Faulty Parallelism

*Faulty parallelism* is a common grammatical error for writers. Whenever elements of a sentence perform similar or equal functions, they should have the same form. Consider the following faulty sentences; they are missing necessary words.

*Examples:*

At most colleges, the dominant attitude among students is that gaining admission to professional graduate school is more important than to obtain a well-rounded education. ✖

To demand that additional seasonings be placed on the table is insulting the chef's judgment on the proper balance of ingredients. ✖

The review was critical of the film, citing the poor photography, the weak plot, and the dialogue was stilted. ✖

In the first example, "gaining admission" and "to obtain" must both have the same form. Either both must be in the gerund form or both must be in the infinitive form. For example: "gaining admission…is more important than obtaining…."

In the second example, the subject ("to demand") and the predicated complement ("insulting") must both have the same form: "To demand…is to insult…."

In the last example, the last element of the list of film criticisms is not of the same form as the other two elements. The sentence should read: "…citing the poor photography, the weak plot, and the stilted dialogue."

---

### CHECK THAT ALL ELEMENTS OF A SENTENCE ARE PARALLEL

 Check that all elements of a sentence are parallel—including verb forms, noun forms, and word pairs such as "this…that," "either…or," and "neither…nor."

---

*Examples:*

He spends his time playing cards, swimming, going to the theater, and at school. ✖

He spends his time playing cards, swimming, going to the theater, and going to school. ✓

He manages his business affairs with knowledge, ease, and confidently. ✖

He manages his business affairs with knowledge, ease, and confidence. ✓

He was required by the instructor to go to the library, to take out several books on the Vietnam War, and that he should report to the class on what he had learned. ✘

He was required by the instructor to go to the library, to take out several books on the Vietnam War, and <u>to report</u> to the class on what he had learned. ✓

I am studying the sources of educational theory and how educational theory has evolved. ✘

I am studying the sources and <u>the evolution</u> of educational theory. ✓

He was not only sympathetic but also knew when to be considerate. ✘

He was not only sympathetic but also <u>considerate</u>. ✓

Not only did he enjoy the movie but also the play. ✘

<u>He enjoyed</u> not only the movie but also the play. ✓

I was concerned about the price of the car and if it was comfortable. ✘

I was concerned about the price and <u>the comfort</u> of the car. ✓

Neither does he speak Spanish nor Helen. ✘

Neither he nor Helen <u>speaks</u> Spanish. ✓

## Incomplete Split Constructions

**Split constructions** refer to phrases in which a thought, interrupted by intervening material, is completed later in the sentence.

*Example:*

The officials were not only aware of, but actually encouraged, the misreporting of scores. ✓

This sentence contains a perfectly acceptable split construction. Ordinarily, the object of a preposition closely follows the preposition: "aware of the misreporting." Here, the object of the preposition is separated from the preposition by the phrase "but actually encouraged." This is unobjectionable as long as the thought is properly completed. There is a danger, however, that the intervening material will throw something off in the sentence.

---

### CHECK THAT SPLIT CONSTRUCTIONS ARE COMPLETED

 A split construction is a sentence structure in which two otherwise separate ideas are joined together by a later element. Be alert for split constructions and check that any interrupted thought is correctly completed.

---

Consider the following faulty sentences; they are incomplete split constructions.

*Examples:*

Her colleagues always speak of Professor Collins as a person who has and will always be sensitive to the needs of younger students. ✘

Judging from the pricing policies of many large corporations, maintaining a stable share of the market is as important, if not more important than, making a large profit. ✘

In the first sentence, the error is in the verb. The auxiliary verb "has" needs the verb "been," but "been" does not appear in the sentence. The sentence could be corrected by completing the construction: "…has been and will always be…." In the second sentence, the error is an incomplete comparison. The sentence should read: "…as important as, if not more important than,…."

---

### RULE FOR CHECKING FOR SPLIT CONSTRUCTIONS

 The intervening material makes it difficult to spot errors of split construction. Therefore, when checking for split constructions, read the sentence without the intervening material—it should make sense, be grammatically correct, and be a complete sentence.

---

## Verb Tense

The same *verb tense* should be used whenever possible within a sentence or paragraph. Avoid shifts in verb tense unless there is a valid reason.

*Example:*

Joan <u>came</u> home last week and <u>goes</u> to her summer cottage where she <u>spends</u> the last weekend of her vacation. ✘

Joan <u>came</u> home last week and <u>went</u> to her summer cottage where she <u>spent</u> the last weekend of her vacation. ✓

### Principal Parts of Verbs

Verb tense is indicated by changing the verb or by combining certain verb forms with auxiliary verbs. The *principal parts* are the verb tenses from which all verb forms are derived: present, past, present perfect, future perfect, and past perfect.

---

### VERB PRINCIPAL PARTS

1. *Present Tense:* talk, write

2. *Past Tense:* talked, wrote

3. *Present Perfect Tense:* have talked, has written

4. *Future Perfect Tense:* will have talked, will have written

5. *Past Perfect Tense:* had talked, had written

---

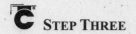 

Verbs are classified as regular (or weak) and irregular (or strong), according to the way in which their principal parts are formed. Regular verbs form their past, present perfect, future perfect, and past perfect tenses by the addition of "-ed" to the infinitive.

*Examples:*

| Present Tense | Past Tense | Present Perfect Tense | Future Perfect Tense | Past Perfect Tense |
|---|---|---|---|---|
| talk | talked | has (have) talked | will have talked | had talked |
| help | helped | has (have) helped | will have helped | had helped |
| walk | walked | has (have) walked | will have walked | had walked |

The principal parts of irregular verbs are formed by changes in the verb itself:

*Examples:*

| Present Tense | Past Tense | Present Perfect Tense | Future Perfect Tense | Past Perfect Tense |
|---|---|---|---|---|
| see | saw | has (have) seen | will have seen | had seen |
| say | said | has (have) said | will have said | had said |
| go | went | has (have) gone | will have gone | had gone |

*Examples:*

*Present Tense*

We were taught that vitamins <u>were</u> important for our well-being. ✘

We were taught that vitamins <u>are</u> important for our well-being. ✔

*Past Tense*

When he spoke, all the people <u>cheer</u> him. ✘

When he spoke, all the people <u>cheered</u> him. ✔

Since he <u>is</u> late, he did not receive a gift. ✘

Since he <u>was</u> late, he did not receive a gift. ✔

*Present Perfect Tense*

I am told that you <u>had completed</u> the job. ✘

I am told that you <u>have completed</u> the job. ✔

*Future Perfect Tense*

I <u>have</u> earned enough money for the car by the end of the month. ✘

I <u>will have earned</u> enough money for the car by the end of the month. ✔

*Past Perfect Tense*

I was told that you <u>have completed</u> the job before you left. ✘

I was told that you <u>had completed</u> the job before you left. ✔

In the first example, the verb tense "are" is used because when expressing a permanent fact, the present tense is used.

The following chart contains a summary of the present tense, past tense, and past participles of many common irregular verbs. The past participle is a word that typically expresses completed action, that is traditionally one of the principal parts of the verb, and that is traditionally used in the formation of the perfect tenses in the active voice and of all tenses in the passive voice.

## PRINCIPAL PARTS OF COMMON IRREGULAR VERBS

| Present | Past | Past Participle |
|---|---|---|
| arise | arose | arisen |
| be | was, were | been |
| bear | bore | borne |
| become | became | become |
| begin | began | begun |
| bid | bade | bid, bidden |
| blow | blew | blown |
| break | broke | broken |
| bring | brought | brought |
| build | built | built |
| buy | bought | bought |
| catch | caught | caught |
| choose | chose | chosen |
| cling | clung | clung |
| come | came | come |
| cut | cut | cut |
| do | did | done |
| draw | drew | drawn |
| drink | drank | drunk |
| drive | drove | driven |
| eat | ate | eaten |
| fall | fell | fallen |
| feed | fed | fed |
| feel | felt | felt |
| fight | fought | fought |
| find | found | found |
| flee | fled | fled |
| fling | flung | flung |
| fly | flew | flown |
| forget | forgot | forgotten |
| forgive | forgave | forgiven |
| freeze | froze | frozen |
| get | got | gotten |
| give | gave | given |
| go | went | gone |
| grow | grew | grown |
| hang (a person) | hanged | hanged |
| hang (an object) | hung | hung |
| hear | heard | heard |
| hide | hid | hidden |
| hold | held | held |
| hurt | hurt | hurt |
| keep | kept | kept |
| know | knew | known |
| lay | laid | laid |

| Present | Past | Past Participle |
|---|---|---|
| lead | led | led |
| leave | left | left |
| lend | lent | lent |
| lie | lay | lain |
| light | lit, lighted | lit, lighted |
| lose | lost | lost |
| make | made | made |
| meet | met | met |
| read | read | read |
| ride | rode | ridden |
| ring | rang | rung |
| rise | rose | risen |
| run | ran | run |
| see | saw | seen |
| send | sent | sent |
| sew | sewed | sewn |
| shake | shook | shaken |
| sit | sat | sat |
| shoot | shot | shot |
| shrink | shrank, shrunk | shrunk, shrunken |
| slay | slew | slain |
| sleep | slept | slept |
| slide | slid | slid |
| speak | spoke | spoken |
| spend | spent | spent |
| spin | spun | spun |
| spring | sprang, sprung | sprung |
| stand | stood | stood |
| steal | stole | stolen |
| sting | stung | stung |
| swear | swore | sworn |
| swing | swung | swung |
| swim | swam | swum |
| take | took | taken |
| teach | taught | taught |
| tear | tore | torn |
| tell | told | told |
| think | thought | thought |
| throw | threw | thrown |
| wake | waked, woke | waked, woken |
| wear | wore | worn |
| weave | wove | woven |
| win | won | won |
| wring | wrung | wrung |
| write | wrote | written |

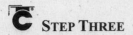
### When to Use the Perfect Tenses

Use the *present perfect* for an action begun in the past and extended to the present.

*Example:*

> I cannot have any more turkey or stuffing; already I <u>have eaten</u> too much food. ✓

In this case, ate would be incorrect. The action have eaten (present perfect) began in the past and extended to the present.

Use the *past perfect* for an action begun and completed in the past before some other past action.

*Example:*

> The foreman asked what <u>had happened</u> to my eye. ✓

In this case, "happened" would be incorrect. The action "asked" and the action "had happened" (past perfect) are used because one action (regarding the speaker's eye) is "more past" than the other action (the foreman's asking).

Use the *future perfect* for an action begun at any time and completed in the future. When there are two future actions, the action completed first is expressed in the future perfect tense.

*Example:*

> When I reach Chicago tonight, my uncle <u>will have left</u> for Los Angeles. ✓

The action "will have left" is going to take place before the action "reach," although both actions will occur in the future.

### The Subjunctive Mood

The *subjunctive* expresses a condition contrary to a fact, a wish, a supposition, or an indirect command.

---

**WHEN TO USE THE SUBJUNCTIVE MOOD**

1. To express a wish not likely to be fulfilled or impossible to realize

2. In a subordinate clause after a verb that expresses a command, a request, or a suggestion

3. To express a condition known or supposed to be contrary to fact

4. After "as if" or "as though"

---

The most common subjunctives are "were" and "be." "Were" is used instead of the indicative form "was," and "be" is used instead of the indicative form "am."

*Examples:*

I wish it <u>were</u> possible for us to approve his transfer at this time. ✔

If I <u>were</u> in St. Louis, I should be glad to attend. ✔

If this <u>were</u> a simple case, we would easily agree on a solution. ✔

If I <u>were</u> you, I should not mind the assignment. ✔

He asked <u>that</u> the report <u>be</u> submitted in duplicate. ✔

It is recommended <u>that</u> this office <u>be</u> responsible for preparing the statements. ✔

We suggest <u>that</u> he <u>be</u> relieved of the assignment. ✔

In formal writing and speech, "as if" and "as though" are followed by the subjunctive since they introduce as supposition something not factual. In informal writing and speaking, the indicative is sometimes used.

*Examples:*

He talked <u>as if</u> he <u>were</u> an expert on taxation. ✔ (He is not.)

This report looks <u>as though</u> it <u>were</u> the work of a college freshman. ✔

Avoid shifts in mood. Once you have decided on the mood that properly expresses your message, use that mood throughout the sentence or the paragraph. A shift in mood is confusing to the listener or reader; it indicates that the speaker or writer himself has changed his way of looking at the conditions.

*Example:*

It is requested that a report of the proceedings <u>be</u> prepared and copies <u>should be</u> distributed to all members. ✘ ("Be" is subjunctive; "should be" is indicative.)

It is requested that a report of the proceedings <u>be</u> prepared and that copies <u>be</u> distributed to all members. ✔

# Analyzing Sentence Structure

**DIRECTIONS:** In sentences #1–30, circle the correct verb choice. Answers are on page 1007.

1. Each year, many people who did not graduate from high school (receive, receives) GED diplomas.

2. The books on the top shelf (was, were) all written by Emily Brontë.

3. The stores in the downtown sector's newly renovated mall (offer, offers) brand name fashions at reduced prices.

4. Only a few dust-covered bottles of the vintage wine (remain, remains) in the cellar.

5. Each tourist who visits the caverns (is, are) given a guidebook.

6. Underneath the leaf covering (was, were) several different species of insects.

7. The young boys, who had never before been in trouble with the law, (was, were) worried about what their parents would say.

8. Several barrels containing a highly toxic liquid (has, have) been discovered at the abandoned factory.

9. The sponsors of the arts and crafts fair (hope, hopes) that it will attract several thousand visitors.

10. Dawn, Harriet, and Gloria, who have formed their own singing group, (is, are) auditioning for jobs.

11. According to insiders, the mayor, whose administration has been rocked by several crises, (worry, worries) that more layoffs are inevitable.

12. There (has, have) been several acts of vandalism in the cemetery in recent months.

13. Rock musicians who perform in front of large speakers often (loses, lose) part of their hearing.

14. The leaves from the branches of the tree that hang over the fence (falls, fall) into the neighbor's yard.

15. The computer and the printer, which are sitting on James' desk, (has, have) never been used.

16. Theresa, wearing her hip-length waders, (was, were) fishing in the middle of the stream.

17. The film critic for the *New York Times* (write, writes) that the film is very funny and entertaining.

18. Several of the ingredients that are used in the dish (has, have) to be prepared in advance.

19. The computer that controls the temperature of the living quarters of the ship (was, were) malfunctioning.

20. There (has, have) been some support for a proposal to build a new courthouse in the center of town.

21. Bill and Jean (is, are) going to the game tomorrow.

22. There (was, were) several students absent last week.

23. I hope that no one has left (his or her, their) homework at home.

24. Each of the sisters celebrated (her, their) birthday at the Plaza.

25. The music of Verdi's operas (is, are) filled with dramatic sweep.

26. All the musicians tuned (his, their) instruments.

27. Either Mrs. Martinez or Carlos (go, goes) to church each week.

28. I told you to (have, have had) the dog walked and fed by the time I got home from work.

29. Last month, the storekeeper, having lost most of his business to a conglomerate retail store, (can, could) not pay the monthly rent bill.

30. Once the weather (became, becomes) cold, Jim could no longer ride his bicycle to work.

**DIRECTIONS:** For items #31–58, choose the verb form that completes the sentence correctly. Answers are on page 1009.

31. A gentleman is _____ to see you.

   (A) comes
   (B) came
   (C) come
   (D) coming
   (E) will come

32. Bill was _____ to telephone you last night.

   (A) to suppose
   (B) supposed
   (C) suppose
   (D) supposing
   (E) will suppose

33. My friend has _____ to get impatient.

   (A) to begin
   (B) began
   (C) begin
   (D) beginning
   (E) begun

34. He has _____ a serious cold.

   (A) catched
   (B) caught
   (C) catch
   (D) catching
   (E) will catch

35. He could _____ before large groups if he were asked.

   (A) sing
   (B) sang
   (C) sung
   (D) singed
   (E) singing

36. She has _____ before large groups several times.

   (A) sing
   (B) sang
   (C) sung
   (D) singed
   (E) singing

37. They have already _____ to the theater.

   (A) go
   (B) goes
   (C) going
   (D) gone
   (E) will go

38. He has _____ me excellent advice.

    (A) give
    (B) gave
    (C) gived
    (D) giving
    (E) given

39. He is _____ to his parents.

    (A) to devote
    (B) devote
    (C) devoted
    (D) devoting
    (E) will devote

40. The engineer has designed and _____ his own home.

    (A) to build
    (B) builds
    (C) building
    (D) built
    (E) had built

41. He _____ as he ran onto the stage following the clown and the magician.

    (A) to laugh
    (B) laughing
    (C) laughed
    (D) laughs
    (E) had laughed

42. She _____ the high-jump so well at trials that she is going to the Olympics this summer.

    (A) had jumped
    (B) to jump
    (C) jumping
    (D) jumps
    (E) jumped

43. It _____ that she continued to blame me even after she knew it wasn't my fault.

    (A) hurt
    (B) hurts
    (C) has hurt
    (D) hurting
    (E) will hurt

44. The man _____ the murder occur if he had really been on that street corner when he said he was.

    (A) see
    (B) sees
    (C) would have saw
    (D) seen
    (E) would have seen

45. The child _____ everywhere now that she is able to stand up by herself.

    (A) to walk
    (B) walks
    (C) walked
    (D) walking
    (E) had walked

46. Tomorrow morning, Sam _____ his sister.

    (A) was calling
    (B) called
    (C) calling
    (D) has called
    (E) will call

47. After she had completed her investigation, the state trooper _____ her report.

    (A) was writing
    (B) wrote
    (C) has written
    (D) writes
    (E) will write

48. When I was growing up, we _____ every summer at my grandmother's home in the country.

    (A) spend
    (B) will spend
    (C) have spent
    (D) were spending
    (E) spent

49. Whenever we get a craving for a late night snack, we _____ a pizza.

    (A) order
    (B) ordered
    (C) had ordered
    (D) have ordered
    (E) were ordering

50. For years now, John _____ his milk at the corner grocery.

    (A) buys
    (B) will buy
    (C) has bought
    (D) is buying
    (E) bought

51. We were just leaving when the telephone _____.

    (A) rang
    (B) will ring
    (C) was ringing
    (D) has rung
    (E) had rung

52. We arrived at the house by noon, but the wedding _____ over.

    (A) is
    (B) will be
    (C) had been
    (D) has been
    (E) was

53. We _____ to drive to the game, but the car stalled.

    (A) plan
    (B) will plan
    (C) had planned
    (D) are planning
    (E) have planned

54. The roofers were putting the last shingles on the house while the plumber _____ the water lines.

    (A) is testing
    (B) was testing
    (C) tests
    (D) will test
    (E) had tested

55. A large flock of Canadian Geese _____ over the meadow and landed in the pond.

    (A) will fly
    (B) were flying
    (C) fly
    (D) flew
    (E) are flying

56. Hui worked very hard to complete her coursework before the baby _____ due.

    (A) is
    (B) are
    (C) was
    (D) will be
    (E) were

57. We _____ to drive from Wisconsin to Washington in two days, but we were late.

    (A) want
    (B) are wanting
    (C) were wanted
    (D) wants
    (E) had wanted

58. Earl and I _____ to eat lunch together outside if it doesn't rain.

    (A) will hope
    (B) had hoped
    (C) hope
    (D) did hope
    (E) hoped

**DIRECTIONS:** For items #59–81, circle the letter of the underlined part of the sentence containing the error. Answers are on page 1012.

59. The owner of the collection <u>requested that</u> the
                                   A
    museum <u>require</u> <u>all people with a camera</u> <u>to leave</u>
            B            C                  D
    them at the door.

60. The young comic <u>found</u> that capturing the
                    A
    audience's attention was easy, <u>but to maintain</u>
                                  B
    <u>their</u> interest <u>was</u> difficult.
      C           D

61. The whale had been <u>laying</u> on the beach for over
                    A
    two hours before the rescue teams <u>were able to</u>
                                B
    <u>begin</u> <u>moving</u> it <u>back into</u> the water.
     B    C       D

62. The praying mantis <u>is welcomed by</u> homeowners
                      A
    for <u>its</u> ability <u>to control</u> destructive garden pests,
       B       C
    <u>unlike the cockroach, which serves no useful</u>
                       D
    <u>function</u>.
     D

63. The <u>newly</u> <u>purchased</u> picture was <u>hanged</u> on the
        A    B              C
    back wall <u>nearest</u> the bay window.
            D

64. The <u>opening scene</u> of the film was a <u>grainy,</u>
          A                   B
    <u>black-and-white</u> shot of an empty town square <u>in</u>
        B                            C
    <u>which</u> an outlaw was <u>hung</u>.
     C          D

65. <u>We spent</u> an exhausting day <u>shopping we</u> could
      A                B      C
    <u>hardly</u> wait <u>to get</u> home.
      C      D

66. The fact that she is bright, articulate, and <u>has</u>
                                A
    <u>charisma</u> <u>will serve</u> her well in her campaign for
      A      B
    governor, <u>particularly</u> since her opponent <u>has</u>
            C                  D
    <u>none</u> of those qualities.
     D

67. Puritans such as William Bradford <u>displaying</u> the
                              A
    courage and piety <u>needed to survive</u> in the New
                  B
    World, a world <u>both</u> promising and threatening,
               C
    <u>which</u> offered unique challenges to their faith.
     D

68. The woman to <u>whom</u> I take my clothes <u>for</u>
               A                B
    <u>tailoring</u> has <u>sewed</u> the hem on this skirt
      B      C
    <u>perfectly</u>.
     D

69. Unfortunately, <u>before</u> cures are found for diseases
                 A
    such as cancer, many lives <u>would have been</u> lost
                        B
    and million of dollars in medical services <u>spent to</u>
                                      C
    treat symptoms <u>rather than to</u> provide a cure.
               D

70. The <u>house on</u> the corner was <u>completely</u> <u>empty</u>,
     A                      B         C
<u>no one</u> <u>came</u> to the door.
  C    D

71. For many people, it is difficult <u>to accept</u>
                               A
compliments graciously and <u>even more difficult</u>
                               B
<u>taking</u> criticism <u>graciously</u>.
  C          D

72. <u>Due</u> to the <u>extremely warm</u> weather this winter,
   A       B
the water has not <u>froze</u> on the pond <u>sufficiently</u>.
                C              D

73. The French poet Artaud <u>believed</u> <u>that,</u> <u>following</u>
                    A    B     C
the climax of a drama, the audience <u>experienced</u> a
 A         B
violent catharsis and is thereby "reborn."

74. <u>Where</u> had <u>everyone</u> <u>gone all</u> the lights were <u>off</u>.
  A       B     C                D

75. <u>Rather</u> than <u>declaring</u> bankruptcy, he <u>applied</u> for a
  A      B                  C
loan, and the bank <u>loaned</u> him the money.
              D

76. <u>Wagering</u> on the Kentucky Derby favorite <u>is</u> a
  A                            B
bad <u>betting</u> proposition, for in the last fifteen
     C
years, the horse that has been the crowd favorite
at post time of the Kentucky Derby <u>loses</u> the race.
                              D

77. We entered the cave <u>very</u> <u>slowly almost</u> afraid of
                   A     B
what we <u>might find</u> <u>there</u>.
        C    D

78. After he <u>had learned of</u> her suicide, he <u>drunk</u> all
         A    B                  C
of the poison <u>from the vial</u>.
            D

79. <u>During the years</u> she spent <u>searching for a cure</u>
     A                         B
for the disease, Dr. Thompson interviewed
hundreds of patients, ran thousands of tests, and
<u>cross-checking</u> <u>millions of bits of data</u>.
     C              D

80. <u>After struggling with the problem</u> for most of the
                A
afternoon, he finally <u>flinged</u> the papers <u>on</u> the
                   B             C
desk and <u>ran out of the room</u>.
          D

81. <u>Suddenly</u>, I felt that something <u>was going to</u>
  A                           B
<u>happen my</u> heart began to <u>beat furiously</u>.
  C                D

**DIRECTIONS:** For sentences #82–96, correct the faulty parallelism if one exists. Answers are on page 1013.

82. When at school, he studies, goes to the library, and he works on the computer.

_____

_____

83. In order to get eight hours of sleep, the student prefers sleeping in late in the morning to go to bed early in the evening.

_____

_____

84. I still need to pass Math 252, English 301, and return two overdue books before I am allowed to graduate.

_____

_____

85. You need to talk to either the teacher or the counselor.

_____

_____

86. Dr. Smydra is not only a captivating lecturer, but also an engaging conversationalist.

_____

_____

87. I will either graduate this fall or lose out on a great opportunity with IBM.

_____

_____

88. Our instructor suggested that we study the assignment carefully, go to the library to research the topic extensively, and we should conduct a survey among 20 subjects.

_____

_____

_____

89. The increase of attrition among community college students is caused by a lack of family support and students have a limited income while attending school.

_____

_____

_____

90. Many non-smokers complained about the health risks associated with second-hand smoke; as a result, smoking is banned in the library, in the cafeteria, and smokers have to leave the building to light a cigarette.

_____

_____

_____

91. After talking to financial aid and see your advisor, return to the registrar's office.

_____

_____

92. Professor Walker not only helped me, but many of my classmates as well.

_____

_____

93. In his communications class, he can either work in groups or in pairs.

_____

_____

94. I prefer that other geography textbook because of the clear explanations, numerous exercises, and Mrs. Patrick's vivid teaching style.

_____

_____

_____

_____

95. The question is whether to study tonight or should I get up earlier tomorrow morning?

_____

_____

96. Reasons for the latest tuition increase are the upgraded computers, new library and, last but not least, inflation has increased to 6.5%.

_____

_____

_____

_____

# Problems of Logical Expression

Ask yourself the following five questions when checking the logical expression of a sentence.

---

**CHECKLIST FOR LOGICAL EXPRESSION ERRORS**

1. Does the sentence contain a faulty or illogical comparison?

2. Does the sentence maintain consistent verb tenses?

3. Does the sentence actually convey the intended meaning?

4. Is the sentence clear and concise?

5. Does the sentence contain any misplaced modifiers?

---

## Faulty or Illogical Comparisons

One problem of logical expression is faulty or illogical comparisons. A faulty comparison is the attempt to compare two things that cannot logically be compared. Consider the following faulty examples.

*Examples:*

> Today, life expectancies of both men and women are much higher compared to the turn of the century when living conditions were much harsher. ✘

> The average salary of a professional basketball player is higher than the top-level management of most corporations. ✘

A comparison can only be made between like items. Yet, in the first sentence we see an attempt to compare "life expectancies" with "the turn of the century"—two dissimilar concepts. The sentence is corrected by simply adding the phrase "those of" before "the turn of the century." Now we have life expectancies compared to life expectancies, and that is a logical comparison.

The same error occurs in the second sentence. An attempt is made to compare "average salary" to "management." The error can be corrected in the same way as in the first example: "…is higher than those of the top-level management…."

---

**WATCH FOR ILLOGICAL COMPARISONS**

Be alert for sentences that attempt to make an illogical comparison between two dissimilar concepts.

---

When two things are being compared, the comparative form of the adjective is used. The comparative is formed in one of the two following ways.

**RULES FOR COMPARISONS BETWEEN TWO OBJECTS**

1. Two objects can be compared by adding "-er" to the adjective.

2. Two objects can be compared by placing "more" before the adjective.

*Examples:*

She is <u>more prettier</u> than her sister. ✘
She is <u>more pretty</u> than her sister. ✔
She is <u>prettier</u> than her sister. ✔

Jeremy is <u>more wiser</u> than we know. ✘
Jeremy is <u>wiser</u> than we know. ✔
Jeremy is <u>more wise</u> than we know. ✔

If three or more things are being compared, then the superlative form of the adjective is used. The superlative is formed in one of the two following ways.

**RULES FOR COMPARISONS AMONG THREE OR MORE OBJECTS**

1. Three or more objects can be compared by adding "-est" to the adjective.

2. Three or more objects can be compared by placing "most" before the adjective.

*Examples:*

Mary is the <u>shorter</u> of all of her friends. ✘
Mary is the <u>shortest</u> of all of her friends. ✔

This is the <u>most sharpest</u> knife I have. ✘
This is the <u>sharpest</u> knife I have. ✔

Calculus is the <u>most difficult</u> class that I have this year. ✔

Some comparative and superlative modifiers require changing the words themselves. A few of these irregular comparisons are given below; consult your dictionary whenever you are in doubt about the comparisons of any adjective or adverb.

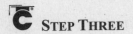 

---

## MODIFIERS THAT DO CHANGE

| Positive | Comparative | Superlative |
|----------|-------------|-------------|
| good | better | best |
| well | better | best |
| bad (evil, ill) | worse | worst |
| badly | worse | worst |
| far | farther, further | farthest, furthest |
| late | later, latter | latest, last |
| little | less, lesser | least |
| many, much | more | most |

Some adjectives and adverbs express qualities that go beyond comparison. They represent the highest degree of a given quality and, as a result, they cannot be improved. Some of these words are listed below.

## MODIFIERS THAT DO NOT CHANGE

| | | | | |
|---|---|---|---|---|
| complete | preferable | horizontally | supreme | totally |
| correct | round | secondly | immortally | unique |
| dead | deadly | square | infinitely | uniquely |
| perfectly | exact | squarely | perfect | universally |
| perpendicularly | | | | |

The use of the comparative in such an expression as "This thing is better than any other" implies that "this thing" is separate from the group or class to which it is being compared. In these expressions, a word such as "other" or "else" is required to separate the thing being compared from the rest of the group of which it is a part.

*Example:*

Our house is cooler than any house on the block. ✖

Since "our house" is one of the houses on the block, it should not be included in the comparison. The sentence should read:

Our house is cooler than any other house on the block. ✔

*Example:*

He has a better record than any salesman in our group. ✖

Since "he" is himself one of the salesmen in the group, the comparison must separate him from the group. The sentence should read:

He has a better record than any <u>other</u> salesman in our group. ✔

Finally, be aware of incomplete comparisons. The result is illogical and confusing.

*Examples:*

The plays of Shakespeare are as good as Marlowe. ✘

The plays of Shakespeare are as good as <u>those</u> of Marlowe. ✓

His skill in tennis is far better than other athletes his age. ✘

His skill in tennis is far better than <u>that</u> of other athletes his age. ✓

His poetry is as exciting, if not more exciting than, the poetry of his instructor. ✘

His poetry is as exciting <u>as</u>, if not more exciting than, the poetry of his instructor. ✓

## Sequence and Verb Tense

A second common problem of logical expression is poor choice of verb tense. The choice of *verb tense* in a correctly written sentence reflects the *sequence* of events described. The following examples contain verb tense errors.

*Examples:*

As soon as Linda finished writing her dissertation, she <u>will take</u> a well-earned vacation in Paris. ✘

A recent study shows that many mothers re-enter the labor force after their children <u>left</u> home. ✘

In the first example, both "writing" and "vacation" must be placed in the same time frame. As written, the sentence places the two actions in different, unconnected time frames. Depending on whether Linda has already completed the dissertation, the sentence could be corrected in either of two ways:

As soon as Linda <u>finishes</u> writing her dissertation, she will take a well-earned vacation in Paris. ✓

As soon as Linda finished writing her dissertation, she <u>took</u> a well-earned vacation in Paris. ✓

The first corrected version of the first example states that neither event has yet occurred and that the writing will precede the vacation. The second corrected version of the first example states that the events are completed and that the writing preceded the vacation.

In the second example, the verb "left" is incorrect because the verb "re-enter" is describing a present, ongoing action. The sentence can be corrected by making it clear that "children leaving home" is also a present phenomenon:

A recent study shows that many mothers re-enter the labor force after their children <u>leave</u> home. ✓

A recent study shows that many mothers re-enter the labor force after their children <u>have left</u> home. ✓

Either sentence is acceptable since both make it clear that leaving home is not a completed past action but an ongoing phenomenon.

---

**WATCH FOR SHIFTING VERB TENSES**

 Make sure that verb tenses properly reflect the sequence, as well as the duration, of any action described in the sentence.

---

*Examples:*

Charles came to town last week and <u>goes</u> to a resort where he <u>rests</u> for three days. ✘

Charles came to town last week and <u>went</u> to a resort where he <u>rested</u> for three days. ✓

Joan came home last week and <u>goes</u> to her summer cottage where she <u>spends</u> the last weekend of her vacation. ✘

Joan came home last week and <u>went</u> to her summer cottage where she <u>spent</u> the last weekend of her vacation. ✓

## Unintended Meanings

Another problem in the category of logical expression relates to whether the sentence actually says what it intends to say. Often, sentences will intend to say one thing but actually say another.

*Examples:*

A childless charwoman's daughter, Dr. Roberts was a self-made woman. ✘

If the present interest rates fall, the dollar will lose some of its value on the foreign exchange. ✘

At first, both of these sentences may seem plausible, but a closer reading will show that each contains an error of logical expression. The first example is actually self-contradictory. As written, it asserts that Dr. Roberts was the daughter of a childless charwoman. In that case, Dr. Roberts would indeed have been a self-made woman! The sentence intends to say that Dr. Roberts was both childless and the daughter of a charwoman: "A charwoman's daughter and childless, Dr. Roberts was a self-made woman."

The second example is a bit subtler. It suggests that present interest rates can change, but that is internally inconsistent, since if the interest rates change, the result is new interest rates, not changed "present" rates. The sentence is corrected by deleting the word "present."

In this category, there are as many possible examples as there are possible errors in human reasoning. Therefore, when checking for intended meaning, just ask yourself what the logic of the sentence implies.

---

**CHECK THAT THE SENTENCE STRUCTURE HAS INTENDED MEANING**

 Determine if the sentence says what it intends to say from the sentence's logical structure.

---

## Conciseness

There are endless possibilities for conciseness errors. Several examples are illustrated below.

### *Avoid Awkward Sentences and Passive Verbs*

A sentence may be grammatically and logically correct yet be in need of correction because it is awkward.

*Examples:*

> The giant condor is able to spread its wings up to 25 feet. ✘
>
> The giant condor has a wingspan of up to 25 feet. ✓
>
> Although most students would benefit from further study of the sciences, doing so is frightening to most of them in that science courses are more difficult than liberal arts courses. ✘
>
> Although most students would benefit from further study of the sciences, most of them are afraid to take science courses because they are more difficult than liberal arts courses. ✓
>
> Given that the Incas lacked the wheel, the buildings at Machu Picchu are more astonishing than any Greek temples that are comparable as an achievement. ✘
>
> Given that the Incas lacked the wheel, the buildings at Machu Picchu are more astonishing than any comparable Greek temple. ✓

In each case, the second sentence is less awkward and more clearly renders the intended thought by being more direct and concise.

A common error among writers is the use of the passive verb. Each of the following examples illustrates that by replacing weak passive verbs, sentences are rendered both clear and concise.

*Examples:*

> One-fourth of the market <u>was captured</u> by the new computer firm. ✘
>
> The new computer firm <u>captured</u> one-fourth of the market. ✓
>
> The lottery prize <u>being</u> $110 million, there are almost as many tickets sold as there are prize dollars. ✘
>
> When the lottery prize <u>is</u> $110 million, there are almost as many tickets sold as there are prize dollars. ✓
>
> The teacher, <u>having finished</u> the day's lesson, let us leave class early. ✘
>
> Because the teacher <u>finished</u> the day's lesson, she let us leave class early. ✓

---

### AVOID PASSIVE VERBS

 Any verb construction using a form of the verb "be" or "have" in addition to the active verb is called a passive verb. Passive verbs are not often used and should be avoided. The active voice is stronger and more direct.

---

### Avoid Needlessly Wordy Sentences

Occasionally, an original sentence will be incorrect simply because it is needlessly wordy.

*Examples:*

> The protracted discussion over what route to take continued for a long time. ✘
>
> The discussion over what route to take continued for a long time. ✓
>
> An aim of the proposal is chiefly to ensure and guarantee the academic freedom of students. ✘
>
> An aim of the proposal is to guarantee the academic freedom of students. ✓

To be protracted is to be continued for a long time; an aim is a chief concern, and to ensure is to guarantee. Therefore, each original is needlessly wordy.

## Misplaced Modifiers

Another error of logical expression is the infamous misplaced modifier. Generally, a modifier should be placed as close to what it modifies as possible. A modifier that is too far from what it intends to modify or too close to some other important element will seem to modify the wrong part of the sentence. Consider the following faulty sentences.

*Examples:*

> Stuffed with herb dressing, trussed neatly, and baked to a golden hue, Aunt Fannie served her famous holiday turkey. ✘
>
> The doctor said gently to the patient that there was nothing wrong with a smile. ✘
>
> At the party, Fred served cold lemonade to his thirsty guests in paper cups. ✘

Consider the first example—poor Aunt Fannie! The proximity of the introductory modifier to Aunt Fannie suggests that she was stuffed, trussed, and baked. The sentence can be corrected by relocating the modifying phrase: "Aunt Fannie served her famous holiday turkey, stuffed with herb dressing, trussed neatly, and baked to a golden hue."

The second example is ambiguous and it could mean either that there is nothing wrong with smiling or that the doctor said, with a smile, that nothing was wrong with the patient. The corrected sentence reads: "With a smile, the doctor said gently to the patient that there was nothing wrong."

Finally, in the third example, the location of the prepositional phrase "in paper cups" implies that the guests are actually inside the paper cups! The sentence is corrected by moving the modifying phrase so that it is closer to what it is intended to modify: "At the party, Fred served cold lemonade in paper cups to his thirsty guests."

---

**WATCH FOR MISPLACED MODIFIERS**

 Be alert for sentences with ambiguous or incorrect modification. Correct misplaced modifiers by placing them as close as possible to what they modify.

---

*Examples:*

> I bought a piano from an old lady with intricate carvings. ✘
>
> I bought a piano with intricate carvings from an old lady. ✓
>
> I read about the destruction of Rome in my history class. ✘
>
> In my history class, I read about the destruction of Rome. ✓

The word "only" often causes confusion. Examine the following confusing sentences.

*Examples:*

> <u>Only</u> he kissed her. ✓
>
> He <u>only</u> kissed her. ✓
>
> He kissed <u>only</u> her. ✓

All three sentences are possible, but a different meaning is conveyed in each, depending on the positioning of "only."

Finally, problems may be created by the placement of a participle phrase.

*Example:*

Answering the doorbell, the cake remained in the oven. ✗

It sounds as though the cake answered the doorbell! Correct this sentence by adding a subject to which the phrase can refer:

Answering the doorbell, we forgot to take the cake from the oven. ✓

*Example:*

Falling on the roof, we heard the sound of the rain. ✗
We heard the sound of the rain falling on the roof. ✓

# Problems of Logical Expression

**DIRECTIONS:** Read the following passage. In items #1–14, choose the best answer that corrects the sentence without changing its meaning or intent. When correcting the sentences, look at them in the context of the passage in order to check for consistency and logical expression. If the sentence is correct as written, choose (A). Answers are on page 1015.

(1) When I was a child, my grandmother's kitchen was the scene of feverish activity during the early fall. (2) Each morning, she would go to the farmers' market and returns with baskets of fruits and vegetables. (3) Then, she would spend the rest of the day preparing the food for the wide-mouthed canning jars that would preserve them through the winter. (4) By late fall, the pantry shelves are lined with rows of jars containing pickled peaches, creamed corn, and many varieties of jams and jellies.

(5) Today, we are able to buy fresh fruits and vegetables at the local grocery store even during the winter. (6) Indeed, years ago, home-canning was a practical solution to one of nature's dilemmas. (7) On the one hand, the harvest produced more fruits and vegetables than could be consumed immediately, so without some way to preserve the produce, they would spoil. (8) On the other hand, during the winter months, fresh produce was not available, so it was important to have preserved foods available.

(9) There are nothing mysterious about home-canning. (10) Fruits or vegetables are packed into special canning jars, fitted with self-sealing lids, and you submerge them in boiling water. (11) The sustained high heat kills dangerous organisms causing the food to spoil. (12) As it gradually cools, a vacuum pulls the lid down against the mouth of the jar to make an airtight seal. (13) Unless the seal is broken, no organisms can enter the jar to cause spoilage.

(14) Although we no longer depend on home-canning, home-canning can be fun. (15) Jams and jellies spread over hot toast on a cold winter morning seems to taste better when you have made them yourself. (16) You also enjoy giving homemade preserves to friends and relatives as gifts. (17) All one needs to do to get started is to find a book about home-canning at the local library or bookstore and follow the directions.

1. Sentence (2): Each morning, she would go to the farmers' market and <u>returns</u> with baskets of fruits and vegetables.

   (A) NO CHANGE
   (B) is returning
   (C) would return
   (D) was returning
   (E) have returned

2. Sentence (3): Then, she would spend the rest of the day preparing the food for the wide-mouthed canning jars that <u>would preserve them</u> through the winter.

   (A) NO CHANGE
   (B) would preserve it
   (C) preserved them
   (D) was preserving them
   (E) preserves it

3. Sentence (4): By late fall, the pantry shelves <u>are lined</u> with rows of jars containing pickled peaches, creamed corn, and many varieties of jams and jellies.

   (A) NO CHANGE
   (B) is lined
   (C) were lined
   (D) was lined
   (E) might be lined

4.  Sentence (6): <u>Indeed,</u> years ago, home-canning was a practical solution to one of nature's dilemmas.

    (A) NO CHANGE
    (B) Indeed
    (C) Furthermore,
    (D) Moreover,
    (E) However,

5.  Sentence (7): On the one hand, the harvest produced more fruits and vegetables than could be consumed immediately, so without some way to preserve the produce, <u>they would spoil.</u>

    (A) NO CHANGE
    (B) it would spoil
    (C) they spoil
    (D) it spoils
    (E) it spoiled

6.  Sentence (8): On the other hand, during the winter months, fresh produce was not available, so it <u>was</u> important to have preserved foods available.

    (A) NO CHANGE
    (B) is
    (C) has been
    (D) could be
    (E) can be

7.  Sentence (9): There <u>are</u> nothing mysterious about home-canning.

    (A) NO CHANGE
    (B) is
    (C) was
    (D) were
    (E) has been

8.  Sentence (10): Fruits or vegetables are packed into special canning jars, fitted with self-sealing lids, and <u>you submerge them</u> in boiling water.

    (A) NO CHANGE
    (B) you submerge it
    (C) you submerged them
    (D) you submerged it
    (E) submerged

9.  Sentence (11): The sustained high heat kills dangerous organisms <u>causing</u> the food to spoil.

    (A) NO CHANGE
    (B) that caused
    (C) that could cause
    (D) to cause
    (E) which caused

10. Sentence (12): <u>As it gradually cools,</u> a vacuum pulls the lid down against the mouth of the jar to make an airtight seal.

    (A) NO CHANGE
    (B) As they gradually cool,
    (C) Gradually cooling,
    (D) Gradually cooled,
    (E) As the jars gradually cool,

11. Sentence (13): Unless the seal is broken, no organisms <u>can enter</u> the jar to cause spoilage.

    (A) NO CHANGE
    (B) are entering
    (C) entered
    (D) have entered
    (E) had entered

12. Sentence (15): Jams and jellies spread over hot toast on a cold winter morning <u>seems to taste</u> better when you have made them yourself.

    (A) NO CHANGE
    (B) seem to taste
    (C) seems tasting
    (D) will seem to taste
    (E) seemed to taste

13. Sentence (16): You also <u>enjoy giving</u> homemade preserves to friends and relatives as gifts.

    (A) NO CHANGE
    (B) will enjoy giving
    (C) enjoyed giving
    (D) enjoy to give
    (E) enjoys giving

14. Sentence (17): All <u>one needs</u> to do to get started is to find a book about home-canning at the local library or bookstore and follow the directions.

    (A) NO CHANGE
    (B) your needs
    (C) you need
    (D) people need
    (E) the reader needs

**DIRECTIONS:** In items #15–29, circle the letter of the underlined part of the sentence containing the error. Answers are on page 1016.

15. <u>Written in almost total isolation from the world,</u>
    ⠀⠀⠀⠀⠀⠀⠀⠀⠀A
    Emily Dickinson <u>spoke of</u> love <u>and</u> death in <u>her</u>
    ⠀⠀⠀⠀⠀⠀⠀⠀⠀B⠀⠀⠀⠀⠀C⠀⠀⠀⠀⠀⠀D
    poems.

16. <u>Early in his career</u>, the pianist entertained
    ⠀⠀⠀A
    thoughts <u>of becoming</u> a composer; but after
    ⠀⠀⠀⠀⠀⠀B
    receiving bad reviews for his own work, <u>he</u> <u>had</u>
    ⠀⠀⠀⠀⠀⠀⠀⠀⠀⠀⠀⠀⠀⠀⠀⠀⠀⠀⠀⠀⠀⠀C⠀D
    <u>given up</u>.
    ⠀D

17. <u>The</u> baseball game was halted due to rain and
    ⠀A
    <u>rescheduled</u> for the following day, <u>even though</u>
    ⠀⠀B⠀⠀⠀⠀⠀⠀⠀⠀⠀⠀⠀⠀⠀⠀⠀⠀⠀⠀⠀⠀C
    <u>the fans would not leave</u> the stadium.
    ⠀⠀⠀⠀⠀⠀D

18. <u>Being highly qualified for the position</u>, the bank
    ⠀⠀⠀⠀⠀⠀⠀⠀A
    president <u>will conduct</u> a final interview of the
    ⠀⠀⠀⠀⠀⠀B
    new candidate tomorrow, <u>after which</u> <u>he will</u>
    ⠀⠀⠀⠀⠀⠀⠀⠀⠀⠀⠀⠀⠀⠀⠀⠀C⠀⠀⠀⠀⠀D
    <u>make</u> her a job offer.
    ⠀D

19. The literature of Native <u>Americans</u> <u>has been</u>
    ⠀⠀⠀⠀⠀⠀⠀⠀⠀⠀⠀⠀⠀⠀A⠀⠀⠀⠀⠀B
    <u>overlooked</u> by most scholars, and the reason is
    ⠀B
    <u>because</u> most university courses in literature <u>are</u>
    ⠀C⠀⠀⠀⠀⠀⠀⠀⠀⠀⠀⠀⠀⠀⠀⠀⠀⠀⠀⠀⠀⠀⠀D
    <u>taught</u> in departments that also teach a language,
    ⠀D
    such as French.

20. <u>In broken English</u>, the police officer patiently
    ⠀A
    Listened to the tourist ask for directions to Radio
    City Music Hall, <u>after which</u> she <u>motioned</u> the
    ⠀⠀⠀⠀⠀⠀⠀⠀⠀⠀B⠀⠀⠀⠀⠀⠀⠀⠀C
    tourist and his family into the squad car and drove
    <u>them</u> to their destination.
    ⠀D

21. Bullfighting <u>remains a controversial</u> sport and
    ⠀⠀⠀⠀⠀⠀⠀⠀⠀⠀A
    <u>many</u> are repulsed by it, <u>since</u> Hemingway was an
    ⠀B⠀⠀⠀⠀⠀⠀⠀⠀⠀⠀⠀⠀⠀C
    aficionado of the sport and glorified <u>it</u> in his
    ⠀⠀⠀⠀⠀⠀⠀⠀⠀⠀⠀⠀⠀⠀⠀⠀⠀⠀⠀⠀⠀D
    writing.

22. <u>Following the recent crash of the stock market,</u>
    ⠀⠀⠀⠀⠀⠀⠀⠀⠀⠀⠀A
    Peter <u>bought</u> a book on portfolio management <u>in</u>
    ⠀⠀⠀⠀⠀B⠀⠀⠀⠀⠀⠀⠀⠀⠀⠀⠀⠀⠀⠀⠀⠀⠀⠀⠀C
    <u>order to learn</u> methods to protect his investments
    ⠀C
    <u>from a well-known investment banker</u>.
    ⠀⠀⠀⠀⠀⠀D

23. <u>Since</u> we have a <u>broader</u> technological base,
    ⠀A⠀⠀⠀⠀⠀⠀⠀⠀B
    American scientists believe that our space
    program <u>will ultimately prove</u> superior <u>to the</u>
    ⠀⠀⠀⠀⠀⠀C⠀⠀⠀⠀⠀⠀⠀⠀⠀⠀⠀⠀⠀⠀⠀D
    <u>Soviet Union</u>.
    ⠀D

24. Although a person may always represent <u>himself</u>
                                              A
in a judicial proceeding, licensed lawyers <u>only</u>
                                             B
may represent <u>others</u> in <u>such</u> proceedings for a
                 C          D
fee.

25. <u>Unlike the pale and delicately built ballerinas of</u>
                            A
<u>romantic ballet</u>, Judith Jamison's movement
        B
<u>seems more African than</u> European-American,
              C
and her physical appearance <u>reinforces</u> the
                                      D
contrast.

26. Market experts <u>predict</u> that in ten years, when the
                       A
harmful effects of caffeine become <u>more</u>
                                      B
<u>generally known</u>, the number of tons of
        B
decaffeinated coffee <u>consumed by</u> Americans
                          C
each year will exceed <u>coffee containing caffeine</u>.
                              D

27. Illiteracy, <u>a widespread problem in the United</u>
                              A
<u>States</u>, <u>undermines</u> productivity because many
   A          B
mistakes <u>are</u> made by workers who do not know
              C
how to read <u>on the job</u>.
                  D

28. As sailors <u>are often assigned</u> to ships <u>that remain</u>
                     A                              B
at sea for months at a time, men in the Navy

<u>spend</u> more time away from home <u>than any</u>
   C                                      D
<u>branch of the service</u>.
        D

29. <u>Like A. J. Ayer</u>, much of Gilbert Ryle's
        A
philosophical argumentation <u>relies</u> on analysis of
                                  B
the way <u>people</u> <u>ordinarily</u> use language.
           C          D

**DIRECTIONS:** For sentences #30–44, correct the faulty comparison if one exists. Answers are on page 1017.

30. The life of my generation is easier than my parents.

_____

_____

31. My two daughters enjoy different TV shows; the oldest watches game shows, while the youngest prefers talk shows.

_____

_____

32. Her present instructor is better of all the ones she has had so far.

_____

_____

33. In the technology lab, I choose the computer with the more greater memory.

_____

_____

34. According to the counselor, taking these classes in this order is much beneficial than the other way around.

_____

_____

35. Our school is very unique in many aspects.

_____

_____

36. The fraternity he joined is better than all fraternities.

_____

_____

37. Professor Baker's explanations are not as clear as Professor Thomas' explanations.

_____

_____

38. You can learn just as much, if not more, online as in a regular classroom.

_____

_____

39. Which of these three sections is better?

_____

_____

40. I am spending more time on the assignments in my management class than all my other classes combined.

_____

_____

41. You will receive your grades no latest than tomorrow at 2 p.m.

_____

_____

42. There is no need for farther negotiation.

_____

_____

43. She is doing so badly in her art class that she could not do any worst.

_____

_____

44. This exercise seems more difficult than all of them.

_____

_____

**DIRECTIONS:** Rewrite sentences #45–54 so that the modified word in each is clear. Answers are on page 1019.

45. He tripped on a crack in the pavement going to school.

_____

_____

46. Mary only failed the test; everyone else in her class passed.

_____

_____

47. Did you see the film about the five people on the boat on television?

_____

_____

48. The police officer ordered the man to stop in his patrol car.

_____

_____

49. Upon picking up the phone, the noise became muted.

_____

_____

50. While swimming, a fish nibbled on my toe.

_____

_____

51. He went to the old church to pray for the people on Cemetery Hill.

_____

_____

52. Of all his admirers, his wife only loved him.

_____

_____

53. Upon entering the class, the blackboard came into view.

_____

_____

54. The baby was pushed by his mother in a stroller.

_____

_____

**DIRECTIONS:** Some of sentences #55–64 are correct, but most are incorrect. Rewrite each incorrect sentence correctly. Answers are on page 1021.

55. She likes tennis, golf, and to go swimming.

_____

_____

56. He could not deliver the supplies. Because the roads had not yet been plowed.

_____

_____

57. If you want to succeed, one must be willing to work hard.

_____

_____

58. Jeff is taller than any boy in his class.

_____

_____

59. To get to school, we nearly walked two miles.

_____

_____

60. The heroine was unbelievable naive.

_____

_____

61. Drive carefully. There may be ice on the roads.

_____

_____

62. Leaning out the window, the garden could be seen below.

_____

_____

63. The hotel room was clean and comfortable that we had reserved.

_____

_____

64. This book is heavier in weight than that one.

_____

_____

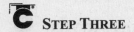 

# Idioms and Clarity of Expression

Standard English contains numerous idioms and two-word verbs that are perfectly acceptable to use. The following is a list of commonly accepted idioms and two-word verbs.

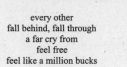

## IDIOMS AND TWO-WORD VERBS

| | | |
|---|---|---|
| about time, about to | every other | make sense of, make way for |
| above all | fall behind, fall through | make up, make up one's mind |
| act up | a far cry from | mark up, mark down |
| add up (*make sense*) | feel free | may as well, might as well |
| a good deal of | feel like a million bucks | mean to |
| an arm and a leg | feel up to | move on, move up |
| at the drop of a hat | few and far between | next to nothing |
| back out (of) | fill in (for) | nose something out |
| bank on | fly off the handle | now and then |
| be about to | follow in someone's footsteps | odds and ends |
| be an old hand (at) | for good | on a shoestring, on its last leg |
| be a question of | get the hang of | on the go |
| beat around the bush | get in one's blood | on one's last leg, on one's toes |
| be bound to | get in the way | on pins and needles |
| be broke | get off, get on, get over, get to | on second thought |
| be fed up (with) | get rid of | on the mend, on the road, on the run |
| be off | get the better of | on the tip of one's tongue |
| be out of something | get under way | on the whole |
| be out of the question | give a hand (to, with) | open up |
| be over | go on (with) | out of order, out of sorts |
| be short for, be short of | go without saying | out of this world, out to win |
| be the picture of | hand in, hand out | over and over |
| be up to someone | hang up | part with |
| be warm | have a heart | pass up |
| bite off more than one can chew | have in mind | pat oneself on the back |
| break down, break the ice | have over | pay off, pay someone a visit |
| break the news (to) | hear first hand (from) | pick out, pick up (*learn*) |
| bring about | hear from, hear of | pick up the tab (for) |
| broken English | hit it off | a piece of cake |
| brush up on | hold on (to), hold still, hold up | play by ear |
| by and large | how come? | point out |
| by heart, by no means | in the dark, in hot water | pull one's leg |
| call off | in the long run, in no time | put aside, put off |
| call on | jump to conclusions | put one's best foot forward |
| care for | keep an eye on, keep an eye out (for) | put together, put up (with) |
| catch on, catch up (with) | keep from, keep on one's toes | rave about |
| come across, come down with | keep on (with), keep up (with) | rough it |
| come out smelling like a rose | knock it off | rule out |
| cost an arm and a leg | lay off | run into, run out of, run short (of) |
| count on, count out | learn the ropes | save one's breath |
| cut down on, cut it close | leave out | search me |
| cut out, cut out for | let (somebody) alone, let (somebody) know | see off, see to |
| day in and day out | let go of | serve one right |
| die down | look after, look for, look forward to | set out |
| do over, do with, do without | look into, look out (for) | settle down, settle on |
| dream up | look up (to) | sing another tune |
| drop in (on), drop off | make a difference, make a point of | show around, show up |
| size up | make ends meet, make out | shut down |
| sleep on it | take it easy, take off (*leave*) | up against |
| snap out of | take one's mind off, take one's time | ups and downs |
| speak up (*say something, speak more loudly*) | take over, take pains, take turns | up-to-date |
| spell out (for) | talk over | use up |
| stand a chance | tangle with | wait for, wait on |
| stand for | tell apart | warm up (to) |
| stand out | think much of | watch out (for) |
| start up | think over | wear out |
| stay out, stay up | throw cold water on | a whole new ballgame |
| a stone's throw (from) | tie up, tie into | with flying colors |
| straighten up | trade in | without a hitch |
| take a chance, take advantage (of) | turn down, turn up, turn into | work out (*exercise, solve*) |
| take after, take in, take into account | turn off, turn on, turn out, turn in | write out |
| | under the weather | zero in (on) |

An expression that is not idiomatic is one that is not acceptable standard written English for any of the following reasons.

---

### CHECKLIST FOR IDIOMATIC EXPRESSION ERRORS

1. Wrong Prepositions

2. Diction

3. Gerunds vs. Infinitives

4. Ambiguity in Scope

5. Low-Level Usage

---

## Wrong Prepositions

In standard written English, only certain prepositions can be used with certain verbs. You should know which prepositions to use with which verbs as a result of daily conversation and writing in standard written English.

*Example:*

I asked him repeatedly if he was from <u>about</u> here, but he never answered me. ✘

The phrase "was from about here" is not correct. You should recognize the correct phrase from daily conversation: "he was from around here."

## Diction
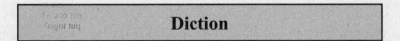

The second category of idiomatic expression errors involves diction, i.e., word choice. Sometimes, a word is used incorrectly, which leads to a construction that is simply not idiomatic or not acceptable according to standard usage.

*Example:*

The techniques of empirical observation in the social sciences are different <u>than</u> those in the physical sciences. ✘

This example is improved by replacing "than" with "from." Rewritten, the sentence reads: "The techniques of empirical observation in the social sciences are different "from" those in the physical sciences."

A variation on this theme uses pairs of words that are often incorrectly used, as the following examples illustrate.

*Examples:*

John expressed his intention to make the trip, but <u>if</u> he will actually go is doubtful. ✖

John expressed his intention to make the trip, but <u>whether</u> he will actually go is doubtful. ✓

Herbert divided the cake <u>among</u> Mary and Sally. ✖

Herbert divided the cake <u>between</u> Mary and Sally. ✓

Herbert divided the cake <u>between</u> Mary, Sally, and himself. ✖

Herbert divided the cake <u>among</u> Mary, Sally, and himself. ✓

The <u>amount</u> of students in the class declined as the semester progressed. ✖

The <u>number</u> of students in the class declined as the semester progressed. ✓

There are <u>less</u> students in Professor Smith's class than there are in Professor Jones' class. ✖

There are <u>fewer</u> students in Professor Smith's class than there are in Professor Jones' class. ✓

Some sentences are incorrect because they use a word that does not convey the intended meaning. The confusion is understandable because of the similarity between the correct word and the chosen word.

> ### WATCH FOR INAPPROPRIATE DICTION
>
> Be alert for non-idiomatic usage and commonly misused words.

The following list is an extended summary of commonly confused word groups.

---

## CONFUSING WORD GROUPS

**accede**—*to agree with* ............................................ They will *accede* to your request for more information.
**exceed**—*to be more than* ........................................ Unfortunately, her expenditures now *exceed* her income.
**concede**—*to yield* (not necessarily in agreement) .......... They *concede* that more information is necessary.

**accept**—*to receive*, or ............................................ I'll *accept* the gift from you.
    *to agree to something* ............................................ I will lend you the money if you *accept* my conditions.
**except**—*to exclude* or *excluding* ............................ Everyone *except* my uncle went home.

**access**—*availability*, or ........................................ The lawyer was given *access* to the grand jury records.
    *to get at* ............................................................ I could not *access* the files without the proper password.
**excess**—*state of surpassing specified limits* (noun), or ...... Expenditures this month are far in *excess* of income.
    *more than usual* (adjective) .................................... The airline charged him fifty dollars for *excess* baggage.

**adapt**—*to adjust or change* .................................... Children can *adapt* to changing conditions very easily.
**adept**—*skillful* ........................................................ Proper instruction makes children *adept* in various games.
**adopt**—*to take as one's own* .................................... The war orphan was *adopted* by the general and his wife.

**adapted to**—*original or natural suitability* ................ The gills of the fish are *adapted to* underwater breathing.
**adapted for**—*created suitability* ............................ Atomic energy is constantly being *adapted for* new uses.
**adapted from**—*changed to be made suitable* .............. Many of Wagner's librettos were *adapted from* Norse sagas.

**addition**—*the act or process of adding* .................... In *addition* to a dictionary, he always used a thesaurus.
**edition**—*a printing of a publication* ........................ The first *edition* of Shakespeare's plays appeared in 1623.

**advantage**—*a superior position* ............................ He had an *advantage* in experience over his opponent.
**benefit**—*a favor conferred or earned* ...................... The rules were changed for his *benefit*.

**adverse**—*unfavorable* ............................................ He was very upset by the *adverse* decision.
**averse**—*having a feeling of repugnance or dislike* ........ Many writers are *averse* to criticism of their work.

**advice**—*counsel, opinion* (noun) ............................ Let me give you some free *advice*.
**advise**—*to offer advice* (verb) ................................ I'd *advise* you to see your doctor.

**affect**—*to influence* (verb) .................................... The pollution *affected* our health.
**effect**—*to cause or bring about* (verb), or ................ Our lawsuit *effected* a change in the law.
    *a result* (noun) .................................................... The *effect* of the storm could not be measured.

**all ready**—*everybody or everything ready* ................ They were *all ready* to write when the test began.
**already**—*previously* .............................................. They had *already* written the letter.

**all together**—*everybody or everything together* .......... The boys and girls stood *all together* in line.
**altogether**—*completely* .......................................... His action was *altogether* strange for a person of his type.

**allude**—*to make a reference to* ................................ In his essay, he *alludes* to Shakespeare's puns.
**elude**—*to escape from* ............................................ The burglar *eluded* the police.

**allusion**—*an indirect reference* .............................. The poem is an *allusion* to one of Shakespeare's sonnets.
**illusion**—*an erroneous concept or perception* ............ My mirror created the *illusion* of space in the narrow hall.

**alongside of**—*side by side with* .............................. Bill stood *alongside of* Henry.
**alongside**—*parallel to the side* .............................. Park the car *alongside* the curb.

**among**—*a term used with more than two persons or things* ...... The inheritance was equally divided *among* the four kids.
**between**—*a term used with two persons or things* ........ The inheritance was divided *between* the two kids.

**angel**—*a heavenly creature* .................................... She has been an *angel* in these difficult times.
**angle**—*a point at which two lines meet*, or ................ A line perpendicular to another line forms a right *angle*.
    *an aspect seen from a particular point of view* .......... From that *angle*, the picture looks completely different.

**ante**—*a prefix meaning before* ................................ The *ante*chamber is the small room before the main room.
**anti**—*a prefix meaning against* .............................. He is known to be *anti*-American.

**assistance**—*the act of assisting, aid* ...................... I needed his *assistance* when I repaired the roof.
**assistants**—*helpers, aides* .................................... The chief surgeon has four *assistants*.

**breadth**—*width* .................................................... The canvas was twice greater in length than in *breadth*.
**breath**—*an intake of air* ........................................ Before you dive in, take a very deep *breath*.
**breathe**—*to draw air in and give it out* .................... It is difficult to *breathe* when you have a bad cold.

---

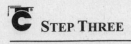 

# CONFUSING WORD GROUPS

**build**—*to erect, construct* (verb), or .............................................. I want to *build* a sandcastle.
   *the physical makeup of a person* (noun)................................... She has a very athletic *build*.
**built**—*the past tense of build* ............................................... We *built* a moat around the sandcastle.

**buy**—*to purchase* ................................................................... I want to *buy* a new tie.
**by**—*near,* ............................................................................. My bloodhound likes to sleep *by* the door at night.
   *by means of, or* ................................................................. He comes to school *by* public transportation.
   *not later than* ................................................................... Mary said that she would be back at work *by* noon.
**bye**—*free pass to next round* ............................................. She had a *bye* in the tournament.

**canvas**—*a heavy, coarse material* ................................... The *canvas* sails were very heavy.
**canvass**—*to solicit, conduct a survey* ............................. The politicians are going to *canvass* our neighborhood.

**capital**—*place of government, or* ..................................... Paris is the *capital* of France.
   *wealth*.................................................................................. It takes substantial *capital* to open a restaurant.
**capitol**—*building that houses legislatures* ....................... Congress convenes in the *Capitol* in Washington, D.C.

**carat**—*a unit of weight*........................................................ The movie star wears a ten-*carat* diamond ring.
**caret**—*a proofreading symbol, indicating where* ............................ He added a phrase in the space above the *caret*.
   *something is to be inserted*
**carrot**—*a vegetable* ............................................................ Does he feed his pet rabbit a *carrot* every other day?

**click**—*a brief, sharp sound* ............................................... The detective drew his gun when he heard the lock *click*.
**clique**—*an exclusive group of people or set* ..................... In high school, I was not part of any *clique*.

**cease**—*to end*....................................................................... Please *cease* making those sounds.
**seize**—*to take hold of* .......................................................... *Seize* him by the collar as he comes around the corner.

**choice**—*a selection* ............................................................ My *choice* for a career is teaching.
**choose**—*to select* ................................................................ We may *choose* our own advisors.
**chose**—*the past tense of choose* ..................................... I finally *chose* my wedding dress.

**cite**—*to quote* ...................................................................... He enjoys *citing* Shakespeare to illustrate his views.
**sight**—*seeing, what is seen* ............................................... The *sight* of the accident was appalling.
**site**—*a place where something is located or occurs* ......................... We are seeking a new *site* for the baseball field.

**cloth**—*fabric or material* ..................................................... The seats were covered with *cloth*, not vinyl.
**clothe**—*to put on clothes, to dress*.................................... Her job is to *clothe* the actors for each scene.

**coarse**—*vulgar, or* .............................................................. He was shunned because of his *coarse* behavior.
   *harsh* .................................................................................. The sandpaper was very *coarse*.
**course**—*a path, or*............................................................... The ship took its usual *course*.
   *a plan of study*.................................................................. How many *courses* are you taking this term?

**complement**—*a completing part*......................................... His wit was a *complement* to her beauty.
**compliment**—*an expression of praise or admiration* .................... He received many *compliments* for his fine work.

**confidant**—*one to whom private* ......................................... His priest was his only *confidant*.
   *matters are confided* (noun)
**confidence**—*a feeling of assurance or certainty* (noun) ................. The ballplayer is developing *confidence* in his ability.
**confident**—*having confidence in oneself* (adjective)...................... Her success in business has given her a *confident* manner.

**conscience**—*the ability to recognize the difference* ........................ The attorney said the criminal lacked a *conscience*.
   *between right and wrong*
**conscious**—*aware* ............................................................... He was *conscious* that his actions had consequences.

**consul**—*a government representative* ................................ Americans abroad should keep in touch with the *consuls*.
**council**—*an assembly that meets for deliberation* ......................... The student *council* met to discuss a campus dress code.
**counsel**—*advice* (counselor) ............................................. The defendant heeded the *counsel* of his friends.

**decent**—*suitable*.................................................................. The *decent* thing to do is to admit your error.
**descent**—*going down*........................................................... The *descent* into the cave was dangerous.
**dissent**—*disagreement* ....................................................... Two of the justices filed a *dissenting* opinion.

**desert** (DEZZ-ert)—*an arid area*........................................ I have seen several movies set in the Sahara *desert*.
**desert** (di-ZERT)—*abandon, or* .......................................... The soldier was warned not to *desert* his company.
   *a reward or punishment*.................................................... We're certain that execution is a just *desert* for his crime.
**dessert** (di-ZERT)—*the final course of a meal* ............................ We had strawberry shortcake for *dessert*.

**disburse**—*to pay out* .......................................................... This week the bank has *disbursed* a million dollars.
**disperse**—*to scatter, distribute widely*.............................. The defeated army began to *disperse*.

**discomfit**—*to upset* ............................................................ The general's plan was designed to *discomfit* the enemy.
**discomfort**—*lack of ease* .................................................. This starched collar causes *discomfort*.

**dual**—*double*....................................................................... Dr. Jekyll had a *dual* personality.
**duel**—*a contest between two persons or groups* ......................... Aaron Burr and Alexander Hamilton engaged in a *duel*.

**elicit**—*to draw forth, evoke*................................................ Her performance *elicited* tears from the audience.
**illicit**—*illegal, unlawful* ....................................................... He was arrested because of his *illicit* business dealings.

**emigrate**—*to leave a country* ............................................. They *emigrated* from Norway in the nineteenth century.
**immigrate**—*to enter a country*............................................ Many Irish *immigrated* to the United States.

## CONFUSING WORD GROUPS

**eminent**—*of high rank, prominent, outstanding* ............................ He was the most *eminent* physician of his time.
**imminent**—*about to occur, impending* ........................................ His nomination to the board of directors is *imminent*.

**epitaph**—*an inscription on a tombstone or monument* .................. His *epitaph* was taken from a section of the Bible.
**epithet**—*a term used to describe or characterize*........................... The drunk was shouting *epithets* at the passersby.
    *the nature of a person or thing*

**expand**—*to spread out* .............................................................. As the staff increases, we can *expand* our office space.
**expend**—*to use up* .................................................................... Don't *expend* all your energy on one project.

**fair**—*light in color,*................................................................... I have a very *fair* complexion.
    *reasonable,* or ..................................................................... Your attitude is not a *fair* one.
    *beauty*.................................................................................. The *fair* princess rode her horse off into the sunset.
**fare**—*a set price*....................................................................... The *fare* is reduced for senior citizens.

**farther**—*used to express distance* ............................................... John ran *farther* than Bill walked.
**further**—*used to express time or degree*...................................... Please go no *further* in your argument.

**faze**—*to worry or disturb*........................................................... I tried not to let his mean look *faze* me.
**phase**—*an aspect*....................................................................... A crescent is a *phase* of the moon.

**find**—*to locate* ......................................................................... Can you *find* the keys?
**fine**—*good,*............................................................................... He is a *fine* cook.
    *well,* ..................................................................................... After being very sick for two weeks, now I feel absolutely *fine*.
    *precise,* or ........................................................................... The calibration of the scale requires very *fine* measurements.
    *a penalty*............................................................................... I received a parking *fine* for an expired meter.
**fined**—*penalized* ....................................................................... The judge *fined* him twenty dollars.

**formally**—*in a formal way* ........................................................ He was dressed *formally* for the dinner party.
**formerly**—*at an earlier time* ...................................................... He was *formerly* a delegate to the convention.

**fort** (fort)—*a fortified place*...................................................... A small garrison was able to hold the *fort*.
**forte** (FOR-tay)—*a strong point*................................................. Conducting Wagner's music was Toscanini's *forte*.
**forte** (FOR-tay)—*a musical term that means loudly*...................... The musical composition was meant to be played *forte*.

**idle**—*unemployed or unoccupied* ............................................... He didn't enjoy remaining *idle* while he recuperated.
**idol**—*image or object of worship* ............................................... Rock musicians are the *idols* of many teenagers.

**in**—indicates *inclusion or location,* or ........................................ The spoons are *in* the drawer.
    *motion within limits* ............................................................. We were walking *in* the room.
**into**—*motion toward one place from another* ............................... I put the spoons *into* the drawer.

**incidence**—*to the extent or frequency of an occurrence* ................. The *incidence* of rabies has decreased since last year.
**incidents**—*occurrences, events*................................................... Luckily, the accidents were just minor *incidents*.

**it's**—the contraction of *it is,* or ................................................ *It's* a very difficult assignment.
    the contraction of *it has* ....................................................... *It's* been a very long day.
**its**—possessive pronoun meaning *belonging to it* ......................... We tried to analyze *its* meaning.

**knew**—the past tense of *know* .................................................... I *knew* her many years ago.
**new**—*of recent origin* ............................................................... I received a *new* bicycle for my birthday.

**know**—*to have knowledge or understanding*................................. I *know* your brother.
**no**—*a negative used to express denial or refusal* ......................... There are *no* more books available.

**later**—*after a certain time* ......................................................... I'll see you *later*.
**latter**—*the second of two*........................................................... Of the two speakers, the *latter* was more interesting.

**lay**—*to put* ............................................................................... I (*lay, laid, have laid*) the gift on the table.
**lie**—*to recline*........................................................................... I (*lie, lay, have lain*) on my blanket on the beach.

**lets**—the third person singular present of *let*............................... He *lets* me park my car in his garage.
**let's**—contraction for *let us* ...................................................... *Let's* go home early today.

**lightening**—*making less heavy* ................................................... Removing the books will succeed in *lightening* your bag.
**lightning**—*electric discharge in the atmosphere,* or...................... Thunderstorms often produce startling *lightning* bolts.
    *moving with great speed* ....................................................... The horse raced *lightning* fast.

**loose**—*not fastened or restrained,* or........................................... The dog got *loose* from the leash.
    *not tight-fitting*.................................................................... After my diet, the new pants were too *loose* on me.
**lose**—*to mislay,* ....................................................................... Try not to *lose* your umbrella.
    *to be unable to keep,* or ....................................................... She *lost* her mind.
    *to be defeated*....................................................................... They can't *lose* with their new strategy.

**mind**—*human consciousness* (noun),........................................... Make up your *mind* which record you want.
    *to object* (verb), or............................................................... We don't *mind* if you bring a friend.
    *to watch out for*.................................................................... I cannot go to the movies because I have to *mind* the children.
**mine**—*a possessive, showing ownership*...................................... Use your own sled; that one is *mine*.

**moral**—*good or ethical* (adjective), or ........................................ The trust administrator had a *moral* obligation to the heirs.
    *a lesson to be drawn* (noun) ................................................. The *moral* of the story is that it pays to be honest.
**morale**—*spirit*........................................................................... The team's *morale* improved after the coach's speech.

**passed**—the past tense of *to pass* ............................................... The week *passed* very quickly.
**past**—*just preceding or an earlier time,* or.................................... The *past* week was a very exciting one.
    *in a direction going close to and then beyond*........................... We walked down the block and *past* the old mansion.

## 📖 CONFUSING WORD GROUPS 📖

**patience**—*enduring calmly with tolerant understanding* ............... He has very little *patience* with fools.
**patients**—*people under medical treatment* ...................... There are twenty *patients* waiting to see the doctor.

**personal**—used to describe *an individual's character,* .................. He took a *personal* interest in each of the students.
    *conduct, or private affairs*
**personnel**—*an organized body of individuals* ............................... The store's *personnel* department is on the third floor.

**precede**—*to come before* ........................................ What events *preceded* the fight?
**proceed**—*to go ahead* ............................................ We can *proceed* with our next plan.

**principal**—*chief or main* (adjective), ............................................. His *principal* support comes from the real estate industry.
    *a leader,* or ............................................... The school *principal* called a meeting of the faculty.
    *a sum of money* (noun) ........................................ He earned 10% interest on the *principal* he invested.
**principle**—*a fundamental truth or belief* ......................... As a matter of *principle,* he didn't register for the draft.

**prophecy**—*prediction* (noun, rhymes with *sea*) ........................... What is the fortune-teller's *prophecy?*
**prophesy**—*to predict* (verb, rhymes with *sigh*) .............................. What did the witches *prophesy?*

**quiet**—*silent, still* ................................................ My brother is very shy and *quiet.*
**quit**—*to give up or discontinue* ..................................... I *quit* the team last week.
**quite**—*very, exactly, or to the greatest extent* ............................... His analysis is *quite* correct.

**raise**—*to lift, to erect* .......................................... The neighbors helped him *raise* a new barn.
**raze**—*to tear down* ............................................. The demolition crew *razed* the old building.
**rise**—*to increase in value,* or ..................................... The price of silver will *rise* again this month.
    *to get up or move from a lower to a higher position* .............. If a judge enters a room, everyone must *rise* from their seats.

**seem**—*to appear* ................................................. He *seems* to be sleeping.
**seen**—*the past participle of see* .................................. Have you *seen* your sister lately?

**set**—*to place something down* (mainly) ........................................ He (*sets, set, has set*) the lamp on the table.
**sit**—*to seat oneself* (mainly) ..................................... He (*sits, sat, has sat*) on the chair.

**stationary**—*standing still* ....................................... Long ago, people thought that the earth was *stationary.*
**stationery**—*writing material* ..................................... We bought our school supplies at the *stationery* store.

**suppose**—*to assume or guess* ..................................... I *suppose* you will be home early.
**supposed**—*past tense and past participle of suppose* ..................... I (*supposed, had supposed*) you would be home early.
**supposed**—*ought to or should* (followed by *to*) .............................. I am *supposed* to be in school tomorrow.

**than**—*used to express comparison* ..................................... Jim ate more *than* we could put on the large plate.
**then**—*used to express time,* or ..................................... I knocked on the door, and *then* I entered.
    *a result or consequence* ..................................... If you go, *then* I will go too.

**their**—*belonging to them* ......................................... We took *their* books home with us.
**there**—*in that place* .............................................. Your books are over *there* on the desk.
**they're**—*the contraction of they are* ................................. *They're* coming over for dinner.

**though**—*although* or ...................................................... *Though* he's my friend, I can't recommend him.
    *as if* (preceded by *as*) ........................................... He acted *as though* nothing had happened.
**thought**—*past tense of to think* (verb), or ......................... I *thought* you were serious!
    *an idea* (noun) .............................................. It is the *thought* that counts.
**through**—*in one side and out another,* ........................... We enjoyed running *through* the snow.
    *by way of,* or ............................................... They met each other *through* a mutual friend.
    *finished* ................................................... My boyfriend and I are completely *through* with one another.

**to**—*in the direction of* (preposition), or ........................... We shall go *to* school.
    used before a verb to indicate the *infinitive* .................... I like *to* swim.
**too**—*very, also* ................................................... It is *too* hot today.
**two**—*the numeral 2* ............................................... I ate *two* sandwiches for lunch.

**use**—*to employ or put into service* ................................. I want to *use* your chair.
**used**—*past tense and the past participle of to use* .......................... I *used* your chair.
**used**—*in the habit of or accustomed to,* ........................... I am *used* to your comments.
    (followed by *to*)
**used**— *an adjective meaning not new* ........................... I bought a *used* car.

**weather**—*atmospheric conditions* .................................. I don't like the *weather* in San Francisco.
**whether**—*introduces a choice* ..................................... He inquired *whether* we were going to the dance.
    (*whether* should not be preceded by *of* or *as to*)

**were**—*a past tense of to be* ....................................... They *were* there yesterday.
**we're**—*the contraction of we are* .................................. *We're* in charge of the decorations.
**where**—*place or location* ......................................... *Where* are we meeting your brother?

**who's**—*the contraction of who is,* or ............................... *Who's* the next batter?
    the contraction of *who has* ................................... *Who's* already gone to this movie?
**whose**—*of whom, implying ownership* ............................. *Whose* notebook is on the desk?

**your**—*a possessive showing ownership* ........................... Please give him *your* notebook.
**you're**—*the contraction of you are* ................................. *You're* very sweet.

## Gerunds vs. Infinitives

The *infinitive* is the "to" form of a verb and the *gerund* is the "-ing" form of a verb. Both the infinitive and the gerund forms of a verb may be used as nouns. In some circumstances, use of either verb form is correct.

*Examples:*

<u>Adding</u> an extra room to the house is the next project. ✓

<u>To add</u> an extra room to the house is the next project. ✓

In this example, each sentence is correct. However, in some circumstances, gerunds and infinitives are NOT interchangeable.

---

### WATCH FOR GERUND-INFINITIVE SWITCHING

 Watch for situations in which the infinitive form of the verb has been switched with the gerund form, or vice versa, when it is not appropriate usage in standard written English.

---

The following list is a summary of common verbs that are often followed by infinitives.

---

### VERBS OFTEN FOLLOWED BY "*TO*" VERB FORMS

| | | | | | |
|---|---|---|---|---|---|
| advise** | care | encourage** | implore** | prefer* | teach** |
| afford | cause** | endeavor | instruct** | prepare | teach…how** |
| agree | caution** | expect* | intend* | pretend | tell** |
| allow** | challenge** | fail | invite** | proceed | tend |
| appear | claim | forbid** | learn | promise* | threaten |
| appoint** | come | force** | manage | prove | urge** |
| arrange | command** | forget | mean | refuse | use** |
| ask* | compel** | get (manage, | motivate** | remind** | volunteer |
| attempt | consent | have the opportunity) | need* | request** | wait |
| be | convince** | get** (persuade) | oblige** | require** | want* |
| be supposed | dare* | happen | offer | seem | warn** |
| beg* | decide | help* | order** | serve | wish* |
| begin | demand | hesitate | pay* | show…how** | would like* |
| believe** | deserve | hire** | permit** | struggle | would love* |
| can't afford | direct** | hope | persuade** | swear | would prefer* |
| can't wait | enable** | hurry | plan | | |

\* verb + infinitive, or verb + (noun *or* pronoun) + infinitive    \*\* verb + (noun *or* pronoun) + infinitive

---

*Examples:*

Our new physics professor <u>prefers to teach</u> by example; that is, by laboratory experience, rather than by theory. ✓

Our dinner reservations were at such an exclusive restaurant, the host <u>required</u> my date <u>to wear</u> a coat and tie. ✓

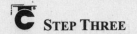 

The following list is a summary of common verbs that are often followed by gerunds.

---

### 📖 VERBS OFTEN FOLLOWED BY "-*ING*" VERB FORMS 📖

| | | | | |
|---|---|---|---|---|
| acknowledge | defer | escape | keep (continue) | recommend |
| admit | delay | excuse | mention | regret |
| anticipate | deny | explain | mind (object to) | report |
| appreciate | detest | feel like | miss | resent |
| avoid | discontinue | finish | postpone | risk |
| be worth | discuss | forgive | practice | spend time |
| cannot help | dislike | give up (stop) | prevent | suggest |
| cannot stand | dispute | go | prohibit | tolerate |
| celebrate | dread | imagine | quit | understand |
| complete | endure | involve | recall | |
| consider | enjoy | justify | | |

---

*Examples:*

My brother <u>recommended bicycling</u> to relieve the knee pain normally caused by running. ✔

In the final written settlement, the company agreed to <u>discontinue testing</u> on animals. ✔

Either infinitives or gerunds may follow certain verbs without changing the original meaning of the verb.

---

### 📖 VERBS FOLLOWED BY EITHER INFINITIVES OR GERUNDS WITHOUT CHANGE IN MEANING 📖

| | | | |
|---|---|---|---|
| attempt | cannot stand | intend | neglect |
| begin | continue | like | prefer |
| cannot bear | hate | love | start |

---

*Examples:*

Following the divorce, she <u>attempted to bring</u> her ex-husband to court on charges of failure to pay alimony. ✔

I had to admit, I <u>preferred eating</u> at a restaurant rather than eating at home when he was cooking! ✔

However, the meanings of certain other verbs do change when followed by infinitives or gerunds.

---

### 📖 VERBS FOLLOWED BY EITHER INFINITIVES OR GERUNDS WITH CHANGE IN MEANING 📖

| | | | |
|---|---|---|---|
| forget | propose | regret | stop |
| mean | quit | remember | try |

---

*Examples:*

You can <u>forget having</u> the party here. ✔

I <u>forgot to have</u> the electricity connected by the time we moved into the new house. ✔

## Ambiguity in Scope

Watch for ***ambiguity in scope***. This occurs when there is no clear division between two ideas, so that the ideas seem to merge.

*Examples:*

> After the arrest, the accused was charged with resisting arrest and criminal fraud. ✘

> The recent changes in the tax law will primarily affect workers who wait tables in restaurants, operate concessions in public places, and drive taxis. ✘

In the first example, the scope of "resisting" is not clear. The sentence can be interpreted to mean that the accused was charged with resisting criminal fraud. The intended scope is made clear by inserting "with": "…charged with resisting arrest and with criminal fraud." The corrected sentence indicates that there are two separate ideas, not one.

In the second example, the use of "and" seems to tie three separate ideas together; that is, it is those workers who do all three jobs who will be affected—clearly not the intent of the sentence. These are three separate ideas that can be clarified by changing "and" to "or," or by making a series of parallel ideas: "…workers who wait tables in restaurants, workers who operate concessions in public places, and workers who drive taxis."

---

**WATCH FOR AMBIGUITY IN SCOPE**

 Be alert for sentences that run two or more ideas together. Usually the error can be corrected by adding words to clarify the two ideas as distinct and to separate them from one another.

---

## Low-Level Usage

There are a few expressions heard frequently in conversation that are regarded as ***low-level usage*** and are unacceptable in standard written English. The exam measures the ability to recognize the difference between standard and non-standard writing.

*Example:*

> She <u>sure</u> is pretty! ✘
> She <u>certainly</u> is pretty! ✓

## AVOID LOW-LEVEL USAGE

| *Instead of:* | *Say:* |
|---|---|
| ain't | am not; are not; is not |
| aren't I | am I not |
| around (2 p.m.) | about (2 p.m.) |
| being that | since |
| between you and I | between you and me |
| bunch (of people) | group (of people) |
| but that | that |
| cannot seem | seems unable |
| different than | different from |
| else than | other than |
| equally as good | equally good; just as good |
| have got | have |
| having took | having taken |
| in back of | behind |
| kind of | somewhat; rather |
| worst kind | very badly |

| *Instead of:* | *Say:* |
|---|---|
| would of | would have |
| may of | may have |
| might of | might have |
| must of | must have |
| off of | off |
| on account of | because |
| plan on | plan to |
| put in | spend, make, or devote |
| quite a few | many |
| same as | in the same way as; just as |
| sort of | somewhat; rather |
| theirselves | themselves |
| try and | try to |
| unbeknownst to | without the knowledge of |
| upwards of | more than |
| should of | should have |

# Idioms and Clarity of Expression

**DIRECTIONS:** In sentences #1–99, circle the correct word choice. Answers are on page 1022.

1. He is the (principal, principle) backer of the play.

2. I hope your company will (accept, except) our offer.

3. We hope to have good (weather, whether) when we are on vacation.

4. Put the rabbit back (in, into) the hat.

5. The attorney will (advice, advise) you of your rights.

6. She is far taller (than, then) I imagined.

7. Are they (all ready, already) to go?

8. She answered the letter on shocking pink (stationary, stationery).

9. What is the (affect, effect) you are trying to achieve?

10. I want to (set, sit) next to my grandfather.

11. He's going to (lay, lie) down for a nap.

12. I'm (all together, altogether) tired of his excuses.

13. He saluted when the flag (passed, past) by.

14. I'd like another portion of (desert, dessert).

15. Try not to (loose, lose) your good reputation.

16. How much will the final examination (effect, affect) my grade?

17. What is it (you're, your) trying to suggest?

18. She's not (use, used) to such cold weather.

19. The cost of the coat will (raise, rise) again.

20. You are (suppose, supposed) to be home at six o'clock.

21. Her cat ran straight for (its, it's) bowl of food.

22. Are you (conscience, conscious) of what you are doing?

23. It will (seen, seem) that we are afraid.

24. His essays are filled with literary (allusions, illusions).

25. This wine will be a good (complement, compliment) to the meal.

26. It's (later, latter) than you think!

27. My cousin has a swimmer's (build, built).

28. I never (knew, new) him before today.

29. She asked her a (personal, personnel) question.

30. The golf (coarse, course) was very crowded.

31. The costume was made from old (cloth, clothe) napkins.

32. The ball carrier was trying to (allude, elude) the tacklers.

33. There are (know, no) more exhibitions planned.

34. I will wait for you in the (ante, anti) room.

35. Her (moral, morale) is very low.

36. Begin the sentence with a (capital, capitol) letter.

37. The fact that he nearly had an accident did not even (faze, phase) him.

38. He earns royalties in (access, excess) of a million dollars a year.

39. Now, may we (precede, proceed) with the debate?

40. Her (fort, forte) is writing lyrics for musical comedy.

41. They wondered how they were going to (disburse, disperse) the huge crowd.

42. Everyone was dressed (formally, formerly) for the dinner party.

43. I am not (adverse, averse) to continuing the discussion at another time.

44. Can something be done to retard the (incidence, incidents) of influenza in that area?

45. "Seeing the film in class will serve a (dual, duel) purpose," he explained.

46. I'm not sure I want to (expand, expend) so much energy on that project.

47. Imagine my (discomfit, discomfort) when she showed up at the party too!

48. He was a famous matinee (idle, idol) many years ago.

49. When did they (emigrate, immigrate) from New York to Paris?

50. I think she is part of a (click, clique) of snobs and creeps.

51. She paid little attention to the fortune-teller's (prophecy, prophesy).

52. The lights went out when the (lightning, lightening) hit the house.

53. I'll provide you (what ever, whatever) assistance you require.

54. We are in (eminent, imminent) danger of losing our reservations.

55. Will she be able to (adapt, adopt) to our way of performing the operation?

56. As we went through the old cemetery, we were fascinated by some of the (epitaphs, epithets).

57. He shared the riches (between, among) Laura, Millie, and Ernestine.

58. The housing law was rewritten for his (advantage, benefit).

59. (Alot, A lot) of the time, he falls asleep at nine o'clock.

60. It was difficult to keep track of the (amount, number) of people who visited him last week.

61. I see him in the park (almost, most) every day.

62. Are you certain that he is (alright, all right) now?

63. She is just beginning to (aggravate, annoy) her mother.

64. He is the school's oldest living (alumni, alumnus).

65. He spotted the riverbank and then guided the canoe up (alongside, alongside of).

66. (Being as, Since) it is Wednesday, we are going to a Broadway matinee.

67. He is (anxious, eager) to be finished with the dental treatment.

68. Where do you want to (meet, meet at)?

69. My aunt just went inside to rest (awhile, a while).

70. It was (about, around) noon when we met for lunch.

71. I brought a (couple, couple of) books for you; both are historical novels.

72. Between (you and I, you and me), I think that her hat is very unbecoming.

73. The (continual, continuous) ticking of the clock was very disconcerting.

74. She (cannot seem, seems unable) to get up early enough to eat breakfast with him.

75. I (assume, expect) that you really earned your salary today.

76. I'm (disinterested, uninterested) in seeing that movie.

77. You must be (every bit as, just as) sleepy as I am.

78. I doubt (that, whether) it will snow today.

79. Sam, Joe, Lou, and Artie have worked with (each other, one another) before.

80. She asked him (if, whether) he wanted to have lunch with her or with her sister.

81. All (humans, human beings) need to take a certain amount of water into their bodies every week.

82. We hope to (conclude, finalize) the deal this month.

83. We were upset when she (flaunted, flouted) her mother's orders.

84. His girlfriend only eats (healthful, healthy) foods.

85. He said such terrible things about her that she is suing him for (libel, slander).

86. I would like to see you in (regard, regards) to the apartment you plan to rent.

87. She is always late for work, (irregardless, regardless) of how early she wakes up in the morning.

88. He'll (loan, lend) you a hand carrying the groceries.

89. The media (are, is) doing the job poorly.

90. The art director was taken (off, off of) the most profitable gallery show.

91. I hope that she will (quit, stop) sending us the job applications.

92. The reason the baby is crying is (because, that) she is hungry.

93. Does he (manage, run) the department efficiently?

94. Anyone who wants to have (his or her, their) conference with me today is invited to meet in my office at ten o'clock.

95. She scored more points than (any, any other) player on the team.

96. His room is very neat (but, while) hers is very messy.

97. He will (try and, try to) be more pleasant to his sister.

98. I shall give it to (whoever, whomever) arrives first.

99. This time, we will not wait (for, on) you for more than ten minutes.

**DIRECTIONS:** In sentences #100–114, determine whether the gerund choice (A), the infinitive choice (B), or BOTH the gerund and the infinitive (C), is the correct answer to fill in the blank. Answers are on page 1031.

100. After the break, the teacher continued _____.

    (A) lecturing
    (B) to lecture
    (C) BOTH

101. He forgot _____ me at the party last year, so he introduced himself again.

    (A) meeting
    (B) to meet
    (C) BOTH

102. Please remember _____ five minutes early on the day of the test.

    (A) arriving
    (B) to arrive
    (C) BOTH

103. He hesitated _____ for the assignment.

    (A) volunteering
    (B) to volunteer
    (C) BOTH

104. After her speech, the lecturer proceeded _____ questions.

    (A) taking
    (B) to take
    (C) BOTH

105. The politician continued _____ soft money contributions during his campaign.

    (A) accepting
    (B) to accept
    (C) BOTH

106. "I will not tolerate _____," the professor said.

    (A) talking
    (B) to talk
    (C) BOTH

107. Taking sixteen credit hours, the student has neglected _____ some of her essays.

    (A) writing
    (B) to write
    (C) BOTH

108. She has not even begun _____ for the exam even though it is tomorrow.

    (A) preparing
    (B) to prepare
    (C) BOTH

109. The applicant tried _____ for an extension of the deadline, but his request was turned down.

    (A) asking
    (B) to ask
    (C) BOTH

110. The class has been warned not _____.

    (A) cheating
    (B) to cheat
    (C) BOTH

111. The senior anticipates _____ next month.

    (A) graduating
    (B) to graduate
    (C) BOTH

112. Knowing that the deadline is tomorrow has forced me _____ on the project.

    (A) concentrating
    (B) to concentrate
    (C) BOTH

113. Cats cannot stand _____ the sound of a vacuum cleaner.

    (A) hearing
    (B) to hear
    (C) BOTH

114. I do not want to spend any more time _____ these equations.

    (A) solving
    (B) to solve
    (C) BOTH

**DIRECTIONS**: For items #115–129, circle the letter of the underlined part of the sentence containing the error and write the correct word or phrase. Answers are on page 1032.

115. Economists have established that there is a
               A
    relation—albeit an indirect one—between the
       B
    amount of oil imported into this country and the
       C
    number of traffic accidents.
       D

    Correct Word/Phrase: _____

116. Ironically, today Elizabeth I and her rival for the
                                        A
    English throne, Mary Stuart, whom Elizabeth had
                                    B              C
    executed, lay side by side in Westminster Abbey.
              D

    Correct Word/Phrase: _____

117. Although the script is interesting and well-

    written, it is not clear <u>whether</u> it can be <u>adopted</u>
                                    A                      B
    for television since the original story contains

    scenes that <u>could not be broadcast</u> <u>over</u> the public
                              C                      D
    airwaves.

    Correct Word/Phrase: _____

118. If he <u>had known</u> how difficult law school would
            A
    be, he <u>would of chosen</u> a different profession or
                B
    perhaps even <u>have followed</u> the <u>tradition</u> of going
                          C                      D
    into the family business.

    Correct Word/Phrase: _____

119. When shopping malls and business complexes <u>get</u>
                                                            A
    <u>built</u>, quite often the needs of the handicapped <u>are</u>
    A                                                          B
    not considered; as a result, it later becomes

    necessary to make <u>costly</u> modifications to
                              C
    structures to make them <u>accessible</u> to persons of
                                  D
    impaired mobility.

    Correct Word/Phrase: _____

120. Researchers <u>have found</u> that children <u>experience</u>
                        A                              B
    twice as much deep sleep <u>than</u> adults, <u>a fact</u>
                                    C              D
    <u>which may</u> teach us something about the
          D
    connection between age and learning ability.

    Correct Word/Phrase: _____

121. <u>Despite</u> the ample evidence that smoking <u>is</u>
      A                                                B
    <u>hazardous</u> to one's health, <u>many</u> people seem to
          B                              C
    find the warnings neither frightening <u>or</u>
                                                D
    convincing.

    Correct Word/Phrase: _____

122. No matter how <u>many</u> encores the audience
                        A
    demands, Helen Walker <u>is always willing</u> to sing
                                      B
    <u>yet</u> another song <u>which pleases</u> the audience.
      C                          D

    Correct Word/Phrase: _____

123. In light of <u>recent</u> translations of stone carvings
                      A
    <u>depicting</u> scenes of carnage, scholars are now
        B
    questioning <u>as to whether</u> the Incas were <u>really</u> a
                      C                                  D
    peace-loving civilization.

    Correct Word/Phrase: _____

124. In galleries containing works of both Gauguin

    and Cézanne, you will find an equal <u>number</u> of
                                                A
    admirers <u>in front of</u> the works of <u>each</u>, but most
                  B                              C
    art critics agree that Gauguin is not of the same

    artistic stature <u>with</u> Cézanne.
                          D

    Correct Word/Phrase: _____

125. The Board of Education <u>will never be</u> <u>fully</u>
                                  A              B
    <u>responsive</u> to the needs of Hispanic children in
        C
    the school system so long <u>that</u> the mayor refuses
                                  D
    to appoint a Hispanic educator to the Board.

    Correct Word/Phrase: _____

126. The judge <u>sentenced</u> the president of the
         A
    corporation to ten years in prison for <u>embezzling</u>
                                              B
    corporate funds but <u>gave</u> his partner in crime <u>less</u>
                          C                                 D
    <u>of a sentence</u>.
         D

    Correct Word/Phrase: _____

127. Scientists <u>have recently discovered</u> that mussels
                       A
    <u>secrete</u> a powerful adhesive that allows them
       B
    <u>attaching</u> themselves to rocks, concrete pilings,
       C
    and <u>other</u> stone or masonry structures.
          D

    Correct Word/Phrase: _____

128. Wall paintings found recently in the caves of

    Brazil are <u>convincing</u> evidence that cave art
                  A
    <u>developed</u> in the Americas at an earlier time <u>as it</u>
       B                                                 C D
    did on other continents.

    Correct Word/Phrase: _____

129. The <u>drop</u> in oil prices and the slump in the
         A
    computer industry <u>account for</u> the recent <u>raise</u> in
                          B                           C
    unemployment in Texas and the <u>associated</u> decline
                                       D
    in the value of real estate in the region.

    Correct Word/Phrase: _____

# Punctuation

Although ***punctuation*** is stressed less than other aspects of standard written English on the exam, it is important to be aware of the principal rules governing punctuation. This section is not intended to give the definitive set of punctuation rules, but rather to provide a basic framework for correct usage.

## Commas

### USE A COMMA BEFORE COORDINATING CONJUNCTIONS

 Coordinating conjunctions ("and," "but," "nor," "or," "for," "yet," "so") join two independent clauses. Use a comma before coordinating conjunctions unless the two clauses are very short.

*Examples:*

The boy wanted to borrow a book from the library, <u>but</u> the librarian would not allow him to take it until he had paid his fines. ✓

Joe has been diligent about completing his work, <u>but</u> he has had many problems concerning his punctuality. ✓

I sincerely hope that these exercises prove to be of assistance to you, <u>and</u> I believe that they will help you to make a better showing on your examinations. ✓

Generally, a comma is not used before a subordinate clause that ends a sentence. However, in long, unwieldy sentences, it is acceptable.

If there is no subject following the conjunction, then a comma cannot be used, as this would create a sentence fragment. If there is a subject following the conjunction, but the two clauses are very short, the separating comma may be omitted.

*Examples:*

She went to the cafe <u>and</u> bought a cup of coffee. ✓

Roy washed the dishes <u>and</u> Helen dried them. ✓

I saw him <u>and</u> I spoke to him. ✓

A restrictive phrase or clause is vital to the meaning of a sentence and cannot be omitted. Do NOT set apart restrictive phrases or clauses with commas.

*Example:*

A sailboat, without sails, is useless. ✗

A sailboat without sails is useless. ✓

---

**USE COMMAS FOR CLARITY**

1. Use a comma if the sentence might be subject to different interpretations without it.

2. Use a comma if a pause would make the sentence clearer and easier to read.

---

The following examples show how commas change the interpretation of the sentences.

*Examples:*

The banks that closed yesterday are in serious financial trouble. (Some banks closed yesterday, and those banks are in trouble.)

The banks, which closed yesterday, are in serious financial trouble. (All banks closed yesterday, and all banks are in trouble.)

My cat Leo fell down the laundry chute. (The implication is that I have more than one cat.)

My cat, Leo, fell down the laundry chute. (Here, Leo is an appositive. Presumably, he is the only cat.)

Inside the people were dancing. ✗

Inside, the people were dancing. ✓

After all crime must be punished. ✗

After all, crime must be punished. ✓

Pausing is not infallible, but it is the best resort when all other rules governing use of the comma seem to fail.

---

**USE COMMAS TO SEPARATE COORDINATE ADJECTIVES,
WORDS IN A SERIES, AND NOUNS IN DIRECT ADDRESS**

1. Coordinate adjectives are adjectives of equal importance that precede the noun that they describe. If the word "and" can be added between the adjectives without changing the sense of the sentence, then use commas.

2. Use a comma between words in a series when three or more elements are present. In such a series, use a comma before "and" or "or." If the series ends in "etc.," use a comma before "etc." Do not use a comma after "etc." in a series, even if the sentence continues.

3. Use commas to set off nouns in direct address. The name of the person addressed is separated from the rest of the sentence by commas.

---

*Examples:*

The jolly, fat man stood at the top of the stairs. ✔

He is a wise, charming man. ✔

She is a slow, careful reader. ✔

Coats, umbrellas, and boots should be placed in the closet at the end of the hall. ✔

Pencils, scissors, paper clips, etc. belong in your top desk drawer. ✔

Bob, please close the door. ✔

I think, José, that you are the one who was chosen. ✔

---

### USE A COMMA TO SEPARATE QUOTATIONS AND INTRODUCTORY PHRASES

1. Use a comma to separate a short, direct quotation from the speaker.

2. Use a comma after an introductory phrase of two or more words.

3. Use a comma after an introductory phrase whenever the comma would aid clarity.

4. Use a comma after introductory gerunds, participles, and infinitives, regardless of their length.

---

On the other hand, if the subordinate clause follows the main clause, it is not necessary to set it off with a comma.

*Examples:*

She said, "I must leave work on time today." ✔

"Tomorrow I begin my summer job," he told us. ✔

As a child, she was a tomboy. ✔

She was a tomboy as a child. ✔

To Dan, Phil was a friend as well as a brother. ✔

Phil was a friend as well as a brother to Dan. ✔

In 1998, 300 people lost their lives in an earthquake. ✔

300 people lost their lives in an earthquake in 1998. ✔

When you come home, please ring the bell before opening the door. ✔

Please ring the bell before opening the door when you come home. ✔

Because the prisoner had a history of attempted jailbreaks, he was put under heavy guard. ✔

The prisoner was put under heavy guard because he had a history of attempted jailbreaks. ✔

Finally, commas must be used to set off a phrase or to interrupt the flow of the sentence.

> ## USE PAIRS OF COMMAS TO SET OFF
> ## APPOSITIVE, PARENTHETICAL, AND NON-RESTRICTIVE ELEMENTS
>
> 1. An appositive phrase follows a noun or pronoun and has the same meaning as that noun or pronoun.
>
> 2. Parenthetical expressions are words that interrupt the flow of the sentence ("however," "though," "for instance," "by the way," "to tell the truth," "believe me," "it appears to me," "I am sure," "as a matter of fact") without changing the meaning of the sentence.
>
> 3. A non-restrictive element introduces material that is not essential to the sentence and, if removed, will not change the meaning of the original sentence.

*Examples:*

Mr. Dias, <u>our lawyer</u>, gave us some great advice. ✓

Bob, <u>an industrious and hard-working student</u>, will run for class treasurer. ✓

This book, <u>I believe</u>, is the best of its kind. ✓

Julie and her three dogs, <u>I am sure</u>, will not easily find an apartment to rent. ✓

Sam, <u>who is a very well behaved dog</u>, never strays from the front yard. ✓

Millie, <u>who is a fine student</u>, has a perfect attendance record. ✓

Test for placement of commas in a parenthetical expression by reading the sentence aloud. If you would pause before and after such an expression, then commas should set it off. In general, if you can omit the material without changing the meaning of the main clause, then the material is non-restrictive and it should be set off by commas.

> ## USE COMMAS TO SEPARATE DATES, ADDRESSES, AND SPECIFIC LOCATIONS
>
> Commas, including a comma after the last item, separate the different parts of a date and address.

*Examples:*

The train will arrive on Friday, February 13, 2003, if it is on schedule. ✓

My new address is: 2040 Winnebago Ave., Apt. #2, Madison, WI. ✓

My daughter traveled from Cambridge, Massachusetts, to Albany, New York, in three hours. ✓

The above rules summarize the most important uses of commas. If you use them in just these situations, then you will not make a serious comma usage mistake.

---

> **SITUATIONS IN WHICH NOT TO USE COMMAS**
>
> 1. Do not use a comma to separate a subject from its verb.
>
> 2. Do not use commas to set off restrictive or necessary clauses or phrases.
>
> 3. Do not use a comma in place of a conjunction.

## Semicolons

> **USE A SEMICOLON TO SEPARATE TWO COMPLETE IDEAS**
>
>  A semicolon may be used to separate two complete ideas (independent clauses) in a sentence when the two ideas have a close relationship, and they are NOT connected with a coordinating conjunction.

*Example:*

The setting sun caused the fields to take on a special glow; all was bathed in a pale light. ✓

The *semicolon* is often used between two or more independent clauses connected by conjunctive adverbs such as "consequently," "therefore," "also," "furthermore," "for example," "however," "nevertheless," "still," "yet," "moreover," and "otherwise." (Note: A comma must follow the adverb.)

> **USE SEMICOLONS ONLY FOR INDEPENDENT CLAUSES**
>
>  Unless each clause can function as an independent sentence, it is probably wrong to use a semicolon.

*Examples:*

He waited at the station for well over an hour; however, no one appeared. ✓
He waited at the station for well over an hour. However, no one appeared. ✓

Anne is working at the front desk on Monday; Ernie will take over on Tuesday. ✓
Anne is working at the front desk on Monday. Ernie will take over on Tuesday. ✓

She waited for her check to arrive in the mail for two weeks; however, the check never appeared. ✓
She waited for her check to arrive in the mail for two weeks. However, the check never appeared. ✓

However, DO NOT use a semicolon between an independent clause and a phrase or subordinate clause.

*Example:*

She worked extra hours every night; yet, was not able to finish the project on time. ✗

She worked extra hours every night yet was not able to finish the project on time. ✓

To summarize, two main clauses should be separated by a conjunction, by a semicolon, or by a period (two sentences). The same two clauses may be written in any one of three ways, as the following example shows.

*Example:*

Autumn had come and the trees were almost bare. ✓

Autumn had come; the trees were almost bare. ✓

Autumn had come. The trees were almost bare. ✓

If you are uncertain about how to use a semicolon to connect independent clauses, write two sentences instead.

---

**USE A SEMICOLON TO SEPARATE A SERIES OF
PHRASES CONTAINING COMMAS OR A SERIES OF NUMBERS**

1. Use a semicolon to separate a series of phrases or clauses, each of which contains commas.

2. Use a semicolon to avoid confusion with numbers.

---

*Examples:*

The old gentleman's heirs were Margaret Whitlock, his half-sister; James Bagley, the butler; William Frame, companion to his late cousin, Robert Bone; and his favorite charity, the Salvation Army. ✓

Add the following prices: $.25; $7.50; and $12.89. ✓

---

## Colons

The *colon* is always used in the following situations.

---

**RULES FOR SITUATIONS REQUIRING A COLON**

1. A colon should be placed after the salutation in a business letter.

2. Use a colon to separate hours from minutes.

3. The colon is used to precede a list of three or more items or a long quotation.

4. A colon should be used to introduce a question.

5. A colon is generally used in places where a full stop would leave the beginning of the sentence unchanged in meaning.

---

*Examples:*

Dear Board Member: ✓

The eclipse occurred at 10:36 A.M. ✓

There are three branches of government: executive, judicial, and legislative. ✓

My question is this: are you willing to punch a time clock? ✓

Avoid using the colon directly after a verb or when it interrupts the natural flow of language.

*Examples:*

We played: volleyball, badminton, football, and tag. ✗

We played volleyball, badminton, football, and tag. ✓

We purchased: apples, pears, bananas, and grapes. ✗

We purchased apples, pears, bananas, and grapes. ✓

---

### DO NOT USE COLONS TO CALL ATTENTION IF ALREADY SIGNALED

 A colon may be used to introduce or to call attention to elaboration or explanation. However, do not use colons after expressions such as "like," "for example," "such as," and "that is." In fact, colons are intended to replace these terms.

---

Be careful not to use a colon to introduce or call attention to material that is already signaled by some other element of the sentence.

*Example:*

We did many different things on our vacation, such as: hiking, camping, biking, canoeing, and kayaking. ✗

We did many different things on our vacation, such as hiking, camping, biking, canoeing, and kayaking. ✓

We did many different things on our vacation: hiking, camping, biking, canoeing, and kayaking. ✓

## Periods

---

### RULES FOR SITUATIONS REQUIRING A PERIOD

1. Use a period at the end of a sentence that makes a statement, gives a command, or makes a "polite request" in the form of a question that does not require an answer.

2. Use a period after an abbreviation and after the initial in a person's name.

---

*Examples:*

He is my best friend. ✓

There are thirty days in September. ✓

Would you please hold the script so that I may see if I have memorized my lines. ✓

Gen. Robert E. Lee led the Confederate forces. ✓

Note: DO NOT use a period in postal service name abbreviations such as AZ (Arizona) or MI (Michigan).

## Exclamation and Question Marks

### RULES FOR SITUATIONS REQUIRING EXCLAMATION MARKS

 Use exclamation marks after expressions showing strong emotion or issuing a command. Use an exclamation mark only to express strong feeling or emotion or to imply urgency.

*Examples:*

Wonderful! You won the lottery! ✓

Oh no! I won't go! ✓

### RULES FOR SITUATIONS REQUIRING QUESTION MARKS

 Use a question mark after a request for information. A question mark is used only after a direct question. A period is used after an indirect question.

Note: A question must end with a *question mark* even if the question does not encompass the entire sentence.

*Examples:*

At what time does the last bus leave? ✓

"Daddy, are we there yet?" the child asked. ✓

Did you take the examination on Friday? ✓

The instructor wanted to know if you took the examination on Friday. ✓

## Dashes

The material following the *dash* usually directs the reader's attention to the content that precedes it. Unless this material ends a sentence, dashes, like parentheses, must be used in pairs.

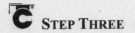 

---

> **RULES FOR SITUATIONS REQUIRING A DASH**
>
> 1. Use a dash for emphasis or to set off an explanatory group of words.
>
> 2. Use a dash before a word or group of words that indicates a summation or reversal of what preceded it.
>
> 3. Use a dash to mark a sudden break in thought that leaves a sentence unfinished.

*Examples:*

The tools of his trade—probe, mirror, and cotton swabs—were neatly arranged on the dentist's tray. ✔

Patience, sensitivity, understanding, and empathy—these are the marks of a friend. ✔

He was not pleased with—in fact, he was completely hostile toward—the takeover. ✔

Dashes in sentences have a function that is similar to commas when they are used to set off parenthetical remarks. The difference between the two is a matter of emphasis. The dashes mark a more dramatic shift or interruption of thought. Do not mix dashes and commas.

## Hyphens

> **RULES FOR SITUATIONS REQUIRING A HYPHEN**
>
> 1. Use a hyphen with a compound modifier that precedes the noun.
>
> 2. Use a hyphen with fractions that serve as adjectives or adverbs.

The following examples demonstrate situations in which it is correct to use a *hyphen* and situations in which it is correct to NOT use a hyphen.

*Examples:*

There was a sit-in demonstration at the office. ✔

We will sit in the auditorium. ✔

I purchased a four-cylinder car. ✔

I purchased a car with four cylinders. ✔

## Quotation Marks

### WHEN TO USE QUOTATION MARKS

1. Use quotation marks to enclose the actual words of the speaker or writer.

2. Use quotation marks to emphasize words used in a special or unusual sense.

3. Use quotation marks to set off titles of short themes or parts of a larger work.

*Examples:*

Jane said, "There will be many people at the party." ✔

He kept using the phrase "you know" throughout his conversation. ✔

"Within You, Without You" is my favorite song on the *Sgt. Pepper's Lonely Hearts Club Band* album by The Beatles. ✔

### WHEN NOT TO USE QUOTATION MARKS

1. Do not use quotation marks for indirect quotations.

2. Do not use quotation marks to justify a poor choice of words.

*Examples:*

He said that "he would be happy to attend the meeting." ✘

He said that he would be happy to attend the meeting. ✔

I gave her research summary article a low score because I didn't think she "got it right." ✘

I gave her research summary article a low score because I didn't think she understood the methods or results. ✔

### PUNCTUATION RULES FOR SITUATIONS WITH QUOTATIONS

1. Always place periods and commas inside quotation marks.

2. Place question marks inside quotation marks if it is part of a quotation. If the entire sentence, including the quotation, is a question, place the question mark outside the quotation marks.

3. Place exclamation marks inside quotation marks if it is part of a quotation. If the entire sentence, including the quotation, is an exclamation, place the exclamation mark outside the quotation marks.

4. Always place colons and semicolons outside quotation marks.

*Examples:*

The principal said, "Cars parked in the fire lane will be ticketed." ✓

The first chapter of *The Andromeda Strain* is entitled "The Country of Lost Borders." ✓

My favorite poem is "My Last Duchess," a dramatic monologue written by Robert Browning. ✓

Three stories in Kurt Vonnegut's *Welcome to the Monkey House* are "Harrison Bergeron," "Next Door," and "EPICAC." ✓

Mother asked earlier tonight, "Did you take out the garbage?" ✓

Do you want to go to the movies and see "Jurassic Park"? ✓

The sentry shouted, "Drop your gun!" ✓

Save us from our "friends"! ✓

My favorite poem is "My Last Duchess"; this poem is a dramatic monologue written by Robert Browning. ✓

He was quoted as supporting the investigation in the "Washington Post": "I don't know of any proof of misappropriation of funds; however, I support a full investigation into any possible wrongdoing by government officials." ✓

## Apostrophes

Errors of **apostrophe** usage usually occur when a paper is not proofread or when a writer isn't sure how to use an apostrophe correctly. The apostrophe is used for possession and contraction.

---

### USE APOSTROPHES FOR POSSESSION

 Use apostrophes to indicate the possessive case of nouns. Do NOT use apostrophes with possessive pronouns (e.g., "yours," "hers," "ours," "theirs," and "whose").

---

*Examples:*

lady's = belonging to the lady ✓

ladies' = belonging to the ladies ✓

To test for correct placement of the apostrophe, read the apostrophe as "of the."

*Examples:*

childrens' = of the childrens ✗

children's = of the children ✓

The placement rule applies at all times, even with regard to compound nouns separated by hyphens and with regard to entities made up of two or more names.

*Examples:*

> Lansdale, Jackson, and Smith's law firm = the law firm belonging to Lansdale, Jackson, and Smith ✓
>
> Brown and Sons' delivery truck = the delivery truck of Brown and Sons ✓

If the noun does not end in "s"—whether singular or plural—add "'s"; if the noun ends in "s," simply add the apostrophe.

*Examples:*

> Socrates's philosophy ✗
>
> Socrates' philosophy ✓
>
> Johnsons's house ✗
>
> Johnsons' house ✓

---

### USE APOSTROPHES FOR CONTRACTIONS

 Use an apostrophe to indicate a contraction; insert the apostrophe in place of the omitted letter(s). It is NOT acceptable in standard written English to begin a paragraph with a contraction.

---

*Examples:*

> haven't = have not ✓
>
> o'clock = of the clock ✓
>
> class of '85 = class of 1985 ✓

Be careful with "its" and "it's." "It's" is the contraction of "it is." "Its" is the third person possessive pronoun. Also, DO NOT confuse "they're" ("they are"), "their" (possessive), and "there" (preposition).

*Example:*

> The cat knows when <u>it's</u> time for <u>its</u> bath. ✓
>
> They're happy to be done with <u>their</u> work. ✓

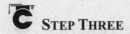 

# Punctuation

**DIRECTIONS:** Punctuate sentences #1–55 with additional commas, semicolons, periods, exclamation marks, question marks, quotation marks, dashes, hyphens, and apostrophes *if necessary.* Answers are on page 1033.

1. He was not aware that you had lost your passport

2. Did you report the loss to the proper authorities

3. I suppose you had to fill out many forms

4. What a nuisance

5. I hate doing so much paper work

6. Did you ever discover where the wallet was

7. I imagine you wondered how it was misplaced

8. Good for you

9. At least you now have your passport

10. What will you do if it happens again

11. I dont know if they are coming though I sent them an invitation weeks ago

12. Neurology is the science that deals with the anatomy physiology and pathology of the nervous system

13. Nursery lore like everything human has been subject to many changes over long periods of time

14. Bob read Joyces Ulysses to the class everyone seemed to enjoy the reading

15. In order to provide more living space we converted an attached garage into a den

16. Because he is such an industrious student he has many friends

17. I dont recall who wrote A Midsummer Nights Dream

18. In the writing class students learned about coordinating conjunctions and but so or yet for and nor

19. Those who do not complain are never pitied is a familiar quotation by Jane Austen

20. Howard and his ex wife are on amicable terms

21. Her last words were call me on Sunday and she jumped on the train

22. He is an out of work carpenter

23. This is what is called a pregnant chad

24. Come early on Monday the teacher said to take the exit exam

25. The dog mans best friend is a companion to many

26. The winner of the horse race is to the best of my knowledge Silver

27. Every time I see him the dentist asks me how often I floss

28. The officer was off duty when he witnessed the crime

29. Anna Karenina is my favorite movie

30. Red white and blue are the colors of the American flag

31. Stop using stuff in your essays its too informal

32. She was a self made millionaire

33. The Smiths who are the best neighbors anyone could ask for have moved out

34. My eighteen year old daughter will graduate this spring

35. Dracula lived in Transylvania

36. The students were told to put away their books

37. Begun while Dickens was still at work on Pickwick Papers Oliver Twist was published in 1837 and is now one of the authors most widely read works

38. Given the great difficulties of making soundings in very deep water it is not surprising that few such soundings were made until the middle of this century

39. Did you finishing writing your thesis prospectus on time

40. The root of modern Dutch was once supposed to be Old Frisian but the general view now is that the characteristic forms of Dutch are at least as old as those of Old Frisian

41. Moose once scarce because of indiscriminate hunting are protected by law and the number of moose is once again increasing

42. He ordered a set of books several records and a film almost a month ago

43. Perhaps the most interesting section of New Orleans is the French Quarter which extends from North Rampart Street to the Mississippi River

44. Writing for a skeptical and rationalizing age Shaftesbury was primarily concerned with showing that goodness and beauty are not determined by revelation authority opinion or fashion

45. We tried our best to purchase the books but we were completely unsuccessful even though we went to every bookstore in town

46. A great deal of information regarding the nutritional requirements of farm animals has been accumulated over countless generations by trial and error however most recent advances have come as the result of systematic studies at schools of animal husbandry

47. Omoo Melvilles sequel to Typee appeared in 1847 and went through five printings in that year alone

48. Go to Florence for the best gelato in all of Italy said the old man to the young tourist

49. Although the first school for African Americans was a public school established in Virginia in 1620 most educational opportunities for African Americans before the Civil War were provided by private agencies

50. As the climate of Europe changed the population became too dense for the supply of food obtained by hunting and other means of securing food such as the domestication of animals were necessary

51. In Faulkners poetic realism the grotesque is somber violent and often inexplicable in Caldwells writing it is lightened by a ballad like humorous sophisticated detachment

52. The valley of the Loire a northern tributary of the Loire at Angers abounds in rock villages they occur in many other places in France Spain and northern Italy

53. The telephone rang several times as a result his sleep was interrupted

54. He has forty three thousand dollars to spend however once that is gone he will be penniless

55. Before an examination do the following review your work get a good nights sleep eat a balanced breakfast and arrive on time to take the test

# Planning an Essay

## Understand the Assignment

### Let the Prompt Be Your Topic

When presented with a prompt, always read it several times until you are completely familiar with the material. Sometimes, it may be helpful to underline key words or phrases that are important.

Usually, the prompt is intended to be your topic and an inspiration to writing. If you pay careful attention to the language of the prompt, it can actually help you to get started.

Consider this sample essay prompt:

> *Human beings are often cruel, but they also have the capacity for kindness and compassion. In my opinion, an example that demonstrates this capacity is ——.*

> **Assignment:** Complete the statement above with an example from current affairs, history, literature, or your own personal experience. Then, write a well-organized essay explaining why you regard that event favorably.

This topic explicitly invites you to choose an example of kindness or compassion from history, current events, literature, or even personal experience. Thus, you could write about the end of a war (history), a mission of humanitarian aid (current events), the self-sacrifice of a fictional character (literature), or even about the day that your family helped a stranded motorist (personal experience). Remember that what you have to say is not as important as how you say it.

### Develop a Point of View

Sometimes an essay prompt will invite you to present your opinion on an issue. When you encounter such prompts, you must decide whether you are in agreement or disagreement with the statement given.

### Write Only on the Assigned Topic

While the types of prompts may differ among assignments or tests, the directions all agree on this point: you must write on the assigned topic. The assigned topic is often "open-ended," so you should have no problem coming up with something to write.

## Organize Your Thoughts

### Limit the Scope of Your Essay

The requirements of your writing assignment should determine the length and scope of your essay. Always remember to define the coverage of an essay before setting pen to paper; this will improve the focus of an essay so that the essay sets out to accomplish only the assigned task, whether it is to defend a controversial position or to provide a definition. The more limited and specific your topic, the more successful your essay is likely to be: you will be able to supply the specific details that add depth and sophistication to an essay. You will also reduce the possibility of straying onto a tangent point or under-developing a specific claim.

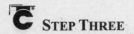 

*Develop a Thesis*

A thesis statement solidifies the scope, purpose, and direction of an essay in a clear and focused statement. This thesis statement usually includes your claims or assertions and the reasoning and evidence that support them. If possible, try to formulate the thesis of your composition in a single sentence during the pre-writing stage. When developing a thesis, keep in mind the following ideas:

---

**IMPORTANT POINTS FOR DEVELOPING A THESIS**

1. The thesis must not be too broad or too narrow.

2. The thesis must be clear to both you and the essay reader.

3. Everything in the essay must support your thesis.

4. Use specific details and examples rather than generalizations to support your thesis.

---

*Identify Key Points*

An effective essay sets out to prove the claims and assertions of the thesis statement presented in the introductory paragraph. It is important in the early pre-writing stage to identify the key points or warrants that support your thesis. For a short essay prompt, aim for three to four key points. Then, decide on the order of presentation for those points.

*Write an Outline*

Once you gain a clear understanding of the assignment and its requirements, it is then important to organize the major points of your essay in a written outline. The purpose of outline is to develop a logical structure to your arguments and to streamline the focus of your essay. An outline should include your thesis statement, the key points of your argument, and the concluding statement of your essay. A sample outline structure is presented below for your reference.

---

**SAMPLE OUTLINE**

I. Introduction
   A. Thesis Statement

II. First Key Point
   A. Sub-Point 1
   B. Sub-Point 2

III. First Key Point
   A. Sub-Point 1
   B. Sub-Point 2

IV. First Key Point
   A. Sub-Point 1
   B. Sub-Point 2

V. Conclusion
   A. Restatement of Thesis

---

# Composition

## Organize Ideas into Paragraphs

It is the hallmark of a good writer to use paragraphs effectively. Paragraphs are important because they provide a structure through which the writer can convey meaning. To illustrate this point with an analogy, imagine a grocery store in which items are not organized into sections. In this store, there is no fresh produce section, no canned goods section, no baked goods section, and no frozen foods section. Consequently, a single bin holds bunches of bananas, cans of beans, loaves of bread, and frozen turkeys; this disorganization characterizes every bin, shelf, rack, and refrigerated case in the store, making shopping in our imaginary store very difficult. Likewise, essays without paragraphs, or with poorly organized paragraphs, are very difficult—if not impossible—to understand.

Decide on how many paragraphs you are going to write. Your essay should contain two to four important points that develop or illustrate your thesis. Each important point should be treated in its own paragraph.

Do not write simply to fill up pages and make it seem that you have many ideas. This approach can result in repetition and wordiness, which is a sign of disorganization and unclear thinking. Write enough to sufficiently demonstrate your writing ability and to prove your thesis. Five paragraphs (an introduction paragraph, three main body paragraphs, and a concluding paragraph) are usually sufficient.

## Write the Essay

Many students become frustrated before they even begin to write. They sit and stare at the blank page and complain that they are "blocked": they cannot think of anything to write. The secret to successfully beginning an essay is to simply start writing after you have completed the pre-writing stage, even if the first few sentences of the essay may need revision. Follow this simple essay structure:

---

**BASIC ESSAY STRUCTURE**

I. Introduction: State the thesis of your essay.
   A. Make sure your position is clearly phrased.
   B. Include the warrants for your thesis.

II. Body: Each paragraph in the body of your essay will be devoted to each of the warrants presented in the introduction.

III. Conclusion: Summarize your position and the reasons for your position.

---

### The Introduction

You have already analyzed the question in your pre-writing stage. Now, you will use the introduction (first paragraph) to write clear and concise sentences, describing the topic that you are writing about and indicating to the reader what you plan to say in your essay to back up your position or to illustrate, with examples, the main point. The general idea of the introduction is to indicate to the reader the direction that your essay will take. However, do not spend too much time on the introduction. This is not the place to expound on the ideas and examples.

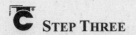 

When writing your introduction, keep these points in mind:

---

### WRITING INTRODUCTORY PARAGRAPHS

1. Always remain focused on the essay prompt. Never stray from the intended essay thesis.

2. Avoid being cute or funny, ironic or satiric, overly emotional or too dramatic. Set the tone or attitude in your first sentence. Your writing should be sincere, clear, and straightforward.

3. Do not repeat the question word for word. A paraphrase in your own words is far better than just copying the words of the exam question.

4. In your first paragraph, tell the reader the topic of your essay and the ideas that will guide the essay's development and organization. A clear topic sentence accomplishes this task.

5. Each sentence should advance your topic and be interesting to your reader.

---

An effective introduction often refers to the subject of the essay, explains the value of the topic, or attracts the attention of the reader by giving a pertinent illustration. Ineffective beginnings often contain unrelated material, ramble, and lack clarity.

### *The Body*

The heart of the essay is the development, or the middle paragraph(s). Here, the writer must attempt, in paragraph form, to support the main idea of the essay through illustrations, details, and examples. The developmental paragraphs must serve as a link in the chain of ideas and contribute directly to the essay's central thought. All the sentences of the development must explain the essential truth of the thesis or topic sentence without digression.

Each paragraph should start with a transitional statement or phrase that describes the relationship of the paragraph to the previous paragraphs. The length of any one of these body paragraphs can be variable, but each paragraph should only cover one main idea with adequate detail. You may do this through a style that is descriptive, narrative, or expository, using a factual or an anecdotal approach. Whatever approach you choose and whatever style you adopt, your writing must be coherent, logical, unified, and well-ordered.

When writing your essay, avoid the following common mistakes:

---

### AVOID THESE COMPOSITION ERRORS

1. Do not use sentences that are irrelevant and contain extraneous material.

2. Do not use sentences that have no sequence of thought or logical development of ideas.

3. Do not use sentences that do not relate to the topic sentence or do not flow from the preceding sentence.

---

*Transitions*

The good writer makes use of transitional words or phrases to connect thoughts, to provide for a logical sequence of ideas, and to link paragraphs. On the next page is a list of some of these transitions and the logical relationships that they indicate.

---

### TRANSITIONAL WORDS AND PHRASES FOR ESSAY DEVELOPMENT

| | | | | |
|---|---|---|---|---|
| *Addition:* | also | in addition | first, second, third | besides |
| | moreover | similarly | furthermore | likewise |
| | again | and | not only…but (also) | |
| | both…and | finally | | |
| | | | | |
| *Alternation:* | or | nor | either…or | neither…nor |
| | | | | |
| *Cause/effect/ purpose:* | therefore | as | consequently | because |
| | since | for | accordingly | hence |
| | so that | so | as a consequence | for this purpose |
| | as a result | | | |
| | | | | |
| *Conditions:* | if | as if (as though) | once…then | unless |
| | | | | |
| *Contrast:* | however | still | all the same | although |
| | but | on the other hand | on the contrary | nevertheless |
| | even though | yet | instead | otherwise |
| | though | | | |
| | | | | |
| *Space:* | here | opposite to | next to | where |
| | there | to the left/right | wherever | nearby |
| | in the middle | | | |
| | | | | |
| *Support:* | for example | such as | for instance | in fact |
| | in general | | | |
| | | | | |
| *Summary:* | as shown above | | to sum up | in other words |
| | in short | | in brief | in conclusion |
| | in summary | | in general | |
| | | | | |
| *Time:* | later | after (noun) | meanwhile | finally |
| | since (clause) | until (clause) | while (clause) | before (noun) |
| | then | during | after (clause) | whenever |
| | as soon as | when | at the present time | eventually |
| | in (month, year) | | before (clause) | |

---

*The Conclusion*

The successful writer must know when and how to end an essay. To effectively conclude your essay, you should draw together comments in a strong, clear concluding paragraph. This paragraph should give the reader the feeling that the essay has made its point, that the thesis has been explained, or that a point of view has been established. This can be accomplished in about three to six sentences in one of the following ways:

---

> **EFFECTIVE METHODS FOR CONCLUDING AN ESSAY**
>
> 1. Restate the main idea.
>
> 2. Summarize the material covered in the essay.
>
> 3. Conclude with a clear statement of your opinion on the issue(s) involved and discussed in the essay.

There are good techniques and there are some very ineffective methods for drawing a composition to a close. Avoid the following mistakes:

> **INEFFECTIVE METHODS FOR CONCLUDING AN ESSAY**
>
> 1. DO NOT apologize for your inability to discuss all the issues in the allotted time.
>
> 2. DO NOT complain that the topic did not interest you or that you do not think it was fair to be asked to write on so broad a topic.
>
> 3. DO NOT introduce material that you will not develop, stray off topic, or use trite or unrelated examples.

Keep in mind that a good conclusion is related to the thesis of the essay and is an integral part of the essay. It may be a review or a restatement, or it may lead the reader to do his or her own thinking, but the conclusion must be strong, clear, and effective.

An effective concluding paragraph may restate the thesis statement, summarize the main idea of the essay, draw a logical conclusion, or offer a strong opinion about what the future holds. An ineffective final paragraph often introduces new material in a scanty fashion, apologizes for the ineffectiveness of the material presented, or is illogical or unclear.

## Principles of Good Writing

While writing, keep the three principles of good writing in mind: write grammatically; punctuate and spell correctly; and write concisely, clearly, and legibly. Following these conventions will allow you to communicate your ideas clearly and effectively, improving the overall quality of your essay.

### Write Grammatically

At a minimum, you should be sure of the following principles of grammar when writing your essay:

---

### CORRECT GRAMMAR IS A MUST FOR EFFECTIVE ESSAYS

1. Does each sentence have a conjugated (main) verb that agrees with its subject?

2. Does each pronoun have a referent (antecedent) with which it agrees?

3. Do similar elements in each sentence have parallel form?

4. Do the modifiers make sense?

5. Does each sentence say what it means to say in a direct and concise way?

*Punctuate and Spell Correctly*

In addition to writing grammatically, concisely, and formally (without using slang and other low-level usage language), you must punctuate and spell correctly. Since you are in charge of writing the essay, you can choose to avoid punctuation and spelling errors. If you are unsure about how to punctuate a particular construction or spell a particular word, choose an alternative.

*Write Concisely, Clearly, and Legibly*

Simple, direct sentences are less likely to get you into trouble than complex, convoluted ones. In writing an essay for a standardized test, any sentence that is more complicated than a sentence with two independent clauses joined by a conjunction such as "and" or "but" or a sentence with one dependent and one independent clause joined by a conjunction such as "while" or "although" is an invitation to error. Unless you are confident in your ability to keep all of the elements of a more complicated sentence under control, use a simpler method of expression. Additionally, avoid using unnecessary and wordy phrases, such as those illustrated in the chart on the following page.

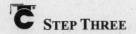

---

### AVOID THESE UNNECESSARY AND WORDY PHRASES

| *Instead of:* | *Say:* |
| --- | --- |
| In my opinion, I believe that | I believe that |
| In the event of an emergency | In an emergency |
| On the possibility that it may | Since it may |
| close to the point of | close to |
| have need for | need |
| with a view to | to |
| in view of the fact that | because |
| give consideration to | consider |
| mean to imply | imply |
| disappear from view | disappear |
| in this day and age | today |
| the issue in question | issue |

Also, while neatness is not graded, it is almost certainly true that an illegible essay will not receive a good grade. Even if you cannot perform calligraphy, you should at least be able to write legibly.

# Revision and Scoring

## Proofread Your Essay

Proofreading is an essential part of the writing process. The first draft of an essay usually will not be free of errors. This means that you will need to reread the essay and correct any grammatical errors or logical inconsistencies in your paper. There are two categories of errors that generally manifest in essays: structural errors and mechanics and usage errors.

### Proofread for Structural Errors

When proofreading, first consider the structural elements of an essay, as these are of primary importance in establishing your argument. The three most important structural factors that should be considered when editing an essay are unity, coherence, and support. Essays are judged by how well they meet these three basic requirements. To improve your essay, ask yourself the following questions:

---

**UNITY, COHERENCE, AND SUPPORT ARE
VITAL FOR AN EFFECTIVE ESSAY**

1. Do all of the details in the essay support and develop the main thesis?

2. Do all of the illustrations relate to the main point and add to the general effectiveness of the essay?

3. Have irrelevant ideas been deleted?

4. Does the essay show a sense of organization?

5. Is the material presented logically?

6. Does the essay include transitional words or phrases that allow the reader to move easily from one idea to the next?

7. Does the essay use details that make it interesting and vivid?

8. Is the main idea supported with concrete and specific illustrations?

9. Does the essay contain sufficient supporting details to clarify and persuade?

---

### Proofread for Mechanics and Usage Errors

Next, look for any mechanics and usage errors. Although these errors are less important than structural errors, they may distract the reader from the substance of your arguments, decreasing the overall ease and readability of your essay. As you proofread, you may also consider altering a word or adjusting a phrase to make your essay more effective.

---

### COMMON WRITING ERRORS ELIMINATED BY PROOFREADING

1. Omission of words—especially "the," "a," and "an"

2. Omission of final letters on words

3. Careless spelling errors

4. Incorrect use of capital letters

5. Faulty punctuation

---

## Scoring Rubric

Review the following rubric (scoring guide) so that you are familiar with the qualities that distinguish an "above average" essay response from a "below average" essay response.

| *Score* | *Essay Qualities* |
|---|---|
| **Above Average** | • demonstrates *reasonably consistent competence* <br> • makes occasional errors or lapses in quality <br> • addresses the writing task effectively <br> • is generally well-organized and adequately developed <br> • uses appropriate examples to support ideas <br> • demonstrates a competent grasp of grammar and style, employs some syntactic variety, and uses appropriate vocabulary |
| **Below Average** | • demonstrates *some incompetence* <br> • is flawed by one or more of the following weaknesses: poor organization; thin development; little or inappropriate detail to support ideas; and frequent errors in grammar, diction, and sentence structure |

# Sample Essay 1

**DIRECTIONS:** You have 25 minutes to plan and write an essay on the topic assigned below. DO NOT WRITE ON ANY OTHER TOPIC. AN ESSAY ON ANOTHER TOPIC IS NOT ACCEPTABLE. Think carefully about the issue presented in the following excerpt and the assignment below. Sample essays and analyses are on page 1042.

> *Residents of rural areas often wonder why people would voluntarily choose to live in a large city and insist that rural life—with its open spaces, relative freedom from worries about crime, and healthful living conditions—is preferable. Conversely, residents of urban areas say that city life—with access to public transportation, cultural amenities, and many entertainment opportunities—is preferable.*

**Assignment:** Which do you find more compelling, the belief that the quality of life is greater in urban areas or the belief that the quality of life is greater in rural areas? Plan and write an essay in which you develop your point of view on this issue. Support your position with reasoning and examples taken from your reading, studies, experience, and observations.

# Sample Essay 2

**DIRECTIONS:** You have 25 minutes to plan and write an essay on the topic assigned below. DO NOT WRITE ON ANY OTHER TOPIC. AN ESSAY ON ANOTHER TOPIC IS NOT ACCEPTABLE. Think carefully about the issue presented in the following excerpt and the assignment below. Sample essays and analyses are on page 1044.

> *The Internet, originally seen as a savior to many, is now seen as an unexpected plague. Media companies are losing millions in revenue to Internet pirates. Cyber thieves are stealing identities and ruining lives. Companies have overextended themselves by pouring capital down the drain with nothing in return. The Internet has not lived up to its initial billing.*

**Assignment:** Has the Internet been a positive technological advance or have its negative effects on society outweighed the positives? Plan and write an essay in which you develop your point of view on this issue. Support your position with reasoning and examples taken from your reading, studies, experience, and observations.

# Sample Essay 3

**DIRECTIONS:** You have 25 minutes to plan and write an essay on the topic assigned below. DO NOT WRITE ON ANY OTHER TOPIC. AN ESSAY ON ANOTHER TOPIC IS NOT ACCEPTABLE. Think carefully about the issue presented in the following excerpt and the assignment below. Sample essays and analyses are on page 1046.

> *Although there is a strong push around the globe to eliminate so-called "Frankenfoods," agricultural products that have been bio-engineered, these protests are by and large unfounded. Through advances in food technology, famine and world hunger will some day be a thing of the past.*

**Assignment:** In your view, should bio-engineered foods have a greater access to the marketplace or should these foods be kept from the public awaiting more testing? Plan and write an essay in which you develop your point of view on this issue. Support your position with reasoning and examples taken from your reading, studies, experience, and observations.

# Analytical Writing Test Mechanics

# CAMBRIDGE TESTPREP™

## Test Mechanics
# ANALYTICAL WRITING

## ANATOMY OF THE ANALYTICAL WRITING TEST SECTION:

The computer-adaptive GRE has one Analytical Writing test section. This section consists of two separately timed writing tasks: a 45-minute Issue task and a 30-minute Argument task. You will be given a choice of two Issue topics, but you will NOT be given a choice of Argument topics. (All topics are selected from published topics.) You must type your essays into the computer for them to be scored. ETS has stated that the GRE Analytical Writing section was developed to assess the following skills:

- Ability to articulate complex ideas clearly and effectively
- Ability to examine claims and accompanying evidence
- Ability to support ideas with relevant reasons and examples
- Ability to sustain a well-focused, coherent discussion
- Ability to control the elements of standard written English

The two Analytical Writing essays are scored by readers on a scale from 0 (unacceptable) to 6 (outstanding). As we discuss in detail in the Writing Core Lesson, the scoring procedure rewards both writing mechanics and logical analysis. A brilliant logical analysis is not sufficient to earn a 6 unless presented using writing that exhibits a strong command of the language. Conversely, a flawlessly executed piece is not going to earn a good score unless there is some meat in the essay. To a certain extent, the time limits force you to balance these two considerations. If you have a schedule in mind and stick to it, you will have the best chances of satisfying both demands.

## ANALYTICAL WRITING PACING TECHNIQUES:

Do NOT try to do too much. During the fairly restrictive time limits, you must not only read and evaluate the topic but also formulate and outline a critique and then write and edit the essay. You must save time at the end to proofread your essay. Although occasional typographical, spelling, or grammatical errors will not affect your score, severe and persistent errors will detract from the overall quality of your essay.

A four- or five-paragraph essay is the extent to which most examinees will have time to write. An essay will create a better impression if it has a beginning, a middle, and an end than if it consists of only a single paragraph full of grand promises that are never fulfilled. And it will be more impressive if it is finished and conveys to the reader a sense of cool completeness rather than becoming increasingly rushed and ending with a makeweight conclusion such as, "Therefore, I have my reasons."

On the following page are general guidelines for allocating writing task time limits.

---

**GRE ISSUE ESSAY TIME ALLOTMENT**
**45 minutes**

🕐 *5–7 minutes:* Carefully read the directions and each essay prompt. Choose the topic that you can discuss more easily and for which you can clearly explain and defend your position with examples and reasons. Choose your position.

🕐 *3–5 minutes:* Make a list (either mental or on paper) of some ideas that you will use to support your position. Create an outline (either mental or on paper) of the essay.

🕐 *25–35 minutes:* Write the essay. Follow your outline, stating your position, reasons, and examples. Eliminate needless "cutting," "pasting," and retyping by composing each sentence in your head before typing. Avoid typos.

🕐 *5 minutes:* Proofread and edit your essay. Make corrections where necessary.

---

**GRE ARGUMENT ESSAY TIME ALLOTMENT**
**30 minutes**

🕐 *2 minutes:* Carefully read the directions and the topic. Make sure that you completely understand the issue as presented and the arguments made in the prompt.

🕐 *3–7 minutes:* Make a list (either mental or on paper) of the answers to the four content questions that will be the basis of the essay:

"Is this really a problem?"

"Is there not a simpler solution?"

"Can we be sure this would work?"

"Would this not create other problems?"

Create an outline (either mental or on paper) of the essay.

🕐 *20–25 minutes:* Write the essay. Follow your outline, stating your position, reasons, and examples. Eliminate needless "cutting," "pasting," and retyping by composing each sentence in your head before typing. Avoid typos.

🕐 *5 minutes:* Proofread and edit your essay. Make corrections where necessary.

# Analytical Writing Concepts
# and Strategies

# Writing

# CAMBRIDGE TESTPREP™

## WRITING OUTLINE

# CORE LESSON

**DIRECTIONS:** The items in this section accompany the in-class review of the concepts and skills, such as grammar, sentence structure, word usage, and punctuation, necessary for success on the GRE Analytical Writing essays. Each of the following sentences contains an error of grammar, sentence structure, usage, or punctuation. Circle the letter of the underlined part of the sentence containing the error. Answers are on page 1049.

1. Her and the other members of the team spoke
   A                                        B
   to the press after their final victory.
   C          D

2. In early America, there has been very little
                    A          B
   to read except for the books sent from Europe.
   C                          D

3. Still remaining in the ancient castle are the
   A                              B
   Duke's collection of early Dutch paintings,

   which will be donated to a museum.
   C     D

4. After having took the entrance examination, she
   A
   was absolutely sure that she would be admitted to
      B              C    D
   the college.

5. Most students preferred courses in the liberal arts
                 A
   to courses in science—unless they are science
   B                     C    D
   majors.

6. The point of the coach's remarks were obviously
                                 A    B
   to encourage the team and to restore its
                           C    D
   competitive spirit.

7. When Mozart wrote "The Marriage of Figaro," the
                 A
   Emperor was shocked at him using mere servants
           B                C
   as main characters.
   D

8. Since he was called back for a third reading, the
   A    B
   actor expected being chosen for the part.
         C       D

9. For a young woman who is ready to join the
                     A
   work force, there now exists many more
                        B      C
   opportunities than existed for her mother.
                   D

10. Movie fans claim there is no greater director than
                A                 B
    him, although most critics would mention the
    C                           D
    names of Bergman or Kurosawa.

11. When the Senate meeting was televised, the
    A            B       C
    first issue to be discussed were federal grants and
                            D
    loans for higher education.

12. Although the average person watches a news
    A                          B
    program every day, they do not always
                        C
    understand the issues discussed.
               D

13. It was said of the noted author Marcel Proust

    that he goes out only at night.
    A   B        C    D

14. Most people do not realize that sparkling wines,
                    A          B
    including champagne, can be made of red and
    C                               D
    white grapes.
    D

15. The earliest architecture in the New World

    resembled neither that of the European
    A         B
    Renaissance or that of the Early Baroque period,
                C
    but rather the medieval architecture of European
    D
    towns.

16. Like many composers of the period, Debussy
    A
    was familiar and admired contemporary poetry
    B    C
    and used it as the inspiration for his music.
        D

17. Americans used to go to the movies as often as
                                        A
    they watched television; however, now that they
                                                 B
    can watch movies in their homes, they are doing
                            C              D
    more of it.
    D

18. After hearing Joan Sutherland perform live at the
    A                                    B
    Metropolitan Opera on December 1, 1984, I am

    convinced that she is greater than any prima
                          C
    donna of the 20ᵗʰ century.
    C          D

19. Like Andy Warhol, the "pop art" of Roy
    A
    Lichtenstein is filled with familiar images such as
                 B                  C     D
    cartoon characters.

20. Because the project had been a team effort, we
    A
    had divided the bonus equally among the five of
    B                            C
    us.
    D

21. Postponing marriage and having little or no
                 A                B
    children are not revolutionary choices for women;
             C
    they were choices made by the grandmothers of
    D
    many postwar women.

22. Being that black bears are large and powerful,
    A                    B
    most people fear them even though the bears
                      C
    are really quite shy.
    D

23. Because consumers believe there to be a
    A                  B          C
    correlation between price and quality, the cost of

    computer software is steadily raising.
                       D

24. Travel to countries with less than ideal sanitary
    A                         B
    conditions increases the amount of victims of
               C            D
    hepatitis.

25. The fuel truck overturned on the highway,
                   A               B
    stopped traffic for over four hours during the
    B                                 C
    busiest part of the day.
    D

26. <u>Primarily found in the remote mountainous</u>
<br>A
<u>regions of the southeastern states,</u> very few
<br>A
people <u>die</u> of the bite of the copperhead or
<br>B
highland moccasin because <u>very few</u> people come
<br>C
into contact with <u>them.</u>
<br>D

27. When <u>Peter started the business</u> in 1982, it was
<br>A
<u>hardly nothing</u> more than a one-room operation
<br>B
with a single telephone line, <u>but</u> today Peter <u>has</u>
<br>C      D
offices in six different states.

28. Unlike <u>the 1960s, when</u> drugs were used
<br>A
primarily by "hippies," cocaine <u>is used</u> today
<br>B
<u>by people</u> in all walks of life, <u>including</u> lawyers.
<br>C                      D

29. While the <u>Reagan-Gorbachev summit</u> cannot be
<br>A
<u>described as</u> a complete waste of time, <u>nothing</u>
<br>B                                   C
<u>particular significant</u> was accomplished during
<br>D
the ten-day meeting.

30. <u>There are some people</u> <u>who are unusually</u> sensitive
<br>A                  B
to bee stings and who may experience allergic
<br>reactions <u>including</u> swelling, chills, nausea, fever,
<br>C
and <u>they may even become delirious.</u>
<br>D

31. <u>When</u> Robert introduced the guest <u>speaker he</u>
<br>A                                B
described <u>his</u> accomplishments in great detail but
<br>C
then forgot <u>to mention</u> the speaker's name.
<br>D

32. The fog <u>was</u> very <u>dense, they</u> were unable
<br>A            B
<u>to make out</u> the beacon light <u>on the opposite shore.</u>
<br>C                              D

33. Gordon <u>told</u> the clerk <u>that he wanted</u> to order
<br>A            B
three bottles of <u>Beaujolais two</u> bottles of <u>port, and</u>
<br>C                              D
one bottle of claret.

34. "Guernica," one of Picasso's many <u>masterpieces</u>
<br>A
<u>was</u> <u>exhibited</u> in the New York Museum of Modern
<br>A    B
Art <u>until,</u> as specified in Picasso's will, it
<br>C
<u>was returned</u> to Spain once democracy was reinstated.
<br>D

35. Mary <u>Alice who is the dean's choice</u> has
<br>A
indicated <u>that she</u> would be willing to serve <u>as</u>
<br>B                                          C
chairperson *pro tem* only on the condition that a
<br>search committee <u>be formed</u> within the next three
<br>D
weeks.

**DIRECTIONS:** Your instructor will read through the following passage in class without and with the appropriate pauses. Fill in the correct punctuation.

36. On Monday Mark received a letter of acceptance from State College he immediately called his mother herself a graduate of State College to tell her about his acceptance when he told her he had also been awarded a scholarship she was very excited after hanging up Mark's mother decided to throw a surprise party for Mark she telephoned his brother his sister and several of his friends because the party was supposed to be a surprise she made them all promise not to say anything to Mark Mark however had a similar idea a party for his mother to celebrate his acceptance at her alma mater he telephoned his brother his sister and several of his parents' friends to invite them to a party at his house on Saturday night and he made them all promise to say nothing to his mother on Saturday night both Mark and his mother were surprised

**DIRECTIONS:** This section contains the GRE Analytical Writing Issue prompt that will be used during the in-class lesson to illustrate proper essay development and writing skills. Follow along with your teacher to outline and develop a sample response to the prompt below.

### Present Your Perspective on an Issue

### 45 Minutes

You will be presented with an Issue topic, which will be summarized in a brief quotation. The topic describes an issue of general interest. Read the topic carefully.

You have 45 minutes to plan, write, and edit your essay. Your essay should present your perspective on the topic. In addressing the claim made in the quotation, you can accept the quotation, reject it outright, or accept it in part and reject it in part as long as the points you make are clearly relevant to the topic. An essay on any other topic will receive a score of zero. Support your position with reasons and examples that are drawn from your everyday reading, personal experience, direct observations, or academic studies.

Your essay will be read by college and university teachers who will evaluate its overall quality, specifically taking into account how well you:

- develop and treat the complexities of the topic;
- organize, develop, and state your ideas;
- support your ideas with relevant examples and reasons;
- control the elements of standard written English.

It may be useful to take a few minutes of your time to think about the issue and to plan or even outline a response before you actually begin to write. Make sure that you organize your ideas into a coherent essay and develop them in some detail. Reserve some of your time to proofread and edit your response.

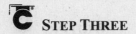 

## PRESENT YOUR PERSPECTIVE ON AN ISSUE
*Time—45 minutes*

*People often complain that manufacturers consciously follow a policy of planned obsolescence and make products that are designed to wear out quickly. Planned obsolescence, they insist, wastes both natural and human resources. They fail to recognize, however, that the use of cheaper materials and manufacturing processes keeps costs down for the consumer and stimulates demand.*

_____

_____

_____

_____

_____

_____

_____

_____

_____

_____

_____

_____

_____

_____

_____

_____

_____

_____

_____

_____

_____

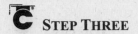 

**DIRECTIONS:** This section contains the GRE Analytical Writing Argument prompt that will be used during the in-class lesson to illustrate proper essay development and writing skills. Follow along with your teacher to outline and develop a sample response to the prompt below.

### Analysis of an Argument

### 30 Minutes

You have 30 minutes to organize and write a critique of the argument presented in the short passage below. A critique of an argument other than the one presented will be given a score of zero.

Analyze the line of reasoning in the argument; identify what, if any, questionable premises are made by the argument; and evaluate how well the evidence presented supports the conclusion of the argument. In evaluating the evidence, you can consider what kinds of proof would weaken or strengthen the argument and what additional information might tend to prove or disprove the conclusion.

Importantly, you are not being asked to present your own personal point of view on the subject.

Your essay will be read by college and university teachers who will evaluate its overall quality, specifically taking into account how well you:

- identify and analyze the important features of the argument;
- organize, develop, and state your points;
- support your critique with relevant examples and reasons;
- control the elements of standard written English.

It may be useful to take a few minutes of your time to think about the issue and to plan or even outline a response before you actually begin to write. Make sure that you organize your ideas into a coherent essay and develop them in some detail. Reserve some of your time to proofread and edit your response.

## ANALYSIS OF AN ARGUMENT
*Time—30 minutes*

*All commercial airliners operating in the United States should be required to carry a computerized on-board warning system that can receive signals from the transponders of other aircraft. (A transponder is a radio device that signals a plane's course.) The system would be able to alert pilots to the danger of a collision and recommend evasive action. Installation of the system would virtually eliminate the danger of mid-air collisions.*

**DIRECTIONS:** The sentences below will be used in class to illustrate strategies to improve the clarity and conciseness of your writing. Read the following sentences and rewrite them concisely, clearly, and free of grammatical and mechanical errors. Answers are on page 1049.

37. Although it might be argued that some students will be distracted by windows, but there is no proof of this presented, it is still the case that many students would benefit from the relaxing effect of open scenery, and that could even help them learn.

_____

_____

_____

_____

38. Even if a student is somewhat distracted, they may be even better able to concentrate when their attention returns to the teacher.

_____

_____

_____

_____

39. This distraction, which occurs in students with more limited attention spans, are easily avoided by arranging desks so that the eyes of a student is directed away from the window.

_____

_____

_____

_____

_____

40. The easiest solution is to have the teacher order each student to keep their eyes directed toward the blackboard.

_____

_____

_____

_____

_____

41. Under this seating arrangement, all of the people in the classroom, except the class monitor and she, will face the blackboard, not the windows.

_____

_____

_____

_____

42. While strolling through Central Park, a severe thunderstorm required my companion and me to take shelter in the band shell.

_____

_____

_____

43. Paul told Mary that he would wed her down by the old mill.

_____

_____

_____

44. When the notice was received by me I immediately reported to the manager's desk.

_____

_____

_____

_____

45. The cake was baked by the chef to please his favorite niece on her wedding day.

_____

_____

_____

46. Let the kids do their own thing. It's too heavy a trip to always have the teacher, the man, laying this guilt business on you. No window would be a head trip. Some of the kids would wind up at the shrink's. So, just lay off, and let them be themselves.

_____

_____

_____

_____

# TIMED-PRACTICE QUIZZES

**QUIZ I, PART A** (Issue Essay, 45 minutes)

**DIRECTIONS:** You will be presented with an Issue topic, which will be summarized in a brief quotation. The topic describes an issue of general interest. Read the topic carefully.

You have 45 minutes to plan, write, and edit your essay. Your essay should present your perspective on the topic. In addressing the claim made in the quotation, you can accept the quotation, reject it outright, or accept it in part and reject it in part as long as the points you make are clearly relevant to the topic. An essay on any other topic will receive a score of zero. Support your position with reasons and examples that are drawn from your everyday reading, personal experience, direct observations, or academic studies.

Your essay will be read by college and university teachers who will evaluate its overall quality, specifically taking into account how well you:

- develop and treat the complexities of the topic;

- organize, develop, and state your ideas;

- support your ideas with relevant examples and reasons;

- control the elements of standard written English.

It may be useful to take a few minutes of your time to think about the issue and to plan or even outline a response before you actually begin to write. Make sure that you organize your ideas into a coherent essay and develop them in some detail. Reserve some of your time to proofread and edit your response.

---

**ISSUE TASK**
**PRESENT YOUR PERSPECTIVE ON AN ISSUE**
*Time—45 minutes*

*Many people reminisce about the "good old days," insisting that the quality of life was much better twenty or thirty years ago. Other people insist that while conditions have changed, they have changed for the better, and that the quality of life today is actually considerably improved over that of twenty or thirty years ago.*

---

**QUIZ I, PART B** (Argument Essay, 30 minutes)

**DIRECTIONS:** You have 30 minutes to organize and write a critique of the argument presented in the short passage below. A critique of an argument other than the one presented will be given a score of zero.

Analyze the line of reasoning in the argument; identify what, if any, questionable premises are made by the argument; and evaluate how well the evidence presented supports the conclusion of the argument. In evaluating the evidence, you can consider what kinds of proof would weaken or strengthen the argument and what additional information might tend to prove or disprove the conclusion.

<u>Importantly, you are not being asked to present your own personal point of view on the subject.</u>

Your essay will be read by college and university teachers who will evaluate its overall quality, specifically taking into account how well you:

- identify and analyze the important features of the argument;

- organize, develop, and state your points;

- support your critique with relevant examples and reasons;

- control the elements of standard written English.

It may be useful to take a few minutes of your time to think about the issue and to plan or even outline a response before you actually begin to write. Make sure that you organize your ideas into a coherent essay and develop them in some detail. Reserve some of your time to proofread and edit your response.

---

**ARGUMENT TASK**
**ANALYSIS OF AN ARGUMENT**
*Time—30 minutes*

*The Springwater Regional Library System (SRLS) consists of a main library and twelve branch libraries. In the past, the main library and all but two branches have been open to the public six days a week with the two exceptions open only three days a week. Budget constraints, however, make it impossible to continue this policy. Therefore, in order to ensure that the main library will continue to operate six days a week, some branches should be closed permanently and the operating hours of others should be trimmed as needed.*

## QUIZ II, PART A (Issue Essay, 45 minutes)

**DIRECTIONS:** You will be presented with an Issue topic, which will be summarized in a brief quotation. The topic describes an issue of general interest. Read the topic carefully.

You have 45 minutes to plan, write, and edit your essay. Your essay should present your perspective on the topic. In addressing the claim made in the quotation, you can accept the quotation, reject it outright, or accept it in part and reject it in part as long as the points you make are clearly relevant to the topic. An essay on any other topic will receive a score of zero. Support your position with reasons and examples that are drawn from your everyday reading, personal experience, direct observations, or academic studies.

Your essay will be read by college and university teachers who will evaluate its overall quality, specifically taking into account how well you:

- develop and treat the complexities of the topic;

- organize, develop, and state your ideas;

- support your ideas with relevant examples and reasons;

- control the elements of standard written English.

It may be useful to take a few minutes of your time to think about the issue and to plan or even outline a response before you actually begin to write. Make sure that you organize your ideas into a coherent essay and develop them in some detail. Reserve some of your time to proofread and edit your response.

---

**ISSUE TASK**
**PRESENT YOUR PERSPECTIVE ON AN ISSUE**
*Time—45 minutes*

*Recently, a 98-year old farmer was asked what he thought was the greatest technological advancement of the past 125 years. He responded, "Electricity, because it made so many chores much easier and faster." A 35-year old executive was asked the same question, and she responded, "Computers, because they make so many chores much easier and faster."*

---

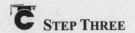 

**QUIZ II, PART B** (Argument Essay, 30 minutes)

**DIRECTIONS:** You have 30 minutes to organize and write a critique of the argument presented in the short passage below. A critique of an argument other than the one presented will be given a score of zero.

Analyze the line of reasoning in the argument; identify what, if any, questionable premises are made by the argument; and evaluate how well the evidence presented supports the conclusion of the argument. In evaluating the evidence, you can consider what kinds of proof would weaken or strengthen the argument and what additional information might tend to prove or disprove the conclusion.

Importantly, you are not being asked to present your own personal point of view on the subject.

Your essay will be read by college and university teachers who will evaluate its overall quality, specifically taking into account how well you:

- identify and analyze the important features of the argument;

- organize, develop, and state your points;

- support your critique with relevant examples and reasons;

- control the elements of standard written English.

It may be useful to take a few minutes of your time to think about the issue and to plan or even outline a response before you actually begin to write. Make sure that you organize your ideas into a coherent essay and develop them in some detail. Reserve some of your time to proofread and edit your response.

---

**ARGUMENT TASK**
**ANALYSIS OF AN ARGUMENT**
*Time—30 minutes*

*The Village of Twin Forks draws its drinking water directly from Lake Watchakobie. Although the water is filtered to remove solid impurities, it is not treated with chemicals. Many cities, towns, and villages treat water with chlorine and other chemicals to kill bacteria and other organisms that may cause illness and even death. If the Twin Forks filtration plant was reconfigured to include a chemical treatment stage, the health of village residents would be better protected.*

---

## QUIZ III, PART A (Issue Essay, 45 minutes)

**DIRECTIONS:** You will be presented with an Issue topic, which will be summarized in a brief quotation. The topic describes an issue of general interest. Read the topic carefully.

You have 45 minutes to plan, write, and edit your essay. Your essay should present your perspective on the topic. In addressing the claim made in the quotation, you can accept the quotation, reject it outright, or accept it in part and reject it in part as long as the points you make are clearly relevant to the topic. An essay on any other topic will receive a score of zero. Support your position with reasons and examples that are drawn from your everyday reading, personal experience, direct observations, or academic studies.

Your essay will be read by college and university teachers who will evaluate its overall quality, specifically taking into account how well you:

- develop and treat the complexities of the topic;
- organize, develop, and state your ideas;
- support your ideas with relevant examples and reasons;
- control the elements of standard written English.

It may be useful to take a few minutes of your time to think about the issue and to plan or even outline a response before you actually begin to write. Make sure that you organize your ideas into a coherent essay and develop them in some detail. Reserve some of your time to proofread and edit your response.

---

**ISSUE TASK**
**PRESENT YOUR PERSPECTIVE ON AN ISSUE**
*Time—45 minutes*

*Residents of rural areas often wonder why people would voluntarily choose to live in a large city and insist that rural life—with its open spaces, relative freedom from worries about crime, and healthful living conditions—is preferable. Residents of urban areas, on the other hand, say that city life—with access to public transportation, cultural amenities, and many entertainment opportunities—is preferable.*

---

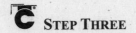 

**QUIZ III, PART B** (Argument Essay, 30 minutes)

**DIRECTIONS:** You have 30 minutes to organize and write a critique of the argument presented in the short passage below. A critique of an argument other than the one presented will be given a score of zero.

Analyze the line of reasoning in the argument; identify what, if any, questionable premises are made by the argument; and evaluate how well the evidence presented supports the conclusion of the argument. In evaluating the evidence, you can consider what kinds of proof would weaken or strengthen the argument and what additional information might tend to prove or disprove the conclusion.

Importantly, you are not being asked to present your own personal point of view on the subject.

Your essay will be read by college and university teachers who will evaluate its overall quality, specifically taking into account how well you:

- identify and analyze the important features of the argument;

- organize, develop, and state your points;

- support your critique with relevant examples and reasons;

- control the elements of standard written English.

It may be useful to take a few minutes of your time to think about the issue and to plan or even outline a response before you actually begin to write. Make sure that you organize your ideas into a coherent essay and develop them in some detail. Reserve some of your time to proofread and edit your response.

---

**ARGUMENT TASK**
**ANALYSIS OF AN ARGUMENT**
*Time—30 minutes*

*All buses used to transport children to and from public schools should be equipped with both lap and harness seat belts. The restraining system would virtually eliminate the danger that a child would be tossed from the seat and injured in the event of an accident.*

---

## QUIZ IV, PART A (Issue Essay, 45 minutes)

**DIRECTIONS:** You will be presented with an Issue topic, which will be summarized in a brief quotation. The topic describes an issue of general interest. Read the topic carefully.

You have 45 minutes to plan, write, and edit your essay. Your essay should present your perspective on the topic. In addressing the claim made in the quotation, you can accept the quotation, reject it outright, or accept it in part and reject it in part as long as the points you make are clearly relevant to the topic. An essay on any other topic will receive a score of zero. Support your position with reasons and examples that are drawn from your everyday reading, personal experience, direct observations, or academic studies.

Your essay will be read by college and university teachers who will evaluate its overall quality, specifically taking into account how well you:

- develop and treat the complexities of the topic;
- organize, develop, and state your ideas;
- support your ideas with relevant examples and reasons;
- control the elements of standard written English.

It may be useful to take a few minutes of your time to think about the issue and to plan or even outline a response before you actually begin to write. Make sure that you organize your ideas into a coherent essay and develop them in some detail. Reserve some of your time to proofread and edit your response.

---

### ISSUE TASK
### PRESENT YOUR PERSPECTIVE ON AN ISSUE
*Time—45 minutes*

*Many people complain that today's workers no longer take any pride in the work that they do and that, as a result, the products that are made today are not as good as those made years ago. Other people maintain that though the processes used to make products have changed, workers still take just as much pride in what they do and that today's products are just as good as, if not better than, those made years ago.*

---

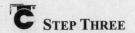 

**QUIZ IV, PART B** (Argument Essay, 30 minutes)

**DIRECTIONS:** You have 30 minutes to organize and write a critique of the argument presented in the short passage below. A critique of an argument other than the one presented will be given a score of zero.

Analyze the line of reasoning in the argument; identify what, if any, questionable premises are made by the argument; and evaluate how well the evidence presented supports the conclusion of the argument. In evaluating the evidence, you can consider what kinds of proof would weaken or strengthen the argument and what additional information might tend to prove or disprove the conclusion.

Importantly, you are not being asked to present your own personal point of view on the subject.

Your essay will be read by college and university teachers who will evaluate its overall quality, specifically taking into account how well you:

- identify and analyze the important features of the argument;

- organize, develop, and state your points;

- support your critique with relevant examples and reasons;

- control the elements of standard written English.

It may be useful to take a few minutes of your time to think about the issue and to plan or even outline a response before you actually begin to write. Make sure that you organize your ideas into a coherent essay and develop them in some detail. Reserve some of your time to proofread and edit your response.

---

**ARGUMENT TASK**
**ANALYSIS OF AN ARGUMENT**
*Time—30 minutes*

*Central High School has a computer lab. It is available to students Monday through Friday from 8:00 am until 3:00 pm. Other schools make their computer facilities available during extended hours. If Central High School students are to be able to compete effectively for college admission, scholarships, and jobs, the computer lab must remain open late afternoons and evenings Monday through Friday.*

---

# CAMBRIDGE TESTPREP™

## Strategy Summary Sheet
# WRITING

**FOUR TESTING AREAS:** Content, Organization, Style, and Mechanics are the four areas tested in the writing assessment. These fall under the task of "how to say it" and are essential to a good essay. The task of "what to say" will ease with practice.

**STRATEGIES FOR PRESENTING YOUR PERSPECTIVE ON AN ISSUE:**

1. *Position:* The first step to developing a strong essay is to take a position. You must decide which position to support, state this position at the start of your essay, and continue to support that position with examples.

2. *Question Cues:* The Issue essay question will provide additional stimulus for essay material from "cues" in the question's wording—providing the direction and basis for development of examples.

3. *Essay Organization:* Because of the 45-minute time limit, essays should be restricted to about four or five paragraphs. The first paragraph should state a position and introduce the examples that support that position. The two or three paragraphs that follow should develop the examples in further detail, following development suggested by question "cues." The final paragraph should summarize the essay development and may include an optional statement of conclusion.

4. *Writing the Essay:* Use provided scratch paper to briefly outline your essay; time spent outlining is included in the 45-minute time limit. When writing the actual essay, do not attempt too much—incomplete essays will receive very low scores. Essays should be concise, avoiding generalities and trite positions. Be sure to save time to proofread your essay.

**STRATEGIES FOR ANALYSIS OF AN ARGUMENT:**

1. *Argument Analysis:* Chances are that the Argument essay will be a policy topic of some sort. Policy topics cite a problem and propose a solution. The task is to critique the given argument, offering evidence as to why the proposed solution is (or is not) flawed. The answers to the following content questions should make up the heart of the essay, detailing why the proposed solution is (or is not) flawed.

   - *Quantification:* Does the argument establish a serious problem?

   - *Inherency:* Is the problem sufficiently inherent to warrant radical change?

   - *Feasibility:* Are proposed changes possible? Will they work?

   - *Disadvantages:* Do the advantages outweigh the disadvantages?

2. *Essay Organization:* Again, because of the 30-minute time limit, the essay will be no longer than about five paragraphs. The first paragraph should state the four reasons why the argument is (or is not) flawed (quantification, inherency, feasibility, and disadvantages). The following four paragraphs should develop each of the four reasons in more detail, giving examples and providing alternative solutions. The last paragraph should summarize the essay's development and provide a statement of conclusion.

3. *Writing the Essay:* Again, use the provided scratch paper to briefly outline your essay; time spent outlining is included in the 30-minute time limit. When writing the actual essay, do not attempt too much—incomplete essays will receive very low scores. Essays should be concise—avoid generalities and trite positions. Be sure to save time

to proofread your essay.

NOTES: _____

_____

_____

_____

_____

_____

_____

_____

_____

_____

_____

_____

_____

_____

_____

_____

_____

_____

_____

_____

_____

_____

_____

_____

_____

# Overcoming Test Anxiety

# OVERCOMING TEST ANXIETY

Test anxiety can manifest itself in various forms—from the common occurrences of "butterflies" in the stomach, mild sweating, or nervous laughter, to the more extreme occurrences of overwhelming fear, anxiety attacks, and unmanageable worry. It is quite normal for students to experience some mild anxiety before or during testing without being greatly affected. On the other hand, more intense worry, fear, or tension can prevent students from performing successfully on standardized tests. Some experts who study human performance propose that light stress may actually help to focus a person's concentration on the task at hand. However, stress that reaches beyond minimum levels and remains for a long period of time can block a student's ability to quickly recall facts, remember strategies, analyze complex problems, and creatively approach difficult items. When taking a test, being calm and collected promotes clear and logical thinking. Therefore, a relaxed state of mind is essential to you as a test-taker. The following strategies provide practical hints and methods to help alleviate debilitating test anxiety.

## PLAN—HAVE A STUDY PLAN AND STICK TO IT

Putting off important test review assignments until the last minute naturally causes high stress for anyone who is seriously anxious about test day. Even the brightest student experiences nervousness when he or she walks into a test site without being fully prepared. Therefore, stress reduction methods should begin weeks or even months in advance. Prepared test-takers are more relaxed, confident, and focused, so you should begin to review materials earlier rather than later in order to reduce anxiety.

Be warned that it is almost impossible to successfully cram for standardized tests. Waiting until the day or week before the test to begin studying will only serve to elevate your anxiety level. While cramming at the last minute may have worked for you in the past with quizzes or less comprehensive tests, it will not work to prepare you for long, comprehensive, standardized tests. Such comprehensive tests require extended and intensive study methods. Trying to cram will leave you feeling frustrated, unprepared, overwhelmed, and nervous about the pending test day.

So, the key to combating test anxiety is to plan ahead so that you are not unprepared. Do not procrastinate—develop a study plan, start early, and stick to it. A study plan is a written set of daily goals that will help you track the content and the sequence of your test review. This plan will help you tell yourself what, when, where, and how much you will study. (See the Time Management section on page 24 for a further description of how to organize your time effectively.)

By planning your work and working your plan, you can alleviate any unnecessary anxiety. Here are some tips on how to produce your study plan.

> ### *Record a Plan on Paper*

A written study plan is more concrete and dependable than one that simply rattles around in your head. So, you should use a piece of paper and a pencil to write out a plan for reviewing all of the materials that are necessary to succeed on the test. Record important items and dates on your calendar (Time Management), and post the study plan in a place where you will see it often (e.g., your bedroom door or your refrigerator). When you accomplish one of the goals on your plan (e.g., taking a timed practice exam or reviewing a certain number of items), designate its completion with a checkmark. This system of recording your goals will give you a sense of achievement.

> ### *Break the Test into Pieces*

Standardized tests are segmented into multiple sections according to subject-area. However, you should not try to learn all of the material related to a particular subject-area in one sitting. The subject matter that is covered is far too broad to learn in a few short minutes, so you should not try to learn every test strategy at once or review the whole test in one

day. Instead, you should break the test into smaller portions and then study a portion until you are confident that you can move on to another. You should also vary the sections that you study in order to ward off boredom. For example, on Monday, study a reasoning section, and on Tuesday, study the reading section.

In addition to breaking the test into smaller portions, you should always remember to review sections that you have already studied. This review will keep all of the sections fresh in your mind for test day. No two students are capable of learning at an identical rate. Some students can learn huge chunks of information at once, while other students need to review smaller amounts of information over a greater period of time. Determine the amount of material that you can comfortably and adequately cover in one day; then, attack that amount of material on each day.

For most students, the study plan is determined by the Cambridge Review Course schedule. The class schedule and sequence have been developed to help you improve your test score. So, follow the guidance of your class instructor and mold your personal study plan around the schedule.

> ### *Do Some Studying or Preparation Every Day*

Yes. It is very important that you study something every single day. Once you get the "study snowball" rolling, the momentum will help you overcome the temptation to quit. Be consistent. It is far better to study sixty minutes per day for seven straight days than to study seven straight hours only once per week.

> ### *Study at the Same Time and Place*

Find somewhere quiet to study, where there are few distractions, the lighting is good, and you feel comfortable. Since the GRE is given at computer terminals, avoid studying in bed or in a lounge chair. Simulate the test conditions by studying at a desk or table. Turn off the television or the radio. Shut down the computer, unless of course you are using it as a study tool. Give yourself uninterrupted quality time to study. Find a consistent time when you can study and lock it into your schedule. Do not let yourself off the hook. Study each day at the same time and place so that you can become accustomed to your work environment.

> ### *Set Goals and Reward Yourself*

Set a weekly goal for the amount of time that you will study and the amount of material that you will review. When you meet these weekly goals, reward yourself. Offer yourself special incentives that will motivate you to reach your next goal.

> ### *Find a Study Partner or Someone to Hold You Accountable for Your Progress*

There really is strength in numbers. Find at least one person who will help you stay on course with your goals. Have this person ask you, every few days, whether or not you are sticking to your plan. Consider finding a "study buddy." Push each other to set and reach high test preparation goals.

Early and consistent test preparation means that you will walk calmly and confidently into the testing center on test day, knowing that you have done your very best to prepare for the test.

## PREPARE POSITIVELY—REPLACE ANXIETY WITH POSITIVITY

Positive thinking helps overcome test anxiety. For years, psychologists have studied how attitudes affect and alter achievement. These studies suggest that students with positive attitudes consistently score higher than students with negative attitudes.

Here are some practical ways to create a positive mindset:

➤ **Talk Positively to Yourself**

Success comes in a "can," not a "cannot." So, learn to think positively by mentally replacing "cannot" with "can." Negative statements such as "I will never pass this test," "I know I can't get this," or "I'm not smart enough to get a good score," are counterproductive, and they hinder both studying and the test-taking process. In order to eliminate negative thoughts, you must first take note of them when they occur and then take steps to remove them from your mind. As soon as you recognize a negative thought, immediately replace it with a positive thought. It is quite easy. Whenever you hear phrases such as "I can't do this" or "I'm not smart enough," think to yourself, "I *can* do this," "I *will* understand this," or "I *am* smart enough." Furthermore, as you walk into the classroom on the day of the test, repeatedly say to yourself, "I have studied, I will do my best, and I will succeed."

➤ **Think Positively About Yourself**

Think positively with the help of visualization. Try this: while in a relaxed mood, close your eyes and envision yourself walking into the test room, perfectly calm and confident. Now, imagine yourself taking each section of the test without any difficulty and with great calmness. See yourself answering the items quickly and correctly. Watch yourself exiting the test area with confidence because you know that you performed extremely well. With these visualization techniques, you can mentally and emotionally practice taking the test in a confident and calm manner. You can practice visualizing yourself at any time and for any given situation. Many students find that it works well close to bedtime. Coaches encourage their peak performing athletes to use daily visualization exercises in order to increase their abilities in running, jumping, shooting, etc. Every single day, from now until the test day, practice visualization and picture yourself taking the test quickly, easily, confidently, and calmly. Visualization can help you exude a positive attitude and overcome test anxiety. Get the picture?

➤ **Act Positively Toward Yourself**

On the day of the test, act positively. Even if you do not "feel" completely confident, you should stride into the test site with your head held high and a bounce in your step. Show both yourself and your peers that you are at ease and in complete control of the situation. Present yourself as someone who knows that he or she will be successful. Acting confidently will actually help you feel confident.

Practice these strategies in order to instill a positive mental attitude. Positive thinking means believing in yourself. Believe that you can achieve your highest goal under any circumstances. Know that you can do it. Dare to try.

## PUT AWAY NEGATIVE THOUGHTS—THEY FUEL TEST ANXIETY

Since you will be practicing positive thinking, you should also learn to recognize and eliminate distorted, or twisted, thinking. Avoid thinking any of the following distorted things about yourself:

*"I must always be perfect."* The reality is that everyone makes mistakes. In testing situations, perfectionists mentally fuss and fume about a single mistake instead of celebrating all of the items that they answered correctly. Dwelling on mistakes wastes time and creates more tension. Push mistakes behind you and move forward to the next set of items. Remember that we all reserve the right to learn and grow.

*"I failed the last time, so I'll fail this time."* Past failure does not lead to future failure. People do get better the more that they practice. Because you did poorly on something in the past does not guarantee a poor performance either this time or in the future. Use this test as an opportunity for a fresh start. Forget yesterday's failures and realize that today is a brand new beginning.

*"People won't like me if I do poorly."* It is preferable to have good relations with people and to have them approve of you or even to love you—but it is not necessary. You will not be unhappy unless you make yourself unhappy. Rely on self-approval, not on the approval of others. Do your best because you want to and you can, not because you want to please someone else.

*"I have been anxious when taking tests before; therefore, I'll always be anxious."* This twisted logic implies that you have no control over your behavior; however, that is not the case. You can change and learn to control your anxiety. It might take time and hard work to build calmness and confidence, but it is certainly within your reach.

## POWER UP PHYSICALLY—RELEASE STRESS WITH PHYSICAL EXERCISE

Physical exercise is an excellent way to both reduce anxiety levels and cope with the effects of stress. Start a regular program of physical fitness that includes stretching and cardiovascular activities. If necessary, check with a doctor or a health professional in order to develop a customized fitness program.

## PRACTICE BEING CALM—LEARN TO MENTALLY AND PHYSICALLY RELAX

You may not realize that mental and physical relaxation play significant parts in the studying process. By setting aside time for clearing your mind and body of stress and anxiety, you will refresh your mental and physical energy reserves. Spend quality time studying and reviewing for the test. Then, spend time relaxing your mind and body so that you are re-energized for your next study session.

Practice the following relaxation exercises to calm the body and mind.

➢ **Physical Relaxation Exercise**

Pick a quiet room where there are few distractions. Shut off all intrusive lights. Sit in a chair or lie down in a bed. If you wear glasses, take them off. Get comfortable, loosening any tight or binding clothing. Close your eyes, and take a deep breath. Blow out all of the air in your lungs, and then breathe in deeply. Now, focus on your tense muscles and consciously relax them. Start by focusing on your toes, your feet, and your calves. Tense and release your muscles to fully relax them. Move upward through each muscle group in your body, up to and including your facial muscles. Continue to breathe slowly, steadily, and fully during this exercise. Repeat this process, while consciously relaxing tense muscles, until you relax your entire body. Rest in this state for a few minutes. When you are finished, open your eyes, and remain still for another minute or two before rising.

➢ **Breathing Exercise**

Deep and relaxed breathing will calm your nerves and reduce stress. Whenever you start feeling anxious, take time out to perform this simple breathing exercise. Place your hands upon your stomach and breathe in slowly and deeply through your nose, feeling your rib cage rise. Pause and hold your breath for a second, thinking to yourself, "I am calm." Release your breath slowly and fully, blowing it out through your mouth. Repeat this exercise eight to ten times. Perform this exercise whenever you feel nervous or anxious.

➢ **Mental Relaxation Exercise**

Meditation, in various forms, has been practiced to allow the mind to release stressful thoughts. Many types of meditation can be learned and then practiced on a regular basis. A popular type of meditation is the passive form. Begin meditating after your body is in a relaxed state. Concentrate on something monotonous until your mind becomes quiet. You may choose to concentrate on a sound, a word, or an object. Observe your thoughts without controlling them.

Gently refocus on the sound, word, or object. Passively observe your thoughts when they come, then gently refocus back upon the sound, word, or object.

## PREPARE—DO NOT LEAVE IMPORTANT ITEMS UNTIL THE LAST MINUTE

You are going to want to remain as relaxed as possible on the day of the test. In order to eliminate the last-minute, frantic rush to find that "one thing" that you cannot locate, make a list of the items that you need for the day of the test. Set out those important items the night before in order to efficiently and effectively speed you on your way toward the testing center.

➤ *Determine the Items that You Are Expected to Bring*

Carefully read the test materials distributed ETS so that you know exactly what you should and should not bring to the test center.

➤ *Gather the Items that You Need*

On the night before the test, gather all of the necessary items so that you can avoid the anxiety of trying to find them at the last minute.

➤ *Know the Directions to the Test Center*

If you have not been to the test center before, make sure that you are provided with clear and specific directions as soon as possible. If you are at all confused about how to get to the test center, call the center immediately and clarify the directions.

➤ *Decide Whether to Study the Night Before the Test*

Should you study the night before the test? Well, as mentioned earlier, you certainly should not attempt to cram for the test. You may want to review a few strategies, but you do not want to attempt to learn large amounts of new material. Instead, take some time to review, and then find some entertaining activity to occupy your time. Go to the gym or see a movie with friends. Laughing is always a great way to reduce stress, so you may want to find something humorous to do or watch.

➤ *Sleep Well*

A good night of sleep will help reduce stress on the test day. Do not stay out late on the night before the test.

➤ *Get to the Test Site Early*

Your anxiety level will increase if you arrive at the test center late. So, arrive early. Take a few minutes to relax and compose yourself. You may also need time to locate the restrooms and drinking fountains. However, do not arrive at the test center too early. Students typically get nervous and anxious when they have to wait for a long period of time with nothing to do except think about the upcoming test. So, find the balance between "too early" and "too late" that works best for you.

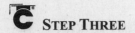 

➤ *Watch Your Diet*

What you choose to eat can be a physical cause of stress. Therefore, control your eating habits in order to maintain lower stress levels. Eat a healthy meal on the day of the test. Restrict your intake of sugar, salt, and caffeine. Remember that sugar and caffeine are found in coffee, cola, cocoa, and tea. These substances trigger a stress response in your body. High levels of sugar and caffeine are associated with nervousness, dizziness, irritability, headaches, and insomnia. Additionally, smoking has been found to decrease a person's ability to handle stress. Cigarettes act as a stimulant because of their nicotine content and will serve to increase stress levels.

➤ *Dress Comfortably*

The good news is that you are going to a test, not a fashion show. So, wear comfortable clothes to the testing center; choose clothes that are not overly binding or tight. Dressing in layers is always a good idea since testing rooms are notoriously either too hot or too cold.

## PAUSE—RELEASE PHYSICAL AND MENTAL ANXIETY BEFORE THE TEST

As already stated, relaxation allows you to focus your full attention and energy on the task at hand, rather than be distracted by tension and stress. Release as much tension and anxiety as possible right before taking the test.

➤ *Release and Relax*

Having arrived early at the test site, take the last few minutes to relax. Do not attempt to study or review at this point. Instead, use a simple relaxation technique. Close your eyes, and breathe in deeply through your nose. Hold that breath for a few seconds. Next, release that breath through your mouth. Repeat this "in-and-out" breathing cycle. Try to gradually slow the pace of the "in-and-out" motion of your breathing. Visualize yourself at a place that you find peaceful and relaxing, such as the beach, the woods, or some other favorite spot. Continue this technique for a few minutes until you feel yourself becoming relaxed and calm.

➤ *Do Some Low-Level Physical Exercise*

Take a brisk walk. For many people, walking helps lower high stress levels, while positively easing the mind from worrying about the upcoming test. Others find that stretching exercises help loosen tense muscles. Just be sure to be at the testing center in time.

➤ *Massage Tension Away*

While waiting for the test, sit comfortably in your chair. Notice places in your body that feel tense—generally the shoulders, neck, or back. Gently massage tense areas for a few minutes.

## PRESS ON—CONCENTRATE ON THE CURRENT ITEM, NOT THE LAST OR NEXT

Dwelling on answers to previous items will only elevate test anxiety, so do not worry about those sections or items that you have finished.

➤ *Focus on One Item at a Time*

Your task on any test is to correctly answer each item, one item at a time. Good test-takers focus only on the item with which they are currently working. Poor test-takers worry about items that they just completed or about items in the upcoming section. Try to stay "in the moment" by concentrating on one item at a time.

## PROUDLY DEPART—WALK OUT WITH YOUR HEAD HELD HIGH

➤ *Know that You Have Done Your Best*

If you have followed the strategies listed in this section, attended test preparation classes, and spent time reviewing and studying on your own, you have most likely done your very best to prepare for the test. As you walk out of the test site, remind yourself that you have indeed put forth your best effort.

➤ *Watch the Labels*

After the test, never label yourself as a "failure," "loser," or "underachiever." Instead, if you do not feel that you did as well as you expected, use the experience to learn about the test and about yourself. Students are able to retake standardized tests, so reflect upon what you can do better next time, not upon how poorly you think you did this time.

## PERSPECTIVE—KEEP LIFE IN PERSPECTIVE

Yes, the test you will take is important, but other things in life are important too. Remember that this test is a means to an end—getting into graduate school—and not the end itself.

NOTE: Some test-takers, even after applying all of the above strategies, still experience debilitating stress. Intense anxiety or stress that causes nausea, headaches, overwhelming emotional fears, or other severe symptoms may need special attention and care that goes beyond the strategies in these pages. If you suffer from these debilitating stress symptoms, ask your counseling office about what resources are available to help overcome severe test anxiety.

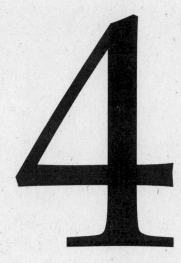

# Step Four: Practice and Reinforcement

Complete the four full-length GRE practice tests to reinforce everything you have learned in the course.

Work through the tests either all at once or by section to highlight specific skills and concepts.

## Step Four Overview:

In this step, you will have the opportunity to apply everything that you have learned throughout the course. Each of the four practice tests has been arranged in an order and with a frequency that approximates the real GRE. Completing these practice tests will help reinforce the test content, help you become more comfortable with timing and pacing, reduce your test anxiety, and give you the chance to practice using alternative test-taking strategies. If you are taking these tests on your own, complete the first two without time restrictions to practice the application of the concepts that you have learned. Then, complete the second two tests with the appropriate timing to practice your pacing.

# Practice Test I

# CAMBRIDGE TESTPREP™

## PRACTICE TEST I OUTLINE

# PRACTICE TEST I

Start with number 1 for each new section. If a section has fewer items than answer spaces, leave the extra answer spaces blank. Be sure to erase any errors or stray marks completely.

**Section 2**

| 1 Ⓐ Ⓑ Ⓒ Ⓓ Ⓔ | 9 Ⓐ Ⓑ Ⓒ Ⓓ Ⓔ | 17 Ⓐ Ⓑ Ⓒ Ⓓ Ⓔ | 25 Ⓐ Ⓑ Ⓒ Ⓓ Ⓔ |
| 2 Ⓐ Ⓑ Ⓒ Ⓓ Ⓔ | 10 Ⓐ Ⓑ Ⓒ Ⓓ Ⓔ | 18 Ⓐ Ⓑ Ⓒ Ⓓ Ⓔ | 26 Ⓐ Ⓑ Ⓒ Ⓓ Ⓔ |
| 3 Ⓐ Ⓑ Ⓒ Ⓓ Ⓔ | 11 Ⓐ Ⓑ Ⓒ Ⓓ Ⓔ | 19 Ⓐ Ⓑ Ⓒ Ⓓ Ⓔ | 27 Ⓐ Ⓑ Ⓒ Ⓓ Ⓔ |
| 4 Ⓐ Ⓑ Ⓒ Ⓓ Ⓔ | 12 Ⓐ Ⓑ Ⓒ Ⓓ Ⓔ | 20 Ⓐ Ⓑ Ⓒ Ⓓ Ⓔ | 28 Ⓐ Ⓑ Ⓒ Ⓓ Ⓔ |
| 5 Ⓐ Ⓑ Ⓒ Ⓓ Ⓔ | 13 Ⓐ Ⓑ Ⓒ Ⓓ Ⓔ | 21 Ⓐ Ⓑ Ⓒ Ⓓ Ⓔ | 29 Ⓐ Ⓑ Ⓒ Ⓓ Ⓔ |
| 6 Ⓐ Ⓑ Ⓒ Ⓓ Ⓔ | 14 Ⓐ Ⓑ Ⓒ Ⓓ Ⓔ | 22 Ⓐ Ⓑ Ⓒ Ⓓ Ⓔ | 30 Ⓐ Ⓑ Ⓒ Ⓓ Ⓔ |
| 7 Ⓐ Ⓑ Ⓒ Ⓓ Ⓔ | 15 Ⓐ Ⓑ Ⓒ Ⓓ Ⓔ | 23 Ⓐ Ⓑ Ⓒ Ⓓ Ⓔ | |
| 8 Ⓐ Ⓑ Ⓒ Ⓓ Ⓔ | 16 Ⓐ Ⓑ Ⓒ Ⓓ Ⓔ | 24 Ⓐ Ⓑ Ⓒ Ⓓ Ⓔ | |

**Section 3**

| 1 Ⓐ Ⓑ Ⓒ Ⓓ Ⓔ | 11 Ⓐ Ⓑ Ⓒ Ⓓ Ⓔ | 21 Ⓐ Ⓑ Ⓒ Ⓓ Ⓔ | 31 Ⓐ Ⓑ Ⓒ Ⓓ Ⓔ |
| 2 Ⓐ Ⓑ Ⓒ Ⓓ Ⓔ | 12 Ⓐ Ⓑ Ⓒ Ⓓ Ⓔ | 22 Ⓐ Ⓑ Ⓒ Ⓓ Ⓔ | 32 Ⓐ Ⓑ Ⓒ Ⓓ Ⓔ |
| 3 Ⓐ Ⓑ Ⓒ Ⓓ Ⓔ | 13 Ⓐ Ⓑ Ⓒ Ⓓ Ⓔ | 23 Ⓐ Ⓑ Ⓒ Ⓓ Ⓔ | 33 Ⓐ Ⓑ Ⓒ Ⓓ Ⓔ |
| 4 Ⓐ Ⓑ Ⓒ Ⓓ Ⓔ | 14 Ⓐ Ⓑ Ⓒ Ⓓ Ⓔ | 24 Ⓐ Ⓑ Ⓒ Ⓓ Ⓔ | 34 Ⓐ Ⓑ Ⓒ Ⓓ Ⓔ |
| 5 Ⓐ Ⓑ Ⓒ Ⓓ Ⓔ | 15 Ⓐ Ⓑ Ⓒ Ⓓ Ⓔ | 25 Ⓐ Ⓑ Ⓒ Ⓓ Ⓔ | 35 Ⓐ Ⓑ Ⓒ Ⓓ Ⓔ |
| 6 Ⓐ Ⓑ Ⓒ Ⓓ Ⓔ | 16 Ⓐ Ⓑ Ⓒ Ⓓ Ⓔ | 26 Ⓐ Ⓑ Ⓒ Ⓓ Ⓔ | 36 Ⓐ Ⓑ Ⓒ Ⓓ Ⓔ |
| 7 Ⓐ Ⓑ Ⓒ Ⓓ Ⓔ | 17 Ⓐ Ⓑ Ⓒ Ⓓ Ⓔ | 27 Ⓐ Ⓑ Ⓒ Ⓓ Ⓔ | 37 Ⓐ Ⓑ Ⓒ Ⓓ Ⓔ |
| 8 Ⓐ Ⓑ Ⓒ Ⓓ Ⓔ | 18 Ⓐ Ⓑ Ⓒ Ⓓ Ⓔ | 28 Ⓐ Ⓑ Ⓒ Ⓓ Ⓔ | 38 Ⓐ Ⓑ Ⓒ Ⓓ Ⓔ |
| 9 Ⓐ Ⓑ Ⓒ Ⓓ Ⓔ | 19 Ⓐ Ⓑ Ⓒ Ⓓ Ⓔ | 29 Ⓐ Ⓑ Ⓒ Ⓓ Ⓔ | |
| 10 Ⓐ Ⓑ Ⓒ Ⓓ Ⓔ | 20 Ⓐ Ⓑ Ⓒ Ⓓ Ⓔ | 30 Ⓐ Ⓑ Ⓒ Ⓓ Ⓔ | |

## SECTION 1
## PRESENT YOUR PERSPECTIVE ON AN ISSUE
### 45 minutes

You will be presented with an Issue topic, which will be summarized in a brief quotation. The topic describes an issue of general interest. Read the topic carefully.

You have 45 minutes to plan, write, and edit your essay. Your essay should present your perspective on the topic. In addressing the claim made in the quotation, you can accept the quotation, reject it outright, or accept it in part and reject it in part as long as the points you make are clearly relevant to the topic. An essay on any other topic will receive a score of zero. Support your position with reasons and examples that are drawn from your everyday reading, personal experience, direct observations, or academic studies.

Your essay will be read by college and university teachers who will evaluate its overall quality, specifically taking into account how well you:

- develop and treat the complexities of the topic;
- organize, develop, and state your ideas;
- support your ideas with relevant examples and reasons;
- control the elements of standard written English.

It may be useful to take a few minutes of your time to think about the issue and to plan or even outline a response before you actually begin to write. Make sure that you organize your ideas into a coherent essay and develop them in some detail. Reserve some of your time to proofread and edit your response. A sample essay is on page 1055.

> Great people should be remembered for their accomplishments in their fields—politics, science, art, or business—and not for their shortcomings as human beings.

**ISSUE TASK**

# S T O P

IF YOU FINISH BEFORE TIME IS CALLED, YOU MAY CHECK YOUR WORK ON THIS ESSAY ONLY.
DO NOT TURN TO ANY OTHER PORTION OF THE TEST.

## ANALYSIS OF AN ARGUMENT
### 30 minutes

You have 30 minutes to organize and write a critique of the argument presented in the short passage below. A critique of an argument other than the one presented will be given a score of zero.

Analyze the line of reasoning in the argument; identify what, if any, questionable premises are made by the argument; and evaluate how well the evidence presented supports the conclusion of the argument. In evaluating the evidence, you can consider what kinds of proof would weaken or strengthen the argument and what additional information might tend to prove or disprove the conclusion.

Importantly, you are not being asked to present your own personal point of view on the subject.

Your essay will be read by college and university teachers who will evaluate its overall quality, specifically taking into account how well you:

- identify and analyze the important features of the argument;

- organize, develop, and state your points;

- support your critique with relevant examples and reasons;

- control the elements of standard written English.

It may be useful to take a few minutes of your time to think about the issue and to plan or even outline a response before you actually begin to write. Make sure that you organize your ideas into a coherent essay and develop them in some detail. Reserve some of your time to proofread and edit your response. A sample essay is on page 1055.

---

The City Parks Department has authority over all of the City's recreational facilities. The City opens the swimming pools on the Memorial Day Weekend and closes them on Labor Day. During the summer, however, all of the City's indoor facilities are closed. In response to a survey question that asked "Do you want children to have the opportunity to play sports such as basketball and handball during the summer?," 98 percent of City residents answered yes. It is clear, then, that City residents want all of the City's recreational facilities open during the summer. So, the City should adopt a new policy that keeps the indoor facilities open during the same months the swimming pools are open.

---

## ARGUMENT TASK

**STOP**

IF YOU FINISH BEFORE TIME IS CALLED, YOU MAY CHECK YOUR WORK ON THIS ESSAY ONLY.
DO NOT TURN TO ANY OTHER PORTION OF THE TEST.

## SECTION 2
### 30 Minutes
### 30 Items

Directions: Each sentence or paragraph in this part of the verbal section has one or more missing elements, as indicated by a blank or blanks. Choose the word or set of words that best fits the meaning of the text. Answers are on page 1056.

1. Execution by lethal injection, although horrifying, is certainly more civilized than the —— penalty of death by torture or dismemberment.

   (A) pervasive
   (B) viler
   (C) humane
   (D) prolific
   (E) complacent

2. Although vitamins are helpful for maintaining good health, alcohol, caffeine, and other drugs severely —— their effectiveness, leaving the body's defenses ——.

   (A) augment. .weakened
   (B) reduce. .indelible
   (C) inhibit. .impaired
   (D) confuse. .allied
   (E) duplicate. .activated

3. Since there are so few conservative thinkers on the committee, their influence on its recommendations is ——.

   (A) monumental
   (B) negligible
   (C) discriminatory
   (D) impractical
   (E) cathartic

4. Laboratory tests which often maim animals and depend solely on observation to determine results are not only —— but highly —— since no two people see the same thing.

   (A) safe. .consistent
   (B) patented. .conclusive
   (C) controversial. .valuable
   (D) gratifying. .explosive
   (E) cruel. .unreliable

5. The victim confronted his attacker in the courtroom calmly, with —— and without apparent —— although he had been severely traumatized by the incident.

   (A) woe. .composure
   (B) ineptitude. .obstinacy
   (C) tempering. .philanthropy
   (D) equanimity. .rancor
   (E) scorn. .malingering

6. The politician hungered for power; as a result of this ——, he succeeded in winning the election but in —— his closest friends and supporters.

   (A) furtiveness. .dissuading
   (B) winsomeness. .disgruntling
   (C) malevolence. .mesmerizing
   (D) acerbity. .seducing
   (E) cupidity. .alienating

GO ON TO THE NEXT PAGE.

Directions: Each of the following items consists of a related pair of words or phrases presented in capital letters, followed by five lettered pairs of words or phrases presented in lowercase letters. For each item, choose the lettered pair that expresses a relationship that is most nearly like that expressed in the capitalized pair. Answers are on page 1056.

7. CONTENT : EUPHORIC ::

 (A) puzzled : candid
 (B) abrasive : satisfactory
 (C) afraid : bold
 (D) sad : morose
 (E) sincere : calm

8. TRIVIAL : IMPORTANCE ::

 (A) tiny : magnitude
 (B) repetitious : pattern
 (C) portable : mobility
 (D) miraculous : faith
 (E) urgent : fallibility

9. MOTE : DUST ::

 (A) summit : mountain
 (B) drizzle : flood
 (C) gable : eave
 (D) bead : water
 (E) grain : particle

10. CLANDESTINE : SECRECY ::

 (A) personal : servant
 (B) imaginative : narrative
 (C) tumultuous : quiet
 (D) predictable : precision
 (E) confidential : privacy

11. REDOLENT : ODOR ::

 (A) recurrent : expenditure
 (B) savory : taste
 (C) passive : aggression
 (D) constricted : vacuum
 (E) harmful : injury

12. ADULTERATE : PURITY ::

 (A) relax : liberation
 (B) inform : knowledge
 (C) transfer : recklessness
 (D) mastermind : plot
 (E) dilute : concentration

13. MIASMA : NOXIOUS ::

 (A) tranquility : worried
 (B) liquid : gaseous
 (C) malignancy : benign
 (D) orchard : barren
 (E) poison : toxic

GO ON TO THE NEXT PAGE.

<u>Directions</u>: Each reading selection in this group is followed by questions based on its content. Answer the questions following a selection on the basis of what is <u>stated</u> or <u>implied</u> in that selection, choosing the best answer to each question. Answers are on page 1057.

The National Security Act of 1947 created a national military establishment headed by a single Secretary of Defense. The legislation had been a year-and-a-half in the making—beginning when President
5  Truman first recommended that the armed services be reorganized into a single department. During that period, the President's concept of a unified armed service was torn apart and put back together several times; the final measure to emerge from Congress was
10 a compromise. Most of the opposition to the bill came from the Navy and its numerous civilian spokesmen, including Secretary of the Navy James Forrestal. In support of unification (and a separate air force that was part of the unification package) were the Army air
15 forces, the Army, and, most importantly, the President of the United States.

Passage of the bill did not bring an end to the bitter inter-service disputes. Rather than to unify, the act served only to federate the military services. It
20 neither halted the rapid demobilization of the armed forces that followed World War II nor brought to the new national military establishment the loyalties of officers steeped in the traditions of the separate services. At a time when the balance of power in
25 Europe and Asia was rapidly shifting, the services lacked any precise statement of United States foreign policy from the National Security Council on which to base future programs. The services bickered unceasingly over their respective roles and missions,
30 already complicated by the Soviet nuclear capability that, for the first time, made the United States subject to devastating attack. Not even the appointment of Forrestal as First Secretary of Defense allayed the suspicions of naval officers and their supporters that
35 the role of the U.S. Navy was threatened with permanent eclipse. Before the war of words died down, Forrestal himself was driven to resignation and then suicide.

By 1948, the United States military establishment
40 was forced to make do with a budget approximately 10 percent of what it had been at its wartime peak. Meanwhile, the cost of weapons procurement was rising geometrically as the nation came to put more and more reliance on the atomic bomb and its delivery
45 systems. These two factors inevitably made adversaries of the Navy and the Air Force as the battle between advocates of the B-36 and the supercarrier so amply demonstrates. Given severe fiscal restraints on the one

hand, and on the other the nation's increasing reliance
50 on strategic nuclear deterrence, the conflict between these two services over roles and missions was essentially a contest over slices of an ever-diminishing pie.

Yet if in the end neither service was the obvious
55 victor, the principle of civilian dominance over the military clearly was. If there had ever been any danger that the United States military establishment might exploit, to the detriment of civilian control, the goodwill it enjoyed as a result of its victories in World
60 War II, that danger disappeared in the inter-service animosities engendered by the battle over unification.

14. With which of the following statements about defense unification would the author most likely agree?

(A) Unification ultimately undermined United States military capability by inciting inter-service rivalry.
(B) The unification legislation was necessitated by the drastic decline in appropriations for the military services.
(C) Although the unification was not entirely successful, it had the unexpected result of ensuring civilian control of the military.
(D) In spite of the attempted unification, each service was still able to pursue its own objectives without interference from the other branches.
(E) Unification was in the first place unwarranted, and in the second place ineffective.

GO ON TO THE NEXT PAGE.

15. According to the selection, the political situation following the passage of the National Security Act of 1947 was characterized by all of the following EXCEPT

    (A) a shifting balance of power in Europe and in Asia
    (B) fierce inter-service rivalries
    (C) lack of strong leadership by the National Security Council
    (D) shrinking postwar military budgets
    (E) a lame-duck President who was unable to unify the legislature

16. The author cites the resignation and suicide of Forrestal in order to

    (A) underscore the bitterness of the inter-service rivalry surrounding the passage of the National Security Act of 1947
    (B) demonstrate that the Navy eventually emerged as the dominant branch of service after the passage of the National Security Act of 1947
    (C) suggest that the nation would be better served by a unified armed service under a single command
    (D) provide an example of a military leader who preferred to serve his country in war rather than in peace
    (E) persuade the reader that Forrestal was a victim of political opportunists and an unscrupulous press

GO ON TO THE NEXT PAGE.

About twice every century, one of the massive
stars in our galaxy explodes. The shock waves heat
interstellar gas, evaporate small clouds, and compress
larger clouds so they collapse under their own gravity
5  to form new stars.

Throughout its evolution, a star is like a leaky
balloon. It keeps its equilibrium by a balance of
internal pressure against the tendency to collapse under
its own weight. The pressure is generated by nuclear
10  reactions in the core of the star which supply energy to
balance the energy leaking out in the form of radiation.
Eventually the nuclear fuel is exhausted and pressure
drops in the core. With nothing to hold it up, the matter
in the center of the star collapses, creating higher and
15  higher densities and temperatures, until nuclei and
electrons are fused into a superdense lump of matter
known as a neutron star.

As overlying layers rain down on the surface of
the neutron star, the temperature rises until, in a
20  blinding flash of radiation, the collapse reverses. A
thermonuclear shock wave runs through the now
expanding stellar envelope, fusing lighter elements into
heavier ones and producing a brilliant burst as intense
as the light of 10 billion suns. The exploding shell of
25  matter plows through the surrounding gas, producing
an expanding bubble of hot gas with temperatures in
the millions of degrees. This gas emits most of its
energy at x-ray wavelengths, and more than twenty
supernova remnants have now been detected in x-ray
30  studies.

Recent discoveries of meteorites with anomalous
concentrations of certain isotopes indicate that a
supernova might have precipitated the birth of our
solar system more than four and a half billion years
35  ago. Although the cloud that collapsed to form the Sun
and the planets was composed primarily of hydrogen
and helium, it also contained carbon, nitrogen, and
oxygen, elements essential for life as we know it.
Elements heavier than helium are manufactured deep
40  in the interior of stars and would, for the most part,
remain there if it were not for the cataclysmic
supernova explosions that blow giant stars apart.
Additionally, supernovas produce clouds of high-
energy particles called cosmic rays. These high energy
45  particles continually bombard the Earth and are
responsible for many of the genetic mutations that are
the driving force of the evolution of species.

17.  According to the passage, all of the following are
true of supernovas EXCEPT

(A) they are extremely bright
(B) they are an explosion of some sort
(C) they emit large quantities of x-rays
(D) they result in the destruction of a neutron star
(E) they are caused by the collision of large
galaxies

18.  It can be inferred from the passage that the
meteorites mentioned by the author in line 31

(A) contain dangerous concentrations of
radioactive materials
(B) give off large quantities of x-rays
(C) include material not created in the normal
development of our solar system
(D) are larger than the meteors normally found in
a solar system like ours
(E) contain pieces of a supernova that occurred
several billion years ago

GO ON TO THE NEXT PAGE.

Considerable advances have been made in the area of healthcare services, including better access to healthcare and improvements in physical plants, but there is mounting criticism of unbridled cost inflation
5 and excessive indulgence in wasteful high-technology "gadgeteering." In recent years, panaceas have proliferated at a feverish pace and disappointments have multiplied at almost the same rate. This has led to an increased pessimism—"everything has been tried
10 and nothing works"—which sometimes borders on cynicism or even nihilism.

The automatic "pass through" of rapidly spiraling costs to government and insurance carriers produced a sense of unlimited resources and encouraged the notion
15 that every practitioner and institution could operate without concern for the "Medical Commons." Full-cost reimbursement encouraged capital investment, and now the industry is overcapitalized. Cities have hundreds of excess hospital beds; hospitals have a
20 superabundance of high-technology equipment; and structural ostentation and luxury have been the order of the day. One-fourth of all beds are vacant; expensive equipment is underused or, worse, used unnecessarily. Capital investment brings rapidly rising operating
25 costs.

Yet, in part, this pessimism derives from expecting too much. Healthcare is usually a painful experience, often accompanied by fear and unwelcome results. Moreover, the capacities of medical science are
30 limited. Humpty Dumpty cannot always be put back together again. Too many physicians are reluctant to admit their limitations to patients; too many patients and families are unwilling to accept such realities. Nor is it true that everything has been tried and nothing
35 works, as shown by prepaid group practice plans. In the main, however, such undertakings have been drowned by a flood of public and private moneys which have supported and encouraged the continuation of conventional practices and subsidized their
40 shortcomings on a massive, almost unrestricted scale. For the most part, there have been no incentives to practice self-restraint or frugality. In this atmosphere, it is not fair to condemn as failures all attempted experiments; it may be more accurate to say many
45 never had a fair trial.

19. The author mentions all of the following as consequences of full-cost reimbursement EXCEPT

(A) rising operating costs
(B) underused hospital facilities
(C) overcapitalization
(D) unnecessary use of expensive equipment
(E) lack of essential services

20. According to the author, the "pessimism" mentioned in line 9 is partly attributable to the fact that

(A) there has been little real improvement in healthcare services
(B) expectations about healthcare services are sometimes unrealistic
(C) large segments of the population find it impossible to get access to healthcare services
(D) advances in technology have made healthcare services unaffordable
(E) doctors are now less concerned with patient care

21. The author cites the prepaid plans in line 35 as

(A) proof of the theory that no plan has been successful
(B) examples of healthcare plans that were over-funded
(C) evidence that healthcare services are fragmented
(D) counterexamples to the claim that nothing has worked
(E) experiments that yielded disappointing results

GO ON TO THE NEXT PAGE.

Directions: Each of the following items consists of a word printed in capital letters, followed by five lettered words or phrases in lowercase letters. Choose the lettered word or phrase that is most nearly <u>opposite</u> in meaning to the word in capital letters. Answers are on page 1057.

22. HACKNEYED:

   (A) trivial
   (B) derogatory
   (C) original
   (D) intense
   (E) inclined

23. DISCONSOLATE:

   (A) resolved
   (B) strong
   (C) compelled
   (D) cheerful
   (E) involved

24. MALEDICTION:

   (A) oblique reference
   (B) incarceration
   (C) blessing
   (D) specific detail
   (E) sophistication

25. ACERBIC:

   (A) sweet
   (B) magical
   (C) healthy
   (D) separate
   (E) distinguished

26. LUGUBRIOUS:

   (A) pliable
   (B) residual
   (C) disreputable
   (D) incorrigible
   (E) joyful

27. PROFLIGATE:

   (A) rank
   (B) proficient
   (C) virtuous
   (D) obstreperous
   (E) mediocre

28. INCHOATE:

   (A) saccharine
   (B) fully developed
   (C) barely heard
   (D) transient
   (E) known to many

29. CRAVEN:

   (A) insubordinate
   (B) courageous
   (C) derelict
   (D) avid
   (E) benign

30. SATURNINE:

   (A) indubitable
   (B) complacent
   (C) viscous
   (D) joyful
   (E) minute

# S T O P

IF YOU FINISH BEFORE TIME IS CALLED, YOU MAY CHECK YOUR WORK ON THIS SECTION ONLY.
DO NOT WORK ON ANY OTHER SECTION IN THE TEST.

**SECTION 3**

30 Minutes

28 Items

In this section, solve each problem using any available space on the page for scratch work. Then, decide which is the best of the choices given and fill in the corresponding oval on the answer sheet.

All numbers used are real numbers.

All angle measures are positive.

A figure accompanying a question is included to provide information useful in answering that question. However, unless a note explicitly states that a figure is drawn to scale, you should answer a question not by estimating the magnitudes of various aspects, but by using your knowledge of the principles of mathematics. You can assume, however, that the positions of points, angles, regions, etc. are in the order shown, that lines shown as straight are straight, and that all figures lie in the plane unless otherwise noted.

Directions: Each of the questions 1 through 14 consists of two quantities, one in Column A and one in Column B. Choose:

    A if the quantity in Column A is greater

    B if the quantity in Column B is greater

    C if the two quantities are equal

    D if the relationship cannot be determined from the information given

Notes: If information is centered above the two quantities to be compared, then that information is true of both quantities.

A symbol that appears in both columns represents the same thing in both columns.

The only possible choices are (A), (B), (C), and (D). Do not choose (E).

Answers are on page 1058.

| | Column A | Column B |
|---|---|---|
| | | |
| 1. | $x + y$ | $z$ |
| 2. | $5^7 - 2^4$ | $5^7 - 2^5$ |
| | $x \neq 0$ | |
| 3. | $\sqrt{x^2}$ | $\sqrt{x^2 + 1}$ |

| | Column A | Column B |
|---|---|---|
| | | |
| | $l_1 \parallel l_2$ | |
| 4. | $x$ | $180 - y$ |
| 5. | $1 \cdot \frac{15}{16}$ | $2 \cdot \frac{15}{16}$ |

GO ON TO THE NEXT PAGE.

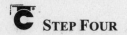 

| Column A | Column B |
|----------|----------|

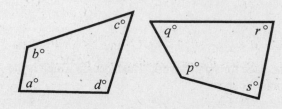

**6.** $a+b+c+d$     $p+q+r+s$

**7.** $-3\div(-1)$     $-3\cdot-1$

$$x > \frac{y}{2} > 0$$

**8.** $x$     $y$

In Town T, merchants must collect a sales tax equal to $p$ percent of the selling price of an item. The sales tax on an item costing \$360 is \$25.20.

**9.** The sales tax on an item costing \$420     \$30

$x$, $y$, and $z$ are three consecutive *even* integers, and $x < y < z$.

**10.** $x+y+1$     $y+z-1$

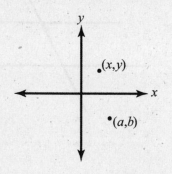

**11.** $x+y$     $a+b$

| Column A | Column B |
|----------|----------|

$[x]=0$ if $x$ is a negative integer.
$[x]=1$ if $x$ is a positive integer.

$p$ and $q$ are integers, $3p$ is negative, and $q-3$ is positive.

**12.** $[p]$     $[q]$

$$\frac{x}{y}=1$$

**13.** $x-y$     $y-x$

The volume of a cube is 8 cubic centimeters.

**14.** The number of square centimeters on the surface of the cube     8

GO ON TO THE NEXT PAGE.

Directions: Each of the following questions has five answer choices. Select the best of the available choices. Answers are on page 1059.

15. If $2^x = 16$ and $x = \frac{y}{2}$, then $y =$

(A) 2
(B) 3
(C) 4
(D) 6
(E) 8

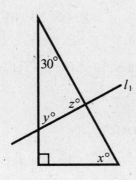

16. In the figure above, if $x = y$, then $z =$

(A) 30
(B) 45
(C) 60
(D) 75
(E) 90

17. If $6 \le x \le 30$, $3 \le y \le 12$, and $2 \le z \le 10$, then what is the least possible value of $\frac{(x+y)}{z}$?

(A) $\frac{9}{10}$
(B) $\frac{9}{5}$
(C) $\frac{21}{5}$
(D) $\frac{9}{2}$
(E) 21

GO ON TO THE NEXT PAGE.

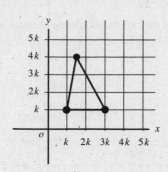

20. After *trimming*, a sapling has $\frac{9}{10}$ of its original height. If it must grow $\frac{9}{10}$ foot to regain its original height, what was its original height?

    (A) 8
    (B) 9
    (C) 10
    (D) 16
    (E) 18

18. If the area of the triangle in the figure above is 12, then $k =$

    (A) 1
    (B) 2
    (C) 3
    (D) 4
    (E) 6

GO ON TO THE NEXT PAGE.

19. If $x$ and $y$ are two different positive integers and $x^3 y^2 = 200$, then $xy =$

    (A) 5
    (B) 6
    (C) 10
    (D) 25
    (E) 40

Items 21–22 refer to the following graphs.

## Sales and Earnings of Company X

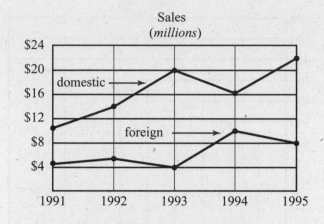

Sales
(*millions*)

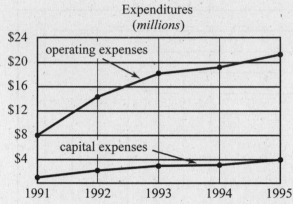

Expenditures
(*millions*)

21. Which of the following pie graphs best represents the division of total sales between foreign and domestic sales for 1994?

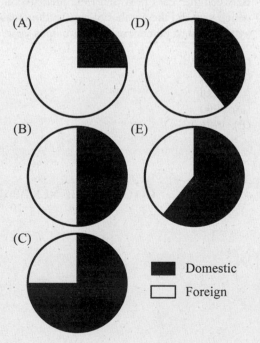

(A)

(D)

(B)

(E)

(C)

■ Domestic
□ Foreign

22. If Company X considers its profit to be the difference between total sales (foreign and domestic) and total expenses (capital and operating), in how many of the years shown were profits more than 20 percent of total sales?

(A) 0
(B) 1
(C) 2
(D) 3
(E) 4

GO ON TO THE NEXT PAGE.

Items 23–25 refer to the following graphs.

## REVENUE AND SALES FIGURES FOR THE RED ROSE CAR DEALERSHIP

Revenues (*millions*)

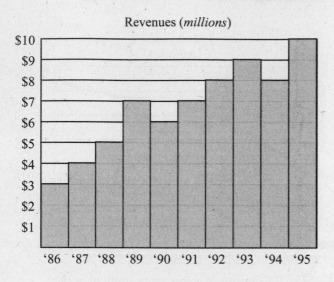

Cars Sold

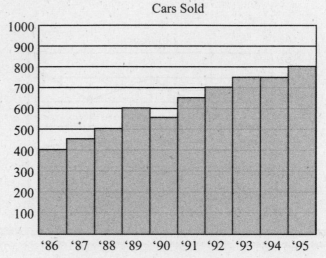

23. From 1988 to 1992 inclusive, the greatest increase in revenues over the previous year was

  (A)  $200,000
  (B)  $750,000
  (C)  $1,500,000
  (D)  $1,750,000
  (E)  $2,000,000

24. In 1993, what was the average price of a car sold by the Red Rose Dealership?

  (A)  $8,500
  (B)  $9,250
  (C)  $10,250
  (D)  $11,500
  (E)  $12,000

25. Between the years 1987 and 1992 inclusive, in which year did the number of cars sold increase by the greatest percent over the previous year?

  (A) 1987
  (B) 1988
  (C) 1989
  (D) 1990
  (E) 1991

GO ON TO THE NEXT PAGE.

26. A tank contains $g$ gallons of water. Water flows into the tank by one pipe at the rate of $m$ gallons per minute, and water flows out by another pipe at the rate of $n$ gallons per minute. If $n > m$, how many minutes will it take to empty the tank?

(A) $\frac{(g-m)}{n}$

(B) $\frac{g}{(m-n)}$

(C) $\frac{(n-g)}{m}$

(D) $\frac{(n-m)}{g}$

(E) $\frac{g}{(n-m)}$

27. If $\frac{13t}{7}$ is an integer, then $t$ could be any of the following EXCEPT

(A) -91
(B) -7
(C) 3
(D) 70
(E) 91

28. If $\frac{(x+y)}{x} = 4$ and $\frac{(y+z)}{z} = 5$, what is the value of $\frac{x}{z}$?

(A) $\frac{1}{4}$

(B) $\frac{1}{3}$

(C) $\frac{3}{4}$

(D) $\frac{4}{3}$

(E) $\frac{3}{1}$

# S T O P

IF YOU FINISH BEFORE TIME IS CALLED, YOU MAY CHECK YOUR WORK ON THIS SECTION ONLY.
DO NOT WORK ON ANY OTHER SECTION IN THE TEST.

# Practice Test II

# CAMBRIDGE TESTPREP™
## PRACTICE TEST II OUTLINE

# PRACTICE TEST II

Start with number 1 for each new section. If a section has fewer items than answer spaces, leave the extra answer spaces blank. Be sure to erase any errors or stray marks completely.

**Section 2**

| 1 Ⓐ Ⓑ Ⓒ Ⓓ Ⓔ | 9 Ⓐ Ⓑ Ⓒ Ⓓ Ⓔ | 17 Ⓐ Ⓑ Ⓒ Ⓓ Ⓔ | 25 Ⓐ Ⓑ Ⓒ Ⓓ Ⓔ |
| 2 Ⓐ Ⓑ Ⓒ Ⓓ Ⓔ | 10 Ⓐ Ⓑ Ⓒ Ⓓ Ⓔ | 18 Ⓐ Ⓑ Ⓒ Ⓓ Ⓔ | 26 Ⓐ Ⓑ Ⓒ Ⓓ Ⓔ |
| 3 Ⓐ Ⓑ Ⓒ Ⓓ Ⓔ | 11 Ⓐ Ⓑ Ⓒ Ⓓ Ⓔ | 19 Ⓐ Ⓑ Ⓒ Ⓓ Ⓔ | 27 Ⓐ Ⓑ Ⓒ Ⓓ Ⓔ |
| 4 Ⓐ Ⓑ Ⓒ Ⓓ Ⓔ | 12 Ⓐ Ⓑ Ⓒ Ⓓ Ⓔ | 20 Ⓐ Ⓑ Ⓒ Ⓓ Ⓔ | 28 Ⓐ Ⓑ Ⓒ Ⓓ Ⓔ |
| 5 Ⓐ Ⓑ Ⓒ Ⓓ Ⓔ | 13 Ⓐ Ⓑ Ⓒ Ⓓ Ⓔ | 21 Ⓐ Ⓑ Ⓒ Ⓓ Ⓔ | 29 Ⓐ Ⓑ Ⓒ Ⓓ Ⓔ |
| 6 Ⓐ Ⓑ Ⓒ Ⓓ Ⓔ | 14 Ⓐ Ⓑ Ⓒ Ⓓ Ⓔ | 22 Ⓐ Ⓑ Ⓒ Ⓓ Ⓔ | 30 Ⓐ Ⓑ Ⓒ Ⓓ Ⓔ |
| 7 Ⓐ Ⓑ Ⓒ Ⓓ Ⓔ | 15 Ⓐ Ⓑ Ⓒ Ⓓ Ⓔ | 23 Ⓐ Ⓑ Ⓒ Ⓓ Ⓔ | |
| 8 Ⓐ Ⓑ Ⓒ Ⓓ Ⓔ | 16 Ⓐ Ⓑ Ⓒ Ⓓ Ⓔ | 24 Ⓐ Ⓑ Ⓒ Ⓓ Ⓔ | |

**Section 3**

| 1 Ⓐ Ⓑ Ⓒ Ⓓ Ⓔ | 11 Ⓐ Ⓑ Ⓒ Ⓓ Ⓔ | 21 Ⓐ Ⓑ Ⓒ Ⓓ Ⓔ | 31 Ⓐ Ⓑ Ⓒ Ⓓ Ⓔ |
| 2 Ⓐ Ⓑ Ⓒ Ⓓ Ⓔ | 12 Ⓐ Ⓑ Ⓒ Ⓓ Ⓔ | 22 Ⓐ Ⓑ Ⓒ Ⓓ Ⓔ | 32 Ⓐ Ⓑ Ⓒ Ⓓ Ⓔ |
| 3 Ⓐ Ⓑ Ⓒ Ⓓ Ⓔ | 13 Ⓐ Ⓑ Ⓒ Ⓓ Ⓔ | 23 Ⓐ Ⓑ Ⓒ Ⓓ Ⓔ | 33 Ⓐ Ⓑ Ⓒ Ⓓ Ⓔ |
| 4 Ⓐ Ⓑ Ⓒ Ⓓ Ⓔ | 14 Ⓐ Ⓑ Ⓒ Ⓓ Ⓔ | 24 Ⓐ Ⓑ Ⓒ Ⓓ Ⓔ | 34 Ⓐ Ⓑ Ⓒ Ⓓ Ⓔ |
| 5 Ⓐ Ⓑ Ⓒ Ⓓ Ⓔ | 15 Ⓐ Ⓑ Ⓒ Ⓓ Ⓔ | 25 Ⓐ Ⓑ Ⓒ Ⓓ Ⓔ | 35 Ⓐ Ⓑ Ⓒ Ⓓ Ⓔ |
| 6 Ⓐ Ⓑ Ⓒ Ⓓ Ⓔ | 16 Ⓐ Ⓑ Ⓒ Ⓓ Ⓔ | 26 Ⓐ Ⓑ Ⓒ Ⓓ Ⓔ | 36 Ⓐ Ⓑ Ⓒ Ⓓ Ⓔ |
| 7 Ⓐ Ⓑ Ⓒ Ⓓ Ⓔ | 17 Ⓐ Ⓑ Ⓒ Ⓓ Ⓔ | 27 Ⓐ Ⓑ Ⓒ Ⓓ Ⓔ | 37 Ⓐ Ⓑ Ⓒ Ⓓ Ⓔ |
| 8 Ⓐ Ⓑ Ⓒ Ⓓ Ⓔ | 18 Ⓐ Ⓑ Ⓒ Ⓓ Ⓔ | 28 Ⓐ Ⓑ Ⓒ Ⓓ Ⓔ | 38 Ⓐ Ⓑ Ⓒ Ⓓ Ⓔ |
| 9 Ⓐ Ⓑ Ⓒ Ⓓ Ⓔ | 19 Ⓐ Ⓑ Ⓒ Ⓓ Ⓔ | 29 Ⓐ Ⓑ Ⓒ Ⓓ Ⓔ | |
| 10 Ⓐ Ⓑ Ⓒ Ⓓ Ⓔ | 20 Ⓐ Ⓑ Ⓒ Ⓓ Ⓔ | 30 Ⓐ Ⓑ Ⓒ Ⓓ Ⓔ | |

## SECTION 1
## PRESENT YOUR PERSPECTIVE ON AN ISSUE
### 45 minutes

You will be presented with an Issue topic, which will be summarized in a brief quotation. The topic describes an issue of general interest. Read the topic carefully.

You have 45 minutes to plan, write, and edit your essay. Your essay should present your perspective on the topic. In addressing the claim made in the quotation, you can accept the quotation, reject it outright, or accept it in part and reject it in part as long as the points you make are clearly relevant to the topic. An essay on any other topic will receive a score of zero. Support your position with reasons and examples that are drawn from your everyday reading, personal experience, direct observations, or academic studies.

Your essay will be read by college and university teachers who will evaluate its overall quality, specifically taking into account how well you:

- develop and treat the complexities of the topic;
- organize, develop, and state your ideas;
- support your ideas with relevant examples and reasons;
- control the elements of standard written English.

It may be useful to take a few minutes of your time to think about the issue and to plan or even outline a response before you actually begin to write. Make sure that you organize your ideas into a coherent essay and develop them in some detail. Reserve some of your time to proofread and edit your response. A sample essay is on page 1065.

> In this age of computers, some people complain that our lives are being controlled by machines. But, in reality, computers actually improve the quality of our lives.

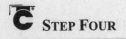 

## ISSUE TASK

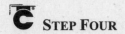
# S T O P

**IF YOU FINISH BEFORE TIME IS CALLED, YOU MAY CHECK YOUR WORK ON THIS ESSAY ONLY.**
**DO NOT TURN TO ANY OTHER PORTION OF THE TEST.**

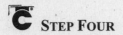 

## ANALYSIS OF AN ARGUMENT
### 30 minutes

You have 30 minutes to organize and write a critique of the argument presented in the short passage below. A critique of an argument other than the one presented will be given a score of zero.

Analyze the line of reasoning in the argument; identify what, if any, questionable premises are made by the argument; and evaluate how well the evidence presented supports the conclusion of the argument. In evaluating the evidence, you can consider what kinds of proof would weaken or strengthen the argument and what additional information might tend to prove or disprove the conclusion.

Importantly, you are not being asked to present your own personal point of view on the subject.

Your essay will be read by college and university teachers who will evaluate its overall quality, specifically taking into account how well you:

- identify and analyze the important features of the argument;
- organize, develop, and state your points;
- support your critique with relevant examples and reasons;
- control the elements of standard written English.

It may be useful to take a few minutes of your time to think about the issue and to plan or even outline a response before you actually begin to write. Make sure that you organize your ideas into a coherent essay and develop them in some detail. Reserve some of your time to proofread and edit your response. A sample essay is on page 1065.

> A recent review of the records of the Putnam Township volunteer rescue squad shows that its average response time is 6 minutes greater than that of the Empire Ambulance Service, a for-profit company operating in the Putnam area. Putnam should disband the rescue squad, sell the equipment, and contract ambulance services out to Empire. We'd get much better emergency care for our citizens.

**ARGUMENT TASK**

**S T O P**

IF YOU FINISH BEFORE TIME IS CALLED, YOU MAY CHECK YOUR WORK ON THIS ESSAY ONLY.
DO NOT TURN TO ANY OTHER PORTION OF THE TEST.

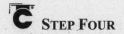 

## SECTION 2

30 Minutes

28 Items

In this section, solve each problem using any available space on the page for scratch work. Then, decide which is the best of the choices given and fill in the corresponding oval on the answer sheet.

> All numbers used are real numbers.
> All angle measures are positive.
> A figure accompanying a question is included to provide information useful in answering that question. However, unless a note explicitly states that a figure is drawn to scale, you should answer a question not by estimating the magnitudes of various aspects, but by using your knowledge of the principles of mathematics. You can assume, however, that the positions of points, angles, regions, etc. are in the order shown, that lines shown as straight are straight, and that all figures lie in the plane unless otherwise noted.

Directions: Each of the questions 1 through 14 consists of two quantities, one in Column A and one in Column B. Choose:

> A if the quantity in Column A is greater
> B if the quantity in Column B is greater
> C if the two quantities are equal
> D if the relationship cannot be determined from the information given

Notes: If information is centered above the two quantities to be compared, then that information is true of both quantities.

> A symbol that appears in both columns represents the same thing in both columns.
> The only possible choices are (A), (B), (C), and (D). Do not choose (E).

Answers are on page 1066.

| | Column A | Column B |
|---|---|---|

A triangle with a $70°$ angle at the top, $4x°$ and $110°$ at the bottom left, and $2x°$ at the bottom right.

**1.** $\quad x \qquad\qquad 30$

---

**2.** $\quad \sqrt{6} \cdot \sqrt{10} \qquad \sqrt{3} \cdot \sqrt{20}$

---

$$x < 0$$

**3.** $\quad x^{15} \qquad\qquad x^{16}$

| | Column A | Column B |
|---|---|---|

Number line: $0 \quad x \quad 50 \quad 100$

**4.** $\quad 50 + x \qquad\qquad 100$

---

The average of $x$, $y$, and $z$ is $y$.

**5.** $\quad x \qquad\qquad z$

GO ON TO THE NEXT PAGE.

| Column A | Column B |
|---|---|

**y**

II      I

•$(x,z)$

→ x

•$(z,y)$

III      IV

Points $(x,z)$ and $(z,y)$ are in
Quadrants I and IV, respectively.

6.      $x$          $y$

---

Peanuts cost $1.25 per pound and
cashews cost $2.25 per pound.

7.    The number of pounds     1
of peanuts in 2 pounds
of a mix of peanuts
and cashews that costs
$1.75 per pound

---

8.    The sum of the      The sum of the
three greatest       three greatest
odd integers        even integers
less than 100       less than 100

---

Old City is 5 kilometers from
New Town, and New Town
is 3 miles from Middlebury.

9.    The distance in      3
kilometers from Old
City to Middlebury

---

0.2    0.3    0.4    0.5    0.6

←—o—|—|—|—|—|—o—|—→
   $x$               $y$

$X$ and $Y$ are points on the number line.

10.     $\overline{XY}$          0.30

---

| Column A | Column B |
|---|---|

11.   The average of     The average of
three numbers     three numbers
the greatest of     the greatest of
which is 15        which is 46

---

$$x + 3y = 6$$

12.    $\dfrac{2x+6y}{5}$        $\dfrac{13}{5}$

---

$k$, $x$, and $y$ are positive
integers, and $xy = k$.

13.     $x$           $k$

---

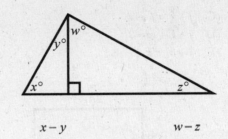

14.    $x - y$         $w - z$

GO ON TO THE NEXT PAGE.

Directions: Each of the following questions has five answer choices. Select the best of the available choices. Answers are on page 1067.

15. $121,212 + (2 \cdot 10^4) =$

   (A) 321,212
   (B) 141,212
   (C) 123,212
   (D) 121,412
   (E) 121,232

16. Jack, Ken, Larry and Mike are $j$, $k$, $l$, and $m$ years old, respectively. If $j < k < l < m$, which of the following *could* be true?

   (A) $k = j + l$
   (B) $j = k + l$
   (C) $j + k = l + m$
   (D) $j + k + m = l$
   (E) $j + m = k + l$

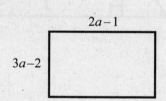

17. What is the perimeter of the rectangle shown above?

   (A) $10a - 6$
   (B) $10a - 3$
   (C) $6a - 2$
   (D) $5a - 6$
   (E) $5a - 3$

18. If $x$ is 80 percent of $y$, then $y$ is what percent of $x$?

   (A) $133\frac{1}{3}\%$
   (B) 125%
   (C) 120%
   (D) 90%
   (E) 80%

19. From which of the following statements can it be deduced that $m > n$?

   (A) $m + 1 = n$
   (B) $2m = n$
   (C) $m + n > 0$
   (D) $m - n > 0$
   (E) $mn > 0$

20. If for *any* number $n$, ⟨$n$⟩ is defined as the least integer that is greater than or equal to $n^2$, then ⟨$-1.1$⟩ =

   (A) $-2$
   (B) $-1$
   (C) $0$
   (D) $1$
   (E) $2$

GO ON TO THE NEXT PAGE.

Items 21–22 refer to the following graphs.

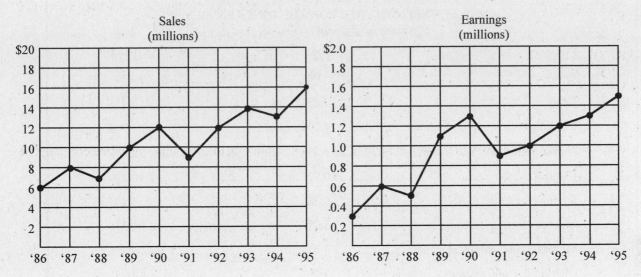

SALES AND EARNINGS OF COMPANY K

21. From 1986 to 1995, earnings of Company K increased by what percent?

    (A) 150%
    (B) 200%
    (C) $233\frac{1}{3}\%$
    (D) 400%
    (E) 500%

22. In how many of the years shown were earnings equal to or greater than 10 percent of sales?

    (A) 3
    (B) 4
    (C) 5
    (D) 6
    (E) 7

GO ON TO THE NEXT PAGE.

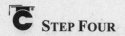
Items 23–25 refer to the following graph.

### ANNUAL EXPENDITURES FOR THE JONES FAMILY
*(percent of disposable income)*

| Category | 1995 | 1996 |
|---|---|---|
| Rent | 23.0% | 19.3% |
| Food | 17.6% | 18.2% |
| Clothing | 14.2% | 15.1% |
| Automobile | 11.3% | 12.3% |
| Utilities | 10.9% | 10.2% |
| Savings | 6.2% | 5.1% |
| Entertainment | 5.2% | 5.3% |
| Medical and Dental Care | 4.0% | 3.7% |
| Charitable Contributions | 3.2% | 3.9% |
| Household Furnishings | 2.9% | 3.1% |
| Other | 1.5% | 3.8% |
| | 100.0% | 100.0% |
| Total Expenditures: | $34,987.00 | $40,012.00 |

23. Approximately how much money did the Jones family spend on medical and dental care in 1995?

(A) $1,200
(B) $1,400
(C) $1,520
(D) $2,250
(E) $4,000

24. By approximately what percent did expenditures by the Jones family increase from 1995 to 1996?

(A) 8.5%
(B) 11.2%
(C) 14.2%
(D) 18.1%
(E) 22.0%

25. If the categories in the table are rank ordered from one to eleven in each year, for how many categories would the rank ordering change from 1995 to 1996?

(A) 2
(B) 3
(C) 4
(D) 5
(E) 6

GO ON TO THE NEXT PAGE.

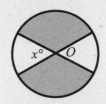

26. The circle with center $O$ has a radius of length 2. If the total area of the shaded regions is $3\pi$, then $x =$

(A)  270
(B)  180
(C)  120
(D)   90
(E)   45

27. If a bar of metal alloy consists of 100 grams of tin and 150 grams of lead, what percent of the entire bar, by weight, is tin?

(A) 10%
(B) 15%
(C) $33\frac{1}{3}$%
(D) 40%
(E) $66\frac{2}{3}$%

28. If $S$ is 150 percent of $T$, then $T$ is what percent of $S+T$?

(A) $33\frac{1}{3}$%
(B) 40%
(C) 50%
(D) 75%
(E) 80%

# S T O P

IF YOU FINISH BEFORE TIME IS CALLED, YOU MAY CHECK YOUR WORK ON THIS SECTION ONLY.
DO NOT WORK ON ANY OTHER SECTION IN THE TEST.

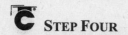 

**SECTION 3**

30 Minutes

30 Items

Directions: Each of the following items consists of a related pair of words or phrases presented in capital letters, followed by five lettered pairs of words or phrases presented in lowercase letters. For each item, choose the lettered pair that expresses a relationship that is most nearly like that expressed in the capitalized pair. Answers are on page 1069.

1. INCISION : SCALPEL ::

   (A) hospital : patient
   (B) playground : swing
   (C) kitchen : knife
   (D) electricity : wire
   (E) cut : saw

2. ALTIMETER : HEIGHT ::

   (A) speedometer : velocity
   (B) observatory : constellation
   (C) racetrack : furlong
   (D) vessel : knots
   (E) metronome : tempo

3. CARAVAN : PROCESSION ::

   (A) merchant : commerce
   (B) wedding : ceremony
   (C) menagerie : animal
   (D) hunter : prey
   (E) forum : argument

4. SLANDER : PEJORATIVE ::

   (A) ingratiate : miraculous
   (B) revere : condemnatory
   (C) extol : laudatory
   (D) ruminate : unexpected
   (E) inculcate : plaintive

5. UNGAINLY : ELEGANCE ::

   (A) stately : majesty
   (B) suitable : propriety
   (C) vacuous : temerity
   (D) feckless : sobriety
   (E) perfunctory : attention

6. CONSERVATOR : WASTE ::

   (A) sentinel : vigilance
   (B) monarch : subject
   (C) demagogue : benevolence
   (D) chaperon : transgression
   (E) minister : profanity

7. POLEMICIST : CONTROVERSY ::

   (A) dilettante : virtuosity
   (B) visionary : dream
   (C) pundit : sophistry
   (D) zealot : benevolence
   (E) bigot : equanimity

GO ON TO THE NEXT PAGE.

<u>Directions</u>: Each of the following items consists of a word printed in capital letters, followed by five lettered words or phrases in lowercase letters. Choose the lettered word or phrase that is most nearly <u>opposite</u> in meaning to the word in capital letters. Answers are on page 1069.

8. INCIPIENT:

   (A) completed
   (B) serious
   (C) opaque
   (D) transcendent
   (E) ineffectual

9. SANCTIFY:

   (A) surrender
   (B) amplify
   (C) sever
   (D) defile
   (E) portend

10. DISSIPATE:

    (A) renounce
    (B) benefit
    (C) court
    (D) confide
    (E) gather

11. ASPERITY:

    (A) smoothness
    (B) fabrication
    (C) duplicity
    (D) indolence
    (E) intercession

12. IGNOMINIOUS:

    (A) melancholy
    (B) cantankerous
    (C) symmetrical
    (D) honorable
    (E) calamitous

13. EVANESCENT:

    (A) indulgent
    (B) obsequious
    (C) permanent
    (D) illimitable
    (E) serendipitous

14. VILIFY:

    (A) thwart
    (B) purport
    (C) abound
    (D) circumscribe
    (E) laud

15. TENDER:

    (A) demote
    (B) truncate
    (C) retract
    (D) emancipate
    (E) besiege

16. FUNGIBLE:

    (A) corrosive
    (B) iridescent
    (C) unique
    (D) retrograde
    (E) discursive

GO ON TO THE NEXT PAGE.

Directions: Each sentence or paragraph in this part of the verbal section has one or more missing elements, as indicated by a blank or blanks. Choose the word or set of words that best fits the meaning of the text. Answers are on page 1069.

17. Because of the —— of acupuncture therapy in China, Western physicians are starting to learn the procedure.

    (A) veracity
    (B) manipulation
    (C) liquidity
    (D) effectiveness
    (E) inflation

18. The conclusion of the program was a modern symphony with chords so —— that the piece produced a sound similar to the —— one hears as the individual orchestra members tune their instruments before a concert.

    (A) superfluous. .melody
    (B) pretentious. .roar
    (C) melodious. .applause
    (D) versatile. .harmony
    (E) discordant. .cacophony

19. Black comedy is the combination of that which is humorous with that which would seem —— to humor: the ——.

    (A) apathetic. .ignoble
    (B) heretical. .salacious
    (C) inferior. .grandiose
    (D) extraneous. .innocuous
    (E) antithetical. .macabre

20. The press conference did not clarify many issues since the President responded with —— and —— rather than clarity and precision.

    (A) sincerity. .humor
    (B) incongruity. .candor
    (C) fervor. .lucidity
    (D) animation. .formality
    (E) obfuscation. .vagueness

21. It is difficult for a modern audience, accustomed to the —— of film and television, to appreciate opera with its grand spectacle and —— gestures.

    (A) irreverence. .hapless
    (B) sophistication. .monotonous
    (C) minutiae. .extravagant
    (D) plurality. .subtle
    (E) flamboyance. .inane

22. Behaviorism was a protest against the —— psychological tradition which held that the proper data of psychology were ——, which reflected one's consciousness or state of mind.

    (A) redoubtable. .superficial
    (B) moralistic. .irrelevant
    (C) rudimentary. .material
    (D) newfangled. .preposterous
    (E) orthodox. .mentalistic

GO ON TO THE NEXT PAGE.

Directions: Each reading selection in this group is followed by questions based on its content. Answer the questions following a selection on the basis of what is <u>stated</u> or <u>implied</u> in that selection, choosing the best answer to each question. Answers are on page 1070.

The founders of the Republic viewed the revolution in political rather than economic or social terms. They spoke of education as essential to the public good—a goal taking precedence over
5  knowledge as occupational training or as a means to self-fulfillment. Both liberals and conservatives felt that the welfare of the Republic rested upon an educated citizenry and that free public schools were the best means of educating the citizenry in civic values
10  and the obligations needed for a republican society. All agreed that the principal ingredients of a civic education were literacy and the inculcation of patriotic and moral virtues.

The founders and their successors were long on
15  rhetoric, but it fell to the textbook writers to distill the essence of those values for school children. The earliest textbook writers were mostly conservatives, more likely Federalist than Jeffersonian, and they almost universally agreed that political virtue rests
20  upon moral and religious precepts. Since most were New Englanders, texts were infused with Protestant and, above all, Puritan outlooks.

In the first half of the Republic, education in the schools emphasized civic values and made little attempt
25  to develop participatory political skills. That task was left to political parties, town meetings, and churches. Additionally, the press did more to disseminate realistic as well as partisan knowledge of government than the schools. The goal of education was to achieve a higher
30  form of *unum* for the new Republic.

In the middle nineteenth century, political values taught in school were not substantially different from those of the first fifty years of the Republic. Their rosy hues if anything became golden. To the resplendent
35  values of liberty, equality, and a benevolent Christian morality were now added the middle-class virtues— especially of New England—of hard work, honesty, integrity, the rewards of individual effort, and obedience to parents and legitimate authority. But of
40  all the political values taught in school, patriotism was preeminent; and whenever teachers explained to school children why they should love their country above all else, the idea of liberty assumed pride of place.

23. The passage deals primarily with the

(A) origin and development of the Protestant work ethic in modern America
(B) role of education in late eighteenth- and early to mid-nineteenth-century America
(C) influence of New England Puritanism on early American values
(D) content of early textbooks on American history and government
(E) establishment of universal, free public education in America

24. Which of the following would LEAST likely have been the subject of an early American textbook?

(A) Basic rules of English grammar
(B) The American Revolution
(C) Patriotism and other civic virtues
(D) Vocational education
(E) Principles of American government

GO ON TO THE NEXT PAGE.

25. The passage provides information that would be helpful in answering which of the following questions?

    (A) Why were a disproportionate share of early American textbooks written by New England authors?
    (B) Was the Federalist party primarily a liberal or conservative force in early American politics?
    (C) How many years of education did the founders believe were sufficient to instruct young citizens in civic virtues?
    (D) What were the names of some of the Puritan authors who wrote early American textbooks?
    (E) Did most citizens of the early Republic agree with the founders that public education was essential to the welfare of the Republic?

26. The author implies that an early American Puritan would likely insist that

    (A) moral and religious values are the foundation of civic virtue
    (B) textbooks should instruct students in political issues of vital concern to the community
    (C) textbooks should give greater emphasis to the value of individual liberty than to the duties of patriotism
    (D) private schools with a particular religious focus are preferable to public schools with no religious instruction
    (E) government and religion are separate institutions and the church should not interfere in political affairs

GO ON TO THE NEXT PAGE.

Ultrasonography works much like sonar. High-frequency sound waves are bounced off surfaces to compose a two-dimensional picture of anatomical structures. Since it became generally available about
5  ten years ago, diagnostic ultrasound has gained increasing acceptance in the American medical community. Its low cost and apparent safety have made it one of the most frequently used methods of imaging in the United States, rivaling conventional radiography
10 in popularity. Because ultrasonography does not utilize ionizing radiation, diagnostic ultrasound is particularly attractive to obstetricians and gynecologists who are concerned with protecting the fetus or the patient's fertility. This aspect of ultrasound, however, can also
15 be a disadvantage.

Because x-rays pass through every type of tissue, images show the varying absorption of the radiation— more for bones, less for soft tissue. But virtually all of the ultrasonic waves that encounter bone or an air
20 pocket are reflected. Therefore, the adult brain cannot be imaged because ultrasound cannot penetrate the completely formed skull. Similarly, the lungs cannot be imaged because ultrasonic waves are almost totally reflected by the air passages called bronchi,
25 bronchioles, and alveoli.

Nevertheless, ultrasound can provide information that is as good or better than that supplied by x-radiography when imaging certain tissues, including those of the heart, abdomen, and fetus. It can be used to
30 guide amniocentesis to assess gestational age and to evaluate bleeding during pregnancy, as well as to determine the location of the fetus and monitor fetal presentation, growth, and anatomy.

27. The author's primary concern is to

(A) define medical terminology
(B) defend the use of radiography
(C) encourage the use of ultrasonography
(D) discuss a new medical technology
(E) warn about a health hazard

28. It can be inferred from the passage that some physicians prefer to use ultrasound when a patient is pregnant because

(A) x-rays are absorbed by the skull
(B) ultrasound is inexpensive
(C) x-rays cannot penetrate the womb
(D) ultrasound is more widely available
(E) x-rays pose a hazard to the fetus

GO ON TO THE NEXT PAGE.

One continuing problem in labor-management relations is the "us/them" mentality. In addition to fiscal constraints, continuing problems with the Fair Labor Standards Act, bad faith negotiations, bad management practices, poor union leadership, and a continued loss of management prerogatives will all combine to produce forces which will cause a significant increase in disruptive job actions in the near future. Neither side is blameless. The tragedy of the situation is that the impact of poor labor-management relations is relatively predictable and is thus avoidable.

Since the economic situation will not improve significantly in the next few years, the pressure on the part of union leaders to obtain more benefits for their members will be frustrated. As a result of the PATCO strike, management has learned that times are conducive to regaining prerogatives lost during the previous decade. The stage for confrontation between labor and management in the public sector is set, and in many areas, only requires an incident to force disruptive job actions. The only solution to this seemingly intractable problem lies in the area of skilled negotiations and good faith bargaining. This requires commitment on the part of management and labor to live up to the terms of existing contracts.

29. It can be inferred that the PATCO strike

(A) was an example of bad faith negotiations
(B) lasted only a brief period
(C) was the fault of incompetent management
(D) violated the provisions of the Fair Labor Standards Act
(E) resulted in a victory for management

30. The author implies that if the economic conditions improve,

(A) management will lose much of its power
(B) labor leaders will not seek more benefits
(C) labor-management tensions will decline
(D) the Fair Labor Standards Act will be repealed
(E) labor will win a voice in management

# S T O P

IF YOU FINISH BEFORE TIME IS CALLED, YOU MAY CHECK YOUR WORK ON THIS SECTION ONLY.
DO NOT WORK ON ANY OTHER SECTION IN THE TEST.

# Practice Test III

# CAMBRIDGE TESTPREP™

## PRACTICE TEST III OUTLINE

# PRACTICE TEST III

Start with number 1 for each new section. If a section has fewer items than answer spaces, leave the extra answer spaces blank. Be sure to erase any errors or stray marks completely.

**Section 2**

| 1 Ⓐ Ⓑ Ⓒ Ⓓ Ⓔ | 9 Ⓐ Ⓑ Ⓒ Ⓓ Ⓔ | 17 Ⓐ Ⓑ Ⓒ Ⓓ Ⓔ | 25 Ⓐ Ⓑ Ⓒ Ⓓ Ⓔ |
| 2 Ⓐ Ⓑ Ⓒ Ⓓ Ⓔ | 10 Ⓐ Ⓑ Ⓒ Ⓓ Ⓔ | 18 Ⓐ Ⓑ Ⓒ Ⓓ Ⓔ | 26 Ⓐ Ⓑ Ⓒ Ⓓ Ⓔ |
| 3 Ⓐ Ⓑ Ⓒ Ⓓ Ⓔ | 11 Ⓐ Ⓑ Ⓒ Ⓓ Ⓔ | 19 Ⓐ Ⓑ Ⓒ Ⓓ Ⓔ | 27 Ⓐ Ⓑ Ⓒ Ⓓ Ⓔ |
| 4 Ⓐ Ⓑ Ⓒ Ⓓ Ⓔ | 12 Ⓐ Ⓑ Ⓒ Ⓓ Ⓔ | 20 Ⓐ Ⓑ Ⓒ Ⓓ Ⓔ | 28 Ⓐ Ⓑ Ⓒ Ⓓ Ⓔ |
| 5 Ⓐ Ⓑ Ⓒ Ⓓ Ⓔ | 13 Ⓐ Ⓑ Ⓒ Ⓓ Ⓔ | 21 Ⓐ Ⓑ Ⓒ Ⓓ Ⓔ | 29 Ⓐ Ⓑ Ⓒ Ⓓ Ⓔ |
| 6 Ⓐ Ⓑ Ⓒ Ⓓ Ⓔ | 14 Ⓐ Ⓑ Ⓒ Ⓓ Ⓔ | 22 Ⓐ Ⓑ Ⓒ Ⓓ Ⓔ | 30 Ⓐ Ⓑ Ⓒ Ⓓ Ⓔ |
| 7 Ⓐ Ⓑ Ⓒ Ⓓ Ⓔ | 15 Ⓐ Ⓑ Ⓒ Ⓓ Ⓔ | 23 Ⓐ Ⓑ Ⓒ Ⓓ Ⓔ | |
| 8 Ⓐ Ⓑ Ⓒ Ⓓ Ⓔ | 16 Ⓐ Ⓑ Ⓒ Ⓓ Ⓔ | 24 Ⓐ Ⓑ Ⓒ Ⓓ Ⓔ | |

**Section 3**

| 1 Ⓐ Ⓑ Ⓒ Ⓓ Ⓔ | 11 Ⓐ Ⓑ Ⓒ Ⓓ Ⓔ | 21 Ⓐ Ⓑ Ⓒ Ⓓ Ⓔ | 31 Ⓐ Ⓑ Ⓒ Ⓓ Ⓔ |
| 2 Ⓐ Ⓑ Ⓒ Ⓓ Ⓔ | 12 Ⓐ Ⓑ Ⓒ Ⓓ Ⓔ | 22 Ⓐ Ⓑ Ⓒ Ⓓ Ⓔ | 32 Ⓐ Ⓑ Ⓒ Ⓓ Ⓔ |
| 3 Ⓐ Ⓑ Ⓒ Ⓓ Ⓔ | 13 Ⓐ Ⓑ Ⓒ Ⓓ Ⓔ | 23 Ⓐ Ⓑ Ⓒ Ⓓ Ⓔ | 33 Ⓐ Ⓑ Ⓒ Ⓓ Ⓔ |
| 4 Ⓐ Ⓑ Ⓒ Ⓓ Ⓔ | 14 Ⓐ Ⓑ Ⓒ Ⓓ Ⓔ | 24 Ⓐ Ⓑ Ⓒ Ⓓ Ⓔ | 34 Ⓐ Ⓑ Ⓒ Ⓓ Ⓔ |
| 5 Ⓐ Ⓑ Ⓒ Ⓓ Ⓔ | 15 Ⓐ Ⓑ Ⓒ Ⓓ Ⓔ | 25 Ⓐ Ⓑ Ⓒ Ⓓ Ⓔ | 35 Ⓐ Ⓑ Ⓒ Ⓓ Ⓔ |
| 6 Ⓐ Ⓑ Ⓒ Ⓓ Ⓔ | 16 Ⓐ Ⓑ Ⓒ Ⓓ Ⓔ | 26 Ⓐ Ⓑ Ⓒ Ⓓ Ⓔ | 36 Ⓐ Ⓑ Ⓒ Ⓓ Ⓔ |
| 7 Ⓐ Ⓑ Ⓒ Ⓓ Ⓔ | 17 Ⓐ Ⓑ Ⓒ Ⓓ Ⓔ | 27 Ⓐ Ⓑ Ⓒ Ⓓ Ⓔ | 37 Ⓐ Ⓑ Ⓒ Ⓓ Ⓔ |
| 8 Ⓐ Ⓑ Ⓒ Ⓓ Ⓔ | 18 Ⓐ Ⓑ Ⓒ Ⓓ Ⓔ | 28 Ⓐ Ⓑ Ⓒ Ⓓ Ⓔ | 38 Ⓐ Ⓑ Ⓒ Ⓓ Ⓔ |
| 9 Ⓐ Ⓑ Ⓒ Ⓓ Ⓔ | 19 Ⓐ Ⓑ Ⓒ Ⓓ Ⓔ | 29 Ⓐ Ⓑ Ⓒ Ⓓ Ⓔ | |
| 10 Ⓐ Ⓑ Ⓒ Ⓓ Ⓔ | 20 Ⓐ Ⓑ Ⓒ Ⓓ Ⓔ | 30 Ⓐ Ⓑ Ⓒ Ⓓ Ⓔ | |

## SECTION 1
## PRESENT YOUR PERSPECTIVE ON AN ISSUE
### 45 minutes

You will be presented with an Issue topic, which will be summarized in a brief quotation. The topic describes an issue of general interest. Read the topic carefully.

You have 45 minutes to plan, write, and edit your essay. Your essay should present your perspective on the topic. In addressing the claim made in the quotation, you can accept the quotation, reject it outright, or accept it in part and reject it in part as long as the points you make are clearly relevant to the topic. An essay on any other topic will receive a score of zero. Support your position with reasons and examples that are drawn from your everyday reading, personal experience, direct observations, or academic studies.

Your essay will be read by college and university teachers who will evaluate its overall quality, specifically taking into account how well you:

- develop and treat the complexities of the topic;

- organize, develop, and state your ideas;

- support your ideas with relevant examples and reasons;

- control the elements of standard written English.

It may be useful to take a few minutes of your time to think about the issue and to plan or even outline a response before you actually begin to write. Make sure that you organize your ideas into a coherent essay and develop them in some detail. Reserve some of your time to proofread and edit your response. A sample essay is on page 1075.

> The sole function of public schools should be to teach academic and practical skills and not to inculcate ethical values.

**ISSUE TASK**

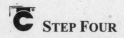
# S T O P

IF YOU FINISH BEFORE TIME IS CALLED, YOU MAY CHECK YOUR WORK ON THIS ESSAY ONLY.
DO NOT TURN TO ANY OTHER PORTION OF THE TEST.

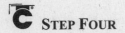 

## ANALYSIS OF AN ARGUMENT
### 30 minutes

You have 30 minutes to organize and write a critique of the argument presented in the short passage below. A critique of an argument other than the one presented will be given a score of zero.

Analyze the line of reasoning in the argument; identify what, if any, questionable premises are made by the argument; and evaluate how well the evidence presented supports the conclusion of the argument. In evaluating the evidence, you can consider what kinds of proof would weaken or strengthen the argument and what additional information might tend to prove or disprove the conclusion.

<u>Importantly, you are not being asked to present your own personal point of view on the subject.</u>

Your essay will be read by college and university teachers who will evaluate its overall quality, specifically taking into account how well you:

- identify and analyze the important features of the argument;
- organize, develop, and state your points;
- support your critique with relevant examples and reasons;
- control the elements of standard written English.

It may be useful to take a few minutes of your time to think about the issue and to plan or even outline a response before you actually begin to write. Make sure that you organize your ideas into a coherent essay and develop them in some detail. Reserve some of your time to proofread and edit your response. A sample essay is on page 1075.

> Two years ago, the Fort Ann School purchased twelve new computers and implemented a requirement that all students take at least two hours of computer instruction each week. The Hudson Falls School, which is near Fort Ann School and has about the same number of students, does not have such a requirement. Over the past two years, the number of Fort Ann School seniors going on to college has increased by 20 percent while the number of Hudson Falls seniors going on to college has remained constant. Therefore, if Hudson Falls wants to give its students the opportunities they deserve, it should buy new computers and teach students how to use them.

**ARGUMENT TASK**

STOP

IF YOU FINISH BEFORE TIME IS CALLED, YOU MAY CHECK YOUR WORK ON THIS ESSAY ONLY.
DO NOT TURN TO ANY OTHER PORTION OF THE TEST.

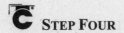
## SECTION 2

30 Minutes

30 Items

Directions: Each of the following items consists of a word printed in capital letters, followed by five lettered words or phrases in lowercase letters. Choose the lettered word or phrase that is most nearly <u>opposite</u> in meaning to the word in capital letters. Answers are on page 1076.

1. REVERE:

(A) collide
(B) succumb
(C) threaten
(D) divide
(E) despise

2. BOORISH:

(A) juvenile
(B) well-mannered
(C) weak-minded
(D) unique
(E) concealed

3. NASCENT:

(A) fully developed
(B) extremely valuable
(C) well-regarded
(D) informative
(E) measurable

4. PENURY:

(A) exploitation
(B) wealth
(C) contingency
(D) void
(E) vindication

5. IMPERVIOUS:

(A) nervous
(B) long-lived
(C) penetrable
(D) orderly
(E) conclusive

6. SURREPTITIOUS:

(A) mighty
(B) plausible
(C) meaningful
(D) unplanned
(E) overt

7. INURED:

(A) authoritative
(B) dissolute
(C) bereft
(D) sensitive
(E) taxing

8. IRASCIBLE:

(A) even-tempered
(B) well-informed
(C) repetitious
(D) motionless
(E) synchronous

9. ALACRITY:

(A) skullduggery
(B) reluctance
(C) interment
(D) bellicosity
(E) specificity

GO ON TO THE NEXT PAGE.

Directions: Each sentence or paragraph in this part of the verbal section has one or more missing elements, as indicated by a blank or blanks. Choose the word or set of words that best fits the meaning of the text. Answers are on page 1076.

10. Despite the millions of dollars spent on improvements, the telephone system in India remains —— and continues to —— the citizens who depend on it.

(A) primitive. .inconvenience
(B) bombastic. .upset
(C) suspicious. .connect
(D) outdated. .elate
(E) impartial. .vex

11. Unlike the images in symbolist poetry which are often vague and ——, the images of surrealist poetry are startlingly —— and bold.

(A) extraneous. .furtive
(B) trivial. .inadvertent
(C) obscure. .concrete
(D) spectacular. .pallid
(E) symmetrical. .virulent

12. A good trial lawyer will argue only what is central to an issue, eliminating —— information or anything which might —— the client.

(A) seminal. .amuse
(B) extraneous. .jeopardize
(C) erratic. .enhance
(D) prodigious. .extol
(E) reprehensible. .initiate

13. Psychologists and science fiction writers argue that people persist in believing in extraterrestrial life, even though the federal government —— all such beliefs, because people need to feel a personal sense of —— in a godless universe.

(A) decries. .morbidity
(B) endorses. .despair
(C) creates. .guilt
(D) discourages. .spirituality
(E) debunks. .alienation

14. Pollen grains and spores that are 200 million years old are now being extracted from shale and are —— the theory that the breakup of the continents occurred in stages; in fact, it seems that the breakups occurred almost ——.

(A) refining. .blatantly
(B) reshaping. .simultaneously
(C) countermanding. .imperceptibly
(D) forging. .vicariously
(E) supporting. .haphazardly

15. The period of the fall of the Roman Empire was a dark period for —— as well as for the other arts, for men had forgotten how to cook; in fact it seemed as if they had lost all interest in —— matters.

(A) gastronomy. .culinary
(B) astrology. .sedentary
(C) histrionics. .scientific
(D) numismatics. .cultural
(E) aesthetics. .clandestine

GO ON TO THE NEXT PAGE.

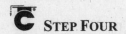 

Directions: Each reading selection in this group is followed by questions based on its content. Answer the questions following a selection on the basis of what is <u>stated</u> or <u>implied</u> in that selection, choosing the best answer to each question. Answers are on page 1077.

Both behavior and innate mechanisms regulate body temperature. Humans rely primarily on the first to provide a hospitable micro-climate for themselves. Thermoregulatory behavior anticipates hyperthermia:
5 removing layers of clothing, going for a cool swim, etc. An organism also responds to changes in the temperature of the body core, as during exercise; but such responses result from the direct stimulation of thermoreceptors distributed widely within the central
10 nervous system, and the ability of these mechanisms to help the organism adjust to gross changes in its environment is limited.

It was once assumed that organisms respond to microwave radiation in the same way they respond to
15 temperature changes caused by other forms of radiation. After all, the argument runs, microwaves heat body tissues. This theory ignores the fact that the stimulus to a behavioral response is a temperature change that occurs at the surface of the organism.
20 Thermoreceptors that prompt behavioral changes are located in the first millimeter of the skin's surface, but the energy of a microwave field may be selectively deposited in deep tissues, bypassing the thermoreceptors. Since the heat is not conducted
25 outward to the surface to stimulate the receptors, the organism does not "appreciate" this stimulation in the same way that it "appreciates" heating and cooling of the skin. In theory, the internal organs could be cooked before the organism even realizes that the balance of its
30 thermomicroclimate has been disturbed.

Until recently, microwave irradiations at densities of about 100 mW/cm$^2$ were considered unequivocally to produce "thermal" effects, irradiations within the range of 10 to 100 mW/cm$^2$ possibly to produce
35 "thermal" effects, and power densities below 10 mW/cm$^2$ to be "nonthermal." Experiments have shown this to be an oversimplification. When the heat generated in the tissues by an imposed radio frequency exceeds the heat-loss capabilities of the organism, the
40 thermoregulatory system has been compromised. Yet surprisingly, not long ago, an increase in the internal body temperature was regarded merely as "evidence" of a thermal effect.

16. The author makes which of the following points about innate mechanisms for heat production?

    I. They are governed by thermoreceptors inside the body of the organism rather than at the surface.
    II. They are a less effective means of compensating for gross changes in temperature than behavioral strategies.
    III. They are not affected by microwave radiation.

    (A) I only
    (B) I and II only
    (C) I and III only
    (D) II and III only
    (E) I, II, and III

17. The author's strategy in lines 27–29 is to

    (A) introduce a hypothetical example to dramatize a point
    (B) propose an experiment to test a scientific hypothesis
    (C) cite a case study to illustrate a general contention
    (D) produce a counterexample to disprove an opponent's theory
    (E) speculate about the probable consequences of a scientific phenomenon

GO ON TO THE NEXT PAGE.

Art, like words, is a form of communication. Words, spoken and written, render accessible to humans of the latest generations all the knowledge discovered by the experience and reflection, both of
5 preceding generations and of the best and foremost minds of their own times. Art renders accessible to people of the latest generations all the feelings experienced by their predecessors, and those already felt by their best and foremost contemporaries. Just as
10 the evolution of knowledge proceeds by dislodging and replacing that which is mistaken, so too the evolution of feeling proceeds through art. Feelings less kind and less necessary for the well-being of human kind are replaced by others kinder and more essential to that
15 end. This is the purpose of art, and the more art fulfills that purpose the better the art; the less it fulfills it, the worse the art.

18. The author develops the passage primarily by

(A) theory and refutation
(B) example and generalization
(C) comparison and contrast
(D) question and answer
(E) inference and deduction

19. The style of the passage can best be described as

(A) speculative
(B) argumentative
(C) expository
(D) poetic
(E) sarcastic

GO ON TO THE NEXT PAGE.

In the 1950s, the development of antipsychotic drugs called neuroleptics radically changed the clinical outlook for patients in mental institutions who had previously been considered hopelessly psychotic. Daily
5 medication controlled delusions and made psycho-therapy possible. Many who otherwise might never have left institutions returned to society. Now physicians have learned that there is a price to be paid for these benefits. Approximately 10 to 15 percent of
10 patients who undergo long-term treatment with antipsychotic drugs develop a cluster of symptoms called tardive dyskinesia, the most common symptoms of which are involuntary repetitive movement of the tongue, mouth, and face, and sometimes the limbs and
15 trunk.

Neuroleptic drugs interfere with the action of dopamine, an important neurotransmitter in the brain, by binding to the dopamine receptors of nerve cells, and dopamine is a prime suspect in the
20 pathophysiology of schizophrenia. Large doses of drugs such as amphetamines, which stimulate secretion of dopamine, produce a psychosis resembling schizophrenia. Reducing the activity of this neurotransmitter alleviates the delusions that cause
25 psychotic behavior. Although the inhibition of dopamine activity can control psychotic behavior, researchers now believe that the central nervous system of some patients adapts to long-term therapy by increasing the number of specific dopamine binding
30 sites. The net result is dopamine hypersensitivity that is correlated with the subsequent appearance of tardive dyskinesia.

The risk of developing tardive dyskinesia is not so great that doctors have considered abandoning the
35 use of antipsychotic drugs. Patients generally are bothered only slightly by the physical side effects, though the abnormal movements are troubling and may hinder social adjustment. Additionally, early diagnosis and prompt discontinuation of the neuroleptics might
40 decrease the incidence of the movement disorders. Unfortunately, without neuroleptic drugs, psychotic behavior returns. So, researchers have tried to achieve a satisfactory balance between the two effects, lowering dosage to a level that minimizes movement
45 disorders yet controls psychosis. In a five-year study of twenty-seven psychiatric patients treated with neuroleptics representing all classes of antipsychotic drugs, researchers attempted to decrease drug doses to their lowest effective levels. Patient responses
50 suggested that low to moderate doses of antipsychotic drugs could control psychoses just as well as high

doses, and tardive dyskinesia symptoms stabilized and gradually diminished or completely disappeared.

The fact that psychoses can be controlled at the
55 same time that tardive dyskensia symptoms are reduced suggests that a drug more specifically affecting the mechanism of psychoses might not cause movement disorders. Sulpiride, a drug not available in the United States but widely used in Europe, where it was
60 developed, may be one such alternative. The drug selectively blocks D–2 dopamine receptors, perhaps especially those in the limbic area of the brain, which is involved in emotion and behavior. It does not adversely affect the adenylate cyclase-linked D–1 dopamine
65 receptors. Sulpiride has proven effective in the short term, but whether it suppresses tardive dyskenesia over a long period of treatment is not yet known.

20. Which of the following titles best describes the content of the passage?

(A) The Therapeutic Value of Antipsychotic Drugs
(B) The Tradeoff in the Use of Neuroleptic Drugs
(C) The Connection between Psychotherapy and Neuroleptic Drugs
(D) Recent Developments in the Treatment of Mental Illness
(E) Techniques for Treating Tardive Dyskinesia

GO ON TO THE NEXT PAGE.

21. It can be inferred that neuroleptic drugs control psychosis by

    (A) suppressing the production of dopamine in the brain
    (B) blocking the nerve impulses transmitted to the muscles
    (C) preventing the absorption of dopamine by brain cells
    (D) creating a hypersensitivity to dopamine
    (E) counteracting the effect of other prescription drugs

22. If a patient shows symptoms of tardive dyskinesia, a doctor would probably

    (A) discontinue the use of all antipsychotic drugs
    (B) increase the dosage of dopamine
    (C) confine the patient to an institution
    (D) reduce the dosage of any neuroleptic drug
    (E) recommend psychotherapy and counseling

23. The author cites the effects of large doses of drugs such as amphetamines in order to

    (A) demonstrate that dopamine may be the cause of some psychotic behavior
    (B) prove that neuroleptic drugs produce symptoms of tardive dyskenesia
    (C) give an example of a neuroleptic drug that does not necessarily cause tardive dyskenesia
    (D) show that smaller dosages of neuropleptic drugs can effectively control psychotic behavior
    (E) persuade the reader that the drug sulpiride should be available in the United States

GO ON TO THE NEXT PAGE.

–795–

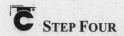 

Directions: Each of the following items consists of a related pair of words or phrases presented in capital letters, followed by five lettered pairs of words or phrases presented in lowercase letters. For each item, choose the lettered pair that expresses a relationship that is most nearly like that expressed in the capitalized pair. Answers are on page 1079.

24. CHAPTER : NOVEL ::

(A) piano : instrument
(B) diamond : gem
(C) scene : drama
(D) poetry : prose
(E) fraction : portion

25. IMPLY : AVER ::

(A) reject : announce
(B) hint : proclaim
(C) encourage : absolve
(D) remind : contradict
(E) embolden : accept

26. PONDEROUS : WEIGHT ::

(A) eternal : temporality
(B) final : decision
(C) gargantuan : size
(D) ancient : value
(E) prototypical : affection

27. FEBRILE : ILLNESS ::

(A) tenacious : astonishment
(B) juvenile : maturity
(C) classic : cultivation
(D) eccentric : discrimination
(E) delusional : insanity

28. INCOMMUNICADO : CONTACT ::

(A) sequestered : company
(B) pretentious : affectation
(C) submissive : compromise
(D) perpetual : adventure
(E) severed : replacement

29. ASBESTOS : FIRE ::

(A) formaldehyde : decay
(B) candle : flame
(C) alcohol : intoxication
(D) caffeine : stimulant
(E) glue : erosion

30. IMPREGNABLE : PENETRATION ::

(A) munificent : extravagance
(B) inscrutable : understanding
(C) incoherent : confusion
(D) symbiotic : malignancy
(E) mesmerizing : consequence

# S T O P

IF YOU FINISH BEFORE TIME IS CALLED, YOU MAY CHECK YOUR WORK ON THIS SECTION ONLY.
DO NOT WORK ON ANY OTHER SECTION IN THE TEST.

## SECTION 3

30 Minutes

28 Items

In this section, solve each problem using any available space on the page for scratch work. Then, decide which is the best of the choices given and fill in the corresponding oval on the answer sheet.

All numbers used are real numbers.

All angle measures are positive.

A figure accompanying a question is included to provide information useful in answering that question. However, unless a note explicitly states that a figure is drawn to scale, you should answer a question not by estimating the magnitudes of various aspects, but by using your knowledge of the principles of mathematics. You can assume, however, that the positions of points, angles, regions, etc. are in the order shown, that lines shown as straight are straight, and that all figures lie in the plane unless otherwise noted.

Directions: Each of the questions 1 through 14 consists of two quantities, one in Column A and one in Column B. Choose:

    A if the quantity in Column A is greater

    B if the quantity in Column B is greater

    C if the two quantities are equal

    D if the relationship cannot be determined from the information given

Notes: If information is centered above the two quantities to be compared, then that information is true of both quantities.

A symbol that appears in both columns represents the same thing in both columns.

The only possible choices are (A), (B), (C), and (D). Do not choose (E).

Answers are on page 1079.

| Column A | Column B |
|----------|----------|

$$x = 2$$
$$y = 5$$

1.     $x^y$        $y^x$

2.     $\overline{KL}$        5

$$xy \neq 0$$

3.     $\dfrac{x}{y}$        $\dfrac{y}{x}$

| Column A | Column B |
|----------|----------|

4.     $D$        6.5

GO ON TO THE NEXT PAGE.

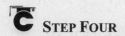
Column A | Column B

In a shipment of six packages, five of the packages weigh exactly 25 pounds each, and the sixth package weighs more than one pound but less than 20 pounds.

5. | Average weight, in pounds, of the six packages. | 22.5

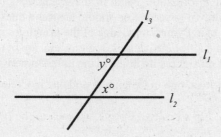

$l_1 \parallel l_2$

6. | $2x$ | $x + y$

Tina has more than twice as many marbles as Chuck and Luis have together.

7. | Number of marbles Tina has | Three times the number of marbles Chuck has

8. | $x + y$ | $p + q$

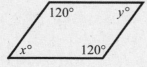

9. | $x$ | $y$

10. | $\sqrt{2}$ | $\dfrac{2}{\sqrt{2}}$

---

Column A | Column B

$xy \neq 0$

11. | $\dfrac{1}{x} + \dfrac{1}{y}$ | $x + y$

$r$ and $s$ are radii of the circles.

12. | Area of the smaller circle of the figure | Area of the shaded portion of the figure

A jar contains 32 red marbles and 16 blue marbles. Seventy-five percent of the red marbles and 50 percent of the blue marbles are removed from the jar.

13. | The fraction of the original number of marbles still remaining in the jar | $\dfrac{2}{3}$

A student purchased a total of 17 pens and pencils. The pens cost \$0.35 each, and the pencils cost \$0.20 each. The total cost of the pens and pencils was \$4.60.

14. | The number of pens purchased by the student | The number of pencils purchased by the student

GO ON TO THE NEXT PAGE.

Directions: Each of the following questions has five answer choices. Select the best of the available choices. Answers are on page 1082.

15. If $12 + x = 36 - y$, then $x + y =$

   (A) $-48$
   (B) $-24$
   (C)  $3$
   (D)  $24$
   (E)  $48$

16. Depending on the value of $k$, the expression $3k + 4k + 5k + 6k + 7k$ may or may not be divisible by 7. Which of the terms, when eliminated from the expression, guarantees that the resulting expression is divisible by 7 for every positive integer $k$?

   (A) $3k$
   (B) $4k$
   (C) $5k$
   (D) $6k$
   (E) $7k$

17. If $n$ is a positive integer, which of the following must be an even integer?

   (A) $n+1$
   (B) $3n+1$
   (C) $3n+2$
   (D) $n^2+1$
   (E) $n^2+n$

18. In a certain group of 36 people, only 18 people are wearing hats and only 24 people are wearing sweaters. If six people are wearing neither a hat nor a sweater, how many people are wearing both a hat and a sweater?

   (A) 30
   (B) 22
   (C) 12
   (D)  8
   (E)  6

19. Motorcycle X averages 40 kilometers per liter of gasoline while Motorcycle Y averages 50 kilometers per liter. If the cost of gasoline is $2 per liter, what will be the difference in the cost of operating the two motorcycles for 300 kilometers?

   (A)  $3
   (B)  $6
   (C) $12
   (D) $15
   (E) $20

20. For a positive integer $k$, which of the following equals $6k + 3$?

   (A) $\frac{1}{2}(k+1)$
   (B) $\frac{1}{k}+4$
   (C) $2k+1$
   (D) $3(k+1)$
   (E) $3(2k+1)$

GO ON TO THE NEXT PAGE.

Items 21–23 refer to the following graphs.

### SELECTED DATA ON HANDGUNS FOR THE UNITED STATES

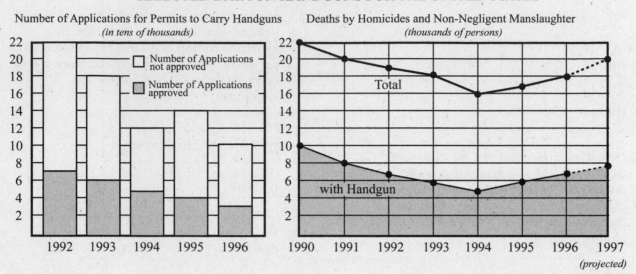

Number of Applications for Permits to Carry Handguns *(in tens of thousands)*

Deaths by Homicides and Non-Negligent Manslaughter *(thousands of persons)*

21. The total number of deaths in the United States due to homicide and non-negligent manslaughter in 1996 was how much greater than that for 1994?

    (A)    300
    (B)    2,000
    (C)    3,000
    (D)    10,000
    (E)    30,000

22. In 1993, approximately what percent of the applications for permits to carry handguns were NOT approved?

    (A)  12%
    (B)  25%
    (C)  $33\frac{1}{3}$%
    (D)  50%
    (E)  $66\frac{2}{3}$%

23. For the period 1993 through 1996, inclusive, in how many years did both the total number of deaths by homicide and non-negligent manslaughter increase, and the number of applications for permits to carry a handgun increase?

    (A) 0
    (B) 1
    (C) 2
    (D) 3
    (E) 4

**GO ON TO THE NEXT PAGE.**

Items 24–25 refer to the following graphs.

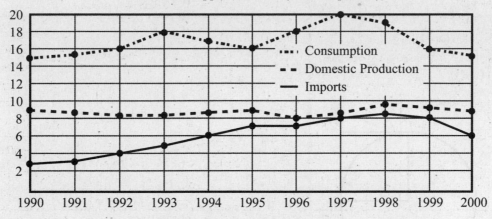

UNITED STATES CONSUMPTION OF OIL

*Demand and Supply (Millions of Barrels per Day)*

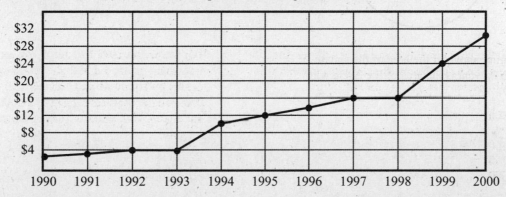

Price per Barrel of Imported Oil

24. In 2000, the average cost of oil imported into the United States each day was approximately

(A) $180,000,000
(B) $150,000,000
(C) $120,000,000
(D)  $90,000,000
(E)  $50,000,000

25. From 1991 through 2000, inclusive, in how many years did both the quantity and price of imported oil increase?

(A) 4
(B) 5
(C) 6
(D) 7
(E) 8

GO ON TO THE NEXT PAGE.

26. To mail a letter costs $x$ cents for the first ounce and $y$ cents for every additional ounce or fraction of an ounce. What is the cost, *in cents*, to mail a letter weighing a whole number of ounces, $w$?

(A) $w(x+y)$
(B) $x(w-y)$
(C) $x(w-1)+y(w-1)$
(D) $x+wy$
(E) $x+y(w-1)$

28. How many positive integers less than 30 are equal to 3 times an *odd* integer?

(A) 10
(B) 7
(C) 5
(D) 4
(E) 3

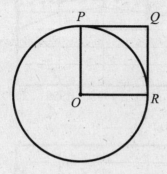

27. In the figure above, if the area of the square $OPQR$ is 2, what is the area of the circle with center $O$?

(A) $\frac{\pi}{4}$
(B) $\pi\sqrt{2}$
(C) $2\pi$
(D) $2\sqrt{2\pi}$
(E) $4\pi$

# STOP

IF YOU FINISH BEFORE TIME IS CALLED, YOU MAY CHECK YOUR WORK ON THIS SECTION ONLY.
DO NOT WORK ON ANY OTHER SECTION IN THE TEST.

# Practice Test IV

# CAMBRIDGE TESTPREP™

## PRACTICE TEST IV OUTLINE

# PRACTICE TEST IV

Start with number 1 for each new section. If a section has fewer items than answer spaces, leave the extra answer spaces blank. Be sure to erase any errors or stray marks completely.

**Section 2**

| 1 Ⓐ Ⓑ Ⓒ Ⓓ Ⓔ | 9 Ⓐ Ⓑ Ⓒ Ⓓ Ⓔ | 17 Ⓐ Ⓑ Ⓒ Ⓓ Ⓔ | 25 Ⓐ Ⓑ Ⓒ Ⓓ Ⓔ |
| 2 Ⓐ Ⓑ Ⓒ Ⓓ Ⓔ | 10 Ⓐ Ⓑ Ⓒ Ⓓ Ⓔ | 18 Ⓐ Ⓑ Ⓒ Ⓓ Ⓔ | 26 Ⓐ Ⓑ Ⓒ Ⓓ Ⓔ |
| 3 Ⓐ Ⓑ Ⓒ Ⓓ Ⓔ | 11 Ⓐ Ⓑ Ⓒ Ⓓ Ⓔ | 19 Ⓐ Ⓑ Ⓒ Ⓓ Ⓔ | 27 Ⓐ Ⓑ Ⓒ Ⓓ Ⓔ |
| 4 Ⓐ Ⓑ Ⓒ Ⓓ Ⓔ | 12 Ⓐ Ⓑ Ⓒ Ⓓ Ⓔ | 20 Ⓐ Ⓑ Ⓒ Ⓓ Ⓔ | 28 Ⓐ Ⓑ Ⓒ Ⓓ Ⓔ |
| 5 Ⓐ Ⓑ Ⓒ Ⓓ Ⓔ | 13 Ⓐ Ⓑ Ⓒ Ⓓ Ⓔ | 21 Ⓐ Ⓑ Ⓒ Ⓓ Ⓔ | 29 Ⓐ Ⓑ Ⓒ Ⓓ Ⓔ |
| 6 Ⓐ Ⓑ Ⓒ Ⓓ Ⓔ | 14 Ⓐ Ⓑ Ⓒ Ⓓ Ⓔ | 22 Ⓐ Ⓑ Ⓒ Ⓓ Ⓔ | 30 Ⓐ Ⓑ Ⓒ Ⓓ Ⓔ |
| 7 Ⓐ Ⓑ Ⓒ Ⓓ Ⓔ | 15 Ⓐ Ⓑ Ⓒ Ⓓ Ⓔ | 23 Ⓐ Ⓑ Ⓒ Ⓓ Ⓔ | |
| 8 Ⓐ Ⓑ Ⓒ Ⓓ Ⓔ | 16 Ⓐ Ⓑ Ⓒ Ⓓ Ⓔ | 24 Ⓐ Ⓑ Ⓒ Ⓓ Ⓔ | |

**Section 3**

| 1 Ⓐ Ⓑ Ⓒ Ⓓ Ⓔ | 11 Ⓐ Ⓑ Ⓒ Ⓓ Ⓔ | 21 Ⓐ Ⓑ Ⓒ Ⓓ Ⓔ | 31 Ⓐ Ⓑ Ⓒ Ⓓ Ⓔ |
| 2 Ⓐ Ⓑ Ⓒ Ⓓ Ⓔ | 12 Ⓐ Ⓑ Ⓒ Ⓓ Ⓔ | 22 Ⓐ Ⓑ Ⓒ Ⓓ Ⓔ | 32 Ⓐ Ⓑ Ⓒ Ⓓ Ⓔ |
| 3 Ⓐ Ⓑ Ⓒ Ⓓ Ⓔ | 13 Ⓐ Ⓑ Ⓒ Ⓓ Ⓔ | 23 Ⓐ Ⓑ Ⓒ Ⓓ Ⓔ | 33 Ⓐ Ⓑ Ⓒ Ⓓ Ⓔ |
| 4 Ⓐ Ⓑ Ⓒ Ⓓ Ⓔ | 14 Ⓐ Ⓑ Ⓒ Ⓓ Ⓔ | 24 Ⓐ Ⓑ Ⓒ Ⓓ Ⓔ | 34 Ⓐ Ⓑ Ⓒ Ⓓ Ⓔ |
| 5 Ⓐ Ⓑ Ⓒ Ⓓ Ⓔ | 15 Ⓐ Ⓑ Ⓒ Ⓓ Ⓔ | 25 Ⓐ Ⓑ Ⓒ Ⓓ Ⓔ | 35 Ⓐ Ⓑ Ⓒ Ⓓ Ⓔ |
| 6 Ⓐ Ⓑ Ⓒ Ⓓ Ⓔ | 16 Ⓐ Ⓑ Ⓒ Ⓓ Ⓔ | 26 Ⓐ Ⓑ Ⓒ Ⓓ Ⓔ | 36 Ⓐ Ⓑ Ⓒ Ⓓ Ⓔ |
| 7 Ⓐ Ⓑ Ⓒ Ⓓ Ⓔ | 17 Ⓐ Ⓑ Ⓒ Ⓓ Ⓔ | 27 Ⓐ Ⓑ Ⓒ Ⓓ Ⓔ | 37 Ⓐ Ⓑ Ⓒ Ⓓ Ⓔ |
| 8 Ⓐ Ⓑ Ⓒ Ⓓ Ⓔ | 18 Ⓐ Ⓑ Ⓒ Ⓓ Ⓔ | 28 Ⓐ Ⓑ Ⓒ Ⓓ Ⓔ | 38 Ⓐ Ⓑ Ⓒ Ⓓ Ⓔ |
| 9 Ⓐ Ⓑ Ⓒ Ⓓ Ⓔ | 19 Ⓐ Ⓑ Ⓒ Ⓓ Ⓔ | 29 Ⓐ Ⓑ Ⓒ Ⓓ Ⓔ | |
| 10 Ⓐ Ⓑ Ⓒ Ⓓ Ⓔ | 20 Ⓐ Ⓑ Ⓒ Ⓓ Ⓔ | 30 Ⓐ Ⓑ Ⓒ Ⓓ Ⓔ | |

## SECTION 1
## PRESENT YOUR PERSPECTIVE ON AN ISSUE
### 45 minutes

You will be presented with an Issue topic, which will be summarized in a brief quotation. The topic describes an issue of general interest. Read the topic carefully.

You have 45 minutes to plan, write, and edit your essay. Your essay should present your perspective on the topic. In addressing the claim made in the quotation, you can accept the quotation, reject it outright, or accept it in part and reject it in part as long as the points you make are clearly relevant to the topic. An essay on any other topic will receive a score of zero. Support your position with reasons and examples that are drawn from your everyday reading, personal experience, direct observations, or academic studies.

Your essay will be read by college and university teachers who will evaluate its overall quality, specifically taking into account how well you:

- develop and treat the complexities of the topic;
- organize, develop, and state your ideas;
- support your ideas with relevant examples and reasons;
- control the elements of standard written English.

It may be useful to take a few minutes of your time to think about the issue and to plan or even outline a response before you actually begin to write. Make sure that you organize your ideas into a coherent essay and develop them in some detail. Reserve some of your time to proofread and edit your response. A sample essay is on page 1087.

> With improvements in transportation making travel easier and less expensive and advances in technology facilitating communication, individuals increasingly come into contact with more and more people; but as a result, individuals are less likely to form long-lasting and intimate relationships.

**ISSUE TASK**

# S T O P

IF YOU FINISH BEFORE TIME IS CALLED, YOU MAY CHECK YOUR WORK ON THIS ESSAY ONLY.
DO NOT TURN TO ANY OTHER PORTION OF THE TEST.

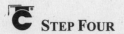 

## ANALYSIS OF AN ARGUMENT
### 30 minutes

You have 30 minutes to organize and write a critique of the argument presented in the short passage below. A critique of an argument other than the one presented will be given a score of zero.

Analyze the line of reasoning in the argument; identify what, if any, questionable premises are made by the argument; and evaluate how well the evidence presented supports the conclusion of the argument. In evaluating the evidence, you can consider what kinds of proof would weaken or strengthen the argument and what additional information might tend to prove or disprove the conclusion.

Importantly, you are not being asked to present your own personal point of view on the subject.

Your essay will be read by college and university teachers who will evaluate its overall quality, specifically taking into account how well you:

- identify and analyze the important features of the argument;

- organize, develop, and state your points;

- support your critique with relevant examples and reasons;

- control the elements of standard written English.

It may be useful to take a few minutes of your time to think about the issue and to plan or even outline a response before you actually begin to write. Make sure that you organize your ideas into a coherent essay and develop them in some detail. Reserve some of your time to proofread and edit your response. A sample essay is on page 1087.

> A recent news article reported that a motorist, angered by the driving of another motorist, rammed the other vehicle, pulled the driver from the car causing serious injury, and then shot a passerby who tried to intervene with a pistol. This is yet another example of road rage, and the best way to combat this rising trend is to require all licensed drivers to attend a one-day clinic on road rage to learn how to recognize its symptoms in themselves and in others and to how to control their own rage and avoid becoming the victims of someone else's.

**ARGUMENT TASK**

**S T O P**

IF YOU FINISH BEFORE TIME IS CALLED, YOU MAY CHECK YOUR WORK ON THIS ESSAY ONLY.
DO NOT TURN TO ANY OTHER PORTION OF THE TEST.

## SECTION 2

### 30 Minutes

### 28 Items

In this section, solve each problem using any available space on the page for scratch work. Then, decide which is the best of the choices given and fill in the corresponding oval on the answer sheet.

All numbers used are real numbers.

All angle measures are positive.

A figure accompanying a question is included to provide information useful in answering that question. However, unless a note explicitly states that a figure is drawn to scale, you should answer a question not by estimating the magnitudes of various aspects, but by using your knowledge of the principles of mathematics. You can assume, however, that the positions of points, angles, regions, etc. are in the order shown, that lines shown as straight are straight, and that all figures lie in the plane unless otherwise noted.

Directions: Each of the questions 1 through 14 consists of two quantities, one in Column A and one in Column B. Choose:

A if the quantity in Column A is greater
B if the quantity in Column B is greater
C if the two quantities are equal
D if the relationship cannot be determined from the information given

Notes: If information is centered above the two quantities to be compared, then that information is true of both quantities.

A symbol that appears in both columns represents the same thing in both columns.

The only possible choices are (A), (B), (C), and (D). Do not choose (E).

Answers are on page 1088.

| Column A | Column B |
|---|---|
| $x = 18 + 19 + 20 + 21 + 22$ | |
| $y = 22 + 21 + 20 + 19 + 18$ | |

1.  $x$  $-y$

---

$x = 4$
$y = 1$

2.  $\dfrac{x+y}{xy}$  $\dfrac{xy}{x+y}$

---

3.  The number of laps in a 50-mile race if each lap is $\frac{1}{5}$ of a mile  100

| Column A | Column B |
|---|---|
| $3(x+2) = 7$ | |

4.  $x$  1

GO ON TO THE NEXT PAGE.

Column A          Column B

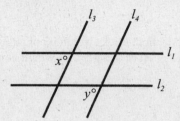

$l_1 \parallel l_2$
$l_3 \parallel l_4$

5.          $x$                    $y$

Cheese costs $2.00 per pound.

6.   The amount of          $\frac{3}{5}$ pound
     cheese that can be
     purchased for $1.50

Rectangular solid X has a volume of 24.
Rectangular solid Y has a volume of 20.

7.   Area of the          Area of the
     base of X            base of Y

8.   $\sqrt{9}$                $\sqrt{6} + \sqrt{3}$

9.   Surface area of        Area of a
     a sphere with         circle with
     radius 1              radius 1

$2x^2 + 4x + 3 = 0$

10.  $2x^2 + 4x$              $-3$

11.  $(111 + 111)^2$    $111^2 + 2(111)^2 + 111^2$

12.  The number of          The number of
     integers between        integers between
     101 and 199            201 and 299
     that are squares        that are squares
     of integers            of integers

Column A          Column B

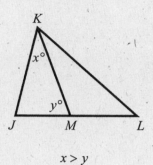

$x > y$

13.   $\overline{JK} + \overline{LM}$          $\overline{JM} + \overline{KM}$

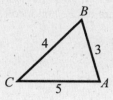

14.   Area of region $ABC$          6

GO ON TO THE NEXT PAGE.

Directions: Each of the following questions has five answer choices. Select the best of the available choices. Answers are on page 1090.

15. If $\frac{1}{x} + \frac{1}{x} = 8$, then $x =$

   (A) $\frac{1}{4}$
   (B) $\frac{1}{2}$
   (C) 1
   (D) 2
   (E) 4

16. In a certain school, there are 600 boys and 400 girls. If 20 percent of the boys and 30 percent of the girls are on the honor roll, how many of the students are on the honor roll?

   (A) 120
   (B) 175
   (C) 240
   (D) 250
   (E) 280

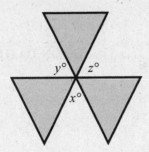

17. In the figure above, three equilateral triangles have a common vertex. $x + y + z =$

   (A)  60
   (B)  90
   (C) 120
   (D) 180
   (E) 240

18. If 100 identical bricks weigh $p$ pounds, then in terms of $p$, 20 of these bricks weigh how many pounds?

   (A) $\frac{p}{20}$
   (B) $\frac{p}{5}$
   (C) $20p$
   (D) $\frac{5}{p}$
   (E) $\frac{20}{p}$

19. For any integer $n$, which of the following represents three consecutive odd integers?

   (A) $n, n+1, n+2$
   (B) $n, n+1, n+3$
   (C) $n, n+2, n+4$
   (D) $2n+1, 2n+2, 2n+3$
   (E) $2n+1, 2n+3, 2n+5$

20. A group of 15 students took a test that was scored from zero to 100. If exactly ten students scored 75 or more on the test, what is the *lowest* possible value for the average of the scores of all 15 students?

   (A) 25
   (B) 50
   (C) 70
   (D) 75
   (E) 90

GO ON TO THE NEXT PAGE.

Items 21–23 refer to the following graphs.

## Advertising Expenditures of Three Candidates
### *(For the 1997 Campaign)*

Candidate P

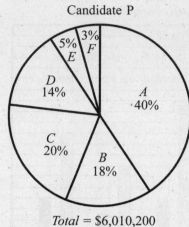

Total = $6,010,200

Candidate Q

Total = $4,501,379

Candidate R

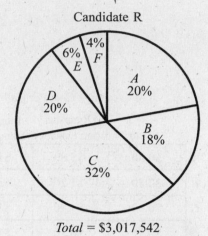

Total = $3,017,542

A = Television    D = Direct Mail
B = Radio    E = Magazines
C = Newspaper    F = Other

21. During the campaign, candidate Q spent approximately how much more money on advertising that candidate R?

 (A) $3,000,000
 (B) $2,750,000
 (C) $2,225,000
 (D) $1,900,000
 (E) $1,500,000

22. During the campaign, candidate P spent approximately how much more money on television advertising than candidate Q?

 (A) $1,500,000
 (B) $1,100,000
 (C) $900,000
 (D) $165,000
 (E) $125,000

23. Approximately what percent of the money spent on advertising by the three candidates combined was spent on television advertising?

 (A) 29%
 (B) 31%
 (C) 33%
 (D) 35%
 (E) 37%

GO ON TO THE NEXT PAGE.

Items 24–25 refer to the following graphs.

Average Number of Calls Made Daily and Average Cost of Calls for Five Offices of Corporation X

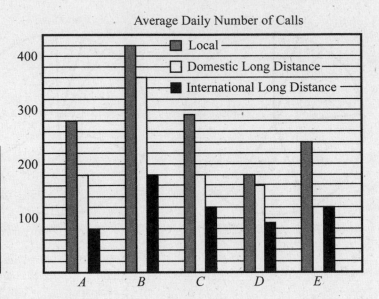

Average Cost Per Call

| | Local | Domestic Long Distance | International Long Distance |
|---|---|---|---|
| A | $0.50 | $5.80 | $19.90 |
| B | $0.80 | $7.20 | $22.40 |
| C | $0.63 | $4.80 | $16.40 |
| D | $0.75 | $6.20 | $18.50 |
| E | $0.40 | $6.80 | $17.20 |

24. For which of the five regional offices does the number of international long distance calls account for the greatest proportion of calls of all types?

(A) A
(B) B
(C) C
(D) D
(E) E

25. The ratio $\frac{\text{daily cost of call at office A}}{\text{daily cost of call at office D}}$ is most nearly

(A) $\frac{1}{6}$
(B) $\frac{1}{3}$
(C) $\frac{4}{7}$
(D) $\frac{5}{6}$
(E) 1

GO ON TO THE NEXT PAGE.

26. If a machine produces $x$ units in $t$ minutes and 30 seconds, what is its average operating speed in units per minute?

(A) $\frac{t+30}{x}$

(B) $\frac{x}{t+30}$

(C) $tx + \frac{1}{2}x$

(D) $\frac{t}{x+\frac{1}{2}}$

(E) $\frac{x}{t+\frac{1}{2}}$

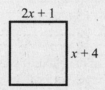

27. If the figure above is a square, what is the perimeter of the figure?

(A) 28
(B) 16
(C) 12
(D) 9
(E) 3

28. If a certain rectangle has a length that is twice its width, what is the ratio of the area of the rectangle to the area of an isosceles right triangle with hypotenuse equal to the width of the rectangle?

(A) $\frac{1}{8}$

(B) $\frac{1}{4}$

(C) $\frac{1}{2}$

(D) $\frac{4}{1}$

(E) $\frac{8}{1}$

# S T O P

IF YOU FINISH BEFORE TIME IS CALLED, YOU MAY CHECK YOUR WORK ON THIS SECTION ONLY.
DO NOT WORK ON ANY OTHER SECTION IN THE TEST.

## SECTION 3
30 Minutes

30 Items

<u>Directions</u>: Each sentence or paragraph in this part of the verbal section has one or more missing elements, as indicated by a blank or blanks. Choose the word or set of words that best fits the meaning of the text. Answers are on page 1093.

1. Although leprosy is not a highly contagious disease, those who have contracted it have always been pariahs who are —— by others.

   (A) ostracized
   (B) accepted
   (C) sheltered
   (D) admonished
   (E) lauded

2. Although the novel was generally boring and awkwardly written, there were —— passages of power and lyricism that hinted at the author's ——.

   (A) occasional. .potential
   (B) frequent. .malevolence
   (C) static. .style
   (D) ill-conceived. .superficiality
   (E) contrived. .ignorance

3. Portraits painted in Colonial America are quite charming but —— and demonstrate the isolation of the American painter; they show little or no —— of the development of painting in Europe.

   (A) grotesque. .concern
   (B) frivolous. .affirmation
   (C) deliberate. .domination
   (D) sophisticated. .consideration
   (E) primitive. .knowledge

4. Although the manager of the corporation was wrong, his stubborn refusal to —— or even to compromise —— an already tense situation.

   (A) arbitrate. .thwarted
   (B) capitulate. .exacerbated
   (C) censure. .rectified
   (D) mandate. .violated
   (E) scrutinize. .contained

5. The design of the building was magnificent, but its classical lines seemed almost —— and out of place in the business district which was —— ultramodern steel and glass skyscrapers.

   (A) garish. .beleaguered by
   (B) anachronistic. .replete with
   (C) untoward. .bereft of
   (D) grotesque. .enhanced by
   (E) sanguine. .populated by

6. Animal behaviorists theorize that dogs are more —— than cats because they are pack animals; whereas cats, solitary hunters, are more independent and —— and therefore less likely to try to please their owners.

   (A) precocious. .complex
   (B) aggressive. .obsequious
   (C) tractable. .obdurate
   (D) intelligent. .resilient
   (E) formidable. .reliable

GO ON TO THE NEXT PAGE.

Directions: Each of the following items consists of a word printed in capital letters, followed by five lettered words or phrases in lowercase letters. Choose the lettered word or phrase that is most nearly <u>opposite</u> in meaning to the word in capital letters. Answers are on page 1094.

7.  BRIDGE:

    (A) separate
    (B) recall
    (C) deflate
    (D) encourage
    (E) exceed

8.  NEBULOUS:

    (A) clear
    (B) tactful
    (C) reluctant
    (D) ill-mannered
    (E) untimely

9.  GARRULOUS:

    (A) conventional
    (B) bizarre
    (C) silent
    (D) forlorn
    (E) intact

10. COUNTENANCE:

    (A) demonstrate
    (B) abound
    (C) fulfill
    (D) classify
    (E) disapprove

11. SANGUINE:

    (A) deceived
    (B) resigned
    (C) refuted
    (D) muddled
    (E) enamored

12. GERMANE:

    (A) engrossed
    (B) extremely sophisticated
    (C) irrelevant
    (D) rewarding
    (E) spurious

13. TRENCHANT:

    (A) readily available
    (B) dimwitted
    (C) easily pleased
    (D) sanguine
    (E) abundant

14. EVINCE:

    (A) regulate
    (B) sanction
    (C) obscure
    (D) aver
    (E) extrapolate

15. CONTEMN:

    (A) invoke
    (B) stupefy
    (C) solicit
    (D) bequeath
    (E) admire

GO ON TO THE NEXT PAGE.

Directions: Each of the following items consists of a related pair of words or phrases presented in capital letters, followed by five lettered pairs of words or phrases presented in lowercase letters. For each item, choose the lettered pair that expresses a relationship that is most nearly like that expressed in the capitalized pair. Answers are on page 1094.

16. RUTHLESS : COMPASSION ::

(A) verbose : conversation
(B) mature : offspring
(C) animated : interest
(D) sublime : perfection
(E) lethargic : energy

17. LEOPARD : CAT ::

(A) zebra : zoo
(B) hawk : prey
(C) parrot : jungle
(D) monkey : chimpanzee
(E) chameleon : lizard

18. ANGER : RABID ::

(A) hunger : ravenous
(B) concern : careless
(C) modernity : contemporary
(D) petulance : mournful
(E) wisdom : hoary

19. BLAMEWORTHY : REPROACH ::

(A) recalcitrant : praise
(B) humorous : approval
(C) sympathetic : rejection
(D) meritorious : reward
(E) noxious : censure

20. PEDESTRIAN : ORIGINALITY ::

(A) monotonous : compulsion
(B) ethereal : mysticism
(C) reclusive : misanthropy
(D) indulgent : forbearance
(E) timorous : cowardice

21. INTERESTED : RAPT ::

(A) amenable : enthusiastic
(B) corrupt : fulfilled
(C) disinclined : concerned
(D) quarrelsome : intemperate
(E) valueless : prescribed

22. RAPACIOUS : GREED ::

(A) zealous : passion
(B) ferocious : timidity
(C) contemptuous : reticence
(D) precocious : admiration
(E) copious : dearth

GO ON TO THE NEXT PAGE.

Directions: Each reading selection in this group is followed by questions based on its content. Answer the questions following a selection on the basis of what is stated or implied in that selection, choosing the best answer to each question. Answers are on page 1095.

Speaking casually, we call *Nineteen Eighty-Four* a novel; but more exactly, it is a fable. True, the book focuses on Winston Smith, who suffers from a varicose ulcer, and it includes Julia, Mr. Charrington, and
5  O'Brien. They exist, however, mainly in their relation to a political system. In a novel, they would have to be imagined in a far more diverse set of relations. A fable is a narrative relieved of much contingent detail so that it stands forth in an unusual degree of clarity and
10  simplicity. A fable is a structure of types, each simplified lest a sense of difference and heterogeneity reduce the force of the typical.

Since a fable is predicated upon a typology, the author cannot afford the sense of familiarity which is
15  induced by detail and differentiation. A fable is a caricature, not a photograph. In a political fable there is tension between a political sense, which deals in the multiplicity of social and personal life, and a sense of fable, which is committed to simplicity of form and
20  feature. If the political sense were to prevail, the narrative would be drawn away from fable into the novel, at some cost to its simplicity. If the sense of fable were to prevail, the narrative would appear unmediated, free or bereft of conditions. A reader
25  might feel that the fabulist had lost interest in the variety of human life and fallen back upon an unconditioned sense of its types. The risk is greater still if the fabulist projects the narrative into the future: the reader can't question by appealing to the conditions
30  of life but is asked to believe that the future is another country where "they just do things differently." Thus, *Nineteen Eighty-Four* is a political fable, projected into a near future.

23. In drawing an analogy between a fable and a caricature (lines 15-16), the author would most likely regard which of the following pairs of ideas as also analogous?

(A) The subject of a caricature and the main character in *Nineteen Eighty-Four*
(B) The subject of a fable and the artist who draws the caricature
(C) The subject of a caricature and the topic of a fable
(D) The artist who draws the caricature and a novelist
(E) The minor characters in a fable and a photographer

GO ON TO THE NEXT PAGE.

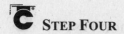
24. Which of the following would be the most appropriate title for the passage?

   (A) A Critical Study of the Use of Characters in *Nineteen Eighty-Four*
   (B) *Nineteen Eighty-Four*: Political Fable Rather Than Novel
   (C) *Nineteen Eighty-Four*: Reflections on the Relationship of the Individual to Society
   (D) The Use of Typology in the Literature of Political Fables
   (E) Distinguishing a Political Fable from a Novel

25. Which of the following best explains why the author mentions that Winston Smith suffers from a varicose ulcer?

   (A) To demonstrate that a political fable must emphasize type over detail
   (B) To show that Winston Smith has some characteristics that distinguish him as an individual
   (C) To argue that Winston Smith is no more important than any other character in *Nineteen Eighty-Four*
   (D) To illustrate one of the features of the political situation described in *Nineteen Eighty-Four*
   (E) To suggest that *Nineteen Eighty-Four* is too realistic to be considered a work of fiction

GO ON TO THE NEXT PAGE.

The uniqueness of the Japanese character is the result of two seemingly contradictory forces: the strength of traditions, and selective receptivity to foreign achievements and inventions. As early as the
5 1860s, there were counter movements to the traditional orientation. Yukichi Fukuzawa, the most eloquent spokesman of Japan's "Enlightenment," claimed "The Confucian civilization of the East seems to me to lack two things possessed by Western civilization: science
10 in the material sphere and a sense of independence in the spiritual sphere." Fukuzawa's great influence is found in the free and individualistic philosophy of the Education Code of 1872, but he was not able to prevent the government from turning back to the canons of
15 Confucian thought in the Imperial Rescript of 1890. Another interlude of relative liberalism followed World War I, when the democratic idealism of President Woodrow Wilson had an important impact on Japanese intellectuals and, especially, students; but more
20 important was the Leninist ideology of the 1917 Bolshevik Revolution. Again, in the early 1930s, nationalism and militarism became dominant, largely as a result of failing economic conditions.

Following the end of World War II, substantial
25 changes were undertaken in Japan to liberate the individual from authoritarian restraints. The new democratic value system was accepted by many teachers, students, intellectuals, and old liberals, but it was not immediately embraced by the society as a
30 whole. Japanese traditions were dominated by group values, and notions of personal freedom and individual rights were unfamiliar.

Today, democratic processes are clearly evident in the widespread participation of the Japanese people
35 in social and political life; yet, there is no universally accepted and stable value system. Values are constantly modified by strong infusions of Western ideas, both democratic and Marxist. School textbooks expound democratic principles, emphasizing equality
40 over hierarchy and rationalism over tradition; but in practice these values are often misinterpreted and distorted, particularly by the youth who translate the individualistic and humanistic goals of democracy into egoistic and materialistic ones.

45 Most Japanese people have consciously rejected Confucianism, but vestiges of the old order remain. An important feature of relationships in many institutions such as political parties, large corporations, and university faculties is the *oyabun-kobun* or parent-child
50 relation. A party leader, supervisor, or professor, in return for loyalty, protects those subordinate to him and takes general responsibility for their interests

throughout their entire lives, an obligation that sometimes even extends to arranging marriages. The
55 corresponding loyalty of the individual to his patron reinforces his allegiance to the group to which they both belong. A willingness to cooperate with other members of the group and to support without qualification the interests of the group in all its external
60 relations is still a widely respected virtue. The *oyabun-kobun* creates ladders of mobility which an individual can ascend, rising as far as abilities permit, so long as he maintains successful personal ties with a superior in the vertical channel, the latter requirement usually
65 taking precedence over a need for exceptional competence. As a consequence, there is little horizontal relationship between people even within the same profession.

26. Which of the following is most like the relationship of the *oyabun-kobun* described in the passage?

(A) A political candidate and the voting public
(B) A gifted scientist and his protégé
(C) Two brothers who are partners in a business
(D) A judge presiding at the trial of a criminal defendant
(E) A leader of a musical ensemble who is also a musician in the group

GO ON TO THE NEXT PAGE.

27. It can be inferred that the Imperial Rescript of 1890

    (A) was a protest by liberals against the lack of individual liberty in Japan
    (B) marked a return in government policies to conservative values
    (C) implemented the ideals set forth in the Education Code of 1872
    (D) was influenced by the Leninist ideology of the Bolshevik Revolution
    (E) prohibited the teaching of Western ideas in Japanese schools

28. Which of the following best states the central thesis of the passage?

    (A) The value system of Japan is based upon traditional and conservative values that have, in modern times, been modified by Western and other liberal values.
    (B) Students and radicals in Japan have used Leninist ideology to distort the meaning of democratic, Western values.
    (C) The notions of personal freedom and individual liberty did not find immediate acceptance in Japan because of the predominance of traditional group values.
    (D) Modern Japanese society is characterized by hierarchical relationships in which a personal tie to a superior is often more important than merit.
    (E) The influence on Japanese values of the American ideals of personal freedom and individual rights is less important than the influence of Leninist ideology.

GO ON TO THE NEXT PAGE.

Open government statutes in California have proved both beneficial and harmful. In the energy commission for example, as in other government commissions, nearly all decisions must be made in
5    public session for which at least seven days' notice must be given. Which decisions can be made by the executive director and which are strictly reserved for the commission becomes quite important in this context. If something is a matter for the commission,
10   there must be a public notice with attendant publicity and preparation of materials for distribution at the meeting. Furthermore, a commissioner may not meet informally with another commissioner nor with the executive director or any member of his staff to discuss
15   commission activities. Such behavior would be a violation of open government statutes. Staff briefings are conducted individually by each commissioner or through each commissioner's advisors. More frequently, commissioners or their advisors contact the
20   staff for information, but all such requests must be submitted in writing.

An example of the impact of open government on the operating procedures of a commission was illustrated by the energy commission's budgetary
25   process. The budget for the commission, unlike that prepared in other state agencies, was prepared in public session by the five commissioners. The session was not simply a "review and comment" session since the commissioners had not previously discussed the
30   budget. Every item proposed for the budget could be commented upon by anyone who attended the session.

Perhaps open government's effect has been greatest in the promulgation of rules and regulations. Complaints have arisen from several legislators and
35   news media about the slowness of the energy commission in setting regulations. If, however, a commission attempts to handle fewer matters without input from state agencies and interested groups in open meetings, it will be criticized for circumventing the
40   open government intentions. If present practices continue, the commission will continue to be criticized for moving too slowly.

29. The passage implies the open government statute is intended to accomplish all of the following EXCEPT

(A) to minimize the likelihood of secret political deals
(B) to allow an opportunity for the public to influence government decisions
(C) to ensure that government officials are held accountable for their policies
(D) to guarantee that a government agency can respond quickly to a problem
(E) to publicize governmental functions

30. The passage most strongly supports which of the following conclusions about a decision that is within the authority of the executive director of an agency?

(A) It would be made more quickly than a decision reserved for a commission.
(B) It would be made with the assistance of the agency's commissioners.
(C) It would be a highly publicized event attended by members of the media.
(D) It would deal with a matter of greater importance than those handled by the commission.
(E) It would be made only after the director had notified commissioners and their aides in writing.

# S T O P

IF YOU FINISH BEFORE TIME IS CALLED, YOU MAY CHECK YOUR WORK ON THIS SECTION ONLY.
DO NOT WORK ON ANY OTHER SECTION IN THE TEST.

# 5

# Step Five: Evaluating Progress (Post-Assessment)

## Step Five Highlights:

See how far you have come and measure your improvement with this second, official test.

Put into action all of the content knowledge and test-taking strategies that you have learned.

Redirect your study plan with a new snapshot of your performance.

Make sure that you are able to work through the test quickly without losing accuracy.

## Step Five Overview:

It's time to measure your progress. You will put into action everything that you have learned during this second "dress rehearsal." After taking this final exam, you will be able to compare your pre- and post-assessment scores and see how much you have improved. You will have a chance to identify any remaining areas of weakness so that you know where to focus your studies prior to the actual test.

Name: _____    Date: _____

Student ID Number: _____

# POST-ASSESSMENT

Start with number 1 for each new section. If a section has fewer items than answer spaces, leave the extra answer spaces blank. Be sure to erase any errors or stray marks completely.

## Section 1

| | | | |
|---|---|---|---|
| 1 (A) (B) (C) (D) (E) | 11 (A) (B) (C) (D) (E) | 21 (A) (B) (C) (D) (E) | 31 (A) (B) (C) (D) (E) |
| 2 (A) (B) (C) (D) (E) | 12 (A) (B) (C) (D) (E) | 22 (A) (B) (C) (D) (E) | 32 (A) (B) (C) (D) (E) |
| 3 (A) (B) (C) (D) (E) | 13 (A) (B) (C) (D) (E) | 23 (A) (B) (C) (D) (E) | 33 (A) (B) (C) (D) (E) |
| 4 (A) (B) (C) (D) (E) | 14 (A) (B) (C) (D) (E) | 24 (A) (B) (C) (D) (E) | 34 (A) (B) (C) (D) (E) |
| 5 (A) (B) (C) (D) (E) | 15 (A) (B) (C) (D) (E) | 25 (A) (B) (C) (D) (E) | 35 (A) (B) (C) (D) (E) |
| 6 (A) (B) (C) (D) (E) | 16 (A) (B) (C) (D) (E) | 26 (A) (B) (C) (D) (E) | 36 (A) (B) (C) (D) (E) |
| 7 (A) (B) (C) (D) (E) | 17 (A) (B) (C) (D) (E) | 27 (A) (B) (C) (D) (E) | 37 (A) (B) (C) (D) (E) |
| 8 (A) (B) (C) (D) (E) | 18 (A) (B) (C) (D) (E) | 28 (A) (B) (C) (D) (E) | 38 (A) (B) (C) (D) (E) |
| 9 (A) (B) (C) (D) (E) | 19 (A) (B) (C) (D) (E) | 29 (A) (B) (C) (D) (E) | |
| 10 (A) (B) (C) (D) (E) | 20 (A) (B) (C) (D) (E) | 30 (A) (B) (C) (D) (E) | |

## Section 2

| | | | |
|---|---|---|---|
| 1 (A) (B) (C) (D) (E) | 9 (A) (B) (C) (D) (E) | 17 (A) (B) (C) (D) (E) | 25 (A) (B) (C) (D) (E) |
| 2 (A) (B) (C) (D) (E) | 10 (A) (B) (C) (D) (E) | 18 (A) (B) (C) (D) (E) | 26 (A) (B) (C) (D) (E) |
| 3 (A) (B) (C) (D) (E) | 11 (A) (B) (C) (D) (E) | 19 (A) (B) (C) (D) (E) | 27 (A) (B) (C) (D) (E) |
| 4 (A) (B) (C) (D) (E) | 12 (A) (B) (C) (D) (E) | 20 (A) (B) (C) (D) (E) | 28 (A) (B) (C) (D) (E) |
| 5 (A) (B) (C) (D) (E) | 13 (A) (B) (C) (D) (E) | 21 (A) (B) (C) (D) (E) | 29 (A) (B) (C) (D) (E) |
| 6 (A) (B) (C) (D) (E) | 14 (A) (B) (C) (D) (E) | 22 (A) (B) (C) (D) (E) | 30 (A) (B) (C) (D) (E) |
| 7 (A) (B) (C) (D) (E) | 15 (A) (B) (C) (D) (E) | 23 (A) (B) (C) (D) (E) | |
| 8 (A) (B) (C) (D) (E) | 16 (A) (B) (C) (D) (E) | 24 (A) (B) (C) (D) (E) | |

## Section 3

| | | | |
|---|---|---|---|
| 1 (A) (B) (C) (D) (E) | 11 (A) (B) (C) (D) (E) | 21 (A) (B) (C) (D) (E) | 31 (A) (B) (C) (D) (E) |
| 2 (A) (B) (C) (D) (E) | 12 (A) (B) (C) (D) (E) | 22 (A) (B) (C) (D) (E) | 32 (A) (B) (C) (D) (E) |
| 3 (A) (B) (C) (D) (E) | 13 (A) (B) (C) (D) (E) | 23 (A) (B) (C) (D) (E) | 33 (A) (B) (C) (D) (E) |
| 4 (A) (B) (C) (D) (E) | 14 (A) (B) (C) (D) (E) | 24 (A) (B) (C) (D) (E) | 34 (A) (B) (C) (D) (E) |
| 5 (A) (B) (C) (D) (E) | 15 (A) (B) (C) (D) (E) | 25 (A) (B) (C) (D) (E) | 35 (A) (B) (C) (D) (E) |
| 6 (A) (B) (C) (D) (E) | 16 (A) (B) (C) (D) (E) | 26 (A) (B) (C) (D) (E) | 36 (A) (B) (C) (D) (E) |
| 7 (A) (B) (C) (D) (E) | 17 (A) (B) (C) (D) (E) | 27 (A) (B) (C) (D) (E) | 37 (A) (B) (C) (D) (E) |
| 8 (A) (B) (C) (D) (E) | 18 (A) (B) (C) (D) (E) | 28 (A) (B) (C) (D) (E) | 38 (A) (B) (C) (D) (E) |
| 9 (A) (B) (C) (D) (E) | 19 (A) (B) (C) (D) (E) | 29 (A) (B) (C) (D) (E) | |
| 10 (A) (B) (C) (D) (E) | 20 (A) (B) (C) (D) (E) | 30 (A) (B) (C) (D) (E) | |

## Section 4

| | | | |
|---|---|---|---|
| 1 (A) (B) (C) (D) (E) | 9 (A) (B) (C) (D) (E) | 17 (A) (B) (C) (D) (E) | 25 (A) (B) (C) (D) (E) |
| 2 (A) (B) (C) (D) (E) | 10 (A) (B) (C) (D) (E) | 18 (A) (B) (C) (D) (E) | 26 (A) (B) (C) (D) (E) |
| 3 (A) (B) (C) (D) (E) | 11 (A) (B) (C) (D) (E) | 19 (A) (B) (C) (D) (E) | 27 (A) (B) (C) (D) (E) |
| 4 (A) (B) (C) (D) (E) | 12 (A) (B) (C) (D) (E) | 20 (A) (B) (C) (D) (E) | 28 (A) (B) (C) (D) (E) |
| 5 (A) (B) (C) (D) (E) | 13 (A) (B) (C) (D) (E) | 21 (A) (B) (C) (D) (E) | 29 (A) (B) (C) (D) (E) |
| 6 (A) (B) (C) (D) (E) | 14 (A) (B) (C) (D) (E) | 22 (A) (B) (C) (D) (E) | 30 (A) (B) (C) (D) (E) |
| 7 (A) (B) (C) (D) (E) | 15 (A) (B) (C) (D) (E) | 23 (A) (B) (C) (D) (E) | |
| 8 (A) (B) (C) (D) (E) | 16 (A) (B) (C) (D) (E) | 24 (A) (B) (C) (D) (E) | |

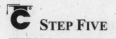 

## ISSUE TASK

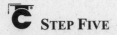 

# S T O P

IF YOU FINISH BEFORE TIME IS CALLED, YOU MAY CHECK YOUR WORK ON THIS ESSAY ONLY.
DO NOT TURN TO ANY OTHER PORTION OF THE TEST.

## ARGUMENT TASK

**S T O P**
IF YOU FINISH BEFORE TIME IS CALLED, YOU MAY CHECK YOUR WORK ON THIS ESSAY ONLY.
DO NOT TURN TO ANY OTHER PORTION OF THE TEST.

# Step Six: What to Do After the Course

## Step Six Highlights:

With the post-assessment data, create a focused post-course study plan so you know what to review.

Make sure you understand all the GRE-specific information concerning the computer-adaptive "ladder of difficulty," item-types, and content before the real test.

Do not waste time on areas you have already mastered; target your remaining areas of weakness to maximize your GRE score.

Determine the parts of the textbook on which you need to spend more time: skills review, test mechanics, test-taking strategies, or pacing with practice tests.

Learn how to prepare your graduate school application and succeed in school when you get there!

## Step Six Overview:

Based on the results of the post-assessment, you will develop a post-course study plan. You may need to return to items you have already reviewed but have not yet mastered in Steps Three and Four. If there are any items you have not yet completed, this is the time to return to those items. You may need to review specific test-taking strategies, focus on pacing techniques, or address other weaknesses. A post-course study plan will target your weaknesses in order to help you reach your true potential and ability.

# POST-COURSE STUDY PLAN

Up until this point, you have spent a great deal of time preparing for the test both in class and on your own. After receiving the results of your final assessment (Step Five) and finishing your GRE preparation course, you will most likely have some spare time before the day of the actual test. Spend this time wisely to make your best effort in preparation for the exam. This study plan section is included as a short guide on how to use that remaining time to your best advantage.

A post-course study plan is critical in order to reinforce and maintain the skills that you have learned throughout the course. Depending on whether several weeks or several days remain before the official exam date, you will want to plan your study differently. If there are several weeks remaining before the day of the test, you should plan to review more material than if there are only a few days remaining. If only a few days remain, a quick summary review is a better choice.

Many topics that are related to creating your post-course study plan have already been covered in the Overcoming Test Anxiety section (Step Three) of this textbook. It is important for you to review the material in that section when designing your study plan. In particular, you should balance a plan that will leave you not only confident but also calm and rested for the day of the exam.

The largest problem that most students face on the official exam is not a lack of subject knowledge but poor management of time. One way to improve your pacing is to take the practice tests included in Step Four of this textbook. These practice tests not only serve to reinforce skills and strategies, but they also emphasize the importance of time management since the third and fourth are to be administered with time restrictions. These time restrictions are put in place to simulate the experience of the actual test. Therefore, when taking these two practice tests, hold rigorously to the allotted times. It is always worthwhile to return to a practice test to address skipped or unfinished items, but you should do so only at the conclusion of the allotted time.

Besides helping your pacing and preparedness, the practice tests are also an excellent guide to targeting your study plan. Look for topics on which your performance could have been improved with access to your course notes. These are likely targets for review as you approach the day of the exam. Listing a few topics for review sets a firm starting ground for your study plan.

The most significant aspect of a post-course study plan is that it is a written plan. A written study plan is more concrete than one that you simply draw on from memory. So, when creating a post-course study plan, write out a day-by-day schedule for reviewing all of the materials that are necessary to succeed on the test. This written format will provide a clear and dependable guide for study. The schedule should be prioritized according to the time that you will devote to each of the different subject-areas based on the amount of time that you have remaining before the day of the official exam. Plan to review all of the materials equally several weeks before test day. Then, when the test date approaches, start focusing on the subject-areas that are giving you the most difficulty. Divide your time proportionally among the test sections based on your assessment of the difficulty of the subject-areas. Although subject-area preparation is extremely important, the amount of time that you have remaining before the exam will determine how strongly you should focus on reviewing certain subject-area material. In the final days before the test, you will not be able to learn a great deal of new material. Therefore, unless there is a long span of time between the end of your review course and the date of the exam, you should focus on practicing the skills that you have already learned (e.g., time management, coding of item stems, the process of elimination strategy).

The following sample schedules are provided for your reference. Remember that these schedules are only examples and that you should devise your own schedule to target the areas that you find most challenging. After you have designed a basic study plan, ask your teacher for insight. Your teacher may be able to suggest further strategies or a subtle re-allotment of your time.

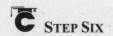 

If you are satisfied with your Verbal Reasoning scores but have not attained your goals for the Quantitative Reasoning test section, you might consider designing a study plan that emphasizes math. Your plan for the week might appear as follows:

| Day of the Week | Assignment | Location in Student Text |
|---|---|---|
| SUNDAY | Review algebraic equations and inequalities. | Quantitative Reasoning Skills Review (Step Three) |
| MONDAY | Revisit formulas. | Quantitative Reasoning Express Skills Review (Step Three) |
| TUESDAY | Review story problems. | Quantitative Reasoning Skills Review (Step Three) |
| WEDNESDAY | Self-administer a Quantitative Comparisons quiz or the Quantitative Comparisons items in Practice Tests III and IV. | Step Three or Step Four |
| THURSDAY | Review Quantitative Reasoning explanations for Practice Tests III and IV. | Answers and Explanations: Step Four |
| FRIDAY | Relax. Use test anxiety reduction strategies. Get a good night's sleep. | Overcoming Test Anxiety (Step Three) |
| SATURDAY (TEST DAY) | Eat a healthy breakfast and remain confident. | — |

On the other hand, if you are more comfortable with the Quantitative Reasoning section of the test, you may want to review the Verbal Reasoning and Analytical Writing material. Focusing on concepts is the best use of your time. A plan that emphasizes reading and writing might appear as follows:

| Day of the Week | Assignment | Location in Student Text |
|---|---|---|
| SUNDAY | Review Careful Reading of Item Stems. | Verbal Reasoning Skills Review (Step Three) |
| MONDAY | Revisit basic grammar and vocabulary lists. | Analytical Writing Skills Review and Verbal Reasoning Skills Review, respectively (Step Three) |
| TUESDAY | Review Coding of Item Stems. | Verbal Reasoning Skills Review (Step Three) |
| WEDNESDAY | Self-administer a Reading Comprehension quiz or the Reading Comprehension items in Practice Tests III and IV. | Step Three or Step Four |
| THURSDAY | Review Verbal Reasoning explanations for Practice Tests III and IV. | Answers and Explanations: Step Four |
| FRIDAY | Relax. Use test anxiety reduction strategies. Get a good night's sleep. | Overcoming Test Anxiety (Step Three) |
| SATURDAY (TEST DAY) | Eat a healthy breakfast and remain confident. | — |

Once you have determined your rubric for study, stick to it without fail. Such discipline will surely reward you on the day of the test. However, do not study too much. An hour or two of studying each day will be more productive than a severe study schedule that leaves you physically and mentally exhausted when the time comes to take the actual exam. Think of this process as training for a sport. While it is necessary to practice every day, it is counterproductive to overexert yourself and to practice too much.

## APPLICATION PREPARATION

The title of this section echoes our analysis of the admission process in Step One (Setting a Test Score Target). To maximize your chances of success, you must create an application that satisfies the needs of the school to which you are applying. This does not mean that you create an application out of whole cloth, but it does mean that you organize and present your experiences in a way that depicts you in the most favorable light.

## CREATING YOUR APPLICATION

On a graduate application, most of the questions you will be asked need only short answers. "Did you work while you were in school?" "What clubs did you join?" "What honors or awards did you receive?" You do not have much room to maneuver here. However, you should try to communicate as much information as possible in your short answers. Compare the following pairs of descriptions:

> *Member of College Orchestra*
> *Second Violinist of the College Orchestra*

> *Played Intra-Mural Volleyball*
> *Co-captain of the Phi Kappa Volleyball Team*

> *Member of the AD's CSL*
> *One of three members on the Associate Dean's Committee on Student Life*

> *Worked at Billy's Burger Barn*
> *Assistant Manager at Billy's Burger Barn (25 hours/week)*

In addition to the short answer questions, most applications invite you to make a personal statement. Some applications ask for very little additional information. For example: "In a paragraph, explain to us why you want to go to graduate school." Other applications are open-ended: "On a separate sheet of paper, tell us anything else you think we ought to know about you." The point of the question is for you to give the admissions committee any information that might not be available from test scores, GPA, and short-answer questions.

You should consider the personal statement to be the most important part of your application for two reasons. First, the personal statement should be your argument to the admissions committee for your acceptance. It should give them reasons to accept you. Second, the personal statement is the one aspect of the application over which you can exercise any real control. Your GPA is already settled; your work experience was accumulated over the years; your GRE has been scored. These aspects of the application cannot easily be manipulated. The personal statement, however, is under your control.

What should go into a personal statement? You should include arguments that interpret your academic, employment, and personal history in such a way as to indicate that you have the ability to complete graduate school and that you are committed to studying and later to pursuing a career in your chosen area of study. Most importantly, the personal statement must not be a simple restatement of facts already in the application. Imagine, for example, a personal statement that reads as follows:

> *I went to State University where I received a 3.5 GPA. I was a member of the Associate Dean's Committee on Student Life, and I worked as the assistant manager on the night shift at Billy's Burger Barn. Then, I took the GRE and scored a 550. I know I will be a good PhD candidate and will enjoy my job.*

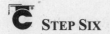 

This is not very interesting. Furthermore, all of that information is already included in your answers to the standard questions on the application. There is no point in simply repeating it.

Instead, you *interpret* the facts of your life to make them *reasons* for accepting you. You should start with your GPA. Try to bring out facts that suggest that the GPA is really better than it looks. Did you have one particularly bad semester, during which you took physics, calculus, and Latin, which pulled your average down? Was there a death in the family or some other difficult time that interfered with your studies? How many hours did you work in an average week? What extracurricular or family commitments took time away from your studies? Did you follow an unusual course of study, such as an honors program or a double major? Was your college major particularly challenging? Did you participate in any unusual courses, such as field research?

These are the points that the admissions committee wants to hear. For example:

> *The committee will see that my final GPA is 3.5. I should point out that the average would have been higher had I not needed to work 20 hours each week to finance my education. Additionally, my grades in the first semester of my junior year were disappointing because my grandmother, who lived with my family and with whom I was very close, died. Finally, in order to fulfill the requirements for the honors program, I wrote a 50-page honors thesis on the Dutch fishing industry of the 18th century. I have included a copy of the introduction to my thesis with this application.*

You should take the same approach to your work experience. For example:

> *During my junior and senior years in college, I worked an average of 20 hours per week at Billy's Burger Barn as the manager on the night shift. I would report to work at midnight and get off at four a.m. As night manager, I supervised eight other employees and was responsible for making emergency repairs on kitchen equipment. For example, once I was able to keep the deep fryer in operation by using a length of telephone cable to repair a faulty thermostat. The night manager was also responsible for maintaining order. It is not an easy job to convince intoxicated students who become too rowdy to leave without calling the police. Moreover, we were robbed at gunpoint not once but twice.*

Of course, if you have considerable work experience, e.g., if you graduated from college several years ago, you will want to go into that experience in more detail than if you had only student work experience.

Can you say anything about the GRE score? Probably not much—the GRE score is straightforward and not usually open to interpretation. However, there are some exceptions. One such exception is a history of poor scores on standardized exams. Consider the following:

> *I believe that my GRE score of 160 understates my real ability, for I have never had much success on aptitude tests. My SAT score was only 925. Yet, I finished college with a 3.6 GPA.*

> *The committee will see that I have two GRE scores: 400 and 550. During the first test, I had the flu and a fever and simply could not concentrate.*

These are the two most common excuses for a disappointing GRE score.

Finally, you must also persuade the admissions committee that you are serious about obtaining your graduate school degree. You must be able to show the committee something in your background that explains why you want to go to graduate school. In addition, it will help your case if you can suggest what you might do with a graduate school degree. For example:

*As a chemistry major, I joined the Student Environmental Association. Working with private company executives, who had themselves satisfied E.P.A. admissions standards, we convinced the University to stop polluting the Ten-Mile Run Creek. From this experience, I learned how business helps to protect our environment. I plan to make environmental resources my area of study, and I hope to work for the government or a private agency to protect the environment.*

A word of warning is in order here. Your career objectives have to be believable. It is not sufficient to write, "I plan to solve the environmental problems of American industry." That is much too abstract. Nor are graduate school admissions officers interested in a general discourse on the advantages of democracy or the hardship of poverty. If you write, "I want to eliminate damage to the planet and to help private industries help themselves environmentally" then there had better be something in your experience that makes this believable.

Finally, with regard to motivation, do not imagine that there is a preferred political position that you should adopt. Graduate school admissions officers span the political spectrum. To be sure, some are political liberals, but there are also conservatives. You do not have to make up a "tear-jerker" essay in order to be accepted.

Thus far, we have discussed the issues of ability and motivation. You may also wish to include in your personal statement information that shows that you have something that will help the school create a diverse student body. This additional information can be something dramatic:

*One morning, a patron choked on a burger and lost consciousness. I used the Heimlich maneuver to dislodge the food and performed CPR until a team of paramedics arrived. The patron recovered fully, in large part, according to her doctors, because of my first aid.*

Conversely, the information may not be dramatic:

*My parents are Armenian immigrants, so I am fluent in Armenian as well as English. I would enjoy meeting others who share an interest in the politics, legal developments, and culture of that part of the world.*

However, do not overestimate the value of this kind of information. It is, so to speak, the icing on the cake. It makes you a more interesting individual and might tip the scale in your favor when all other things are equal. It will not, however, get you an acceptance at a school for which you are not otherwise competitive in terms of GRE and GPA.

Now we turn our attention to matters of style. When you marshal your arguments for acceptance, you need to present them in an organized fashion. There is no single preferred format, but you might start with the outline on the following page:

I. I have the ability
  A. My college studies are good
    1. I had one bad semester
    2. I was in the honors program
    3. I wrote a thesis
  B. My work experience is good
    1. I worked while in college
    2. I was promoted to shift leader at my job
II. I want to earn my graduate degree
  A. I worked with PhD students on the pollution problem
  B. I would become a specialist in environmental chemistry
III. There is something interesting about me

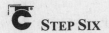 

The prose you use should be your own natural style of writing. Do not try something cute. Admissions officers detest essays that try to look like manuscripts and footnote "documentary evidence." You should create your outline, using all the arguments of which you can think. Then, you must begin to edit. For most people, the final document should not be more than a page to a page and a half—typed of course! During the editing process, you will strive for an economy of language, so that you can convey as much information as possible. Additionally, you will be forced to make considered judgments about the relative importance of various points. You will be forced to delete those ideas that are not that compelling. To obtain a superior personal statement, it may be necessary to reduce five or six pages to a single page, and the process may require more than 20 drafts.

## LETTERS OF RECOMMENDATION

Perhaps the best advice that we can give you about so-called letters of recommendation is to think of them as evaluations rather than recommendations. Indeed, many admissions officers refer to letter-writers as evaluators. These letters can be very important factors in an application, so who should write them?

First, some schools require a letter from the dean of students (or some similar functionary) at your college. This is not optional on your part. Even if you have never met the dean, you must get this letter. However, graduate schools do not really expect the dean to have much to say. The requirement is in essence an inquiry to the school about your behavior. It is intended to evoke any information about disciplinary problems that might not otherwise surface. So, the best letter from a dean, and the one most people get, is just a statement to the effect that there is nothing to say about you. In addition to the dean's letter, most schools require or at least permit you to submit two or three letters of evaluation from other sources. Who should write these? First, let us dispose of a common misunderstanding. A letter of evaluation does not have to come from a famous person. How effective is the following letter?

*William Hardy, Chief Judge*
*Chairperson of the Board*

*To the Admissions Committee:*

*I am recommending Susan Roberts for graduate school. Her mother is a member of our board of directors. Susan's mother earned her doctorate at the University of Chicago and she regularly makes significant contributions to our corporate meetings. Susan, following her mother's example, will make a fine graduate school candidate.*

*Sincerely,*
*William Hardy*

The letterhead holds great promise, but then the letter itself is worthless. It is obvious that the letter-writer does not really have any basis for his conclusion that the candidate will make a good graduate school candidate.

The best letters of evaluation will come from people who know you very well: a professor with whom you took several courses, your immediate supervisor at work, or a business associate with whom you have worked closely. A good evaluation will incorporate personal knowledge into the letter and reference specific events and activities. For example:

*Mary P. Weiss*
*White, Weiss, and Blanche*

*To the Admissions Committee:*

*White, Weiss, and Blanche is a consulting firm that advises corporations on environmental concerns. Susan Roberts has worked for us for the past two summers. Her work is outstanding, and she is an intelligent and genial person.*

*Last summer, as my assistant, Susan wrote a 25-page report that outlined a way of altering a client's exhaust stack to reduce sulfur emissions. The report was organized so that it was easy to follow and written in a style that was clear and easy to understand. Additionally, Susan gave a live presentation during a meeting with the client's board of directors and engineers. She was confident and handled some very difficult questions in an easy manner. I should note that we have used Susan's innovation in several other plants.*

*Finally, Susan made an important contribution to our company softball team. The team finished in last place, but Susan played in every game. Her batting average was not anything to brag about, but her enthusiasm more than made up for it.*

*Sincerely,*
*Mary Weiss*

To get a letter such as this one, you will have to ask someone who knows you well.

## OTHER SOURCES

Using the information in this section, you will create an application that will position you for acceptance—that is, an application that will give a graduate school an affirmative reason for accepting you. In addition to this section, you may also want to consider some other sources. For general information about accredited graduate schools in the United States, either check the reference materials at your school's library or perform an online search. Then, for each school in which you have even a passing interest, request the appropriate bulletin or catalog. Read these publications carefully. They provide listings of faculty members and their qualifications, descriptions of any special programs, information about student activities and campus life, catalogues of financial aid, and much more.

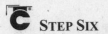 

# SUCCEEDING IN GRADUATE SCHOOL

## INTRODUCTION

As a successful student, you have invested many years of your life climbing the winding stairway of the academic multi-storied tower. Each step upward elevated you toward a new level of opportunity to learn and develop advanced skills, further knowledge, and deeper analytical abilities. The fact that you have conquered the lower levels of academia and now are ascending to a level known as "graduate school" clearly suggests that you are bright, talented, and motivated. Congratulations!

Having been among the brightest and best of high school and undergraduate students may leave you with an impression that stepping into graduate school requires but a slight incremental increase over your undergraduate knowledge and abilities. Unfortunately, this impression is false. Graduate school programs are qualitatively different than undergraduate programs. Faculty throws higher expectations on graduate students' efforts. Papers and exams are graded with a more critical eye. Universities, which often financially subsidize graduate programs and graduate students, anticipate higher levels of personal and professional achievements from graduate school students. And employers who hire students from various graduate school programs demand more knowledge and greater skill for the higher wages that those graduates desire and deserve.

What are the differences between undergraduate and graduate programs? Across the university, graduate programs of course differ in their concentration and character. A graduate program in history will differ greatly from a graduate program in chemistry; a graduate program in education will differ from a graduate degree in mathematics; and a graduate program in music performance will differ from a graduate program in business. But even across the diverse university curricula, there remain core differences between academic expectations for undergraduate and graduate programs. Undergraduate programs are based on a desire to help undergraduate students memorize information, recall foundational content, understand basic relationships and apply a knowledge or skill base within an academic discipline (e.g., chemistry, mathematics, music, history, etc.). In contrast, graduate programs require students to deconstruct and analyze existing information; synthesize broad ranges of content in order to build new content and theories; and assess, evaluate, and even criticize complex relationships. While as an undergraduate student you were expected to absorb and accept information from various sources, as a graduate student you will be expected to not only absorb and accept information from other sources, but also to critically examine this information and innovatively create new ideas and concepts of your own.

In short, by entering graduate school, you take more than a small step into a new academic space—you climb onto an entire new floor of the academic life with new expectations. To your successfully learned box of knowledge and skills you will need to add an entirely new set of skills to become a successful graduate student. Here are a few critical keys to success in graduate school.

➤ *Consider Life Beyond Graduation Right Now*

Remember your early freshman days in college. Everything was new. Possibilities were endless. You created and re-created you vision for your future frequently. You may have changed programs or even changed colleges. While most undergraduate programs allowed, even encouraged this type of academic and personal exploration, graduate programs are more highly focused and intentional in their academic or research pursuits. Thus most successful students, immediately upon entering a program, become focused and intentional regarding the ultimate results they desire from their graduate studies.

To succeed in graduate school, you must well understand for what ultimate purpose you are attending graduate school. When you consider the following four statements, which one most describes your desire for a graduate program?

- After graduation, I want to immediately pursue a professional vocation in my field of study and will immediately search for employment in my field.

- After graduation, I want to continue with further educational opportunities in a doctoral or post-doctoral program of study in my academic area.
- After graduation, I want to continue my education in a different field (e.g., go on to law school, medical school, or another complementary research area).
- After graduation, I want to pursue an academic career in higher education (e.g., become a professor or work in higher education administration).

Each statement above requires you to take a slightly different approach to a graduate school program. Your end goal should directly influence the classes you take, the professors you seek as mentors, the research projects you request, the internships you approach, and even the other students with whom you network.

In a short statement, can you describe what you want for yourself immediately following your graduation from your graduate program? When you can do this, set up a meeting with your academic advisor or faculty mentor and together begin to plan how your graduate program can help you meet this goal.

➢ *Attend and Learn from Orientation*

Because you've successfully navigated a solid number of experiences surrounding university life during your undergraduate years, your first reaction may be to ignore those early orientation meetings associated with your graduate program. Your time, you assume, is much too valuable to waste listening to faculty and administrators provide the perfunctory introductions to student life. In contrast to your assumptions, graduate school orientations provide a wealth of vital information that will help you bridge from life as an undergraduate student to life as a graduate student.

Take note of the following items covered by most graduate school orientations:

- Securing assistantships and internships
- Meeting graduation requirements
- Finding technological resources
- Understanding academic policies and procedures
- Knowing your rights as a student
- Preparing for your thesis, dissertation, or research project
- Exploring the surrounding community
- Meeting key faculty, advisors, and administrators
- Finding housing and transportation
- Obtaining financial support or research funding
- Hearing "inside advice" from previous graduate students
- Paying tuition and fees
- Knowing about health insurance and other university benefits
- Understanding the university calendar, major deadlines, and schedules
- Gaining an overview of the campus layout, parking, and safety factors
- Getting to know other students

Some of this information is more personal in nature while some is more academic. But all of it is important for you to be successful. Invest your time and energy wisely by listening and learning well at your graduate school orientation sessions.

➢ *Network Above, Around, and Beyond*

Graduate school provides you a unique opportunity to explore and research at deeper levels a particular academic area (e.g., physics, art history, accounting, sociology). But successful graduate students know that it is not simply *what* they study that pays dividends, but also *with whom* they study. A key connection with the right person or persons can launch your academic or career path forward in untold ways.

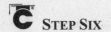 

Networking is the fine art of establishing and maintaining relationship with others who may provide valuable resources in the future. By building relationship with other people, you plant relational seeds that grow into a valuable harvest of future opportunities.

With whom should you network?

- Professors—Seek to find at least two or three professors in your program to serve as mentors to you. Networking with professors is essential since they typically provide a wealth of experience and knowledge both about the academic world (e.g., what class should you take next, how you can find an assistantship, what research will likely get published) and the professional world through their own network of alumni and friends. Ask for their advice on classes, research projects, internships, and career goals.
- Professionals—Often, graduate schools offer lectures or seminars presented by "outside" professionals in your particular area of study. Look to build relationships with "outside" presenters since they may serve as a great source for internship or future job contacts.
- Other Students—While most undergraduates "socialize" with other students, spend time networking with other students in your program. A relationship with a student who graduates a year or two before you may prove a valuable contact later when you are looking for a job.
- University Administrators—Though this may be difficult, seek a solid relationship with those who can help you within the university, such as financial aid administrators or academic advisors. A friendly relationship with a "gatekeeper" (a secretary or administrative assistant) to a university administrator may help open the door when others find it shut.
- Alumni—Don't forget to build relationship with the school's alumni. These individuals who financially support the university often want to help graduates obtain good jobs and further educational opportunities.

How do you network?

- Attend academic functions—Go to departmental socials, workshops, or special lectures.
- Go to conferences—Attend annual meetings in your field where other faculty and students gather.
- Never eat lunch alone—Connect with professors and other students as often as possible during meals.
- Send thank you notes—Show gratitude to those who have helped you.
- Let people know you are interested—Listen well and remember names.
- Take the initiative—Step out of your comfort zone and make the appointment to talk with a key contact in your area of study.
- Ask for advice—Professors and professionals often respond well to graduate students who are seeking genuine advice.

➢ *Go to Seminars Prepared*

The staple diet of many undergraduate programs is the lecture. Professors stand before classes and provide a monologue of information and analysis that students record in the form of notes and outlines. Class reading assignments often supplement or support the professor's lecture. Discussion is minimal. Students are assessed on how well they recall and reconstruct the information on tests or exams.

Many graduate students will experiences classes where professors lecture using a one-way communication style. But graduate students will also most likely experience a variety of classes that utilize a graduate "seminar" approach. Seminars may vary in exact approach, but generally there is an expectation in a seminar class that students will fully participate in class dialogue both with the professors and other students. In some seminars, the professor may intensively question students on the nuances of assigned reading, arguments, or research findings. In others, students may read and then debate papers they themselves have written. In still others, student may be required to present and defend new research findings or methods. Whatever the particular style of the seminar, graduate students are expected to fully engage in the discussion, explain or debate merits of other's arguments, and present thoughtful questions and answers.

How do you succeed in a seminar class environment?

- Always go to class prepared, since there is little chance of faking your way through the intensity of these dialogues. Don't call attention to yourself if, for some reason, you have not adequately prepared (e.g., don't raise your hand).
- Anticipate what your professor will ask and discuss. Know what types of questions, research areas, or findings your professor typically utilizes.
- Form a study group with other students. Before going to class, ask questions of each other, debate critical material, and anticipate discussion areas. Preview with others the particular theme of the seminar.
- Stay sharp. Get rest the night before these types of classes. These classes require students to think on their feet.

➢ **Learn to Write Well for Your Field**

For most programs, especially those that ultimately require a thesis, major final project, or dissertation, excellent writing skills are essential. Each program has a writing style and tone unique to it. Some styles are direct and factual. A few styles call for creativity. Many expect particular vocabulary. Successful students prepare to write well for their particular program.

- Take a refresher course in writing prior to beginning your graduate program.
- Read the journals or articles written in your field. Learn the unique writing style for your field.
- Learn the accepted methods for citing references and for avoiding plagiarism.
- Get advice from professors if you think your writing is below standard.
- Brush up on your vocabulary. Memorize the words essential to your field.
- Find a tutor or proofreader for your papers who can give recommendations for more acceptable writing.

➢ **Read Critically**

At the undergraduate level, professors assign reading often for the purposes of passing on foundational information. At the graduate level, it is expected that you already know the foundational content in your area and are now ready to critically assess the merits of an author's findings, arguments, or methodologies.

Here are some foundational questions to ask when reading critically:

*Who is the author and with what biases does he or she write?*

- What is the author's background and how does this influence his or her arguments or opinions (e.g., nationality, economic status, gender, education)?
- What are the author's credentials and does the author have a vested reason to argue his or her opinion (e.g., certifications, titles, degrees, positions held)?
- What are the author's direct or indirect biases and how do they appear in his or her opinions (e.g., strong likes, dislikes, prejudices)?
- What positive or negative experiences have flavored the author's point of view?

*Why did the author write this?*

- Is the author attempting to inform or persuade?
- What side of the issues did this author take? Are there other sides?
- What does the author ultimately want you to believe?
- Why is the author passionate about this issue?

*Are the author's research findings and arguments valid?*

- Are the research methods used by the author generally accepted in his or her field of research?

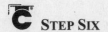 

- Do the conclusions that he or she reached directly support his or her findings or arguments?
- Are there alternative conclusions that he or she could have reached given his or her findings?
- Are the arguments complete or do they lack logical consistency?

The skill of critical reading is necessary in graduate school. If you want to work on this skill, begin by reading broadly from academic journals, journal your thoughts as you deconstruct and reconstruct various authors' work, learn acceptable research methodologies, and review the basics of logical argumentation.

➤ *Time Management is Self-Management*

Successful graduate learners maintain their forward momentum as students by managing to accomplish a multitude of tasks in an efficient and effective manner. To juggle the many responsibilities that fall to them, they learn that time management is really self-management.

Here are some important steps to self-management:

- Prioritize—Always do the most important tasks for your success first.
- Prime time—Learn what time of day you enter your peak performance stage and do your most critical work then.
- Push the non-essentials aside—Learn to say "no" and mean it.
- Piece together the puzzle—Use those ten- to fifteen-minute "open" slots to accomplish smaller but necessary tasks (e.g., review notes, memorize important facts, proofread a paper).
- Pull away—Don't forget to find time to rest and relax. Stress is a factor that all graduate students must acknowledge and manage.

## CONCLUSION

No graduate program guarantees that all students who enter their particular program will be successful. Instead, you as a beginning graduate student must take those important and critical steps to help yourself succeed. Be proactive. Take initiative. Be tenacious. Go succeed!

# Answers and Explanations:
## Step One

# FORM CODE GR 92-2

## SECTION 1—VERBAL REASONING

1. **(A)** This is a Thought Reversal item, as indicated by the coordinate conjunction "but," which sets up a contrast between how young members of the British theater are received onstage versus how they are received offstage. Offstage, they have been "relegated to relative obscurity," which means that onstage they must have gained some measure of recognition. Therefore, they would not have "had much *trouble* getting recognition." So, (A) is the best answer choice. As for (C) and (B), someone involved in the world of theater would certainly be "curious about" and ultimately "satisfied with," respectively, gaining public recognition. (D) is wrong because not being successful at gaining recognition parallels the idea of being relegated to obscurity. Finally, (E) is wrong because those persons involved in the theater would not be afraid of receiving recognition.

2. **(D)** This is a Thought Extension item, as indicated by the subordinate conjunction "because," which suggests a causal relationship between the first and second parts of the sentence. If an institution's reputation is "at the mercy of the actions of its members," then the misdeeds of such members would "discredit" ("injure") said reputation. So, (D) is the best answer choice. (A) and (C) are wrong because the misdeeds of an institution's members would serve neither to "reform" nor "honor" that institution. As for (B) and (E), while the misdeeds of individuals might be used to "coerce" or "intimidate," it is not made clear to what ends. Additionally, the term "discredit" most appropriately captures the idea of a tarnished reputation.

3. **(A)** This is a Combined Reasoning item, as indicated by two key logical signals that are important in understanding the overall structure of the sentence. First, a reversal of thought is indicated by the adverb "not" in the elliptical phrase "do not." So, the first blank must be filled with a word that means the opposite of "casual." All of the first word choices satisfy this meaning. Second, an extension of thought is indicated by the subordinate conjunction "since." If the first part of the sentence sets up a contrast between two groups of people, one that develops lung cancer and one that does not develop lung cancer, then the second blank must be filled with a word that describes in what way these two groups differ. They would differ in their "susceptibility to," or "sensitivity to," cancer-causing agents. So, (A) is the best answer choice. None of the other second word choices provide the necessary meaning. Do not be distracted by the *seemingly* illogical statement that casual smokers develop cancer and heavy smokers do not develop cancer; this comparison serves to prove a point: that individuals differ in their susceptibility.

4. **(C)** This is a Thought Extension item, as indicated by the logical structure of the sentence. The sentence describes a causal chain, so each element must follow logically from the previous element. The idea of being "independent" is synonymous with the idea of "freedom." So, if staunch independence makes one feel "isolated" and "lonely," then freedom would logically be perceived as a *negative* condition. (C) is the best answer choice; if freedom becomes "a negative" condition, then people will attempt to "escape" such freedom. Do not be distracted by (E); freedom as an "irreparable" ("impossible to repair") condition does not make sense; additionally, if such an idea did in fact make sense, it would not logically follow from isolation and loneliness.

5. **(E)** This is a Thought Extension item, as indicated by the second comma (punctuation clue) in conjunction with the material that follows. So, the blank must be filled with a word describing a bird that is "blithe" ("carefree") and leaves the mothering duties of incubating and nurturing to other birds. "Feckless," which means "having no sense of responsibility; indifferent; lazy" is the best answer choice. As for (D), "lackluster," which means "dull or without spirit," does not capture the character of behavior as does "feckless." Finally, as for the remaining answer choices, they all provide opposite meanings: "mettlesome" means "spirited; courageous"; "industrious" means "hard-working"; and "domestic" means "devoted to motherly affairs."

6. **(B)** This is a Thought Extension item, as indicated by the phrase "by denigrating" as well as the colon (punctuation clue) in conjunction with the material that follows. The first blank must be filled with a word that describes for what reason a company would "denigrate" a rival company in an ad campaign. Most likely, such tactics would be used to "tout" ("solicit" or "promote") one's own product. As for the second blank, "foolhardy" describes behavior that might backfire and be counterproductive to the advertiser. Do not be distracted by (A); a company might "criticize" a rival product in order to denigrate that rival campaign, but they would not criticize their own product.

7. **(D)** This is a Thought Reversal item, as indicated by the adverb "instead." While the semicolon signals a logical connection between the first and second parts of the sentence, the adverb "instead" suggests that the second blank must be filled with a word that has a meaning *opposite* to the first missing word. If a person's "imperturbability" ("ability to remain unfazed or unbothered") *fails* to reassure even his supporters, then his "probity," or "honesty," must be put into question. "Guile," which means "cunning dishonesty or manipulation," provides the appropriate opposite meaning. Of the remaining answer choices, only (E) provides a pair of near opposites; however, their meanings are inappropriate in this context.

8. **(C)** This is a Tools item. A GAVEL is a tool used by a JUDGE to maintain order in the courtroom; likewise, a "whistle" is a tool used by a "referee" to maintain order on the playing field. So, (C) is the correct answer choice. As for (A) and (D), while a "uniform" and an "insignia" might be defining characteristics of a "detective" and a "soldier," respectively, neither of these things functions as a tool. Do not be distracted by (B); while a "stethoscope" is a tool used by a "doctor," it is not used to maintain order. Finally, as for (E), while a "podium" is a place for a lecturer to stand, it is certainly not a tool used to maintain order.

9. **(B)** This is a Type Of item. A KIDNEY is a type of ORGAN; likewise, a "rib" is a type of "bone." So, (B) is the correct answer choice. As for (A) and (D), while a "kneecap" is part of a "skeleton" and a "stomach" is part of an "abdomen," respectively, neither of these pairs demonstrates a "type of" relationship. (C) is wrong because a "synapse" is not a type of "neuron" but instead the point of connection *between* two neurons. Finally, as for (E), while the "aorta" is a place for "blood," it is certainly not a type of blood.

10. **(E)** This is a Sequence item. Sequence analogies tend to indicate a cause and effect relationship. SOOT is the waste-product (effect) of COMBUSTION; likewise, "sawdust" is the waste-product (effect) of "woodcutting." So, (E) is the correct answer choice. As for (A) and (D), the sequences are inverted: "brushing" would occur in response to the presence of "lint," and "housecleaning" would occur in response to the presence of "rubbish," respectively. Do not be distracted by (B); while "gravel" would be the result of "crushing" rock, it cannot be inferred that it is simply the result of "crushing" (in general). Finally, as for (C), there is no clear logical relationship between "gristle" and "tenderizing." Meat is tenderized and meat contains gristle, but these relationships are not relevant to this item.

11. **(D)** This is a Tools item. To PURIFY something is the means for (tool for) removing IMPERFECTION; likewise, to "verify" something is the means for (tool for) removing "doubtfulness." So, (D) is the correct answer choice. As for (A), the relationship is not analogous; an "adjustment" is performed to "align" vertebrae. As for (B) and (C), while "weariness" is a sign of or defining characteristic of "boredom" and "disagreement" is a sign of or defining characteristic of "controversy," respectively, neither of the former is a means for removing the latter. Finally, as for (E), to "hone" something is not the means for removing "sharpness" but instead the means for creating "sharpness."

12. **(D)** This is a Tools item. A CENTRIFUGE is the tool used to SEPARATE one thing *from* another; likewise, a "colander" is the tool used to "drain" one thing *from* another. So, (D) is the correct answer choice. As for (A) and (B), while one would "calibrate" a "thermometer" or "chisel" a "statue," respectively, a "thermometer" is not a tool used to "calibrate," and a "statue" is certainly not a tool used to "chisel." As for (C), a "floodgate" is a tool used to *prevent* "overflow," not a tool used to *create* "overflow." Finally, as for (E), while a "television" is in fact a tool used to "transmit" signals, it is not used to separate signals.

13. **(E)** This is a Degree item. To MOCK someone is more extreme (in the negative direction) than to IMITATE someone; likewise, to "taunt" someone is more extreme (in the negative direction) than to CHALLENGE someone. So, (E) is the correct answer choice. As for (A), this pair of words does not exhibit a clear logical relationship; while "satire" is extreme, it would not be considered an extreme form of "charm." As for (B) and (C), while these pairs of words exhibit synonymous relationships, they do not involve matters of degree. Finally, as for (D), "adapt" and "duplicate" exhibit an inverted synonymous relationship. To "adapt" something is to make it *similar* to something else, and to "duplicate" something is to make an *exact* copy of something.

    Alternatively, this item can be categorized as Spurious Form. MOCKING might be considered a spurious form of IMITATION. Likewise, "taunting" might be considered a spurious form of "challenging."

14. **(D)** This is a Lack of Defining Characteristic item; the two words might be considered opposites. To be MALADROIT is to lack the defining characteristic of SKILL; likewise, to be "glib" is to lack the defining characteristic of "profundity." So, (D) is the correct answer choice. (A), (C), and (E) are wrong because these pairs of words exhibit synonymous relationships. Do not be distracted by (B); while reason and intuition are comparable ideas, "unreasonable" and "intuition" do not exhibit a clear logical relationship.

15. **(C)** This is a Defining Characteristic item. A defining characteristic of an EQUIVOCATION is that it is AMBIGUOUS; likewise, a defining characteristic of a "platitude" is that it is "banal." So, (C) is the correct answer choice. (A) and (E) are wrong because they are opposites. As for (A), "mitigation" is meant to resolve differences, so it would not be characterized as "severe." As for (E), an "explanation" would be considered "intelligible." (B) is wrong because the defining characteristic of a "contradiction" is that it is NOT "peremptory." Finally, while a "precept" is a tool that is put in place to make someone "obedient," a defining characteristic of a "precept" is NOT that it is "obedient."

16. **(B)** This is a Defining Characteristic item. A defining characteristic of a TEMPER is that it is VOLATILE; likewise, a defining characteristic of "wit" is that it is "ready." So, (B) is the correct answer choice. As for the remaining answer choices, while the first word in each pair might be used to describe the second word, in none of these cases is the former a defining characteristic of the latter.

17. **(B)** This is a Main Idea item. The primary purpose of the passage is to predict how all-volunteer military service will affect women's rights. (B), which refers to a reasoned "prognosis," or "prediction," of women's status in an all-volunteer military best captures this idea. As for (A), the passage does not refer to different types of assignments. As for (C), the passage suggests that an all-volunteer military would not be a model case of equal employment. (D) is wrong because the passage does not go so far as to analyze reforms necessitated by an all-volunteer military. Finally, as for (E), while "functional equivalence" is mentioned, its analysis is not the focus of the passage.

18. **(E)** This is a Specific Detail item. For this item, the phrase "occupational equality" functions as key material for locating the correct answer. In lines 7–8, that precise phrase is mentioned. In the next sentence, the passage states that the difficulty with such an institutional change is that women may not be assigned to combat jobs. Since combat jobs are military tasks that are typically assigned to men, (E) must be the correct answer choice.

19. **(A)** This is an Implied Idea item. In the first sentence of the passage, the author states that the present "all-volunteer armed forces…will eventually produce a gradual increase in the proportion of women [and women's assignments] in the armed forces." So, it can be inferred that this all-volunteer aspect is a factor conducive to a more equitable representation of women in the armed forces. As for (B), the author indicates that equality *will be* based on functional equivalence (lines 13–14). (C) is wrong because the author states that "a significant portion of the larger society remains uncomfortable" (lines 11–12) with extending equality to women in the armed forces. As for (D), the author states that a "growing emphasis on deterrence" will result in a more equitable representation. Finally, (E) is wrong because "restrictive" policies would not be conducive to equality.

20. **(B)** This is a Logical Structure item. This item asks specifically for the logical relationship between two ideas expressed by the author of the passage. In lines 4–6, the author suggests that "dramatic gains for women" in the military have not been made as expected. Then, as mentioned in the previous explanation, he or she states in lines 11–12 that "a significant portion of the larger society remains uncomfortable" with extending equality to women in the armed forces. So, it can be inferred that the lack of dramatic gains is a product of society's resistance to the equality of women in this particular arena. (B) best expresses this relationship between the two ideas.

21. **(A)** This is an Implied Idea item. For this item, locate the instances of the word "shergottites," and then make inferences about the given statements based on the adjacent material. Note that the second statement appears in all but one of the five answer choices. So, if this statement can be proven false, the correct answer becomes evident. In lines 23–26, the author states that the "shergottites" exhibit properties indicating that their source was a planet comparable in size to that of Mars. Since Earth is larger than Mars, the second statement is indeed false. So, (A) must be the correct answer choice. In lines 32–33, the author states that "shergottites" are speculated to have derived from an environment of volcanic activity, Io. As for the third statement, the author says in lines 34–37 that the chemical composition of Io's volcanic products is probably unlike that of the "shergottites," suggesting that they are not derived from a similar planetary body.

22. **(C)** This is a Specific Detail item. In lines 26–31, the author indicates that large planets are an unlikely source for meteorites because the gravitational pull of even a smaller body would prevent meteorites from escaping its orbit. (C) best captures this idea.

23. **(B)** This is an Implied Idea item. In lines 18–20, the author says that shergottites formed "3.5 billion years later than typical achondrites," so it can be inferred that their age is less than that of most achondrites, (B).

24. **(C)** This is a Specific Detail item. In the first paragraph, the author states the following: that igneous meteorites have undergone melting; that these same meteorites lack "chondrules"; and that "chondrules" are found in meteorites that were composed at the origin of the solar system. Therefore, the presence of chondrules in a meteorite indicates that it has not been melted since the formation of the solar system, (C).

25. **(E)** This is a Specific Detail item. In lines 41–42, the author states that there is photographic evidence of giant volcanoes on the Martian surface. So, (E) is the correct answer choice. As for the remaining questions, none of them are answered in the passage. The only reference to age in the passage appears in relation to the formation of shergottites (lines 19–20). In the second paragraph, while the author states that shergottites are the name given to anomalous achondrites, he or she fails to provide the origin of this name. As for (C), while the author states that there is a chemical similarity between Martian soil and the shergottites (last sentence of the passage), the specific shared properties are not mentioned. Finally, as for (D), the author refers to the volcanic activity of one of Jupiter's moons, Io.

26. **(D)** This is an Implied Idea item. For this item, a reversal of thought is indicated by the word "EXCEPT." So, the correct answer is *not* a consideration in determining if a planet is a source of shergottites. Of the five answer choices provided, the one not mentioned in relation to the possible source of shergottites is (D), the proximity of a planet to its moons. While one of Jupiter's moons (Io) is mentioned in relation to chemical composition, (E), its proximity to Jupiter is not. As for (A) and (B), a planet's size and proximity to Earth are considerations mentioned in lines 48–52. Finally, (C) is wrong because the strength of a planet's gravitational pull is considered in the third and fourth paragraphs.

27. **(B)** This is an Implied Idea item. In the first paragraph, the author states that only about 100 of the thousands of meteorites found on Earth are igneous. Then, he or she proceeds to explain that these igneous meteorites lack chondrules. So, it can be inferred that most of these meteorites contain chondrules, (B). As for (A), the author refers to shergottites, which are "crystallized" from molten rock; however, only three of these shergottites have thus far been discovered on Earth. As for (C), the passage makes no reference to "metals." Finally, (D)

and (E) are wrong because "sodium" and "sulfur," respectively, are mentioned in reference to the chemical composition of Io's surface.

28. **(B)** In this context, LIMP functions as an adjective that means "not firm"; therefore, "firm" provides the best opposite meaning. So, (B) is the correct answer choice.

29. **(A)** GLOBAL means "all-encompassing" or "far-reaching"; therefore, "local," which means "limited in scope" or "restricted," provides the best opposite meaning. So, (A) is the correct answer choice.

30. **(B)** STABILITY means "changelessness" or "constancy"; therefore, "inconstancy," which literally means "not constant" or "not stable," provides the best opposite meaning. So, (B) is the correct answer choice.

31. **(A)** DILATE means "to widen" (e.g., DILATED pupils); therefore, "narrow" provides the best opposite meaning. So, (A) is the correct answer choice.

32. **(C)** In this context, CONSOLE functions as a verb that means "to soothe pain"; therefore, "aggravate grief" provides the best opposite meaning. So, (C) is the correct answer choice. Do not be distracted by (B); while CONSOLING involves the reduction of suffering, the opposite of this idea is not to "reveal suffering."

33. **(A)** EXCULPATE means "to prove to be innocent"; therefore, "attribute guilt," which means the same thing as "to prove guilty," provides the best opposite meaning. So, (A) is the correct answer choice.

34. **(D)** ACCRETION means "to build slowly"; therefore, an anticipated opposite might move in one of two directions: "to reduce slowly" or "to build quickly." "Reduction in substance caused by erosion" describes a substance that is being slowly reduced over time. So, (D) provides the best opposite meaning.

35. **(D)** CADGE is a peculiar vocabulary word that means "to obtain something by imposing on another's generosity or friendship"; therefore, "earn," which means "to obtain something honestly and as a result of hard work," provides the best opposite meaning. So, (D) is the correct answer choice.

36. **(C)** ABJURE means "to renounce or retract"; therefore, "espouse," which means "to adopt or embrace," provides the best opposite meaning. So, (C) is the correct answer choice.

37. **(C)** SPECIOUS means "fallacious" or "false" and is typically related to an argument that is based on thin evidence or weak logic; therefore, "valid," which means "accurate" or "true" and is typically related to having strong or sound evidence, provides the best opposite meaning. So, (C) is the correct answer choice.

38. **(A)** QUOTIDIAN means "ordinary" or "common"; therefore, "extraordinary" provides the best opposite meaning. So, (A) is the correct answer choice.

## SECTION 2—QUANTITATIVE REASONING

1. **(B)** This is an Arithmetic Comparison item. Perform the indicated operation in Column B and convert the result to a decimal:

$$\frac{1}{2} + \frac{1}{3} = \frac{5}{6} = .8333$$

$.8333 > 8$, so (B) is the correct answer choice.

Alternatively, rather than finding a common denominator, convert the given fractions into equivalent decimals and then find their sum:

$$\tfrac{1}{2} + \tfrac{1}{3} = .5 + .333 = .8333$$

2. **(D)** This is an Arithmetic Comparison item. If Pat is older than Lee, and Lee is younger than Maria, it can be inferred that Lee is younger than both Pat and Maria. However, this information indicates nothing of the relationship between Pat's age and Maria's age. So, (D) is the correct answer choice.

3. **(A)** For this Algebra Comparison item, the most direct approach is to reason informally. If a value is divided by both 16 and 20, the result of the former division would be greater than the result of the latter division. So, (A) is the correct answer choice.

   Alternatively, if the above fact is not so obvious, assume a value for the area of the plots (e.g., 160) and then divide by the respective number of parcels to determine the number of acres in each plot:

   $$n = \tfrac{160}{16} = 10 \text{ acres}$$
   $$m = \tfrac{160}{20} = 8 \text{ acres}$$

4. **(D)** The best way to solve this Algebra Comparison item is to plug in some values for $x$ in Column A. Since $x > 1$, try 2 and 3:

   2: $2 - 4 = -2$, which is equal to Column B
   3: $3 - 4 = -1$, which is greater than Column B

   So, since Column A can either be equal to or greater than Column B, the relationship is indeterminate.

5. **(B)** This is a Geometry Comparison item. $\text{Area}_{\text{rectangle}} = l \cdot w$, where $l$ represents the length and $w$ represents the width. Since the rectangle has a perimeter of 40 and a width of 8, its perimeter can be expressed as $8 + 8 + l + l = 40 \Rightarrow 2l + 16 = 40$. Solve for $l$:

   $$2l + 16 = 40$$
   $$2l = 24$$
   $$l = 12$$

   Now, find the area of the rectangle:

   $$\text{Area}_{\text{rectangle } R} = 12 \cdot 8 = 96$$

   $256 > 96$, so (B) is the correct answer choice.

6. **(A)** This is an Algebra Comparison item. Use the FOIL (First, Outer, Inner, Last) method to simplify the expression in Column B:

   $$(2n+1)(2n-1) = 4n^2 - 2n + 2n - 1 = 4n^2 - 1$$

   Then, eliminate the like element from both columns ($4n^2$), which results in 0 in Column A and $-1$ in Column B. So, (A) is the correct answer choice.

   Alternatively, assume a few values for $n$, plugging them into each of the expressions and then comparing the columns. If $n = 1$:

   <u>Column A:</u> $4(1)^2 = 4$
   <u>Column B:</u> $[2(1)+1][2(1)-1] = (3)(1) = 3$

If $n = 0$:

Column A:  $4(0)^2 = 0$
Column B:  $[2(0)+1][2(0)-1] = (1)(-1) = -1$

If $n = -1$:

Column A:  $4(-1)^2 = 4$
Column B:  $[2(-1)+1][2(-1)-1] = (-1)(-3) = 3$

In each case, Column A is greater than Column B.

7. **(B)** This is an Algebra Comparison item. Since $0 < a < 1$ and $0 < b < 1$, $a$ and $b$ must be fractional values. Since the result of a fraction squared is a lesser fraction, the sum of two fractions must be greater than the sum of their squares. So, (B) is the correct answer choice.

Alternatively, if the above fact is not so obvious, substitute $\frac{1}{2}$ for each of the variables and then compare columns:

$(\frac{1}{2})^2 + (\frac{1}{2})^2 = \frac{1}{4} + \frac{1}{4} = \frac{1}{2}$ and $\frac{1}{2} + \frac{1}{2} = 1$

8. **(A)** This is a Geometry Comparison item. There is no information given regarding the dimensions of the triangle. However, a fundamental rule of triangles is that the sum of any two sides is always greater than the third side. So, $x + z$ must be greater than $y$, $y + z$ must be greater than $x$, and $x + y$ must be greater than $z$. So, (A) is the correct answer choice.

9. **(D)** For this Arithmetic Comparison item, there are no restrictions given for the value of $x$. If $x = 0$, the columns are both equal to 1. If $x < 0$, Column A is larger than Column B (e.g., $3^{-1} = \frac{1}{3}$ and $4^{-1} = \frac{1}{4}$). And if $x > 0$, Column B is larger than Column A (e.g., $3^1 = 3$ and $4^1 = 4$). So, (D) is the correct answer choice.

10. **(A)** This is a Geometry Comparison item. The opposite angles of a parallelogram must be equal since the figure consists of two sets of parallel sides. So, $3x = 4y$, and $x$ must therefore be greater than $y$.

Alternatively, set the opposite angles equal to each other and solve for $x$ and then $y$:

$3x = 4y \Rightarrow x = \frac{4}{3}y$
$3x = 4y \Rightarrow y = \frac{3}{4}x$

11. **(C)** This is an Arithmetic Comparison item. For a set of consecutive integers, the sum of the integers is equal to the mean of the integers multiplied by the number of integers. In the case of consecutive integers, the mean is equal to the median. Although time-consuming, the most straightforward and reliable approach to determining the number of integers and their median is to simply write them all down and count them. On the other hand, the following shortcut is much more efficient. In an inclusive consecutive set, the number of integers is simply the difference between the highest value and one less than the lowest value. Since the median is halfway between the lowest and highest values, it is twice the lowest value. So, in the case of Column A, the number of integers is $59 - (19-1) = 59 - 18 = 41$, and the median is $19 \cdot 2 = 38$. As for Column B, the number of integers is $60 - (22-1) = 60 - 21 = 39$, and the median is $22 \cdot 2 = 44$. $39 \cdot 44$ is clearly greater than $38 \cdot 41$, so Column B is greater.

Alternatively, since the two sets of numbers are nearly identical, compare only the differences between the two sets. Column A contains three numbers that are not in Column B: 19, 20, and 21. As for Column B, it contains one number that is not in Column A: 60. So, since $19 + 20 + 21 = 60$, it can be concluded that the two columns are equal.

12. **(B)** This is a Geometry Comparison item. If $y$ were equal to 0, then one would solve for $x$ in the equation to determine the coordinates. Likewise, if $x$ were equal to 0, then one would solve for $y$. This item essentially asks for a comparison to be made between the $x$-coordinate when $y$ is equal to 0, and the $y$-coordinate when $x$ is equal to zero. ($\overline{PO}$ is simply the distance to the center when $x = 0$, and $\overline{RO}$ is the distance to the center when $y = 0$.) Solve for $x$ and then for $y$:

$$y = \tfrac{8x}{9} + 3: \; 0 = \tfrac{8x}{9} + 3 \Rightarrow -3 = \tfrac{8x}{9} \Rightarrow -27 = 8x \Rightarrow x = -\tfrac{27}{8} = -3\tfrac{3}{8}$$
$$y = \tfrac{8x}{9} + 3: \; y = \tfrac{8(0)}{9} + 3 \Rightarrow y = 0 + 3 = 3$$

Remember that distance is always positive. So, since $3\tfrac{3}{8}$ is greater than 3, $\overline{RO}$ is greater than $\overline{PO}$.

Alternatively, since the given equation is written in the slope-intercept form $y = mx + b$ (where $m = $ slope), and the slope is equal to $\tfrac{\text{rise}}{\text{run}}$, $\tfrac{8}{9}$ is equal to $\tfrac{\overline{PO}}{\overline{RO}}$. Therefore, $\overline{RO}$ (horizontal change) is greater than $\overline{PO}$ (vertical change).

13. **(D)** This is an Algebra Comparison item. According to the given inequality, $a$ and $b$ are both negative. Remember, however, that they could be two negative fractions or two negative integers. If both values are negative fractions, then both columns are positive but Column A is greater:

Column A: $\;(-\tfrac{1}{4})(-\tfrac{1}{2}) = \tfrac{1}{8}$
Column B: $\;[(-\tfrac{1}{4})(-\tfrac{1}{2})]^2 = (\tfrac{1}{8})^2 = \tfrac{1}{64}$

If both values are negative integers, then both columns are positive but Column B is greater:

Column A: $\;(-1)(-2) = 2$
Column B: $\;[(-1)(-2)]^2 = (2)^2 = 4$

So, (D) must be the correct answer choice.

14. **(B)** For this Geometry Comparison item, first use the Pythagorean theorem ($a^2 + b^2 = c^2$) to determine the distance along the vertical wall before and after the 20-foot ladder is pulled 2 feet farther out from its base. Let $a$ equal the distance along the ground, let $b$ equal the distance along the vertical wall from the ground to the top of the ladder, and let $c$ equal the length of the ladder. Before the ladder is pulled, $a = 10$, $b$ is unknown, and $c = 20$. So:

$$10^2 + b^2 = 20^2$$
$$100 + b^2 = 400$$
$$b^2 = 300$$
$$b = \sqrt{300} = \sqrt{100} \cdot \sqrt{3} = 10\sqrt{3}$$

Since this item requires finding the difference between two distances ($x$), reason informally to approximate the decimal equivalent to $10\sqrt{3}$. $\sqrt{3}$ is between $\sqrt{1}=1$ and $\sqrt{4}=2$, but it is closer to $\sqrt{4}$. Therefore, it can be inferred that $\sqrt{3}$ is approximately equal to 1.7. So:

$$b = 10\sqrt{3} \approx 10 \cdot 1.7 = 17$$

After the ladder is pulled, $a = 12$, $b$ is unknown, and $c = 20$. So:

$$12^2 + b^2 = 20^2$$
$$144 + b^2 = 400$$
$$b^2 = 256$$
$$b = \sqrt{256} = 16$$

$x$ represents the difference between $b$ before the ladder is pulled and $b$ after the ladder is pulled. So, $x \approx 17 - 16 = 1$. Since $2 > 1$, (B) is the correct answer choice.

15. **(C)** This is an Arithmetic Comparison item. Factor Column A:

$$\frac{99^9}{9^{99}} : \frac{(9 \cdot 11)^9}{9^{99}} = \frac{9^9 \cdot 11^9}{9^9 \cdot 9^{90}} = \frac{11^9}{9^{90}}$$

So, the two columns are equal.

16. **(D)** This is an Arithmetic item. An appliance priced at \$300 with a sales tax of 5 percent costs $300 + (300 \cdot .05) = 300 + 15 = \$315$, and an appliance of the same price with a sales tax of 8 percent costs $300 + (300 \cdot .08) = 300 + 24 = \$324$. So, if the sales tax falls between 5 and 8 percent, the cost of the appliance could be between \$315 and \$324. (D) is the only answer choice that satisfies this condition.

17. **(D)** This is an Algebra item. Simplify the given expression:

$$2[2x + (3x + 5x)] - (3x + 5x)$$
$$2(2x + 8x) - 8x$$
$$2(10x) - 8x$$
$$20x - 8x = 12x$$

18. **(C)** This is an Arithmetic item. If $x$ and $y$ are positive integers and their sum is 3, then they must represent some combination of the integers 1 and 2 (either/or). The product of 1 and 2 is 2.

19. **(B)** This is an Algebra item. If $x - y = x$, then $y = 0$. So, if $x - y > x$, then $y < 0$. So, (B) is the correct answer choice.

Alternatively, assume a value for $x$ (e.g., 5):

$$5 - y > 5$$
$$-y > 0$$
$$y < 0$$

20. **(D)** For this Geometry item, what is important to understand is that the diameter of a circle is the maximum possible distance from one side of the circle to the other. If the radius of the circle is 2, then the diameter must be 4. And since 4 is the maximum possible distance from one side to the other, it is also the maximum possible distance between two points along a line that intersects the circle.

21. **(A)** According to the first pie graph, contributed commodities make up 19.5% of $60 million. Use 20% as an approximate percentage: $(60,000,000)(.20) = 12,000,000$. So, (A) is the closest answer choice.

22. **(D)** Since there are ten categories of expenditures, the average (arithmetic mean) expenditures per category is one-tenth of 100%, or 10%. At 10.1%, "new investments" is the closest to 10%.

23. **(B)** If 10% of $60 million is $6 million, then $2.9 million is a little less than 5% of $60 million. At 4.9%, "freight reimbursement" is the closest to 5%.

24. **(E)** For this item, simply find the sum of the four fractions of percents (rounded off for purposes of approximation):

    For "refugee housing," round 12.4% to 12%: $\frac{1}{3}(12\%) = 4\%$

    For "emergency workers," round 20.3% to 20%: $\frac{1}{5}(20\%) = 4\%$

    For "commodities," round 19.5% to 20%: $\frac{1}{4}(20\%) = 5\%$

    For "post-disaster assistance," round 13.1% to 13%: $\frac{2}{3}(13\%) \approx 9\%$

    $4 + 4 + 5 + 9 = 22\%$

    So, if 20% of $60 million is $12 million, then 22% of $60 million must be greater than $12 million. (E) is the only answer choice that satisfies this condition.

25. **(B)** Since each of the pie graphs represents the same value ($60 million), simply compare the percent values of the two categories mentioned rather than first finding their numeric value. Freight reimbursements make up 4.9% of the agency's income, and freight makes up 6.8% of its expenditures. So, $\frac{4.9}{6.8} = \frac{49}{68} = 0.72 = 72\%$ of the freight expenditures is covered by freight reimbursements, which means that $100\% - 72\% = 28\%$ of the freight expenditures is not covered.

26. **(C)** For this Geometry item, notice that $z°$ is part of $y°$. So, the figure can be simplified into a single equation: $x° + y° - z° = 180°$. Now, substitute the given values and solve for $z$:

    $x + y - z = 180$
    $110 + 120 - z = 180$
    $230 - z = 180$
    $230 = 180 + z$
    $z = 50$

27. **(A)** This is a Geometry item. The triangular region is a right triangle with a hypotenuse that equals 10 and a base that equals 6. These measurements indicate that the triangle is a 3-4-5 right triangle, so its height must be $4 \cdot 2 = 8$. $\text{Area}_{triangle} = \frac{b \cdot h}{2}$, so the area of the triangular region is $\frac{6 \cdot 8}{2} = \frac{48}{2} = 24$.

28. **(C)** This is an Algebra item. The widow received $\frac{1}{3}$ of her husband's estate, so the balance remaining for her sons was $1 - \frac{1}{3} = \frac{2}{3}$ of the original amount. Each of her sons received $\frac{1}{3}(\frac{2}{3}) = \frac{2}{9}$ of that original amount. In order to determine the amount of the estate, first find the common denominator between the widow's portion and each of the son's portions. As already stated, each son received $\frac{2}{9}$ of the estate, so the widow's $\frac{1}{3}$-share can be converted to $\frac{3}{9}$. Now, with common denominators, set up an equation to solve for the whole estate, $x$:

    $\frac{3}{9}x + \frac{2}{9}x = 60,000$

$$\frac{5}{9}x = 60,000$$

$$x = \frac{60,000}{\frac{5}{9}}$$

$$x = 60,000 \cdot \frac{9}{5}$$

$$x = \frac{540,000}{5}$$

$$x = 108,000$$

29. **(E)** This is an Algebra item. Remember that dividing by 0 is undefined. So, if $\frac{x+2}{y-3} = 0$, it must be that $x + 2 = 0$ and $y - 3 \neq 0$, in which case $x = -2$. (A), (B), and (C) can therefore be eliminated. As for $y$, since the denominator cannot be equal to 0, $y \neq 3$.

30. **(E)** For this Algebra item, the relationship between $x$, $y$, and $z$ may best be recognized by understanding certain similarities between fractions and decimals. The fractional equivalent of any decimal between 0 and 1 has the same properties as that decimal: the square of such a value always decreases in size, and the square root of such a value always increases in size. So, the inequality may be expressed as $(0.888)^2 < 0.888 < \sqrt{0.888}$, or $z < x < y$.

## SECTION 3—VERBAL REASONING

1. **(C)** This is a Combined Reasoning item, as indicated by two key logical signals that are important in understanding the overall structure of the sentence. First, a reversal of thought is indicated by the subordinate conjunction "although." Second, an extension of thought is indicated by the coordinate conjunction "and." The first blank must be filled with a word describing chimpanzees that are "easier to study." If the animals are less "shy," then they are easier to study. As for the remaining answer choices, if they are easier to study, they would most likely be *more* "interesting," *more* "manageable," *more* "poised," or *more* "accessible," respectively. "Although" indicates that while feeding wild chimpanzees makes them less shy and easier to study, there is also a negative result: "it is also known to disrupt their normal social patterns." While "upset," "inhibit," and "retard" provide meanings similar to that of "disrupt," (C) is the only answer choice that satisfies the first word choice.

2. **(D)** This is a Combined Reasoning item, as indicated by two key logical signals that are important in understanding the overall structure of the sentence. First, a reversal of thought is indicated by the subordinate conjunction "while." Second, an extension of thought is indicated by the coordinate conjunction "and" in conjunction with the phrase clue "consequently declining." "While" suggests that the second blank must be filled with a word that has a meaning opposite to that of "proliferate" ("to grow" or "to increase in number"). Additionally, the coordinate conjunction "and" signals that the second missing word must parallel the idea of a "decline." So, (A), (B), and (E) can immediately be eliminated. As for the first blank, the logical structure of the sentence dictates that it must be filled with a word indicating the *imbalance* between proliferation and decline; "incongruous," which means "inconsistent" or "not harmonious," is the best second word choice. So, (D) is the correct answer choice. The "diminishment" of religious ardor and consequential decline of church building in most of the eighteenth-century Western world was "incongruous" with the proliferation of monasteries in Bavaria at that time.

3. **(A)** This is a Combined Reasoning item, as indicated by two key logical signals that are important in understanding the overall structure of the sentence. In the first part of the sentence, an extension of thought is indicated by the subordinate conjunction "because," and a reversal of thought is indicated by the adverb "not." So, it can be inferred that the first blank must be filled with a word that means the opposite of "various meanings." "Univocal," which literally means "one voice," is the only first word choice that satisfies this meaning. The semicolon logically connects the first part of the sentence to the second part of the sentence. In the second part of the sentence, an extension of thought is indicated by the adverb "thus." So, if "mechanism"

and "vitalism" should *not* be considered "univocal" terms, the idea that they have single definitions would "thus" be considered "erroneous," or "incorrect."

4. **(E)** This is a Thought Extension item, as indicated by the coordinate conjunction "and," which logically joins the idea that follows it with the idea that precedes it. By definition, an "entrepreneur" is a person who exhibits "individual initiative." So, if such initiative "epitomized," or "defined," Americans in the 1890's, then the entrepreneur must have "personified," or "represented," the values of that age. So, (E) is the correct answer choice. Do not be distracted by (A); a "caricature" usually refers to a distorted image of a person or thing.

5. **(C)** This is a Combined Reasoning item, as indicated by two key logical signals that are important in understanding the overall structure of the sentence. First, an extension of thought is indicated by the semicolon (punctuation clue), which logically connects the first part of the sentence to the second part of the sentence. Second, a reversal of thought is indicated by the adverb "in fact." If neither philosophers nor ordinary people can do something by themselves (in this case, "change reality," as can be inferred from the second part of the sentence), then they ("in fact") can do it together. So, the second blank must be filled with a word that means something similar to "working together." As for the first blank, it must be filled with a word that has a meaning parallel to that of "change." Since "transform" and "alter" are the only first word choices that satisfy this meaning, (A), (B), and (D) can be eliminated. As for "interplay" and "intervention," only the former has the same meaning as "working together." So, (C) is the correct answer choice.

6. **(E)** This is a Thought Extension item, as indicated by the key word clues "revise" and "eliminate" in conjunction with the dash (punctuation clue). This sentence demonstrates a progression of thought regarding the extent to which art historians have tended to approach the concept of the Renaissance. They have not merely wanted to "revise," or "adjust," the concept but they have sought to "eliminate" its existence entirely. The material that follows the dash must therefore be an extension of this idea. "Contest," which means "to challenge with the hope of invalidating something," is the best answer choice. Art historians have sought to "contest" not only the uniqueness of the Renaissance but also its very existence.

7. **(B)** This is a Thought Extension item, as indicated by the subordinate conjunction "that." The missing word must therefore proceed from the idea of being "inured to…caprices." (Note the difficulty level of these vocabulary words.) "Inured" means "accustomed to" and "caprices" means "flighty, impulsive actions." If the employees had become accustomed to unpredictable personnel policies, then they would most likely greet the announcement of a dress code policy with something akin to indifference. "Impassivity," which means "an absence of emotion; apathy," is the best answer choice. None of the other answer choices provide the appropriate meaning.

8. **(E)** This is a Defining Characteristic item. A defining characteristic of a SURGEON is his or her DEXTERITY; likewise, a defining characteristic of an "acrobat" is his or her "agility." So, (E) is the correct answer choice. As for (A), there is no clear logical relationship between "engineer" and "clarity." As for (B), while a "sailor" would have an understanding of "navigation," the latter is not a defining characteristic of the former. As for (C) and (D), while a "magistrate" would set a "precedent" and an "industrialist" would most certainly possess "capital," the latter are not defining characteristics of the former.

9. **(B)** This is a Sequence item. To PRUNE (cause) a HEDGE is to neaten or beautify (effect) that HEDGE; likewise, to "trim" (cause) someone's "hair" is to neaten or beautify (effect) that person's "hair." So, (B) is the correct answer choice. Notice that both of these relationships involve grooming and maintenance. As for (A) and (D), to "shuck" ("remove the shell from") "corn" is to remove it from its husk for purposes of consumption and to "reap" a "crop" is to cut it for a harvest. In both cases, the result is practical, not aesthetic. As for (C), to "cut" a "bouquet" is to cut flowers for the purposes of arrangement, not to cut and groom the flowers themselves. Finally, do not be distracted by (E); to "shave" a "mustache" is different than to "trim" a mustache; the former implies removing the mustache altogether while the latter implies grooming.

10. **(C)** This is a Tools item. LIGHT is one of the resources (tools) by which a PHOTOGRAPH is created; likewise, "sound" is one of the resources (tools) by which a recording is made. So, (C) is the correct answer choice. As for (A) and (E), a "scene" is part of a "script," and a "song" might be part of a "concert," respectively; a "scene" is NOT a tool used to create a "script," and a "song" is NOT a tool used to create a "concert." As for (B) and (D), a "negative" is a type of "film," and a "rehearsal" is a type of "practice."

11. **(D)** This is a Tools item. An ANTIBIOTIC is a medicinal tool used to reduce an INFECTION; likewise, a "coagulant" is a medicinal tool used to reduce "bleeding." So, (D) is the correct answer choice. As for (A), a "hormone" is a substance that might undergo "modification." As for (B), an "enzyme" would be part of the "digestion" process. Finally, as for (C) and (E), "dependency" is a defining characteristic of "narcotic" use, and lack of "relaxation" is a defining characteristic of "stimulant" use, respectively.

Alternatively, this item can be categorized as Sequence. After an ANTIBIOTIC is administered, an INFECTION is reduced. Likewise, after a "coagulant" is administered, the "bleeding" is reduced.

12. **(D)** This is a Defining Characteristic item. A defining characteristic of a EULOGY ("funeral speech") is that it takes the form of PRAISE for someone who is deceased; likewise, a defining characteristic of an "elegy" ("funeral song") is that it takes the form of "lament" ("mourning") for someone who is deceased. So, (D) is the correct answer choice. Do not be distracted by (A); while "laughter" is a defining characteristic of "comedy," these ideas do not relate to respecting the deceased. As for (B) and (C), neither of these pairs of words exhibits a clear logical relationship. Finally, as for (E), a "parody" is defined by its lack of respect for something.

13. **(E)** This is a Sequence item. To DAMP is to reduce, or cause a reduction in, VIBRATION; likewise, to "stanch" is to reduce, or cause a reduction in, "flow" (e.g., the flow of water). So, (E) is the correct answer choice. As for (A), to "drench" is to cause an increase, not a reduction, in "moisture." As for (B), an "extraction" is a "concentrated" form of something. As for (C), one does not typically "boil" a "liquid" in order to cause a reduction in that liquid. Finally, as for (D), while one might "seal" a "perforation" or "perforate" something that is "sealed," this relationship does not exhibit the same quality of *reduction* as does that of the item stem.

14. **(E)** This is a Sequence item. ABRADED means "worn down"; FRICTION means "the rubbing together of two surfaces." So, something to which has been applied FRICTION (cause) becomes ABRADED (effect); and likewise, something to which has been applied "heat" (cause) becomes "vaporized" (effect). So, (E) is the correct answer choice. As for (A), "refined" is the defining characteristic of a "distillate" ("purified form"). As for (B), "anodized" is a type of "metal" that has been coated with a protective oxide. As for (C), while "gas" can be "diluted" ("made thinner") by mixing it with another liquid (e.g., water), "gas" is not the cause of the "diluted" mixture. Finally, (D) is wrong because the application of "pressure" results in a weakened, not a "strengthened," state of matter.

15. **(A)** This is a Sequence item. To QUARRY is the action by which STONE is produced at an actual quarry site; likewise, to "fell" a tree is the action by which "timber" is produced. (Note: QUARRY is used as a verb in this context as opposed to the more commonly used noun form.) So, (A) is the correct answer choice. As for the remaining answer choices, none of these relationships involve the idea of production; instead, they involve the idea of manipulation: to "dredge" a "canal" is to deepen the body of water; to "assay" is to analyze; to "bale" is to wrap for purposes of packaging; and to "mold" is to sculpt into a new shape.

16. **(B)** This is a Defining Characteristic item. A defining characteristic of someone who is a DUPE is that he or she is CREDULOUS ("believes anything"); likewise, a defining characteristic of a "boor" is that he or she is "insensitive." So, (B) is the correct answer choice. As for (A), (C), and (D) a "monarch," a "lawyer," and an "extrovert" may or may not be "wealthy," "argumentative," and "spontaneous," respectively. Finally, as for (E), a defining characteristic of a "miser" is that he or she is NOT "extravagant."

17. **(E)** This is a Logical Structure item. This item asks for the way in which the author develops the passage to treat the accepted generalizations made about organ transplantation. The author presents findings regarding liver transplants in rats, which serve to qualify the statements made at the beginning of the passage. So, (E) is the correct answer choice. As for (A) and (C), the author does not discuss the features of the generalizations themselves. (B) and (D) are wrong because the author neither suggests an alternative nor criticizes the generalizations but instead qualifies them with scientific findings.

18. **(C)** This is an Implied Idea item. In line 16, the author refers to "strains of rats" in reference to his or her hypothesis, which focuses on the immune-response reactions of rats. So, (C) is the best answer choice. (A) is wrong because the author makes no reference to the size of rats' livers. As for (B), "skin" is mentioned only as an example of a successful transplant when administered subsequent to that of the liver. (D) is wrong because "antigens" are mentioned only at the beginning of the passage in relation to the generalizations made about organ transplantation. Finally, (E) is wrong because the author refers to the concentration of, not the adaptability of, lymphocytes.

19. **(D)** This is a Specific Detail item. In lines 11–15, the author refers to the success of other organ transplants subsequent to that of the liver. In the second point of the proceeding hypothesis, the author theorizes that the focus of the immune-response system's attention is at the site of the liver transplant. (D) best captures this idea. As for the remaining answer choices, they do not offer reasons for the success of subsequent organ transplants.

20. **(A)** This is a Further Application item. This item asks for new data that would support the author's hypothesis. As for the first statement, the author makes no mention of stomach transplants. Likewise, as for the fourth statement, the author makes no mention of lymphocyte concentrations. The third statement would not support the author's hypothesis since the passage discusses only transplants from the same donor, and the theory revolves around why that specific donor's organs become accepted by the immune-response system. So, (A) is the correct answer choice. The second statement would strengthen the author's hypothesis. The author theorizes that the liver is especially effective at fighting off rejection by the immune-response system. So, increasing the strength of the immune-response reaction would logically induce rejection of the liver.

21. **(A)** This is a Main Idea item. The passage presents a neutral discussion of the director, David W. Griffith. So, (A) is the best answer choice. While all of the other answer choices are mentioned, none of them serve as the primary purpose of the passage.

22. **(D)** This is an Implied Idea item. For this item, a reversal of thought is indicated by the word "EXCEPT." The author makes no mention of Griffith's impact on "sound editing." So, (D) is the correct answer choice. As for the remaining answer choices, the author does indeed mention Griffith's impact on creative editing, camera shots, composition, and directing.

23. **(A)** This is an Implied Idea item. The author indicates that the conventional length of a film in 1911 was one reel (lines 45–47). He or she then proceeds to explain that Griffith's *Judith of Bethulia* in 1913 reached the unprecedented length of four reels, which was equal to one hour of running time (lines 49–52). From this information, two pieces of information can be deduced. First, one reel is equal to 15 minutes of running time. Second, prior to 1911 (and therefore prior to 1910), the typical film had a length of one reel and was therefore at most fifteen minutes in duration. So, (A) is the correct answer choice.

24. **(E)** This is a Specific Detail item. Just as with item #22, this item involves a reversal of thought, as indicated by the word "EXCEPT." As for (A) and (B), the author mentions that Griffith's early work dealt with social issues and included adaptations from Browning and Tennyson (lines 39–43), respectively. As already suggested in the explanation for item #22, Griffith introduced creative editing techniques, such as the flashback (line 29), (C). Finally, although the author mentions that Griffith was influenced by Victorian painting (lines 8–9), (D), and the Victorian novel (lines 34–35), there is no mention that he was influenced by Victorian theater. So, (E) is the correct answer choice.

25. **(B)** This is an Implied Idea item. As for the first statement, the author does not suggest that Griffith's use of the Victorian novel made it a popular source for film subjects. Instead, he or she states that Griffith implemented certain devices of the Victorian novel. As for the second statement, there is no reference made to the experimentations of other film directors. So, (B) must be the correct answer choice. As is offered in the third statement, Griffith proved false the apparent limitations of filmmaking through his artistic innovations.

26. **(C)** This is a Further Application item. This item asks for a statement with which Griffith would agree. Based on the information provided in the passage, (C) is the best answer choice. In the first paragraph, the author establishes that camera work is a foundational element in good filmmaking. As for (A), Griffith would most likely not agree with the idea of exploring new ideas as quickly as possible. (B) is wrong because Griffith seems to focus more on the technical aspects of filmmaking. (D) is wrong because the author points out that Griffith's work was quite eclectic (third paragraph). Finally, as for (E), Griffith seems to value both composition and editing.

27. **(D)** This is an Attitude/Tone Item. In the first paragraph, the author suggests that photography in the cinema before Griffith "consisted of little more than placing the actor before a stationary camera." So, the author would have a negative attitude toward such photography. (A), (B), and (C) can therefore be eliminated. (D), "condescending," best captures the author's tone. As for (E), the author does not exhibit an attitude as extreme as "hostility."

28. **(A)** ADHERE means "to hold or cling to something"; therefore, "detach," which means "to let go of something," provides the best opposite meaning. So, (A) is the correct answer choice.

29. **(D)** UNCONVENTIONALITY means "not conventional" or "not traditional"; therefore, "fidelity to custom," which means "faithful to tradition," provides the best opposite meaning. So, (D) is the correct answer choice.

30. **(C)** In this context, PINCH functions as a noun that means "a very small amount"; therefore, "abundant amount," which means "a great amount," provides the best opposite meaning. So, (C) is the correct answer choice. (Note: The noun PINCH can also be used to refer to a difficult or stressful period. The verb PINCH means "to squeeze.")

31. **(E)** OUTSET means "beginning"; therefore, "termination," which means "end," provides the best opposite meaning. So, (E) is the correct answer choice.

32. **(D)** RAREFY means "to make thin" or "to refine"; therefore, "make more dense" provides the best opposite meaning. So, (D) is the correct answer choice.

33. **(B)** EFFRONTERY means "an assertiveness that is considered to be rude"; therefore, "deference," which means "passivity" or "extreme politeness," provides the best opposite meaning. So, (B) is the correct answer choice.

34. **(B)** SCURVY typically functions as a noun that refers to a disease cause by a lack of vitamin C. In this context, however, it functions as an adjective that means "contemptible" or "corrupt"; therefore, "above reproach," which means "without fault" or "honest," provides the best opposite meaning. So, (B) is the correct answer choice.

35. **(A)** OBDURATE means "stubborn" (especially with regard to resisting persuasion); therefore, "complaisant," which means "willing to please and compliant to orders or commands," provides the best opposite meaning. So, (A) is the correct answer choice.

36. **(D)** AVER means "to assert something as true"; therefore, "deny," which means "to state that something is not true," provides the best opposite meaning. So, (D) is the correct answer choice.

37. **(E)** PITH means "the important or essential part of something"; therefore, "superficial element," or "insignificant element," provides the best opposite meaning. So, (E) is the correct answer choice.

38. **(A)** SUPINE means "relaxed and indifferent"; therefore, "vigilant," which means "alert and wary," provides the best opposite meaning. So, (A) is the correct answer choice.

## SECTION 4—QUANTITATIVE REASONING

1. **(A)** This is an Arithmetic Comparison item. Use the "flying-x" method to perform the indicated operations; then, compare columns:

   Column A: $\frac{4}{5} - \frac{4}{7} = \frac{4(7) - 5(4)}{5(7)} = \frac{28 - 20}{35} = \frac{8}{35}$

   Column B: $\frac{4}{7} - \frac{2}{5} = \frac{4(5) - 2(7)}{5(7)} = \frac{20 - 14}{35} = \frac{6}{35}$

   $\frac{8}{35} > \frac{6}{35}$, so (A) is the correct answer choice.

2. **(C)** This is an Arithmetic Comparison item. The arithmetic mean (average) of a group of values is the sum of those values divided by their number. For this item, recognize that one of the three values in each column is the same, one of the three values in Column A is 1 unit greater than one of the values in Column B, and one of the three values in Column B is 1 unit greater than one of the values in Column A. So, the sum and therefore the average of each group of values is the same.

   Alternatively, since each column seeks to find the average of three values, simply find the sum of the values in each column and then compare results:

   Column A: $87 + 95 + 130 = 312$
   Column B: $88 + 95 + 129 = 312$

3. **(B)** For this Arithmetic Comparison item, use the formula for distance (distance = rate • time) to solve for time. Since distance and rate are given, let $t$ represent time:

   Column A: $300 = 52 \cdot t \Rightarrow t = \frac{300}{52} = 5.8$
   Column B: $240 = 40 \cdot t \Rightarrow t = \frac{240}{40} = 6$

4. **(A)** This is an Arithmetic Comparison item. Column A contains a negative integer with an even exponent; therefore, the resulting quantity is positive. Column B contains a negative number with an odd exponent; therefore, the resulting quantity is negative. So, (A) is the correct answer choice.

5. **(C)** This is an Arithmetic Comparison item. Column A is the total amount paid by Ms. Rogers after the $120 down payment and 12 monthly payments of $28 each. The reference to "in excess of" simply indicates that she ultimately paid more than the cash price, which is $400. So, calculate the amount that she paid and then subtract 400 from that value:

   $120 + 12(28) = 120 + 10(28) + 2(28) = 120 + 280 + 56 = 456$
   $456 - 400 = 56$

6. **(B)** This is a Geometry Comparison item. The best way to solve this item is to recognize some properties of chords. A chord is a straight line from one point on a circle to another point on the circle. The longest possible chord is the diameter of the circle, which is also the greatest possible distance between two points on a circle. A chord becomes smaller as the points move closer together, and the points move closer together the further

the chord is from the center of the circle. All of these facts are made visible in the diagram. So, the larger of the two chords is the one closest to the center, which is $\overline{XY}$.

7.  **(B)** This is an Algebra Comparison item. Factor $n$ out of each equation so that $x$ and $y$ more comparable:

$$\frac{n}{x} = 428 \Rightarrow n = 428x$$
$$\frac{n}{y} = 107 \Rightarrow n = 107y$$

Now, notice that 107 can be factored out of both of the equations:

$$n = 428x \Rightarrow n = 4x$$
$$n = 107y \Rightarrow n = y$$

So, since $y = 4x$, $y$ is larger.

Alternatively, recognize that when dividing a value by a larger number, the quotient is smaller than when dividing it by a smaller number. Since the quotient in Column B (107) is smaller than that in Column A (428), $y$ must be larger than $x$.

8.  **(D)** This is a Geometry Comparison item. At first glance, since it is given that the two lines are parallel, it appears that the "big angle/little angle" theorem could be put into use. However, even though $r + s = 180$, their individual measures are unknown. Therefore, since $s$ could be greater than, less than, or equal to 60, the relationship cannot be determined.

9.  **(A)** This is an Algebra Comparison item. Simply perform the necessary calculations for each statement:

6 is $x$ percent of 24: $x = \frac{6}{24} = \frac{1}{4} = .25 = 25\%$

$y$ is 25 percent of 96: $y = \frac{1}{4}(96) = \frac{96}{4} = 24$

So, (A) is the correct answer choice.

10. **(B)** This is an Algebra Comparison item. For this item, assume some values for $x$ and then plug them into the first expression. Since $x > 2$, try 3:

$$2(3) + y < 3 \Rightarrow 6 + y < 3 \Rightarrow y < -3 \text{ (If } y < -3, \text{ then } y \text{ must be less than 0.)}$$

Now, try 4:

$$2(4) + y < 3 \Rightarrow 8 + y < 3 \Rightarrow y < -5 \text{ (If } y < -5, \text{ then } y \text{ must be less than 0.)}$$

So, if the value of $y$ decreases as the value of $x$ increases, $y$ will always be less than 0. Therefore, (B) is the correct answer choice.

Alternatively, if $x > 2$, then $2x > 4$. If $2x$ were equal to 4, then $4 + y < 3$, which would imply that $y < -1$. So, $y$ must be less than 0.

11. **(C)** This is a Geometry Comparison item. If the perimeter of square $S$ is equal to the perimeter of the given rectangle, then the perimeter of the square is:

$$2(x) + 2(x + 6) = 2x + 2x + 12 = 4x + 12$$

And one of its four equal sides is:

$$\frac{4x+12}{4} = x+3$$

So, the two columns are equal.

12. **(D)** For this Algebra Comparison item, first assume some obvious whole number values for $a$, $b$, and $c$ (e.g., $0 < 2 < 3 < 4$) and compare columns:

Column A:  $\frac{b}{a} = \frac{3}{2} = 1\frac{1}{2}$

Column B:  $\frac{c}{b} = \frac{4}{3} = 1\frac{1}{3}$

In this case, Column A is greater than Column B. Note, however, that different assumed whole number values (e.g., $0 < 2 < 3 < 15$) can change the comparison:

Column A:  $\frac{b}{a} = \frac{3}{2} = 1\frac{1}{2}$

Column B:  $\frac{c}{b} = \frac{15}{3} = 5$

In this case, Column B is greater than Column A. If increasing the value of $c$ is not so obvious, assume some fractional values for the three variables (e.g., $0 < \frac{1}{4} < \frac{1}{3} < \frac{1}{2}$) and compare columns:

Column A:  $\frac{b}{a} = \frac{\frac{1}{3}}{\frac{1}{4}} = \frac{1}{3}(4) = \frac{4}{3} = 1\frac{1}{3}$

Column B:  $\frac{c}{b} = \frac{\frac{1}{2}}{\frac{1}{3}} = \frac{1}{2}(3) = \frac{3}{2} = 1\frac{1}{2}$

Again, in the case of the assumed fractional values, Column B is greater than Column A. Therefore, (D) is the correct answer choice.

13. **(A)** This is a Geometry Comparison item. This item deals with the relationship of $\pi$ to the circumference and diameter of a circle. $\pi$ is defined as the ratio of the diameter of a circle to the circumference. The circumference is equal to the product of the diameter and $\pi$, or twice the radius and $\pi$ ($2\pi r$). The circle in the centered information has a radius of 3, so it has a diameter of 6 and a circumference of $6\pi$. The ratio is expressed as $\frac{6\pi}{6}$, which is simply reduced to $\pi$. Since $\pi$ is approximately 3.14, Column A is greater.

14. **(D)** This is an Algebra Comparison item. First, use the "flying-x" method to simplify Column A:

$$\frac{3}{r} + \frac{4}{t} = \frac{3t + 4r}{rt}$$

Since both quantities have the same numerator, cancel it out by dividing each of them by $3t + 4r$. The result is a comparison between $rt$ and $r + t$. Since no information is provided for either $r$ or $t$, the relationship cannot be determined.

15. **(C)** This is a Geometry Comparison item. Consider the properties of the given figure. First, the angle opposite $x$ is also equal to $x$. Second, the angle adjacent to $z$ creates a line that measures 180 degrees. The measure of this angle can be written as $180 - z$. Finally, the sum of the measures of the three interior angles in the triangle is equal to 180.

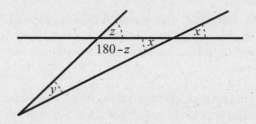

Therefore:

$$y + x + 180 - z = 180$$
$$y + x - z = 0$$
$$y + x = z$$
$$y = z - x$$

Alternatively, solve this item by recognizing two particular geometric properties. First, vertical angles are equal, so the angle vertical to that with measure $x$ is also of measure $x$ (see figure above). Second, the measure of an exterior angle of a triangle is equal to the sum of the remote interior angles. So, in this case, $z = x + y \Rightarrow y = z - x$.

16. **(E)** This is an Arithmetic item. For this item, simply perform the indicated operations:

$$\frac{9^2 - 6^2}{3} = \frac{81 - 36}{3}$$

Then, factor to ease the manipulation:

$$\frac{81 - 36}{3} = \frac{27(3) - 12(3)}{1(3)} = \frac{27 - 12}{1} = \frac{15}{1} = 15$$

17. **(C)** This is an Arithmetic item. The units to the left of the decimal are the tenths, hundredths, thousandths, ten thousandths, etc. Thus, the thousandths place is the third number to the right of the decimal. In this case, the thousandths place rounds up from 3 to 4. (Note that the number to the right of the thousandths place is greater than 5.)

18. **(A)** This is an Algebra item. Distribute and then solve for $x$:

$$3(x + 2) = x - 4$$
$$3x + 6 = x - 4$$
$$2x + 6 = -4$$
$$2x = -10$$
$$x = -5$$

19. **(E)** This is an Algebra item. $(x + y)^4$ can be understood as $(x + y)^2 \cdot (x + y)^2$. Using the FOIL method, $(x + y)^2$ can be rewritten as $x^2 + 2xy + y^2$. Since the item stem states that this expression is equal to 9, the whole thing can be written as $(x + y)^4 = 9 \cdot 9 = 81$.

20. **(B)** This is a Geometry item. Although this item references the coordinate system, in actuality, it asks for a direct proportion: as $x$ increases, $y$ increases proportionally. So, set up the proportion and cross-multiply:

$$\frac{3}{4.8} = \frac{2}{y} \Rightarrow 3y = 9.6 \Rightarrow y = 3.2$$

21. **(C)** For this item, refer to the upper left-hand graph, which deals with public and private health expenditures. Find the number of years when the percent for private expenditures was at least twice what it was for public

expenditures. In 1975 and 1976, the private expenditures were in the vicinity of 70% and the public expenditures were in the vicinity of 30%. In 1977, however, the private expenditures were *less* than twice the public expenditures, and the difference between the two continued to narrow as the years went on. So, (C) is the correct answer choice.

22. **(B)** For this item, refer to the bottom left-hand graph, which deals with national health expenditure per capita. In 1984, per capita spending appears to have been about $490. So, find the year when per capita spending was roughly half of $490, or $245. In 1977, it appears to have been just below $250. So, (B) is the correct answer choice.

23. **(D)** This item requires the percent change formula, which is $\frac{\text{Change}}{\text{Original}}$. The difference in the national health expenditure per capita between 1981 and 1982 appears to have been about $420 - \$380 = \$40$. Since per capita spending for 1981 was about $380, the percent increase between those two years was $\frac{40}{380} = .105 \approx 10\%$.

24. **(A)** This item asks for the amount of public expenditures (in billions of dollars) in 1980. According to the upper left-hand graph, the percent of public expenditures that year was about 36%. According to the right-hand graph, the national expenditures that year totaled about $68 billion. So, $68 \cdot .36 = 24.48 \approx 25$.

25. **(C)** This item requires some understanding of the general terminology used. Basically, "per capita" refers to the average per person. So, the population of Country $X$ in 1977 can be determined by dividing the per capita average into the total expenditures for that year. In 1977, the per capita average was about $250 (per person). The total expenditures for that year were about $47 billion. Therefore, the country's population in 1977 was approximately $\frac{47,000,000,000}{250} = 188,000,000$. (C) is the closest answer choice.

26. **(C)** This is an Arithmetic item. There is a difference of 10 between 5 and fifteen, and the number that is twice as far from 5 as from 15 will be equal to $5 + (\frac{2}{3} \cdot 10) \Rightarrow 5 + 6\frac{2}{3} = 11\frac{2}{3}$.

27. **(E)** This is an Arithmetic item. The total number of stamps in Jane's collection must be divisible by the sum of its parts. If she has "3 times as many" Canadian stamps than she does non-Canadian stamps, the ratio of the former to the latter is $3 : 1$, and the sum of the ratio parts is $3 + 1 = 4$. So, the correct answer is the number that CANNOT be divided evenly by 4, which is 54.

28. **(A)** This is a Geometry item. Based on the given information, the area of the larger square is $1 \cdot 1 = 1$. So, the area of the smaller square is $\frac{1}{2}$, which means that each of its sides is $\sqrt{\frac{1}{2}}$. Since $\sqrt{1} = 1$, $\sqrt{\frac{1}{2}} = \frac{1}{\sqrt{2}}$. Now, since the diagonal of a square is also the hypotenuse of an isosceles right triangle, the diagonal is equal to the product of one of the triangle's sides and $\sqrt{2}$. For the larger triangle, one of its sides is equal to 1, so its diagonal is $1 \cdot \sqrt{2} = \sqrt{2}$. For the smaller triangle, one of its side is equal to $\frac{1}{\sqrt{2}}$, so its diagonal is $\frac{1}{\sqrt{2}} \cdot \sqrt{2} = \frac{\sqrt{2}}{\sqrt{2}} = 1$. So, the difference between the two diagonals is $\sqrt{2} - 1$.

Alternatively, based on the given information, assume that the area of the larger square is $1 \cdot 1 = 1$. Therefore, the area of the smaller square is $\frac{1}{2}$, which means that each of its sides is $\sqrt{\frac{1}{2}}$. Next, use the Pythagorean theorem $(a^2 + b^2 = c^2)$ to determine the length of each diagonal, which is also the hypotenuse of a right triangle. The diagonal of the larger square is:

$$1^2 + 1^2 = c^2$$
$$2 = c^2$$
$$c = \sqrt{2}$$

The diagonal of the smaller square is:

$$(\sqrt{\tfrac{1}{2}})^2 + (\sqrt{\tfrac{1}{2}})^2 = c^2$$
$$\tfrac{1}{2} + \tfrac{1}{2} = c^2$$
$$1 = c^2$$
$$c = 1$$

And the difference between the two diagonals is $\sqrt{2} - 1$.

29. **(D)** This is an Algebra item. This item is essentially a distance problem. To determine the rate of flow out at spout $B$, use the distance formula ($\text{distance} = \text{rate} \cdot \text{time}$), where the volume of the drum (64 gallons) represents the distance; the time is 96 hours; and the rate is the difference between the rate of flow through spout $A$ ($\text{rate}_{\text{spout } A}$), which is 2 gallons per hour, and the rate of flow out at spout $B$ ($\text{rate}_{\text{spout } B}$):

$$\text{distance} = (\text{rate}_{\text{spout } A} - \text{rate}_{\text{spout } B}) \cdot 96$$
$$64 = (2 - \text{rate}_{\text{spout } B}) \cdot 96$$
$$64 = 192 - 96(\text{rate}_{\text{spout } B})$$
$$64 + 96(\text{rate}_{\text{spout } B}) = 192$$
$$96(\text{rate}_{\text{spout } B}) = 128$$
$$\text{rate}_{\text{spout } B} = \tfrac{128}{96}$$

Simplify by dividing both the numerator and the denominator by 2 until the fraction can be reduced no further:

$$\text{rate}_{\text{spout } B} = \tfrac{128}{96} = \tfrac{64}{48} = \tfrac{32}{24} = \tfrac{16}{12} = \tfrac{8}{6} = \tfrac{4}{3}$$

Alternatively, reason informally to solve this item. If spout $A$ flows at a rate of 2 gallons per hour for 96 hours, then a total of 192 gallons flow into the drum. Since the drum contains 64 gallons of distillate after 96 hours, subtract this amount from the total gallons that flow into the drum in order to determine the total amount pumped out of the drum: $192 - 64 = 128$ gallons. Then, divide this amount by the total pumping time to determine the rate of flow at spout $B$: $\tfrac{128}{96} = \tfrac{4}{3}$.

30. **(C)** This is a Geometry item. The area of the smaller field, or $K$, can be represented as $LW$, where $L = \text{length}$ and $W = \text{width}$. Therefore, the larger field could be represented as $2L \cdot 4W$. Since $2 \cdot 4 = 8$, the area of the larger field must be 8 times larger than the smaller field, or $8K$. So, the area of the larger field is greater than the area of the smaller field by $8K - K = 7K$.

# Answers and Explanations:
## Step Three

# Verbal Reasoning

# VERBAL REASONING SKILLS REVIEW

**EXERCISE 1—CREATING DIAGNOSTIC SENTENCES** (p. 36)

1. A CRUSADER fights for or defends a CAUSE.

2. **X**

3. A DEBUT is the BEGINNING of something.

4. To act out of IMPULSE is to act without DELIBERATION.

5. **X**

6. **X** (Although someone might predict a disaster, it is not part of the meaning of DISASTER that it must be predicted. Nor is it a part of the meaning of PREDICTION that it must be a PREDICTION of a DISASTER.)

7. **X** (Although a NOMAD might live in the MOUNTAINS, it is not necessary to live in the MOUNTAINS to be a NOMAD. Conversely, MOUNTAINS are still MOUNTAINS without a NOMAD living on it.)

8. **X**

9. IMITATION is the lack of ORIGINALITY.

10. VAPORIZATION is the process that characterizes something that is VOLATILE.

11. The place for a SPEAKER is on the DAIS.

12. **X** (PHOTOSYNTHESIS is characteristic of plants, and though there may be many plants in the TROPICS, PHOTOSYNTHESIS is not confined to the TROPICS.)

13. The SHOULDER is the place for an EPAULET.

14. A COMPLIMENT shows APPROBATION.

15. Someone who is INTREPID is without FEAR.

16. OPULENCE is great WEALTH.

17. **X**

18. Someone who is MALADROIT is totally lacking in SKILL.

19. **X** (Although CONFUSION might sometimes be funny [as in a play or a movie], there is no necessary connection between CONFUSION and LEVITY.)

20. Something that is MOTLEY is characterized by VARIETY.

21. **X**

22. **X** (Although a REVOLUTION might overthrow a MONARCH, there is no tight connection between these ideas. A REVOLUTION might or might not be aimed at a MONARCH, and a MONARCH might or might not have to deal with a REVOLUTION.)

23. **X**

24. To EQUIVOCATE is to be unclear in one's meaning, so equivocation is defined by a lack of CLARITY.

25. That which is ODIOUS inspires disgust or REPULSION.

26. A SOOTHSAYER predicts events of the FUTURE.

27. **X**

28. Something that is EXCRUCIATING is PAINFUL to a very great degree.

29. **X**

30. A SINECURE is a position or office that brings compensation to its holder without the need of EMPLOYMENT.

31. An OAR is the tool used to propel a BOAT.

32. **X**

33. **X**

34. A CASINO is a place where GAMBLING occurs.

35. **X** (Although there is a possible connection here [one might put SYRUP on APPLES], there is no tight connection.)

36. **X**

37. A LISP is a type of SPEECH.

38. A SPRINT is a faster form of running than a JOG.

39. **X** (Although DRAWER may mean either a storage bin or a person who sketches, neither meaning has a necessary connection with PAINT.)

40. A QUARRY is the place where ROCK is mined.

41. To SCRIBBLE is a way to WRITE.

42. **X**

43. **X**

44. A PASTEL is a kind of COLOR.

45. **X**

46. **X** (Although TARGET and WOUND might seem to have something to do with weapons, there is no necessary connection between TARGET and WOUND themselves.)

47. The KEYSTONE is a part of an ARCH.

48. **X**

49. **X** (Although both of these are character traits, there is no necessary connection between BRAZEN and TRUSTWORTHY themselves.)

50. **X**

51. A QUIVER is the place where an ARROW is stored.

52. To MELT something forms a LIQUID.

53. CHAOS is the total absence of ORDER.

54. **X** (Although both are geographical features, there is no necessary connection between a PLATEAU and a RIVER.)

55. **X**

56. **X** (One might or might not ADMIRE a COMPETITOR.)

## EXERCISE 2—UNDERSTANDING ANALOGY RELATIONSHIPS (p. 41)

1. **S**: A person is first CONDEMNED and then EXECUTED.

2. **DC**: ORIGINALITY is a defining characteristic of an INVENTION.

3. **DC**: A lack of CITIZENSHIP is a defining characteristic of an ALIEN.

4. **DC**: The defining characteristic of an ERROR is that it is FALLACIOUS.

5. **D**: MORTIFICATION is a more extreme level of EMBARRASSMENT.

6. **LO**: One cannot EXPRESS something that is INEFFABLE (by definition).

7. **DC**: The defining characteristic of something that will PERISH is that its life is EPHEMERAL ("not lasting").

8. **TO**: A TARANTULA is a type of ARACHNID.

9. **LO**: The behavior of a person who exhibits a lack of HASTE would be characterized as PROCRASTINATION.

10. **S**: A person will PROSELYTIZE about something in order to create a CONVERSION in someone else's thinking.

11. **DC**: The defining characteristic of a PARIAH is that he or she is the recipient of SCORN.

12. **LO**: A lack of SENSE is a defining characteristic of one who experiences DELERIUM.

13. **TO**: A PROTAGONIST ("hero") is a type of CHARACTER.

14. **LO**: A lack of CARE is the defining characteristic of NEGLIGENCE.

15. **S**: After a patient makes a RECOVERY, he or she may RELAPSE into illness.

16. **LO**: A lack of CARE is a defining characteristic of one who is IDLE ("lazy").

17. **DC**: The defining characteristic of someone who is GARRULOUS is that he or she will TALK a great deal.

18. **S**: If a consumer were to DEFAULT on his or her payments, then there would be a FORECLOSURE on his or her assets.

19. **D**: MANIA is a greater degree of ENTHUSIASM.

20. **DC**: Making PROPHECY is a defining characteristic of a SOOTHSAYER.

21. **LO**: Lack of CONSCIOUSNESS is the defining characteristic of a COMA.

22. **DC**: KNOWLEDGE is a defining characteristic of a PUNDIT ("learned person").

23. **DC**: A defining characteristic of a PHILANTHROPIST is that he or she shows BENEVOLENCE to humankind.

24. **LO**: Lack of ORNAMENTATION is the defining characteristic of AUSTERITY.

25. **S**: EVICTION from a place follows RESIDENCE in that place.

26. **PF**: A COURTROOM is a place for a JUDGE.

27. **PO**: A STAR is a part of a GALAXY.

28. **PO**: A NOTE is a part of a SCALE.

29. **T**: A CHISEL is a tool used by a SCULPTOR.

30. **PF**: A SNIFTER is a goblet in which to serve BRANDY.

31. **D**: OBSEQUIOUSNESS ("servile compliance") is a more extreme form of OBEDIENCE.

32. **SO**: To GRIMACE is to show a sign of PAIN.

33. **S**: A VACCINATION is administered to a person in order to provide him or her with IMMUNITY to a disease.

34. **T**: A BUFFER is a tool used to reduce SHOCK.

35. **PO**: LUNCH is one part of a WORKDAY.

36. **D**: To GUZZLE ("to drink a great deal at a rapid rate") is more extreme than to SIP ("to drink a very small amount").

37. **T**: An AX is a tool used by a LUMBERJACK to cut wood.

38. **D**: A BATTLE is more extreme than a TIFF ("small disagreement").

39. **PO**: A MAST is the part of a SHIP used to support the sails.

40. **PF**: A CITADEL ("fortress") is a place for which to protect oneself from ATTACK.

41. **S**: An APPETIZER is served before the meal, and DESSERT is served after the meal.

42. **TO**: JOY is a type of EMOTION.

43. **T**: A BOW is the tool used to play a CELLO.

44. **PF**: A SEMINARY is the place for a THEOLOGIAN in training.

45. **S**: To SAND wood, for example, is to create SMOOTHNESS along the wood's surface.

46. **S**: A cat, for example, will first CROUCH and then SPRING after a mouse.

47. **S**: As time passes, the process of EROSION will eventually create a GULLY.

48. **T**: A COLANDER is a tool used by a CHEF to separate food from water.

49. **TO**: A TERMITE is a type of INSECT.

## EXERCISE 3—CREATING PARALLEL RELATIONSHIPS (p. 44)

1. speak, talk
2. clock, watch
3. patient
4. bat
5. fire, flame
6. feather
7. success
8. funds, money
9. migrate
10. student
11. cheerfulness
12. thrift, frugality
13. condemnatory
14. witness
15. mortified
16. plant
17. doctor
18. paper
19. raincoat
20. arm
21. weight
22. moth
23. frigid, frozen
24. people
25. cup, pot
26. fur
27. blueprint
28. animal
29. substance
30. farewell, goodbye

## EXERCISE 4—UNDERSTANDING WORD PARTS (p. 52)

1. **asymptomatic**—showing no symptoms
   **asexual**—without sexual orientation
   **anaerobic**—able to live without air

2. **benefit**—advantage
   **benevolent**—characterized by acts of kindness
   **benefactor**—one who does good deeds

3. **cooperate**—work together
   **collapse**—fall together
   **concentrate**—bring closer together

4. **dyslexia**—poor reading
   **dysrhythmia**—abnormal rhythm
   **dystopia**—society with extremely bad conditions

5. **extraterrestrial**—from beyond the earth
   **extracurricular**—outside of the regular schedule
   **extraneous**—non-essential or outside element

6. **forecast**—tell ahead of time
   **foreleg**—front leg
   **foreshadow**—indicate the future

7. **homophonic**—sounding the same
   **homogenous**—not varied
   **homosexual**—same-sex sexual orientation

8. **intrastate**—within a state
   **intravenous**—with or administered into a vein
   **introvert**—to turn inward

9. **maladjusted**—poorly adjusted
   **malevolent**—evil or ill-wishing
   **malefactor**—evildoer

10. **Neolithic**—of the New Stone Age
    **neoconsesrvatism**—social conservatist movement that began in the 1960s (relatively recent)
    **neo-expressionism**—expressionist art movement that began in the 1980s (relatively recent)

11. **obstruct**—stand against
    **obverse**—counterpart or complement
    **obviate**—prevent

12. **periscope**—device for seeing all around
    **perimeter**—outer limits around an area
    **periodontal**—surrounding a tooth

13. **rethink**—think again
    **reimburse**—pay back
    **regenerate**—form anew

14. **subscribe**—write underneath
    **suffer**—undergo
    **suspend**—hang down

15. **defendant**—one who defends himself
    **confidant**—one who is confided in
    **president**—one who presides over

16. **presidency**—position of president
    **decency**—state of being decent
    **ascendancy**—state of being raised up

17. **wisdom**—state of being wise
    **martyrdom**—state of being a martyr
    **kingdom**—territory that belongs to a king

18. **dependence**—state of depending
    **absence**—state of being away
    **fluorescence**—state of emitting visible radiation

19. **pacify**—make peaceful
    **nullify**—to invalidate
    **rectify**—to make right

20. **civil**—having to do with citizens
    **tactile**—having to do with touch
    **infantile**—like a child

21. **monologue**—speech made by one person
    **colloquy**—conversation
    **soliloquy**—act of speaking to oneself

22. **patrimony**—trait inherited from one's father
    **matrimony**—state of being married
    **testimony**—act of offering a declaration of fact

23. **kindness**—quality of being kind
    **wretchedness**—quality of being wretched
    **lifelessness**—quality of being dead

24. **glamorous**—full of glamour
    **clamorous**—making a loud outcry
    **verbose**—having an excessive number of words

25. **horsemanship**—skill in riding horses
    **leadership**—state of being a leader
    **ownership**—state of being an owner

26. **rectitude**—state of being morally upright
    **aptitude**—state of being apt or appropriate
    **certitude**—state of being certain or sure of something

27. **homeward**—in the direction of home
    **heavenward**—toward heaven
    **downward**—toward a lower position

28. **wily**—full of wiles
    **crafty**—marked by deception
    **juicy**—full of juice

29. **anarchy**—without government
    **matriarch**—a woman ruler
    **arch-nemesis**—main enemy

30. **captive**—held in bondage
    **accept**—to willingly take
    **receipt**—act of receiving

31. **endure**—to carry on through hardship
    **duration**—persistence in time
    **obdurate**—hardhearted or stubborn

32. **err**—to make a mistake
    **error**—a mistake
    **aberrant**—deviant

33. **fidelity**—faithfulness
**perfidious**—faithless
**bona fide**—undertaken in good faith

34. **gradation**—a degree in a progression of steps or stages
**transgression**—the act of overstepping a boundary
**regress**—to go backward

35. **heliocentric**—having the sun as a center
**aphelion**—point farthest from the sun
**heliotrope**—a plant that turns toward the sun

36. **isotope**—having the same atomic number
**isometric**—having equal measurement
**isomorphic**—having a similar structure

37. **conjugal**—related to marriage
**conjunction**—the act of joining
**adjunct**—a dependent attachment

38. **legible**—able to be read
**eligible**—qualified for selection
**lecture**—an instructive speech

39. **medieval**—of the Middle Ages
**mediate**—to resolve from a middle position
**intermediary**—existing between

40. **nascent**—coming into existence
**native**—by birth or origin
**innate**—inborn

41. **operational**—working
**cooperative**—a group that works together
**inoperable**—not functioning

42. **telepathy**—extrasensory communication
**patient**—feeling in a calm manner
**compassion**—feelings for another's suffering

43. **query**—a question
**inquiry**—a question
**inquisitive**—inclined to investigation

44. **regulate**—to manage with rules
**dirigible**—having an unyielding structure
**corrective**—that which corrects

45. **sequel**—a follow up
**consequence**—result
**consecutive**—to immediately follow in order

46. **disturb**—to bother
**turbulence**—disruptive flow
**perturbation**—agitation

47. **umbrella**—a device that provides shade from the sun
**penumbra**—partial shadow
**umbrage**—shadow

48. **volunteer**—a person who willingly performs a duty
**volition**—will
**involuntary**—not under one's control

## EXERCISE 5—VOCABULARY IN CONTEXT (p. 69)

1. **(E)** (A), (B), (C), and (D) are all possible meanings of the word "heartily"; however, (E) is the only answer choice that is appropriate in this context. Thomas Jefferson was "completely" tired from the daily conflicts, leading to his resignation from office.

2. **(C)** The "public" life that is the subject of this passage is a life in politics or government—an "official" life.

3. **(E)** The word "final" has many related meanings, including "last" (e.g., "final" day), "closing" (e.g., "final" statement), "ultimate" (e.g., "final" offer), "eventual" (e.g., "final" home), and "conclusive" (e.g., "final" authority). In this context, the appropriate meaning is "conclusive." Jefferson insisted that his retirement would conclude his participation in public life.

4. **(B)** The word "allowed" can be used to mean "permitted" (e.g., The manager "allowed" them to enter the store.) in this context, however, "allowed" means "admitted." Jefferson "admitted" that he had been forced to examine his true feelings on the subject of his retirement.

5. **(B)** The word "anticipating" can be used to mean "expecting," or "looking forward to" (e.g., The boy was "anticipating" the arrival of his father.); in this context, however, "anticipating" means "presaging," or "predicting." The Republican party presaged the campaign tactics of the opposing party.

6. **(B)** The word "uniform" can be used to mean "standard" (e.g., her "uniform" response to a question); in this context, however, the intended meaning of "uniform" is "unchanging." The newspapers presented Jefferson as "unchanging" in his advocacy of equal rights.

7. **(E)** The word "champion" can be used to mean "victor" (e.g., the "champion" at the Olympics); in this context, however, the intended meaning of "champion" is "advocate," or "defender." The newspapers portrayed Adams as an "advocate" for, or a "defender" of, rank, titles, heredity, and distinctions.

8. **(B)** The word "senior" can be used to mean "older in age" (e.g., He is four years my "senior."); in this context, however, "senior" means "higher in rank." The phrase "in public office" clarifies the intended meaning of the author. With regard to public office, Adams had always been a person of higher rank than Jefferson.

9. **(B)** A "luminary" is literally a bright object in the sky, but the word is also used to refer to a famous person. In this context, the extremely famous George Washington is compared to a less "famous person."

10. **(E)** The primary meaning of "diminution" is "a lessening in size" (e.g., the "diminution" of the crowd); in this context, however, the concept is extended to mean "a lessening in esteem," or "degradation." Jefferson believed that Adams had never suffered a "lessening in esteem."

## EXERCISE 6—VOCABULARY COMPLETIONS (p. 71)

| | | | | | |
|---|---|---|---|---|---|
| 1. **C** | 3. **E** | 5. **A** | 7. **C** | 9. **D** | 11. **A** |
| 2. **B** | 4. **D** | 6. **B** | 8. **D** | 10. **C** | 12. **B** |

13. exceed, surpass

14. climax, high point, zenith

15. boring, dull, uninspiring

16. serious, severe, large-scale

17. complete, comprehensive

18. complete, total, authoritarian

19. hides, camouflages, conceals

20. wanted, infamous, notorious

21. dazed, confused, disoriented

22. generate, spark, increase

23. The survivors had been drifting for days in the lifeboat, and in their weakness, they appeared to be _____ rather than living beings.

The blank must be filled with a word that means the opposite of something that is alive. "Dead," "spirits," and "ghosts" are possible completions. Notice that the missing word can either be an adjective (e.g., "dead"), modifying the noun "beings," or a noun (e.g., "spirits"), paralleling the phrase "living beings."

24. The guillotine was introduced during the French Revolution as a(n) _____, an alternative to other less humane means of execution.

The blank must be filled with a noun that extends the idea of something that is an "alternative to" a "less humane" practice. "Reform" and "improvement" are possible completions.

25. Because of the _____ nature of the chemical, it cannot be used near an open flame.

The blank must be filled with an adjective that extends the idea of a chemical that "cannot be used near an open flame." "Flammable," which means "easily capable of burning," is one obvious completion.

26. The Mayor's proposal for a new subway line, although a(n) _____, is not a final solution to the city's transportation needs.

The blank must be filled with a noun that both extends the idea of something that is "new" and reverses the idea of something that is "final." "Start" and "beginning" are possible completions.

27. In a pluralistic society, policies are the result of compromise, so political leaders must be _____ and must accommodate the views of others.

The blank must be filled with an adjective that extends the idea of a "compromise" and parallels the idea of accommodation. "Tolerant" and "understanding" are possible completions.

28. The committee report vigorously expounded the bill's strengths but also acknowledged its _____.

The blank must be filled with a plural noun that means the opposite of "strengths." "Weaknesses" and "shortcomings" are possible completions.

29. Because there is always the danger of a power failure and disruption of elevator service, high-rise buildings, while suitable for younger persons are not recommended for _____.

The sentence suggests that high-rise buildings are suitable for "younger persons" but not for a different group of people. So, the blank must be filled with a word or phrase that means the opposite of "younger persons." "The elderly" and "senior citizens" are possible completions.

30. For a child to be <u>happy</u>, his day must be very <u>structured</u>; when his routine is _____, he becomes <u>nervous and irritable.</u>

    The "if-then" logical structure of the sentence indicates that if the child is to be happy, his day must be structured. However, the word clue, nervous and irritable, after the semicolon suggests that the parallel structure in the second clause of the sentence must be the reverse of the first. If "structured" activity makes a child "happy," then unstructured activity would make a child "nervous and irritable." So, the blank must be filled with a verb that suggests the idea of unstructured activity. "Disrupted" and "interrupted" are possible completions.

31. The current spirit of _____ among different religions <u>has led to</u> a number of meetings that their leaders hope will lead to better <u>understanding</u>.

    The blank must be filled with a noun that satisfies the following construction: The spirit of _____ has led to understanding. "Cooperation" and "accord" are possible completions.

32. Our modern industrialized societies have been responsible for the greatest <u>destruction of nature and life</u>; indeed, it seems that more civilization <u>results in greater</u> _____.

    The blank must be filled with a noun that extends the idea of the "destruction of nature and life," thereby satisfying the following construction: If "modern industrialized societies" are "responsible for" the "destruction of nature and life," then "more civilization" "results in greater" _____. "Annihilation" and "death" are possible completions.

## EXERCISE 7—CAREFUL READING OF VERBAL REASONING ITEM STEMS, PT. I (p. 77)

1. **(A)** (A) is correct because the original asks for the main idea, which is the central theme, or primary focus, of the passage.

   (B) is wrong because the original asks for the main idea, which is the overarching theme, entailing much more than just a specific detail. Also, without any additional information, it is not possible to know whether the main idea is found in the first sentence.

   (C) is wrong because the main idea is not necessarily found in the last sentence of the passage; it could be found anywhere in the passage.

   (D) is wrong because the original asks for the main idea, not a supporting detail. A supporting detail is usually a specific detail that supports the main idea.

2. **(D)** (A) is wrong because the author's statement regarding words and art does not necessarily involve how the two subjects relate to one another.

   (B) is wrong because the original does not simply ask for a statement that pertains to both words and art but asks for a statement that the author holds to be true regarding both words and art.

   (C) is wrong because the original asks for a statement that the author would hold to be true regarding both words and art, not just words.

   (D) is correct because, as stated above, the original asks for a statement that the author would hold to be true regarding both words and art.

3. **(C)** (A) is wrong because the original asks for the contextual definition of "address," not the most common definition.

    (B) is wrong because the original asks for a contextual definition of "address," not the only definition (The word "address" has more than one definition.)

    (C) is correct because the original asks for the definition of "address" as it is used in the context of the passage.

    (D) is wrong because the original does not ask for who the author addresses in the passage; rather, it asks for the contextual meaning of the word "address."

4. **(D)** (A) is wrong because the original asks for the primary (central) purpose of the passage, not the primary (first) specific detail mentioned in the passage.

    (B) is wrong because the original asks for the primary purpose of the passage, not the author's tone.

    (C) is wrong because the original does not ask for how the passage makes you feel as a reader.

    (D) is correct because the original asks for the primary purpose, or main objective, of the passage.

5. **(C)** (A) is wrong because the original asks for the main point of the storyteller's interpretation, not the storyteller's interpretation of the main point.

    (B) is wrong because the original asks for the main point of the storyteller's interpretation, not for one of many potential interpretations made by the storyteller.

    (C) is correct because the original asks for the main point, or central focus, of the storyteller's interpretation.

    (D) is wrong because the original asks for the main point of an interpretation, not for one of many potential interpretations made by the storyteller.

6. **(A)** (A) is correct because the original asks for the meaning, or definition, of the term "Monocrats."

    (B) is wrong because the original asks the reader to make an inference about the meaning of the term "Monocrats"; it does not ask for the author's interpretation of the term.

    (C) is wrong because the original does not ask for the reason why the author uses the term "Monocrats" in the passage.

    (D) is wrong because the original asks for the definition of the term "Monocrats," not the location of the term in the passage.

7. **(B)** (A) is wrong because the original asks for an inference about the author, not for the reason behind the Hudson Bay Company reference.

    (B) is correct because the original asks the reader to infer from the passage the author's regard towards or feelings about the Hudson Bay Company.

    (C) is wrong because the original does not ask about the author's association with the Hudson Bay Company.

    (D) is wrong because the original asks for an inference about the author, not for an inference about the Hudson Bay Company.

8. **(B)** (A) is wrong because the original asks why it is difficult to formulate a general historical law about revolution, not why the author finds it difficult to formulate plans for revolution.

    (B) is correct because the original asks why it is difficult to formulate a general historical law about revolution.

    (C) is wrong because the original does not ask why the author of Passage 1 formulates a general law.

    (D) is wrong because the original does not state that it is easy to formulate a general law.

9. **(C)** (A) is wrong because the original asks for the contextual, not the general, meaning of the phrase.

   (B) is wrong because the original asks for a meaning of the phrase "adequately articulated," not for a phrase that adequately articulates a line in the passage.

   (C) is correct because the original asks for the contextual meaning of the phrase "adequately articulated."

   (D) is wrong because the original does not ask for a specific phrase that is adequately articulated in the passage.

10. **(C)** (A) is wrong because the original does not ask for specific laws but for the cause of disappointment.

    (B) is wrong because the original states that general laws fail to explain historical events.

    (C) is correct because the original asks for the cause of disappointment at the failure of laws to explain events.

    (D) is wrong because the original asks for the cause of disappointment at the failure, not for the cause of the failure itself.

11. **(B)** (A) is wrong because the original asks for something that can be studied by means of a certain technique, not for a person (historian) who can explain this technique.

    (B) is correct because the original asks for something that can be studied by means of the Verstehen technique.

    (C) is wrong because the original does not ask for something that cannot be studied by means of the Verstehen technique.

    (D) is wrong because the original does not ask for a particular technique. The technique is known; the object of study is unknown.

12. **(B)** (A) is wrong because the original does not state that the author of Passage 1 necessarily refers to the "inside" of a historical event.

    (B) is correct because the original asks for something that the author of Passage 1 would reference to account for the "inside" of a historical event.

    (C) is wrong because the original simply states that the author of Passage 2 refers to the "inside" of a historical event; it does not ask why the author of Passage 2 makes this reference.

    (D) is wrong because the original asks for something that would be referenced by the author of Passage 1, but not by the author of Passage 2.

13. **(B)** (A) is wrong because the original asks for an assumption that can be made by virtue of the list, not for a reason as to the contents of the list.

    (B) is correct because the original asks for an assumption that can be made by virtue of the author's list of regions.

    (C) is wrong because the original asks for an assumption that can be made by virtue of the list of regions, not for a specific region that is included on the list.

    (D) is wrong because the original asks for an assumption that can be made by virtue of the list of regions, not for an assumption that can be made about the cultivation of maize.

14. **(D)** (A) is wrong because the original does not ask what the wheat and barley exemplify; instead, it asks why the author mentions wheat and barley.

    (B) is wrong because the original does not ask for the author's sequence of reference.

    (C) is wrong because the original does not ask where in the passage the author discusses wheat and barley but why the author refers to them in the passage.

    (D) is correct because the original asks why the author mentions wheat and barley in the passage.

15. **(D)** (A) is wrong because the original asks for the author's primary (main or chief) purpose, not for the purpose that is mentioned in the first sentence.

(B) is wrong because the original asks for the author's primary, not secondary, purpose.

(C) is wrong because the original asks for the author's main purpose, not for the purpose that the reader first detects when reading the passage.

(D) is correct because the original asks for the author's primary purpose in (reason for) writing the passage.

## EXERCISE 8—CAREFUL READING OF QUANTITATIVE REASONING ITEM STEMS, PT. I (p. 79)

1. **(D)** (A) is wrong because the original asks for the number of minutes that it takes to make 30, not 270, thingamabobs at a particular per-hour rate. (A) is distracting because it simply adds together the two values given in the item stem.

(B) is wrong because the original does not ask for the number of minutes that it takes to produce 8 sets of 30 thingamabobs, or 240 thingamabobs.

(C) is wrong because the original does not ask for the number of minutes that it takes to produce 240 thingamabobs at a particular rate. (C) is also distracting because it switches the two values given in the item stem.

(D) is correct because the original asks for the number of minutes that it takes to produce 30 thingamabobs at a rate of 240 thingamabobs per hour.

2. **(A)** (A) is correct because the original asks for the price of the item before the decrease, which is the same as the original price of the item.

(B) is wrong because the original refers to a 20-percent decrease in price, not to an 80-percent decrease.

(C) is wrong because the original asks for the price of the item before the decrease, not for the price after the decrease.

(D) is wrong because the original asks for the price of the item before the 20-percent decrease, not for the price before an 80-percent increase.

3. **(C)** (A) is wrong because the original asks how much *less* candy can be purchased for $3.50 at the new price, not at the old price.

(B) is wrong because the original does not ask how much total candy can be purchased for $3.50 at the new price but how much *less* candy.

(C) is correct because the original asks how much *less* candy can be purchased for $3.50 at the new price.

(D) is wrong because the original does not ask how much total candy can be purchased for $3.50 at the old price but how much *less* candy can be purchased for $3.50 at the new price.

4. **(D)** (A) is wrong because the original asks for the percentage of marbles in the jar that are black, not white.

(B) is wrong because the original does not ask for the difference between black and white marbles in the jar. The original asks for a percentage.

(C) is wrong because the original does not ask for the percentage of marbles in the jar that are not black (white).

(D) is correct because the original asks for the percentage of the marbles in the jar that are black (not white).

5. **(C)** (A) is wrong because the original asks for the ratio (expressed in percent) of Tuesday's total number of students to Monday's total number of students, not for the ratio of the combined total number of students to Monday's total number of students.

(B) is wrong because the original does not ask for the ratio of the combined total number of students to Tuesday's total number of students.

(C) is correct because the original asks for the ratio (expressed in percent) of Tuesday's total number of students to Monday's total number of students.

(D) is wrong because the original does not ask for the ratio of Monday's total number of students to Tuesday's total number of students.

6. **(C)** (A) is wrong because although the mode is a type of average, unless specified, the term "average" refers to the mean average.

(B) is wrong because the mode of a series of values is that value which occurs most frequently, not least frequently.

(C) is correct because the mode of a series of values is that which occurs most frequently.

(D) is wrong because the median of a series of values is not the same as the mode. The median is the middle value in a series of numbers.

7. **(C)** (A) is wrong because the original asks for the amount of chocolate that can be purchased for $12 at the given price, not for the difference between the amount that can be purchased for $12 and the amount that can be purchased for $10.

(B) is wrong because the original asks for the amount of chocolate that can be purchased for $12, not for the cost of 12 pounds of chocolate.

(C) is correct because the original asks for the amount of chocolate that can be purchased for $12 at the given price.

(D) is wrong because the original does not ask for the amount of chocolate that can be purchased for $10.

8. **(B)** (A) is wrong because the original asks for the number of students that did not buy a yearbook, not for the number of students that did buy a yearbook.

(B) is correct because the original asks for the number of students that did not buy a yearbook based on the fact that 45%, or 540, did buy a yearbook.

(C) is wrong because the original states that 540 students bought yearbooks, not that a percentage of 540 students bought yearbooks.

(D) is wrong because the original states that 540 students bought yearbooks, not that a percentage of 540 students did not buy yearbooks.

9. **(C)** (A) is wrong because the original states that it takes Jill 1 hour to walk home at 4 miles per hour, not that it takes 4 hours to walk home at a rate of 5 miles per hour.

(B) is wrong because the original states that it takes Jill 1 hour to walk home at 4 miles per hour, not that it takes 1 hour to walk home at a rate of 5 miles per hour.

(C) is correct because the original states that it takes Jill 1 hour to walk home at 4 miles per hour.

(D) is wrong because the original states that it takes Jill 1 hour to walk home at 4 miles per hour, not that it takes 4 hours to walk home at a rate of 1 mile per hour.

10. **(D)** (A) is wrong because the original asks for the smallest integer of 5 consecutive integers totaling 40, and (A) does not specify that these integers must be consecutive.

(B) is wrong because the original asks for the smallest of 5 consecutive integers, not for the smallest of 10 consecutive integers.

(C) is wrong because the original asks for the smallest of 5 consecutive integers, not for the largest of 5 consecutive integers.

(D) is correct because the original asks for the smallest integer of 5 consecutive integers totaling 40.

11. **(A)** (A) is correct because the original asks for an equation that best describes, or expresses, the relationship between $x$ and $y$ in the table.

(B) is wrong because the original asks for an equation, not for a value that expresses how much $y$ is greater than $x$.

(C) is wrong because the original asks for an equation, not for a value that expresses how much $x$ is greater than $y$.

(D) is wrong because the original does not ask about the relationship between $x$ and $z$; $z$ is not even mentioned in the item stem.

12. **(C)** (A) is wrong because the original asks for the complete solution to the equation $x^2 - 3x = 4$, not to the equation $x^2 - 4x = 3$. (A) rearranges the values in the original equation.

(B) is wrong because the original asks for the complete solution to the given quadratic equation, not for the complete solution to the quadratic formula. There is no solution to the quadratic formula; it is used to solve quadratic equations.

(C) is correct because the original asks for the complete solution to the equation $x^2 - 3x = 4$.

(D) is wrong because the original asks for the complete solution to the given equation, not for a partial solution to the given equation. The complete solution would include two values for $x$, not just one value for $x$.

13. **(D)** (A) is wrong because the original asks for the number of points that were scored on the first, not the fifth, turn.

(B) is wrong because the original does not ask for the number of points that were scored after the fifth turn (total points). That information is already given: 465 total points were scored after five turns.

(C) is wrong because the original asks for the number of points that were scored on the first turn, not after the first turn. The correct answer to (C) would be the total number of points scored from the second, third, fourth, and fifth turns.

(D) is correct because the original asks for the number of points that the player scored on the first turn.

14. **(C)** (A) is wrong because the original asks for a number of days, not for a number of trucks. Also, the original uses the variable $d$ to represent gallons of fuel needed per day for each truck, not to represent actual days.

(B) is wrong because the original asks for the number of days that $g$ gallons of fuel will supply $t$ trucks, not for the number of days that d gallons of fuel will supply t trucks.

(C) is correct because the original asks for the number of days that $g$ gallons of fuel will supply $t$ trucks.

(D) is wrong because the original does not ask for the number of days that both $g$ and $d$ gallons combined will supply $t$ trucks. Both variables do not represent total gallon amounts: $g$ represents a rate and $d$ represents the total.

15. **(C)** (A) is wrong because the original states that the $25 price is increased and then the resulting price is decreased, not the other way around.

    (B) is wrong because the original states that there is one item, not ten items.

    (C) is correct because the original states that the $25 price is increased and then the resulting price is decreased.

    (D) is wrong because the original asks for a final price after an increase and decrease, not for a percentage of the original price. (D) is distracting because it inappropriately adds the two 10% values together.

16. **(D)** (A) is wrong because the original asks for an average speed, not for a length of time.

    (B) is wrong because the original uses $m$ to represent miles and $h$ to represent hours, not the other way around.

    (C) is wrong because the original uses the value 45 to specify time (minutes), not distance (miles). Also, the original uses $m$ to represent miles, not minutes.

    (D) is correct because the original asks for an average speed based on a rate of $m$ miles in $h$ hours and 45 minutes.

17. **(B)** (A) is wrong because the original specifically asks for the hypotenuse of a right isosceles triangle, not for the hypotenuse of a right triangle. A right triangle does not necessarily have two equal sides, as does an isosceles triangle.

    (B) is correct because the original asks for the hypotenuse of a right isosceles triangle, or a right triangle in which two sides are equal.

    (C) is wrong because the original does not ask for the hypotenuse of an isosceles triangle in which all three sides are equal, or an equilateral triangle. In such a triangle, all three angles would measure 60° each. A right triangle, by definition, has one 90° angle.

    (D) is wrong because the original does not ask for the hypotenuse of a 30°-60°-90° triangle. In such a triangle, each of the three sides would be of a different length.

18. **(D)** (A) is wrong because the original asks for the slope of one line, not for two slopes of two lines. Also, to find the slope of a given line, two points on that line must be given. (A), however, provides only one point for each of its two referenced lines.

    (B) is wrong because the original asks for the slope of a line with four positive coordinates, not for the slope of a line with three positive coordinates and one negative coordinate. This negative coordinate would position the line in a different quadrant on the graph.

    (C) is wrong because it reverses the $x$- and $y$-coordinates for each of the given points. With these points reversed, a different line is created.

    (D) is correct because the original asks for the slope of a line with specific $x$- and $y$-coordinates: (3,6) and (7,9).

19. **(B)** (A) is wrong because the original does not ask for the average of 8 numbers. This information is already given. The original, rather, asks for the average of 14 numbers.

    (B) is correct because the original asks for the average of all 14 numbers: the additive total of 8 numbers, plus the additive total of the other 6 numbers, divided by 14.

    (C) is wrong because the original asks for the average of all 14 numbers, not for the average of 8 numbers plus the average of the other 6 numbers. These two formulations would produce different results.

    (D) is wrong because the original does not ask for the average of the other 6 numbers. This information is already given. The average of the other 6 numbers is 8.

20. **(B)** (A) is wrong because the original asks about a geometric sequence, not a periodic sequence.

(B) is correct because the original asks for a value that is represented by the second (between first and third) term in a geometric sequence.

(C) is wrong because the original asks for a term (which represents a value) in a geometric sequence; it does not ask for a geometric term (geometric terminology) such as "isosceles triangle" or "supplementary."

(D) is wrong because the original asks for a value that is represented by the second term in a geometric sequence that possesses the values 3,125 and 125; the original does not ask for the difference between these two given values.

## EXERCISE 9—CAREFUL READING OF VERBAL REASONING ITEM STEMS, PT. II (p. 83)

1. **(B)** (A) is wrong because the original asks for the contextual meaning of a certain word, not the tacit (unspoken) meaning of a certain line in the passage.

(B) is correct because the original asks for the meaning of the word "tacitly" in the context of a certain line in the passage.

(C) is wrong because the original does not ask for a contextual meaning of the word "tacit."

(D) is wrong because the original asks for the contextual meaning of a certain word, not the tacit (unspoken) meaning of the first word in a certain line in the passage.

2. **(A)** (A) is correct because the original asks for a description of how Stanton's tone changes between the two paragraphs.

(B) is wrong because the original does not ask for a description of Stanton's initial tone but for a description of how Stanton's tone changes.

(C) is wrong because the original states that Stanton's tone changes but does not specify the quality (positive or negative) of the tone.

(D) is wrong because the original states that Stanton's tone changes, not that it remains unchanged.

3. **(D)** (A) is wrong because the original asks for a description of a way in which Madame de Staël and Dante are not alike.

(B) is wrong because the original asks for a description of a way in which Madame de Staël is different from Dante, not a description of a way in which she dislikes Dante.

(C) is wrong because the original does not ask whether Madame de Staël likes or dislikes Dante.

(D) is correct because the original asks for a description of a way in which Madame de Staël and Dante are not alike.

4. **(B)** (A) is wrong because the original does not ask whether Sun Yat-sen is from Hong Kong.

(B) is correct because the original asks for something that Sun Yat-sen uses Hong Kong to exemplify.

(C) is wrong because the original asks for something that Sun Yat-sen uses Hong Kong to exemplify; it does not state that Sun Yat-sen uses Hong Kong to exemplify Chinese culture.

(D) is wrong because the original states that Sun Yat-sen uses Hong Kong as an example; it does not ask for an example of Sun Yat-sen's relationship to Hong Kong.

5. **(D)** (A) is wrong because the original does not ask whether Gandhi's charges are "on the level" (legitimate); instead, it asks for a description of how Gandhi feels about the charge leveled (directed) against him.

(B) is wrong because the original does not state whether Gandhi exhibited any opposition to the charges leveled against him.

(C) is wrong because the original asks for a description of how Gandhi feels about the charge leveled against him, not for a description of how he would feel about leveling charges against others.

(D) is correct because the original asks for a description of how Gandhi feels about the charge leveled against him.

6. **(C)** (A) is wrong because the original does not ask for a reason why Rousseau complains to Madame d'Épinay.

(B) is wrong because the original does not ask for a description of how Rousseau feels about Madame d'Épinay's complaints but vice versa.

(C) is correct because the original asks for a description of how Madame d'Épinay feels about Rousseau's complaints.

(D) is wrong because the original does not ask for a comparison between Rousseau's and Madame d'Épinay's complaints.

7. **(B)** (A) is wrong because the original does not ask about Rousseau's feelings toward Madame d'Épinay's philosophy.

(B) is correct because the original asks for a summary of the difference (distinction) between Rousseau's and Madame d'Épinay's philosophies of friendship.

(C) is wrong because the original asks for the difference, not the similarity, between Rousseau's and Madame d'Épinay's philosophies of friendship.

(D) is wrong because the original does not ask about a philosophy of rivalry.

8. **(A)** (A) is correct because the original asks for Galileo's reason behind including the second paragraph.

(B) is wrong because the original does not ask about the relationship between the second paragraph and the remainder of the passage.

(C) is wrong because the original does not ask about the order (sequence) in which the lines are arranged in the second paragraph; instead, it asks why Galileo includes the second paragraph.

(D) is wrong because the original does not state whether Galileo is mentioned in the passage; Galileo wrote the passage.

9. **(C)** (A) is wrong because the original asks for a point on which Chekhov does not express a definite opinion. If "not based on fact" can be taken to mean "opinion," answer choice (A) asks nearly the opposite of the original.

(B) is wrong because the original meaning is reversed. It looks similar to the original, but the key reversal word "EXCEPT" is missing.

(C) is correct because the original asks for a point on which Chekhov does not express a definite opinion.

(D) is wrong because the original focuses on identifying where Chekhov has expressed opinions. (D) shifts the focus to an evaluation of whether Chekhov has support for what he has expressed.

10. **(D)** (A) is wrong because the original asks about slaveholders' cruelty, not Sojourner Truth's cruelty.

(B) is wrong because the original does not specify whether Sojourner Truth belongs to any slaveholders.

(C) is wrong because the original asks about the basis of slaveholders' cruelty, not the basis for justify that cruelty.

(D) is correct because the original asks about the basis of slaveholders' cruelty.

11. **(D)** (A) is wrong because the original does not ask whether Sojourner Truth actually approved of the Declaration of Sentiments.

    (B) is wrong because the original asks for a description of what the reader would expect, not for a description of what Sojourner Truth would have expected.

    (C) is wrong because the original does not ask about the Declaration of *Sentience* but about the Declaration of Sentiments. (Note: Pay careful attention to the spelling of words that are phonetically similar.)

    (D) is correct because the original asks about whether the reader would expect Sojourner Truth to have approved of the Declaration of Sentiments.

12. **(B)** (A) is wrong because the original does not ask for the main point of only the second paragraph but asks for the main point of the entire passage, which may or may not also be the main point of the second paragraph.

    (B) is correct because the original asks for the main point, or main idea, of the passage.

    (C) is wrong because the original asks for the overarching purpose of the passage, not for a specific detail that is mentioned in the passage.

    (D) is wrong because the original asks for a point that is necessary to understanding the passage. A point that is not mentioned in the passage is unlikely to facilitate such an understanding.

13. **(C)** (A) is wrong because the original states that Vignes and Wolfskill are two names that refer to one site, not two names for two different sites.

    (B) is wrong because the original does not imply that the author values the Vignes/Wolfskill site more or less than any other site.

    (C) is correct because the original asks for the primary reason why the author values the Vignes/Wolfskill site.

    (D) is wrong because the original does not imply that the author values the Vignes/Wolfskill site more or less than any other site.

14. **(D)** (A) is wrong because the original asks for the meaning of a vocabulary word ("appropriate"); it does not ask about the appropriateness of a quote.

    (B) is wrong because the original asks about the word "appropriate" in line 52; it does not ask about another word in that line.

    (C) is wrong because the original does not ask about the appropriateness of line 52 in the context of the passage; instead, it asks about the meaning of a word in the context of line 52.

    (D) is correct because the original asks about the meaning of the word "appropriate" in the context of line 52.

15. **(A)** (A) is correct because the original asks for the chief characteristic (main quality) of Lady Bertram that is exposed in the excerpt.

    (B) is wrong because the original asks for Lady Bertram's main characteristic, not whether she is the main character.

    (C) is wrong because the original asks whether Lady Bertram's chief characteristic is exposed, not whether she exposes a different character's chief characteristic.

    (D) is wrong because the original asks for the chief characteristic of Lady Bertram that is exposed in the excerpt.

16. **(C)** (A) is wrong because the original asks about an analogy (comparison), not a contrast.

    (B) is wrong because the original asks about what the author of Passage 1 makes analogous to a novel, not about what the author of Passage 2 makes analogous to a novel.

    (C) is correct because the original asks about what the author of Passage 1 makes analogous to a novel.

    (D) is wrong because the original does not specify what is made analogous to a novel; the analogy is not necessarily made between two novels.

17. **(B)** (A) is wrong because the original asks for a statement with which both (not neither) authors would agree.

    (B) is correct because the original asks for a statement with which both authors would agree.

    (C) is wrong because the original asks for a statement with which both authors (not just one) would agree.

    (D) is wrong because the original asks for a statement with which both authors would agree, not disagree.

18. **(D)** (A) is wrong because the original asks for a characteristic of an allergen that makes it different from antigens, not vice versa. Although the difference is the same, the answer would be a trait representative of an allergen, rather than of antigens.

    (B) is wrong because the original does not ask about how antigens and an allergen are similar.

    (C) is wrong because the original does not ask about similarity but about difference. Also, the original refers to "allergen" in the singular form and "antigens" in the plural form, not vice versa.

    (D) is correct because the original asks for a characteristic of an allergen that makes it different from antigens.

19. **(D)** (A) is wrong because the original refers to Mrs. Norris's many occupations, not Austen's many occupations.

    (B) is wrong because the original asks about how Austen depicts Mrs. Norris, not about one of Mrs. Norris's many occupations.

    (C) is wrong because the original asks about how Austen depicts Mrs. Norris, not about the number of Mrs. Norris's occupations.

    (D) is correct because the original asks about how Austen depicts Mrs. Norris in describing her many occupations.

20. **(A)** (A) is correct because the original asks for a description of something that is metaphorically associated with an immune response.

    (B) is wrong because the original does not ask for a contextual definition of an immune response.

    (C) is wrong because the original states that the passage relies upon an extended metaphor, which means that it most likely extends throughout more than one paragraph. However, the original does not ask about the number of paragraphs through which this metaphor might extend.

    (D) is wrong because the original asks about an immune response, not about the author's response to a metaphor.

21. **(B)** (A) is wrong because the original does not ask about what would convince a child that television violence is real but about what would deter a child from regarding such violence as real.

    (B) is correct because the original asks about what would deter (prevent) a child from regarding television violence as real.

    (C) is wrong because the original does not ask about a specific type of television violence.

    (D) is wrong because the original does not ask about what would deter a child from actually watching television violence but about what would deter a child from regarding it as real.

22. **(C)** (A) is wrong because the original asks about the function of the final paragraph, not about the content of the final paragraph. Function and content are not necessarily the same thing.

    (B) is wrong because the original asks about the function of the final paragraph, not about the function of the paragraph that precedes it.

    (C) is correct because the original asks about the function (purpose) of the final paragraph.

    (D) is wrong because the original asks about the function of the final paragraph, not about the function of the first paragraph.

23. **(D)** (A) is wrong because the original asks for a statement about dialogue in novels, not about dialogue in general.

    (B) is wrong because the original asks for a statement with which the author of Passage 2 would agree, not disagree.

    (C) is wrong because the original asks for a statement with which the author of Passage 2, not Passage 1, would agree.

    (D) is correct because the original asks for a statement about dialogue in novels with which the author of Passage 2 would agree. This answer choice is more specific than (A): dialogue in novels rather than dialogue in general. If (D) were not one of the given answer choices, then (A) would be considered the best restatement of the question that is being asked.

24. **(C)** (A) is wrong because the original states that Austen undercuts her description of the Miss Bertrams, not vice versa.

    (B) is wrong because the original states that Austen undercuts her own description; it does not state that the Miss Bertrams undercut Austen's description.

    (C) is correct because the original asks for a description of how Austen undercuts (undermines) her own description of the Miss Bertrams.

    (D) is wrong because the original states that the description is made of the Miss Bertrams, not of Austen.

25. **(D)** (A) is wrong because the original asks for the meaning of a vocabulary term ("asserting"); it does not ask about a particular statement that is asserted in the context of the passage.

    (B) is wrong because the original asks for the contextual meaning of a word, not the most common meaning of a word.

    (C) is wrong because the original asks about the implicit meaning of a word as it relates to the context of line 30; it does not ask about an explicit meaning that is actually provided in line 30.

    (D) is correct because the original asks for the contextual meaning of the word "asserting."

26. **(C)** (A) is wrong because the original asks for the meaning behind someone's use of a saying, not for the meaning behind the actual saying itself.

    (B) is wrong because the original refers to a saying made by Gertrude Stein, not Dolores Hayden.

    (C) is correct because the original asks for the meaning behind Dolores Hayden's use of Gertrude Stein's saying.

    (D) is wrong because the original refers to a saying made by Gertrude Stein, not Dolores Hayden.

27. **(B)** (A) is wrong because the original asks for the author's primary (chief) concern; in this case, the word "primary" is not intended to refer to the primacy of the first paragraph.

    (B) is correct because the original asks for the author's primary (chief) concern (regard) in the passage.

    (C) is wrong because although the word "concern" is used with the same general intent, the original provides no evidence that the author's concern is necessarily directed toward a dilemma.

    (D) is wrong because the original asks for the author's primary (chief) concern, not the author's primary (initial) topic of reference.

**EXERCISE 10—CAREFUL READING OF QUANTITATIVE REASONING ITEM STEMS, PT. II** (p. 87)

1. **(C)** (A) is wrong because the original asks about a number that is increased by 25, not about a number that is twice 25.

   (B) is wrong because the original asks about a number that is increased by 25, not about a number that is half of 25.

   (C) is correct because the original asks about a number that yields the same result when either increased by 25 or multiplied by 2.

   (D) is wrong because the original asks about a number that yields the same result when either increased by 25 or multiplied by 2, not vice versa.

2. **(B)** (A) is wrong because the original asks for a fraction of a fraction, which would require the multiplication, not division, of those two given fractions.

   (B) is correct because the original asks for a fraction of a fraction, which would require the multiplication of those two given fractions.

   (C) is wrong because the original asks for a fraction of a fraction, which would require the multiplication, not division, of those two given fractions.

   (D) is wrong because the original asks for a fraction of a fraction, which would require the multiplication, not addition, of those two given fractions.

3. **(C)** (A) is wrong because the original does not include the variable $y$ in the group of values that is to be averaged.

   (B) is wrong because the original states that the average of a given group of values is 11, not 15.

   (C) is correct because the original asks for the value of $x$ in a group of values that yields 11 when averaged; the group of values in (C), while arranged in a different order, are the same group of values that is provided in the original. Remember, the sequence of values in a group to be averaged is of no consequence.

   (D) is wrong because the original does not include the value 11 in the group of values that is to be averaged.

4. **(A)** (A) is correct because the original asks for Jane's age when Hector was twice her age; when Hector was 12, Jane was 6.

   (B) is wrong because the original does not ask for Jane's future age but for Jane's past age.

   (C) is wrong because this information is given in the original: When Hector was 36, Jane was 30.

   (D) is wrong because the original does not ask for Hector's age but for Jane's age.

5. **(D)** (A) is wrong because the original asks for the percent increase in price of a book, not the percent decrease in price of a book; also, the book originally cost $10.00 and now costs $12.50, not vice versa.

   (B) is wrong because the original states that the book now costs $12.50, not $22.50.

   (C) is wrong because the original asks for the percent increase in price, which requires determining a percentage of the original price, not the new price.

   (D) is correct because the original asks for the percent increase in price, which requires determining a percentage of the old price (original price).

6. **(B)** (A) is wrong because the original states that there are 36 people in the club, not 51 people.

   (B) is correct because the original states that there are 15 girls in a club with 36 people, which means that there are 21 boys; the original also asks for the fraction of the club (in lowest terms) that is boys (not girls).

   (C) is wrong because the original asks for the fraction of the club that is boys, not girls.

   (D) is wrong because the original asks for the fraction of the club that is boys, not girls.

7. **(A)** (A) is correct because the original asks for the least (smaller) of two consecutive integers that when added together total 29.

   (B) is wrong because the original is concerned with two consecutive integers, not two non-consecutive integers.

   (C) is wrong because the original is concerned with the smaller of two consecutive integers, not the larger of two consecutive integers.

   (D) is wrong because the original is concerned with two consecutive integers that when added together total 29, not 92.

8. **(B)** (A) is wrong because the original asks for the percentage of marbles that is black, not white. (If there are 300 total black and white marbles in the jar and there are 156 white marbles, then there are 144 black marbles.)

   (B) is correct because the original asks for the percentage of marbles that is black. (144 of the 300 marbles are black.)

   (C) is wrong because the original states that there are 300 total marbles in the jar, not 456 total marbles.

   (D) is wrong because the original states that there are 300 total marbles in the jar, not 456 total marbles.

9. **(D)** (A) is wrong because the original asks for the number of digits that change when a given decimal is rounded off to the nearest hundredth, not to the nearest tenth.

   (B) is wrong because the original asks for the number of digits that change when a given decimal is rounded off to the nearest hundredth, not to the nearest thousandth. Also, the given decimal is 0.129914, not 0.129414.

   (C) is wrong because in the original, the given decimal is 0.129914, not 0.129941.

   (D) is correct because the original asks for the number of digits that change when 0.129914 is rounded off to the nearest hundredth.

10. **(B)** (A) is wrong because the original asks for how old Cindy is now, not for how old she will be 8 years from now.

    (B) is correct because the original asks for how old Cindy is now (current age).

    (C) is wrong because the original states that Ray is currently 10 years older than Cindy, not 8 years older.

    (D) is wrong because the original asks for how old Cindy is now, not for old she will be in the future.

11. **(A)** (A) is correct because the original states that the "JOSH" of a particular number is defined as 3 less than 3 times that number. If $x$ were to represent the number, then the original would be asking for the value of $x$ that is equal to $3x - 3$.

    (B) is wrong because the original states that the "JOSH" of a particular number is defined as 3 less than 3 times that number, not 3 more than 3 times that number.

    (C) is wrong because the original states that the "JOSH" of a particular number is defined as 3 less than 3 times that number, not 3 more than 3 times another number. (The variables on either side of the equation must be the same.)

    (D) is wrong because the original states that the "JOSH" of a particular number is defined as 3 less than 3 times that number, not 3 less than 3 times another number. (The variables on either side of the equation must be the same.)

12. **(B)** (A) is wrong because in the original, $O$ represents the center point of the circle, not the circle itself.

(B) is correct because the original asks for the area of a circle with center $O$.

(C) is wrong because the original does not ask for the area of the center point. A point is one-dimensional and therefore does not have an area.

(D) is wrong because the original asks for the area of a circle, not for the circumference of a circle. Remember that although the circumference would be sufficient information to solve for the area, that is not the objective of this exercise.

13. **(C)** (A) is wrong because the original asks for the number of globs that is equivalent to 2 glops, not for the number of globs that is equivalent to 4 glips; that information is given in the original: 4 glips are 5 globs.

(B) is wrong because the original asks for the number of globs that is equivalent to 2 glops, not a particular number of glups. (Glup is the name of the country, not the name of one of the given quantifiable things.)

(C) is correct because the original asks for the number of globs that is equivalent to 2 glops.

(D) is wrong because the original does not ask for the number of globs that is equivalent to 3 glips.

14. **(C)** (A) is wrong because the original asks for the result of $\frac{4}{5}$ subtracted from its reciprocal (inverted fraction), not for the result of the given fraction's reciprocal ($\frac{5}{4}$) subtracted from the given fraction ($\frac{4}{5}$).

(B) is wrong because the original does not ask for the result of $\frac{4}{5}$ subtracted from itself.

(C) is correct because the original asks for the result of $\frac{4}{5}$ subtracted from its reciprocal (inverted fraction), $\frac{4}{5}$.

(D) is wrong because the original asks for the result of $\frac{4}{5}$ subtracted from its reciprocal. (The reciprocal is not defined as the difference between 1 and the given fraction.)

15. **(B)** (A) is wrong because the original asks for the difference between two fractions but it does not specify that the answer must necessarily be in decimal form.

(B) is correct because the original asks for the value of $\frac{2}{3} - \frac{5}{8}$ ($\frac{5}{8}$ subtracted from $\frac{2}{3}$).

(C) is wrong because the original does not ask for the value of $\frac{5}{8} - \frac{2}{3}$ ($\frac{2}{3}$ subtracted from $\frac{5}{8}$).

(D) is wrong because the original asks for the value of $\frac{5}{8}$ subtracted from $\frac{2}{3}$, not for the value of $\frac{8}{5}$ subtracted from $\frac{3}{2}$. ($\frac{8}{5}$ and $\frac{3}{2}$ are the reciprocals of the original given fractions.)

16. **(D)** (A) is wrong because the original asks for the average of three numbers, not the median average of three numbers.

(B) is wrong because in the original, 7.5 is not one of the given numbers.

(C) is wrong because the original asks for the average of three numbers, which requires dividing the sum total of those three numbers by 3, not multiplying the sum total by 3.

(D) is correct because the original asks for the average of three numbers (8.5, 7.8, and 7.7), which requires dividing the sum total of those numbers by 3. When adding numbers, sequence is of no consequence; the result will always be the same.

17. **(D)** (A) is wrong because the original asks for the area of a square with four points $P$, $Q$, $R$, and $S$ that trace the square in that particular order. Based on this sequence, square $QSPR$ would not be the same figure as square $PQRS$.

    (B) is wrong because the original asks for the area of a given square, not for the area of a given parallelogram. Although both shapes are quadrilaterals, only the square has four equal sides and four right angles.

    (C) is wrong because the original asks for the area of a given square, not for the area of a given rectangle. Although both shapes are quadrilaterals, only the square has four equal sides.

    (D) is correct because the original asks for the area of a square with four points $P$, $Q$, $R$, and $S$ that trace the square in that particular order. Based on this sequence, only square $SRQP$ (traced in reverse order) would be the same figure as square $PQRS$.

18. **(A)** (A) is correct because the original asks for the result of $z - y$ given two different averages of two different groups of values. Remember that when adding numbers, sequence is of no consequence; the result will always be the same.

    (B) is wrong because the original states that the average of 4, 5, $x$, and $y$ is 6 and that the average of $x$, $z$, 8, and 9 is 8, not vice versa.

    (C) is wrong for the same reason that (B) is wrong. (C) is slightly more confusing because the values in each group are rearranged.

    (D) is wrong because the original asks for the result of $z - y$, not for the result of $y - z$.

19. **(C)** (A) is wrong because the original states that 0.01 is the resultant ratio of 0.1 to another value, not that 0.1 is the resultant ratio of 0.01 to another value.

    (B) is wrong because the original asks for an unknown value that is determined by dividing 0.1 by 0.01, not vice versa.

    (C) is correct because the original states that 0.01 (or .01) is the resultant ratio of 0.1 (or .1) to another value.

    (D) is wrong because in the original, .001 is not one of the given values.

20. **(D)** (A) is wrong because the original states that $\overline{CB}$ is equal, not parallel, to $\overline{CA}$ and that $\overline{DE}$ is parallel, not equal, to $\overline{BA}$. Remember that the two points in a line can be in either order.

    (B) is wrong because the original states that $\angle BED = 50°$, not that $\angle EDB = 50°$. $\angle BED$ and $\angle EDB$ are not the same angle.

    (C) is wrong because the original does not state either that $\overline{AB}$ is parallel to $\overline{AC}$ or that $\overline{ED}$ is equal to $\overline{BC}$.

    (D) is correct because the original asks for a value based on all of the same conditions that are provided in this answer choice. $\angle DEB$ and $\angle BED$ are the same angle.

**EXERCISE 11—COMPREHENSION LEVEL CODING** (p. 92)

1. **SP** This is a Specific Points item. The item stem asks you for a specific detail that is made by the author regarding certain locator material ("tears and laughter"), as indicated by the phrase "according to the passage." Note also that the word "EXCEPT" indicates a reversal of thought, suggesting that all but one of the answer choices is found in the passage.

2. **E** This is an Evaluation item. The item stem asks you for an implied idea that is made by the author regarding a specific detail (an ability that animals lack).

3. **E** This is an Evaluation item. The item stem asks you for the meaning of a vocabulary word ("ludicrous") as it is used in the context of the passage ("line #").

4. **SP** This is a Specific Points item. The item stem asks you for the manner with which the author develops the overall structure of the passage.

5. **SP** This is a Specific Points item. The item stem asks you for a specific detail regarding something specifically mentioned by the author in the second paragraph of the passage.

6. **GT** This is a General Theme item. The item stem asks you for a description that summarizes the overall content, or central theme, of the passage.

7. **GT** This is a General Theme item. The item stem asks you for a description of the author's primary concern, or central focus, in the passage.

8. **SP** This is a Specific Points item. The item stem asks you for a specific detail that is made by the author regarding certain locator material ("the open government statute is intended to accomplish"), as indicated by the phrase "the passage states." Note also that the word "EXCEPT" indicates a reversal of thought, suggesting that all but one of the answer choices is found in the passage.

9. **E** This is an Evaluation item. The item stem asks you to draw a conclusion about something ("a decision") that is supported by the details of the passage. To answer this item, you must apply those details to a new situation.

10. **SP** This is a Specific Points item. The item stem asks you for a specific detail regarding something that is specifically mentioned by the author in the final paragraph of the passage.

11. **SP** This is a Specific Points item. The item stem asks you for a specific detail that is made by the author regarding certain locator material ("the rules governing the commission"). Note also that the word "EXCEPT" indicates a reversal of thought, suggesting that all but one of the answer choices is found in the passage.

12. **E** This is an Evaluation item, as indicated by the phrase "it can be inferred from the passage." It asks you to identify an implied idea that is made by details in the passage.

13. **E** This is an Evaluation item, as indicated by the structure of the item stem ("Which of the following statements…can be inferred…"). Specifically, the item stem asks you to identify an implied idea that is made by the author regarding "a 'review and comment' session."

14. **SP** This is a Specific Points item. The item stem asks you for a specific detail that is made by the author regarding certain locator material ("metamorphic rock"), as indicated by the phrase "according to the passage." Note also that the word "EXCEPT" indicates a reversal of thought, suggesting that all but one of the answer choices is found in the passage.

15. **SP** This is a Specific Points item. The item asks you for a specific detail that is made by the author regarding certain locator material ("the sequence of events leading to the present landscape"), as indicated by the phrase "as described by the selection."

16. **E** This is an Evaluation item. The item stem asks you to determine how the author regards his own explanation for something. To answer this item, you must further assess the details presented in the passage.

17. **SP** This is a Specific Points item. The item stem asks you for a particular term that can be defined by specific information that is provided by the author of the passage.

18. **E** This is an Evaluation item. The item stem asks you to choose a statement with which the author would most likely agree. In order to answer this item, you must have an understanding of the author's position and be able to extrapolate that information to determine the author's view on related issues.

19. **E**   This is an Evaluation item. The item stem asks you to draw a conclusion about something ("the writings of Yevgeny Zamyatin") that is supported by the details of the passage. To answer this item, you must apply those details to a new situation.

20. **E**   This is an Evaluation item. The item stem asks you to determine the author's attitude toward something ("James Burnham's writing"), as indicated by the phrase "the author's treatment of."

21. **E**   This is an Evaluation item. The item asks you to determine the implicit meaning of a statement made by the author: "Burham inverted the logical priority of the individual over the state."

22. **SP**   This is a Specific Points item. The item stem asks you for a specific detail regarding something that is specifically mentioned by the author in the passage (the nature of his or her criticism of Burnham).

## EXERCISE 12—ITEM-TYPE CODING (p. 94)

1. **SD**   This is a Specific Detail item. The item stem asks you for a specific detail regarding something that is specifically mentioned by the author in the passage (why Burnham thinks that history will come to an end in a completely autocratic state). Notice that the phrase "according to Burnham" is interchangeable with either "according to the author" or "according to the passage."

2. **II**   This is an Implied Idea item. The item stem asks you for an implied idea that is made by the author regarding a specific detail, as indicated by the phrase "it can be inferred from the passage."

3. **II**   This is an Implied Idea item. The item stem asks you for an implied idea that is made by the author regarding a specific detail (the nature of "currently accepted theories on galaxy formation").

4. **SD**   This is a Specific Detail item. The item stem asks you for a specific detail that is made by the author regarding certain locator material ("a cluster with a central, supergiant galaxy"), as indicated by the phrase "according to the passage."

5. **SD**   This is a Specific Detail item. The item stem asks you for a specific detail that is made by the author regarding certain locator material ("the outcome of a collision between galaxies"), as indicated by the phrase "according to the passage."

6. **SD**   This is a Specific Detail item. The item stem asks you for a specific detail that is made by the author regarding certain locator material ("a galaxy falls inward toward the center of a cluster"), as indicated by the phrase "according to the passage."

7. **SD**   This is a Specific Detail item. The item stem asks you for a specific detail that is made by the author regarding certain locator material ("our Sun would probably not be found in a cluster such as Virgo"), as indicated by the phrase "according to the passage."

8. **FA**   This is a Further Application item. The item stem asks you to determine the meaning of a quote by Emerson based on what you have learned from the rest of the passage. Therefore, you are making a further assessment based on given details.

9. **II**   This is an Implied Idea item. The item stem asks you for an implied idea that is made by the author regarding a specific detail ("the difference between farms and the landscape").

10. **II**   This is an Implied Idea item. The item stem asks you to determine the meaning of a vocabulary word ("property") as it is used in the context of a phrase ("property in the horizon") in the passage (line #).

11. **II**   This is an Implied Idea item. The item stem asks you for the meaning of a phrase ("color of the spirit") as it used in the context of the passage (line #).

12. **MI**   This is a Main Idea item. The item stem asks you for a description of the author's main purpose, or central theme, of the passage.

13. **FA**   This is a Further Application item. The item asks you to determine the difference between things that are described in the passage ("a life circumstance and a life event"). To answer this item, you must further assess the details presented in the passage.

14. **LS**   This is a Logical Structure item. The item stem asks you to recognize a technique that the author does not use to develop the overall structure of the passage. Note also that the word "EXCEPT" indicates a reversal of thought, suggesting that all but one of the answer choices is found in the passage.

15. **LS**   This is a Logical Structure item. The item stem asks you to recognize the relationship between two consecutive paragraphs in the passage, which in turn indicates how the author develops the overall structure of the passage.

16. **SD**   This is a Specific Detail item. The item stem asks you for a particular term that can be defined by specific information that is provided by the author of the passage.

17. **SD**   This is a Specific Detail item. The item stem asks you for a specific detail that is made by the author regarding certain locator material (geographical features of Wineland), as indicated by the phrase "according to the passage."

18. **II**   This is an Implied Idea item. The item stem asks you for an implied idea that is made by the author regarding a specific detail, as indicated by the phrase "it can be inferred from the passage." Note also that the word "EXCEPT" indicates a reversal of thought, suggesting that all but one of the answer choices is found in the passage.

19. **LS**   This is a Logical Structure item. The item stem asks you for the logical role played by a specific part of the passage (the author's mention of "the two high mountains"), as indicated by the structure "the author mentions…in order to."

20. **SD**   This is a Specific Detail item. The item stem asks you for a specific detail that is made by the author regarding certain locator material (similarities between Leif Erikson's voyage and Biarni's voyage), as indicated by the phrase "all of the following are mentioned." Note also that the word "EXCEPT" indicates a reversal of thought, suggesting that all but one of the answer choices is found in the passage.

21. **II**   This is an Implied Idea item. The item stem asks you for an implied idea that is made by the author regarding a specific detail (the historicity of the Biarni narrative), as indicated by the phrase "it can be inferred that the author."

22. **AT**   This is an Attitude/Tone item. The item stem asks you to determine the author's attitude toward someone ("the Aleuts").

# VERBAL REASONING CONCEPTS AND STRATEGIES

## ANALOGIES—CORE LESSON (p. 107)

| | | | |
|---|---|---|---|
| 1. E | 13. E | 25. B | 37. E |
| 2. B | 14. B | 26. E | 38. B |
| 3. A | 15. E | 27. E | 39. A |
| 4. B | 16. A | 28. D | 40. E |
| 5. A | 17. B | 29. C | 41. C |
| 6. C | 18. D | 30. C | 42. C |
| 7. A | 19. D | 31. A | 43. E |
| 8. C | 20. C | 32. D | 44. A |
| 9. A | 21. C | 33. C | 45. B |
| 10. A | 22. C | 34. D | |
| 11. B | 23. A | 35. E | |
| 12. A | 24. B | 36. A | |

## ANALOGIES—REVIEW (p. 111)

| | | | |
|---|---|---|---|
| 1. B | 14. B | 27. C | 40. D |
| 2. C | 15. B | 28. D | 41. B |
| 3. B | 16. A | 29. B | 42. A |
| 4. B | 17. B | 30. D | 43. C |
| 5. E | 18. A | 31. B | 44. B |
| 6. C | 19. B | 32. C | 45. E |
| 7. E | 20. C | 33. A | 46. C |
| 8. E | 21. C | 34. A | 47. B |
| 9. A | 22. E | 35. C | 48. D |
| 10. D | 23. B | 36. D | 49. A |
| 11. A | 24. B | 37. B | 50. E |
| 12. E | 25. B | 38. E | |
| 13. B | 26. C | 39. D | |

## ANALOGIES—TIMED-PRACTICE QUIZZES (p. 116)

| *QUIZ I* | *QUIZ II* | *QUIZ III* |
|---|---|---|
| 1. A | 1. B | 1. D |
| 2. B | 2. E | 2. B |
| 3. A | 3. C | 3. C |
| 4. A | 4. D | 4. C |
| 5. A | 5. A | 5. C |
| 6. E | 6. B | 6. B |
| 7. A | 7. B | 7. E |
| 8. E | 8. D | 8. C |
| 9. B | 9. A | 9. A |
| 10. C | 10. E | 10. E |
| 11. B | 11. B | 11. A |
| 12. C | 12. D | 12. C |
| 13. B | 13. D | 13. D |
| 14. B | 14. C | 14. B |
| 15. B | 15. D | 15. A |
| 16. C | 16. C | 16. E |
| 17. E | 17. B | 17. E |
| 18. A | 18. C | 18. B |
| 19. D | 19. E | 19. C |
| 20. A | 20. A | 20. B |
| 21. C | 21. D | 21. D |
| 22. A | 22. E | 22. B |

## ANTONYMS—CORE LESSON (p. 129)

| | | | |
|---|---|---|---|
| 1. B | 9. B | 17. A | 25. B |
| 2. D | 10. D | 18. C | 26. D |
| 3. A | 11. E | 19. A | 27. C |
| 4. B | 12. A | 20. A | 28. B |
| 5. E | 13. E | 21. D | 29. C |
| 6. A | 14. C | 22. B | 30. E |
| 7. C | 15. B | 23. B | |
| 8. C | 16. E | 24. C | |

# ANSWERS AND EXPLANATIONS

## ANTONYMS—REVIEW (p. 132)

| | | | |
|---|---|---|---|
| 1. A | 11. A | 21. D | 31. B |
| 2. B | 12. D | 22. B | 32. C |
| 3. C | 13. E | 23. D | 33. D |
| 4. A | 14. C | 24. C | 34. D |
| 5. C | 15. C | 25. C | 35. E |
| 6. A | 16. A | 26. D | 36. D |
| 7. C | 17. E | 27. B | 37. B |
| 8. A | 18. B | 28. C | 38. D |
| 9. A | 19. C | 29. A | |
| 10. A | 20. A | 30. B | |

## ANTONYMS—TIMED-PRACTICE QUIZZES (p. 136)

| *QUIZ I* | *QUIZ II* | *QUIZ III* |
|---|---|---|
| 1. E | 1. E | 1. C |
| 2. C | 2. D | 2. A |
| 3. B | 3. C | 3. C |
| 4. A | 4. D | 4. A |
| 5. A | 5. C | 5. B |
| 6. E | 6. D | 6. E |
| 7. D | 7. A | 7. E |
| 8. D | 8. A | 8. E |
| 9. A | 9. E | 9. A |
| 10. D | 10. A | 10. C |
| 11. C | 11. E | 11. B |
| 12. E | 12. D | 12. C |
| 13. D | 13. A | 13. B |
| 14. B | 14. A | 14. E |
| 15. C | 15. E | 15. B |
| 16. E | 16. A | 16. D |
| 17. A | 17. D | 17. A |
| 18. E | 18. B | 18. B |
| 19. A | 19. B | 19. C |
| 20. C | 20. B | 20. E |

## SENTENCE COMPLETIONS—CORE LESSON (p. 149)

| | | | |
|---|---|---|---|
| 1. **C** | 12. **E** | 23. **D** | 34. **labyrinth;** **manipulation** |
| 2. **A** | 13. **D** | 24. **D** | 35. **false;** **competition** |
| 3. **E** | 14. **B** | 25. **B** | 36. **arcane;** **classical;** **advocating** |
| 4. **E** | 15. **C** | 26. **A** | 37. **attenuated;** **unimpaired;** **complex** |
| 5. **B** | 16. **B** | 27. **B** | |
| 6. **B** | 17. **C** | 28. **E** | |
| 7. **B** | 18. **A** | 29. **D** | |
| 8. **A** | 19. **E** | 30. **E** | |
| 9. **C** | 20. **A** | 31. **E** | |
| 10. **B** | 21. **E** | 32. **C** | |
| 11. **B** | 22. **D** | 33. **B** | |

## SENTENCE COMPLETIONS—REVIEW (p. 154)

| | | | |
|---|---|---|---|
| 1. **B** | 15. **B** | 29. **B** | 43. **B** |
| 2. **C** | 16. **D** | 30. **D** | 44. **A** |
| 3. **A** | 17. **B** | 31. **B** | 45. **A** |
| 4. **B** | 18. **B** | 32. **D** | 46. **A** |
| 5. **C** | 19. **A** | 33. **A** | 47. **A** |
| 6. **A** | 20. **C** | 34. **C** | 48. **C** |
| 7. **E** | 21. **D** | 35. **A** | 49. **E** |
| 8. **C** | 22. **B** | 36. **C** | 50. **A** |
| 9. **A** | 23. **D** | 37. **D** | 51. **A** |
| 10. **B** | 24. **C** | 38. **D** | 52. **A** |
| 11. **E** | 25. **D** | 39. **E** | 53. **C** |
| 12. **A** | 26. **D** | 40. **C** | 54. **C** |
| 13. **D** | 27. **B** | 41. **C** | |
| 14. **A** | 28. **B** | 42. **C** | |

## SENTENCE COMPLETIONS—TIMED-PRACTICE QUIZZES (p. 160)

| *QUIZ I* | *QUIZ II* | *QUIZ III* |
|---|---|---|
| 1.  B | 1.  E | 1.  B |
| 2.  C | 2.  D | 2.  B |
| 3.  B | 3.  A | 3.  D |
| 4.  D | 4.  D | 4.  B |
| 5.  A | 5.  D | 5.  E |
| 6.  E | 6.  A | 6.  E |
| 7.  E | 7.  E | 7.  B |
| 8.  D | 8.  D | 8.  C |
| 9.  B | 9.  E | 9.  D |
| 10.  C | 10.  B | 10.  D |
| 11.  E | 11.  A | 11.  C |
| 12.  D | 12.  C | 12.  B |
| 13.  D | 13.  C | 13.  C |
| 14.  B | 14.  B | 14.  C |
| 15.  E | 15.  A | 15.  D |
| 16.  C | 16.  C | 16.  C |
| 17.  B | 17.  B | 17.  B |
| 18.  E | 18.  D | 18.  D |
| 19.  B | 19.  B | 19.  B |
| 20.  D | 20.  B | 20.  A |

## READING COMPREHENSION—CORE LESSON (p. 177)

| | | | |
|---|---|---|---|
| 1. **B** | 8. **C** | 15. **A** | 22. **D** |
| 2. **D** | 9. **E** | 16. **E** | 23. **B** |
| 3. **A** | 10. **E** | 17. **A** | 24. **D** |
| 4. **E** | 11. **A** | 18. **D** | 25. **A** |
| 5. **C** | 12. **C** | 19. **E** | 26. **D** |
| 6. **C** | 13. **C** | 20. **C** | |
| 7. **A** | 14. **B** | 21. **C** | |

## READING COMPREHENSION—REVIEW (p. 185)

| | | | |
|---|---|---|---|
| 1. **A** | 10. **B** | 19. **B** | 28. **C** |
| 2. **E** | 11. **A** | 20. **A** | 29. **E** |
| 3. **D** | 12. **B** | 21. **C** | 30. **B** |
| 4. **B** | 13. **D** | 22. **B** | 31. **A** |
| 5. **E** | 14. **A** | 23. **A** | 32. **D** |
| 6. **C** | 15. **A** | 24. **D** | |
| 7. **C** | 16. **E** | 25. **E** | |
| 8. **D** | 17. **E** | 26. **B** | |
| 9. **A** | 18. **C** | 27. **A** | |

## READING COMPREHENSION—TIMED-PRACTICE QUIZZES (p. 196)

| *QUIZ I* | *QUIZ II* | *QUIZ III* |
|---|---|---|
| 1. **B** | 1. **C** | 1. **E** |
| 2. **C** | 2. **B** | 2. **D** |
| 3. **B** | 3. **E** | 3. **E** |
| 4. **D** | 4. **D** | 4. **D** |
| 5. **A** | 5. **B** | 5. **B** |
| 6. **E** | 6. **D** | 6. **D** |
| 7. **C** | 7. **D** | 7. **D** |
| 8. **D** | 8. **C** | 8. **C** |

# Quantitative Reasoning

# QUANTITATIVE REASONING SKILLS REVIEW

**EXERCISE 1—NUMBERS** (p. 228)

1. **(B)** To decrease the value of the number 12,345 by 1,000, simply subtract 1 from the digit in the thousands column (2).

2. **(B)** To increase the value of the number 736,124 by 30,000, simply add 3 to the digit in the ten thousands column (3).

3. **(B)** Adding 1 to each digit of the number 222,222 is the same as adding 111,111 to that number $(222,222+111,111)$. Therefore, adding 1 to each digit of 222,222 will increase the value of the number by 111,111.

4. **(C)** $(1 \cdot 10,000)+(2 \cdot 1,000)+(3 \cdot 100)+(4 \cdot 10)+(5 \cdot 1)=10,000+2,000+300+40+5=12,345$.

   Alternatively, recognize that the item stem is designed in the form of the column system. So, there is a 1 in the ten thousands place, a 2 in the thousands place, a 3 in the hundreds place, a 4 in the tens place, and a 5 in the units place. These digits can therefore be arranged as 12,345.

5. **(C)** $(1 \cdot 1)+(1 \cdot 10)+(1 \cdot 100)+(1 \cdot 1,000)+(1 \cdot 10,000)=1+10+100+1,000+10,000=11,111$.

   Alternatively, recognize that this particular item stem is designed in the form of an inverted column system (starting with the units place and moving up to the ten thousands place). So, there is a 1 in the units place, a 1 in the tens place, a 1 in the hundreds place, a 1 in the thousands place, and a 1 in the ten thousands place. These digits can therefore be arranged as 11,111.

6. **(D)** $(1 \cdot 100,000)+(2 \cdot 10,000)+(3 \cdot 1,000)=100,000+20,000+3,000=123,000$.

   Alternatively, recognize that this item stem too is designed in the form of the column system. So, there is a 1 in the hundred thousands place, a 2 in the ten thousands place, and a 3 in the thousands place. These digits can therefore be arranged as 123,000.

7. **(C)** $(2 \cdot 1,000)+(3 \cdot 100)+(1 \cdot 10,000)+(2 \cdot 10)+1=2,000+300+10,000+20+1=12,321$.

   Alternatively, note that there is a 1 in the ten thousands place, a 2 in the thousands place, a 3 in the hundreds place, a 2 in the tens place, and a 1 in the units place. These digits can therefore be arranged as 12,321.

8. **(E)** $(9 \cdot 10,000)+(9 \cdot 100)=90,000+900=90,900$.

   Alternatively, note that there is a 9 in the ten thousands place and a 9 in the hundreds place. These digits can therefore be arranged as 90,900.

9. **(E)** $(2 \cdot 10,000)+(8 \cdot 1,000)+(4 \cdot 10)=20,000+8,000+40=28,040$.

   Alternatively, note that there is a 2 in the ten thousands place, an 8 in the thousands place, and a 4 in the tens place. These digits can therefore be arranged as 28,040.

10. **(B)** $2+3=5$.

11. **(C)** $5+7+8=12+8=20$.

12. **(D)** $20 + 30 + 40 = 50 + 40 = 90$.

13. **(D)** $8 - 3 = 5$.

14. **(C)** $28 - 14 = 14$.

15. **(D)** $2 \cdot 8 = 16$.

16. **(C)** $20 \cdot 50 = 1,000$.

17. **(C)** $12 \cdot 10 = 120$.

18. **(B)** $(5+1) + (2+3) = 6 + 5 = 11$.

19. **(B)** $(5+2) - (3 \cdot 2) = 7 - 6 = 1$.

20. **(C)** $(2+3) \cdot (3+4) = 5 \cdot 7 = 35$.

21. **(C)** $(2 \cdot 3) + (3 \cdot 4) = 6 + 12 = 18$.

22. **(C)** $(3 \cdot 4) - (2 \cdot 3) = 12 - 6 = 6$.

23. **(E)** $12 \div 7 = 1$, with a remainder of 5.

24. **(A)** $18 \div 2 = 9$, with a remainder of 0.

25. **(A)** $50 \div 2 = 25$, with a remainder of 0.

26. **(D)** $15 \div 8 = 1$, with a remainder of 7.

27. **(B)** $15 \div 2 = 7$, with a remainder of 1.

28. **(B)** $8 \div 5 = 1$, with a remainder of 3. $13 \div 5 = 2$, with a remainder of 3. To solve this item, first subtract 3 from both 8 and 13, resulting in 5 and 10, respectively. Then, figure out if 5 and 10 can be divided by any of the answer choices without yielding a remainder. Both 5 and 10 are evenly divisible by 5.

29. **(A)** $33 \div 4 = 8$, with a remainder of 1. $37 \div 4 = 9$, with a remainder of 1. To solve this item, first subtract 1 from both 33 and 37, resulting in 32 and 36, respectively. Then, figure out if 32 and 36 can be divided by any of the answer choices without yielding a remainder. Both 32 and 36 are evenly divisible by 4.

30. **(D)** $12 \div 7 = 1$, with a remainder of 5. $19 \div 7 = 2$, with a remainder of 5. To solve this item, first subtract 5 from both 12 and 19, resulting in 7 and 14, respectively. Then, figure out if 7 and 14 can be divided by any of the answer choices without yielding a remainder. Both 7 and 14 are evenly divisible by 7.

31. **(D)** $(4 \cdot 3) + 2 = 12 + 2 = 14$.

32. **(C)** $(2 \cdot 3) \div (2 + 1) = 6 \div 3 = 2$.

33. **(C)** $[2 \cdot (12 \div 4)] + [6 \div (1 + 2)] = (2 \cdot 3) + (6 \div 3) = 6 + 2 = 8$.

34. **(E)** $[(36 \div 12) \cdot (24 \div 3)] \div [(1 \cdot 3) - (18 \div 9)] = (3 \cdot 8) \div (3 - 2) = 24 \div 1 = 24$. Remember to work inside out.

35. **(B)** $[(12 \cdot 3) - (3 \cdot 12)] + [(8 \div 2) \div 4] = (36 - 36) + (4 \div 4) = 0 + 1 = 1.$ Solve the inside parentheses first; then work outwards.

36. **(A)** $(1 \cdot 2 \cdot 3 \cdot 4) - [(2 \cdot 3) + (3 \cdot 6)] = 24 - (6 + 18) = 24 - 24 = 0.$

37. **(D)** Solve I, II, and III to see if the left side of the equation is equal to the right side.

    I: $(4 + 3) - 6 = 4 + (6 - 2) \Rightarrow 7 - 6 = 4 + 4 \Rightarrow 1 \neq 8.$
    II: $3(4 + 5) = (3 \cdot 4) + (3 \cdot 5) \Rightarrow 3(9) = 12 + 15 \Rightarrow 27 = 27.$
    III: $(3 + 5) \cdot 4 = 4 \cdot (5 + 3) \Rightarrow 8 \cdot 4 = 4 \cdot 8 \Rightarrow 32 = 32.$

    II and III are true statements.

38. **(B)** Factor out 12 from 12, 24, and 36 to get $12(1 + 2 + 3).$

39. **(D)** Factor out 25 from 25, 50, and 100 to get $25(1 + 2 + 4).$

40. **(B)** Factor out the 99 in the numerator; then, simplify. $\frac{99(121) - 99(120)}{33} = \frac{99(121 - 120)}{33} = \frac{99(1)}{33} = 3.$

41. **(A)** Factor out 1,234; then, simplify. $1,234(96) - 1,234(48) = 1,234(96 - 48) = 1,234 \cdot 48.$

42. **(C)** 23 and 29 are the only two numbers between 20 and 30 that are not divisible by any number other than themselves and 1.

43. **(C)** 50 and 60 are the only two numbers between 50 and 60 that are not divisible by any number other than themselves and 1.

44. **(A)** 11 is not divisible by any number other than 1 and itself. 111 is divisible by 3. 1,111 is divisible by 11. So, only I is prime.

45. **(E)** 12,345 is divisible by 5. 999,999,999 is divisible by 3. 1,000,000,002 is divisible by 2. None of the three Roman numerals are prime.

46. **(A)** First, list all the prime factors of each number. Then, multiply together the common prime factors from both numbers. This will be the greatest common factor between the two numbers. $25 = 5 \cdot 5.$ $40 = 2 \cdot 2 \cdot 2 \cdot 5.$ 5 is the greatest common factor of 25 and 40.

47. **(B)** First, list all the prime factors of each number. The product of the common prime factors will be the greatest shared factor: $6 = 2 \cdot 3.$ $9 = 3 \cdot 3.$ 3 is the greatest common factor of 6 and 9.

48. **(A)** First, list all the prime factors of each number. Then, multiply together the common prime factors from both numbers. This will be the greatest common factor between the two numbers. $12 = 2 \cdot 3 \cdot 3.$ $18 = 2 \cdot 3 \cdot 3.$ $2 \cdot 3 = 6$ is the greatest common factor of 12 and 18.

49. **(A)** First, list all the prime factors of each number. Then, multiply together the common prime factors from all the numbers. This will be the greatest common factor among the three numbers. $18 = 2 \cdot 3 \cdot 3.$ $24 = 2 \cdot 2 \cdot 2 \cdot 3.$ $36 = 2 \cdot 2 \cdot 3 \cdot 3.$ $2 \cdot 3 = 6$ is the greatest common factor of 18, 24, and 36.

50. **(B)** First, list all the prime factors of each number. Then, multiply together the common prime factors from all the numbers. This will be the greatest common factor among the three numbers. $7 = 1 \cdot 7.$ $14 = 2 \cdot 7.$ $21 = 3 \cdot 7.$ 7 is the greatest common factor of 7, 14, and 21.

51. **(B)** The smallest multiple of two numbers is the smallest number that shares all of the prime factors of those two numbers. Since 5 and 2 are both prime, their product, 10 is the smallest common multiple.

52. **(A)** First, list all the prime factors of each number. Then, multiply all the prime factors that occur in either list. $12 = 2 \cdot 2 \cdot 3$. $18 = 2 \cdot 3 \cdot 3$. The prime factors that occur in either list are 2, 2, 3 and 3. So, the lowest common multiple of 12 and 18 is $2 \cdot 2 \cdot 3 \cdot 3 = 36$.

53. **(C)** Even numbers are evenly divisible by 2. 12 can be evenly divided by 2 twice. 36 can be evenly divided by 2 twice. Only 101 cannot be evenly divided by 2. Therefore, only I and II are even.

54. **(C)** According to the principles of odd and even numbers, multiplying an even number by an odd number will always result in an even number. However, multiplying an odd number by another odd number will always result in an odd number. Therefore, only III results in an odd number.

55. **(C)** According to the principles of odd and even numbers, multiplying an even number by an odd number will always result in an even number. Also, adding an odd number to another odd number will always result in an even number. However, multiplying an odd number by another odd number will always result in an odd number. Therefore, both I and II will yield even numbers.

56. **(E)** There are no rules in the principles of odd and even numbers for division, therefore it is highly likely that answer choice (E) may not always be even. Test this out by substituting an even number for n, 2: $\frac{2}{2} = 1$, which is odd. Furthermore, the product of two even numbers is even, the sum of two even numbers is even, and the product of an even number and an odd number is even.

57. **(C)** I may be even if n is odd. II may be even if n is even. III is the only one that must be odd no matter what n, because any number times two will be even, and any even number minus an odd number, in this case one, will result in an odd number.

58. **(C)** Start by defining the item stem. It asks for the first number in a series of three consecutive whole numbers, where the third is equal to 8. So, there are three variables: $n$, $n+1$, and $n+2$. $n+2 = 8 \Rightarrow n = 8-2 = 6$. The first of the three consecutive whole numbers is n, and n is equal to 6. Or, just count backwards twice from 8.

59. **(D)** Start by defining the item stem. It asks for the third number in a series of five consecutive odd numbers, where the fifth is equal to 15. So, there are five variables: $n$, $n+2$, $n+4$, $n+6$, and $n+8$. $n+8 = 15 \Rightarrow n = 15-8 = 7$. The third of the five consecutive whole numbers is $n+4$, and that is equal to 11, $7+4 = 11$.

Alternatively, count backwards from 15.

60. **(C)** Start by defining the item stem. It asks for the largest of three consecutive whole numbers, where the total of all three numbers is equal to 15. So, there are three variables: $n$, $n+1$, and $n+2$, which also refer to $m$, $n$, and $o$, respectively. $n+(n+1)+(n+2) = 15 \Rightarrow 3n+3 = 15 \Rightarrow n = \frac{15-3}{3} = 4$. The largest of the three consecutive whole numbers is $n+2$, and that is equal to 6, $4+2 = 6$.

61. **(A)** First, find the exponents of each of the prime factors in the equation. Then add one to each and multiply them together. The exponents of $2^2$, 3, and 7 are 2, 1, and 1, respectively. $(2+1)(1+1)(1+1) = 3 \cdot 2 \cdot 2 = 12$. $A$ has 12 positive factors including 1 and 84.

62. **(D)** First, find the exponents of each of the prime factors in the equation. Then add one to each and multiply them together. The exponents of 5, $2^3$, and 11 are 1, 3, and 1, respectively. $(1+1)(3+1)(1+1) = 2 \cdot 4 \cdot 2 = 16$. $B$ has 16 positive factors including 1 and 440. The above is a method of finding all of the possible combinations of the prime factors of a number. Including the exponent zero, 5 can be taken to two powers, 0 and 1, 2 to 4 powers, 0, 1, 2, and 3, and 11 to 2 powers, 0 and 1. So, the total number of combinations will be equal to the product of the number of possibilities for each prime.

63. **(A)** First, perform all the operations inside the parentheses; then, multiply $ab$ by the result of these operations. If either $a$ or $b$ is 0 then the whole equation would also be 0. Therefore, neither $a$ nor $b$ can be 0 since the right side of the equation is not 0 but $-6$.

64. **(E)** First, perform all the operations inside the brackets; then, multiply $e$ by the result of these operations. If $e$ is 0 then the whole equation would also be 0. And since the right side of the equation is 3, $e$ cannot be 0.

65. **(E)** $3 + 1 = 4$. The original position is 3. Moving it 1 unit in the positive direction would result in 4.

66. **(D)** $5 - 2 = 3$. The original position is 5. Moving it 2 units in the negative direction would result in 3.

67. **(D)** $5 + (-2) = 5 - 2 = 3$. The original position of the counter is 5. Moving it 2 units in the negative direction would result in 3.

68. **(A)** $3 + 2 + (-7) = 5 - 7 = -2$. The original position of the counter is 3. Moving it 2 units in the positive direction would result in a 5. Moving the counter 7 units from the 5 in a negative direction would result in $-2$.

69. **(B)** $2 + (-4) = 2 - 4 = -2$. The original position of the counter is 2. Moving it 4 units in the negative direction would result in $-2$.

70. **(A)** $-2 + (-2) = -2 - 2 = -4$. The original position of the counter is $-2$. Moving it 2 units in the negative direction would result in $-4$.

71. **(C)** $4 + (-2) + (-2) = 4 - 2 + (-2) = 2 - 2 = 0$. The original position of the counter is 4. Moving it 2 units in the negative direction would result in 2. Moving it 2 more units in the negative direction would result in 0.

72. **(A)** $-4 + (-1) + (-1) = -4 - 1 + (-1) = -5 - 1 = -6$. The original position of the counter is $-4$. Moving it 1 unit in the negative direction would result in $-5$. Moving it 1 more unit in the negative direction would result in $-6$.

73. **(D)** $-4 + 8 = 8 - 4 = 4$. The original position of the counter is $-4$. Moving it 8 units in the positive direction would result in 4.

74. **(D)** $-2 + 2 + (-1) = 0 - 1 = -1$.

75. **(E)** $2 - (-1) = 2 + 1 = 3$.

76. **(E)** $5 - (-2) = 5 + 2 = 7$.

77. **(D)** $0 - (-4) = 0 + 4 = 4$.

78. **(C)** $-2 - (-1) = -2 + 1 = 1 - 2 = -1$.

79. **(D)** $-3 - (-1) - (-2) = -3 + 1 - (-2) = -2 + 2 = 0$.

80. **(C)** $5 + 8 + (-2) + (-1) = 13 - 2 + (-1) = 11 - 1 = 10$.

81. **(C)** $12 - 7 + 6 + (-1) = 5 + 6 + (-1) = 11 - 1 = 10$.

82. **(C)** $3 + (-3) = 3 - 3 = 0$.

83. **(A)** $0 + (-12) = 0 - 12 = -12$.

84. **(B)** $-3 + 1 = 1 - 3 = -2$.

85. **(A)** $-2+(-6)=-2-6=-8$.

86. **(B)** $-2+(-3)+(-4)=-2-3+(-4)=-5-4=-9$.

87. **(D)** $100+(-99)=100-99=1$.

88. **(A)** $14-(-2)=14+2=16$.

89. **(A)** $2-(-5)=2+5=7$.

90. **(D)** $0-(-4)=0+4=4$.

91. **(D)** $-2-(-3)=-2+3=1$.

92. **(B)** $-5-(-1)-1=-5+1-1=-5$.

93. **(C)** $(5-1)+(1-5)=4+(-4)=4-4=0$.

94. **(E)** $[2-(-6)]-[-2+(-1)]=(2+6)-(-2-1)=8-(-3)=8+3=11$.

95. **(A)** $1\cdot(-2)=-2$. An odd number of negatives will result in a negative answer.

96. **(A)** $-8\cdot6=-48$. An odd number of negatives will result in a negative answer.

97. **(E)** $-10\cdot(-10)=100$. An even number of negatives will result in a positive answer.

98. **(D)** $-2\cdot(-1)\cdot1=2$. An even number of negatives will result in a positive answer.

99. **(A)** $-10\cdot(-10)\cdot(-10)=-1,000$. An odd number of negatives will result in a negative answer.

100. **(D)** $-2\cdot(-2)\cdot(-2)\cdot(-2)=16$. An even number of negatives will result in a positive answer.

101. **(D)** $-1\cdot(-1)\cdot(-1)\cdot(-1)\cdot(-1)\cdot(-1)\cdot(-1)\cdot(-1)\cdot(-1)\cdot(-1)=1$. An even number of negatives will result in a positive answer.

102. **(B)** $4\div(-2)=-2$. An odd number of negatives will result in a negative answer.

103. **(B)** $-12\div4=-3$. An odd number of negatives will result in a negative answer.

104. **(C)** $-12\div(-12)=1$. An even number of negatives will result in a positive answer.

105. **(C)** $[7-(-6)]+[3\cdot(2-4)]=(7+6)+[(3\cdot(-2)]=13+(-6)=13-6=7$.

106. **(A)** $[2\cdot(-3)][1\cdot(-4)][2\cdot(-1)]=(-6)(-4)(-2)=-48$.

107. **(C)** $[(6\cdot(-2)]\div[(3\cdot(-4)]=-12\div(-12)=1$.

108. **(B)** $[4-(-3)]+[7-(-1)][-3-(-2)]=[(4+3)+(7+1)](-3+2)=(7+8)(-1)=15\cdot(-1)=-15$.

109. **(D)** $\{[2\cdot(-1)]+[4\div(-2)]\}[(-6+6)-(2-3)]=[-2+(-2)][0-(-1)]=(-2-2)(0+1)=-4\cdot1=-4$.

110. **(B)** $(2-3)(3-2)(4-3)(3-4)(5-4)(4-5)=(-1)(1)(1)(-1)(1)(-1)=-1$.

111. **(D)** $[2(3-4)]+\{[125 \div (-25)][1 \cdot (-2)]\} = [2(-1)]+[(-5)(-2)] = -2+10 = 8$.

112. **(C)** $-\frac{1}{2} \cdot 2 \cdot (-\frac{1}{2}) \cdot 2 \cdot (-\frac{1}{2}) \cdot 2 = -1 \cdot (-1) \cdot (-1) = -1$.

113. **(B)** $[(2 \cdot 3) \div (-6 \cdot 1)][(21 \div 7) \cdot \frac{1}{3}] = (-\frac{6}{6})(\frac{3}{3}) = -1$.

114. **(A)** $[-5 \cdot (-2)]-[-2 \cdot (-5)] = 10-10 = 0$.

115. **(A)** $6 \div (-\frac{1}{3}) = 6 \cdot (-3) = -18$.

116. **(C)** $[-3-(-3)]-[-2-(-2)]-[-1-(-1)] = (-3+3)-(-2+2)-(-1+1) = 0$.

117. **(A)** I is correct because the sum of two or more negative numbers must result in a negative number. II is incorrect because the product of an even number of negative numbers must result in a positive number. Finally, III is incorrect because $-n+n = 0$ (e.g., $-1+1 = 0$).

118. **(A)** I is correct because the product of a negative number and a positive number must result in a negative number. II is incorrect because the product of any number of positive numbers must result in a positive number. Finally, III is incorrect because $n-n = 0$ (e.g., $-1-(-1) = -1+1 = 0$).

119. **(C)** I is correct because the product of a positive number and a negative number must result in a negative number. II is correct because the sum of two negative numbers must result in a negative number. Finally, III is incorrect because the sum of two positive numbers must result in a positive number.

120. **(E)** I is incorrect because $-n+n = 0$ (e.g., $-1+1 = 0$). II is correct because the product of an even number of negative numbers must result in a positive number. Finally, III is correct because a positive number divided by another positive number must result in a positive number.

121. **(B)** I is incorrect because it is equal to $n^6$: $-n \cdot (-n) \cdot (-n) \cdot (-n) \cdot (-n) \cdot (-n) = (-n)^6 = n^6$; therefore, $n \neq 0$. II is correct because it is equal to 0: $[(n-n)-n]-[(n-n)-n] = (0-n)-(0-n) = -n-(-n) = -n+n = 0$. Finally, III is incorrect because it is equal to $n^2$: $n \div [(n \div n) \div n] = n \div (1 \div n) = n \div \frac{1}{n} = n \cdot n = n^2$; therefore, $n \neq 0$.

122. **(D)** Point $x$ between $A$ and $B$ is two times as far from $A$ as from $B$. This means that $x-A$ is twice the distance of $B-x$. Solve the equation for $x$: $x-A = 2(B-x) \Rightarrow x-(-10) = 2(41-x) \Rightarrow x+10 = 82-2x \Rightarrow x+2x = 82-10 \Rightarrow 3x = 72 \Rightarrow x = \frac{72}{3} = 24$.

123. **(B)** Point $x$ between $A$ and $B$ is three times as far from $A$ as from $B$. This means that $x-A$ is three times the distance of $B-x$. Solve the equation for $x$: $x-A = 3(B-x) \Rightarrow x-(-12) = 3(28-x) \Rightarrow x+12 = 84-3x \Rightarrow x+3x = 84-12 \Rightarrow 4x = 72 \Rightarrow x = \frac{72}{4} = 18$.

124. **(E)** $|1|+|-2|+|3|+|-4|+|5|+|-6|+|7|+|-8|+|9|+|-10|+|11|+|-12| = 1+2+3+4+5+6+7+8+9+10+11+12 = 78$.

## EXERCISE 2—FRACTIONS (p. 241)

1. **(E)** $\frac{(5 \cdot 8)+3}{8} = \frac{40+3}{8} = \frac{43}{8}$.

2. **(D)** $\frac{(2 \cdot 3)+3}{4} = \frac{8+3}{4} = \frac{11}{4}$.

3. **(B)** $\frac{(3 \cdot 12)+1}{12} = \frac{36+1}{12} = \frac{37}{12}$.

4. **(C)** $\frac{(1 \cdot 65) + 1}{65} = \frac{65 + 1}{65} = \frac{66}{65}$.

5. **(C)** $\frac{(5 \cdot 7) + 2}{7} = \frac{35 + 2}{7} = \frac{37}{7}$.

6. **(D)** Divide 12 by 8 to get 1 with a remainder of 4. The whole number part of the mixed number is 1 and the fraction is the remainder 4 over 8, which can be reduced to 1 over 2: $\frac{12}{8} = 12 \div 8 = 1\frac{4}{8} = 1\frac{1}{2}$.

7. **(A)** Divide 20 by 6 to get 3 with a remainder of 2. The whole number part of the mixed number is 3 and the fraction is the remainder 2 over 6, which can be reduced to 1 over 3: $\frac{20}{6} = 20 \div 6 = 3\frac{2}{6} = 3\frac{1}{3}$.

8. **(C)** Divide 23 by 13 to get 1 with a remainder of 10. The whole number part of the mixed number is 1 and the fraction is the remainder 10 over 13: $\frac{23}{13} = 23 \div 13 = 1\frac{10}{13}$.

9. **(E)** Divide 25 by 4 to get 6 with a remainder of 1. The whole number part of the mixed number is 6 and the fraction is the remainder 1 over 4: $\frac{25}{4} = 25 \div 4 = 6\frac{1}{4}$.

10. **(C)** Divide 201 by 100 to get 2 with a remainder of 1. The whole number part of the mixed number is 2 and the fraction is the remainder 1 over 100: $\frac{201}{100} = 201 \div 100 = 2\frac{1}{100}$.

11. **(B)** Divide both the numerator and denominator by the common factor of 3 to get 1 over 4: $\frac{3 \div 3}{12 \div 3} = \frac{1}{4}$.

12. **(C)** Divide both the numerator and denominator by the common factor of 27 to get 1 over 3: $\frac{27 \div 27}{81 \div 27} = \frac{1}{3}$.

13. **(B)** Divide both the numerator and denominator by the common factor of 125 to get 1 over 5: $\frac{125 \div 125}{625 \div 125} = \frac{1}{5}$.

14. **(E)** Divide both the numerator and denominator by the common factor of 13 to get 3 over 4: $\frac{39 \div 13}{52 \div 13} = \frac{3}{4}$.

15. **(E)** Divide both the numerator and denominator by the common factor of 11 to get 11 over 12: $\frac{121 \div 11}{132 \div 11} = \frac{11}{12}$.

16. **(A)** For each answer, determine the number that the numerator, four, of $\frac{4}{25}$ would have to be multiplied by to equal the numerators of the answer fractions. Then, multiply 25 by that number to see if it equals the denominators. Luckily, the first is the answer: $4 \cdot 2 = 8 \Rightarrow 25 \cdot 2 = 50$.

17. **(C)** All of the answer choices, except for (C), can be reduced to 3 over 8. Because 31 is prime, $\frac{31}{81}$ is irreducible. $\frac{6}{16} = \frac{3}{8}$, $\frac{15}{40} = \frac{3}{8}$, $\frac{31}{81} \neq \frac{3}{8}$, $\frac{33}{88} = \frac{3}{8}$, and $\frac{120}{320} = \frac{12}{32} = \frac{3}{8}$.

18. **(C)** All of the answer choices, except for (C), can be reduced to 3 over 4. $\frac{6}{8} = \frac{3}{4}$, $\frac{12}{16} = \frac{3}{4}$, $\frac{20}{24} = \frac{5}{6} \neq \frac{3}{4}$, $\frac{36}{48} = \frac{9}{12} = \frac{3}{4}$, and $\frac{300}{400} = \frac{3}{4}$.

19. **(B)** All of the answer choices, except for (B), can be reduced to 5 over 6: $\frac{25}{30} = \frac{5}{6}$, $\frac{45}{50} = \frac{9}{10} \neq \frac{5}{6}$, $\frac{50}{60} = \frac{5}{6}$, $\frac{55}{66} = \frac{5}{6}$, and $\frac{100}{120} = \frac{50}{60} = \frac{5}{6}$.

20. **(E)** All of the answer choices, except for (E), can be reduced to 1 over 6: $\frac{2}{12} = \frac{1}{6}$, $\frac{3}{18} = \frac{1}{6}$, $\frac{4}{24} = \frac{1}{6}$, $\frac{5}{30} = \frac{1}{6}$, and $\frac{6}{40} = \frac{3}{20} \neq \frac{1}{6}$.

21. **(B)** $\frac{1}{7} + \frac{2}{7} = \frac{1+2}{7} = \frac{3}{7}$.

22. **(B)** $\frac{5}{8} + \frac{1}{8} = \frac{5+1}{8} = \frac{6}{8} = \frac{3}{4}$.

23. **(D)** $\frac{12}{13} + \frac{12}{13} = \frac{12+12}{13} = \frac{24}{13}$.

24. **(B)** $\frac{3}{8} + \frac{5}{8} = \frac{3+5}{8} = \frac{8}{8} = 1$.

25. **(C)** $\frac{1}{11} + \frac{2}{11} + \frac{7}{11} = \frac{1+2+7}{11} = \frac{10}{11}$.

26. **(C)** Use the "flying-x" method to solve this item. Remember to reduce the result. $\frac{3}{8} + \frac{5}{6} = \frac{3 \cdot 6}{8 \cdot 6} + \frac{5 \cdot 8}{6 \cdot 8} = \frac{18+40}{48} = \frac{58}{48} = \frac{29}{24}$.

27. **(E)** Use the "flying-x" method to solve this item: $\frac{1}{8} + \frac{1}{7} = \frac{1 \cdot 7}{8 \cdot 7} + \frac{1 \cdot 8}{7 \cdot 8} = \frac{7+8}{56} = \frac{15}{56}$.

28. **(A)** Use the "flying-x" method to solve this item: $\frac{1}{12} + \frac{1}{7} = \frac{1 \cdot 7}{12 \cdot 7} + \frac{1 \cdot 12}{7 \cdot 12} = \frac{7+12}{84} = \frac{19}{84}$.

29. **(B)** Use the "flying-x" method to solve this item: $\frac{3}{5} + \frac{2}{11} = \frac{3 \cdot 11}{5 \cdot 11} + \frac{2 \cdot 5}{11 \cdot 5} = \frac{33+10}{55} = \frac{43}{55}$.

30. **(C)** Use the "flying-x" method to solve this item. Only apply this method to the first two fractions since the third fraction is already a common multiple of the first two. Then, add to solve. $\frac{1}{2} + \frac{1}{3} + \frac{1}{6} = \frac{1 \cdot 3}{2 \cdot 3} + \frac{1 \cdot 2}{3 \cdot 2} + \frac{1}{6} = \frac{3+2+1}{6} = \frac{6}{6} = 1$.

31. **(D)** The common denominator for this item is 6. Multiply the first fraction by $\frac{2}{2}$ to achieve a common denominator throughout the entire item: $\frac{2}{3} + \frac{3}{6} + \frac{4}{6} = \frac{2 \cdot 2}{3 \cdot 2} + \frac{3}{6} + \frac{4}{6} = \frac{4+3+4}{6} = \frac{11}{6}$.

32. **(B)** $\frac{2}{3} - \frac{1}{3} = \frac{2-1}{3} = \frac{1}{3}$.

33. **(D)** $\frac{5}{7} - \frac{4}{7} = \frac{5-4}{7} = \frac{1}{7}$.

34. **(A)** The common denominator for this item is 10. Multiply the second fraction by $\frac{2}{2}$ to achieve a common denominator throughout the entire item: $\frac{9}{10} - \frac{1}{5} = \frac{9}{10} - \frac{1 \cdot 2}{5 \cdot 2} = \frac{9-2}{10} = \frac{7}{10}$.

35. **(A)** The common denominator for this item is 4. Multiply the first fraction by $\frac{2}{2}$ to achieve a common denominator throughout the entire item: $\frac{3}{2} - \frac{1}{4} = \frac{3 \cdot 2}{2 \cdot 2} - \frac{1}{4} = \frac{6-1}{4} = \frac{5}{4}$.

36. **(C)** Convert the mixed fraction into an improper fraction: $2\frac{1}{2} = \frac{(2 \cdot 2)+1}{2} = \frac{5}{2}$. Then, multiply the first fraction by $\frac{4}{4}$ to achieve a common denominator throughout the entire item: $\frac{5 \cdot 4}{2 \cdot 4} = \frac{20}{8}$. $\frac{20}{8} - \frac{7}{8} = \frac{20-7}{8} = \frac{13}{8}$.

37. **(C)** Convert the mixed fractions into improper fractions: $2\frac{2}{3} = \frac{(2 \cdot 3)+2}{3} = \frac{8}{3}$, and $1\frac{1}{6} = \frac{(1 \cdot 6)+1}{6} = \frac{7}{6}$. Then, multiply the first fraction by $\frac{2}{2}$ to achieve a common denominator throughout the entire item: $\frac{8 \cdot 2}{3 \cdot 2} = \frac{16}{6}$. Solve: $\frac{16}{6} - \frac{7}{6} = \frac{9}{6} = 1\frac{3}{6} = 1\frac{1}{2}$.

38. **(B)** For this item, simplify by canceling the 2s: $\frac{1}{\cancel{2}} \cdot \frac{\cancel{2}}{3} = \frac{1}{3}$.

39. **(B)** For this item, simplify by dividing the 2 in the numerator of the first fraction and the 4 in the denominator of the second fraction by 2: $\frac{2}{7} \cdot \frac{1}{4} = \frac{2 \cdot 1}{7 \cdot 4} = \frac{2}{28} = \frac{1}{14}$.

40. **(A)** $\frac{1}{3} \cdot \frac{1}{3} = \frac{1 \cdot 1}{3 \cdot 3} = \frac{1}{9}$.

41. **(B)** $\frac{1}{2} \cdot \frac{1}{2} \cdot \frac{1}{2} = \frac{1 \cdot 1 \cdot 1}{2 \cdot 2 \cdot 2} = \frac{1}{8}$.

42. **(A)** For this item, simplify by dividing the 3 in the denominator of the first fraction and the 3 in the numerator of the second fraction by 3. Simplify further by dividing the 4 in the denominator of the second fraction and the 4 in the numerator of the third fraction by 4: $\frac{2}{\cancel{3}} \cdot \frac{\cancel{3}}{\cancel{4}} \cdot \frac{\cancel{4}}{5} = \frac{2}{5}$.

43. **(A)** $\frac{1}{4} \cdot \frac{1}{8} \cdot 3 = \frac{1 \cdot 1 \cdot 3}{4 \cdot 8} = \frac{3}{32}$.

44. **(B)** For this item, simplify by dividing the 6 in the denominator of the second fraction and 12 by 6: $\frac{1}{3} \cdot \frac{1}{6} \cdot 12 = \frac{1}{3} \cdot 1 \cdot 2 = \frac{2}{3}$.

45. **(A)** Dividing by a fraction is the same by multiplying by its reciprocal, so invert the divisor, the second fraction, and then multiply. Simplify by dividing the 8 in the denominator of the first fraction and the 4 in the numerator of the second fraction by 4: $\frac{7}{8} \div \frac{3}{4} = \frac{7}{\cancel{8}} \cdot \frac{\cancel{4}}{3} = \frac{7}{2} \cdot \frac{1}{3} = \frac{7}{6}$.

46. **(C)** Invert the divisor, the second fraction, and then multiply. Simplify by dividing the 7 in the denominator of the first fraction and the 7 in the numerator of the second fraction by 7: $\frac{5}{7} \div \frac{1}{7} = \frac{5}{7} \cdot \frac{7}{1} = 5$.

47. **(B)** Dividing by a fraction is the same by multiplying by its reciprocal, so invert the divisor, the second fraction, and then multiply. Simplify by dividing the 12 in the denominator of the first fraction and the 12 in the numerator of the second fraction by 12: $\frac{1}{12} \div \frac{1}{12} = \frac{1}{12} \cdot \frac{12}{1} = \frac{12}{12} = 1$.

48. **(A)** Invert the divisor, the second fraction, and then multiply: $2 \div \frac{1}{11} = 2 \cdot 11 = 22$.

49. **(A)** Invert the divisor, the second fraction, and then multiply: $\frac{8}{9} \div \frac{7}{8} = \frac{8}{9} \cdot \frac{8}{7} = \frac{64}{63}$.

50. **(A)** Invert the divisor, the second fraction, and then multiply. Simplify by dividing the 10 in the denominator of the first fraction and the 5 in the numerator of the second fraction by 5: $\frac{1}{10} \div \frac{3}{5} = \frac{1}{10} \cdot \frac{5}{3} = \frac{1}{2} \cdot \frac{1}{3} = \frac{1}{6}$.

51. **(D)** $(\frac{1}{4} + \frac{2}{3}) \cdot (\frac{3}{2} + \frac{1}{4}) = (\frac{1 \cdot 3}{4 \cdot 3} + \frac{2 \cdot 4}{3 \cdot 4}) \cdot (\frac{3 \cdot 4}{2 \cdot 4} + \frac{1 \cdot 2}{4 \cdot 2}) = \frac{3+8}{12} \cdot \frac{12+2}{8} = \frac{11 \cdot 14}{12 \cdot 8} = \frac{11 \cdot 7}{12 \cdot 4} = \frac{77}{48}$.

52. **(C)** $(\frac{2}{3} \cdot \frac{1}{6}) \div (\frac{1}{2} \cdot \frac{1}{4}) = \frac{2}{18} \div \frac{1}{8} = \frac{1}{9} \cdot \frac{8}{1} = \frac{8}{9}$.

53. **(A)** $[(\frac{1}{3} + \frac{1}{2}) \cdot (\frac{2}{3} - \frac{1}{3})] \cdot 18 = [(\frac{1 \cdot 2}{3 \cdot 2} + \frac{1 \cdot 3}{2 \cdot 3}) \cdot (\frac{1}{3})] \cdot 18 = [\frac{5}{6} \cdot \frac{1}{3}] \cdot 18 = \frac{5}{6} \cdot 6 = 5$. Note that this item is no more difficult than any of the other similar items; it is simply longer. Solve from the inside out, one step at a time.

54. **(A)** $[(\frac{1}{3} \div \frac{1}{6}) \cdot (\frac{2}{3} \div \frac{1}{3})] \cdot (\frac{1}{2} + \frac{3}{4}) = [(\frac{1}{3} \cdot 6) \cdot (\frac{2}{3} \cdot 3)] \cdot (\frac{1 \cdot 2}{2 \cdot 2} + \frac{3}{4}) = (2 \cdot 2) \cdot \frac{5}{4} = 5$. Do not panic at the size of this item. It is actually composed of many smaller problems that can be solved first before combining the answers to find the final solution.

55. **(E)** $8(\frac{1}{3}+\frac{3}{4}) = 8(\frac{1 \cdot 4}{3 \cdot 4}+\frac{3 \cdot 3}{4 \cdot 3}) = 8 \cdot \frac{4+9}{12} = \frac{2 \cdot 13}{3} = \frac{26}{3}$.

56. **(C)** Use the "flying-x" method to solve this item: $\frac{1}{4}-\frac{1}{5} = \frac{1 \cdot 5}{4 \cdot 5}-\frac{1 \cdot 4}{5 \cdot 4} = \frac{5-4}{20} = \frac{1}{20}$.

57. **(E)** Invert the divisor, the bottom fraction, and then multiply. Simplify by dividing the 4 in the numerator of the first fraction and the 2 in the denominator of the second fraction by 2: $\frac{\frac{4}{9}}{\frac{2}{5}} = \frac{4}{9} \cdot \frac{5}{2} = \frac{2}{9} \cdot 5 = \frac{10}{9} = 1\frac{1}{9}$.

58. **(A)** $(-\frac{1}{2})^2 + (\frac{1}{4})^2 + (-2)(\frac{1}{2})^2 = (-\frac{1}{2})(-\frac{1}{2}) + (\frac{1}{4})(\frac{1}{4}) + (-2)(\frac{1}{2})(\frac{1}{2}) = \frac{1}{4} + \frac{1}{16} - \frac{2}{4} = \frac{1}{16} - \frac{1}{4} = \frac{1-4}{16} = -\frac{3}{16}$.

59. **(D)** The fastest way to solve this item is to convert all the fractions into decimals, and then compare them. $\frac{9}{16} = 0.5625$, $\frac{7}{10} = 0.7$, $\frac{5}{8} = 0.625$, $\frac{4}{5} = 0.8$, and $\frac{1}{2} = 0.5$. The largest fraction in this list is (D), $\frac{4}{5} = 0.8$.

60. **(D)** Jughead eats $\frac{2}{5}$ of a pound of cake each day, and he eats this amount each day for three weeks, which is 21 days. $\frac{2 \text{ pounds}}{5 \text{ days}} \cdot 21 \text{ days} = \frac{42}{5} = 8\frac{2}{5}$ pounds.

61. **(E)** Chompa eats $\frac{3}{8}$ of a bag of candy each day, which means that he eats $\frac{21}{8}$ bags of candy each week. If the equation is inverted, it is understood that Chompa eats 21 bags every 8 weeks. Since 42 is twice 21, 42 bags would last 16 weeks.

62. **(A)** Bruce eats $2\frac{1}{2} = \frac{(2 \cdot 2)+1}{2} = \frac{5}{2}$ bananas per day, which means he eats $\frac{35}{2}$ bananas per week. So, Bruce can eat 70 bananas in 4 weeks: $\frac{35}{2} \cdot 4 = 35 \cdot 2 = 70$.

63. **(B)** $3\frac{5}{16} + 2\frac{3}{4} = \frac{3 \cdot 16 + 5}{16} + \frac{2 \cdot 4 + 3}{4} = \frac{53}{16} + \frac{11}{4} = \frac{53}{16} + \frac{11 \cdot 4}{4 \cdot 4} = \frac{53+44}{16} = \frac{97}{16} = 6\frac{1}{16}$.

64. **(E)** $10\frac{1}{2} \div \frac{1}{2} = \frac{21}{2} \div \frac{1}{2} = \frac{21}{2} \cdot \frac{2}{1} = 21$.

65. **(D)** $5\frac{3}{4} \cdot 3 = \frac{23}{4} \cdot \frac{3}{1} = \frac{69}{4} = 17\frac{1}{4}$.

66. **(A)** The lowest common denominator for the first week is 24. Thus, $3\frac{1}{2} = 3\frac{12}{24}$, $1\frac{1}{4} = 1\frac{6}{24}$, $1\frac{1}{6} = 1\frac{4}{24}$, and $2\frac{3}{8} = 2\frac{9}{24}$. The total miles traveled in the first week is $3\frac{12}{24} + 1\frac{6}{24} + 1\frac{4}{24} + 2\frac{9}{24} = 7\frac{31}{24} = 8\frac{7}{24}$. The least common denominator for the second week is 16. Thus, $\frac{1}{4} = \frac{4}{16}$, $\frac{3}{8} = \frac{6}{16}$, $\frac{9}{16} = \frac{9}{16}$, $3\frac{1}{16} = 3\frac{1}{16}$, $2\frac{5}{8} = 2\frac{10}{16}$, $3\frac{3}{16} = 3\frac{3}{16}$. The total miles traveled in the second week is $\frac{4}{16} + \frac{6}{16} + \frac{9}{16} + 3\frac{1}{16} + 2\frac{10}{16} + 3\frac{3}{16} = 8\frac{33}{16} = 10\frac{1}{16}$. The common denominator for the first and second weeks is 48. Thus, $10\frac{1}{16} = 10\frac{3}{48}$ and $8\frac{7}{24} = 8\frac{14}{48}$. The difference between the second and the first weeks is $10\frac{3}{48} - 8\frac{14}{48} = 2\frac{3-14}{48} = 1\frac{51-14}{48} = 1\frac{37}{48}$.

67. **(C)** The best way to approach this item is to compare the answers. Each 6-foot board yields one $5\frac{1}{2}$-foot board with one-half foot of waste. Each 12-foot board yields two $5\frac{1}{2}$-foot boards with one foot of waste. Each 22-foot board yields four $5\frac{1}{2}$-foot boards, with no waste. Each 24-foot board yields four $5\frac{1}{2}$-foot boards with two feet of waste. No 26-foot boards are sold.

68. **(D)** $\frac{15}{16} = \frac{\$7,500}{x} \Rightarrow 15x = 16 \cdot \$7,500 = \$120,000 \Rightarrow x = \frac{\$120,000}{15} = \$8,000$.

69. **(D)** The increase in populations is equal to: $\frac{2}{3} \cdot 54,000 = 2 \cdot \frac{54,000}{3} = 2 \cdot 18,000 = 36,000$. Thus, the present population is $54,000 + 36,000 = 90,000$.

70. **(C)** Let $x$ equal the final amount of liquid: $x = (1 - \frac{1}{3})(1 - \frac{3}{4})$(original amount) $= (\frac{2}{3})(\frac{1}{4})$(original amount) $= \frac{1}{6}$ of original amount.

71. **(C)** $\frac{7}{8}$ of capacity is 14 gallons. Thus, the tank's total capacity is $14 \div \frac{7}{8} = 14 \cdot \frac{8}{7} = 16$ gallons.

## EXERCISE 3—DECIMALS (p. 252)

1. **(C)** $\frac{7}{10} = 0.7$.

2. **(C)** For each zero in the denominator, move the decimal one place to the left in the numerator: $\frac{73}{100} = 0.73$.

3. **(B)** For each zero in the denominator, move the decimal one place to the left in the numerator: $\frac{21}{1,000} = 0.021$.

4. **(B)** Start to the right of the numerator, 557, and count one digit to the left for each zero in the denominator, 3. $\frac{557}{1,000} = 0.557$.

5. **(B)** Start to the right of the numerator, 34, and count one digit to the left for each zero in the denominator, 4. $\frac{34}{10,000} = 0.0034$.

6. **(E)** Start to the right of the numerator, 1, and count one digit to the left for each zero in the denominator, 6. $\frac{1}{1,000,000} = 0.000001$.

7. **(B)** Start to the right of the numerator, 30, and count one digit to the left for each zero in the denominator, 2. $\frac{30}{100} = 0.3$. Note that $\frac{30}{100}$ can first be reduced before converting it to a decimal. $\frac{30}{100} = \frac{30 \div 10}{100 \div 10} = \frac{3}{10} = 0.3$.

8. **(A)** $\frac{1,000}{4,000} = \frac{1,000 \div 1,000}{4,000 \div 1,000} = \frac{1}{4} = 0.25$.

9. **(E)** $\frac{1}{10} = 0.1$. I is incorrect because it does not have the decimal in the proper place. It has the decimal place one unit to the right of 1. II is correct because the decimal point is in the proper place (one decimal place to the left of 1). Finally, III is also correct because the decimal point is in the proper position relative to the numerator number (one decimal place to the left of 1). The trailing zeros do not affect the value of the number.

10. **(A)** $\frac{25}{100} = 0.25$. Only I has the decimal in the correct position.

11. **(B)** $\frac{257}{100} = 2.57$.

12. **(B)** $\frac{57}{10} = 5.7$.

13. **(B)** First, convert the fraction so that the denominator is a multiple of ten. Since it is often difficult to determine what that number should be, use several steps: $\frac{5}{8} = \frac{5}{5} \cdot \frac{5}{8} = \frac{25}{40} \cdot \frac{5}{5} = \frac{125}{200} \cdot \frac{5}{5} = \frac{625}{1,000} = 0.625$. Then, multiply each time by the smallest number possible to put another zero at the end of the denominator, until the denominator is a multiple of ten, and no other number: $8 \rightarrow 40 \rightarrow 200 \rightarrow 1,000$.

14. **(C)** Convert the fraction so that the denominator is a multiple of ten, then reduce: $\frac{4}{5} = \frac{4}{5} \cdot \frac{2}{2} = \frac{8}{10} = 0.8$.

15. **(A)** Convert the fraction so that the denominator is a multiple of ten, then reduce: $\frac{1}{20} = \frac{1}{20} \cdot \frac{5}{5} = \frac{5}{100} = 0.05$.

16. **(B)** Convert the fraction so that the denominator is a multiple of ten, then reduce: $\frac{1}{50} = \frac{1}{50} \cdot \frac{2}{2} = \frac{2}{100} = 0.02$.

17. **(B)** Convert the fraction so that the denominator is a multiple of ten, then reduce: $\frac{3}{200} = \frac{3}{200} \cdot \frac{5}{5} = \frac{15}{1,000} = 0.015$.

18. **(D)** Convert the fraction so that the denominator is a multiple of ten, then reduce: $\frac{9}{500} = \frac{9}{500} \cdot \frac{2}{2} = \frac{18}{1,000} = 0.018$.

19. **(B)** Convert the fraction so that the denominator is a multiple of ten, then reduce: $\frac{17}{500} = \frac{17}{500} \cdot \frac{2}{2} = \frac{34}{1,000} = 0.034$.

20. **(A)** Convert the fraction so that the denominator is a multiple of ten, then reduce: $\frac{123}{200} = \frac{123}{200} \cdot \frac{5}{5} = \frac{615}{1,000} = 0.615$.

21. **(C)**
$$\begin{array}{r} 0.1 \\ +\ 0.1 \\ \hline 0.2 \end{array}$$

22. **(E)**
$$\begin{array}{r} 0.27 \\ 0.13 \\ +\ 0.55 \\ \hline 0.95 \end{array}$$

23. **(A)**
$$\begin{array}{r} 0.528 \\ 0.116 \\ +\ 0.227 \\ \hline 0.871 \end{array}$$

24. **(A)**
$$\begin{array}{r} 0.700 \\ 0.013 \\ +\ 0.028 \\ \hline 0.741 \end{array}$$

25. **(C)**
$$\begin{array}{r} 1.23000 \\ +\ 0.00001 \\ \hline 1.23001 \end{array}$$

26. **(B)**
$$\begin{array}{r} 57.100 \\ 23.300 \\ +\ 35.012 \\ \hline 115.412 \end{array}$$

27. **(D)**
$$\begin{array}{r} 0.01000 \\ 0.00100 \\ 0.00010 \\ +\ 0.00001 \\ \hline 0.01111 \end{array}$$

28. **(A)**     0.9000
                0.0900
                0.0090
            +   0.0009
                0.9999

29. **(B)**     0.27000
                0.36000
                2.11170
                3.77777
            +   1.42000
                7.93947

30. **(D)**    12,279.10
                3,428.01
            +   3,444.99
               19,152.1

31. **(E)**     0.7
            −   0.3
                0.4

32. **(C)**     0.75
            −   0.25
                0.50

33. **(A)**     1.35
            −   0.35
                1.00

34. **(A)**    25.125
            −   5.357
               19.768

35. **(E)**     1.00000
            −   0.00001
                0.99999

36. **(D)** First, multiply as if the decimals are whole numbers: $0.2 \cdot 0.1 \Rightarrow 2 \cdot 1 = 2$. Then, count the total number of decimal places in the numbers that are being multiplied, 0.2 and 0.1. There is one place in each number, so move the decimal in the result of 2, to the right by two places: $2 \Rightarrow 0.02$.

37. **(D)** Multiply as if the decimals are whole numbers: $0.1 \cdot 0.1 \cdot 0.1 \Rightarrow 1 \cdot 1 \cdot 1 = 1$. Then, count the total number of decimal places in the numbers that are being multiplied, 0.1, 0.1, and 0.1. There are 3 decimal places. So, place the decimal three units to the left in the answer, starting from the right side of the last digit: 0.001.

38. **(A)** First, multiply as if the decimals are whole numbers: $1.1 \cdot 1.1 \cdot 1.1 \Rightarrow 11 \cdot 11 \cdot 11 = 1,331$. Then, count the total number of decimal places in the numbers that are being multiplied, 1.1, 1.1, and 1.1. There is a total of 3 decimal places in the item. So, place the decimal point three units to the left in the answer, starting from the right side of the last digit: 1.331.

39. **(B)** Multiply as if the decimals are whole numbers: $0.11 \cdot 0.33 \Rightarrow 11 \cdot 33 = 363$. Count the total number of places in the numbers that are being multiplied, 0.11, 0.33. There is a total of 4 decimal places in the item. Place the decimal four units to the left in the answer, starting from the right side of the last digit: 0.0363.

40. **(B)** First, multiply as if the decimals are whole numbers: $0.2 \cdot 0.5 \cdot 0.2 \cdot 0.5 \Rightarrow 2 \cdot 5 \cdot 2 \cdot 5 = 100$. Then, count the total number of decimal places in the numbers that are being multiplied, 0.2, 0.5, 0.2 and 0.5. There is a total of 4 decimal places in the item. So, place the decimal point four units to the left in the answer, starting from the right side of the last digit: 0.01.

41. **(A)** First, multiply as if the decimals are whole numbers: $5 \cdot 0.25 \Rightarrow 5 \cdot 25 = 125$. Then, count the total number of decimal places in the numbers that are being multiplied, 5 and 0.25. There is a total of 2 decimal places in the item. So, place the decimal point two units to the left in the answer, starting from the right side of the last digit: 1.25.

42. **(A)** First, multiply the numbers that have decimal components by a multiple of ten large enough that no numbers remain to the right: $0.000001 \cdot 1,000,000 = 1$. Remember the number you used. Now, multiply the numbers as normal: $10 \cdot 1 = 10$. Now, divide by the multiple of ten you used: $\frac{10}{1,000,000} = 0.00001$.

43. **(B)** First, multiply as if the decimals are whole numbers: $100 \cdot 0.00052 \Rightarrow 100 \cdot 52 = 5,200$. Then, count the total number of decimal places in the numbers that are being multiplied, 100 and 0.00052. There is a total of 5 decimal places in the item. So, place the decimal point five units to the left in the answer, starting from the right side of the last digit: 0.052.

44. **(B)** First, multiply as if the decimals are whole numbers: $1.2 \cdot 1.2 \Rightarrow 12 \cdot 12 = 144$. Then, count the total number of decimal places in the numbers that are being multiplied, 1.2 and 1.2. There is a total of 2 decimal places in the item. So, place the decimal point two units to the left in the answer, starting from the right side of the last digit: 1.44.

45. **(A)** None of the numbers right of the decimals are significant: $1.000 \cdot 1.000 \cdot 1.000 \cdot 1.000 = 1 \cdot 1 \cdot 1 \cdot 1 = 1$.

46. **(D)** $6 \div 0.2 = 60 \div 2 = 30$.

47. **(B)** $0.2 \div 5 = 2 \div 50 = 4 \div 100 = 0.04$.

48. **(B)** $1 \div 0.001 = 1 \div \frac{1}{1,000} = 1 \cdot \frac{1,000}{1} = 1,000$.

49. **(B)** $25.1 \div 2.51 \Rightarrow 25.1 = 2.51 \cdot 10 \Rightarrow \frac{25.1}{2.51} = 10$.

50. **(C)** $0.25 \div 8 = \frac{0.25}{8} \cdot \frac{4}{4} = \frac{1}{32} \cdot \frac{5}{5} = \frac{5}{160} \cdot \frac{5}{5} = \frac{25}{800} \cdot \frac{5}{5} = \frac{125}{4,000} \cdot \frac{5}{5} = \frac{625}{20,000} \cdot \frac{5}{5} = \frac{3,125}{100,000} = 0.03125$.

51. **(A)** That numbers are fractional does not change the fact that a number divided by itself will equal 1.

52. **(C)** $2 \div 2.5 = 20 \div 25 = \frac{20}{25} \cdot \frac{4}{4} = \frac{80}{100} = 0.8$.

53. **(E)** It is clear that the second number is the same as the first, except with the decimal point moved three places to the left. So, $0.111 \cdot 1,000 = 111$.

54. **(B)** Note that the second number is the same as the first, but with an extra zero before the decimal point. Thus, they differ by a factor of 10.

55. **(A)** $(0.002 \div 0.00002) \cdot 1,000 = 2 \div 0.02 = 20 \div 0.2 = 200 \div 2 = 100$.

56. **(C)** First, add the fractions together using the "flying-x" method: $\frac{3}{5} + \frac{5}{8} = \frac{3 \cdot 8}{5 \cdot 8} + \frac{5 \cdot 5}{8 \cdot 5} = \frac{24}{40} + \frac{25}{40} = \frac{49}{40} \cdot \frac{5}{5} \cdot \frac{5}{5} = \frac{1,225}{1,000} = 1.225$

57. **(C)** An average of two numbers is the sum of the two numbers divided by two. Since the answer choices are all given in fractions, start by converting 0.75 into a fraction: $0.75 = \frac{3}{4}$. Then, add the two fractions: $\frac{2}{3} + \frac{3}{4} = \frac{2 \cdot 4}{3 \cdot 4} + \frac{3 \cdot 3}{4 \cdot 3} = \frac{8+9}{12} = \frac{17}{12}$. Next, divide by 2: $\frac{17}{12} \div 2 = \frac{17}{24}$.

58. **(B)** An average of three numbers is the sum of the three numbers divided by three. Since all of the answer choices are given in decimals, start by converting $\frac{1}{4}$ into a decimal: $\frac{1}{4} = 0.25$. Then, add the three decimals together: $0.1 + 0.01 + 0.25 = 0.36$. Next, divide by 3: $0.36 \div 3 \Rightarrow 36 \div 3 = 12 \Rightarrow 12 \div 100 = 0.12$.

59. **(D)** Convert the mixed number numerator into an improper fraction and the decimal denominator into a fraction: $12\frac{1}{3} = \frac{(12 \cdot 3) + 1}{3} = \frac{37}{3}$ and $0.2 = \frac{2}{10} = \frac{1}{5}$. So, $\frac{37}{3} \div \frac{1}{5} = \frac{37}{3} \cdot \frac{5}{1} = \frac{185}{3}$.

60. **(B)** $0.1 = \frac{1}{10}$. Starting with the parentheses, solve the equation following basic orders of operations: $\frac{1}{10}[\frac{1}{3} - 2(\frac{1}{2} - \frac{1}{4})] = \frac{1}{10}[\frac{1}{3} - 2(\frac{1 \cdot 2}{2 \cdot 2} - \frac{1}{4})] = \frac{1}{10}(\frac{1}{3} - \frac{2}{4}) = \frac{1}{10}(\frac{1 \cdot 4}{3 \cdot 4} - \frac{2 \cdot 3}{4 \cdot 3}) = \frac{1}{10}(-\frac{2}{12}) = -\frac{2}{120} = -\frac{1}{60}$.

61. **(D)** Add together the savings for each month: $\$4.56 + \$3.82 + \$5.06 = \$13.44$.

62. **(C)** Add to find the total deductions: $\$3.05 + \$5.68 = \$8.73$. Subtract the total deductions from the salary to determine the check amount: $\$190.57 - \$8.73 = \$181.84$.

63. **(B)** The outer radius minus the inner radius is equal to the thickness of the metal: $2.84 - 1.94 = 0.90$ inches.

64. **(C)** Add the daily earnings to find the total earnings: $\$20.56 + \$32.90 + \$20.78 = \$74.24$. Divide the total earnings by 2 to find out what Pete has left: $\$74.24 \div 2 = \$37.12$.

65. **(C)** Find the cost of $3\frac{1}{2}$ pounds of meat: $\$1.69 \cdot 3.5 \approx \$5.92$. Find the cost of 20 lemons: $\$0.60 \div 12 = \$0.05$ for 1 lemon and $\$0.05 \cdot 20 = \$1.00$ for 20 lemons. Add the cost of meat and the cost of lemons: $\$5.92 + \$1.00 = \$6.92$.

66. **(A)** Subtract the weight of the empty reel from the total weight to find the weight of the cable: $1,279 - 285 = 994$ pounds. Each foot of cable weighs 7.1 pounds. Therefore, to find the number of feet of cable on the reel, divide 994 by 7.1: $994 \div 7.1 = 9,940 \div 71 = 140$.

67. **(D)** Each fastener costs: $\$4.15 \div 100 = \$0.0415$. Thus, 345 fasteners cost: $345 \cdot 0.0415 = \$14.32$.

## EXERCISE 4—PERCENTS (p. 261)

1. **(E)** To express a decimal as a percent, move the decimal point two units to the right and add a percent sign at the right of the number: $0.79 = 79\%$.

2. **(A)** To express a decimal as a percent, move the decimal point two units to the right and add a percent sign at the right of the number: $0.55 = 55\%$.

3. **(B)** To express a decimal as a percent, move the decimal point two units to the right and add a percent sign at the right of the number: $0.111 = 11.1\%$.

4. **(B)** To express a decimal as a percent, move the decimal point two units to the right and add a percent sign at the right of the number: $0.125 = 12.5\%$.

5. **(C)** To express a decimal as a percent, move the decimal point two units to the right and add a percent sign at the right of the number: $0.5555 = 55.55\%$.

6. **(A)** To express a decimal as a percent, move the decimal point two units to the right and add a percent sign at the right of the number: $0.3 = 30\%$.

7. **(C)** To express a decimal as a percent, move the decimal point two units to the right and add a percent sign at the right of the number: $0.7500 = 75\%$.

8. **(B)** To express a decimal as a percent, move the decimal point two units to the right and add a percent sign at the right of the number: $2.45 = 245\%$.

9. **(A)** To express a decimal as a percent, move the decimal point two units to the right and add a percent sign at the right of the number: $1.25 = 125\%$.

10. **(A)** To express a decimal as a percent, move the decimal point two units to the right and add a percent sign at the right of the number: $10 = 1,000\%$.

11. **(B)** To express a decimal as a percent, move the decimal point two units to the right and add a percent sign at the right of the number: $0.015 = 1.5\%$.

12. **(B)** To express a decimal as a percent, move the decimal point two units to the right and add a percent sign at the right of the number: $0.099 = 9.9\%$.

13. **(A)** To express a decimal as a percent, move the decimal point two units to the right and add a percent sign at the right of the number: $0.0333 = 3.33\%$.

14. **(A)** To express a decimal as a percent, move the decimal point two units to the right and add a percent sign at the right of the number: $0.001 = 0.1\%$.

15. **(A)** To express a decimal as a percent, move the decimal point two units to the right and add a percent sign at the right of the number: $0.0100 = 1\%$.

16. **(C)** To express a percent as a decimal, remove the percent sign and move the decimal point two units to the left: $25\% = 0.25$.

17. **(B)** To express a percent as a decimal, remove the percent sign and move the decimal point two units to the left: $56\% = 0.56$.

18. **(D)** To express a percent as a decimal, remove the percent sign and move the decimal point two units to the left: $10\% = 0.1$.

19. **(C)** To express a percent as a decimal, remove the percent sign and move the decimal point two units to the left: $100\% = 1$.

20. **(C)** To express a percent as a decimal, remove the percent sign and move the decimal point two units to the left: $250\% = 2.5$.

21. **(C)** To express a percent as a decimal, remove the percent sign and move the decimal point two units to the left: $1,000\% = 10.0$.

22. **(D)** To express a percent as a decimal, remove the percent sign and move the decimal point two units to the left: $0.25\% = 0.0025$.

23. **(E)** To express a percent as a decimal, remove the percent sign and move the decimal point two units to the left: $0.099\% = 0.00099$.

24. **(D)** To express a percent as a decimal, remove the percent sign and move the decimal point two units to the left: $0.0988\% = 0.000988$.

25. **(D)** To express a percent as a decimal, remove the percent sign and move the decimal point two units to the left: $0.00100\% = 0.00001$.

26. **(B)** To solve this item, first, convert the fraction into a decimal number. Then, move the decimal point two units to the right and add a percent sign at the end of the number: $\frac{1}{10} = 0.1 = 10\%$.

27. **(C)** To solve this item, first, convert the fraction into a decimal number. Then, move the decimal point two units to the right and add a percent sign at the end of the number: $\frac{3}{100} = 0.03 = 3\%$.

28. **(A)** To solve this item, first, convert the fraction into a decimal number. Then, move the decimal point two units to the right and add a percent sign at the end of the number: $\frac{99}{100} = 0.99 = 99\%$.

29. **(C)** To solve this item, first, convert the fraction into a decimal number. Then, move the decimal point two units to the right and add a percent sign at the end of the number: $\frac{100}{1,000} = \frac{1}{10} = 0.1 = 10\%$.

30. **(A)** To solve this item, first, convert the fraction into a decimal number. Then, move the decimal point two units to the right and add a percent sign at the end of the number: $\frac{333}{100} = 3.33 = 333\%$.

31. **(B)** To solve this item, first, convert the fraction into a decimal number. Then, move the decimal point two units to the right and add a percent sign at the end of the number: $\frac{9}{1,000} = 0.009 = 0.9\%$.

32. **(E)** To solve this item, first, convert the fraction into a decimal number. Then, move the decimal point two units to the right and add a percent sign at the end of the number: $\frac{3}{4} = 0.75 = 75\%$.

33. **(D)** To solve this item, first, convert the fraction into a decimal number. Then, move the decimal point two units to the right and add a percent sign at the end of the number: $\frac{4}{5} = 0.8 = 80\%$.

34. **(B)** To solve this item, first, convert the fraction into a decimal number. Then, move the decimal point two units to the right and add a percent sign at the end of the number: $\frac{3}{50} = 0.06 = 6\%$.

35. **(D)** To solve this item, first, convert the fraction into a decimal number. Then, move the decimal point two units to the right and add a percent sign at the end of the number: $\frac{3}{75} = 0.04 = 4\%$.

36. **(C)** To solve this item, first, convert the fraction into a decimal number. Then, move the decimal point two units to the right and add a percent sign at the end of the number: $\frac{6}{500} = 0.012 = 1.2\%$.

37. **(D)** To solve this item, first, convert the fraction into a decimal number. Then, move the decimal point two units to the right and add a percent sign at the end of the number: $\frac{111}{555} = 0.2 = 20\%$.

38. **(B)** To solve this item, first, convert the fraction into a decimal number. Then, move the decimal point two units to the right and add a percent sign at the end of the number: $\frac{8}{5,000} = 0.0016 = 0.16\%$.

39. **(A)** To solve this item, first, convert the fraction into a decimal number. Then, move the decimal point two units to the right and add a percent sign at the end of the number: $1\frac{1}{10} = 1.1 = 110\%$.

40. **(A)** To solve this item, first, convert the fraction into a decimal number. Then, move the decimal point two units to the right and add a percent sign at the end of the number: $9\frac{99}{100} = 9.99 = 999\%$.

41. **(D)** To solve this item, first, convert the fraction into a decimal number. Then, move the decimal point two units to the right and add a percent sign at the end of the number: $3\frac{1}{2} = 3.5 = 350\%$.

42. **(A)** To solve this item, first, convert the fraction into a decimal number. Then, move the decimal point two units to the right and add a percent sign at the end of the number: $1\frac{3}{4} = 1.75 = 175\%$.

43. **(E)** To solve this item, first, convert the fraction into a decimal number. Then, move the decimal point two units to the right and add a percent sign at the end of the number: $10\frac{1}{5} = 10.2 = 1,020\%$.

44. **(A)** To solve this item, first, convert the fraction into a decimal number. Then, move the decimal point two units to the right and add a percent sign at the end of the number: $3\frac{1}{50} = 3.02 = 302\%$.

45. **(B)** To solve this item, first, convert the fraction into a decimal number. Then, move the decimal point two units to the right and add a percent sign at the end of the number: $\frac{111}{100} = 1.11 = 111\%$.

46. **(D)** To solve this item, first, convert the fraction into a decimal number. Then, move the decimal point two units to the right and add a percent sign at the end of the number: $\frac{7}{2} = 3.5 = 350\%$.

47. **(A)** To solve this item, first, convert the fraction into a decimal number. Then, move the decimal point two units to the right and add a percent sign at the end of the number: $\frac{13}{5} = 2.6 = 260\%$.

48. **(B)** To solve this item, first, convert the fraction into a decimal number. Then, move the decimal point two units to the right and add a percent sign at the end of the number: $\frac{9}{8} = 1.125 = 112.5\%$.

49. **(A)** To solve this item, first, convert the fraction into a decimal number. Then, move the decimal point two units to the right and add a percent sign at the end of the number: $\frac{22}{5} = 4.4 = 440\%$.

50. **(A)** To solve this item, first, convert the fraction into a decimal number. Then, move the decimal point two units to the right and add a percent sign at the end of the number: $\frac{33}{6} = 5.5 = 550\%$.

51. **(C)** First, convert the percent to a fraction. Remember that a percent just means that the denominator is 100: $18\% = \frac{18}{100}$.

52. **(C)** Convert the percentage into a decimal number by removing the percent sign and moving the decimal point two units to the left: $80\% = 0.8$.

53. **(B)** First, convert the percent to a fraction. Remember that a percent just means that the denominator is 100: $45\% = \frac{45}{100}$. Then, simplify the fraction: $\frac{45}{100} = \frac{45 \div 5}{100 \div 5} = \frac{9}{20}$.

54. **(B)** Convert the percentage into a decimal number by removing the percent sign and moving the decimal point two units to the left: $7\% = 0.07$.

55. **(B)** Convert the percentage into a decimal number by removing the percent sign and moving the decimal point two units to the left: $13.2\% = 0.132$.

56. **(B)** Convert the percentage into a decimal number by removing the percent sign and moving the decimal point two units to the left: $1.111\% = 0.01111$.

57. **(C)** Convert the percentage into a decimal number by removing the percent sign and moving the decimal point two units to the left: $10.101\% = 0.10101$.

58. **(B)** Convert the percent to a fraction. Remember that a percent just means that the denominator is 100: $33\% = \frac{33}{100}$.

59. **(C)** First, convert the percent to a fraction. Remember that a percent just means that the denominator is 100: $80.1\% = \frac{80.1}{100} = \frac{80.1 \cdot 10}{100 \cdot 10} = \frac{801}{1,000}$. Then, convert it to a decimal number: $80.1\% = 0.801$. (C) is the only answer choice that is an equivalent form of 80.1%.

60. **(D)** First, convert the percent to a fraction. Remember that a percent just means that the denominator is 100: $0.02\% = \frac{0.02}{100} = \frac{0.02 \cdot 100}{100 \cdot 100} = \frac{2}{10,000}$. Then, simplify the fraction: $\frac{2}{10,000} = \frac{2 \div 2}{10,000 \div 2} = \frac{1}{5,000}$.

61. **(D)** First, convert the percent to a fraction. Remember that a percent just means that the denominator is 100: $250\% = \frac{250}{100}$. Then, convert it to a decimal number: $250\% = 2.5$. (D) is the only answer choice that is an equivalent form of 250%.

62. **(C)** First, convert the percent to a fraction. Remember that a percent just means that the denominator is 100: $1,000\% = \frac{1,000}{100}$. Then, convert it to a decimal number: $1,000\% = 10$. (C) is the only answer choice that is an equivalent form of 1,000%.

63. **(B)** Add the percents as if they are regular numbers. Remember to add the percent sign at the end of the answer: $37\% + 42\% = 79\%$.

64. **(B)** Add the percents as if they are regular numbers. Remember to add the percent sign at the end of the answer: $210\% + 21\% = 231\%$.

65. **(B)** Add the percents as if they are regular numbers. Remember to add the percent sign at the end of the answer: $8\% + 9\% + 10\% + 110\% = 137\%$.

66. **(B)** Add the percents as if they are regular numbers. Remember to add the percent sign at the end of the answer: $254\% + 166\% + 342\% = 762\%$.

67. **(E)** Add the percents as if they are regular numbers. Remember to add the percent sign at the end of the answer: $0.02\% + 0.005\% = 0.025\%$.

68. **(C)** Subtract the percents as if they are regular numbers. Remember to add the percent sign at the end of the answer: $33\% - 25\% = 8\%$.

69. **(D)** Subtract the percents as if they are regular numbers. Remember to add the percent sign at the end of the answer: $100\% - 0.99\% = 99.01\%$.

70. **(B)** Subtract the percents as if they are regular numbers. Remember to add the percent sign at the end of the answer: $222\% - 22.2\% = 199.8\%$.

71. **(B)** This is an addition word item, just add the percentages of the pages he read on Monday and Tuesday together: $15\% + 25\% = 40\%$.

72. **(D)** This is an addition word item. Add the percentages of the lawn she mowed from 9-12 and 12-3 together: $35\% + 50\% = 85\%$.

73. **(C)** On Monday, 8% of the project is scheduled to be completed. On Tuesday, another 17% is scheduled to be completed. And, on Wednesday, another 25% is scheduled to be completed. The combined percentages of the project scheduled to be completed for these three days is 50%: $8\% + 17\% + 25\% = 50\%$. So, by the end of Wednesday one half, 50%, of the work is scheduled to be completed.

74. **(C)** This is an addition item. Add the percent of the project scheduled to be completed Monday with the percent of the project scheduled to be completed Tuesday to arrive at the answer: $8\% + 17\% = 25\%$.

75. **(D)** You know that at the end of Wednesday one half of the project is scheduled to be completed: $8\% + 17\% + 25\% = 50\%$. And, at the end of Thursday, 83% of the project is scheduled to be completed: $8\% + 17\% + 25\% + 33\% = 83\%$. This means that, if the production is on schedule, $\frac{2}{3}$, 66.6%, of the work will be completed sometime Thursday.

76. **(D)** This is an addition item. First, convert the added amount of water, $\frac{1}{4}$ of the bucket's capacity, into a percent: $\frac{1}{4} = 0.25 = 25\%$. Next, add the amount of water already in the bucket to the amount of water just added: $33\% + 25\% = 58\%$.

77. **(D)** First, find the amount of allowance that Edward spent: $15\% + 25\% = 40\%$. Next, subtract this amount from his total allowance to find out how much allowance he has left. The total amount of allowance Edward has is equal to 100%. So, $100\% - 40\% = 60\%$.

78. **(C)** To multiply percentages, first, convert the percents to decimals. Multiply the decimals together and then convert the answer back into a percent: $50\% \cdot 50\% = 0.5 \cdot 0.5 = 0.25 = 25\%$.

79. **(C)** To multiply percentages, first, convert the percents to decimals. Multiply the decimals together and then convert the answer back into a percent: $1\% \cdot 100\% = 0.01 \cdot 1 = 0.01 = 1\%$.

80. **(C)** This is a "What is X Percent of Some Quantity" item. Set up the equation. Remember that "of" indicates multiplication: $66\% \cdot 100 = 0.66 \cdot 100 = 66$. So, 66 of the marbles in the jar are red.

81. **(D)** This is a "What is X Percent of Some Quantity" item. Set up the equation. Remember that "of" indicates multiplication: $75\% \cdot 240 = 0.75 \cdot 240 = 180$. So, there are 180 sedans in this particular parking lot.

82. **(C)** This is a "What is X Percent of Some Quantity" item. Set up the equation. Remember that "of" indicates multiplication: $0.1\% \cdot 100 = 0.001 \cdot 189,000 = 189$. So, 189 of the names have the initials "B.D."

83. **(C)** This is a "What Percent Is This of That" item. Note that $of = 10$ and $is = 1$. Set up the "is over of" equation to solve: $\frac{is}{of} = \frac{\%}{100} \Rightarrow \frac{1}{10} = 0.1 = \frac{\%}{100} \Rightarrow \% = 100 \cdot 0.1 = 10\%$.

84. **(C)** This is a "What Percent Is This of That" item. Note that $of = 12$ and $is = 3$. Set up the "is over of" equation to solve: $\frac{is}{of} = \frac{\%}{100} \Rightarrow \frac{3}{12} = \frac{1}{4} \Rightarrow .25 = \frac{\%}{100} \Rightarrow \% = .25 \cdot 100 = 25\%$.

85. **(A)** This is a "What Percent Is This of That" item. Note that $of = 40$ and $is = 50$. Set up the "is over of" equation to solve: $\frac{is}{of} = \frac{\%}{100} \Rightarrow \frac{50}{40} = 1.25 = 125\%$.

86. **(D)** This is a "What Percent Is This of That" item. Note that $of = 100$ and $is = 10$. Set up the "is over of" equation to solve: $\frac{is}{of} = \frac{\%}{100} \Rightarrow \frac{is}{100} = \frac{10}{100} \Rightarrow is = 100 \cdot 0.1 = 10$.

87. **(D)** This is a "What Percent Is This of That" item. Note that $of = 12$ and $is = 250$. Set up the "is over of" equation to solve: $\frac{is}{of} = \frac{\%}{100} \Rightarrow \frac{is}{12} = \frac{250}{100} \Rightarrow is = 12 \cdot 2.5 = 30$.

88. **(C)** This is a "What Percent Is This of That" item. Note that $of = $ Patty's age $= 48$ and $is = $ Al's age $= 36$. Set up the "is over of" equation to solve: $\frac{is}{of} = \frac{\%}{100} \Rightarrow \frac{36}{48} = \frac{3}{4} = 0.75 = \frac{\%}{100} \Rightarrow \% = 0.75 \cdot 100 = 75\%$.

89. **(D)** First, find out the total number of employees at the bank: $25 + 15 = 40$. This item stem can be simplified to "What percent is 25 women out of 40 employees?" Set up the "is over of" equation to solve: $\frac{is}{of} = \frac{\%}{100} \Rightarrow \frac{25}{40} = \frac{5}{8} = 0.625 = 62.5\%$.

90. **(E)** This is a "What Percent Is This of That" item. Note that $of = $ old price $= 5$ and $is = $ new price $= 8$. Set up the "is over of" equation to solve: $\frac{is}{of} = \frac{\%}{100} \Rightarrow \frac{8}{5} = 1.6 = \frac{\%}{100} \Rightarrow \% = 1.6 \cdot 100 = 160\%$.

91. **(C)** This is a "What Percent Is This of That" item. Note that $of = $ new price $= 8$ and $is = $ old price $= 5$ Set up the "is over of" equation to solve: $\frac{is}{of} = \frac{\%}{100} \Rightarrow \frac{25}{40} = \frac{5}{8} = 0.625 = 62.5\%$.

92. **(D)** This is a "What Percent Is This of That" item. Note that $of$ equals the old price ($200) and $is$ equals the new price ($160). Set up the "is over of" equation to solve: $\frac{is}{of} = \frac{\%}{100} \Rightarrow \frac{160}{200} = \frac{4}{5} = 0.8 = \frac{\%}{100} \Rightarrow \% = 0.8 \cdot 100 = 80\%$.

93. **(E)** This is a "What Percent Is This of That" item. Note that $of$ equals the new price ($160) and $is$ equals the old price ($200). Set up the "is over of" equation to solve: $\frac{is}{of} = \frac{\%}{100} \Rightarrow \frac{200}{160} = \frac{4}{5} = 0.8 = \frac{\%}{100} \Rightarrow \% = 1.25 \cdot 100 = 125\%$.

94. **(A)** This is a percent change word item. Set up the equation: $\frac{\text{change}}{\text{original}} = \frac{200 - 160}{200} = \frac{40}{200} = \frac{20}{100} = 20\%$.

95. **(B)** This is a "What Percent Is This of That" item. Note that $of$ equals the number of enrollees for the second week (25) and $is$ equals the number of enrollees for the first week (10). Set up the "is over of" equation to solve: $\frac{is}{of} = \frac{\%}{100} \Rightarrow \frac{10}{25} = \frac{2}{5} = 0.4 = 40\%$.

96. **(C)** This is a "What Percent Is This of That" item. Note that $of$ equals the number of enrollees for the fifth week (30) and $is$ equals the number of enrollees for the fourth week (15). Set up the "is over of" equation to solve: $\frac{is}{of} = \frac{\%}{100} \Rightarrow \frac{15}{30} = \frac{1}{2} = 0.5 = 50\%$.

97. **(E)** This is a "What Percent Is This of That" item. Note that $of$ equals the number of enrollees for the fourth week (15) and $is$ equals the number of enrollees for the fifth week (30). Set up the "is over of" equation to solve: $\frac{is}{of} = \frac{\%}{100} \Rightarrow \frac{30}{15} = 2 = 200\%$.

98. **(D)** This is a percent change word item. Set up the equation: $\frac{\text{change}}{\text{original}} = \frac{25 - 10}{10} = \frac{15}{10} = 1.5 = 150\%$.

99. **(A)** This is a percent change word item. Set up the equation: $\frac{\text{change}}{\text{original}} = \frac{20 - 15}{20} = \frac{5}{20} = \frac{1}{4} = 0.25 = 25\%$.

100. **(D)** This is a "What is X Percent of Some Quantity" item. This item stem can be reworded as "What is 8% of $30?" Set up the equation. Remember that "of" indicates multiplication. $8\% \cdot 35 = 0.08 \cdot 35 = 2.8$. So, the sales tax on the textbook is $2.80.

101. **(D)** This is a "What is X Percent of Some Quantity" item. Set up the equation. First, find the cost of an 8.5% sales tax. Then, add that tax to the textbook cost. $8.5\% \cdot 30 = 0.085 \cdot 30 = 2.55$. So, the sales tax on the textbook is $2.55. Therefore, the total cost of this one textbooks is $32.55, $30 + $2.55 = $32.55$.

102. **(C)** This is a "What is X Percent of Some Quantity" item. Remember that "of" indicates multiplication. $25\% \cdot 80 = 0.25 \cdot 80 = 20$.

103. **(B)** This is a "What is X Percent of Some Quantity" item. Remember that "of" indicates multiplication. $2.3\% \cdot 90 = 0.023 \cdot 90 = 2.07$.

104. **(A)** First, find out how many questions Gertrude got right on the entire test. This would be 80% of 50 questions, which is a "What is X Percent of Some Quantity" item. Then, find the difference between how many questions she answered correctly on the first 40 questions of the test to how many questions she answered correctly on the entire test to find out how many of the last 10 questions she answered correctly. $80\% \cdot 50 = 0.8 \cdot 50 = 40$. $40 - 34 = 6$.

105. **(C)** This is a "What Percent Is This of That" item. Note that $of = 1,000$ and $is = 105$. Set up the "is over of" equation to solve: $\frac{is}{of} = \frac{\%}{100} \Rightarrow \frac{105}{1000} = 0.105 = 10.5\%$.

106. **(C)** This is a "What Percent Is This of That" item. Note that $of = 50$ and $is = 40$. Set up the "is over of" equation to solve: $\frac{is}{of} = \frac{\%}{100} \Rightarrow \frac{40}{50} = \frac{4}{5} = 0.8 = 80\%$.

107. **(E)** This is a "What Percent Is This of That" item. Note that $of = 20$ and $is = 80$. Set up the "is over of" equation to solve: $\frac{is}{of} = \frac{\%}{100} \Rightarrow \frac{80}{20} = 4 = 400\%$.

108. **(C)** First, find the total number of students in the junior class: $300 + 500 = 800$. Then, set up the "is over of" equation and solve. Note that this item stem can be reworded to say "What percent is 500 out of 800 students?" Note that $of = 800$ and $is$ equals the number of junior high students who did not enroll in test prep (500). $\frac{is}{of} = \frac{\%}{100} \Rightarrow \frac{500}{800} = \frac{5}{8} = 0.625 = 62.5\%$.

109. **(E)** This is a percent change word item. Set up the equation: $\frac{change}{original} = \frac{0.05 - 0.02}{0.02} = \frac{0.03}{0.02} = \frac{3}{2} = 1.5 = 150\%$.

110. **(D)** First, find the number of students who did not receive A's: $30 - 6 = 24$. Note that this item stem can be reworded to say "What percent is 24 out of 30 students in the class. Set up the "is over of" equation and solve.?" $\frac{is}{of} = \frac{\%}{100} \Rightarrow \frac{24}{30} = \frac{4}{5} = 0.8 = 80\%$.

111. **(D)** This is a "What Percent Is This of That" item. This item stem can be reworded as "What is 10 out of 12 games?" Note that $of$ equals the total number of games (12) and $is$ equals the total number of games that the Wildcats won (10). Set up the "is over of" equation to solve: $\frac{is}{of} = \frac{\%}{100} \Rightarrow \frac{10}{12} = \frac{5}{6} = 0.8\overline{3} = 83\%$.

112. **(E)** Find the total number of free throws attempted and the total number of free throws made. Divide the number of those made by those attempted: $\frac{86 + 46}{100 + 50} = \frac{132}{150} = 88\%$.

113. **(D)** This item stem can be simplified into "$256 is 80% of what?" Note that since it is discounted by 20%, the discounted price is the same as 80% of the original price: $100\% - 20\% = 80\%$. Set up a "This is X Percent of What" equation. Note that $\% = 80$ and $is$ equals the discounted price of the stereo ($256). Set up the "is over of" equation to solve: $\frac{is}{of} = \frac{\%}{100} \Rightarrow \frac{256}{x} = \frac{80}{100} \Rightarrow 80x = 256 \cdot 100 = 25,600 \Rightarrow x = \frac{25,600}{80} = 320$. The original price of the stereo was $320.

114. **(B)** This item stem can be simplified into "136 is equal to 85% of the total number of jellybeans." Since the bag contains only red and black jellybeans, if 15% are red, then, 85% must be black: $100\% - 15\% = 85\%$. Set up an "is over of" equation and solve. Note that $\% = 85$ and $is$ equals the number of red jellybeans (136). $\frac{is}{of} = \frac{\%}{100} \Rightarrow \frac{136}{x} = \frac{85}{100} \Rightarrow 85x = 136 \cdot 100 = 13,600 \Rightarrow x = \frac{13,600}{85} = 160$. There is a total of 160 jellybeans in the bag.

115. **(D)** $\$118.80 \cdot 0.20 = \$23.76$. $\$118.80 - \$23.76 = \$95.04$.

Alternatively, $\$118.80 \cdot 0.80 = \$95.04$.

116. **(E)** Add the figures given for housing, food, clothing, and taxes: $26.2\% + 28.4\% + 12.0\% + 12.7\% = 79.3\%$. Subtract this total from 100% to find the percent for miscellaneous items: $100.0\% - 79.3\% = 20.7\%$.

117. **(C)** The price of the shuttlecocks is: $24(\$0.35) = \$8.40$. The price of the rackets is: $4(\$2.75) = \$11.00$. The total price is: $\$8.40 + \$11.00 = \$19.40$. Because the discount is 30% of the total, the actual cost is $100\% - 30\% = 70\%$ of the total. Thus, the actual cost is: $70\% \cdot \$19.40 = 0.7 \cdot \$19.40 = \$13.58$.

118. **(E)** Subtract the weight of the wood after drying from the original weight of the wood to find amount of moisture in wood: $10 - 8 = 2$ ounces. Therefore, the moisture content is equal to: $\frac{2 \text{ ounces}}{10 \text{ ounces}} = 0.2 = 20\%$.

119. **(A)** Find the number of each kind of coin: there are $10\% \cdot 800 = 0.1 \cdot 800 = 80$ dimes, $30\% \cdot 800 = 0.3 \cdot 800 = 240$ nickels, and $(100\% - 10\% - 30\%) \cdot 800 = 60\% \cdot 800 = 0.6 \cdot 800 = 480$ quarters. Therefore, the total dollars in the bag is: $(80 \cdot 0.10) + (240 \cdot 0.05) + (480 \cdot 0.25) = 8.00 + 12.00 + 120.00 = \$140.00$.

120. **(C)** The first solution contains 20% of 6 quarts of alcohol; so the alcohol content is equal to: $0.20 \cdot 6 = 1.2$ quarts. The second solution contains 60% of 4 quarts of alcohol; the alcohol content is equal to: $0.60 \cdot 4 = 2.4$ quarts. The mixture contains $1.2 + 2.4 = 3.6$ quarts of alcohol and $6 + 4 = 10$ quarts of liquid. The mixture's alcoholic strength of mixture is: $3.6 \div 10 = 36\%$.

121. **(D)** $2\frac{1}{2}\%$ of the insured value is $\$348$. The insured value is equal to: $\$348 \div 2\frac{1}{2}\% = \$348 \div 0.025 = \$13,920$. Since $\$13,920$ is 80% of the total value, the total value is equal to: $\frac{\$13,920}{80\%} = \frac{\$13,920}{0.8} = \$13,920 \div \frac{4}{5} = \$13,920 \cdot \frac{5}{4} = \$13,920 \cdot 1.25 = \$17,400$.

122. **(D)** $\frac{1}{5} \cdot 35 = 7$ hours sorting mail; $\frac{1}{2} \cdot 35 = 17\frac{1}{2}$ hours filing; $\frac{1}{7} \cdot 35 = 5$ hours reception. Thus, $29\frac{1}{2}$ hours are accounted for, leaving $5\frac{1}{2}$ hours spent on messenger work. The percent that is messenger work is: $5\frac{1}{2} \div 35 = \frac{11}{2} \div \frac{35}{1} = \frac{11}{2} \cdot \frac{1}{35} = \frac{11}{70} = 0.15\frac{5}{7} = 15\frac{5}{7}\%$.

123. **(C)** $\frac{1,152 \text{ boys}}{80\%} = \frac{1,152}{0.8} = 1,152 \div \frac{4}{5} = 1,152 \cdot \frac{5}{4} = 1,440$ boys are enrolled. Thus, the total number of students is: $\frac{1,440}{40\%} = 1,440 \div \frac{2}{5} = 1,400 \cdot \frac{5}{2} = 3,600$.

124. **(B)** The percent of raise is: $\frac{\$27,500 - \$25,000}{\$25,000} = \frac{\$2,500}{\$25,000} = 0.1 = 10\%$.

125. **(B)** The percent of population increase is: $\frac{100,000 - 80,000}{80,000} = \frac{20,000}{80,000} = 0.25 = 25\%$.

126. **(D)** The percent of decrease is: $\frac{\$25 - \$21}{\$25} = \frac{\$4}{\$25} = \frac{16}{100} = 16\%$.

127. **(A)** This item can be answered without any calculation. Whenever something is doubled, the percent of increase is 100%.

128. **(A)** The percent of decrease is: $\frac{200 - 150}{200} = \frac{50}{200} = 0.25 = 25\%$.

129. **(C)** The increase is by 9,000. Find the percent of increase by dividing the change (increase) in enrollment by the original enrollment: $\frac{9,000}{3,000} = 3 = 300\%$.

## EXERCISE 5—STATISTICAL MEASURES (p. 272)

1. **(A)** This is a basic average item; just take the sum of all the numbers and divide that by the number of quantities involved: $\frac{8+6+16}{3} = \frac{30}{3} = 10$.

2. **(D)** This is a basic average item; just take the sum of all the numbers and divide that by the number of quantities involved: $\frac{0+50}{2} = \frac{50}{2} = 25$.

3. **(C)** This is a basic average item; just take the sum of all the numbers and divide that by the number of quantities involved: $\frac{5+11+12+8}{4} = \frac{36}{4} = 9$.

4. **(B)** This is a basic average item; just take the sum of all the numbers and divide that by the number of quantities involved: $\frac{25+28+21+30+36}{5} = \frac{140}{5} = 28$.

5. **(C)** This is a basic average item; just take the sum of all the numbers and divide that by the number of quantities involved: $\frac{\frac{1}{4}+\frac{3}{4}+\frac{5}{8}+\frac{1}{2}+\frac{3}{8}}{5} = \frac{\frac{2}{8}+\frac{6}{8}+\frac{5}{8}+\frac{4}{8}+\frac{3}{8}}{5} = \frac{\frac{20}{8}}{5} = \frac{20}{40} = \frac{1}{2}$.

6. **(E)** This is a basic average item; just take the sum of all the numbers and divide that by the number of quantities involved: $\frac{\$0.78+\$0.45+\$0.36+\$0.98+\$0.55+\$0.54}{6} = \frac{\$3.66}{6} = \$0.61$.

7. **(A)** This is a basic average item; just take the sum of all the numbers and divide that by the number of quantities involved: $\frac{0.03+0.11+0.08+0.5}{4} = \frac{0.72}{4} = 0.18$.

8. **(C)** This is a basic average item; just take the sum of all the numbers and divide that by the number of quantities involved: $\frac{1,001+1,002+1,003+1,004+1,005}{5} = \frac{5,015}{5} = 1,003$.

9. **(E)** This is a basic average item; just take the sum of all the numbers and divide that by the number of quantities involved: $\frac{(-8)+(-6)+(-13)}{3} = -\frac{27}{3} = -9$.

10. **(A)** This is a basic average item; just take the sum of all the numbers and divide that by the number of quantities involved: $\frac{79+85+90+76+80}{5} = \frac{410}{5} = 82$.

11. **(E)** This is a basic average item; just take the sum of all the numbers and divide that by the number of quantities involved: $\frac{\$4.51+\$6.25+\$3.32+\$4.48+\$2.19}{5} = \frac{\$20.75}{5} = \$4.15$.

12. **(B)** This is a basic average item; just take the sum of all the numbers and divide that by the number of quantities involved: $\frac{8.5+9.3+8.2+9.0}{4} = \frac{35}{4} = 8.75$.

13. **(B)** This is a basic average item; just take the sum of all the numbers and divide that by the number of quantities involved: $\frac{44+33+45+44+29}{5} = \frac{195}{5} = 39$.

14. **(A)** The sum of all staff hours need to process 120 building permit applications is 360, so the average time it takes to process these 120 building permit applications is just the sum of all the staff hours divided by the quantity of permit applications: $\frac{360}{120} = 3$. The average processing time for each application is 3 hours.

15. **(C)** This is a basic average item; just take the sum of all the numbers and divide that by the number of quantities involved: $\frac{84\% + 89\% + 87\% + 90\% + 80\%}{5} = \frac{430\%}{5} = 86\%$.

16. **(D)** This item asks for a missing element in an average. First, set up the equation for finding the average, then solve for $x$: $\frac{21 + 23 + x}{3} = 24 \Rightarrow \frac{44 + x}{3} = 24 \Rightarrow 44 + x = 72 \Rightarrow x = 28$.

17. **(E)** This item asks for a missing element in an average. First, set up the equation for finding the average, then solve for $x$: $\frac{0 + 0 + x}{3} = 5 \Rightarrow x = 15$.

18. **(A)** This item asks for a missing element in an average. First, set up the equation for finding the average, then solve for $x$: $\frac{150 + 200 + 180 + x}{4} = 166 \Rightarrow 530 + x = 664 \Rightarrow x = 134$.

19. **(D)** This item asks for a missing element in an average. First, set up the equation for finding the average, then solve for $x$: $\frac{81 + 79 + 85 + 90 + x}{5} = 83 \Rightarrow 335 + x = 415 \Rightarrow x = 80$.

20. **(D)** This item asks for a missing element in an average. First, set up the equation for finding the average, then solve for $x$: $\frac{\$30 + 2x}{10} = \$3.60 \Rightarrow \$30 + 2x = \$36 \Rightarrow 2x = \$6 \Rightarrow x = \$3$.

21. **(D)** First, find the total weight of the twelve books, $w_{\text{total } 12}$: $\frac{w_{\text{total } 12}}{12} = 2.75 \Rightarrow w_{\text{total } 12} = 33$ pounds. Second, find the total weight of the eleven books, $w_{\text{total } 11}$: $\frac{w_{\text{total } 11}}{11} = 2.70 \Rightarrow w_{\text{total } 11} = 29.7$ pounds. Third, find the difference between the two, this will be the weight of the removed book: $33 - 29.7 = 3.3$ pounds.

22. **(E)** First, find the sum of the seven scores, $s_{\text{total } 7}$: $\frac{s_{\text{total } 7}}{7} = 80 \Rightarrow s_{\text{total } 7} = 560$. Second, find the sum of the scores after the lowest and highest have been removed, $s_{\text{w/o low/high}}$: $\frac{s_{\text{w/o low/high}}}{5} = 78 \Rightarrow s_{\text{w/o low/high}} = 390$. Thus, the sum of the lowest and highest scores is: $560 - 390 = 170$. Therefore, the average of the lowest and highest score is: $\frac{170}{2} = 85$.

23. **(E)** This is a weighted average item. Solve by setting up the equation for a weighted average. Note that the quantities contributing to the average is the total number of children in the group: $12 + 8 = 20$. $\frac{(12 \cdot 10) + (8 \cdot 15)}{20} = \frac{120 + 120}{20} = \frac{240}{20} = 12$ years.

24. **(B)** This is a weighted average item. Note that the quantities contributing to the average is the total number of deposits Robert made in his savings account: $4 + 2 + 4 = 10$. Solve by setting up the equation for a weighted average: $\frac{(4 \cdot \$15) + (2 \cdot \$20) + (4 \cdot \$25)}{10} = \frac{\$60 + \$40 + \$100}{10} = \frac{\$200}{10} = \$20$.

25. **(B)** First, find the total weight of the six people, $w_{\text{total } 6}$: $\frac{w_{\text{total } 6}}{6} = 145 \Rightarrow w_{\text{total } 6} = 870$ pounds. Second, find the total weight of all seven people, $w_{\text{total } 7}$: $\frac{w_{\text{total } 7}}{7} = 147 \Rightarrow w_{\text{total } 7} = 1,029$ pounds. Third, find the weight of the seventh person by taking the difference of the two totals: $1029 - 870 = 159$ pounds.

26. **(C)** This is a basic average item. Remember that mean is a synonym for average. So, to solve, just take the sum of all the numbers and divide that by the number of quantities involved: $\frac{2 + 3 + 13 + 15 + 1}{5} = \frac{34}{5} = 6.8$.

27. **(B)** This is a basic average item. Remember that mean is a synonym for average. So, to solve, just take the sum of all the numbers and divide that by the number of quantities involved: $\frac{-3 + 2 + 6 + 5 + 2 + 0}{6} = \frac{12}{6} = 2$.

28. **(E)** This item asks for a missing element in an average. First, set up the equation for finding the average, then solve for $x$: $\frac{-3 + 5 + 6 + 13 + 17 + x}{6} = 10 \Rightarrow 38 + x = 60 \Rightarrow x = 22$.

29. **(B)** First, find the sum of the five numbers, $s_5 : \frac{s_5}{5} = 56 \Rightarrow s_5 = 280$. Second, find the sum of the seven numbers, $s_7 : \frac{s_7}{7} = 58 \Rightarrow s_7 = 406$. The sum of the two added numbers is the difference between the two totals: $406 - 280 = 126$. Their average is that number divided by 2. Thus, their average is 63.

30. **(B)** This item is a variation of the basic average item. First, set up the average equation. Then solve for $x$: $\frac{(3x+1) + (2x+4) + (x+10)}{3} = 13 \Rightarrow 6x + 15 = 39 \Rightarrow 6x = 24 \Rightarrow x = 4$.

31. **(C)** This is a weighted average item. Note that the quantities contributing to the average is the total number of female corporate officers interviewed, 100. Solve by setting up the equation for a weighted average: $\frac{(34 \cdot 55) + (28 \cdot 45) + (26 \cdot 35) + (12 \cdot 25)}{100} = \frac{1{,}870 + 1{,}260 + 910 + 300}{100} = \frac{4{,}340}{100} = 43.4$ years.

32. **(D)** To find the median for this item, first list the numbers in ascending order. Then, since there is an even number of data points, average the two middle values: $\{26, 29, 30, 33, 33, 35, \mathbf{37}, \mathbf{38}, 40, 42, 42, 42, 47, 51\}$. Thus, the median is: $\frac{37 + 38}{2} = \frac{75}{2} = 37.5$.

33. **(D)** To find the mode for this item, first list the numbers in ascending order. Then, look for the number that occurs with the most frequency. For this item, it is 42, and it occurs 3 times in the set: $\{26, 29, 30, 33, 33, 35, 37, 38, 40, \mathbf{42}, \mathbf{42}, \mathbf{42}, 47, 51\}$.

34. **(A)** This item asks for a missing element in an average. First, set up the equation for finding the average, then solve for $x$: $\frac{26 + 29 + 30 + 33 + 33 + 35 + 37 + 38 + 40 + 42 + 42 + 42 + 47 + 51 + x}{15} = 37 \Rightarrow \frac{525 + x}{15} = 37 \Rightarrow 525 + x = 555 \Rightarrow x = 30$.

35. **(C)** To find the median for this item, first list the numbers in ascending order. Then, since there is an odd number data points, the middle value is the median. $\{1, 2, \mathbf{3}, 7, 8\}$. The median is 3.

36. **(C)** To find the median for this item, first list the numbers in ascending order. Then, since there is an odd number data points, the middle value is the median: $\{-16, -3, 0, 1, 2, \mathbf{2}, 4, 4, 8, 9, 12\}$. The median is 2.

37. **(D)** To find the median for this item, first list the numbers in ascending order. Then, since there is an even number data points, average the two middle values: $\{-16, -3, 2, 2, \mathbf{4}, \mathbf{4}, 8, 8, 9, 12\}$. Thus, the median is: $\frac{4 + 4}{2} = 4$.

38. **(B)** To find the mode for this item, first list the numbers in ascending order. Then, look for the number that occurs with the most frequency. For this item, it is 8, and it occurs 2 times in the set: $\{4, \mathbf{8}, \mathbf{8}, 10, 15\}$.

39. **(D)** To find the mode for this item, first list the numbers in ascending order. Then, look for the number that occurs with the most frequency. For this item, it is 2: $\{-2, \mathbf{2}, \mathbf{2}, \mathbf{2}, 4, 6, 8, 8, 10\}$.

40. **(A)** In order for the mode to be a negative even number, then at least two of the three unknown values must be equal as well as being negative even numbers. Therefore, set each unknown number equal to another, solve for $x$ (thus producing a mode—at least the two numbers of interest are equal, creating a mode), and then plug $x$ back into to the unknowns to determine if the result really is a negative even number. $2x + 8 = x - 4 \Rightarrow x = -12$; $2x + 8 = 7x - 4 \Rightarrow 5x = 12 \Rightarrow x = \frac{12}{5}$; $x - 4 = 7x - 4 \Rightarrow 6x = 0 \Rightarrow x = 0$. Thus, the three combinations of equations yield three possibilities for $x$. Now, find the one that makes at least two of the equations equal a negative, even number: Of the three values of $x$, only zero appears as an answer. Check your answer by evaluating the three equations with $x = 0$: $2x + 8 = 2(0) + 8 = 8$; $x - 4 = (0) - 4 = -4$; $7x - 4 = 7(0) - 4 = -4$. Thus, zero does indeed produce two values that are negative and even.

41. **(B)** $100 + 55 + 75 + 80 + 65 + 65 + 95 + 90 + 80 + 45 + 40 + 50 + 85 + 85 + 85 + 80 + 80 + 70 + 65 + 60 = 1{,}450$. So, the average grade is: $\frac{1{,}450}{20} = 72.5$.

42. **(B)** $\frac{75 \cdot 0.15 + 100 \cdot 0.30 + 50 \cdot 0.72}{75 + 100 + 50} = \frac{11.25 + 30 + 36}{225} = \frac{77.25}{225} = 34\frac{1}{3}$ cents.

43. **(E)** Multiply the grade in each course by its weight in the final average: $90(4) + 84(3) + 75(3) + 76(1) = 360 + 252 + 225 + 76 = 913$. The total weight is: $4 + 3 + 3 + 1 = 11$. Therefore, the average is: $\frac{913}{11} = 83$.

44. **(D)** Average $= \frac{3+4+4+0+1+2+0+2+2}{9} = \frac{18}{9} = 2$.

45. **(B)** Arrange the numbers in order: $\{0, 0, 1, 2, 2, 2, 3, 4, 4\}$. Of the nine numbers, the fifth (middle) number is 2.

46. **(C)** The most frequent data value in the set is 2.

47. **(C)** The range of measurements for a rod of diameter $1.51 \pm 0.015$ inches is $1.510 - 0.015 = 1.495$ inches to $1.510 + 0.015 = 1.525$ inches.

48. **(E)** To find which statement cannot be true, it is easiest to assume specific number sets for $A$ and $B$ and show which statements can be true. Let $A = \{1, 2, 3, 4, 5\}$ and $B = \{1, 2, 4, 5\}$. The mean and median of $A$ are both 3; the mean and median of $B$ are both 3 as well. Furthermore, since the range of a set is the difference between the greatest and smallest numbers in the set, $A$ and $B$ also have the same range, $5 - 1 = 4$. Therefore, (A), (B), and (C) can all be true. If $A = \{1, 2, 3, 4, 5\}$ and $B = \{1, 2, 3, 4\}$, then the mean of $A$ (3) is greater than the mean of $B$ (2.5). Thus, (D) can be true. The correct answer must be (E). To see that this statement CANNOT be true, suppose that $x$ denotes the number in $A$ that is not in $B$. If $x$ is either the smallest or the greatest number in $A$, then the range of $T$ would be less than the range of $B$. However, if $x$ is between the smallest number and the greatest number in $A$, then the range in $B$ would be equal to the range in $A$. Either way, the range of $A$ cannot be less than the range of $B$.

49. **(C)** To be more than 1.0 standard deviations from the mean of the data set, a value must be either more than 1.0 standard deviations above the mean or more than 1.0 standard deviations below the mean. Thus, to be more than 1.0 standard deviations from the mean of 10.0, the value must be either greater than $10.0 + 1.0(1.5) = 11.5$, or less than $10.0 - 1.0(1.5) = 8.5$. Since the question asks for the value that is *more than* 1.0 standard deviations, (B) and (D) are incorrect. The only answer choice that falls between 8.5 and 11.5 is (C), 9.5

50. **(E)** Since the mean is 15.5 and the standard deviation is 3.0, 1.5 standard deviations less than the mean is: $15.5 - 1.5(3.0) = 11$.

51. **(D)** Note that the frequency distributions for both $A$ and $C$ are symmetric about 3, which implies that both variables have mean = median = 3. Calculate the mean and median for $B$ to determine if it should be included in the answer. Mean for $B$ is: $\frac{(1 \cdot 3) + (2 \cdot 5) + (3 \cdot 2) + (4 \cdot 6) + (5 \cdot 4)}{20} = \frac{3 + 10 + 6 + 24 + 20}{20} = \frac{63}{20} \frac{63}{20} = 3\frac{3}{20}$. Median for $B$ is $3\frac{1}{2}$. Therefore, $A$ and $C$ are the only frequency distributions for which the mean equals the median.

## EXERCISE 6—RATIOS AND PROPORTIONS (p. 280)

1. **(B)** There are 3 blue marbles and 8 red marbles; thus, the ratio between them is 3:8, or $\frac{3}{8}$.

2. **(A)** The ratio between the teachers and the students is $\frac{24}{480} = \frac{6 \cdot 4}{10 \cdot 6 \cdot 4 \cdot 2} = \frac{1}{20}$, or 1:20.

3. **(D)** The ratio between works of fiction and works of non-fiction is $\frac{12,000}{3,000} = \frac{12}{3} = \frac{4 \cdot 3}{3} = \frac{4}{1}$, or 4:1.

4. **(C)** Since we want to find fractions equivalent to 1:3, ask yourself in which ratio, I – III, is the denominator three times as large as the numerator. I: $120 = 3 \cdot 40$; II: $100 \neq 3 \cdot 75$; III: $360 = 3 \cdot 120$. Thus, I and III are both equivalent to 1:3.

5. **(A)** There are 90 seventh-grade girls and a total of $90 + 80 = 170$ girls in Tyler Junior High. Thus, the ratio of seventh-grade girls to the total number of girls in Tyler Junior High is $\frac{90}{170} = \frac{9}{17}$.

6. **(A)** There are 80 eighth-grade girls and a total of $90 + 85 + 80 + 75 = 330$ students in Tyler Junior High. The ratio between the eighth-grade girls and the total number of students in Tyler Junior High is then $\frac{80}{330} = \frac{8}{33}$.

7. **(D)** The item asks for the average mileage per gallon of an airplane that flies 275 miles on 25 gallons of fuel. Our goal, then, is to find, from the information given, the distance the plane flies on a single gallon of fuel. Therefore, the miles per gallon is equal to: $\frac{275}{25} = \frac{11 \cdot 25}{25} = 11 \frac{miles}{gallon}$.

8. **(B)** The ratio of chocolates to caramels to mints is 12:6:9. These are all divisible by three; the ratio can be simplified to 4:2:3.

9. **(B)** Let Lucy's money $= x$; Ricky's money $= y$; Ethel's money $= z$. The item gives us the following ratios: $x : 2y$ and $y : 3z$. We substitute $3z$ for $y$ in the first ratio, leaving us with $x : 2 \cdot (3z) \Rightarrow x : 6z$. Lucy has 6 times as much money as Ethel. So, the ratio of the amount of money Ethel has to the amount of money Lucy has is 1:6.

10. **(D)** 3 farkels : 2 kirns and 3 kirns : 5 pucks. First, we need to find a common element: kirns. Second, we must relate farkels and pucks to the same number of kirns. The lowest number that captures both ratios is 6 kirns. Then, 9 farkels : 6 kirns : 10 pucks. So, 9 farkels buys 10 pucks.

11. **(D)** First, set up the equations: $X : 2Y$; $Y : \frac{2}{3}Z$. Then, multiply the second equation by 2 to relate the first equation to the second equation. Now, we have $X : 2Y : \frac{4}{3}Z$. Thus, the ratio of the rate of operation of machine $X$ to that of machine $Z$ is $1 : \frac{4}{3}$ or $\frac{1}{\frac{4}{3}} = \frac{3}{4}$.

12. **(C)** First, we find the total number of 'parts' into which the marbles need to be divided. We can think of Bill as having 3 parts, and Carl as having 5 parts. Thus, there are 8 total parts. Second, we divide 48 into 8 equal parts to obtain 6 marbles per part. Since Bill has 3 parts, he should have 18 marbles, $3 \cdot 6 = 18$.

13. **(B)** We can express the division of shares between Nelix and Janeway as $J : 4N$. Thus, we see that there is a total of five parts. $\frac{\$10.00}{5} = \$2.00$. Janeway's share is 4 parts, so $\$2.00 \cdot 4 = \$8.00$.

14. **(C)** To divide something into unequal parts, we must first express those parts as fractions of a single whole. We can use the imagery of a pie. If the pie is distributed in a ratio of $2 : 3 : 5$, we can add the parts, $2 + 3 + 5 = 10$. Next, we can cut the pie into ten equal pieces and give each person his or her share of the pie, one piece of pie for each part of the ratio. Thus we give 2 pieces, 3 pieces, and 5 pieces of pie. Now, applying that to the item at hand, we divide $\$1,000$ by 10; each part of the 'pie' equals $\$100$. The recipient of the largest "piece of the pie", will receive $5 \cdot \$100 = \$500$.

15. **(D)** $\frac{6}{8} = \frac{x}{4} \Rightarrow x = 4 \cdot \frac{6}{8} \Rightarrow x = \frac{6}{2} = 3$.

16. **(D)** $\frac{14}{x} = \frac{2}{7} \Rightarrow x \cdot \frac{14}{x} = x \cdot \frac{2}{7} \Rightarrow 14x = x\frac{2}{7} \Rightarrow 14 \cdot \frac{7}{2} = x = 49$.

17. **(E)** $\frac{3}{4} = \frac{4}{x} \Rightarrow \frac{4}{3} = \frac{x}{4} \Rightarrow x = 4 \cdot \frac{4}{3} = \frac{16}{3}$.

18. **(D)** $\frac{\$36}{240 \text{ widgets}} = \frac{x}{180 \text{ widgets}} \Rightarrow x = \$36 \cdot \frac{180}{240} = \$36 \cdot \frac{18}{24} = \$36 \cdot \frac{3}{4} = \$27$.

19. **(D)** $\frac{\$9.60}{1 \text{ kilogram}} = \frac{x}{450 \text{ grams}} \cdot \frac{1,000 \text{ grams}}{1 \text{ kilogram}} \Rightarrow x = \$9.60 \cdot \frac{450}{1,000} = \$9.60 \cdot \frac{45}{100} = \$9.60 \cdot \frac{9}{20} = \$0.48 \cdot 9 = \$4.32$.

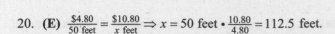

20. **(E)** $\frac{\$4.80}{50 \text{ feet}} = \frac{\$10.80}{x \text{ feet}} \Rightarrow x = 50 \text{ feet} \cdot \frac{10.80}{4.80} = 112.5 \text{ feet}$.

21. **(C)** If one quarter of a population has red hair, then three quarters does not. So the ratio of red haired people in the population to the remainder of the population is $1:3$. Let $z$ signify those without red hair. Then, $\frac{3}{1} = \frac{z}{100} \Rightarrow z = 300$.

22. **(B)** Let $x$ be the amount raised when 50% of the goal has been reached: $\frac{x}{50} = \frac{\$12,000}{20} \Rightarrow 50 \cdot \$600 = \$30,000 = x$.

23. **(C)** $\frac{y}{50 \text{ kilograms}} = \frac{72 \text{ liters}}{48 \text{ liters}} = \frac{3}{2} \Rightarrow y = \frac{3}{2}(50) = 75 \text{ kilograms}$.

24. **(C)** Be careful with this item. You might be tempted to do the following: $\frac{x}{5 \text{ miles/hour}} = \frac{2 \text{ hours}}{4 \text{ miles/hour}} \Rightarrow$ $x = \frac{5 \text{ miles}}{\text{hour}} \cdot \frac{1 \text{ hour}}{2 \text{ miles/hour}} = 2.5 \text{ hours}$. But, reflection will show that the first relationship is incorrect. The way it is set up above, the hours will *increase* in proportion to the increase in speed; however, if the rate increases the trip should take less time. Note that this is answer A. A clear pitfall. When dealing with inverse proportions, group like objects, in this case hours and miles per hour, and invert one side of the proportion. Now lets try: $\frac{x}{2 \text{ hours}} = \frac{4 \text{ miles/hour}}{5 \text{ miles/hour}} \Rightarrow x = 2 \cdot \frac{4}{5} = 1.6 \text{ hours}$.

25. **(B)** This is an inverse relationship item. Group like terms: $\frac{x}{200 \text{ gallons/hour}} = \frac{5 \text{ hours}}{8 \text{ hours}}$. Now, invert the right side: $\frac{x}{200 \text{ gallons/hour}} = \frac{8 \text{ hours}}{5 \text{ hours}}$. Then, solve for $x$: $x = 200 \cdot \frac{8}{5} = 40 \cdot 8 = 320$ gallons per hour.

26. **(C)** $\frac{3}{8} = 0.375$.

27. **(D)** $\frac{3}{4} = \frac{15}{x} \Rightarrow \frac{4}{3} = \frac{x}{15} \Rightarrow x = 15 \cdot \frac{4}{3} = 5 \cdot 4 = 20$.

28. **(B)** Let $x$ be the number of problems Annika can solve in 48 minutes: $\frac{x}{10} = \frac{48}{30} \Rightarrow x = 10 \cdot \frac{48}{30} = 16$ problems.

29. **(E)** Let $x$ signify the flights of stairs Seung can mount in 18 minutes: $\frac{x}{18} = \frac{6}{4} \Rightarrow x = \frac{18 \cdot 6}{4} = \frac{108}{4} = 27$ flights of stairs.

    Alternatively, recognize that 4 goes 4.5 times into 18. If Seung can ascend 6 flights of stairs in 4 minutes, in 18 minutes he should be able to ascend $4.5 \cdot 6 = 27$ flights of stairs.

30. **(C)** Let $x$ represent the cost of 6 candy bars: $\frac{x}{6} = \frac{\$1.04}{4} \Rightarrow x = 6 \cdot \$0.26 = \$1.56$.

31. **(D)** Let $x$ represent the number of steps Baby Andrew takes to walk 5 yards: $\frac{x}{8} = \frac{5}{2} \Rightarrow x = \frac{40}{2} = 20$ steps.

32. **(C)** $3:5$ implies 8 parts. $\frac{40}{8} = 5$ and $5 \cdot 3 = 15$.

33. **(B)** Let $x$ represent the number of ounces popped from 5 bags of popcorn: $\frac{28}{3} = \frac{x}{5} \Rightarrow x = \frac{5 \cdot 28}{3} = \frac{140}{3} = 46\frac{2}{3}$.

34. **(A)** $\frac{x}{60,000,000} = \frac{420}{1,000} = \frac{42}{100} = \frac{21}{50} \Rightarrow x = \frac{60,000,000 \cdot 21}{50} = 1,200,000 \cdot 21 = 25,200,000$ people.

35. **(D)** Think of this in terms of growth, not of total length. Thus, for the first four days, we want to use $12 - 5 = 7$ in the ratio: $\frac{x}{6} = \frac{7}{4} \Rightarrow x = \frac{6 \cdot 7}{4} = \frac{3 \cdot 7}{2} = 10.5$ centimeters. Now, we must remember to add this to the length after four days: $10.5 + 12 = 22.5$ centimeters.

36. **(C)** Let $x$ be the time in minutes Elan needs to mow 5 lawns: $\frac{x}{85} = \frac{5}{3} \Rightarrow \frac{85 \cdot 5}{3} = \frac{425}{3} = 141$ minutes, 40 seconds.

37. **(B)** Let $x$ signify the fraction of a job Sarah does in 10 minutes: $\frac{x}{10} = \frac{\frac{1}{5}}{6} \Rightarrow 10 \cdot \frac{1}{30} = \frac{1}{3}$.

38. **(B)** $\frac{2\frac{1}{2}}{4} = \frac{1\frac{7}{8}}{s} \Rightarrow s = \frac{4 \cdot 1\frac{7}{8}}{2\frac{1}{2}} = \frac{1 \cdot \frac{15}{2}}{\frac{5}{2}} = \frac{15}{2} \cdot \frac{2}{5} = \frac{30}{10} = 3$ inches.

39. **(C)** Let $p$ equal the cost per dozen handkerchiefs: $\frac{3}{12} = \frac{\$2.29}{p} \Rightarrow p = \frac{12 \cdot \$2.29}{3} = \frac{4 \cdot \$2.29}{1} = \$9.16$.

40. **(A)** Let $f$ equal the height of the first pole: $\frac{f}{24} = \frac{3}{4} \Rightarrow f = \frac{24 \cdot 3}{4} = \frac{6 \cdot 3}{1} = 18$ feet.

41. **(D)** Let $y$ equal the unknown length: $\frac{3\frac{1}{2}}{\frac{1}{8}} = \frac{y}{1} \Rightarrow y = \frac{3\frac{1}{2} \cdot 1}{\frac{1}{8}} = 3\frac{1}{2} \div \frac{1}{8} = \frac{7}{2} \cdot \frac{8}{1} = \frac{7}{1} \cdot \frac{4}{1} = 28$ feet.

42. **(B)** If only two parts of a proportion are known, the item must be solved by the ratio method. The ratio 10:1 means that if the alloy were separated into equal parts, 10 of those parts would be copper and 1 would be aluminum, for a total of $10 + 1 = 11$ parts. $77 \div 11 = 7$ pounds per part. The alloy contains 1 part aluminum. $7 \cdot 1 = 7$ pounds aluminum.

43. **(C)** The cost, $c$, is proportional to the number of square feet: $\frac{\$0.31}{c} = \frac{1}{180} \Rightarrow c = \frac{\$0.31 \cdot 180}{1} = \$55.80$.

44. **(B)** The amount earned is proportional to the number of days worked: $\frac{\$352}{a} = \frac{16}{117} \Rightarrow a = \frac{\$352 \cdot 117}{16} = \$2,574$.

45. **(D)** Let $n$ equal the unknown length: $\frac{\frac{1}{8}}{3\frac{3}{4}} = \frac{12}{n} \Rightarrow n = \frac{12 \cdot 3\frac{3}{4}}{\frac{1}{8}} = 45 \div \frac{1}{8} = 45 \cdot \frac{8}{1} = 360$.

46. **(B)** The ratio of investment is: $9,000 : 7,000 : 6,000$ or $9 : 7 : 6$. $9 + 7 + 6 = 22$. $\$825 \div 22 = \$37.50$ for each share of the profit. James' share of the profit is $7 \cdot \$37.50 = \$262.50$. James spends $230, so he is left with $\$262.50 - \$230.00 = \$32.50$.

47. **(A)** $\frac{1\frac{5}{8} \text{ inches}}{10 \text{ miles}} = \frac{2.25 \text{ inches}}{x \text{ miles}} \Rightarrow x = 2.25 \text{ inches} \cdot \frac{10 \text{ miles}}{1\frac{5}{8} \text{ inches}} = 2\frac{1}{4} \cdot \frac{10}{\frac{13}{8}} = 2\frac{1}{4} \cdot \frac{80}{13} = \frac{9}{4} \cdot \frac{80}{13} = \frac{9 \cdot 20}{13} = \frac{180}{13}$ miles.

48. **(C)** $\frac{72 \text{ inches tall}}{48 \text{ inches shadow}} = \frac{66 \text{ inches tall}}{x \text{ inches shadow}} \Rightarrow x = 66 \cdot \frac{48}{72} = \frac{66 \cdot 2}{3} = 44$ inches of shadow.

49. **(B)** $\frac{1 \text{ inch}}{12 \text{ feet}} = \frac{7 \text{ inches}}{x \text{ yards}} \Rightarrow x \text{ yards} = 7 \text{ inches} \cdot \frac{12 \text{ feet}}{1 \text{ inch}} \cdot \frac{1 \text{ yard}}{3 \text{ feet}} = \frac{7 \cdot 4}{1} = 28$ yards. Note that if 1 inch represents 12 feet, it also represents 4 yards. All we need to do now is to multiply the ratio 1 inch : 4 yards by 7. That is, 7 inches : 28 yards.

50. **(E)** $\frac{4 \text{ units}}{7 \text{ inches}} = \frac{5 \text{ units}}{x \text{ inches}} \Rightarrow x \text{ inches} = 5 \text{ units} \cdot \frac{7 \text{ inches}}{4 \text{ units}} = \frac{35}{4} = 8\frac{3}{4} = 8.75$ inches.

## EXERCISE 7—EXPONENTS AND RADICALS (p. 293)

1. **(E)** $3^3 = 3 \cdot 3 \cdot 3 = 9 \cdot 3 = 27$.

2. **(D)** $2^4 = 2 \cdot 2 \cdot 2 \cdot 2 = 4 \cdot 2 \cdot 2 = 8 \cdot 2 = 16$.

3. **(E)** Any number taken to the first power is equal to itself: $x^1 = x$. Thus, $1,000,000^1 = 1,000,000$.

4. **(B)** Any number taken to the power of zero is equal to 1: $x^0 = 1$. Thus, $100^0 = 1$.

5. **(C)** $2^3 \cdot 2^2 = 2^{3+2} = 2^5$. When two numbers with the same base are multiplied, the result is equal to that base taken to the sum of the original exponents.

6. **(E)** I: $3^{10} \cdot 10^3 = 3^3 \cdot 3^7 \cdot 10^3 = 3^7 \cdot (3^3 \cdot 10^3) = 3^7 \cdot (3 \cdot 10)^3 = 3^7 \cdot 30^3$. We have manipulated the equation, so that we can compare like quantities. To accomplish this, we separated out the number of times 30 occurs in the base expression. Now, we compare it to the figure in I: $3^7 \cdot 30^3 = 30^{30} \Rightarrow 3^7 = \frac{30^{30}}{30^3} = 30^{30-3} = 30^{27}$. Clearly, $3^7 \neq 30^{27}$, so I is not true. As for II, $3^{10} \cdot 10^3 = 300 \cdot 1000 \Rightarrow 3^{10} = 300 \Rightarrow 3^9 = 100$. But, 3 doesn't further divide 100, so II is false. III: Since $10^3 = 1000 > 30 + 30 = 60$, III is also false.

7. **(C)** Use the product rule of exponents; add the exponents of like terms: $5^4 \cdot 5^9 = 5^{4+9} = 5^{13}$.

8. **(A)** Use the product rule of exponents; add the exponents of like terms: $2^3 \cdot 2^4 \cdot 2^5 = 2^{3+4+5} = 2^{12}$.

9. **(A)** $(2+3)^{20} = (5)^{20} = 5^{20}$.

10. **(A)** $\frac{2^5}{2^3} = 2^{5-3} = 2^2$. The quotient of two numbers with the same base is equal to that base taken to the difference of the exponent of the numerator and the exponent of the denominator.

11. **(B)** Use the quotient rule of exponents; subtract the exponents of like terms: $\frac{3^{10}}{3^8} = 3^{10-8} = 3^2$.

12. **(C)** Use the quotient rule of exponents; subtract the exponents of like terms: $\frac{5^2}{5^2} = 5^{2-2} = 5^0 = 1$. Thus, II and III are true.

13. **(C)** Use the quotient rule of exponents; subtract the exponents of like terms: $\frac{3^2}{3^3} = 3^{2-3} = 3^{-1} = \frac{1}{3^1} = \frac{1}{3}$. Thus, I and II are both true.

14. **(B)** Use the power rule of exponents; multiply the exponents: $(2^2)^3 = 2^{2 \cdot 3} = 2^6$.

15. **(B)** Use the power rule of exponents; multiply the exponents: $(5^2)^6 = 5^{2 \cdot 6} = 5^{12}$.

16. **(C)** Use the power rule of exponents; multiply the exponents: $(7^7)^7 = 7^{7 \cdot 7} = 7^{49}$.

17. **(E)** $(3 \cdot 2)^2 = 3^2 \cdot 2^2 = 3 \cdot 3 \cdot 2 \cdot 2 = 36$. So, I, II, and III are true.

18. **(D)** Look at I and III. They cannot both be true: $15^2 \neq 8^2$ Now, $(5 \cdot 3)^2 = 5^2 \cdot 3^2 = 15^2$. Thus, I and II are true.

19. **(C)** $(\frac{8}{3})^2 = \frac{8^2}{3^2} = \frac{64}{9} \neq 11^2$. I and II only are true.

20. **(C)** $(\frac{4}{9})^2 = \frac{4^2}{9^2} = \frac{16}{81}$.

21. **(C)** Use the product rule and the power rule: $(2 \cdot 2^2 \cdot 2^3)^2 = (2^{1+2+3})^2 = (2^6)^2 = 2^{6 \cdot 2} = 2^{12}$.

22. **(A)** Use the quotient rule, then the power rule: $(\frac{2^4 \cdot 5^4}{2^2 \cdot 5^2})^2 = (2^{4-2} \cdot 5^{4-2})^2 = (2^2 \cdot 5^2)^2 = 2^{2 \cdot 2} \cdot 5^{2 \cdot 2} = 2^4 \cdot 5^4$. It is usually easier in the long run to first simplify the inside of a fraction before operating on it.

23. **(E)** Use the quotient rule: $\frac{3^6 \cdot 5^3 \cdot 7^9}{3^4 \cdot 5^3 \cdot 7^8} = 3^{6-4} \cdot 5^{3-3} \cdot 7^{9-8} = 3^2 \cdot 5^0 \cdot 7^1 = 3^2 \cdot 1 \cdot 7 = 3^2 \cdot 7$

24. **(A)** Use the quotient rule, then the power rule: $(\frac{5^{12} \cdot 7^5}{5^{11} \cdot 7^5})^2 = (5^{12-11} \cdot 7^{5-5}) = (5^1 \cdot 7^0)^2 = 5^{1 \cdot 2} \cdot 7^{0 \cdot 2} = 5^2 \cdot 7^0 = 5^2 \cdot 1 = 25$.

25. **(D)** Use the quotient rule, then the power rule: $(\frac{12^{12} \cdot 11^{11} \cdot 10^{10}}{12^{12} \cdot 11^{11} \cdot 10^9})^2 = (\frac{10^{10}}{10^9})^2 = (10^{10-9})^2 = (10^1)^2 = 10^{1 \cdot 2} = 100$.

26. **(A)** $\sqrt{36} = x \Rightarrow x^2 = 36$. We can immediately eliminate II, because the radical sign always denotes a positive number unless preceded by $\pm$. Now, we try placing I and III into $x$: $6^2 = 36$; $(3\sqrt{3})^2 = 9 \cdot 3 = 27$. Thus, only I is true.

27. **(C)** Remember, you can't add the insides of radicals when the radicals are added: $\sqrt{81} + \sqrt{4} \neq \sqrt{85}$. $\sqrt{81} + \sqrt{4} = 9 + 2 = 11$. Only III is true.

28. **(B)** Factor out perfect squares: $\sqrt{27} = \sqrt{9 \cdot 3} = 3\sqrt{3}$.

29. **(C)** Try to think of the number inside a radical as a composite containing a perfect square: $\sqrt{52} = \sqrt{13 \cdot 4} = 2\sqrt{13}$.

30. **(C)** $\sqrt{\frac{9}{4}} = \frac{\sqrt{9}}{\sqrt{4}} = \frac{3}{2}$.

31. **(A)** Rewriting this item is the easiest way to solve it: $\frac{\sqrt{81}}{\sqrt{27}} = \sqrt{\frac{81}{27}} = \sqrt{3}$.

32. **(A)** $2\sqrt{2} = \sqrt{8} \Rightarrow \sqrt{4} < \sqrt{8} < \sqrt{9} \Rightarrow 2 < \sqrt{8} < 3$. But, $\sqrt{8}$ is much closer to 3 since 8 is much closer to 9. Thus, 2.8 is the best answer.

33. **(D)** $\sqrt{25} < \sqrt{27} < \sqrt{36} \Rightarrow 5 < \sqrt{27} < 6$. Because 27 is closer to 25 than to 36, $\sqrt{27}$ is closer to 5 than to 6. The only answer that fits these criteria is 5.1.

34. **(B)** 12 is closer to 9 than to 16, so $\sqrt{12}$ is closer to $\sqrt{9} = 3$ than to $\sqrt{16} = 4$. Since, $3 < \sqrt{12} < 4$, 3.4 is the best answer. The best way to approach these types of items is to find the nearest two perfect squares, one above and one below, in this case 9 and 16. By taking their square roots we can wedge the unknown root between two known values. Then, we can determine which the unknown root is closer to by how close it is to the perfect squares we chose.

35. **(B)** $\sqrt{16} < \sqrt{23} < \sqrt{25} \Rightarrow 4 < \sqrt{23} < 5$. Considering that $\sqrt{23}$ is much closer to $\sqrt{25}$ than to $\sqrt{16}$, 4.8 is the best answer.

36. **(C)** $\sqrt{36} < \sqrt{45} < \sqrt{49} \Rightarrow 6 < \sqrt{45} < 7$. Since 45 is closer to 49 than to 36, $\sqrt{45}$ is closer to 7 than to 6. Thus, 6.6 is the best answer.

37. **(D)** For these types of items, use the FOIL method: $(7 + \sqrt{5})(3 - \sqrt{5}) = 7 \cdot 3 - 7\sqrt{5} + 3\sqrt{5} - (\sqrt{5})^2 = 21 - 4\sqrt{5} - 5 = 16 - 4\sqrt{5}$.

38. **(B)** Use the FOIL method: $(5 - \sqrt{2})(3 - \sqrt{2}) = 15 - 5\sqrt{2} - 3\sqrt{2} + (\sqrt{2})^2 = 15 - 8\sqrt{2} + 2 = 17 - 8\sqrt{2}$.

39. **(C)** Use the FOIL method: $(\sqrt{3} + 1)(2 - \sqrt{3}) = 2\sqrt{3} - (\sqrt{3})^2 + 2 - \sqrt{3} = \sqrt{3} - 3 + 2 = -1 + \sqrt{3}$.

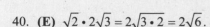 

40. **(E)** $\sqrt{2} \cdot 2\sqrt{3} = 2\sqrt{3 \cdot 2} = 2\sqrt{6}$.

41. **(D)** $\sqrt{8} + \sqrt{50} = \sqrt{4 \cdot 2} + \sqrt{25 \cdot 2} = 2\sqrt{2} + 5\sqrt{2} = 7\sqrt{2}$.

42. **(B)** $\sqrt{3^2 + 5^2} = \sqrt{9 + 25} = \sqrt{34}$.

43. **(D)** $\sqrt{(2\sqrt{3})^2 + 2^2} = \sqrt{(2^2 \cdot 3) + 4} = \sqrt{12 + 4} = \sqrt{16} = 4$. Do not be intimidated by the size of this item; simply solve from the inside out.

44. **(A)** Simplify to find out if the expression is rational: $(5 + \sqrt{2})(5 - \sqrt{2}) = 25 - 5\sqrt{2} + 5\sqrt{2} - (\sqrt{2})^2 = 25 - 2 = 23$. Note that because the two expressions in the parentheses are of the form $(a + b)(a - b) = a^2 - b^2$, the $\sqrt{2}$ will be squared and will equal 2, so there will be no radicals left in the expression.

45. **(B)** Because $\sqrt{2}$ is irrational, and we know that the sum or difference of a rational number and an irrational number is also irrational, we know that we are dealing with the quotient of two irrational numbers. Such a quotient is always irrational.

46. **(A)** Use the distributive law: $\frac{\sqrt{2}}{2}(\sqrt{6} + \frac{\sqrt{2}}{2}) = \frac{\sqrt{12}}{2} + \frac{\sqrt{4}}{4} = \frac{\sqrt{4 \cdot 3}}{2} + \frac{1}{2} = \frac{2\sqrt{3}}{2} + \frac{1}{2} = \sqrt{3} + \frac{1}{2}$.

47. **(D)** $\frac{15\sqrt{96}}{5\sqrt{2}} = 3\sqrt{48} = 3\sqrt{16 \cdot 3} = 12\sqrt{3}$.

48. **(C)** In order to take the square root of a decimal, it must have an even number of decimal places so that its square root will have exactly half as many. In addition, the digits must form a perfect square (e.g. $\sqrt{0.09} = 0.3$).

49. **(B)** $(-\frac{1}{3})^4 = (-\frac{1}{3})(-\frac{1}{3})(-\frac{1}{3})(-\frac{1}{3}) = \frac{1}{81}$.

50. **(A)** $-4^4 = -(4)(4)(4)(4) = -256$.

51. **(D)** $\sqrt[12]{x^6} = x^{\frac{6}{12}} = x^{\frac{1}{2}}$.

52. **(E)** $\sqrt[k]{6^{2km}} = 6^{\frac{2km}{k}} = 6^{2m}$. If $m$ is any non-negative integer such as 0, 1, 2, etc., then $6^{2m}$ must be a positive integer.

53. **(E)** $n$ is the number of decimal places that the decimal point in 0.012345 will move to the right in the product $0.012345 \times 10^n$. By inspection, $n = 6$ is the value for which $0.012345 \times 10^n$ becomes larger than 10,000: $0.012345 \times 10^6 = 12,345$.

### EXERCISE 8—ALGEBRAIC OPERATIONS (p. 306)

1. **(A)** Like terms are terms that contain exactly the same variable taken to the same power. Thus, while II contains $x$ and $xy$, and III contains $x^3$ and $x$, I contains only one variable type: $x$.

2. **(E)** When two terms have the same variables taken to the same powers, they are said to be like terms. I contains only the variable $x$. II contains no variables, thus the terms are like. If you like, you could think of II as containing the variable $x^0$. III contains a single variable as well: $x^2$.

3. **(C)** Combine like terms by adding and subtracting the coefficients: $x + 2x + 3x = (1 + 2 + 3)x = 6x$.

4. **(C)** Combine like terms by adding and subtracting the coefficients: $2x + 3x - x + 4x = (2 + 3 - 1 + 4)x = 8x$.

5. **(E)** Because none of the terms $a^3$, $a^2$, or $a$ are like terms, the expression cannot be reduced. Thus, $a^3 + a^2 + a$.

6. **(B)** Combine like terms by adding and subtracting the coefficients: $z^2 + 2z^2 - 5z^2 = (1 + 2 - 5)z^2 = -2z^2$.

7. **(A)** Combine like terms by adding and subtracting the coefficients: $a^3 - 12a^3 + 15a^3 + 2a^3 = (1 - 12 + 15 + 2)a^3 = 6a^3$.

8. **(E)** Combine like terms by adding and subtracting the coefficients: $3c + 2a - 1 + 4c - 2a + 1 = (3 + 4)c + (2 - 2)a - 1 + 1 = 7c$.

9. **(B)** Combine like terms by adding and subtracting the coefficients: $-7nx + 2nx + 2n + 7x = (-7 + 2)nx + 2n + 7x = -5nx + 2n + 7x$.

10. **(B)** Combine like terms by adding and subtracting the coefficients: $c^2 + 2c^2d^2 - c^2 = 2c^2d^2$.

11. **(C)** Combine like terms by adding and subtracting the coefficients: $2x^2 + 2x^2 + 2x^2 = (2 + 2 + 2)x^2 = 6x^2$.

12. **(C)** Combine like terms by adding and subtracting the coefficients: $3xy + 3x^2y - 2xy + y = 3x^2y + xy + y$.

13. **(E)** Do not be intimidated by the length of this item. It is no harder; it only requires more steps to complete. Combine like terms by adding and subtracting the coefficients: $x^2 + 2xy - 3x + 4xy - 6y + 2y^2 + 3x - 2xy + 6y = x^2 + 2y^2 + (2 + 4 - 2)xy + (-3 + 3)x + (-6 + 6)y = x^2 + 2y^2 + 4xy$.

14. **(A)** Combine like terms: $8p + 2p^2 + pq - 4p^2 - 14p - pq = (2 - 4)p^2 + (1 - 1)pq + (8 - 14)p = -2p^2 - 6p$.

15. **(E)** Because no term shares a variable with any of the other terms, there is no way to simplify the given expression.

16. **(D)** Use the product rule of exponents: $(x^2)(x^3) = x^{2+3} = x^5$.

17. **(D)** Use the product rule of exponents: $(a)(a^2)(a^3)(a^4) = a^{1+2+3+4} = a^{10}$.

18. **(D)** Use the quotient rule of exponents: $y^5 \div y^2 = \frac{y^5}{y^2} = y^{5-2} = y^3$.

19. **(B)** Use the product rule of exponents: $(x^2y)(xy^2) = x^{2+1}y^{1+2} = x^3y^3$.

20. **(C)** Use the product rule of exponents: $(abc)(a^2bc^2) = a^{1+2}b^{1+1}c^{1+2} = a^3b^2c^3$.

21. **(C)** $(xy^2)(x^2z)(y^2z) = (x^{1+2}y^2z)(y^2z) = (x^3y^{2+2}z^{1+1}) = x^3y^4z^2$ or $(xy^2)(x^2z)(y^2z) = x^{1+2}y^{2+2}z^{1+1} = x^3y^4z^2$.

22. **(B)** Use the quotient rule of exponents: $\frac{x^2y^4}{xy} = x^{2-1}y^{4-1} = xy^3$.

23. **(A)** Use the quotient rule of exponents: $\frac{a^3b^4c^5}{abc} = a^{3-1}b^{4-1}c^{5-1} = a^2b^3c^4$.

24. **(C)** Use the power rule of exponents: $(x^2y^3)^4 = x^{2 \cdot 4}y^{3 \cdot 4} = x^8y^{12}$.

25. **(B)** Use the power rule of exponents: $(\frac{a^2}{b^3})^3 = \frac{a^{2\cdot3}}{b^{3\cdot3}} = \frac{a^6}{b^9}$.

26. **(C)** Use the quotient rule of exponents: $\frac{x^3y^4z^5}{x^4y^2z} = x^{3-4}y^{4-2}z^{5-1} = x^{-1}y^2z^4 = \frac{y^2z^4}{x}$.

27. **(C)** Use the quotient rule of exponents; then use the power rule: $(\frac{c^4d^2}{c^2d})^3 = (c^{4-2}d^{2-1})^3 = (c^2d)^3 = $ $= c^{2\cdot3}d^{1\cdot3} = c^6d^3$.

28. **(C)** Use the quotient rule of exponents; then use the product rule: $(\frac{x^2y^3}{xy})(\frac{x^3y^4}{xy}) = (xy^2)(x^2y^3) = x^{1+2}y^{2+3} = x^3y^5$.

29. **(C)** Use the quotient rule of exponents; then use the product rule: $(\frac{abc^2}{abc^3})(\frac{a^2b^2c}{ab}) = c^{-1}(abc) = ab$.

30. **(C)** Use the quotient rule of exponents; then use the product rule: $(\frac{x^5y^3z^2}{x^4y^2z})^2(\frac{x^2y^3z^5}{xy^2z^4})^3 = (xyz)^2(xyz)^3 = (xyz)^{2+3} = (xyz)^5 = x^5y^5z^5$. Remember that this item is not more difficult; it is simply longer. Work from the inside out; complex items will always be composed of smaller, more familiar problems.

31. **(B)** $\frac{a}{c} + \frac{b}{c} = \frac{a+b}{c}$.

32. **(A)** $\frac{x}{2} + \frac{y}{2} + \frac{z}{2} = \frac{x+y+z}{2}$.

33. **(C)** $\frac{ab}{x} + \frac{bc}{x} + \frac{cd}{x} = \frac{ab+bc+cd}{x}$. The numerator cannot be combined any further. Recall that only like terms can be combined.

34. **(D)** $\frac{x^2}{k} + \frac{x^3}{k} + \frac{x^4}{k} = \frac{x^2+x^3+x^4}{k}$. Because the denominators are equal, the terms can be added. However, since the numerator does not contain like terms, each containing the same variable, but taken to different powers, they cannot be more closely combined.

35. **(A)** $\frac{2x}{z} - \frac{y}{z} = \frac{2x-y}{z}$.

36. **(E)** Multiply to find a common denominator: $\frac{x}{y} + \frac{y}{x} = (\frac{x}{x})(\frac{x}{y}) + (\frac{y}{y})(\frac{y}{x}) = \frac{x^2}{xy} + \frac{y^2}{yx} = \frac{x^2+y^2}{xy}$.

37. **(E)** Multiply to find a common denominator: $\frac{a}{b} - \frac{b}{a} = (\frac{a}{a})(\frac{a}{b}) - (\frac{b}{b})(\frac{b}{a}) = \frac{a^2-b^2}{ab}$.

38. **(E)** Multiply to find a common denominator: $\frac{x^2}{y} + \frac{x^3}{z} = (\frac{z}{z})(\frac{x^2}{y}) + (\frac{y}{y})(\frac{x^3}{z}) = \frac{x^2z+x^3y}{yz}$.

39. **(C)** Multiply to find a common denominator: $\frac{x}{a} + \frac{y}{b} + \frac{z}{c} = (\frac{b}{b})(\frac{c}{c})(\frac{x}{a}) + (\frac{a}{a})(\frac{c}{c})(\frac{y}{b}) + (\frac{a}{a})(\frac{b}{b})(\frac{z}{c}) = \frac{xbc+yac+zab}{abc}$.

40. **(D)** Multiply to find a common denominator: $\frac{x^2}{y^2} - \frac{y^3}{x^3} = (\frac{x^3}{x^3})(\frac{x^2}{y^2}) - (\frac{y^2}{y^2})(\frac{y^3}{x^3}) = \frac{x^5-y^5}{x^3y^2}$.

41. **(B)** Distribute: $2(x+y) = 2x+2y$.

42. **(B)** Distribute: $a(b+c) = ab+ac$.

43. **(C)** Distribute: $3(a+b+c+d) = 3a+3b+3c+3d$.

44. **(D)** Distribute: $2x(3x+4x^2) = 6x^2+8x^3$.

45. **(D)** Distribute: $3a^2(ab+ac+bc) = 3a^3b+3a^3c+3a^2bc$.

46. **(E)** FOIL and simplify: $(x+y)(x+y) = x^2+xy+yx+y^2 = x^2+2xy+y^2$. This form occurs so frequently it should be memorized.

47. **(E)** FOIL and simplify: $(a+b)^2 = (a+b)(a+b) = a^2+ab+ba+b^2 = a^2+2ab+b^2$. This form occurs so frequently it should be memorized.

48. **(C)** FOIL and simplify: $(x-y)^2 = (x-y)(x-y) = x^2-xy-yx+y^2 = x^2-2xy+y^2$. This form occurs so frequently it should be memorized.

49. **(A)** FOIL and simplify: $(a+b)(a-b) = a^2-ab+ba-b^2 = a^2-b^2$. This form occurs so frequently it should be memorized.

50. **(D)** FOIL and simplify: $(x-2)^2 = (x-2)(x-2) = x^2-2x-2x+4 = x^2-4x+4$.

51. **(D)** FOIL and simplify: $(2-x)^2 = (2-x)(2-x) = 4-2x-2x+x^2 = x^2-4x+4$.

52. **(A)** FOIL and simplify: $(ab+bc)(a+b) = a^2b+ab^2+abc+b^2c = a^2b+ab^2+b^2c+abc$.

53. **(D)** FOIL and simplify: $(x-y)(x+2) = x^2+2x-yx-2y = x^2-xy+2x-2y$.

54. **(D)** FOIL and simplify: $(a+b)(c+d) = ac+ad+bc+bd$.

55. **(E)** FOIL and simplify: $(w+x)(y-z) = wy-wz+xy-xz$.

56. **(B)** FOIL and simplify: $(x+y)(w+x+y) = xw+x^2+xy+yw+yx+y^2 = x^2+y^2+wx+wy+2xy$.

57. **(D)** FOIL and simplify: $(2+x)(3+x+y) = 6+2x+2y+3x+x^2+xy = x^2+xy+5x+2y+6$.

58. **(C)** FOIL and simplify: $(x+y)^3 = (x+y)(x^2+2xy+y^2) = x^3+2x^2y+xy^2+x^2y+2xy^2+y^3 = x^3+3x^2y+3xy^2+y^3$.

59. **(A)** FOIL and simplify: $(x-y)^3 = (x-y)(x^2-2xy+y^2) = x^3-2x^2y+xy^2-x^2y+2xy^2-y^3 = x^3-3x^2y+3xy^2$.

60. **(D)** FOIL and simplify: $(a+b)(a-b)(a+b)(a-b) = (a^2-b^2)(a^2-b^2) = a^4-a^2b^2-a^2b^2+b^4 = a^4-2a^2b^2+b^4$.

61. **(A)** Find the common factor: $2a+2b+2c = 2(a+b+c)$.

62. **(D)** Find the common factor: $x+x^2+x^3 = x(1+x+x^2)$.

63. **(A)** Find the common factor: $2x^2+4x^3+8x^4 = 2x^2(1+2x+4x^2)$.

64. **(D)** Find the common factor: $abc+bcd+cde = c(ab+bd+de)$.

65. **(D)** Find the common factor: $x^2y^2 + x^2y + xy^2 = xy(xy + x + y)$.

66. **(B)** $p^2 + 2pq + q^2 = (p+q)(p+q)$. Know this backwards and forwards.

67. **(B)** $144^2 - 121^2 = (144 + 121)(144 - 121)$. Remember that $(a+b)(a-b) = a^2 - ab + ba - b^2 = a^2 - b^2$.

68. **(A)** $x^2 - y^2 = x^2 - xy + xy - y^2 = (x+y)(x-y)$.

69. **(B)** $x^2 + 2x + 1 = (x+1)(x+1)$.

70. **(C)** $x^2 - 1 = (x+1)(x-1)$.

71. **(B)** First, what are the factors that will produce $x^2$? $x$ multiplied by $x$. Then, what are the factors that will produce 2? 2 and 1. Finally, what factors when added together through FOIL will produce $3x$? 2 times $x$ and 1 times $x$. Therefore, $x^2 + 3x + 2 = (x+2)(x+1)$.

72. **(B)** First, what are the factors that will produce $a^2$? $a$ multiplied by $a$. Then, what factors will yield $-2$? $(+1,-2)$ and $(-1,+2)$. Finally, which of those terms when added together through FOIL will create $-a$? $+1$ and $-2$. Therefore, $a^2 - a - 2 = (a-2)(a+1)$.

73. **(A)** $p$ times $p$ equals $p^2$. The last term, 3, can be produced from either $(+3,+1)$ or $(-3,-1)$. The middle term, $4p$, however, can only be the sum of $+3p$ and $+1p$. Thus, $p^2 + 4p + 3 = (p+3)(p+1)$.

74. **(A)** Given a quadratic, find two numbers, $m$ and $n$ such that their sum is equal to the coefficient of the middle term, in this case 6, and their product is equal to the last term. $c^2 + 6c + 8 = c^2 + 4c + 2c + 8 = (c+2)(c+4)$.

75. **(A)** $x^2 + x - 20 = x^2 + 5x - 4x - 20 = (x+5)(x-4)$.

76. **(C)** $p^2 + 5p + 6 = p^2 + 2p + 3p + 6 = (p+2)(p+3)$.

77. **(E)** We find two numbers, $m$ and $n$, such that their product is equal to 16 and their sum is equal to 8. $x^2 + 8x + 16 = x^2 + 4x + 4x + 16 = (x+4)(x+4)$.

78. **(D)** $x^2 - 5x - 6 = x^2 - 6x + x - 6 = (x-6)(x+1)$.

79. **(A)** $a^2 - 3a + 2 = a^2 - 2a - a + 2 = (a-2)(a-1)$.

80. **(C)** We find two numbers, $m$ and $n$ such that their product is equal to $-12$ and their sum is equal to 1. $x^2 + x - 12 = x^2 + 4x - 3x - 12 = (x+4)(x-3)$.

81. **(D)** $x^2 - 8x + 16 = x^2 - 4x - 4x + 16 = (x-4)(x-4) = (x-4)^2$.

82. **(D)** We solve the following equation: $x^2 + 12x + a^2 = (x+a)^2$. Now, since $2ax = 12x$, $a = 6$. Thus, $a^2 = 36$.

83. **(C)** A quadratic is a perfect square when it has only one root. The quadratic equation give us $x = \frac{-b \pm \sqrt{b^2 - 4ac}}{2a}$.
    Now, this will yield only one number only when the square root is equal zero. Thus, we need to solve $b^2 = 4ac$ where, in this case, $a = 4$, and $b = 12$. Thus, $12^2 = 4(4)c \Rightarrow 144 = 16c \Rightarrow c = 9$.

84. **(D)** $x^2 - 8x + 15 = x^2 - 5x - 3x + 15 = (x - 5)(x - 3)$.

85. **(B)** For this item, note that the first term is $2x^2$. Thus, one of the first terms of our factors is $x$ and the other is $2x$ (or they could be the negatives of the same terms). So, (A), (D), and (E) can be eliminated. Since the last terms of both (B) and (C) are each equal to $-3$, the decisive factor will be the middle term: $+5x$. For (C), we have $-6x + x = -5x$. Therefore, (B) must be the correct answer through process of elimination. Also, $-x + 6x = +5x$.

86. **(A)** First, rearrange the expression: $10x^2 + 21x - 10$. The factors that will produce the first term, $10x^2$, are $(10x, x)$, $(5x, 2x)$, and those terms in the negative. Similarly, the factors that will produce the last term, $-10$, are $(10, -1)$, $(-10, 1)$, $(5, -2)$, and $(-5, 2)$. We can get $21x$ by choosing $(5x, 2x)$ to produce the first terms and $(5, -2)$ to produce the last terms: $10x^2 + 21x - 10 = (5x - 2)(2x + 5)$.

87. **(C)** Find the common factor: $ax^2 + 3ax = ax(x + 3)$.

88. **(B)** $2x^2 - 8x + 3 - (x^2 - 3x + 9) = x^2 - 5x - 6 = x^2 - 6x + x - 6 = (x - 6)(x + 1)$.

89. **(C)** $15x^2 + ax - 28 = (5x - 4)(3x + 7) = 15x^2 + 35x - 12x - 28 = 15x^2 + 23x - 28$. Thus, $a = 23$.

90. **(D)** $x^2 - 9 = (x + 3)(x - 3)$. This factor is fundamental, so it should be memorized.

91. **(A)** Whenever you see the difference of two squared terms in an expression, you can always factor it as follows: $x^2 - 9y^4 = x^2 + 3xy^2 - 3xy^2 - 9y^4 = (x + 3y^2)(x - 3y^2)$.

92. **(E)** $x^2 + 6x - 27 = x^2 + 9x - 3x - 27 = (x + 9)(x - 3)$.

93. **(D)** $\frac{8x^{-4}}{2x} = \frac{4}{x^{1+4}} = \frac{4}{x^5}$.

94. **(B)** $\frac{3^{-1}x^5y^2}{2xy} = \frac{x^{5-1}y^{2-1}}{3^1 \cdot 2} = \frac{x^4 y}{6}$.

95. **(D)** $\frac{6x^{-5}y^2}{3^{-1}x^{-4}y} = \frac{6y^2}{3^{-1}x^{-4+5}y} = \frac{3^1 \cdot 6y}{x^1} = \frac{18y}{x}$.

96. **(A)** $\frac{9^2 x^3 y}{3^{-1}x^{-4}y} = 3^1 \cdot 81x^{3+4} = 243x^7$.

97. **(B)** $(-2)^2 = (-2)(-2) = 4$.

98. **(C)** $(-3)^2 \cdot 5 = 9 \cdot 5 = 45$.

99. **(C)** $(-2)^2 - 4(-2)(-3) - (-2) = 4 - 24 + 2 = -18$.

100. **(A)** $(x - y)(x^2 - 2x + 5) = x^3 - 2x^2 + 5x - x^2y + 2xy - 5y$.

101. **(E)** $(2x+\sqrt{3})^2 = (2x+\sqrt{3})(2x+\sqrt{3}) = 4x^2 + 4x\sqrt{3} + 3$.

102. **(C)** $2(-2)^2 - (-2)(3) = 8 + 6 = 14$.

103. **(E)** $(\frac{x^2 y^3 x^5}{2^{-1}})^2 = (2x^7 y^3)^2 = 4x^{14} y^6$.

104. **(C)** Choose any two low numbers to test this, say 1 and 1. $\sqrt{1^2 + 1^2} = \sqrt{2} \ne 1 + 1 = 2$. Thus, it could be no. Now, consider 0 and 0: $\sqrt{0^2 + 0^2} = 0 + 0 = 0$. Thus, it could be yes. So, we can't determine the answer from the information given.

105. **(A)** Remember that both sides of an equation can be squared while still preserve its equality. Since the square roots do not matter, it is obvious that this is our well known basic FOIL: $(x+y)(x+y) = x^2 + xy + yx + y^2 = x^2 + 2xy + y^2$.

106. **(C)** $\frac{x}{\sqrt{2x-y}} = x\sqrt{2x+y} \Rightarrow \frac{x}{x} = \sqrt{2x-y}\sqrt{2x+y} \Rightarrow 1 = \sqrt{4x^2 - y^2} \Rightarrow 1^2 = 4x^2 - y^2$. Let $x = 1$. Then, $1 = 4 - y^2 \Rightarrow -3 = -y^2 \Rightarrow y^2 = 3 \Rightarrow y = \sqrt{3}$. So, it can be true, for at least one pair $(x, y)$. Now, consider $x = 3, y = 4$. Then, $1 = 4 \cdot 9 - 16 = 20$; this is obviously false.

107. **(A)** $\frac{6}{\sqrt{2a-3c}} = \frac{6\sqrt{2a-3c}}{(2a-3c)} \Rightarrow \frac{6}{6} = \frac{\sqrt{2a-3c}\sqrt{2a-3c}}{(2a-3c)} = \frac{(\sqrt{2a-3c})^2}{(2a-3c)} = \frac{2a-3c}{2a-3c} = 1$. So, for all $a$ and $b$, the expression is true.

108. **(D)** $\frac{n}{6} + \frac{2n}{5} = \frac{5n + 12n}{30} = \frac{17n}{30}$.

109. **(B)** $\frac{1}{1} - \frac{x}{y} = \frac{y-x}{y}$.

110. **(B)** $\frac{x-y}{x+y} \div \frac{y-x}{y+x} = \frac{x-y}{x+y} \cdot \frac{y+x}{y-x}$. Since addition is commutative, you can cancel $x+y$ with $y+x$, as they are the same quantity. However, subtraction is not commutative, so you cannot cancel $x-y$ with $y-x$, as they are not the same quantity. Change the form of $y-x$ by factoring out $-1$. So, $y-x = (-1)(x-y)$. In this form, cancel $x-y$, leaving $\frac{1}{-1} = -1$.

111. **(A)** Simplify by multiplying every term in the fraction by $x$: $\frac{1 + \frac{1}{x}}{\frac{y}{x}} \cdot \frac{x}{x} = \frac{x+1}{y}$.

112. **(E)** $\frac{2x^2}{y} \cdot \frac{2x^2}{y} \cdot \frac{2x^2}{y} = \frac{8x^6}{y^3}$.

113. **(D)** Simplify by multiplying every term of the fraction by $xy$: $\frac{\frac{1}{x} + \frac{1}{y}}{3} \cdot \frac{xy}{xy} = \frac{y+x}{3xy}$.

114. **(C)** If $b \ge 0$, then $\frac{\sqrt{32b^3}}{\sqrt{8b}} = \sqrt{4b^2} = 2b$.

115. **(B)** $\sqrt{\frac{16x^2 + 9x^2}{144}} = \sqrt{\frac{25x^2}{144}} = \frac{5x}{12}$.

116. **(E)** The terms cannot be combined, and it is not possible to take the square root of separated terms.

117. **(D)** $\sqrt{\dfrac{100x^2 - 64x^2}{6,400}} = \sqrt{\dfrac{36x^2}{6,400}} = \dfrac{6x}{80} = \dfrac{3x}{40}$.

118. **(A)** $\sqrt{\dfrac{9y^2 - y^2}{18}} = \sqrt{\dfrac{8y^2}{18}} = \sqrt{\dfrac{4y^2}{9}} = \dfrac{2y}{3}$.

119. **(E)** It is not possible to find the square root of separate terms.

120. **(A)** Since $x < 0$ and $y < 0$, $|x| = -x$ and $|xy| = xy$. Thus, $\dfrac{x}{|x|} + \dfrac{xy}{|xy|} = \dfrac{x}{-x} + \dfrac{xy}{xy} = -1 + 1 = 0$.

121. **(D)** $16x^4 - 81y^{16} = (4x^2 + 9y^8)(4x^2 - 9y^8) = (4x^2 + 9y^8)(2x + 3y^4)(2x - 3y^4)$.

## EXERCISE 9—ALGEBRAIC EQUATIONS AND INEQUALITIES (p. 327)

1. **(C)** Divide by the coefficient of the variable $x$: $3x = 12 \Rightarrow x = \dfrac{12}{3} = 4$.

2. **(C)** Combine like terms, and divide by the coefficient of the variable: $2x + x = 9 \Rightarrow 3x = 9 \Rightarrow x = \dfrac{9}{3} = 3$.

3. **(C)** Combine like terms, and divide by the coefficient of the variable: $7x - 5x = 12 - 8 \Rightarrow 2x = 4 \Rightarrow x = 2$.

4. **(B)** Combine like terms, and divide by the coefficient of the variable: $3x + 2x = 15 \Rightarrow 5x = 15 \Rightarrow x = 3$.

5. **(E)** Combine like terms, and divide by the coefficient of the variable: $a - 8 = 10 - 2a \Rightarrow a + 2a = 10 + 8 \Rightarrow 3a = 18 \Rightarrow a = 6$.

6. **(E)** Combine like terms, and divide by the coefficient of the variable: $p - 11 - 2p = 13 - 5p \Rightarrow p - 2p + 5p = 13 + 11 \Rightarrow 4p = 24 \Rightarrow p = 6$.

7. **(D)** Combine like terms, and divide by the coefficient of the variable: $12x + 3 - 4x - 3 = 8 \Rightarrow 8x = 8 \Rightarrow x = 1$.

8. **(B)** Combine like terms, and divide by the coefficient of the variable: $5x - 2 + 3x - 4 = 2x - 8 + x + 2 \Rightarrow 2x - 6 = 3x - 6 \Rightarrow 0 = x$.

9. **(D)** Combine like terms, and divide by the coefficient of the variable: $a + 2b - 3 + 3a = 2a + b + 3 + b \Rightarrow 4a - 2a = 2b - 2b + 3 + 3 \Rightarrow 2a = 6 \Rightarrow a = 3$.

10. **(C)** Combine like terms, and divide by the coefficient of the variable: $4y + 10 = 5 + 7y + 5 \Rightarrow 4y - 7y = 10 - 10 \Rightarrow -3y = 0 \Rightarrow y = 0$.

11. **(A)** Combine like terms, and divide by the coefficient of the variable: $-4 - x = 12 + x \Rightarrow -16 = 2x \Rightarrow -8 = x$.

12. **(D)** Combine like terms, and divide by the coefficient of the variable: $\dfrac{x}{2} + x = 3 \Rightarrow \dfrac{3x}{2} = 3 \Rightarrow x = \dfrac{2}{3} \cdot 3 = 2$.

13. **(D)** Combine like terms, and divide by the coefficient of the variable: $\dfrac{2x}{3} + \dfrac{x}{4} + 4 = \dfrac{x}{6} + 10 \Rightarrow \dfrac{2x}{3} + \dfrac{x}{4} - \dfrac{x}{6} = 6 \Rightarrow \dfrac{4 \cdot 2x + 3x - 2x}{12} = 6 \Rightarrow 9x = 72 \Rightarrow x = 8$.

14. **(E)** Combine like terms, and divide by the coefficient of the variable: $\dfrac{a}{2} - \dfrac{a}{4} = 1 \Rightarrow \dfrac{2a - a}{4} = 1 \Rightarrow \dfrac{a}{4} = 1 \Rightarrow a = 4$.

15. **(E)** Combine like terms, and divide by the coefficient of the variable: $\dfrac{1}{p} + \dfrac{2}{p} + \dfrac{3}{p} = 1 \Rightarrow \dfrac{6}{p} = 1 \Rightarrow 6 = p$.

16. **(D)** Combine like terms, and divide by the coefficient of the variable: $\frac{2x-6}{3}=8 \Rightarrow 2x-6=24 \Rightarrow 2x=30 \Rightarrow x=15$.

17. **(C)** Combine like terms, and divide by the coefficient of the variable: $\frac{5-x}{5}=1 \Rightarrow 5-x=5 \Rightarrow -x=0 \Rightarrow x=0$.

18. **(A)** Combine like terms, and divide by the coefficient of the variable: $\frac{2-x}{10}=1 \Rightarrow 2-x=10 \Rightarrow -x=8 \Rightarrow x=-8$.

19. **(B)** Combine like terms, and divide by the coefficient of the variable: $\frac{5}{x+1}+2=5 \Rightarrow \frac{5}{x+1}=3 \Rightarrow 5=3(x+1) \Rightarrow 5=3x+3 \Rightarrow 3x=2 \Rightarrow x=\frac{2}{3}$.

20. **(C)** A moment's reflection will serve to convince you that $x=1$. Note that the right side of the equation looks exactly like the left side, but with 1 in place of $x$.

21. **(B)** When given two equations with two unknowns, first solve for one unknown in terms of the other: $x+y=6 \Rightarrow y=6-x$. Then, substitute that into the other equation: $3x+(6-x)=10 \Rightarrow 2x=4 \Rightarrow x=2$. Make sure to use both equations. If you substitute the results of the first equation back into the first equation, you will always get $0=0$.

22. **(B)** Solve for $x$ in terms of $y$: $2x+y=10 \Rightarrow x=\frac{10-y}{2}$. Now, substitute that into the other equation: $(\frac{10-y}{2})+y=7 \Rightarrow 10-y+2y=14 \Rightarrow y=4$.

23. **(A)** Solve for $y$ in terms of $x$: $2x-y=3 \Rightarrow -y=3-2x \Rightarrow y=2x-3$. Now, replace the $y$ in the first equation with the result from the first equation: $x+3y=5 \Rightarrow x+3(2x-3)=5 \Rightarrow x+6x-9=5 \Rightarrow 7x=14 \Rightarrow x=2$.

24. **(C)** Here we will add the two equations together:

$$\begin{array}{r} x+y=2 \\ +\quad x-y=2 \\ \hline 2x=4 \\ x=2 \end{array}$$

Now, replace $x$ in one of the given equations with the numeric value of $x$: $2+y=2 \Rightarrow y=0$.

Alternatively, recognize that it does not matter whether $y$ is added or subtracted; both equations equal 2. This suggests that $y=0$.

25. **(B)** Solve for $a$ in terms of $b$: $a+b=5 \Rightarrow a=5-b$. Plug that result into the second equation: $2(5-b)+3b=12 \Rightarrow 10-2b+3b=12 \Rightarrow b=2$.

26. **(A)** Solve for $x$: $2x=4 \Rightarrow x=2$. Insert that result into the first equation: $5(2)+3y=13 \Rightarrow 3y=3 \Rightarrow y=1$.

27. **(E)** Whenever the two given equations contain terms that are exactly opposite each other, it is easiest to add the two equations:

$$\begin{array}{r} k-n=5 \\ +\quad 2k+n=16 \\ \hline 3k=21 \\ k=7 \end{array}$$

28. **(C)** We can easily manipulate the first equation so that it contains $(-t)$: $t = k - 5 \Rightarrow 5 = k - t \Rightarrow k - t = 5$. Now, we can add the two equations together to cancel out the $t$ variables:

$$\begin{array}{r} k - t = 5 \\ +\quad k + t = 11 \\ \hline 2k = 16 \\ k = 8 \end{array}$$

29. **(B)** Use the second equation to solve for $b$ in terms of $a$: $a - b = 3 \Rightarrow a - 3 = b$. Now, plug that result into the first equation: $a + 5(a - 3) = 9 \Rightarrow a + 5a - 15 = 9 \Rightarrow 6a = 24 \Rightarrow a = 4$.

30. **(B)** The first equation is already a solution of $y$ in terms of $x$. Thus, we can enter that directly into the second equation to solve for $x$: $2(8 + x) + x = 28 \Rightarrow 16 + 2x + x = 28 \Rightarrow 3x = 12 \Rightarrow x = 4$.

31. **(D)** If we multiply the first equation by 2, we get an equation which will, when added to the second equation, cancel out the $y$ terms:

$$2(\tfrac{x+y}{2} = 4)$$
$$x + y = 8$$

$$\begin{array}{r} x + y = 8 \\ +\quad x - y = 4 \\ \hline 2x = 12 \\ x = 6 \end{array}$$

32. **(D)** If we multiply the first equation by 2 and the second by 3, we get two equations that, when added together, will yield an equation without $y$ terms. Solve for $x$:

$$2(\tfrac{x+y}{2} = 7)$$
$$x + y = 14$$

$$3(\tfrac{x-y}{3} = 2)$$
$$x - y = 6$$

$$\begin{array}{r} x + y = 14 \\ +\quad x - y = 6 \\ \hline 2x = 20 \\ x = 10 \end{array}$$

33. **(D)** Do not let the extra variable distract you:

$$\begin{array}{r} x + y + z = 10 \\ +\quad x - y - z = 4 \\ \hline 2x = 14 \\ x = 7 \end{array}$$

34. **(C)** Since the equations have two terms that are opposites of each other, solve by linear combination. To do this, add the equations and solve for $x$:

$$\begin{array}{r} x+2y-z=4 \\ +\ 2x-2y+z=8 \\ \hline 3x=12 \\ x=4 \end{array}$$

35. **(C)** Note that the first two equations have opposite terms: $\pm z$. Thus, we can add the first two equations together to produce an equation with just $x$ and $y$ terms. We can then use that equation with the third equation to solve for $x$:

$$\begin{array}{r} x+y+z=6 \\ +\ x+y-z=4 \\ \hline 2x+2y=10 \\ x+y=5 \end{array}$$

$$\begin{array}{r} x+y=5 \\ +\ x-y=3 \\ \hline 2x=8 \\ x=4 \end{array}$$

36. **(B)** Approach these types of items by first factoring and then finding the two values of $x$, such that each factor equals 0: $x^2-5x+4=0 \Rightarrow x^2-4x-x+4=(x-4)(x-1)=0$. The left side will equal zero when $x=4$ or $x=1$.

37. **(D)** Use the quadratic formula: $x=\dfrac{-b\pm\sqrt{b^2-4ac}}{2a}=\dfrac{-(-3)\pm\sqrt{(-3)^2-4(1)(-4)}}{2(1)}=\dfrac{3\pm\sqrt{9+16}}{2}=\dfrac{3\pm5}{2}=\{4,-1\}$. Or, simply factor: $x^2-3x-4=0 \Rightarrow x^2-4x+x-4=(x-4)(x+1)=0$. The left side will equal zero when $x=4$ or $x=-1$.

38. **(A)** Factor to solve: $x^2+5x+6=0 \Rightarrow x^2+3x+2x+6=(x+3)(x+2)=0$. Thus, $x=-3$ or $x=-2$.

39. **(C)** Use the quadratic formula: $x=\dfrac{-b\pm\sqrt{b^2-4ac}}{2a}=\dfrac{-(-3)\pm\sqrt{(-3)^2-4(1)(2)}}{2(1)}=\dfrac{3\pm\sqrt{9-8}}{2}=\dfrac{3\pm1}{2}=\{1,2\}$. Or, simply factor: $x^2-3x+2=0 \Rightarrow x^2-2x-x+2=(x-2)(x-1)=0$. The left side will equal zero when $x=2$ or $x=1$.

40. **(E)** When given a list of choices, it is still wisest to factor the equation, as it is more accurate. If that is impossible, then substitute the values from the list back into the equation. $x^2+3x+2=0 \Rightarrow x^2+2x+x+2=(x+2)(x+1)$. So, $x=-1$ or $x=-2$. So, I is false, and II and III are true.

41. **(A)** This item is simply a quadratic problem with the form $ax^2+bx+c=0$. Solve by factoring and equating both factors to zero: $x^2+5x=-4 \Rightarrow x^2+5x+4=0 \Rightarrow x^2+4x+x+4=(x+4)(x+1)=0$. So, $x=-1$ or $x=-4$.

42. **(C)** This item is just a reformulation of a quadratic problem with the form $ax^2+bx+c=0$. First, reorganize the equation to conform to the standard quadratic form; then, factor and solve each set of factors by setting them equal to zero: $x^2-8=7x \Rightarrow x^2-7x-8=0 \Rightarrow x^2-8x+x-8=(x-8)(x+1)=0$. So, $x=-1$ or $x=8$.

43. **(E)** Factor to solve: $k^2-10=-3k \Rightarrow k^2+3k-10=0 \Rightarrow k^2+5k-2k-10=(k+5)(k-2)=0$. So, $k=2$ or $k=-5$.

44. **(B)** Factor to solve: $x^2=12-x \Rightarrow x^2+x-12=0 \Rightarrow x^2+4x-3x-12=(x+4)(x-3)=0$. So, $x=-4$ or $x=3$.

45. **(B)** Clearly, $x=0$ would satisfy the equation. We search for a second value: $3x^2=12x \Rightarrow 3x=12 \Rightarrow x=4$.

46. **(A)** $4(5-x)=2(10-x^2) \Rightarrow \frac{4(5-x)}{2}=\frac{2(10-x^2)}{2} \Rightarrow 2(5-x)=(10-x^2) \Rightarrow 10-2x=10-x^2 \Rightarrow x^2=2x \Rightarrow x=0$ or $x=2$.

47. **(C)** $3+4x<28 \Rightarrow 4x<25 \Rightarrow x<\frac{25}{4}=6.25$.

48. **(A)** $5(3x-2)\geq 50 \Rightarrow (3x-2)\geq \frac{50}{5} \Rightarrow 3x-2\geq 10 \Rightarrow 3x\geq 12 \Rightarrow x\geq 4$.

49. **(D)** $8-3x>35 \Rightarrow -3x>27 \Rightarrow 3x<-27 \Rightarrow x<-9$. Remember to reverse the direction of the inequality when dividing by a negative number, in this case, $-1$.

50. **(D)** Factor to solve: $x^2=6x-8 \Rightarrow x^2-6x+8=0 \Rightarrow x^2-4x-2x+8=(x-4)(x-2)=0$. So, $x=2$ or $x=4$.

51. **(D)** The equation is true when either $(x-8)$ or $(x+2)$ equals 0. Thus, $x=8$ or $x=-2$.

52. **(E)** $9-3(6-x)=12 \Rightarrow 9-18+3x=12 \Rightarrow 3x=21 \Rightarrow x=7$. (A) and (B) can be eliminated since an equation will have two solutions *only* if $x$ is squared.

53. **(C)** Combine like terms, and divide by the coefficient of the variable: $\frac{x+5}{4}=17 \Rightarrow x+5=4\cdot 17 \Rightarrow x=68-5=63$.

54. **(B)** Combine like terms, and divide by the coefficient of the variable: $\frac{x}{2}-\frac{x-2}{3}=0.4 \Rightarrow \frac{3x}{6}-\frac{2(x-2)}{6}=0.4 \Rightarrow 3x-2x+4=2.4 \Rightarrow x=2.4-4=-1.6$.

55. **(A)** Combine like terms, and then divide by the coefficient of the variable: $0.02x+1.44=x-16.2 \Rightarrow 1.44+16.2=x-0.02x \Rightarrow 0.98x=17.64 \Rightarrow x=\frac{17.64}{0.98}=18$.

56. **(C)** Combine like terms, and divide by the coefficient of the variable: $3-2(x-5)=3x+4 \Rightarrow 13-4=3x+2x \Rightarrow 5x=9 \Rightarrow x=\frac{9}{5}$.

57. **(D)** Factor to solve: $x^2-9x-22=0 \Rightarrow x^2-11x+2x-22=(x-11)(x+2)=0$. Thus, $x=11$ or $x=-2$.

58. **(E)** $(x+8)(x+1)=78 \Rightarrow x^2+9x+8=78 \Rightarrow x^2+9x-70=0 \Rightarrow x^2+14x-5x-70=(x+14)(x-5)$. Thus, $x=-14$ or $x=5$. We now test those two values in the second equation: $(5)^2+9(5)=25+45=70$; $(-14)^2+9(-14)=196-126=70$.

59. **(C)** Replace $x$ in the equation by $-6$ and solve for $y$: $2(-6)+3y=12 \Rightarrow -12+3y=12 \Rightarrow 3y=24 \Rightarrow y=8$.

60. **(D)** When a line intersects the $x$-axis, $y=0$. Thus, replace $y$ in the equation by 0: $5x+2(0)=20 \Rightarrow 5x=20 \Rightarrow x=4$. So, the point is $(4,0)$.

61. **(E)** $3x+5y=10 \Rightarrow 5y=10-3x \Rightarrow y=-0.6x+2$.

62. **(B)** $x=ay+3 \Rightarrow ay=x-3 \Rightarrow y=\frac{x-3}{a}$.

63. **(A)** $8x+16=(x+2)(x+5) \Rightarrow 8(x+2)=(x+2)(x+5)$. If $x=-2$, both sides will equal zero. But, we can also divide each side by $(x+2)$: $8=(x+5) \Rightarrow x=3$. Or, you can solve this equation formally: $8x+16=(x+2)(x+5)$ $8(x+2)=(x+2)(x+5) \Rightarrow 8(x+2)-(x+2)(x+5)=0 \Rightarrow (x+2)[8-(x+5)] \Rightarrow (x+2)(3-x)$. So, $x=-2$ or $x=3$.

64. **(C)** $\frac{x+5}{0.2} = \frac{x+5}{\frac{1}{5}} = 5(x+5) = 0.3x \Rightarrow 5x + 25 = 0.3x \Rightarrow 4.7x = -25 \Rightarrow 47x = -25 \cdot 10 = -250 \Rightarrow x = -\frac{250}{47}$.

65. **(D)** Combine like terms, and divide by the coefficient of the variable: $\frac{0.2+x}{3} = \frac{\frac{5}{6}}{4} \Rightarrow 0.2 + x = \frac{3 \cdot 5}{6 \cdot 4} \Rightarrow x = \frac{15}{24} - \frac{2}{10} = \frac{5}{8} - \frac{1}{5} = \frac{25-8}{40} = \frac{17}{40}$.

66. **(C)** The statements $6 < x$ and $x$ is an integer imply that $x$ is an integer equal to or greater than 7. The additional statement $x < 8$ says that $x$ is an integer equal to or smaller than 7. The three statements taken together show that $x = 7$.

67. **(E)** $5 \leq x \leq 7$ is true for 5, 6, and 7. The inequality can be broken down into three relationships: $5 = x$, $5 < x < 7$, and $x = 7$.

68. **(C)** Since $x$ and $y$ are integers, we know from the two inequalities that $x = 3$ and $y = 7$. Thus, $xy = 3 \cdot 7 = 21$.

69. **(A)** The minimum value of $xy$ will equal the product of the smallest possible values of each $x$ and $y$. From the first inequality, we see that $x = 2$ is the smallest possible $x$. From the second, we see that $y = 7$ is the smallest possible $y$. Thus, $xy = 2 \cdot 7 = 14$ is the minimum value of $xy$.

70. **(D)** $\frac{5}{2} = 2.5$, $\frac{7}{2} = 3.5$, and $\frac{3}{2} = 1.5$. Thus, only I and III are true.

71. **(E)** To solve for $x$ in the equation $3^{8x+4} = 27^{2x+12}$, we need to get the variable out of the exponents. The trick here is to notice that $27 = 3 \cdot 3 \cdot 3$, so that $27^{2x+12} = 3^{2x+12} \cdot 3^{2x+12} \cdot 3^{2x+12} = 3^{3(2x+12)} = 3^{6x+36}$. Therefore, $3^{8x+4} = 3^{6x+36} \Rightarrow 8x + 4 = 6x + 36 \Rightarrow 2x = 32 \Rightarrow x = 16$.

72. **(D)** $(3+x)x = 2x + x + 16 \Rightarrow (3+x)x = 3x + x^2 = 2x + x + 16 \Rightarrow x^2 = 16 \Rightarrow x = \pm 4$.

73. **(A)** $10x^2 = 30 \Rightarrow x^2 = 3$ and $(6+y)y = 6y + 52 \Rightarrow 6y + y^2 = 6y + 52 \Rightarrow y^2 = 52$. So, $2x^2 + 2y^2 = 2 \cdot 3 + 2 \cdot 52 = 110$.

74. **(B)** $|x| = 5 \Rightarrow |-5| = 5 \Rightarrow |5| = 5$. Thus, $x = \pm 5$.

75. **(B)** The key to this item is in the wording of the item stem: The authors define commutativity, and then ask about it in relation to addition. Only two of the answers have anything to do with addition, so you can eliminate the others. The definition of commutativity is that the order of objects does not matter in a 2-variable function. Addition is a 2-variable function: $a + b$. The commutative property merely states that $a + b = b + a$. But, it only holds for terms that are the same. So, $2a + b \neq 2b + a$ for all $a$ and $b$.

76. **(B)** Just replace $x$ with $3a$ in the second equation: $y = 5(3a) + 6 = 15a + 6$.

77. **(A)** Solve for $x$ in terms of $a$: $2(x+3) = 18a + 10 \Rightarrow 2x + 6 = 18a + 10 \Rightarrow 2x = 18a + 4 \Rightarrow x = 9a + 2$.

78. **(A)** $F = 1.8C + 32 \Rightarrow 41° = 1.8C + 32 \Rightarrow 9° = \frac{9}{5}C \Rightarrow \frac{5}{9}9° = C \Rightarrow C = 5°$.

79. **(E)** Using the second equation, substitute $x^4$ for $y$: $x^5 = 8x^4 \Rightarrow x = 8$.

Alternatively, divide the first equation by the second to directly obtain the answer: $\frac{x^5 = 8y}{x^4 = y} \Rightarrow x = 8$.

80. **(A)** This item asks about commutativity with respect to multiplication. So, only (A) and (C) should be considered since they involve multiplication. (C) is false, in general, because $2b \neq 2a$. Therefore, (A) is the correct answer

choice. Note that $xy = yx$ expresses exactly the defined property: The order of the procedure (multiplication) does not affect the result (e.g., $2 \cdot 1 = 1 \cdot 2$).

81. **(E)** Since $1^2 = 1$, $1^2 = 1$, $2^2 = 4$, $3^2 = 9$, and $4^2 = 16$, the given sequence is the sequence of squares of integers. Therefore, the tenth term is $10^2 = 100$.

82. **(D)** Since $a_1 = 1$, $a_2 = (1-3)^2 = (-2)^2 = 4$, and $a_3 = (4-3)^2 = 1^2 = 1$. Therefore, $a_4 = (1-3)^2 = 4$.

83. **(D)** To find the constant, divide any term in the sequence by the term before it, so $\frac{8}{2} = \frac{128}{32} = 4$. To find the next term, multiply 128 by 4: $128 \cdot 4 = 512$.

84. **(E)** To answer this item, first note that $f(x) = x^3 + x^2 - 2x + 1$. Next, realize that the phrase "consecutive whole numbers" in the question stem infers the set of numbers $\{1, 2, 3, 4, \ldots\}$. Essentially, you want to plug in each whole number for $x$. By doing this you will get the sequence given: $\{1, 9, 31, 73, \ldots\}$. For example, $f(1) = 1^3 + 1^2 - 2(1) + 1 = 1$; $f(1) = 1^3 + 1^2 - 2(1) + 1 = 1$, $f(2) = 2^3 + 2^2 - 2(2) + 1 = 9$, and so on. To determine the next term in the sequence, simply plug in the next "consecutive whole number"—that is, plug 5 into $f(x)$. So, $f(5) = 5^3 + 5^2 - 2(5) + 1 = 125 + 23 - 10 + 1 = 141$. Hence, the answer is 141.

85. **(A)** From the quadratic formula, $x = \frac{-b \pm \sqrt{b^2 - 4ac}}{2a}$, we know that the nature of the values of $x$ depends most fundamentally on the terms inside the square root. For there to be two real solutions for $x$, the difference inside the square root must be positive. If it is zero there will be only one real solution. If it is negative, the solutions will be imaginary. Thus, $b^2 - 4ac > 0 \Rightarrow b^2 > 4ac \Rightarrow (8)^2 > 4(1)c = 4c \Rightarrow 64 > 4c \Rightarrow 16 > c \Rightarrow c < 16$. Only $-20$ fulfills that criterion.

86. **(A)** From the quadratic formula, $x = \frac{-b \pm \sqrt{b^2 - 4ac}}{2a}$, we know that the nature of the values of $x$ depends most fundamentally on the terms inside the square root. For there to be two real solutions for $x$, the difference inside the square root must be positive. If it is zero there will be only one real solution. If it is negative, the solutions will be imaginary. So, $b^2 - 4ac > 0 \Rightarrow b^2 > 4ac \Rightarrow b^2 > 4(1)(8) = 32 \Rightarrow b^2 > 32 \Rightarrow b > \sqrt{32} = 4\sqrt{2}$. Only 6 fulfills that requirement.

87. **(D)** An inch is one thirty-sixth of a yard, so the cost of $x$ yards and $y$ inches is equal to: $xk + \frac{yk}{36}$.

88. **(B)** $x^2 - 14k^2 = 5kx \Rightarrow x^2 - 5kx - 14k^2 = x^2 - 7kx + 2kx - 14k^2 = (x - 7k)(x + 2k)$. Thus, the two solutions for $x$ in terms of $k$ are $x = -2k$ and $x = 7k$.

89. **(E)** There is a general formula for the $n$th term of an arithmetic sequence: $a_n = a_1 + (n-1)c$, where $a_n$ is the value of the $n$th term in the series, $a_1$ is the value of the first term in the series, and $c$ is the constant designating the common difference between consecutive terms. Thus, with $n = 9$, $a_1 = 1$, and $c = 3$, we get $a_9 = 1 + (9-1)3 = 1 + 8 \cdot 3 = 25$.

90. **(D)** $\frac{1}{a^2} - \frac{1}{b^2}$ is equivalent to $(\frac{1}{a} + \frac{1}{b})(\frac{1}{a} - \frac{1}{b})$. Therefore, $\frac{1}{a^2} - \frac{1}{b^2} = (7)(3) = 21$.

91. **(D)** Solve for $x$: $\frac{3x}{4} = 1 \Rightarrow 3x = 4 \Rightarrow x = \frac{4}{3}$. Substitute this value for $x$ in the expression $\frac{2x}{3}$: $\frac{2x}{3} = \frac{2}{3}(x) = \frac{2}{3}(\frac{4}{3}) = \frac{8}{9}$.

92. **(D)** Substitute $\frac{y}{7}$ for $x$ in the second equation: $7x = 12 \Rightarrow 7(\frac{y}{7}) = 12 \Rightarrow y = 12$.

93. **(E)** Two equations are actually given: $x = k + \frac{1}{2}$ and $k + \frac{1}{2} = \frac{k+3}{2}$. Solve for $k$: $k + \frac{1}{2} = \frac{k+3}{2} \Rightarrow 2k + 1 = k + 3 \Rightarrow$ $k = 2$. Substitute 2 for $k$ and solve for $x$: $x = k + \frac{1}{2} = 2 + \frac{1}{2} = \frac{5}{2}$.

94. **(C)** Solve for $x$ in the first equation: $7 - x = 0 \Rightarrow x = 7$. Substitute 7 for $x$ in the second equation: $10 - x = 10 - 7 = 3$.

95. **(D)** $xy = (7 - \sqrt{3})(7 + \sqrt{3}) = 49 + 7\sqrt{3} - 7\sqrt{3} - 3 = 49 - 3 = 46$. Therefore, (I) is rational. (II) is also rational: $(7 - \sqrt{3}) + (7 + \sqrt{3}) = 14$.

96. **(E)** $\frac{2^{x+4} - 2(2^x)}{2(2^{x+3})} = 1 - 2^{-3} = 1 - \frac{1}{2^3} = 1 - \frac{1}{8} = \frac{7}{8}$.

97. **(A)** $w = 8^x = 2y$, so $8^x = 2(2^x)$. Since $8^x = (2 \cdot 2 \cdot 2)^x = 2^{3x}$ and $2(2^x) = 2^{x+1}$, $2^{3x} = 2^{x+1} \Rightarrow 3x = x + 1 \Rightarrow$ $2x = 1 \Rightarrow x = \frac{1}{2}$.

98. **(D)** $105 \; \cancel{\text{months}} \cdot \frac{1 \text{ year}}{12 \; \cancel{\text{months}}} = \frac{35}{4}$ years. Therefore, $16 \cdot 2^{\frac{2x}{5}} = 16 \cdot 2^{\frac{2(\frac{35}{4})}{5}} = 16 \cdot 2^{\frac{70}{20}} = 16 \cdot 2^{\frac{7}{2}} = 16 \cdot 2^{3\frac{1}{2}} =$ $16 \cdot 8 \cdot \sqrt{2} = 128\sqrt{2}$.

99. **(E)** The equality holds true for all values in the set: $\frac{1+2+\cdots+n}{2+4+\cdots+2n} = \frac{\frac{n(n+1)}{2}}{n(n+1)} = (\frac{n(n+1)}{2})(\frac{1}{n(n+1)}) = \frac{1}{2}$.

Alternatively, substitute values from the set for $n$. Only a few substitutions are necessary to demonstrate that the equality is true for all values in the set.

100. **(B)** Eliminate (A) by substituting $x = -1$ or any value such that $-1 < x < 0$. Eliminate (C) by multiplying the right side of the equation to obtain $x^3 + 8$. Eliminate (D), since $36 < 72$. Eliminate (E), since $\frac{2^x}{2^{x-1}} = 2^{x-(x-1)} = 2^1 = 2$.

101. **(A)** $3^3$ is odd, as are $5^5$, $7^7$, and $11^{11}$. Since the sum of four odd numbers is an even number, and an even number is divisible by 2, 2 is the smallest prime number that the divides the sum of $3^3 + 5^5 + 7^7 + 11^{11}$.

102. **(A)** If $x = 1$, $3^{\frac{1}{4}} < 2^1$. If $x = 3$, $3^{\frac{1}{4} + \frac{3}{4}} < 2^3$. If $x = 5$, $3^{\frac{1}{4} + \frac{3}{4} + \frac{5}{4}} = 3^{\frac{9}{4}} < 2^5$. If $x = 7$, $3^{\frac{1}{4} + \frac{3}{4} + \frac{5}{4} + \frac{7}{4}} = 3^4 < 2^7$. If $x = 9$, $3^{\frac{1}{4} + \frac{3}{4} + \frac{5}{4} + \frac{7}{4} + \frac{9}{4}} = 3^{\frac{25}{4}} > 2^9$. $x = 9$, which is a multiple of three.

103. **(C)** $x^{128} = 16^{32} = 8^{64} = 4^{128} \Rightarrow x = \pm 2$.

104. **(C)** $8^0 = 1$; $9^{-2} = \frac{1}{9^2} = \frac{1}{81}$; $(\frac{1}{9})^{-2} = \frac{1}{(\frac{1}{9})^2} = \frac{1}{\frac{1}{81}} = 81$; $(\frac{1}{8})^{\frac{2}{3}} = (\sqrt[3]{\frac{1}{8}})^2 = (\frac{1}{2})^2 = \frac{1}{4}$; $(\frac{1}{16})^{-\frac{1}{4}} = \frac{1}{\sqrt[4]{\frac{1}{16}}} = \frac{1}{\frac{1}{2}} = 2$. Therefore, three of the given numerical expressions represent whole numbers.

105. **(D)** $3^{x+2} = 3^x \cdot 3^2 = y \cdot 9 = 9y$.

106. **(B)** $x = \sqrt{x} + 20 \Rightarrow x - 20 = \sqrt{x} \Rightarrow x^2 - 40x + 400 = x \Rightarrow x^2 - 41x + 400 = 0 \Rightarrow (x - 25)(x - 16) = 0 \Rightarrow x = 25$ or $x = 16$. Since this reduction required taking the square of each side of the equation, check both values for $x$ in the

equation. Let $x = 25$: $25 - 20 = x = \sqrt{25} \Rightarrow 5 = 5$. Let $x = 16$: $16 - 20 = x = \sqrt{16} \Rightarrow -4 \neq 4$. Therefore, $x$ is equal to only one value, 25.

107. **(E)** Since $x = 3k$, and $k$ is an integer, the values of $x$ that must be tested are: $-6$, $-3$, 0, 6, and 12. If $x = -6$, $\sqrt{2x+8} = \sqrt{-4}$; this equality is invalid for any value of $y$. If $x = -3$, $\sqrt{2x+8} = \sqrt{2}$, which is valid for $y = 2$. If $x = 0$, $\sqrt{2x+8} = \sqrt{8}$, which is valid for $y = 8$. If $x = 6$, $\sqrt{2x+8} = \sqrt{14}$, which is valid for $y = 14$. If $x = 12$, $\sqrt{2x+8} = \sqrt{28}$, which is valid for $y = \sqrt{28}$. The sum of the valid values for $y$ is: $-3 + 0 + 6 + 12 = 15$.

108. **(B)** If $k = 12$, $\sqrt{8x} + 12 = 18 \Rightarrow 8x = 36 \Rightarrow x = 4.5$. If $k = 13$, $\sqrt{8x} + 13 = 18 \Rightarrow 8x = 25 \Rightarrow x = \frac{25}{8}$. If $k = 14$, $\sqrt{8x} + 14 = 18 \Rightarrow 8x = 16 \Rightarrow x = 2$. Therefore, only one value of $k$ meets the stated requirements.

109. **(D)** The numerator, $x - 2$, is less than zero whenever $x < 2$ and the denominator, $2x - 13$, is less than zero whenever $x < 6.5$. However, for $f(x) < 0$, the numerator must be positive and the denominator must be negative. Therefore, $2 < x < 6.5$, and so 6 is the largest whole number that $x$ can be, (D).

Alternatively, simply substitute the answer choices into the function to find the largest value of $x$ for which $f(x) < 0$: $\frac{x-2}{2x-13} = \frac{6-2}{2(6)-13} = -4$.

110. **(C)** To generate two equations with two unknowns, substitute the given values for $x$ into $f(x)$: $f(x) = kx + w$, so $f(2) = 8 = 2k + w$ and $f(6) = 20 = 6k + w$. To eliminate $w$, subtract $f(2)$ from $f(6)$:

$$6k + w = 20$$
$$- \quad 2k + w = 8$$
$$\overline{\phantom{xxxxxxxxxxxxxxx}}$$
$$6k + w - 2k - w = 20 - 8$$
$$4k = 12$$
$$k = 3$$

To determine $w$, substitute $k = 3$ into either equation and solve for $w$: $8 = 2k + w \Rightarrow w = 8 - 2(3) = 2$. Thus, $k + w = 3 + 2 = 5$.

111. **(B)** The absolute value of any real number $k$ is $k$ if $k \geq 0$ and $-k$ if $k < 0$. Since $-5 < x < -1$, $1 + 2x < 0$. Therefore, $|1 + 2x| = -1 - 2x$. $f(x) = |14 - |1 + 2x|| = |14 - (-1 - 2x)| = |15 + 2x|$. Finally, $15 + 2x > 0$, so $|15 + 2x| = 15 + 2x$.

112. **(B)** $f(2) + g(3) = (3 + 2^2) + (2 + 3)^3 = 3 + 4 + 5^3 = 7 + 125 = 132$.

113. **(E)** If $f(f(x)) = x$, then $f(x)$ is its own inverse. This means that if $y = \frac{kx}{3x+5}$ is solved for $x$ as a function of $y$, then $x = f(y)$: $y = \frac{kx}{3x+5} \Rightarrow 3xy + 5y - kx = 0 \Rightarrow x(3y - k) = -5y \Rightarrow x = \frac{-5y}{3y-k}$. $f(y) = \frac{ky}{3y+5}$, and since $x = f(y)$, $\frac{ky}{3y+5} = \frac{-5y}{3y-k}$. Thus, $k = -5$.

114. **(A)** The range is the set of all values for $y$, and the domain is the set of all values for $x$. If $y = 0$, $4x = 0 \Rightarrow x = 0$. If $y = 9$, $4x = 9^2 \Rightarrow x = \frac{81}{4} = 20.25$. If $y = 16$, $4x = 16^2 \Rightarrow 4x = 256 \Rightarrow x = 64$. Thus, the domain is $\{0, 20.25, 64\}$.

115. **(D)** The domain is $\{0, 1, 2, 3, 4, 5, 6, \ldots\}$. Substitution of the first six numbers yields the values 1, 3, 5, 7, 9, and 11 for $y$. Therefore, the range for $y$ is the set of all positive odd integers.

116. **(E)** $7x + 4y = 218 \Rightarrow 4y = 218 - 7x \Rightarrow y = \frac{218 - 7x}{4}$. Beginning with 1, substitute consecutive whole numbers for $x$ until two whole number values for $y$ are generated. If $x = 1$, then $y = \frac{218 - 7}{4}$, which is not a whole number. If

$x = 2$, then $y = \frac{218 - 7(2)}{4} = 51$, which is the largest value for $y$. The next largest value for $y$ is for $x = 6$, $y = \frac{218 - 7(6)}{4} = 44$. Thus, the answer is $51 + 44 = 95$.

117. **(B)** Since dividing by zero is not possible, if $x^2 - 11x + 30 = 0$, then $(x-5)(x-6) = 0$, and $x = 5$ or $x = 6$. Therefore, 5 and 6 are the only whole numbers not in the domain of values for $x$.

118. **(A)** $f(x) = 17x + 14 \Rightarrow f(2) = 17(2) + 14 = 48$; $f(3) = 17(3) + 14 = 65$; $f(4) = 17(4) + 14 = 82$. Therefore, adding together the functions evaluated for the three values of $x$ gives: $f(2) + f(3) + f(4) = 48 + 65 + 82 = 195$.

119. **(E)** If $x = 2$, then $g(2) = 3(2) + 8 = 14$. Thus, two points that belong to $f(x)$ are represented by $(1,5)$ and $(2,14)$. Since $f(x)$ is linear, $f(x) = mx + b$. Substitute $(1,5)$ and $(2,14)$ into $f(x) = mx + b$: $f(1) = 5 = m + b$ and $f(2) = g(2) = 14 = 2m + b$. From these two equations, $m = 9$. Substitute $b = 5 - m = 5 - 9 = -4$. Thus, $f(x) = 9x - 4$. Therefore, $f(4) = mx + b = (9)(4) - 4 = 32$.

## EXERCISE 10—GEOMETRY (p. 350)

1. **(C)** There are $360°$ in a circle. Thus, $x = 360 - 270 = 90$.

2. **(D)** Again, every circle has $360°$. Thus, $x = 360 - (2 \cdot 120) = 120$.

3. **(C)** Every circle has $360°$. Thus, $x = 360 - 240 = 120$.

4. **(B)** A line has $180°$. Thus, when met by another line, the sum of the two new angles is $180°$. $x = 180 - 150 = 30$.

5. **(E)** A straight line measures $180°$ on each side. $x = 180 - 60 = 120$.

6. **(A)** The sum of the angles around a given point is always $360°$. So, the sum of the degrees of two angles created by two lines emanating from a given point will always equal $360°$. Thus, $x = 360 - 150 = 210$.

7. **(E)** The little box in the figure indicates a $90°$ angle. Since a line measures $180°$ to a side, $x = 180 - 90 = 90$. This is such a common calculation and shorthand for representing right angles that it should be memorized. It is also the basis for many of the more advanced calculations that will be required for this test.

8. **(D)** $l_1$ and $l_2$ are perpendicular, thus the angles they form are each $90°$. Now, $x = 90 - 30 = 60$.

9. **(B)** When two lines intersect, the opposite angles are congruent, or equal. Thus, we have four angles, two measuring $120°$ and two measuring $x°$. The sum of these angles is equal to $360°$. $2x = 360 - (2 \cdot 120) = 120 \Rightarrow x = 60$.

   Alternatively, recognize that line 2 is $180°$ on both sides. Therefore, $x = 180 - 120 = 60$.

10. **(A)** Opposite angles created by the intersection of two lines are equal. Thus, $x = 30$.

11. **(B)** The statement $\overline{AB} \cong \overline{BC}$ means that the lengths of these two sides are the same. Because two angles of the triangle in question are equal, the triangle is isosceles. In such a case, the sides opposite the angles are equal in length. Thus, II is true. For a special class of isosceles triangle, the equilateral triangle, where all three angles are equal, the measure of all three sides is the same. For such a triangle, however, since the sum of the three angles must equal $180°$, each angle must be $60°$. Since that is not the case for this triangle, we can conclude that I and III are false.

12. **(B)** The diagram given shows two parallel lines, intersected by a third line. In the special case when that intersecting line is perpendicular to the parallel lines, all of the eight angles created are equal. That is not true

generally. However, it is always true for cases represented by the diagram that each angle falls into one of two categories, and there are four angles for each intersection point. On the diagram, all of the opposite angles are equal. Thus, $a = d = e = h$ and $b = c = f = g$. Only II is true.

13. **(A)** $a = d = e = h$ and $b = c = f = g$ since this is the general case of the intersection of two parallel lines by another line. Thus, only I is true.

14. **(C)** As always, if two angles lie on the same side of an intersected line, then their sum is 180°. So, I and II are true. As for III, $b$ and $g$ are similar and thus, except for the exceptional case of a perpendicular intersecting line, unequal.

15. **(A)** $g = 180 - 120 = 60$.

16. **(A)** $h$ and $d$ are similar, thus $d = 60$.

17. **(C)** In a triangle, two angles are equal if and only if their opposite sides are equal. Thus, $z = x$.

18. **(E)** The measure of two sides of a triangle are equal if and only if their opposite angles are equal. Thus, $\overline{PQ} \cong \overline{QR} \cong \overline{PR}$. Also, since all the internal angles of this triangle are congruent and each equal to 60°, this must be an equilateral triangle. Therefore, all the sides must be congruent.

19. **(E)** Because the sides of this triangle are all equal, all of the angles are equal as well: $x = y = z$.

20. **(C)** The perimeter of any closed polygon (e.g., a triangle) is equal to the sum of its sides: $P = 3 + 5 + 7 = 15$.

21. **(A)** The perimeter of a triangle is the sum of its three sides. In this instance: $P = 4 + 8 + 8 = 20$.

22. **(C)** The perimeter of the given triangle is the sum of the lengths of its sides: $P = 6 + 6 + 6 = 18$.

23. **(C)** The area of a triangle is equal to one-half the product of its width and its height. The width can be the length of any side, while the height is not necessarily the length of a side, but the length of a perpendicular line originating from the triangle's vertex. This line is called the altitude. In this instance, $A = \frac{3 \cdot 8}{2} = 12$.

24. **(E)** A triangle's area is equal to one-half of the product of its altitude and its width. Thus, $A = \frac{5 \cdot 10}{2} = 25$.

25. **(D)** The area of a triangle is equal to the one-half the product of its altitude and its width. Thus, $A = \frac{4 \cdot 9}{2} = 18$.

26. **(B)** For right triangles, the sum of the squares of the lengths of the two legs adjacent to the right angle is equal to the square of the length of the hypotenuse. Thus, $(\overline{RS})^2 = 3^2 + 4^2 = 9 + 16 = 25 \Rightarrow \overline{RS} = 5$. This is a 3-4-5 right triangle. It shows up often on the test, so memorize it.

27. **(B)** Use the Pythagorean theorem: $(\overline{AB})^2 + (\overline{BC})^2 = (\overline{AC})^2 \Rightarrow (\overline{AB})^2 + 6^2 = 10^2 \Rightarrow (\overline{AB})^2 + 36 = 100 \Rightarrow (\overline{AB})^2 = 64 \Rightarrow \overline{AB} = 8$.

28. **(A)** Use the Pythagorean theorem: $(\overline{PR})^2 + (\overline{PQ})^2 = (\overline{QR})^2 \Rightarrow (\overline{PR})^2 + 5^2 = 13^2 \Rightarrow (\overline{PR})^2 = 169 - 25 = 144 \Rightarrow \overline{PR} = 12$.

29. **(D)** This item can be approached in two ways. One way is to recognize that for a 45°-45°-90° isosceles triangle, the length of the hypotenuse is equal to the length of a side (the two sides besides the hypotenuse are equal) times $\sqrt{2}$. Thus, we can arrive immediately at $\overline{AC} = 4\sqrt{2}$. This is certainly worth committing to memory.

Alternatively, use the Pythagorean theorem: $(\overline{AC})^2 = 4^2 + 4^2 = 16 + 16 = 32 \Rightarrow \overline{AC} = \sqrt{32} = \sqrt{16 \cdot 2} = 4\sqrt{2}$.

30. **(E)** Use the Pythagorean theorem to solve this item. $(\overline{JL})^2 = 3^2 + 5^2 = 9 + 25 = 34 \Rightarrow \overline{JL} = \sqrt{34}$.

31. **(B)** This item is a good example of how test-writers place 'noise' in the problem. Noise is information that isn't actually required to solve the item. For example, in this item, the test-writers give you the length of the right side of the parallelogram; it is additional information that is not needed to solve the item. The area of a parallelogram is equal to the product of its base (the length of its bottom (or top) side) and its height, as obtained by an altitude line. The line that makes a right angle with the base of the parallelogram is the altitude. Thus, $A = 20 \cdot 6 = 120$.

32. **(B)** The area of a parallelogram can be calculated by multiplying the length of the altitude with the length of the base. To solve this item, we need to determine the length of the altitude that forms the right side of the triangle in the parallelogram. This can be accomplished by realizing that the altitude forms a 30°-60°-90° triangle with the base. Using the properties of 30°-60°-90° triangles, we can determine the length of the altitude (the side opposite the 30° angle) to be equal to one-half the length of the hypotenuse. Thus, the length of the altitude is: $\frac{10}{2} = 5$. Alternatively, the length of the altitude can be computed by using trigonometry: $\sin 30° = \frac{x}{10}$, where $x$ is the altitude. Therefore, $x = 10 \sin 30° = 5$. Once the length of the altitude is calculated, the area of the parallelogram can be solved: $A = 5 \cdot 16 = 80$.

33. **(C)** First, we need to find the length of the parallelogram's altitude. We start by finding the angle of the triangle formed by drawing an altitude through the left side of the diagram. The angle opposite to that is equal to 135°; therefore, since this is a parallelogram, the angle encompassing the altitude line is also 135°. We can also see that the part of that angle inside the triangle will be equal to $135° - 90° = 45°$. Since the triangle is a right triangle, we know that both of its non-right angles are 45°. Since both legs of a 45°-45°-90° triangle are equal to one-half the product of the length of the hypotenuse and $\sqrt{2}$, the length of the altitude, $l$, is: $8\sqrt{2} \cdot \frac{\sqrt{2}}{2} = \frac{8 \cdot 2}{2} = 8$. Knowing the length of the altitude, we can now compute the area: $A = l \cdot b = 8 \cdot 16 = 128$, where $b$ is the length of the base.

34. **(C)** $\angle ABO = \angle ABD = 70°$. $\angle ABD$ is an *inscribed angle*. The measure of such an angle is equal to one half of the angle of the arc it intercepts, in this case, $\overset{\frown}{AD}$, which is the perimeter of the circle from point $A$ to point $D$. The angle measure of that arc is thus $\overset{\frown}{AD} = 2 \cdot \angle ABD = 2 \cdot 70° = 140°$. Now, since $\overline{BD}$ is a diameter, $\angle \overset{\frown}{BD} = 180°$. But, $\angle \overset{\frown}{BD} = \angle \overset{\frown}{BA} + \angle \overset{\frown}{AD}$. Thus, $\angle \overset{\frown}{BA} = 180° - 140° = 40°$. $\overset{\frown}{BA}$ is intercepted by $\angle BOA$, which is similar to its opposite angle, $\angle COD$. Thus, $\angle COD = 40°$.

35. **(B)** That $\overline{AC}$ and $\overline{DE}$ bisect each other, implies that $\overline{AB} \cong \overline{BC}$ and $\overline{EB} \cong \overline{BD}$. Since we know additionally that $\angle ABE = \angle DBC$, we can conclude that $\overline{AE} \cong \overline{DC}$. Therefore, the two triangles are similar. Thus, $\angle C = \angle A = 20°$. So, $\angle DBC + \angle D + \angle C = 180° \Rightarrow \angle DBC = 180° - 86° - 20° = 74°$.

36. **(A)** The longest side of a triangle is always opposite the triangle's largest angle. To compare, we need to find the measure of $\angle C$: $\angle C = 180° - \angle A - \angle B = 180° - 23° - 84° = 73°$. Therefore, $\angle B$ is the largest angle. The side opposite $\angle B$ is the side that connects the other two points. Thus, the longest side is $\overline{AC}$.

37. **(D)** $\angle C = 180° - \angle A - \angle B = 180° - 40° - 70° = 70°$. The longest side is the angle opposite the largest angle, but here we do not have a largest angle. We only have two longer angles that are equal to each other. So, in this instance, the two longer sides are the ones opposite those two angles: $\overline{AC} \cong \overline{AB}$.

38. **(C)** The smallest angle of a triangle is the angle opposite its shortest side. $\overline{AB}$ is the shortest side, thus $\angle C$ is the smallest angle.

39. **(B)** The edges of the square's sides will also be edges of the cube. Since $A_{\text{side}}$ = area of side $= 49 = l^2 \Rightarrow l = 7$. Now, $A_{\text{cube}}$ =area of the cube $= l^3 = 7^3$.

40. **(D)** A cube has six surfaces, each a square, all equal in dimensions. Therefore, $SA_{\text{cube}}$ = surface area of the cube = $54 = 6 \cdot A_{\text{square}} \Rightarrow A_{\text{square}} = 9$, where $A_{\text{square}}$ is the area of each surface square. Each side of the squares, and thus the cube itself, has a length of 3 inches. So, $V = 3^3 = 27$.

41. **(D)** To solve this equation, we can divide the trapezoid into three sections, by dropping two perpendicular lines from the top two vertices of the trapezoid to the base. Because they are perpendicular to the base, and the base and the top are parallel, they are identical in length to the given altitude. Now, to find the length of the bottom edge of the right triangle, we use the Pythagorean theorem: $x^2 + 6^2 = 10^2 \Rightarrow x^2 = 64 \Rightarrow x = 8$. Since the upper and lower edges are parallel, the bottom edge of the left triangle is thus $26 - 8 - 12 = 6$. Thus, the total area is equal to: $A_{\text{left}\triangle} + A_{\text{right}\triangle} + A_{\text{rectangle}} = \frac{6 \cdot 6}{2} + \frac{6 \cdot 8}{2} + 6 \cdot 12 = 18 + 24 + 72 = 114$.

Alternatively, use the equation $A_{\text{total}} = \frac{h(b_1 + b_2)}{2} = \frac{6(12 + 26)}{2} = 114$.

42. **(B)** We can create two triangles and a rectangle within the trapezoid by dropping altitudes from the upper vertices of the trapezoid. These altitudes are perpendicular to the lower side. Thus, they are equal in length to the given altitude. To determine the length of the bottom side of the left triangle, use the Pythagorean theorem: $l^2 = 20^2 - 16^2 = 400 - 156 = 144 \Rightarrow l = 12$. The equation would be no different for the triangle on the right, so the upper base is $b_2 = 30 - 12 - 12 = 6$. Thus, $P = 30 + 20 + 20 + 6 = 76$.

43. **(D)** To solve this item, you must know the formula for the surface area of a sphere: $SA_{\text{sphere}} = 4\pi r^2$, where $r$ is the radius of the sphere. So, $SA_{\text{sphere}} = 324\pi = 4\pi r^2 \Rightarrow r^2 = \frac{324\pi}{4\pi} = 81 \Rightarrow r = 9$. Use this radius in the equation given for the volume of a sphere: $V_{\text{sphere}} = \frac{4}{3}\pi r^3 = \frac{4}{3}\pi(9^3) = \frac{4 \cdot 81 \cdot 9}{3}\pi = 4 \cdot 81 \cdot 3\pi = 972\pi$.

44. **(D)** $P = 2s_1 + 2s_2 = 2 \cdot 2 + 2 \cdot 4 = 4 + 8 = 12$, where $s_1$ and $s_2$ are two different, non-parallel sides of the rectangle.

45. **(E)** $P = 2s_1 + 2s_2 = 2 \cdot 3 + 2 \cdot 5 = 6 + 10 = 16$, where $s_1$ and $s_2$ are two different, non-parallel sides of the rectangle.

46. **(E)** $A = s_1 \cdot s_2 = 4 \cdot 5 = 20$, where $s_1$ and $s_2$ are two different, non-parallel sides of the rectangle.

47. **(C)** $A = s_1 \cdot s_2 = 3 \cdot 4 = 12$, where $s_1$ and $s_2$ are two different, non-parallel sides of the rectangle.

48. **(C)** $A = s_1 \cdot s_2 = 2 \cdot 7 = 14$, where $s_1$ and $s_2$ are two different, non-parallel sides of the rectangle.

49. **(D)** $A = s^2 = 5^2 = 25$, where $s$ is the length of one of the square's sides.

50. **(D)** The diameter of a circle is twice its radius. Thus, the diameter of a circle with a radius of 2 is 4.

51. **(B)** A circle's radius is equal to one-half the length of the circle's diameter. Thus, for a circle with a diameter of 10, the radius is 5.

52. **(C)** $C = 2\pi r = 2\pi(3) = 6\pi$, where $r$ is the radius.

53. **(B)** $C = 2\pi r = 2\pi(5) = 10\pi$, where $r$ is the radius.

54. **(A)** $C = \pi d = \pi(8) = 8\pi$, where $d$ is the diameter of the circle.

55. **(D)** $A = \pi r^2 = \pi(3)^2 = 9\pi$, where $r$ is the radius of the circle.

56. **(A)** $A = \pi r^2 = \pi(5)^2 = 25\pi$, where $r$ is the radius of the circle.

57. **(A)** $r = \frac{d}{2} = \frac{8}{2} = 4 \Rightarrow A = \pi r^2 = \pi(4)^2 = 16\pi$, where $r$ and $d$ are the radius and the diameter of the circle, respectively.

58. **(E)** $r = \frac{d}{2} = \frac{12}{2} = 6 \Rightarrow A = \pi r^2 = \pi(6)^2 = 36\pi$, where $r$ and $d$ are the radius and the diameter of a circle, respectively.

59. **(B)** A special property of 30°-60°-90° triangles is that the side opposite the 30° angle is equal to one half the length of the hypotenuse. Thus, $2 = \frac{b}{2} \Rightarrow b = 4$. Another special property of this type of triangle is that the side adjacent to the 30° angle is equal to the length of the hypotenuse multiplied by $\frac{\sqrt{3}}{2}$. Thus, $a = 4 \cdot \frac{\sqrt{3}}{2} = 2\sqrt{3}$.

60. **(C)** Because this is a 30°-60°-90° triangle, $c = \frac{8}{2} = 4$ and $d = \frac{8\sqrt{3}}{2} = 4\sqrt{3}$.

61. **(E)** Since this is a 30°-60°-90° triangle, $7\sqrt{3} = f\frac{\sqrt{3}}{2} \Rightarrow f = 7\sqrt{3} \cdot \frac{2}{\sqrt{3}} = 14$. Now, $e = \frac{f}{2} = \frac{14}{2} = 7$.

62. **(C)** In a 30°-60°-90° triangle, the side adjacent to the 30° angle is equal to the hypotenuse times $\frac{\sqrt{3}}{2}$. Thus, $6 = h\frac{\sqrt{3}}{2} \Rightarrow h = \frac{12}{\sqrt{3}} = 12 \cdot 3^{-\frac{1}{2}} = 4 \cdot 3^1 \cdot 3^{-\frac{1}{2}} = 4 \cdot 3^{\frac{1}{2}} = 4\sqrt{3}$. Now, in such a triangle, the side opposite the 30° angle is equal to half the length of the hypotenuse. Therefore, $g = \frac{h}{2} = \frac{4\sqrt{3}}{2} = 2\sqrt{3}$.

63. **(B)** The lengths of the three sides of an equilateral triangle with $P = 24$ are each 8. If we drop an altitude from one point to the opposite side, we will have bisected the triangle, creating two 30°-60°-90° triangles (note that the top angle was split into two, so it is 30°). Now, the side adjacent to the 30° angle is equal to the length of the hypotenuse, 8, times $\frac{\sqrt{3}}{2}$. Thus, $a = 8\frac{\sqrt{3}}{2} = 4\sqrt{3}$.

64. **(A)** This is a 45°-45°-90° triangle. It is also isosceles. Thus, the sides equal to the two right angles are equal. Thus, $i = 3$. Now, using the Pythagorean theorem, we can arrive at the length of the hypotenuse: $j^2 = 3^2 + 3^2 = 18 \Rightarrow j = \sqrt{18} = 3\sqrt{2}$. The last equation demonstrates a result worth remembering. That is, if $i$ is the length of one leg of a 45°-45°-90° triangle, then the hypotenuse is equal to the length of that side times $\sqrt{2}$.

65. **(D)** We use a general result: $k = m = 9\sqrt{2}\frac{\sqrt{2}}{2} = 9$. This is evident from a general property of 45°-45°-90° triangles: $s = \frac{h\sqrt{2}}{2}$, where $h$ is the length of the hypotenuse, and $s$ is the length of one of the sides.

66. **(B)** There are two ways to do this. First, use the Pythagorean theorem: $(\overline{AC})^2 = (\overline{AB})^2 + (\overline{BC})^2 = (\sqrt{6})^2 + (\sqrt{6})^2 = 6 + 6 = 12 \Rightarrow \overline{AC} = \sqrt{12} = 2\sqrt{3}$. Second, note that since $\overline{AB} = \overline{BC}$, the triangle $ABC$ is a 45°-45°-90° triangle. A general property of such triangles is that $h = s\sqrt{2}$, where $h$ is the hypotenuse, and $s$ is one of the sides. Thus, $\overline{AC} = \sqrt{6}\sqrt{2} = \sqrt{12} = 2\sqrt{3}$.

67. **(A)** $P = 40 = 4s \Rightarrow s = 10$. The diagonal divides the square into two similar, 45°-45°-90° isosceles triangles. The diagonal is the hypotenuse of those triangles, so $d = h = s\sqrt{2} = 10\sqrt{2}$.

68. **(E)** Here we must use properties of both 30°-60°-90° triangles and 45°-45°-90° triangles. The hypotenuse of the lower triangle is equal to twice the length of the side opposite to the 30° angle. Thus, $h = 12 \cdot 2 = 24$. Now, $p = s\sqrt{2} = 24\sqrt{2}$.

69. **(C)** The measure of the inscribed angle $PQR$ is 30°, so the measure of minor arc $PR$ is 60°. Since $RS$ is parallel to $PQ$, the measure of the inscribed angle $QRS$ is 30°, and the measure of minor arc $QS$ is 60°. Thus, the measure of minor arc $RS$ is $180° - 60° - 60° = 60°$, and the length of minor arc $RS$ is $\frac{60}{360} = \frac{1}{6}$ of the length of the circumference of the circle. Since the diameter $PQ$ has length 12, the circumference is $\pi d = 12\pi$. Therefore, the length of minor arc $RS$ is: $\frac{1}{6}(12\pi) = 2\pi$.

70. **(D)** Divide the circle into minutes: $\frac{360}{60} = 6$. Thus, each minute measures 6°. Twenty minutes after is 120°. There are 30° between each hour. Since it is one-third past the hour, the hour hand is one-third of the way to three. It thus measures: $(2 \cdot 30) + (\frac{1}{3} \cdot 30) = 70$. The difference between the two is 50°.

71. **(C)** $A = \pi r^2 = 49 \Rightarrow r^2 = \frac{49}{\pi} \Rightarrow r = \frac{7}{\sqrt{\pi}}$.

72. **(B)** $C = \frac{22\pi}{3} = 2\pi r \Rightarrow r = \frac{11}{3} \Rightarrow A = \pi r^2 = \pi\left(\frac{11}{3}\right)^2 = \frac{121\pi}{9}$.

73. **(B)** $A = \pi r^2 = 36\pi^3 \Rightarrow r^2 = 36\pi^2 \Rightarrow r = 6\pi$.

74. **(E)** $C = 2\pi r = 2\pi(8) = 16\pi$.

75. **(A)** The coordinates indicate that the radius is 8. Thus, $A_{\text{shaded}} = \frac{A}{4} = \frac{\pi r^2}{4} = \frac{\pi(8)^2}{4} = 16\pi$.

76. **(B)** $A = A_B - A_A = \pi r_B^2 - \pi r_A^2 = \pi(3^2 - 2^2) = 5\pi$.

77. **(A)** First, we find the radius of the circle. The lengths of the sides of the square will be twice that radius. $A_{\text{circle}} = 144\pi = \pi r^2 \Rightarrow r = 12$. $A_{\text{square}} = (2 \cdot 12)^2 = 576$. The area of the shaded area is $A_{\text{shaded}} = A_{\text{square}} - A_{\text{circle}} = 576 - 144\pi$.

78. **(A)** Each side of the first square measures 10. We must find the diameter of the inscribed circle: $A = 64\pi = \pi r^2 \Rightarrow r = 8 \Rightarrow d = 2r = 16$. The ratio of the first square to the second is: $\frac{10}{16} = \frac{5}{8}$.

79. **(A)** $A = s^2 = 64x^2y^{16} \Rightarrow s = \sqrt{64x^2y^{16}} = 8xy^8$.

80. **(B)** For this item, use the Pythagorean theorem: $A = l^2 = 4^2 - 3^2 = 16 - 9 = 7$. Therefore, each side of the square is equal to $\sqrt{7}$, and the area of the square is $\sqrt{7} \cdot \sqrt{7} = 7$.

81. **(B)** In a right triangle, one leg serves as the base and the other leg serves as the height. Therefore, $A = \frac{l_1 l_2}{2} = \frac{4 \cdot 5}{2} = 10$, where $l_1$ and $l_2$ are the legs of the triangle.

82. **(D)** While the inscribed figure is drawn to resemble a 90° triangle, it is not a foregone conclusion. To prove that it is a 90° triangle, first, extend the line $\overline{AO}$ down to the other side of the circle to a new point, say $C$. Since $\overline{AC}$ is a diameter, $\overarc{AC}$ measures 180°. $\angle OAB$ is an inscribed angle. Hence it is half as large as the arc it intercepts, $\overarc{BC}$. Thus, $\overarc{BC}$ measures 90°. But, $\angle \overarc{AB} + \angle \overarc{BC} = 180° \Rightarrow \angle \overarc{AB} = 180° - 90° = 90°$. $\angle AOB$ is a central angle; therefore, it possesses the same number of degrees as the angle of the arc that it intercepts, $\overarc{AB}$. Thus, $\angle AOB$ is indeed a right angle. Now we know too that $\angle OAB$ is a 45°-45°-90° triangle. Thus, $\overline{OA} = \overline{OB} = 4\sqrt{2}$. So,

$A_{\text{shaded}} = \frac{A_{\text{circle}}}{4} - A_{\text{triangle}} = \frac{\pi(4\sqrt{2})^2}{4} - \frac{(4\sqrt{2})^2}{2} = 8\pi - 16$.

83. **(C)** First, find the length of the second leg in $\triangle ABC$ from the area of the rectangle: $A = 15 = (\overline{AB})(\overline{BC}) = 6(\overline{BC}) \Rightarrow \overline{BC} = \frac{15}{6}$. Then, find the length of diagonal $\overline{AC}$ by applying the Pythagorean theorem to $\triangle ABC$:

$(\overline{AC})^2 = 6^2 + (\frac{15}{6})^2 = 36 + (\frac{5}{2})^2 = 36 + \frac{25}{4} = \frac{144+25}{4} = \frac{169}{4} \Rightarrow \overline{AC} = \sqrt{\frac{169}{4}} = \sqrt{\frac{169}{4}} = \frac{13}{2} = 6.5$.

84. **(D)** (D) is the only answer choice that provides a true statement of the Pythagorean theorem. Do not be confused because the usual order of variables has been rearranged.

85. **(A)** $41^2 - 40^2 = x^2 \Rightarrow x = \sqrt{1681 - 1600} = 9$. So, $A = 9 \cdot 40 = 360$. Therefore, the cost is equal to: $360 \cdot \frac{12}{100} = 12 \cdot 3.6 = \$43.20$.

86. **(B)** $(\overline{BD})^2 = 23 + 13 \Rightarrow \overline{BD} = \sqrt{36} = 6$. So, $(\overline{BC})^2 = 6^2 - (4\sqrt{2})^2 = 36 - 32 = 4 \Rightarrow \overline{BC} = 2$.

87. **(C)** The diagonal of a square is the hypotenuse of the two 45°-45°-90° triangles created inside the square by the presence of the diagonal. Thus, $s = \frac{h\sqrt{2}}{2} = \frac{5\sqrt{2}\sqrt{2}}{2} = 5$, where $s$ is one of the square's sides and $h$ is the length of the diagonal. Therefore, $A = s^2 = 5^2 = 25$.

88. **(E)** $x^2 = 13^2 - 12^2 = 139 - 144 = 25 \Rightarrow x = 5$. Thus, $A = s_1 s_2 = 5 \cdot 12 = 60$.

89. **(D)** $x^2 = (\sqrt{29})^2 - 5^2 = 29 - 25 = 4 \Rightarrow x = 2$.

90. **(A)** $s^2 + s^2 = 2s^2 = (2\sqrt{3})^2 = 12 \Rightarrow s^2 = 6 \Rightarrow s = \sqrt{6} \Rightarrow P = 4s = 4\sqrt{6}$.

91. **(C)** $\frac{P_{\triangle ABC}}{P_{\triangle DEF}} = \frac{3 \cdot 10}{2 \cdot 10 + 12} = \frac{30}{32} = \frac{15}{16}$, or 15:16.

92. **(D)** $A = \pi r^2 = \pi(2\sqrt{5})^2 = 20\pi$.

93. **(C)** $A = 12\pi = \pi r^2 \Rightarrow r^2 = 12 \Rightarrow r = 2\sqrt{3}$.

94. **(D)** $C = 2 \cdot \sqrt{6}\pi = 2\pi\sqrt{6} = 2\pi r \Rightarrow r = \sqrt{6}$.

95. **(B)** $h^2 = l_1^2 + l_2^2 = 2^2 + 5^2 = 4 + 25 = 29 \Rightarrow h = \sqrt{29}$.

96. **(C)** $h^2 = l_1^2 + l_2^2 \Rightarrow 37^2 = 35^2 + l_2^2 \Rightarrow l_2^2 = 1369 - 1225 = 144 \Rightarrow l_2 = 12$.

97. **(C)** $V = l_1 \cdot l_2 \cdot l_3 = 2\sqrt{12} \cdot 3\sqrt{6} \cdot 4\sqrt{3} = 24\sqrt{12 \cdot 6 \cdot 3} = 24\sqrt{2 \cdot 2 \cdot 3 \cdot 2 \cdot 3 \cdot 3} = 24 \cdot 2 \cdot 3\sqrt{6} = 144\sqrt{6}$.

98. **(B)** $C = \sqrt{128}\pi = 2\pi r \Rightarrow r = \frac{\sqrt{128}}{2} = \frac{2\sqrt{32}}{2} = \sqrt{32} = 4\sqrt{2} \Rightarrow V = Ah = \pi r^2 h = \pi(4\sqrt{2})^2 10 = 320\pi$.

99. **(C)** Let the third angle in the triangle on the right be $y°$. Now, we set up a system of equations: $x + y + 50 = 180 \Rightarrow x + y = 130$. The third angle in the left triangle must be $180 - y$. Thus, $x + 60 + (180 - y) = 180 \Rightarrow x - y = -60$. Add these two equations together and solve for $x$:

$$\begin{aligned} x + y &= 130 \\ + \quad x - y &= -60 \\ \hline 2x &= 70 \\ x &= 35 \end{aligned}$$

100. **(A)** Since $\sqrt{3}$ and 2 are both more than one, as we move right in the three-part ratio, the terms increase in size. Thus, $x$ is the smallest side. So, the largest side is $2x$, or 10.

101. **(C)** The hypotenuse of a $30°$-$60°$-$90°$ triangle is equal to twice the length of the side opposite to the $30°$ degree angle. Thus, $\overline{JK} = 12m$.

102. **(C)** In a right isosceles triangle, the two legs are equal. Thus, $(\overline{DF})^2 = (\overline{FE})^2 \Rightarrow 2(\overline{DF})^2 = (\overline{DE})^2 = (\sqrt{6})^2 = 6$. Therefore, $2(\overline{DF})^2 = 6 \Rightarrow (\overline{DF})^2 = 3 \Rightarrow \overline{DF} = \sqrt{3}$.

103. **(C)** The longest side of any right triangle is the hypotenuse. Thus, the legs are equal to one-half the hypotenuse and the hypotenuse times $\frac{\sqrt{3}}{2}$. Thus, $A = \frac{s_1 \cdot s_2}{2} = \frac{\frac{h}{2} \cdot \frac{h\sqrt{3}}{2}}{2} = \frac{h^2\sqrt{3}}{8} = \frac{(2\sqrt{3})^2 \cdot \sqrt{3}}{8} = \frac{12\sqrt{3}}{8} = 1.5\sqrt{3}$.

104. **(B)** $(\overline{AD})^2 = 2 \cdot 4^2 = 32 \Rightarrow (\overline{AC})^2 = 2(\overline{AD})^2 = 2 \cdot 32 = 64 \Rightarrow \overline{AD} = 8$.

105. **(C)** $\angle ABC$ is an interior angle. Such angles are equal to one half of the angle of the arc they intercept, in this instance $\overset{\frown}{BC}$. Therefore, $\angle ABC = 30°$. So, $\overline{BC} = \frac{AC}{2} = 4$ and $\overline{AB} = \frac{AC\sqrt{3}}{2} = 4\sqrt{3}$. Thus, $A_{\text{triangle}} = \frac{\overline{AB} \cdot \overline{BC}}{2} = \frac{4 \cdot 4\sqrt{3}}{2} = 8\sqrt{3}$.

106. **(D)** The angle opposite to $2x$ is also equal to $2x$. Therefore, $x + 2x + 60 = 180 \Rightarrow x = 40 \Rightarrow 2x - 60 = 20$.

107. **(E)** Since $a$ is opposite to $y$, $a = y$. Next, $a + 30 + x = 180 \Rightarrow a = 150 - x$. Similarly, $c = 30$, so $a + b + c = 180 \Rightarrow a = 180 - b - c = 150 - b$. So, (A), (B), (C), and (D) are all true. Therefore, (E) must be the correct answer choice.

108. **(C)** Because $\overline{EC} \parallel \overline{AB}$, $\angle EAB \cong x$, and $\angle CBA \cong y$. $\angle BCE + \angle A + \angle B = (180 - y)° + x° + y° = (180 + x)°$.

109. **(D)** $\overline{AD} \parallel \overline{BD}$. Thus, $\angle DBC = \angle DCB = 80°$. So, $\angle BDC = 180° - 80° - 80° = 20°$.

110. **(A)** When a line intersects a parallel line, there are two sets of four angles, each angle in the set is congruent. Those angles are opposite each other. The angles opposite to $d$ are $a$, $e$, and $h$.

111. **(B)** $3y + y = 180 \Rightarrow y = \frac{180}{4} = 45$. Since $x$ and $y$ are opposite each other, $x = y = 45$.

112. **(A)** $\angle BAC = 37° \Rightarrow \angle ABC = 180° - 90° - 37° = 53°$. Given two sides of a triangle, the larger side will be opposite the larger angle. Thus, $AC > BC$.

113. **(B)** $\angle CGM = \angle GHJ = 126° \Rightarrow \angle CGO = 180° - 126° = 54° \Rightarrow \angle EGC = \angle EGF + \angle FGC = \frac{54°}{3} + \frac{54°}{3} = 36°$.

114. **(D)** This is a ratio item. Since the smaller triangle is similar to the larger triangle, $\frac{\overline{AC}}{\overline{AB}} = \frac{\overline{CD}}{\overline{BE}} \Rightarrow \frac{6}{2} = \frac{\overline{CD}}{5} \Rightarrow \overline{CD} = 15$.

115. **(B)** The smallest perimeter will occur when the triangle is smallest. In this item, 40 should be set as the largest length. Since the ratio between the two triangles is 1:2, the other two sides will have lengths 24 and 28. Thus, the smallest possible perimeter that can be obtained under the constraints of the problem is 92.

116. **(E)** $V = Ah = \pi(\frac{8x}{2})^2 \cdot 3y = 48\pi x^2 y$.

117. **(E)** Begin by converting the given width to yards: $48 \ \text{feet} \cdot \frac{1 \ \text{yard}}{3 \ \text{feet}} = 16 \ \text{yards}$. Then, apply the perimeter formula to solve: $P_{\text{rectangle}} = 2l + 2w$, where $w$ is the width and $l$ is the length. Thus, the correct answer is $68 = 2l + 2(16) \Rightarrow 2l = 68 - 32 = 36 \Rightarrow l = 18 \ \text{yards} = 54 \ \text{feet}$.

118. **(E)** Again, $P_{\text{rectangle}} = 2l + 2w$. Therefore: $P = 2(46) + 2(34) = 92 + 68 = 160 \ \text{feet} \cdot \frac{1 \ \text{yard}}{3 \ \text{feet}} = 53\frac{1}{3} \ \text{yards}$.

119. **(E)** The umbrella would be the hypotenuse of a right triangle whose legs are the dimensions of the trunk.

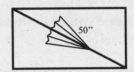

From the Pythagorean theorem, the sum of the dimensions of the trunk squared must at least equal the length of the umbrella squared, which is $50^2$ or 2,500. Only (E) works: $40^2 + 30^2 = 1,600 + 900 = 2,500$.

120. **(A)** The new road is the hypotenuse of a right triangle, and the legs are the old road.

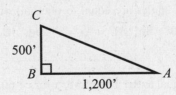

Use the Pythagorean theorem: $(\overline{AC})^2 = 500^2 + 1200^2 = 250,000 + 1,440,000 = 1,690,000 = 1,300^2 \Rightarrow \overline{AC} = 1,300$ feet. The old road was 1,700 feet. Thus, the difference is $1,700 - 1,300 = 400 \ \text{feet}$.

121. **(C)** Since $6^2 + 8^2 = 10^2$, the triangle is a right triangle. The area of the triangle is $\frac{6 \cdot 8}{2} = \frac{48}{2} = 24$. Therefore, the area of the rectangle is 24. If the width of the rectangle is 3, the length is $\frac{24}{3} = 8$. The perimeter of the rectangle is $2(3 + 8) = 2 \cdot 11 = 22$.

122. **(C)** The ladder forms a right triangle with the wall and the ground.

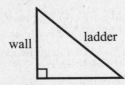

First, find the height that the ladder reaches when the lower end of the ladder is 25 feet from the wall: $25^2 + x^2 = 65^2$; $x^2 = 3,600 \Rightarrow x = 60$. The ladder reaches 60 feet up the wall when its lower end is 25 feet from the wall. If the upper end is moved down 8 feet, the ladder will reach a height of $60 - 8 = 52 \ \text{feet}$. The new triangle formed has a hypotenuse of 65 feet and one leg of 52 feet. Find the length of the other leg: $52^2 + x^2 = 65^2 \Rightarrow x^2 = 1,521 \Rightarrow x = 39$. The lower end of the ladder is now 39 feet from the wall. This $39 - 25 = 14$ feet farther than it was before.

123. **(C)** Convert the dimensions of the bin to inches: $4\text{ feet} = 48\text{ inches}$, $3\text{ feet} = 36\text{ inches}$, and $2\text{ feet} = 24\text{ inches}$. Thus, the total volume of the bin is: $V_{\text{bin}} = 48 \bullet 36 \bullet 24 = 41,472$ cubic inches. The volume of each brick is: $V_{\text{brick}} = 8 \bullet 4 \bullet 2 = 64$ cubic inches. Note that the bricks' dimensions evenly divide the dimensions of the bin. Thus, the total number of bricks is: $\frac{V_{\text{bin}}}{V_{\text{brick}}} = \frac{41,472}{64} = 648$ bricks.

124. **(D)** The trench contains $2\text{ yards} \bullet 5\text{ yards} \bullet 4\text{ yards} = 40$ cubic yards. Thus, the cost of digging the trench is: $40 \; \cancel{\text{cubic yards}} \bullet \frac{\$2.12}{\cancel{\text{cubic yard}}} = \$84.80$.

125. **(C)** Find the dimensions of the square: if the area of the square is 121 square inches, each side is $\sqrt{121} = 11$ inches, and the perimeter is $4 \bullet 11 = 44$ inches. Next, find the dimensions of the rectangle: the perimeter of the rectangle is the same as the perimeter of the square, since the same length of wire is used to enclose either figure. Therefore, the perimeter of the rectangle is 44 inches. If the two lengths are each 13 inches, their total is 26 inches, and $44 - 26$ inches, or 18 inches, remain for the two widths. Each width is equal to $18 \div 2 = 9$ inches. Thus, the area of a rectangle 13 inches long and 9 inches wide is: $13 \bullet 9 = 117$ square inches.

126. **(B)** A drawing of the information contained in the question stem makes it clear that this is really just a shaded area problem.

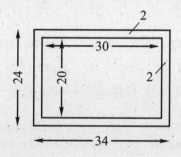

The area of the walk is equal to the difference between the area of the large rectangle and the area of the small rectangle. Therefore: $A_{\text{walk}} = A_{\text{large rectangle}} - A_{\text{small rectangle}} = (34 \bullet 24) - (30 - 20) = 816 - 600 = 216$ square feet.

127. **(A)** If the area of a circle is $49\pi$, its radius is $\sqrt{49} = 7$. The circumference is equal to $2 \bullet 7 \bullet \pi = 14\pi$.

128. **(D)** In one hour, the minute hand rotates $360°$. In two hours, it rotates $2 \bullet 360° = 720°$.

129. **(C)** Find the area of each surface of the box: $A_{\text{top}} = 12 \bullet 16 = 192$ square inches; $A_{\text{bottom}} = 12 \bullet 16 = 192$ square inches; $A_{\text{front}} = 6 \bullet 16 = 96$ square inches; $A_{\text{back}} = 6 \bullet 16 = 96$ square inches; $A_{\text{right side}} = 6 \bullet 12 = 72$ square inches; $A_{\text{left side}} = 6 \bullet 12 = 72$ square inches. The total surface area of the box is the sum of these surface areas: $A_{\text{total}} = 2(192) + 2(96) + 2(72) = 720$ square inches.

130. **(A)** For a cube, $V = e^3$. If the volume is 64 cubic inches, each edge is $\sqrt[3]{64} = 4$ inches. A cube has 12 edges. If each edge is 4 inches, the sum of the edges is $4 \bullet 12 = 48$ inches.

131. **(C)** The unlabeled angle inside the triangle is equal to $x$: $(x + 15) + (x + 15) + x = 180 \Rightarrow 3x + 30 = 180 \Rightarrow 3x = 150 \Rightarrow x = 50$.

132. **(C)** $A_{\text{square w/ side5}} - A_{\text{square w/ side 4}} = 5^2 - 4^2 = 25 - 16 = 9$.

133. **(D)** A triangle with sides of 4, 6, and 8 has a perimeter of $4 + 6 + 8 = 18$. An equilateral triangle with the same perimeter has three sides of length $18 \div 3 = 6$.

134. **(B)** Since $\overline{AB} \cong \overline{BC}$, $\Delta ABC$ is a 45°-45°-90° triangle. $\angle BAD = 45° + 15° = 60°$, so $x = 180 - 90 - 60 = 30$.

135. **(C)** $A_{\text{rectangle}} = l \cdot w \Rightarrow 1 = l \cdot \frac{3}{4} \Rightarrow l = \frac{4}{3}$.

136. **(C)** The three arcs together are a semicircle, or half the perimeter length of the entire circle. Since $P = 2\pi r$, the sum of the three arcs equals $\frac{P}{2} = \pi r$. Thus, $2\pi + 6\pi + 14\pi = \pi r \Rightarrow r = 2 + 6 + 14 = 22$.

137. **(B)** The unmarked angle plus the 120° angle form a straight line: $120 + x = 180 \Rightarrow x = 60$. Then, since the unmarked angle is part of a right triangle, $90 + 60 + y = 180 \Rightarrow y = 30$.

138. **(C)** If two angles of a triangle are congruent, then the two sides of the triangle that are opposite those two angles are also congruent. $\overline{BC}$ is opposite $\angle A$, and $\overline{AC}$ is opposite $\angle B$, so $\overline{AC} \cong \overline{BC}$.

139. **(C)** A ray extends infinitely in one direction: in the figure, $\overrightarrow{AB}$ is incomplete. As $\overrightarrow{AB}$ is extended through $B$, the ray will intersect the circle at two points.

140. **(C)** Since both pairs of opposite angles of $ABCD$ are congruent, $ABCD$ is a parallelogram. In a parallelogram, the opposite sides must be congruent. Thus, $\overline{AB} \cong \overline{DC}$ and $\overline{AD} \cong \overline{DC}$.

141. **(D)** Use the Pythagorean theorem to find the length of the base $\overline{BC}$ and the length of the altitude $\overline{AB}$. Let $\overline{BC} = b$ and $\overline{AB} = h$: $b + h = 3\sqrt{38} \Rightarrow (b+h)^2 \Rightarrow b^2 + h^2 + 2bh = 9(38) = 342$. Since $\overline{AC} = 10\sqrt{2}$, $b^2 + h^2 = (10\sqrt{2})^2 = 200$. Thus, $b^2 + h^2 + 2bh = 342 \Rightarrow 200 + 2bh = 342 \Rightarrow 2bh = 142 \Rightarrow bh = 71$. $A_{\text{triangle}} = \frac{bh}{2} = \frac{(AB)(BC)}{2} = \frac{71}{2} = 35.5$.

142. **(A)** Let $\angle A = x$, so $\angle AFB = x$. An exterior angle of a triangle is equal to the sum of the two remote interior angles. From $\Delta ABF$, $\angle CBF = 2x$; and $\overline{BF} \cong \overline{CF}$, so $\angle BCF = 2x$. From $\Delta AFC$, $\angle CFE = 3x$, and $\overline{CF} \cong \overline{CE}$, so $\angle CEF = 3x$. From $\Delta ACE$, $\angle DCE = 4x$; $\overline{CE} \cong \overline{DE}$, so $\angle CDE = 4x$; and $\overline{AD} \cong \overline{AE}$, so $\angle DEA = 4x$. Thus, in $\Delta ADE$, $4x + 4x + x = 180 \Rightarrow x = 20$.

143. **(C)** Based on the properties of tangents, the radius of a circle at the point of tangency is perpendicular to the tangent line. Use the Pythagorean theorem to find the length of the radius: $(\overline{AO})^2 + 8^2 = 10^2 \Rightarrow \overline{AO} = 6$. Thus, $A_{\text{circle}} = \pi r^2 = \pi(6)^2 = 36\pi$.

144. **(E)** A radius is perpendicular to a tangent at the point of tangency; thus, both $\angle OBC$ and $\angle OAC$ are right angles. Thus, $\angle AOB$ must be a right angle. Since $\overline{OA} \cong \overline{OB}$, $OACB$ is a square. The area of the shaded region is the area of the square minus one-fourth of the area of the circle: $A_{\text{shaded region}} = s^2 - \frac{\pi r^2}{4} = 10^2 - \frac{\pi \cdot 10^2}{4} = 100 - 25\pi$.

145. **(C)** Draw a line from $P$ to $\overline{AO}$ intersecting $\overline{AO}$ at $C$ so that $\overline{PC} \parallel \overline{AB}$:

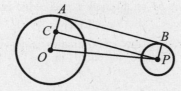

Since a tangent and a radius are perpendicular to each other, $\angle ACP$ and $\angle OCP$ are right angles. Because of the parallel lines, $ABPC$ must be a rectangle. Thus, $\overline{AC} = 3$ and $\overline{OC} = 10$. $\angle OCP$ is a right angle, so use the Pythagorean theorem to find the length of $\overline{PC}$ in $\triangle PCO$: $10^2 + (\overline{PC})^2 = 26^2 \Rightarrow \overline{PC} = 24$. Since $ABPC$ is a rectangle, $\overline{AB} = 24$.

146. **(E)** A radius is perpendicular to a tangent at the point of tangency, so a right triangle is formed. Use the Pythagorean theorem to find the length of the hypotenuse of this right triangle: $h^2 = x^2 + y^2 = 12^2 + 16^2 = 144 + 256 = 400 \Rightarrow h = 20$.

147. **(A)** Draw perpendicular lines from $T$ and $R$ to $\overline{PA}$. $\overline{PA}$ is then divided into three lengths, from left to right, of 16, 12, and 16:

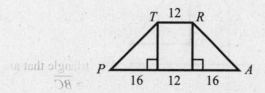

Given the properties of a 45°-45°-90° triangle, the altitude of the trapezoid (perpendicular line from $T$ to $\overline{PA}$) is 16. Therefore, the area of the trapezoid is: $\frac{h}{2}(b_1 + b_2) = \frac{16}{2}(12 + 44) = 448$.

148. **(C)** $\frac{\overline{AB}}{\overline{BC}} = 1 \Rightarrow \frac{10}{\overline{BC}} = 1 \Rightarrow \overline{BC} = 10$. Since both legs of the triangle are equal in length, $\angle BAC = \angle ACB = 45°$. Therefore, using the properties of a 45°-45°-90° triangle or the Pythagorean theorem, $\overline{AC} = 10\sqrt{2}$.

149. **(D)** Since the length of $\overline{BC}$ is equal to one-half the length of $\overline{CD}$, $\angle BDC = 30°$.

150. **(E)** Label the given angles $A$, $B$, $C$, $D$, and $E$. Write a list of all possible combinations created using two angles: $AB$, $AC$, $AD$, $AE$, $BC$, $BD$, $BE$, $CD$, $CE$, and $DE$. So, there are ten possible combinations. Only $AB$, $AC$, and $BC$ are combinations resulting in acute angles. Therefore, the probability of the new angles being acute is: $\frac{3}{10}$.

151. **(C)** Use the formula given in the item stem solve: $P = 6s = 6 \cdot 3 = 18$. The key to solving this item it to realize that a regular hexagon (or a regular polygon) has equal sides. So, knowing the length of one side is to know the length of all the sides of the hexagon. The perimeter can then be calculated.

152. **(E)** $\frac{\pi r^2 h}{3} \Rightarrow \frac{\pi(3)^2 12}{3} = 36\pi$.

## EXERCISE 11—COORDINATE GEOMETRY (p. 377)

1. **(B)** (B) is the only graph in which $x$ can be any real number, and $y$ can be any real number that is equal to or greater than zero.

2. **(A)** To find which letter is a possible value of $\frac{F}{X}$, determine the range of possible values. $X$ might be any value between $-3$ and $-2$, and $F$ appears to be 4. Therefore, if $X = -3$, $\frac{F}{X} = \frac{4}{-3} = -1\frac{1}{3}$, and if $X = -2$, $\frac{F}{X} = \frac{4}{-2} = -2$. $A$ is the only letter that lies between the values of $-2$ and $-1\frac{1}{3}$.

3. **(A)** Find the midpoint of $\overline{AB}$ by averaging the $x$-coordinates and averaging the $y$-coordinates: $(\frac{6+2}{2}, \frac{2+6}{2}) = (4, 4)$.

4. **(C)** $O$ is the midpoint of $\overline{AB}$. $\frac{x+4}{2} = 2 \Rightarrow x + 4 = 4 \Rightarrow x = 0$. $\frac{y+6}{2} = 1 \Rightarrow y + 6 = 2 \Rightarrow y = -4$. Therefore, $(x, y)$ is $(0, -4)$.

5. **(A)** $d = \sqrt{(8-4)^2 + (6-3)^2} = \sqrt{4^2 + 3^2} = \sqrt{16+9} = \sqrt{25} = 5$.

6. **(D)** Sketch the triangle. $A_{\text{triangle}} = \frac{b \cdot h}{2} = \frac{3 \cdot 4}{2} = 6$.

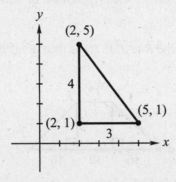

7. **(A)** Since the area of a circle is $\pi r^2$, $16\pi = \pi r^2 \Rightarrow r = 4$. (B), (C), (D), and (E) are all points that are 4 units from the origin, so the circle passes through each of these points. Therefore, (A) is the correct answer choice. $(4, 4)$ is not on a circle of radius 4 centered on the origin.

8. **(A)** Slope $= m = \frac{y_2 - y_1}{x_2 - x_1} = \frac{27 - (-5)}{8 - 0} = \frac{32}{8} = 4$.

9. **(E)** Slope $= \frac{1}{3} = \frac{y-7}{12-3} \Rightarrow y - 7 = 3 \Rightarrow y = 10$.

10. **(B)** From the slope-intercept form of a line equation, we know that the coefficient on the variable $x$, 5, is the slope.

11. **(C)** Slope $= m = \frac{y_2 - y_1}{x_2 - x_1} = \frac{2k - 8}{w - 3}$.

12. **(C)** Lines that are parallel have the same slope and point $(0, y)$ corresponds to the $y$-intercept. Write the given equation in slope-intercept form: $4x + 2y = 17 \Rightarrow y = \frac{-4x + 17}{2} = -2x + \frac{17}{2}$. Therefore, $m = -2$ for the two parallel lines. The given $y$-intercept point is $(0, 13)$, so $b = 13$. The equation is: $y = -2x + 13$.

13. **(B)** Perpendicular lines have reciprocal slopes with opposite signs. The slope of the given line is $-\frac{1}{2}$, so the perpendicular line has a slope of 2. The $y$-intercept point given for the perpendicular line is $(0, -5)$, so $b = -5$. The line equation is $y = 2x - 5$.

14. **(B)** Since no drawing is provided, sketch the coordinate system and enter points $P$ and $Q$:

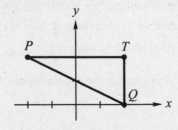

Find the distance between the two points by using the Pythagorean theorem: $(\overline{PT})^2 + (\overline{QT})^2 = (\overline{PQ})^2 \Rightarrow 4^2 + 2^2 = 16 + 4 = 20$. Therefore, $\overline{PQ} = \sqrt{20} = \sqrt{4 \cdot 5} = 2\sqrt{5}$.

Alternatively, use the distance formula: $d = \sqrt{(x_2 - x_1)^2 + (y_2 - y_1)^2} = \sqrt{(2 - (-2))^2 + (0 - 2)^2} = \sqrt{4^2 + (-2)^2} = \sqrt{20} = 2\sqrt{5}$.

15. **(A)** Use the distance formula: $d = \sqrt{(x_2 - x_1)^2 + (y_2 - y_1)^2} = \sqrt{(x + 1 - x)^2 + (y + 1 - y)^2} = \sqrt{1^2 + 1^2} = \sqrt{2}$.

16. **(C)** A quick sketch of the information provided in the item stem shows that we need to employ the Pythagorean theorem:

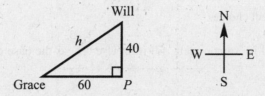

The shortest distance from Will to Grace is the hypotenuse of this right triangle: $h^2 = 60^2 + 40^2 = 3{,}600 + 1{,}600 = 5{,}200$. $h = \sqrt{5{,}200} = \sqrt{4 \cdot 1{,}300} = \sqrt{4 \cdot 4 \cdot 325} = \sqrt{16 \cdot 25 \cdot 13} = 20\sqrt{13}$.

17. **(A)** Use the distance formula to determine the distance between the two points $(5, 6)$ and $(6, 7)$: $d = \sqrt{(x_2 - x_1)^2 + (y_2 - y_1)^2} = \sqrt{(6 - 5)^2 + (7 - 6)^2} = \sqrt{1^2 + 1^2} = \sqrt{2}$.

18. **(A)** The coordinates of point $A$ are $(x, y)$. Regardless of the $y$-coordinate of point $B$, it is 7 units to the left, or in the negative direction, of point $A$. Therefore, the $x$-coordinate of point $B$ is that of point $A$, minus 7 units, or $x - 7$.

19. **(E)** The $x$-coordinate of point $S$ is the same as that of point $R$, $x$, while the $y$-coordinate is three times that of point $(R, 3y)$. Thus, point $S$ has the coordinates $(x, 3y)$.

20. **(C)** To move 7 units to the right on the coordinate plane, add 7 to the original $x$-coordinates; to move 5 units downward, subtract 5 from the original $y$-coordinates.

21. **(E)** Since the graph is of a straight line, plug the values given in the item stem into the straight line equation, $y = mx + b$ ($m$ is the slope and $b$ is the $y$-intercept when $x$ is zero), and solve for $y$. One point on the graph is $(0, 0)$, so the $y$-intercept, $b$, is 0. A second point on the graph is $(2, 3)$, so $m = \frac{3 - 0}{2 - 0} = \frac{3}{2}$. Thus, $y = \frac{3x}{2}$. Substitute 4.2 for $x$: $y = \frac{3(4.2)}{2} = 6.3$.

22. **(B)** If $(x, -4)$ is in Quadrant III, then $x$ is negative. If $(-1, y)$ is in Quadrant II, then $y$ is positive. Therefore, $(x, y)$ or $(-, +)$ is in Quadrant II.

23. **(E)** Since a figure is not provided, draw one:

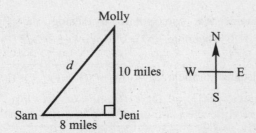

Use the Pythagorean theorem to find the approximate distance between Molly's house and Sam's house: $d = \sqrt{8^2 + 10^2} = \sqrt{64 + 100} = \sqrt{164}$. Since $\sqrt{144} = 12$ and $\sqrt{169} = 13$, $\sqrt{164}$ is between 12 and 13. Therefore, the approximate difference between the two paths is: $18 - 2 = 6$ miles, or $18 - 13 = 5$ miles. Since 5 miles is the largest answer choice, (E) is the correct choice.

24. **(D)** Since the figure provided is not complete, fill it in. Use $\overline{AC}$ as the base of $\triangle ABC$ because it lies on the $x$-axis. $A = \frac{bh}{2} = \frac{4 \cdot 4}{2} = 8$.

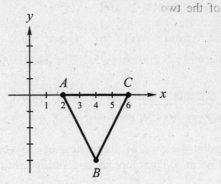

25. **(C)** Use the distance formula to determine the distance between the two points $(-1, 4)$ and $(2, 8)$: $d = \sqrt{(x_2 - x_1)^2 + (y_2 - y_1)^2} = \sqrt{(2 - (-1))^2 + (8 - 4)^2} = \sqrt{3^2 + 4^2} = \sqrt{25} = 5$.

26. **(B)** Slope $= m = \frac{rise}{run} = \frac{y}{18} \Rightarrow y = 18m$.

27. **(B)** Midpoint $= (\frac{x_1 + x_2}{2}, \frac{y_1 + y_2}{2}) = (\frac{-2 + 8}{2}, \frac{15 + 17}{2}) = (\frac{6}{2}, \frac{32}{2}) = (3, 16)$.

28. **(D)** Use a form of the midpoint formula: $\frac{3 + x}{2} = 7$ (the $x$-coordinate of the center of the circle); $\frac{2 + y}{2} = 5$ (the $y$-coordinate of the center of the circle). Then, solve for the missing coordinates: $\frac{3 + x}{2} = 7 \Rightarrow 3 + x = 14 \Rightarrow x = 11$; $\frac{2 + y}{2} = 5 \Rightarrow 2 + y = 10 \Rightarrow y = 8$. So, (D) is the correct answer choice.

29. **(C)** The first, fourth, and fifth graphs are each part or all of a non-vertical line, so each represents a linear function. Both the second and third graphs represent parts of two lines, so they do not represent a linear function. The correct answer is (C).

30. **(C)** The four equations for the four sets can be found using the equation for the slope of a line, $m = \frac{y_2 - y_1}{x_2 - x_1}$ and the form of a linear equation, $y = mx + b$: $y = 2x + 1$, $y = -10x + 2$, $y = 3x - 11$, and $y = 4x - 7$. Substituting the $y$-value from each of the ordered pairs in which $x$ is unknown into the respective equation returns the following values for $x$: $-\frac{1}{2}$, $-1$, $8$, $5$. Therefore, $x$ is less than zero for two of the sets of ordered pairs.

31. **(D)** Substitute the given values for $(x, y)$ into the linear equation, $y = mx + b$. For $(5, 20)$, $20 = 5m + b$; for $(9, 32)$, $32 = 9m + b$. Determine the value for $m$ by subtracting the first equation from the second equation: $32 - 20 = 12 = (9m + b) - (5m + b) = 4m \Rightarrow m = 3$. Determine the value for $b$ by substituting $m = 3$ into either of the two equations: $20 = 5m + b \Rightarrow b = 20 - 5(3) = 5$. Therefore, $m + b = 5 + 3 = 8$.

32. **(E)** For both of the given equations, $y = 0$ for $x = 0$. As a result, $(0, 0)$ must lie on both of the plotted functions. So, (A), (C), and (D) can be eliminated. Since neither of the two equations yields multiple $y$-values for a given value of $x$, (B) can also be eliminated. Therefore, (E) is the correct answer choice.

33. **(C)** Equations with both $y$ and $x^2$ terms represent parabolas that open up or down. The general equation for such parabolas is $y = a(x - h)^2 + k$, where the vertex is located at $(h, k)$. To determine the vertex coordinates, rewrite the given equation in the standard form by completing the square: $y = -2x^2 + 16x - 1 = -2(x^2 - 8x + 16) - 1 + 32 = -2(x - 4)^2 + 31$. Therefore, the vertex, or highest point on the curve, is $(4, 31)$.

34. **(C)** This item is solved directly by setting the two equations equal to one another and solving for $x$: $4x^2 = x^2 + 3x \Rightarrow 4x^2 - x^2 - 3x = 0 \Rightarrow 3x^2 - 3x = 0 \Rightarrow 3x(x - 1) = 0$. Therefore, $x = 1$ or $x = 0$. Substitute these values for $x$ into either of the two given equations to find the value of $y$ at these points: $y = 4(1)^2 = 4$ and $y = 4(0)^2 = 0$. Therefore, the two graphs intersect at two points: $(1, 4)$ and $(0, 0)$.

35. **(B)** Substitute the given $x$-values to determine which equation returns the closest approximation for the $y$-value. If $x = 2$: (A) $y = x^2 + 6 = 10$; (B) $y = x^2 + 3x + 2 = 12$; (C) $y = 2x^2 + x + 4 = 14$; (D) $y = x^2 - x + 8 = 10$; (E) $y = 2x^2 + x + 4 = 16$. If $x = 5$, the $y$-values for (A), (B), (C), (D), and (E) are 31, 42, 59, 28, and 64, respectively. Therefore, (B) is the correct equation for the curve.

36. **(A)** Using the given order pairs, determine the approximate value of the slope $(m = \frac{y_2 - y_1}{x_2 - x_1})$: $m_{21} = \frac{23 - 18}{2 - 1} = 5$; $m_{32} = \frac{27 - 23}{3 - 2} = 4$; $m_{43} = \frac{32 - 27}{4 - 3} = 5$; $m_{54} = \frac{38 - 32}{5 - 4} = 6$. Thus, the slope is approximately equal to 5, and $y = 5x + b \Rightarrow b = y - 5x$. Substitute the ordered pairs into this equation to determine $b$: $b(1, 18) = y - 5x = 18 - 5 = 13$; $b(2, 23) = 23 - 10 = 13$; $b(3, 27) = 27 - 15 = 12$; $b(4, 23) = 32 - 20 = 12$; $b(5, 38) = 38 - 25 = 13$. Therefore, 13 is the best approximation of $b$.

37. **(D)** The distance traveled is directly proportional to insect length; so, for the shapes in (A), (B), (C), (D), and (E), a 1-inch long insect would travel 4 inches, 3 inches, 3.14 inches, 1.57 inches, and 5 inches, respectively. Only (D) comes close to the observed distances traveled.

38. **(A)** Parallel lines have equal slopes. Since $\frac{0 - (-2)}{4 - 0} = \frac{2}{4} = \frac{1}{2}$, the slope of each line is $\frac{1}{2}$.

39. **(C)** The center of the circle is also the midpoint of the diameter. This allows for solutions determining the $x$ and $y$ points of the second end of the diameter. Solving for $x$: $19 = \frac{4 + x}{2} \Rightarrow 38 = 4 + x \Rightarrow x = 34$. Solve for $y$: $7 = \frac{6 + y}{2} \Rightarrow 14 = 6 + y \Rightarrow y = 8$. The second end of the diameter is located at $(34, 8)$.

40. **(D)** Each corner of a square is a right angle. Since $\angle FGH \cong \angle A$, $\angle FGH = 90°$. Thus, the slope of $\overline{FG}$ must be the opposite reciprocal of the slope of $\overline{GH}$. The slope of $\overline{FG}$ is $\frac{8 - 4}{3 - 5} = \frac{4}{-2} = -2$. Therefore, the slope of $\overline{GH}$ is $\frac{1}{2}$.

Alternatively, substitute the four given points to determine the slope of $\overline{GH}$. $(8, 6)$: $m = \frac{6 - 4}{8 - 5} = \frac{2}{3}$; $(9, 6)$: $\frac{6 - 4}{9 - 5} = \frac{1}{2}$; $(11, 7)$: $m = \frac{7 - 4}{11 - 5} = \frac{1}{2}$; $(13, 8)$: $m = \frac{8 - 4}{13 - 5} = \frac{1}{2}$. Thus, three of the four ordered pairs could represent point $H$.

41. **(E)** Parallel lines have equal slopes. The slope of the first line is: $\frac{17-5}{-2-1} = \frac{12}{-3} = -4$. Thus, $\frac{y-6}{13-17} = -4 \Rightarrow$ $y = (-4)(-4) + 6 = 22$.

42. **(C)** Use the distance formula: $d = \sqrt{(7-(-2))^2 + (-7-5)^2} = \sqrt{9^2 + (-12)^2} = \sqrt{81+144} = \sqrt{225} = 15$.

43. **(D)** $A_{\text{circle}} = \pi r^2 = 9\pi \Rightarrow r = 3$. Thus, the center of the circle is at $(0,3)$, and the constant function, $y = k$, intersects the circle at $(0,6)$. Therefore, $k = 6$.

44. **(A)** Since $y$ is equal to a constant value divided by something, $y \neq 0$. Complete the square: $x^2 + 6x + 7 = (x+3)^2 - 2$. Thus, the part of the graph below the $x$-axis reaches a peak or maximum at $(-3,-2)$ and $y \neq -1$. Therefore, there are two integer values for $y$ that are not a part of the graph: 0 and $-1$.

45. **(B)** The lowest point on the upper function plot occurs when $x = 1$: $(1,4)$. The highest point on the bottom function plot occurs when $x = -5$: $(-5,2)$. Thus, $2 < y < 4$ are the values for $y$ that are not on plot of the function.

46. **(E)** The equation of the transformed graph is: $y = (x-2+4)^2 + 3 = (x+2)^2 + 3$. To find the point of intersection, set the two equations equal to each other: $(x+2)^2 + 3 = (x-2)^2 + 3 \Rightarrow x^2 + 4x + 4 = x^2 - 4x + 4 \Rightarrow 8x = 0 \Rightarrow x = 0$. By substitution, $y = 3$. Therefore, the point of substitution is $(0,3)$.

47. **(A)** Complete the square for $y = 2x^2 = 12x + 1$: $y = 2(x^2 + 6x + 9) + 1 - 2(9) = 2(x+3)^2 - 17$. From this last equation, the three transformations can be determined: (1) vertical stretch by a factor of two; (2) horizontal shift of three units to the left; and (3) vertical shift of 17 units down.

48. **(D)** (A) and (B) can be immediately eliminated since for these equations each $y$-value is more than the corresponding value for $x$. For the remaining answer choices, determine the residuals. That is, the actual $y$-values minus the $y$-values as predicted by a possible line. The residuals (actual $y$-values minus the $y$-values as predicted by a possible line) for (C), (D), and (E), respectively, are: $\{6,4,0,-22,-38,-33,-45\}$, $\{2,5,5,-6,-7,8,6\}$, and $\{-6,-18,-24,-74,-120,-135,-167\}$ $-120,-135,-167\}$. The set with the smallest variance is the second from last, (D).

49. **(D)** The point $(0,0)$ is the center of the original circle, so $(4,2)$ must be the center of the transformed circle. So, (A), (B), and (C) can be eliminated. The point $(0,-4)$ is on the original circle, so $(0+4,-4+2) = (4,-2)$ must be on the transformed circle, so (E) can also be eliminated. Therefore, (D) is the correct answer choice. In general, solve this type of item by moving a few key coordinate points in accordance with the transformation(s).

### EXERCISE 12—SOLVING STORY PROBLEMS (p. 401)

1. **(A)** The amount of the discount is \$12. The rate of discount is figured on the original price: $\frac{12}{80} = \frac{3}{20} \Rightarrow \frac{3}{20} \cdot 100 = 15\%$.

2. **(C)** Lilian spent $\frac{1}{3}$ of \$60, or \$20, at the supermarket, leaving her with \$40. Of the \$40 she spent $\frac{1}{2}$, or \$20, at the drugstore, leaving her with \$20 when she returned home.

3. **(A)** $\overline{OP}$ is made up of the radius of circle $O$ and the radius of circle $P$. To find the length of $\overline{OP}$, you need to know the lengths of the two radii. Since the length of the radius is equal to one-half the length of the diameter, the radius of the circle $O$ is $\frac{8}{2} = 4$, and the radius of circle $P$ is $\frac{6}{2} = 3$. Thus, $\overline{OP} = 3 + 4 = 7$.

4. **(C)** \$70 represents 80% of the marked price: $70 = 0.80x \Rightarrow 700 = 8x \Rightarrow x = \$87.50$.

5. **(B)** If we let $x$ equal the number of quarters, then $2x$ equals the number of nickels and $35 - 3x$ equals the number of dimes. Convert the money values to cents: $25(x) + 5(2x) + 10(35 - 2x) = 400 \Rightarrow 25x + 10x + 350 - 30x = 400 \Rightarrow 5x = 50 \Rightarrow x = 10$.

6. **(E)** $r\% = \frac{r}{100}$. The commission is $\frac{r}{100} \cdot s = \frac{rs}{100}$.

7. **(D)** If we let $x$ equal the first integer, then $x + 2$ is the second integer and $x + 4$ is the third integer. Next, translate the question stem into an equation: $3x = 3 + 2(x + 4) = 3 + 2x + 8 \Rightarrow x = 11$. Therefore, the third integer is equal to: $11 + 4 = 15$.

8. **(B)** \$273 represents 130% of the cost: $1.30x = \$273 \Rightarrow 13x = \$2,730 \Rightarrow x = \$210$. Thus, the cost is \$210. To yield 10% profit on the cost, the refrigerator should be sold for: $1.10 \cdot \$210 = \$231$.

9. **(B)** The more feet, the more pounds—this is a *direct variation*: $\frac{60 \text{ feet}}{80 \text{ pounds}} = \frac{6 \text{ feet}}{x \text{ pounds}} \Rightarrow \frac{3}{4} = \frac{6}{x} \Rightarrow 3x = 24 \Rightarrow x = 8$.

10. **(D)** Work with a simple figure, such as \$100: first sale price is 90% of \$100, or \$90; final sale price is 85% of \$90, or \$76.50; total discount was $\$100 - \$76.50 = \$23.50$. Therefore, the percent of discount is: $\frac{\$23.50}{\$100} = 0.235 = 23.5\%$.

11. **(C)** Let: $b = $ Stan's age now; $b + 15 = $ Robert's age now; $b - y = $ Stan's age $y$ years ago; $b + 15 - y = $ Robert's age $y$ years ago. Therefore, $b + 15 - y = 2(b - y) \Rightarrow b + 15 - y = 2b - 2y \Rightarrow 15 = b - y$.

12. **(B)** If we let $m$ equal the marked price, then the first sale price is equal to $0.85m$ and the net price is equal to $0.90(0.85m) = 0.765m$. Therefore, $0.765m = \$306 \Rightarrow m = \$400$. In this case, it would be easy to work from the answers: 15% of \$400 is \$60, making a first sale price of \$340; 10% of this price is \$34, making the net price \$306. (A), (C), and (D) would not give a final answer in whole dollars.

13. **(D)** The larger the gear, the fewer revolutions per time period. Therefore, this is an *inverse variation*: (50 inches)(15 revolutions) = (30 inches)($x$ revolutions) $\Rightarrow 750 = 30x \Rightarrow x = 25$.

14. **(C)** Let \$100 be the selling price. If the profit is 20% of the selling price, or \$20, then the cost is \$80. Thus, the profit based on cost is: $\frac{20}{80} = \frac{1}{4} = 25\%$.

15. **(B)**

|          | ounces | $\times$ | $\frac{\% \text{ acid}}{100}$ | = | Amount of Acid |
|----------|--------|----------|------------------------------|---|----------------|
| Original | 20     |          | 0.05                         |   | 1              |
| Added    | $x$    |          | 1.00                         |   | $x$            |
| Mixture  | $20 + x$ |        | 0.24                         |   | $0.24(20 + x)$ |

$1 + x = 0.24(20 + x)$. Multiply by 100 to eliminate the decimals: $100 + 100x = 480 + 24x \Rightarrow 76x = 380 \Rightarrow x = 5$.

16. **(B)** The more men there are working, the fewer days the job will take. Therefore, this is an *inverse variation problem*: ($x$ men)($h$ days) = ($y$ men)(? days) $\Rightarrow$ ? days $= \frac{xh}{y}$.

17. **(C)** If profit is to be 20% of selling price, cost must be 80% of selling price: $\$72 = 0.80x \Rightarrow \$720 = 8x \Rightarrow x = \$90$.

18. **(A)** The $a$ lbs. of nuts are worth a total of $ab$ cents. The $c$ lbs. of nuts are worth a total of $cd$ cents. The value of the mixture is $(ab + cd)$. Since there are $(a + c)$, each pound is worth $(\frac{ab + cd}{a + c})$. Since the dealer wants to add 10 cents to each pound for profit, and the value of each pound is in cents, add 10 to the value of each pound: $\frac{ab + cd}{a + c} + 10$.

19. **(A)** The more days that the furnace burns, the more oil that it uses. Therefore, this is a *direct variation problem*:
$\frac{40 \text{ gallons}}{7 \text{ days}} = \frac{x \text{ gallons}}{10 \text{ days}} \Rightarrow 7x = 400 \Rightarrow x = 57\frac{1}{7}$, or 57.

20. **(E)** If Nell invests $x$ additional dollars at 8%, then her total investment will amount to $\$2,400 + x$ dollars. $0.05(2,400) + 0.08(x) = 0.06(2,400 + x) \Rightarrow 5(2,400) + 8x = 6(2,400 + x) \Rightarrow 12,000 + 8x = 14,400 + 6x \Rightarrow 2x = 2,400 \Rightarrow x = \$1,200$.

21. **(B)** The team must win 75%, or $\frac{3}{4}$, of the games played during the entire season. With 60 games played and 32 more to play, the team must win $\frac{3}{4} \cdot 92 = 69$. Since 40 games have already been won, the team must win 29 additional games.

22. **(D)** The more sugar used in the recipe, the more flour that must be used. Therefore, this is a *direct variation problem*: $\frac{13 \text{ ounces sugar}}{18 \text{ ounces flour}} = \frac{10 \text{ ounces sugar}}{x \text{ ounces flour}} \Rightarrow 13x = 180 \Rightarrow x = 13\frac{11}{13}$, or 14.

23. **(B)** Total time elapsed is $5\frac{1}{2}$ hours. However, one hour was used for dinner. Therefore, Ivan drove at 30 miles per hour for $4\frac{1}{2}$ hours, covering 135 miles.

24. **(E)** Gross receipts is equal to price times sales. Therefore, if $p$ equals the original price and $s$ equals the original sales, then the original gross receipts is equal to $ps$. The new price is the original price reduced by 25%, so the new price is equal to $0.75p$. The new sales is the original sales increased by 20%, so the new sales is equal to $1.20s$. Therefore, the new gross receipts is: $(0.75p)(1.20s) = (\frac{3p}{4})(\frac{6s}{5}) = \frac{9ps}{10} = 0.90ps$. Thus, the new gross receipts are 90% of the original gross receipts, which is a 10% decrease.

25. **(A)** The more miles the car drives, the more gasoline it uses. Therefore, this is a *direct variation problem*: $\frac{25 \text{ miles}}{2 \text{ gallons}} = \frac{150 \text{ miles}}{x \text{ gallons}} \Rightarrow 25x = 300 \Rightarrow x = 12$.

26. **(B)** The time spent traveling is equal to the distance divided by the rate of speed: $t = \frac{30 \text{ miles}}{60 \text{ miles/hour}} = \frac{1}{20}$ hour, or 3 minutes. Therefore, the arrival time is 5:01 p.m.

27. **(B)** 5% of sales between $200 and $600 is: $0.05(\$600 - \$200) = \$20$. 8% of sales over $600 is: $0.08(\$200) = \$16$. Therefore, the total commission is: $\$20 + \$16 = \$36$.

28. **(E)** The more children there are, the fewer days the bread will last—this is an *inverse variation problem*: (30 children)(4 days) = (40 children)($x$ days) $\Rightarrow 120 = 40x \Rightarrow x = 3$.

29. **(C)** Dave takes twice as long as Mr. Bridges to wash the car alone, or 30 minutes. Therefore, the time the job takes if they work together is: $\frac{x}{15} + \frac{x}{30} = 1 \Rightarrow 2x + x = 30 \Rightarrow 3x = 30 \Rightarrow x = 10$ minutes.

30. **(C)** If $m$ represents the number of miles between Madison and Chicago, then the train trip to Chicago took $\frac{m}{50}$ hours, and the return train trip took $\frac{m}{40}$ hours. The average speed for the trip is the total number of miles $(2m)$ divided by the total time $(\frac{m}{50} + \frac{m}{40})$: $\frac{2m}{\frac{m}{50} + \frac{m}{40}} = \frac{2m}{\frac{40}{40} \cdot \frac{m}{50} + \frac{50}{50} \cdot \frac{m}{40}} = \frac{2m}{\frac{40m}{200} + \frac{50m}{200}} = \frac{2m}{\frac{90m}{200}} = \frac{400}{90} \approx 44.4$ mph.

31. **(D)** The larger the quantity of salami purchased, the greater the cost—this is an *inverse variation*: $\frac{c \text{ cents}}{16 \text{ ounces salami}} = \frac{x \text{ cents}}{a \text{ ounces salami}} \Rightarrow x = \frac{ac}{16}$.

32. **(C)** The more miles, the more kilometers—this is a *direct variation*: $\frac{3 \text{ miles}}{4.83 \text{ kilometers}} = \frac{x \text{ miles}}{11.27 \text{ kilometers}} \Rightarrow 4.83x = 33.81 \Rightarrow x = 7$.

33. **(B)** Since 4 workers took an hour, each worker does $\frac{1}{4}$ of the job in an hour. So 12 workers will work at the rate of $\frac{12}{4}$ of the job per hour. Thus, if $T$ is the total time it takes for 12 workers to do the job, $\frac{12}{4} \cdot T = 1$ job and so $T = \frac{4}{12} = \frac{1}{3}$ hour.

34. **(B)** By paying attention to how the units cancel so as to leave the desired value, it is easy to find the necessary equation: $\frac{6 \text{ papers}/s \text{ seconds}}{1 \text{ machine}} \cdot m \text{ machines} \cdot x \text{ seconds} = 18,000 \text{ papers}$. Now, solve the equation for $x$: $x = \frac{18,000s}{6m} = \frac{3,000s}{m}$ seconds. Note, however, that the item asks for $x$ in terms of minutes: $x = \frac{3,000s \text{ seconds}}{m} \cdot \frac{1 \text{ minute}}{60 \text{ seconds}} = \frac{50s}{m}$ minutes.

35. **(B)** The more pencils bought, the greater the cost—this is a *direct variation problem*: $\frac{p \text{ pencils}}{d \cdot 100 \text{ cents}} = \frac{x \text{ pencils}}{c \text{ cents}} \Rightarrow x = \frac{pc}{100d}$.

36. **(A)** Gerard works at a rate of $\frac{1}{6}$ of the job per hour and Leo works at a rate of $\frac{1}{8}$ of the job per hour. Using the formula for work problems, we have $\frac{1}{6} + \frac{1}{8} = \frac{1}{T}$, where $T$ is total time it takes Gerard and Leo working together to complete the job. Solve for $T$: $\frac{1}{6} + \frac{1}{8} = \frac{1}{T} \Rightarrow \frac{1}{6}(48T) + \frac{1}{8}(48T) = \frac{1}{T}(48T) \Rightarrow 8T + 6T = 48 \Rightarrow 14T = 48 \Rightarrow T = \frac{48}{14} = \frac{24}{7} = 3\frac{3}{7}$ hours.

37. **(D)** Drain 1 and drain 2 together take 20 minutes to empty the pool, so together they drain the pool at a rate of $\frac{1}{20}$ of the pool per minute. Drain 2 takes 30 minutes to empty the pool by itself, so it drains the pool at the rate of $\frac{1}{30}$ of the pool per minute. Let $r$ be the rate at which drain 1 will empty the pool by itself. Then $\left(r + \frac{1}{30}\right)$ of the pool per minute is the rate at which both drains together will empty the pool, so $r + \frac{1}{30} = \frac{1}{20}$. Therefore, $r = \frac{1}{20} - \frac{1}{30} = \frac{1}{60}$, and drain 1 empties the pool at a rate of $\frac{1}{60}$ of the pool per minute, so it will take 60 minutes to drain the pool if drain 2 is closed.

38. **(D)** Use the formula for combined rates to find the time, $T$, that it takes machines $Y$ and $Z$ to do the job together: $\frac{1}{5} + \frac{1}{6} = \frac{1}{T} \Rightarrow \frac{1}{5}(30T) + \frac{1}{6}(30T) = \frac{1}{T}(30T) \Rightarrow 6T + 5T = 30 \Rightarrow 11T = 30 \Rightarrow T = \frac{30}{11}$. Therefore, it takes machines $Y$ and $Z$ a total of $\frac{30}{11}$ hours to complete the job together. Finally, the ratio of the time it takes machine $X$ to do the job (3 hours) to the time required for machines $Y$ and $Z$ working together to do the job is: $\frac{3}{\frac{30}{11}} = \frac{3 \cdot 11}{30} = \frac{33}{30}$.

39. **(D)** If the price of a newspaper is \$1, then the number $n$ of newspapers that would be sold is $n = 40 - 3(1) = 37$. Thus, the total revenue from the sale of 37 newspapers at \$1 each would be \$37.

40. **(D)** Write two equations based on the given information. First, the discount price is equal to the list price minus 20%: $d = l - 0.20l$, where $d$ is the discount price and $l$ is the list price. Second, the discount price is equal to the profit plus the cost: $d = p + c$, where $p$ is the profit and $c$ is the cost. Since the cost is \$4,800, and the profit is equal to 25% of the cost, or $0.25c$, $d = 0.25c + c$. $0.80l = 1.25c \Rightarrow l = \frac{1.25 \cdot \$4,800}{0.80} = \$7,500$.

41. **(E)** If the manufacturer will sell each bar for $d$ dollars, and the cost to manufacture each bar is \$0.25, then the profit per bar is equal to the selling price minus the cost, or $d - \$0.25$. To attain a profit of at least \$420 on the production and sale of all 400 bars, $400(d - \$0.25) \geq \$420$, or $x > \$1.30$.

42. **(C)** Profit is equal to selling price minus cost: $P = S - C$. If $n$ is the number of items produced, then $S = \$12 \cdot n$, $C = \$120,000 + (\$6 \cdot n)$, and so $P = 12n - (120,000 + 6n) = 12n - 120,000$. Since $P = \$60,000$, $12n - 120,000 = 60,000 \Rightarrow 12n = 180,000 \Rightarrow n = 15,000$.

43. **(A)** The variable $m$ varies directly as $t^2$: $\frac{m_1}{t_1^2} = \frac{m_2}{t_2^2} \Rightarrow \frac{7}{1^2} = \frac{m}{2^2} \Rightarrow m = 28$.

44. **(D)** $16\frac{2}{3}\% = \frac{16\frac{2}{3}}{100} = \frac{\frac{(16 \cdot 3) + 2}{3}}{100} = \frac{\frac{50}{3}}{100} = \frac{50}{300} = \frac{1}{6}$. Thus, since $16\frac{2}{3}\%$ of $x$ equals 6: $6 = \frac{x}{6} \Rightarrow x = 36$. Therefore, the number of students who passed the course is: $36 - 6 = 30$.

45. **(D)** First, create an equation for the new property value: $v_2 = v_1 - 0.10v_1 = 0.90v_1$, where $v_1$ is the original property value and $v_2$ is the new property value. Next, create an equation for the new tax rate: $r_2 = r_1 + 0.10r_1 = 1.10r_1$, where $r_1$ is the original tax rate and $r_2$ is the new tax rate. Finally, tax is equal to tax rate times property value, so $t_1 = r_1v_1$ and $t_2 = r_2v_2$, where $t_1$ is the original tax rate and $t_2$ is the new tax rate. Therefore: $t_2 = r_2v_2 = (1.10r_1)(0.90v_1) = 0.99r_1v_1 = 0.99t_1$, or a 1% decrease.

46. **(B)** The variable $m$ varies jointly as $r$ and $l$: $\frac{m_1}{r_1l_1} = \frac{m_2}{r_2l_2} \Rightarrow \frac{8}{(1)(1)} = \frac{m}{(2)(2)} \Rightarrow m = 32$.

47. **(E)** $40\% = \frac{2}{5} \Rightarrow \frac{2}{5} \cdot 95\% = 38\%$.

48. **(C)** Create a formula. Anna was born three years after $1980 - x$, so she was born in $1980 - x + 3$. 20 years later the year will be $1980 - x + 3 + 20 = 2003 - x$.

49. **(B)** $500 + 0.05x = \$2,400 \Rightarrow 0.05x = \$1,900 \Rightarrow 5x = \$190,000 \Rightarrow x = \$38,000$.

50. **(B)** The correct answer must be smaller than the shortest time given, for no matter how slow a helper may be, he does do part of the job and therefore it will be completed in less time. $\frac{time\ spent}{total\ time\ needed\ to\ do\ job\ alone} = \frac{x}{3} + \frac{x}{5} = 1$. Multiply by 15 to eliminate fractions: $5x + 3x = 15 \Rightarrow 8x = 15 \Rightarrow x = 1\frac{7}{8}$ hours.

51. **(E)** Average speed in miles per hour is defined as distance in miles divided by time in hours. Weber travels a total of $x + y$ miles in $h + h$ hours. Therefore, the average speed in miles per hour for the entire marathon can be represented by $\frac{x+y}{2h}$.

52. **(C)** This item is easily solved by using a Venn diagram. Use circles to represent students taking the SAT and students taking the ACT. The overlap of the two circles represents students taking both tests; students not taking either test are represented outside of the circles.

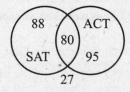

Thus, the total number of students is: $88 + 80 + 95 + 27 = 290$.

53. **(C)** Count the subsets that meet the requirements: $\{3\}$, $\{5\}$, $\{7\}$, $\{9\}$, $\{3,5\}$, $\{3,6\}$, $\{3,7\}$, $\{3,9\}$, $\{5,6\}$, $\{5,7\}$, $\{5,9\}$, $\{6,7\}$, $\{6,9\}$, $\{7,9\}$, $\{3,5,6\}$, $\{3,5,7\}$, $\{3,5,9\}$, $\{3,6,7\}$, $\{3,6,9\}$, $\{3,7,9\}$, $\{5,6,7\}$, $\{5,6,9\}$, $\{5,7,9\}$, $\{6,7,9\}$, $\{3,5,6,7\}$, $\{3,5,6,9\}$, $\{3,5,7,9\}$, $\{3,6,7,9\}$, and $\{5,6,7,9\}$. Therefore, there are 29 possible subsets of 1, 2, 3, or 4 elements containing one or more odd numbers.

54. **(D)** Draw a Venn diagram of the information provided. The four unlabeled parts of the circles in the Venn diagram must total to 14 $(51 - 10 - 12 - 15 = 14)$. Notice that the unlabeled parts of the circles can be assigned various numbers, as the following two extreme cases indicate.

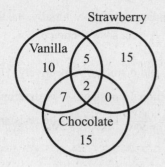

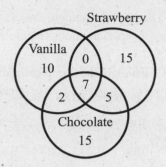

In the first of the two extreme cases above, two students liked both chocolate and strawberry. In the second of the two extreme cases above, twelve students liked both chocolate and strawberry. So, (D) is the correct answer choice.

55. **(B)** If we add 45, 35, and 20, the people enrolled in exactly two of the courses will be counted twice and the people in all three courses will be counted three times. If $x$ equals the number enrolled in exactly two courses, then $60 = 45 + 35 + 20 - x - 2(15) = 70 - x$. Therefore, $x = 70 - 60 = 10$, and there are 10 students enrolled in exactly two of the three courses.

56. **(D)** There are 3 different ways to go from Seattle to Olympia. Once you are in Olympia, there are 4 different ways to get to Portland. So, using the multiple principle of counting, there are $3 \cdot 4 = 12$ different ways to get from Seattle to Portland going through Olympia.

57. **(D)** The least common multiple of 6 and 8 is 24. The intersection is $\{24, 48, 72, 96, 120, ...\}$, which is the set of all positive integral multiples of 24.

58. **(E)** First, find the number of possible combinations for seating the four men in four seats: $4! = 4 \cdot 3 \cdot 2 \cdot 1 = 24$. Next, find the number of possible combinations for seating the 3 women: $3! = 3 \cdot 2 \cdot 1 = 6$. Since for each arrangement of the men, there are 6 arrangements of the women, there are $24 \cdot 6 = 144$ ways in which the 4 men and the 3 women can be seated.

59. **(B)** The number of children assigned to softball will be $0.40 \cdot 50 = 20$, and so 30 will be assigned to baseball. The number of children who prefer softball is $0.70 \cdot 50 = 35$, and the rest, 15, prefer baseball. Therefore, to minimize the number who will not be assigned to the sport they prefer, let the 15 who prefer baseball be assigned to baseball. That leaves 35 children who prefer softball, but only 20 of them can be assigned to softball, leaving only 15 children who will not be assigned to the sport they prefer.

60. **(D)** Use the combination formula, where $C$ is the number of color codes (12), $n$ is the total number of colors, and $k$ is the number of colors chosen for each code (2). Since we are solving for $n$ in the combination formula, it is simpler to test the values of $n$ given in the answer choices. To minimize the number of tests, begin with the middle value. Using 5 colors ($n = 5$), we have $\frac{5!}{3!(5-3)!} = \frac{5 \cdot 4 \cdot \cancel{3}!}{\cancel{3}! \cdot 2 \cdot 1} = 10$ possible color codes. Since we need a minimum of 12 possible color codes, try 6 colors ($n = 6$): $\frac{6!}{3!(6-3)!} = \frac{\cancel{6} \cdot 5 \cdot 4 \cdot \cancel{3}!}{\cancel{3}! \cdot \cancel{3} \cdot \cancel{2} \cdot 1} = 20$ possible color codes. Therefore, 6 colors is the minimum number needed to represent at least 12 different color codes.

61. **(D)** If $y$ varies directly as $x$, then $\frac{y}{x}$ is always the constant of variation. In the example, $\frac{12.3}{4.1} = 3$, so 3 is the constant of variation. In this case, the constant of variation is: $\frac{6.72}{4.2} = 1.6$.

62. **(C)** Direct variation relationships are expressed as $y = kx$, and inverse variation relationships are expressed as $xy = k$; in both cases, $k$ is a constant real number. The first equation in (C) relates a direct variation:

$x = \frac{y}{3} \Rightarrow y = 3x$. The second equation, $xy = 7$, relates an inverse variation. Finally, the third equation, $x^2 + y^2 = \frac{x}{5}$ is neither direct nor inverse variation. Therefore, (C) is the correct answer choice.

63. **(C)** Let $R$, $x$, and $d$ represent the wire's resistance, length, and diameter, respectively. The item stem states that the resistance of a wire is expressed as $R = \frac{kx}{d^2}$. The proportional constant, $k$, is determined from the information provided for the first wire: $R = \frac{kx}{d^2} \Rightarrow k = \frac{Rd^2}{x} = \frac{(0.1)(0.1)^2}{50} = \frac{(0.1)^3}{50}$. Therefore, the resistance for the second wire is: $R = \frac{kx}{d^2} = \frac{0.1^3 \cdot 9{,}000}{50 \cdot 0.3^2} = 2$.

64. **(C)** $y = kx \Rightarrow 10 = k(1.25) \Rightarrow k = 8$; thus, $y = 8x$. $w = cx^2 \Rightarrow 8 = (c\sqrt{2})^2 \Rightarrow c = 4$; thus, $y = 4x^2$. $4x^2 = 8x \Rightarrow 4x^2 - 8x = 0 \Rightarrow 4x(x-2) = 0$; thus, $x = 0$ or $x = 2$.

65. **(B)** The formula for the circumference of a circle is: $C = 2\pi r$, where $r$ is the radius of the circle. Therefore, the constant of variation is $2\pi$.

66. **(E)** The graphs in (A), (B), (C), and (D) all have at least one point for which either $x$ or $y$ is zero, and thus at these points, $xy = 0$, whereas $xy \neq 0$ at all other points where neither $x$ nor $y$ are zero. Therefore, $xy$ is not a constant value for these four graphs. (E) is the only answer choice that represents a possible inverse variation relationship.

67. **(E)** Substitute 1, 2, 4, 6, and 12, respectively, for $n$ to find the approximate values after 1 year: $10,416$, $10,420.33$, $10,422.53$, $10,423.28$, and $10,424.02$. Trying the other years also indicates that $n$ is approximately 12.

68. **(D)** $I = prt = \$1,000 \cdot 0.06 \cdot 2 = \$120$. Remember to convert the percentage to a decimal. Thus, $6\% = 0.06$.

69. **(C)** There is a total of 8 digits, and there are 2 digits that equal 4. Thus, the probability of Helen selecting a 4 is $\frac{\text{digits that equal 4}}{\text{total digits}} = \frac{2}{8} = \frac{1}{4}$.

70. **(C)** Let $d$ equal the time of Dave's arrival. Let $k$ equal the time of Kathy's arrival. Since they agreed to wait 15 minutes for each other to arrive before leaving, $|d - k| \leq \frac{15}{60} = \frac{1}{4}$. The following graph represents this equation for the two hours between 10:00 p.m. and midnight in units of hours:

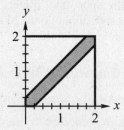

Based on this figure, the probability that Dave and Kathy were at Pizza Palace at the same time is equal to the area of the shaded region divided by the area of the square. $A_{\text{square}} = s^2 = 2^2 = 4$. To determine the area of the shaded region, subtract the area of the two triangles on either side of the shaded region from the area of the square: $A_{\text{shaded}} = 4 - 2(\frac{1}{2} \cdot \frac{7}{4} \cdot \frac{7}{4}) = \frac{15}{16}$. Thus, the probability of Dave and Kathy being at Pizza Palace together is equal to: $\frac{A_{\text{shaded}}}{A_{\text{square}}} = \frac{\frac{15}{16}}{4} = \frac{15}{64}$.

71. **(C)** You can set this up as the product of two ratios expressed in fractional terms: $(\frac{1}{6})(\frac{1}{5}) = \frac{1}{30}$. George can choose from 6 pencils and 5 pens, which results in 30 possible combinations.

72. **(D)** The probability of picking a "D" letter is: $\frac{\text{number of "D"s in name}}{\text{total number of letters in name}} = \frac{2}{5}$.

73. **(B)** The probability of picking an "M" letter is: $\frac{\text{number of distinct letters in the word "MATHEMATICS"}}{\text{number of letters in the alphabet}} = \frac{8}{26} = \frac{4}{13}$.

74. **(B)** The number of possible selections from $X$ is 5 and the number of possible selections from $Y$ is 4. Therefore, the number of different pairs of numbers, one from each set, is $5 \cdot 4 = 20$. Of these 20 pairs of numbers, there are 3 possible pairs that sum to 11: 4 and 7, 8 and 3, and 9 and 2. Thus, the probability that the sum of the 2 integers selected will equal 11 is $\frac{3}{20} = 0.15$.

75. **(D)** The 6 books could be lined up in $6! = 120$ ways. If the oldest book must be at the left and the newest at the right, there are $4! = 24$ ways that the remaining books can be lined up between them. Thus, 24 line-ups are favorable to the event in question. Hence, the probability is $\frac{24}{120} = \frac{1}{5}$.

76. **(D)** This problem involves a multiple-event probability where the individual events can have different outcomes, or are independent. Therefore, the probability that on at least one of the tosses the coin will turn up heads is equal to 1 minus the probability that it will turn up tails on all three tosses. The probability of getting 3 tails is $\frac{1}{2} \cdot \frac{1}{2} \cdot \frac{1}{2} = \frac{1}{8}$, since the probability of tails on each toss is $\frac{1}{2}$. Thus, the probability of getting at least one heads is $1 - \frac{1}{8} = \frac{7}{8}$.

77. **(D)** $\overline{AF} + \overline{FE} = 9 + 1 = 10$. Since $ACDE$ is a square, $\overline{AB} = \overline{AC} - \overline{BC} = 10 - 8 = 2$. $A_{\text{rectangle}} = \overline{AF} \cdot \overline{AB} = 9 \cdot 2 = 18$. $A_{\text{square}} = (\overline{AC})^2 = 10^2 = 100$. Therefore, the probability of a point chosen at random in the interior of the square also being in the interior of the rectangle is $\frac{A_{\text{rectangle}}}{A_{\text{square}}} = \frac{18}{100} = \frac{9}{50}$.

78. **(D)** The points in the scatter plot in (D) are the only ones that generally represent a curvilinear relationship.

79. **(C)** The net change in the daily weather temperature for the week, in degrees Celsius, is the sum of all the change values for the week: $5.5 + 1.7 - 3.9 - 3.3 - 0.5 + 0.8 - 0.2 = 0.10$.

80. **(E)** The table shows number of voters in the general election in millions and the percent change from the primary election. Since the question asks for the county with the greatest net increase in voters, eliminate counties $M$ and $O$ since these both had a decrease in the number of voters. Let $n$ equal the number of voters in the primary election. Consider county $N$: since 2.34 (million) voters is an increase of 14% in the number of voters in the primary, $\frac{2.34}{1.14} = 2.05$, and the net increase is $2.34 - 2.05 = 0.29$ million voters. For county $P$, $n = \frac{4.56}{1.04} = 4.38$, and the net increase is $4.56 - 4.38 = 0.18$ million voters. For county $Q$, $n = \frac{6.23}{1.08} = 5.77$, and the net increase is $6.23 - 5.77 = 0.46$ million voters. Therefore, the county with the greatest net increase in voters is county $Q$.

81. **(C)** The easiest method for solving a set problem such as this is to use a Venn diagram. The following diagram shows the distribution of the students according to the given information.

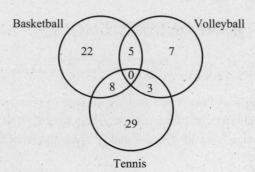

Therefore, the total number of students that participate only in basketball or tennis is $22 + 29 = 51$.

# QUANTITATIVE REASONING CONCEPTS AND STRATEGIES

**DISCRETE QUANTITATIVE—CORE LESSON** (p. 445)

| | | | | | | | |
|---|---|---|---|---|---|---|---|
| 1. | **8** | 23. | **50** | 45. | B | 67. | E |
| 2. | C | 24. | D | 46. | B | 68. | B |
| 3. | D | 25. | C | 47. | D | 69. | E |
| 4. | D | 26. | C | 48. | A | 70. | A |
| 5. | B | 27. | A | 49. | D | 71. | E |
| 6. | C | 28. | C | 50. | D | 72. | D |
| 7. | D | 29. | B | 51. | D | 73. | C |
| 8. | E | 30. | C | 52. | E | 74. | B |
| 9. | D | 31. | E | 53. | D | 75. | C |
| 10. | E | 32. | A | 54. | C | 76. | B |
| 11. | D | 33. | D | 55. | C | 77. | C |
| 12. | D | 34. | B | 56. | C | 78. | A |
| 13. | E | 35. | D | 57. | E | 79. | D |
| 14. | C | 36. | E | 58. | $-\frac{1}{4}$ | 80. | C |
| 15. | B | 37. | **80** | 59. | A | 81. | D |
| 16. | D | 38. | **90** | 60. | E | 82. | C |
| 17. | C | 39. | **10** | 61. | D | 83. | C |
| 18. | B | 40. | C | 62. | **6** | 84. | D |
| 19. | C | 41. | E | 63. | **30** | 85. | D |
| 20. | D | 42. | A | 64. | D | 86. | B |
| 21. | $\frac{12}{47}$ | 43. | C | 65. | **20** | 87. | B |
| 22. | E | 44. | A | 66. | D | 88. | C |

**DISCRETE QUANTITATIVE—REVIEW** (p. 458)

| | | | | | | | |
|---|---|---|---|---|---|---|---|
| 1. | C | 15. | C | 29. | C | 43. | B |
| 2. | D | 16. | E | 30. | C | 44. | C |
| 3. | C | 17. | B | 31. | D | 45. | E |
| 4. | C | 18. | B | 32. | D | 46. | C |
| 5. | B | 19. | B | 33. | E | 47. | E |
| 6. | C | 20. | C | 34. | C | 48. | A |
| 7. | C | 21. | C | 35. | D | 49. | A |
| 8. | E | 22. | B | 36. | A | 50. | E |
| 9. | B | 23. | A | 37. | B | 51. | B |
| 10. | D | 24. | B | 38. | C | 52. | A |
| 11. | C | 25. | A | 39. | C | 53. | C |
| 12. | D | 26. | B | 40. | B | 54. | E |
| 13. | E | 27. | B | 41. | E | 55. | E |
| 14. | A | 28. | C | 42. | A | 56. | E |

| 57. | A | 66. | A | 75. | A | 84. | A |
|-----|---|-----|---|-----|---|-----|---|
| 58. | D | 67. | A | 76. | B | 85. | B |
| 59. | A | 68. | D | 77. | E | 86. | D |
| 60. | D | 69. | C | 78. | B | 87. | A |
| 61. | C | 70. | C | 79. | D | 88. | B |
| 62. | D | 71. | D | 80. | D | 89. | D |
| 63. | E | 72. | E | 81. | B | 90. | E |
| 64. | D | 73. | E | 82. | A | | |
| 65. | E | 74. | E | 83. | D | | |

## DISCRETE QUANTITATIVE—TIMED-PRACTICE QUIZZES (p. 474)

| *QUIZ I* | | *QUIZ II* | | *QUIZ III* | |
|----------|---|-----------|---|------------|---|
| 1. | C | 1. | E | 1. | E |
| 2. | A | 2. | E | 2. | B |
| 3. | E | 3. | D | 3. | C |
| 4. | C | 4. | C | 4. | E |
| 5. | D | 5. | D | 5. | C |
| 6. | C | 6. | C | 6. | C |
| 7. | D | 7. | A | 7. | C |
| 8. | A | 8. | C | 8. | E |
| 9. | E | 9. | B | 9. | B |
| 10. | D | 10. | C | 10. | D |
| 11. | B | 11. | B | 11. | B |
| 12. | C | 12. | A | 12. | A |
| 13. | D | 13. | B | 13. | D |
| 14. | E | 14. | D | 14. | E |
| 15. | B | 15. | D | 15. | D |
| 16. | C | 16. | C | 16. | B |
| 17. | B | 17. | E | 17. | A |
| 18. | C | 18. | A | 18. | D |
| 19. | A | 19. | A | 19. | B |
| 20. | D | 20. | A | 20. | B |

## QUANTITATIVE COMPARISONS—CORE LESSON (p. 491)

| | | | |
|---|---|---|---|
| 1. A | 26. C | 51. D | 76. C |
| 2. B | 27. A | 52. D | 77. C |
| 3. C | 28. C | 53. D | 78. A |
| 4. A | 29. A | 54. B | 79. C |
| 5. B | 30. D | 55. A | 80. C |
| 6. C | 31. A | 56. B | 81. C |
| 7. D | 32. C | 57. C | 82. A |
| 8. A | 33. C | 58. B | 83. B |
| 9. B | 34. D | 59. B | 84. B |
| 10. C | 35. C | 60. A | 85. C |
| 11. D | 36. C | 61. B | 86. C |
| 12. B | 37. A | 62. C | 87. C |
| 13. D | 38. D | 63. D | 88. D |
| 14. B | 39. C | 64. A | 89. D |
| 15. C | 40. A | 65. D | 90. D |
| 16. D | 41. A | 66. D | 91. D |
| 17. C | 42. C | 67. C | 92. D |
| 18. A | 43. A | 68. B | 93. D |
| 19. B | 44. B | 69. B | 94. C |
| 20. D | 45. B | 70. C | 95. A |
| 21. D | 46. D | 71. C | 96. C |
| 22. D | 47. D | 72. A | |
| 23. C | 48. D | 73. A | |
| 24. C | 49. D | 74. C | |
| 25. A | 50. B | 75. A | |

## QUANTITATIVE COMPARISONS—REVIEW (p. 501)

| | | | |
|---|---|---|---|
| 1. A | 16. A | 31. C | 46. C |
| 2. D | 17. D | 32. B | 47. A |
| 3. D | 18. D | 33. D | 48. C |
| 4. D | 19. D | 34. D | 49. D |
| 5. C | 20. B | 35. D | 50. B |
| 6. D | 21. D | 36. C | 51. C |
| 7. D | 22. D | 37. C | 52. C |
| 8. A | 23. C | 38. A | 53. D |
| 9. B | 24. B | 39. B | 54. A |
| 10. A | 25. D | 40. A | 55. A |
| 11. C | 26. D | 41. D | 56. B |
| 12. D | 27. B | 42. C | 57. A |
| 13. C | 28. D | 43. D | 58. B |
| 14. A | 29. C | 44. B | 59. C |
| 15. A | 30. D | 45. B | 60. C |

| | | | | | | | |
|---|---|---|---|---|---|---|---|
| 61. | **C** | 66. | **D** | 71. | **C** | 76. | **A** |
| 62. | **A** | 67. | **D** | 72. | **C** | | |
| 63. | **C** | 68. | **B** | 73. | **C** | | |
| 64. | **C** | 69. | **C** | 74. | **B** | | |
| 65. | **A** | 70. | **B** | 75. | **C** | | |

## QUANTITATIVE COMPARISONS—TIMED-PRACTICE QUIZZES (p. 510)

| *QUIZ I* | | *QUIZ II* | | *QUIZ III* | |
|---|---|---|---|---|---|
| 1. | **B** | 1. | **A** | 1. | **D** |
| 2. | **C** | 2. | **D** | 2. | **C** |
| 3. | **C** | 3. | **D** | 3. | **D** |
| 4. | **B** | 4. | **B** | 4. | **C** |
| 5. | **B** | 5. | **D** | 5. | **B** |
| 6. | **C** | 6. | **D** | 6. | **D** |
| 7. | **D** | 7. | **A** | 7. | **A** |
| 8. | **B** | 8. | **B** | 8. | **A** |
| 9. | **A** | 9. | **A** | 9. | **D** |
| 10. | **D** | 10. | **C** | 10. | **C** |
| 11. | **A** | 11. | **D** | 11. | **B** |
| 12. | **C** | 12. | **D** | 12. | **A** |
| 13. | **B** | 13. | **B** | 13. | **C** |
| 14. | **C** | 14. | **C** | 14. | **C** |
| 15. | **A** | 15. | **B** | 15. | **C** |
| 16. | **A** | 16. | **A** | 16. | **B** |
| 17. | **D** | 17. | **B** | 17. | **A** |
| 18. | **C** | 18. | **B** | 18. | **C** |
| 19. | **C** | 19. | **C** | 19. | **B** |
| 20. | **D** | 20. | **C** | 20. | **A** |
| 21. | **C** | 21. | **D** | 21. | **A** |
| 22. | **A** | 22. | **A** | 22. | **A** |

**GRAPHS—CORE LESSON** (p. 527)

| | | | |
|---|---|---|---|
| 1. **D** | 9. **A** | 17. **B** | 25. **B** |
| 2. **C** | 10. **C** | 18. **C** | 26. **A** |
| 3. **D** | 11. **B** | 19. **D** | 27. **C** |
| 4. **D** | 12. **A** | 20. **B** | 28. **B** |
| 5. **C** | 13. **D** | 21. **E** | 29. **A** |
| 6. **D** | 14. **C** | 22. **B** | |
| 7. **A** | 15. **B** | 23. **B** | |
| 8. **E** | 16. **C** | 24. **D** | |

**GRAPHS—REVIEW** (p. 533)

| | | | |
|---|---|---|---|
| 1. **C** | 11. **C** | 21. **D** | 31. **D** |
| 2. **E** | 12. **E** | 22. **B** | 32. **E** |
| 3. **B** | 13. **A** | 23. **B** | 33. **E** |
| 4. **E** | 14. **D** | 24. **B** | 34. **D** |
| 5. **D** | 15. **D** | 25. **E** | 35. **E** |
| 6. **D** | 16. **D** | 26. **C** | 36. **A** |
| 7. **A** | 17. **B** | 27. **D** | 37. **D** |
| 8. **C** | 18. **D** | 28. **B** | |
| 9. **B** | 19. **A** | 29. **C** | |
| 10. **B** | 20. **C** | 30. **A** | |

**GRAPHS—TIMED-PRACTICE QUIZZES** (p. 545)

| *QUIZ I* | *QUIZ II* | *QUIZ III* |
|---|---|---|
| 1. **B** | 1. **A** | 1. **C** |
| 2. **C** | 2. **C** | 2. **A** |
| 3. **B** | 3. **A** | 3. **D** |
| 4. **C** | 4. **B** | 4. **E** |
| 5. **D** | 5. **C** | 5. **A** |

# Analytical Writing

# ANALYTICAL WRITING SKILLS REVIEW

**EXERCISE 1—COMMON GRAMMATICAL ERRORS** (p. 572)

1. **(A)** The adjective "harsh" is intended to modify the verb "deals." However, an adjective cannot be used to modify a verb. So, the adverb "harshly" should be used instead.

2. **(D)** "Them" is intended to be a pronoun substitute for "advertising," but "advertising" is singular, not plural. "It" should replace "them."

3. **(D)** "You" is intended to refer to "one," but "one" is in the third person while "you" is in the second person. The sentence could be corrected simply by omitting the underlined portion altogether: "...and read a book."

4. **(C)** "That" has no clear referent. "That" might refer either to "horrifying conditions" or to "English boarding schools." The ambiguity could be avoided by rewording the sentence: "...about the horrifying conditions in the English boarding schools, conditions that he learned about...."

5. **(C)** "It" has no clear referent. "It" might refer either to "movement" or to "manifesto." The sentence can be corrected by including an appropriate noun to clarify the speaker's meaning: "...of a manifesto, a work that incorporated...."

6. **(D)** "Capable" is intended to modify "played," a verb. Thus, the adverb form must be used: "...played capably."

7. **(B)** "Who" and "whom" are the correct pronouns to use for people: "...countryside who sheltered...."

8. **(B)** "We" cannot be used as the object of "to." The correct choice of pronoun is "us."

9. **(A)** When a pronoun is used to modify a gerund, the pronoun must be in the possessive case: "Your taking the initiative...."

10. **(C)** "Which" has no clear antecedent. Had the speaker hoped to avoid the conference or just being selected to be the representative of the group at the conference? To avoid the ambiguity, the sentence will have to be substantially revised: "...at the conference, and I had hoped to avoid the conference altogether."

11. **(C)** "Whom" should be used here instead of "which," since the pronoun refers to a person.

12. **(D)** The subject of the main clause is "few," a plural pronoun, so the verb should be "are" rather than "is."

13. **(B)** The subject of the sentence is "differences," a plural noun, so the verb should be "help" rather than "helps."

14. **(B)** "Hardly no" is a double negative. The sentence should read "hardly any."

15. **(B)** The subject of the sentence is "diaries," a plural noun. The verb should be "provide" rather than "provides."

16. **(D)** "Its" intends to refer to "whales," so the sentence should use the plural pronoun "their."

17. **(A)** A pronoun used to modify a gerund must be in the possessive case: "His being at the rally...."

18. **(D)** "Satisfactory" is intended to modify "system." Therefore, another verb is required: "...and is more than satisfactory."

19. **(B)** "Who" is intended to be the object of the verb "recommended," so the objective case pronoun "whom" is required.

20. **(B)** "Recent" is intended to modify "constructed," an adjective. However, an adjective cannot be used to modify another adjective. Here the adverb "recently" should be used.

21. **(D)** "Which" does not have a clear referent. It is unclear whether the faculty was angry because the resolution passed or because it passed with few dissenting votes. The sentence must be rewritten to clarify the speaker's intention. One acceptable rewrite is as follows: "Many faculty members grew angry when the student senate passed the resolution banning smoking in the cafeteria with scarcely any dissenting votes."

22. **(D)** "Your" is intended to refer to "one's," so you need some kind of third person pronoun, for example, "his or her."

23. **(D)** "It" lacks a referent. "It" seems to refer to something like "insurance," but there is no such noun in the sentence. The sentence could be corrected by using the noun "insurance" in place of the pronoun "it."

24. **(C)** "Candid" is intended to modify the verb "wrote," so the sentence must use the adverb "candidly."

25. **(A)** The sentence commits the error of the "ubiquitous they." The sentence can be corrected by using a noun such as "the team" or "the management" in place of "they." Note that changing the plural noun to a singular noun, such as "the team," requires that the verb also be singular.

26. The adverb "slowly" is the correct answer choice. The verb "does" is being modified, and verbs are modified by adverbs.

27. The adverb phrase "really well" is the correct answer choice. The verb "understand" is being modified, and verbs are modified by adverbs.

28. The adjective "polite" is the correct answer choice. "Be" is a linking verb, and linking verbs are modified by adjectives. Although the blank follows the verb, the sense of "polite" more clearly qualifies the subject. Since nouns are qualified by adjectives, "polite" is the correct choice.

29. The adverb "well" is the correct answer choice. The verb "doing" is being modified, and verbs are modified by adverbs.

30. The adjective "good" is the correct answer choice. The pronoun "it" is being modified, and pronouns (like nouns) are modified by adjectives. In this sentence, the sense of goodness qualifies the noun, not the verb. Therefore, the adjective "good" is the correct completion.

31. The adjective "terrible" is the correct answer choice. The noun "mess" is being modified, and nouns are modified by adjectives.

32. The adjective "awful" is the correct answer choice. "Felt" is a linking verb, and linking verbs are modified by adjectives. When describing the subject, and not the manner in which some action is being undertaken, adjectives are used.

33. The adverb "terribly" is the correct answer choice. The adjective "exciting" is being modified, and adjectives are modified by adverbs.

34. The adverb "well" is the correct answer choice. The verb "doing" is being modified, and verbs are modified by adverbs.

35. The adverb "well" is the correct answer choice. The verb "smell" is being modified, and verbs are modified by adverbs.

36. This item primarily tests diction. Both "hard" and "hardly" are adverbs, however "hard" expresses effort, while "hardly" means "barely." Mrs. Chang would not be proud of her son because he hardly worked in class.

37. The adverb "fast" is the correct answer choice. The verb "biked" is being modified, and verbs are modified by adverbs. This question is tricky because "fast" can function either as an adjective or an adverb. In this context, it functions as an adverb. On the other hand, "quick" can only function as an adjective. The adverb "quickly" would also be acceptable in this context, but that is not one of the answer choices.

38. The adjective "near" is the correct answer choice. The noun "college" is being modified, and nouns are modified by adjectives.

39. The adverb "slowly" is the correct answer choice. The verb "appeared" is being modified, and verbs are modified by adverbs.

40. The adjective "healthy" is the correct answer choice. "Remain" is a linking verb, and linking verbs are followed by adjectives. When attempting to ascribe a characteristic to a subject, an adjective is used, even if it follows a verb.

41. The adjective "heavy" is the correct answer choice. "Felt" is a linking verb, and linking verbs are followed by adjectives. The quality of weight is more applicable to the subject, thus an adjective is appropriate.

## EXERCISE 2—ANALYZING SENTENCE STRUCTURE (p. 584)

1. The plural subject "many people" requires the plural form "receive."

2. The plural subject "books" requires the plural form "were." The plural subject is modified by a prepositional phrase that contains a singular noun ("on the top shelf"). However, the object of a prepositional phrase ("shelf") cannot serve as the subject of the sentence.

3. The plural subject "stores" requires the plural form "offer." The plural subject is modified by a prepositional phrase that contains a singular noun ("in the downtown sector's newly renovated mall"). However, the object of a prepositional phrase ("mall") cannot serve as the subject of the sentence.

4. The plural subject "bottles" requires the plural form "remain." The plural subject is modified by a prepositional phrase that contains a singular noun ("of the vintage wine"). However, the object of a prepositional phrase ("wine") cannot serve as the subject of the sentence.

5. The singular subject "tourist" requires the singular form "is." The singular subject is modified by a clause that contains a plural noun ("who visits the caverns"). However, this is not the subject of the main clause.

6. The plural subject "several different species" requires the plural form "were." This is a tricky sentence because it uses an inverted structure in which the verb ("were") precedes the subject ("several different species"). In addition, the sentence begins with a prepositional phrase that contains a singular noun ("Underneath the leaf covering"). However, the object of a prepositional phrase ("leaf covering") cannot serve as the subject of the sentence.

7. The plural subject "young boys" requires the plural form "were." This is a tricky sentence because the subject and verb are separated by a long clause ("who had never before been in trouble with the law"). In addition, the last word of this clause ("law") is a singular noun, which could easily be misinterpreted as the subject of the sentence. However, this is not the subject of the main clause.

8. The plural subject "several barrels" requires the plural form "have." Again, the subject and verb are separated by intervening material ("containing a highly toxic liquid"), and the last word of this intervening material is a singular

noun ("liquid"), which could easily be misinterpreted as the subject of the sentence. However, this is not the subject of the main clause.

9. The plural subject "sponsors" requires the plural form "hope." The plural subject is modified by a prepositional phrase that contains a singular noun ("of the arts and crafts fair"). However, the object of a prepositional phrase ("fair") cannot serve as the subject of the sentence.

10. The plural subject "Dawn, Harriet, and Gloria" requires the plural form "are." This is a tricky sentence because the subject is a compound subject made up of singular elements. Remember that a compound subject consists of two or more elements that are joined together by the conjunction "and." Compound subjects always require plural forms, even when each of the elements is singular.

11. The singular subject "the mayor" requires the singular form "worries." The subject and verb are separated by intervening material that contains a plural noun ("whose administration has been rocked by several crises"). However, this is not the subject of the main clause.

12. The plural subject "acts" requires the plural form "have been." This sentence is difficult for two reasons. First, it uses an inverted structure in which the verb ("have been") precedes the subject ("several acts") Remember that "here" and "there" do not typically act as the subjects of sentences. Second, the plural subject is modified by a prepositional phrase that contains a singular noun ("of vandalism"). However, the object of a prepositional phrase ("vandalism") cannot serve as the subject of the sentence.

13. The plural subject "rock musicians" requires the plural form "lose."

14. This sentence contains a long prepositional phrase: "from the branches of the tree that hang over the fence." When attempting to determine the correct agreement for a sentence, ignore prepositional phrases. The remaining sentence is "the leaves fall into the neighbor's yard," where it is clear that we need the plural form "fall" to agree with "the leaves."

15. The plural subject "The computer and the printer" requires the plural form "have." This sentence is difficult for two reasons. First, the subject of the sentence is a compound subject made up of singular elements ("the computer" and "the printer"). Even though this compound subject consists of singular subjects, a compound subject always requires a plural form. Second, the subject and verb are separated by a modifying clause ("which are sitting on James' desk"), and the last word in this clause is a singular noun ("desk"). However, this is not the subject of the main clause.

16. The singular subject "Theresa" requires the singular form "was." The subject and verb are separated by a qualifying phrase that contains a plural noun ("waders"). However, this is not the subject of the main clause.

17. Attention should not be paid to prepositional clauses. They in no way affect subject-verb agreement. Eliminating the prepositional phrase, the sentence reads: "the film critic writes that the film is very funny and entertaining." At this point, the correct verb-choice is clear.

18. This sentence contains a clause introduced by "that", which can be ignored. The new sentence becomes "several of the ingredients have to be prepared in advance."

19. The singular subject "The computer" requires the singular form "was." This sentence is difficult because the subject and verb are separated a large group of words that modifies the subject of the sentence ("The computer").Focus only on those parts of the sentence that are required to have a complete sentence, since clauses and phrases do not enter into subject-verb agreement considerations.

20. The singular subject "support" requires the singular form "has." This sentence is difficult because it uses an inverted structure in which the verb ("has been") precedes the subject ("support"). This inverted structure can

make subject-verb agreement more difficult to understand. Remember that "here" and "there" do not typically act as the subjects of sentences.

21. The plural subject "Bill and Jean" requires the plural form "are." "Bill and Jean" is a compound subject. Even though this compound subject consists of singular elements ("Bill" and "Jean"), a compound subject always requires a plural form.

22. The plural subject "several students" requires the plural form "were." This sentence uses an inverted structure (as noted by the word "there"), which can make subject-verb agreement more difficult to understand. However, a plural subject always requires a plural form.

23. The singular pronoun "his or her" is the correct answer choice. A pronoun must always agree with its antecedent: If the antecedent is singular, then the pronoun must be singular. The antecedent in this sentence is the singular "no one."

24. The singular pronoun "her" is the correct answer choice. A pronoun must always agree with its antecedent: If the antecedent is singular, then the pronoun must be singular. In this sentence, the antecedent is the singular "each," not the plural noun "sisters." "Sisters" is part of the prepositional phrase that modifies "each." Ignore phrases and clauses; they do not affect subject-verb agreement.

25. The singular subject "music" requires the singular form "is." This sentence might be confusing because the singular subject is modified by a prepositional phrase that contains a plural noun ("of Verdi's operas"). Secondary phrases and clauses should not be considered in subject-verb agreement items.

26. The plural pronoun "their" is the correct choice. The antecedent ("All the musicians") is plural. So, the pronoun must be plural.

27. The subject of this sentence ("Either Mrs. Martinez or Carlos") is a disjunctive subject. Disjunctive subjects consist of multiple elements that are introduced by the pronoun "either." When a disjunctive subject is used, the verb in the sentence must agree with the last element in the disjunctive subject. The last element in this disjunctive subject is the singular "Carlos." So, the singular form "goes" is required.

28. "Have" is the correct answer choice. "Have had" would imply that the speaker wanted the tasks done before she asked. But, the stipulation "by the time I got home from work" puts the actions that the speaker desires after she asks, but before she returns from work.

29. "Could" is the correct answer choice. It correctly establishes the sequence of events. First, the storekeeper lost most of his business to a conglomerate retail store. As a result, he "could" not pay his bill last month. It is important to recognize that the entire sequence of events took place and concluded in the past. The present tense auxiliary verb "can" is wrong because it incorrectly suggests that the storekeeper is still unable to pay his monthly rent bill. "Can" should also arouse suspicion because the resulting "can not" is low-level; "cannot" is always preferred.

30. "Became" is the correct answer choice. It correctly establishes the sequence of events. First, the weather "became" cold. Then, Jim "could" not ride his bicycle to work. Both events took place in the past, and the change in weather preceded Jim's inability to ride his bicycle. The present tense verb "becomes" is wrong because it suggests that the future condition of the weather will affect Jim's past ability to ride.

31. **(D)** (C) is wrong because the correct verb must agree with the singular, 3rd person subject "gentleman." (B) and (E) are wrong because the correct verb must also be in the present tense since the activity is happening in the present. Finally, (A) is wrong because the correct verb must also complement the auxiliary verb "is." (D) is the only answer choice that satisfies all of these conditions.

32. **(B)** The correct verb must be in the past tense since the activity happened last night. Therefore, (B) "supposed" is the correct answer choice. (A), (C), (D), and (E) can all be eliminated since none of these answer choices are in the past tense.

33. **(E)** The correct verb must be in the past tense since the "My friend has...to" construction indicates past activity. So, (A), (C), and (D) can be eliminated. As for (B), although "began" is a past tense verb, it creates an incorrect present perfect construction ("has began"). (E) creates a correct present perfect construction ("has begun").

34. **(B)** The correct verb must be in the past tense since "He has" indicates past activity. So, (C), (D), and (E) can be eliminated. (A) appears to be a past tense verb. However, "catched" is not a correct conjugation of "catch" in any circumstance. "Caught" is the past tense form of "catch."

35. **(A)** The correct verb must be in the present tense, since "he could" suggests something that is based on a condition ("if he were asked"). "Sing" is the correct verb form.

36. **(C)** The correct verb must be in the past tense since "she has" indicates past activity. So, (A) and (E) can be eliminated. (D) can be eliminated because it is an incorrect attempt to form the past tense of "sing". As for (B), although "sang" is a past tense verb, it creates an incorrect present perfect construction ("has sang"). (C) creates a correct present perfect construction ("has sung").

37. **(D)** The correct verb must be in the past tense since "They have already" indicates past activity. Therefore, (A), (B), (C), and (E) can be eliminated.

38. **(E)** The correct verb must be in the past tense since "He has" indicates past activity. So, (A) and (D) can be eliminated. (C) can be eliminated because it is an incorrect attempt to form the past tense of "give"; "gived" is not a word. As for (B), although "gave" is a past tense verb, it creates an incorrect present perfect construction ("has gave"). (E) creates a correct present perfect construction ("has given").

39. **(C)** (A) and (D) are wrong because they suggest an object that does not exist in the sentence. What is he "to devote" to his parents? What is he "devoting" to his parents? (B) and (E) are wrong because they cannot be used after "He is"; they result in sentences that are grammatically incorrect. Therefore, (C) is the correct answer choice.

40. **(D)** The correct verb must parallel the verb that already exists in the sentence ("designed"). So, (A), (B), (C), and (E) can be eliminated. Therefore, (D) is the correct answer choice.

41. **(C)** The correct verb must indicate past activity since this activity happened at the same time as when "he ran onto the stage." So, (A), (B), and (D) can be eliminated. As for (E), although "had laughed" does indicate past activity, it is the past perfect form of "laugh." The past perfect is used to describe activity that was undertaken and completed before another past activity. In this sentence, the two activities happened at the same time. Therefore, (C) is the correct answer choice.

42. **(E)** The correct verb must indicate past activity since this activity allowed her to make the upcoming Olympics. So, (B), (C), and (D) can be eliminated. As for (A), although "had jumped" does indicate past activity, it is the past perfect form of "jump." The past perfect is used to describe activity that was undertaken and completed before another past activity. In this sentence, the Olympics are still in the future. So, the past perfect "had jumped" is incorrect. Therefore, (E) is the correct answer choice.

43. **(A)** The correct verb must indicate past activity since the cause of the pain is in the past ("she continued to blame me"). (E) is wrong because it suggests that the cause of the pain is in the future. (D) is wrong because the resulting sentence is grammatically incorrect. (A), (B), and (C) all sound like they might be correct answer choices. However, (B) is ultimately wrong because the resulting sentence suggests that the pain is ongoing; there is no concrete evidence in the sentence to confirm that this is the case. (C) is wrong because the resulting sentence suggests that the pain fluctuates (e.g., "It has hurt. Then it did not hurt. Weeks later, though, it hurt again."); there

is no concrete evidence in the sentence to confirm that this is the case either. Therefore, (A) is the correct answer choice.

44. **(E)** The correct verb must include a subjunctive because the second half of the sentence ("if he had really...") describes a condition that is either known or supposed to be contrary to fact. So, (A), (B), and (D) can be eliminated. Finally, (C) is wrong because the past participle of "see" is "seen," not "saw." Therefore, (E) is the correct answer choice.

45. **(B)** (A) and (D) are wrong because the correct verb must agree with the singular, 3rd person subject "child." (C) and (E) are wrong because they distort the sequence of events. First, the child learned how to stand. Then, she walked. The word "now" indicates present activity, as well as parallelism with "is able".

46. **(E)** The correct verb must be in the future tense since the activity will take place "tomorrow morning." So, (A), (B), (C), and (D) can be eliminated. Therefore, (E) is the correct answer choice.

47. **(B)** The first part of the sentence includes a past perfect construction ("After she had completed her investigation"). A past perfect construction describes activity that was undertaken and completed before another past activity. So, the correct answer choice must also indicate past activity. Accordingly, (A), (D), and (E) can be eliminated. As for (C), "has written" indicates something that happened before the moment of speech, but fails to place the event after the investigation. Only (B) follows the logic of the sentence.

48. **(E)** The correct verb must indicate past activity since this activity happened at the same time as "When I was growing up." (A) and (B) are wrong because they indicate present and future activity, respectively; they distort the sequence of events. (C) is wrong because a present perfect construction describes activity that was undertaken but not concluded in the past; however, the speaker describes something that is firmly set in the past, not an ongoing activity. Finally, (D) is wrong because it too fails to indicate that the past activity has concluded. Therefore, (E) is the correct answer choice: The past tense "spent" indicates something that is firmly set in the past.

49. **(A)** The correct verb will be parallel to "get," which is a present form. Only "order" is also in the present tense.

50. **(C)** The correct verb must indicate past activity since the activity has happened "for years now." So, (A), (B), and (D) can be eliminated. (E) is wrong because the word "now" also indicates that the activity is ongoing. Therefore, (C) is the correct answer choice.

51. **(A)** "We were just leaving" indicates past activity, so the correct verb must also indicate past activity. (B) is wrong because it incorrectly suggests that the telephone has not yet rung. (C) is wrong because it distorts the sequence of events; in other words, it fails to establish the fact that they first tried to leave and then the telephone started to ring. (D) is wrong because it uses a present perfect construction, which describes activity that started but did not finish in the past; there is no evidence in the sentence to suggest that the telephone is still ringing. Finally, (E) is wrong because it uses a past perfect construction, which describes an activity that started and finished before another past activity. In this sentence, though, the activity (the telephone ringing) does not start and finish before some other past activity. Rather, the telephone prevents the other activity in the sentence (leaving) from happening. Therefore, (A) is the correct answer choice.

52. **(E)** "We arrived at the house" indicates past activity, so the correct verb must also indicate past activity. (A) and (B) are wrong because they indicate present and future activity, respectively. (C) is wrong because it uses a past perfect construction, which describes activity that started and finished before another past activity. However, this sentence does not identify another past activity that occurred prior to the wedding. Finally, (D) is wrong because it uses a present perfect construction, which describes activity that started but did not finish in the past; there is no evidence in the sentence to suggest that the wedding was not entirely finished. Therefore, (E) is the correct answer choice.

53. **(C)** (A), (B), and (D) can be eliminated because they distort the sequence of events. The resulting sentences suggest that first the car stalled and then the plans were made. (E) is wrong because it uses a present perfect construction, which describes activity that occurred anterior to the present. But, we need a form that expresses anteriority to a past event. Therefore, (C) is the correct answer choice.

54. **(B)** The word "while" indicates that the events described by two clauses were happening simultaneously. Only "was" testing agrees with "were putting."

55. **(D)** Because this sentence describes a simple sequence of events, the verbs should be in the same tense. Only "flew" agrees with "landed."

56. **(C)** (B) and (E) are wrong because they are plural forms that do not agree with the singular noun "baby." (A) and (D) are wrong because they incorrectly imply that the baby has not yet arrived. Therefore, (C) is the correct answer choice.

57. **(E)** (A) and (B) are wrong because they distort the fact that the desire to drive from Wisconsin to Washington preceded the fact that they were late. In other words, the resulting sentences do not accurately reflect the sequence of events; a present activity cannot precede a past activity ("we were late"). (D) is incorrectly conjugated. (C) is wrong because the sentence requires an active verb construction ("We wanted"), but (C) results in an incomplete passive verb construction ("We were wanted") that never answers who wanted them. Therefore, (E) is the correct answer choice.

58. **(C)** The condition "if it doesn't rain" is in the present tense, so the completion should also be in the present tense. So, (A), (B), (D), and (E) can all be eliminated because they indicate either past or future activity.

59. **(C)** The sentence commits an error of logical expression, because it implies that all the people coming into the museum have but a single camera. It could be corrected by changing "a camera" to "cameras."

60. **(B)** The sentence is flawed by faulty parallelism. It could be corrected by changing "to maintain" to "maintaining."

61. **(A)** The sentence contains the incorrect form of the irregular verb "to lay" and is corrected by changing "laying" to "lying."

62. **(D)** The final phrase is out of place. As written, the sentence implies that the cockroach is unlike destructive garden pests, but the speaker means to say that the cockroach is not like the praying mantis. The sentence can be corrected by relocating the phrase closer to the noun it modifies: "The praying mantis, unlike the cockroach, which serves no useful function, is welcomed by homeowners…."

63. **(C)** The incorrect form of the verb "to hang" is used. Instead, the sentence should read: "…picture was hung…."

64. **(D)** Unlike in the previous item in which the correct sentence read: "…picture was hung…," when one is talking about the hanging of a person, the correct verb form is "hanged," not "hung."

65. **(B)** The original sentence is a run-on sentence. It can be corrected by adding end-stop punctuation: "We spent an exhausting day shopping. We could hardly wait to get home."

66. **(A)** The sentence is flawed by a lack of parallelism, an error that can be corrected by substituting the adjective "charismatic" for the phrase "has charisma."

67. **(A)** This item is a sentence fragment that lacks a conjugated verb. The fragment can be changed into a complete sentence by substituting "displayed" for "displaying."

68. **(C)** The improper form of "to sew" is used. The sentence should read: "The woman…has sewn the hem…."

69. **(B)** The use of the subjunctive "would have been" is illogical. The use of the subjunctive incorrectly implies that the loss of lives and money is contingent upon some event, but no such event is mentioned in the sentence. The sentence can be corrected by substituting "will have been."

70. **(C)** This is a run-on sentence. It should read: "The house on the corner was completely empty. No one came to the door."

71. **(C)** The sentence suffers from a lack of parallelism. This deficiency can be corrected by changing "taking" to "to take." (In any event, the use of the gerund "taking" instead of the infinitive "to take" is not idiomatic.)

72. **(C)** The incorrect verb tense of "to freeze" is used. The sentence can be corrected by substituting "frozen" for "froze."

73. **(D)** The tense of the first verb is not sequentially consistent with the tense of the second verb. The sentence can be corrected by substituting "experiences" for "experienced."

74. **(C)** This is a run-on sentence. It can be corrected by adding a question mark: "Where had everyone gone? All the lights were off."

75. **(B)** The original sentence contains an incorrect verb form. The sentence should read: "Rather than declare bankruptcy...."

76. **(D)** The use of the present tense "loses" is illogical and inconsistent with the use of the past tense "was" earlier in the sentence. The error can be corrected by substituting "lost" for "loses."

77. **(B)** This is a run-on sentence. The sentence is correct if a comma is added between "slowly" and "almost." The correct sentence reads: "We entered the cave very slowly, almost afraid of what we might find there."

78. **(C)** The original sentence contains the incorrect form of the verb "to drink." The corrected sentence reads: "...he drank all of the poison from the vial."

79. **(C)** The elements of the sentence are not parallel. It would be correct if "cross-checking" were changed to "cross-checked."

80. **(B)** The sentence contains an incorrect form of the verb "to fling." It can be corrected by changing "flinged" to "flung."

81. **(C)** The sentence is a run-on sentence. The sentence may be corrected in one of two ways, both changes occurring between "happen" and "my." First, end-stop punctuation may be added: "...was going to happen. My heart...." Second, an exclamation mark could be used instead of a period: "...was going to happen! My heart...."

82. "When at school, he studies, goes to the library, and works on the computer."

In the original, the final element in the series incorrectly begins with the word "he," which disrupts the parallelism of the sentence. In the corrected sentence, each element in the series agrees with the pronoun "he," but it is not necessary to repeat that pronoun at any point.

83. "In order to get eight hours of sleep, the student prefers sleeping in late in the morning to going to bed early in the evening."

In the corrected sentence, the two verbs that follow "prefers" are both gerunds ("sleeping...going"). As a result, the sentence is parallel.

84. "I still need to pass Math 252 and English 301 and return two overdue books before I am allowed to graduate."

In the corrected sentence, the two verbs that describe what the student needs to do are parallel ("pass...return"). Pass, in turn, has a parallel construction containing two nouns. These two levels of parallelism should not be mixed.

85. The original is correct. The objects of "either" are correctly paralleled.

86. The original is correct. The subject-verb agreement across the main and subordinate clauses is correctly paralleled.

87. The original is correct. The original exhibits the correct parallelism of verb-subject agreement between the two clauses joined by "either...or...."

88. "Our instructor suggested that we study the assignment carefully, go to the library to research the topic extensively, and conduct a survey among 20 subjects."

    In the original, the final element in the series incorrectly begins with the words "we should." These words disrupt the parallelism of the sentence. In the corrected sentence, each element of the series begins with a parallel verb form ("study...go...conduct"). It is unnecessary to repeat the subject at any point in such a series. In fact, such a repetition is ungrammatical.

89. "The increase of attrition among community college students is caused by a lack of family support and a limited income while attending school."

    The original not only suffers from faulty parallelism, but its second element is a complete sentence unto itself ("students have a limited income while attending school"). In the corrected sentence, the causes of increased attrition are parallel noun forms ("a lack of family support...a limited income").

90. "Many non-smokers complained about the health risks associated with second-hand smoke; as a result, smoking is banned in the library and the cafeteria, and smokers have to leave the building to light a cigarette."

    In the original, the first and second elements in the series suggest a parallel series. The third element, however, disrupts the parallelism. The corrected sentence simply eliminates the series to create the needed parallelism.

91. "After talking to financial aid and seeing your advisor, return to the registrar's office."

    In the corrected sentence, the two tasks detailed at the beginning of the sentence are now expressed in parallel gerund verb forms ("talking...seeing").

92. "Professor Walker helped not only me, but many of my classmates as well."

    In the corrected sentence, "not only" is moved to its proper place. As a result, what is intended to be parallel is made clear (Professor Walker's help to "me" and Professor Walker's help to "my classmates").

93. "In his communications class, he can work either in groups or in pairs."

    In the corrected sentence, "either" is moved to its proper place. As a result, what is intended to be parallel is made clear (a choice to work "in groups" or a choice to work "in pairs").

94. "I prefer that other geography class because of the clear explanations and numerous exercises in the textbook, as well as Mrs. Patrick's vivid teaching style."

    The original suffers from faulty parallelism; as a result, it incorrectly implies that "Mrs. Patrick's vivid teaching style" was a feature of the geography textbook. The correct sentence makes clear that the textbook and Mrs. Patrick's teaching style are both features of the preferred geography class.

95. "The question is whether to study tonight or to get up earlier tomorrow morning."

In the original, the second element incorrectly begins with the words "should I." These words disrupt the parallelism of the sentence. Specifically, the second element is a complete sentence unto itself (Should I get up earlier tomorrow morning?). In the corrected sentence, both elements have parallel verb forms ("to study" and "to get up").

96. "Reasons for the latest tuition increase are the upgraded computers, the new library, and the 6.5% inflation."

The original not only suffers from faulty parallelism, but the third element in the series is a complete sentence unto itself (Inflation has increased to 6.5%.). In the corrected sentence, the three causes for the tuition increase are parallel noun forms ("the upgraded computers…the new library…the 6.5% inflation").

## EXERCISE 3—PROBLEMS OF LOGICAL EXPRESSION (p. 600)

1. **(C)** The original suffers from faulty parallelism. "Would return" creates the necessary parallelism ("would go…would return"). Also, it firmly establishes the correct sequence of events—first, she "would go"; then, she "would return." (A), (B), (D), and (E) do not create the necessary parallelism. They place the grandmother's actions in different and unconnected time frames.

2. **(B)** The original has a problem of pronoun-antecedent agreement. Remember that a pronoun must agree in number with its antecedent, or referent. According to this sentence, the canning jars preserve "the food." "Food" is a singular noun. Singular pronouns refer to singular nouns, so the plural pronoun "them" should be replaced by the singular pronoun "it." (C) and (D) are wrong because they do not solve the problem of pronoun-antecedent agreement. (E) solves the problem of pronoun-antecedent agreement, but it incorrectly substitutes the singular form "preserves" for the plural form "preserve"; the singular form "preserves" does not agree with the plural noun "jars." (B) is the only answer choice that uses the correct pronoun and provides a plural form for the plural noun "jars" ("would preserve it").

3. **(C)** "By late fall" indicates activity that is complete, so the correct verb must be in the past tense. (A), (B), and (E) can therefore be eliminated. As for (D), although "was lined" is in the past tense, the singular "was" does not agree with the plural subject "shelves." (C) is the correct answer choice because it is a past tense verb, and it agrees in number with the subject.

4. **(E)** This item requires the use of contextual information. Sentence 6 describes something that contrasts what is stated in sentence 5. As a result, sentence 6 needs to begin with a word that signals such a contrast. "However" accomplishes this task. The other answer choices do not suggest contrast; in fact, they suggest that sentence 6 will offer a logical continuation of the idea that is expressed in sentence 5.

5. **(B)** The original has a problem of pronoun-antecedent agreement. According to this sentence, "the produce" is at risk of spoiling. "Produce" is a singular noun. Singular pronouns refer to singular nouns, so the plural pronoun "they" should be replaced by the singular pronoun "it." (A) and (C) are wrong because they do not solve the problem of pronoun-antecedent agreement. (D) and (E) fail to use the conditional "would." (B) is the only answer choice that both maintains the conditional parallel and solves the problem of pronoun-antecedent agreement.

6. **(A)** The original is correct. (B), (D), and (E) are wrong because they incorrectly introduce the present tense into a sentence that clearly describes past activity ("during the winter months"). (C) is wrong because it uses a present perfect construction. A present perfect construction describes activity anterior to the moment of speech. What the speaker wants to express here, however, is that the preservation of food was important at the same time as the past winter months. (C) does not express that subtlety.

7. **(B)** The original has a problem of subject-verb agreement. The singular noun "nothing" requires a singular form. So, (A) and (D) can be eliminated. (C) and (E) solve the problem of subject-verb agreement, but they incorrectly

indicate past activity. In the third paragraph, the discussion of home-canning takes place in the present tense. (B) is the only answer choice that supplies a singular form and keeps the discussion in the present tense.

8. **(E)** The original suffers from faulty parallelism. The three elements in the series are not expressed in the same form ("packed...fitted...you submerge them"). In order to solve this problem, the final verb in the series must be made parallel with the preceding verbs ("packed...fitted...submerged"). (E) accomplishes this task.

9. **(C)** The original implies that the killing of dangerous organisms causes food to spoil. (B) and (E) indicate that the organisms had already caused spoilage at the time of the heating. Finally, (D) incorrectly asserts that the goal of the killing is spoilage.

10. **(E)** As written, the original incorrectly implies that the vacuum does the cooling. (C) and (D) are wrong for the same reason; they incorrectly imply that the vacuum gradually cools. (B) is wrong because it begins the sentence with a pronoun that has no clear antecedent. (E) is correct because it provides a noun and correctly asserts that jars, not a vacuum, are being cooled.

11. **(A)** The original is correct. (C), (D), and (E) are wrong because they indicate that the organisms already have entered, or are in the process of entering. They incorrectly imply that organisms can enter the jar prior to the breaking of the seal. (B) is wrong because it suggests current activity rather than conditional activity.

12. **(B)** The original suffers from a problem of subject-verb agreement. The singular form "seems" does not agree with the plural subject of the sentence ("jams and jellies"). (C) is wrong for the same reason. The last paragraph takes place in the present tense, so (D) and (E) are wrong because they incorrectly introduce future and past activity, respectively. (B) is the only answer choice that solves both the problem of subject-verb agreement and the discrepancy of tense.

13. **(B)** The last paragraph is descriptive. It describes home-canning, homemade jams and jellies, and how you will enjoy giving these homemade preserves as gifts. The original is wrong because it incorrectly indicates present activity and implies that "you" already enjoy the practice of giving homemade preserves as gifts. However, the last paragraph actually assumes that you have not yet made preserves (Sentence 17 suggests finding a book about home-canning.). In fact, you first need to make the preserves before you can give them away; so, the future tense is required. (C), (D), and (E) are wrong because they do not indicate future activity.

14. **(C)** The original suffers from a shift in pronoun case. The last paragraph establishes that the author is addressing a 2nd person audience ("when you have made them yourself" and "You also enjoy"). However, the original unnecessarily switches from addressing "you" to addressing "one." (B) is wrong because it creates a grammatically incorrect sentence without a proper subject. (D) and (E) are wrong for the same reason as the original.

15. **(A)** The sentence has a dangling modifier. As written, the sentence implies that Emily Dickinson herself was written. To correct this error, it would have to be rewritten to bring the introductory modifier closer to the noun it modifies (poems): "Emily Dickinson's poems, written in almost total isolation from the world, spoke of love and death."

16. **(D)** The use of the perfect tense "had given up" is not consistent with the use of the past tense "entertained," for the use of the perfect tense implies that the pianist gave up his attempt to become a composer before he even entertained the idea of becoming one. The sentence can be corrected by substituting "gave up" for "had given up."

17. **(B)** The sentence commits an error of illogical expression, for, as written, it implies that the fans' leaving the stadium would ordinarily be sufficient to halt a game and reschedule it for later. The problem of illogical expression can be corrected by substituting the conjunction "but" for "even though."

18. **(A)** The sentence has a dangling modifier. It implies that the bank president is highly qualified for the position. The sentence needs major revision: "The bank president will conduct a final interview of the new candidate tomorrow. Since the candidate is highly qualified for the position, the president will make her a job offer after the interview."

19. **(C)** The sentence commits an error of logical expression by implying that the "reason" is an effect of some other cause, when the speaker really means to say that the reason and the cause are the same thing, the explanation for the phenomenon. The error can be corrected by substituting "that" for "because." (Note: This use of "because" to introduce a noun clause can also be considered an example of an expression that is not acceptable in English usage.)

20. **(A)** The sentence contains a dangling modifier. As written, it implies that the police officer is listening in broken English (not listening to broken English). The sentence can be corrected by relocating the modifier: "The police officer patiently listened to the tourist ask in broken English for directions to Radio City Music Hall,...."

21. **(C)** The choice of "since" is illogical, because "since" implies that there is a causal or explanatory connection between Hemingway's view of bullfighting and the fact that bullfighting is a controversial sport that repulses some people. The problem of illogical subordination can be corrected by substituting "but" for "since."

22. **(D)** The sentence contains a misplaced modifier. As written, it implies that Peter hopes to learn how to protect his investments from the threat posed by a well-known investment banker. The sentence must be rewritten: "...in order to learn from a well-known investment banker methods to protect his investments."

23. **(D)** The sentence makes an error of logical expression, for it seems to compare our space program to the Soviet Union. The error is eliminated by using the phrase "to that of" instead of "to" after "superior."

24. **(B)** The sentence contains a misplaced modifier. The placement of "only" seems to imply a restriction on the verb rather than on the subject. The sentence is easily corrected by moving "only" and placing it just before "licensed lawyers."

25. **(A)** The sentence contains a dangling modifier and seems to compare ballerinas of the romantic ballet with the movement of Judith Jamison. To correct this error, the sentence would have to be substantially rewritten: "Judith Jamison's movement seems more African than European-American, and her physical appearance, which is unlike that of the pale and delicately built ballerinas of romantic ballet, reinforces the contrast."

26. **(D)** The sentence contains an error of logical expression. It attempts to compare an amount of decaffeinated coffee with coffee containing caffeine. The sentence can be corrected by inserting clarifying phrases: "...the number of tons of coffee containing caffeine consumed by Americans."

27. **(D)** The sentence contains a misplaced modifier. As written, it implies that the workers are illiterate because they do not know how to read on the job. The sentence can be corrected by relocating the offending phrase so that it is closer to the noun it modifies: "... many mistakes are made on the job by workers...."

28. **(D)** The sentence makes an illogical statement. It attempts to compare "men" and "branch of the service." The sentence can be corrected by inserting a clarifying phrase: "...than do men in any other branch...."

29. **(A)** The sentence contains a dangling modifier. It implies a comparison between A.J. Ayer, the person, and the writings of Gilbert Ryle. The error can be corrected in the following way: "Like the writing of A.J. Ayer, much of...."

30. "The life of my generation is easier than that of my parents."

   The original suffers from a faulty comparison. It attempts to compare "The life of my generation" with "my parents." However, unlike items cannot logically be compared; a comparison can only be made between like items. In the corrected sentence, the phrase "that of" is inserted before "my parents" in order to make a logical comparison. Now, one life (of a generation) is compared to another life (of parents).

31. "My two daughters enjoy different TV shows; the older one watches game shows, while the younger one prefers talk shows."

The original is wrong because it incorrectly uses the superlative forms of the adjectives "old" and "young" ("oldest" and "youngest"). The superlative form is only used when three or more items are compared. In the original, however, only two items (two daughters) are compared. In the corrected sentence, the comparative forms of the adjectives "old" and "young" ("older" and "younger") are used.

32. "Her present instructor is the best of all the ones she has had so far."

The original is wrong because it incorrectly uses the comparative form of the adjective "good" ("better"). The comparative form is only used when two items are compared. In the original, however, the "present instructor" is compared to all previous instructors. In other words, at least three items are compared. In the corrected sentence, the superlative form of the adjective "good" ("best") is used.

33. "In the technology lab, I choose the computer with the greatest memory."

The original is wrong for two reasons. First, it incorrectly uses two techniques to express a comparison when only technique is required. Two items can either be compared by adding "-er" to the adjective or by placing "more" before the adjective. "More greater" is grammatically incorrect. Second, the original incorrectly uses the comparative form. The comparative form is used when two items are compared. However, it is logical to assume that there are more than two computers in the technology lab. In the corrected sentence, the superlative form of the adjective "great" ("greatest") is used in place of "more greater."

34. "According to the counselor, taking these classes in this order is much more beneficial than the other way around."

In the original, two items are compared (taking classes "in this order" and taking classes "the other way around," or in the opposite order). When two items are compared using an adjective, the comparative form of that adjective is required. However, the original fails to use the comparative form. Since "beneficialer" is not a word, the word "more" must be used. In the corrected sentence, "more" is placed before "beneficial."

35. "Our school is unique in many aspects."

The original is wrong because it unnecessarily uses an adverb to modify the adjective "unique." "Unique" already expresses the highest degree of individuality; there are no comparative or superlative forms of this adjective. In the corrected sentence, the adverb "very" is omitted.

36. "The fraternity he joined is better than all other fraternities."

The original is wrong because it illogically compares a "fraternity" to itself. When the comparative form of an adjective ("better") is used in an expression to compare one item to any other item of that kind, an adjective such as "other" or "else" is required to separate the initial item from the rest of the items. For example, the statement "Tom is better than any boy" is illogical because it incorrectly implies that Tom is also better than himself. However, the statement "Tom is better than any other boy" makes a logical comparison between Tom and other boys. In the corrected sentence, the adjective "other" is placed before "fraternities."

37. The original is correct. Two items are compared, and they are expressed as like items ("Professor Baker's explanations" and "Professor Thomas' explanations").

38. The original is correct. Two experiences are compared (learning "online" and learning "in a regular classroom"), and the sentence correctly uses the comparative form of "many/much" ("more").

39. "Which of these three sections is best?"

The original is wrong because it uses the comparative form ("better") when the superlative form ("best") should be used. Three items are compared ("three sections"). When more than two items are compared, the superlative form of the adjective is required. In the corrected sentence, "better" is replaced with "best."

40. "I am spending more time on the assignments in my management class than on those in all my other classes combined."

The original suffers from a faulty comparison. It attempts to compare "assignments in my management class" with "all my other classes combined." However, unlike items cannot logically be compared; a comparison can only be made between like items. In the corrected sentence, the phrase "those in" is inserted before "all my other classes combined" in order to make a logical comparison. Now, assignments (in management class) are compared to other assignments (in all other classes combined).

41. "You will receive your grades no later than tomorrow at 2 p.m."

The original is wrong because it uses the superlative form of "late" ("latest") when the comparative form ("later") should be used. Two items are compared (an unspecified time when grades will be issued and the specific time of 2 p.m. tomorrow). When two items are compared, the comparative form of the adjective is required. In the corrected sentence, "latest" is replaced with "later."

42. "There is no need for further negotiation."

The original uses the wrong comparative form of the adjective "far." "Farther" is the form that is typically used to describe distance (e.g., "farther down the road"). "Further" is the form that is typically used to describe extent or degree (e.g., "further negotiations" or "further studies"). In the original, the extent of current negotiations is discussed. Therefore, the comparative form "further" is required.

43. "She is doing so badly in her art class that she could not do any worse."

The original is wrong because it uses the superlative form of "bad" ("worst") when the comparative form ("worse") should be used. Two items are compared (the woman's current performance in art class and her possible performance in art class). When two items are compared, the comparative form of the adjective is required. In the corrected sentence, "worst" is replaced with "worse."

44. "This exercise seems more difficult than all of the others."

The original is wrong because it illogically compares an "exercise" to itself. When the comparative form of an adjective ("more difficult") is used in an expression to compare one item to any other item of that kind, an adjective such as "other" or "else" is required to separate the initial item from the rest of the items. In the corrected sentence, "more difficult than all of them" is changed to "more difficult than all of the others."

45. "Going to school, he tripped on a crack in the pavement."

The original suffers from a misplaced modifier ("going to school"). Remember that a modifier should be placed as close as possible to what it modifies. Otherwise, the modifier might appear to modify some other element in the sentence. In the original, "going to school" is intended to modify "tripped." However, these two elements appear at opposite ends of the sentence. As a result, it sounds as though the pavement is going to school. In the corrected sentence, "going to school" is placed at the beginning of the sentence.

46. "Only Mary failed the test; everyone else in her class passed."

Simply by its placement, the word "only" can drastically change the entire meaning of a sentence. In the original, "only" is placed before "failed." As a result, it sounds as though Mary failed the test but did not fail anything else. However, the second half of the sentence clearly states that all of her classmates passed the test. Therefore, the original intends to say that Mary was the only student in her class who failed the test. In the corrected sentence, "only" is placed before "Mary" so that the intended meaning is made clear.

47. "Did you see the film on television about the five people on the boat?"

The original suffers from a misplaced modifier ("on television"). Remember that a modifier should be placed as close as possible to what it modifies. Otherwise, the modifier might appear to modify some other element in the sentence. In the original, "on television" is intended to modify "see" (the film is actually being shown on television). However, these two elements appear nearly at opposite ends of the sentence. As a result, it sounds as though the film is about a television program involving five people on a boat. In the corrected sentence, "on television" is placed immediately after "the film."

48. "The police officer, in his patrol car, ordered the man to stop."

The original suffers from a misplaced modifier ("in his patrol car"). In the original, "in his patrol car" is intended to modify "the police officer." However, these two elements appear at opposite ends of the sentence. As a result, it sounds either as though "the man" (rather than "the police officer") is in his own patrol car or he is in the police officer's patrol car. In the corrected sentence, "in his patrol car" is placed after "the police officer."

49. "When you picked up the phone, the noise became muted."

The original is unclear because the modifier ("Upon picking up the phone") modifies a subject that does not actually appear in the sentence. Who picked up the phone? As a result of this absence, the modifier incorrectly modifies the noun that is closest to it ("the noise"). In the corrected sentence, an actual subject ("you") is introduced, indicating that a person picked up the phone.

50. "While I was swimming, a fish nibbled on my toe."

The original is unclear because the modifier ("While swimming") modifies a subject that does not actually appear in the sentence. Who was swimming? As a result of this absence, the modifier incorrectly modifies the noun that is closest to it ("a fish"). Of course, we can be quite certain that the fish was swimming when it bit the toe; after all, fish are always swimming. Also, the possessive pronoun "my" indicates that the toe belongs to a person. Therefore, the modifier could not have been intended to modify "a fish." In the corrected sentence, an actual subject ("I") is introduced, indicating that a person was swimming.

51. The original is correct, unless the author intends to say that the church is on Cemetery Hill. The proximity of "on Cemetery Hill" to "people" suggests that the people are on Cemetery Hill, not the church.

52. "Of all his admirers, only his wife loved him."

Simply by its placement, the word "only" can drastically change the entire meaning of a sentence. In the original, "only" is placed before "loved." As a result, it sounds as though the wife had limited affection for her husband (she only loved him). However, "Of all his admirers" makes it clear that this is not the intended meaning. The original intends to say that although he had many admirers, only his wife actually loved him. In the corrected sentence, "only" is placed before "his wife" so that the intended meaning is made clear.

53. "When we entered the class, the blackboard came into view."

The original is unclear because the modifier ("Upon entering the class") modifies a subject that does not actually appear in the sentence. Who entered the class? As a result of this absence, the modifier incorrectly modifies the noun that is closest to it ("the blackboard"). In the corrected sentence, an actual subject ("we") is introduced, indicating that a group of persons entered the class.

54. "The baby was in a stroller pushed by his mother."

The original suffers from a misplaced modifier ("in a stroller"). In the original, "in a stroller" is intended to modify "the baby." However, these two elements are separated by the phrase "was pushed by his mother." As a result, it sounds as though the mother was in the stroller. In the corrected sentence, "in a stroller" is placed closer to "the baby," indicating that the baby is in the stroller.

55. "She likes tennis, golf, and swimming."

The original suffers from faulty parallelism. The three elements in the series are not expressed in the same form ("tennis…golf…to go swimming"). The first two items are nouns ("tennis" and "golf"), but the third item is a verb ("to go swimming"). In the corrected sentence, the verb "to go swimming" is replaced by the noun "swimming."

56. "He could not deliver the supplies because the roads had not yet been plowed."

The original is wrong because it treats a dependent clause ("because the roads had not yet been plowed") as an independent clause. A dependent clause cannot stand by itself. By definition, a dependent clause depends on another clause for its meaning and completeness. In the original, "because the roads had not yet been plowed" does not have any clear meaning as a separate sentence. What was the result of the roads not being plowed? In the corrected version, the period between "supplies" and "Because" is omitted, forming two separate sentences. Now, the dependent clause "because the roads had not yet been plowed" functions properly.

57. "If you want to succeed, you must be willing to work hard."

"If one wants to succeed, one must be willing to work hard."

The original suffers from a shift in pronoun case. It switches from addressing "you" to addressing "one." Pronoun case should remain consistent.

58. "Jeff is taller than any other boy in his class."

The original is wrong because it illogically compares "Jeff" to himself. When the comparative form of an adjective ("taller") is used in an expression to compare one item to any other item of that kind, an adjective such as "other" or "else" is required to separate the initial item from the rest of the items. The original intends to say that Jeff is taller than any other boy in his class. In the corrected sentence, the adjective "other" is simply placed before "boy."

59. "To get to school, we walked nearly two miles."

The original suffers from a misplaced modifier ("nearly"). Remember that a modifier should be placed as close as possible to what it modifies. Otherwise, the modifier might appear to modify some other element in the sentence. In the original, "nearly" is intended to modify "two miles." However, these two elements are separated by the verb "walked." As a result, it sounds as though they nearly, but did not actually, walk. In the corrected sentence, "nearly" is placed before "two miles," indicating how far they walked.

60. "The heroine was unbelievably naive."

The original is wrong because it uses an adjective ("unbelievable") to modify another adjective ("naïve"). Adverbs should be used to modify adjectives. In the corrected sentence, the adjective "unbelievable" is replaced by the adverb "unbelievably."

61. The original is correct. The adverb "carefully" is used to modify the verb "drive." Also, the two independent clauses are punctuated as two separate sentences.

62. "Leaning out the window, she could see the garden below."

The original is unclear because the modifier ("leaning out the window") modifies a subject that does not actually appear in the sentence. Who leaned out the window? As a result of this absence, the modifier incorrectly modifies the noun that is closest to it ("the garden"). In the corrected sentence, an actual subject ("she") is introduced, indicating that a female person leaned out the window.

63. "The hotel room that we had reserved was clean and comfortable."

The original suffers from a misplaced modifier ("that we had reserved"). In the original, "that we had reserved" is intended to modify "The hotel room." However, these two elements are separated by the clause "was clean and comfortable." As a result, "that we had reserved" modifies the adjective "comfortable," but this relationship makes no sense and the resulting sentence is grammatically incorrect. In the corrected sentence, "that we reserved" is placed after "The hotel room," indicating that they had reserved the hotel room.

64. "This book is heavier than that one."

The original is needlessly wordy. The comparative form of "heavy" ("heavier") clearly indicates that the weights of two books are compared. Therefore, the phrase "in weight" is redundant. In the corrected sentence, the phrase "in weight" is omitted.

## EXERCISE 4—IDIOMS AND CLARITY OF EXPRESSION (p. 617)

1. The adjective "principal" is the correct answer choice. "Principal" means "chief" or "main," which is the intended meaning in this context. ("He is the main backer of the play.") The noun "principle" means "truth" or "rule." Since an adjective is required to successfully complete the sentence, the noun "principle" is the wrong word choice in this context because it is not an adjective.

2. The verb "accept" is the correct answer choice. "Accept" means "to agree to," which is the intended meaning in this context. ("I hope your company will agree to our offer.") The verb "except" means "to leave out" or "to object to." However, someone does not typically hope that another company will object to their offer. The preposition "except" means "other than," but since a verb is required to successfully complete the sentence, the preposition "except" is the wrong word choice in this context.

3. The noun "weather" is the correct answer choice. "Weather" means "atmospheric conditions," which is the intended meaning in this context. The conjunction "whether" means "if." Since a noun is required to successfully complete the sentence, the conjunction "whether" is the wrong word choice in this context because it cannot be modified by the adjective "good."

4. The preposition "into" is the correct answer choice. "Into" indicates something that moves from one place to the inside or interior of another place. The sentence intends to say that the rabbit moves from outside of the hat back "into" the hat. The preposition "in" does not indicate the necessary facet of movement.

5. The verb "advise" is the correct answer choice. "Advise" means "to offer advice," which is the intended meaning in this context. The noun "advice" means "information about what should be done in a particular situation." Furthermore, a verb is required to successfully complete the sentence, the noun "advice" is the wrong word choice in this context.

6. The conjunction "than" is the correct answer choice. "Than" is used after comparative adjectives or adverbs in order to introduce the second item in a comparison. The sentence intends to make a comparison between

someone's actual height and her imagined height. The adverb "then" is used to indicate when something happened or the result/consequence of an event (e.g., "If you knock, then I will enter."). Since a conjunction is required to successfully complete the sentence, the adverb "then" is the wrong word choice in this context.

7. The phrase "all ready" is the correct answer choice. As a self-contained phrase, this noun ("all") and adjective ("ready") combination means "completely prepared." As two separate words, the phrase "all ready" means "all of them are prepared." In either case, the phrase expresses the intended meaning and properly modifies "they." The adverb "already" means "by a certain time." Since an adverb cannot modify a pronoun ("they"), "already" is the wrong word choice in this context.

8. The noun "stationery" is the correct answer choice. "Stationery" means "writing paper," which is the intended meaning in this context. ("She answered the letter on shocking pink writing paper.") The adjective "stationary" means "standing still." Since a noun is required to successfully complete the sentence, the adjective "stationary" is the wrong word choice in this context.

9. The noun "effect" is the correct answer choice. As a noun, "effect" means "result," which is the intended meaning in this context. ("What is the result you are trying to achieve?") The verb "affect" means "to produce an effect in." Since a noun is required to successfully complete the sentence, the verb "affect" is the wrong word choice in this context.

10. The verb "sit" is the correct answer choice. "Sit" means "to seat oneself," which is the intended meaning in this context. ("I want to seat myself next to my grandfather.") The verb "set" means "to place something down," and it is the wrong word choice in this context. The speaker does not want to set something next to his or her grandfather.

11. The verb "lie" is the correct answer choice. As a verb, "lie" means "to recline," which is the intended meaning in this context. The verb "lay" means "to put," and it is the wrong word choice in this context.

12. The adverb "altogether" is the correct answer choice. "Altogether" means "entirely," which is the intended meaning in this context. The speaker says that he or she is entirely tired of someone else's excuses. The phrase "all together" is used to describe a group that is acting in unison. Since an adverb is required to successfully complete the sentence, the phrase "all together" is the wrong word choice in this context.

13. The past tense verb "passed" is the correct answer choice. "Pass" means "to move past something," which is the intended meaning in this context. The adjective "past" means "at an earlier time." Since a verb is required to successfully complete the sentence, the adjective "past" is the wrong word choice in this context.

14. The noun "dessert" is the correct answer choice. "Dessert" means "the final course of a meal," which is the intended meaning in this context. Since a noun is required to successfully complete the sentence, the verb "desert," which means "to abandon," is the wrong word choice in this context. The noun "desert" means "an arid area," but that is not the intended meaning in this context.

15. The verb "lose" is the correct answer choice. "Lose" means "to misplace" or "to be unable to keep," and "to be unable to keep," which is the intended meaning in this context. The adjective "loose" means "not fastened or restrained." Since a verb is required to successfully complete the sentence, the adjective "loose" is the wrong word choice in this context.

16. The verb "affect" is the correct answer choice. "Affect" means "to change" or "to influence," which is the intended meaning in this context. The speaker wants to know how much the final examination will influence his or her grade. "Effect" can function as either a verb or a noun, and a verb is required to successfully complete the sentence. However, the verb "effect" means "to cause" or "to bring about," and neither of these meanings is intended in this context.

17. The contraction "you're" is the correct answer choice. "You're" is a shortened version of the phrase "you are," and it successfully completes the sentence. The possessive pronoun "your" is the wrong word choice in this context because it results in a sentence without a verb.

18. "Used" is the correct answer choice. "Used to" is an idiomatic expression that means "accustomed to," which is the intended meaning in this context. ("She's not accustomed to such cold weather.") "Use" can function as either a verb or a noun. The verb "use" means "to employ" or "to put into service," and the noun "use" means "the manner of using, or usage." "Use to," however, is a the correct idiomatic expression.

19. The verb "rise" is the correct answer choice. "Rise" means "to increase," which is the intended meaning in this context. The verb "raise" means "to lift" or "to erect." The cost of the coat will increase; however, the sentence does not emphasize anyone acting to "raise" the price.

20. "Supposed" is the correct answer choice. "Supposed to" is an idiomatic expression that means "ought to" or "should"; in this context, "supposed" successfully completes the sentence. The verb "suppose" means "to assume" or "to guess." "Suppose to," however, is not a correct idiomatic expression.

21. The possessive pronoun "its" is the correct answer choice. A possessive pronoun is used before a noun to indicate that the noun belongs to someone or something else. In this context, the pronoun "its" indicates that the bowl belongs to the cat. The contraction "it's" is a shortened version of the phrase "it is," which is the wrong word choice in this context.

22. The adjective "conscious" is the correct answer choice. "Conscious" means "aware," which is the intended meaning in this context. ("Are you aware of what you are doing?") The noun "conscience" means "the ability to recognize the difference between right and wrong." Since an adjective is required to successfully complete the sentence, the noun "conscience" is the wrong word choice in this context because it is not an adjective.

23. The verb "seem" is the correct answer choice. "Seem" means "to appear," which is the correct meaning in this context. The past participle "seen" does not work grammatically in this sentence. A correct sentence could be formed with "be seen", but that is not an answer choice.

24. The plural noun "allusions" is the correct answer choice. "Allusions" means "references," which is the intended meaning in this context. "Literary allusions" are references to other works of literature. The plural noun "illusions" means "wrong ideas" or "wrong perceptions," and it is the wrong word choice in this context. While an entirely possible word choice, "literary allusions" is an idiomatic expression, and thus should be preferred.

25. The noun "complement" is the correct answer choice. "Complement" means "a completing part," which is the intended meaning in this context. The noun "compliment" means "an expression of praise or admiration," and it is the wrong word choice in this context. While a bottle of wine might be worthy of a compliment, a bottle of wine itself cannot be a compliment.

26. The adjective "later" is the correct answer choice. "Later" is a comparative adjective that compares two times, in this instance the time of speech and the time thought. The adjective "latter" means "the second of two," which is the wrong word choice in this context. "Latter" incorrectly implies that the sentence is about two things, two choices, or two persons. Furthermore, it cannot be used in conjunction with the comparative "than." Something cannot be more "latter" than something else.

27. The noun "build" is the correct answer choice. As a noun, "build" means "physical makeup" or "body," which is the intended meaning in this context. ("My cousin has a swimmer's body.") As a verb, "build" means "to construct," and "built" is the past tense form of this verb. Since a noun is required to successfully complete the sentence, the verb "built" is the wrong word choice in this context.

28. The past tense verb "knew" is the correct answer choice. "Know" means "to be familiar with" or "to understand," and "to be familiar with," which is the intended meaning in this context. ("I was never familiar with him before today.") The adjective "new" means "of recent origin." Since a verb is required to successfully complete the sentence, the adjective "new" is the wrong word choice in this context.

29. The adjective "personal" is the correct answer choice. "Personal" means "of or relating to a person's character, conduct, or affairs," which is the intended meaning in this context. The noun "personnel" means "an organized body of individuals," and it is the wrong word choice in this context. While it is possible to ask a "personnel question," or a question regarding personnel, "personal question" is idiomatic, and thus should be preferred.

30. The noun "course" is the correct answer choice. "Course" means "path," and a "golf course" is a place where people play golf. The adjective "coarse" means "vulgar" or "harsh," which is the wrong word choice in this context.

31. The adjective "cloth" is the correct answer choice. The noun "cloth" means "a type of fabric used for a specific purpose." The verb "clothe" means "to put on clothes" or "to dress," and it is the wrong word choice in this context.

32. The verb "elude" is the correct answer choice. "Elude" means "to escape from" or "to avoid," which is the intended meaning in this context. ("The ball carrier was trying to avoid the tacklers.") The verb "allude" means "to make reference to," which is the wrong meaning in this context.

33. The adverb "no" is the correct answer choice. "No" is a negative that indicates denial, refusal, absence, or lack. The sentence intends to say that there was a lack of exhibitions. The verb "know" means "to have knowledge" or "to understand." Since an adverb is required to successfully complete the sentence, the verb "know" is the wrong word choice in this context.

34. The prefix "ante" is the correct answer choice. "Ante" means "before." An "anteroom" is a room that is located before, or in front of, another room. The prefix "anti" means "against." However, there is no such room as an "anti room."

35. The noun "morale" is the correct answer choice. "Morale" means "spirit," which is the intended meaning in this context. Since a noun is required to successfully complete the sentence, the adjective "moral," which means "ethical," is the wrong word choice in this context. The noun "moral" means "lesson," but that is not the intended meaning in this context.

36. The adjective "capital" is the correct answer choice. "Capital" can function as either a noun or an adjective. As a noun, "capital" means "place of government" or "wealth." As an adjective, "capital" means "upper case," which is the intended meaning in this context. The noun "capitol" means "a building where government or legislatures are located." Since an adjective is required to successfully complete the sentence, the noun "capitol" is the wrong word choice in this context.

37. The verb "faze" is the correct answer choice. "Faze" means "to worry" or "to disturb," which is the intended meaning in this context. "Phase" can function as either a verb or a noun, and a verb is required to successfully complete the sentence. However, the verb "phase" means "to carry out in stages," which is not the intended meaning in this context.

38. "Excess" is the correct answer choice. "In excess of" means "a state surpassing specified limits," which is the intended meaning in this context; therefore, "excess" successfully completes the sentence. "Access" can function as either a noun or a verb. The noun "access" means "availability," and the verb "access" means "to get at." However, neither of these meanings successfully completes the sentence.

39. The verb "proceed" is the correct answer choice. "Proceed" means "to go ahead" or "to continue," which is the intended meaning in this context. ("Now, may we continue with the debate?") The verb "precede" means "to come or go before," and it is the wrong word choice in this context.

40. The noun "forte" is the correct answer choice. "Forte" means "strength," which is the intended meaning in this context. ("Her strength is writing lyrics for musical comedy.") The noun "fort" means "a fortified place," which is an incorrect word choice in this context.

41. The verb "disperse" is the correct answer choice. "Disperse" means "to scatter," which is the intended meaning in this context. ("They wondered how they were going to scatter the huge crowd.") The verb "disburse" means "to pay out," and it is the wrong word choice in this context. While it is possible to disburse something (e.g., money) to a huge crowd, the sentence as it stands implies that the payment would be comprised of the crowd, which is unlikely.

42. The adverb "formally" is the correct answer choice. "Formally" means "in a formal way." The sentence intends to say that everyone was wearing formal attire for the dinner party. So, everyone was most likely dressed in tuxedos, evening gowns, etc. The adverb "formerly" means "before" or "at an earlier time;" placed before "dressed", "formerly" could be idiomatic, but at the insertion point, it would not be.

43. The adjective "averse" is the correct answer choice. "Averse" means "having a feeling of opposition or dislike," which is the intended meaning in this context; it is used to describe a person or group of persons. ("I am not opposed to continuing the discussion at another time.") The adjective "adverse" means "serving to oppose" or "unfavorable," and it is the wrong word choice in this context; it is used to describe circumstances (e.g., "they fought the battle under adverse conditions").

44. The noun "incidence" is the correct answer choice. "Incidence" means "the frequency of occurrence," which is the intended meaning in this context. The speaker asks if something can be done to diminish the frequency with which influenza occurs. The plural noun "incidents" means "events," but it does not make sense for events to be diminished.

45. The adjective "dual" is the correct answer choice. "Dual" means "double, " which is the intended meaning in this context. The speaker says that seeing the film in class will serve two purposes. The noun "duel" means "a contest between two persons or groups," and it is the wrong word choice in this context.

46. The verb "expend" is the correct answer choice. "Expend" means "to use up," which is the intended meaning in this context. ("I'm not sure I want to use up so much energy on that project.") The verb "expand" means "to spread out," which is the wrong word choice in this context.

47. The noun "discomfort" is the correct answer choice. "Discomfort" means "lack of ease," which is the intended meaning in this context. ("Imagine my lack of ease when she showed up at the party too!) The verb "discomfit" means "to upset." Since a noun is required to successfully complete the sentence, "discomfit" is the wrong word choice in this context.

48. The noun "idol" is the correct answer choice. "Idol" means "image or object of worship," which is the intended meaning in this context, as indicated by the adjective "famous." The adjective "idle" means "unemployed or unoccupied." Since a noun is required to successfully complete the sentence, "idle" is the wrong word choice in this context.

49. The verb "emigrate" is the correct answer choice. "Emigrate" means "to leave a country," which is the intended meaning in this context. The verb "immigrate" means "to enter a country," and it is the wrong word choice in this context. The position of the preposition "from" in relationship to the verb "emigrate" indicates the intended meaning of the sentence. If the two prepositions were inverted, then "immigrate" would be the correct answer choice.

50. The noun "clique" is the correct answer choice. "Clique" means "an exclusive group of people," which is the intended meaning in this context. ("I think she is part of an exclusive group of snobs and creeps.") The noun "click" means "a brief, sharp sound," and it is the wrong word choice in this context.

51. The noun "prophecy" is the correct answer choice. "Prophecy" means "prediction, which is the intended meaning in this context. ("She paid little attention to the fortune-teller's prediction.") The verb "prophesy" means "to predict." "Prophecy" and "prophesy" have similar meanings; however, since a noun is required to successfully complete the sentence, "prophesy" is the wrong word choice in this context.

52. The noun "lightning" is the correct answer choice. "Lightning" means "the electric discharge in the atmosphere that precedes or accompanies rain." The sentence intends to say that the lights go out when the house is struck by an electric bolt or discharge. The progressive verb "lightening" means "making less heavy." Since a noun is required to successfully complete the sentence, the verb "lightening" is the wrong word choice in this context.

53. The adjective "whatever" is the correct answer choice. "Whatever" means "any or anything," which is the intended meaning in this context. The speaker offers to provide any assistance that is required. "What ever" is simply a misspelled version of "whatever."

54. The adjective "imminent" is the correct answer choice. "Imminent" means "impending" or "immediate," which is the intended meaning in this context. ("We are in immediate danger of losing our reservations.") The adjective "eminent" means "prominent" or "outstanding," and it is the wrong word choice in this context. It would not be idiomatic to describe the loss of reservations as a prominent or outstanding danger.

55. The verb "adapt" is the correct answer choice. "Adapt" means "to change" or "to adjust," which is the intended meaning in this context. ("Will she be able to adjust to our way of performing the operation?") The verb "adopt" means "to take in as one's own," and it is the wrong word choice in this context.

56. The noun "epitaphs" is the correct answer choice. "Epitaph" means "an inscription on a tombstone," which is the intended meaning in this context. ("As we went through the old cemetery, we were fascinated by some of the inscriptions on the tombstones." The noun "epithet" means "a term used to describe or characterize the nature of a thing or person," and it is the wrong word choice in this context. While it is quite possible for an epithet (e.g., "The Great Emancipator") to be part of an epitaph, the noun "cemetery" indicates that "epitaphs" is the better word choice in this context.

57. The preposition "among" is the correct answer choice. "Among" is used when referring to three or more people or things. The sentence intends to say that he shared the riches with three people ("Laura," "Millie," and "Ernestine"). The preposition "between" is used when referring to either two people or two things, which is not the case in this context.

58. The noun "benefit" is the correct answer choice. As a noun, "benefit" means "an advantage." Interestingly enough, the noun "advantage" means "benefit." However, "for his advantage" is not an idiomatic expression. The correct idiomatic expression is "for his benefit." The preposition "for" indicates the intended meaning of the sentence. If the preposition "for" were changed to the preposition "to," then "advantage" would be the correct answer choice ("to his advantage").

59. The adverb "a lot" is the correct answer choice. "A lot" means "a great number of" or "much," which is the intended meaning in this context. ("Much of the time, he falls asleep at nine o'clock.") "Alot" is simply a misspelled version of "a lot."

60. The noun "number" is the correct answer choice. "Number" is used when describing things that can be counted accurately, which is the intended meaning in this context since people can be counted accurately. The noun "amount" is used when describing things that cannot be counted accurately (e.g., "the amount of pain" or "the amount of effort"), and it is the wrong word choice in this context.

61. The adverb "almost" is the correct answer choice. "Almost" means "nearly," which is the intended meaning in this context. ("I see him in the park nearly every day.") The adjective "most" means "the majority of," and it is the wrong word choice in this context. "Most every day" is not an idiomatic expression.

62. The adjective "all right" is the correct answer choice. "All right" means "fine," which is the intended meaning in this context. ("Are you sure that he is fine now?") "Alright" is simply a misspelled version of "all right."

63. The verb "annoy" is the correct answer choice. "Annoy" means "to bother," which is the intended meaning in this context. ("She is just beginning to bother her mother.") The verb "aggravate" means "intensify an already troublesome situation." Because we cannot assume that the situation is already vexing, "annoy" is a more fitting choice.

64. The singular noun "alumnus" is the correct answer choice. "Alumnus" means "a graduate of a school," which is the intended meaning in this context. ("He is the school's oldest living graduate.") The plural noun "alumni" is the wrong word choice in this context because only one person is mentioned in the sentence.

65. The adverb "alongside" is the correct answer choice. "Alongside" means "to the side," which is the intended meaning in this context. ("He spotted the riverbank and then guided the canoe up to the side.") In this case, "alongside" properly modifies "guided." The preposition "alongside of" means "side by side with." Since an adverb is required to successfully complete the sentence, the preposition "alongside of" is the wrong word choice in this context; a sentence cannot end with a preposition.

66. The conjunction "since" is the correct answer choice. As a conjunction, "since" is another way to say "because," which is the intended meaning in this context. ("Because it is Wednesday, we are going to a Broadway matinee.")

67. The adjective "eager" is the correct answer choice. "Eager" means "having a great interest in" or "enthusiastic," and it is used when describing a thing that is desired. The sentence intends to say that he has a great desire to be finished with his dental treatment. The adjective "anxious" means "worried," and it is used when describing a thing that is not desired. We can be certain that he desires the conclusion of his dental treatment.

68. The verb "meet" is the correct answer choice. "Meet" means "to come into the presence of someone or something," which is the intended meaning in this context. "Meet at" is an example of low-level (informal) usage that might appear in casual conversation. It is the wrong word choice in this context because it creates a sentence that ends with a preposition.

69. The adverb "awhile" is the correct answer choice. "Awhile" means "for a short time," which is the intended meaning in this context. ("My aunt just went inside to rest for a short time.") "A while" is the proper form only when preceded by a preposition. Thus, "my aunt just went inside to rest for a while."

70. The adverb "about" is the correct answer choice. "About" means "approximately," which is the intended meaning in this context. ("It was approximately noon when we met for lunch.") As an adverb, "around" also means "approximately," but it is more suited for describing movement and position.

71. "Couple of" is the correct answer choice because it creates the appropriate adjective ("a couple of") to modify "books." The noun "couple" means "two persons or things." Since an adjective is required to successfully complete the sentence, the noun "couple" is the wrong word choice in this context.

72. "You and me" is the correct answer choice. Since both pronouns in this context are objects of the preposition "between," they should be in the objective case ("you" and "me"). The pronoun "I" is an example of the nominative (or subjective) case, so "you and I" is the wrong word choice in this context.

73. The adjective "continuous" is the correct answer choice. "Continuous" means "non-stop" or "proceeding without stopping," which is the intended meaning in this context. ("The non-stop ticking of the clock was very

disconcerting.") The adjective "continual" means "at frequent intervals," and it is the wrong word choice in this context. The clock does not tick at frequent intervals (with breaks in-between); instead, it ticks without any breaks at all.

74. "Seems unable" is the correct answer choice. The verb "seems" means "appears," which is the intended meaning in this context. ("She appears unable to get up early enough to eat breakfast with him.") "Cannot seem" is the wrong word choice in this context because the resulting sentence is vague and confusing. The verb "seem" means "appear." How can it be impossible for her to appear to get up early?

75. The verb "assume" is the correct answer choice. "Assume" means "to suppose," which is the intended meaning in this context. ("I suppose that you really earned your salary today.") The verb "expect" can also mean "to suppose," but it is an example of low-level (informal) usage that might appear in casual conversation; therefore, it is less acceptable in standard written English.

76. The adjective "uninterested" is the correct answer choice. "Uninterested" means "to have no interest," and that is the intended meaning in this context. The speaker has no interest in seeing the movie. The adjective "disinterested" means "unbiased by personal interest or advantage," and it is the wrong word choice in this context

77. "Just as" is the correct answer choice. "Just as" means "in the same way as," which is the intended meaning in this context. "Every bit as" is an example of low-level (informal) usage that might appear in casual conversation; therefore, it is less acceptable in standard written English. "Every bit as" is also needlessly wordy.

78. The conjunction "that" is the correct answer choice. As a conjunction, "that" is used to introduce a relative clause. In this context, "that" introduces "it will snow today." The conjunction "whether" is typically used to introduce the first of two or more alternatives, and it is incorrect in this context because the sentence is not about two or more alternatives.

79. The pronoun "one another" is the correct answer choice. "One another" is used when describing the relationship among three or more people. The sentence intends to say that four people ("Sam," "Joe," "Lou," and "Artie") worked together. The pronoun "each other" is used when describing the relationship between two people.

80. The conjunction "whether" is the correct answer choice. "Whether" is typically used to introduce the first of two or more alternatives. The sentence intends to introduce two alternatives ("to have lunch with her or to have lunch with her sister"). Interestingly enough, the conjunction "if" means "whether," but it is the wrong word choice in this context because it cannot be used to introduce the first of two or more alternatives. If "if" were used, the response to the question would be "yes" or "no." It would not present the choice between the sisters correctly.

81. The plural noun "human beings" is the correct answer choice. "Humans" can function as a plural noun, but the word "human" typically functions as an adjective rather than a singular noun. Therefore, "human beings" is the best word choice in this context.

82. The verb "finalize" is the correct answer choice. "Finalize" means "to agree on final details" or "to put into final form," which is the intended meaning in this context. ("We hope to put the deal into final form this month.") The verb "conclude" means "to end." However, someone does not typically hope to end a business deal; he or she typically hopes to begin a deal once the final details have been resolved. Therefore, "conclude" is the wrong word choice in this context.

83. The past tense verb "flouted" is the correct answer choice. "Flout" means "to disregard in a disrespectful way," which is the intended meaning in this context. ("We were upset when she disregarded her mother's orders.") The verb "flaunt" means "to show off" or "to display in an ostentatious manner," it would be unlikely to see someone showing off his or her mother's orders.

84. The adjective "healthful" is the correct answer choice. "Healthful" means "conducive to good health." The sentence intends to say that she eats foods that are conducive to (or likely to produce) good health. The adjective "healthy" means "possessing good health," and it is the wrong word choice in this context. Foods are typically not said to be in good health; instead, people or animals are said to be in good health.

85. The noun "slander" is the correct answer choice. "Slander" means "the attack of someone's reputation with spoken words," which is the intended meaning in this context ("He said such terrible things about her"). The noun "libel" means "the attack of someone's reputation with written words," and it is the wrong word choice in this context.

86. "Regard" is the correct answer choice. "In regard to" is an idiomatic expression that means "about," which is the intended meaning in this context. ("I would like to see you about the apartment you plan to rent.") "Regards" can function as either a plural noun or a singular verb. The plural noun "regards" means "sentiments of esteem or affection," and the singular verb "regards" means "observes" or "looks upon." "In regards to," however, is not an idiomatic expression.

87. The adverb "regardless" is the correct answer choice. "Regardless" means "without regard" or "in spite of." The sentence intends to say that she is always late for work in spite of the fact that she wakes up early in the morning. "Irregardless" is considered non-standard or low-level usage, and it is the wrong word choice in this context. It is redundant to add the negative prefix "ir-" to the root word "regardless."

88. The verb "lend" is the correct answer choice. "To lend a hand" is an idiomatic expression that means "to help." The sentence intends to say that he will help carry the groceries. "To loan a hand" is not an idiomatic expression.

89. The singular verb "is" is the correct answer choice. "Media" can function as either a plural noun or a singular noun. "Media" is the plural form of the singular noun "medium." However, the singular noun "media" means "a group of people who make up the communications industry," which is the intended meaning in this context. A group is singular; thus, the plural verb "are" is the wrong word choice in this context.

90. The preposition "off" is the correct answer choice. As a preposition, "off" means "so as to be removed from," which is the intended meaning in this context. "Off of" is an example of low-level (informal) usage that might appear in casual conversation; therefore, it is less acceptable in standard written English.

91. The verb "stop" is the correct answer choice. "To stop sending" is the correct idiomatic expression. "To quit sending" is not an idiomatic expression.

92. The conjunction "that" is the correct answer choice. As a conjunction, "that" can be used to introduce a noun clause ("she is hungry"). The conjunction "because" should not be used to introduce a noun clause.

93. The verb "manage" is the correct answer choice. "Manage" means "to direct," which is the intended meaning in this context. ("Does he direct the department efficiently?") The verb "run" has several definitions, one of which is "to operate" (e.g., "run a lawnmower"). However, the verb "run" cannot be used in this manner to describe people ("the department"). In this context, "run" is an example of low-level (informal) usage that might appear in casual conversation; therefore, it is less acceptable in standard written English.

94. The singular pronoun "his or her" is the correct answer choice. The antecedent, or referent, in this sentence is the singular "anyone." The plural pronoun "their" does not agree in number with the singular antecedent, and it is the wrong word choice in this context.

95. "Any other" is the correct answer choice. When comparing someone to the rest of a group, a word such as "other" or "else" is required to separate that person from the other members of the group. The sentence intends to say that she scored more points than every player on the team (except, of course, herself). In this context, the use of "any" would imply that she scored more points than herself, a logical impossibility.

96. The conjunction "but" is the correct answer choice. "But" is used to indicate the contrast between two things. The sentence intends to say that his very neat room stands in contrast to her very messy room. The conjunction "while" is also used to indicate contrast; however, it further suggests a causal connection between the two things (e.g., The reason for the neatness is in some way related to the reason for the messiness.). This causal connection, however, is not justified in this context.

97. "Try to" is the correct answer choice. "Try to" makes clear the fact that he will undertake only one activity ("being more pleasant to his sister"). On the other hand, "try and" incorrectly suggests that he will undertake two separate activities ("he will try" and "he will be more pleasant to his sister"). What will he try?

98. "Whoever" is the correct answer choice. This is a very difficult question. At first, it would appear that "whomever" is the correct answer choice since it comes after the verb and is the object of the preposition "to." Both of these reasons would typically justify using the objective case ("whomever"). However, in this instance, the object of the preposition "to" is the entire clause that follows. This clause requires a subject, and subjects are always expressed in the nominative case ("whoever").

99. The preposition "for" is the correct answer choice. The preposition "on" inadvertently creates the verb phrase "wait on." This verb phrase is used when talking about service or servants (e.g., "I will wait on your table tonight."), and it is the wrong word choice in this context.

100. **(C)** Either the gerund "lecturing" or the infinitive "to lecture" successfully completes the sentence.

101. **(A)** The meaning of the verb "forgot" changes, depending on whether it is followed by an infinitive or a gerund. In the case of the infinitive ("he forgot to meet me"), the sentence implies that he neglected to meet the speaker. In the case of the gerund ("he forgot meeting me"), the sentence implies that he failed to remember meeting the speaker. Since he reintroduced himself to the speaker, the gerund is required in this context.

102. **(B)** The meaning of the verb "remember" changes, depending on whether it is followed by an infinitive or a gerund. In the case of the infinitive ("please remember to arrive"), the sentence implies that the day of the test is in the future. In the case of the gerund ("please remember arriving"), the sentence implies that the day of the test is in the past. However, it is unlikely that a teacher would ask his or her students to remember when they arrived five minutes early to a test that they took in the past. Therefore, the infinitive is required in this context.

103. **(B)** The verb "hesitate" is almost always followed by an infinitive.

104. **(B)** The verb "proceed" is almost always followed by an infinitive.

105. **(C)** Either the gerund "accepting" or the infinitive "to accept" successfully completes the sentence.

106. **(A)** The verb "tolerate" is almost always followed by a gerund.

107. **(C)** Either the gerund "writing" or the infinitive "to write" successfully completes the sentence.

108. **(C)** Either the gerund "preparing" or the infinitive "to prepare" successfully completes the sentence.

109. **(A)** The meaning of the verb "tried" changes, depending on whether it is followed by an infinitive or a gerund. In the case of the infinitive ("The applicant tried to ask"), the sentence implies that applicant attempted but failed to ask for an extension. In the case of the gerund ("The applicant tried asking"), the sentence implies that the applicant asked for an extension but was rejected. Since the sentence says that the applicant's request was turned down, the gerund is required in this context.

110. **(B)** The verb "warn" is almost always followed by an infinitive.

111. **(A)** The verb "anticipate" is almost always followed by a gerund.

112. **(B)** The verb "force" is almost always followed by an infinitive.

113. **(C)** Either the gerund "hearing" or the infinitive "to hear" successfully completes the sentence.

114. **(A)** The verb phrase "spend time" is almost always followed by a gerund.

115. **(B)** The noun "relation" means "family member." The noun "relationship" means "connection," which is the intended meaning in this context; there is a connection between the amount of imported oil and the number of traffic accidents. Therefore, "relation" should be replaced with "relationship."

116. **(D)** The verb "lay" means "to put." The verb "lie" means "to recline," which is the intended meaning in this context; Westminster Abbey is a place where English notables and royalty are buried. Therefore, "lay" should be replaced with "lie."

117. **(B)** The verb "adopt" means "to take in as one's own." The verb "adapt" means "to change," which is the intended meaning in this context; the speaker is unsure whether the script can be changed to meet certain requirements. Therefore, "adopted" should be replaced with "adapted."

118. **(B)** The phrase "would of" is not acceptable in standard written English. This phrase is commonly confused with the contraction of "would have" ("would've") because they sound the same as one another. Therefore, "would of chosen" should be replaced with "would have chosen."

119. **(A)** "Get built" is low-level, or informal, usage that might appear in casual conversation. However, it is not acceptable in standard written English. The correct verb phrase is "are built."

120. **(C)** The expression "as much than" is not idiomatic. The correct idiomatic expression is "as much as." Therefore, "than" should be replaced with "as."

121. **(D)** The expression "neither...or..." is not idiomatic. When a negative statement is made about two separate things, the correct idiomatic expression is "neither...nor...." Therefore, "or" should be replaced with "nor."

122. **(D)** The original is wrong for two reasons. First, it suggests that Helen Walker's willingness to sing pleases the audience. While her willingness most certainly contributes to the audience's pleasure, the sentence intends to say specifically that Helen Walker's songs please the audience; an audience typically demands encores when it enjoys the actual performance. The infinitive "to please" would make it perfectly clear that it is her songs (rather than her willingness) that please the audience. Second, the original is incorrectly punctuated; there should be a comma between "song" and "which." Therefore, "which pleases" should be replaced with "to please."

123. **(C)** The original is needlessly wordy. The phrase "as to whether" should be replaced with "whether." The resulting sentence is more concise and less vague.

124. **(D)** The expression "not of the same...with..." is not idiomatic. The correct idiomatic expression is "not of the same...as...." Therefore, "with" should be replaced with "as."

125. **(D)** The expression "so long that" is not idiomatic. The correct idiomatic expression is "so long as." Therefore, "that" should be replaced with "as."

126. **(D)** The original is awkward and needlessly wordy. The phrase "less of a sentence" should be replaced with "a lesser sentence." The resulting sentence is less awkward and more concise.

127. **(C)** The verb "allows" is almost always followed by an infinitive. Therefore, "attaching" should be replaced with "to attach."

128. **(C)** The expression "an earlier time as" is not idiomatic. The correct idiomatic expression is "an earlier time than." Therefore, "as" should be replaced with "than."

129. **(C)** The verb "raise" means "to lift" or "to erect." The verb "rise" means "to increase," which is the intended meaning in this context. Unemployment is not something that can be physically lifted; however, it is quantifiable and therefore subject to both increase and decrease. So, "raise" should be replaced with "rise."

## EXERCISE 5—PUNCTUATION (p. 636)

1. He was not aware that you had lost your passport.

   A period is required after "passport" since the sentence is an independent clause and a statement.

2. Did you report the loss to the proper authorities?

   A question mark is required after "authorities" since the sentence is an independent clause and a direct request for information. A sentence that asks a question is an interrogative sentence.

3. I suppose you had to fill out many forms.

   A period is required after "forms" since the sentence is an independent clause and a statement. Do not be distracted by the nature of uncertainty in this statement, as indicated by the word "suppose"; this sentence is not a direct request for information (interrogative).

4. What a nuisance!

   An exclamation mark is required after "nuisance" since the statement is an expression of strong emotion, as indicated by the "What a…" structure.

5. I hate doing so much paper work!

   An exclamation mark is required after "work" since the statement is an expression of strong emotion, as indicated by the verb "hate."

6. Did you ever discover where the wallet was?

   A question mark is required after "was" since the sentence is an independent clause and a direct request for information. A sentence that asks a question is an interrogative sentence.

7. I imagine you wondered how it was misplaced.

   A period is required after "misplaced" since the sentence is an independent clause and a statement Do not be distracted by the nature of uncertainty in this statement, as indicated by the word "imagine"; this sentence is not a direct request for information (interrogative).

8. Good for you!

   An exclamation mark is required after "you" since the statement is an expression of strong emotion.

9. At least you now have your passport.

   A period is required after "passport" since the sentence is an independent clause and a statement. A comma is not required after the phrase "At least"; it would introduce an awkward and unnecessary pause. Read the sentence aloud to double-check this pause.

10. What will you do if it happens again?

A question mark is required after "again" since the sentence is an independent clause and a direct request for information. A sentence that asks a question is an interrogative sentence.

11. I don't know if they are coming, though I sent them an invitation weeks ago.

The original is missing three pieces of punctuation. First, a period is required after "ago" since the sentence is a combination of two independent clauses that are statements. Second, a comma is required before "though." Remember that a comma is required before a coordinating conjunction (e.g., "and," "or," "but," "though") that joins two independent clauses. Finally, in the first independent clause, an apostrophe is required to create the contraction of "do not"; the apostrophe should be inserted between the letter "n" and the letter "t" ("don't"). Note that the apostrophe is properly located in place of the letter that was contracted.

12. Neurology is the science that deals with the anatomy, physiology, and pathology of the nervous system.

The original is missing two pieces of punctuation. First, a period is required after "nervous system" since the sentence is an independent clause and a statement. Second, two commas are required to set off the three elements in the series ("anatomy," "physiology," and "pathology"). Remember that commas are always used to separate elements in a series (as long as there are three or more elements in the series).

13. Nursery lore, like everything human, has been subject to many changes over long periods of time.

Nursery lore—like everything human—has been subject to many changes over long periods of time.

The original is missing two pieces of punctuation. First, a period is required after "time" since the sentence is an independent clause and a statement. Second, either two commas or two dashes are required (one before "like" and the other after "human") to set off the non-restrictive element ("like everything human"). Remember that a non-restrictive element contains non-essential information and can therefore be removed (as indicated by either commas or dashes) without changing the meaning of the original. When choosing between commas and dashes, remember that dashes are for stronger breaks and are less formal.

14. Bob read Joyce's Ulysses to the class; everyone seemed to enjoy the reading.

The original is missing three pieces of punctuation. First, a period is required after "reading" since the sentence is a combination of two independent clauses that are statements. Second, in the first independent clause, a possessive apostrophe is required to indicate that Joyce wrote *Ulysses*; the apostrophe should be inserted between the letter "e" and the letter "s" ("Joyce's"). Finally, "end-stop" punctuation is required after "class" to separate the two independent clauses that make up the sentence ("Bob read Joyce's *Ulysses* to the class" and "everyone seemed to enjoy the reading"). Either a period or a semicolon could be used to separate these clauses; however, if a period were used, "everyone" would need to be capitalized. Remember that this exercise does not test capitalization; therefore, a semicolon is required. A semicolon also emphasizes the connection between the two closely related independent clauses.

15. In order to provide more living space, we converted an attached garage into a den.

The original is missing two pieces of punctuation. First, a period is required after "den" since the sentence is an independent clause and a statement. Second, a comma is required after "living space" to more clearly set off short introductory phrase ("In order to provide more living space").

16. Because he is such an industrious student, he has many friends.

The original is missing two pieces of punctuation. First, a period is required after "friends" since the sentence is an independent clause and a statement. Second, a comma is required after "student" to more clearly set off the introductory subordinate clause ("Because he is such an industrious student"). Remember that if the subordinate clause were to follow the main clause, then a comma would not be required ("He has many friends because he is such an industrious student.").

17. I don't recall who wrote *A Midsummer Night's Dream*.

The original is missing three pieces of punctuation. First, an apostrophe is required in the title of the play to indicate the possessive case; the apostrophe should be inserted between the letter "t" and the letter "s" ("*Night's*"). Second, a period is required after "*A* Midsummer *Night's Dream*" since the sentence is an independent clause and a statement. Finally, an apostrophe is required to create the contraction of "do not"; the apostrophe should be inserted between the letter "n" and the letter "t" ("don't").

18. In the writing class, students learned about coordinating conjunctions—and, but, so, or, yet, for, and nor.

The original is missing several pieces of punctuation. First, a period is required after "nor" since the sentence is an independent clause and a statement. Second, a comma is required after "class" to more clearly set off the short introductory phrase ("In the writing class"). Third, a dash is required after "conjunctions" to set off the explanatory group of words that follows. Finally, six commas are required to set off the seven elements in the series (the list of coordinating conjunctions). Remember that commas are always used to separate elements in a series (as long as there are three or more elements in the series). Also, be careful not to confuse the functional coordinating conjunction in the sentence ("and") with the coordinating conjunction "and" that occurs as an element of the series.

19. "Those who do not complain are never pitied" is a familiar quotation by Jane Austen.

The original is missing two pieces of punctuation. First, a period is required after "Jane Austen" since the sentence is an independent clause and a statement. Second, quotation marks are required around the words written by Jane Austen ("Those who do not complain are never pitied"). Remember that quotation marks are used to enclose the actual words of a speaker or writer.

20. Howard and his ex-wife are on amicable terms.

The original is missing two pieces of punctuation. First, a period is required after "terms" since the sentence is an independent clause and a statement. Second, a hyphen is required between "ex" and "wife" to create the compound noun "ex-wife."

21. Her last words were, "call me on Sunday," and she jumped on the train.

The original is missing several pieces of punctuation. First, a period is required after "train" since the sentence is a combination of independent clauses that are statements. Second, in the first independent clause, quotation marks are required around the words that are spoken by the woman ("call me on Sunday"). Third, in the first independent clause, a comma is required after "were" to set off this brief quotation. Finally, a comma is required before "and." Remember that a comma is required before a coordinating conjunction (e.g., "and," "or," "but," "though") that joins two independent clauses. However, remember to insert the comma before the second inserted quotation mark.

22. He is an out-of-work carpenter.

The original is missing two pieces of punctuation. First, a period is required after "carpenter" since the sentence is an independent clause and a statement. Second, two hyphens are required (one before and one after "of") to create the compound adjective "out-of-work."

23. This is what is called a "pregnant chad."

The original is missing two pieces of punctuation. First, a period is required after "pregnant chad" since the sentence is an independent clause and a statement. Second, quotation marks are required (one before "pregnant" and the other after the inserted period) to emphasize words that are used in a special or unusual way ("pregnant chad"); the chad is not literally pregnant.

24. "Come early on Monday," the teacher said, "to take the exit exam."

    The original is missing three pieces of punctuation. First, a period is required after "exam" since the sentence is an independent clause and a statement. Second, quotation marks are required around both sets of words that are spoken by the teacher ("Come early on Monday" and "to take the exit exam"). Remember that the fourth quotation mark should appear after the inserted period. Finally, two commas are required (one before the second inserted quotation mark and the other after "said") to set off the teacher's spoken words.

25. The dog, man's best friend, is a companion to many.

    The dog—man's best friend—is a companion to many.

    The original is missing three pieces of punctuation. First, a period is required after "many" since the sentence is an independent clause and a statement. Second, an apostrophe is required to indicate the possessive case of "man"; the apostrophe should be inserted between the letter "n" and the letter "s" ("man's"). Finally, either two commas or two dashes are required (one before "man's" and the other after "friend") to set off the non-restrictive element ("man's best friend"). Remember that a non-restrictive element contains non-essential information and can therefore be removed (as indicated by either commas or dashes) without changing the meaning of the original. When choosing between commas and dashes, remember that dashes are for stronger breaks and are less formal.

26. The winner of the horse race is, to the best of my knowledge, Silver.

    The winner of the horse race is—to the best of my knowledge—Silver.

    The original is missing two pieces of punctuation. First, a period is required after "Silver" since the sentence is an independent clause and a statement. Second, either two commas or two dashes are required (one before "to" and the other after "knowledge") to set off the non-restrictive element ("to the best of my knowledge"). Remember that a non-restrictive element contains non-essential information and can therefore be removed (as indicated by either commas or dashes) without changing the meaning of the original. When choosing between commas and dashes, remember that dashes are for stronger breaks and are less formal.

27. Every time I see him, the dentist asks me how often I floss.

    The original is missing two pieces of punctuation. First, a period is required after "floss" since the sentence is an independent clause and a statement. Second, a comma is required after "him" to more clearly set off the introductory clause ("Every time I see him").

28. The officer was off-duty when he witnessed the crime.

    The original is missing two pieces of punctuation. First, a period is required after "crime" since the sentence is an independent clause and a statement. Second, a hyphen is required between "off" and "duty" to create the compound modifier "off-duty."

29. *Anna Karenina* is my favorite movie.

    A period is required after "movie" since the sentence is an independent clause and a statement.

30. Red, white, and blue are the colors of the American flag.

The original is missing two pieces of punctuation. First, a period is required after "flag" since the sentence is an independent clause and a statement. Second, two commas are required to set off the three elements in the series ("Red," "white," and "blue"). Remember that commas are always used to separate elements in a series (as long as there are three or more elements in the series).

31. Stop using "stuff" in your essays; it's too informal.

The original is missing several pieces of punctuation First, a period is required after "informal" since the sentence is a combination of two independent clauses that are statements. Second, in the first independent clause, quotation marks are required around the word that is recurring in the essays ("stuff") since it is a direct quotation from the essays. Third, in the second independent clause, an apostrophe is required to create the contraction of "it is"; the apostrophe should be inserted between the letter "t" and the letter "s" ("it's"). Finally, "end-stop" punctuation is required after "essays" to separate the two independent clauses that make up the sentence ("Stop using 'stuff' in your essays" and "it's too informal"). Either a period or a semicolon could be used to separate these clauses; however, if a period were used, "it's" would need to be capitalized. Remember that this exercise does not test capitalization; therefore, a semicolon is required. A semicolon also emphasizes the connection between the two closely related independent clauses.

32. She was a self-made millionaire.

The original is missing two pieces of punctuation. First, a period is required after "millionaire" since the sentence is an independent clause and a statement. Second, a hyphen is required between "self" and "made" to create the compound modifier "self-made."

33. The Smiths, who are the best neighbors anyone could ask for, have moved out.

The Smiths—who are the best neighbors anyone could ask for—have moved out.

The original is missing two pieces of punctuation. First, a period is required after "out" since the sentence is an independent clause and a statement. Second, either two commas or two dashes are required (one before "who" and the other after "for") to set off the non-restrictive element ("who are the best neighbors anyone could ask for"). Remember that a non-restrictive element contains non-essential information and can therefore be removed (as indicated by either commas or dashes) without changing the meaning of the original. When choosing between commas and dashes, remember that dashes are for stronger breaks and are less formal.

34. My eighteen-year-old daughter will graduate this spring.

The original is missing two pieces of punctuation. First, a period is required after "spring" since the sentence is an independent clause and a statement. Second, two hyphens are required (one before and one after "year") to create the compound modifier "eighteen-year-old."

35. Dracula lived in Transylvania.

A period is required after "Transylvania" since the sentence is an independent clause and a statement.

36. The students were told to put away their books.

A period is required after "books" since the sentence is an independent clause and a statement.

37. Begun while Dickens was still at work on *Pickwick Papers*, *Oliver Twist* was published in 1837 and is now one of the author's most widely read works.

The original is missing three pieces of punctuation. First, a period is required after "works" since the sentence is an independent clause and a statement. Second, a possessive apostrophe is required to indicate that Dickens wrote *Pickwick Papers*; the apostrophe should be inserted between the letter "r" and the letter "s" ("author's"). Finally, a comma is required after "*Pickwick Papers*" to more clearly set off the introductory clause ("Begun while Dickens was still at work on *Pickwick Papers*").

38. Given the great difficulties of making soundings in very deep water, it is not surprising that few such soundings were made until the middle of this century.

    The original is missing two pieces of punctuation. First, a period is required after "century" since the sentence is an independent clause and a statement. Second, a comma is required after "deep water" to set off the introductory clause ("Given the great difficulties of making soundings in very deep water").

39. Did you finish writing your thesis prospectus on time?

    A question mark is required after "time" since the sentence is an independent clause and it is a direct request for information (interrogative).

40. The root of modern Dutch was once supposed to be Old Frisian, but the general view now is that the characteristic forms of Dutch are at least as old as those of Old Frisian.

    The original is missing two pieces of punctuation. First, a period is required after "Old Frisian" since the sentence is a combination of independent clauses that are statements. Second, a comma is required before "but." Remember that a comma is required before a coordinating conjunction (e.g., "and," "or," "but," "though") that joins two independent clauses.

41. Moose, once scarce because of indiscriminate hunting, are protected by law, and the number of moose is once again increasing.
    Moose—once scarce because of indiscriminate hunting—are protected by law, and the number of moose is once again increasing.

    The original is missing three pieces of punctuation. First, a period is required after "increasing" since the sentence is a combination of independent clauses that are statements. Second, in the first independent clause, either two commas or two dashes are required (one before "once" and the other after "hunting") to set off the non-restrictive element ("once scarce because of indiscriminate hunting"). Remember that a non-restrictive element contains non-essential information and can therefore be removed (as indicated by either commas or dashes) without changing the meaning of the original. Finally, a comma is required before "and." Remember that a comma is required before a coordinating conjunction (e.g., "and," "or," "but," "though") that joins two independent clauses. "End-stop" punctuation is not an option in this case since "and" can neither be capitalized (in the case of a period) nor removed (in the case of a semicolon).

42. He ordered a set of books, several records, and a film almost a month ago.

    The original is missing two pieces of punctuation. First, a period is required after "ago" since the sentence is an independent clause and a statement. Second, two commas are required to set off the three elements in the series ("a set of books," "several records," and "a film"). Remember that commas are always used to separate elements in a series (as long as there are three or more elements in the series).

43. Perhaps the most interesting section of New Orleans is the French Quarter, which extends from North Rampart Street to the Mississippi River.

    The original is missing two pieces of punctuation. First, a period is required after "Mississippi River" since the sentence is an independent clause and a statement. Second, a comma is required before "which" for the sake of clarity. Without a comma, the sentence implies that the most interesting section of New Orleans is the part of the French Quarter between North Rampart Street and the Mississippi River. However, the sentence intends to say that the French Quarter, in its entirety, extends from North Rampart Street to the Mississippi River.

44. Writing for a skeptical and rationalizing age, Shaftesbury was primarily concerned with showing that goodness and beauty are not determined by revelation, authority, opinion, or fashion.

The original is missing three pieces of punctuation. First, a period is required after "fashion" since the sentence is an independent clause and a statement. Second, a comma is required after "age" to more clearly set off the introductory clause ("Writing for a skeptical and rationalizing age"). Finally, three commas are required to set off the four elements in the series ("revelation," "authority," "opinion," and "fashion"). Remember that commas are always used to separate elements in a series (as long as there are three or more elements in the series).

45. We tried our best to purchase the books, but we were completely unsuccessful even though we went to every bookstore in town.

The original is missing two pieces of punctuation. First, a period is required after "town" since the sentence is a combination of independent clauses that are statements. Second, a comma is required before "but." Remember that a comma is required before a coordinating conjunction (e.g., "and," "or," "but," "though") that joins two independent clauses.

46. A great deal of information regarding the nutritional requirements of farm animals has been accumulated over countless generations by trial and error; however, most recent advances have come as the result of systematic studies at schools of animal husbandry.

The original is missing three pieces of punctuation. First, a period is required after "animal husbandry" since the sentence is a combination of independent clauses that are statements. Second, in the second independent clause, a comma is required after the parenthetical expression "however." Finally, "end-stop" punctuation is required after "trial and error" to separate the two independent clauses that make up the sentence ("A great deal of information regarding the nutritional requirements of farm animals has been accumulated over countless generations by trial and error" and "however, most recent advances have come as the result of systematic studies at schools of animal husbandry"). Either a period or a semicolon could be used to separate these clauses; however, if a period were used, "however" would need to be capitalized. Remember that this exercise does not test capitalization; therefore, a semicolon is required. A semicolon also emphasizes the connection between the two closely related independent clauses.

47. *Omoo*, Melville's sequel to *Typee*, appeared in 1847 and went through five printings in that year alone.

*Omoo*—Melville's sequel to *Typee*—appeared in 1847 and went through five printings in that year alone.

The original is missing three pieces of punctuation. First, a period is required after "alone" since the sentence is an independent clause and a statement. Second, a possessive apostrophe is required to indicate that Melville wrote *Omoo* and *Typee*; the apostrophe should be inserted between the letter "e" and the letter "s" ("Melville's"). Finally, either two commas or two dashes are required (one before "Melville's" and the other after *Typee*) to set off the non-restrictive element ("Melville's sequel to *Typee*"). Remember that a non-restrictive element contains non-essential information and can therefore be removed (as indicated by either commas or dashes) without changing the meaning of the original. When choosing between commas and dashes, remember that dashes are for stronger breaks and are less formal.

48. "Go to Florence for the best gelato in all of Italy," said the old man to the young tourist.

The original is missing three pieces of punctuation. First, a period is required after "tourist" since the sentence is an independent clause and a statement. Second, quotation marks are required around the words that are spoken by the old man ("Go to Florence for the best gelato in all of Italy"). Finally, a comma is required after "Italy" to set off the quotation.

49. Although the first school for African Americans was a public school established in Virginia in 1620, most educational opportunities for African Americans before the Civil War were provided by private agencies.

The original is missing two pieces of punctuation. First, a period is required after "private agencies" since the sentence is an independent clause and a statement. Second, a comma is required after "1620" to more clearly set off the introductory clause ("Although the first school for African Americans was a public school established in Virginia in 1620").

50. As the climate of Europe changed, the population became too dense for the supply of food obtained by hunting, and other means of securing food, such as the domestication of animals, were necessary.

   As the climate of Europe changed, the population became too dense for the supply of food obtained by hunting, and other means of securing food—such as the domestication of animals—were necessary.

   The original is missing several pieces of punctuation. First, a period is required after "necessary" since the sentence is a combination of independent clauses that are statements. Second, in the first independent clause, a comma is required after "changed" to more clearly set off the introductory clause ("As the climate of Europe changed"). Third, in the second independent clause, either two commas or two dashes are required (one before "such" and the other after "animals") to set off the non-restrictive element ("such as the domestication of animals"). Remember that a non-restrictive element contains non-essential information and can therefore be removed (as indicated by either commas or dashes) without changing the meaning of the original. Finally, a comma is required before "and." Remember that a comma is required before a coordinating conjunction (e.g., "and," "or," "but," "though") that joins two independent clauses. "End-stop" punctuation is not an option in this case since "and" can neither be capitalized (in the case of a period) nor removed (in the case of a semicolon). When choosing between commas and dashes, remember that dashes are for stronger breaks and are less formal.

51. In Faulkner's poetic realism, the grotesque is somber, violent, and often inexplicable; in Caldwell's writing, it is lightened by a ballad-like, humorous, sophisticated detachment.

   The original is missing several pieces of punctuation. First, a period is required after "detachment" since the sentence is a combination of independent clauses that are statements. Second, two apostrophes are required (one to indicate the possessive case of "Faulkner" and the other to indicate the possessive case of "Caldwell"); the first apostrophe should be inserted between the letter "r" and the letter "s" ("Faulkner's"), and the second apostrophe should be inserted between the letter "l" and the letter "s" ("Caldwell's"). Third, in the second independent clause, a hyphen is required between "ballad" and "like" to create the compound modifier "ballad-like." Fourth, in the first independent clause, a comma is required after "poetic realism" to more clearly set off the introductory clause ("In Faulkner's poetic realism"). Fifth, in the second independent clause, a comma is required after "writing" to more clearly set off the introductory clause ("in Caldwell's writing"). Sixth, two commas are required to set off the three elements in the series that describes Faulkner's concept of the grotesque ("somber," "violent," and "often inexplicable"). Seventh, two commas are required to set off the three elements in the series that describes Caldwell's concept of the grotesque ("ballad-like," "humorous," and "sophisticated"). Note that this series of three adjectives modifies the noun "detachment." Finally, "end-stop" punctuation is required after "inexplicable" to separate the two independent clauses that make up the sentence ("In Faulkner's poetic realism, the grotesque is somber, violent, and often inexplicable" and "in Caldwell's writing, it is lightened by a ballad-like, humorous, sophisticated detachment"). Either a period or a semicolon could be used to separate these clauses; however, if a period were used, "in" would need to be capitalized. Remember that this exercise does not test capitalization; therefore, a semicolon is required. A semicolon also emphasizes the connection between the two closely related independent clauses.

52. The valley of the Loire, a northern tributary of the Loire at Angers, abounds in rock villages; they occur in many other places in France, Spain, and northern Italy.

   The valley of the Loire—a northern tributary of the Loire at Angers—abounds in rock villages; they occur in many other places in France, Spain, and northern Italy.

   The original is missing several pieces of punctuation. First, a period is required after "northern Italy" since the sentence is a combination of independent clauses that are statements. Second, in the first independent clause, either two commas or two dashes are required (one before "a" and the other after "Angers") to set off the non-restrictive element ("a northern tributary of the Loire at Angers"). When choosing between commas and dashes, remember that dashes are for stronger breaks and are less formal. Third, in the second independent clause, two commas are required to set off the three elements in the series ("France," "Spain," and "northern Italy"). Finally, "end-stop" punctuation is required after "rock villages" to separate the two independent clauses that make up the sentence ("The valley of the Loire, a northern tributary of the Loire at Angers, abounds in rock villages" and "they occur in many other places in France, Spain, and northern Italy"). Either a period or a semicolon could be used to separate these clauses; however, if a period were used, "they" would need to be capitalized. Remember that this exercise does not test capitalization; therefore, a semicolon is required. A semicolon also emphasizes the connection between the two closely related independent clauses.

53. The telephone rang several times; as a result, his sleep was interrupted.

The original is missing three pieces of punctuation. First, a period is required after "interrupted" since the sentence is a combination of independent clauses that are statements. Second, in the second independent clause, a comma is required after "result" to more clearly set off the introductory clause ("as a result"). Finally, "end-stop" punctuation is required after "times" to separate the two independent clauses that make up the sentence ("The telephone rang several times" and "as a result, his sleep was interrupted"). Either a period or a semicolon could be used to separate these clauses; however, if a period were used, "as" would need to be capitalized. Remember that this exercise does not test capitalization; therefore, a semicolon is required. A semicolon also emphasizes the connection between the two closely related independent clauses.

54. He has forty-three thousand dollars to spend; however, once that is gone, he will be penniless.

The original is missing several pieces of punctuation. First, a period is required after "penniless" since the sentence is a combination of independent clauses that are statements. Second, a hyphen is required between "forty" and "three" because every whole number from twenty-one to ninety-nine (even when it is used as part of a larger number) is always hyphenated. Third, in the second independent clause, a comma is required after the parenthetical expression "however." Fourth, in the second independent clause, a comma is required after "gone" to more clearly set off the clause ("once that is gone") that precedes the main clause ("he will be penniless"). Finally, "end-stop" punctuation is required after "spend" to separate the two independent clauses that make up the sentence ("He has forty-three thousand dollars to spend" and "however, once that is gone, he will be penniless"). Either a period or a semicolon could be used to separate these clauses; however, if a period were used, "however" would need to be capitalized. Remember that this exercise does not test capitalization; therefore, a semicolon is required. A semicolon also emphasizes the connection between the two closely related independent clauses.

55. Before an examination, do the following: review your work, get a good night's sleep, eat a balanced breakfast, and arrive on time to take the test.

The original is missing several pieces of punctuation. First, a period is required after "test" since the sentence is a command. Second, a comma is required after "examination" to more clearly set off the introductory clause ("Before an examination"). Third, a colon is required after "following" to precede the list of items that follows. Fourth, an apostrophe is required to indicate the possessive case of "night"; the apostrophe should be inserted between the letter "t" and the letter "s" ("night's"). Finally, three commas are required to set off the four elements in the series ("review your work," "get a good night's sleep," "eat a balanced breakfast," and "arrive on time to take the test"). Remember that commas are always used to separate elements in a series (as long as there are three or more elements in the series).

## EXERCISE 6— SAMPLE ESSAY 1 (p. 649)

### Essay 1—Below Average

Residents of rural areas insist that their life is better. People living in urban city areas prefer the lively life that they lead. Each has a viewpoint, but I feel that the city life is much better. Urban areas have good streets and roads and many things to do.

A city is closer together than rural areas. Everything can be reached pretty quickly by car, bus, or even bicycle. The streets are maintained by the city in winter and summer. My Aunt in the mountains is snowed in each winter for days at a time. Sometimes traffic is a problem in urban areas, but that's the price you pay.

The urban areas have so many activities to do. Lots of movies, concerts, and sports events are always going on. Because the urban areas have more people and money, more famous artists visit and perform there.

Some really important things in cities include good hospitals and healthcare. With lots of people there is a need for specialist doctors and great hospitals, even for children. I feel that I can find people in the city that share my interests whatever I decide on.

In conclusion, urban areas are the best places to live. Americans, and people around the world are moving from rural areas more each day to get to the excitement and opportunity of urban areas.

### Writing skill and position on issue:

This essay demonstrates developing writing skills. Although the writer's position on the issue is clear, he or she fails to provide an adequate introduction to the issue. The writer discusses both sides of the argument, but he or she is unsuccessful in describing the relationship between the two sides. The writer's thesis is not broad enough to sufficiently cover the point raised in the fourth paragraph regarding "hospitals and healthcare."

### Development of ideas and organization of essay:

The ideas presented are good but lack sufficient elaboration. The writer does not include clear topic sentences in any of the three body paragraphs, and there are random statements that are not organized in any coherent pattern throughout the essay. This lack of coherence distracts the reader from obtaining a clear understanding of the argument. For example, the writer mentions that he or she "can find people in the city that share my interests" in the same paragraph (fourth) that he or she discusses "hospitals and healthcare"; however, no logical connection is made between these two ideas. Since the essay prompt asks the writer to compare two living conditions, the development of such an essay would require the use of comparisons and contrasts. However, the writer does not adequately use either of these tools to support his or her thesis. Overall, the writer presents a list of the qualities that he or she prefers in cities but does not explain why this list adds up to a higher quality of life.

### Structure of essay, paragraphs, and transitions:

The writer has a grasp of the basic structure of an essay: an introduction, a body, and a conclusion. However, the paragraphs are too short; they are not supported or expanded sufficiently; and they become unfocused. The essay also lacks transitions; its content is presented in a choppy fashion, with random introductions of the writer's main points. The only transitional phrase ("In conclusion"), which appears in the last paragraph, is contrived and low-level usage.

### Language usage, sentence structure, and punctuation:

The essay is understandable, but it contains many errors in grammar and mechanics that distract the reader from its content. In the first paragraph, for example, the writer states that "Urban areas have…many things to do." However, "areas" cannot "have things to do." The proper phrase would be "There are many things to do in urban areas." Also, in the second paragraph, the writer omits the word "living" from the sentence "My Aunt in the mountains…." Overall, an excess of low-level language (e.g., "pretty quickly," "that's the price you pay", and "Lots of") mars the quality of the essay. In the last paragraph, the comma after "Americans" is unnecessary. Stylistically, the writer does not vary the sentence structure and resorts to simple sentences and lists.

### Summary and conclusions:

The essay lacks sufficient support and reasoning to make a compelling argument.

### Essay 2—Above Average

The question of the quality of the rural life versus the life of a city dweller is an interesting one that faces each adult making a decision about their life activities. Plainly, United States citizens "voted with their feet" and have flocked to the cities in the 20th century. But recently there has been some movement back to rural areas and the "simple life" that they represent. I feel that a more rural area offers the best quality of life in the beginning of the 21st century. This opinion is based on the issues of emotional health, community involvement and opportunity, and best usage of my time.

Life in urban areas can be very stressful and difficult. Noise and traffic go on 24 hours a day. "Street people" who may need intervention may be outside your door in a downtown area. Traffic may make your voyage to work or entertainment difficult and lengthy. In rural areas the noise level is lessened, the roads less crowded, and more humane contact is likely.

In a more rural area, each person can have more of an impact within the community. The problems and challenges may be shared community wide and not just in your own neighborhood as in a large city. You can more easily be known and make a difference in a rural area. A contrary view contends that newcomers are sometimes not part of the "community family" in a small town. Gaining acceptance can be harder than in cities used to an influx of new people.

A rural area places less demands on my personal time: less traffic, less commuting, and fewer lines of people waiting to get services. I could get home faster from work and pursue my own interests.

In conclusion, I prefer rural areas. Keeping in communication and accessing healthcare used to be a problem there. But the Internet and satellite dishes helped alleviate the first concern. Regional health centers and rapid transportation have helped make "big city" healthcare available to rural areas.

### Writing skill and position on issue:

This essay shows good facility with written English, clear organization, and mostly consistent writing skills. The writer's position on the issue is presented clearly and the thesis is well developed. In the third paragraph, the writer presents a contrary viewpoint, which is a strong and persuasive technique. However, he or she fails to refute this opposing viewpoint, which is important when presenting evidence that is contrary to the thesis.

### Development of ideas and organization of essay:

The initial paragraph effectively details both sides of the issue. Reference to social trends gives the writer a voice of authority. Examples are well presented and elaborated upon with sufficient detail. The arguments are laid out in a logical order and structured closely after the thesis statement. Each supporting paragraph begins with an organizing topic sentence and continues with an in-depth discussion of the writer's major points.

*Structure of essay, paragraphs, and transitions:*

In the introduction, the writer previews the evidence that he will use to support his or her thesis, and the structural set-up in the opening paragraph is closely followed throughout the essay. The supporting paragraphs are appropriate, and each deals with an argument or position of the writer. The transition that is used to move from the second paragraph to the third paragraph ("In a more rural area") is very effective; however, transition usage in general is low. For example, "In conclusion" is a low-level usage transitional phrase.

*Language usage, sentence structure, and punctuation:*

The analogy "voted with their feet" is effective in this essay, and the supporting details hold the reader's interest. Minor errors in grammar and mechanics do not distract the reader from understanding the essay and are likely present due to time restrictions that are placed on the writer.

*Summary and conclusions:*

The essay is clearly written and demonstrates a firm command of the language.

## EXERCISE 7—SAMPLE ESSAY 2 (p. 651)

*Essay 1—Below Average*

The Internet is used daily by millions of citizens and businesses around the world. However, I feel that the Internet has invaded people's lives and our society. It has caused bad effects on business, people in smaller countries, and on home life in the USA.

The first problem the Internet is the expense and the need for knowledge to use it. If you do not know how to effectively use a computer. Or, if you don't have the money for the computer, the software and the Internet support, then you are considered backward. Many people and families do not have these resources or the money needed. Airlines are now even charging more to call them for reservations, than if you use the Internet.

If you do have the computer, and have Internet access, then there is the problem of the content. Just a few people with prejudice can have their writings accessed all over the world. There is no fact checking or editing of information, as there is for newspapers or magazines. Also some content is gross and suited only for adults. Parents have a problem watching out for what their children access.

Home life is hurt when family members get addicted to using the Internet. Games and chat rooms can take up many hours each day. Online shopping can easily run up large debts. And worse, you can connect with dangerous people who mask their identity and planned activities.

I agree that controlled Internet activity can be useful and a valuable information resource. But the Internet has mainly caused problems that are worse than its usefulness.

*Writing skill and position on issue:*

The essay illustrates developing skills. The writer's position is clearly, though awkwardly, presented in the introductory paragraph. The introduction, though adequate in presenting a thesis statement, does not introduce the topic effectively, mentioning only briefly the proliferation of the Internet. The writer fails to address the scope of the issue by providing both sides of the argument.

*Development of ideas and organization of essay:*

The thesis statement in the initial paragraph attempts to set up the structure that is to be followed in the essay. However, only one of its three claims is actually developed. Neither injury to "business" nor injury to "people in smaller countries" is elaborated upon in the paragraphs that follow. The negative impact of the Internet on "home life in the USA" is the only point that is developed. Unfortunately, each of its supporting paragraphs lacks a consistent internal structure. In the second paragraph, for example, the writer begins by discussing how people are unable to afford Internet access (as well as resources, support, and training for such a service) but then lapses into an example about airlines charging more for non-Internet reservation assistance. There may be a connection between these two ideas, but the writer fails to make this connection. The essay wanders, introducing several new, non-supportive points. Finally, the conclusion is too brief and fails to summarize the major points of the essay.

*Structure of essay, paragraphs, and transitions:*

The basic three-part essay structure (an introduction, a body, and a conclusion) is present but weak. Only the second paragraph flows smoothly from the introduction because of the use of a transitional phrase ("The first problem…."). Transition usage is absent in the remainder of the essay. Only the fourth paragraph has a clear topic sentence; the other body paragraphs lack structure and focus.

*Language usage, sentence structure, and punctuation:*

The sentence fragment in the second paragraph needs repair. Low-level language usage, such as "bad," "hurt," and "gross," detract from the quality of the writing. The writer needs to work on making better word choices to increase the readability and interest of the essay.

*Summary and conclusions:*

This essay lacks the necessary qualities of an effective essay.

### Essay 2—Above Average

The usage of the Internet is increasing daily. Citizens in most countries have daily access to a vast array of information. Much of the information and the usage is valuable, and I feel this outweighs the problems. What are some of the significant beneficial uses of the Internet to you and me, to businesses, and for government agencies?

The Internet provides us with instant access to almost infinite arrays of information. This access can be used for education, entertainment, or even our daily shopping. Challenges include spurious sites, gross inappropriate content and actual criminal stealing of personal information. The Internet has given us a direct contact with businesses. I help my parents make travel plans, and book affordable plane trips and hotels using travel sites on the Internet.

Businesses are able to reach out directly to consumers and to other business via the Internet. This gives both a much wider range of choice in products and services. However, the Internet has also had its downside with Internet based businesses blazing and then failing like a shooting star. These failures cost investors billions of dollars, and lost the workers their jobs.

Governmental agencies using the Internet can offer residents faster services such as license renewals, at lower cost to the agencies. The democratic governmental goals of "transparency" and "public access" can be better met if we can read every document and attend every meeting using the Internet.

The value of the Internet is increased if all citizens can have access to it, not just the well-off.

Therefore, computers and access from libraries and other public sites is essential, and some cities are pursuing this goal.

I feel the Internet is valuable and will increase in usefulness as we learn more about the best uses for it.

*Writing skill and position on issue:*

This essay illustrates solid writing skills, and the writer's position is made very clearly. The introduction adequately presents the topic in an interesting way, employing an atypical inversion of the thesis statement into a question. The overall flow and structure of the essay is consistent and logical. Instances that are opposed to the writer's position are presented appropriately and add interest.

*Development of ideas and organization of essay:*

Ideas are generally presented and developed effectively; appropriate examples are used and explored in detail. A couple of minor points are misplaced and confusing, such as when the writer recommends that we all "read every document and attend every meeting using the Internet." However, these errors do not detract from the overall strength of the essay. The writer effectively introduces opposing arguments; however, he or she does not explicitly refute these claims. This slight oversight undermines the writer's argument, but it is permissible since the writer presents an essay in which the "pros" outweigh the "cons."

*Structure of essay, paragraphs, and transitions:*

The initial paragraph is clear and provides an atypical thesis in the form of a question. The supporting paragraphs are appropriate, and they are integral to the writer's argument. Each supporting paragraph is predicated upon its own topic sentence as well as the thesis. The examples are compelling and varied. The closing paragraph offers an appropriate and conclusive summary but could use further development.

*Language usage, sentence structure, and punctuation:*

The essay shows varied and strong language usage. The few errors noted will not distract the reader and are likely due to the time restrictions placed on the writer. The sentences vary in length and style and are effective in presenting the writer's arguments.

*Summary and conclusions:*

The writer successfully makes an intelligent point of social commentary regarding the need for free Internet access to all.

**EXERCISE 8— SAMPLE ESSAY 3** (p. 653)

*Essay 1—Below Average*

My position is that bio-engineered foods should be accepted and not be called "Frankenfoods." An insulting term like that causes conflict and I feel is incorrect. Sure there are concerns that bio-engineered foods could change other natural foods. But there are advantages to bio-engineered foods.

With the growing populations around the world, more food will be needed each year. But the land is going away due to new houses and businesses being built. Bio-engineered crops can produce more in a given field. So food production can meet our appetites.

The fresh water is getting more salty in the San Francisco Bay area. Bio-engineered crops could be made resistant to some salt problems and let crops still be grown.

What if food scientists could add vitamins, or other helpful components to crops such as corn? Then some illnesses from deficiencies of vitamins would be lower in the country. Many of the bio-engineered crops are being developed in the USA. Our agriculture businesses could really be helped by increased trade in these seeds and plants.

Sure, scientific progress must watched for dangers. But I think bio-engineered foods can help us like so many other scientific developments have in the past.

### Writing skill and position on issue:

The essay illustrates some developing skills. A restatement of the essay prompt and an introduction to the issue would be more effective than beginning the essay with "My position...." The writer's position is stated in a roundabout way, arguing about language more than substance. The writer fails to provide a thesis statement that explains his or her position and how the rest of the essay is to be organized.

### Development of ideas and organization of essay:

The essay should be better focused; supporting paragraphs should include transitions and topic sentences. Most of the points are valid and supportive of the writer's position; however, they are not well developed and require further elaboration. Specific examples, rather than hypothetical ones ("What if...."), would strengthen the writer's overall argument.

### Structure of essay, paragraphs, and transitions:

The supporting paragraphs are generally appropriate for the ideas expressed in them, but the essay would flow better if transitions were used. The writer moves abruptly from one idea to the next. The essay does possess the basic structural elements: an introduction, a body, and a conclusion. However, the concluding paragraph is too short and requires more development.

### Language usage, sentence structure, and punctuation:

Low-level language usage and a number of language errors detract from the essay's overall readability and presentation. How does "food production meet our appetites"? It would be better to write: "Food production can meet the nutritional needs of a growing population." Rather than write "let crops be grown," write "enable crops to be grown." "Going away" is a poor choice of words. The land is not "going away"; the use of the land is just "changing" from agricultural to other uses. Grammatical errors, such as "must watched for dangers" instead of "must watch for dangers," distract the reader from the content of the essay. Some sentences are too brief, not completing their ideas effectively for the reader. The use of "sure" in the introduction and conclusion is colloquial and inappropriate for an essay such as this one.

### Summary and conclusions:

More information on the ideas listed would better support the writer's position.

### Essay 2—Above Average

Bio-engineered foods have been discussed frequently in the media in the last few years. The European community and the USA have even had major trade disputes over the issue. The term "Frankenfood" fits the opinion of many activists in the USA and Europe. The activists fear the effects of bio-engineering on the world's food supply. I agree with the concerned activists, and contend that the effects can be negative. We and our food supply will suffer, as will world trade and people in less developed countries.

As "Frankenfoods" with their altered genetics are planted widely, they may crossbreed with native plants. For example, the genetic changes could proliferate through all wheat plants starting from a small number of bio-engineered wheat fields. If the genetic change proves to be injurious to some people, or bad for crop survival, then farmers could not "back-out" the genetic changes.

When I visited a relative's farm in the Midwest, I learned that bio-engineered crops resistant to weed killer has caused a problem. The weed killer resistance has passed into some weeds, and now they are facing "Frankenweeds." These weeds cannot be controlled by the chemicals that were previously effective. This leads to more chemicals being used to eliminate even more hardy weeds.

Bio-engineered crops may be patented and owned by large companies. These companies can charge high fees for the seeds. Less-developed countries will be at even more of an economic disadvantage as more crops are bio-engineered. If the European community continues to resist American bio-engineered foods, our trade in farm goods with them will suffer greatly.

Looking at the contrary argument, a strong case has been made by scientists for the advantages of bio-engineered crops. Scientists note increased production, resistance to pests, and added nutrients. Useful drugs may even be produced by these bio-engineered crops. But the problems of crossbreeding and contamination of the food supply are very important. Therefore I believe bio-engineered crops must be strongly controlled and tested over a few years before widespread usage is allowed.

### Writing skill and position on issue:

This essay shows solid and strong expression and writing skills. Each side of the issue is presented well in the beginning of the essay. The essay could be improved with a better thesis statement, detailing the major points that the writer intends to cover throughout the rest of the essay. The writer presents his or her opinion clearly and even offers a standard for qualifying the use of bio-engineered crops.

### Development of ideas and organization of essay:

Ideas introduced in the initial paragraph are clearly presented and supported with arguments. Good personal experience examples and scientific explanations are used to support the writer's position. The essay could be improved with better explanations in some of the supporting paragraphs. For example, in the fourth paragraph, the writer could explain how increased costs for bio-engineered seeds would lead to an economic disadvantage for less-developed countries. Overall, the development of ideas is logical and consistent with the subject matter. The writer even presents a contrary position and refutation to this position, which add to the richness of content and argument.

### Structure of essay, paragraphs, and transitions:

The essay has a clear structure, and good transitions help the reader to understand the positions that are argued. The supporting paragraphs are appropriate, and each paragraph deals with an argument or position of the writer. The fourth paragraph is the only paragraph that lacks a transition. This lapse is probably due to the time restrictions that are placed on the writer. The concluding paragraph is effectively introduced by referencing the contrary argument.

**Language usage, sentence structure, and punctuation:**

Language usage is appropriate and the vocabulary is sophisticated (e.g., "contend," "proliferate," and "injurious"). The few punctuation errors do not distract the reader and are likely due to the time restrictions that are placed on the writer.

**Summary and conclusions:**

The writer's control of language usage is strong. The few language errors do not detract significantly from the presentation of the ideas.

# ANALYTICAL WRITING CONCEPTS AND STRATEGIES

## WRITING—CORE LESSON (p. 665)

| | | | |
|---|---|---|---|
| 1. **A** | 12. **C** | 21. **B** | 30. **D** |
| 2. **A** | 13. **C** | 22. **A** | 31. **B** |
| 3. **B** | 14. **D** | 23. **D** | 32. **B** |
| 4. **A** | 15. **C** | 24. **D** | 33. **C** |
| 5. **A** | 16. **C** | 25. **B** | 34. **A** |
| 6. **A** | 17. **D** | 26. **A** | 35. **A** |
| 7. **C** | 18. **C** | 27. **B** | |
| 8. **D** | 19. **A** | 28. **A** | |
| 9. **B** | 20. **B** | 29. **D** | |
| 10. **C** | | | |
| 11. **D** | | | |

36. On Monday, Mark received a letter of acceptance from State College. He immediately called his mother—herself a graduate of State College—to tell her about his acceptance. When he told her he had also been awarded a scholarship, she was very excited. After hanging up, Mark's mother decided to throw a surprise party for Mark. She telephoned his brother, his sister, and several of his friends. Because the party was supposed to be a surprise, she made them all promise not to say anything to Mark. Mark, however, had a similar idea: a party for his mother to celebrate his acceptance at her alma mater. He telephoned his brother, his sister, and several of his parents' friends to invite them to a party at his house on Saturday night, and he made them all promise to say nothing to his mother. On Saturday night, both Mark and his mother were surprised.

37. This sentence is improved by having each sentence express a single thought: "There is no proof presented that students are distracted by windows. Even assuming some students are distracted, many other students might find the view relaxing. A relaxed student should be a better learner than one who is tense—and learning is the goal of the classroom."

38. This sentence contains a grammatical error. The pronoun "they," which begins the main clause of the sentence, is plural. But it refers to "student," which is singular. This type of error usually occurs when writers do not have the complete thought or sentence in mind when they begin to write. They lose track of what they have said and shift from the singular to the plural. The best way for you to avoid such errors is to have a good idea of what the completed sentence will say before you begin to write it down.

39. Errors in subject-verb agreement occur here: "distraction…are" and "eyes…is." A clause including two prepositional phrases comes between the first subject and verb, and it is therefore likely that one of the two nouns, "students" or "spans," was mistaken for the subject when the writer chose a verb. A prepositional phrase—"of a student"—comes between the second subject and verb, and the writer has mistaken "student" for the subject of the verb and written "is."

40. The choice of the pronoun "their" is wrong. The pronoun must refer to "student," which is singular—"their" is plural.

41. The pronoun "she" is incorrect because it is in the wrong case. The pronoun here functions as the object of a preposition ("except"), and it should therefore be in the objective case ("her"). One sure way of avoiding errors in the use of pronouns is to avoid unnecessary pronouns. This sentence is corrected by writing: "Under this seating arrangement, all of the people in the classroom, except the class monitor and the teacher, will…."

42. Given the construction of the sentence, it is made to appear that the severe thunderstorm was strolling through the park. When a modifying idea starts a sentence and is set off with a comma, the modifier must be taken to modify the first noun or noun phrase after the comma. A related error to be avoided is the squinting modifier, which is placed so that it may modify either one of two things, producing ambiguity in the sentence.

43. Did Paul tell Mary down by the old mill that he would wed her, or did Paul tell Mary that he would wed her and the wedding would take place down by the old mill?

44. The correct structure of this sentence is: "When I received the notice I immediately reported to the manager's desk."

45. The correct structure of this sentence is: "The chef baked the cake to please his favorite niece on her wedding day."

46. This paragraph is full of slang. How would you rewrite this to avoid using the slang present? One way is as follows: "Let the kids do things their own way. It is too hard having the teacher always make them feel guilty. No windows would have a negative effect on the kids. They might need counseling as a result. So, relax the pressure on kids and let them be themselves."

# Answers and Explanations:
## Step Four

# Practice Test I

## SECTION 1—ANALYTICAL WRITING (p. 723)

### *'PRESENT YOUR PERSPECTIVE ON AN ISSUE' SAMPLE ESSAY RESPONSE*

Great people are always remembered for their accomplishments. Thomas Jefferson is remembered as a patriot and a profound political thinker who wrote the Declaration of Independence. Albert Einstein is remembered as the brilliant physicist who developed the Theory of Relativity. Were it not for these accomplishments, these great people would not be considered great and likely would not be remembered at all.

It is currently fashionable, however, to try to bring great people down a notch or two by parading out their shortcomings to show that they really were not so great after all. Evidence has recently become available to prove that Thomas Jefferson carried on an affair with a woman who was his slave and that he fathered a child or children by her. A popular way of scoring points in trivia is to point out that Einstein was notoriously poor at math and got Cs in high school algebra. But do these shortcomings make them any less great? Only if one has an unrealistic definition of greatness. Would Jefferson have been as deep a thinker had he been less complex? Would Einstein have grasped the fundamental intuition of relativity had he been enslaved to mathematics?

It seems likely, then, that great people will always be remembered for their shortcomings as well as their accomplishments. It is a way of making them seem human and not so distant from the rest of us. And, in a real sense, balancing a person's shortcomings with their accomplishments is appropriate. That is because a great person is also, by definition, a person. As Hegel said of Napoleon, whom he idolized but realized had faults, "No man is a hero to his valet."

### *'ANALYSIS OF AN ARGUMENT' SAMPLE ESSAY RESPONSE*

The evidence provided does not support the recommendation regarding indoor facilities for three reasons. First, it is not clear that residents support the plan. Second, there is no proof that children are lacking any recreational opportunities. Third, implementing the ambitious plan could actually undermine the recreational programs.

First, it is not clear that residents think that children need other opportunities. The wording of the question includes the phrase "such as." Many of those who responded "yes" might have interpreted the question to include swimming.

Second, there is no evidence that children are denied the opportunity to play basketball or racquetball. Presumably, the City also has outdoor recreational facilities with hoops and walls. Those can certainly be used during the summer months. Plus, many other activities such as softball and soccer are available during the summer months.

Third, the attempt to keep the indoor facilities open year-round might actually undermine the quality of the City recreational programs. Obviously, there will be an attendant cost for hiring more workers to staff the additional facilities. Money spent on indoor facilities during the summer might draw needed money away from outdoor facilities that are traditionally used only during those months. Additionally, it is logical to schedule maintenance tasks on the indoor facilities during the summer months when the weather will not interfere with work. Trying to keep the facilities open year-round could make it more difficult to keep them in top condition. Finally, some indoor facilities may not even be useable during the hot summer months due to lack of suitable ventilation.

While everyone would agree that, in principle, children should be given the widest range of recreational opportunities possible, sometimes hard decisions have to be made about what is realistic. Without further evidence that there is a real need for the indoor recreational facilities to remain open, the City should continue its policies.

**SECTION 2—VERBAL REASONING** (p. 732)

1. **(B)** *Thought Reversal.* For this item, a reversal of thought is indicated by the subordinate conjunction "although." Although something is "horrifying," something else is worse. The answer choices are easy vocabulary words. What word is stronger than "horrifying"? (A) and (D) make no sense. (C) and (E) are not adjectives one would use to describe torture or dismemberment. (B), "viler," is the only possibility.

2. **(C)** *Combined Reasoning.* There are two key logical signals in this item that are important in understanding the overall structure of the sentence. A reversal of thought is indicated by the subordinate conjunction "although," which tells you that what comes after the comma will be an idea that is the opposite of "good health." You can eliminate (D) and (E) on the grounds of usage. You can eliminate (A) because "augment" means "to increase," extending rather than reversing the thought. This leaves you with (B) and (C). The second part of the sentence is an extension of the first blank, as indicated by the comma (punctuation clue). You can immediately eliminate (B) because a body's defenses cannot be "indelible." This leaves you with (C). The body's defenses are "impaired" if the effectiveness of vitamins is "inhibited."

3. **(B)** *Thought Extension.* For this item, an extension of thought is indicated by the word "since." You know that because of something, something else will be true. The next important word is "few." Since there are only a few conservatives, their influence must be ——. So, you might anticipate a choice such as "slight" or "insignificant." Eliminate (D) and (E) on the grounds of usage. (A) makes no sense, because it is not logical that only a few would have a monumental influence. (C), "discriminatory," does not have anything to do with the fact that there are only a few conservatives. You are left with (B). It does make perfect sense to say that the influence of a few would be "negligible."

4. **(E)** *Thought Extension.* For this item, an extension of thought is indicated by the "not only *this* but *that*" structure, which suggests that the two missing words are parallel in tone. (Note that, by itself, the coordinate conjunction "but" typically indicates a reversal of thought.) The first blank requires an adjective that extends the idea of a test that maims animals. (D) is not a possible choice because one would not be gratified by the maiming of animals. Although (A) and (B) make some sense, the word "maim" gives you a clue that the adjective will have a negative connotation. This leaves you with (C) and (E). Now, you have to look at the second blank, which requires an adjective that summarizes what comes after. Since no two people see the same thing, the test is something. Only the second element of (E), "unreliable," works.

5. **(D)** *Combined Reasoning.* There are two key logical signals in this item that are important in understanding the overall structure of the sentence. The first blank is an extension of the word "calmly." Eliminate (A), (B), and (C) on the grounds of usage. This leaves you with (D) and (E). "Scorn" does not extend the idea of calm, but "equanimity" does. Test the second element of (D). It should reverse the idea of "equanimity," and it does.

6. **(E)** *Thought Extension.* For this item, an extension of thought is indicated by the singular pronoun "this," which refers to the politician's hunger for power. So, the first blank requires a word that describes someone who is hungry for power. If you know that the word is "cupidity," you have the question answered. Otherwise, you will have to eliminate choices containing words you do know cannot be correct and make your guess.

7. **(D)** *Degree.* EUPHORIA is a more intense form of CONTENTMENT; likewise, "moroseness" is a more intense degree of "sadness."

8. **(A)** *Lack of Defining Characteristic.* Something lacking IMPORTANCE is TRIVIAL; likewise, something lacking "magnitude" is "tiny."

9. **(D)** *Part of.* A MOTE is a single unit of DUST; likewise, a "bead" is a single unit of "water." So, (D) is the correct answer choice. Do not be distracted by (E); had the second word in this answer choice been "sand" instead of "particle," it would have been a better option.

10. **(E)** *Defining Characteristic.* Something CLANDESTINE must be SECRET, and something "confidential" must be "private."

11. **(B)** *Defining Characteristic.* Part of the definition of REDOLENT is ODOR. (REDOLENT means "having a pleasing ODOR.") Likewise, part of the definition of "savory" is "taste." ("Savory" means "having a pleasing taste.")

12. **(E)** *Lack of Defining Characteristic.* Something that is ADULTERATED lacks PURITY, and something which is "diluted" lacks "concentration."

13. **(E)** *Defining Characteristic.* A MIASMA is NOXIOUS, and "poison" is "toxic."

14. **(C)** *Further Application.* In the closing paragraph, the author states that an unexpected result of the unification battle was that the military would never be able to establish itself as a power independent of and outside civilian control.

15. **(E)** *Specific Detail.* This is a Specific Detail item with a thought-reverser. Four of the five ideas are mentioned in the selection. The one that is not is the correct choice. (A) and (C) are mentioned in the second paragraph. (D) is mentioned in the third paragraph. (B) is mentioned at several points in the selection. (E), however, is not mentioned.

16. **(A)** *Logical Structure.* In the second paragraph, the author is describing the bitter rivalries that surrounded the passage of the NSA, and it is at the end of that paragraph that he mentions the resignation and suicide of Forrestal. The reason he mentioned Forrestal, therefore, must have been to underscore the bitterness of the inter-service fighting.

17. **(E)** *Specific Detail.* This is a Specific Detail item with a thought-reverser. Although the word galaxy is used in the selection, the author does not say that supernovas are caused by colliding galaxies. So, (E) is the one detail not mentioned in the selection.

18. **(C)** *Implied Idea.* The key word for this item is "anomalous." The author states that the unexpected makeup of the meteorites is evidence that a supernova helped form our solar system. However, this evidence supports the conclusion only if the strange content is foreign to our solar system. So, (C) is a correct inference. None of the other choices explains the connection between the theory of the origin of our solar system and the strange makeup of the meteors.

19. **(E)** *Specific Detail.* This is a Specific Detail item with a thought-reverser. The author describes the consequences of full-cost reimbursement, specifically mentioning rising costs, underused facilities, overcapitalization, and unnecessary use of expensive equipment.

20. **(B)** *Specific Detail.* The author states that some problems do remain and gives some examples. The second paragraph discusses some of the causes of the problems. The third paragraph says that the problems are not as bad as they sometimes seem. Some of the disappointment in healthcare services must be attributable to the fact that people expect too much from health care. (A) specifically contradicts the first paragraph where the author states there have been improvements. As for (C), (D), and (E), even if these statements were true (ultimately they seem inconsistent with the first paragraph), they are not responsive to this question.

21. **(D)** *Logical Structure.* In the first paragraph, the author states that there have been disappointments which have led to pessimism. The second paragraph explains why this pessimism is at least in part unfounded. The third paragraph says that it is not true that nothing works. At this point, the prepaid plans are mentioned. So, they must be examples of the ideas that worked. As for (B), this is a problem with other experiments. As for (C), this is never mentioned in the passage. (A) and (E) are contradicted by our analysis of the correct answer.

22. **(C)** *Antonyms.* Since HACKNEYED means "much used" or "trite," "original" is an exact opposite.

23. **(D)** *Antonyms.* DISCONSOLATE means "sorrowful or sad," so "cheerful" is a precise opposite.

24. **(C)** *Antonyms.* A MALEDICTION is a cursing or an invocation of evil. "Blessing" is a good opposite.

25. **(A)** *Antonyms.* Since ACERBIC means "sour" or "harsh," "sweet" is a straightforward opposite.

26. **(E)** *Antonyms.* LUGUBRIOUS means "mournful," so "joyful" is a good opposite.

27. **(C)** *Antonyms.* PROFLIGATE means "shamelessly wicked" or "abandoned to vice." "Virtuous" is a good antonym.

28. **(B)** *Antonyms.* INCHOATE means "just begun" or "only partially in existence or operation," so "fully developed" is a good opposite.

29. **(B)** *Antonyms.* CRAVEN means "cowardly" or "base," so "courageous" is a good antonym.

30. **(D)** *Antonyms.* SATURNINE means "gloomy or morose," so "joyful" is a perfect opposite.

## SECTION 3—QUANTITATIVE REASONING (p. 739)

1. **(C)** *Geometry Comparison.* Let the unlabeled angle of the triangle be $w$:

$$x + y + w = 180$$
$$- \quad z + w = 180$$
$$x + y + w = z + w$$
$$x + y = z$$

2. **(A)** *Arithmetic Comparison.* Simplify across the comparison by subtracting $5^7$ from both sides and by adding $2^4$ and $2^5$ to both sides. Column A becomes $2^5$ and Column B becomes $2^4$. So, Column A is larger.

3. **(B)** *Algebra Comparison.* Square both sides: Column A becomes $x^2$, and Column B becomes $x^2 + 1$. Then, subtract $x^2$ from both sides. The final comparison is zero in Column A with 1 in Column B.

4. **(C)** *Geometry Comparison.* Use the "big angle/little angle" theorem: $x + y = 180 \Rightarrow x = 180 - y$.

5. **(B)** *Arithmetic Comparison.* When the indicated operation is simple, just do it. In Column B: $2(\frac{15}{16}) = \frac{30}{16} = 1\frac{14}{16}$. So, $\frac{30}{16}$ is larger than $\frac{15}{16}$.

6. **(C)** *Geometry Comparison.* Although the figures have different shapes, they are both quadrilaterals. And the sum of the measure of the interior angles of any quadrilateral is $360°$.

7. **(C)** *Arithmetic Comparison.* Here, the indicated operations are simple, so do them:

Column A: $-3 \div -1 = 3$
Column B: $-3 \cdot -1 = 3$

So, the two columns are equal.

8. **(D)** *Algebra Comparison.* Multiply the inequality by 2: $2x > y$. Does that help you make the comparison between $x$ and $y$? No. The inequality asserts only that 2 times $x$ is larger than $y$, but the inequality does not determine the relationship between $x$ and $y$. Of course, you can reach the same conclusion by substituting some numbers. If $x = 2$, then $y$ must be less than 4—but how much less? $y$ could be 3 (in which case $y > x$) or 2 (in which case $y = x$) or 1 (in which case $y < x$).

9. **(B)** *Arithmetic Comparison.* Find the percent at which items are taxed: $\frac{\$25.20}{\$360} = 0.07 = 7\%$. So, the sales tax on $420 would be: $0.07 \cdot \$420 = \$29.40$.

10. **(B)** *Algebra Comparison.* One way of making this comparison would be to redefine the two larger integers in terms of the smallest integer. Since these are consecutive even integers, $y = x + 2$ and $z = x + 4$. Using these values for $y$ and $z$ in Column A and B, we have:

    Column A: $x + (x + 2) + 1 = 2x + 3$
    Column B: $(x + 2) + (x + 4) - 1 = 2x + 5$

    So, no matter what the value of $x$, Column B is two larger than Column A. Of course, you could also reach the same conclusion by picking values for the variables, for example, $x = 2$, $y = 4$, and $z = 6$.

11. **(D)** *Geometry Comparison.* Remember that the figures in this section are not necessarily drawn to scale. Here, you know that $x$ and $y$ are both positive. (Both coordinates in the first quadrant are positive.) And you know that $a$ is positive and $b$ is negative. (In the fourth quadrant the $x$ coordinate is positive and the $y$ coordinate is negative.) However, this information is not sufficient to determine whether the *sum* of $x$ and $y$ is more than the *sum* of $a$ and $b$.

12. **(B)** *Algebra Comparison.* This is a defined function problem. Since $3p$ is negative, $p$ must be negative and Column A is zero. Since $q - 3$ is positive, $q$ must be positive, and Column B is 1.

13. **(C)** *Algebra Comparison.* The equation can be rewritten as $x = y$, so Column A becomes 0 and Column B becomes 0; so the two columns are equal. Of course, you could reach the same conclusion by picking some numbers.

14. **(A)** *Geometry Comparison.* To calculate the volume of any rectangular solid, you just multiply the three dimensions. To calculate the volume of a cube (which is the special case of a rectangular solid in which all three dimensions are the same), you just multiply:

    $$\text{Volume}_{\text{cube}} = \text{edge} \cdot \text{edge} \cdot \text{edge}$$
    $$8 = \text{edge}^3 \Rightarrow \text{edge} = 2$$

    The area of each face of a cube with an edge of 2 is $2 \cdot 2 = 4$; and since the cube has six faces, the total surface area of the cube is $6 \cdot 4 = 24$ square centimeters.

15. **(E)** *Arithmetic.* You can arrive at the correct answer by reasoning that since $2^x = 16$, $x = 4$. Therefore, $4 = \frac{y}{2}$ and $y = 8$. Or, you can work backwards by substituting answers. If $y = 8$, then $x = 4$, and it is true that $2^4 = 16$.

16. **(E)** *Geometry.* There are two triangles in the given figure: the large right triangle and the smaller triangle within that triangle formed by $30°$, $y°$, and $z°$. For the large right triangle, $x + 30 + 90 = 180 \Rightarrow x = 60$. Then, for the smaller triangle, since $x = y$, $y = 60$. So, $60 + 30 + z = 180 \Rightarrow z = 90$.

17. **(A)** *Algebra.* The least possible value for the expression $\frac{x+y}{z}$ will occur when $x$ and $y$ are the least and $z$ is greatest: $\frac{(6+3)}{10} = \frac{9}{10}$.

18. **(B)** *Geometry.* The base of the triangle is $3k - k = 2k$, and the altitude of the triangle is $4k - k = 3k$. Since the area of a triangle is equal to $\frac{1}{2}(\text{altitude})(\text{base})$, the area is $\frac{1}{2}(2k)(3k) = 12 \Rightarrow 3k^2 = 12 \Rightarrow k^2 = 4 \Rightarrow k = 2$.

19. **(C)** *Algebra.* Since $x$ and $y$ are integers, just try substituting numbers. $y$ must be 5 and $x$ must be 2.

20. **(B)** *Algebra.* Set up an equation. Let $h$ be the original height of the sapling and solve for $h$: $h = \frac{9h}{10} + \frac{9}{10} \Rightarrow 10h = 9h + 9 \Rightarrow h = 9$. You can also test the answer choices.

21. **(E)** *Graphs.* Total sales were $26 million. Domestic sales accounted for $\frac{16}{26} = \frac{8}{13}$, or just more than 60 percent; therefore, foreign sales account for about 40 percent of total sales.

22. **(B)** *Graphs.* The arithmetic needed to answer this question is not in and of itself difficult. You need to create a fraction: $\frac{\text{sales} - \text{expenses}}{\text{expenses}}$. Work with the fractions directly, instead of converting them to percents. Since $20\% = \frac{1}{5}$, any fraction that is larger than $\frac{1}{5}$ is a year which meets the conditions specified in the item stem.

$\quad$ 1991: $\frac{14-9}{14} = \frac{5}{14}$ ($\frac{5}{14}$ is approximately $\frac{1}{3}$, so it is greater than $\frac{1}{5}$.)

$\quad$ 1992: $\frac{19-16}{19} = \frac{3}{19}$ ($\frac{3}{19}$ is slightly less than $\frac{1}{8}$, so it is less than $\frac{1}{5}$.)

$\quad$ 1993: $\frac{24-21}{24} = \frac{3}{24} = \frac{1}{8}$ ($\frac{1}{8}$ is less than $\frac{1}{5}$.)

$\quad$ 1994: $\frac{26-22}{26} = \frac{4}{26} = \frac{2}{13}$ (Since $\frac{2}{14} < \frac{2}{13} < \frac{2}{12}$, $\frac{1}{7} < \frac{2}{13} < \frac{1}{6}$; so, $\frac{2}{13}$ is less than $\frac{1}{5}$.)

$\quad$ 1995: $\frac{30-25}{30} = \frac{5}{30} = \frac{1}{6}$ ($\frac{1}{6}$ is less than $\frac{1}{5}$.)

So, only in 1991 were profits more than 20 percent of total sales.

23. **(E)** *Graphs.* During the period specified, the greatest increase in revenues occurred from 1988 to 1989: $1989 - 1988 = \$7,000,000 - \$5,000,000 = \$2,000,000$.

24. **(E)** *Graphs.* Divide total sales for the year in question by the number of units sold to get the average price per unit: average price = revenue $\div$ units $= \$9,000,000 \div 750 = \$12,000$.

25. **(C)** *Graphs.* Since this question asks about percent change, you should use the "change-over" formula. Since you will be creating fractions of the form "$\frac{\text{Change}}{\text{Original}}$," try to compare fractions directly to determine which is larger. (In that way, you avoid the necessity of converting the fractions to percents.)

$\quad$ (A): $\frac{1987 - 1986}{1986} = \frac{450 - 400}{400} = \frac{50}{400} = \frac{1}{8}$

$\quad$ (B): $\frac{1988 - 1987}{1987} = \frac{500 - 450}{450} = \frac{50}{450} = \frac{1}{9}$

$\quad$ (C): $\frac{1989 - 1988}{1988} = \frac{600 - 500}{500} = \frac{100}{500} = \frac{1}{5}$

$\quad$ (D): $\frac{1990 - 1989}{1989} = \frac{550 - 600}{600} = -\frac{50}{600} = -\frac{1}{12}$ (decrease)

$\quad$ (E): $\frac{1991 - 1990}{1990} = \frac{650 - 550}{550} = \frac{100}{550} = \frac{2}{11}$

26. **(E)** *Algebra.* Since $n > m$, the net drain from the tank per minute will be $n - m$. So, the time required to empty the tank is $\frac{g}{n-m}$. You can arrive at the same conclusion by substituting numbers.

27. **(C)** *Arithmetic.* The easiest way to attack this problem is to "test-the-test." Each of the numbers given in the choices will produce an integer except for the value given in (C): $\frac{13(3)}{7} = \frac{39}{7}$, which is not an integer.

Alternatively, note that for $\frac{13t}{7}$ to be and integer, the numerator must be a multiple of the denominator. Since 13 is not a multiple of 7, $t$ must be a multiple of 7.

28. **(D)** *Algebra.* Rewrite the equations:

$$\frac{(x+y)}{x} = 4 \Rightarrow 4x = x + y \Rightarrow 3x = y$$

$$\frac{(y+z)}{z} = 5 \Rightarrow y + z = 5z \Rightarrow 4z = y$$

Since $3x$ and $4z$ are both equal to $y$: $3x = 4z \Rightarrow \frac{x}{z} = \frac{4}{3}$.

# Practice Test II

## SECTION 1—ANALYTICAL WRITING (p. 753)

### *'PRESENT YOUR PERSPECTIVE ON AN ISSUE' SAMPLE ESSAY RESPONSE*

Computers are so ubiquitous that it sometimes seems as though they control every aspect of our lives. Certainly, they handle a lot of very important tasks that are literally matters of life and death. For example, large government and private computers keep track of air traffic, tracking individual airplanes, plotting safe routes, and monitoring the skies for emergencies. Or, to take another example, computers are also essential for doing advanced medical research. Whether we get a new drug or treatment seems to depend on whether a university computer concluded in a study that the therapy improved the chances for treatment of a certain disease. Computers also are responsible for a lot of small but useful tasks: they open and close doors automatically, regulate the temperature of buildings, and operate various appliances like VCRs and microwaves. And they seem to do this all behind our backs and without our asking for it or consent. Sometimes, computers are really intrusive. Who has not been interrupted during dinner by the computerized dialer of some telemarketer? Also, most of us worry that computers have so much information about us that we cannot control.

On the other hand, in spite of all of this, computers do not really control us. We control them. In the first place, computers depend on us for their very existence. We manufacture them, and then we program them. Moreover, we can always escape from them. We can go camping in the wilderness or even just take a walk in the country without the help of a computer. In the final analysis, we can always pull the plug if we want to. If you do not want to program your VCR, you do not have to.

On balance, while it may seem that computers control us, a closer look at things shows that we really control them. If there are ways that computers adversely affect us when we do not want them to, it is not really the computer's doing. It is the person behind the computer. The telemarketing computer did not tell itself to call me during dinner; the salesperson did. So, if there is any blame to be assigned, it belongs to people, not inanimate machines.

### *'ANALYSIS OF AN ARGUMENT' SAMPLE ESSAY RESPONSE*

The argument to abolish the volunteer rescue squad in favor of a professional ambulance service is not persuasive for three reasons. First, the evidence cited does not prove the existence of a serious problem. Second, any problem that does exist can perhaps be solved with less drastic measures. Third, the radical plan called for might have serious side-effects.

First, the six-minute difference in response time does not, in and of itself, prove the existence of a serious problem. The evidence refers simply to a review of records but says nothing more about how that review was conducted. It would be important to determine that a representative time-slice was taken and that representative cases were reviewed. A single difficult case, for example during a snowstorm, could skew the statistics. Additionally, the information given in the argument does not prove that the six-minute difference is an important difference. It is entirely possible that the volunteer squad responds to calls according to their survey. For example, a minor traffic accident does not call for break-neck speed.

Second, if a problem does exist, Putnam should consider ways of improving the performance of the rescue squad. At minimum, it should look at the equipment now being used. Is the squad properly equipped? Is its dispatch and radio equipment reliable? Are its vehicles in good working order? Beyond that, it should look at training procedures, perhaps compare them with those of similar rescue squads elsewhere. If improvement is needed, more training would be in order. Finally, it could even consider working more closely with Empire, calling on Empire to answer those calls when it is unable to respond.

Third, Putnam should also consider the possibility that eliminating its rescue squad may cause new problems. Of course, it has to determine what the cost of such a move would be. Additionally, it has to realize that a private company might not be as cooperative as volunteers from the community. Further, if the new plan should be a complete failure, it might be difficult to reinstate the old system. People might be reluctant to volunteer again; leadership might be lacking; equipment might not be available or available only at a prohibitive cost.

In conclusion, there are at least three good reasons why Putnam should proceed cautiously and get more information before it makes a decision.

## SECTION 2—QUANTITATIVE REASONING (p. 762)

1. **(C)** *Geometry Comparison.* Since the sum of the measures of the interior angles of a four-sided figure is 360, $2x+4x+70+110=360 \Rightarrow 6x+180=360 \Rightarrow 6x=180 \Rightarrow x=30$. So, the two columns are equal.

2. **(C)** *Arithmetic Comparison.* Do the indicated operations. Column A is $\sqrt{6} \cdot \sqrt{10} = \sqrt{60}$. Column B is $\sqrt{3} \cdot \sqrt{20} = \sqrt{60}$. The "good enough" principle says that this is as far as you need to go. The two columns are equal.

3. **(B)** *Algebra Comparison.* $x$ is negative and a negative number raised to an odd power is negative while a negative number raised to an even power is positive.

4. **(B)** *Arithmetic Comparison.* Subtract 50 from both sides. Column A becomes $x$ and Column B becomes 50. The centered information establishes that $x$ is less than 50, so Column B is greater.

5. **(D)** *Arithmetic Comparison.* Set up an equation that expresses algebraically the centered information: $\frac{(x+y+z)}{3} = y \Rightarrow x+y+z = 3y \Rightarrow x+z = 2y$. That is one equation with three variables, so it is not possible to determine the value of any one of the variables. You can also reach the same conclusion just by substituting some values.

6. **(A)** *Geometry Comparison.* Since $(x,z)$ is in Quadrant I, $x$ must be positive. (In that quadrant, both coordinates are positive.) Since $(z,y)$ is in Quadrant IV, $y$ must be negative. (In that quadrant, the $x$ coordinate is positive and the $y$ coordinate is negative.) Therefore, $x$ must be larger than $y$, and Column A greater than Column B.

7. **(C)** *Arithmetic Comparison.* One way of solving this comparison is to set up simultaneous equations to find the numbers of pounds of peanuts in the mixture. Let $x$ be the number of pounds of peanuts and $y$ the number of pounds of cashews: $x+y=2 \Rightarrow 1.25x+2.25y=3.5$. (Note: The mix costs $1.75 per pound, but there are 2 pounds, so the cost of the mix is $3.50.) Using the first equation, express $y$ in terms of $x$: $y=2-x$. Substitute this value for $y$ in the second equation: $1.25x+2.25(2-x)=3.5 \Rightarrow 1.25x+4.5-2.25x=3.5 \Rightarrow -x=-1 \Rightarrow x=1$.

Alternatively, recognize that $1.75 (the price per pound of the mix) is the average of $1.25 and $2.25, the price of peanuts and cashews, respectively. This means that there must be equal amounts of each in the mix. Another alternative is to work backwards. Assume that there is exactly one pound of peanuts in the mix. That would mean one pound of cashews, and the total cost of the mix would be $1.25+$2.25=$3.50 for 2 pounds, or $1.75 per pound. This proves that the mix contains one pound of peanuts.

8. **(A)** *Arithmetic Comparison.* One way to make the comparison is simply to perform the indicated operations:

Column A: $99+97+95=291$
Column B: $98+96+94=288$

Alternatively, make the comparison by reasoning that the largest odd integer less than 100, which is 99, is one more than the largest even integer less than 100, which is 98. Then, since the next less odd integer will be greater than the next less even integer and so on, the sum of the odd integers must be greater than the sum of the even integers.

9. **(D)** *Arithmetic Comparison.* Although the centered statement provides information about distances, it provides no information about direction ($OC$ = Old City; $NT$ = New Town; $M$ = Middlebury):

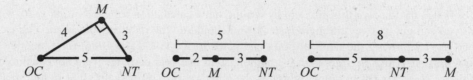

These figures demonstrate that the distance in kilometers from Old City to Middlebury is indeterminate.

10. **(A)** *Arithmetic Comparison.* $\overline{XY}$ is longer than $0.55 - 0.25 = 0.30$. So, Column A is greater.

11. **(D)** *Arithmetic Comparison.* The other numbers in the averages could be anything, so the comparison is indeterminate. If you are not certain of this conclusion, try working with some numbers. For example, use only positive numbers for Column A, and use two negative numbers for Column B.

12. **(B)** *Algebra Comparison.* The numerator of Column A can be factored: $2x + 6y = 2(x + 3y)$. Since the centered information provides that $x + 3y = 6$, the numerator of Column A is equal to 12, and $\frac{12}{5}$ is smaller than $\frac{13}{5}$.

13. **(D)** *Algebra Comparison.* The easiest way to miss this question is to reason that $k$, a positive integer, is the product of $x$ and $y$, both positive integers as well, and that $k$ must therefore be larger than $x$. Although it is true that $k$ might be larger than $x$ (e.g., if $x = 2$, $y = 3$, and $k = 6$), it is also true that $y$ might be 1, in which case $x$ and $k$ are equal: $x(1) = k$.

14. **(D)** *Geometry Comparison.* You can deduce that $x + y = 90$ and that $w + z = 90$, but this is not sufficient to find a value for $x - y$ and $w - z$. If the algebra does not persuade you of this conclusion, try distorting the figures. If you distort the figure, the sizes of the angles change—$x$ might be larger than $y$ (in which case $x - y$ is positive), equal to $y$ (in which case $x - y = 0$), or smaller than $y$ (in which case $x - y$ is negative).

15. **(B)** *Arithmetic.* $2 \cdot 10^4 = 20,000$, and $121,212 + 20,000 = 141,212$.

16. **(E)** *Algebra.* You can reason in general terms to the correct answer. As for (A), since $k$ is less than $l$, $k$ cannot be equal to $l$ plus something. The same reasoning applies to (B), (C), and (D). (E), however, could be true. For example, if Jack is five, and Ken is ten, and Larry is 15, and Mike is 20, then $5 + 20 = 10 + 15$.

17. **(A)** *Geometry.* The perimeter is: $2(3a - 2) + 2(2a - 1) = 6a - 4 + 4a - 2 = 10a - 6$. That is a fairly simple algebraic manipulation, but if you insist on avoiding algebra altogether, you could assume a value for $a$. For example, if $a = 2$ then the length of the figure is $3(2) - 2 = 4$, and the width of the figure is $2(2) - 1 = 3$. The perimeter would be $4 + 4 + 3 + 3 = 14$. Substituting 2 for $a$ into the correct formula yields the value 14. Only (A) does that.

18. **(B)** *Arithmetic.* Since $x$ is 80 percent of $y$, $x = 0.8y$, and $y = \frac{x}{0.8} = 1.25x$. So, $y$ is 125 percent of $x$. Or, you can just use some numbers. Assume that $y$ is 100. If $y = 100$, then $x = 80$ percent of $y = 80$. Finally, find what percent $y$ is of $x$: $\frac{100}{80} = \frac{5}{4} = 1.25 = 125$ percent.

19. **(D)** *Algebra.* You can rewrite $m - n > 0$ by adding $n$ to both sides: $m > n$. As for (A), this proves that $m < n$. As for (B), this proves nothing about $m$ and $n$, since $m$ and $n$ might be either negative or positive. The same is true of (C), which is equivalent to $m > -n$. Finally, as for (E), you have relative values for neither $m$ and $n$ nor their signs.

20. **(E)** *Algebra.* Here, we have a defined function. Just do the indicated operation. $(-1.1)^2 = 1.21$, and the smallest integer greater than that is 2.

21. **(D)** *Graphs.* Since this question asks for percent change, use the "change-over" strategy. $\frac{1995-1986}{1986} \Rightarrow \frac{1.5-0.3}{0.3} = \frac{1.2}{0.3} = 4$, or 400%.

22. **(B)** *Graphs.* If you try to solve this problem by writing out a calculation for each of the years, you will run out of time before you can get halfway through. Instead, you should do the math in your head. You can find 10 percent of a number just by moving the decimal point one place to the left. Take 1986, for example. Ten percent of 6 million is 0.6 million, which is larger than 0.3 million, so in that year earnings were not equal to or greater than 10 percent of sales. Work your way quickly through the other years. You will find that in four years, earnings were either equal to or greater than 10 percent of sales: 1989, 1990, 1991, and 1994.

23. **(B)** *Graphs.* In 1995, medical and dental care accounted for 4.0% of expenditures. Since the question specifically asks for an approximation, we will use $35,000 as the value of expenditures in 1995: $0.04 \cdot \$35,000 = \$1,400$.

24. **(C)** *Graphs.* To answer this question, use the "change-over" strategy. Percent Increase $= \frac{\text{Change}}{\text{Original}} = \frac{(\$40,000-\$35,000)}{\$35,000} = \frac{\$5,000}{\$35,000} = \frac{1}{7} = 14.2\%$.

25. **(E)** *Graphs.* To answer this question, just rank order the categories in each year:

| 1995 | 1996 |
|------|------|
| 1. Rent | 1. Rent |
| 2. Food | 2. Food |
| 3. Clothing | 3. Clothing |
| 4. Automobile | 4. Automobile |
| 5. Utilities | 5. Utilities |
| 6. Savings | 6. Entertainment |
| 7. Entertainment | 7. Savings |
| 8. Medical, etc. | 8. Charity |
| 9. Charity | 9. Other |
| 10. Furnishings | 10. Medical, etc. |
| 11. Other | 11. Furnishings |

So, six categories (Savings, Entertainment, Medical, Charity, Furnishings, and Other) changed ranks from 1995 to 1996.

26. **(E)** *Geometry.* First, find the area of the circle: $\pi r^2 = \pi(2)^2 = 4\pi$. Since the shaded area is equal to $3\pi$, it accounts for $\frac{3\pi}{4\pi} = \frac{3}{4}$ of the circle. So, the unshaded area accounts for $\frac{1}{4}$ of the circle. This means that angle $x$ plus the angle vertically opposite $x$ are equal to $\frac{1}{4}(360°) = 90°$. So, $2x = 90$, and $x = 45$. Or, you could have relied on estimation.

27. **(D)** *Arithmetic.* Use the "this-of-that" strategy: $\frac{\text{this}}{\text{of that}} = \frac{\text{tin}}{\text{entire bar}} = \frac{100}{100+150} = \frac{100}{250} = \frac{2}{5} = 40\%$.

28. **(B)** *Arithmetic.* You can solve this problem using $S$ and $T$ as unknowns. Since $S$ is 150 percent of $T$, $S = 1.5T$. Then, the question asks you to express $\frac{T}{S+T}$ as a percent. Just substitute $1.5T$ for $S$: $\frac{T}{1.5T+T} = \frac{T}{2.5T} = \frac{1}{2.5} = 40\%$. If you do not like working with letters, the pick some numbers. Let $S$ be 10 and $T$ be 15. Then, $\frac{T}{S+T} = \frac{15}{10+15} = \frac{10}{25} = 40\%$.

## SECTION 3—VERBAL REASONING (p. 768)

1. **(E)** *Tools.* An INCISION is made with a SCALPEL, or a SCALPEL is the tool used to make an INCISION. A "cut" is made with a "saw," or a "saw" is the tool used to "cut."

2. **(A)** *Tools.* This analogy is fairly straightforward. An ALTIMETER is a tool used to measure HEIGHT, and a "speedometer" is a tool used to measure "velocity."

3. **(B)** *Type of.* A CARAVAN is a type of PROCESSION, and a "wedding" is a type of "ceremony."

4. **(C)** *Defining Characteristic.* A defining characteristic of speech that SLANDERS is its PEJORATIVE content, and a defining characteristic of speech that "extols" is its "laudatory" content.

5. **(E)** *Lack of Defining Characteristic.* That which is UNGAINLY lacks ELEGANCE, and that which is "perfunctory" lacks "attention."

6. **(D)** *Defining Characteristic.* A CONSERVATOR is one who prevents WASTE, and a "chaperon" is one who prevents "transgression."

7. **(B)** *Defining Characteristic.* A POLEMICIST is involved in CONTROVERSY, and a "visionary" in a "dream."

8. **(A)** *Antonyms.* INCIPIENT means "beginning" or "in the first stage"; therefore, a good opposite is "completed."

9. **(D)** *Antonyms.* To SANCTIFY is to "make holy" or to "purify"; therefore, a straightforward antonym is "defile."

10. **(E)** *Antonyms.* To DISSIPATE is to "scatter or disperse"; therefore, its opposite is "gather."

11. **(A)** *Antonyms.* ASPERITY means "roughness" or "unevenness"; therefore, a good antonym is "smoothness."

12. **(D)** *Antonyms.* IGNOMINIOUS means "dishonorable" or "disgraceful." "Honorable" is a precise antonym.

13. **(C)** *Antonyms.* EVANESCENT means "vanishing, fleeting, or passing away." A good opposite is "permanent."

14. **(E)** *Antonyms.* To VILIFY means to "slander, defile, or defame." "Laud," which means to "praise," is a fine opposite.

15. **(C)** *Antonyms.* As a verb, TENDER means "to present for acceptance" or "to offer." Therefore, "retract" is a good antonym.

16. **(C)** *Antonyms.* Since FUNGIBLE means "capable of being used in place of something else," "unique" is a good opposite.

17. **(D)** *Thought Extension.* For this item, an extension of thought is indicated by the subordinate conjunction "because." The sentence tells you that Western physicians are learning a procedure. Logically, they are doing this "because" it is desirable, so you should look for the noun that has a positive connotation. This eliminates (B) and (E). If you substitute (A) or (C), you have a meaningless sentence. So, (D) must be the correct answer choice.

18. **(E)** *Thought Extension.* For this item, an extension of thought is indicated by the logical structure of the sentence. The second missing word must extend the idea expressed by the first missing word ("the chords [were] so —— that [they] produced... ——"). You can eliminate (A) because the idea of hearing a melody does not explain why a chord is superfluous. You can eliminate (B) because the idea of hearing a roar does not explain why a chord might be pretentious. You can eliminate (C) because the idea of hearing applause does not explain why a chord might be melodious. And you can eliminate (D) because hearing harmony does not explain why a chord might be

versatile. (E) preserves the sense and logic of the sentence. The phrase "hearing cacophony" indicates that the chord is "discordant."

19. **(E)** *Thought Extension.* For this item, substitute each pair until you find one that works. You can immediately eliminate (A) on the grounds of usage, as "*apathetic* to humor" makes no sense. Next, the "salacious" is not "heretical" to humor, so eliminate (B). The "grandiose" is not "inferior" to humor, so eliminate (C). The "innocuous" is not "extraneous" to humor, so eliminate (D). You are left with (E), which does make sense. The "macabre" might be "antithetical" to humor.

20. **(E)** *Thought Reversal.* For this item, a reversal of thought is indicated by the word "rather." The President responded with something other than clarity and precision. You should immediately look for opposites of these words for the blanks. (E), "obfuscation" and "vagueness," does the job.

21. **(C)** *Combined Reasoning.* There are two key logical signals in this item that are important in understanding the overall structure of the sentence. The first blank requires a word to reverse the idea of grand spectacle, since we know that the modern audience has learned to appreciate the opposite of grand spectacle. The second blank requires a word to extend the idea of grand spectacle. (A) is not possible, since "irreverence" is not the opposite of grand spectacle and "hapless" does not extend that idea. (B) seems plausible, since one could say that film and television are "sophisticated," but "monotonous" is hardly the word one would use to describe grand spectacle. (C) is correct because the idea of "minutiae," or details, is opposite to the idea of something large or grand like opera. The second word also fits nicely, since "extravagant" extends the idea of grand spectacle. As for (D), the first word fails to make a meaningful sentence, and (E) cannot be correct since "flamboyance" extends the idea of grand spectacle instead of reversing it.

22. **(E)** *Thought Extension.* The first blank obviously requires a word that means something like "standard" or "popular," since it states that behaviorism was a protest against what already existed. The second blank requires something that has to do with the mind. (A) is not correct because although "redoubtable" might be a possible choice, the second word does not fit the logic of the sentence. (B) is wrong because although one might make a case for the first word, the second word also violates the logic of the sentence. (C) is also wrong because the second word fails to create a logical sentence. (D) creates an illogical sentence; something "new-fangled" would not be related to a tradition. (E) is correct because "orthodox" is related to the idea of tradition, and "mentalistic" is related the idea of the mind.

23. **(D)** *Main Idea.* The passage is primarily a discussion of what was contained in school textbooks in the late eighteenth and early nineteenth centuries. (D) correctly summarizes this. You can eliminate (A) because this is not the main point of the discussion. Though you do learn something about the origin of the work ethic by reading the passage, that is not the author's goal. You can eliminate (B) because the passage is more focused than (B) suggests. It does not discuss the role of education generally, except to mention in passing that its main objective was to teach civic virtue. (C) makes the mistake of elevating one part of the passage to the status of main idea. Finally, (E) is incorrect because the focus of the passage is not the establishment of schools but what material was included in textbooks.

24. **(D)** *Further Application.* There is ample support for (A) (literacy), (B) (American history), (C) (patriotic and moral virtues), and (E) (principles of republican government) in the first two paragraphs. As for (D), the first paragraph specifically states that at that time education would not have included occupational training.

25. **(B)** *Specific Detail.* In the second paragraph the author equates the Federalists with conservatives, so the passage contains information that would answer the question posed by (B). As for (A), though the passage does state that most early textbooks were written by New Englanders, the author does not explain why this happened. As for (C), the passage does state that the founders believed education to be important to the welfare of the Republic, but the passage does not say how much education the founders wanted children to have. As for (D), the passage does not mention any authors by name. Finally, as for (E), the passage does not talk about the attitudes of the majority of citizens—as opposed to the attitudes of the founders themselves.

26. **(A)** *Implied Idea.* In the second paragraph, the author states that the textbook writers, most of whom were Puritans, believed that political virtue rests upon moral and religious precepts. We can infer, therefore, that other Puritans would agree with this position as well.

27. **(D)** *Main Idea.* You can eliminate (E) because the first word is not descriptive of the selection. The selection is not intended to warn. Then, (A) can be eliminated because the main point of the passage is not to define terms. Although the author does define ultrasonography in the opening paragraph, that is a small part of the passage. You can eliminate (B) because the focus of the passage is ultrasonography, not radiography. (C) should be eliminated because the author's main purpose is not to encourage the use of ultrasonography. When the author describes the advantages of ultrasonography, he is not trying to sell the reader on the technique; he is informing the reader. This is why (D) best describes the overall theme of the passage. The author discusses this new medical technology.

28. **(E)** *Implied Idea.* In the second to last sentence of the first paragraph the author states that doctors who are concerned about the health of a fetus use ultrasound rather than radiography. Although the passage does not specifically state that x-rays are hazardous, we may infer from this statement that they are. As for (A), while it is true that x-rays are absorbed by bone and therefore by the skull, that does not explain why a doctor uses one technique over the other on a pregnant patient. As for (B), the author does say that ultrasonography is not expensive, but cost is not the reason the technique is particularly attractive to doctors attending to pregnant women. (C) is incorrect because x-rays penetrate the womb, thereby posing a threat to the fetus. Finally, (D) like (B) is contradicted by the first paragraph of the selection.

29. **(E)** *Implied Idea.* The author states that a result of the PATCO strike is that management can now expect to regain some of the power it gave up to labor in earlier decades. You may infer that the outcome of that strike was favorable to management. This is the description given by (E). As for (A), though the author mentions bad faith negotiations in the first paragraph, there is nothing to connect that concept with the example mentioned in the second paragraph. As for (B), nothing in the passage supports a conclusion one way or the other about the length of the strike, as opposed to its outcome. (C) and (D) make the same mistake as (A). Though they are ideas mentioned in the passage, there is nothing to connect them with the example of the PATCO strike.

30. **(C)** *Implied Idea.* The first sentence of the second paragraph states that *since* the economic situation will not improve, union leaders will be frustrated. So, the stage is set for confrontation. We may infer, therefore, that if economic conditions were better, labor would be happier, and tensions would be lessened. This is (C). (A) carries this line of reasoning too far. We can infer that better economic conditions would prevent management from recouping its losses, but we cannot infer that better economic conditions will cause further erosion of management's position. As for (B), the opposite conclusion seems inferable. When economic circumstances are good, labor demands more. As for (E), there is nothing to connect this idea mentioned in the first paragraph with the line of reasoning in the second. Finally, (D) makes the same mistake as (A).

# Practice Test III

## SECTION 1—ANALYTICAL WRITING (p. 781)

### *'PRESENT YOUR PERSPECTIVE ON AN ISSUE' SAMPLE ESSAY RESPONSE*

Providing a public school education to children is one of the most important functions of government because most children (except those in private schools) have to attend public school until they are at least 16 years old. Children are in school several hours every day, so the content of the curriculum influences them in some important ways. But what should be the limits of a public school curriculum in a democracy where freedom of conscience is so important?

On the one hand, it might be thought that the sole function of public schools should be to teach academic and practical skills and to avoid ethical issues altogether. Certainly, government through public education should avoid dictating religious views. It is no business of the schools to tell children that they should be Protestant, Catholic, Jewish, Muslim, or any other religion. And related issues such as abortion and sexual activity should be left to parents.

On the other hand, it seems impossible to avoid such issues altogether. While it might be possible to teach pure math without ethical overtones, history and even literature are about human activities. It is impossible to teach about the Holocaust without saying that it was morally wrong. Teaching the history of western expansion would be one-sided if it did not raise questions about the actions of the white settlers. Hamlet would not be Hamlet without the dilemma of "to be or not to be." And even in the so-called *hard* sciences, questions about the environment and the appropriate use of and conservation of resources raise ethical issues that just cannot be avoided. Biology and human reproduction are legitimate academic subjects that also start to raise ethical questions including evolution.

It is easy in theory to say that government should not be in the business of teaching ethics in the public schools. But in practice, the ethical issues are impossible to avoid. Instead of pretending that schools can avoid morality altogether, we should insist that when such issues come up, they are presented from a variety of perspectives so that children are exposed to different viewpoints but not told what to believe.

### *'ANALYSIS OF AN ARGUMENT' SAMPLE ESSAY RESPONSE*

The argument is interesting but not entirely persuasive. It will obviously appeal to many people who uncritically accept the idea that *computers* are a silver bullet for all of our educational woes. A closer look, however, shows that much more would be needed to support the conclusion.

First, it is necessary to determine in what respects, if any, the education at Hudson Falls School is deficient. The argument does not say that Hudson Falls students are prevented from going to college because they do not learn about computers. For all we know, Hudson Falls already has all of the computer equipment that it needs and gives its students instruction in computers. Additionally, the number of students who go to college is not the only measure of a school's effectiveness. Not every student wants to go to college. It would also be important to learn whether Hudson Falls effectively serves the needs of students who want vocational training using computers.

Second, it would be important to ask whether or not the computers used at Fort Ann School made the difference in the number of college-bound students. Perhaps Fort Ann already had enough computers to begin with, and the twelve new computers were really just extra resources that did not have a real impact. And what was taught during the two hours of computer instruction? Word processing, graphics, bookkeeping, internet research? Some computer skills are more relevant to college preparation than others. Nothing in the argument draws a causal connection between the computer instruction and the number of students going to college.

Third, it is necessary to consider what would be the overall effect of investing in new computer equipment and requiring computer study. We do not know anything about the size of the student body at Hudson Falls School, but new computer equipment may mean a substantial investment compared to the overall budget. That could mean money not available for texts, library books, newspaper subscriptions, field trips, and even sports. Additionally, time spent in a computer lab is time not spent learning a second language or working in the chemistry lab. These other activities may be even more important for college preparation than learning a little about computers.

In summary, the argument fails to prove the conclusion. It does not establish that there is a problem at Hudson Falls; it does not identify the real cause of the supposed problem; and it does not consider the overall effect of spending more money on computers. The word "computers" has a nice ring to it; but a lot more research would have to be done before it could be concluded that new computers and required courses are needed at Hudson Falls School.

## SECTION 2—VERBAL REASONING (p. 790)

1. **(E)** *Antonyms.* To REVERE is to "regard with deep awe" or "respect." A straightforward opposite is "despise."

2. **(B)** *Antonyms.* BOORISH means "rude" or "ill-mannered." A precise opposite, then, is "well-mannered."

3. **(A)** *Antonyms.* NASCENT means "coming into being" or "beginning to form." A clear opposite, then, is "fully developed."

4. **(B)** *Antonyms.* Since PENURY means "extreme poverty," the precise opposite is "wealth."

5. **(C)** *Antonyms.* IMPERVIOUS means "incapable of being penetrated," so "penetrable" is a good opposite.

6. **(E)** *Antonyms.* SURREPTITIOUS means "done in stealth; clandestine." "Overt" is the best opposite.

7. **(D)** *Antonyms.* To be INURED means to "become accustomed to something painful." "Sensitive" is a good opposite.

8. **(A)** *Antonyms.* Since IRASCIBLE means "irritable" or "easily provoked to anger," "even-tempered" is a perfect antonym.

9. **(B)** *Antonyms.* ALACRITY means "cheerful willingness to act or serve," so "reluctance" is a good opposite.

10. **(A)** *Combined Reasoning.* There are two key logical signals in this item that are important in understanding the overall structure of the sentence. The sentence starts with a thought-reverser, so we know that the correct choice will describe something unexpected given the amount of money invested. The second blank will be a logical continuation of the first blank, as indicated by the verb "continues." (B), (C), and (E) can be eliminated immediately because they do not create meaningful phrases when substituted into the first blank. (A) and (D) are possibilities because a phone system can be both primitive or outdated. Next, we eliminate (D) because an outdated phone system would hardly elate those who depend on it. (A) creates a logical sentence. The system is primitive, despite the money spent on it, and it continues to inconvenience those who use it.

11. **(C)** *Combined Reasoning.* There are two key logical signals in this item that are important in understanding the overall structure of the sentence. The first blank needs a word that continues the idea of vagueness; the second blank is "unlike" the first and must therefore be something close to an opposite. All of the choices make sense since they can all be used to describe images, but only one parallels vague and that is obscure. The second element, concrete, is an opposite of obscure and completes the sentence nicely. The second elements of (A), (B), (D), and (E) are not things that could be said of images and make no sense when substituted in the sentence.

12. **(B)** *Combined Reasoning.* There are two key logical signals in this item that are important in understanding the overall structure of the sentence. The sentence says that the lawyer argues only what is central, eliminating something. Logically, what is eliminated is what is not central, so you should look for a word that means not central. (A) and (B) are both possibilities. We can eliminate (C), (D), and (E) because they do not make sense in this context. The second element is the deciding factor here. The lawyer would not want to "jeopardize" her client; therefore, (B) is the best answer. It makes no sense to say that the lawyer would not want to "amuse" her client.

13. **(D)** *Combined Reasoning.* There are two key logical signals in this item that are important in understanding the overall structure of the sentence. The thought-reverser is signaled by the phrase "even though." Since people persist, "even though" the government does something, the government must be trying to stop the belief in extraterrestrial life. The second blank requires a thought-extender—something that extends the idea of "personal," and reverses the idea of "godless." Although (A) seems correct at first, since "decry" means "to condemn," the second word of the pair disqualifies it. To say that people need a personal sense of morbidity makes little sense. (B) is incorrect as it fails to reverse the idea that people persist in believing. To say that they persist even though the government endorses their actions is not logical. (C) is not correct for the same reason. If the government creates all such theories, it would not be surprising for people to believe in them. (E) appears to be a possibility since "debunk" has the right negative overtones and it explains why the persistent belief is surprising. The second word of (E), however, does not create a logical thought. People would not need a personal sense of alienation in a godless universe—in fact, that is what this sentence suggests they are trying to avoid.

14. **(B)** *Combined Reasoning.* There are two key logical signals in this item that are important in understanding the overall structure of the sentence. The "in fact" in the second part of the sentence is the clue that tells you that the theory of the breakup of the continents is somehow changed. We are therefore looking for the opposite of "occurring in stages" or something close to it. The second blank requires an extension of that idea. (A) is not correct because although "refining" suggests a change in the theory, the second word, "blatantly," does not reverse the idea of occurring in stages. (C) certainly suggests a strong reversal of the theory, but the second word is practically synonymous with "in stages." (D) appears plausible, since the idea of forging a theory might suggest something new, but the second word does not make a meaningful sentence. (E) is wrong because it does not reverse the theory, but rather "supports" it; and the idea that the breakup was "haphazard" does not reverse the idea of "gradual." (B) is correct because the theory is "reshaped," and the word "simultaneously" reverses the idea that the continents broke up in stages.

15. **(A)** *Thought Extension.* For this item, an extension of thought is indicated not only by the phrase "as well as" but also by the semicolon (punctuation clue). The best strategy here is to eliminate anything that cannot be considered an "art," and to look for a word which has something to do with cooking, as indicated by the semicolon. The first choice, (A) appears to be correct. "Gastronomy" is the art or science of good eating, and "culinary" is an adjective that is related to cooking. The best thing to do is to look at the other choices to be sure that (A) is the correct choice. (B) is wrong because "sedentary" has nothing to do with cooking. (C) is wrong because scientific has nothing to do with cooking. (D) is incorrect because "numismatics" (coin collecting) is not an art. (E) cannot be correct because "clandestine" has nothing to do with cooking.

16. **(B)** *Specific Detail.* In the opening sentence, the author establishes that there are two general responses available to warm-blooded animals for regulating body temperature: behavior and innate mechanisms. The author goes on to state that humans rely primarily on the first type of response but adds that the organism also responds to changes in temperature in the core of the body (the second type of response) and that these changes are triggered by thermoreceptors distributed throughout the central nervous system. Thus, statement (I) must be part of the correct answer choice. In the final sentence of the first paragraph, the author states that the second type of mechanism for regulating temperature is less effective for adjusting to gross changes in temperature than the first type. Thus, (II) must be part of the correct response. Finally, the author does not state that the internal thermoreceptors are not affected by microwave radiation. The problem cited by the author is not that internal thermoreceptors do not respond to changes in the temperature of the core of the body but that they do not trigger the type of response needed to counteract gross changes in environmental temperatures.

17. **(A)** *Logical Structure.* In the lines indicated, the author states that it is possible that an organism could be cooked by microwave radiation (because the radiation penetrates into the core) before it even realizes its temperature is rising. The verb tense here (could) clearly indicates that the author is introducing a hypothetical possibility. Given the shocking nature of the example, we should conclude that the author has introduced it to dramatize a point.

18. **(C)** *Logical Structure.* This is a Logical Structure item that asks about the overall development of the selection. The main organizational principle of the passage is the comparison and contrast of art and knowledge. The author

points to similarities and differences between the two. (A) is incorrect. Though you may think the author has proposed his own theory of the purpose of art, there is no refutation of anything in the passage. As for (B), though some general conclusions are offered, the author does not make any generalizations based on examples. As for (D), though the passage can be viewed as an answer to the question "What is art for?" the author does not make question and answer the organizational principle of the selection. Finally, as for (E), the author states bold conclusions but does not deduce or infer those conclusions from other premises or information.

19. **(C)** *Attitude/Tone.* You can easily eliminate (E) because there is no hint of sarcasm in the passage. As for (D), while poetry and art seem to go together, the author's method of presenting ideas is not poetry. As for the remaining choices, (C) best describes the confident and neutral tone of the passage. As for (A), though the purpose of art may be an important philosophical question (and therefore related to speculation in one sense of the word), the tone of the passage is not speculative. The author makes statements with confidence. (B) goes too far. To assert with confidence is not necessarily to be argumentative.

20. **(B)** *Main Idea.* This is a Main Idea item that asks for an appropriate title. The strategy is to find a title that describes the main point of the passage. The author discusses the use of neuroleptic drugs, their benefits and some disadvantages of their use. Finally, the author suggests possible solutions to the dilemma created by the unwanted effects. (B) correctly describes this development; the word "tradeoff" is particularly well-chosen. (A) is too narrow. The description of the benefits of the drugs is only one-half of the selection. (C) is wrong because it takes one relatively minor point from the passage and elevates that point to the status of main idea. The author does mention that these drugs make psychotherapy possible, but that is not the main point of the selection. (D) is overly broad. The author focuses on the tradeoff in the use of neuroleptic drugs, one particular kind of drug. So, the passage is not a general discussion of recent developments in treatments for mental illness. Finally, (E) is too narrow. It is true that the author mentions a technique for minimizing the effects of tardive dyskenesia, but that is not the main point of the passage.

21. **(C)** *Implied Idea.* The word "inferred" indicates that this is an Implied Idea item. The author does not specifically describe the mechanism by which neuroleptic drugs have their effect, but we can deduce some conclusions about that mechanism. The second paragraph describes the functioning of neuroleptic drugs. Such drugs interfere with the action of dopamine by binding to the dopamine receptors. We can infer that this means the drugs *coat* the receptors so the dopamine cannot be absorbed, the process described by (C). (A) is incorrect. The passage does not state that less dopamine is produced, only that the existing dopamine is rendered relatively ineffective. (B) is incorrect because neuroleptic drugs block the absorption of dopamine by the nerve cells, not the impulses going to the muscles. (D) is incorrect since this is an unwanted side effect of the drugs, not the method by which psychosis is controlled. Finally, as for (E), the passage describes the operation of the drugs in terms of dopamine, a chemical produced by the brain itself. Dopamine is not a drug introduced from outside the body.

22. **(D)** *Further Application.* In the third paragraph, the author suggests that a possible solution to the dilemma is finding an optimal dosage, one that controls psychosis while minimizing the symptoms of tardive dyskinesia. This idea of balancing is the key to this question. Given that a balance must be struck, the most reasonable course of action in the given situation is to reduce the drug dosage, hoping that the lower dosage will be effective and will result in a reduction of the unwanted side effects. (A) is incorrect since the course of action it suggests completely ignores the idea of finding an appropriate balance. (B) is wrong as increasing the dosage would likely result in worse symptoms of tardive dyskinesia. (C) and (E) are related to the general idea of psychosis, but neither suggests a course of action that addresses the dilemma created by the use of neuroleptic drugs.

23. **(A)** *Logical Structure.* The item stem cites an idea mentioned in the passage and then asks *why* that idea was introduced. In the second paragraph, where the author is discussing the effect of neuroleptic drugs, the author states that dopamine is considered a likely cause of schizophrenia. The author says that amphetamines cause the secretion of dopamine and are associated with psychosis. We conclude that the author mentions the effect of amphetamines in order to show that dopamine is related to schizophrenia. (B) is an idea mentioned in the passage, but (B) is not responsive to the question. As for (C), the author does mention a drug that does not necessarily cause tardive dyskinesia (sulpiride), but sulpiride is not said to be an amphetamine. As for (D), this too is a point

mentioned in the selection, but this idea is not responsive to the question asked. Finally, as for (E), though the author might agree with this conclusion, this is not the reason that the author mentions the effects of amphetamines.

24. **(C)** *Part of.* A CHAPTER is part of a NOVEL and a "scene" is part of a "drama." Do not be deceived by the mention of other literary terms such as "poetry" and "prose" or by other words such as "fraction" and "portion," which actually mean "part of."

25. **(B)** *Degree.* To IMPLY is to indicate or suggest something, while to AVER is to affirm something with confidence. Likewise, to "hint" is to imply, while to "proclaim" is to declare.

26. **(C)** *Defining Characteristic.* By definition, something that is PONDEROUS has a lot of WEIGHT, and something that is "gargantuan" is large or "sizable."

27. **(E)** *Sign of.* To be FEBRILE is a sign of ILLNESS and to be "delusional" is a sign of "insanity."

28. **(A)** *Lack of Defining Characteristic.* Lack of CONTACT is a defining characteristic of being INCOMMUNICADO, and lack of "company" is a defining characteristic of being "sequestered."

29. **(A)** *Lack of Defining Characteristic.* This item is a variation on the "lack of" relationship. ASBESTOS is not exactly a lack of FIRE, but it does prevent fire, just as "formaldehyde" prevents "decay." Do not be distracted by (C)—"alcohol" causes "intoxication"; it does not prevent it.

30. **(B)** *Defining Characteristic.* That which is IMPREGNABLE cannot be PENETRATED, and that which is "inscrutable" cannot be "understood."

## SECTION 3—QUANTITATIVE REASONING (p. 797)

1. **(A)** *Algebra Comparison.* Just substitute the values for $x$ and $y$ into the expressions in the columns and perform the indicated operations. Column A becomes: $x^y = 2^5 = 32$, and Column B becomes $5^2 = 25$.

2. **(B)** *Geometry Comparison.* As you learned in the chapter on quantitative comparisons, the figures in this part of the math sections are not necessarily drawn to scale. Try distorting this figure. You will see that the length of $\overline{KL}$ can approach zero:

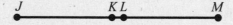

Further, the length of $\overline{KL}$ can approach 5.

But $\overline{KL}$ cannot be equal to or exceed 5 (since points $K$ and $L$ are both between points $J$ and $M$). Therefore, Column B is larger.

3. **(D)** *Algebra Comparison.* Here, you would probably want to use the strategy of assuming some numbers. The centered information states that neither $x$ nor $y$ is zero. Aside from that restriction, $x$ and $y$ could be any values. Start, for example, with $x = 1$ and $y = 2$. On those assumptions Column A is: $\frac{x}{y} = \frac{1}{2}$. Column B is: $\frac{y}{x} = \frac{2}{1} = 2$.

Column B is larger. Now, reverse the assumptions and let $x = 2$ and $y = 1$. You get the opposite result. This shows that the relationship is indeterminate, and so the answer is (D).

4. **(A)** *Geometry Comparison.* In a right triangle with angles of 90 degrees, 60 degrees, and 30 degrees, the length of the side opposite the 60-degree angle is equal to one-half the length of the hypotenuse multiplied by the square root of 3. Therefore:

$$D = (\tfrac{1}{2})(13)(\sqrt{3}) = (\tfrac{13}{2})(\sqrt{3})$$

Since $\frac{13}{2} = 6.5$, $\frac{13}{2}(\sqrt{3}) = 6.5(\sqrt{3})$, and Column A is larger.

5. **(D)** *Arithmetic Comparison.* Use the extremes of the weight range for the sixth package to test the range of the average. If the sixth package weighs 1 pound (the lower limit), the average for the six packages is: $\frac{5(25)+1}{6} = \frac{126}{6} = 21$. If the sixth package weighs 20 pounds (the upper limit) the average of the six is: $\frac{5(25)+20}{6} = \frac{145}{6} = 24\frac{1}{6}$. So, the relationship between the two columns is indeterminate.

6. **(C)** *Geometry Comparison.* Since parallel lines intersected by a transversal (third line) create congruent alternate interior angles, it can be established that $x = y$. So, Column A, which is equivalent to $x + x$, could be written as $x + y$. This shows the two columns are equal.

7. **(D)** *Arithmetic Comparison.* Assume some numbers. For example, if Chuck and Luis each have one marble and Tina has 100 marbles, then Column A is larger. If Chuck has ten marbles, Luis one, and Tina 25, then Column B is greater.

8. **(A)** *Geometry Comparison.* Even though the figures are not necessarily drawn to scale, everything that you need to make a comparison is provided: $x + y + 60 = 180 \Rightarrow x + y = 120$. Further, $p + q + 90 = 180 \Rightarrow p + q = 90$.

9. **(D)** *Geometry Comparison.* For this item, the story is different: everything that you need to make a comparison is not provided. Since the sum of the measures of the interior angles of a quadrilateral is 360: $x + y + 120 + 120 = 360 \Rightarrow x + y + 240 = 360 \Rightarrow x + y = 120$. However, you are stuck with an equation that contains two variables. So, there is no way to find a value for $x$ or $y$ individually.

10. **(C)** *Arithmetic Comparison.* Simplify across the comparison. $\sqrt{2}$ is positive, so multiply both sides of the comparison by $\sqrt{2}$. The result is:

Column A: $\sqrt{2} \cdot \sqrt{2} = 2$
Column B: $(\frac{2}{\sqrt{2}})(\sqrt{2}) = 2$

Alternatively, simply rationalize the denominator in Column B:

Column A: $\sqrt{2}$
Column B: $(\frac{2}{\sqrt{2}})(\frac{\sqrt{2}}{\sqrt{2}}) = \frac{2\sqrt{2}}{2} = \sqrt{2}$

Either approach shows that the two columns are equal.

11. **(D)** *Algebra Comparison.* You might start by performing the operation indicated in Column A: $\frac{1}{x} + \frac{1}{y} = \frac{(y+x)}{xy}$. But you cannot simplify the comparison any further. It would be a mistake to multiply or divide across the columns

because you do not know the signs of $x$ and $y$. At this point, you can reach the conclusion that the relationship is indeterminate.

Alternatively, select some numbers. Start with $x = 1$ and $y = 1$. (Nothing says that $x$ and $y$ are different numbers.) On this assumption, the two columns are equal. Next, try $x = 2$ and $y = 2$. On this assumption, Column A is 1 and Column B is 4, which proves that the relationship is indeterminate.

12. **(D)** *Geometry Comparison.* This comparison can be solved by using the technique of distorting the figure:

In the first distorted figure, the area of the smaller circle appears to be larger than the area of the shaded part of the figure; however, in the other distorted figure, the area of the smaller circle appears to be less than the area of the shaded part of the figure.

13. **(B)** *Arithmetic Comparison.* Reasoning that 75% of one type of marble and 50% of the other type are removed means that only 25% of the one type and 50% of the other remain in the jar. So, fewer than $\frac{1}{2}$ of the original number of marbles remain.

Alternatively, you may be more comfortable with a concrete analysis of the quantities involved. 75% of 32 is 24, so $32 - 24 = 8$ red marbles remain in the jar. 50% of 16 is 8, so $16 - 8 = 8$ blue marbles remain in the jar. $8 + 8 = 16$ marbles out of an original total of $32 + 16 = 48$ marbles remain in the jar. So, the fraction of the number of marbles originally in the jar that remain in the jar is $\frac{16}{48} = \frac{1}{3}$.

14. **(B)** *Algebra Comparison.* One way of attacking this comparison is to set up simultaneous equations to find how many pens and pencils were purchased. Let $x$ be the number of pens purchased, and $y$ the number of pencils purchased. Set up the two equations:

$$x + y = 17 \text{ and } 0.35x + 0.20y = 4.60$$

Use the first equation to redefine $x$ in terms of $y$: $x = 17 - y$. Substitute this value for $x$ in the second equation: $0.35(17 - y) + 0.20y = 4.60$. Solve for $y$:

$$5.95 - 0.35y + 0.20y = 4.60$$
$$-0.35y + 0.20y = 4.60 - 5.95$$
$$-0.15y = -1.35$$
$$0.15y = 1.35$$
$$y = 9$$

Substitute this value for $y$ back into the first equation: $x + 9 = 17 \Rightarrow x = 8$. The student bought nine pencils and eight pens. Therefore, Column B is larger. If you need to make a guess, you should NOT guess (D). You know that the number of pens and pencils can be calculated using equations—even though that process may take some time. Since the comparison can be made, do NOT guess (D).

Alternatively, you can also solve the comparison by working backwards. For example, assume that the number of pencils purchased was eight and the number of pens, nine. On that assumption, the student spent:

$8(\$0.20) + 9(\$0.35) = \$1.60 + \$3.15 = \$4.75$. That, however, is too much money, but in what way is our assumption wrong? Since the assumption generates a total cost of more than $4.60, we must have assumed too many pens were purchased. (The pens are more expensive.) So, we should invert our assumption so that the number of pens is eight and the number of pencils is nine. But at this point, the comparison is already made. We have already established that the student purchased at *least* nine pencils, which means she purchased more pencils than pens.

15. **(D)** *Algebra.* Here, you have one equation with two variables. It is not possible to solve for *x* or *y* individually, but you do not need to. Just rewrite the equation so that you have it in the form $x + y$:

$$12 + x = 36 - y$$
$$x + y = 36 - 12 = 24$$

16. **(B)** *Algebra.* You can analyze the problem as follows: the sum of $3k$, $4k$, $5k$, $6k$, and $7k$ is $25k$, a number that will be divisible by 7 only if *k* is divisible by 7. If, however, the coefficient of *k* were divisible by 7, then that number would be divisible by 7 regardless of value of *k*. If we drop the term $4k$ from the group, the sum of the remaining terms is $21k$. Since 21 is divisible by 7, $21k$ will be divisible by 7 regardless of the value of *k*. Assume a value for *k*, say $k = 1$. Then, the total of the five terms is $3 + 4 + 5 + 6 + 7 = 25$. Eliminating which term will yield a sum that is divisible by 7? The answer is to get rid of the 4, because 21 is divisible by 7.

17. **(E)** *Algebra.* If *n* is even, then $n^2$ is even and $n^2 + n$ is also even. If *n* is odd, then $n^2$ is odd, but $n^2 + n$ is even.

Alternatively, since *n* is a positive integer, plug in an even integer (e.g., 2) and an odd integer (e.g., 3) for *n* and test each answer choice. Only (E) results in an even integer for both possibilities.

18. **(C)** *Algebra.* Here, we can use the overlapping circles diagram we have used before:

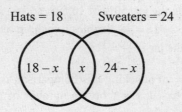

Hats = 18       Sweaters = 24

$18 - x$   $x$   $24 - x$

The twist here is that the diagram is not intended to represent all 36 people in the group. Six of the 36 are wearing neither a hat nor a sweater. So, the total represented by the diagram is $36 - 6 = 30$:

$$18 - x + x + 24 - x = 30$$
$$-x + x - x + 18 + 24 = 30$$
$$-x + 42 = 30$$
$$-x = -12$$
$$x = 12$$

19. **(A)** *Arithmetic.* Proportions make this calculation easy. First, do the calculation for Motorcycle X: $\frac{\text{Fuel Used X}}{\text{Fuel Used Y}} = \frac{\text{Miles Driven X}}{\text{Miles Driven Y}}$. (The X and Y here refer to the two different situations, not the motorcycles.) $\frac{1}{x} = \frac{40}{300} \Rightarrow 300 = 40x \Rightarrow x = 7.5$. So, Motorcycle X uses 7.5 liters of fuel for the 300-kilometer trip. Now, do the same for Motorcycle Y: $\frac{1}{x} = \frac{50}{300} \Rightarrow 300 = 50x \Rightarrow x = 6$. So, Motorcycle Y uses 6 liters of fuel for the trip. Since Motorcycle X uses $7.5 - 6 = 1.5$ liters more than Motorcycle Y, the fuel for Motorcycle X costs $1.5 \cdot \$2 = \$3$ more.

Alternatively, reason informally. If Motorcycle X averages 40 kilometers per liter of gasoline, and the cost of gasoline is $2 per liter, then Motorcycle X rides $\frac{40}{2} = 20$ kilometers for each $1 spent on gasoline. Now, if

Motorcycle Y averages 50 kilometers per liter of gasoline, then Motorcycle Y rides $\frac{50}{2} = 25$ kilometers for each $1 spent on gasoline. Therefore, Motorcycle X spends $\frac{300}{20} = \$15$ for a 300-kilometer trip, and Motorcycle Y spends $\frac{300}{25} = \$12$ for a 300-kilometer trip. The difference in cost is $\$15 - \$12 = \$3$.

20. **(E)** *Algebra.* You can factor $6k + 3$: $6k + 3 = 2(3k + 1)$, which is (E). If you miss that insight, you can assume some numbers to substitute into the choices. Assume that $k = 2$. Then, $6k + 3 = 6(2) + 3 = 12 + 3 = 15$. Now, substitute 2 for $k$ into each of the answer choices. The correct one will yield the value 15.

Alternatively, distribute each of the answer choices until finding the one that equals $6k + 3$.

21. **(B)** *Graphs.* The question asks for the following: $\text{total}_{1996} - \text{total}_{1994}$. Consult the second graph and find the appropriate values: $\text{total}_{1996} - \text{total}_{1994} = 18,000 - 16,000 = 2,000$.

22. **(E)** *Graphs.* One way of attacking this item is to use the "this percent of that" formula: $\frac{\text{approved applications}}{\text{total applications}} = \frac{6}{18} = \frac{1}{3} = 33\frac{1}{3}\%$. Therefore, the percent NOT approved was $66\frac{2}{3}\%$.

23. **(B)** *Graphs.* During the period 1993 through 1996, inclusive, in only two years did total deaths increase: 1995 and 1996. During that period, in only one year, 1995, did applications for permits increase. So, in only one year did both measures increase.

24. **(A)** *Graphs.* To answer this question, you will have to use information from both graphs. From the upper graph, we get the number of barrels imported each day in 2000: 6,000,000. From the lower graph we get the price per barrel: $30. So, the average daily cost of imported oil during 2000 was $6,000,000 \cdot \$30 = \$180,000,000$.

25. **(B)** *Graphs.* To answer this question, you must use information from both graphs:

| | Price | Quantity |
|------|-------------|-------------|
| 1991 | Increase | Increase |
| 1992 | Increase | Increase |
| 1993 | No Increase | Increase |
| 1994 | Increase | Increase |
| 1995 | Increase | Increase |
| 1996 | Increase | No Increase |
| 1997 | Increase | Increase |
| 1998 | No Increase | Increase |
| 1999 | Increase | Decrease |
| 2000 | Increase | Decrease |

So, from 1991 to 2000, inclusive, both quantity and price of imported oil increased in five years: 1991, 1992, 1994, 1995, and 1997.

26. **(E)** *Algebra.* You can devise the formula to be $x$, the cost for the first ounce, plus some expression to represent the additional postage for weight over $x$ ounces. The postage for the additional weight is $y$ cents per ounce, and the additional weight is $w$ minus the first ounce, or $w - 1$. So, the additional postage is $y(w - 1)$, and the total postage is $x + y(w - 1)$.

Alternatively, you can reach the same conclusion by assuming some numbers to be substituted into the answer choices. Make the ridiculous assumption that the first ounce costs one cent and every additional ounce is free. If $x = 1$ and $y = 0$, then a letter of say 10 ounces ($w = 10$) will cost one cent. Substitute 1 for $x$, zero for $y$, and 10 for $w$ into the answer choices. The correct formula will generate the value 1. Even on these silly assumptions, you can eliminate every choice but (D) and (E). Make another set of assumptions, and you will have the answer.

27. **(C)** *Geometry.* Here, we have another composite figure. The side of the square is also the radius of the circle. Since the square has an area of 2, its side is: $s \cdot s = 2 \Rightarrow s^2 = 2 \Rightarrow s = \sqrt{2}$. $\sqrt{2}$ is the radius of the circle, so the area of the circle is $\pi r^2 = \pi(\sqrt{2})^2 = 2\pi$.

28. **(C)** *Arithmetic.* You can solve this problem mathematically by reasoning that the eligible integers must meet two requirements. They must be between zero and 30, and they must equal 3 times an odd integer. So, the eligible numbers are 3 multiplied by the sequence of odd numbers, with the last eligible number being the one before the one which, when multiplied by 3, generates a product greater than 30.

Alternatively, just start counting. The first such number is 3 ($3 \cdot 1 = 3$). Then, you skip 6 ($3 \cdot 2 = 6$, but 2 is even). The next eligible number is 9 ($3 \cdot 3 = 9$). The next is 15 ($3 \cdot 5 = 15$). The next is 21 ($3 \cdot 7 = 21$). The last is 27 ($3 \cdot 9 = 27$). So, there are five of them.

# Practice Test IV

## SECTION 1—ANALYTICAL WRITING (p. 809)

### *'PRESENT YOUR PERSPECTIVE ON AN ISSUE' SAMPLE ESSAY RESPONSE*

Because technological advancement has made travel and "virtual travel" easier, people today are better able to form long-lasting and intimate relationships. In the first place, quantity does not necessarily mean a diminution of quality. Second, having access to a wider variety of human experiences makes it more likely that individuals will find other people with whom to share experiences. And third, ease of contact helps people nurture relationships.

First, an increase in the number and variety of people that we know does not necessarily mean that we care less for those with whom we are closest. To be sure, we may meet many more people whom we only get to know casually and with whom we never form lasting bonds. But the fact that we have more casual acquaintances than our parents did does not mean that we cannot have long-lasting and intimate friendships. Indeed, the very fact that many contacts remain superficial means that they cannot possibly overtax our emotional resources. We are still left with a reserve on which to draw to nourish those relations that seem particularly important.

Second, the fact that people today come into contact with so many other people makes it more likely that they will build successful long-lasting and deep relationships—like cross-pollination. For example, 50 years ago, someone who grew up on a farm in Iowa might have had a circle of friends that was limited to people in that immediate area whose experiences were all very similar. Today, the same person might attend a university 1,000 miles away, or spend a summer traveling in other countries, or chat with friends on the internet from around the world. The sheer number of these contacts makes it likely that something will "click" between two people.

Third, if anything, these advances make it easier to nurture long-lasting relationships. The adage "absence makes the heart grow fonder" sounds too much like rationalization: you cannot do anything about separation, so make the best of it. But now if you are away from friends, you can call them on the telephone, exchange e-mail, or even arrange for a special gift over the internet.

### *'ANALYSIS OF AN ARGUMENT' SAMPLE ESSAY RESPONSE*

The argument is an oversimplification in many respects and does not really support the sweeping change called for. First, it fails to quantify the magnitude of the "road rage" problem. Second, it offers no evidence that a one-day clinic will be effective in combating road rage. And third, it may be that such an approach would not be cost-effective and might actually be counterproductive.

First, while "road rage" is a hot topic for the news media, most of what we actually hear is purely anecdotal, like the example included in support of the argument. After all, how many people carry a loaded weapon in their car and are likely to use one? The news media report this or that example of extreme behavior primarily because it is extreme and makes headlines. Before acting on such a suggestion, it would be essential to have some hard data about "road rage": how many incidents occur in a typical period, is the incidence increasing, are encounters really becoming more violent, are the incidents really caused by "road rage" or by some other factor such as job frustration or substance abuse. One just cannot leap from the fact that the incident took place on a roadway to the conclusion that it was caused by driving, any more than one can conclude that a fight caused by too much alcohol was triggered by "bar rage" simply because that is where it occurred.

Second, even assuming that road rage is quantified and documented as a serious syndrome, what reason is there to believe that a one-day workshop would have any beneficial effect? After all, the causes of this sort of violence seem to be deeply rooted, e.g., traumatic childhoods, adult stresses, and many other factors that might respond to long-term professional counseling but probably would not be corrected by a one-day clinic.

Third, the money spent on such clinics might be better spent in other areas. We do not have unlimited resources, and if there is a problem, we need to create policies that will deal with it effectively, for example, perhaps better policing of our highways with more tickets for bad driving would reduce the level of (legitimate) frustration. Additionally, a one-day clinic poorly done might very well trivialize the issue and make already anger-prone people more likely to erupt because they would get the message that the very concept of "road rage" is a joke that no one takes seriously.

## SECTION 2—QUANTITATIVE REASONING (p. 818)

1. **(C)** *Arithmetic Comparison.* Do the indicated operations:

$$x = 18 + 19 + 20 + 21 + 22 = 100$$
$$y = 22 + 21 + 20 + 19 + 18 = 100$$

So, $x = y$, and the two columns are equal. A better solution is just to see that $x$ and $y$ are the sum of the same five numbers, even though those numbers are presented in a different order for $x$ than for $y$.

2. **(A)** *Algebra Comparison.* Substitute and perform the indicated operations for both columns:

Column A: $\frac{4+1}{(4)(1)} = \frac{5}{4}$

Column B: $\frac{(4)(1)}{4+1} = \frac{4}{5}$

So, Column A is greater.

3. **(A)** *Arithmetic Comparison.* If each lap is $\frac{1}{5}$ of a mile, then a 50-mile race will include $50 \div \frac{1}{5} = 50 \cdot 5 = 250$ laps. Column A, therefore, is 250, and Column B is only 100.

4. **(B)** *Algebra Comparison.* Find the value of $x$ in the center equation:

$$3(x+2) = 7 \Rightarrow 3x + 6 = 7 \Rightarrow 3x = 1 \Rightarrow x = \frac{1}{3}$$

So, Column B is greater.

5. **(C)** *Geometry Comparison.* Since the figure consists of intersecting pairs of parallel lines, use the "big angle/little angle" theorem. In the figure, all of the "big" angles are the same size, and all of the "little" angles are the same size. Since $x$ and $y$ are both the measures of "little" angles, they must be equal.

6. **(A)** *Arithmetic Comparison.* The easiest approach to this item is "supermarket math." If cheese costs $2.00 per pound, for $1.50 you can buy $\frac{\$1.50}{\$2.00} = \frac{3}{4}$ of a pound. Since $\frac{3}{4}$ is larger than $\frac{3}{5}$, Column A is greater.

7. **(D)** *Geometry Comparison.* The centered information states:

$$\text{Volume}_{\text{solid X}} = 24 = \text{height}_{\text{solid X}} \cdot \text{base area}_{\text{solid X}}$$
$$\text{Volume}_{\text{solid Y}} = 20 = \text{height}_{\text{solid Y}} \cdot \text{base area}_{\text{solid Y}}$$

With two different equations, each with two different variables, there is no way to solve for the base of either. Do not make the error of assuming that the larger volume has the larger base. Solid X could have a base of 1 by 1 and a height of 24, and Solid Y could have a base of 5 by 4 and a height of 1.

8. **(B)** *Arithmetic Comparison.* First, $\sqrt{6} + \sqrt{3}$ is not equal to $\sqrt{9}$. (The radicals do not work that way.) Second, you do not need to try to find an exact value for $\sqrt{6}$. Since 6 is more than 4, $\sqrt{6}$ is more than $\sqrt{4}$, and $\sqrt{6}$ is more than 2. And you know that $\sqrt{3}$ is about 1.7, so Column B is more than 3.7, which makes it more than $\sqrt{9}$.

9. **(A)** *Geometry Comparison.* Do not worry; for this item, the formula for finding the surface area of a sphere is not necessary. Just visualize a circle, or disk, as a two-dimensional section of a sphere, or ball. Since the area of the section of the sphere must be less than the area of the sphere itself, Column A is greater.

10. **(C)** *Algebra Comparison.* Look first at what is required by the two columns, then rewrite the centered equation: $2x^2 + 4x = -3$.

11. **(C)** *Arithmetic Comparison.* You could do the indicated operation, but since those operations are tedious, you would be better advised to try an alternative attack strategy: factoring. The right column has the general form: $x^2 + 2xy + y^2$ which, as you know, can be factored as $(x+y)(x+y)$, or $(x+y)^2$. Here, $x$ and $y$ are the same. So, $(111+111)^2$ can be rewritten as $111^2 + 2(111)^2 + 111^2$.

12. **(A)** *Arithmetic Comparison.* This problem reminds us that when a solution seems too difficult, there must be a more direct one. At first you might think that you will have to test each number from 101 to 199 and from 201 to 299 to find the number of perfect squares. That, however, would be too time-consuming, so you look for an alternative solution. The better solution is to work from the other direction. Instead of trying to decide whether 102, 103, 104, and so on are perfect squares, start with the number 10 and work forward. Ten squared is 100, which is less than 101. So, the next integer, when squared, will be greater than 100:

| Column A | Column B |
|---|---|
| $11^2 = 121$ | $15^2 = 225$ |
| $12^2 = 144$ | $16^2 = 256$ |
| $13^2 = 169$ | $17^2 = 289$ |
| $14^2 = 196$ | $18^2 = 324$ |

So, the perfect squares between 101 and 199 are 121, 144, 169, and 196, and the perfect squares between 201 and 299 are 225, 256, and 289. So, there are more perfect squares between 101 and 199 than between 201 and 299.

13. **(D)** *Geometry Comparison.* Here, you can use the technique of distorting the figure. For example, $\overline{LM}$ might be very long, making Column A greater:

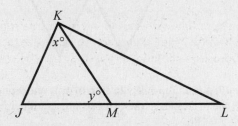

Or, $\overline{LM}$ might be very short, in which case, Column B would be greater:

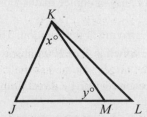

So, the relationship cannot be determined from the information given.

14. **(C)** *Geometry Comparison.* You should always be looking for opportunities to use the special instance of the Pythagorean theorem in which the lengths of the sides of a right triangle are 3, 4, and 5:

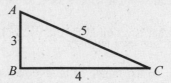

$$\text{Area}_{\triangle ABC} = \tfrac{1}{2}(3)(4) = 6.$$

15. **(A)** *Algebra.* Here, you have a single equation with one variable, so you might as well solve for $x$: $\frac{1}{x} + \frac{1}{x} = 8 \Rightarrow \frac{2}{x} = 8 \Rightarrow x = \frac{1}{4}$. Or, you might have reasoned that $\frac{1}{x}$ and $\frac{1}{x}$ are equal, and since their sum is 8, $\frac{1}{x}$ must be 4. So, the value of $x$ must be $\frac{1}{4}$. Of course, you could have substituted numbers, but this is such a simple equation, one of the two techniques just described is more effective.

16. **(C)** *Arithmetic.* This question asks about percents. You must take a percent of a number:

    20% of 600 boys = 120 boys on the honor roll
    30% of 400 girls = 120 girls on the honor roll

    120 boys + 120 girls = 240 students on the honor roll.

17. **(D)** *Geometry.* Let us label the unlabeled angles:

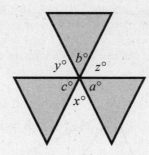

Since the measure of the degrees in a circle is 360, the sum of $x$, $y$, and $z$ plus the sum of $a$, $b$, and $c$ is 360. What is the value of the angles inside the triangles? Since those are equilateral triangles, each of the angles is 60°: $3(60) + x + y + z = 360 \Rightarrow x + y + z = 180$.

Alternatively, you could have "guestimated" the size of $x$, $y$, and $z$. Each one appears to be about 60°, so they should total about 180°. (D) is the only answer choice that is close to 180°.

18. **(B)** *Algebra.* There are three ways of arriving at the solution. The simplest and most direct way is to reason that if 100 bricks weigh $p$ pounds, 20 bricks, which is $\frac{1}{5}$ of 100, must weight $\frac{1}{5}$ of $p$.

Another approach is to express this reasoning using a direct proportion. The more bricks the greater the weight, so: $\frac{100}{20} = \frac{p}{x} \Rightarrow 100x = 20p \Rightarrow x = \frac{20p}{100} = \frac{p}{5}$.

Finally, a third approach is to substitute numbers. Assume that 100 bricks weigh 100 pounds, which is one pound apiece. Twenty bricks weigh 20 pounds. On the assumption that $p = 100$, $\frac{p}{5}$ will generate the number 20.

19. **(E)** *Algebra.* You can eliminate (A), (B), and (C) because $n$ might or might not be odd ($n$ can be any integer). $2n+1$, however, must be odd. ($2n$ is even, so $2n+1$ is odd.) Then, the next odd integer will be 2 more, or $2n+3$, and the next 2 more than that, or $2n+5$.

Alternatively, you could have substituted numbers. Of course, if you pick an odd number for substitution, (C) and (E) both work. In which case you should try an even number.

20. **(B)** *Algebra.* This question is a variation on the theme of an average with missing elements. Ten students have scores of 75 or more, so their score total is at minimum $10 \cdot 75 = 750$. Then, even assuming the other five students each scored zero, the average for the 15 would be at least $750 \div 15 = 50$.

21. **(E)** *Graphs.* Simply subtract the total for the "pie" for Q from the total for the "pie" for R. Since the question calls for an approximation, you can round off the numbers: $\$4,500,000 - \$3,000,000 = \$1,500,000$.

22. **(C)** *Graphs.* You must find the amount spent by P and the amount spent by Q on television. For P, the amount is approximately:

$$40\% \text{ of } \$6,000,000 = 0.40 \cdot \$6,000,000 = \$2,400,000$$

For Q, the amount is approximately:

$$33\% \text{ of } \$4,500,000 = 0.33 \cdot \$4,500,000 = \$1,500,000$$

And the difference is: $\$2,400,000 - \$1,500,000 = \$900,000$.

23. **(C)** *Graphs.* Do not make the mistake of simply averaging the percents spent by each candidate on television advertising. The candidates spent different totals. The correct method for solving this item is to use the "this percent of that" principle: $\frac{\text{total television ad}}{\text{total expenditures}}$. First, find the total amount spent by the candidates on television advertising:

$$P: 40\% \text{ of } \$6,000,000 = \$2,400,000$$
$$Q: 33\% \text{ of } \$4,500,000 = \$1,500,000$$
$$R: 20\% \text{ of } \$3,000,000 = \$600,000$$

So, the total amount spent on television advertising is $\$4,500,000$.

Next, find the total amount spent by the three candidates on all forms of advertising: $\$6,000,000 + \$4,500,000 + \$3,000,000 = \$13,500,000$. Finally, use the "this percent of that" principle: $\frac{\$4,500,000}{\$13,500,000} = \frac{1}{3} = 33\frac{1}{3}\%$.

24. **(E)** *Graphs.* To find the office in which international calls accounted for the greatest proportion, create a fraction: $\frac{\text{international calls}}{\text{total calls}}$. The question is answered by finding the largest such fraction. Keep in mind that in comparing fractions, you should use benchmarks and approximation.

Office A: $\frac{80}{540}$ is slightly more than $\frac{8}{56}$ and therefore slightly more than $\frac{1}{7}$.
Office B: $\frac{180}{960} = \frac{3}{16}$; $\frac{3}{16}$ is halfway between $\frac{1}{8}$ and $\frac{1}{4}$ and therefore considerably more than $\frac{1}{7}$. (Eliminate (A).]
Office C: $\frac{120}{590} = \frac{12}{59}$, which is slightly more than $\frac{12}{60}$ and therefore slightly more than $\frac{1}{5}$.

So, which is larger, (C) or (B)? If you remember the fraction and decimal equivalents, you can reason as follows: $\frac{3}{16}$ is equal to $\frac{1}{8}$ plus $\frac{1}{16}$; $\frac{1}{8}$ is equivalent to 0.125 and $\frac{1}{16}$ must be half of that or 0.0625; so $\frac{3}{16}$ is equal to

$0.125 + 0.0625 = 0.1875$, which is less than $\frac{1}{5}$. So, (C) is larger. Or, you can simply bracket this comparison and work through the remaining choices, hoping that one will be clearly larger than either (B) or (C).

Office $D$: $\frac{90}{430} = \frac{9}{43}$, which is slightly more than $\frac{9}{45}$ and so slightly more than $\frac{1}{5}$. [Again, you can bracket the comparison hoping that (E) is larger than (B), (C), or (D).]

Office $E$: $\frac{120}{480} = \frac{1}{4}$, which is clearly larger than $\frac{1}{5}$.

So, (E) must be larger than (B), (C), and (D).

25. **(E)** *Graphs.* Since the item stem uses the phrase "most nearly," you can calculate the cost of calls at each office using estimates for some of the average costs per call:

Office $A$ (Local Calls): $\$0.50 \cdot 280 = \$140$
Office $A$ (Domestic Long Distance Calls): $\$6 \cdot 180 = \$1,080$
Office $A$ (International Long Distance Calls): $\$20 \cdot 80 = \$1,600$
Office $A$ (Total Calls): $\$2,820$
Office $D$ (Local Calls): $\$0.75 \cdot 180 = \$135$
Office $D$ (Domestic Long Distance Calls): $\$6 \cdot 160 = \$960$
Office $D$ (International Long Distance Calls): $\$19 \cdot 90 = \$1,710$
Office $D$ (Total Calls): $\$2,805$

The ratio $\frac{2,820}{2,805}$ is very close to 1.

26. **(E)** *Algebra.* The operating speed is expressed in units per minute. The machine produces $x$ units in $t$ minutes plus $\frac{1}{2}$ minute. So, the average operating speed is $\frac{x}{t + \frac{1}{2}}$. Or, you could have tried substituting some numbers.

27. **(A)** *Geometry.* Since the figure is a square, the two sides are equal: $2x + 1 = x + 4 \Rightarrow x = 3$. So, each side is $x + 4 = 3 + 4 = 7$, and the perimeter is $4(7) = 28$, (A).

28. **(E)** *Geometry.* You can work this out algebraically. Let $w$ be the width of the rectangle. The length of the rectangle is twice that or $2w$. So, the rectangle has an area of $w \cdot 2w = 2w^2$. Then, $w$ is also the length of the hypotenuse of a 45-45-90 triangle. (All isosceles right triangles are 45-45-90.) Each of the other two sides (the ones that form the right angle) is $\frac{1}{2} \cdot w \cdot \sqrt{2} = \frac{\sqrt{2} \cdot w}{2}$. (Since the two sides form a right angle, they can be the altitude and base). So, the area of the triangle is $\frac{1}{2} \cdot$ altitude $\cdot$ base $= \frac{1}{2}(\frac{\sqrt{2} \cdot w}{2})(\frac{\sqrt{2} \cdot w}{2}) = \frac{1}{2}(\frac{2w^2}{4}) = \frac{w^2}{4}$. And the ratio of the area of the rectangle to that of the triangle is $(2w^2 \div \frac{w^2}{4}) \cdot (2 \cdot \frac{1}{4}) = \frac{8}{1}$.

Alternatively, draw a diagram:

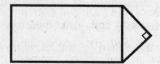

In the first place, the rectangle is obviously bigger than the triangle. So, (A), (B), and (C) can be eliminated. Next, a quick addition to the figure shows that the area of the triangle is less than $\frac{1}{4}$ of the area of the rectangle:

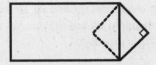

So, by the process of elimination, (E) must be the correct answer choice.

## SECTION 3—VERBAL REASONING (p. 824)

1. **(A)** *Thought Extension.* This question is pretty much a test of vocabulary. The last part of the sentence (including the blank) is an explanation of what it means to be a pariah. A pariah is an outcast, so (A) must be the correct choice.

2. **(A)** *Combined Reasoning.* You can eliminate both (C) and (E) on the ground that their first elements, when substituted into the passage, do not create meaningful phrases. Next, "although" sets up a contrast between "generally boring and awkwardly written" and "—— passages of power and lyricism," the former a negative judgment and the latter a positive judgment. On this ground, eliminate (B). To create a contrast, the good parts must have been relatively few. (D) also fails to provide a contrast. If the passage were ill-conceived, then the second idea would reinforce the first, rather than contrast with it.

3. **(E)** *Combined Reasoning.* There are two logical clues in the sentence. In the first clause, we have a reversal: "charming but ——." So, the first word of the correct choice will complete a contrast. Then, the entire second clause extends and explains the idea presented in the first clause. Eliminate (C) and (D) because they do not provide a contrast with "charming." The first words of the other choices are possibilities, so examine their second elements. Eliminate (B) because "affirmation of the development of painting" is not a meaningful phrase. As for (A), although "grotesque" contrasts with "charming," the idea of grotesqueness does not set up a thought to be explained by the second clause. The fact that American painters were not concerned with European painting does not explain why American painting might have been grotesque. This is why (E) is correct. American painting was primitive because American painters were ignorant of European painting.

4. **(B)** *Combined Reasoning.* There are two important logical features in this item. One, the first blank sets up a thought-extender that is completed by "compromise": "the manager did not —— and did not even compromise." The only choice that sets up this extension is (B). Of the available choices, only "capitulate" is an action like compromise. You might also have arrived at the correct answer by focusing on the second elements. The second blank must be filled by a word that explains the outcome of the manager's refusal to compromise. A refusal to compromise is most likely to result in a confrontation or conflict. Thus, (B) provides a good completion for that second blank.

5. **(B)** *Combined Reasoning.* The conjunction "but" here signals a reversal. The second clause must express an idea that contrasts with the idea that the design of the building is magnificent, which means that the first blank must be completed by a word with negative connotations. On this ground, you can immediately eliminate (E). (E) fails for the additional reason that it is people, not buildings, that populate an area. The first elements of the remaining choices have the appropriate negative overtones. The first blank must be completed by a word that also sets up a contrast with the idea of ultra-modern steel and glass skyscrapers (otherwise, the building would not be out of place). Only (B) accomplishes this. You should notice how well the two elements of (B) work together: the classical lines belonged to a different time period and were therefore out of place in an area filled with modern structures.

6. **(C)** *Combined Reasoning.* A good way to analyze this sentence is to see that the second blank extends the idea of "solitary" and echoes the idea of independence. On this basis, you can eliminate (B), and (C) looms as the correct choice. You could, however, probably make an argument for the second element of (A), (D), or (E), so we will pursue the analysis. The "more —— than" construction sets up a contrast between some characteristic of dogs and different traits of cats. Then, the second clause describes cats as independent and unlikely to try to please their owners. So, the first blank must be completed by a word that creates an idea that contrasts with independence, and (C) does this nicely. "Tractable" means "easily managed."

7. **(A)** *Antonyms.* Although we usually use BRIDGE as a noun to refer to a structure, here the word functions as a verb. (Check the part of speech of the choices.) To BRIDGE means to "build a bridge, thereby joining." So, the best opposite is "separate."

8. **(A)** *Antonyms.* NEBULOUS means "cloudy" or "hazy" (in a physical sense) or "unclear" or "ill-defined" (as a thought or an idea). "Clear" responds nicely as an opposite to both of these uses.

9. **(C)** *Antonyms.* GARRULOUS means "very talkative," so "silent" is an exact opposite.

10. **(E)** *Antonyms.* Although COUNTENANCE is often a noun (meaning "the face" or "an expression of the face"), here it is a verb meaning "to give approval to something."

11. **(B)** *Antonyms.* SANGUINE means "optimistic," "cheerful," or "hopeful." To resign oneself to something is to submit passively and to accept it. "Resigned" means "characterized by a willingness to give up."

12. **(C)** *Antonyms.* GERMANE means "closely connected to or related to." A good opposite is "irrelevant." Here is another case in which you might have been able to answer with only a vague idea of the meaning of the word. Perhaps you know the phrase "GERMANE to the issue." Whatever GERMANE means in the phrase, it has something to do with an issue. On this ground, (C) would appear the most likely choice.

13. **(B)** *Antonyms.* TRENCHANT originally meant "cutting" or "sharp" and so by extension is applied to things like arguments or words to mean penetrating or incisive. So, a good opposite is "dimwitted."

14. **(C)** *Antonyms.* EVINCE means "to show in a clear manner; to make something manifest or evident." To "obscure" means "to hide from view."

15. **(E)** *Antonyms.* To CONTEMN means to "scorn," to "despise," or to "disdain," so a very nice opposite is "admire."

16. **(E)** *Lack of Defining Characteristic.* Adjusting the parts of speech to make our diagnostic sentence read more smoothly, we might say that RUTHLESSNESS is characterized by a lack of COMPASSION and "lethargy" is characterized by a lack of "energy."

17. **(E)** *Type of.* A LEOPARD is a type of CAT, and a "chameleon" is a type of "lizard."

18. **(A)** *Degree.* To be RABID is to be extremely ANGRY, and to be "ravenous" is to be extremely "hungry."

19. **(D)** *Defining Characteristic.* This analogy is based on the "defining characteristic" connection, but getting a correctly formulated sentence is a little tricky: Something that is REPROACHED is BLAMEWORTHY, and something that is "rewarded" is "meritorious."

20. **(D)** *Lack of Defining Characteristic.* The analogy relationship here is "lack of"; the analogy itself is fairly simple, but the vocabulary is difficult. PEDESTRIAN means a lack of ORIGINALITY. So, something that is PEDESTRIAN is lacking in ORIGINALITY, and someone who is "indulgent" is lacking in "forbearance."

21. **(A)** *Degree.* To be RAPT is to be extremely INTERESTED in something. To be "amenable" is to be willing to do something, but to be "enthusiastic" is to be extremely willing to do something.

22. **(A)** *Defining Characteristic.* GREED is the defining characteristic of RAPACIOUSNESS, and "passion" is the defining characteristic of "zealousness."

23. **(C)** *Implied Idea.* The author draws an analogy between a political fable and a caricature because the political fable emphasizes certain points over others; it paints with a very broad brush, dealing in types rather than characters. Similarly, a caricature emphasizes certain personal characteristics over others. Thus, this is the analogy: society is to political fable as person is to caricature.

24. **(B)** *Main Idea.* This is a Main Idea item that asks you to "pick the best title." The author begins by announcing that *Nineteen Eighty-Four* is not a novel in the strict sense of that term but really a political fable. (B) echoes the author's statement of his own purpose. (A) is incorrect because it is too narrow. The author barely mentions in passing some of the characters in the book. (C) also is too narrow. Although it is true that the author does state that one of the characteristics of a political fable is that characters are defined in relation to their society, that is but one of many points made in the selection. (D) suffers from the same defect. There are several other points made by the author in the passage. In addition, (D) is in a sense too broad, for the author takes as the focus for his discussion the particular work *Nineteen Eighty-Four*—not political fables in general. Finally, (E) suffers from both of the ills that afflict (D). (E) is both too narrow because the distinction between novel and political fable is but one part of the discussion and too broad because it fails to acknowledge that the author has chosen to focus on a particular work.

25. **(B)** *Logical Structure.* Why does the author mention this characteristic of Winston Smith? The answer to this question does not become clear until you have read the entire selection. One important feature of a political fable is that characters are reduced to mere types. They do not have the idiosyncrasies that they would have in a novel. The first sentence preempts a possible objection: Winston Smith is described in some detail. So, the author mentions this to let the reader know that that this makes no difference to the argument. Given this analysis, (A) must be incorrect. Small details like an ulcer would not be characteristic of a type but of an individual. (C) simply represents a confused reading of that section of the passage. The author implies there that Winston Smith is the main character of the work. As for (D) and (E), not only do these have no basis in the passage, they are not responsive to the question.

26. **(B)** *Further Application.* You must take what you have learned about the *oyabun-kobun* and apply it to a new situation. What are the defining characteristics of this relationship? First, the *oyabun-kobun* is like a parent-child relationship; one person is superior to the other. On this ground, you can eliminate both (C) and (E). They describe situations in which people behave more or less as equals. Another aspect of the parent-child relation is intimacy. So, you can eliminate (A), which is a relationship between one and many. Although (D) describes a one-on-one situation in which one party is in charge, the situation lacks the element of intimacy. This leaves (B). And (B) describes a relationship that is personal, in which the interests of the parties are similar, and in which one party is superior to the other.

27. **(B)** *Implied Idea.* This is an Implied Idea item based on the first paragraph. The key sentence is the one that reads "[Fukuzawa] was not able to prevent the government from turning back to the canons of Confucian thought in the Imperial Rescript of 1890." Since Fukuzawa represented liberal thought and Confucianism was the source of traditional values, we can infer that the Imperial Rescript represented a return to traditional values. Thus, (A) and (C) both reach clearly wrong conclusions. (D) represents a confused reading of the selection. The Bolshevik Revolution did not occur until 1917. Finally, (E) represents the second most attractive answer. It at least notes that the Imperial Rescript represented a reaction to liberal ideas. The difficulty with (E) is that it goes too far beyond the explicit text. While we can infer the general conclusion that the Imperial Rescript represented a reaction to liberal thinking, there is nothing in the selection to support the very specific conclusion given in (E).

28. **(A)** *Main Idea.* This is a Main Idea item that asks you to find a description of the selection that is neither too broad nor too narrow. (A) best captures this idea. The very first sentence summarizes the author's thesis. Japanese values are the product of two seemingly contradictory forces, traditional values and modern values. (B) and (E) are incorrect because they refer to but minor points in the development of the selection. (C) and (D) make the same mistake, though less egregiously. (D) refers only to the final paragraph of the selection. (C) seems to be the second most attractive answer for it is one of the important points the author makes. But the description of the *initial* reception of the new values is not the main point of the selection.

29. **(D)** *Implied Idea.* This is an Implied Idea item that covers virtually the whole passage. The term "open government" provides a clue. The general idea of the law is to ensure that the workings of an agency are open to public scrutiny. So, (C) and (E) must surely be purposes of the law. Beyond that, the second paragraph mentions that the law is so strict it prohibits private meetings between members of the commission. This fact, coupled with the general intent of an "open government" law, implies that it is intended to prevent private deals. So, (A) is implied by the selection. (B) is supported by the last sentence of the second paragraph. A consequence of the law is that the public is given an opportunity to participate in the decision-making process. (D), however, is not implied by the passage. In fact, according to the last paragraph, the procedures required to implement the law have actually slowed the decision-making process.

30. **(A)** *Further Application.* You must use what you have learned from the passage about the administrative process. In the first paragraph, the author says decisions can be classified according to whether they can be made by the executive director or must be reserved for the commission. If the matter can only be decided by the commission, then it must be done publicly. Later, the author points out that the requirements of publicity and public meetings slow the administrative process. We may conclude, therefore, that the executive director, because he or she is not bound by the open government requirements, can act more swiftly. (B) and (C) are incorrect since a decision solely within the discretion of the executive director is made without the participation of the commission and the attendant publicity. As for (D), the "big decisions," like the entire budget, are the ones that must be done publicly. Finally, (E) is just a misreading of the passage. The passage mentions that requests for information from commissioners to staff must be in writing.